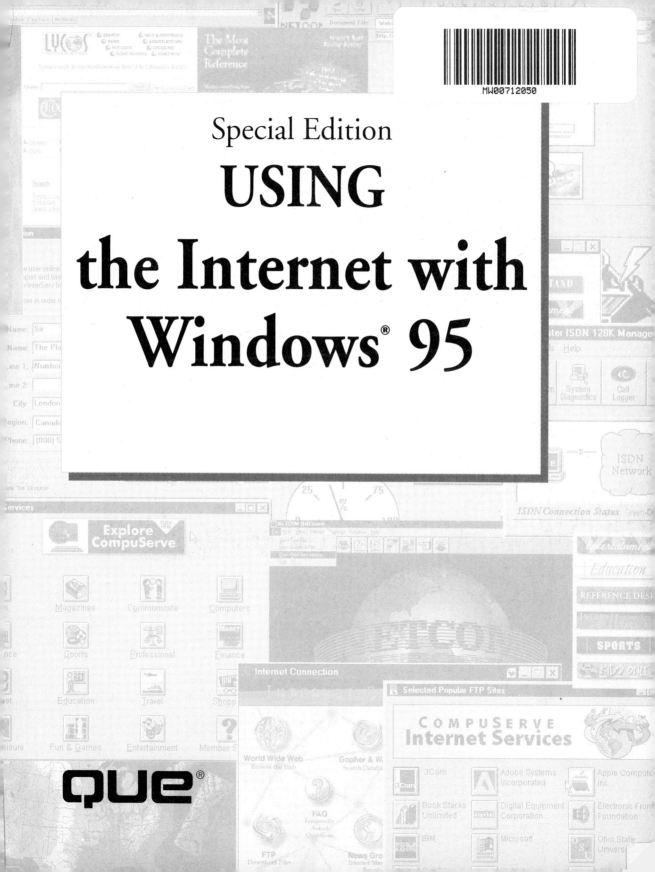

Special Edition

USING
the Internet with
Windows® 95

Que®

Special Edition

USING

the Internet with

Windows® 95

Written by Mary Anne Pike

with

Mark R. Brown	Jim Minatel	Contributions by:
James Bryce	James O'Donnell	Scott Berkun
Dick Cravens	Tod Pike	David Cook
Heather Fleming	Eric Richardson	Robin Hohman
Faisal Jawdat	J. Michael Roach	Bill Kirkner
John Jung	Joe Schepis	Marian Myerson
Pam Kane	Sarah Tourville	Tim Parker
Ralph Losey		Rosalind Resnick
		John Taschnek

que®

Special Edition Using the Internet with Windows® 95

Library of Congress Catalog No.: 95-72572

ISBN: 0-7897-0646-6

98 97 96   6 5 4 3 2 1

Interpretation of the printing code: the rightmost double-digit number is the year of the book's printing; the rightmost single-digit number, the number of the book's printing. For example, a printing code of 96-1 shows that the first printing of the book occurred in 1996.

All terms mentioned in this book that are known to be trademarks or service marks have been appropriately capitalized. Que cannot attest to the accuracy of this information. Use of a term in this book should not be regarded as affecting the validity of any trademark or service mark.

Screen reproductions in this book were created using Collage Plus from Inner Media, Inc., Hollis, NH.

Credits

President
Roland Elgey

Publisher
Stacy Hiquet

Editorial Services Director
Elizabeth Keaffaber

Managing Editor
Sandy Doell

Director of Marketing
Lynn E. Zingraf

Senior Series Editor
Chris Nelson

Publishing Manager
Jim Minatel

Acquisitions Editor
Doshia Stewart

Product Director
Mark Cierzniak

Production Editor
Heather Kaufman Urschel

Editors
Kelli Brooks
Noelle Gasco
Mitzi Gianakos
Susan Moore
Kelly Oliver
Nanci Sears Perry

Assistant Product Marketing Manager
Kim Margolius

Technical Editors
Chris Nelson
Greg Newman
Brian-Kent Proffitt
Tony Schafer

Technical Specialist
Nadeem Muhammad

Acquisitions Coordinator
Ruth Slates

Operations Coordinator
Patty Brooks

Editorial Assistant
Andrea Duvall

Book Designer
Ruth Harvey

Cover Designer
Dan Armstrong

Production Team
Steve Adams, Brian Buschkill, Heather Butler, Jason Carr, Kim Cofer, Terri Edwards, Bryan Flores, DiMonique Ford, Trey Frank, Jason Hand, George Hanlin, Sonja Hart, Damon Jordan, Daryl Kessler, Clint Lahnen, Bob LaRoche, Glenn Larsen, Stephanie Layton, Michelle Lee, Erika Millen, Beth Rago, Erich Richter, Kaylene Riemen, Laura Robbins, Bobbi Satterfield, Tim Taylor, Michael Thomas, Scott Tullis, Christine Tyner, Karen Walsh, Suzanne Whitmer, Paul Wilson, Karen York

Indexer
Chris Cleveland

Composed in *Stone Serif* and *MCPdigital* by Que Corporation.

About the Authors

Mary Ann Pike has a B.S. in electrical engineering and an M.A. in professional writing from Carnegie Mellon University. She has experience in software design and development, and is currently working as a techinical writer at the Software Engineering Institute at Carnegie Mellon University. She has authored several other Que Internet books, including *Special Edition Using the Internet*, Second Edition, *Using Mosaic*, and *Special Edition Using the World Wide Web and Mosaic*. Several of her books have won awards from the Society for Technical Communication. (Chapters 1, 2, 20, 22, 23, 24, and 35, and appendixes A, B, C, and D)

Mark R. Brown has been writing computer magazine articles, books, and manuals for over 13 years. He was Managing Editor of *.info* magazine when it was named one of the six Best Computer Magazines of 1991 by the Computer Press Association, and was nominated by the Software Publisher's Association for the 1988 Software Reviewer of the Year award. He is currently the Manager of Technical Publications for Neural Applications Corporation, a major player in applying cutting-edge artificial intelligence techniques to industrial control applications, such as steel making and food processing. A bona-fide personal computing pioneer, he hand-built his first PC in 1977, taught himself to program it in hexadecimal, and has since dabbled in dozens of different programming languages. He has been telecomputing since 1983, and is currently Webmaster of two World Wide Web sites: **http:// www.neural.com**, and a personal Web site on the topic of airships, which will have moved to a new URL by the time this is published.

Mark is a life-long resident of Iowa, and offers of magazine editing jobs in California and New York City have not appealed to him in the least. He enjoys reading and writing, gaming, Iowa Hawkeye Big 10 football, walks in the park with his dog, Bosco, and day trips through the Iowa countryside with his wife, Carol. (Chapters 41 and 42)

James Y. Bryce is a writer, speaker, and consultant on communications systems and future technologies. He worked with the early phases of integrated circuits on the Minuteman ICBM project having learned electronics hands-on in amateur radio. He has a B.A. in philosophy and mathematics and a J.D. in law. He practiced law for 10 years prior to studying computer science and installing the first commercial Ethernet using IBM PCs. He has worked with many of the major network operating systems from their inception. James travels extensively consulting and presenting issues of high technology to executive and user audiences. He is currently speaking, writing, and consulting on convergence of computer and telephone technology as illustrated by explosive growth of the Internet and ISDN. He resides in Austin, Texas. His Internet address is **bryce@bryce.com**. (Chapters 4, 7, 8, and 9)

Dick Cravens lives and works in Columbia, Missouri, where he is a product manager designing the Next Big Thing from DATASTORM TECHNOLOGIES, Inc., a publisher of fax, data, and TCP/IP communications software for Windows PCs. In previous lives he designed training programs for support technicians, answered gazillions of questions about modems, worked as production manager for an advertising agency, sold television programming to evil cable TV empires, managed a chain of one-hour photo shops, ran a commercial photographic studio, and chased Angus cows, kind of in that order. Since he just bought the classic fixer-upper bungalow and has an addiction to way-cool-wicked-fast computer stuff, he writes the occasional computer book, too. His son, Jesse, budding MUD freak, abuses the hand-me-down computers, slops the cats, and orders the pizzas. (Chapters 13, 22, 34, 36, 37, and 38)

Faisal Jawdat is an Internet business consultant with TeleGlobal Media. In his copious free time he does freelance technical writing, and is a general creative media hack. He wishes to thank Shin, Josh, Scott, Christy, and several anonymous cats. He can be reached on the Internet at **faisal@obscure.org**. (Chapter 43)

Heather A. Fleming received her first lessons on a computer when she was given an Apple IIe for a Christmas present at the age of 12. After working her way to a Stephens College graduation with a B.A. in mathematics and computer science, she landed a job working at a lumber mill in Oregon, where, besides pulling green chain, she studied machinery automation. The next year was spent studying human and computer interaction at the University of Nebraska—Lincoln, University of Missouri—Columbia, and Stephens College, and set her on a career path that has kept her in mid-Missouri writing training manuals for DATASTORM TECHNOLOGIES, Inc., ever since. (Chapters 10, 11, and 17)

John Jung is an alumni from the University of Southern California with a degree in computer science. He became interested in computers over 16 years ago and has been on the Net for over eight years. He wastes his time watching TV, surfing the Net, and playing video games. John can be reached at **jjung@netcom.com**. (Chapters 14 and 16)

Pam Kane is a best-selling computer book author and Contributing Editor of *HomePC* magazine. She and Andy Hopkins are co-developers of the PANDA family of anti-virus and security products. They have given presentations around the world on computer viruses and security issues. (Chapters 12, 44, and 45)

Ralph C. Losey is an attorney and legal counselor with an office in Orlando, Florida, and in cyberspace at **http://seamless.com/rcl/rcl.html**. He is also the provider of the Information Law Web located on the Internet at **http://seamless.com/rcl/infolaw.html**. Ralph is a partner in the law firm of Subin, Shams, Rosenbluth, Moran, Losey & Brennan, P.A., 111 North Orange Avenue, Suite 900, Orlando, Florida 32801; Telephone: (407) 841-7470; Facsimile: (407) 648-4995. Losey has been using computerized legal research and practice tools since his days in law school in 1978. Over the years he has worked to apply these technical skills to serve his law clients, including businesses in and out of the computer industry. An early legal explorer of cyberspace, Ralph is one of those rare attorneys fluent in both "legalese" and "computerese." With the help of his 16-attorney law firm, he has put together many deals and projects, particularly software-related transactions. He is also no stranger to the courtroom, where he has tried a number of different cases and appeals. Ralph has been a member of the Florida Bar since 1980 and has been certified by the Bar as a mediator of computer law–related disputes, and an arbitrator of state Circuit Court cases. He is the author of numerous legal articles, including *The Practical and Legal Protection of Computer Databases,* published originally by the Florida Bar Journal and now available in updated form at **http://seamless/rcl/article.html**.

When not working or attempting "quality time" with his wife, Molly, and their two kids, Eva and Adam, Ralph studies, writes, and teaches philosophy. In this role he is the moderator of the popular School of Wisdom Web site and mailing list found at **http://www.webcom.com/~metanoic/wisdom/**. (Chapter 3)

Jim Minatel is a Title Manager working for Que. His areas of expertise include the Internet and new technologies. He is the author of Que's *Easy World Wide Web with Netscape* and has contributed to several other books. Before coming to Que, he developed college math texts, earned a M.S. in mathematics from Chicago State University, and a B.A. in mathematics and physics from Wabash College. (Chapters 46, 47, 48, 49, 50, and 51)

Jim O'Donnell was born on October 17, 1963 (you may forward birthday greetings to **odonnj@rpi.edu**), in Pittsburgh, Pennsylvania. After a number of unproductive years, he began his studies in electrical engineering at Rensselaer Polytechnic Institute. He liked it so much that he spent 11 years there getting three degrees, graduating for the third (and final) time in the summer of 1992. He can now be found plying his trade at the NASA Goddard Space Flight Center (which takes a tolerant, though hardly enthusiastic, view of his writing endeavors). He's not a rocket scientist, but he's close.

Mr. O'Donnell's first experience with a "personal" computer was in high school with a Southwest Technical Products computer using a paper tape storage device, quickly graduating up to a TRS-80 Model II with cassette tape storage. His fate as a computer geek was sealed when Rensselaer gave him an Atari 800 as part of a scholarship. Mr. O'Donnell doesn't actually own a Windows PC, but expects to take the plunge, soon. Wish him luck. (Chapters 18, 19, 30, 31, 32, and 40)

Tod Pike is a graduate of Carnegie Mellon University, where he first became familiar with the Internet. A system administrator for almost 10 years, he works daily with UNIX, UseNet, and Internet mail. He can be reached on the Internet at **tgp@cmu.edu**. (Chapters 5, 6, 21, and 33)

Eric C. Richardson is an Internet consultant and freelance writer who resides in Northeastern Pennsylvania with his wife, Stacie. He grew up around computers and realized at an early age that they were far easier to take apart than to put back together. He now spends most of his professional time helping businesses explore the possibilities of using the Internet via training and corporate set up. He enjoys reading, mountain biking, and writing. With his wife he is a co-owner of Richardson Consulting. He can be reached at **rchcnslt@epix.net**. (Chapters 41 and 42)

J. Michael Roach, a native of St. Louis, Missouri, now lives in Columbia, Missouri, where he works as a teacher, trainer, and course developer for DATASTORM, publisher of the award-winning PROCOMM PLUS line of communications software.

J. Michael started working with the Internet about two years ago, and helped to develop the company-wide Internet training for DATASTORM. Since that time, he has shared his enthusiasm for the Internet with friends, family, and colleagues. *Special Edition Using the Internet with Windows 95* is his third Internet-related project with Que. (Chapters 15 and 28)

Joseph Schepis has been involved with computing, programming, and engineering since 1979. He began working with Digital Equipment Corp's DEC 10 at the Catholic University of America's Computer Center while earning a B.S. in mechanical engineering there. Since 1982, he has been employed at NASA's Goddard Space Flight Center. At NASA, he develops structures and mechanisms for Earth orbiting satellites and Space Shuttle payloads, and acts as his Branch's network administrator. He is married to a woman who tolerates his computing hobbies (especially during the writing of this book), the father of two children with whom he prolongs his own childhood, and enjoys woodworking and music. He can be reached by e-mail on the Internet at **jschepis@div720.gsfc.nasa.gov**. (Chapters 26, 27, and 29)

Sarah G.E. Tourville is Founder, President, and CEO of SAGRELTO Enterprises, Inc., 5107 Inverness Drive, Durham, NC 27712-1813, **sagrelto@sagrelto.com**, **http://www.sagrelto.com/sget/home.htm & home.sgm**.

SAGRELTO Enterprises, Inc., is a company dedicated to solving the problems of infoglut and assisting users and providers of information for the highways. SAGRELTO, one of the first companies to focus on preparing information for SGML on the Web, provides consulting, training, information preparation, server management, and software development services related to SGML, HTML, Internet, and the World Wide Web. SAGRELTO is a small business sponsor member of SGML Open, the SGML vendor consortium, and the Netscape Development Partner Program. (Chapter 30)

Acknowledgments

A lot of effort goes into producing a book like this. It was great working with all the other authors, and I would like to thank them for the wonderful job they did sharing their expertise. As always, the crew at Que put in a lot of hard work to get this project done. And, finally, this book would not be possible without the technical and moral support of my husband Tod, and the patience of Megan and Sharon, who are tired of having Mom hog the computer.

We'd Like to Hear from You!

As part of our continuing effort to produce books of the highest possible quality, Que would like to hear your comments. To stay competitive, we *really* want you, as a computer book reader and user, to let us know what you like or dislike most about this book or other Que products.

You can mail comments, ideas, or suggestions for improving future editions to the address below, or send us a fax at (317) 581-4663. For the online inclined, Macmillan Computer Publishing has a forum on CompuServe (type **GO QUEBOOKS** at any prompt) through which our staff and authors are available for questions and comments. The address of our Internet site is **http://www.mcp.com** (World Wide Web).

In addition to exploring our forum, please feel free to contact me personally to discuss your opinions of this book: I'm **76245,476** on CompuServe, and I'm **mcierzniak@que.mcp.com** on the Internet.

Thanks in advance—your comments will help us to continue publishing the best books available on computer topics in today's market.

Mark Cierzniak
Product Development Specialist
Que Corporation
201 W. 103rd Street
Indianapolis, Indiana 46290
USA

Contents at a Glance

Introduction	1

About the Internet   **7**
1. How the Internet Works   9
2. The Various Parts of the Internet   25
3. Your Cyber Rights and Responsibilities: Law and Etiquette   47

About the Internet

Getting Connected   **99**
4. The Various Ways to Connect to the Internet: Which One Is Right for You?   101
5. Connecting Through a LAN with Windows 95   125
6. Connecting to a PPP or SLIP Account with Windows 95   137
7. Other Software for Connecting to the Internet   157
8. Setting Up an ISDN Connection   177
9. Setting Up a High-Speed Internet Connection   215
10. Connecting Through CompuServe   231
11. Connecting Through America Online   263
12. Connecting Through Prodigy   287
13. Connecting Through Microsoft Network   309

Getting Connected

Using Internet E-Mail   **327**
14. How Internet E-Mail Works   329
15. Using Microsoft Exchange   349
16. Using Eudora   379
17. E-Mailing Outside the Internet and with Online Services   401
18. Using Internet Mailing Lists   417
19. Encoding and Decoding Files   439

Using Internet E-Mail

The World Wide Web   **455**
20. How the World Wide Web Works   457
21. Using Microsoft Internet Explorer   473
22. Using Netscape   497
23. Using Mosaic   539
24. Using Helper Apps   577
25. Planning Your Own WWW Home Pages   597
26. Using HTML to Build Your Home Page   621
27. Using Microsoft Internet Assistant to Build Web Pages   667
28. Using Netscape Navigator Gold and HotDog to Create Web Pages   699
29. New Web Technologies   723

The World Wide Web

UseNet Newsgroups   **747**

30   How UseNet Works   749

31   Using NewsXpress   775

32   Using Agent   791

Locating and Retrieving Information   **817**

33   Using Telnet   819

34   Using FTP and Popular FTP Programs   837

35   Using Gopher and Popular Gopher Programs   867

36   Using WAIS   897

37   Searching on the Internet   911

Interactive Communications   **939**

38   How IRC Works   941

39   Using mIRC and Netscape Chat   949

40   Talking on the Net: Internet Phone and Internet Voice Chat   971

41   Video Conferencing on the Net   995

42   Games on the Net: MUDs, MOOs, and MUSHes   1011

Internet Security   **1031**

43   Privacy and Security on the Net   1033

44   Protecting Yourself from Viruses   1053

NetReference: Hot Internet Sites   **1071**

45   Top Internet Mailing Lists   1073

46   Top World Wide Web Sites   1091

47   Top FTP Sites   1139

48   Top UseNet Newsgroups   1155

49   Top Gopher Sites   1175

Using NetCD95   **1179**

50   Installing and Using NetCD95   1181

Appendixes   **1189**

A   Country Codes   1191

B   Time Zone Code Table   1199

C   Vendor Contacts for Selected Internet Software and Services   1205

D   Glossary   1219

Index   1239

UseNet Newsgroups

Locating and Retrieving

Interactive Communications

Internet Security

NetReference Hot Sites

Using NetCD95

Appendixes

Contents

Introduction   **1**

What's Changed in This Edition 2

What This Book Is 3

NetCD95—Your Free Source for Internet Software 4

Conventions Used in This Book 5

I About the Internet   **7**

1 How the Internet Works   **9**

A Brief History of the Internet 9

    The Development of the ARPANET 10

    The Structure of the Internet 10

    The National Information Infrastructure.......................... 13

    Internet-Related Organizations 13

The Culture of the Internet 15

    The Community Expands 15

    Cultural Pitfalls 16

The Growth of the Internet 17

    Traffic Growth 17

    Host Growth 19

How Do I Use the Internet? 19

    How Do I Get Connected to the Internet? 19

    What Is Available on the Internet? 21

    How Do I Use Internet Resources? 22

2 The Various Parts of the Internet   **25**

File Transfers—Downloading with FTP 26

    What Are FTP Servers? 26

    What Are Anonymous FTP Servers? 27

Retrieving Information Using Gopher 31

    What Is Gopherspace? 32

    Locating Files Using Veronica 32

Locating Documents Using WAIS 33

Connecting to Host Resources Using Telnet 34

World Wide Web (WWW) 35

    What Are WWW Documents? 36

    Finding WWW Documents... 37

    Future Web Developments 38

Electronic Mail (E-Mail) 38
    Mailing Lists 39
    Getting E-Mail to Work for You 40
Interactive Internet Communications 41
    Internet Relay Chat 41
    Live Video Conferencing 42
    Interactive Games 42
    Live Voice 42
    Phone by Net 42
Internet Newsgroups (UseNet) 43
    What Is UseNet? 43
    Newsgroups and Topics 43
Commercial Online Services 44

3 Your Cyber Rights and Responsibilities: Law and Etiquette   47

Law on the Internet 48
First Amendment 48
A Few Common-Sense Limitations on Free Speech 51
The Slander and Libel Limitation 53
Are Computer Networks Information Distributors
    or Publishers? 54
    Obscenity Limitations on Free Expression 59
    U.S. v. Robert and Carleen Thomas 61
    Child Pornography Limitations 63
    To Inspect or Not to Inspect? 65
Pending Federal Legislation 67
Your Rights and Responsibilities of Privacy on the Internet 68
    E-Mail Privacy—Who Else Can Read Your E-Mail? 68
    Federal Computer Privacy Laws 69
    Cryptology, Secret Codes, and the Clipper Chip 71
Your Rights and Responsibilities of Copyright
    on the Internet 72
    The ABCs of Copyright Law 75
    Playboy Enterprises, Inc. v. Frena 80
    Scientology v. NETCOM (and just about everyone else) 81
Your Rights and Responsibilities of Fair Trade
    on the Internet 82
    When Is a Deal a Deal? 83
    Network Use Agreements 85
    Software License Agreements 86
Trademarks and Internet Domain Names 87
Your Rights and Responsibilities of Protection from
    Crime on the Internet 90
The Growing Problem of Computer Viruses 95

II Getting Connected   99

4 The Various Ways to Connect to the Internet: Which One Is Right for You?   101

Considerations on How to Connect 102
   Company Access 103
   Personal Access 104
   Domain Names 105
Services You Need 107
Direct Connection Through a Gateway 109
Connecting Through Another Gateway 110
Using an Internet Service Provider 110
   Telephone Line Options 110
   Protocol Options 112
   Service Options 114
   Frontdoors and Backdoors 116
Online Services 117
Other Ways to Connect 120
Important Considerations 121
   Services 121
   Availability 121
   Cost 122
   Access 122
   Software 123
   Security 123
   Technical Support 124

5 Connecting Through a LAN with Windows 95   125

A Brief Introduction to TCP/IP 126
Installing TCP/IP Support in Windows 95 127
Configuring the Windows 95 TCP/IP Protocol 129
   The IP Address Page 130
   The WINS Configuration Page 131
   The Gateway Page 132
   The DNS Configuration Page 133
   The Advanced and Bindings Pages 134
Testing Your TCP/IP Connection 135

6 Connecting to a PPP or SLIP Account with Windows 95   137

Installing Dial-Up Networking Support 138
Installing Network Protocols 139
Installing SLIP and Scripting Support 140
Setting Up a Dial-Up Networking Connection 141
Configuring Your Dial-Up Connection 145
Connecting to Your Internet Service Provider 147

Using Dial-Up Scripting 148
   Getting the Dial-Up Scripting Software 149
   Setting Up a Script for an Internet Connection.............. 149
   Using the Scripting Language 149
Connecting with Trumpet Winsock 151
   Upgrading to the Windows 95 Version of Trumpet 152
   Using Trumpet Winsock 153
The RoboDUN Dialing Software 153
Troubleshooting Your Dial-Up Connection 155
   If Your Modem Does Not Dial 155
   Your Modem Dials, but the Other Modem Doesn't
     Answer 155
   The Other Modem Answers, but the Connection Fails ... 156
   Internet Applications Don't Work 156

7 Other Software for Connecting to the Internet   157

Threshold Problems of Microsoft and Other TCP/IP Stacks 158
   Brute Force Solution to TCP/IP Stack Conflicts 158
   Brute Force Solution to Dialer Conflicts 159
   Generic Stack and Dialer Solution 159
Internet in a Box 160
   Installation and Configuration 160
   The Members of the Suite 167
NetManage's Chameleon Family 168
   Installation and Configuration 168
NetCruiser 172
Other Software 175

8 Setting Up an ISDN Connection   177

Digital and Analog 177
   Noise 179
   Attenuation 180
The Advantages of ISDN 182
   Telephone Systems 183
   Transmission 184
   Switching 185
   Narrowband ISDN 187
Ordering ISDN Service 194
Wiring for ISDN 196
Cautions When Wiring 197
ISDN Hardware 199
   External Terminal Adapters 199
   Internal Card Terminal Adapters 208
   Routers for ISDN 213
   Which Is Best? 214

9 Setting Up a High-Speed Internet Connection   215

Why a High-Speed Connection? 216
When ISDN Basic Rate Interface Isn't Enough 218
ISDN Primary Rate Interface (PRI) 218
The Hitch in Switched-56 219
Frame Relay 220
    Frame Relay and X.25 220
    How Frame Relay Works 221
T-Carrier Connections 224
The Highest of High-Speed Connections 226
The Internet on Cable TV, Dishes, Power Lines, and Pipes? ... 226
SONET and ATM 227
Digital Dilemmas: Which Type Do I Need? 229
The Cost of Being on the Internet 229

10 Connecting Through CompuServe   231

An Introduction to CompuServe 232
    An Overview of CompuServe and Its Pricing 232
    About CompuServe Information Manager for
    Windows (WinCIM 2.0.1) 233
CompuServe's Internet Gateway 234
Using Internet E-Mail 235
    Using WinCIM to Send E-Mail Messages 236
    Using WinCIM's Address Book to Store E-Mail
    Addresses 237
Joining Internet Mailing Lists 238
    Subscribing to (and Unsubscribing from)
    a Mailing List 238
    Posting to a Mailing List 240
Participating in UseNet Newsgroups 240
    Accessing Newsgroups Through WinCIM 241
    Accessing Newsgroups in Terminal Emulation Mode 246
Using File Transfer Protocol (FTP) 251
Telneting with WinCIM 253
Surfing the World Wide Web 254
    Downloading NetLauncher 255
    Installing NetLauncher 256
    Using CompuServe Mosaic 257
    Working with CompuServe's Hotlist 259
    Sending Mail with Your Web Browser 260
    Using UseNet News with Your Web Browser 260
    Searching Gopher Sites Through the Web 261
    Accessing FTP Sites Through the Web 261
Further Reference: CompuServe's Internet Forums 262
Looking Ahead: The Future According to CompuServe 262

11 Connecting Through America Online   263

What Is America Online? 264
    America Online for Windows 265
    America Online's Internet Gateway 266
Using Internet E-Mail 267
    Using America Online to Send E-Mail Messages 268
    Using America Online's Address Book to Store
      E-Mail Addresses 269
Joining Internet Mailing Lists 270
    Subscribing to (and Unsubscribing from)
      a Mailing List 270
    Posting to a Mailing List 272
Participating in UseNet Newsgroups 272
    Subscribing to Newsgroups 273
    Reading Newsgroup Messages 275
    Posting Newsgroup Articles 276
    Responding to Newsgroup Articles 277
Accessing Gopher and WAIS Databases 278
    Using Gopher 279
    Using Veronica 280
Using File Transfer Protocol (FTP) 281
Using the World Wide Web 283
Looking Ahead: The Future According to America Online 285

12 Connecting Through Prodigy   287

What Is Prodigy? 287
    What Services Are Offered? 289
    Pricing 289
Connecting to Prodigy 290
    Installing Prodigy 290
    Starting Prodigy 290
    Logging On 291
How Prodigy Is Organized 292
    The Bottom Line 294
    GoTo 294
Prodigy's Internet Services 296
    How to Get to the Internet Area 296
    Using the World Wide Web on Prodigy 297
Using Prodigy's World Wide Web Browser 297
    Home Page 298
    Your Own Home Page 298
    Speed Limits on the Information Highway 298
Using Gopher and FTP on Prodigy 299
    Gopher 299
    FTP 300
UseNet News on Prodigy 301
    Subscribing to UseNet Newsgroups 302
    Reading Newsgroup Messages 302

Posting to Newsgroups 303
Unreadable Messages 303
Internet Mail 305
Getting Mail from the Internet 305
Sending Mail on the Internet 305
Address Book 306
How to Get More Information on the Internet
Through Prodigy 306

13 Connecting Through Microsoft Network 309

What Is the Microsoft Network? 309
Basic Requirements for MSN 310
Setting Up Your Modem 311
Installing Plus! and the Internet Jumpstart Kit 313
Establishing Your MSN Account 315
Choosing an Access Method 318
Using the Internet with MSN 319
Getting On- and Offline with MSN 320
Using the Internet Explorer with MSN 321
Using Internet Mail with MSN 322
Using Internet UseNet Newsgroups with MSN 324

III Using Internet E-Mail 327

14 How Internet E-Mail Works 329

Simple Mail Transfer Protocol (SMTP) 330
X.400 and X.500 331
Finding Someone's E-Mail Address 332
Finger 333
WHOIS 334
Netfind 336
Knowbot Information Service 337
UseNet User List 338
Files 339
ASCII Format Only 339
File Compression 340
Legal Issues and E-Mail 343
Encryption 344
E-Mail Etiquette 345
Handling Unwanted E-Mail 346

15 Using Microsoft Exchange 349

What Makes Microsoft Exchange Unique? 350
Installing Microsoft Exchange 351
Where to Find Microsoft Exchange 351
Is Microsoft Exchange Installed Already? 352
Installing from the Windows 95 Installation
Disks or CD-ROM 353

Using Internet Mail 355
    Internet Mail Requirements 355
    Installing Internet Mail 356
The Quick Tour 359
    Starting and Exiting Microsoft Exchange 360
    The Toolbars 360
    The Mailbox Window 361
    The Message Window 362
Sending and Receiving Messages 362
    Sending a Message 363
    Adding People to Your Address Book 365
    Using the Personal Address Book 366
    Receiving Messages 367
    Viewing a Message 367
    Replying to a Message 368
    Forwarding a Message 369
Saving and Organizing Messages 369
    Creating Folders 370
    Moving and Copying Messages 371
Show Me the Really Cool Stuff! 372
    Configuring Basic Options 372
    General Options 372
    Read Options 373
    Send Options 375
    Delivery Options 375
Using Profiles 376
    Creating a New Profile 376
    Using Microsoft Exchange with More Than One User 376

16 Using Eudora   **379**

Downloading and Installing PC Eudora 380
Adapting Eudora for Several Users 382
Entering a Password 382
Configuring Eudora 383
Customizing Eudora 384
Creating Mail 385
    Making Nicknames 386
    Using Nicknames 387
Using the Quick Recipient List 387
    Removing a Recipient 388
    Creating a Signature 388
Saving Mail 389
    Editing Mail 389
    Working with In, Out, Trash, and Transfer 390
Sending Mail 391
    Attaching Files to Mail 392
    Queuing Messages 393

Retrieving Mail 394
Retrieving Mail with Attached Files 395
Creating Folders and Mailboxes 396
Rerouting Mail 397
Deleting Mail 398
Upgrading to Eudora 2.1.2 399

17 E-Mailing Outside the Internet and with Online Services   401

Direct and Indirect Service Providers 402
Direct Service Providers 402
Indirect Service Providers 403
Mail Message Contents 404
Messages to UUNET Users 405
Online Services 406
America Online 406
CompuServe 408
Delphi 409
GEnie 409
MCI Mail 410
Prodigy 411
The Microsoft Network 412
List of Services 413

18 Using Internet Mailing Lists   417

What Are Internet Mailing Lists? 418
Mastering a Mailing List 419
Working with LISTSERV Mailing Lists 420
Subscribing to and Unsubscribing from LISTSERV
Mailing Lists 421
Available Lists 423
Using Other LISTSERV Commands 426
Sending Messages to a LISTSERV Mailing List 428
LISTSERV Miscellany 429
Using Majordomo Mailing Lists 430
Sending Majordomo Commands 430
Getting Majordomo Help 430
Subscribing to and Unsubscribing from
Majordomo Lists 431
Finding Majordomo Lists 431
Majordomo Miscellany 432
Accessing Private or Other Mailing Lists 432
Understanding Different Mailing List Types 433
Working with Moderated and Unmoderated Lists 433
Working with Digestified and Undigestified Lists 433
Using Netiquette 433
Understanding Bandwidth or Signal-to-Noise Ratio 434
Avoiding Flame Wars 435

Changing Your E-Mail Address or Going on Vacation 435
Anonymous Mailing Services 436
Internet Mailing Lists and UseNet 437

19 Encoding and Decoding Files 439

What Is File Encoding/Decoding, and Why Is It Needed? 440
What Types of Encoding and Decoding Are There? 441
File Encoding and Decoding with Microsoft Exchange
    and Eudora 441
Sending Encoded Files Using Microsoft Exchange 442
Sending Encoded Files Using Eudora 444
Recognizing Different Encoding Schemes 445
Encoding and Decoding Files from Windows 95 446
Installing Wincode 447
Using Wincode to Encode a File 449
Using Wincode to Decode a File 451
Other Features of Wincode 452
File Encoding and Decoding on UseNet 453
Recognizing Macintosh BINHEX 453

IV The World Wide Web 455

20 How the World Wide Web Works 457

History of the WWW 457
Important WWW Concepts 458
Browsers 458
Hypertext (and Hypermedia) 459
HTML 460
Links 461
URLs 463
HTTP 465
Home Pages 465
Clients and Servers 466
Future Developments on the Web 466
VRML 466
Live Communications 466
Built-In Multimedia 467
Learning More about WWW 467
UseNet Newsgroups 467
Electronic Mailing Lists 468
WWW Interactive Talk 470
The WWW Itself 470
Books 471

21 **Using Microsoft Internet Explorer** 473

Setting Up Internet Explorer 473
    Installing Internet Explorer from the Plus! Pack 474
    Installing Internet Explorer without the Plus! Pack 475
Starting and Configuring Internet Explorer 475
    Understanding the Internet Explorer Display 476
    Configuring Internet Explorer 478
Using the Internet Explorer Interface 482
    Using Links to Move Between Documents 483
    Opening URLs Directly 483
    Using the History List 484
    Using the Favorites List 486
Mailing, Saving, and Printing Documents 487
Reading UseNet News with Internet Explorer 488
Viewing Multimedia Files with Internet Explorer 491
    Viewing Graphics Images with Internet Explorer 492
    Viewing Animations with Internet Explorer 492
    Playing Background Sounds with Internet Explorer 493
    Viewing VRML Sites with Internet Explorer 493
Other Internet Explorer Features 494

22 **Using Netscape** 497

Getting Netscape Up and Running 497
    Will Your Computer Run Netscape? 497
    Where to Get Netscape 498
    Obtaining Auxiliary Software for Netscape 500
Installing Netscape on Your System 500
Using the Netscape Interface 502
    Starting Netscape 502
    The Netscape Window 502
    What Is a Home Page? 505
    Telling Netscape What Home Page to Load 505
Moving Between Documents 507
    Using Links to Move Between Documents 507
    Customizing the Hyperlink Indicators 508
    Moving Backward and Forward 509
    Using URLs to Move Between Documents 510
    Opening Multiple Documents 510
    Caching Documents 510
    Setting Netscape's Color Scheme 511
    What You See When a Document Is Loaded 512
    Looking for Information in a Document 515
    Saving Documents 516
    Printing Documents 517
    Customizing the Displayed Window Areas 517

Working with Local Files 518
Effective Browsing Techniques 519
   How to Keep Track of Where You've Been 519
   How to Get Where You Were 520
Create Lists of Your Favorite URLs 522
   Setting Your Current Bookmark File 522
   Creating and Editing Bookmarks 523
   Using Bookmarks 525
   Sharing Bookmarks 525
Security 526
Plug-In Applications 528
   RealAudio 528
   Shockwave 530
   Acrobat Amber 530
   WebFX 532
Other Internet-Related Features 533
   Internet E-Mail 533
   Reading UseNet Newsgroups 535
   Java Compatibility 536

23 Using Mosaic   **539**

Getting Mosaic for Windows Running 539
   Can Your Computer System Run Mosaic
     for Windows? 540
   Where to Get Mosaic for Windows.................................. 541
Installing the Mosaic for Windows 95 Software 542
Using the Mosaic Interface 543
   Starting Mosaic.. 543
   What Is a Home Page? 544
   The Mosaic Window 544
Moving Between Documents 547
   Moving Between Documents Using Links 547
   Moving Backward and Forward 548
   Moving Between Documents Using URLs 550
   What You See When a Document Is Loading 550
   Looking for Information in a Document...................... 551
   Saving Documents 552
   Printing Documents 553
Customizing Your Mosaic Window 553
   Customizing the Hyperlink Indicators in Windows........ 554
   Document Customization.................................... 555
   Window Customization 555
   Customizing the Displayed Fonts in Windows 556
Viewing Multimedia Files 558
Working with Local Files 558
Effective Browsing Techniques 559
   How to Keep Track of Where You've Been 559
   How to Get Where You Were 560

Using Advanced Hotlist Manager to Track URLs 562
    Creating a New Folder 563
    Adding Items to a Folder 564
    Adding the Current Document to the Current Folder 565
    Adding the URLs from the Current Document
        to Your Hotlist 565
    Editing Hotlists 565
    Creating a New Hotlist 567
    Saving Your Hotlists 567
Quick Access to Your Favorite URLs 568
    Loading a Hotlist 568
    Accessing Items in a Hotlist 568
    Sharing Hotlists 570
    Using Built-In Hotlists 570
Other Internet-Related Features 571
    Internet E-Mail 571
    Collaborative Sessions 572
    Reading UseNet Newsgroups 572
Problems that Occur While Navigating the WWW 574
    User Errors 574
    Network Errors 575

24 Using Helper Apps   577

Read, Listen, and Watch: Multimedia Is Here 578
    Graphics Galore: Images on the Web 578
    Let's Hear It—How to Enable Sound 580
    Lights, Camera, Action—How to Enable Movies 581
    MIME—A Multimedia Standard 582
Finding and Installing Multimedia Viewers 583
    Retrieving Multimedia Viewers 583
    Installing Multimedia Viewers 584
    Popular Multimedia Viewers 585
Viewing Multimedia Files from Internet Explorer 587
Viewing Multimedia Files from Netscape 588
    Defining Helper Applications for Recognized
        MIME Types 588
    Adding a New MIME Type 590
    Loading a File with an Unknown Viewer 590
    Specifying Netscape's Temporary Directory 592
Viewing Multimedia Files from Mosaic 592
    Configuring Mosaic to Use Viewers 593
    Configuring Application Viewers 594
Using Viewers 595

25 Planning Your Own WWW Home Pages   597

Getting Started: Basic Decisions 597
    Planning for Your Audience 601
    Housing Your Home Page 603

What Will It Cost? 605
  Storage Charge 606
  Throughput Charge 607
File versus HTTP Storage Mechanisms 607
Text versus Graphic Browsers 608
Home Page Options 609
  Simple Text 609
  Links 610
  Inline Images 611
  Sound 613
  Forms 614
  Pictures, Movies, and Binaries 614
  Custom Options 615
What Goes into a Good Home Page 615
Generating and Keeping Interest 617
HTML Editors and Filters 618
  Editors 618
  Filters 619
  Where to Find Editors 620
  Pros and Cons 620

26 Using HTML to Build Your Home Page   621

HTML Basics 622
  How HTML Works: An Overview 622
  The HTML Element 622
  How HTML Deals with Spaces and Carriage Returns 624
  Reserved Words in HTML 625
  File Extensions and HTML 627
  URL Naming Convention 627
  HTML Document Organization 630
HTML Elements 630
  Elements that Effect Text Size 630
  Elements that Affect Text Positioning 631
  Elements that Effect Text Emphasis 633
  Elements that Insert Inline Images 634
  Elements that Insert Lists and Indentation 636
  Elements that Are Anchors and Links............................ 637
  Browser Control Elements 640
  Combining Elements 641
Creating a Simple Home Page 642
Enhancing Your Page by Creating Interactive Forms 644
  How Forms Are Processed 645
  The Basic Form Element.. 645
  The INPUT Element 647
  Using the TEXTAREA Element 656
  Using the SELECT Element to Create a List 658
  Creating a Complete Form 661

Understanding How Forms Are Submitted 663
A Brief Look at CGI-bin 665
Conclusion 666

27 Using Microsoft Internet Assistant to Build Web Pages   667

What Is Internet Assistant? 667
    Internet Assistant Requirements 668
    The Correct Version of Word 669
Downloading and Installing Internet Assistant 669
    Where to Find Internet Assistant 669
    Installing Internet Assistant 671
Using Internet Assistant to Browse the Web 672
    Opening a Web Document 673
    Surfing the Net 673
Using Internet Assistant to Build Web Pages 677
    A Review of HTML 678
    Using the Word Styles to Create HTML Formatting
        Codes 679
    Inserting a Hyperlink 680
    Adding Graphics 684
    Creating Rules 686
    Inserting Unsupported HTML Code 687
Creating Forms 688
    Creating Form Fields 689
    Using CGI Programs 693
Web Pages and Word Documents 694
    Building a Web Page from an Existing Page 694
    Building Web Pages from Word Documents 695
    Creating a Word Document from a Web Page 697

28 Using Netscape Navigator Gold and HotDog to Create Web Pages   699

Getting to Know Netscape Navigator Gold 699
Downloading and Installing Netscape Navigator Gold 702
Getting to Know HotDog 703
Installing HotDog 705
Reviewing HTML Basics 709
    HEAD, TITLE, and BODY Elements 710
    Heading Levels 710
    Text Entry and Formatting 710
    Text Attributes 711
    Separators and Graphics 711
    Indented Text and Lists 713
    Anchors 714
Creating Advanced Pages 715
    Adding Tables 715

Adding Forms 717
Setting Page Colors and Adding Background Graphics ... 718
Mailto Links 719
Testing and Publishing Your Page in HotDog 720
Configuring a Viewer and Previewing Your Page 720
Publishing the Page 721

29 New Web Technologies   723

SGML on the Web 724
What Are SGML and HTML? 724
What Is a DTD? 725
The Benefits of SGML 725
SGML Viewer: Panorama FREE and Panorama Pro 725
Installing Panorama FREE 726
SGML Example versus HTML Example 728
Other SGML Applications 730
Enhancing Your Web Browser On-the-Fly 731
What Is Java? 731
A Java Example 732
What Is Hyper-G? 733
VRML: The WWW in Three Dimensions 733
What Is VRML? 734
Installing WebFX, a VRML Plug-In for Netscape 734
Configuring WebFX 735
Example VRML World on the World Wide Web 735
VRML Resources on the Internet 738
Video Applications on the Web 739
Installing Shockwave 739
Using Shockwave 740
Audio Applications on the Web 741
Installing RealAudio 741
Using RealAudio 742
Keeping Up with New Technology 743

V UseNet Newsgroups   747

30 How UseNet Works   749

What Is UseNet? 750
A Very Brief History of UseNet 751
UseNet Behavior 752
Newsgroup Names 752
New and Bogus Newsgroups 755
Moderated Newsgroups 755
Threads 756
What Do I Need to Know? 756
Getting Started in a Newsgroup 757

Posting Articles 758
   Signatures 760
   Anonymous Postings 762
   Cross-Posting 763
   Who Gets Your Article?—Distribution 763
   Replying to an Article 764
   Copyrights 764
   Posting Files 765
Filtering and Searching for News 765
   News Filtering 766
   News Searching 767
Netiquette 770
   Abbreviations 771
   Flames 771
   Shouting 772
   Surfing and Lurking 772
   Smileys 773
Writing Postings: A Checklist 773

31 Using NewsXpress   **775**

Why Use NewsXpress? 775
Setting Up 776
   Installing the Software 776
   Connecting to the News Server 778
   Configuring NewsXpress 778
   Connecting to UseNet 779
Retrieving Newsgroup Names 780
Subscribing to and Unsubscribing from Newsgroups 780
Selecting and Reading Articles 783
Saving and Replying to Articles and Posting Your Own 785
   Saving Articles 785
   E-Mail Options 786
   UseNet Options 787
Posting and Retrieving Non-Text Information 788

32 Using Agent   **791**

Getting and Installing Agent 792
Starting and Configuring Agent 792
   Setting Agent Preferences 794
   Setting Up Signatures in Agent 800
   Setting Up Inbound E-Mail 801
   Setting Up Your Fonts 803
   Setting Up Your Window Layout 803
   Setting Group Options 804
Subscribing to and Unsubscribing from Newsgroups 805
Reading Articles in Newsgroups 806
Following Article Threads 808
Posting Articles 810

Extracting Files from Articles 811
Managing E-Mail 812
    Sending New E-Mail Messages 812
    Reading E-Mail Messages............................... 813

VI Locating and Retrieving Information 817

33 Using Telnet 819

What Is Telnet? 819
Why Use Telnet? 820
Some Quick Background Information 821
    What's a VT100? Or an ANSI? Or a TTY? 821
    What to Expect When You Connect 822
    A Brief Word about Addresses..................... 823
Running the Telnet Program from a Command-Line
    Account 825
    Connecting to a Remote Computer Using Telnet 826
    A Second Way of Starting Telnet from a
        Command-Line Account 827
    Using UNIX to Do Two (or More) Things at Once 828
    Closing a Connection to a Remote Computer 829
    Running Out of Time 829
    Connecting to a Telnet Address with a Port 829
    Telnetting for Fun 830
Using Telnet on a SLIP/PPP Account 831
    Using Windows 95 Telnet 831
Using Telnet Through a Local Area Network (LAN) 834
Don't Be Afraid to Ask for Help 835

34 Using FTP and Popular FTP Programs 837

What Is FTP? 837
    What Are Client/Server Services? 838
    Anonymous FTP 838
    Using FTP from the Command Line 839
    Windows-Based FTP Clients.......................... 841
    Locating Files 841
    Downloading and Uploading Files 842
Installing WS_FTP32 843
Using WS_FTP 844
    Connecting to a Host 844
    Working in Directories................................. 848
    Customizing WS_FTP 855
    Exiting WS_FTP 865

35 Using Gopher and Popular Gopher Programs 867

What Is Gopher? 867
Why Use Gopher? 868

Understanding Gopher Terminology 869
    What Is Gopher+? 869
Using HGopher 870
    Installing HGopher 870
    Configuring HGopher 872
    Navigating with HGopher 873
    Transferring Files with HGopher 876
    Marking the Gopher Trail with Bookmarks 878
    Using Other HGopher Features 883
Searching Gopherspace with Veronica 888
    What Is Veronica? 888
    Using Veronica to Search Gopherspace 889
    What Is Jughead? 891
    Searching with Jughead 892
Sites of Interest: The Best of Gopher 895

36 Using WAIS   **897**

Using WinWAIS 898
    Installing WinWAIS 899
Searching for WAIS Information 900
    Using Relevance Feedback 902
    Saving Information to the Clipboard 903
    What the WAIS Finds Tell You 903
Using WAIS Manager 3.1 904
    Installing WAIS Manager 3.1 904
    Searching with WAIS Manager 3.1 905
    Using Relevance Feedback 906
    Saving WAIS Information 907
    Saving Queries for Future Use 907
    Using Viewers 907
    WAIS Searches with E-Mail 908

37 Searching on the Internet   **911**

Available Information 912
What Are Search Engines? 912
    Popular Web Search Engines 913
Using Lycos 915
Using WebCrawler 919
Using Yahoo! 922
    Gathering Information with Telnet 925
Using WSArchie 927
    Archie 927
    Setting Up WSArchie to Work with WS_FTP 929
    Doing a Search 930
    Getting the Results 932
    Retrieving Files 935
    Setting Your Default Search Parameters 936
    Exiting WSArchie 937
Gopher 937

VII Interactive Communications   939

38 How IRC Works   941

The Basics of IRC 941
    What Is the Purpose of IRC? 942
    History of IRC 942
How Internet Relay Chat Works 943
    IRC Clients 943
    IRC Servers 944
    Telneting to IRC 945
    Net Splits 946
Talking on IRC 947
    Nicknames 947
    IRC Channels 947
The Undernet 948
Other Sources of Information on IRC 948

39 Using mIRC and Netscape Chat   949

Why Use mIRC or Netscape Chat? 950
Installing mIRC 950
Setting Up mIRC 951
Accessing the IRC Using mIRC 953
    Connecting to IRC 953
    Joining the Discussion 953
    Private Conversations 955
    A Little More Privacy Using DCC 957
Setting mIRC Options 959
    General Options 959
    Fonts 963
    Popup Menus 964
Netscape Chat and IRC 964
    Installing Chat 965
    Connecting to IRC Using Chat 965
    Netscape Chat versus mIRC 969

40 Talking on the Net: Internet Phone and
Internet Voice Chat   971

Using the Internet as a "Phone" 971
System Requirements 972
    Your Sound Card 973
    Your Modem 975
Internet Telephone Software 976
The Internet Phone 977
    Installation and Configuration 978
    Making a Call 981
Digiphone 983
    Installation and Configuration 984
    Making a Call 986

Internet Global Phone 987
   Speak Freely 987
   WebTalk 988
   WebPhone 988
   PowWow 989
   Cyberphone 990
   TS Intercom 991
Real-Time Audio Player Programs 992
TrueSpeech 992
Changes Voice Communication Is Making on the Net 993
The Future 994

41 Video Conferencing on the Net   995

Communications and Video Conferencing 995
The History of Video Conferencing 996
The Advantages of Video Conferencing 997
The Problem of Bandwidth 998
Hardware for Video Conferencing 999
   Your Computer 999
   Video Capture Board 1000
   Camera 1000
   Sound Card 1001
   Monitor 1001
CU-SeeMe: A "Free" Video Conferencing Program 1002
   Installation 1003
   Configuration 1004
   Operation 1005
   Limitations 1008
The Future of Video Conferencing 1008
   The MBONE 1008
   The Virtual Meeting Room 1009
   Holographic Video Conferencing 1009
What to Do 1009

42 Games on the Net: MUDs, MOOs, and MUSHes   1011

What Are MUDs? 1012
   A History of MUDs 1013
   Types of MUDs 1013
   How MUDs Work 1013
MUD Culture 1015
   MUD Jargon 1015
   MUD Clients for Windows 95 1017
   Joining a MUD 1018
   Getting Help 1020
   Exploring the MUD 1020
   Dealing with Other Users 1021
   Objects, Possessions, and Money 1022
   Combat 1023

Leaving the MUD 1023
Advanced Concepts 1024
More Information on MUDs 1024
Netrek 1024
How Netrek Works 1025
Netrek on Windows 95 1025
Joining a Game 1026
Getting Killed 1027
More Information on Netrek 1028
DOOM and Beyond 1028
Stars! 1028
More Information on Online Games 1030

VIII   Internet Security   1031

43 Privacy and Security on the Net   1033

Internet Security Overview 1033
Classic Hacking Methods 1034
Password Attacks 1034
Data Interception 1035
Keyboard Logging 1036
Firewalls 1036
Password Security 1037
Your Risk 1038
Risks from Common Internet Utilities 1039
World Wide Web 1039
FTP 1041
Gopher 1041
Telnet 1042
Mail 1042
Keeping Your Communications Private 1042
For the Truly Paranoid 1043
Encryption Programs 1044
Cypher Keys 1044
Public Key 1045
PGP 1045
WINPGP4 1046
Network Security 1050
NetWare 1052

44 Protecting Yourself from Viruses   1053

What Is a Virus? 1054
Program Infectors 1054
Boot Sector Infectors 1055
Macro Viruses 1055
What a Virus Is Not 1056

A History Lesson—The Virus Wars 1057
    War Games 1058
    Apocalypse Now 1058
    Armageddon 1059
    Hype or Help? 1059
Representing the Defense 1060
    Known Virus Scanning 1060
    Validity Checks 1060
    Behavior Blockers 1061
When You're at Risk 1061
What to Do When the Worst Happens 1062
    Back Up! 1062
    Back Up!! 1063
    Back Up!!! 1063
Restoring a Virus-Infected Computer 1063
Windows 95 and Computer Viruses 1064
    Boot Sector Self Check 1064
    File Viruses under Windows 95 1065
Protecting Your Computer 1066
    Which Anti-Virus Programs Are Best? 1067
    Getting Reliable Virus Information 1068
    A Couple of Recommendations 1068

IX NetReference: Hot Internet Sites   1071

45 Top Internet Mailing Lists   1073

Mailing Lists about the Internet 1074
Mailing Lists about Computers and Software 1081
Where to Find More Mailing Lists 1089

46 Top World Wide Web Sites   1091

Computer Systems 1091
Component and Peripheral Hardware 1094
Computer Productivity Software 1100
Fun and Games 1105
Where to Buy Computer Stuff Online 1109
Lots of Free (or Really Inexpensive) Software 1112
Web Browsers, Servers, and Add-Ons 1116
HTML Creation 1120
Java, VRML, and RealAudio Heat Up the Net 1121
Combo Deals: Web Browsers, E-Mail Readers,
    and the Kitchen Sink Rolled into One 1125
Other Internet Software 1127
Internet Service Providers 1129
Online Services 1130
Searches and Directories 1131
The Best of the Rest 1136

47 Top FTP Sites   **1139**

    Collections of Free Software 1139
    Internet Software and Information 1144
    Commercial Software and Computer Hardware 1148
    Other Sites of Interest 1152
    FTP Lists and Directories 1153

48 Top UseNet Newsgroups   **1155**

    A Look at Some Popular Groups 1156
    UseNet News and Software Groups 1160
    General Computing Issues 1162
    Internet Services and Software 1163
    Computer Hardware 1167
    Computer Software 1169
    Miscellaneous Computing Topics 1172
    Where to Find More Groups 1173
        Use Your Newsreader Group List 1173
        Look at David Lawrence's Lists of Groups 1173
        If All Else Fails... 1174

49 Top Gopher Sites   **1175**

    Gopher Sites that Correspond to Servers
       in Other Chapters 1175
    Other Gophers 1176

X Using NetCD95   **1179**

50 Installing and Using NetCD95   **1181**

    All-in-One Suites 1183
    E-Mail 1184
    UseNet News 1184
    FTP and Archie 1184
    World Wide Web 1184
    HTML Editors 1185
    Multimedia Editors and Viewers 1186
    IRC 1186
    Utilities and Other Software 1187
    Internet Documents 1187

XI Appendixes   1189

A Country Codes   1191

B Time Zone Code Table   1199

C Vendor Contacts for Selected Internet
Software and Services   1205

Internet Applications 1205
Internet Service Providers 1210
Internet Connections Hardware and Software 1211

D Glossary   1219

Index   1239

Introduction

In the past several years, the Internet has exploded on the computer scene as a topic of national interest. What used to be a computer network reserved for a select few scientists, government workers, and educational institutions has become available to corporations—large and small—and even individual users.

If you bought, or are considering buying, *Special Edition Using the Internet with Windows 95,* chances are you want to know what the Internet is all about and how to access all the powerful capabilities it promises to bring to your computer. (You can retrieve files, search for information, exchange e-mail, keep up-to-date on current events, and chat with other users anywhere in the world.)

We know the Internet can be a frustrating place for newcomers. There is so much information out there, but how can you find it and use it? The Internet was originally designed by academic and research scientists, and wasn't particularly easy to understand for the casual computer user.

As the Internet opened up to commercial and private accounts, people who had heard about the great resources available on the Internet discovered that you needed to be a rocket scientist to find and use those resources. So, some of the almost-rocket scientists who had access to the Internet began designing easy-to-use interfaces to those useful but cryptic Internet resources like FTP, Gopher, WAIS, and Telnet. These resources are great, but what's really propelled the Internet into popularity is the World Wide Web, a service that lets you access linked documents that incorporate graphics, sound, and other media along with text.

Now, almost anyone can begin using the Internet within hours of being connected. If you have a PC or other computer that has a windowing environment, getting access to Internet resources is as easy as pointing and clicking.

The incredible network with the cryptic interfaces is now a set of interconnected roadways easily accessible to almost anyone.

The Internet and all its resources are explored in more depth in the body of this book. Que's NetCD95 has lots of useful software and information to help get you up-and-running quickly on the Information Superhighway.

What's Changed in This Edition

A year has gone by since the last edition of this book, and the Internet phenomenon just keeps on growing. More and more individuals and companies are connecting to the Net. Internet providers are not only in the major cities, but are also moving into the smaller markets now, giving almost everyone the option of accessing the Net, often at less than the cost of cable TV.

On top of that, online services like America Online, CompuServe, and Prodigy have opened the floodgates to the Internet. Users of these services are quickly becoming a large part of the Net's social fabric. You can now easily access almost all the available Internet services from the commercial online services.

Last year, shareware offered the primary source of software interfaces for the Internet. A few commercial companies were offering beta versions of their products for users to try out. Now that the Internet is becoming more mainstream, there are real products that give you supported Internet software. You can buy complete packages of Internet interfaces, or you can get low-cost, easy-to-use interfaces for individual Internet services from different sources. (And there's still lots of good shareware out there.)

One of the biggest changes in the last year, however, was the release of Windows 95. With previous versions of Windows, it could be tricky getting your computer to talk to the Internet and use the 32-bit applications that were needed to use some of the Internet services. Now, Windows 95 has the Internet communications protocols built right in to the operating system—so you don't need to add anything to get your computer connected to the Internet on a network or over the phone. And because Windows 95 is a 32-bit operating system, the 32-bit applications run without any additional software.

Because Windows 95 has made it even easier to connect to the Internet and use the full power of your computer, this edition of the book focuses on the applications that take advantage of Windows 95. Many of the applications that were discussed in the last edition, like Mosaic and Netscape, work even better under Windows 95. And, of course, the application developers are constantly adding new features to their Internet interfaces, so you'll learn about all the great new things you can do with the latest versions of your favorite interfaces.

Another thing you'll notice about this edition is the expanded coverage of World Wide Web information. With tens of thousands of Web sites, both commercial and personal, the amount of information you can find is mind-boggling. We've devoted chapters to the most popular Web browsers, and the search tools that let you find the Web sites that interest you. In addition, most Internet providers let you put your own pages out on the Web. You can pay someone to design a Web page for you, but it's not too difficult to design one of your own. So we've included discussion of good Web page design, an explanation of HTML—the language of Web pages, and several of the most popular tools you can use to help you quickly put together your Web page.

Like the last edition, we've included over 100 pages that list the best Internet sites available, with additional long lists of resources on NetCD95. With this approach, you get the best information about how to use the Internet, the best places to visit, and the best things to do. If you need a complete list of mailing lists or newsgroups, you can look at the unabridged lists on NetCD95—it's really the best of both worlds.

What This Book Is

This book is intended to provide a comprehensive overview of the Internet. All of the available Internet services are discussed, along with popular interfaces to the services.

The Internet has a great variety of resources; this book tells you the best way to find the resources of most use to you. Here is a glimpse of the contents of the book, with short descriptions of each part:

- Part I, "About the Internet," provides a brief history of the Internet and an overview of Internet services. The Internet services discussed in this book are introduced here.

- Part II, "Getting Connected," tells you how to get connected to the Internet. This part discusses the different types of Internet accounts, along with the pros and cons of using each particular type of Internet service provider.

- Part III, "Using Internet E-Mail," shows you how to use Internet e-mail, the service that lets you communicate with more than 40 million people around the world. Learn about the most popular Internet mail programs and how to connect your business e-mail system to the Internet.

- Part IV, "The World Wide Web," discusses the World Wide Web, one of the most exciting Internet services yet developed. If you want to learn the easiest way to interface with the Internet, don't miss this section.

- Part V, "UseNet Newsgroups," provides information about the largest collection of discussion groups in cyberspace. You can talk to people all over the world about almost any subject you can imagine.

- Part VI, "Locating and Retrieving Information," delves into the Internet's wealth of information. Learn how to look for the information of interest to you and get it to your computer.

- Part VII, "Interactive Communications," talks about how the Internet connects you to people all over the world—live. Learn how to use Internet Relay Chat and WebChat to have real-time online conferences with others who have the same interests. See how you can use the Net to phone home and send live video.

- Part VIII, "Internet Security," discusses how the Internet's capability to provide access to a tremendous amount of information has created security issues. The Internet was designed originally as an academic/ research network, and security measures were not part of its initial development. Learn about security problems you may encounter, and what you can do to make your data and communications safe.

- Part IX, "NetReference: Hot Internet Sites," provides addresses and descriptions of the most interesting, unique, and useful Internet sites. These chapters direct you to the best of the best.

- Part X, "Using NetCD95," tells you how to use NetCD95, which comes with this book. This CD contains almost everything you need to get started on the Internet—communications programs, interfaces to the most useful Internet services (FTP, Gopher, Telnet, WWW), lists of Internet resources, and software to make your Internet services more useful. (See the next section for more details about NetCD95.)

NetCD95—Your Free Source for Internet Software

What is NetCD95? If you turn to the inside back cover of the book, you'll find Que's NetCD95. It's designed to provide you with all the software and documentation that you need to get started on the road to Internet success.

You'll find a wide variety of software for use with the Internet on NetCD95. We've spent hours online over the past few months to gather the best freeware, shareware, and public domain software available. Hopefully, these efforts will save you online time and money.

In addition to software that is available on the Net, we've made special arrangements to bring you commercial products that aren't available for downloading on the Net. Included is an enhanced version of Mosaic, the software to connect to several major Internet service providers, and some special versions of shareware that were tweaked especially for this book. In some cases, this software can't be obtained for free anywhere other than on NetCD95. In other cases, it may be free, but not easy to get.

Finally, we've included a large collection of useful documents about the Internet. You'll find RFCs, STDs, and FYIs on NetCD. We've also included lists of service providers, some selected FAQs, and other documents of special interest.

Conventions Used in This Book

This book uses various conventions designed to make it easier to use. That way, you can quickly and easily learn to use the Internet and locate the Internet resources you want.

With most programs, you can use the mouse or keyboard to perform operations. The keyboard procedures may include shortcut key combinations or *mnemonic* keys. In this book, key combinations are joined with plus signs (+). For example, Ctrl+X means hold down the Ctrl key and press the X key (then release both keys). Some menu and dialog box options have underlined or highlighted characters that indicate mnemonic keys. To choose such an option using the mnemonic key, you press the Alt key plus the indicated mnemonic key. In this book, mnemonic keys are underlined: for example, File.

The book uses several other typeface enhancements to indicate special text, as indicated in the following table.

Typeface	Meaning
Italic	Italic is used to indicate variables in commands or addresses, and terms used for the first time.
Bold	Bold is used for text you type and to indicate actual addresses for Internet sites, newsgroups, mailing lists, WWW pages, and more. (Don't worry, all these terms are explained in chapter 2, "The Various Parts of the Internet.")
`monospace`	This special type is used for commands (such as the DOS COPY or UNIX cp command). It is also used to indicate text that appears on-screen (such as a `File does not exist` error alert).

Tip

Tips suggest easier or alternative methods of executing a procedure.

Note

Notes provide additional information that may help you avoid problems or offer advice or general information related to the topic at hand.

Caution

Cautions warn you of hazardous procedures and situations that can lead to unexpected or unpredictable results, including data loss or system damage.

Troubleshooting

Troubleshooting sections anticipate common problems...

...and then provide you with practical suggestions for solving those problems.

▶ See "Section Title," p. xx

Marginal cross-references direct you to related information in other parts of the book. Right-facing triangles indicate later chapters, and left-facing triangles point you back to information earlier in the book.

You'll also see the NetCD95 icon in the margins throughout the book indicating that the text is discussing software or a document on the NetCD95.

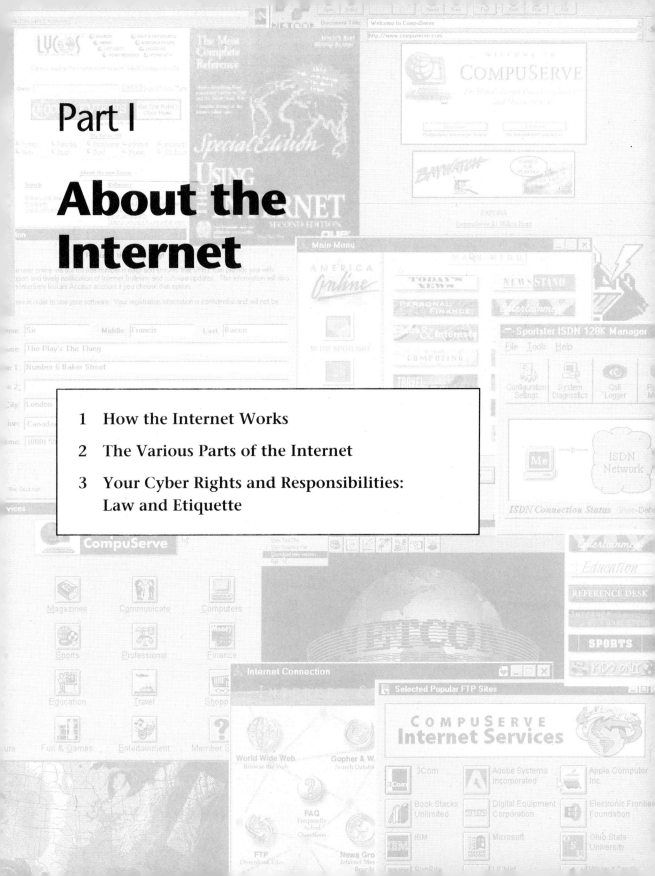

Part I

About the Internet

1   How the Internet Works

2   The Various Parts of the Internet

3   Your Cyber Rights and Responsibilities:
    Law and Etiquette

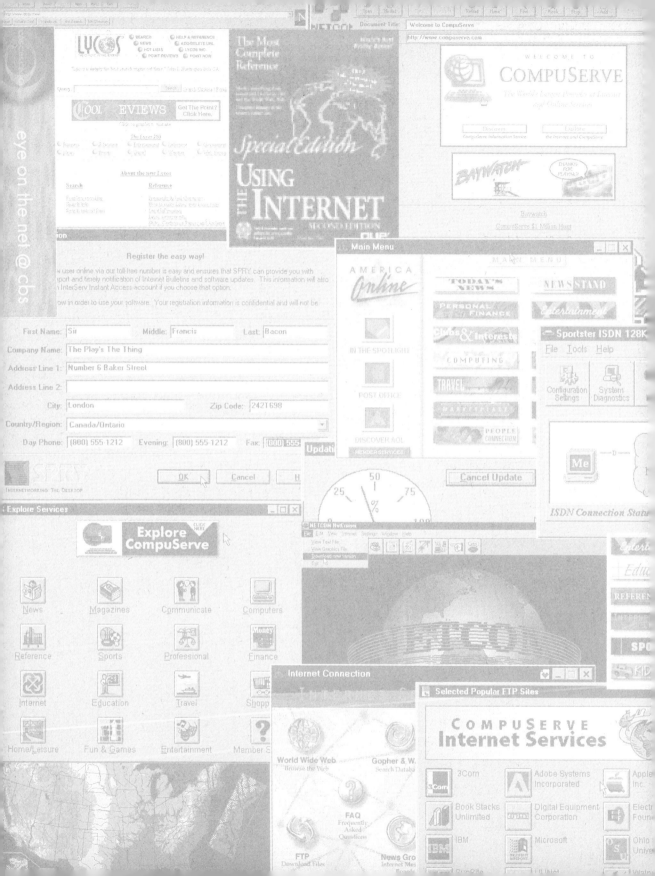

CHAPTER 1

How the Internet Works

The use of remote computer resources is as common today as the use of type-writers was 20 years ago. There are commercial online services, such as CompuServe and Prodigy; there are automatic teller machines that communi-cate with banks in other states; and there are companies with nationwide (or even worldwide) offices that transfer information between these offices al-most instantaneously. What is common to all of these resources is that they involve accessing a *network*, communicating over long-distance lines (often phone lines) to enable remote computers and terminals to send information back and forth.

The Internet is the oldest long-distance network in the country, if not the world. Rather than limiting remote computing to terminals accessing a cen-tral computing site (as the online services of today do), the Internet provides a way for remote computer centers to communicate and share services and resources.

This chapter discusses the history and growth of the Internet, including the following topics:

- A brief history of the Internet
- The culture of the Internet
- The growth of the Internet
- An overview of how to use the Internet

A Brief History of the Internet

Almost as soon as computers were developed, the need to transfer informa-tion between machines became apparent. Initially, this was done by writing the information to an intermediate medium (such as magnetic tape or punched cards) and physically carrying that medium to the new machine.

In the early 1960s, computer scientists across the country began exploring ways of directly connecting remote computers and their users. In the mid-to-late 60s, the United States government began to realize the impact computers would have on education and military research and development. So, the government decided to fund an experimental network that would enable remote research and development sites to exchange information. This network, funded by the U.S. Advanced Research Projects Agency, was christened the *ARPANET*.

The Development of the ARPANET

One of the main goals of the ARPANET research was to develop a network on which communications would not be seriously impaired if physical sections of the network were lost. Also, the network needed to allow the addition and removal of new nodes with minimal impact, and allow computers of many different types to communicate easily.

▶ See "A Brief Introduction to TCP/IP," p. 126

One of the major impacts of the ARPANET research, and the one that led to today's Internet, was the development of the *TCP/IP* (Transmission Control Protocol/Internet Protocol) *network protocol*, the language that computers connected to the network use to talk to one another. During the 1970s, TCP/IP became the standard network protocol for the ARPANET. Also during this time, the government began encouraging the educational community to take advantage of the ARPANET. The increasing number of users led to the development of many of the services available on the Internet today, including electronic mail (e-mail), file transfer (FTP), and remote login (Telnet).

The Structure of the Internet

During the early 1980s, all the interconnected research networks were converted to the TCP/IP protocol, and the ARPANET became the *backbone* (the physical connection between the major sites) of the new Internet, which comprised all TCP/IP-based networks connected to the ARPANET. This conversion to TCP/IP was completed by the end of 1983—and the Internet was born.

When the Internet first came into existence in the early 80s, there were only 213 registered *hosts* (computers that provided services) connected to the network. By February of 1986, there were 2,308 hosts. Today, the Internet is undergoing tremendous growth, with over 5 million hosts connected worldwide.

Internet Administration

The Internet is not "owned" by anyone, in the usual sense of the word. It is simply a collection of networks that communicate with each other. Until recently, the Internet backbone in the U.S. was managed by the National Science Foundation (*NSF*); however, now the infrastructure of the Internet is completely commercial. There are regional and international segments of the network that have their own funding and administration.

Any network connected to the Internet agrees to the decisions and standards set forth by the Internet Architecture Board (*IAB*). Anyone who is willing to help may participate in the process of devising and setting standards. The IAB administrates several committees that provide technical support for the Internet, the main one being the Internet Engineering Task Force (*IETF*). The IETF is a committee of scientists and experts that work to resolve technical and related support issues for the Internet.

▶ See "Important WWW Concepts," p. 458

The reports of the IAB are made public through the publication of Request for Comment (*RFC*) documents. Some of these RFCs document Internet standards, but many of them are meant to introduce new ideas and stimulate discussion about future developments on the Internet. Past and current RFCs can be found at a number of places on the Internet. The NetCD95 included with this book gives you quick access to all the RFCs. Another way to read RFCs is to use the anonymous FTP (File Transfer Protocol) service to retrieve them (a good place to look for them is **ftp.internic.net**). Or, you can read them from the Internic Web page at **http://www.internic.net/ds/dspg1intdoc.html**.

NetCD95

> **Note**
>
> You can learn a lot about the Internet by reading the informational RFCs (the informational RFCs also are known as FYI documents). Among other things, these documents discuss the culture of the Internet, give a glossary of Internet terms, and answer commonly asked questions about the Internet.

The NSF Manages the Internet Backbone

In the mid-1980s, the National Science Foundation established a number of supercomputer centers around the country. To give universities and research centers around the country remote access to these supercomputer centers, NSF funded a backbone network (*NSFNET*) that connected these supercomputer centers, and also provided funding for connections to the backbone for regional networks.

In the late 1980s, NSF awarded a contract to a single organization (MERIT, a consortium of educational institutions in Michigan) to be responsible for maintaining and upgrading the physical network and the network administration for the NSFNET. In the early 1990s, MERIT proposed allowing the Internet to carry commercial traffic. Initially, the NSF was opposed to the conveyance of commercial traffic on what was intended as an educational and research network. An agreement was reached that required the profits from commercial traffic to be used to improve the national and regional network infrastructure.

The NSF decided to allow the commercial sector to provide the infrastructure for the Internet because there was growing interest in commercial use of the Internet. By mid-1995, the Internet had become completely commercial; a number of networks connected to high-speed backbones. In this arrangement, regional networks pay connection fees to use the high-speed backbones, and commercial and educational institutions who want to connect to the regional networks pay network usage fees. Rather than the NSF directly funding the network, they instead provide funds for NSF-sponsored research projects to pay for the projects' network usage fees.

Network Information Services Providers

In April of 1993, the NSF awarded five-year cooperative agreements for the management of the Network Information Services. The recipients of these agreements together manage the *InterNIC (Internet Network Information Center)*. They are responsible for providing information about getting connected to and using the Internet. Although it no longer funds the infrastructure of the Internet, the NSF does still provide these Internet support services.

Network Solutions was chosen to provide the Internet registration services, including the assignment of IP addresses (the unique identifier for each computer on the Internet) and registration of domain names. (See the section "What Is an IP Address?" later in this chapter for an explanation of IP addresses, and the section "What Is a Host Name?" for an explanation of domain names.) Network Solutions also provides NIC support services for the research and educational community (providing general information about the Internet and educational services).

AT&T was chosen to maintain lists of FTP sites, lists of various types of servers available on the Internet, lists of white- and yellow-page directories, library catalogs, and data archives. AT&T also will offer database design, management, and maintenance services to groups for material available to the Internet community.

The National Information Infrastructure

Because the government recognized the importance of a national information infrastructure (*NII*), it began to set in place the funds for the development of the high-speed, cutting-edge communications network. This network
is a research project involving collaboration between government and
industry, and is meant to encourage the continued expansion of network
technology. By developing a stable, widely used network technology, the
government hopes to encourage the commercial development of similar
networking technology and services.

The development of the information infrastructure of the country could be as
important to the educational climate and economy as the development of
the automobile highway infrastructure was in the 1950s. Eventually, connections to the Information Superhighway should be as common as telephone
connections are today. The Superhighway will provide access to retail mer-
chants, information services (such as personalized newspapers and online
magazines), commercial databases, public information (such as library hold-
ings and government documents), and many other services.

Access to a common network will facilitate the concept of telecommuting
(working at home, using the network to access information, have video
conferences, and so on) and teleschooling (having students attend classes
remotely, using a two-way live video conference, in addition to video broadcasts and online multimedia information and exercises). Companies are already beginning to take customer complaints and inquiries by e-mail, and
distribute marketing materials and product updates online. All financial
transactions could take place online, with currency becoming almost unnecessary. Eventually, the Information Superhighway could completely change
the structure of our society.

Some of these things are already available through commercial online services (such as CompuServe, Prodigy, and America Online), but the potential
for information access through a common network like the Internet is almost
unlimited. In addition to business and educational activities, social forums
on the Internet provide interaction among millions of people around the
world, allowing people to explore other cultures and exchange information
about topics of common interest.

Internet-Related Organizations

There are a number of organizations whose members are involved with
educating people about the Internet or exploring topics important to the
Internet. Some of these organizations are listed here. Information about these

organizations' Internet sites can be found in Part IX, "NetReference: Hot Internet Sites."

Corporation for National Research Initiatives

The Corporation for National Research Initiatives (*CNRI*) is a non-profit organization that was formed to encourage the cooperation of government, academic, and private industry in the development of a national data network. CNRI is involved in organizing many research projects, including faster transmission lines that will be able to carry live video broadcasts and graphics simulations; and *knowbots*, programs similar to good computer viruses that will be able to search through the Internet for information of interest to the knowbots' "owner."

Internet Society

The Internet Society (*ISOC*) is a non-profit organization that seeks to encourage the use and evolution of the Internet and to provide educational materials, and a forum for discussion of the Internet. The Internet Society is the secretariat of the Internet Architecture Board and the Internet Engineering Task Force. It holds an annual meeting that includes workshops and symposia on topics of interest to the membership. In addition, the Internet Society supports organizations involved in network security and Internet educational activities.

Computer Professionals for Social Responsibility

The Computer Professionals for Social Responsibility (*CPSR*) is an organization of people concerned about the ethical use of computers. Originally formed in 1983 by people concerned about the reliability of software developed for military applications, CPSR members are concerned about many social issues that involve computers. Some of these issues include the following:

- The privacy of personal online information, such as medical records and income tax returns.
- The reliability of software that controls possibly life-threatening processes, such as nuclear reactors.
- The relationship of computers to the workplace, concerning issues such as the replacement of workers by computers and the pollution caused by the manufacture and use of computers.

Electronic Frontier Foundation

The Electronic Frontier Foundation (*EFF*) is another organization concerned about the social effects of computers on society. It, however, is particularly concerned about the legal rights of computer users. Most current laws do not specifically apply to electronic communications and are sometimes inappropriately applied to activities of computer users. EFF wants to help shape public policy in the emerging area of computer-based communications.

The Culture of the Internet

When researchers first began to explore the concept of a large-scale network, few envisioned the uses to which the network would be put or the eventual size of the network. The initial designers of the ARPANET imagined that it would facilitate cooperation among researchers by giving them access to easy information exchange and remote processing. Most of those initial network developers were surprised when one of the most-used network services turned out to be electronic mail.

Before computer networks became so widespread, researchers depended on printed materials (journals, technical reports, letters, and so on), conferences, and face-to-face meetings to exchange information about their research. Researchers were very isolated, having infrequent contact with any but their closest colleagues. Researchers in different parts of the country could be pursuing the same goal, with no way of knowing that their efforts were being duplicated, or sharing the information that might have allowed them to collaborate or compare results.

One of the main goals of the ARPANET was to allow researchers to exchange information in a more timely and convenient manner. Through the file-exchange facilities, reports and data could be easily transferred from one researcher to another within a matter of hours, if not minutes. Programs that were developed at one site could be shared with others who were doing similar work. The resources of a powerful computer could be made available to labs that were too small to be able to afford to purchase such a machine for themselves.

All of this has become a reality on the Internet. But the Internet has become something much more than this.

The Community Expands

Back in the early days of the ARPANET (even as late as 1981), the Internet community was so small that people literally knew almost everyone on the network. Most of the sites were either government or university research centers. If a researcher received a request for information from a colleague at another site, he or she generally would know the colleague (or know of him), and would be able to spend a few hours (or more) of his time answering the request.

With the growth of the Internet, this type of personal response has become more difficult. It can be compared with a small town suddenly acquiring a large industry and expanding to 25 times its original size. People in the small town all used to know each other and be on speaking terms with most of their neighbors. Their children went to the same schools and grew up together. In the big city, people keep their houses shut and only come out to drive to work or for other necessities. They don't have time to know their neighbors, except perhaps one or two they have something in common with.

In a way, the Internet has become like this. There are so many people on the Internet now that it is difficult to know even the people in your own organization (if it is large), let alone others on the network. Perhaps people know a few dozen others who participate in a discussion group, or people who they have met at conferences or whose papers they have read in journals.

Even though this smallness has been lost, there is still a community of sorts in the Internet. Right now, access to the Internet is still relatively restricted. Compared to the hundreds of millions of people in the United States, the approximately 10 million or so that have Internet access is still a small number. Most use the Internet for its intended purpose—to exchange information or use remote computer resources unavailable to them locally. Usually this is done in a friendly and honest manner.

Cultural Pitfalls

One interesting thing about communicating over the Internet is that it removes many preconceived notions that you form about people when you meet them in person. When you communicate with individuals over the network, you don't know (unless they tell you) their age, race, height, weight, or even their gender sometimes. You don't know if they're the president of a company, or a high-school student. The only thing you have to judge them by is their words.

For this reason, it's important to carefully choose the words you use in your Internet communications. The Internet, for the most part, is a friendly, open community. However, because there is little chance of any real retribution, some people make vicious attacks on others. These people quickly lose credibility in the community and may find themselves in trouble if they ever do need to have dealings with someone they insulted or someone who was unimpressed by their abuse. This ability to attack people without fear of retribution is one of the few drawbacks of the Internet community, but it is one that has grown as the number of users on the Internet has grown.

The Internet community has features that physical communities have, but on a much larger scale. Two people from different parts of the country may strike up a friendship that eventually leads to a romantic relationship, or even marriage. There are online conferences using services, such as the Internet Relay Chat or Web Chat, that allow many people to converse in real-time about subjects they have in common. There are all types of people on the Internet—shy people, aggressive people, friendly people, and even abusive people. It is truly representative of today's society.

The Growth of the Internet

The increase of activity on the Internet has been absolutely phenomenal, particularly over the last five years. The number of machines connected and the amount of traffic carried has grown tremendously.

Traffic Growth

While the Internet backbone was managed by the NSF, statistics on traffic were collected on a monthly basis. Now that the Internet infrastructure is completely commercial and more distributed, it is not possible to collect these types of statistics. The charts shown in figures 1.1 and 1.2 use the last statistics available from the NSF to give you a feel for the explosive growth of the information that was carried over that network.

> **Note**
>
> You will notice in the charts in this section, the values for January of 95 seem to indicate a leveling off of Internet traffic. The reason for this is that by that time, some of the traffic was already being picked up by commercial providers and was no longer being carried by the NSFNET backbone.

The number of data packets that flowed through the NSFNET went from 1,153 million in July of 1989 to 60,399 million packets in January of 1995 (see fig. 1.1).

Fig. 1.1
Growth of
NSFNET packet
traffic from July
1989 to January
1995.

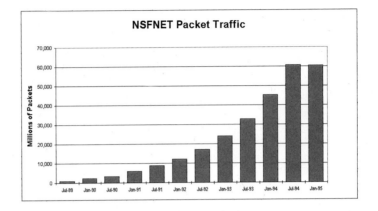

The byte traffic increased from 1,594 billion bytes of data in July of 1991 to around 13,196 billion bytes of data in January of 1995 (see fig. 1.2).

Fig. 1.2
Growth of
NSFNET byte
traffic from July
1991 through
January 1995.

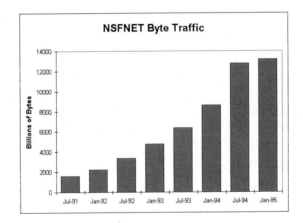

As of the final statistics that were collected, approximately 26 percent of the network traffic involved WWW activity. Approximately 21 percent involved file exchange (FTP activity). Approximately 13 percent involved e-mail and UseNet traffic, although this had dropped considerably from a high of almost 30 percent four years ago. Telnet traffic averaged about 2.5 of the total. Gopher traffic ran about two percent of the total.

Host Growth

The number of hosts on the Internet has grown from 213 in August of 1981 to approximately 6.6 million hosts in July of 1995 (see fig. 1.3). This was the first year that the com domain, which is for commercial organizations, had more hosts than the edu domain, which is for educational and research organizations. The com domain had about 1.7 million hosts, while the edu domain had about 1.4 million. (Domains are groupings of addresses explained later in this chapter in the section "What Is a Host Name?")

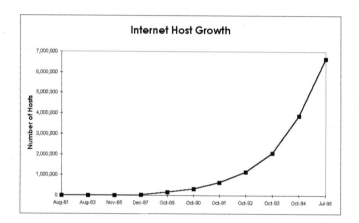

Fig. 1.3
Internet Host Growth from August of 1981 to July of 1995.

How Do I Use the Internet?

There are some basic concepts that you need to understand in order to get connected to the Internet and use the various Internet services. First, you need to know about the different types of Internet connections available—what their features and limitations are. Next, you need to know what is available on the Internet. Finally, you need to know how to get to the services you want to use.

How Do I Get Connected to the Internet?

Until the Internet became open to commercial traffic, the only way that you could reach the Internet was to work for part of the government or an organization that was connected to the Internet or attend a school that had an Internet connection. Now, there are many different ways that you can get connected to the Internet. Almost any type of computer can be used on the Internet. Your computer could connect directly to the Internet, or you could use a modem to access an Internet account over the phone lines. Part II, "Getting Connected," gives an in-depth discussion of the different types of Internet accounts that are available and the pros and cons of each type.

If you work for a company that is an Internet site, you may be able to get an account through work. Usually, companies or organizations that are Internet sites have full access to all Internet services. If you work at a place that has machines with graphical user interfaces (either PCs with Windows, Macintoshes, or X Windows–based UNIX machines), you can access many Internet services through graphical interfaces. If the company or organization has only terminals, you will have to use command-line or menu-based interfaces to access the Internet.

▶ See "The Various Ways to Connect to the Internet: Which One Is Right for You?" p. 101

The advantage of having an account with your employer is that you can use all Internet services directly from your computer at work. This means that you can transfer files to and from your computer, receive electronic mail on your computer, and so on.

If your company does not have access to the Internet, there are many commercial Internet providers now. There are menu-based bulletin board systems that allow you to access Internet services by selecting items from a menu. There are command-line-based accounts that let you have full Internet access using command-line interfaces. Both of these accounts usually require that you dial in to their computer to use your account. Although these accounts generally provide comprehensive Internet access, there are a number of limitations to them. You are usually limited in the amount of file storage that you have, and possibly the amount of data that you can transfer over the Internet. Your files all exist on the computers of your provider, and you need to have a way to transfer them to your home or business computer if you want to keep them for any length of time.

Another way of accessing the Internet is from some of the commercial online services like CompuServe, America Online, and Prodigy. These services now provide access to a number of Internet services. Like the menu-based and command-line accounts, the online services have a number of drawbacks. You are often charged extra to access Internet services, and may be limited in the amount of Internet data you can store. You will need to transfer files to your personal or business computer if you want to keep them for any length of time. Also, you may not be able to access all Internet services, or may not have full access to services. But these services also offer many other features that may be important to you.

Many Internet providers offer SLIP (Serial Line Internet Protocol) or PPP (Point to Point Protocol) accounts, which allow your home or business computer to become an Internet host over a standard phone line. These accounts allow you to use Internet services directly from your home or business computer. If your computer can run a *GUI* (graphical user interface) like Windows

95, you can use graphical interfaces to all the services available on the Internet. This gives you the ability to easily read electronic mail, participate in discussion groups, transfer files, and view multimedia documents.

A SLIP or PPP account has the advantage that any data you retrieve or electronic mail your receive is stored directly on your computer. One of the main limitations of these accounts is that data transfers are usually slow because your communications speed is limited by your modem and phone line.

If you need it, you can get a high-speed Internet connection directly to your home or business. This type of connection requires that you know how to set up and maintain an Internet site (or hire someone who can do this). Also, a high-speed connection is generally very expensive. But it is the fastest, most complete connection to the Internet you can have.

What Is Available on the Internet?

Now that you have some background about the Internet and know how you can get connected, what can you do on the Internet? The Internet was originally developed with the idea of providing a means for transferring information and using remote-computer resources. You can still do this—a number of Internet resources allow you to upload and download files, and to use programs that are running on remote Internet hosts. Electronic mail allows you to communicate with anyone who is connected to the Internet.

▶ See "The Various Parts of the Internet," p. 25

The main "product" that the Internet gives you access to is information. Information is usually contained in files on an Internet host, and can be presented in many different formats depending on what Internet service you are using and whether you are using that service through a GUI or through a terminal command-line interface. An Internet host can be a PC, Macintosh, UNIX-based workstation, or any computer that can speak TCP/IP. If you look at the information available on a host through a simple command-line interface, you will probably need to know something about the underlying file structure for that type of host to find the information you are looking for. If you have a GUI interface, you will probably not even know what type of host you are connecting to because the GUI interfaces tend to hide all the low-level information about a host, making the access to information uniform for all machines.

Now that commercial organizations are connecting to the Internet, the number of services available are exploding. The World Wide Web is a recent Internet service that makes using the Internet as easy as clicking your mouse button. Many organizations are using the World Wide Web to provide access to their products and services. A number of businesses currently allow you to peruse their catalogs and order merchandise over the Internet. Some manu-facturers have already begun providing product information over the Internet. The potential for information access is almost unlimited.

One of the only drawbacks to communication over the Internet is the lack of security. Because the original users of the Internet were academic and re-search organizations, there was little need for security on the Internet. Now that organizations are using the network for business purposes, security is a major concern. There are some commercial packages that are being developed to provide secure communications. But most of what travels the Internet is decipherable by anyone who has access to the networks that your informa-tion passes through. Part VIII, "Internet Security," tells you what to look out for and how you can keep your information secure.

How Do I Use Internet Resources?

Internet *addresses* are the key to using the Internet. You use *mail addresses* to send messages to other Internet users, and you use *host addresses* (or *host names*) to retrieve files and connect to hosts that provide Internet services. This section discusses what makes up an Internet address.

What Is a Host Name?

All Internet sites are identified by a unique *domain name* (such as bigcorp.com). The domain name is made up of several pieces that identify the organization and the domain hierarchy to which it belongs. A host name contains the domain name in addition to a name identifying a particular computer (see fig. 1.4). This section describes the various parts of a host name.

Fig. 1.4
An Internet host name tells you the name of the computer and the domain name of the organization to which it belongs.

Host names are found in e-mail addresses and also are used when connecting to Internet hosts to use Internet services (such as the World Wide Web) or retrieve files. A host name is made up of several words separated by periods. You can examine these words to find out information about the host. The host name bigmachine.bigcorp.com is used here to illustrate the parts of a host name. The rightmost word, for example, specifies the *domain* of the machine. In this case, the word com means that the machine belongs to a commercial entity—a company of some kind. The major domains are listed in table 1.1. Also, each country that is connected to the Internet has a domain assigned to it; for example fr is the domain name for France (appendix A contains a table of country codes).

Table 1.1 **The Major Internet Domains**	
Domain	**Description**
com	Commercial organizations
edu	Educational institutions
gov	Non-military U.S. government organizations
mil	U.S. military organizations
net	Network organizations
org	Other organizations

Note

There is an ISO standard document that lists the country codes used in Internet host names. You can get a copy of this document from a number of different places on the Internet. The file can be retrieved by anonymous FTP or through a WWW browser (these services are discussed elsewhere in this book). One place to find the file iso3166-countrycodes is at **rs.internic.net** in the directory netinfo.

Working to the left in the host name, you come to the word bigcorp. This part of the host name defines the institution that owns the machine. When an institution connects to the Internet, they must register the name of their organization with the Internet registration services. In this case, the name bigcorp.com has been registered to a fictitious company called Big Corporation (this name can be used only for machines connected to Big

Corporation's network). Examples of real-life institution names (including the domain name) are ibm.com for International Business Machines, mit.edu for the Massachusetts Institute of Technology, and nasa.gov for the National Aeronautics and Space Administration.

Any words to the left of the institution name are assigned within the institution. Small organizations usually have only a single word (specifying the name of an individual machine at the organization) to the left of the institution name. Sometimes, the host name for large organizations has more words, which usually designate departments within the organization. For example, you may see a name such as amachine.cs.mit.edu, which indicates that the machine amachine is within the cs (probably Computer Science) department within MIT, an educational institution. With host names, the leftmost word is always the name of a machine.

What Is an IP Address?

▶ See "A Brief Introduction to TCP/IP," p. 126

Host names are used to access individual hosts on the Internet. The host name is really just a convenient way for people to refer to hosts. The host name represents the *IP address* (or host address) of the host, which is the address that Internet software needs to get information to or from the host. The *IP address* is a unique number assigned to identify a host on the Internet. This address is usually represented as four numbers between 1 and 254 separated by periods—for example, 192.58.107.230.

Most software translates automatically between the host name and the IP address so that you don't have to remember which numbers represent which machine.

CHAPTER 2

The Various Parts of the Internet

In the early days of the Internet there were a small number of hosts, and most people who were on the Internet knew where to find the information they needed (often data or programs connected with their research). Today, there are many thousands of personal and commercial sites on the Internet. These sites provide services that businesses and individuals can use on a daily basis if they know they exist (for example, database searches and product ordering information). How do you find and retrieve the information you need?

A number of different services have been developed over the years to facilitate the sharing of information among the many sites on the Internet. Because the Internet was originally research-oriented, many of these services were hard to use and poorly documented. Now that the Internet has been opened to commercial and private sites, new services are being developed that are easier to use, and new interfaces to the older services make them more friendly.

This section familiarizes you with the common Internet services, including the following:

- Information retrieval services (FTP and Gopher)
- Information search services (WAIS, Archie, Veronica)
- Communication services (e-mail, Telnet, UseNet, IRC)
- Multimedia information services (World Wide Web, video conferencing, virtual chat)
- Recreational services (MUDs, MOOs, MUSHes)

File Transfers—Downloading with FTP

▶ See "What Is FTP?" p. 837

One of the first developed Internet services allows users to move files from one place to another—the file transfer protocol (FTP) service. This service is designed to enable you to connect to a computer on the Internet (using an FTP program on your local machine), browse through the list of files that are available on the remote computer, and retrieve files. FTP lets you transfer any type of files—programs, text, pictures, sound, or any other file format.

> **Note**
>
> FTP also allows you to upload files to a remote host, as long as you are allowed to write to that host. If you are connected to your personal account on the remote host, this should be no problem. If you are connected to an anonymous FTP site, many of these sites provide an incoming directory to allow you to contribute to the collection on the server.

What Are FTP Servers?

FTP is an example of a client-server system. In this kind of system, you use a program on your local computer (called a *client*) to talk to a program on a remote computer (called a *server*). (Fig. 2.1 shows an example of a graphical FTP client.) In the case of FTP, the server on the remote computer is designed to let you download and upload files. Many other client-server services are available on the Internet. Some of these services, such as Gopher and Archie, are discussed later in this chapter.

> **Tip**
>
> Windows 95 comes with a basic command-line FTP client.

To connect to a computer system using an FTP program, the remote system must have an FTP server running on it. This server must be set up by the administrators of the machine, and the administrators decide which files and information are made available through the FTP server.

Using FTP once involved entering cryptic commands to a UNIX command line. Now that more PCs and Macintoshes are connected directly to the Internet, new graphical interfaces have been developed to make FTP easier to use. Many of the Windows-based FTP programs provide interactive browsers that allow you to quickly change directories and select the files that you want to transfer on your local machine and on the remote machine.

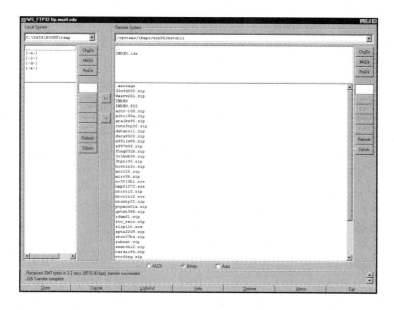

Fig. 2.1
WS_FTP allows you to easily view directories on your local machine and a remote Internet host and to transfer files between the two machines.

When you connect to a remote machine using FTP, you must log in to an account on the remote machine. If you have an account on the machine, you can use FTP to log in to your account and upload and download files between your local machine and your account on the remote machine. This allows you to easily move files between one Internet host and another.

What Are Anonymous FTP Servers?

One common type of FTP server is an anonymous FTP server. This server connects to a remote host and downloads files without having an account on the machine. You still need to log in when you connect to a machine that has an anonymous FTP server. However, you use the special user name "anonymous" when you connect. This anonymous user name lets you log in by providing any password you want.

Tip

It is considered common courtesy on the Internet to use your e-mail address as the password when logging in at an anonymous FTP site. Many FTP sites display a message requesting you to do this when you connect to the site.

Anonymous FTP servers are one of the major means of distributing software and information across the Internet. There is a large amount of software available on anonymous FTP servers. Much of the software is shareware, which means that you can try the software for free and pay the author if you decide to keep it. Some of the software is freeware—the author provides the software for anyone to use free of charge. Software is available for many different types of computer systems, such as UNIX, IBM PC, and Macintosh systems. You can find a wide assortment of programs, such as games, communications software, and system utilities. You can also find a lot of other files, such as recipes, movie reviews, pictures—almost anything you can think of.

Locating Files at FTP Sites

One of the most frustrating problems with the Internet is the difficulty of finding information such as the location of FTP sites, host resources, sources of information, and so on. Imagine going into your local public library and finding books in piles on the floor rather than arranged on shelves according to a book-classification scheme. And instead of a central card catalog, there are notes placed on some of the piles stating what people had found in that pile. Well, this is how the Internet has been for most of its existence; there are many resources, but no way to easily locate them.

Most FTP sites do not have a listing of all their available files. Sometimes the only way to locate a file or find interesting files is to click the folders to show the contents of the directories, and then look through them.

Because the format of the file and directory names depends on the machine that is being used as the FTP server, what you see depends on the type of system you connect to. If the server is running on a UNIX system, for example, the file names appear with any combination of uppercase or lowercase letters, and can be of any length.

If, on the other hand, the system you connect to is a VMS system (from Digital Equipment Corporation), the file names will be only uppercase. Other systems, such as PCs and Macintoshes, display files and directory names in their standard formats.

Tip

You should always download the README files and read the contents—the files are put there for a reason.

On some machines (especially the very large archive sites), the site maintainers keep an index of available files with brief descriptions of what the files contain. This is very helpful, and makes finding useful files much easier. When you enter a directory, you should look for a file called INDEX (either in uppercase or lowercase). You also should look for a file called README (or perhaps readme, or read.me). These README files are descriptions of the contents of the directories, or information about the server system.

If you have a question about an FTP server, or about the contents of the files there, you can send an e-mail message to the "postmaster" of the FTP machine. For example, if you connected to the machine rs.internic.net, you should send e-mail to the address postmaster@rs.internic.net. Some FTP servers have a different person to contact; in this case, the name of the contact person is displayed when you connect to the machine, or is in a README file in the first directory you see when you connect.

Locating Files Using Archie

Information retrieval systems are being explored as a way to locate information resources on the Internet. Even though a complete central list of all the resources on the Internet does not exist, the various information retrieval systems go a long way toward making a resource easy to find.

▶ See "Archie," p. 927

Archie was the first of the information retrieval systems developed on the Internet. The purpose of Archie is simple—to create a central index of files that are available on anonymous FTP sites around the Internet. To do this, the Archie servers periodically connect to anonymous FTP sites that participate and download lists of all the files that are on these sites. These lists of files are merged into a database, which then can be searched by users.

To use Archie, you must either have an Archie client (such as WSArchie, shown in fig. 2.2) running on your local machine, or use Telnet to connect to one of the Archie servers and search the database there.

When you have connected to one of the Archie database machines, you can search the database for a program or file. Because the database only knows the names of the files, you must know at least part of the file name for which you are looking. For example, if you are looking for a program that compresses files (makes them smaller), you would search the database for the word *compress*. The Archie program returns the location of all the files that are named "compress."

About the Internet

Fig. 2.2
WSArchie provides a graphical interface that you can use to search the Archie databases for files.

Now, this search returns only those files exactly named "compress," so it wouldn't return the location of a file named "uncompress" (which undoes the work of the compress program). Archie, though, lets you search for a string of characters that is anywhere in the file name. If you tell the Archie program that you want to do a *substring search*, it looks for files that have your search string anywhere in the file name. Similarly, you can tell the Archie program to match the file name even if it has different capitalization than your search string.

The Archie server provides the machine name and location of the files that match the string for which you are searching. You can use the FTP program to connect to the machine and download the file to your local machine. The main limitation of Archie is that you have to know at least something about the name of the file to search for it; if you don't have any idea what the file is called (for example, you want a program that searches for viruses on your machine and don't know that it is called scanv), you may have to try several searches using different strings before you find something that looks useful.

Another limitation of Archie is that not all sites on the Internet that have anonymous FTP servers participate in the Archie database. There may be a file that fits your specifications at a non-participating site, but Archie cannot find it because it is not in the database. Despite these limitations, however, Archie is a very useful tool for locating files to download through FTP.

> **Note**
>
> As the World Wide Web has grown over the past few years, people have put together Web pages that link to large collections of software and collections of files related to particular topics. You can use one of the Web search engines discussed in chapter 37, "Searching on the Internet," to look for software and files in these collections. One of the advantages of Web search engines is that you can often search for topic words, not just file names, because the Web pages often have comments about the files and these comments are also searched.

Retrieving Information Using Gopher

Gopher is another information distribution service within the Internet. Sites on the Internet that distribute information through the Gopher system set up and run Gopher servers to enable people with Gopher clients to display and download files and directories. Gopher provides a menu-based interface to the resources available from the Gopher server, eliminating the need to enter cryptic commands to move between directories and retrieve files.

▶ See "What Is Gopher?" p. 867

> **Tip**
>
> Connect to **gopher.unl.edu** and select Archie from the Internet Resources menu for a simple interface to Archie.

The functionality of Gopher is similar to FTP, but Gopher can connect you to other Internet services in addition to displaying and retrieving directories and files. Displaying or downloading a file is as easy as selecting an item from a menu (see fig. 2.3). This ease-of-use, plus the ability to put descriptive titles on the menu items, makes Gopher a much easier method of browsing files than simply using FTP.

One of the big advantages of the Gopher system is that you can include menu items on a server that, when selected, move the user to other Gopher servers on the Internet. For example, one menu item on machine A's Gopher server may say Connect to Machine B Gopher. When that menu item is selected, your Gopher client connects to machine B's Gopher server, just as if you had connected to it when you ran your Gopher client.

▶ See "Why Use Gopher?" p. 868

Fig. 2.3

WSGopher
provides a GUI
that you can use
to connect to
Gopher servers.

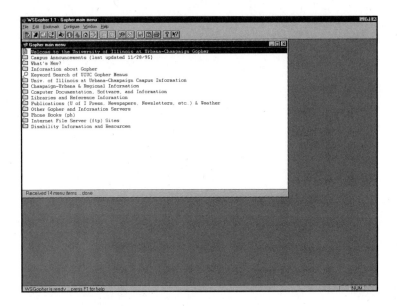

What Is Gopherspace?

This ability to link Gopher sites together makes it easy to examine the files available at one site and then move to other interesting Gopher sites. All Gopher servers are at some point interconnected—this network of Gopher servers is known as Gopherspace. When a new Gopher site becomes available on the Internet, the administrators send an e-mail message to the maintainers of the Gopher software (at the University of Minnesota) to have their site included in the master list of all Gopher sites worldwide. Many organizations run Gopher servers; universities and colleges, companies, and government agencies all have information available through Gopher.

The Gopher maintainers run a Gopher server (located at the address **gopher.tc.umn.edu**) that lists all the known Gopher servers and lets you connect to them. This gives you a good starting place to browse through all the Gopher servers and discover the wealth of information available on the Internet. Some of the top Gopher servers are listed in chapter 49, "Top Gopher Sites," but the main Gopher server at **gopher.tc.umn.edu** is the best place to begin exploring the information on Gopher because you can get to every Gopher server that exists from there.

Locating Files Using Veronica

▶ See "Searching Gopherspace with Veronica," p. 888

With all the Gopher sites available, though, it may be hard to locate a site that carries the information and files you want. You probably want to search the Gopher sites for a document you want. A service, called Veronica, is available to do this.

Just as Archie is a service that searches file names and directories on anonymous FTP servers, Veronica searches menu items on Gopher servers. To use Veronica, you have to be connected to a Gopher server that gives you access to a Veronica server. The Veronica database is built by scanning the Gopher menus on servers around the world, and can be searched by selecting Search Gopherspace using Veronica, which is found on the Other Gopher and Information Servers menu of the Gopher site **gopher.tc.umn.edu**.

Because Gopher menu items can be descriptive phrases (more than just file names), it can be easier to find information of interest through Veronica than it is through Archie. The entries in a Gopher menu can say something relevant about the contents of a file or directory (Topographical Maps, for example), rather than just listing the exact name of a file or directory. Veronica may find a file at an FTP site that Archie wouldn't because you can use Veronica to search for information on topics (maps, for example), rather than just searching for file names.

When Veronica has finished searching Gopherspace, it builds a Gopher menu that contains all the items it has found to match your search. You can then examine those items by selecting them, just as you would from any Gopher menu.

Locating Documents Using WAIS

Whereas Gopher is a good system to use for exploring the files and systems available on the Internet, suppose you want to find all documents available on a particular subject. The *WAIS (Wide Area Information Server)* is a system that searches for your subject through documents on servers all over the world. WAIS (pronounced "ways") searches a set of databases that has been indexed with keywords, and returns addresses where you can locate documents that would be of interest to you.

▶ See "Using WAIS," p. 898

The heart of the WAIS system is the use of client software running on your local computer that lets you ask for information in simple, English-like language. The client takes your question and sends it off to the WAIS server you select. The server takes your question and searches all the documents it knows about for the information you want. If it finds documents that match your question, it returns indexes to these documents, which you can then use to download the documents and display them on your local system.

One of the key features of the WAIS system is the capability of a WAIS server to have indexes that actually point to other WAIS servers. A central site on the Internet maintains indexes to all known WAIS servers on the Internet;

you can use this central site as a starting point for your searches. For example, say you want to find out all the times that President Clinton mentioned the city of Atlanta, Georgia, in his speeches.

You can set your search database to be directory-of-servers, which is located on the machine **quake.think.com**. As a quick example of how WAIS works, using this database, you search for "president clinton," and it returns (among others) a database resource marked "clinton-speeches." You can now use this database to search for "atlanta georgia." This search returns some number of documents, and the first ones are the ones that best match your question. These speeches, when retrieved, are the ones that mention Atlanta, Georgia.

Connecting to Host Resources Using Telnet

▶ See "What Is Telnet?" p. 819

▶ See "Some Quick Background Information," p. 821

Just as a host can run an FTP server to allow you to transfer files, a computer on the Internet can be set up to run any program automatically when you connect to that computer. There are a wide variety of hosts providing this type of service (also called host resources) on the Internet with information about everything from agriculture to space research. Some of these host resources are similar to bulletin board systems, which you may be familiar with. But instead of dialing into one of these systems using a telephone line and modem, you can connect to these systems over the Internet using a program called Telnet. Other host resources are programs that run automatically when Telnet connects to the host. For example, some host resources let you get weather forecasts, find out team schedules for different sports, or play a game of chess.

> **Tip**
>
> Windows 95 comes with a Telnet application.

Although Telnet does let you access host resources quickly, the primary use of Telnet is much more basic. Telnet is a method used to connect two computers together; it provides a terminal connection to the remote machine. This connection enables you to type commands to the remote machine, just as if you had a terminal hooked into it. You are probably already familiar with the idea of a terminal program; if you have a modem connected to a personal computer that you use to dial into computer systems, you use a terminal program to talk to the modem and remote system.

Just as you use a local FTP program to connect to an FTP server on another machine on the Internet, you use a Telnet program on your local machine to talk to the Telnet server on another machine anywhere on the Internet. The main difference between FTP and Telnet is that when you connect to the remote machine with FTP, the FTP server only lets you do things related to transferring files. When you connect to a machine using Telnet, what you see really depends on what the host resource provides. You may see a bulletin board menu system, or a simple command-line interface, or you may just receive some output without typing anything. It all depends on what the resource provides.

World Wide Web (WWW)

The World Wide Web (WWW) is one of the newest client-server based Internet services. In the late 1980s, CERN (the European Laboratory for Particle Physics) began experimenting with a service that would allow anyone to easily access and display documents that were stored on a server anywhere on the Internet. To do this, they developed a standard format for the documents that enabled them to be easily displayed by any type of display device, and allowed links to other documents to be placed within documents. (Part IV, "The World Wide Web," covers the Web in detail.)

Although the WWW was developed for the CERN researchers to use, after the service was made public it became tremendously popular. A number of different client applications (the ones that actually display the documents on-screen) were developed to read WWW documents. There are graphical-based clients (some of the most popular of these are Netscape, Mosaic, and the Microsoft Web browser, Internet Explorer), and terminal-based clients. Figure 2.4 shows an example of a graphical Web browser.

Most WWW clients also allow you to use the same interface to access other Internet services, such as FTP and Gopher. In addition, some WWW clients display multimedia files (such as movies and sounds) through multimedia player programs that you have installed on your computer.

Fig. 2.4
Netscape is one of the more popular Web browsers, allowing you to view, save, and print Web documents.

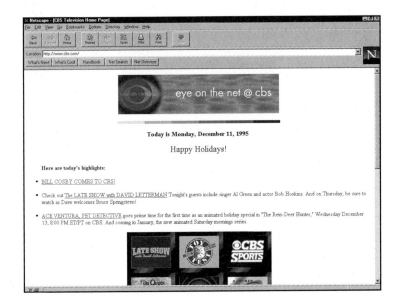

What Are WWW Documents?

▶ See "Important WWW Concepts," p. 458

WWW documents are not ASCII text documents. They are ASCII documents that contain commands from a language called HTML (HyperText Markup Language). HTML commands allow you to tag passages of text (see fig. 2.5). This tagging allows each WWW client to format the text in a way that is appropriate for the display that the client is using, providing for effective use of text formatting (larger text for heading, bold or italic text for emphasis, and so on). HTML also enables you to include inline images (pictures) in documents that can be displayed by the graphical WWW clients.

One of the main features of HTML is its capability to insert hypertext links into a document. Hypertext links enable you to load another WWW document into your WWW client simply by clicking a link area on-screen. A document may contain links to many other related documents. The related documents may be on the same computer as the first document, or they may be on a computer halfway around the world. A link area may be a word or group of words, or even a picture. And the document that you retrieve can be a text file, a graphic file, a sound file, an animation, or almost any other type of file.

HTML lets you
create Web
documents that
can be displayed
differently
depending on the
Web browser you
are using.

Finding WWW Documents

There are thousands of WWW servers on the Internet today. Some have personal information on them, some have academic or government information on them, and many now have commercial information on them. You can find recipes for chicken casserole or fact sheets for a new printer. Many universities are putting their campus directories on the Web, and the government has everything from the text of congressional legislation to a tour of the White House. But how do you find these things?

▶ See "Searching
on the
Internet,"
p. 911

If you know where you want to look for something, one thing that you can do is simply guess at the name of the WWW server. The convention for naming Web servers is to start the server name with "www." If, for example, you want to look for information about products from Kodak, you could try looking at the site www.kodak.com. That's great if you know where you can find the information that you want.

When the Web started to expand so dramatically in the mid-90s, a number of people realized that it was fast becoming impossible to keep track of everything that's out there. So they designed programs to go out and search the Web, find all of the servers that exist, and build databases of the information that's on those servers (see fig. 2.5). These Web search facilities (such as Yahoo! and Lycos) are great resources.

Fig. 2.6
Lycos is one of the most popular of the World Wide Web search facilities.

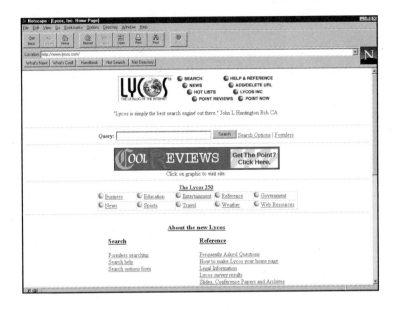

Note

Many people are trying to collect and organize the overwhelming amount of information you can access from the Web. You can find a number of Web pages that are devoted to a particular topic. For example, at **http://www.interlog.com/~ohi/www/writesource.html**, you can find links to resources for all types of writers.

Future Web Developments

▶ See "New Web Technologies," p. 723

Hypermedia is only the beginning of the exciting onslaught of information that will be brought to us on the Web. Developments in current Web technology include a language that will allow three-dimensional images to be included in Web documents, and the inclusion of live audio and video over the Web. One new application allows you to walk into a room, see a representation of another person in the room, and carry on a conversation with the person. Other applications under development will allow you to do things like take a walking tour through a 3D representation of a building.

Electronic Mail (E-Mail)

E-mail was one of the first Internet services developed. Although the original intent of having a network connecting physically remote sites was to exchange files and to use computing resources, the designers of the network discovered that one of the most popular services involved personal communications (e-mail). Today, e-mail is an important service on any computer network, not just the Internet. (Part III, "Using Internet E-Mail," covers Internet e-mail in considerable detail.)

E-mail involves sending a message from one computer account to another. It enables people to quickly communicate across vast distances. E-mail can be used to send important information about projects or products, or it can be used to say hello to your cousin. It can even be used to send files directly to someone, although if the files are executable, they must be encoded into ASCII with one of many encoding programs available because Internet e-mail can only handle ASCII information.

▶ See "Files," p. 339

Mailing Lists

One of the most popular Internet services is based on e-mail. The mailing list is a way for a group of people with a common interest to have discussions. There are several ways of running a mailing list. The original way of doing it (and the way you can still do it if your list is small) is to have each person keep a list of the members of the mailing list. Then, when someone wants to submit a message for discussion, that person just sends the message to everyone on the list. The disadvantage to this method of having a mailing list is that everyone on the list has to remember to add and delete people from the list as the membership changes. Also, the machine of each person sending a message is tied up while the message is sent to everyone on the list.

Better ways of managing mailing lists have developed over the years. There are now several programs that automate the administration of mailing lists. The members of a list can number in the hundreds or thousands, but now the master list of e-mail addresses can be kept on the host that runs the mailing list program. All requests for information, or to subscribe (participate) or unsubscribe (drop out), are automatically handled by the mailing-list software. All messages to the participants are sent to the central host, where the mailing-list software then distributes them to all the members of the list (thus limiting the workload to that central machine). Mailing lists still have human administrators, but they only need to take care of unusual problems that arise.

Most mailing lists consist of people who have agreed to discuss a particular topic, so there is no need to restrict the distribution of messages, and every message sent to the list is simply re-sent to every member of the list. Some mailing lists that discuss controversial topics (such as religion or politics) are moderated. In a moderated mailing list, a person reads every message that is sent to the list to make sure the contents of the messages are within the agreed-upon guidelines for that list. If a message is within the guidelines, it is sent on to the members. If not, it is deleted.

> **Tip**
>
> Ask your friends with similar interests if they belong to any mailing lists. It's an easy way to find one.

▶ See "Available Lists," p. 423

▶ See "Finding Majordomo Lists," p. 431

There are thousands of mailing lists that you can subscribe to. Some of them discuss topics that are also found in the UseNet discussion groups, because not everyone who has an e-mail address has access to UseNet (UseNet is explained in the section "Internet Newsgroups (UseNet)" later in this chapter).

Getting E-Mail to Work for You

▶ See "Using Microsoft Exchange," p. 349

There are many different e-mail standards developed for different types of networks or large self-contained user communities such as the commercial online services. This variety of standards makes it difficult to write a general-purpose application to read and send e-mail, because the application would have to understand every different e-mail standard. However, there are a number of companies coming out with e-mail gateways that handle mail from many different e-mail systems (such as between cc:Mail and the Internet). Windows 95 comes with Microsoft Exchange, a mail client that allows you to send Microsoft Mail or Internet mail.

E-mail can be exchanged between the Internet and all the commercial online services, including America Online, CompuServe, and Prodigy. Gateways have been set up so that you can send e-mail to people on these services as easily as you can send e-mail to another Internet user. Chapter 17, "E-Mailing Outside the Internet and with Online Services," tells you how to address your e-mail to these online services and other non-Internet destinations.

E-mail is becoming a popular way to conduct business over long distances. People can now use e-mail to report problems or request information about products and services. Using e-mail to contact a business associate can be better than using the phone because the recipient can read it at a convenient time, and the sender can include as much information as needed to explain the situation.

Care must be taken, though, to express yourself clearly, because all the recipient has to go on is your words. All subtle communication clues such as voice inflection and facial expression are missing in written communications. And the Internet may not be the best means of sending sensitive information because security on the Net is still under development. However, the Internet does provide one of the fastest ways to communicate with someone halfway around the world.

Interactive Internet Communications

In the early days of the Internet, communication speeds were relatively slow (comparable to today's modem speeds). This limited how information was exchanged to physically moving files from one computer to another. With today's lightning-fast communications speeds, real-time transfer of audio data is very practical, and real-time video is quickly becoming practical. These two capabilities open the door to many types of applications that benefit from live communications.

Internet Relay Chat

Internet Relay Chat (IRC) is a service that was developed in the late 1980s, originally as a replacement for the UNIX talk program. IRC enables multiple people to "talk" simultaneously (by typing, of course). Like many other Internet services, IRC is a client/server application. People who want to talk with each other must be running an IRC client, and they must connect to an IRC server (see fig. 2.7). Once on the server, they select the channel on which they want to talk (channels often are named for the topic they discuss, if they restrict themselves to a particular topic). For example, the hot-tub channel is supposed to simulate conversations that would occur between occupants of a hot tub.

▶ See "The Basics of IRC," p. 941

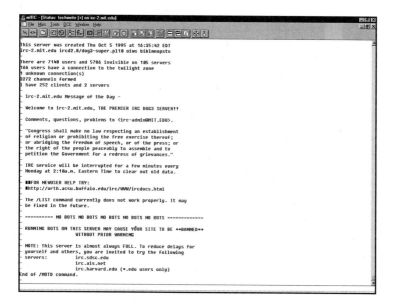

Fig. 2.7
mIRC lets you chat in real time with people around the world.

When you are involved in an IRC channel, you can type to the other participants from your terminal while you see what others are typing on theirs. This is an interesting way of having a real-time conference, but the speed of communication is rather slow, because typing something is much slower than speaking. It does, however, allow everyone to participate equally, preventing any one person from taking over the conversation by "shouting" or "talking" continuously.

Live Video Conferencing

▶ See "Video Conferencing on the Net," p. 995

As research into expanding the amount of information that can be carried on our data highways continues, people are developing hardware and programs that will allow live video to be broadcast from one computer to another. At this time, good quality live video is not commonplace because of the communication speeds needed to transfer the huge amount of information involved. But as the bandwidth increases, it should be possible to hold remote meetings and attend classes electronically, among other things.

Interactive Games

▶ See "Games on the Net: MUDs, MOOs, and MUSHes," p. 1011

There are a number of servers on the Net that allow you to participate live in multi-player games. Games known as MUDs, MOOs, and MUSHes have been developed over the last few years to allow people from all over the world to have some live recreational interaction. In addition, the designers of a number of the popular graphical games developed for PCs in the last few years are planning to add Internet access capabilities to the games so that these commercial games can be played interactively over the Net.

Live Voice

▶ See "Talking on the Net: Internet Phone and Internet Voice Chat," p. 971

Carrying audio over the Internet is a lot simpler than carrying video, because there isn't as much information involved. In the past year or so, several services have sprung up that let Internet users have live conversations.

Phone by Net

▶ See "Using the Internet as a 'Phone'," p. 971

When real-time audio became practical on the Net, someone figured out that it would be just as easy (and a lot cheaper) to talk to someone using the Internet instead of your long-distance phone company. Although it's not quite the same as talking to someone on the phone, there are a lot of advantages to conversing over the Internet.

Internet Newsgroups (UseNet)

Internet newsgroups are online discussions (via posted messages) on thousands of different topics. In addition to the mechanics of reading and posting to newsgroups, you should be aware of some of the social aspects of participating in newsgroup discussions. (Part V, "UseNet Newsgroups," provides extensive coverage of UseNet newsgroups.)

What Is UseNet?

UseNet (which is short for users' network) is made up of all the machines that receive network newsgroups, which are computer discussion groups or forums. The network news (commonly referred to as netnews) is the mechanism that sends the individual messages (called articles) from your local computer to all the computers that participate in UseNet.

While you don't have to understand the exact details of how UseNet works, a broad outline helps you to understand what makes UseNet a powerful means for reaching lots of people. The basic idea with UseNet is that when you post an article on your local computer, the article is stored on your computer's disk, and then the article is sent to other computers that have agreed to exchange netnews articles with your computer. These machines, in turn, then send your article to other machines, who send it to others; this continues until your article has reached every computer that participates in UseNet. Because each machine can send articles to many other machines, your article can reach the majority of UseNet computers within a few hours.

▶ See "What Do I Need to Know?" p. 756

A news article is very similar to an e-mail message. It has some information at the top of the article in the header lines and the content of the article in the message body. Just as in an e-mail message, the header lines give information to the netnews software that puts the article in the right newsgroup or groups (an article can appear in more than one group at the same time—this is called cross-posting the article) and to identify the sender of the article.

The message body of the article contains the information that the sender of the article wrote. In many cases, the article ends with a signature; this is often a witty comment or some information about the author. Many newsreaders allow you to set up a file that contains your signature; this file is automatically included by your newsreader at the end of each article you post.

Newsgroups and Topics

The information carried by UseNet is divided into newsgroups, which are areas of discussion that can be compared to bulletin boards (the cork kind) with messages tacked all over them. Each newsgroup is devoted to a particular

▶ See "Newsgroup Names," p. 752

topic, although the discussion in these groups can be far-reaching (see fig. 2.8). There is a newsgroup for almost every topic you can imagine—many large UseNet sites carry well over 15,000 newsgroups!

Fig. 2.8

Free Agent is a very popular UseNet interface, allowing you to read and post articles, reply to the newsgroup or the author of an article, and save and print articles.

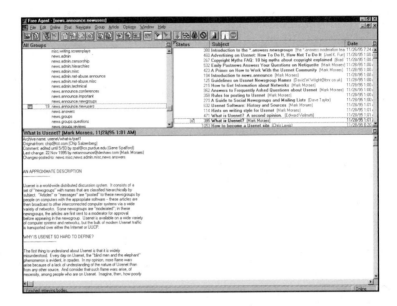

To get an idea of how discussion happens in newsgroups, you might think of UseNet as a large building, and each newsgroup as a room in that building. Each room has a name on the door, and a brief description of the topic of discussion in that room. In some of these rooms, you'll find a small number of people politely discussing a serious topic. You can come in, ask a question, and join in the discussion.

In other rooms, you may find a loud, raucous group of people discussing a heated topic. Each person is shouting out his or her opinion loudly, with little regard for the shouting from the people around them. You try to enter the conversation, but you either find that your opinions are ignored or you are insulted. Both of these conditions happen everyday (sometimes in the same newsgroup at different times!) on UseNet.

Commercial Online Services

Although not originally part of the Internet, the commercial online services have all connected to the Internet in the past two years. CompuServe, America Online, and Prodigy all have their own interfaces to most of the Internet services discussed in this chapter. In addition, Microsoft now has its own online service, Microsoft Network (MSN). Although you can access most Internet services through the commercial online services, their Internet interfaces may not be as nice as the ones you can buy or obtain free. But the online services do provide a wealth of other services that you might not be able to find on the Internet, so you may prefer to get your Internet access through one of them.

CHAPTER 3

Your Cyber Rights and Responsibilities: Law and Etiquette

You have important legal rights and responsibilities in cyberspace, just like anywhere else. Contrary to popular opinion, the Internet is not some kind of wild west frontier beyond the laws of any country. There is no place in cyberspace—or anywhere else for that mater—where laws somehow magically end. Rest assured—or if you're planning criminal activities on the Internet, be worried—the long arm of the law *does* stretch into cyberspace. Just about everyone connecting to the Internet from a computer located in the U.S. is subject to U.S. law. These laws apply throughout the U.S., even if you are sitting at your keyboard and talking to someone in Timbuktu. Foreign citizens outside of the U.S. are subject to the laws of their own country. (That's another story that we won't get into.)

For the most part, the application of U.S. laws to our cyberspace should be cause for comfort, not alarm. Under U.S. law, we enjoy legal rights and freedoms that people in many other countries only dream about. The law of the Internet is not as complicated as you might think. The laws of the Internet are the same laws that apply to the rest of your life. You are probably already familiar with most of them.

So relax, enjoy your time in cyberspace; you have rights here, just like anywhere else. Outside of cyberspace you don't break the law without knowing it (except perhaps that time you spit on the sidewalk!). You are as unlikely to break the law by mistake on the Internet as you are in real life. With a few spitting-on-the-sidewalk type exceptions that I'll point out to you, the common-sense notions of right and wrong, legal and illegal, apply on the Internet, just like anywhere else, so too do common sense and courtesy. Follow these, and the basic legal principles, tips, and pointers contained in this chapter, and you can stay within the law.

In this chapter, you learn about:

- Your rights and responsibilities of free speech and association on the Internet
- The slander and libel limitation—your protection from "flames" that burn
- The important distinction between Internet publisher and distributor
- Obscenity limitations—the risks of selling porn on the Net
- Your rights and responsibilities of privacy, copyright, and fair trade on the Internet
- Your rights and responsibilities of protection from crime on the Internet

Law on the Internet

With a few important exceptions that I'll spell out later, you have the right to say and write just about anything you want on the Internet. You also have the right to go anywhere on the Net and join almost any group that you want to. Most of these rights are commonplace and expected in our country, and are the same kind of rights you enjoy when not on the computer. These rights all spring from the First Amendment to the United States Constitution.

> **Tip**
>
> For the full text of our Constitution, see **http://seamless.com/rcl/const.txt**.

> **Tip**
>
> For a good listing of over a 1,000 law-related Web sites on the Internet, see the Seamless Website's directory of links at **http://tsw.ingress.com/tsw/road.html**.

First Amendment

Thanks to the First Amendment, and a strong legal culture in the U.S., you now have more rights and personal liberties than at any time in written history. Under the First Amendment's right of free speech, you can believe and think whatever you want, and can publicly say or write just about anything. Free speech means freedom of expression in any form—speech, writings, art, music, dance, movies, and so on. Some governmental limitations on free expression are permitted, but they are on the far fringes, where your speech constitutes fighting words, plots a crime, incites a riot, or is "obscene." We'll discuss some of these limitations as applied to the Internet later. But before we get to the few exceptions to free speech, it helps to understand the strength and importance of the general rule guaranteeing your free speech. As a U.S. citizen on the Internet, you are free to express yourself in just about any way you want to without fear of government retaliation.

For over two centuries the First Amendment has fulfilled its original purpose to give the press and all citizens the freedom to report abuses of power by public officials, to hear news critical of the government, and to exchange information and opinions without interference by government officials. In our culture the lack of government censorship has always been considered vital to our pursuit of happiness and our search for truth, justice, and knowledge. We have always believed that freedom from governmental supervision makes possible and facilitates our search for self fulfillment through art, religion, literature, and music, as well as public debate.

Under the First Amendment you are also guaranteed the right to associate with anyone you please, to peacefully assemble in public groups, and to form and associate any groups that you please. On the Internet this means you can freely assemble in online communities without government interference. Both of the fundamental First Amendment liberties of free speech and free association come into play every day to protect your activities on the Internet.

Tip

For a good introduction to these issues check out the First Amendment Cyber-Tribune at **http://w3.trib.com/FACT/**.

Within the last 75 years the First Amendment has been the subject of tens of thousands of lawsuits, and judges and lawyers have written hundreds of thousands of pages of legal opinions about it. But the First Amendment of the United States Constitution itself is short:

> "Congress shall make no law respecting an establishment of religion, or prohibiting the free exercise thereof; or abridging the freedom of speech, or of the press, or the right of the people peaceably to assemble, and to petition the Government for a redress of grievance."

Since World War I, and especially since around 1960, the courts have created a vast body of written case law that interprets and applies these few words. The appellate decisions interpreting the Constitution constitute legal precedent that courts today, even the Supreme Court, are obliged to follow. There are literally tens of thousands of U.S. Supreme Court and other lower court cases pertaining to the First Amendment and other provisions of the Constitution.

> ### Tip
>
> To find some of the important First Amendment cases online, see **http://www. law.cornell.edu/topics/first_amendment.html**. Check out the collection put together by the Congressional cyber-librarians at **http://www.pls.com:8001/his/ 93.htm.**

The case law interpreting the First Amendment has slowly evolved, so that today, it provides us with a host of rights and liberties. This legal precedent now serves as a bulwark of protection from misguided legislatures and judges, demagogues, and would-be despots of all persuasions. That is because statutes enacted by any legislature, even the U.S. Congress and Senate, which violate the Constitution, are illegal, void, and can be declared invalid and unenforceable by the courts.

> ### Tip
>
> In case you're thinking right about now that all lawyers take themselves and the law too seriously, see the Law Jokes Web site at **http://gnn.com/gnn/bus/nolo/ jokes.html**.

As we will see, there are now several bills pending in Congress pertaining to the Internet that may well be struck down as unconstitutional. This is a normal and natural process in our country. Technologies change but human nature remains the same. New technologies create new areas of culture, and someone in government tries to chill the exercise of first amendment rights there. The process has gone on for centuries. Time and again the law, lawyers, judges, and individual citizens rise to the challenge, and foil the attempts of a few misguided government officials. First the courts adapted to the new technologies of the railroads and telegraphs, then the automobiles and telephones, then radio, television, and video tape recorders. Now the challenge is from computers and the Internet. Society, the courts, and the law will once again adapt to the new technologies. It is critically important to us, and to all future generations, that the legal adaptations continue our traditions of freedom and human rights.

Tip

For a good collection of human rights related Web sites see **http://www.iwc. com/entropy/marks/hr.html**.

A Few Common-Sense Limitations on Free Speech

The right to free expression on the Internet, like anywhere else, is subject to some restrictions and common-sense guidelines. For instance, it doesn't protect perjury, a threat, or a fraud. You are always at risk if you lie, or if you incite people to riot or criminal activities. For instance, there is the famous example given by Supreme Court Justice Oliver Wendell Holmes, of the villain who knowingly lies and shouts "FIRE!" in a crowded theater. If a panic ensues and people are hurt, the villain can be arrested for what he said. Depending upon how bad the people are hurt by the panic he started, he will be subject to various degrees of criminal and civil liability. However, if he shouted an obscenity in the same crowded room, he might get everyone annoyed, and some quite angry, but he is unlikely to be arrested for the speech alone.

The government can't punish a speaker for inflammatory speech unless it can show that the speech "is directed to inciting or producing imminent lawless action, and is likely to incite or produce such action." This is an almost impossible legal standard for the government prosecutors to satisfy. For that reason your speech, no matter how offensive or inflammatory, is very hard for the government to prohibit. You are pretty much free to say what you want, and express whatever crazy ideas you may have, so long as you are not plotting a crime or selling pornography, an important exception for the Internet that we'll get into later.

In spite of the clear laws, there always seem to be a few public officials around who want to try and punish speech that is offensive to voters.

Tip

For a good Web site resource on censorship see **http://fileroom.aaup.uic.edu/ FileRoom/documents/TofCont.html**.

For instance, a University of Michigan student recently posted a sick story on the Internet newsgroup alt.sex.stories, which graphically described torture, rape, and murder. Nothing that unusual so far, but this guy went one step further and gave the fictional victim the real name of one of his female classmates. Then he went still further and started e-mailing messages to a friend that the fantasies no longer did the trick for him, and now he wanted to do it for real. They started exchanging e-mail about the possibility of attacking 13- and 14-year old girls in his neighborhood. They were turned in, and the government arrested the student with the sick story. He spent 29 days in jail as a danger to the community while undergoing psychological evaluation. The evaluation showed there was no evidence he was a danger to himself or the community. The Court threw out the indictment, and questioned the prosecutor's good judgment in bringing the case in the first place. The violent fantasies of the student were simply too far removed from an imminent lawless action to justify his arrest. Amazingly, the government again indicted the guy, this time for a different violation, transmitting a threat in interstate commerce. Again the Court threw it out based on the First Amendment, with harsh words for the prosecutor for so unwisely pursuing what the judge thought was a school disciplinary matter. (The student was expelled from school.) For the full, convoluted story of this case see **http:// www.eff.org/pub/Legal/Cases/Baker_UMich_case/**.

The First Amendment prevents all governments—federal, state, and local— and the police and prosecutors of these governments from prohibiting or restraining your speech based on its content. The fact that your speech offends people, or even disrupts civil order and disturbs the peace, doesn't mean the speaker can be restrained by the government. You can't punish a speaker because his listeners become violent. Indeed in one famous Supreme Court case, *Terminiello v. Chicago* in 1949, the Court noted that free speech may best serve its purpose when it "induces a condition of unrest, creates dissatisfaction with conditions as they are, or even stirs people to anger."

> **Note**
>
> Remember that the First Amendment only prohibits governmental restraints. Your speech may still be legally restrained by non-governmental sources, such as in a commercial setting by contract. For example, a computer network can require you to agree to its rules of censorship as a condition of membership. You don't have to agree, of course; you can take your business elsewhere. But if the agreement requires you to abide by certain speech restrictions, such as no profanities, then the network provider may legally censor your messages that violate the agreement. The provider may even terminate your membership, or otherwise exercise its rights under the

subscription agreement if you break it. There are certain legal risks to the network provider in trying to control the content, which we will get into later, but it has the legal right to try to do so.

Although you can pretty much say what you want on the Internet, even if it's unpopular or outrageous, there is still need for some common-sense restraints and courtesy on the Net. The basic moral persuasions, albeit not legal rules, which normally limit what you can or should say in the real world, apply with equal force on the Internet. Common mutual respect, human decency, and politeness are as needed on the Internet as anywhere else.

Tip

Familiarize yourself with Netiquette and don't do things in cyberspace that you wouldn't do in person.

The Slander and Libel Limitation

Although there is no good Internet equivalent to inciting cyber-panic by shouting fire in a theater, typing **VIRUS** in all caps in a crowded chat room might alarm a few newbies. Still, even if it resulted in an immediate net split, where everyone leaves a chat room immediately, no one's life would be endangered so as to justify making it illegal, and it's unlikely that even the most uptight prosecutor could be persuaded to indict the villain. But before you go around shouting VIRUS because it's the kind of speech that can't be outlawed, remember that you could still be subject to civil lawsuits and damages for your loud lie. For example, if you lied and said a sysop or Webmaster had files in his cyberspace with lots of nasty viruses and worms, that could be libelous. If people believed you, it could damage a good reputation or hurt someone's business. If you write lies about a person or their business, that's *libel*; if you say it, it's *slander*. (Lies about a business are called *trade libel*.) If the libel damages the business—for instance, if people stopped buying their software for fear of viruses—you could be sued and forced to pay the damages, such as the lost profits from lost sales. The law protects the truth, but not a lie.

> **Note**
>
> If you write, for instance, in a mailing list or chat room, that another person is a software thief or his computer files are contaminated with viruses, and it's true, then it's protected free speech. It's only libel or slander if it's not true. You can call someone a crook, if it's true. But you'd better be prepared to prove the truth of your assertions in court if the person sues you! If it's not true, then you are at risk—your flame outburst could end up busting you financially.

A major exception to this libel rule involves public figures, which can be either an elected official or a celebrity. For a person who is a public figure, such as an elected government official like the President, it has to be proven that the disparaging remarks were false, and were made with malice or a reckless disregard for the truth. Sometimes the public figure might be able to prove the statement was false, say for instance, prove that he's not a crook. But malice or recklessness is very hard to prove. If, for instance, you called your mayor a cocaine user, and he responded by suing you for libel, the mayor would not only have to prove it was not true, but he would have to prove that you made the statement out of malice or with reckless disregard as to whether it was true or not. The law requires public figures to put up with a lot of verbal abuse. But without this rule, a publisher could be held liable for the mere reporting of false facts about public officials. The press would be chilled from reporting the news, for fear of being swamped by libel suits by news figures upset by unfavorable stories. This happened in the past and is what led the Supreme Court to make this rule in the famous case of *New York Times v. Sullivan* (**http://www.eff.org/pub/Legal/Cases/ nytvsullivanlibelpubfigures.notes**).

> **Tip**
>
> For more on libel, public figures, and the Net, see **http://www.eff.org/pub/ Legal/**.

Are Computer Networks Information Distributors or Publishers?

The question of libel and flaming in cyberspace has already hit the courts. For instance *Cubby, Inc. v. CompuServe, Inc.*, 776 F.Supp. 135 (S.D.N.Y. 1991) involved a flame in the Journalism forum on CompuServe by a cyber publication called Rumorville. (For more information on this case, see **http://seamless.com/rcl/compu.txt**.) *Cubby v. CompuServe* is a 1991 New York federal district court case. In the context of a libel dispute this case raises a legal question very important to the Internet. It's the question of whether a computer network should be treated as an information distributor or an information publisher. The *Cubby v. CompuServe* case shows how the consequences of this legal distinction can have far-reaching effects upon our life in cyberspace.

The Rumorville publication on CompuServe provided daily cyber reports about broadcast journalism and journalists. Believe it or not, Rumorville had an electronic newsletter competitor somewhere else in cyberspace that also provided such reports called Skuttlebut. Rumorville is alleged to have made defamatory remarks about Skuttlebut and Skuttlebut's owner. Rumorville supposedly said, among other things, that Skuttlebut was a "new start up scam" and its owner had been "bounced" from his last job in broadcast journalism. Skuttlebut, under its corporate name of Cubby, Inc., then sued Rumorville, its individual proprietor, and also sued CompuServe, all for libel, trade libel, and unfair business practices. The fact that Skuttlebut also sued CompuServe is what makes this case so interesting.

CompuServe defended by saying that even if it was true that Rumorville illegally disparaged Skuttlebut, CompuServe could not be held liable for what went on in its forum as a matter of law because it neither knew, nor had reason to know, of the statements; it was just a distributor. Cubby argued to the contrary that CompuServe was a publisher and should be held responsible for what it published on its forums. Under the law a person who publishes, or who repeats or otherwise republishes defamatory statements, is subject to liability as if he had originally said it. Cubby also argued that the forum leader was a CompuServe agent, and so CompuServe was vicariously liable for the actions of its agent. The court agreed with CompuServe and held that it was acting as a vendor or distributor of information/speech, not a publisher, and the forum leaders were not CompuServe agents.

A publisher, such as a newspaper, is responsible for what it publishes. If the contents of a story in a newspaper are libelous, the publisher can be found liable, along with the author. On the other hand, information vendors, such as bookstores, newsstands, or libraries, have long been protected from liability for defamation contained in the materials they distribute, unless they knew, or had reason to know, of the defamation. They are considered to be passive conduits of information, and so are screened from liability unless they are somehow at fault. Any alternative would be disastrous. In the words of the Supreme Court in *Auvil v. CBS 60 Minutes,* it would force distributors to set up:

...full time editorial boards...throughout the country which possess sufficient knowledge, legal acumen and access to experts to continually monitor incoming...(materials)...at every turn. That is not realistic. More than unrealistic in economic terms, it is difficult to imagine a scenario more chilling on the media's right of expression and the public's right to know.

CompuServe Decision

Guided by such Supreme Court decisions, the federal trial judge who decided the *CompuServe* case, Judge Leisure, considered the difference between publishers and distributors. His ruling is now important legal precedent for the Internet. Read for yourself what the Judge had to say:

> CompuServe's CIS product is essentially an electronic, for profit library that carries a vast number of publications and collects usage and membership fees from its subscribers in return for access to the publications. CompuServe and companies like it are at the forefront of the information industry revolution....While CompuServe may decline to carry a given publication altogether, in reality, once it does decide to carry a publication, it will have little or no editorial control over that publication's contents....

> CompuServe has no more editorial control over such a publication than does a public library, book store, or newsstand, and it would be no more feasible for CompuServe to examine every publication it carries for potentially defamatory statements than it would be for any other distributor to do so.... Obviously, the national distributor of hundreds of periodicals has no duty to monitor each issue of every periodical it distributes. Such a rule would be an impermissible burden on the First Amendment....

> Technology is rapidly transforming the information industry. A computerized database is the functional equivalent of a more traditional news vendor, and the inconsistent application of a lower standard of liability to an electronic news distributor such as CompuServe than that which is applied to a public library, book store, or newsstand would impose an undue burden on the free flow of information. Given the relevant First Amendment considerations, the appropriate standard of liability to be applied to CompuServe is whether it knew or had reason to know of the allegedly defamatory Rumorville statements.

The court went on to declare that CompuServe neither knew nor had reason to know of the statements on its forums, and so granted a summary judgment in CompuServe's favor on all counts. The case went on as between Rumorville and Skuttlebut, but nobody much cares about that petty dispute!

Hopefully the *Cubby v. CompuServe* case will be followed by other courts around the country, and computer networks will be classified for First

Amendment purposes as distributors, not publishers. But, in a case involving a different network, Prodigy, at least one court has already gone the other way, and treated a network as a publisher. (*Stratton Oakmont, Inc. v. Prodigy Services Company, a Partnership of IBM Corp. and Sears-Roebuck & Co.*) For more information on this case see **http://www.eff.org/ pub/Legal/Cases/Stratton_Oakmont_Porush_v_Prodigy/ stratton-oakmont_porush_v_prodigy_et-al.decision**. The New York state court judge in the *Prodigy* case, Judge Ain, was well aware of the *CompuServe* and *CBS 60 Minutes* decisions. In fact, he quoted extensively from both of these cases and used them to support his decision. Judge Ain did so by distinguishing the facts of these different cases.

Stratton Oakmont v. Prodigy involves an alleged libelous statement made by an anonymous user in the Money Talks forum on Prodigy. The unknown cyber-poster said, among other things, that Stratton Oakmont, a securities investment banking firm, was a "cult of brokers who either lie for a living or get fired" and said the owner was a "soon to be proven criminal." Stratton Oakmont then sued Prodigy, and John Doe, the unknown villain, for libel, claiming the remarks were untrue and caused severe damages. Stratton claimed that Prodigy was a publisher and the moderator of the Money Talk forum was Prodigy's agent. So far it sounds a lot like the CompuServe case, so why did Judge Ain reach the opposite result?

The answer lies in Prodigy's own statements to the public, and the manner in which it tried to run the network as a "family place" where all offensive material was screened out. The court considered such facts as Prodigy's advertising, its promulgation of "content guidelines" for all of its users, its use of a software screening program that could supposedly prescreen all bulletin board postings for offensive language, and its use of Board Leaders hired to, among other things, police its boards and delete offensive speech. Prodigy protested to the contrary that it had changed its policy, or it didn't really mean what it said, and couldn't possibly police the more than 60,000 messages a day that go through its cyberspace. Judge Ain was unconvinced. He found it was undisputed that Prodigy had set itself up as a private censor that could control the content of everything posted to its network. That is essentially why he found Prodigy to be a publisher whereas CompuServe was not. It's kind of like "live by the sword, die by the sword."

Prodigy Decision

Here is what Judge Ain said when he ruled against Prodigy and found it could be liable for libelous remarks posted in its forums (*Stratton Oakmont v. Prodigy*):

(continues)

(continued)

Prodigy has uniquely arrogated to itself the role of determining what is proper for its members to post and read on its bulletin boards. Based on the foregoing, this Court is compelled to conclude that…Prodigy is a publisher rather than a distributor.

Prodigy has virtually created an editorial staff of Board Leaders who have the ability to continually monitor incoming transmissions and in fact do spend time censoring notes. Indeed, it could be said that Prodigy's current system of automatic scanning, Guidelines, and Board Leaders may have a chilling effect on freedom of communication in cyberspace, and it appears that this chilling effect is exactly what Prodigy wants, but for the legal liability that attaches to such censorship.

Let it be clear that this Court is in full agreement with *Cubby v. CompuServe* and *Auvil v. CBS 60 Minutes.* Computer bulletin boards should generally be regarded in the same context as bookstores, libraries, and network affiliates.

(Citations omitted) It is Prodigy's own policies, technology and staffing decisions which have altered the scenario and mandated a finding that it is a publisher. Prodigy's conscious choice, to gain the benefits of editorial control, has opened it up to greater liability than CompuServe and other network providers that make no such choice.

The consequences of classifying Prodigy as a publisher, not a distributor, are to increase the network's exposure and liability for the contents of everything posted on its forums. Beyond Prodigy, it means that if any cyber network exercises editorial control over content, or even if it just claims it is going to do so, then it may be held legally responsible for all of the information supposedly under its control.

Note

There is federal legislation pending that has already passed the House that addresses this problem, the Internet Freedom and Family Empowerment Act (**http://www.cdt.org/policy/freespeech/cox_wyden.html**). Among other things, it allows providers to police their networks without thereby becoming a publisher.

Many contend that unless the Prodigy opinion is reversed, or neutralized by legislation, it will have a chilling effect over the entire Internet, and impose unrealistic duties upon all networks. But it might just have the opposite effect. The networks may be forced by fear of liability to back off of all censorship. They may be forced to stop any monitoring or editorial control, and start acting more like the telephone company. If you are offended, or libeled in such a free network, you'll have to turn to the particular publisher who libeled you. You won't be able to also sue the electronic library that brought you the offending material. If someone slandered you over the telephone, you'd sue the slanderer. You wouldn't even think of suing the telephone company. Networks that try and go the other way and promise clean, inoffensive Disney-esque content like Prodigy once did will have to act with such strong controls that its expenses and charges will go sky high. Few users are likely to be willing to pay the price for such censored clean networks.

Prodigy got itself into the current legal mess it is now in by holding itself out to the public as a controller of the content of its network. The CompuServe and Prodigy cases read together provide a clear message to all information networks that they are better off not "knowing or having reason to know" the contents of the information in their cyberspace. If they do, they may be treated as the publishers, or republishers, of the information, and be liable for what they publish.

Obscenity Limitations on Free Expression

It's legal to read or look at anything you want in the privacy of your own home, even the most obscene pornography anyone can imagine. But some forms of adult sexual content is considered so offensive, so obscene, that even though it may be legal to possess it in your own home, it's illegal for anyone to sell it to you, or to publicly display it. Obscene expressions can be legally prohibited from public sale and exhibition. The trouble is, people can't agree on what obscene means.

The Supreme Court has struggled with this issue for years. One person's obscenity might be another's art. Tastes and personal values differ so much in this large and multi-cultural country. Some Supreme Court Justices claimed to "know it when they see it" but they still couldn't put a workable legal definition on obscenity. Finally, in 1974, the Supreme Court came up with a flexible, compromise type of illegal obscenity test in *Miller v. California*. Materials are considered legally obscene, and thus, outside of First Amendment protection if:

- The average person, applying contemporary community standards, would find the materials, taken as a whole, appeal to the prurient interest.

- The materials depict or describe, in an obviously offensive way, sexual conduct specifically prohibited under state law.

■ The work, taken as a whole, lacks serious literary, artistic, political, or scientific value.

Under this test "community standards" became the key.

The Miller test allowed for cultural diversity, recognizing the fact that what is shocking and offensive to an ordinary person in a small town, might be ho hum in Las Vegas or New York City. The Miller community standards test avoided what the Supreme Court saw as the evil of the "absolutism of imposed uniformity," which would strangle the diversity of different attitudes and tastes of people in different communities. Under this interpretation of the First Amendment, a movie can be legally sold and displayed in one community, but banned and illegal as pornography in another. The Supreme Court sort of dodged the impossible question of "What is obscenity?" by letting the local communities decide, subject, of course, to certain general parameters. Further, the Court has consistently held that the private possession and viewing of obscene materials remain protected by the First Amendment, no matter where you live.

Under the Miller test of pornography, if you live in that proverbial conservative small town, you might not be able to buy the particularly dirty book you want in any adult book store in your town. But you can still travel to the big city, buy your smut there, and then bring it home and secretly look at it without fear of arrest and imprisonment. A compromise was reached that seemed to work. Then along came the Internet and threw the whole question of "community" into doubt.

> **Note**
>
> Many of the places you visit on the Internet really have no physical location. Where is a newsgroup located: a Web site, a discussion group, a chat room? Is it the particular geographical locale in which the computer temporarily hosting the cyber connections is located? What if there are several such host computers located in different communities? Alternatively, is it the local community of each individual participant in the online community? If so, how can that possibly work when most online communities now have members from all over the place, from both the big city and the small town? The participants in most electronic groups on the Internet are probably from all over the world, not just the U.S. So what community standards should govern the virtual communities of the Internet? They simply don't follow the normal limitations of space and time. When you log on to the Internet you log on to a new kind of space, a computer space that really has no geographical location.

The creation of virtual communities raises the next big obscenity legal issue of our times. It is just now starting to hit the courts and will probably take years before the issue is settled. The Miller test will definitely have to be re-thought because the geographically based community standards don't apply to transmissions over a global network. Today computer networks allow the formation of virtual communities, globally, without any significant impact on local, territorial communities. Eventually the law will catch up with the new technologies and cyber-culture. The courts will begin to recognize virtual communities as having their own independent existence, their own rights to define what is, and is not, acceptable to the community of computer users who voluntarily choose to come together in cyberspace. The First Amendment right to free association demands this. But to a judge and prosecutor who have never used a computer, much less logged on to the Internet, the notion of virtual communities must seem like "pie in the sky" gibberish. The first case to apply the Miller community test in cyberspace seems to have run into just this kind of techno-gap problem.

U.S. v. Robert and Carleen Thomas

The case of *U.S. v. Robert and Carleen Thomas* shows just how messed up things can get in the law when judges first try to deal with new technologies they don't understand. (See **http://www.eff.org/pub/Legal/Cases/ AABBS_Thomases_Memphis/**.) Mr. and Mrs. Thomas, residents of San Francisco, were indicted by a federal grand jury in Memphis, Tennessee (a place they had never even visited) for transporting obscene materials over the Internet. In the words of the government press report that announced their arrest in San Francisco on February 3, 1994: "The Thomas's operated a computer bulletin board service specializing in pornographic material enabling other computer users throughout the country to receive pornographic material via their computer." They were subsequently found guilty by a jury in Memphis, Tennessee and convicted of 11 counts of transmitting obscenity through interstate phone lines via their bulletin board. Each count carries up to five years in prison and a $250,000.00 fine. At present, they are out on bail awaiting a decision on their appeal.

The facts of the case are important to understand the potential negative consequences to the Internet of this decision, and why most legal experts expect that it will be reversed on appeal. The saga began when a postal inspector in Tennessee, acting upon the complaint of an unknown computer user in western Tennessee, logged on to the Thomases "adult only" bulletin board. They ran their BBS from a computer in their home in San Francisco. The BBS had a sign-on warning that it contained adult materials, and it required a password to access. The password was only issued to adults after application and payment of a modest membership fee. The postal inspector applied for membership under a fake name, paid his fee, and commenced his detailed inspection of the in-excess-of 20,000 GIFs and other images on the BBS. Our tireless government worker then selected the worst, kinkiest junk he could find on the board, and downloaded them onto his computer in Memphis. He had caused the Thomases to commit a crime in Tennessee without their even knowing about it! He also ordered the nastiest videos he could find and caused them to be sent to him in the mail. Another crime committed by the Thomases.

Note

I've read some of the original materials in the court file. The postal inspector's search warrant affidavit includes a description of the stuff he selected, all of which he carefully viewed, of course. I couldn't even finish reading the descriptions! Bestiality, rape, torture—perverse, vile, and sick by most people's standards. Make no mistake about it: the board had some very hard core stuff on it.

The Thomases knew very well what was on their board. Their name was on every item, every GIF. They even answered some of the "undercover" postal inspector's questions about the junk. Apparently there is a market for this, and they made money on the downloads and video sales.

Based on the postal inspector's descriptions of some of the videos he ordered, it's easy to understand how a jury in western Tennessee would decide it was all pornography, even the computer GIFs. The question is, should the standards and values of a jury in western Tennessee be imposed on the rest of the country? Should the local standards of the most conservative communities in the country control and decide what everyone else in cyberspace is allowed to see? Should we force all virtual communities to limit their speech so as to conform to the most restrictive physical-world communities?

Back to the facts. Even though the Thomases had never advertised in Tennessee, had no contacts with the state whatsoever, and it was the law enforcement officer in Tennessee, not the Thomases, who took all of the actions required to gain access to the materials and be transported to Tennessee, the Thomases woke up to a knock on their door one day to find themselves under arrest for an indictment in Tennessee. The federal officers had a search warrant and they seized all of the Thomases computers and software, including the private messages of their 3,500 BBS members. Even their backup tapes were taken.

This was not the first time police had seized the Thomases equipment and stopped their BBS. In 1992, all of the Thomases computer equipment was seized by the San Jose Police Department. After inspecting all of the materials on their BBS, the police returned the equipment and did not press charges. The police found no adult or child pornography and determined that the materials were not pornographic under the standards of their community, the San Francisco Bay area. Similar materials could be found in hundreds of adult bookstores throughout that community.

Note

After the arrest and seizure by federal agents from Tennessee, the Thomases were released on bail, but it took them months to get all of their computer equipment back. An excerpt from the motion filed by the Thomases attorney in federal court in San Francisco to try and force the return of their computer equipment gives some flavor as to what this case is about:

> It is hard to determine the reasons the Western District of Tennessee has reached out in an attempt to impose their standards on the Northern District of California. Perhaps it is the simple desire to obtain tens of thousands of dollars worth of computer equipment. Had they applied for a warrant to search an adult book store in San Francisco, they would have been laughed out of court.

Is an electronic version of an adult book store that different?

The Thomases were later tried and convicted in Memphis, Tennessee. The conviction outraged many in the Internet community. It is now under appeal. The reason for the concern is it allows one local geographic community to dictate the standards for the entire cyber community. This is just the kind of "absolutism of imposed uniformity" that the Miller case was designed to avoid. The Thomas decision allows censorship, even though adults could easily have avoided the unwanted materials and prevented their children from accessing them. It will be interesting to see what the appellate court does. You'll no doubt be reading about this case on the Internet.

Child Pornography Limitations

We all want to try and protect our children on the Net from unwanted influences. The question is how to go about doing that without infringing on everyone's First Amendment rights. First of all, the First Amendment does not protect child pornography or child pornographers. That is not the question. As a society, we have already decided that it is a crime, and we have many laws against it. Unlike obscene materials, the mere possession of child pornography may be a crime, even in the privacy of a home.

Under federal law, child pornography is any "visual material" that depicts a child either engaging in explicit sexual acts, or posing in a "lewd and lascivious" manner, when the manufacture of such material involves the actual use of a real child (18 U.S.C. §2251, et seq.; Sexual Exploitation and Other Abuse of Children Act). This is material that is illegal regardless of whether it is obscene. That means you don't have to ask any questions about "community standards."

Note

Child pornography laws are really completely separate and apart from adult obscenity laws. Obscenity laws are aimed at forbidden expression. They assume that some things are socially harmful by virtue of being expressed or depicted. Child pornography laws, in contrast, are not aimed at "expression" at all. They are instead designed to try and protect children from abuse. They try and destroy a market for materials that cannot be produced without sexually abusing children. In fact, if the child in a child-porn movie is a computer animation, and no real child was used in the production, the movie would not violate the child pornography laws (although it would probably still violate the obscenity laws under most community standards). Also, child pornography laws do not apply to any written works at all, since they do not involve the use of children. It's aimed at videos and pictures, and designed to protect the innocent child actors and models.

We have other laws on the books, mostly state laws, that prohibit adults from engaging in sex with a minor, exposing themselves, and so on. Sexual abuse and seduction of children have long been illegal in our country. Child pornographers and pedophiles who use the Net to try and lure children for their perverse crimes are being arrested every day under the existing laws. For instance, in September of 1995 the Justice Department in one fell swoop searched 125 homes across the country, and arrested dozens of people, culminating a two-year investigation of child pornographers and pedophiles on American Online. AOL had started the investigation when it discovered child pornography on its network and notified the FBI. Still, there are real dangers to children cruising unsupervised on the Net, just as there are real dangers to children left alone in their own neighborhoods. We would all like to make the world a safer place for our children.

The question is, do we need additional laws directed at the Net to stop this problem. Many people think not, especially with the development of new software that users can now apply to keep adult areas of the Internet off limits to their children. Let the users police themselves they say—the problem of children on the Net is a non-problem that has been blown way out of proportion by a sensationalizing press, poor research, and vote hunting politicians. (See **http://www2000.ogsm.vanderbilt.edu/cyberporn.debate.cgi**.) We'll address this question when we consider a few of the clean-up-the-Internet type bills now pending in Congress and the trouble they might cause if enacted.

To Inspect or Not to Inspect?

Existing law already presents a troubling question for information providers on the Internet. What happens if someone posts a file to their BBS, Web site, or user group that contains either child pornography, or obscene materials? If you know about it, and it's clearly illegal, the answer is easy. Get rid of it, fast. But should you be on the lookout for it? Should you monitor and inspect the GIFs and other media uploaded on to your turf to keep it clean? If you do monitor, how do you decide if it's obscene or not? How do you determine if a person depicted nude or in a sex act is a minor (under 18) or not? Maybe it's better not to look at all?

As far as disparaging comments go, and the possible liability for republishing libel, we've already seen that under current law (Prodigy), it's probably better not to know, not to inspect, not to act like an editor who prescreens publications. You should have clearly posted policies and agreements that prohibit such speech, but at the same time announce to all users that you do not prescreen, or edit, or in any other way act as a publisher. But does that also hold true for child pornography, or obscenity? Do you say it's prohibited, will not be tolerated, and will be removed if found, and brought to the attention of law enforcement; then also say no effort will be made to prescreen? Do you warn users to beware of illegal postings because you have not inspected the postings, and cannot do so or lose your legal status as a distributor?

This question is still very much in doubt, especially as applied to child pornography. My best guess right now is that it's probably better not to inspect, and to warn every user of that. For if you do inspect, you may once again be found to be a republisher, and held criminally liable for all of the materials in your cyberspace. Under criminal law, including criminal obscenity statutes, the government must prove "scienter" (essentially, "guilty knowledge" on the defendant's part) before a defendant can be found guilty. So, if the government can't prove beyond a reasonable doubt that a system operator knew, or should have known, that there was obscene material on his system, the operator should not be found guilty of an obscenity crime. But if the sysop had a policy of inspection, and he missed one, or wrongly guessed if something was obscene, or someone was under 18, then he might be found guilty under the "should have known" standard. If he did not have an inspection policy, and clearly advised users of this fact, that it wasn't policed by him, and they should proceed at their own risk, it would be much harder to prove "should have known."

The question of child pornography is more difficult because the mere possession may be a crime. If there is a child-porn GIF in a sysop's computer, and he doesn't know it, he might still be criminally guilty for possession alone.

Again, no one knows for sure at this time. Hopefully there would be no criminal liability for unknowing possession of child pornography because there would be no criminal intent, no scienter. If a sysop is held criminally liable, even though he didn't know or have reason to know, then all sysops will be forced to inspect, and to inspect carefully, else shut down. The law can't go in that direction, at least not for long, without changing around a lot of other legal rules. If fear of child pornography forces everyone to inspect, then under current law everyone will in turn be opened to civil liability under defamation and the like. There will be no more computer networks; everyone in cyberspace will be a publisher, like it or not. That would cause quite a negative First Amendment chill on the Net!

> **Note**
>
> There is pending federal legislation that could change the law and take the risks out of providers' attempts to police their networks for pornography—the Internet Freedom and Family Empowerment Act (**http://www.cdt.org/policy/freespeech/cox_wyden.html**).

The legal situation is a little clearer when a sysop somehow knows that there is illegal material in his space, say by accidental perusal, or someone tells him. He then has a duty to delete the obscenity or child pornography, and perhaps even the libel (especially if he knows it to be libel). He may even then have the additional duty to suspend or revoke the privileges of the user who posted the materials. The severity of the sysop's response would depend upon the seriousness of the offense. If it's clearly child pornography, as in the AOL case, the sysop probably also has a duty to alert the police. If the sysop becomes aware of the illegal materials, and does nothing about it, or responds inadequately, that may create the necessary scienter for criminal prosecution. So even if you don't inspect, if you happen to see it or are told about it, delete it and punish the poster.

> **Caution**
>
> As a final legal type disclaimer, remember that all of cyber-law is a murky area of very tricky legal waters where the only constant is change. By the time you read this, new laws may have been enacted, or court cases decided, that change everything. This is especially true of obscenity and child pornography issues. This book does not provide legal advice. When in doubt, consult an attorney. If you are a cyber-network, a sysop, forum leader, newsgroup moderator, Webmaster, or an electronic publisher of any kind, you should have an attorney, and ask them for legal advice on your particular

situation. Even if you are just a user who likes to post (upload) "adult materials" on the Internet, you should probably have the advice of an attorney too, else you may run the risk of finding out later that you were a publisher of pornography and didn't even know it. The uploading of files may constitute publication. Depending on the community in which you live, or the community in which the Courts eventually decide applies to your cyber-activities, you may be surprised to discover that what you thought was cool and socially acceptable, your community finds obscene and criminal.

Pending Federal Legislation

As of November 1995 there are several clean-up-the-Internet type bills pending in Congress. To put it mildly, some are a lot better than others. The mentioned Internet Freedom and Family Empowerment Act may have a favorable impact. It's designed to help protect the Internet by keeping the FCC out, legally classifying providers as distributors, not publishers, and encouraging software that allows parents to screen out areas of the Internet they deem unacceptable for their children.

Other pending legislation could have a chilling, Big Brother effect. The most notable is the Communications Decency Act giving the FCC the power to regulate indecency on the Internet. Indecency is something far less than obscenity and includes such things as comedian George Carlin's "seven dirty words." It's an attempt to extend to the Internet the government regulation we allow over television. The unique governmental rationale for broadcast television censorship just does not apply to cyberspace. The problems for networks and information providers we've discussed with obscenity and child pornography would be magnified a million times if extended to indecent speech. Under the proposed law, if someone posted a note on your Web with certain four-letter words you could be held criminally liable, fined up to $50,000, or jailed for six months. For a list of a few indecent Web sites likely to become illegal if this legislation is passed see **http://thehugelist.com/ malaise.html**.

Obviously, if passed, the U.S. parts of the Internet would be disrupted. Also, just think how ridiculous we would look to the rest of the Internet global community. The law would not last for long. Almost everyone seems to think the law is unconstitutional, even House Speaker Newt Gingrich has publicly said so. But still, the bill passed the Senate by a vote of 84 to 16! The house has not passed the bill, but some modified version may well get through.

It is times like this that the importance of the First Amendment and constitutional government really strikes home. The idea of legislating morality on the Internet seems very appealing to many politicians, especially in an election year. There may be no stopping them outside of the court room. Some groups seem determined to try and make the entire Internet a child-safe "happy Net" where all children can frolic unsupervised by their parents. A place where Big Brother is in charge, and the young—supposedly ever so fragile techno-nerds—could never be offended or find inappropriate materials. The proposed legislation would in effect take the world's largest library and screen out, or burn, all of the books except for the ones in the children's department! Fortunately, there is the ability of the legal system to declare such unconstitutional legislation to be null and void.

Note

For an update on legislation affecting the Internet, as well as most of the cases discussed in this chapter, check out the Web site of the Electronic Frontier Foundation at **http://www.eff.org/**. The EFF keeps abreast of all legal issues affecting the Internet. You'll not only find the latest news, but a wide range of intelligent commentary by Internet leaders and lawyers. Also see the Web site of the Center For Democracy & Technology at **http://www.cdt.org/**, and the Net Politics page in the Path Finders Web site at **http://pathfinder.com/pathfinder/politics/netpol/index.html**.

Your Rights and Responsibilities of Privacy on the Internet

Although the Fourth Amendment prohibits unreasonable searches and seizures by the government, there is no place in the Constitution that explicitly says you have a right to privacy. Still, in the last century the courts have found a fundamental right to privacy implied in the Constitution. Legal decisions and state and federal legislation have set up legal protections to try to guarantee us the right to privacy, to be left alone, and to be secure in our communications. As U.S. citizens, these rights are again carried with us when we enter the Internet.

E-Mail Privacy—Who Else Can Read Your E-Mail?

E-mail is one of the biggest uses of the Internet. How secure and private is it? Aside from the intended recipients, who else, if anyone, can read your mail? E-mail is not legally the same as the U.S. mail, and is not entitled to the same protections. If a network provider wanted to, it could make a condition of network use that you agree to allow it to read your e-mail at any time for any reason. You in turn could agree to disagree and take your business elsewhere! Most Internet providers and networks don't have such an agreement. They keep your e-mail private and don't peek unless required to do so by warrant or subpoena, as we'll discuss later.

The situation is very much different in the workplace with company networks. Management can, and usually does, make it a condition of use of the company's computer network that the employees *do not* have a right to privacy of their e-mail. The justification is that you are only supposed to be using the company computers and e-mail systems for company business. Management has a right to inspect its employee's work. It's the employer's computer system, and so the employer can put whatever restrictions on it that it wants. So far, in the few cases that have hit the courts in this area, when an employer reads an employee's e-mail, and some terrible, embarrassing thing is revealed hurting the employee who subsequently sues, the employer's practice has been upheld as legal. Absent new legislation in this area, e-mail and other computer privacy will probably not be required in the workplace. So don't assume your e-mail at work is private and confidential unless the employer has a policy which expressly makes it private.

Outside of the workplace, read the subscription or user agreement with your networks. You should have a right to privacy of your e-mail, unless the agreement specifically provides to the contrary. There are two federal laws that apply to keep it private.

Federal Computer Privacy Laws

Congress has enacted and revised two laws so that they apply to e-mail and other computer telecommunications: the Electronic Communications Privacy Act, 18 U.S.C. §2501, et seq., and the Stored Wire and Electronic Communications and Transactional Records Act, 18 U.S.C. §2701, et seq. Many other states have their own computer laws and privacy laws that might apply to you. Some are listed later in this chapter.

The Electronic Communications Privacy Act is the federal wiretap law. It was amended in 1986 to clarify its application to computer transmissions. No one can intercept your communications without your authorization—for instance, no one can secretly wiretap your telephone, or your computer data line—except for the government. The government can only do it if it first gets a warrant from a judge. The judge, in turn, is only supposed to issue a wiretap warrant under very limited circumstances spelled out in the law.

The wiretap law applies only to electronic data, be it voice or data, that is in transit. Once the data arrives somewhere, and is stored in a computer for instance, this law no longer applies. (See *Steve Jackson Games, Inc. v. United States Secret Service* at **http://www.io.com/SS/appeal-opinion.html**.)

Tip

For more information on these laws and the intriguing case of the Secret Service's illegal raid on the Steve Jackson Games bulletin board, see the Web sites at **http://www.io.com/SS/** and **http://www.eff.org/pub/Legal/Cases/SJG/**.

That is where the other law kicks in, the Electronic Communications and Transactional Records Act. It protects data, such as e-mail, that is stored somewhere, that's no longer in transit. An example is e-mail stored in your Internet provider's computer before you access and download it onto your computer. E-mail that has arrived at your provider's computer is no longer in transit, even if it hasn't reached its final destination, namely your computer.

Both laws have hefty criminal and civil penalties for their violation. The Electronic Communications and Transactional Records Act has several provisions to protect a sysop or other network provider from substantial liability for inadvertent or necessary interceptions of the private transmissions of its users. A provider is shielded from liability if the interception, disclosure, or use of the communication was done "in the normal course of his employment while engaged in any activity which is a necessary incident to the rendition of his service or to the protection of the rights or property of the provider of that service."

The idea behind this exception is that the provider might inadvertently see your e-mail while working on a technical problem, just like the mailman might see a postcard to you. There are other circumstances spelled out in the law where a provider may access a communication to or from a user, but the provider is prohibited from divulging the contents of the communication to anyone. The only exception to the non-disclosure rule is where there is court-ordered disclosure by warrant or subpoena. Again, the law spells out the circumstances and complex requirements for the government to obtain such court orders.

There is an important arbitrary distinction in the law made for messages that have been stored by the provider for more than 180 days. The law is complicated, and you are urged to read it for yourself to understand the details, but simply put, messages or files stored for less than 180 days are much harder for the government to get to. After 180 days the government can require a provider to produce communications with just a subpoena, a court document far easier for a prosecutor to obtain than a warrant.

> **Tip**
>
> Never leave your messages with an e-mail server for more than 180 days. Download and delete with the server/provider.

Cryptology, Secret Codes, and the Clipper Chip

Another highly controversial Internet privacy law issue concerns the federal laws limiting the use and transmission of coded messages. Certain cryptology software is illegal to use, and very illegal to send out of the country. It is even illegal to publish certain technical data about encryption theory without first getting a license from the government. If you wonder why the government has such extreme paranoia on this subject, just remember World War II. Many believe our greatest secret weapon in the war was not the atom bomb, it was our ability to crack the German and Japanese code, and our contra ability (thanks primarily to Native American languages) to send impenetrable codes. We could read their secret messages; they couldn't read ours. It provided a tremendous military advantage. This is why codes have always been top secret, classified military stuff. Today, codes are primarily a matter of computer science, not esoteric languages. For this reason, the federal government classifies certain cryptology software as military weapons. The software can't be exported without a weapons permit!

A lot of people on the Internet think that the government should stop treating cryptology, the science and study of secret writing, like a dangerous tool that only the military should have. They contend that we have a First Amendment right to freely discuss and use secret codes, and that we need to do so to preserve our privacy. They cite the dangers of Big Brother having a computer record of everything you do and buy, of hackers and criminals reading your e-mail, stealing your credit card numbers, and the like. Perhaps most importantly, they contend that the government's laws on this subject are hindering the development of a private, secure Internet, one not so vulnerable to attack by hackers, criminals, con men, and the like. See for instance the EFF files at **http://www.eff.org/pub/EFF/Frontier_Files/ EFF_Files/Privacy_Crypto/**. Also see the Electronic Privacy Information Center Web site at **http://epic.org/**.

One of the rallying cases in this area is the government's prosecution of a cryptologist, Phil Zimmerman, who invented a software encryption program called Pretty Good Privacy, or PGP for short. Zimmerman posted his software on the Internet, free for the taking by anyone who wanted to keep their communications secure. See **http://www.eff.org/pub/Net_info/Tools/ Crypto/PGP/**.

The problem is, PGP is good, so good that some think even the super secret National Security Agency can't crack it. Naturally there are many in the government who don't want hostile governments or criminals to have such a "weapon." Even though the cold war is over, they want to be able to eavesdrop and crack any codes necessary for "national security purposes" or to fight the never-ending "war on crime."

That's why the government is instead promoting, and may require by law, the use of the so called clipper chip for encoding. Right now that's the government's solution for how to make the Internet and other cyberspace more secure from criminals and hackers. With the clipper chip, the government always has the key to decode any encryption. For more information on the clipper chip see **http://www.eff.org/pub/Privacy/Clipper/**. Needless to say, there are problems with this idea. For one, foreign governments won't buy into a worldwide computer network where the U.S. government always has the keys in its pocket to all encrypted messages.

The likes of Zimmerman's PGP code loose on the Internet, a cyberspace without national boundaries, is perceived by some as a threat. His posting PGP on the Internet may well have violated several federal laws, a possibility Zimmerman knew about when he posted it. Naturally Zimmerman is now the subject of a federal grand jury investigation, and his imminent arrest is expected by many. Zimmerman, with the help of the EFF, has already begun to prepare his defense on First Amendment and privacy grounds. This will be another interesting case to watch.

Your Rights and Responsibilities of Copyright on the Internet

Copyright is the place in cyberspace law where you're most likely to inadvertently break the law. For instance, any time you reply and copy a person's prior message on a newsgroup or mailing list, you are violating copyright law. It's a spitting-on-the-sidewalk type of offense and no one is likely to complain—but still you copied someone's writing without first asking and receiving permission. It violates copyright law to copy anybody's writing, even their public postings on a newsgroup, unless you have consent. The same holds true when you forward someone's e-mail without their permission. It is also a copyright violation to scan someone else's photos, say from a magazine, and post the GIF on the Internet—even if no one pays you anything for it. The same holds true for copying an audio recording or a video.

With a few limited exceptions, which we will talk about later, copyright law prohibits the copying of another person's work (writings, GIFs, audios, movies, whatever) without his permission. If you copy another person's electronic message, then you have violated his copyrights, unless his posting expressly states that you have his consent to copy it. The fact that it's electronic, not paper, or doesn't have a copyright claim or notice on it, has nothing to do with it. It's protected by copyright law whether it be in electronic or paper form, and with or without copyright notice.

Some copyright violations are of the trivial spitting-on-the-sidewalk kind, such as recopying another's note in full when you reply to it in a newsgroup. If that kind of violation ever went to court it would probably be thrown out based upon an implied grant of permission to copy for the limited purpose of reply. You may also have a right to copy a prior posting under the so-called "fair use" exception to copyright, which we'll talk about later. The implied consent would be found from the common practice of the virtual community. People do it all the time, so by participating, you implicitly consent to having your message copied, at least to all participants in that group.

But what if someone took your newsgroup message and posted it to a thousand other groups? This frequently happens on the Net. Usually it's obvious that the writer wants to have her message published as far and wide as possible. But what if she didn't? What if it was hard-copied and sold on the street? In that case, the technical spitting-on-the-sidewalk type of copyright violation might become a lawsuit, especially if the writer who owns the copyright of her work is somehow damaged by the unauthorized copying. What if the copied message libeled someone? What if it caused the author to lose a job? What if the message was, for instance, a short story, and another claimed it as his own? What if someone else made money by selling the story to a movie producer? To be safe, better ask for permission before you transmit a copy outside of the confines of the virtual community in which it was posted. In the context of e-mail, also, it's good practice not to forward a letter to others unless the original author of the e-mail knows and consents. That's not only required by technical copyright law, but also common courtesy and Netiquette, especially if the material is somehow sensitive, or you don't know the sender that well.

> **Tip**
>
> Never claim another's work as your own, or publish or revise that work without permission. When in doubt—ask for permission.

There is also the question of copying on the World Wide Web. As a practical necessity there is an implied grant of permission to copy Web materials onto your own computer, at least into its memory. How else can you see it? Web browsing, like many other Internet uses, is based on copying from one computer to another. When you access a Web site, a copy of the materials on the sender's computer is transmitted to your computer. The World Wide Web is based upon such copying, so a grant is necessarily implicit; but that implied consent to copy is not without limits. It may only extend from RAM onto your hard drive. Absent a specific notice to the contrary on the Web site, the consent to copy Web materials probably does not extend beyond your own computer. For instance, it would be a copyright violation to send a copy to someone else's computer, or to print hard copies and give them away, or worse, sell to others. When you sell it you have almost certainly crossed the line of an author's implied consent to copy materials he posts on the WWW.

> **Note**
>
> The line of implied consent on the WWW, as elsewhere on the Internet, is an ill-defined area of the law. To avoid being a defendant in one of the cases that will surely come along to define that line, and as good Netiquette, always ask for permission from the Webmaster or other information provider before you distribute copies of any of their work. Usually he will be pleased to consent, so long as you provide proper credit to him, leave any copyright notices intact, and don't modify it.

Legally you do not have to ask permission before you put a hyperlink in your own Web site to someone else's Web site. A link doesn't involve copying. It's just a citation. Still, people frequently ask each other for permission to do so, and it never hurts to ask. In fact, it's good Netiquette and Net politics to do so, because it frequently results in reciprocal links back to your Web site. Although the hyperlink itself requires no permission under copyright law, the description you put on the link might run afoul of other laws, such as negligence, fraud, or libel. Be careful not to make an incorrect description of the linked Web site. That might damage the other Web site. If, for any reason, the other Webmaster doesn't want to be linked to your Web site, then don't do it, not as a matter of law, but as Netiquette. Why should you link to someone who doesn't want you to? It's not exactly cyber-rape, but it's offensive none the less.

> **Tip**
>
> For more information on Web copyright issues see **http://www.benedict.com/webiss.htm#can**.

The ABCs of Copyright Law

To help "stay legal" in the little-known waters of copyright law, it helps to have a general handle on the basic rules. These rules can help guide you when you encounter a new situation and are unsure of your rights and responsibilities. Also, for a Web-based primer on copyright law see **http://www.ilt.columbia.edu/projects/copyright/index.html**. Still, remember the old but true sayings: "a little bit of knowledge is a dangerous thing," and "only a fool has himself for a lawyer." Copyright law can get very complicated and very involved, particularly in the area of emerging technologies.

> **Tip**
>
> Ask a lawyer when confused about copyrights, particularly when a commercial transaction is involved. The type of lawyers who should know about copyrights are called *Intellectual Property* lawyers.

Basically, copyright law provides that the "author" of any "original work" has the "exclusive rights" to it, including the sole right to copy the work. *Author* is a copyright term that is broadly applied to mean the creator of any original work, be it a book, a play, a movie, a song, a picture, a computer program, and so on. *Works* are in turn very broadly defined to include all kinds of original expressions, including software and electronic media of all types. Courts have held that the amount of originality required for a work to be original, and so qualify for copyright protection, is very low.

For works created after 1978, the protection is limited in time to the duration of the author's life, plus 50 years after the author dies. The duration of copyright for works created before 1978 under an earlier version of the law is somewhat different, but the old rules that govern pre-1978 works are too complex to try to explain here. The exclusive rights granted to authors include much more than just the right to copy; they include the exclusive right to make modified versions of the work (called *derivative works*), to distribute the work, transmit it, perform it, or run it on a computer.

Copyright law is derived from a short passage in the U.S. Constitution and from lengthy federal legislation which implements that passage. It is governed exclusively by federal law, which means that no state can pass its own copyright laws. Article I, Section 8 of the U.S. Constitution gives Congress (and Congress alone) the power, "To promote the progress of science and useful arts, by securing for limited times to authors and inventors the exclusive right to their respective rights and discoveries." Based on that constitutional passage, Congress has enacted numerous lengthy patent and copyright laws.

Tip

A copy of the complete text of U.S. copyright law can be found on my Information Law Web site at **http://seamless.com/rcl/things.html#statutes**.

Note

Government works lie outside of copyright law. Thus, for instance, all federal laws are not subject to copyright and may be freely copied by anyone. The laws lie in the public domain because the author is the government, and the government is owned by us, "we the people." The same holds true for government pamphlets, reports, photographs, charts, and the like.

It helps to have a general understanding of the distinction between copyright law and patent law. Patents cover innovative inventions that implement ideas. Copyrights cover original works that express ideas. Neither cover the ideas themselves. Thus, you can't patent the idea of a car, only a particular automobile that embodies that idea. Similarly you can't copyright an idea, say the idea of icon-based software interfaces. You can only copyright a particular original expression of the idea. The line between idea and expression can sometimes become blurry in copyright law—judges have written thousands of pages on it, especially in the area of computer software—but the general idea of the distinction is clear enough in most cases. The only way to try to keep an idea to yourself, and keep anyone else from copying the idea, is to keep it secret. Companies sometimes try to do that with trade secrets and agreements, but it is generally impractical. Once the idea has been expressed, someone else is free to express the same idea, so long as they don't copy your particular expression of the idea.

You can't copyright (or patent for that matter) a fact or a law of nature. The fact exception to copyright was recently greatly strengthened by a decision of the Supreme Court *Feist Publications, Inc. v. Rural Telephone Service.* (For more information, see **http://seamless.com/rcl/feist.txt**.) The Feist decision has enormous ramifications for the Internet and for computer databases in general. Feist permits the free copying of facts gathered by others, so long as you don't copy any original selection or arrangement of the facts, and your copying doesn't extend beyond plain facts to include original creative content.

Note

For a full discussion of this fascinating area of the law—fascinating to me anyway—see my article, "The Practical and Legal Protection of Computer Databases" in the Information Law Web site at **http://seamless:com/rcl/article.html**. That article contains a full discussion of Feist.

Government works are not the only ones that are in the public domain and outside of copyright protection. All works whose copyright time has expired fall into the public domain—Shakespeare, for instance—as do particular works that the authors have intentionally dedicated to the public domain. Anyone can decide to relinquish all or part of their exclusive rights. Under prior copyright law it was even possible to unintentionally waive your copyrights by publishing a work with a copyright notice.

Tip

For a Web site with information about works that are supposedly in the public domain see **http://northcoast.com/savetz/pd/pd.html**.

Many people think that you have to apply for a copyright. Wrong! You don't apply for a copyright. You have one automatically by law as soon as you create something. You can elect to register your copyright with the Copyright Office in Washington, D.C., but registration has never been a prerequisite of copyright protection. Still it's a good idea to register your copyright if your work is valuable, and you may need to take legal action to protect it.

Tip

For copyright registration forms, instructions on how to register, and other good information on copyrights, see the Copyright Web site at **http://www.benedict. com/register.htm#register**.

You can't file suit to enforce your copyright unless and until you register. Also, you are not eligible for statutory damages, awards, or attorney fee awards for infringements that occur before registration. Many people also think that you have to put a copyright notice on a work for it to be protected by copyright law. Wrong again! That used to be the law, but now U.S. law follows international copyright treaty and the copyright notice is not necessary. You automatically have a full copyright even if you don't state a claim to one on the work itself. If you say nothing, a full claim to copyright is implied. Still, a notice is a good idea, particularly if your work goes out of the country.

> **Note**
>
> A copyright notice should state the name of the author, the date the work was published, and the word copyright or its abbreviations, copr. or ©. For instance, a notice would read name, date, ©, all together on one line—as in, Ralph Losey © 1995. It also doesn't hurt to add "All Rights Reserved," especially if your work may end up in South America.

If you want to dedicate your work to the public domain, or otherwise relinquish some of your exclusive rights, then you need to say so on the work itself. This reverse type of copyright notice is starting to be known as a *copyless notice*. If you don't see a copyless notice, you should assume that the author claims full copyrights. When in doubt, contact the author.

> **Tip**
>
> There are companies that specialize in obtaining copyright clearances, such as Total Clearance, Inc. at **totalclear@aol.com**. Also try the Copyright Clearance Center's Web site at **http://www.copyright.com/**.

In addition to the general misconceptions about copyright law just discussed, there are some Internet-specific myths. Quite a few people in cyberspace seem to think that copyright somehow does not apply on the Internet. They believe that copyright law is now an archaic vestige of the past. Some will tell you that anything on the Internet has been dedicated to the public domain, and may be freely copied. Another version of the myth is that copyrights don't apply to computer files in general, and the Internet in particular, under some sort of "fair use" exception or another. These notions are not true. They are myths from an earlier era of the Internet when it was the exclusive home of scientists and academics. The Internet is just like anywhere else—you can't take a person's intellectual property, creative works, without his or her permission. Property rights are alive and well on the Internet and ignorance or misconception of the law is no defense.

A legal exception to copyright which is often misunderstood is the fair use exception. It is a much smaller loophole than most people realize. It allows you to take small quotes of another author's work and put them into your work. For instance, you may use short quotes in a book of literary criticism, a short film clip in a movie review, or you may copy an article for classroom discussion. The criteria for the test varies from case to case, but, generally, to qualify you must meet the following five criteria:

- You have to take very little of the copyrighted work.
- The quoted portions have to be a small part of your own work.
- Your quoting can't interfere with sales of the original copyrighted work.
- Your sales don't depend on the copied materials.
- Your use of the copied materials promotes a public objective, like education or commentary. It doesn't have to be nonprofit to qualify, but it helps.

In several Internet copyright cases that have gone to court the defendant tried to use the fair use doctrine. It didn't work.

Tip

For more about the fair use doctrine see **http://www.benedict.com/fair. htm#fair**, and **http://www.eff.org/pub/Legal/fair_use_and_copyright. excerpt**.

As the Internet gets bigger and bigger, and cyberspace becomes an integral part of commerce, more and more claims of copyright infringement are hitting the courts. Copyright infringement that doesn't have a significant impact on someone's pocketbook is frequently tolerated by the owner of the copyright. But when the damages start to hurt, the tolerance of most authors lessens accordingly. That is what is happening now on the Internet, and is likely to continue for the next several years. We'll see more and more Internet copyright infringement suits until the myth of the copyright-free Internet is finally laid to rest. In this chapter we will look at two of these cases, one brought by Playboy magazine and the other by the Church of Scientology.

Make no mistake about it, the damages that can flow from a copyright infringement can be substantial, even if the infringement was not intentional.

The civil remedies include an injunction, seizure and impounding of all illegal copies—which can include seizure of your computers if that is where the copies are stored—an attorney fee award, an award of actual damages or alternatively of statutory damages of between $500 and $20,000 per infringement at the discretion of the judge, or up to $50,000 per infringement if the violation was intentional. Intentional copyright infringement is also a criminal violation; as anyone who watches home videotapes well knows, violation can subject you to imprisonment or fines.

Playboy Enterprises, Inc. v. Frena

Many people have discovered just how easy it is to scan a picture and put it on their computer screen. With super VGA monitors the quality is remarkable. Many have also learned how to upload their favorite pictures into cyberspace. There they can be viewed by other graphics connoisseurs around the world. Tens of thousands or more of such computer graphics are exchanged between computers all the time. Many of the humans who sit in front of these computers like to see provocative pixels of naked people— naked women usually. By now you probably realize that unless you took the pictures, or have the permission of the photographer, that scanning and copying the pictures is a copyright violation. You also probably suspect that this is all a spitting-on-the-sidewalk type infringement that the owner of the photograph's copyright wouldn't care about. Indeed, it has been tolerated for years, but one copyright owner, Playboy magazine, finally had enough.

To be sure Playboy has been a favorite target of computer hobbyists who like naked GIFs. It's so easy to scan its centerfolds and make impressive digital pictures. The practice was widespread, almost commonplace around thousands of BBSs around the country. Somebody at Playboy must have figured this was having an adverse impact on its bottom line. So they picked a blatant BBS infringer to make an example of and sued for copyright and trademark infringement and unfair competition. Playboy won the lawsuit, and defendant George Frena, the small BBS owner, ended up with a $500,000 judgment against him (*Playboy Enterprises, Inc. v. Frena*; see **http:// seamless.com/rcl/playb.txt**).

Frena, the sysop owner, claimed that he didn't know there were Playboy copyrighted GIFs on his board. He said they were all uploaded by subscribers and he had no knowledge of this activity. Playboy didn't contest that the original copies had come from subscribers, not Frena, but they argued that he knew about it, permitted, even encouraged it, and therefore was a republisher. There are several credibility problems with Frena's "ignorance defense." It was undisputed that he had over 170 Playboy files on his not too big board. In many of the GIFs, the Playboy text had been removed and replaced with ads for Frena's BBS. Last but not least, he had used the Playboy trademark to identify and name the files.

It is clear from Judge Schlesinger's opinion that the judge didn't believe Frena when Frena claimed that he didn't know the Playboy photos were on his board. Still, to avoid the credibility issue, the judge ruled that Frena violated copyright law, and was liable, even if he was an innocent infringer. Judge Schlesinger noted that intent to infringe is not needed to find copyright infringement. Intention is only a necessary element of criminal copyright infringement. In civil cases, the only relevance of knowledge and intent is in the judge's equitable determination of the amount of statutory damages to impose.

Frena also tried to defend using the fair use exception to copyright. This defense failed primarily because the judge found that Frena's public display and transmission of Playboys' pictures was for a "clearly commercial" use. The BBS was a for profit enterprise where users paid $25 per month to access his board. Judge Schlesinger also found that Playboy was injured by the copying—deprived of lost revenues from magazine sales by the easy availability of Playboy pictures in cyberspace. The judge did not determine the amount of damages. Before that issue was finally decided the parties reached a $500,000 settlement agreement. It is interesting to note that Playboy has since gone on the Net with its own Web pages. (See **http:// www.playboy.com/**.) Yes, it includes the ability to download files of naked playmates!

Scientology v. NETCOM (and just about everyone else)

Another new copyright case that is getting a lot of attention by legal Net watchers these days is one of the many lawsuits brought by the Church of Scientology. This one is against a well-known Internet provider, NETCOM. *Religious Technology Center v. NETCOM On-Line Communication Services, Inc.* See the EFF pages on this case at **http://www.eff.org/pub/Legal/Cases/ CoS_v_the_Net/**.

This case may be important to the Internet community because it attempts to hold a provider liable for copyright infringement from the mere transmission of infringing materials through its network. Scientology sought an injunction against NETCOM prohibiting its transmission of any materials it claimed violated its copyrights. NETCOM claimed this was not only an illegal request, but an impossible one. If granted, NETCOM said it would effectively shut down its services, and make anyone on the Internet a potential copyright infringer. Scientology has taken action against other people on the Net for similar reasons. See, for instance, **http://www.eff.org/pub/Alerts/ eff_cos.letter** and **http://www.cybercom.net/~rnewman/ scientology/home.html**.

The underlying dispute is between Scientology and one of its former leaders, Dennis Erlich. Erlich left the church and is now a leader of the opposition against Scientology. He uses Scientology's own secret publications to expose Scientology and support his contention that it is a fraud. He sent several internal Scientology documents to a UseNet newsgroup on the Internet (**alt.religion.scientology**). Also see **http://www.yahoo.com/ Society_and_Culture/Religion/Scientology/**. NETCOM was the Internet provider that was used by Erlich to post the allegedly infringing materials to the newsgroup. (There was a BBS intermediary who was also sued).

There is a question as to whether the Scientology works were really infringed or not, and whether the fair use doctrine might apply to Erlich's non-commercial activities. But aside from those questions, NETCOM claims that it cannot be liable because it is a passive distributor of information, not a publisher. This is essentially the same distinction we've seen before in the area of libel and pornography. NETCOM is opposing the well-funded Scientology action against it by arguing that copyright liability should not be extended to passive information conduits like itself who merely transmit data, much like a telephone company. The Playboy case does, however, pose problems for NETCOM because it held that the BBS was liable even if its copyright infringement was innocent. NETCOM argues that it is physically impossible for it to control the content of the information it carries (over 150,000,000 keystrokes of information per day). Scientology argues to the contrary that technical means exist for NETCOM to screen out Scientology materials. NETCOM denies this. There has not yet been a ruling on Scientology's case against NETCOM, but one is expected soon. Look for the latest at **http:// www.eff.org/pub/Legal/Cases/CoS_v_the_Net/**.

Your Rights and Responsibilities of Fair Trade on the Internet

When the government first started the Net and paid for it, there was an "acceptable use policy" which, among other things, banned all commercial activity on the Net. For better or for worse these early days of the Internet as an ivory tower are over. Not only is commercial activity tolerated, the Net is fast becoming a booming center of commerce. As you do business on the Internet just remember its demographics and non-commercial history. The soft sell is definitely the best approach—so too is the provision of bonafide information and free services along with the trade. Pure commercial speech is still frowned on by most Net users.

The freedom to engage in commercial speech, to own property, and to contract are basic constitutional rights which are all carried over onto the Internet. Under the law these freedoms carry responsibilities of honesty, good faith, and fair dealing. The old legal principle of "caveat emptor," let the buyer beware, has been long abandoned by most courts, and will not be resurrected again for the Internet. Fraud, pyramid schemes, bait and switch, misleading advertising, simple negligence, gross negligence, defective products, unconscionable contracts, breach of contract, theft, conspiring to fix prices, unfair trade, trade libel, usury, sale of unregistered securities, unlawful discrimination, and so on—these are all just as illegal on the Net as anywhere else. Any business practices not allowed in your home town would probably also be illegal on the Net.

There is one unfair business practice that has spawned on the Net that is new and unique to the Net. It's the foul art of spamming. *Spamming*—the practice of sending out unsolicited e-mail and news postings to large groups of users— is anathema to everyone. It is junk mail on a grand scale. It wastes Internet resources and even costs some recipients of the junk mail who are charged by the item by their providers. It may be legal, but if you do it, your reputation on the Net is dead. The users themselves will quickly retaliate and put you out of business. Don't believe the bogus get-rich-quick-on-the-Internet schemes you may read about. The spam scams won't work.

When Is a Deal a Deal?

Most contracts or agreements are enforceable as soon as there is a meeting of the minds on the essential terms of a deal. Contrary to popular opinion, most oral agreements are legally enforceable, even though they are often difficult to enforce because the unwritten terms are disputed. To be sure, there are some agreements that must be in writing to be enforceable, like an agreement to sell real property, or to pay the debts of another. The rule is commonly called the Statute of Frauds. Still, in most states even for those kinds of agreements there are many exceptions to the Statute of Frauds, like for instance when there is part performance, or some later writings consistent with the agreement. So if you make a deal on the Internet, don't assume it's not enforceable just because you've never signed your name to a piece of paper. If you make a deal with someone over the Net, plan to stick by it, and expect the other person to, also.

Still, having said that oral agreements are frequently enforceable, it's still recommended that you always confirm your deals in writing. If nothing else, that is the best way for all concerned to know what duties and obligations they have assumed. Otherwise there is likely to be an argument later as to exactly what was agreed to. When things go bad later you will be amazed at how widely recollections can vary of a deal you made on IRC last month. If your deal involves a new business undertaking, or a substantial amount of money, you should probably see a lawyer before the deal is made. It's better to spend a few bucks for assistance up front, instead of waiting until later when things go bad and you have to spend all you've got. A "legal stitch in time can save nine." I've seen it happen a million times. Trust me, I'm a lawyer.

Note

Whenever you make an agreement on the Net, and everyone involved is not a resident of the same state, it's important to decide in advance which state law will govern. The same goes double if a person or company from another country is involved.

You should also decide in advance the forum for any dispute resolution, be it mediation, arbitration, or litigation. If you have to go to court to enforce the deal—say, to get your money—what court will that be, and whose law will govern? These are very important questions when things go sour. Right now, the law has very few answers in the context of cyberspace so you had better decide yourself in advance. If you don't, you could be unpleasantly surprised later when a judge throws out your case and tells you that you have to go to a court in Timbuktu.

So when is a deal confirmed in writing? Does e-mail suffice? It might if a signature is not required by the law of the state or foreign country that governs the agreement. Sometimes it might not be good enough, even if there is no Statute of Frauds or its foreign country equivalent. It can become an evidentiary problem of later proving there was a bona fide meeting of the minds. One person to the agreement could try to wiggle out of it later and claim it was not their letter, that they never agreed to it. E-mail can be easily forged or altered. It might be hard to prove the authenticity of the e-mail and thus of the agreement. Courts are used to dealing with letters and the U.S. mail where it is presumed that a letter posted to someone is received by them, and they have to prove the contrary. Also a written document with a person's signature is presumed to be authentic. Most e-mail today does not have a signature that can be verified by an expert. Lawyers are concerned about the evidentiary problems still inherent in proving e-mail and other electronic deals. That's why most lawyers still recommend that a written document be prepared and signed by the parties. That may well change in the future as electronic signatures become foolproof, and the authenticity of electronic documents can be confirmed by experts. For more on forgery proof electronic signatures and how you can get one, see **http://www.verisign.com/**, and generally on this subject see **http://www.eff.org/pub/Privacy/Digital _signature/**.

> **Tip**
>
> Confirm any important agreements you make on the Net with U.S. snail mail and ink-on-paper signatures.

Network Use Agreements

Most networks and Internet providers require their subscribers and users to agree to their standard form agreement as a condition of use. These agreements usually spell out the provider's acceptable use policy, which is the basic rules of conduct, and set forth terms of payment. Some providers later confirm the agreement with paper and a signature. These agreements are probably enforceable, even if just electronic, and never confirmed with paper and ink. Still, some of their specific terms may be unenforceable if a court finds them to be unconscionable, that is, totally unfair and unreasonable. One court has already done this to the term in CompuServe's agreement that purports to allow CompuServe to sue any of its subscribers in Ohio, instead of the subscribers home state, for any violation of the contract. See **http:// www.eff.org/pub/Legal/Cases/cis_v_patterson.notes**.

A network or other provider has the right to cancel your subscription and terminate your service if you don't comply with their rules, even if their rules violate free speech. Remember the First Amendment protects you from the government, not a private company. Competition and the forces of a free economy are supposed to protect you from oppressive contractual requirements that suppress free speech. Right now there appears to be enough providers to keep this from being a problem. There are tens of thousands of Internet providers, and more coming each day. The competition should continue to protect us from overreaching providers. The network agreements, on the other hand, should protect us from the rude spammers and flamers, and allow the networks to screen them out.

> **Tip**
>
> Read your provider's agreement. If there is something in there you don't like, tell them about it!

Newsgroups and Web sites are also information providers. Most on the Net are now free, but this is likely to change. I suspect that more and more will add premium areas that can only be accessed with a password, for a charge. Some already have agreements as a condition of admittance. More will probably do so in the future, especially if any files are transferred, or if there is any kind of charge to users. These agreements can try to protect the operators from liability from the actions of their users. Written agreements should also be prepared for all of the advertisements now being sold on the Web, but many times today this is not done. The parties have an ill-defined verbal agreement. If you are spending money for a Web site or an ad on somebody else's Web site, you have the right to have the full terms of your agreement spelled out in writing. Confirm it by e-mail or fax, and if enough money is involved, get the ink signature on paper.

Software License Agreements

There is a lot of confusion about all of the different types of software agreements out there—shareware, freeware, free trials with expiration dates, beta tests, licenses in perpetuity, site licenses, license per user, license per computer, software sales, shrink wraps, contracts of adhesion, look and feel. This is a complex subject, and the confusion extends to most lawyers and judges now being called to decide these new questions. I can only touch on the surface of this law, but for those who want more detailed information on software licensing, a good legal article can be found at **http://www.eff.org/ pub/Legal/Intellectual_property/software_licensing.paper**. For information for a software developer trying to protect his work, see **http:// www.island.com/LegalCare/welcome.html**.

The *shrink wrap* type of agreement is now in widespread use for software. This is a license where there is a sticker on the outside of the package that warns you that if you break the seal you agree to the license inside. The license may also say that if you don't agree to all of the terms, then return the software immediately for a full refund. Online equivalents of the shrink wrap have now become commonplace. You come to a screen where an arcane license or other agreement is presented to you and you are asked to indicate yes or no whether you agree to all of the terms. If you say yes, you go on. If you say no, you're out. Windows 95 has such a screen as part of the installation process. You can expect more of the same from everyone else.

Are these types of agreements enforceable? Probably yes. But enforcement against individual consumers is rare and the law is still unsettled. Again, it is largely an evidentiary problem. What if your minor child opened the shrink wrap for you, or entered into the domain for you? A minor can't enter into a legally enforceable contract. If you never saw the agreement how could you have agreed to it? There would be no meeting of the minds necessary for contract formation.

Beyond proof of intent, there is the issue of unconscionability. There is no negotiation over the terms of these agreements. You either accept the form deal or not. Also, the parties have unequal bargaining strength. Legally, these form agreements are called contracts of adhesion. The courts will not enforce a term in a contract of adhesion that they feel is very unfair or overreaching to the consumer. So if you've inadvertently pledged your firstborn in one of those form computer agreements that no one reads, don't worry about it, it's not enforceable.

Software on trial for a limited time is now a commonplace marketing device on the Net. Give the software away at first. People will come to depend on it—get hooked on it—and then they will want the updates and improvements as they come out. They will even be willing to pay for the next version! Eudora and Netscape have used this strategy successfully. It's kind of like shareware. If you end up using a shareware program you try out, then go ahead and pay for it. Send in the few bucks for the shareware—pay for the upgrade. The law requires it. You agreed to do so when you received the software. Sure, you'll never be caught if you don't follow the agreement, but you should do it because it's the right thing to do. It pays someone for their honest labor and efforts, and keeps them in business to develop yet a better version of their product for your computing pleasure. More so than most any other industry, software developers depend upon the honesty and fairness of the consumers to keep afloat.

Trademarks and Internet Domain Names

A *trademark* is a name or design used by a business to identify its product. A *service mark* does the same thing for a service. They are protected by state and federal laws. The basic rule of these laws is to protect the first user of a name from latecomers who try to use the same name to identify their products or services. If the use of a same or similar mark is likely to cause confusion to the consumers, then the law will prohibit the use of the mark by the latecomer. Trademarks can be registered in the Patent and Trademark Office in Washington. This allows people to determine whether a name is available for use or not. For more information on trademark laws see **http:// www.law.cornell.edu/topics/trademark.html**.

Internet domain names are a form of trademark. They frequently identify a commercial service or product. If you have a domain name that is important to you, you'd better try and protect that name from use outside of the Net by a trademark registration. For information on the registration process and forms see **http://www.naming.com/naming/trademark.html**. Hopefully you won't be unpleasantly surprised to find that someone else already has the rights to your name in a similar product or service. If they do, you could be infringing their trademark and they could sue you and force you to stop using their name.

There are many lawsuits now underway concerning trademark infringements on the Internet or against computer companies. We've already seen how Playboy sued the BBS for both copyright infringement and for violation of its trademarks. Singer Bob Dylan has sued Apple Computer for naming a computer language Dylan. It was supposedly an abbreviation for Dynamic Language. Astronomer Carl Sagan also complained to Apple when it started using Sagan as the internal code name of a computer that became the Macintosh 7100. Apple stopped using his name, but instead started calling it the BHA. Sagan sued Apple anyway for trademark infringement, defamation, and invasion of privacy, claiming that it was well known that Apple used BHA as an acronym for Butt-Head Astronomer. The Judge reportedly threw out Sagan's case.

Network Solutions, Inc. is the company that is now responsible for the assignment of domain names on the Internet. It has been caught up in disputes between holders of domain names on the Internet and holders of preexisting trademarks of the same name. For instance, ex-video jockey Adam Curry uses the domain name of MTV and his former employer doesn't like it. MTV has sued him for trademark infringement. Curry claims they gave him permission to do so, that they said they were not interested in the Internet. For a copy of Adam Curry's public statement about the case, see **http://www.eff.org/pub/Legal/Cases/curry_v_mtv.announce**. Assuming MTV did give him permission, it was obviously before it understood the Internet and the potential value and importance of a domain name. Adam Curry's MTV Web site is now visited by an average of 35,000 people a day. There are other cases where a competitor has deliberately reserved the use of its competitor's name as a domain name to try and lock them out. (It didn't work!) Someone has even taken on Microsoft and is using a variation of its name. They have a funny home page about it with extensive Bill Gates satire. See **http://www.micros0ft.com/**.

Network Solutions now recognizes the problem of trademark rights and domain names. For that reason, in May 1995 they instituted a policy wherein they will suspend the use of a domain name if the person using the name does not voluntarily relinquish it after demand from a company that owns a federal trademark to the name. Later, in August 1995 Network Solutions announced a new policy where any company that registers a domain name is required to indemnify it for any expenses it may incur from a lawsuit by someone claiming federal trademark rights on the same name. The next month, Network Solutions announced that it was going to start charging users a fee of $50 per year to maintain their domain names. This outraged many small, long-time domain users who were used to a free ride. But in view of all the disputes in this area, it's easy to see how the revenue is needed by the company stuck in the middle of many of these suits.

Trademark Searches

Before you get an Internet domain name, or before you begin to use any new name to identify your company's product or service, check to see if the name is available. At the present time, the Trademark Office registrations are not computerized and you have to pay a service in Washington to do a manual search for you. It costs $150 or more depending on the scope of the search you order. The search service I use is Government Liaison Services at 1-800-642-6564. If the search report shows that the name you wanted is already taken, then you may be disappointed, but you've saved yourself from a big mess later. You should go back to the drawing boards to come up with a new name.

Once you find a name that is clear, go ahead and register that name in Washington so that someone else won't use it. State registrations are probably useless for any Net-related business because they only apply for protection in that state. Also, don't assume that you have the right to use your own name or company name to identify your product. You don't if the name is already a registered mark. Even Senator Exon couldn't open up a gas station with his own name on it.

Tip

Never use a product or service name until you check to see if the name is already registered.

Your Rights and Responsibilities of Protection from Crime on the Internet

What kind of crime are you at risk of on the Internet? There are the commercial crimes, like intentional copyright infringement, sale of computer counterfeit goods, and good old-fashion fraud—where con men will promise you a deal too good to be true. The Internet has unscrupulous people just like anywhere else. But even more dangerous than the consumer crimes are the more traditional criminal dangers of stalking, burglary, breaking and entering, theft, and vandalism. Cyber-burglary happens all the time on the Net. People who do that—who get into your computers without your permission—are called *crackers,* or sometimes *hackers*. These crackers enjoy finding ways to break into your computer system. Some are harmless—they don't do much once they get inside beyond leave you a cyber equivalent of "Kilroy was here." Some people look up to these benevolent hackers as technical gurus. But many hackers are malicious and dangerous indeed. Once inside they may steal and use valuable information, like credit card numbers, or if they get in a bank, they may transfer funds. They may also engage in acts of vandalism, like erase all your files, or plant viruses, worms, bombs, and the like that will make your computer malfunction in many strange and sometimes undetectable ways.

One famous hacker, Vladimir Levin, a 24 year-old mathematician in St. Petersburg, Russia, reportedly hacked his way into Citibank in New York. He is alleged to have made unauthorized transfers of $40,000,000 and withdrawals of $400,000. U.S. authorities finally caught and arrested him in September 1995 at Heathrow Airport in England. He'll be extradited to New York and stand trial for theft, computer misuse, forgery, and false accounting.

Another famous hacker, Kevin Mitnick, was also finally caught in 1995, after successfully eluding the police for years as a fugitive. Many think he is a benevolent type of hacker and should not go to jail. He was indicted on 23 counts of fraud involving the hacking of computers. He allegedly stole information worth more than a million dollars, including 20,000 credit card numbers, but he never used any of the information, never used the credit card numbers. He claims to have done it just for the challenge, not financial gain. He hacked into the computers of highly regarded computer security experts, who then later helped police track him down.

When cyberspace was first born, the police were easily confused by cyber-crimes and by hackers. They didn't understand the technologies well enough to understand the crimes or to catch the criminals. The prosecutors some-times found that the laws available were inadequate and didn't clearly apply to allow them to get a conviction. Those days appear to be over. Now almost every state in the country has enacted computer crime laws, and the federal government has one too. Some detectives are now streetwise to the Net, and more and more of them are patrolling the cyber-streets undercover. The FBI and many urban police forces now have special squads who specialize in computer crime. The easy early days for computer criminals is definitely over.

> ## Tip
>
> For a good list of Web sites concerning security issues see **http://www.cs. purdue.edu/homes/spaf/hotlists/csec.html**.

Table 3.1 is a state-by-state list of the computer crime laws now in effect across the country. New laws are being enacted every year. Most of these laws can be found on the Net. Try looking at the Web site of a university or lawyer in your state. For a detailed discussion of the various state computer crime laws see **http://www.eff.org/pub/Legal/ prosecuting_computer_criminals.article**.

In addition to clearly criminalizing the unauthorized access, use or interfer-ence with a computer, some states are also enacting special laws prohibiting computer stalking. That's where someone follows you around in cyberspace and harasses you. Of course, there are already many laws on the books, as previously mentioned, to prohibit pedophiles, sexual predators, and child pornographers.

Table 3.1 State Computer Laws

AL	Computer Crime Act, Code of Alabama, Sections 13A-8-100 to 13A-8-103
AK	Statutes, Sections 11.46.200(a)(3), 11.46.484(a)(5), 11.46.740, 11.46.985, 11.46.990
AZ	Revised Statues Annotated, Sections 13-2301(E), 13-2316
CA	Penal Code, Section 502
CO	Revised Statutes, Sections 18-5.5-101, 18-5.5-102
CT	General Statutes, Sections 53a-250 to 53a-261, 52-570b
DE	Code Annotated, Title 11, Sections 931-938

(continues)

About the Internet

Table 3.1   Continued

FL	Computer Crimes Act, Florida Statutes Annotated, Sections 815.01 to 815.07
GA	Computer Systems Protection Act, Georgia Codes Annotated, Sections 16-9-90 to 16-9-95
HI	Revised Statutes, Sections 708-890 to 780-896
ID	Code, Title 18, Chapter 22, Sections 18-2201, 18-2202
IL	Annotated Statutes (Criminal Code), Sections 15-1, 16-9
IN	Code, Sections 35-43-1-4, 35-43-2-3
IO	Statutes, Sections 716A.1 to 716A.16
KS	Statutes Annotated, Section 21-3755
KY	Revised Statutes, Sections 434.840 to 434.860
LA	Revised Statutes, Title 14, Subpart D. Computer Related Crimes, Sections 73.1 to 73.5
ME	Revised Statutes Annotated, Chapter 15, Title 17-A, Section 357
MD	Annotated Code, Article 27, Sections 45A and 146
MA	General Laws, Chapter 266, Section 30
MI	Statutes Annotated, Section 28.529(1)-(7)
MN	Statutes (Criminal Code), Sections 609.87 to 609.89
MI	Code Annotated, Sections 97-45-1 to 97-45-13
MS	Revised Statutes, Sections 569.093 to 569.099
MT	Code Annotated, Sections 45-2-101, 45-6-310, 45-6-311
NE	Revised Statutes, Article 13(p) Computers, Sections 28-1343 to 28-1348
NV	Revised Statutes, Sections 205.473 to 205.477
NH	Revised Statutes Annotated, Sections 638:16 to 638:19
NJ	Statutes, Title 2C, Chapter 20, Sections 2C:20-1, 2C:20-23 to 2C:20-34, and Title 2A, Sections 2A:38A-1 to 2A:38A-3
NM	Statutes Annotated, Criminal Offenses, Computer Crimes Act, Sections 30-16A-1 to 30-16A-4
NY	Penal Law, Sections 155.00, 156.00 to 156.50, 165.15 subdiv. 10, 170.00, 175.00
NC	General Statutes, Sections 14-453 to 14-457
ND	Century Code, Sections 12.1-06.1-01 subsection 3, 12.1-06.1-08
OH	Revised Code Annotated, Sections 2901.01, 2913.01, 2913.04, 2913.81
OK	Computer Crimes Act, Oklahoma Session Laws, Title 21, Sections 1951-1956

OR	Revised Statutes, Sections 164.125, 164.377
PA	Consolidated Statutes Annotated, Section 3933
RI	General Laws (Criminal Offenses), Sections 11-52-1 to 11-52-5
SC	Code of Laws, Sections 16-16-10 to 16-16-40
SD	Codified Laws, Sections 43-43B-1 to 43-43B-8
TN	Code Annotated, Computer Crimes Act, Sections 39-3-1401 to 39-3-1406
TX	Codes Annotated, Title 7, Chapter 33, Sections 33.01 to 33.05
UT	Computer Fraud Act, Utah Code Annotated, Sections 76-6-701 to 76-6-704
VA	Computer Crime Act, Code of Virginia, Sections 18.2-152.1 to 18.2-152.14
WA	Revised Code Annotated, Sections 9A.48.100, 9A.52.010, 9A.52.110 to 9A.52.130
WI	Statutes Annotated, Section 943.70
WY	Statutes, Sections 6-3-501 to 6-3-505

In addition to these state laws, there is a federal law known as The Computer Fraud and Abuse Act—18 U.S.C. §1030. This law, coupled with the federal wiretap laws previously discussed, provides federal agents with powerful legal weapons to fight crime on the Net. The Computer Fraud and Abuse Act makes it illegal to access a computer without proper authorization, or even to exceed your authorized access level, and imposes criminal and civil penalties. The penalties are most severe for unauthorized access of a federal computer or a computer of a financial institution, up to ten years imprisonment per offense. The law also makes it a crime to send a computer virus or other harmful program code into another's computer, to steal a password, or to traffic in passwords. The Secret Service is charged with enforcement.

There have already been many prosecutions and convictions under this law, some of them controversial for the zeal shown by the Secret Service. One case previously mentioned, *Steve Jackson Games, Inc. v. United States Secret Service* (see **http://www.io.com/SS/appeal-opinion.html**), involved an illegal seizure of computers and arrest. The Secret Service didn't properly follow the law and ended up paying damages to Steve Jackson in the civil suit that followed.

Another more successful suit by the Secret Service involved its prosecution of Robert Morris, the infamous perpetrator of the Internet worm. *United States v. Morris*, 928 F.2d 504 (2nd Cir. 1991). (For more information, see **http://**

seamless.com/rcl/worm.txt.) Morris was in a Ph.D. program in computer science at Cornell University. (His father happens to be a famous computer security expert.) As a part of his academic studies, young Morris started work on a kind of computer virus that later became known as the Internet worm. The new virus he created exploited flaws in Internet e-mail design so as to infiltrate computer systems and spread to other systems. His goal was to demonstrate the inadequacies of security measures on the Internet.

He crossed the legal line when he decided to test his code by surreptitiously releasing it onto the Internet on November 2, 1988 from a computer at MIT. His new baby was supposed to be harmless, just get in and spread, but not hurt anything. Nobody was supposed to even know it was in their computer. He just wanted to prove a point. But alas, his baby turned into a Franken-stein. It had unexpected side effects. The Internet worm started reproducing itself and spreading far faster than he expected. Before he knew it, computers around the country were starting to crash or become catatonic.

Morris tried to fix things by sending out an anonymous message, this time from a computer at Harvard, explaining how to kill the worm. But the Internet was already so clogged by the worm that people didn't get his message in time. Computer systems all over the place were shut down, including systems at leading universities, military sites, and medical research facilities. Millions of dollars of damage was done in the form of lost time to deal with the worm.

Morris was discovered, arrested, and found guilty of violation of the Computer Fraud and Abuse Act. He appealed on the basis that he lacked criminal intent, it was all just a horrible accident, a science experiment gone bad. His conviction was upheld by the appellate court. It found that the statute only required intent for unauthorized access of a computer, not intent to damage. He was clearly guilty of unauthorized access.

Another interesting prosecution under both the federal Computer Fraud statute and the Wire Fraud statute (18 U.S.C. §1343) involves a well-known hacker, Robert Riggs, known by his computer handle as the Prophet. *United States v. Riggs*. 743 FedSupp 556 (E.D. Ill. 1990). (For more information, see **http://www.eff.org/pub/Legal/Cases/Phrack_Neidorf_Riggs/**.) The Prophet was charged with devising and implementing a scheme to defraud using computers. Here is the language of the actual amended indictment that describes the scheme:

> To fraudulently obtain and steal private property in the form of computerized files by gaining unauthorized access to other individuals' and corporations' computers, copying the sensitive computerized files in

those computers, and then publishing the information from the computerized files in a hacker publication for dissemination to other computer hackers.

This scheme was supposedly known to the Internet hacker community as the Phoenix Project. The overall purpose of the scheme was to disseminate information that would help other hackers to break into computers and elude law enforcement. The only thing the prosecutors could nail them on, however, was the theft of a supposedly secret file on the 911 telephone system from a Southern Bell computer. In a convoluted story involving issues of trade secret, most of the defendants eventually plead guilty and the Prophet went to jail. See **http://www.eff.org/pub/Legal/Cases/ Phrack_Neidorf_Riggs/phrack_riggs_neidorf_godwin.article**. Still, many computer-oriented police believe that the Phoenix Project continues, in one form or another.

> ### Tip
>
> For inside information on hackers and their interesting above-the-law, "all information should be free" philosophy see Phrack's home page at **http://freeside.com/ phrack.html**, and a hypertext version of the well-known book on the subject, *The Hacker Crackdown*, at **http://www.eecs.nwu.edu/hacker_crackdown/**.

The Growing Problem of Computer Viruses

Something as bad as the Internet worm of 1988 hasn't hit since that time, but plenty of other smaller incidents have occurred. This is a growing problem that is not likely to go away anytime soon. Essentially, a computer virus is an act of vandalism, and under federal law it's a crime to use a virus to infect another's computer, even if no harm is intended. The problem is, it's very hard to know where a virus came from when you detect it on your computer. Sometimes it's even hard to know your computer is infected.

A personal story will help illustrate the problem, and possible solutions to the problem. My law firm's computers were infected for nine months this year before I happened to detect it when I bought a new, improved virus detection program. The old virus detection program supposedly guarding all of our computers had failed to detect the virus. It goes by the glamorous name of the stealth_boot.B virus. It just hung out in high memory, looking for a chance to infect the boot sectors of any floppies it could find. Once on a floppy, it would spread to any other hard drives the floppy was put into. Before we knew it, all of our computers, and thousands of diskettes were infected with the little stealth bugger. The impact of having the hidden program in high memory was not great, just occasional, seemingly random errors of the kind all computer users are all too familiar with. We never suspected a virus!

It wasn't until I installed Windows 95 in August, and decided to upgrade to new virus checkers at the same time, that I happened to find stealth_boot.b. Once found, it was relatively easy to kill, but very time consuming. There were 18 computers to clean, and thousands of diskettes. I knew it would cost thousands of dollars in overtime to cure our disease, so I took a look at our insurance policy, just for the heck of it. Nothing in there about computer viruses, but I went ahead and made a claim anyway. At first they were going to deny the claim; this was the first time anyone in the state had ever made such a claim, but then they checked with the national underwriters. They decided to pay the claims under the vandalism provision of the policy. The expenses incurred to repair the acts of vandalism were covered.

> **Tip**
>
> If you get hit with a virus that causes you damages, submit a claim with your insurance company and ask for coverage under the vandalism clause.

My mistake that allowed this virus to get through was low vigilance. I had a false sense of complacency because we had never been infected before, and I didn't bother to upgrade and keep my existing virus checking software current. (Good programs are updated quarterly.) Now we have the latest software and a strict policy requiring all employees to check any disk before it's run on any of our computers. We treat any new program, even factory issue right out of the shrink wrap, as potentially bugged. You can receive software that is infected, and the sender has absolutely no idea it's infected. I'm sure that's what happened in our case. As additional protection, whenever a new version of our software virus protection program comes out, we'll be among the first to buy it. It's a good investment. Further, all our computers are now fully inoculated and forced virus checking is built into the autoexec.bat files.

> **Note**
>
> Remember that even the most elaborate virus detection systems can't protect you from a new and devilish virus. Back up often to prepare for a crash. Also, try and insure against all kinds of catastrophic computer failure—viruses, lightning strike, theft, fire. Ask your insurer exactly what is covered in advance of trouble and find out what they will do if your system fails. If you are not covered, look for another company that will insure you. Depending upon your business, and what the virus or other unexpected loss does to you, the damages could be overwhelming.

> **Tip**
>
> Assume every new disk or program is infected and don't run it until you've checked for viruses.

There are many good anti-virus Web sites on the Internet that can provide you with a wealth of information. Make time to visit a few of them soon. For instance, see Symantec's Web site at **http://www.symantec.com/virus/ virus.html**, or IBM's anti-virus page at **http://www.brs.ibm.com/ ibmav.html**, or the Web site of the National Computer Security Association at **http://www.ncsa.com/**.

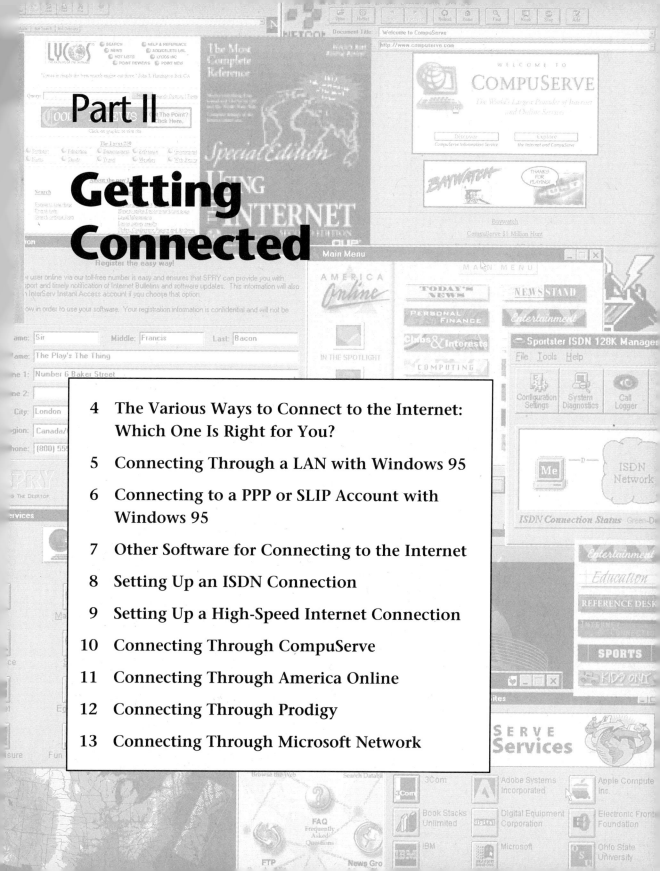

Part II

Getting Connected

4   The Various Ways to Connect to the Internet: Which One Is Right for You?

5   Connecting Through a LAN with Windows 95

6   Connecting to a PPP or SLIP Account with Windows 95

7   Other Software for Connecting to the Internet

8   Setting Up an ISDN Connection

9   Setting Up a High-Speed Internet Connection

10 Connecting Through CompuServe

11 Connecting Through America Online

12 Connecting Through Prodigy

13 Connecting Through Microsoft Network

The Various Ways to Connect to the Internet: Which One Is Right for You?

So you want to get online with the Internet. How should you do it? Which of the methods to access the Internet is right for you? Which will give you the best access to the services you need? Which has the most reasonable cost? This chapter helps you decide how to connect to the Internet by explaining the options and by giving you a set of guidelines you can follow to determine the best access method for your needs.

The next few chapters cover each of the access methods in more detail, but it's worth taking time to consider the alternatives before reading more. That way you'll know which chapters are more relevant to your needs. You also can make sure the details fit within your anticipated requirements.

You'll seldom choose your access method on the basis of cost alone. The services you want to access must be provided and readily available—a simple issue that's often overlooked by newcomers to the Internet. Factors other than cost and services provided may also be important. The line speeds needed to support the traffic you anticipate, as well as the size and overall purpose of the Internet access, must be considered.

In the next few pages you'll see the available alternatives as I discuss the important advantages and disadvantages of each. In this chapter you learn the following:

- Different ways you can connect to the Internet
- Advantages and disadvantages of each method
- Costs involved in hardware and software
- Important considerations to bear in mind when choosing a method

There are several factors to consider. By the end of this chapter you should be able to narrow the choices down considerably and choose the best method for your needs.

Considerations on How to Connect

An overwhelming number of companies offer Internet access or services; all try hard to get your money. Full-page advertisements by online services seem to promise everything you could want, but a careful shop-around shows the promises don't always meet your needs.

You also can run into many strange terms, such as PPP, SLIP, dialup-access, and IP routers. All of these terms are explained in this and the following chapters.

Luckily for newcomers to the Internet, there are really only four ways to connect:

- *Your own direct gateway*—This method uses a dedicated machine (a gateway) to connect into the Internet backbone. This gives you full access to all services but is expensive to set up and maintain. It's really only for large corporations.

- *Internet Service Provider*—These are usually called ISPs. They're direct providers of connection to the Internet. Your machine accesses the ISP's gateway that provides limited or full access to Internet services. These companies are not the same as online services; ISPs only act as gateways to the Internet; online services provide other services and interpose control and filtering between you and the Internet. ISPs often offer dialup and dedicated telephone connections. All offer analog service; many are starting to offer ISDN service. Both ISDN and dedicated services can potentially provide higher data rates and more flexible services. Examples of a direct service provider at the national level include UUNET Technologies and PSI. Local and regional ISPs have sprung up throughout the United States, Canada, and many other countries.

- *Online Services*—This category is designed for the "classic" online services such as CompuServe, Prodigy, and America Online. These are indirect service providers because they interpose their computers between you and the Internet controlling the interface and possibilities for exchange of information far more than the ISP environment. This control is convenient, as it makes connection easy, but it adds considerably to your costs and may remove functions and access you want. Online service Internet connection is chosen by many individuals who are already using an online service. But not all online services offer all Internet features. And the costs associated with this type of connection can be relatively high when compared to ISPs.

- *Access through your company's system*—This may be available for your personal use as more and more companies are recognizing the benefits of having their staff on the Internet and experienced in Internet use.

- *Free use of someone else's direct gateway*—This usually involves getting permission to use someone else's gateway for full access to all services. This is a handy method for students whose Internet access is usually bundled with their general student fees, but those out of school may be out of luck when it comes to finding someone willing to let them use their gateway.

Choosing the connection method that's right for you isn't difficult. Your answers to the following questions will lead you to the most sensible alternative:

- Are you accessing the Internet for your company or for yourself?
- What services do you need?
- How much time are you going to spend using the system each month?
- How much are you're willing to pay?
- What data rate do you want?

If the access is for you, then adding your own gateway doesn't make economic sense. If the access is for your company as a whole, then using online services is too restrictive.

Company Access

If you want company-wide access, online services seldom are able to provide the level of performance or function needed to support company e-mail, FTP, and other Internet services. Online services don't have the throughput larger corporations require, and maintaining a large number of user accounts on someone else's system is not a wise move from a systems administration point of view. In addition, setting up a large number of accounts with online services usually costs considerably more than setting up similar numbers of accounts through a company-owned direct gateway or an Internet service provider.

Most companies should obtain their own domain name, for example supercorporation.com. This provides a professional aspect for their e-mail, Web, and other corporate communications. Equally important, a domain name is the property of its owner. As a result it stays with the owner regardless of the means of connecting to the Internet. Contrast this with the user who does not own a domain name. Then the user or firm must use the domain supplied by the service provider. When providers are changed, the

◀ See "What Is a Host Name?," p. 22

domain name changes, the e-mail address changes, the Web URL changes, and so on. What a mess! We'll cover more on domain names later in this chapter.

> **Caution**
>
> Not all Internet service providers provide domain name services, and none of the large online services provide it. So this rules out the online services for any serious business right away. Using an online service (or anyone else but yourself) for your domain identity is like getting married—easy to get into, hard to get out of.

The list of alternatives can be narrowed more. It's rare to find a company that can "borrow" another company's gateway. Unless the second company is willing to share the costs of the gateway, most companies that have a gateway are reluctant to let outsiders (or competitors) use their system.

A company is left with the choice of either using a direct gateway to the Internet or using an Internet service provider. The choice between these two options usually comes down to an issue of the size of the company and a comparison of the cost to connect for each method. Setting up a gateway is expensive, but may be cheaper than arranging accounts with a service provider if the volume of traffic is high.

Personal Access

If you want access for yourself, or for a very small company, it's unreasonable to have your own dedicated gateway. Not only is the cost high, but the investment will not pay for itself and will require continual administration. For all but the most affluent, the choice for connecting to the Internet is between borrowing someone's gateway, using a service provider, or using an online service.

Finding a gateway you can use is difficult. Give it a shot, if you like; just call local businesses and educational institutions and ask for free access to their Internet gateway—who knows, chutzpah has gotten much bigger things. Usually this type of access is available only if you know someone who can vouch for your reliability. If you're well-connected in the human sense, go for it; you'll get full Internet access at no cost. What have you got to lose? They can only say, "No," and they might say, "Yes."

Setting up an account with an Internet service provider and then making the connection work used to involve a big time startup curve filled with the esoterica of TCP/IP, C, and UNIX. Those days are gone. Any ISP expecting that of its clients is either out of business or soon will be. ISPs either supply users with preconfigured software kits from the free/shareware available on the Internet or sell or support commercial packages.

Most service providers offer a flat-fee rate that provides a certain number of hours free, with a connect-time surcharge after the free hours are used up. This is a cut-throat business and it pays to shop around. It's hard to tell how long we'll be seeing an ISP on every corner. Expect these guys to be gobbled up like mom and pop banks at a meeting of the National Bankers Association.

> **Note**
>
> The near certainty that you'll be changing ISPs either due to the ISP going out of business, being eaten alive by another ISP, or your finding a better deal, drives home the near absolute requirement that you obtain your own domain name. With that name in hand, your bargaining position is substantially better (you're no longer married to the ISP's name) and your printing costs (for your new cards, et al.) are drastically lower.

The last alternative, online services, would seem to be the choice for most individuals. But the proliferation of ISPs both locally and nationally has seriously cut into the online services. Though online services are loath to admit it, it's a little hard for someone who has discovered the full range of resources available on the Internet to take the online services seriously. Let's face it folks, CompuServe, America Online, Prodigy, and Bill's new Microsoft Network are in trouble. They have to come up with some reason for you to use them. If all they're going to do is act as gateways to the Internet, they'd better be ready to compete on price, and they aren't doing that now. If they claim to be providing more than Internet access, you'd better check to see what, if anything, it's worth to you.

▶ See "Connecting Through CompuServe," p. 231

▶ See "Connecting Through America Online," p. 263

▶ See "Connecting Through Prodigy," p. 287

▶ See "Connecting Through Microsoft Network," p. 309

Online services certainly are a good way to start until you're better able to decide what your Internet requirements really are. But most such services don't offer full access to all Internet capabilities. And the expense of using an online service for even a few hours a week can become alarmingly high. You'll see the different online service choices in more detail in later chapters.

Domain Names

A *domain name* is a unique identifier for your company that's used, for example, when mail is addressed to you. Domain names provide two pieces of information separated by a period: your company's online identification, or name, and the type of company or organization you are. For example, Que is

II

Getting Connected

an imprint of the publishing corporation, Macmillan Computer Publishing. The domain name for the corporation is mcp.com; the com indicates it's a commercial enterprise. An editor's mail address might be **aeinstein@que.mcp.com** (Que strives to have well-qualified editors). The que is the name of a sub-domain; usually this is a division, as with Que, or a specific server. In any case, this part is assigned by the corporation. But the mcp.com is assigned by the InterNIC, the part of the Internet in charge of domain names; in late 1995, the actual administration of naming was contracted to a private company.

You apply to InterNIC for the name; they issue and propagate it throughout the Internet to name servers that advise other servers looking for you. These servers translate the name to the IP address that is programmed into a particular device on your network. The whole thing is called the Domain Name System (DNS).

▶ See "A Brief
Introduction to
TCP/IP," p. 126

> **Note**
>
> Names mean something to people. It's far easier to remember an address using DNS than it is to recall 198.45.6.32 or whatever IP address is associated with a given domain name. Besides, you can have several names pointing to a single IP address. This technique allows you to have a single machine with a given IP address handling the business of a number of different domains. And any one of those names may move to another IP address without disrupting the others—lots of flexibility.

The end part of the domain name, called the *domain identifier*, comes after the period. There are six domain identifiers associated with different types of organizations:

.com	Commercial company
.edu	Educational institution
.gov	A governmental body of the United States of America
.mil	Military of the United States of America
.net	An Internet access provider or other network support type organization
.org	Anything that doesn't fall into one of the other categories; this usually includes charitable and trade associations

These identifiers are used by organizations throughout the world, but notice that the .gov and .mil identifiers are generally restricted to the United States. (OK, since you asked, **socks@whitehouse.gov** or

president@whitehouse.gov). However, there is another category of domain names arranged by geographic location. In Austin, Texas, the city has the domain ci.austin.tx.us. To send e-mail to the mayor you use the address **mayor@ci.austin.tx.us**.

▶ See "Country Code Table," p. 1191

> **Tip**
>
> Point your browser to **http://www.internic.net** for more on the domain name system.

> **Note**
>
> This use of the domain name carries over to services other than e-mail: **http://www.mcp.com** and **http://www.ci.austin.tx.us**. Or, in my case, **http://www.bryce.com/~bryce**. All of these are World Wide Web addresses. In the last one, my home page, the /~bryce tells your browser to look in my home directory on the Web server. Actually, this server is under the domain name of my Internet service provider, but through the magic of alias redirection, my domain service, mail service, and Web service are handled on the ISP's server.

Services You Need

While deciding which method to use to access the Internet, you need to consider the types of services you want from the Internet. If all you need is e-mail, then any kind of access will provide it, but some can be ridiculously expensive.

The Internet offers many types of services; each is explained in depth in other chapters. As a starting point, decide which of the following services are necessary and which are less important (you may want to answer this question after you've read the relevant chapters):

- *Electronic mail (e-mail)*—Sending mail to and from other Internet users
- *Telnet*—Remote logins to other machines on the Internet that allow you to work on the remote system or try software
- *FTP*—File transfers between machines that allow you to download software, graphics, and other files
- *World Wide Web (WWW) access*—An interlinked and usually graphical information service

- *UseNet newsgroups*—A set of bulletin boards for conversations on many different subjects
- *Gopher*—An information search and retrieval system
- *Archie*—A method for finding files to transfer
- *Internet Relay Chat (IRC)*—A text conversation system much like a CB
- *Video over the Internet*—This includes multimedia and video conferencing options of all kinds
- *RealAudio*—A newly developing product that can exchange quality audio over the Internet
- *Internet telephone technology*—Allows you to make full duplex phone calls anywhere in the world over the Internet

Tip

Listen for RealAudio at **http://www.realaudio.com** and ring up Internet phones at **http://www.itelco.com**. See a plethora of video at **http://www.yahoo.com/Computers_and_Internet/Video** and **http://www.yahoo.com/Computers_and_Internet/Videoconferencing**.

Any system directly connected to the Internet through a gateway (your company's or a borrowed gateway) can provide complete access to all the services listed above (unless the system administrator blocks them for some reason).

Online services provide e-mail, and most are adding the other services slowly. Not all the services are available with all online providers, though, so check with a representative to see what services they offer. You don't want to be frustrated by lack of support for a service you need.

If you intend to use e-mail frequently, it may be worth finding out if any mail you write is sent immediately (the usual case) or batched for transmission at a later time. Batching is used by some services to cut costs because the Internet link needs to be connected only for a few minutes at regular intervals. However, your e-mail delivery is slowed with a batch system.

Note

In my experience, batching of mail is a major drawback. When I'm working on a project, I'm frequently talking on the phone, faxing, and e-mailing all at once. If the e-mail is delayed at either end, it substantially slows the work. I've noticed batching delay often happens when the classic online services are used.

Direct Connection Through a Gateway

A direct connection (often called a *dedicated connection*) is one in which you or your company attach to the Internet backbone through a dedicated machine called a *gateway* or *IP router*. The connection is over a dedicated telephone line capable of high-speed transfers. The gateway becomes part of the Internet architecture and must remain online at all times. You can then use a computer on the gateway's network to access the Internet services.

> **Note**
>
> The term "dedicated" is used in various ways. In this case, I am referring to a device actually attached to the Internet. Sometimes "dedicated" simply means the Internet service provider has a modem set aside for your use; this does not imply a machine is always reserved for your connection.

Typically, dedicated connections imply high volumes of traffic and require systems with multi-megabit data rates. This type of connection usually is used by a large corporation to provide Internet access to employees. It's unlikely that an individual or small company would have direct gateway access primarily because of the high cost of installation and maintenance.

To create a direct access system, you must work with the Internet Network Information Center (InterNIC) to establish a domain name and IP addresses for your company. Then you must install gateways on the Internet backbone. The capital expense of such a system is high, both for initial hardware and software and for continuing support. Considerable costs may also be involved for dedicated telephone lines capable of supporting high data rates.

Obtain a copy of the Internet RFC (Request for Comment) 1359, "Connecting to the Internet," to see what steps you should follow. This document was developed specifically to help companies attach to the Internet.

> **Note**
>
> You can obtain a copy of this or any other RFC by pointing your Web browser to **http://ds.internic.net**. I also suggest you check out **http://www.ietf.org** to see what the Internet Engineering Task Force is up to; they write the RFCs.
>
> To obtain a printed copy of the RFC, call the Internet Network Information Center at 800-235-3155, have the RFC number at hand.

II

Getting Connected

Connecting Through Another Gateway

An alternative method of connecting to the Internet through a gateway relies on using a "friendly" machine or network. In such a system, a corporation or educational institution that has an Internet gateway may allow you to access the Internet through their system, usually through an attached modem. Because this type of access gives you freedom on their networks, many organizations now refuse this type of piggy-back access.

If you're lucky enough to find a company or school that will let you use their network, you simply call into a communications port on the network or gateway, then route through the gateway to the Internet. In many ways, it's as though you are a machine on the provider's network. Typically, you have unlimited access to the Internet's services, though some companies do set restrictions.

This type of access is usually readily available for students. Most universities have dedicated gateways to the Internet and allow registered students to dial in to the systems for full access. Usually, the Computer Sciences or the Information Technology department has information about access.

> **Note**
>
> If you're a student, connecting through your school's Internet gateway is the most economical and least limiting option. If you've graduated, check out the alumni association, credit union, or other university-affiliated organizations to see if your continued membership includes Internet access. If they don't know what you're talking about, ask to see their PR people and executive director and suggest Internet access be added as a perk to encourage membership.

Using an Internet Service Provider

Internet service providers are companies with an Internet gateway they share among many organizations and individuals. ISPs can be local, regional, national, or international in scope. An ISP offers you options in three distinct categories: telephone line, protocol, and service.

Telephone Line Options

Telephone line options include various ways for you to connect with the ISP over the telephone system. There are more ways than you might think:

- Dialup connection through the telephone system
- Dedicated connection through the telephone system
- Plain Old Telephone Service (POTS, analog)
- Integrated Service Digital Network (ISDN)

A *dialup connection* is established only when you dial the provider and connect. Notice that the most emphasis is on you dialing the provider. But some providers also have the capability to dial you up. This would be useful if you want to have the provider connect when new mail is received, an FTP transfer is requested, or a Web request is made of a server at your location.

A *dedicated connection* is a telephone line that is attached from your location to the provider and is always connected. There's sort of a middle ground of a "quasi-dedicated" connection that uses a dialup line, but the line is never hung up. This sort of line is useful when you don't want to have the delay for connection, or you want greater data rates than an standard telephone line can carry. Dedicated connections can be very expensive.

POTS is plain old telephone service, or, more formally, analog telephone technology. It's been with us for over 100 years. It's the line attached to your phone—that one sitting next to you right now. To use it with your computer, you attach a modem and call up the ISP.

ISDN is the new kid on the block. It's a totally digital technology. As a result, it offers the potential for much higher data rates than POTS. It also is able to set up and tear down connections in a fraction of a second; as a result when your equipment dials up your ISP, you're connected in less than a second—the same for disconnection. ISDN effectively destroys any advantage a dedicated line used to have. More and more ISPs are offering ISDN. Many are charging little if anything more for ISDN than for POTS. Often the ISP has equipment that is totally ISDN and simply "spoofs" POTS calls that use modems so such calls use the same telephone numbers for analog service as ISDN calls.

> **Note**
>
> You'll hear some horror stories about difficulties getting ISDN service from your phone company. Most of these stories are dated. ISDN is invading so rapidly now, you'll probably have little difficulty finding competent help from your "local exchange carrier," telespeak for the phone company. True, you might have to go through two or three people to find someone trained in ISDN, but you will.

▶ See "Setting Up an ISDN Connection," p. 177

Getting Connected

II

Protocol Options

Your ISP may offer you several protocol options that affect what you can do with your Internet connection and how fast you can do it. Now just what do I mean by protocol options? Protocol options are the rules and standards the ISP's computers use to talk to your computers:

- Shell
- Serial Line Internet Protocol (SLIP)
- Point to Point Protocol (PPP)

A *shell protocol* provides a way for your computer to act as a terminal looking into the programs actually running on the computers of your ISP. So if you ask for a file transfer from some computer out on the Internet using FTP, the file will be transferred not to your computer, but to the computer of your ISP; you're simply seated at a dumb terminal connected to the ISP's computer. You'll have to go through some other step to have the ISP's computer transfer the file to you. If you want to use the World Wide Web, you'll probably be limited to a character-based browser, Lynx, for example, which is unable to convey the graphic nature of the Web and often can't handle complex interactions such as interactive forms. In other words, you don't want a shell protocol connection! Well, the only reason you'd want one is that the equipment you have is not powerful enough to run some of the Internet applications or maybe your ISP doesn't offer anything but a shell account. But wait a minute! This is a book about using the Internet with Windows 95; you're equipment is powerful enough. If your ISP doesn't have anything but shell—scratch that ISP. The only real reason for a shell account now is isolation of your system from the Internet. Since you're only running as a terminal, the bad guys out there can't get into your computer.

A *SLIP* connection lets your computer become a real node on the Internet. Now you can execute FTP and really get the file. SLIP allows you to connect your computer over a serial link, such as a telephone line. SLIP also allows your computer to send and receive IP packets using the TCP/IP protocol. But SLIP is an older remote access standard that is typically used by UNIX remote access servers. Use SLIP only if your ISP's site has a UNIX system configured as a SLIP server for Internet connections. The remote access server must be running TCP/IP. SLIP is not in great use today as PPP is taking over. SLIP lets you use the Web and have all the graphics and interactive forms. SLIP is a desirable protocol, but it's getting a little long in the tooth and never was formally adopted as an official Internet protocol, so let's move on to PPP.

A *PPP* connection is the most advanced standardized connection you can get. It's a developing protocol and offers better performance and additional features over SLIP. Current work on PPP includes elements for aggregating multiple communication channels and compression. You want a PPP protocol connection! (But you can settle for SLIP if that's all you can get for a while.)

PPP has become the standard for remote access. Microsoft recommends that you use PPP because of its flexibility and its role as an industry standard and for future flexibility with client and server hardware and software. If a dial-up client is running PPP, it can connect to a network running IPX, TCP/IP, or NetBEUI protocols. PPP is the default protocol for the Microsoft Windows 95 Dial-Up adapter. In short, PPP has the following advantages involving standard protocols:

- PPP supports a standard way of encapsulating datagrams over serial links. This uses the ISO standard protocol High Level Data Link Control (HDLC). Since this is a standard that is nearly universal, IBM's mainframe communications use a relative of HDLC; it provides great flexibility for heterogeneous interconnection.

- PPP uses Link Control Protocol (LCP) to check the integrity of the connection. It sets up such things as compression and various security protocols including Password Authentication Protocol (PAP and Challenge Handshake Authentication Protocol (CHAP) that are standard throughout data communications.

- PPP supports a broad spectrum of network control protocols, including NetBIOS Frames Control Protocol (NBF CP), Internet Protocol Control Protocol (IPCP), and Internet Packet Exchange Control Protocol (IPXCP) that works with the NetWare IPX protocol family.

Tip

For the minutia all Internet standards tune into **http://www.ietf.org** and then to **http://ds.internic.net/rfc/rfc1880.txt**.

Since we're most concerned with Windows 95 you'll probably be hearing about something called *WinSock*, short for *Windows Sockets*. Many people mistake this for a particular implementation called Trumpet WinSock, but that's an error. WinSock is a well-defined application program interface (API) that has become the de facto standard for Windows-based, communications-capable applications. Many software products incorporate the WinSock standard; Microsoft uses it in Windows 95. Trumpet WinSock is just another implementation of the WinSock standard, albeit a widely used and excellent

II

Getting Connected

implementation. Microsoft was a founding member of the WinSock Group of thirty companies launched in 1991. Microsoft's Windows Open Systems Architecture (WOSA) includes WinSock. Version 2 of WinSock supports:

- TCP/IP (and thus PPP)
- IPX/SPX (NetWare)
- AppleTalk
- OSI

▶ See "Connecting to a PPP or SLIP Account with Windows 95," p. 137

Tip

See **http://www.stardust.com** for the latest on WinSock; you can also blow your horn at **ftp.trumpet.com.au**.

Service Options

Now for the good parts. Your ISP can supply you with Internet services that actually do something for you. Look for an ISP that provides the following services:

- E-mail
- Name
- World Wide Web
- News
- Firewall

▶ See "How Internet E-Mail Works," p. 329

▶ See "E-Mailing Outside the Internet and with Online Services," p. 401

▶ See "Encoding and Decoding Files," p. 439

You already know what e-mail is. Your provider should have an e-mail server on the Internet at all times. It should send out all messages you send within a few seconds of your request; that is, it should not batch e-mail for any appreciable period of time. It should be able to deal with all attachments and e-mail.

Name service is vital to you. Your ISP should provide a service that allows you to have your own domain name and have it serviced on the ISP's machines. This way you can be sure the world knows who and where you are. The ISP will have to help you apply for a domain name and participate in periodic renewals. Once you receive the name, the ISP will make sure all Internet traffic addressed to that domain is directed to your mailbox, Web server, or other receiving location and is protected from invasion or corruption by other users.

World Wide Web service means the ISP has a program running on a server that can store hypertext documents you prepare for your own home page. You should be able to change the contents of your own directory and home page at any time and as often as you like. World Wide Web service can include additions such as the ability to read and insert in a database responses to forms you've placed on the Web (Common Gateway Interface, CGI scripts).

News service is provided to receive newsfeeds from the newsgroups on the Internet. There are thousands of such groups. Every day a provider must download additions to the newsgroups, delete old items, and add new items. This takes a considerable amount of disk space. In many cases, a provider will choose not to take all the possible newsfeeds; some feeds will be chopped due to anticipated lack of interest, others for concern over possibly offensive content, and so on. If your ISP doesn't have a newsgroup you want, ask for it; usually the ISP can establish a connection. And should you want to establish a newsgroup, the ISP can help with that as well.

▶ See "Using HTML to Build Your Home Page," p. 621

▶ See "Using Microsoft Internet Assistant to Build Web Pages," p. 667

▶ See "Using Netscape Navigator Gold and HotDog to Create Web Pages," p. 699

▶ See "New Web Technologies," p. 723

Tip

You don't have to use only the news through your ISP; other sites are available over the Internet; just enter the site's URL as your news location.

Firewall service is security maintained by your ISP to block hackers from you and your information. This protects you from virus attacks, theft, and destruction of information. An elaborate collection of techniques is used to provide firewalls. In some cases *proxy servers* are set up to monitor Internet traffic into and out of your network. These servers are application specific—that is, they work only with a particular database or whatever you are seeking to protect. As a result, they can have much more protection built in than a router that must deal with generic forms of network traffic.

Tip

Get your firewall plans from **http://www.iwi.com/pubs/faq.htm**.

As you might suspect, not all, or even most, ISPs provide all these options. But now you have some idea of the range. Of course, the more you get the more you pay. But you'll be pleasantly surprised by the competitive marketplace.

II

Getting Connected

Frontdoors and Backdoors

Let's take another perspective on these services. Telephone line options and protocol options fall into a category I call the frontdoor. Frontdoor options get you into the Internet. You have to have a frontdoor to reach the Internet or nothing will happen. Think of this in a physical way: a frontdoor is the connection of your computer through the phone lines to the Internet service provider's modem or ISDN terminal adapter bank.

On the other hand, backdoor options are the services that are provided once you're on the Internet. These services include mail service, Web service, domain name service. Since these services are provided through the Internet there's some magic possible. Here's the trick: You can have different providers for your frontdoor and backdoor options; in fact you can have a number of backdoor providers, all at the same time! Many people think their mail service must be provided by the same provider they dial into, which is wrong. The same goes for the Web and domain services and any number of other services that might appear on the Internet.

Everything Is Connected to Everything Else

Got it? Since on the Internet everything is connected to everything else, the physical location of a service is irrelevant once you're on. You don't care that someone else's Web page you're reading is on a server on the other side of the planet. Why should you care that the server that receives and stores your e-mail is too?

Why do you care? In shopping around you might find a provider that can give you a great deal on the frontdoor, but either doesn't have what you want in backdoor options or charges too much. For example, you might want to use a national provider like PSI for your frontdoor because they have points of presence in most major cities of the United States and can handle both POTS and ISDN with a single phone number. On the other hand, they may require you to use their domain name or charge too much for domain service. Fine. Use PSI for your frontdoor. Now shop around and find other providers that will cut you a good rate for domain name service, mail service, and all the other backdoor options. You might find you'll need one for domain name and e-mail and another for Web service. The Internet can handle all this; simply configure your software to point to the appropriate location for the service. This book's already saved you its price.

If a provider won't sell you a backdoor service without selling the frontdoor, point out the great reduction in their costs your deal will make; they don't need a line for you, or a modem, and so on. These are really the big costs to an ISP. If they still don't bite, go somewhere else. And remember, unlike frontdoor options, you don't have to get your backdoor services locally; literally anyone in the world can provide them to you!

> **Tip**
>
> Remember, the incremental cost of providing many of these options is minor to an ISP; use this knowledge to get a lot for your money as I've just described, shop around.

> **Note**
>
> The setup procedure for using direct service providers is much easier than it was as the Internet took off with commercial use. Now Windows-based packages are available directly aimed at providing access through these providers. Often the providers have a listing and built-in configuration already in the software; you simply select your provider and enter your name. Internet Chameleon from NetManage, Internet in a Box from Spry/CompuServe, and SuperTCP from Frontier are examples of such programs.

▶ See "Vendor Contacts for Selected Internet Software and Services," p. 1205

Online Services

Online services like CompuServe, America Online, and Prodigy were popular before they offered Internet access. They provided a place for conversation, file transfer, and experimentation with new software. Now online services are rushing to connect to the Internet in an effort to attract new users and avoid mass defection of current ones.

Online (or indirect) service providers have expanded their Internet content dramatically in response to user demands. All online services have e-mail capabilities to and from the Internet; most offer or are in the process of developing UseNet access, FTP capabilities, and World Wide Web facilities. Now the largest providers have these classic Internet services.

Online services are a good choice for the casual Internet user who expects to be on the Internet less than two or three hours a month. If you occasionally want to send e-mail or browse newsgroups, and you don't anticipate spending a lot of time each day on the system, the online services are probably your best alternative. They charge users a basic fee as well as a connect-time rate, so low-volume users are not facing a large monthly bill.

II

Getting Connected

> **Caution**
>
> Beware: the Internet is addictive, and your plan to spend only half an hour a day can quickly change as you scan the UseNet newsgroups and especially the Web! Some services such as CompuServe, America Online, and Prodigy can add a hefty surcharge as your use grows. Check it out; charges change over time in response to demand and competition.
>
> When considering an online service, ask if there's a charge for each message (e-mail or newsgroup article) you send or receive. These charges can quickly add up! If there are charges other than a flat-amount connect time fee, find out if the additional charges are based on characters or messages sent and received. If you plan to download graphics, sound files, or binaries, character-based fees can add up at an alarming rate.

If you want to make use of some of the service's other features, the online service may be your best choice. Some of the other features offered are:

- Large file download areas and technical support (a strength of CompuServe)
- Graphics-based multi-player games and general news (features of Prodigy)
- Online access to magazines and search databases (a good feature of America Online)

For any extensive use of the Internet, without use of the other features, online services have not been a good buy.

Connecting to an online service provider is easy. All you really need is a modem and a communications software package from the service or some software designed for the service from a third party. Unless you've been in deep space for the last ten years, you've probably gotten hundreds of online software disks in the mail or with hardware and software you've bought or been given.

Most online services have access numbers in large urban centers, so long-distance telephone bills are not an issue unless you live in the country or out of the immediate toll-free calling area. Check the availability of a dial-in port; some services may have too few lines (which may mean a lengthy wait to get access, or force you to use inconvenient hours). All major online services have 800 telephone numbers that provide this kind of information, as well as local access telephone numbers.

Caution

Make sure the online service you choose has a local number. Long-distance numbers add to your costs. Some systems that have 800 numbers add their cost to your bill when you use them.

Also, some services require you to access the system through a packet-switched network (such as Tymnet, Datapac, and SprintNet), that adds its own connect charges.

Make sure you understand exactly how much access is going to cost you.

Most online services now offer UseNet newsgroups, although some services filter the newsgroups received. They usually restrict newsgroups both to reduce the overall volume (approximately 90M per day) and to act as a censor to prevent "questionable" material from being available through their family-oriented services. For example, some services restrict any newsgroup with the word *sex* in the title. When asking about these services, find out if a full UseNet feed is available.

▶ See "How UseNet Works," p. 749

The major online services have graphical interfaces for Internet services. Some smaller ones rely on character-based systems, which may not be what you want. Character-based systems also limit the Internet facilities you can access. Use of the World Wide Web is severely hampered by a character-only interface.

Tip

Character-based browsers are available. The most popular is Lynx available at **ftp2.cc.ukans.edu/pub/WWW/DosLynx/DLX0_A.EXE**.

▶ See "Connecting Through CompuServe," p. 231

In the past there was a snobbishness within the Internet's e-mail and UseNet newsgroups; this was directed against those who used online services for access. These users are identified by their user names, which have the online service domain names attached (such as aol.com or compuserve.com). Users who accessed through online services were not considered to be really a part of the Internet community, but more like users sneaking in through a backdoor. Most of the people who expressed such negative sentiments have been put out to some distant pasture where they belong. If you come in through an online service, you should and will be treated with all the respect you show others. Anyone who acts otherwise toward you is not worthy of your concern; ignore them.

▶ See "Connecting Through America Online," p. 263

▶ See "Connecting Through Prodigy," p. 287

▶ See "Connecting Through Microsoft Network," p. 309

II

Getting Connected

Tip

You'll even run into some who feel that Windows, DOS, and Mac users shouldn't be on the Internet and that the Internet should be reserved for the UNIX, C, and TCP/IP elite. Blow off their attempts to cast asparagus.

Other Ways to Connect

There are some connection alternatives that haven't been mentioned so far, primarily because they are difficult to find and usually available only through the good graces of a user.

One of the Internet access methods is through a traditional bulletin board system (BBS). Some BBSs have now added limited Internet access to their services. The most commonly added feature is Internet e-mail capabilities, although a few BBSs also provide some UseNet newsgroup downloads and limited FTP or WWW features. The Internet capabilities tend to be more common on subscriber-based BBSs (where you pay either a flat fee or a connect-time fee) rather than the free-service BBS. To find a BBS in your area that has these services, check with local user groups, other bulletin board systems, or one of the magazines that caters to the BBS market.

Another alternative is to gain access through a professional society or organization that has user services. Some groups have BBS or online systems dedicated to member support, with a wide variety of capabilities available. A few groups have started to offer limited Internet services, especially e-mail that ties in with their professional e-mail service. If you belong to a national or international professional group, you should inquire about their membership services. Also, local organizations, ranging from yachting clubs to bowling teams, offer members access to their computer systems. Check with any groups you may belong to about Internet access.

For the very casual user, there's another choice that is becoming trendy— online bars and cafes. These places let you use a terminal to Net surf while you sip your favorite beverage (using a computer-generated user name or one chosen by you as your login). Although the number of online establishments of this nature is still quite small, the popularity should ensure their spread to many cities.

Libraries and service-oriented businesses such as copy shops are starting to offer Internet access. Libraries often provide at least some limited use for no charge, but they may crack down when you spend ten hours playing Internet games.

Important Considerations

Here are the important points to bear in mind when choosing a service provider. There are numerous stories of users who selected a service provider before carefully considering all the factors and found themselves either severely limited in what they could access or faced with costs far out of proportion to what was expected. It's better to be safe and consider these points carefully again!

Services

Make sure the service you're considering supports the Internet features you want. After you decide what features you want from your Internet access (e-mail, FTP, UseNet newsgroups, WWW, name, and so on), ask your intended service provider if the services are fully supported. Many providers have a habit of telling you they are supported when in fact they only offer a subset or restrict some services in some way. Be direct and ask about limitations.

Some systems restrict access to Internet games such as multi-user dungeons (MUDs) to cut down on heavy Internet usage. If you're planning on using someone else's gateway, ask whether they object to you accessing this type of service.

Ask if the service limits the UseNet newsgroups? Is FTP service fully supported to any machine on the Internet? Is anonymous FTP supported? Does the system support World Wide Web? Are Gopher and Archie available? You get the idea. Decide what you want; then don't accept anything less.

> ### Tip
>
> Remember, through splitting between backdoor and frontdoor options, you can use more than one provider to get the right mix of services.

Availability

If you're choosing an access method for a company or organization, you have to decide if the system should be available 24 hours a day. If so, and you don't want to have any delays in sending or receiving information through the Internet, a direct connection or direct service provider is necessary. Decide how often you want to check the Internet for traffic to you.

The same consideration applies to an individual. Do you want to check the Internet every hour for mail, or is once a day adequate? If you're using an online service and dialing in every hour, the expenses become very high. If you must have frequent access, an online service provider is a poor choice.

Cost

For many users, cost is a primary item in selecting a service. The most economical solution is to find a gateway you're allowed to access free of charge. This is relatively easy for university students, but much more difficult for others. Therefore, you must carefully weigh the costs involved with other services.

Ask your service provider for a detailed fee schedule. Sometimes the charge depends on the services you access and the amount of time you spend on the service. Almost all services have a flat-fee monthly rate; many have a connect fee based on time beyond the flat-fee.

Make sure you know how you'll be billed for Internet access: is it time-, character-, or message-based? Is there a packet-switching network fee on top? If you're using an online service, ask if the Internet service is a "premium" service with additional fees over the usual service fee.

Don't assume high prices are related to better service; conversely, low prices may not mean the best deal. Make a list of the services you need, and estimate your average and highest weekly usage; then shop around for the service that gives you all the services you need at the best price. Remember, some services include more than Internet access in their price, will you be using those additional services?

Access

The access issue ties in with costs to some extent, especially if there is no local number for the service you want to use. Long distance bills add up, especially when you're spending several hours a week reading UseNet newsgroups or navigating the Web. An 800 number is no guarantee of free access. Most online services have a surcharge for use of an 800 line (the line is considered a convenience for the user).

Several of the national providers have *points of presence* (POP) in all the major cites in the United States and Canada and often in Europe and Asia. If you need such coverage, they're worth a careful look.

> **Tip**
>
> Check out **http://www.cybertoday.com/isps** for listings of ISPs and references to other ISP lists throughout the world.

Ask about the number of lines an online service offers. Having a local access number is not a benefit to you if you can't access it when you want. Some online services keep only a few modems available in small population centers; it's worth finding out how easy it will be for you to access the system. It's not good to have to wait until the wee hours of the morning to connect!

Check the speeds supported by the access lines. Currently the fastest generally used modems on POTS lines operate at 28.8 kilobits per second; your provider should offer this rate for most lines, and you should buy a 28.8 kbps modem to enjoy the full advantage of the service. ISDN is becoming widely available and offers data rates in multiples of 64 kbps with fraction of a second set up/tear down times; does the provider have ISDN?

Some systems shut down for a couple of hours late at night for system backups, or are shut down part of some day during the week. Ask your service provider if they have round-the-clock access, limited access during certain hours, or no access at some periods.

▶ See "Setting Up an ISDN Connection," p. 177

Software

If you're using an online service, there may be a special software package needed to access the system. Although these software applications are usually free, you still have to find a copy and learn how to use it. Also, some systems don't work well with some communications packages. Check with the service provider to find out if your favorite communications software will work, or whether you should use their own interface.

As a general rule, the online services provide the software you need to connect. Now that software is almost always Windows-based and new versions are available taking advantage of Windows 95's power. The major online services, CompuServe, America Online, and Prodigy all incorporate Internet software in these packages.

Security

Security is important to protect your activities on the system. You don't want someone else to be able to access your e-mail mailbox or see what newsgroups you're reading. Ask the intended service provider how they manage security and whether they support any kind of encryption for sensitive mail messages. This broaches the issue of firewall services.

Many online systems make it clear in their user agreements that you have no rights to privacy if you use their system. Read your agreement carefully. It may look like mumbo-jumbo, but you could be giving up some important rights to privacy.

II

Getting Connected

Technical Support

Technical support is usually an issue for the individual user. Although most corporations have knowledgeable people on staff to handle gateways and routers, the ins and outs of making everything connect up may make it necessary to use service help from a provider even for the largest of users. It's good to know how much (if any) support you can expect from a service. Beware of promises. One popular online provider touted their help lines as being fully staffed by professionals 24 hours a day; often there was at least a two-hour wait for someone to answer a call; then another long wait for a call back from them with the answer!

Even though you may be an experienced computer user, you'll still need technical support. Many services have a lot of protocol behavior that's transparent to the user, but which can cause anomalous behavior. Having someone to ask about the problem is not only handy but vital to the functioning of your communications.

CHAPTER 5

Connecting Through a LAN with Windows 95

One of the major improvements in the Windows 95 operating system is the built-in support for connecting to the Internet. Although Microsoft built in some support for networking in previous versions of Windows (notably Windows for Workgroups), users who wanted to connect to the Internet often had to add a significant amount of software.

The Windows 95 distribution CD-ROM, however, already includes everything that you need to connect to the Internet (at least in a basic form)—support for Ethernet cards, a TCP/IP protocol stack (including a WINSOCK library), and basic applications such as File Transfer Protocol (FTP) and Telnet. This chapter explains what you need to do to install and configure this software so that you can connect to the Internet from your local area network (LAN)-based PC.

> **Note**
>
> If your computer is not directly connected to a LAN (with an Ethernet card, for example) but instead uses a modem to connect to the Internet, see chapter 6, "Connecting to a PPP or SLIP Account with Windows 95."

This chapter assumes that your computer is already physically connected to your LAN and that your network interface card is already installed and working with other network protocols (such as the Microsoft Network clients). In this chapter, you learn:

- Some basic information about TCP/IP networks
- How to install TCP/IP support in Windows 95
- How to configure the TCP/IP protocol
- How to test and troubleshoot your TCP/IP connection

A Brief Introduction to TCP/IP

TCP/IP (*Transmission Control Protocol/Internet Protocol*) is the basic network protocol that computers connected to the Internet use to communicate with each other. Although Windows 95 supports other communications protocols (such as IPX/SPX to communicate with Novell-compatible servers and NETBEUI to communicate with Windows NT-based servers), your Windows 95 system requires TCP/IP to talk to other computers on the Internet. Programs such as FTP, Telnet, and World Wide Web (WWW) browsers are all based on the TCP/IP protocol.

A unique *IP address* identifies each computer connected to the Internet. This address consists of four numbers, each from 1 to 256, usually separated by periods (for example, 192.58.107.230). When a network is connected to the Internet, these addresses are assigned in groups (usually of 256).

For example, when your company connects to the Internet, you might be assigned a group of IP addresses from 128.50.25.1 through 128.50.25.256. Your network administrator can then use any of these addresses for internal computers that need to talk to other computers on the Internet.

If your LAN is large (or divided into different groups of computers that mostly talk among themselves), your network administrator might set up *subnets*. A subnet defines a group of computers that listen for *broadcast messages* (messages sent to a group of computers rather than a specific computer) from other computers in the group. Subnets are like a radio or television frequency—only computers "listening" on the particular frequency receive the broadcast message.

Along with the unique IP address, each computer on the Internet has a unique *host name*. The Domain Name System automatically translates the host name to the IP address.

A host name consists of groups of characters separated by periods and usually organized from right to left. The *domain name* part of the host name is assigned when your organization applies for a connection to the Internet. This domain name is the rightmost part of the host name; for example, all computers at International Business Machines (IBM) have a domain name of ibm.com.

> **Note**
>
> Network names and IP addresses are assigned by the InterNIC (Internet Network Information Center) Registration Services center, currently operated by Network Solutions, Inc. of Herndon Virginia. They can be reached via e-mail at **mailserv@rs.internic.net** and via the World Wide Web at **http://rs.internic.net**.

The local network administrator assigns the rest of the host name, which can be almost anything. Small organizations might add only one segment to make up the complete host name (for example, host1.ibm.com). Larger organizations might add several other segments (for example, server1.marketing.eastcoast.ibm.com). However long the host name is, it always corresponds to a unique Internet address.

When two networks are connected together (for example, a local area network connecting to the Internet) a gateway machine is used to pass packets between the two networks. A gateway watches the traffic on the two (or more) networks that connect to it. When the gateway sees a packet on one network that is destined for another network, it passes the packet on to that network.

A gateway is also used to connect physically different types of networks; connecting a fiber-optic network to an Ethernet network is accomplished through a gateway.

Installing TCP/IP Support in Windows 95

If your computer system already has an Ethernet card (or any other type of network card for that matter) installed and operational, installing the TCP/IP protocol support in Windows 95 is easy.

To install the Windows 95 TCP/IP protocol, open the Network control panel (by choosing Start, Settings, Control Panel, Network). The first screen, shown in figure 5.1, lists all the network components already installed on your computer. If the control panel already lists TCP/IP, the Windows 95 TCP/IP protocol is already installed, and you need not need install it again (you can proceed to the section "Configuring the Windows 95 TCP/IP Protocol").

II

Getting Connected

Fig. 5.1

The Network control panel lists all available network components.

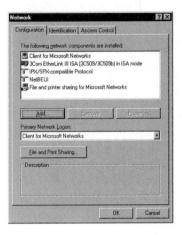

To install the Windows 95 TCP/IP protocol, click the Add button, which displays the Select Network Component Type dialog box. Select the protocol type and then click Add. You then see the Select Network Protocol dialog box, shown in figure 5.2. In this dialog box, you select the manufacturer (in this case Microsoft) and the exact network protocol (in this case TCP/IP).

Fig. 5.2

You select the TCP/IP protocol in the Select Network Protocol dialog box.

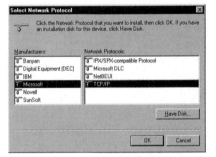

After selecting the TCP/IP protocol from the Network Protocols list, click OK to confirm your selections in each of these dialog boxes. When you click OK on the Network control panel, Windows 95 installs the TCP/IP protocol support from your installation media. At this point, the program might prompt you to insert your Windows distribution CD-ROM or floppy disk.

Note

Most TCP/IP programs that run under Windows (including Windows 95) use a library called WINSOCK (for Windows Sockets, an implementation of the TCP/IP socket library for Windows-based computers). This library enables the programs to set up connections to other computers easily and to communicate with programs on the other computer. Earlier versions of Windows did not include the WINSOCK library, but Windows 95 includes the library as part of the TCP/IP package.

If your network application (such as a WWW browser) is WINSOCK-compatible, it should work fine with Windows 95's built-in WINSOCK library.

Configuring the Windows 95 TCP/IP Protocol

After installing the Windows 95 TCP/IP protocol driver support, you must configure the TCP/IP protocol so that it matches the network configuration of your Internet service provider.

Caution

You should ask your Internet service provider or LAN administrator to provide the correct TCP/IP configuration settings. Using incorrect TCP/IP configuration settings can cause serious problems on your LAN, so you should check first before setting or changing anything.

To configure the TCP/IP protocol, open the Network control panel and select the TCP/IP protocol from the list of installed network components. Click Properties to view (and change) the settings for the TCP/IP protocol. Figure 5.3 shows the first page of the TCP/IP Properties dialog box, IP Address.

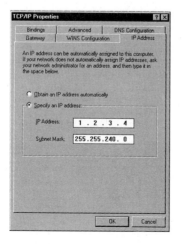

Fig. 5.3
The TCP/IP Properties dialog box enables you to configure the protocol settings.

II

Getting Connected

The IP Address Page

The IP Address page provides two ways to assign an IP address. To specify the address manually, you can click the Specify option and then type the numeric IP address in the boxes provided. Alternatively, you can have Windows 95 obtain an IP address from a server on your network when Windows starts up.

If your computer has a fixed IP address (one that is permanently assigned to the computer), you should enter that IP address into the page's IP Address field. To enter the IP address, type the four sets of digits in the field's four boxes. If you type a three-digit number (such as 128), the cursor automatically moves to the next box. To move to the next box manually, you can click the next box, press Tab, or type a period.

If your network is set up to use subnets, enter the proper subnet mask (for example, 255.255.255.0) into the Subnet Mask field. You enter the subnet mask much like you enter the IP address.

Note

The subnet mask controls what set of IP addresses on your network will receive *broadcasts* from your computer. Broadcasts are packets from your computer that are sent to more than one destination computer.

Caution

Check with your network administrator to ensure that you enter the correct value for the IP address and subnet mask. If you enter the wrong values, you can affect other computers on the LAN as well as your own. For example, if you enter an IP address that another computer on your LAN is using, information that is supposed to go to that computer will instead go to yours.

If your network administrator has set up a server on your network (such as a server for the Dynamic Host Configuration Protocol [DHCP]) that assigns IP addresses automatically, you should select the option Obtain an IP Address Automatically. Ask your network administrator whether this option is appropriate for your site.

The WINS Configuration Page

When you select the TCP/IP Properties dialog box's second tab, you see the WINS Configuration page (figure 5.4). *WINS (Windows Internet Naming Standard)* is a method, similar to the Domain Name System, for translating host names into IP addresses. Computers usually are set up to use the Domain Name System to translate host names to IP addresses, but your administrator might prefer that you use WINS instead.

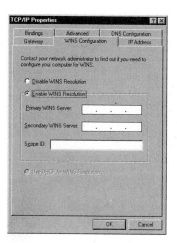

Fig. 5.4

Configuring a WINS server for the TCP/IP protocol.

If your LAN administrator has set up a WINS server on your network, you can set your computer to use the WINS server by selecting the Enable WINS Resolution check box. You must enter the IP address for your network's primary WINS server, and you might also have to enter the secondary WINS server.

You use the Scope ID text box to specify which computers can receive your network traffic. Only computers with the same Scope ID setting as your computer receive your network traffic; likewise, your computer receives messages only from other computers with the same Scope ID setting. Unless your network administrator tells you otherwise, you should leave this infrequently used setting blank.

If your network has a DHCP server set up, that server might automatically provide addresses for the WINS server. Check with your network administrator to see whether this feature is available; if it is, you can select the Use DHCP for WINS Resolution option at the bottom of the page.

II

Getting Connected

> **Note**
>
> DHCP is a service that allows your network administrator to allocate a pool of host names and addresses which can be automatically allocated to computers when they boot. New computers on the network can be automatically assigned a name and address without intervention by the network administrator, and names used by hosts that no longer exist can be automatically returned to the pool. This type of service can greatly simplify the administration of TCP/IP networks.

The Gateway Page

The TCP/IP Properties dialog box's Gateway page (shown in figure 5.5) enables you to configure the gateway machine that connects your LAN to the rest of the Internet. Your network administrator can tell you the proper address to use.

Fig. 5.5

The Gateway page enables you to set your default gateway address.

To set your default gateway address, type your gateway's IP address into the New Gateway field and then click the Add button. This adds the new gateway to the Installed Gateways list. This list can include more than one gateway address. To remove a gateway address from the list, select that address and click the Remove button.

> **Note**
>
> If you can use TCP/IP programs (such as Telnet or FTP) to connect to computers on your LAN but cannot connect to computers outside of your LAN, your Gateway address is probably configured incorrectly or missing.

The DNS Configuration Page

By clicking the next tab on the TCP/IP Properties dialog box, you display the DNS Configuration page (shown in figure 5.6). In this page, you can configure your DNS (Domain Name System) addresses. As with most of the TCP/IP settings, you should talk to your network administrator to ensure that you enter the correct values.

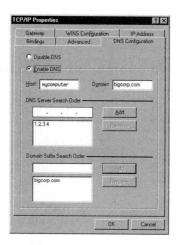

Fig. 5.6

Specify your DNS servers in the DNS Configuration page.

If your network uses DNS to translate from host names to IP addresses, you should select the Enable DNS option and configure the rest of the settings on this page.

In the Host text box, you enter the specific host name for your computer. In the Domain text box, you enter the rest of your computer's host name. For example, if your computer's host name is mycomputer.bigcorp.com, you enter **mycomputer** in the Host text box and **bigcorp.com** in the Domain text box.

In the DNS Server Search Order field, you enter the first server's IP address. Then click the Add button to add the DNS server to the list of servers. If your network has multiple DNS servers, you can enter the IP addresses one at a time and then click Add to add them to the list. If you want to remove an entry from the list of DNS servers, select that entry and then click the Remove button.

At the bottom of the DNS Configuration page, you can create a list of domains to search when you try to access just a host name. For example, if you enter the domain bigcorp.com (by typing **bigcorp.com** into the Domain Suffix Search Order text box and then clicking Add) and then try to connect

II

Getting Connected

to a computer called *server*, your computer would first try to look up the name *server* in the Domain Name System and then try to look up the name server.bigcorp.com.

You can remove an entry from the list of domains to search by selecting the entry and then clicking the Re<u>m</u>ove button.

Tip

If you can connect to computers by typing their IP addresses but not by using their host names, you probably have not set up your DNS servers correctly.

Also, if your computer takes more than 30 seconds to connect to another computer, check whether one of your DNS server entries is incorrect. Such delays are caused by your computer trying the first entry in the list of DNS servers and, if the entry is incorrect (or the DNS server is unavailable), waiting for that server to respond. Eventually, your computer gives up and moves on to the next DNS server—which results in a significant delay while your computer connects to another machine.

Note

If you access a particular site frequently, you should add its domain name into your domain suffix search order. Then you can connect to that host simply by typing only its specific host name rather than its full Internet name.

For example, if you often connect to computers at another.corp.com, add that domain name to the search order; then you can connect to a machine called server.another.corp.com simply by typing the name **server**.

The Advanced and Bindings Pages

The last two pages, Advanced and Bindings, are quite simple. The only setting that the Advanced page offers specifies that the TCP/IP protocol is the default protocol. You can safely leave this setting unselected.

In the Bindings page, you can configure which network clients (such as the client for Microsoft Networks or the client for Novell Networks) use the TCP/IP protocol. You can safely select all available clients to enable each to use the TCP/IP protocol.

Testing Your TCP/IP Connection

After configuring your TCP/IP protocol settings (and reviewing them a couple of times to make sure that they are correct), you should test your connection to ensure that it works correctly.

If your network card already works with other protocols (which you can check by opening your Network Neighborhood from the desktop and seeing whether any other computers are visible), you can check your TCP/IP connection by using the program PING.EXE, which is in your Windows folder.

PING is a DOS program that sends a special IP packet to another computer. This *echo packet* should cause the remote computer to return a packet to your computer. The PING program sends the packet and waits for the echo to return.

From the DOS command line (you might open an MS-DOS command window from Windows 95, for example), type the command **ping** followed by the IP address of another computer on your LAN. For example, if your network administrator tells you that one of your local DNS servers has the address 192.44.55.66, you can enter the command **ping 192.44.55.66**. The PING program then sends an echo packet to the remote computer and reports whether it receives the return packet. If the computers send and receive the packets correctly, your TCP/IP connection is working correctly.

If the PING command fails, check whether your TCP/IP settings are correct. If you cannot get the TCP/IP connections to work correctly, check with your network administrator.

You can check your DNS (or WINS) servers by using the PING program with a host name rather than an IP address. For example, enter the command **ping hostname** (substituting *hostname* with a valid host name on your LAN). If the command completes correctly, your system can translate the host name into an Internet address and contact the remote machine.

Now you can check whether your connection to the Internet as a whole works correctly by using the PING program with a host name outside of your LAN. Pick a computer at a large site that should be available most of the time; for example, you might use the host **ftp.microsoft.com** (which is the FTP server at Microsoft Corporation).

If the PING command fails the first time, don't be too concerned; the remote server might be unavailable when you try it. Try other hosts (check some of the FTP servers listed in chapter 47, "Top FTP Sites," for example). If you cannot contact any hosts outside of your LAN, check your gateway configuration.

II

Getting Connected

Connecting to a PPP or SLIP Account with Windows 95

In addition to the built-in capability to connect to the Internet through a local area network (as described in chapter 5, "Connecting Through a LAN with Windows 95"), Windows 95 has built-in software that allows your computer to connect to the Internet using a modem. Instead of needing additional software to connect to an Internet service provider and Internet applications, Windows 95 has all the software you need to use the Internet at home.

In order to connect to the Internet using the Windows 95 dialing software, you need to set up your modem as a network interface. In addition, you will configure the network software to dial your Internet service provider and connect your computer to its network.

The Windows 95 dial-in networking supports most of the connection protocols required by Internet service providers, including the Serial Line Internet Protocol (SLIP), SLIP with compression, the Point to Point Protocol (PPP), Netware connect, and the Windows NT Remote Access Protocol (RAS). In addition, the Windows 95 dialing software has the ability to automate the connection process using dialing scripts.

In this chapter, you learn how to:

- Install support for dial-up networks
- Configure your dial-up connection
- Connect to your Internet service provider
- Use the Dial-up Scripting tool to automate your connection
- Troubleshoot common dial-up problems

Installing Dial-Up Networking Support

If your computer had a modem installed in it when you installed Windows 95, the dial-up adapter (which acts as a network device working over your modem) and the dial-up networking support should already be installed on your system. Before you can use your modem to connect to the Internet, you have to have both the dial-up networking software and a dial-up adapter installed on your system.

You can check to see if the dial-up networking support is installed on your system by opening the Add/Remove Programs control panel (Start, Settings, Control Panel, Add/Remove Programs). Select the Windows Setup tab and click the Communications item in the list of components. Click the Details button to list all the communications components that are available.

In the list of communications components (as shown in fig. 6.1), the dial-up networking component is shown as already installed (the check box is checked). If the box is not checked, click the check box and click OK to install the dial-up networking software. You may be prompted to insert your distribution CD or floppy during the installation process.

Fig. 6.1
Installing the dial-up networking support is done through the Add/Remove Programs control panel.

You can check to see if the dial-up adapter is installed on your system by opening the Network control panel (Start, Settings, Control Panel, Network). The dial-up adapter should be listed in the list of installed network components.

If the dial-up adapter is not already installed, you can install it from the Network control panel. Click the Add button to open the Select Network Component Type page, which lists all the different types of network components you can install.

Click the Adapter item in the list, and click the Add button. This brings up
the Select Network Adapters page. This page lists all the types of network
adapters supported by Windows 95. On the left side of the page is a list of
manufacturers and on the right side is a list of adapters from that manufacturer.

To install the dial-up adapter, scroll down the list of manufacturers until
you find Microsoft. Click the Microsoft entry and the dial-up adapter
item will be displayed in the list of Network Adapters. Select the dial-up
adapter from the list and click OK. Selecting the dial-up adapter is shown
in figure 6.2.

Fig. 6.2
Install the
Microsoft dial-up
adapter from the
Network control
panel.

Installing Network Protocols

Once you have dial-up networking support installed, you must install support
for the protocols that your Internet connection will require. Because all
Internet applications work with the TCP/IP protocol, you should first install
the Windows 95 TCP/IP network support.

Installing the TCP/IP support in Windows 95 is similar to installing the dial-
up adapter support described previously. Open the Network control panel
(Start, Settings, Control Panel, Network). Click the Add button to bring up
a list of network components to install. Select the Protocol component and
click Add.

This brings up the Select Network Protocol page, which is shown in figure
6.3. Select Microsoft from the list of manufacturers and TCP/IP from the list
of network protocols available. Click OK to install the TCP/IP protocol support. You may be asked for your installation CD or floppies during the installation process.

Now that the TCP/IP protocol is installed on your system, you must tell the
dial-up adapter that you will be using the TCP/IP protocol on connections
through the adapter. Open the properties for the dial-up adapter by selecting
dial-up adapter from the list of network components on the Network control
panel and clicking Properties.

Getting Connected

Fig. 6.3
Installing the TCP/
IP support from
the Network
control panel.

On the Bindings page of the dial-up adapter properties sheet, make sure that the check box next to the TCP/IP protocol is checked. This allows the dial-up adapter to use the TCP/IP protocol.

Installing SLIP and Scripting Support

When you configure your dial-up connection, you must tell the connection software what type of dial-up server you are connecting to. By default, Windows 95 only supports connections using the Point to Point Protocol (PPP), Remote Access Service (RAS), and Netware Connect. Since many Internet service providers support the Serial Line Internet Protocol, you may have to install support for SLIP before using your dial-up connection.

> **Tip**
>
> Many Internet service providers support both SLIP and PPP connections. Because PPP offers error correction and data compression, you should use it if possible. Check with your Internet service provider to see if PPP is available to you before installing SLIP support in Windows 95.

Support for SLIP and dial-up scripting is provided in a separate software package that is included on the Windows 95 CD-ROM distribution in the directory /admin/apptools/slip.

> **Note**
>
> If you have the floppy disk distribution of Windows 95, you can get the SLIP and scripting support from the Microsoft FTP site (**ftp.microsoft.com**) in the file DSCRPT.EXE. This is a self-extracting file; download the file into a temporary directory and run the file there to unpack the files.

To install the SLIP and dial-up scripting support, start the Add/Remove Programs control panel (Start, Settings, Control Panel, Add/Remove Programs). Select the Windows Setup tab and click the <u>H</u>ave Disk button. Enter the directory where the SLIP and dial-up scripting files are located (either on the Windows 95 CD-ROM or your local disk). Select the installation file RNAPLUS.INF and click OK to install the support files.

After you have installed the support for SLIP and dial-up scripting, you can remove these files at any time by opening the Install/Uninstall tab from the Add/Remove Programs control panel. Select the SLIP and Scripting for dial-up networking entry from the list of software that can be uninstalled and click the Add/<u>R</u>emove button to delete the software.

Setting Up a Dial-Up Networking Connection

After you have installed the dial-up networking support in Windows 95, you are ready to set up your networking connection to your Internet service provider. In order to set up your connection, you should obtain the following information from your service provider:

- The type of connection supported (SLIP, PPP, RAS, etc.)
- The telephone number to dial
- Your IP address (if it is permanently assigned)
- Your full Internet domain name
- The IP addresses of all DNS servers
- The IP address of the service provider's gateway machine
- Your login name and password

Generally, your Internet service provider is experienced in helping you set up your dial-up connection; your provider should be able to quickly provide you with the information you need.

To set up a dial-up connection, open the dial-up networking folder found in the My Computer folder on your desktop. This folder (shown in fig. 6.4) contains the Make New Connection wizard, which leads you through the steps necessary to create a new dial-up connection.

Start the Make New Connection wizard by double-clicking on the wizard. This brings up the first page of the wizard, shown in figure 6.5. On this page, you can name your dial-up connection (which makes it easier to remember which system you are connecting to if you have several different systems you use regularly) and specify the modem you will be using to connect.

Fig. 6.4

The Make New Connection wizard is found in the dial-up networking folder.

Fig. 6.5

Setting up your connection with the Make New Connection wizard.

On this page, you can also configure your modem settings for this connection by clicking the Configure button. This brings up the Properties for your modem. On the General tab (shown in fig. 6.6) you can set the volume of the speaker on the modem (if it has one) and the maximum speed that your modem will support. Pick the highest speed from the list that your modem supports (if your modem speed is not listed exactly, such as 14,400 baud, you can safely pick the next highest speed; for example if you have a 14,400 baud modem, pick 19,200 baud). If your modem supports it, you also have the option to force your connection to be made at a particular speed (by checking the Only Connect at This Speed box).

Fig. 6.6

Setting the general modem properties.

The Connection tab on the modem properties (shown in fig. 6.7) allows you to set up options such as the number of data bits, parity, and stop bits for the modem. Unless your Internet service provider tells you otherwise, or you encounter problems with your connection, you should leave these settings alone.

Fig. 6.7
Setting the
connection
modem properties.

The settings listed under Call preferences are useful, however. You should generally leave the Wait for dial tone before dialing box set, but if you have a very long telephone number to dial (for example, you use a calling card or long distance service) or your service provider takes a particularly long time to answer, you may need to change the Cancel the Call if not Connected within settings. Either lengthen the time limit or uncheck this option to entirely disable this feature.

The final option on this page allows you to automatically disconnect your dial-up connection if the connection is idle for a period of time. This is useful to prevent running up long telephone bills if you forget to terminate your connection.

Caution

Note that there is a bug in the release version of the Windows 95 dial-up software such that if you are downloading a large file but not otherwise using your connection, the connection will still time out. We recommend that you disable the timeout feature until this is fixed.

On the Options tab (shown in fig. 6.8) you can set up your connection to bring up a terminal window either before or after the phone number is dialed (or both). Bringing up the terminal window before the number is dialed is useful if you need to set special options in your modem before you connect.

Bringing up the terminal window after dialing allows you to manually type the commands to your Internet service provider to log in and start your connection. This option is discussed further in the section "Connecting to Your Internet Service Provider."

Another option on this page allows you to specify manual or operator assisted calling. This feature is useful if you have to go through an operator to make your call; the system waits for you to click the Connect button before continuing your call.

II

Getting Connected

Fig. 6.8
Setting connection
options for your
modem.

The final option allows you to display the modem status indicator on your task bar. This indicator shows up as a small modem with status lights that blink when sending or receiving data.

Now that the configuration options on the modem have been set, you can continue to set up your dial-up connection. Click the Next button to go on to the second page of the Make New Connection wizard, shown in figure 6.9.

Fig. 6.9
The second page
of the Make New
Connection
wizard.

This page allows you to set the area code, telephone number, and country code for this connection. This is fairly self-explanatory; fill in the full telephone number for your Internet service provider (the number in the figure is just an example). Click the Next button to continue.

The final page of the wizard confirms that your connection is set up with the name you gave it. Click Finish to complete the setup process.

Your new connection appears in the dial-up networking folder, as shown in figure 6.10.

Note
Note that some general modem settings are changed from the Modem control panel. Options such as disabling call waiting, using a calling card, pulse or tone dialing, and others are configured from this control panel.

Fig. 6.10
The newly configured connection in the dial-up networking folder.

Configuring Your Dial-Up Connection

After doing the initial setup of your connection, you will have to set several options to specify the type of connection you are making with your Internet service provider. This configuration is done through the properties sheet for your dial-up connection. Bring up the properties sheet by right-clicking the icon for your connection in the dial-up networking folder and choosing Properties. This properties sheet is shown in figure 6.11.

Fig. 6.11
Setting the properties for your dial-up connection.

The properties sheet lists the important options for your connection on the main page, including the telephone number, area code, and the modem to use. Clicking on the Configure button brings up the modem configuration sheets described previously.

Clicking the Server Type button brings up the Server Types page, as shown in figure 6.12. This page allows you to set up the type of server you are connecting to, the network protocols that will be used over this connection, and several advanced options.

Fig. 6.12
Setting up options on the Server Types page.

The types of servers that are available to select from are:

- *CSLIP:* UNIX Connection with IP Header Compression (this option is only available if you install SLIP support)
- *NRN:* NetWare Connect
- *PPP:* Windows 95, Windows NT 3.5, Internet
- *SLIP:* UNIX Connection (this option is only available if you install SLIP support)
- Windows for Workgroups and Windows NT 3.1

Pick the appropriate connection for your Internet service provider. Most of the time you will pick either PPP or SLIP.

Depending on the server type you select, you will be able to set different advanced options. Checking the Log on to Network tells Windows 95 to try to log onto the network when you connect, using the user name and password provided in the connection page.

Selecting Enable Software Compression allows Windows 95 to compress the data going through your modem, which allows more information to flow through the connection. This option will only work if your modem and the remote modem support compression.

Selecting Require Encrypted Password ensures that your computer will only send out passwords that are encrypted when logging in to remote computers or services. This option only works when the remote computer or service supports encrypted passwords, but using this option decreases the chance that someone may intercept your password.

Under the Allowed Network Protocols, you should select only those protocols that you will use over this connection. Most of the time, you can select just the TCP/IP protocol to use Internet applications. If you are going to be using any of the other protocols, you should select their options.

Clicking the TCP/IP Settings button brings up the page shown in figure 6.13. This page allows you to specify your IP address, DNS servers, and WINS servers if you know these values in advance. For most connections, you can select the Server assigned options, which means that your Internet service provider's software will send these values to you when you connect.

If your Internet service provider can tell you the appropriate settings for your IP address, DNS servers, and WINS servers, you can enter them on this page.

Fig. 6.13
Setting up your
connection's
TCP/IP settings.

Connecting to Your Internet Service Provider

Once you have your connection set up, you can test your connection to your service provider. How the connection proceeds depends on the type of computer or service you are connecting to. This section provides you with some notes on connecting to different types of computers.

When you connect to a remote computer, your system first dials the number you specified in the connection properties. When the remote computer answers, your modem first establishes settings (such as connection speed and error correction) with the remote modem.

Next, your computer's software attempts to talk to the remote software to establish the connection protocol (such as PPP, SLIP, or Netware Connect). How this connection is established depends on the type of remote computer and the protocol.

> **Note**
>
> When connecting with the PPP protocol, there are two options for passing your password to the PPP server. These two options are PAP (Password Authentication Protocol) and CHAP (Challenge Authentication Protocol). If you have selected the Use Encrypted Password option for your connection, it will force the use of the CHAP protocol.
>
> If your service provider requires CHAP, but you have not selected this option, you will be asked to confirm the use of the encrypted password when you connect.

Many Internet service providers use UNIX systems (or terminal servers, which behave similarly) to provide SLIP and PPP access. These systems require you to provide a login name and password. After you are logged in, you often type a command (such as "slip") to start the protocol your connection needs. After these commands are processed, your protocol is established and you can use the connection.

When using this type of connection, you can use the option to bring up a terminal window after dialing (as specified on the options tab of the modem properties). The terminal window allows you to manually type in your user name, password, and the command to start your connection.

At this point, the service provider should display a message giving you the IP address assigned to your computer for this session. You should write this address down, because you will need it in a minute. After the protocol is established, you can click the Continue button to start using the protocol. You will see a dialog box asking you for the IP address assigned to you; type in the number you just wrote down.

Note

After you have made sure your connection works correctly, you can automate the connection process by using dial-up scripting. Using a dial-up script allows you to automatically enter your user name, password, and any commands. Dial-up scripting is discussed later in this chapter.

If you are connecting to a Windows NT server (using the Remote Access Service, for example), you won't need to perform any manual input in order to establish your connection. The dial-up networking software automatically passes along your user name and password and establishes the protocol for you.

Other Internet service providers may require some user input in order to establish your connection. The safest way to use these connections (at least at first) is to specify the option to bring up a terminal window after dialing and manually go through the connection process a few times. Again, you can automate the connection process by using dial-up scripting.

Using Dial-Up Scripting

If your connection requires that you type some information in order to connect (such as your username and password), you can automate this process by using dial-up scripting. Dial-up scripting support is provided in the Microsoft Plus! for Windows 95 package, but is also available (in a somewhat limited version) in the standard Windows 95 package.

> **Note**
>
> The dial-up scripting software provided at no charge on the standard Windows 95 disk or from the Microsoft Web server is not the full package, but it supports the most commonly used commands. Unfortunately, there is no documentation on exactly the differences between the free version and the Plus! pack version.

Getting the Dial-Up Scripting Software

If you do not have the Microsoft Plus! package, but you have the CD-ROM version of Windows 95, you can find the dial-up scripting utility under the Admin directory of the CD-ROM. Follow the instructions on how to install the support using the Add/Remove Programs control panel.

If you do not have the CD-ROM version of Windows 95, you can get the dial-up scripting software from the Microsoft Web page (**http:// www.microsoft.com**) as a self-extracting archive. The name of the package is DSCRIPT.EXE. Put this executable into a temporary directory and execute it. This will unpack the files and allow you to install the software using the "Add/Remove Programs" control panel.

If you have Microsoft Plus! for Windows 95, the dial-up scripting software is installed as part of the installation of the Plus! software.

Setting Up a Script for an Internet Connection

Once you have the dial-up scripting software installed, you can add a script to one of your existing Internet connections by running the scripting tool (which is found under Start, Programs, Accessories, dial-up Scripting Tool).

The dial-up scripting tool lets you assign a script to a particular connection. To assign a script to one of your dial-up connections, select the connection you want the script assigned to, and then type the name of the script file in the File Name box. You can edit the script by clicking the Edit button.

Using the Scripting Language

The basic idea of the dial-up scripting language is to wait for the remote system (the one you are connecting to) to prompt for certain information, and then to automatically provide this information. While there are quite a few advanced commands in the scripting language, the basic ones (the ones you will use frequently) are:

- proc—starts a script procedure or program
- waitfor—waits for the remote computer to output a string

■ transmit—sends a string of characters to the remote computer

■ delay—waits for a specified amount of time

■ getip—sets your Internet address from the remote system

■ endproc—ends a script procedure or program

For an example of using a script, let's assume that the procedure for connecting to your Internet service provider is as follows:

■ The remote computer prompts you with name:, and you type in your login name

■ The remote computer prompts you with password:, and you type in your password

■ The remote computer prompts you with command:, and you type in the command PPP to start up the connection

So, in your script you would use waitfor commands to wait for the remote computer to output each string, and then use transmit commands to send the right information. The scripting language provides several variables that make sending information easier—these variables hold the information you entered on the dial-up connection properties page:

■ $USERID—holds the user name specified in the connection dialog box

■ $PASSWORD—holds the password specified in the connection dialog box

An example script that automates the above procedure might look like this:

```
proc main
waitfor "name:"
transmit $USERID + "^M"
waitfor "password:"
transmit $PASSWORD + "^M"
waitfor "command:"
transmit "PPP^M"
endproc
```

Note

In the above example, the "^M" characters provide a carriage return to send each line. Depending on the type of system you are connecting to, you may need a carriage return and line feed to send each line.

This example script is sufficient (with minor changes, depending on the prompts that your service provider gives you) to log into most Internet service providers. More information about the scripting tool and all the commands it implements is provided with the tool itself.

Since the release of the Windows 95 operating system, several third-party packages have become available that replace or augment the standard Windows 95 dial-up software. The two main packages that are available currently are the 32-bit version of the popular Trumpet Winsock package and the RoboDUN dial-up package.

Connecting with Trumpet Winsock

Trumpet Winsock was one of the most popular programs used to connect to the Internet with Windows 3.1. Trumpet was distributed as shareware on the Internet so it was easily available, it was inexpensive to register, and most every service provider had experience with it and recommended it for their customers. For all of those reasons, many people who used this with Windows 3.1 have been hesitant to use the built-in Internet connectivity features in Windows 95.

> **Note**
>
> Some earlier versions did not have a strict way to enforce the 30-day trial on the unregistered shareware. If you are using an unregistered version, be aware that you will need to register to continue using it beyond 30 days.

However, using the existing versions of Trumpet that were written for Windows 3.1 meant sacrificing some functionality in Windows 95. Although Trumpet 2.0 and 2.1 will run with Windows 95, you can't use any 32-bit applications such as the 32-bit versions of Netscape 2.0 or WinVN with 3.1 versions of Trumpet.

Trumpet has now released some upgrade files that enable current users of Trumpet to continue using Trumpet with Windows 95 and 32-bit applications. Why would you want to do this? If you have been using Trumpet, several reasons could include:

- Old Trumpet login scripts still work with the upgrade so you don't have to create new login scripts as you would with Windows 95 dial-up networking.
- Your service provider still won't provide support for Windows 95.
- You have had problems getting Windows 95's Internet connection to start automatically when you start an Internet application. If this is an important convenience to you, Trumpet seems to handle this better.

■ You are an advanced user and need the use of Trumpet's many diagnostic features.

NetCD95

So, if you need to use Trumpet for those reasons or any others, here is how you do it. You need to get the 32-bit Trumpet files from NetCD95 or some other source. On NetCD95, they are in the \netutils\trump95 directory. You can also find this at most any major FTP site or WWW software site including TUCOWS. The home Web site for Trumpet is at **http://www.trumpet.com.au**. However, since this site is in Australia, if you are in the U.S., try to find a local copy of the program first.

Caution

If you do not have Trumpet currently installed and are attempting to set up your first Internet connection, it is recommended that you use Windows 95 built-in Internet connection rather than Trumpet.

Upgrading to the Windows 95 Version of Trumpet

Upgrading to the Windows 95 version of Trumpet involves renaming some Windows files and copying the new Trumpet versions:

Tip

This is a simple procedure and the chances of anything going wrong are small. But, to be safe and prevent any possible disasters, make a backup copy of everything in your Trumpet directory before proceeding.

---

1. Rename the two Windows 95 internetworking files. The two files you need to rename are

    c:\windows\winsock.dll

    c:\windows\system\wsock32.dll

    Change the extension on both of these files from .DLL to something else, such as .MS (to remind you that these are the Microsoft versions of the winsock files).

2. Extract the following files from the Trumpet for Windows 95 zip file (or copy these files from NetCD95):

    TCPMAN.EXE

    WINSOCK.DLL

    TWSK16.DLL

    WSOCK32.DLL

3. Move these files to your Trumpet directory. You will be prompted to replace existing versions. Confirm all replacements.

4. Verify that your Trumpet directory is in your Path statement in AUTOEXEC.BAT. If you have been using Trumpet and it works, this is already there. If not, add it. If you make any changes, you will need to restart Windows before using Trumpet.

That completes the installation process and you are now ready to run the new version and connect to the Internet.

Note

If you ever decide to stop using Trumpet as your Winsock and want to use Windows 95's built-in Winsock, rename the two files from step one back to their original names and remove the trumpet entry from your path statement. Then see the directions earlier in this chapter for configuring dial-up Windows 95 Internet connectivity.

Using Trumpet Winsock

If you are familar with the Windows 3.1 versions of Trumpet, you already know how to use this version. As a quick refresher, you can start Trumpet and connect to the Internet by:

■ Starting any Internet application such as Netscape or WS_FTP

■ Starting TCPMAN.EXE, which is the executable part of the Trumpet package

Doing either of these will result in Trumpet dialing your ISP and logging you in (if you have automatic login enabled in the Trumpet options). This results in the familiar Trumpet screen shown in figure 6.14.

After this, you should be able to use Trumpet and connect to the Internet just as you always have in the past.

The RoboDUN Dialing Software

The RoboDUN package is a replacement for the Windows 95 dial-up scripting tool. It provides functionality similar to the standard dial-up scripting, but has a somewhat more sophisticated scripting language, and includes a dialing package.

RoboDUN is available freely through many Windows 95 shareware sites (**http://www.windows95.com** is a good source; look for the file RDUN61.ZIP) and was written by Mark Gamber (**markga@epix.net**).

Fig. 6.14

The main Trumpet
Window shows a
log of all activity
such as dialing and
login, as well as
the results of your
login scripts
including your IP
address.

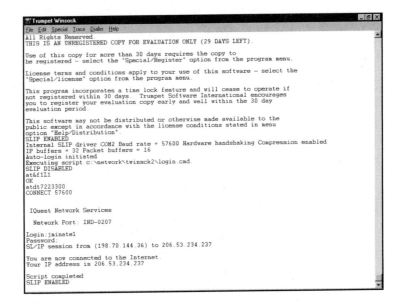

```
Trumpet Winsock
File  Edit  Special  Trace  Dialer  Help
All Rights Reserved.
THIS IS AN UNREGISTERED COPY FOR EVALUATION ONLY (29 DAYS LEFT).

Use of this copy for more than 30 days requires the copy to
be registered - select the "Special/Register" option from the program menu.

License terms and conditions apply to your use of this software - select the
"Special/license" option from the program menu.

This program incorporates a time lock feature and will cease to operate if
not registered within 30 days.  Trumpet Software International encourages
you to register your evaluation copy early and well within the 30 day
evaluation period.

This software may not be distributed or otherwise made available to the
public except in accordance with the license conditions stated in menu
option "Help/Distribution".
SLIP ENABLED
Internal SLIP driver COM2 Baud rate = 57600 Hardware handshaking Compression enabled
IP buffers = 32 Packet buffers = 16
Auto-login initiated
Executing script c:\network\twinsck2\login.cmd.
SLIP DISABLED
at&f1L1
OK
atdt7223300
CONNECT 57600


 IQuest Network Services

  Network Port: IND-0207

Login:jainate1
Password:
SL/IP session from (198.70.144.36) to 206.53.234.237

You are now connected to the Internet.
Your IP address is 206.53.234.237

Script completed
SLIP ENABLED
```

Once you have the RoboDUN archive file, installing the software is as easy as extracting the files from the archive into a folder on your system. The package includes two programs, RDUN32 (which is the software to manage your connections) and ROBODUN (which handles the dialing and scripting support).

To enable the RoboDUN package, run the manager software and click the Start RoboDUN button to start the support software. Select one of the available connections and click Edit to start editing the dial-up script for that connection.

> **Note**
>
> Examples of dial-up scripts are provided in the RoboDUN help file. Most of the commands provided with RoboDUN are similar to those provided with the Windows 95 scripting language.

After you have set up a script, it will be used whenever your connection is started.

Troubleshooting Your Dial-Up Connection

Dial-up connections are harder to troubleshoot than connections through a local area network, because there are more things that can go wrong with the connection. A problem with your modem, telephone line, Internet service provider, or connection setup can all cause your connection to fail or work poorly. This section gives you some things to check if your connection is not working correctly.

If Your Modem Does Not Dial

If your modem does not dial at all when you try to connect to your Internet service provider, you should first check to make sure that you have the correct modem configured for your system. Open the Modems control panel and verify that the modem type reported is the same as the actual modem installed. When you installed the modem, the wrong modem may have been detected; reinstall the modem support with the correct type of modem.

Once you have confirmed that the modem is the correct type, check that the modem is working with the system correctly. Open the System control panel, select the Device Manager tab and select the modem under the Modems item. Click Properties to open the properties sheet for the modem. Make sure that the sheet indicates the modem is working correctly. If the sheet indicates a problem, check your modem and communications port settings.

If the modem is reported as working correctly, check your phone connection to make sure the modem is connected to the phone line. You can also try dialing your modem manually using the Phone dialer application found under Start, Programs, Accessories on your Start Bar.

Your Modem Dials, but the Other Modem Doesn't Answer

First, try the connection a second time to make sure that the problem wasn't only a temporary one. Make sure that you are dialing the correct number for this connection. Verify the area code and any access codes that may be added to the phone number are correct, also. Depending on phone conditions (for example, if the phone system is particularly busy), you might need to add extra time after getting an outside line. Most modems allow you to add a pause by putting a comma (,) into the telephone number.

If the telephone number is correct, check with someone at the remote site to make sure their system is on and the modem is working correctly.

The Other Modem Answers, but the Connection Fails

This is one of the most difficult situations to diagnose, and this is where most problems with dial-up connections happen. The first step is to verify that all your connection and modem settings are correct, especially the settings for the remote server type. Most Internet service providers have information packets for users of Windows 95 systems that list all the correct settings for connections to their systems.

If the settings are correct, turn on the option to display a terminal window after dialing the modem. (This option is found under the properties for the dial-up connection.) This terminal window allows you to see what is happening after the modems connect; any error messages or problems will usually be immediately obvious (such as an invalid user name, password, or server type).

Internet Applications Don't Work

If your connection starts up, but your Internet applications (such as a WWW browser or FTP program) don't work, you should first check your TCP/IP settings to make sure that they are correct.

An easy way to check your TCP/IP settings is to run the program "winipcfg" (found in the Windows directory). This program displays all the information about your current TCP/IP setup, including your IP address, DNS servers, and other network settings. You can easily verify that your TCP/IP settings are correct.

If you cannot connect at all to any Internet service, make sure your IP address is set correctly. This is often a problem when you have to enter the IP address manually during the connection process. If your service provider automatically sets up your IP address when you connect, make sure that your TCP/IP settings for your connection are set up to automatically set your IP address (and DNS servers if applicable).

If you can connect to an Internet service using an IP address but not by using an Internet host name, your DNS servers are set up incorrectly. Check with your service provider for the addresses of their DNS servers so you can manually set them up in your TCP/IP settings.

If you can connect to some Internet services (in particular, ones that are local to your service provider) but not to Internet hosts outside of your local service provider, your gateway address is probably incorrect. Check with your service provider for the address of their Internet gateway machine so you can enter it into your configuration.

CHAPTER 7

Other Software for Connecting to the Internet

Several commercial software packages are available to help you connect to the Internet. Some of these packages include add-ons that set up directories for your e-mail or Web locations. Some add-ons provide electronic directories already full of interesting Internet site information. Often products are tied in with Internet service providers (ISPs) that either supply the products or make deals with the software companies to put the ISP on a list of "approved" ISPs. This chapter reviews several popular software packages that you might use in addition to those packaged with this book and the freeware and shareware available over the Internet itself:

- Microsoft includes a TCP/IP stack with Windows 95. This is a blessing and a curse. I'll describe how you can stay in grace with Bill's offering and deal with conflict among different TCP/IP stacks and dialers.

- Spry's Internet in a Box is a popular package that makes connecting to the Internet easy and integrates several Internet components.

- Internet Chameleon and related family members from NetManage often furnish the basis for large, commercial installations; we'll see how Chameleon provides choices beyond those of the "...in a Box" line.

- ECCO is a personal information manager that integrates with NetManage Internet products that maintain mailing lists and Uniform Resource Locators (URLs); let's see how it looks.

- NetCruiser is an Internet software package from a national ISP; we'll look at it as a good example of what the nationals provide.

- CyberSearch is a CD-based search system that enables you to search the Internet without actually being connected to it. You'll see how it can speed up your searches and slow down your costs.

- NetLink is a CD directory and book that provides thousands of ready-to-use connections to the Internet. The book makes it even easier to visualize what you're looking for.

This chapter begins with a discussion of Microsoft's TCP/IP stack that is included in Windows 95. Then, because Mosaic in a Box is quite a popular program and easy to configure for a simple system, I'll discuss it and its many setup features in much more detail than the other software packages. Similar features are available in competitive programs such as Internet Chameleon and Super TCP, so their unique features are also discussed in detail. The general ideas about configuration given at first also apply to other packages.

Threshold Problems of Microsoft and Other TCP/IP Stacks

◀ See "Installing TCP/IP Support in Windows 95," p. 127

◀ See "Configuring the Windows 95 TCP/IP Protocol," p. 129

▶ See "Connecting Through Microsoft Network," p. 309

Microsoft provides a TCP/IP stack with Windows 95. This is a mixed blessing. It means that you can easily use Microsoft's Internet tools that are optimized for the TCP/IP stack supplied. But it also means you run the risk of seriously hampering and probably disabling Internet products from different manufacturers.

Caution

Internet in a Box and Mosaic in a Box from Compuserve/Spry and Internet Chameleon from NetManage, among others, can run into problems with Microsoft's stack or the stacks of each other. The problems revolve around the close coupling each maker has made between its TCP/IP stack, telephone dialer, and the applications themselves. The products are designed so clicking any particular application icon checks to see if a connection exists. If there is no connection, the product's dialer is activated to establish the connection—you don't have to think about it. The means of doing this varies among all the products and with Microsoft; so, more often than not, things don't work and you have to resort to one particular maker's entire package, including the stack and dialer.

Your solution to this problem rests with finding some way around the conflicts of TCP/IP stacks and their associated dialers.

Brute Force Solution to TCP/IP Stack Conflicts

The most direct way to overcome the conflict problem is to change the WINSOCK.DLL file in your windows subdirectory to the one supplied by the maker of the application you want to use. This isn't quite as easy as it sounds. Usually you find out about these conflict problems only after you've installed the second package of Internet-TCP/IP-Dialer software. You start to use and are greatly pleased with your new programs. Then you decide you'd like to use one of the programs you'd previously installed. It fails and fails and fails.

So you reinstall it. Now it works great, but when you try the other one it fails. Now you know what happened; the different stacks and dialers conflict with the applications.

WINSOCK.DLL is the most important file in this string of failures. And your problem is when you look in your windows directory, you find only one copy. Your best cure is to stop right now and go to your computer. If you have installed Microsoft's or anyone else's TCP/IP stack, you'll find a WINSOCK.DLL file. Make a copy of this file in the windows subdirectory but change the extension to the name of the vendor. For example, if you've last installed Microsoft's TCP/IP, execute the following command:

```
copy winsock.dll winsock.ms
```

Now you have an identical copy of the file protected against overwrite by a subsequent installation. Each time you install a new vendor's product that overwrites the WINSOCK.DLL, be sure to do the same thing with a unique extension; for example: WINSOCK.MS, WINSOCK.NM, WINSOCK.BOX, etc. Put each of these into your windows directory and copy the appropriate one to the name WINSOCK.DLL as needed when you change among applications. You could write a batch file to do this for you from a simple menu.

> ### Tip
>
> Maybe you've already installed a second TCP/IP stack that overwrote your WINSOCK.DLL. If you're lucky, the second program renamed your old WINSOCK.DLL to WINSOCK.001 or something similar, check it out.

Brute Force Solution to Dialer Conflicts

In some cases a dialer gives problems. If a dialer is designed for 16-bit applications and a 32-bit application attempts to use it, the 32-bit application will report it's unable to make the connection. If your favorite applications that are all neatly coupled to a dialer work great, but the new 32-bit application you just downloaded fails, this is probably it. The solution is to disable the dialer and use some other method of dialing such as the dialer that is internal to a terminal program. If the terminal program can be minimized once it has made the connection, chances are it can be used for this purpose.

Generic Stack and Dialer Solution

Until everyone agrees to make their stacks and dialers interchangeable, your best bet, if you want to use a number of different pedigree programs, is to find and use a generic stack and dialer that is not tied to any program. The leading candidate is the Trumpet Winsock stack and associated dialers.

▶ See "Stroud's
Consummate
Winsock List,"
p. 1114

> **Note**
>
> You'll find some of the latest Trumpet Winsock releases at **ftp://
> ftp.enterprise.net/mirror/winsock-l/Windows95/WinSock/twsk95b4.zip**.
> The file name may change as releases are revised. The software has a 30-day trial
> period and a subsequent $25 cost. Also check **http://cwsapps.texas.net/
> 95crit.html** for additional resources.

Internet in a Box

Spry developed Internet in a Box as a consumer market integrated package of
its commercially oriented Air series of products. Version 1 was one of the first
such packages to reach the consumer market. The general idea of all these
products is to provide several Internet applications for the Windows environment and make their installation and use as simple and foolproof as possible.

Although Internet in a Box version 1 was distributed on only three disks, version 2 is supplied on five 3 1/2 inch disks. But much has changed between
version 1 and 2. Of course, Spry improved several functions and features, but
the major changes to Internet in a Box are the result of CompuServe buying
out Spry. Because of the buyout, version 2 adds the Windows CompuServe
Information Manager (WinCIM) as a part of the package—you get both products in the same box. This discussion focuses on the Internet elements.

Installation and Configuration

Installation couldn't be easier. You simply insert the first disk in your machine, click the Start button, choose Settings, and then click the Add/Remove
icon. Windows 95 finds the setup program for Internet in a Box and guides
you through the process of flipping the floppies. During the installation, the
program asks a few questions similar to those that you must answer during
any Internet installation. This section looks at the installation process.

The process is mainly a matter of inserting the floppies in sequence until you
reach the questions about your specific identifications and resources. Figure
7.1 shows the startup screen for the Internet in a Box Setup Wizard that the
program presents after you finish the installation. Click OK to begin.

Fig. 7.1
After the initial installation, Internet in a Box's Setup Wizard helps you begin setting up and registering the program.

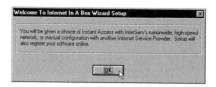

The Setup Wizard presents a selection of ports and speeds for your modem, as shown in figure 7.2. The wizard uses this information to register the software and, if you choose to use the Internet provider InterServ, open your account.

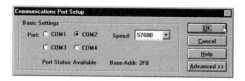

Fig. 7.2
Internet in a Box's communications port and speed settings for registration.

Next you enter registration information as shown in figure 7.3.

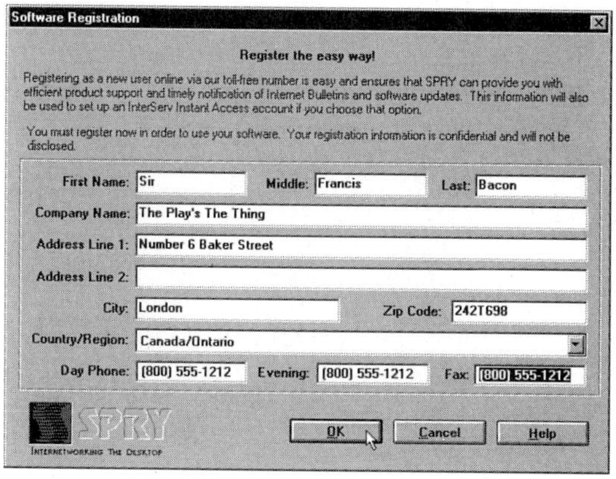

Fig. 7.3
Internet in a Box's Software Registration dialog box enables you to specify registration information.

As shown in figure 7.3, Internet in a Box already has a supplier available, InterServ. When you finish filling out the form and click OK, you're taken to the Select a Pricing and Access Option dialog box (see fig. 7.4) that enables you to choose among the specified supplier's plans or a manual configuration that uses some other ISP. Select Manual Configuration.

Fig. 7.4

Internet in a Box's pricing selection for InterServ and selection of alternative ISPs through the Manual Configuration.

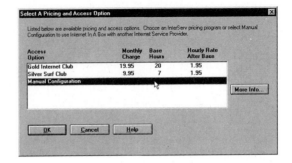

After filling in the information required to register your software, you can click OK on the screen in figure 7.4 to call up and register. The program displays a series of icons indicating the status of your call and connection. For example, figure 7.5 shows the icon that displays while the program is dialing. When the call connects, you see another icon; finally, when everything is ready to go, an icon pops up for a few seconds showing balloons celebrating your success. You can display these icons in many different ways, such as in the status bar at the bottom of your Windows 95 screen.

Fig. 7.5

Internet in a Box's icon to indicate that you are dialing a call.

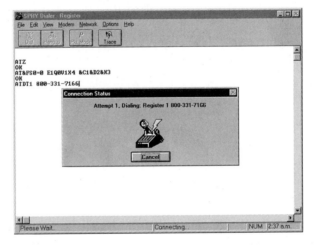

After the server at Internet in a Box accepts your registration, you get into serious configuration. Figure 7.6 shows the Dialer Setup dialog box. If you want to dial a 9 to get an outside line, for example, you enter **9** in the Dial Before text box; the same idea applies to the Dial After text box. However, the other controls involve more important issues.

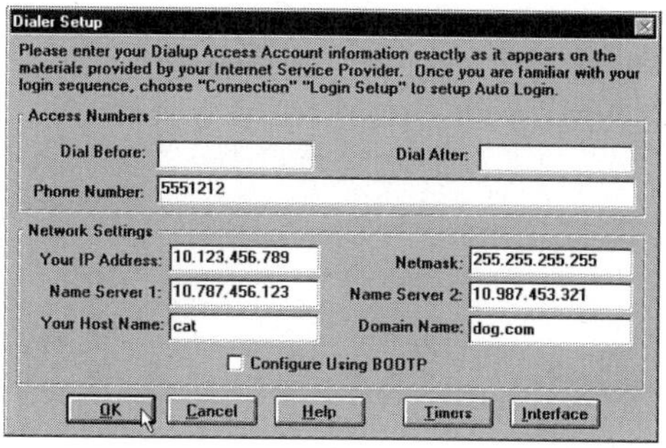

Fig. 7.6
Internet in a Box's
Dialer Setup dialog
box.

In the Phone Number text box, you enter your ISP's number. Be sure to use the exact number that the supplier tells you to use for your setup and account; some ISPs have very different configurations on different numbers.

You then enter your IP address. If your ISP provided a unique IP address for you, enter it in the Your IP Address text box. Otherwise, your ISP probably will tell you to use 0.0.0.0 as the address and enable the provider's equipment to load an address dynamically each time that you call. This system uses the limited supply of addresses available much more efficiently than the assignment of static IP addresses to each and every possible user.

The netmask is a more complex issue than deserves your attention here. Again, your ISP tells you what information to place in the Netmask text box.

The Name Server entries of the Dialer Setup dialog box are much easier to understand. The name servers maintained by your ISP convert the names of objects on the Internet to IP addresses that actually represent physical addresses. Most ISPs have two or more name servers because they're frequently used, and because failure of a single server system would shut down most Internet access. Enter the IP addresses of those name servers. (You don't simply enter the name server's name, because otherwise there still is no IP address to look up for the name server. You must provide at least an IP address for the name server.)

Tip

You can speed things up a bit by using the IP address for an object. The object can then be accessed faster because it doesn't require an intermediate step to a name server for the IP address.

In the Your Host Name text box, you enter the name that you want to give your PC on the Internet. You can enter anything, unless the ISP specifies a

II

Getting Connected

name for you. In the Domain Name text box, you enter the domain of
your ISP.

> **Caution**
>
> The domain name must be that of your ISP, even if you have your own domain name
> aliased back to your ISP. Such an alias name does not work in every case. Try it with
> the Web browser part of Internet in a Box. When I tried such an alias name, the
> browser could find information only on my ISP's Web server and displayed a `server`
> `not connected` error message for all others.

When you click <u>T</u>imers at the bottom of the panel shown in figure 7.6, you
see the Connection Timer Settings dialog box shown in figure 7.7. This dialog
box gives you an opportunity to set the dialer retries and the timeouts for
your connection. If you're paying by the minute either for your phone connection or the ISP use, carefully configuring these settings can save you a lot
of money.

Fig. 7.7
Internet in a Box's
timer settings.

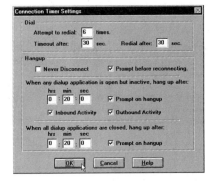

You'll probably have to experiment for several days or weeks to determine
the optimum timer settings, so don't get too concerned if the first ones that
you choose are too short (which forces you to log in several times during a
work session) or too long (which increases your bill). You'll eventually get
what you want. Make the times as short as your daily work needs can
tolerate.

After you set the timers and click OK, you return to the Dialer Setup dialog
box. Click the <u>I</u>nterface button to display the Network Interface dialog box
shown in figure 7.8. This dialog box offers only two choices: PPP (Point to
Point Protocol) and SLIP (Serial Line IP Protocol). Your ISP can tell you which
option to choose.

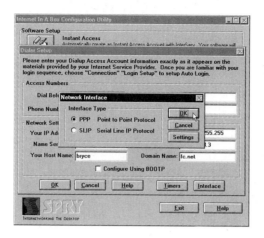

Fig. 7.8
Selecting the
interface for
Internet in a Box.

If you choose SLIP, click the Settings button to display the SLIP Settings dialog box as shown in figure 7.9. In this dialog box, you can review your options for SLIP. You must declare whether your ISP assigns a static IP address or your ISP's equipment assigns a dynamic address each time that you log in. If you choose Static, you must have declared the IP address in the Dialer Setup dialog box's Your IP Address text box. If your choice is Dynamic, you must have entered **0.0.0.0** in the Your IP Address text box. If your ISP provides compression using VJ CSLIP, select the Enable VJ CSLIP check box to improve performance. The maximum transmission unit (MTU) can be as large as 1,500; the larger the number, the faster a large file transfers, but the less efficient small exchanges are; your ISP might provide some ideas for this setting.

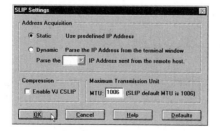

Fig. 7.9
SLIP settings for
Internet in a Box.

Most likely, your ISP uses PPP as your connection's protocol as PPP is the most widely accepted standard and is used throughout the Internet. If so, choose PPP in the Network Interface dialog box. Then when you select Settings and then Advanced, you see the PPP Settings dialog box shown in figure 7.10. The technical nature of these options is imposing. Your ISP should guide you through these settings. Often the defaults are just fine. However, if your ISP provides a secure installation, you must configure the authentication

(PAP or CHAP) portions. You also might find some benefit in experimenting with the size of the maximum receive units (MRU); as with the MTU in SLIP, you can set the MRU as high as 1,500. This setting improves performance of file transfers with large files, but slows down interactive functions such as small Web queries. To set the remainder of this dialog box's settings properly, you need information from your ISP.

Tip

This chapter gives you a glimpse into details of the setup. Frequently, the default settings work just fine; start with them first.

Fig. 7.10
PPP settings for
Internet in a Box.

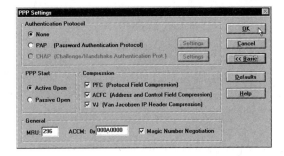

Several other screens let you select modem types and automate your login by writing a script. The dialer provides fairly complete support for the analog modem world. However, the dialer for Internet in a Box (and most other packages) lacks support for any significant portion of the ISDN device world. Although it does list the Motorola TA210, a near cousin to the BitSURFR covered in chapter 8 devoted to ISDN, true ISDN support is not included.

Windows 95, with its built-in telephone interfaces (including a dialer), should soon eliminate the need for dialers in software. Figure 7.11 shows the Windows 95 dialer.

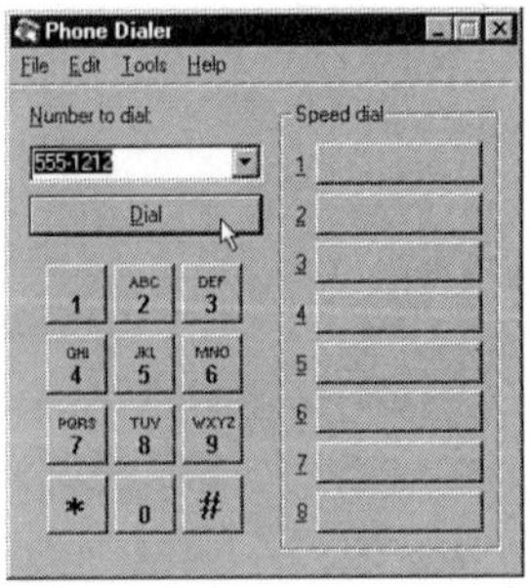

Fig. 7.11
The Windows 95
dialer.

Figure 7.12 shows the Default Hosts dialog box; to arrive here choose the Configuration icon in the Internet in a Box group and then choose Hosts. Because Internet in a Box is an integrated product, accessing all the sources for the Web, mail, FTP, and so on from each of the program's utilities should be fairly easy. Except for the e-mail settings, all the displayed information consists of defaults. Notice that CompuServe directs you to its Web site and to the Gopher and news servers of the built-in ISP, InterServ. You can enter any host that you want in these text boxes; of course, if you don't have access rights to a host that you enter, the setting won't help you much.

Tip

You should usually start with your ISP's default Web and news servers. These settings simply speed up processing. You can change them whenever you want.

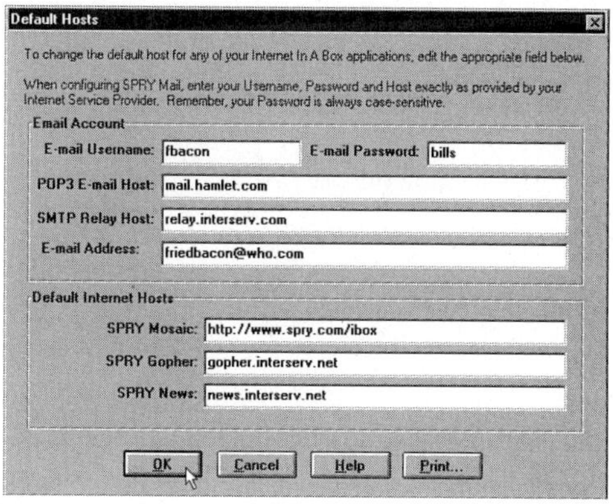

Fig. 7.12
Internet in a Box's Default Hosts dialog box lets you select any Web and news servers that you want for your defaults.

Getting Connected

The Members of the Suite

Internet in a Box consists of seven pieces:

- Web browser: Air Mosaic
- Electronic mail: Air Mail
- Newsreader: Air News
- File transfer protocol: Air FTP
- Gopher: Air Gopher
- Telnet: Air Telnet
- Viewer: ImageView

The Air series that I mentioned earlier is the basis for all these features. As you examine the functionality of these features in depth with much of the software supplied with this book, this chapter doesn't describe them in any great detail. But one thing you will notice about Internet in a Box and several of the other commercial products is the level of integration.

Internet in a Box's browser is convenient and easy to use. Part of the Mosaic line of browser development which has become the basis of many popular Web browsers, Air Mosaic has a feel that most users already understand. It integrates both mail and news from its menu. Several chapters in this book discuss browsers and hypertext, so this section touches on just one feature that you'll be glad to see: security. Figure 7.13 shows Air Mosaic opened with security features. This screen, the New Key Request dialog box, is among those available from the Security selection in the top ribbon. The form defaults to a Persona Certificate that you can obtain from RSA Data Security, Inc. RSA is responsible for much of the security and encryption technology used today. This default enables you to use this technology.

Fig. 7.13
RSA public key encryption is designed into the Air Mosaic browser within Internet in a Box. Here, the new key request form is ready for your information.

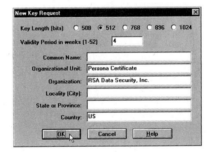

NetManage's Chameleon Family

NetManage makes several versions of its Chameleon family. At the low-priced end competing with Internet in a Box, you'll find Internet Chameleon. At the high end, ChameleonNFS provides an overwhelming suite of programs. This section looks at both ends. Actually, many of the elements are the same for each package. As you progress toward the high-end NFS product, the number of programs and some of the functions expand.

Installation and Configuration

The Chameleon products come on a handful of disks. You go through the usual floppy changing to get them installed. This section describes how the configuration differs.

The biggest difference among Chameleon and many other packages is the complex variety of options for configuring the interfaces. As you can see in figure 7.14, NetManage offers a wide selection of possible interfaces. The network interfaces such as Ethernet, Token Ring, and Fiber Distributed Data Interface (FDDI) aren't available in the Internet Chameleon, but at the other end of the spectrum, ChameleonNFS, you find the total list. Because your interest probably lies with telephone line access, you'll be glad to know that Internet Chameleon supports both connection through the serial port and WinISDN. WinISDN is an application program interface (API) that many ISDN card makers use. NetManage wrote much of the WinISDN specification.

Fig. 7.14
You reach NetManage's Add dialog box by selecting the Custom (connect here) icon in the NetManage group.

In the Add New Interface dialog box, you select the interface that you want. Usually you'll want to choose PPP. In my configuration, the program pops up Serial01 as the interface's default name. In Chameleon, you can have many different interfaces configured and select among them, which is a particularly attractive feature if you frequently move your notebook back and forth between the office and home or take it on the road.

Figure 7.15 shows the selection list for various items that you have to set up. These setup items are similar to those for Internet in a Box. Chameleon offers a greater variety of choices, and that variety makes its configuration a bit more complex and difficult. Once you've chopped through these technical details, you can move on to the good stuff you can really use.

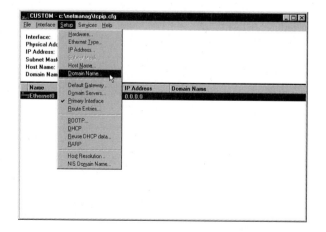

Fig. 7.15
NetManage Chameleon's Setup menu options.

II

Getting Connected

The NetManage family has a terrific set of options available. I'd like to show you how two fit together to really help you make better use of Internet time:

■ NEWTShooter

■ ECCO Internet Address Book

The NEWTShooter is a utility that installs as an icon in your screen's upper-left corner. Get it? Baby chameleons are newts! The NEWTShooter acts sort of like the Windows Clipboard, except the NEWTShooter goes straight to either mail or the WebSurfer browser. Used with the ECCO address book, NEWTShooter makes your Internet work fast and easy. Suppose you're doing research in ancient history and want to find out what's available on the Web. You pop open the ECCO address book and scan down to find a reference to a URL on ancient history, as shown in figure 7.16.

Fig. 7.16
NetManage ECCO finds the Ancient History reference.

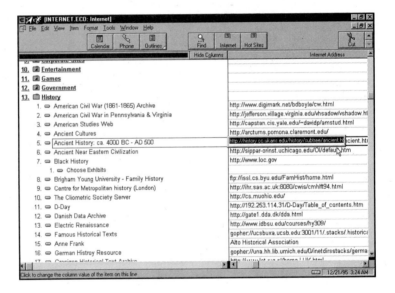

Now that you have the reference, you could write it down, go to your browser, start the browser, enter the URL, and look at the site. But here's the fast way using NEWTShooter. You access the menu by clicking the NEWTShooter icon in your screen's upper-left corner. Then select WebSurf Selected URL as shown in figure 7.17.

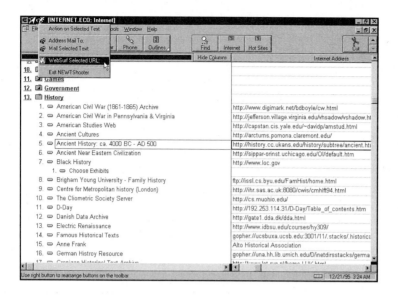

Fig. 7.17
NEWTShooter
selects the URL for
a web search.

NetManage then automatically initiates its Web browser. If the phone line is not dialed into your ISP at the time, NetManage starts the dialer to make the connection, as shown in figure 7.18.

Fig. 7.18
NetManage starts
the dialer after
NEWTShooter
requests to load
the URL into the
web browser when
the connection is
down.

When the connection is made, the browser finds the Web server and delivers the information.

Similarly, NEWTShooter can move text from a word processor to your electronic mail and move a mail address from the ECCO directory to your mail address field.

Internet Chameleon comes with all the utilities mentioned in the discussion about Internet in a Box, including mail, FTP, Telnet, Web, news, Gopher, and image viewer. In addition, you get the following utilities:

■ *Archie* enables you to browse through the various FTP servers for files. The utility connects with Archie servers that keep track of files on FTP sites.

Getting Connected

II

- *Finger* provides information about specific users on known hosts.
- *Ping* enables you to bounce ("ping") a packet transmission from another location to be certain that your equipment and the equipment at the other end of the transmission are both operating properly. The utility also measures the time that it takes for the signal to travel from your machine to the distant machine and return.
- *Talk* gives you a way to engage in real-time conversations with others over the Internet. These conversations consist of text only, not audio communications.
- *Whois* takes the name of a user or domain and checks the Internet for registration information.
- *Name Resolver* provides the IP addresses of a known host. You might want this utility to provide IP addresses for some of your most frequently contacted sites and thus speed up the connection.

All these utilities are native to the command-driven world of the original Internet. NetManage has simply put them in a more usable form for you.

NetManage Chameleon is quite popular. It ships with several products as the operator equipment manufacturer (OEM)-supplied software. The ISDN*tek ISDN cards come with a version of Internet Chameleon. PSI, one of the large, national Internet service providers, supplies Chameleon in its Internet access package.

NetCruiser

NetCruiser is a suite of Internet applications distributed by NetCom Internet Service, a national ISP. The well-integrated package works smoothly with NetCom's Internet access system (but read the caution later in this section).

To install NetCruiser, insert the single issue disk in your 3 1/2 inch disk drive, click Start, choose Settings, then Control Panel, and then double-click Add/ Remove Programs. Then choose Install and Windows 95 will find the setup program on the disk. You first see the setup screen, in which you either accept the default directory or enter one that you prefer (see fig. 7.19).

After filling in the NetCruiser Login dialog box (see fig. 7.20), you'll be asked about your modem. Then determine and enter the telephone number for a local point of presence (POP) for NetCom; the number is on a selection list and includes most major cities in North America.

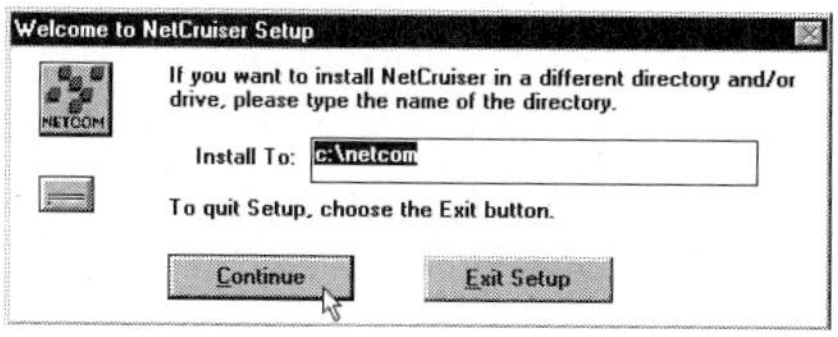

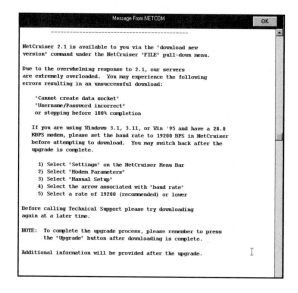

Fig. 7.19
In NetCruiser's initial setup screen, you enter your choice for a directory or accept the default shown.

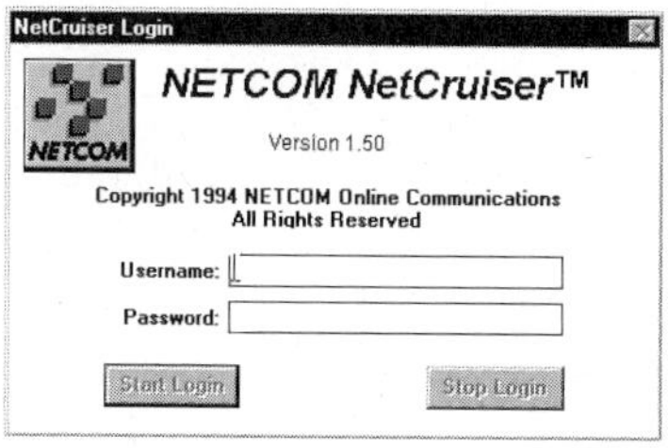

Fig. 7.20
The NetCruiser Login dialog box enables you to enter NetCom.

I used NetCruiser version 1.6, which is supplied with the excellent Artisoft product, Lantastic Power Suite. This local area network supports access to the Internet by creating communications servers with included software and use of the NetCruiser package. When I attempted to log in to NetCom, its server advised me that I needed to update the software that I was using. I selected the option to upgrade and waited about 15 minutes for it to finish (see figs. 7.21 and 7.22).

Fig. 7.21
NetCom's instructions for upgrading NetCruiser software to version 2.0.

Getting Connected

Fig. 7.22
To download a
new version of
NetCruiser
software, choose
Download New
Version from the
File menu.

I then ran several tests on NetCruiser and NetCom. Figure 7.23 shows the
browser checking Que's listing for the previous edition of this book. Figure
7.24 shows the Gopher listing using the geographic approach. By clicking a
state, you set up the URL for the Gopher or Web; the site is usually a university with an extensive home page of information concerning the state.

Fig. 7.23
NetCruiser's Web
browser reading
the Web server at
Macmillan
Computer
Publishing and
showing *Special
Edition Using the
Internet,* Second
Edition.

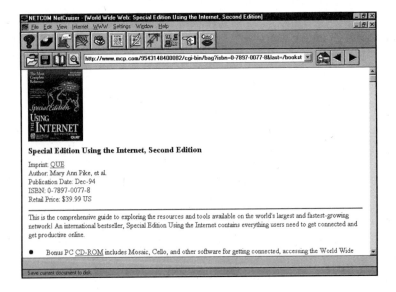

Fig. 7.24
You can choose the nearest Gopher site with the help of a map.

Other Software

Many other commercial programs can help you use the Internet. Among the most useful and interesting are those that help you search the Internet extensively without actually being connected. Frontier Technologies has a well-respected suite of Internet applications called Super TCP and Super TCP Pro. These applications are much like the previously discussed Internet in a Box and NetManage Chameleon applications. Consider using the Frontier package as well.

The Frontier package has a unique feature, CyberSearch. This program has a built-in browser and Lycos search engine. The issue CD includes another feature: thousands of Web sites with URLs and descriptions. Therefore, you can search cyberspace without being connected to the Internet. When you find an interesting site, simply click the URL to connect to the live Internet. Think of the Internet time charges that you'll save. Think of the time that you'll save compared to the speed of a search with an ordinary modem. Figure 7.25 shows the CyberGuide that's also a part of the Frontier package. Frontier Technology frequently updates the CD for subscribers.

II

Getting Connected

Fig. 7.25
Frontier Technologies' CyberSearch gives you a fast, easy way to search the Internet without connecting until you really need to.

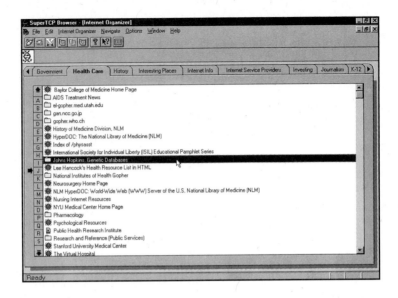

Mitzi Waltz's *Internet International Directory* (Ziff-Davis, 1995) provides a different approach to the same problem. This book contains a CD with the entire text and graphics from the book plus active hyperlinks to all the sites. When you find something interesting, simply click the hyperlink and your browser goes straight to it. The CD also has the most generally useful Internet tools and makes it easy to sign up with a national ISP, NetLink. Figure 7.26 shows a portion of the education listings.

Fig. 7.26
The Internet International Directory by Mitzi Waltz is both a book and a CD with built-in hyperlinks.

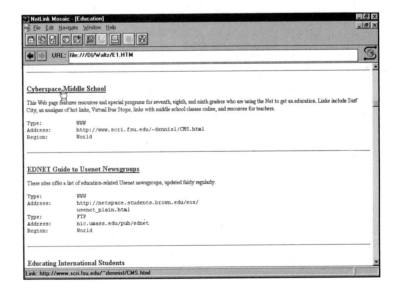

CHAPTER 8

Setting Up an ISDN Connection

ISDN is the acronym for *Integrated Services Digital Network,* not that that tells you very much. ISDN really boils down to a telephone technology that delivers digital signals to your house or business. Plain Old Telephone Service (POTS) is the regular telephone connection you have now; it uses analog signaling. What this means and why it's important to you is the subject of this chapter. You'll learn the answers to the following questions:

- What's the difference between digital and analog signaling and why do you care?
- What is ISDN and where did it come from?
- How do you get ISDN from the phone company?
- How do you wire up your house or business for ISDN?
- What kind of hardware do you need to use ISDN with your computer?

Tip

Keep up with ISDN by reviewing information at **http://alumni.caltech.edu/ ~dank/isdn** and **http://www.bryce.com/~bryce**.

Digital and Analog

The meanings and distinctions between digital and analog are fundamental to an understanding of just what is going on in most of computing and telecommunication.

An analog signal is created and handled in electronic circuits as if one or more of its characteristics, for example strength (amplitude) or pitch (frequency), can be increased or decreased in amounts that are as large or as small as we want. There is *no quantum of quantity in the quality* we are describing as analog.

Okay, that's a little too much alliteration. I'll try again. There is no smallest unit into which we can divide our information. A recording of music would, until very recently, use equipment designed to convert sounds received acoustically into variations in electrical frequency, phase, and amplitude tracking the parallel and continuous variations in the air your ears perceive as sound. If you had sense organs that could detect the electrical variations, you could read those variations directly. You would not need any code, protocol conventions, or higher math to turn the received electrical impulses into what your nervous system perceives as sound. These electrical signals would assume an unlimited number of amplitude levels, phase relationships, and frequencies. An analog transducer such as a microphone creates an analog stream of information in the new medium (electricity) and conveys a continuous replica of the information in electronic form.

A digital signal presumes there is a *quantum of quantity in the quality* you are describing as digital. Translation: there is a smallest unit into which you can divide your information. In its most frequent use with computers, "digital logic," it implies only two states of electrical signals are recognized: one and zero. Regardless of some variations in the electrical signals in a computer or digital transmission line due to faulty components, noise, or whatever, all are resolved into ones and zeros. In many instances this makes a digital system less prone to malfunction than an analog system. As strange as it seems, it is possible to create all of mathematics from this simple "two valued logic."

It's possible to encode sounds, pictures, and other information into a stream of ones and zeros; the whole trick of encoding otherwise analog material such as sound is the fineness of the sampling of that material; the smaller the unit of sampling, the closer the encoding can subsequently be decoded to reproduce the originally analog information. Let's say you want to encode analog sounds into digital information. You build a device that looks at the analog signal and samples it at various times. The more samples taken, the more exactly the digital pulses can carry details of the original analog information.

This seems like a lot of effort to, in effect, actually lose information. The only way you can get an exact replica of the analog signal is by sampling it an unlimited number of times, and this would probably cost you an unlimited amount of money; why not just stick with the analog form in the first place? Why do all of this? You will probably prefer to use the digital form because it solves two very troublesome problems: noise and attenuation.

In broad perspective, a telephone system consists of two functions: transmission and switching. *Transmission* involves the cables, microwave, and so on that are used to get information from one point to another. *Switching* involves the equipment the transmission elements are hooked to that direct signal among desired sources and destinations. It turns out the larger an analog system becomes, the more expensive and complex the transmission and switching problems become. Digital techniques approach transmission and switching in a very different way that results in considerably less cost and complexity for telephone systems of the size you need—global. Let's look at the major problems in an analog system and see how digital approaches overcome them more economically.

Noise

Noise is anything that does not make up the desired communication; the desired communication is called *signal*. Noise is like the marble that a sculptor chips away to release the hidden form within a work of art. An analog system is, by its nature, noisy. The first telephone systems were simple analog designs very limited in the distances they could transmit sounds in large measure by the noise floor of the system. The *noise floor* is the very least noise that exists in your system after you've removed everything else. Your signal must be above this floor or you lose it in the noise. As the wires of those systems grew longer, more and more noise began to be heard. This noise could come from a number of sources:

- Random motion of the molecules making up the wire (heat)
- Electrical disturbances such as lightning
- Other signals flowing in parallel wires being induced onto your wires (crosstalk)
- Electrical power from adjacent equipment.

On a short run, a mile or so, these items tended to stay in the background and were not noticed by, or at least were not of concern to, telephone users. But as the wires became longer the noise level began to approach that of the signal (signal-to-noise ratio) and could no longer be ignored.

A number of techniques were adopted to overcome various types of noise: loading coils, noise canceling circuits that reversed the phase of the noise, shielded, and twisted cables, and coaxial cables. Through it all noise gradually increased, and avoidance and cancellation of noise became the bulk of the cost in long distance transmission.

II

Getting Connected

Attenuation

Worse, as the noise became stronger, the signal became weaker, or *attenuated*, while going through the system. As electrical energy travels through a conductor it encounters resistance to its flow determined by the physical properties of the conductor. This resistance turns some of the electrical energy into heat and random molecular motion, therefore adding to the noise. Scientists and engineers seek to reduce this resistance by selecting materials that have low resistance. Silver has the least resistance of any generally available conductor; copper has a higher resistance but is much cheaper and is the usual choice for cables.

The attenuation that results from the resistance affects different parts of the signal in different ways. The low frequency components are diminished a little, but the high frequency components are severely diminished. This *frequency selective attenuation* ultimately results in voices that lack most of their highs. The high ranges contain a good deal of the information needed to understand speech. As transmission lines become longer and longer, you might hear someone's now overly bass voice sounds at the distant end but be unable to understand the words spoken.

The remedy for a weak, selectively attenuated signal in an analog circuit is the addition of an amplifier that takes the received signal and increases its amplitude; in fact, the amplifier must increase the amplitude of the received high frequencies much more than that of the low frequencies (*slope equalization* is the buzz word) to make the voice intelligible. But, guess what, at the same time your amplifier is increasing the amplitude of the signal, it is increasing the amplitude of the noise. Enter ever more elaborate and expensive techniques to cancel noise and restore naturalness to the signal. Long distance and international carriers worked diligently perfecting ways to make an analog signal go great distances with low distortion and favorable signal to noise ratio. But their efforts always resulted in very expensive and complicated equipment. A way was needed to send the analog voice by digital means.

Sample your voice signal several times each second, then for each sample assign a number representing the characteristics of the analog signal at that instant. The more times you sample, the more numbers you get per second and the closer will be your approximation of the original, analog signal. Then express these numbers in binary form and transmit these binary numbers as strings of ones and zeros over your transmission system. It's a miracle. Most of your transmission problems disappear. Why?

Let's start with noise. Now that you know there are only two possible elements making up your digital signal, ones and zeros, you can design electronic circuits that look for only the unique electrical waveform that represents a one or a zero. This can become quite complicated, but it is at least limited to isolating only two. Contrast this with the analog environment, which must consider everything received as signal unless complex circuits such as noise cancellers give it other information to the contrary.

> ### Note
>
> The general rule is the sampling must be at a rate twice that of the highest frequency you want to transmit. For ordinary speech the highest frequency needed for comfortable intelligibility and fidelity is considered to be 4 kHz (4,000 cycles per a second). The sampling rate is then 8,000 (8,000 times a second).

The same rules regarding attenuation and distortion apply to the digital signal, but you can tolerate a lot of distortion when you are looking for only two states. You can determine an item is a one; it may have been severely distorted and attenuated, but you know for certain it is a one. Rather than amplifying what you received, that is, increasing its strength and thereby retaining and increasing the distortion, you regenerate it; usually the device you use for this is called a *repeater*. Since you know what a perfect one is specified to be, given the standard protocols in your system, and you know this thing you received, though distorted, still falls within the parameters for a one, you can create a perfect one and send it on its way to the next leg of the transmission system. *Presto*, all the distortion is gone from the signal. *Chango*, the noise disappears, because it never gave rise to either a one or a zero in your regeneration device.

Amplifier, Regenerator, Repeater

These terms often are mixed in text or conversation.

An *amplifier* is an analog device that increases the amplitude of a received signal and to a greater or lesser extent, depending on the sophistication of its design, sends it on, noise, distortion, and all.

A *regenerator* is a digital device that determines when a digital one or zero is received, creates a new one or zero, retimes the bit stream, and sends it on its way. Now it gets confused. Sometimes a manual or company will call a box that is a digital regenerator an amplifier.

(continues)

II

Getting Connected

(continued)

Repeaters are even more confusing. Most of the time the term repeater refers to a regenerator; in fact, repeater is the prevalent term. But sometimes repeater is used to describe what is actually an analog amplifier. When in doubt, figure out what the box is actually doing and don't rely on the often arbitrary nomenclature.

A digital signal seeks to render information to be conveyed by analysis of the information into a collection of discrete electrical signals, each either a one or a zero. Even if you had sense organs that could detect variations of electrical signals, you would not be able to perceive the message being sent because the digital signal is by definition not an analog of the original phenomenon. All you could determine would be that a string of marks and spaces, ones and zeros, frequency *x* and frequency *y*, phase 90 degrees and phase 270 degrees, was going by.

In and of itself this stream would make no sense. You must have an agreed upon means of taking the ones and zeros and transforming them into something meaningful to you. You must have a protocol that tells you that 1000001 is to be interpreted as "A" (in the ASCII code set, your protocol). And you must be more sophisticated. You must know when to start counting ones and zeros and when to stop, and what constitutes a package of information. Timing, synchronization, packets, and frames enter the picture. All of this is a part of the standards that make up your communications system. Now let's look at ISDN as it uses these concepts to improve your computer and telephone connections.

The Advantages of ISDN

ISDN, Integrated Services Digital Network, uses these methods of digital technology to give you:

- A faster data rate when you connect your computer to other systems over the phone system

- Faster set up and tear down when you place a data call

- More information about a call in progress

You've probably already heard about the increased data rate ISDN provides (see fig. 8.1). But have you thought about improvements that stem from faster set up and tear down? Think how long it takes a modem to sync up with another modem; remember all the squawks and buzzes? None of this happens with ISDN. The connection is made in a fraction of a second (see fig. 8.2). This can cut down greatly on your connection time. It means you can be cruising the Web, click a hyperlink, call up your Internet service provider, download the information, and disconnect. The next link you click duplicates the process. There's no reason to be connected while you're reading the page! ISDN is much more efficient in use of the telephone connection and demands on the Internet service provider for lines and equipment.

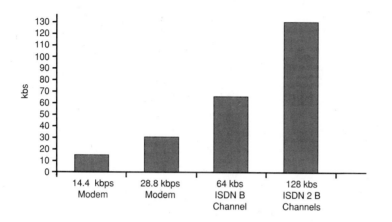

Fig. 8.1
The higher the data rate, the better it is for your use of the connection. ISDN provides 64 kbps B channels for communication. Two B channels can be combined.

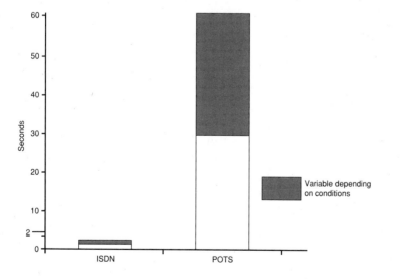

Fig. 8.2
The lower the time, the better it is for you.

Telephone Systems

As I mentioned earlier, telephone systems are composed of two major parts:

- Transmission
- Switching

Each is essential to telephone communication and each plays a big role in the current importance of ISDN to you.

Transmission

Transmission gets a signal from point A to point B. In particular, transmission is concerned with issues surrounding transmission media. Media used in telephony come in four flavors:

- Twisted pair cable
- Coaxial cable
- Fiber optic cable
- Radio

Due to noise and attenuation characteristics, it turns out fiber optic cables carry the most information the greatest distance and twisted pair copper cables carry the least information the shortest distance. Coax falls somewhere in between. Radio is frequently restricted due to the need to share spectrum space with others.

Prior to the wide use of fiber, long-distance carriers relied on coaxial cable supplemented with microwave radio. The two were using fundamentally analog radio technology to carry signals. Fiber and digital technology have proven more economic and capable of carrying vastly more information; therefore, microwave and coax are being phased out.

Today, essentially all the telephone system is based on fiber optic cables carrying digital signals. Cities are connected by interexchange carriers using fiber. Central offices within cities are connected to each other using fiber optics. The only place you'll find much copper twisted pair running analog signals today is the *local loop*, the cable from the central office to your office or house. And guess what. It is the local loop that is the determining factor in the data rate, noise, and errors associated with your use of the telephone system. The local loop is the weak link.

Long ago the local exchange carriers and the interchange carriers (long distance carriers) decided it was in their best interests to use fiber optics for telephone exchange to telephone exchange communication; this decision saved them a lot of money. It also saved them a lot of money to ensure that the signals going down those cables were digital signals since your whole electronic technology has concentrated on perfecting digital transmission for nearly 40 years.

However, you're faced with a twisted pair to the telco (that's telephone talk for telephone company) switch. And that twisted pair places a severe limit on the data rate that can be delivered to you. ISDN helps get the last gasp of use out of that twisted pair because it delivers a digital, rather than analog signal. Soon you'll have to go to fiber, coax, or wireless methods. Twisted pair is the best most of us have so let's get the most out of it. You can anticipate development of a competitive market for improvement in media. Suddenly, capital that was written down over 20 to 40 years by traditional telephone companies will be depreciated out in five, and you'll get vastly more for vastly less.

Switching

The first automated exchanges were collections of magnetically operated rotary switches that stepped through each pulse sent from the dial. A connection was made to another such switch that stepped to the next digit and so on. Hence the name of the equipment, *step by step*. Following this design a more elaborate and flexible, but still electromechanical, design called a *cross-bar switch* began to take over.

As we moved into the 1960s, the initial electronic switches were used. They were based on analog technology since the telephone still was analog. The 1970s saw the development of the first digital switches concurrently with the flow of digital information on the transmission side of the equation. Now there was every economic reason to keep information in digital form throughout the system. Conversion back and forth through switches was expensive. With rare exception it was to the operating companies' advantage to use both digital switches and digital transmission lines. Figure 8.3 shows how we're currently hooked up.

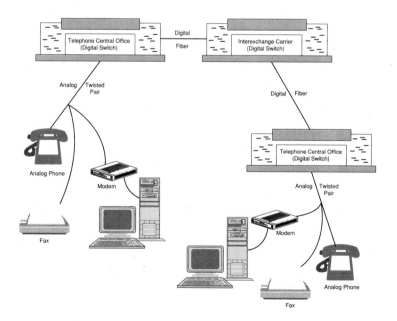

Fig. 8.3
Notice the digital connections among telephone switches along with the fiber optic cables. Now look at the copper twisted pair that carries analog signals to you.

Getting Connected

At the very end, this wonderful digital information system was converted to analog for that last mile or two down the twisted pair copper loop. This conversion was not cheap; it needed codec devices and electronic gear to convert digital to analog and back, but it was deemed cheaper than rewiring the loop or going to a digital technique and placing new digital equipment at the subscriber's location or at the least making the digital to analog conversion there.

Today ISDN finishes the job. It delivers digital information to the subscriber. The subscriber decides whether or not the equipment he connects is digital or analog and supplies the connection devices to make it work.

Note

Although it looks like just about anything can be connected to an ISDN system, be aware it takes special electronics to use ISDN. If you attempt to call an analog modem with your ISDN equipment, it won't connect. If someone with an analog modem attempts to call your ISDN equipment, nothing happens. Although there are some ISDN devices that embed analog modems for such instances and some that go so far as to be able to detect the difference and automatically switch, other equipment is not so agile. In short, moving to ISDN provides no backward compatibility with POTS; don't throw your modems out yet. Figure 8.4 assumes use of ISDN electronics that enables connection of analog gear to use one or more of the digital B channels of ISDN.

Fig. 8.4
With ISDN, the telephone signal is digital all the way to you house or business. You can use your existing analog equipment on ISDN only with appropriate adapters in your ISDN electronics.

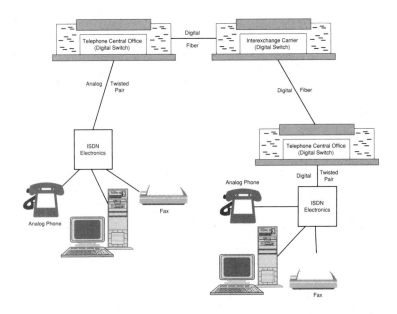

Here are the factors that play into your efforts to make ISDN work for you.

- You must have a local exchange carrier that has ISDN available to your area.

- The carrier may have a digital switch, but that switch may not be ISDN compliant, or it may not be compliant with the new National ISDN standards you need for the equipment you buy.

- The local exchange carrier may be able to get ISDN to a switch for you but still be unable to supply a cable adequate to carry the digital information from the switch to you.

- All of this may be technically possible, but there may not be a tariff filed with the appropriate government regulatory authority allowing the carrier to connect ISDN to you.

- And, finally, the switch may be right, the wires may work, the tariff may be available, but the price to you is horrendous.

Narrowband ISDN

You're concerned with *narrowband ISDN* that carries data rates of a few hundred to a few million bits per second. On the horizon is *wideband ISDN,* delivering tens and hundreds of megabits; that area is outside the scope of this discussion and not yet widely available. Narrowband ISDN comes in two forms:

- Basic Rate Interface (BRI)
- Primary Rate Interface (PRI)

If you're a larger business or an Internet service provider, you may be interested in PRI; it delivers about 1.5 megabits per second service. However, the big emphasis in this book is on BRI; it delivers two B channels of 64 kilobits per second (kbps) and one D channel at 16 kbps. "What is all this B and D stuff," you say? Glad you asked. Here's the word.

Note

A new family of protocols and hardware has the potential to dramatically increase the data rates delivered on the local loop—we're talking megabits, folks. Check out the *DSL technologies (ADSL, HDSL, and SDSL) briefly described under "The Internet on Cable TV, Dishes, Power Lines, and Pipes?" in chapter 9. And look at these Web sites: **http://www.sbexpos.com/sbexpos/association/adsl/home.html**, **http://www.alumni.caltech.com/~dank/isdn**, and **http://www.bryce.com/~bryce**.

II

Getting Connected

ISDN uses the basic rate interface (BRI) to deliver two channels of 64 kbps each. These "B channels" are designed to carry the information the subscriber wants to transmit across the network. There is a third channel running at 16 kbps. This "D channel" is used primarily to control the flow of information through the network. It provides call set up and tear down, network monitoring, and other overhead functions. As the D channel is separate from the B channels, the signaling is called "common channel." This is a form of out of band signaling since it is, by definition, not in the same band as the data bearer channel.

The D channel is common to the B channels controlled. In other services, such as your plain old telephone service (POTS), information for telephone network control is carried within the same channel as that of the subscriber using a technique called *in-band signaling*. You'll see later in this chapter how this influences your actual usage of the circuit.

Once a call is set up, the D channel is not fully utilized and may be made available for user packet traffic. Call control always takes priority over user packets, but the capacity of the D channel is ideal for such things as credit card identification and simple terminal-to-host sessions.

Basic rate interface ISDN delivers three separate channels for your use: 64 kbps, 64 kbps, and 16 kbps (this combination is often called *2B+D*). This is transmitted over the same pair of wires that carried only one channel of comparatively small capacity analog information with POTS.

Basic Rate Interface D Channel

Let's start with the D channel. It's the most radical departure from the analog world. In a way, the two most important things ISDN brings to the table are its inherent digital nature and the D channel.

In the analog world, a telephone call is controlled in band. When you pick up the phone, an "off hook" signal is sent to the central office switch, which detects the condition and connects you to a dial tone indicating you may proceed to use the system. You enter various tones using the "dual tone multiple frequency" (DTMF) in band signaling available from the buttons on the phone. If you have a rotary phone, you make and break the line rapidly creating pulses that are counted at the exchange switch. In the earlier mechanical switches, the pulses actuated stepper relays that selected each successive number. In modern electronic switches the pulses are counted and converted to DTMF signals. In fact, there is a whole mini-industry manufacturing devices to convert the pulses to tones since a great deal of the world is still tied to the rotary dial.

It makes you wonder. Why does it take more equipment to translate the dial pulses than to directly accept the DTMF tones, but many local exchange carriers continue to charge extra for DTMF service? It's sort of like the question of why ISDN often costs more than POTS when it is the POTS analog signal that must be converted to digital for carriage through the otherwise digital switch and telephone network. No one ever said telephone system pricing made sense outside the never-never world of rate regulation, antiquated telephone accounting methods, and the monopoly marketplace.

Anyway, one way or another the pulses or tones set up a path to the phone you are calling. Then a ringing current is placed on the line of the called phone. This is really a strange beast. Suddenly you go from a low voltage direct current line to 90 volts of alternating current to ring the bell. If you happen to be holding on to the line when it is rung, you'll ring too. Take note. This could be dangerous.

> **Caution**
>
> When working on your telephone wiring, be sure it is disconnected from the line coming into your house or office. Ringer current is not as dangerous as the electric power running through your building, but under the wrong conditions, especially your particular physical condition, it could seriously harm or even kill you.
>
> The picture of a movie star taking a bath while using a phone is an invitation to tragedy. Perhaps wireless phones are safe in such circumstances; wired phones never are. Even without ringer current, as is the case with ISDN, transient electrical spikes of hundreds or even thousands of volts may appear on the line from accidental contact with power wiring or lightning strokes. Play it safe.

II

Getting Connected

When the ringer current appears at the called phone, circuitry in the phone directs it to the bell or other attention-getting device and the phone rings. Now at your end (the calling party) you hear the buzz, buzz you have learned to associate with a ringing phone. There is no direct correlation between the "ringing" you hear in the handset and the actual ringing of the bell on the called phone. This is why you frequently encounter a phone being answered "before it has rung." The physical phone rang at the called party end, but the buzz you as the calling party associate with ringing had not been initiated by the central office switch on your end. Now you know the secret; it's all smoke and mirrors. Since the system is really digital and you're using analog devices at both ends, the digital switches fake what you've come to associate with analog calls. When the called party answers, his phone goes "off hook," signaling his central office switch the call has been answered and turning off the ringing current. Your call can now proceed.

You both talk for a while when suddenly you hear a tone in the earpiece of your phone. At the called party's end there is a momentary "click, click" and loss of a syllable or two you were speaking at the time. You explain you must take another call and depress the switchhook; this sends a momentary off condition to your central office switch, which has been programmed to interpret this as a signal to place your original called party on hold and transfer you to the new "call waiting" party. You may now switch back and forth between the two by using the switch hook to signal the central office switch.

I've just outlined the current technology of analog in-band signaling. Any time you want to make a change in the call setup, you must interrupt your ongoing call to advise the central office switch of your desires. The same is true for the switch; to advise you it must signal in band, interrupting your call in progress. Your actions in dialing with a rotary dial, DTMF tones, or switchhook manipulation create analog signals that must be interpreted into digital instructions for the switch. These are complex, expensive, roundabout ways of adapting the analog local loop to an otherwise digital telephone system.

ISDN does away with this. The D channel becomes the vehicle for signaling. This signaling is common channel. Your calls are never interrupted because the signal that a call is waiting, for example, is sent over the D channel. When such a signal arrives at your ISDN phone you have determined what will happen. Perhaps a screen on the phone blinks with the number or name of the calling party. Perhaps your computer monitor detects the call and switches you to a database entry associated with the calling party. In any case there is no need for signaling in the same channel as you are using for talking. In fact, there is no way for signaling to take place in the B channel. All signaling takes place in the D channel:

- When you pick up the handset of an ISDN phone the phone sends a "setup" message on the D channel to the central office switch.

- The switch acknowledges receipt of the message on the D channel and turns on the dial tone for the selected B channel.

- When you dial the phone it sends each digit to the switch on the D channel.

- After the first digit is dialed the switch turns off the dial tone on the B channel.

- When the switch has received enough digits to complete the call, it sends a "call proceeding" message to your phone on the D channel.

- The switch then sends a "setup" message to the phone you are calling on that phone's D channel.

- The called phone sends an acknowledgment to the switch.

- When the called phone handset is removed, that phone sends a "setup" message to the switch on the D channel.

- It is expected that the phone will be a multi-button type so the answering party will now select the button for your call; this sends a "connect" message to the switch on the D channel.

- Now the switch sends a "connect" message to your phone on the D channel and connects your selected B channel with that of the called party.

- Now you talk.

During the call you notice a flash on your phone's viewing panel and hear a beep from the phone; you look at your computer monitor and find it showing an incoming call and offering to retrieve the party's records from your database. Neither you nor the party to whom you are currently speaking are interrupted by tones or clicks; all the signaling for the call waiting is done over the separate D channel while your call proceeds on a B channel. You may select to place your current party on hold by pressing buttons on your phone or making selections on your connected computer. You never use the switchhook. You may leap back and forth between the parties or several other call waiting parties or engage selected ones in conference calling. All this is possible due to the flexibility of D channel signaling.

Notice mention of the connected computer. Although much of the D channel signaling may take place with a fancy ISDN phone, a simple phone, even an old POTS phone with an appropriate terminal adapter and a PC used in conjunction with ISDN, can give even more flexibility. This is the beauty of ISDN. In the past, all the tricks of telephones were contained in the switch or your PBX. Now with ISDN and D channel signaling, a great deal of processing may take place in the equipment on your desk as it is working in what is essentially a peer relationship with the switch.

With ISDN, the telephone industry is making the same sort of transition as the computer industry did in moving from terminal to host networks to peer-to-peer and client/server local area networks. More intelligence is being placed nearer the user with the user in control. You can expect this evolution to continue. With network packet protocols taking on more functions that replace historic switch functions, expect to see simpler central office switches, more complex network protocols, and richer user equipment and choices. All of this results from the move to digital information in the local loop and D channel common channel signaling; these are all elements of ISDN.

OK, so now aren't you ready for the B channels, the real carriers of your information? Not so fast. Remember the D channel is used for signaling and most of that signaling takes place during call set up and tear down. Are you going to waste a 16,000-bit-per-second channel during the remainder of the time? Not at all. You may use the unused capacity of the D channel to transmit packet switched information.

If you live in an area where a special set of standards, called Signaling System #7, has not been implemented, you may find your ISDN is limited to two B channels, each with only 56 kbps capacity. In this case the remaining 8 kbps of each channel have been "robbed" to do signaling duty normally handled by Signaling System #7. This limitation applied to a substantial amount of Pacific Bell's California ISDN system when first implemented; over time the system will be fully compliant and all its B channels will be 64 kbps without bit robbing.

The Interface Between You and the Phone Company

Figure 8.5 shows several terms you need to know to be conversant with ISDN. First notice the box called "NT1." This is an electronic gear that you must have to make ISDN work for you. Often this is a separate device that is connected on one side to the telephone company's single twisted pair cable. The other side has two twisted pair that connect to your equipment. The line from the telephone company provides a "U interface." This is converted to an "S/T interface" for connection to your equipment.

Fig. 8.5

The U interface comes from the telephone company. The S/T interface is required for your equipment.

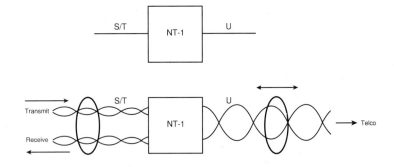

Something happens in the NT1 device converting a one pair signal from the telephone company into two pairs for distribution to your equipment. It is more economical for the telco to use only one pair rather than two, but from your viewpoint there is a major disadvantage. On the one pair U side you may only connect one NT1 device. So if you have half a dozen devices to tie onto your ISDN line, you don't want them to require a U interface; you want an S/T interface because the S/T side allows you to connect a number of additional devices.

Basically the U interface side carries full duplex information on the single pair. This means information travels in both directions simultaneously. Engineering constraints prevent such an arrangement from allowing multidrop connections of the sort you probably want for several devices. Consequently, conversion to the S/T interface breaks the signal into two paths, one transmit, one receive. Which is which depends on whether you are looking from the point of view of the NT1 or a piece of terminal equipment; what is transmission for one is reception for the other. Each signal is now carried on a separate pair, and you are allowed to connect multiple devices. The rules of connection for ISDN are quite different from a POTS installation, but flexibility in the long run is much greater.

A third or even a fourth pair may also be connected to the NT1; each of these additional pairs is used for powering other equipment in your system. In many cases, especially those involving computers, this powering feature in not needed.

One thing becomes clear from the U versus S/T design: equipment that incorporates the NT1 functions internally with no S/T interface connection limits your use of an ISDN line. You'll see this arrangement in computer boards that connect directly to the BRI U interface. Often this arrangement reduces costs; however, flexibility for use of other equipment on your ISDN line is sacrificed. You'll explore a number of practical options later.

> **Note**
>
> Frequently you'll find devices marked with an R interface; usually this is understood to be for connection to analog telephone equipment, phones, modems, and faxes. You can see the advantage of this; with such a connection you can use your existing analog equipment on the ISDN line. But the R interface is not limited to the analog telephone specification. It could be a connection to totally different equipment so long as that equipment is not ISDN compliant.

The B Channel

Now that you've covered the D channel and the interfaces, you'll look at the B channels, the ones that will do most of your work.

A BRI provides two B channels of 64 kbps each. This is like having two independent telephone lines. Each has a different telephone number. The proper term here is *directory number* (DN). In fact you may have several directory numbers for each B channel. This would enable you to have several devices on the S/T multidrop side of your NT1 with each device having a different directory number. For example, you could have a fax machine, a telephone, and a computer all using one B channel, but each with a different directory number. This works through the D channel signaling with each device. Of course these must be ISDN type devices that can communicate with the D channel and make it happen.

Tip

Watch out. We are now entering the world of ISDN numbers. There are two kinds you must remember. I've already mentioned the directory number (DN). Since you're familiar with that from the POTS world, the only thing new to remember is the ability to have different directory numbers for each device using a B channel. But there is more to it. Your equipment is identified with a *terminal endpoint identifier* (TEI). This in turn is wrapped up with the *service profile identifier* (SPID). It is here that things get sticky. How the TEI and SPID numbers are assigned and what they mean can vary from telco to telco and switch to switch. You will need to enter the DN and SPID when you configure your equipment. It is very important to get this information from the telephone company so your configuration goes smoothly.

Ordering ISDN Service

Why a section on ordering telephone service? If you asked this question, the chances are you've not yet attempted to order ISDN, or when you ordered it you were very lucky. It's not as simple as POTS. It's not simple at all. Very strange things have been reported by those attempting this task. Upon reaching one telephone company, a caller was told he couldn't have ISDN. He asked why; the response was, "It's illegal." Be prepared for anything.

Ordering is a word we all understand. If you want something, you order it. So, if you want ISDN, you order it. But what is provisioning? Provisioning is the telephone company's side. A telephone switch must be "provisioned" to supply services. In the case of ISDN the switch must be designed for ISDN and then must be provisioned to provide such ISDN services as the company wants to supply, has tariff approval to supply, and that can be supplied by the switch hardware and software. We've come a long way from the "number please" manual switchboard. There are so many options and possibilities inherent in ISDN generally, and vastly more when combinations are assembled, that making it all work and explaining what it is and how to use it becomes overwhelming.

When you call up for ISDN service, the order person may fill your order promptly and efficiently; the installer may connect you perfectly and test the line to ensure it talks to the switch; your equipment supplier may provide excellent software and hardware, but you may find nothing works. Why? The order was accepted based upon what your telephone company considered "generic" ISDN, but you needed some features or capabilities that are not in that "generic" package. Now comes the hard part; what do you need that you did not get, and what did you get?

This involves us in a litany of standards. In the beginning it was in the interest of switch manufactures to provide features and capabilities unique to their switch and unavailable or inaccessible to their competitors' switches. This was fine as long as all your ISDN went through only that manufacturer's switch and needed nothing that manufacturer lacked. This placed the onus of making a particular piece of customer-provided equipment work on your back and the back of the customer-provided equipment (CPE) maker. It also made it hard to call other ISDN installations if they didn't have the same configuration and equipment as your local exchange carrier. This led to a period of ISDN stagnation that persisted until 1988 when the North American ISDN Users' Group, the National Institute of Standards and Technology, and Bellcore decided to team up and develop the National ISDN series of specifications starting with National ISDN 1 (NI-1) finalized in 1991. This was followed by NI-2 that was released in 1994; NI-3 is expected in 1996.

> ### Tip
>
> You'll find these standards at **http://www.bellcore.com/ISDN/ISDN.html** and **http://www.ocn.com/ocn/niuf_top.html**.

Each NI-x provides specific descriptions of what a telephone switch is to provide within its provisioning to meet the given specification. Now makers of customer premises equipment (CPE) and you can be assured that the hardware and software you have will work with any switch meeting a given NI-x standard if the elements of that standard contain everything needed for your particular applications.

Look at what this really says. It brings the switch makers to the table with various sets of least common denominator features and functions. It says if that collection of features and functions includes all you need, it is technically possible for your equipment to work with the switch. But it doesn't answer the following questions:

II

Getting Connected

- Given that the switch can technically be provisioned to supply what I need, how do I ask for the particular collection of features and functions that make my device work?

- What if the switch supports NI-x, but I need something that is not in NI-x?

- Even if I know how to order the right stuff, and the switch can be provisioned for it, what if there is no tariff for it?

ISDN Ordering Codes

The complexity of ordering became so great that industry specialists designed a collection of "ISDN Ordering Codes." These codes are designated by letters of the alphabet and are designed to cover virtually all the combinations of needs commonly encountered by users of ISDN. Most manufacturers of ISDN equipment now advise buyers of the appropriate codes to use for their equipment. This standardization has simplified the process considerably.

Limited Options

In reality, most of the complexity of ISDN ordering comes not from computer data users, but from voice users. If you're going to use your ISDN connection for data and, at most, simple voice communications, you can probably get by with the limited options approach.

And here are your selections from one of the big local exchange carriers:

- 0B+D   (packet and signaling on D)
- 1B+D   (only signaling on D)
- 1B+D   (packet and signaling on D)
- 2B+D   (only signaling on D)
- 2B+D   (packet and signaling on D)

You get voice or data on demand; this means your customer provided equipment (CPE) requests one or the other through the D channel.

So that's it. What do about 95 percent plus of the ISDN subscribers take? Just exactly what you want: 2B+D (only signaling on D). The cost differences among the selections between one and two B channels are several dollars per month, but not so great as to make most users opt for only one B.

Wiring for ISDN

Wiring? Do you have to consider wiring to use ISDN? Yes. ISDN is designed to deal with much higher data rates than those of POTS. As a result the specifications for wiring are stricter. This applies not only to wiring of the telephone company; it also applies to the wiring in your house or business.

Remember the discussion of noise and attenuation? The greater the distance a signal travels down a cable, the more it is weakened (attenuated) and the more non-signal interference (noise) adds up to confuse or obscure your desired communications. This distorts the digital information reducing the usable data rate and eventually making it impossible to operate within ISDN specifications.

Cautions When Wiring

Now I'm starting to talk about the wiring at your house or business. I expect you may examine it during this discussion. So please read and heed the following warnings:

Caution

Read and heed the cautions in the text. If you don't know how to handle wires and electricity, hire someone who does.

Do not work on your telephone wiring at all if you wear a pacemaker. Telephone lines carry electrical current. To avoid contact with electrical current:

- Never install telephone wiring during a lightning storm.
- Never install telephone jacks in wet locations unless the jack is specially designed for wet locations.
- Use caution when installing or modifying telephone lines.
- Use a screwdriver and other tools with insulated handles.
- You and those around you should wear safety glasses or goggles.
- Be sure that your inside wire is not connected to the access line while you are working on your telephone wiring. If you cannot do this, take the handset of one of your telephones off the hook. This will keep the phone from ringing and reduce, but not eliminate, the possibility of your contacting electricity.
- Do not place telephone wiring or connections in any conduit, outlet, or junction box containing electrical wiring.
- Installation of inside wire may bring you close to electrical wire, conduit, terminals, and other electrical facilities. EXTREME CAUTION must be used to avoid electrical shock from such facilities. You must avoid contact with all such facilities.

- Telephone wire must be at least six feet from bare power wiring or lightning rods and associated wires, and at last six inches from other wire (antenna wires, doorbell wires, wires from transformers to neon signs), steam or hot water pipes, and heating ducts.

- Before working with existing inside wiring, check all electrical outlets for a square telephone dial light transformer and unplug it from the electrical outlet. Failure to unplug all telephone transformers can cause electrical shock.

- Do not place a jack where it would allow a person to use the telephone while in a bathtub, shower, swimming pool, or similar hazardous location.

- Protectors and grounding wire placed by the service provider must not be connected to, removed, or modified by the customer.

This list of warnings is from the North American ISDN Users' Forum (NIUF) as stated in their excellent and detailed *ISDN Wiring and Powering Guidelines (Residence and Small Business)*. Your local building codes, ordinances, and other laws govern over the suggestions made here and throughout this book. Please use common sense when working around electricity. This list and the book provide several suggestions to help you, but it cannot cover all possibilities or dangers. If you really don't have a general knowledge of electricity and methods for working around it, have a professional do the job for you.

Tip

Check out the NIUF at **http://www.ocn.com/ocn/niuf_top.html**.

It's often possible to run ISDN over the existing wiring in your house or business. However, if possible, it is best to install new wiring to ensure maximum performance and future upgradability. You should use Category 3 cable at a minimum; it is best to use Category 5. These categories of twisted pair cable have been developed to carry high data rate digital signals. The details of wiring are too extensive for coverage in this book. In the event you plan to install cabling or modify your existing cabling; refer to the NIUF book *ISDN Wiring and Powering Guidelines (Residence and Small Business)* and to *Special Edition Using ISDN* by James Y. Bryce (Que 1995, ISBN 0-7897-0405-6).

ISDN Hardware

This is the part you've probably been waiting for. Here are some ideas about the actual hardware you can use to connect to ISDN; in ISDN terminology these devices are called *terminal adapters*. There are three types of such devices:

- External terminal adapters
- Internal card terminal adapters
- Routers with built in terminal adapters

I'll go through a detailed configuration for the Motorola BitSURFR, an external terminal adapter that connects through the serial port. The BitSURFR is aimed at the general computer user and is available from many computer "superstores" at prices comparable to higher end modems. The discussion of its configuration gives a flavor of the details you'll need to set up most ISDN terminal adapters. The serial port equipment is fairly similar in its setup. The internal cards differ considerably within breed. By the time you get to routers the setup is so varied and frequently complex, no brief treatment such as this is possible.

> **Note**
>
> The information included about products is subject to very rapid change in this exploding market; check suppliers for the latest details and check out Dan Kegel's ISDN Web site, **http://www.alumni.edu/~dank/isdn**, and mine, **http://www.bryce.com/~bryce**, for additional information and ideas.
>
> Also, the inclusion of a product or the exclusion of some other product is in no way a commendation or condemnation. Choices were made to represent types and concepts. Many products left unmentioned are well worthy of your consideration.

External Terminal Adapters

I'm calling this first category of ISDN hardware "external ISDN terminal adapters." You'll find terms like "ISDN modem" and simply "terminal adapter" also used for these boxes. The distinguishing characteristics are:

- Stand-alone box with its own power supply
- Connection to your computer through the serial port (although closely related equipment using the parallel port is available)
- Use of the AT command set so the device will work with your existing modem programs

Serial Port Issues

As you'll see, this equipment provides a straightforward solution to using ISDN. But, there are drawbacks; there always are. The primary drawback is the serial port itself. These ports are limited in their data rate performance. If you're using Windows 3.x, the native drivers with Windows limit your serial port speeds to considerably less than that supported by ISDN. Your solution is to install a third-party serial port driver. Three very popular programs that perform this function are TurboCom, CyberCom, and KingCom. These are usually supplied as a part of external ISDN adapter software.

These software programs will do you no good if you have an older serial port. It's mandatory that you have a 16550A UART on the serial port you're using for ISDN. Otherwise, you'll be unable to realize the data rate gains of ISDN. If you're using a recently manufactured PC you probably have a 16550A. Older machines don't have them. You can buy a board with one or more 16550A serial ports for less than $50.

Since you've probably moved to Windows 95 you'll be glad to know there's no need for special software drivers for your serial ports. Assuming you have 16550As for serial hardware, Windows 95 comes with support for data rates clear up to and including 921,600 bits per second, as shown in figure 8.6.

Fig. 8.6

Notice the range of date rates extends up to 921,600 bps, far more than the 57,600 bps of Windows 3.x.

Windows 95 also brings UNIMODEM to the world of modem-type devices. It provides a single, universal modem driver. This means you will no longer be selecting a modem type within your applications—Windows 95 takes care of that for you. It's much the same as the move from needing applications to contain drivers for every printer under DOS to being able to write solely to the Windows printer software as it became possible with Windows 3.x. Now, applications that use modems, or ISDN terminal adapters that are addressed as modems, need only write to UNIMODEM. It's easier for the writers, and it's easier for the users.

Windows 95 also provides Windows Telephony API (TAPI) as a part of the Windows Open Services Architecture (WOSA). This greatly simplifies communication and control of telephone interconnection. In particular, the added control available through use of D channel signaling is recognized in versions of Windows 95 that followed the initial release.

Windows 95 also supports the Universal Serial Bus (USB). USB revolutionizes the connection of devices to your computer. It operates at 12 megabits per second and supports up to 63 devices with isochronous and asynchronous data communications. Your keyboard, mouse, modems, ISDN devices, and lots more will use USB. It's here; Windows 95 has it. Check it out at **http://www.teleport.com/~USB**.

> ### Tip
>
> A number of ISDN features were not available in the first release of Windows 95. Be sure to get the most recent release to take full advantage of ISDN. Check **http://www.microsoft.com**.

AT Command Set

A central characteristic of serial port terminal adapters is use of the AT command set originally developed by Hayes. This makes it easy to run modem applications. But watch out for variations. For example, the usual tone dialing command is "ATDT," but some equipment with combination ISDN/analog modem functions reserves "ATDT" for calling with the analog modem and uses "ATD" for calls with the ISDN functions.

> ### Note
>
> A good example of this ATD/ATDT difference is the 3Com Impact; ATD enables ISDN calling; ATDT enables analog modem calling. On the other hand, a similar product from U.S. Robotics, the I Modem, uses ATDT to dial and determines whether to use an analog modem or ISDN from the response sent back from the far end device.

The advantage of the AT command set will diminish over time as development of ISDN specific drivers continues. But for now these developments are just starting, so the AT commands are quite a help. A number of excellent serial port devices are available. I'll use the Motorola BitSURFR as an example.

Motorola BitSURFR

The Motorola BitSURFR was designed to be a plug-and-play device taking full advantage of such features in Windows 95. Figure 8.7 shows the BitSURFR as detected by Windows 95 during hardware installation. All you have to do is connect the BitSURFR to an available serial port and run the Windows 95 hardware installation from the Windows 95 Control Panel. Click Start, click Settings, click Control Panel, and double-click Add New Hardware. Then choose Next and allow Windows 95 to find the plug-and-play (PnP) BitSURFR for you. All of the settings will be done.

Fig. 8.7
Windows 95 with Plug and Play detected the Motorola BitSURFR.

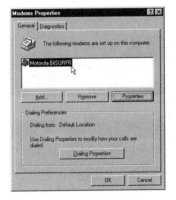

Your next step is to install the BitSURFR configuration software supplied by Motorola. Insert the disk provided and again go to the Control Panel. This time select the Add/Remove Program icon and let Windows 95 find the disk and setup program for you. Then go to Start, choose Programs, and then se-lect the Motorola group; double-click the program icon created for the Motorola BitSURFR software.

From the initial screen (see fig. 8.8), open the Access menu and choose Define Adapter. In the Define Adapter dialog box, as shown in figure 8.9, click the Model drop-down list, click BitSURFR, and then click OK.

Go to the main screen ribbon and choose File, New. You'll have a screen like figure 8.10 showing a number of selection tabs. You're on the right one to start "ISDN Provisioning." Fill in the SPIDs, directory numbers, and switch type supplied by your telephone company. If you have no other information to the contrary from the telco or other sources, leave the TEI entries as "automatic."

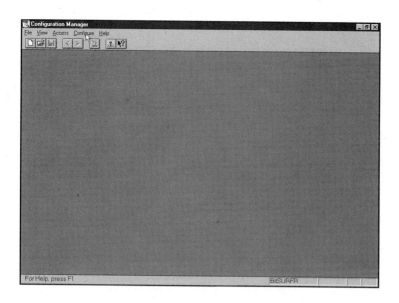

Fig. 8.8
This is the
Motorola BitSURFR
Configuration
Manager Main
Screen. You'll
first select the
BitSURFR under
Access, then
choose New
under File.

Fig. 8.9
Motorola BitSURFR
Define Adapter
selection provides
a way to choose
among Motorola's
ISDN devices. The
photograph at
the right is the
BitSURFR.

Caution

Do not insert dashes or spaces in the SPIDs or directory numbers. Often these characters will cause your configuration to fail.

Choose the Protocols tab (see fig. 8.11). Choose V.120 if you're connecting to an async serial device at your Internet provider. Often, providers use Adtran equipment for V.120; if this is the case, change the frame sizes to 253. If you're connecting to a synchronous device—that usually means a router—choose "PPP." BONDING is a method used to aggregate multiple B channels; chances are you'll have a recent version of the software with a selection for MP, indicating "Multilink PPP" also. If you have the ability to use more than one B channel through your Internet provider agreement, the provider will tell you what should be entered here.

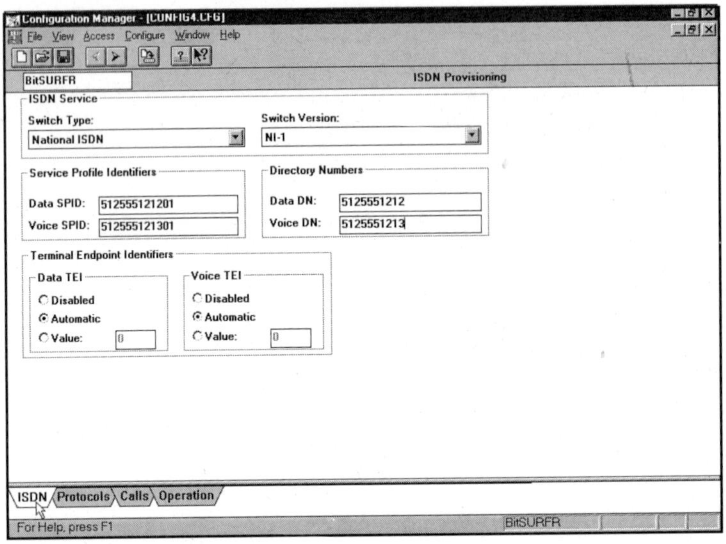

Fig. 8.10
BitSURFR ISDN Provisioning selections are reflected on the table labeled ISDN. Insert SPIDs, directory numbers, and switch type.

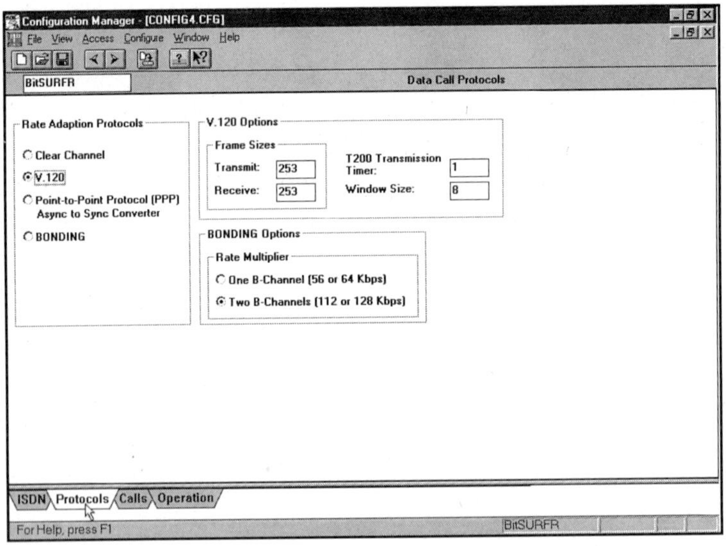

Fig. 8.11
The BitSURFR Protocols tab selection allows you to select from among V.120, clear channel (64 kbps), PPP async to sync and BONDING.

Click the Calls tab (see fig. 8.12), and, after scrolling down, figure 8.13 appears. As a start, I suggest in the "Call Establishment" part you set the channel speed to 56 kbps or 64 kbps depending on what is available from your switch. Leave Speech for the Originate Voice Calls As setting, and Data for the Originate Data Calls As setting.

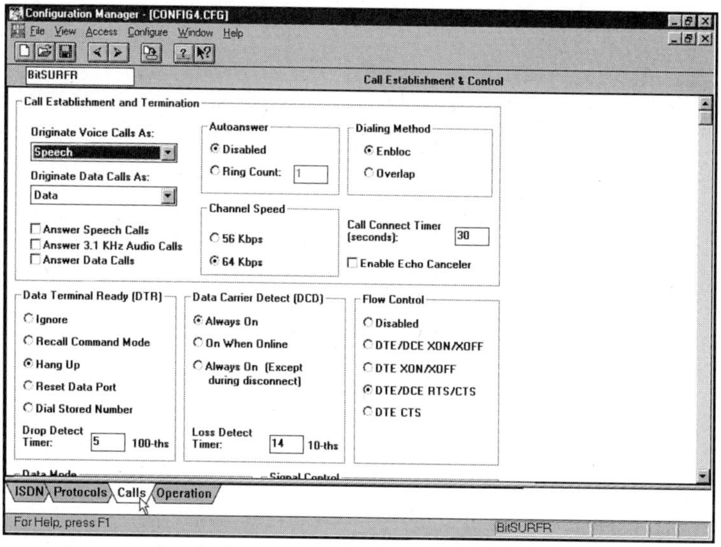

Fig. 8.12
The top half of the BitSURFR Calls tab has a large number of selections for establishing and terminating connections.

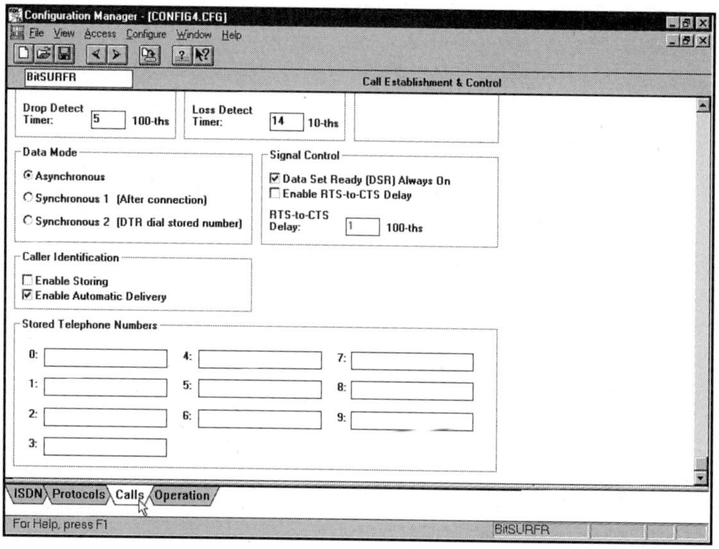

Fig. 8.13
The bottom half of the BitSURFR Calls tab provides a number of selections including caller identification and stored numbers.

In the "DTR" screen start with "Ignore." If your line doesn't hang up, try "Hang Up" or "Reset." Set "Asynchronous" if you're calling another serial device. Set "Synchronous 1" if you're calling a router; if that doesn't work, you may also need to try "Synchronous 2."

Select the next tab, Operations. I suggest you check the Extended Response box to receive more extensive messages, as shown in figure 8.14. With this selection you'll receive more extensive messages while the BitSURFR is placing calls or encountering errors; these will help you diagnose or avoid problems. Enabling local character echo puts the characters you type on your screen, escape sequence guard keeps brief glitches from bringing the device down, and the dial response messages give you an indication of what's going on much the same as the responses from a modem like CONNECT or BUSY.

Fig. 8.14
The BitSURFR Operations tab sets up the AT command operations.

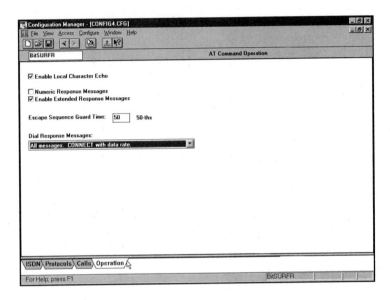

The little button on the ribbon that is all alone, third from the right, is the Update button. Click it and you'll get a window asking if you want to update the device's configuration with the new material. Choose Save and Restart. This does just what it says and brings up a percentage complete meter (see fig. 8.15). If you fail to save you've accomplished nothing. If you want to be able to restore this particular configuration after you've made other changes, save your configuration to a file. Choose File, Save As, and give this configuration a file name. If you attempt to exit the program without saving it should stop you, but just be sure.

Fig. 8.15
The BitSURFR Update in the midst of loading a new config-uration.

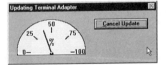

Motorola has provided several options to preconfigure so you don't really have to do anything but enter your switch type and numbers. Choose Con-figure, Quick Setup (see fig. 8.16). One of the four choices for async and sync operation will probably take care of you. Then you might do a little customization such as disabling auto answer, but it's a lot better than trying to figure out what all of the obtuse technical possibilities actually mean and then what to do with each one.

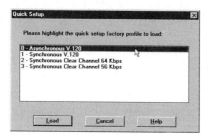

Fig. 8.16
The BitSURFR Quick Setup selection does most of your setup work. Check it out; then customize as needed.

Other External Terminal Adapters

The Motorola BitSURFR is not the only member of this breed. 3Com has the Impact that may have the easiest setup on the market. Adtran offers the ISU Express. US Robotics has a serial port version of the I Modem (it's also avail-able in an internal card version). And Zycel provides a similar unit that takes advantage of the much faster operation of the parallel port. I expect all of these companies and many more to offer Universal Serial Bus products as that standard catches on.

▶ See "Vendor Contacts for Selected Internet Soft-ware and Ser-vices," p. 1205

Options Available

All of the external products I've mentioned and many of the other types ei-ther come with or have options for inclusion of several features:

■ Analog port. This allows you to connect a regular phone, modem or FAX to the device and use a B channel for analog phone calls. Some of these create "ringer current" and can ring a phone or make a modem or FAX answer; some do not have ringer current and can't. Most give pref-erence to the voice call. So if you're using 2 B channels for data and pick up the phone, the device will drop one data channel to allow you to make the call.

■ Support for multilink PPP (MP). This is a very important feature. It means you can put two B channels together and get twice the data rate of one. This only works if your Internet provider supports MP.

- Internal NT1 support is often available. This means you don't have to buy an external NT1; you have a U interface right on the box. But it also means you can only use the ISDN device itself. You can't connect anything else to your ISDN line. An external NT1 allows you to connect other equipment; in this case you should get the S/T interface on your unit.

- Built-in analog fax/modems so you don't have to have another analog device. Some devices require you to issue the proper command to tell the device you want a modem or digital call. Others are able to sense the device calling or being called and switch automatically.

Internal Card Terminal Adapters

These internal card products are computer cards designed to plug into the internal bus of your computer. Such cards are made for the Industry Standard Architecture (ISA), MicroChannel (MCA), or Peripheral Component Interconnect (PCI). For now the ISA bus is so prevalent I'll limit this discussion to it for simplicity. The ideas expressed carry over to most of the other bus structures.

You've already seen some of the details of configuration so in this section you'll see some more ideas of how a product can use the fancy interfaces available with Windows 95.

US Robotics Sportster ISDN 128K

You plug this into an ISA bus machine and run through a configuration similar to the one previously described. It does not support V.120 but does support PPP and multilink PPP so you can use both B channels. It has a connection for analog phones, faxes and modems, but it does not provide ringer current. However, US Robotics has an optional device that will produce ringer current when attached to the card. Now for the good part—the user interface using Windows 95. Take a look at figure 8.17.

Fig. 8.17
The US Robotics ISDN 128K Main Application Window showing the initial connection ISDN has over the D channel in a graphical format.

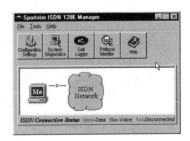

It's too bad you can't see this all in color. The lines representing connections are red and green and blue in various states. In any case, figure 8.16 indicates your ISDN connection is functioning properly. The D channel is always up, regardless of whether or not you're engaged in a call.

Now look at figure 8.18. This shows an ISDN data connection using two B channels. Notice the clear, graphical representation. And then look at figure 8.19 for a data call on one B channel and a voice call on the other. Wow!

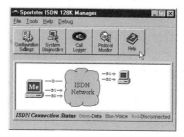

Fig. 8.18
An ISDN data connection using two B channels. Data transmission over the B channels is shown in blue.

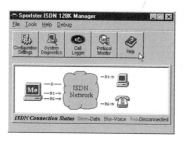

Fig. 8.19
An ISDN voice connection on one B channel is represented by a green line; the remaining B channel in blue carries data.

Getting Connected

Digi International DataFire

Digi International provides the DataFire ISDN board. This board, the USR Sportster ISDN 128K, and other boards are supported by MicroSoft's ISDN additions to Windows 95. These additions make installation and configuration of supported products very easy.

> **Note**
>
> Initially, there was some concern over the complexity of configuration and impenetrability of Digi International's documentation. The DataFire received a "Not Ready for Prime Time" rating as a result. Microsoft has ridden to Digi International's rescue with ISDN support for the DataFire built into Windows 95. This frees manufacturers such as Digi from problems surrounding creation of user interfaces and allows them to concentrate on making better products. As long as they write to Microsoft's interfaces, this will work for them, Microsoft, and you.

Here's all there is to installing the DataFire. First, take a look at the I/O addresses available for the card. Digi gives you the following options:

- 110h
- 140h
- 150h
- 300h
- 310h
- 340h
- 350h

> **Tip**
>
> An "H" or "h" after a number means the number is hexadecimal—base 16. You'll find a lot of hexadecimal numbering around computers.

Open the computer and plug the card in. The card's not really Plug and Play or software configurable. In other words, you have to do the work. If you've made a list of the I/O locations used on the machine, pick one for the DataFire that's not used elsewhere and set the card switch as described in the manual; the switch is on the top edge of the card and made for viewing and changing while the card is in place, but don't throw the switches while the juice is on.

You don't have a listing of the I/O locations already used? Go into Control Panel, select System, and then Device Manager and go through the various devices checking the Resources tab on each to see if any of the I/O addressing conflicts.

If this is too tedious, skip it and pick one of the DataFire selections. If you've got a conflict it'll show up on the Device Manager as an exclamation point in yellow over the DataFire card icon; then you can change the I/O on the DataFire Resources screen until you find one that works. Then turn off the computer and reset the switches on the card.

Go to Control Panel. Choose the Network icon to display the Network tabbed dialog box (see fig. 8.20).

In the Network tabbed dialog box, choose the Configuration tab and then select Adapter. The Select Network Component Type dialog box appears; choose Add. The Select Network Adapters dialog box appears (see fig. 8.21). Choose Digi International and the type of card from the list.

Fig. 8.20
Select the Network icon to start the process of installing the DataFire.

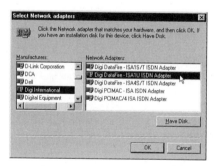

Fig. 8.21
The Select Network Adapters dialog box is where you select the DataFire adapter.

Close the various other dialog boxes and return to the Network tabbed dialog box where you can double-click the DigiDataFire to display the Properties sheet. Choose Resources and enter the I/O you set on the card. Then you'll be sent to the ISDN Configuration dialog box (see fig. 8.22). Here you can select Next and begin the process of switch selection (see fig. 8.23).

You'll finish with dialog boxes asking for directory numbers and SPIDs much like that shown in the Motorola BitSURFR example earlier. Then you simply go to the My Computer icon your desktop, double-click the My Computer icon, choose Dial-Up Networking, and the icon for the DataFire card. Enter your login name and password and choose Connect; then you're on your way (see fig. 8.24).

Fig. 8.22
This is the ISDN
Configuration
dialog box; choose
Next to continue.

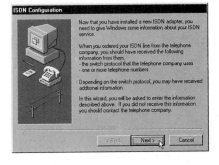

Fig. 8.23
Here are the
ISDN switch
types. Notice that
switches for North
America, Europe,
and Japan are
included.

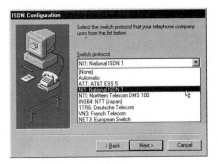

Fig. 8.24
Connecting to the
DataFire: Open My
Computer, select
Dial-Up Network-
ing, DataFire, and
then enter your
login name and
password and click
Connect.

Other ISDN Cards

Many ISDN cards are available. US Robotics also makes its I modem in a card
version. IBM offers the WaveRunner in ISA, Microchannel, and PCMCIA
form; both of these cards have chips on board that can be reprogrammed
with software to completely change the card's personality. They both can
handle V.120, PPP, MP, and function as analog fax and modem devices.
ISDN*Tek makes several cards from the very simple and inexpensive "Com-
muter Card" with a single B channel up through complex multi-channel
cards.

Routers for ISDN

While it may seem far afield to discuss LAN equipment in a book devoted to the general user of Internet and ISDN, it's really not. Think about a LAN connection for a minute. Ethernet offers a data rate of ten megabits. That's quite a lot more than are available through the serial or even the parallel port. And an Ethernet card today can be as cheap as US$50.00 or less!

Therefore, use a router to make your connection. There's little doubt this will give you a fast, if not the fastest, connection possible. However, routers currently cost anywhere from half again to twice as much as the other ways you may connect to ISDN. Those prices are dropping now, however.

Just what is a router? In a few words it's a device that senses traffic on a network and, when it sees traffic bound for a location other than your LAN, routes that traffic to the appropriate place over a wide area connection—ISDN. It's fast because you've already configured it to know what the network addresses are on your network are and what the addresses are on the other network(s) your want to connect with. When it sees those other addresses, it dials the number of the foreign network and passes the traffic.

Now here's where the magic of ISDN comes into play. Since ISDN has such a rapid set up and tear down, you don't need to be connected all the time if you have a fast router. It can connect, pass traffic, and disconnect so quickly you won't even know the line's not up all the time! Of course this requires careful configuration and coordination with your Internet service provider.

Although routers are becoming easier to set up, they're still more daunting by far than external devices or cards. Here are the names of several products and companies that offer routers appropriate for your consideration:

> ### Tip
>
> Remember, this is just a short list. Many more vendors are appearing every day. Check **http://www.alumni.caltech.edu/~dank/isdn** and **http://www.bryce.com/~bryce**.

- Cisco offers the 1003; this is a small router built to the specifications and configuration options of Cisco's larger routers. It's no picnic to configure, but if your company uses Cisco, it's certainly a major contender.

- Ascend provides the Pipeline 25 and 50; Ascend has the lion's share of the Internet service provider market for ISDN equipment. The small routers are fairly easy to set up and, in some versions, include features such as analog ports.

- Combinet offers several models such as the 2060; the most recent versions have software that configures through the Windows interface and finally brings ease of set up to the world of routers.

- 3Com offers some routers for small office and home use in its NetBuilder Line.

- Gandalf has the LANLine 5242I that sets up with DTMF (TouchTone) signals and Windows.

Which Is Best?

"Which is best?" you ask. After all you bought this book looking for THE answer. The answer is all types are good and will get you connected through ISDN. The serial port equipment is simple and inexpensive. The cards are more difficult to set up, but comparably priced. The routers are more expensive and difficult to set up, but often give the best performance. It's time to jump in. You already know in this industry, what you buy this year is seriously obsolete in a couple of years. The real question is: can it help me do what I want to do now and save or make enough money to pay for itself before I replace it. I suggest the answer is always yes for all these items.

CHAPTER 9

Setting Up a High-Speed Internet Connection

Now that you're sure you want to hop onto the Internet, you'll want to ensure you do it in the fastest way possible. After all, you'll never reach superhighway speeds if you're stuck at a traffic light. Fortunately, there are a lot of practical ways to get from here to there, for you and your company.

Getting up to speed on the Internet can be as simple as installing a 28.8 kbps modem; this will double your Internet access speed, if you've been using a standard 14.4 kbps modem. But there are ways to pump up your Internet performance even more. *Integrated Services Digital Network (ISDN)* technology was discussed in chapter 8 and is the most likely choice for many individual and organizational environments. In this chapter I'll cover high-speed methods other than ISDN; these include digital high-speed dedicated lines, such as T1 and T3 connections. The phone and cable companies are constantly improving the current technology and thinking about the future of telecommunications systems—all have a direct influence on your Internet performance.

> **Tip**
>
> Use a 28.8 kbps modem if you can. 14.4 kbps works pretty well. 9.6 kbps really makes you wait, and 2.4 kbps gives you time for lunch.

In this chapter, you learn the following:

- What the phone companies are doing to speed-up Internet access
- Low-cost ways to give your company high-speed Internet access
- Implementations for large organizations
- What will make up the future backbone of the nation's superhighway

Why a High-Speed Connection?

Once you've surfed on the Internet, you realize that there's a lot of information out there. If browsing is the fun part, then downloading demands extreme patience. And that's not the worst part. If you're connected at too slow a speed, you won't even be able to use the best Internet utilities out there, including some on the CD-ROM included with this book.

> **Caution**
>
> If you have less than a 14.4 kbps modem, you'll be disappointed when you use graphical browsers to access the Internet. These utilities—some of which are listed below—demand higher speed connections to handle the constant data transfers necessary to make them work.
>
> | | |
> |---|---|
> | WinWeb | Cello |
> | Mosaic | NETCOM NetCruiser |
> | Netscape | Pipeline |

> **Tip**
>
> Most, probably all, graphical browsers offer an option that turns off downloading of graphics. If you're using slower connections, and often even if you have a fast connection, you'll find turning graphics off helps you find what you want more quickly.

You'll be more productive and have more fun if you have a high-speed connection. Face it; all the really cool stuff for the Internet is only accessible through graphical front ends. Ask any computer pros, and they'll tell you not to run anything with the word graphical in it when connected to a slow modem. Don't misunderstand though; there are some graphical interfaces out there designed to connect at 14.4 kbps and work splendidly, but if you want to cruise in style, you'll need a high-speed connection.

> **Note**
>
> Keep these limited data rate issues in mind when you design hypertext for use over the World Wide Web. It's a good idea to provide a text only option button users can select. It's also helpful to include a text description of images that will appear when viewers have graphics turned off or use text-only browsers. Whatever you do, be sure the meaning of your message and the selections users will make are visible in a text-only browser.

Graphical Internet browsers like Mosaic allow you to see images on-screen, play videos, and listen to sounds. But those images, sounds, and videos are all located somewhere out on the Net, not on your computer. This means that to play these sounds and watch these videos, you must first transfer them to your computer, a sometimes time-consuming process.

▶ See "Planning Your Own WWW Home Pages," p. 597

Say you want to see an image of the Mona Lisa. When you click a button that says "View Mona Lisa," the image in digital format is crammed through your tiny phone lines until it's re-created on your desktop screen. You've swapped time to load for image detail.

> ### Tip
>
> You'll actually save money—if your time is worth anything—with a higher speed modem, ISDN, or the methods in this chapter. How long it takes to recoup your investment depends on how much you use the connection.

That image can be fairly large. You could be waiting several minutes before you see it if you use a 14.4 kbps modem. Just think of driving onto the ramp of an interstate highway and stepping on the accelerator; you want quick acceleration to highway speed, but your five horsepower car is so under powered it takes two minutes to get up to speed. That's the feeling you'll have if you try to view the Mona Lisa with an underpowered connection. Some interesting technology allows an image to be compressed on the host end and blasted to you faster, but it could still be annoying waiting for the image to appear.

Video presents a greater problem as the image is constantly changing. To run full screen, full motion video takes several megabits of data rate. Currently available compression and other techniques can achieve pretty good results with a single ISDN PRI. If you are willing to settle for some jerkiness, 3 BRI lines do a passable job. When you get down to a single BRI, the image is really only acceptable for desktop use. On the desktop, an image is scaled down to a tiny window on-screen and runs at a flickering rate of 10-15 frames per second. Even at this smaller scale, analog transmission is almost useless as a carrier.

II

Getting Connected

◀ See "Setting
Up an ISDN
Connection,"
p. 177

To lessen the effect of delays, and to enable an image to run at all in some cases, programs now compress the image file at the host end, download the file to your local hard disk, and then use your computer's processor to play it back. You're in for a delay, but at least you can do it. But why bother? If you really want performance, there are higher speed options.

When ISDN Basic Rate Interface Isn't Enough

Most small organizations in typical fields will probably be satisfied with the 128 kbps of an ISDN BRI line. If more capacity is needed, additional BRIs can be installed. Up to a point, this is an excellent strategy. Where is the point where adding BRIs isn't the best route? It all depends on the pricing for alternatives in your area. The two most logical alternatives are ISDN primary rate interface (PRI) and T carrier service.

ISDN Primary Rate Interface (PRI)

Chapter 8 dealt mostly with ISDN's basic rate interface, as that is the cheapest method of buying ISDN service. ISDN is also available in the form called primary rate interface (PRI). With PRI instead of the two B channels and one D channel of BRI, you get 23 B channels and an expanded 64 kbps D channel. Do the math and you get 23X64 kbps or nearly 1.5 megabits per second bandwidth. That's nearly as fast as expensive dedicated T1 speeds, and it can be a lot cheaper. Once you have a PRI installed, the next PRI you install at your location can have 24 B channels and no D channel; the D channel on your first PRI can control several additional PRIs—exactly how many lies with your local exchange carrier, tariffs, and switching equipment.

> **Caution**
>
> Well, it seems any time you go to a need for several B channels you should get a PRI. Not so fast. Ironically the pricing of PRI service is sometimes such that it pays you to install multiple BRIs rather than a PRI! Check costs carefully.

The Hitch in Switched-56

Two common technologies for wide-area internetworking are *Switched-56* and *Dedicated-56*. Switched-56 gets its name from its circuit switching technology and its 56 kbps speed.

Switched-56 is a good choice when you want a low-cost, moderate-speed connection that you don't need running all the time. Figure 9.1 shows the layout of a switched-56 system. That's because Switched-56 is a dial-up service. You only pay for what you use, and this is important as we move up the bandwidth scale to T1 and T3 connections discussed in a later section.

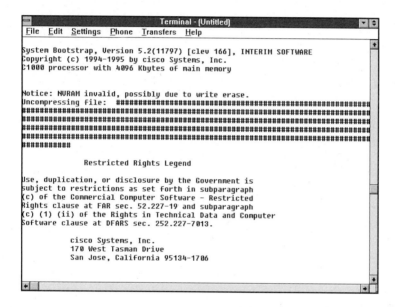

Fig. 9.1

A typical Switched-56 connection.

Dedicated-56 is the same as Switched-56, but it's not switched—it's dedicated. A dedicated line is always connected from one point to another. Both have the same start-up costs of between $700 and $900 for the phone company hook up, about $1,000 for the CSU/DSU, and well over $1,000 for a router for LAN connection. The price scale of routers varies widely depending on the functions needed.

Switched-56 and Dedicated-56 have limited bandwidth and should be used only if your requirements for the connection are light. If you spend more than two or three hours per day on a 56 kbps line, it's time to move up to ISDN.

Getting Connected

> **Caution**
>
> In reality Switched/Dedicated-56 is a dying technology—it's rapidly being killed by ISDN. Most of the time you'll find no economic reason to use Switched/Dedicated-56; in almost every case you'll find the costs several times the cost an ISDN BRI, and offers less than half the data rate and none of the sophistication of D channel control.

Switched/Dedicated-56 also has another problem. It relies on analog/digital switches that are becoming archaic, making it generally more expensive than ISDN. The phone company plans on phasing out this technology in favor of ISDN. Of course the income per line will be less, but the number of ISDN lines will be many times that of Switched/Dedicated-56. ISDN will retain compatibility with 56 kbps connections, albeit at the slower 56 kbps rate.

Like all high-speed connections, to set up a Switched-56 or a Dedicated-56 connection, you must contract with your phone company or your Internet provider. Internet providers typically charge around $125 per month for dial-up service, and $400 a month for dedicated service. Initial hook-up rates are around $1,200 if you already have the router and CSU, and $3,400 if you don't.

Frame Relay

Frame relay is based on a good deal of the work that went into ISDN, yet frame relay is expanding wildly outside the auspices of ISDN development.

Recent reports show frame relay use jumping from about 1,500 sites to over 5,000 from the first of 1994 to the first of 1995; later reports support a similar upward trend. This is a huge leap and shows the value of frame relay in providing a way to take existing communications needs and merging them into a more economical form.

Frame Relay and X.25

So what's frame relay? In a few words, it's a major improvement in the way packet switching has been done under X.25. The difference becomes clear when you realize frame relay is packet switching with most of the overhead removed.

> **Tip**
>
> Frame your questions and set up a relay to **http://cell-relay.indiana.edu** to find out about the Frame Relay Forum.

First off, frame relay eliminates a whole layer of the ISO OSI model. That'll save you tons of cost and time sending your packets around. Take a look at figure 9.2. This shows the three layers required by X.25.

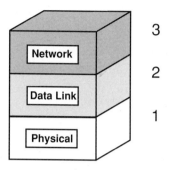

X.25

Fig. 9.2
X.25 layers.

Now look at figure 9.3. There are only two layers used in the frame relay structure, Physical and Data Link. This means that considerably less processing is used along the way from frame handler to frame handler throughout the network. This means reduced time and cost.

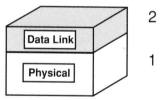

Frame Relay

Fig. 9.3
Frame relay layers.

How Frame Relay Works

How can frame relay throw away a whole layer and still take care of the job? To answer that, let's look at what goes on with X.25. In layer three the protocol handles a number of questions:

- Is this a data packet?
- Is the connection active?
- Have I received a valid layer three acknowledgment?
- What is the next expected sequence number, and does the packet I just received have that number?

If all of these questions are answered yes, an acknowledgment is sent back. If any are answered no, error recovery is undertaken. Here's what happens at layer two:

- Is this a valid frame?
- Is this an information frame?
- Have I received a valid acknowledgment?
- Move window to accommodate information.
- Are all frames acknowledged? If no, restart timer and see if window fits. If yes, request retransmission. If no, recover from error.
- Send acknowledgment of layer two.

If the answer to any of these is no, another error is created at layer two.

> **Tip**
>
> Don't spend your day trying to figure out all of what is going on here. Just notice that there are acknowledgments, connections, and sequence numbers passing through the process.

Here's what goes on in frame relay (see fig. 9.3). Since there is no layer three, "all" of this is at layer two:

- Is this a valid frame?
- Does it use a known data link connection identifier?

That's it. While X.25 requires at least ten frame processing steps across two separate layers, frame relay does the job in two steps within a single layer. Moreover, it's done without acknowledgments or sequence numbers. Frame relay recognizes that its transport will most likely be through a reliable digital network and risks problems that were expected to be remedied by acknowledgments and sequence numbers in X.25.

> **Note**
>
> Is there a risk in using frame relay since it seems to do away with all the protections built into X.25? Not really. Any higher layer protocol you might be using with frame relay will catch what frame relay misses. The real problem might be a substantially diminished performance, contrasted with X.25 in the case of truly poor or noisy conditions. But then our assumptions are that you'll be using frame relay over clean digital circuits.

As a general rule, frame relay runs at from 56/64 kbps up to 512 kbps. It's capable of running at much higher data rates. The data field size is dependent on vendor; the maximum is 4,096 bytes. Since frame relay has a variable data field contrasted with the fixed field of 48 bytes in ATM, as I'll describe below, it has a low overhead compared to ATM.

Frame Relay doesn't compete with Switched-56 or Dedicated-56, nor does it replace high-speed leased lines in general. Instead, frame relay is a protocol that is typically used over high-speed lines; it replaces the older standard, X.25. It allows the large bandwidth of a leased line to be split up into dynamic channels. With dynamic channels, frame relay is able to use all of the bandwidth available from the entire frame relay connection. With the old technology, expensive multiplexers are used to split up the bandwidth into fixed channels. Fixed channels only guarantee that you'll have the bandwidth from one available channel at a time.

Mulitplexers aren't suitable for current technologies such as video conferencing. Frame relay allows the entire bandwidth to be split up into whatever is needed at the moment. This is especially important when Internet connections, video conferencing, and other technologies are used simultaneously. Because frame relay only gives each channel what it needs, it's an elegant cost-effective solution.

The older X.25 standard was used for remote terminal access. The standard doesn't operate well in the high-speed Internet world because X.25 doesn't support the Internet protocol (TCP/IP) well over wide-area networks. Frame relay, on the other hand, is far more intelligent when it comes to purely digital data. Frame relay routers assume that there are no errors in the transmission, and blasts them along to their proper destination. There's no worrying about the possibility that a blip in an analog transmission might slip by.

Connecting with frame relay gives larger organizations a scaleable solution to Internet access. Once again, you connect to the Internet by going through a service provider, such as NETCOM On-Line Communication services.

To implement frame relay, your organization will have to replace its current set of routers and bridges with frame relay-compatible equipment. Frame relay is an excellent solution to the growing problem of not enough bandwidth. It's a significant investment—consult your Internet provider, your information systems department, and the phone company before making this leap.

> **Tip**
>
> Many hardware suppliers are making their equipment modular so you change among frame relay, ISDN, analog, X.25, etc., with minimum expense, while retaining most of your investment. This modularity is worth it to you.

Ironically, as telephone companies install ATM to carry more and more traffic, frame relay will be carried over ATM. The two methods do not conflict; they're complimentary.

T-Carrier Connections

As the telephone system evolved into digital transmission, the industry developed a system of multiplexing information called *T-carrier*. The "T" designations correspond to digital signal (DS) nomenclature as shown in table 9.1.

Table 9.1 T-Carrier System			
T Carrier	**DS Level**	**Data Rate**	**Voice Channels**
T1	DS 1	1.544 Mbps	24
T1C	DS 2	3.152 Mbps	48
T2	DS 2	6.312 Mbps	96
T3	DS 3	44.736 Mbps	672
T4	DS 4	274.176 Mbps	4032

The T1 and T3 lines are generally available to organizations. T1s and T3s handle all kinds of transmissions—voice, fax, video, or data. These lines are also the most costly of the available connections.

Basically, T1 is the all-digital backbone of the telephone infrastructure. It was originally meant to carry voice transmissions from central office to central office, or to connect the phone company's many central offices (COs). T1s are used for connection of telephone customer sites and for high-speed Internet connections.

T1s use *Time Division Multiplexing (TDM)* and Pulse Code Modulation. Based on the research and mathematics developed by H. Nyquist, TDM allows the capacity of the T1 line to be divided up into 64 channels. The Nyquist rule states that it is possible to re-create analog signals—voice, for example—on a digital line. It requires that the sampling rate of the analog signal be twice the highest analog frequency. For voice transmission, the highest frequency carried is 4000 Hertz; therefore, 8000 samples per second are taken. There are 24-total channels on a T1, and each is multiplexed—or divided up—so that each channel carries one sample at any one time.

Pulse Code Modulation is the method used to convert analog samples into digital format. PCM calls for the sample size to be exactly 8 bits. PCM and TDM work together to provide 64,000 bits of bandwidth to each channel, or 8 bits multiplied by 8,000 samples per second equals 64,000 bits per second. Taken together, each T1 connection can have 1.544 megabits per second of bandwidth. Like ISDN, however, some signaling packets are used, bringing the overall transmission bandwidth down to 1.536 megabits per second. This true bandwidth is known as the DS-1, or Digital Signal 1.

T1s are commonly used as the backbone technology in large organization WANs. The T1 line is a physical connection, meaning that the phone company has to come in and physically provide you with the service. The phone company typically connects the T1 directly to your organization's PBX. This is accomplished through a network interface unit connected to the T1, the channel service unit (CSU), the channel bank, and the PBX.

To create an Internet connection, you must arrange all of the details of your connection with a service provider. Most providers will furnish you with all the equipment you need, such as a router and a digital service unit (DSU). Some routers have DSUs built in. This allows the Internet connection to feed directly into your local-area network. In most cases, Internet providers make all the arrangements for you, and you never have to deal with the phone company directly.

Tip

Choose routers that have built-in, modular DSUs. They are more manageable, and it's easier to get support on one unit from a single company; and you can change them as your needs change.

What this means to you is that you'll have the highest-speed Internet connection available. You'll have plenty of bandwidth so that your organization's Internet server won't tax your T1. All that's necessary now is to load the software to allow transport to take place.

The Highest of High-Speed Connections

High-Speed doesn't end with T1. In fact, the T-carrier system extends to T3 and beyond. As you move higher in number up the T-carrier chain, you get faster speeds. For example, T3 lines can pump your data at a rate of about 44.8 Mbps—the capacity of 28 T1 lines.

The main difference between T1 and T3 is that T3 lines require higher bandwidth lines to transport the data at nearly 44.8 Mbps. While T1 typically uses twisted-pair wires, T3 uses fiber-optic cables, digital microwaves, and coaxial cables.

The Internet on Cable TV, Dishes, Power Lines, and Pipes?

The future of Internet high-speed connections is not clear. For the first time, the telephone companies face a challenge from a totally different kind of competitor—cable TV. The telephone companies themselves have been trying to purchase large stakes in the big cable companies. Cable has a lot to offer, including huge penetration into residential areas. The cable itself can handle throughput of about 500 Mbps—that's significantly greater than the twisted pair wires currently coming into your home through phone lines.

The fact that the same cable that brings Showtime into your home may also be your telephone wire is all part of the convergence of computer and telephone technology, *computer telephony integration (CTI)*. Sooner or later your notebook computer, your TV, and your telephone will be tethered by the same cord. Currently, various cable hookup technologies are being tested for Internet access. This is part of the development of a set-top box that is expected to broker communications to your home and business in competition with the telephone company.

Other developments promise more competition. This means more function, higher data rates and lower prices for you. Look for wireless delivery methods including cellular, microwave, and satellite. And don't be surprised if your electric power company, gas company, and water company offer Internet and other communications links using their rights of way, cables, and pipes.

And now for something completely different. AT&T, Motorola, and others have perfected and are beginning to deliver the following acronyms:

- ADSL
- HDSL
- SDSL

This industry is really about selling alphabet soup, but I'll clue you in on what this all means. *Asymmetric digital subscriber line (ADSL)*, *high bit-rate digital subscriber line (HDSL)*, and *symmetric digital subscriber line (SDSL)* all refer to a new technology that delivers data rates of as much as 8 Mbps over a single twisted pair to your house or business. Wow! What's this do to ISDN? We don't know yet, but it could be a boon for using existing twisted pair to deliver multi-megabit data rates almost anywhere.

ADSL is asymmetric in providing much higher data rate from the upstream location (the Internet for our interests) to you than you deliver back. So since most of the time you're downloading files or Web pages, this may be your best bet. SDSL provides the same data rate in both directions and can co-exist with ISDN on the same pair. HDSL takes two pair and gives T1 (or E1) without repeaters over distances that have required repeaters in the past.

Tip

For more info on *DSL line up with **http://www.sbexpos.com/sbexpos/association/adsl/home.html**, **http://www.alumni.caltech/~dank/isdn**, and **http://www.bryce.com/~bryce**.

SONET and ATM

If the telephone companies don't buy into cable TV, or if the regulators don't let them, they've got some interesting alternatives. As it becomes clear that the T-carrier system cannot provide the bandwidth necessary for today's Internet infrastructure, the phone company is grooming SONET as the replacement for the nation's telecommunications backbone.

SONET stands for *Synchronous Optical Network*. It's just a fancy term for an all fiber-optic transport that once and for all rids the nation of slow copper-wire links. Besides super-fast speeds, SONET has the claim to fame that it can run almost all of the current and planned network capabilities, such as broadband ISDN, Asynchronous Transfer Mode (ATM), Switched Multimegabit data services (SMDS), and Fiber distributed data interface (FDDI).

II

Getting Connected

ATM seems like it will be the choice protocol to run over SONET. ATM is a cell relay protocol that uses extremely small 53-byte cells to transport data. Small cells are important as they better handle the bursts and flows that are common in wide-area networks. ATM is probably the only protocol that will allow entire gigabit cinema movies to be transported over the nation's wires. But that's a completely different story.

SONET comes in several implementations, like the T-carrier system. The first is called OC-1 (optical carrier). It can deliver speeds of up to 51.84 Mbps, or 28 DS-1 links. Most of the interest today is in OC-3, which can deliver 155.52 Mbps, the equivalent of 84 T1 connections. That's a lot of bandwidth. But it doesn't stop there. SONET has capabilities that extend it well into the billion-bit-per-second range—or gigabits per second. Figure 9.4 shows how all these technologies fit together.

While there are no plans to sell this technology directly to organizations, it has a large impact on wide-area networking and the Internet.

Fig. 9.4

The Big Picture of everything packed into ATM and then into SONET.

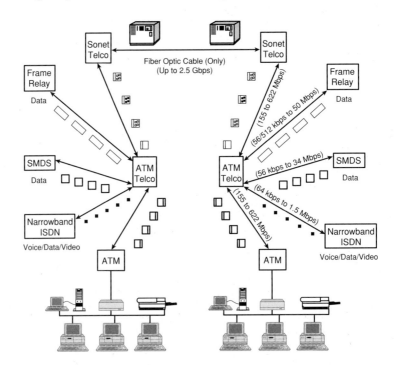

Digital Dilemmas: Which Type Do I Need?

You know all about the various possible connections to the Internet; now you need to know which one is right for you. Unfortunately, there's no easy answer. It depends largely on how much you're willing to spend. If you're a small accounting firm that wants to use the Internet for e-mail, you certainly don't want to waste money on a T1 connection. You'll never recoup the investment. But if you're thinking about whether to go with ISDN or Switched-56, that's a much tougher question. See table 9.2 for some suggestions here.

Table 9.2   Choosing Your Connection Technology

Hours Use per Person per Day	Number of Users	Connections to Consider	Best Bet
0–1	1	BRI, 14.4/28.8 modem	Modem
1–2	1–2	BRI, 14.4/28.8 modem	BRI
2–3	2–10	BRI, Switched–56	BRI
3–5	10–15	BRI, Dedicated–56	BRI
3–5	15–40	PRI, T1, Frame Relay	PRI, FR
3–5	40+	PRI, T1, Frame Relay	PRI, FR
3–5+	100+	PRIs, T1s, T3	T3 (PRI, FR?)

Note

Your mileage will vary, so be careful when choosing an Internet provider. Think about growth in your Internet usage. The wrong investment in hardware can set you back thousands of dollars; consider modular equipment that can be incrementally upgraded. Plan carefully, and consult your Internet provider.

The Cost of Being on the Internet

Your Internet connection doesn't always end with getting your organization on the Internet. You'll often want to let others access your network. This could involve setting up FTP or Telnet access, or creating your own World Wide Web (WWW) home page. If you want your organization to have a

II

Getting Connected

presence on the Internet, you'll need to consider how that affects your bandwidth. Each user who accesses your network is going to nibble away at your available bandwidth.

If you think estimating your own bandwidth need is tough, just imagine estimating everyone else's needs. There will be people accessing your data for business use, personal use, or even by accident. There's no mathematical formula for estimating the connection space that these people will take up—you'll have to make educated guesses and play it by ear.

Connecting Through CompuServe

10

If you're a CompuServe user, one of the easiest ways to connect to the Internet may be through the service you're already using. While CompuServe doesn't provide full Internet access—at least, not yet—its CompuServe Information Manager for Windows (WinCIM) software offers a clean, easy-to-use interface for accessing Internet e-mail, newsgroups, file transfer protocol, Telnet, the World Wide Web, and, soon, Gopher.

While CompuServe isn't the only consumer online service that offers Internet access—rivals America Online, Prodigy, GEnie, and Delphi offer full or partial Internet gateways, too—CompuServe is a good choice if you're looking for a single online service that gives you access to the free stuff available on the Internet, as well as the universe of information for which you have to pay. With over 3.5 million members worldwide, more than 2,000 databases, online shopping and brokerage services, and communications links to practically every other online network, CompuServe is arguably the most complete online service available to consumers today. While CompuServe costs more than its competitors, many business owners and professionals consider it well worth the price to tap into the thousands of news, business, and financial databases CompuServe has to offer. This chapter will show you how to use WinCIM 2.0.1 to access Internet e-mail, newsgroups, and files. You'll also get a glimpse of what CompuServe has in store for the future.

In this chapter, you learn the following:

- What sets CompuServe apart from other online services
- How to use WinCIM to send and retrieve Internet e-mail
- How to use WinCIM as a UseNet newsreader
- How to use WinCIM to retrieve files from other Internet-connected computers (FTP)

- How to use WinCIM to Telnet to other Internet-connected computers
- How to access the World Wide Web through your CompuServe account
- The future of CompuServe's Internet gateway

An Introduction to CompuServe

Of the five major commercial online services, CompuServe is clearly the top choice for business users, especially those who want to network with colleagues and customers worldwide. CompuServe boasts 2.3 million subscribers in the United States and Canada, 900,000 subscribers in the Pacific Rim, 450,000 in Europe, with a few more scattered throughout the rest of the world. CompuServe supports direct dial-up nodes in 40 countries and provides access to over 150 more countries through other networks. Accessing the Internet through CompuServe gives users a chance to expand the international advantage they enjoy already.

An Overview of CompuServe and Its Pricing

CompuServe Information Service is the World Trade Center of the online world. Founded in 1979 and currently owned by H&R Block, CompuServe is an information treasure chest that doubles as one of the world's busiest online communications hubs. The service offers access to more than 2,000 databases, including newspaper and magazine libraries, online editions of publications such as *U.S. News & World Report*, stock market and financial data, an online stock brokerage, a shopping mall and travel agency, plus communications links with the Internet, MCI Mail, AT&TMail, the NetWare MHS Local Area Network, and fax and Telex machines around the world. CompuServe's Executive News Service lets subscribers "clip" news stories from a wide range of news wires.

In addition to the standard online staples of news, weather, sports, and computer games, CompuServe offers hundreds of special-interest bulletin boards called *forums* where its 3.5 million members gather to discuss everything from quilt-making to fantasy baseball to computer programming, and to download free and low-cost software. CompuServe's forums also provide free technical support for many major hardware and software vendors, and its CB Simulator chat area provides a forum for real-time conversations among CompuServe members worldwide.

Recently, CompuServe has moved to bring its pricing more in line with the rest of the online pack by introducing a $9.95-a-month flat-fee plan that includes five hours a month access to forums, mail, and Internet utilities, and unlimited access to 70 of its basic members services. There is an additional charge of $2.95 for each hour you spend on the service after the first five. Though CompuServe still charges by the hour for accessing premium services, the service recently slashed forum rates for flat-fee subscribers to a more affordable $2.95 an hour. The hourly charge is no longer dependent upon the baud rate at which you connect to the service.

About CompuServe Information Manager for Windows (WinCIM 2.0.1)

A few years ago CompuServe created a new interface called CompuServe Information Manager (CIM), a graphical front-end program that makes the service much easier to navigate, allowing subscribers to click icons and pull down boxes and other on-screen options with a mouse, instead of typing hard-to-remember commands at the system prompt. WinCIM 2.0.1, shown in figure 10.1, also lets you compose mail and set up file transfers before logging on, saving time and money. To access the program through Windows 95, open the Start menu, select the Programs option, then the CompuServe folder and choose the CompuServe Information Manager entry.

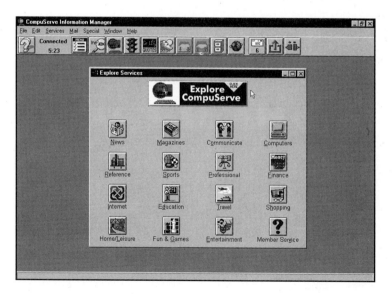

Fig. 10.1
WinCIM 2.0.1's Explore Services screen lets you navigate the service by clicking graphical icons.

II

Getting Connected

WinCIM 2.0.1, the Windows version of CompuServe Information Manager, offers a graphical welcome screen that lets you click icons that automatically log you onto the service and transport you to popular areas such as Computers, News, Reference, Finance, Education, Sports, Shopping, Fun & Games, and the Internet. It also sports a Session Settings window that stores your I.D.

and password so you don't have to type it in every time you log on; the Favorite Places window, which can take you to your favorite forum or database with the click of a mouse; and an offline text editor that lets you create messages to be sent later. You can also use WinCIM 2.0.1's Mail feature to retrieve your mail, ship off any messages you've typed offline, and log you off once the job is done. The program also includes an Address Book, In Basket, Out Basket, Filing Cabinet, and other handy desktop features.

> **Note**
>
> CompuServe is expected to release a Windows 95 version of the CompuServe Information Manager in 1996.

The toolbar that runs across the top of the screen, as shown in figure 10.2, lets you click icons to access Favorite Places, the Go command, the Find command, Weather, Stock Quotes, the Filing Cabinet, and other popular destinations pictured in figure 10.1. You also can click an icon to disconnect from the service and exit the program. In addition, WinCIM 2.0.1 features a *toolbox*—a floating palette of icons—that makes it easier to post messages, download files, and engage in real-time conference sessions on CompuServe's bulletin boards, Executive News Service, and CB Simulator. Click the picture of a hand holding a pen, for example, and a template appears that lets you create a bulletin-board message.

Fig. 10.2
The new WinCIM toolbar makes it easier to access both the message and library sections of a forum.

> **Note**
>
> If you are a regular CompuServe user, you should purchase a copy of *Special Edition Using CompuServe* from Que. This book covers all of the CompuServe features and WinCIM in detail.

CompuServe's Internet Gateway

Spurred by the Internet's phenomenal growth, CompuServe has begun offering its users expanded access to the network, which, until the summer of 1994, consisted solely of e-mail access to the network. As a result, you can now access UseNet newsgroups directly through CompuServe without opening an account with an Internet access provider. You can also read and post newsgroup messages either through text-based menus or through WinCIM 2.0.1.

The recently released 2.0.1 version of WinCIM, developed by CompuServe with the assistance of Spry, provides all CompuServe members with access to many of the most used features of the Internet. CompuServe added file transfer protocol (FTP) capability and a link to the Internet's popular World Wide Web and Gopher servers. The company's Network Services Division offers business customers high-speed dedicated Internet and Internet Protocol access via its FRAME-Net frame relay service, as well as asynchronous access via point-to-point protocol (PPP) for dial-up sessions.

The following is a rundown of CompuServe's current Internet offerings:

- *E-mail*—CompuServe Mail lets you swap messages and files with other CompuServe members, as well as with users of other online networks, such as MCI Mail, AT&TMAIL, and Internet.
- *Mailing Lists*—Through CompuServe Mail, you can sign up for any of the thousands of mailing lists, or e-mail discussion groups, that the Internet has to offer.
- *UseNet Newsgroups*—CompuServe lets you access the full spectrum of UseNet newsgroups through its graphical WinCIM interface or a text-based terminal emulation mode.
- *FTP*—Through CompuServe's FTP client you can access files all across the Internet. You can download shareware programs from all around the world. You can also upload important information to associates in just minutes.
- *World Wide Web*—With the advent of the CompuServe NetLauncher program the World Wide Web became available to all CompuServe members. You can access Web sites all across the globe, retrieving needed information while sitting at your computer. The Web browser also allows you access Gopher and FTP sites.
- *Telnet*—With the introduction of the ability to Telnet from CompuServe to other computers on the Internet, members can easily check their other systems without making multiple calls.

Using Internet E-Mail

With CompuServe's e-mail gateway, you can quickly and easily send e-mail messages to friends, colleagues, and customers all over the world. You also can send ASCII text files.

Using WinCIM to Send E-Mail Messages

Suppose you have an account on CompuServe, but your colleague in California has an account with an Internet access provider, say, Netcom.

To send your colleague a message, follow these steps:

1. Open the Mail menu and choose Create Mail. Type your colleague's first and last name in the Name text box in the Recipient List dialog box (see fig. 10.3).

2. Tab to the Address or User ID box and type your colleague's Internet address. WinCIM 2.0.1 does not require you to type **INTERNET:** before the recipient's Internet address and domain, unlike the previous versions of the software.

3. Tab to the Address Type drop-down list and select Internet. If you are sending a message to one of the other systems listed, you need to select the corresponding option.

Fig. 10.3
WinCIM 2.0.1's Recipient List dialog box lets you address Internet e-mail messages automatically.

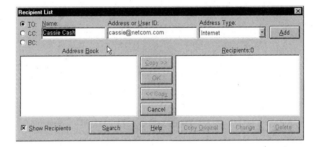

4. Click the Add button or press the Enter key. Then click OK. This brings up a Create Mail window.

> **Tip**
>
> If the individual that you are sending your message to is already listed in the address book window, you can click the Copy>> button to automatically add it to the Recipient List. If the address that you are entering is new, you can use the <<Copy button to automatically add it to the address book for future use.

5. Type the subject of your message at the Subject prompt.

6. Tab to the message blank and type your message.

7. Click Send Now to log onto CompuServe and send it right away, or click Out-Basket to send it later. Other options include File It, Cancel, and Options.

> **Tip**
>
> To send an ASCII (text) file using WinCIM 2.0.1, follow the steps outlined above, except instead of choosing Create Mail in step 1, choose Send File from the Mail menu. This process sends the text file as a standard message. It does not send the file as an attachment.

Using WinCIM's Address Book to Store E-Mail Addresses

If you're planning to send e-mail to colleagues on a regular basis, it's a good idea to enter their names in WinCIM 2.0.1's Address Book. That way, you won't have to root around for their e-mail addresses every time you want to send them a note. The following steps take you through this procedure.

1. Open the Mail menu and choose Address Book (see fig. 10.4). Click the Add button, or press Ctrl+A, to add a name and address to the list.

Fig. 10.4
WinCIM 2.0.1's Address Book stores both CompuServe and Internet addresses for future reference, making addressing messages quick and easy.

2. Type your colleague's first and last names at the Name prompt—for example, Cassie Cash.

3. Tab to the Address or User ID prompt and type her e-mail address—for example, cassie@netcom.com. Then select Internet from the Address Type list.

4. Tab to the Comments prompt and enter any additional information you wish, such as her fax number, postal address, birthday, or children's names. Click the OK button to store the entry, or press Enter. Should your colleague switch his or her Internet account, you can use the Change button to edit the Address Book entry.

5. The next time you want to send Ms. Cash a message, simply open the Mail menu and choose Create Mail, and then select her name from the Address Book. The program fills in her name and e-mail address automatically.

II

Getting Connected

> **Tip**
>
> WinCIM 2.0.1 also lets you "capture" e-mail addresses from any e-mail message that you receive and save them for future reference. Just click the From box and choose OK. The person's name and e-mail address is stored automatically in your Address Book.

Joining Internet Mailing Lists

▶ See "Subscribing to and Unsubscribing from LISTSERV Mailing Lists," p. 421

With WinCIM 2.0.1, joining an Internet mailing list is no harder than using Internet e-mail. Say, for example, that you want to subscribe to com-priv, the mailing list devoted to discussing topics related to the commercialization and privatization of the Internet. (Be aware, however, that signup instructions for mailing lists vary depending on the type of mailing list software the list uses.)

> **Note**
>
> Many mailing lists are stored on machines devoted to the dispersal of mail. These machines are often referred to as List Servers. In some instances you will address your original subscription to **listserv@**_domain.name_, rather than the actual name of the mailing list as shown in the following section. In these instances you will type **subscribe** in the Subject field of your message, and **SUBSCRIBE** _listname Firstname Lastname_ in the body of your message. In this example you would replace _listname_ with the name of the actual list, _firstname_ with your first name, and _lastname_ with your last name. For example:
>
> SUBSCRIBE Greyhound-L Cassie Cash
>
> ListServ is not the only type of mailing list software that is available to run mailing lists. There are systems that use Majordomo and Listproc systems. You will find a more detailed discussion of the various types of mailing lists in chapter 18, "Using Internet Mailing Lists." As this chapter will show, there are many ways to both subscribe to and unsubscribe from mailing lists.

Subscribing to (and Unsubscribing from) a Mailing List

To use WinCIM to join the com-priv list, follow these steps:

1. Open the Mail menu and choose Create Mail, and then type **com-priv** at the Name prompt.

2. Tab to the Address or User ID prompt and type **com-priv-request@psi.com**, then select Internet from the Address Type list box.

3. Click the <u>A</u>dd button, or press the Enter key. Then click OK.

4. Type **subscribe** at the Subject prompt.

5. Tab to the message blank and type the command **SUBSCRIBE**, followed by your name—for example, SUBSCRIBE Cassie Cash (see fig. 10.5).

Tip

On many mailing lists you have to type **SUBSCRIBE** in all capital letters when it is in the body of your message. On other systems, you do not need to worry about the case of your commands.

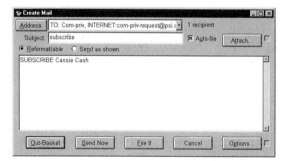

Fig. 10.5
With WinCIM 2.0.1, subscribing to a mailing list is no harder than sending an e-mail message.

Note

On many lists that you may use, you will be asked to return a confirmation message to allow the list to double-check your mail address. Most of these messages must be returned within a specified amount of time or your request will be canceled. After subscribing to a mailing list, check your mail frequently to make sure that you do not miss any confirmation message deadlines.

---

6. Click <u>S</u>end Now to log onto CompuServe and send it right away, or click the <u>O</u>ut-Basket to send it later.

7. To quit the list, follow the same steps and send a message to the same address containing the command **UNSUBSCRIBE**, followed by your name—for example, UNSUBSCRIBE Rob Bixby.

II

Getting Connected

Tip

Unless you fill in the Name and Subject prompts, WinCIM 2.0.1 won't send your message. The Add, Send Now, File It, and Out-Basket buttons are disabled (grayed out) until you fill in those blanks.

Note

Some of the more active Internet mailing lists generate several hundred e-mail messages a day. Because CompuServe charges 15 cents for every Internet message you receive, you can end up burning a hole in your wallet—fast! That's why, if you become an avid mailing list subscriber, it may pay off to sign up for mailing lists through an Internet access provider that charges a flat monthly fee—say, $15 to $20 a month—that allows you to receive an unlimited quantity of Internet e-mail at no extra charge. There are many local Internet service providers across the country that provide this service. Look in your Yellow Pages under Computers, or call your local University Extension to find out about the possible ways to get access to the Internet.

Posting to a Mailing List

You can also use WinCIM 2.0.1 to post a message on an Internet mailing list.

To do this on com-priv, follow these steps:

1. Open the Mail menu and choose Create Mail, and then type **com-priv** at the Name prompt.
2. Tab to the Address or User Name prompt and type **com-priv@psi.com**. Then select Internet from the Address Type list.
3. Click the Add button, or press the Enter key. Then click OK.
4. Type the subject of your message at the Subject prompt.
5. Tab to the message blank and type your message. A copy is then forwarded to every subscriber's e-mail box.
6. Click Send Now to log onto CompuServe and send it right away, or click the Out-Basket to send it later.

Participating in UseNet Newsgroups

CompuServe's newsreader interface isn't jazzy—no cute, little icons here!—but it's clean, fast, and functional, and gets the job done with minimal fuss. It also includes handy features such as quotation (for replying to articles), holding (for reading articles later), ignoring (by subject and/or author), and the ability to create signature files. CompuServe lets you choose between the graphical WinCIM interface or text-based terminal emulation mode—both of which are easy to use. Like CompuServe's forums, access to newsgroups incurs connect time charges, so your bills can run up if you become a newsgroup groupie! For more details on UseNet newsgroups and how to participate, see chapter 30, "How UseNet Works."

▶ See "How UseNet Works," p. 749

Accessing Newsgroups Through WinCIM

WinCIM 2.0.1's full-featured newsreader lets you do practically everything that stand-alone programs can do. With just a click of your mouse, you can subscribe to newsgroups, read newsgroup messages, and post newsgroup articles of your own.

Subscribing to Newsgroups

To subscribe to newsgroups through WinCIM 2.0.1, follow these steps:

1. Open the Services menu and choose Go; or select the Go icon from the toolbar. Type **USENET** at the prompt and select OK. You can also select the Internet tool from the Select dialog window, then the Discussion Groups (USENET) button from the Internet screen.

2. Select USENET Newsreader (CIM) from the menu. Double-click the newsgroup, or click it once and press Select.

> **Note**
>
> If this is your first time using the UseNet newsgroups through CompuServe you will receive a disclaimer message that you must read before you can enter the Newsgroup area. CompuServe will also ask you to read an article on Netiquette before proceeding into the Newsgroup area.

3. A window appears, then select Subscribe to Newsgroups from the menu. Double-click it, or press Enter.

4. To browse for newsgroups, double-click a newsgroup category, or select it and then press Enter (see fig. 10.6).

   You can also subscribe to newsgroups by name (just select the Subscribe By Name button and type the name of the newsgroup you want to join) or search for newsgroups of interest by typing a topic at the Keyword prompt and then selecting the Search command.

II

Getting Connected

Fig. 10.6
WinCIM 2.0.1 lets you subscribe to newsgroups by browsing a list of categories, then selecting the groups you want.

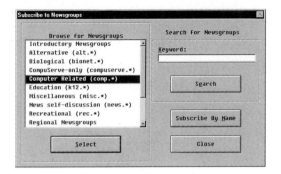

5. A window appears with a listing of newsgroups. To subscribe to a newsgroup, click the box next to the newsgroup's name. Then click Subscribe, or tab to Subscribe and press the Enter key. You can preview newsgroups by selecting the Preview button.

Troubleshooting

I can't find what I am looking for.

If you're browsing through the newsgroup list but can't seem to find what you're looking for, don't blame your eyes. CompuServe purposely makes certain that controversial newsgroups, such as the majority of the alt.sex hierarchy, are difficult to find by not listing them in its browser. However, you can still subscribe to any newsgroup you like by typing in its name.

Reading Newsgroup Messages

After you subscribe to the newsgroups that interest you, you can begin reading the messages, or articles, that are posted to the groups by other Internet users.

To read these messages, follow these steps:

1. Open the Services menu and choose Go; or select the Go icon from the toolbar. Type **USENET** at the prompt and select OK.

2. Select USENET News reader (CIM) from the menu. Double-click it, or press Enter.

3. Select Access Your USENET Newsgroups from the menu. Double-click it, or press the Enter key.

4. Select a newsgroup.

5. To browse the newsgroup, double-click it, or highlight it and then press the Enter key.

6. To read an article posted to the newsgroup, double-click it, or highlight the article and then tab to <u>G</u>et and press the Enter key. The buttons below the article let you Hold the message to reread later, reply to it via private e-mail or a public posting to the newsgroup, forward it to another Internet user or newsgroup, or access More options such as the <u>C</u>reate command, which lets you post an article on a new topic to the group (see fig. 10.7).

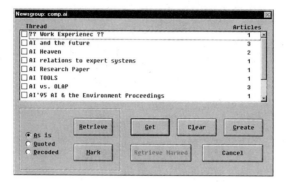

Fig. 10.7
With WinCIM 2.0.1, you can read a newsgroup article now, hold it to read later, reply to it via private e-mail, and more.

Getting Connected

Note

If you want to save a newsgroup message as a file on your hard drive, simply open the <u>M</u>ore menu and choose <u>R</u>etrieve. Then click OK in the Save As dialog box. The file will be stored in your CompuServe Download directory.

You can also save a message directly from your Browse window by clicking the <u>R</u>etrieve button, providing a name for the message, and saving it to your download directory.

Troubleshooting

I can't locate a posting that I have looked at before.

Occasionally, you may want to go back and re-read a posting that you glanced at the day before—only to find that it has disappeared. That's because the WinCIM newsreader, like many other newsreader programs, considers a posting to be "new" only until it is read. To save articles as "new," click the <u>H</u>old button or press the H key from the newsgroup dialog box containing the article you want to re-read.

Posting Newsgroup Articles

After you have a chance to read the articles posted by other newsgroup members, you probably will want to try posting a few of your own.

To post an article to a newsgroup, follow these steps:

> **Note**
>
> If you have never posted a message to a UseNet newsgroup through CompuServe before, you need to enter your name in the USENET Options dialog box. You can reach this window by selecting Set USENET Options in the USENET Newsgroups dialog window. If you forget to set these options before you send your message, WinCIM will prompt you for the USENET Options information before your message is sent. All that is required to send a message is your name.

1. Open the Services menu and choose Go; or select the Go icon from the toolbar. Type **USENET** at the prompt and select OK.

2. Select USENET News reader (CIM) from the menu. Double-click it, or press the Enter key.

3. Select Create an Article from the menu. Double-click it, or press Enter.

> **Tip**
>
> You can also select the Create command from within an individual newsgroup, even if you want to post the article to other newsgroups as well.

4. At the Subject prompt, type the topic of your article.

5. Select the box or boxes next to the newsgroup or groups to which you want to post your article. You must subscribe to a newsgroup before you can post to it.

6. Tab to Message Contents and type your article. When you are finished writing, click Send.

> **Note**
>
> If you want to upload a file to a newsgroup, select the Upload button. At the File: prompt, enter the DOS file name for your posting. (The default is USENET.TXT.) Choose Binary, Text, JPEG, or GIF as the File Type. Then click OK. Your file will then be posted to the group.

Setting UseNet Options

There are five options that can be set on the USENET Options screen. Here is a short run-down on what each of them does:

- *Name*—This field must be filled in before you can send any UseNet messages. You can enter any name you want into this field, although most groups ask that you use your real name.

- *Organization's name*—This field is optional, and simply requests the name of the company or organization that you represent.

- *Default articles for newly subscribed newsgroups*—By default this option is set to 20, although you can change it to any number between 0 and 9,999,999,999 if you want. It controls the number of messages that you will see being posted from a new UseNet group.

- *Display Newsgroups with no articles*—This option allows you to display the names of newsgroups that have no new articles posted. Simply check this box.

- *Signature*—You can set up a signature that will appear at the end of every message.

▶ See "Signatures," p. 760

WinCIM 2.0.1 also makes it easy to attach a signature file to the end of your UseNet postings. To attach a signature file, follow these steps:

1. Open the Services menu and choose Go; or select the Go icon from the toolbar. Type **USENET** at the prompt and select OK.

2. Select USENET News reader (CIM) from the menu. Double-click it, or press the Enter key.

3. Select Set USENET Options from the menu. Double-click it, or press Enter.

4. The Options dialog box appears on your screen (see fig. 10.8). At the Name prompt, type your first and last name. Type your company name, university, or government affiliation at the Organization prompt. At the Signature prompt, type any information that you want to include at the end of your newsgroup postings (such as your company's name and address or a favorite slogan).

Tip

WinCIM 2.0.1 limits you to four lines of text in your signature file.

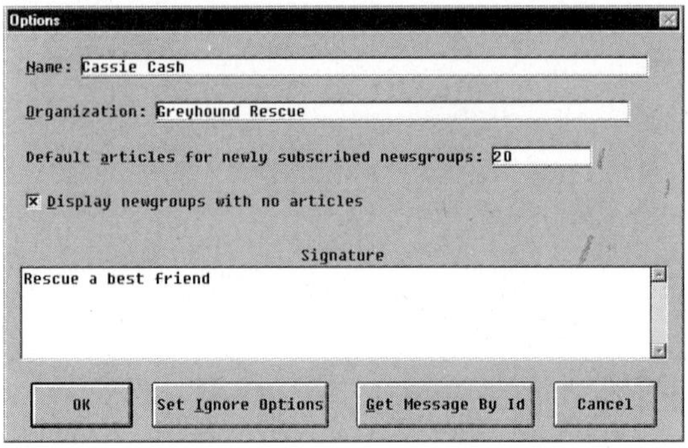

Fig. 10.8

WinCIM 2.0.1 lets you create a signature file to identify yourself and your company in newsgroup postings.

Other Features

CompuServe is continually adding new features to enhance the WinCIM 2.0.1 newsreader. Features now include the following:

- The most recently read newsgroup and thread remain highlighted, saving time and money by allowing you to easily read newsgroups and articles sequentially.

- Articles are not marked as "read" until you exit the newsgroup. This lets you browse articles you've already read without having to select the Hold command.

- Entire threads may be marked for downloading, not just individual articles. Simply mark the threads that interest you, and retrieve them for offline reading when the meter isn't running.

- The Retrieve option lets you indicate whether you want the retrieved text to be quoted or not in your follow-up posting.

- Automatically decodes images during retrieval.

- A new batch file download queue allows members to mark multiple threads in a series of newsgroups and retrieve them in a single download.

Accessing Newsgroups in Terminal Emulation Mode

If you prefer text-based menus to WinCIM's graphical Windows environment, CompuServe also gives you the chance to access newsgroups through what's known as *terminal emulation mode*—a blank screen with ASCII characters. Though terminal emulation (ASCII) mode moves faster than WinCIM 2.0.1, it's a little more difficult for novices to master. The other drawback is that you can't cut and paste between newsgroup messages and your Windows applications.

> **Note**
>
> Flipping from menu to menu in terminal emulation mode requires a little knowledge of CompuServe's text-based command language. Typing the letter **m** at the system prompt brings you back to the previous menu; typing the letter **t** takes you to the UseNet Newsgroups welcome screen.

Subscribing to Newsgroups

To subscribe to newsgroups using terminal emulation mode, follow these steps:

1. Open the Services menu and choose Go; or select the Go icon from the toolbar. Type **USENET** at the prompt and select OK.

2. Select USENET Newsreader (ASCII) from the menu. Double-click it, or press the Enter key.

3. After you enter terminal emulation mode, select item 3, Subscribe to Newsgroups, from the menu by typing **3** at the system prompt. Press the Enter key.

4. If you know the name of the newsgroup you want to subscribe to, select item 1, Subscribe to Newsgroup by Name by typing **1** at the system prompt and pressing the Enter key.

   To subscribe to a newsgroup by browsing, select item 2 from the menu described in step 4; then choose items 1 through 13 from the Browsing Newsgroups menu.

> **Troubleshooting**
>
> *I can't type commands at the prompt.*
>
> Occasionally, CompuServe's terminal emulation mode locks up in mid-session, leaving you unable to type commands at the system prompt. Press **Ctrl+C** and you will be prompted to type **H** for help, **M** to go back to the previous menu, or **T** to return to the top menu.

5. After you make your choice, you can sign up for any of the newsgroups that appear on-screen by typing the numeral at the system prompt and pressing the Enter key (see fig. 10.9).

6. To unsubscribe from a newsgroup, choose item 4 from the Reading UseNet News menu and press the Enter key. Then select a group from the menu by typing its numeral at the system prompt.

Gettting Connected

Fig. 10.9

CompuServe's Terminal Emulation mode lets you subscribe to newsgroups by selecting them from a menu.

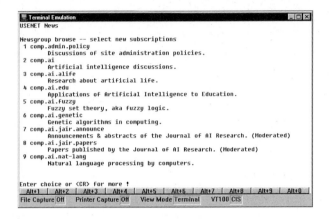

```
Terminal Emulation                                                  _ □ ✕
USENET News

Newsgroup browse -- select new subscriptions
 1 comp.admin.policy
            Discussions of site administration policies.
 2 comp.ai
            Artificial intelligence discussions.
 3 comp.ai.alife
            Research about artificial life.
 4 comp.ai.edu
            Applications of Artificial Intelligence to Education.
 5 comp.ai.fuzzy
            Fuzzy set theory, aka fuzzy logic.
 6 comp.ai.genetic
            Genetic algorithms in computing.
 7 comp.ai.jair.announce
            Announcements & abstracts of the Journal of AI Research. (Moderated)
 8 comp.ai.jair.papers
            Papers published by the Journal of AI Research. (Moderated)
 9 comp.ai.nat-lang
            Natural language processing by computers.


Enter choice or <CR> for more ↑
  Alt+1  |  Alt+2  |  Alt+3  |  Alt+4  |  Alt+5  |  Alt+6  |  Alt+7  |  Alt+8  |  Alt+9  |  Alt+0
File Capture Off      Printer Capture Off    View Mode Terminal    VT100 CIS
```

Reading Newsgroup Messages

After you subscribe to the newsgroups that interest you, you can begin reading the messages, or articles, that are posted to the groups by other Internet users. To read a message, follow these steps:

1. Open the Services menu and choose Go; or select the Go icon from the toolbar. Type **USENET** at the prompt and select OK.

2. Select USENET Newsreader (CIM) from the menu. Double-click it, or press Enter.

3. Select Access Your USENET Newsgroups from the menu by typing **1** at the system prompt and pressing the Enter key.

4. Choose a newsgroup by typing its number at the system prompt and pressing Enter.

5. Then choose the BROWSE, SHOW, READ, SEARCH, CREATE, IGNORE, or CLEAR command (see fig. 10.10). The Browse command shows you the articles' subject lines and lets you pick an article number to see more. The Show command displays each article's author and article number in addition to the subject line. The Read command gives you the full text of each article page by page.

6. To reply to the article that you are currently reading, type **Choices** and press the Enter key at the system prompt and select 1 from the Choices menu. You also have the option of replying with quotations, replying by private e-mail, creating an article, canceling an article, rereading the article, holding the article, flipping to the next article, reading the next article in the thread, returning to the parent article, clearing articles in the newsgroup, ignoring the article, or downloading the article to your hard drive.

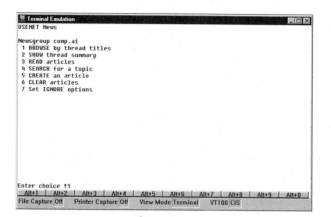

```
Terminal Emulation                                    _ □ ×
USENET News

Newsgroup comp.ai
 1 BROWSE by thread titles
 2 SHOW thread summary
 3 READ articles
 4 SEARCH for a topic
 5 CREATE an article
 6 CLEAR articles
 7 Set IGNORE options




Enter choice !1
 Alt+1 | Alt+2 | Alt+3 | Alt+4 | Alt+5 | Alt+6 | Alt+7 | Alt+8 | Alt+9 | Alt+0
File Capture Off    Printer Capture Off    View Mode Terminal    VT100 CIS
```

Fig. 10.10
CompuServe's Terminal Emulation mode lets you browse, read, show, search, create, and clear newsgroup postings.

> **Note**
>
> CompuServe's ASCII newsreader also works with the TAPCIS, OzCIS, and other offline readers that let you automatically retrieve e-mail and forum messages, which saves time and money. To find out more, download the INTERN.ZIP file from the TAPNEWS/Fact File Section of CompuServe's TAPCIS Forum (**GO TAPCIS**).

Posting Newsgroup Articles

To post an article to a newsgroup, follow these steps:

1. Open the Services menu and choose Go; or select the Go icon from the toolbar. Type **USENET** at the prompt and select OK.

2. Select USENET Newsreader (ASCII) from the menu. Double-click it, or press the Enter key.

3. Select Create an Article (item 6) from the Reading USENET News menu and press the Enter key.

> **Tip**
>
> You also can select the Create command from within an individual newsgroup article by selecting it from the Choices menu.

4. Type the text of your article; then type /EXIT on a separate line when you're through and press the Enter key.

5. You'll be prompted to select those newsgroups to which you want the message posted. (You must subscribe to a newsgroup first before you can post to it.)

II

Getting Connected

6. At the Subject prompt, type the topic of your message and press the Enter key.

7. The next menu lets you POST the article (item 1), EDIT the article text (item 2), ABORT the posting (item 3), PREVIEW this article (item 4), or Set OPTIONS (item 5).

Creating a Signature File

Like WinCIM, the ASCII newsreader makes it easy to attach a signature file to the end of your UseNet postings.

To attach a signature file to the end of your postings, follow these steps:

1. Open the Services menu and choose Go; or select the Go icon from the toolbar. Type **USENET** at the prompt and select OK.

2. Select USENET News reader (ASCII) from the menu. Double-click it, or press Enter.

3. Select Set Options (item 5) from the menu and press the Enter key.

4. At the Name prompt, type your first and last name. Type your company name, university, or government affiliation at the Organization prompt. At the Signature prompt, type any information that you'd like to include at the end of your newsgroup postings, such as your company's name and address or a favorite slogan (see fig. 10.11).

Tip

Like the WinCIM 2.0.1 newsreader, the ASCII newsreader limits you to four lines of text in your signature file.

Fig. 10.11
Like WinCIM 2.0.1, CompuServe's Terminal Emulation mode also lets you create a signature file to accompany your newsgroup postings.

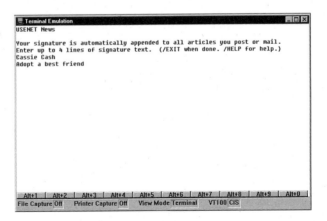

Other Features

Like the WinCIM newsreader, CompuServe's ASCII newsreader continues to be improved with the addition of new features that make the program more functional and easier to use.

In addition to the features described previously, the ASCII news reader offers the following functions:

■ Reminds you to make sure that the "receipt of Internet mail" function is turned on when you post or e-mail an article

■ Attaches signature files you create to e-mail messages as well as UseNet postings

■ Gives you the ability to add comments to forwarded mail

■ Lets you indicate whether you want articles marked as read immediately or read after you exit the newsgroup

Using File Transfer Protocol (FTP)

WinCIM 2.0.1's file transfer protocol (FTP) interface is much jazzier than its Plain Jane newsreader interface, and thanks to a bevy of colorful icons, it's a joy to use (see fig. 10.12). Like newsgroups, FTP downloads do incur connect time charges at $2.95 an hour.

Fig. 10.12
WinCIM 2.0.1's new FTP interface uses icons to make file-hunting a snap. To access a listed site, for example, you just point and click.

II

Gettting Connected

To access a listed FTP site, follow these steps:

1. Open the Services menu and choose Go; or select the Go icon from the toolbar. Type **FTP** at the prompt and select OK. You may also select Internet from the Services window, then FTP from the Internet dialog box.

> **Note**
>
> If this is your first time using the CompuServe Internet utilities you will be greeted with an Alert message pointing out the dangers involved in downloading files from other services—viruses especially.

2. From the FTP welcome screen, click one of four icons that represent the four FTP options: Selected Popular Sites, List of Sites, Access a Specific Site, and Site Descriptions.

3. If you choose a site from the menu, the user name and password are automatically supplied. If you choose a site not on the menu, you are asked to fill in a user name and password. Click OK to continue past this screen and the next.

> **Note**
>
> By default your user name will be entered as "anonymous," and your password will be your CompuServe e-mail address. To access a site that you have a personal account with, you will have to enter your own account information at the prompts.

4. After you gain access to the FTP site, you are presented with a list of the directories and files available on the remote computer at the site you chose as you can see in figure 10.13. You can move from directory to directory to see which files are there. You can even view graphical files (in GIF format) as well as ASCII (text) files.

5. After you locate the files you want to download, just mark the box next to the file name. When you've marked all the files you want to download, select the Retrieve button. You are prompted for the location on your own computer where you want the files stored.

6. When you are done with your FTP session, you can log out of that site by choosing Leave and then log into another, or you can quit FTP and return to the CompuServe menu.

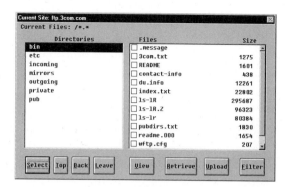

Fig. 10.13
The FTP interface allows you to select files from remote computers and download them to your local system.

> ## Caution
>
> Unlike the files that are uploaded to CompuServe's forums, the FTP files it makes available are not checked for viruses. Just because you're using CompuServe, don't assume that these FTP files are safer than any others on the Internet!

Telneting with WinCIM

CompuServe added Telnet access to its list of services in June 1995, which opened another world of information access to its customers. You can Telnet to some computer sites and run software or work with files as if you were actually sitting at that computer. The following instructions take you through a Telnet session on CompuServe.

1. Open the Services menu and choose Go; or click the Go button on the toolbar. Type **telnet** at the prompt and click OK.

This opens a dialog window showing all the options that are available when using CompuServe's Telnet capabilities. There are quite a few options on this screen that provide you with specific information about Telnet in general, and about Telneting through CompuServe. The three most commonly used options are listed below.

- *Telnet Site Descriptions*—This item allows you to select a specific Telnet site from the list and learn about the information that it has to offer.

- *List of Sites*—CompuServe keeps a short list of Telnet sites that have been made available to CompuServe members. When you use a site selected from this list, you will automatically be logged into the computer and be allowed access to all the information that this site has chosen to make available to CompuServe members.

II

Getting Connected

■ *Access a Specific Site*—This option will take you directly to a site. To use this feature you must know the Internet address of the machine you want to visit. For example, if I wanted to go to Microsoft's Telnet site, I would have to know that their address was **bbs.microsoft.com**. I would not be able to reach them using just **microsoft.com** for my address.

2. After you select the site that you want to Telnet to, you will be greeted with a CompuServe Warning. This message lists CompuServe's liabilities for your actions during these Telnet sessions.

3. The terminal window will then open showing you the introductory screen to the site that you selected to visit. Figure 10.14 shows one possible opening screen for a Telnet site.

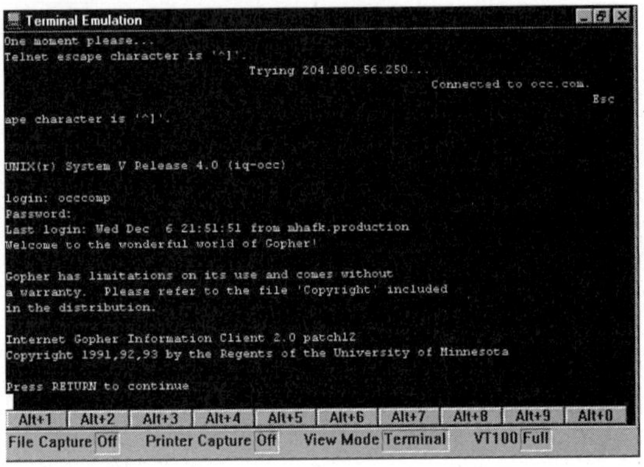

Fig. 10.14
The introductory screen that greets you upon Telneting to the Career Center.

Once you have completed your tasks on the Telnet site, you can hang up your Telnet connection by issuing some sort of hang-up command to the machine that you were connected to, or you can close the Terminal window.

Surfing the World Wide Web

Like rivals Prodigy and America Online, CompuServe is now giving members access to the World Wide Web.

CompuServe is providing World Wide Web access to its members through a dial-up PPP connection using NetLauncher, if you are using WinCIM 1.4, or through a direct link to CompuServe Mosaic for WinCIM 2.0.1 users. NetLauncher is a software package composed of CompuServe's Internet Dialer and Spry's Mosaic Web Browser. The dialer allows CompuServe members to access the Internet through local access numbers, just as they normally access the main CompuServe system. WinCIM 2.0.1 essentially includes all the features of NetLauncher, so there is not a separate installation program.

Note

CompuServe's Internet Dialer opens a PPP connection to the Internet that is accessible by any program. You do not have to use Spry's Browser. You could use another World Wide Web browser, newsreader, or other external FTP client to access these services.

To sneak a peak at CompuServe's own Web site, log on to the Internet through an Internet access provider and type **http:// www.compuserve.com** in your Web browser software. For more information about accessing the World Wide Web, see chapter 20, "How the World Wide Web Works."

Downloading NetLauncher

You can easily download NetLauncher by following these steps:

1. Open the <u>S</u>ervices menu and select <u>G</u>o, or press the Go button.
2. In the Go Services window type **NetLauncher**, then click OK.
3. From the CompuServe NetLauncher for Windows dialog box double-click the Download NetLauncher—CNL.EXE (1.2 MB) entry.
4. On the NetLauncher Liability and Warranty window click <u>R</u>etrieve.
5. In the Save As dialog box, select the directory that you want to download the file into, and then click OK. Figure 10.15 shows you the download dialog box that tracks the progress of the file transfer.

Note

By default WinCIM will direct the downloaded file into c:\cserve\download. This is the directory that is used in the discussion of installing NetLauncher. You could download this file into a temporary directory to make clean-up easier.

II

Gettting Connected

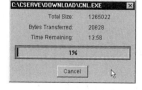

Fig. 10.15
CompuServe's download progress bar showing the download of NetLauncher.

Once you have completed the download you will need to close WinCIM and your connection to CompuServe before you continue on with the installation of the program.

Installing NetLauncher

NetLauncher has a nice installation program that takes you through most of the configuration of CompuServe's dialer and the setup of the service. The following steps should help you complete the installation of NetLauncher with little difficulty:

1. Open the Start menu and select the Run option.

2. In the Run dialog box type **c:\cserve\download\cnl.exe** and click OK.

3. Click the Proceed button to continue with the installation.

4. Click the OK button to accept c:\cserve as the main CompuServe installation directory. Watch as all the files are expanded and copied onto your hard drive.

5. Once the installation is complete, you will be asked if you wish to start Spry Mosaic, as shown in figure 10.16. Click Yes.

Fig. 10.16
When NetLauncher's installation is complete, you will be asked if you want to start CompuServe's Edition of Spry Mosaic.

Caution

You must remove any copies of WINSOCK.DLL that are loaded into your computer's memory before you start the installation of NetLauncher. The installation program overwrites your existing WINSOCK.DLL during installation. You must use the WINSOCK.DLL provided with NetLauncher to use CompuServe's Internet Dialer. If you attempt to use the WINSOCK.DLL that came with Windows 95 you will be asked to replace it with CompuServe's version of that file.

To avoid problems in the future, you will want to rename your existing winsock.dll file to something like winsock.w95 so you know which version was provided with Windows 95 and which version was provided with the CompuServe Dialer. If you rename WinSock rather than replace it, you will be able to use Windows 95's Dial-Up Networking connections when accessing other service providers or when using other Internet software packages.

Once the installation is complete you will see the Spry Mosaic screen open with a dialog box that lets you know you are attempting to connect to CompuServe. Once the connection is made you will see another window that lets you know the service is negotiating for the best transfer rate; then you will be greeted with CompuServe's home page.

Troubleshooting

The Web browser keeps telling me that the connection to CompuServe could not be made. What do I do?

The CompuServe Dialer uses the main Session Settings that WinCIM does when making that first call. If you have continually attempted to make the connection and it has failed, you generally have to correct these settings. To do this, follow these steps:

1. Open the Start menu on the Windows 95 task bar, select Programs, CompuServe, then CompuServe Dialer.

2. Once the dialer is running, open the Settings menu and select Sessions.

3. The Setup Sessions Settings dialog box, as seen in the figure 10.17, appears asking for the specific information you need to use to connect to the CompuServe network. Make sure that the correct phone number, modem speed, modem COM port, Name, User ID, and Password are all correct.

4. Click OK.

5. Click the Dial button.

You should now be connecting to the CompuServe Information Network.

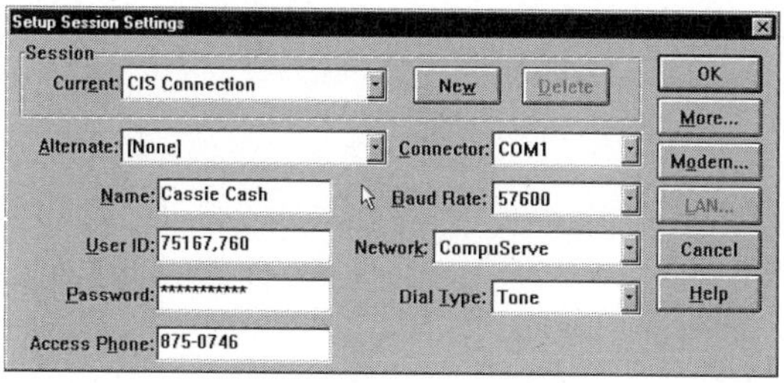

Fig. 10.17
The CompuServe Dialer's Setup Session Settings dialog showing one possible configuration.

Using CompuServe Mosaic

When CompuServe and Spry started working together to create a Web browser that could easily be used by CompuServe members around the globe they came up with one of the best browsers available. This browser includes the following features as shown in figure 10.18:

- Document URL field allowing you to go directly to a site without following a link
- Home Page setting

- Hotlist for keeping track of your favorite sites

- Kiosk mode for doing presentations from a Web site

- Back and Forward buttons allow you to travel through the sites that you have visited during a session

- Find feature allows you to search a particular Web page for specific text

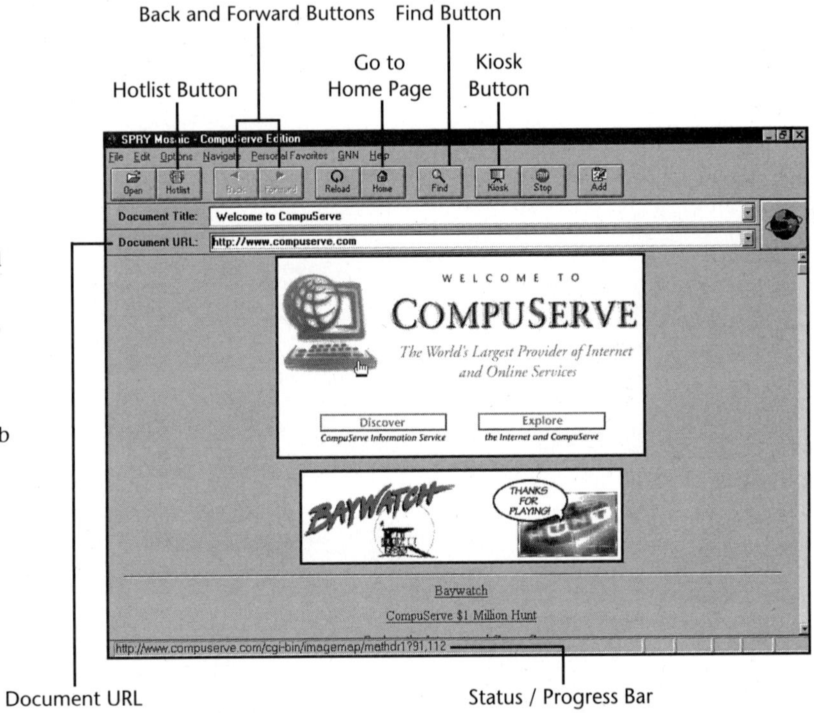

Fig. 10.18

CompuServe's Web browser interface uses the standard tools and layout that you may have seen during your exploration of CompuServe and other Internet Web browsers.

To start the Spry Mosaic browser, open the Start menu, select Programs, CompuServe, then CompuServe Mosaic. After the dialing process is completed you see CompuServe's Web home page which includes a company overview with announcements about CompuServe's future plans, a description of CompuServe's current services, and information about CompuServe CD and CompuServe Magazine. There are many different sites that you can visit out on the Web. You can use some of the following ideas to find them:

- To visit any of the sites on the CompuServe Web server, just click the link to that particular piece of information and Mosaic takes you there. For example, you can click the Join CompuServe graphic on CompuServe's home page to get access to WinCIM 1.4, the latest downloadable version of the CompuServe Information Manager, and the codes required to get your free trial month of membership.

■ The home page button automatically takes you to the CompuServe home page on the Web.

■ The Web Page field allows you to enter the name of a site that you wish to go to without having to find a link that takes you there. For example, if you want to visit the WebCrawler search engine page, you would type **http://www.webcrawler.com** in this field.

■ The Hotlists button opens up your Hotlist screen allowing you to add a new site to this list or go directly to that site. A Hotlist is an organized list of the sites that you find most entertaining, informative, or useful in some fashion. You can add as many site addresses to this list as you want. Controlling your Hotlist is discussed in the following section, titled "Working with CompuServe's Hotlist".

Once you are done surfing the Net with CompuServe Mosaic you can hang up the phone by right-clicking the CompuServe Internet Dialer taskbar button, then clicking the Hangup entry on the shortcut menu.

Working with CompuServe's Hotlist

As mentioned earlier in this chapter, CompuServe Mosaic uses a Hotlist to track your favorite locations. Mosaic also comes with an extensive existing list of sites that might interest CompuServe members. Hotlists serve as one of the fastest ways to maneuver through familiar areas of the Internet. The following list gives a brief overview of the main functions you can perform with your Hotlist:

■ *Add a Hotlist Entry*—Adding an entry can be done in two ways. If you currently have the World Wide Web site loaded that you want to list, simply click the Add button. If you know the address of a site, you can add it to the list by clicking the Hotlist button, selecting the folder that you want to store it in, and then clicking Add. Select Web Page, and then click OK. Type the title of the page in the Title field and enter the address of the Web page in the URL field. Click OK. You should now see your site added to the folder that you selected.

■ *Delete a Hotlist Entry*—To remove an item from your Hotlist, select the item from your list of folders and click the Remove button. Click Yes when asked if you are sure you want to remove the entry. That entry will no longer appear in your Hotlist.

II

Getting Connected

- *Reorganize Your Hotlist*—The only way to reorganize your Hotlist is to remove the entries that you want to move, and then add them again to the folders you want.

- *Go to a Site on your Hotlist*—Once again there are two ways to accomplish this task. The first way is to click the Hotlist button, which opens the list of sites, and then double-click the site that you want to go to.

  The other way is to select the folder in which you have your sites listed. Check the Add to Menu option on the bottom of your Hotlist screen and then click the Close button. You should now see this folder's name appear on your menu bar. You can select this menu option and select your site from it.

Sending Mail with Your Web Browser

CompuServe's Web browser allows you to send mail through CompuServe's mail system. As you can see in figure 10.19, the Send Mail dialog box allows you to specify who the message recipient is, whether anyone will receive a carbon copy of the message, list a subject matter, and the contents and content type of the message.

To send a mail message, simply enter the e-mail address of the person you're sending the message to in the Recipient field, and a subject for the message. After you type your message in the Message Body area, click the Se_nd button.

Fig. 10.19

CompuServe's Mosaic Send Mail window, from which you can send e-mail across the Internet using your CompuServe account.

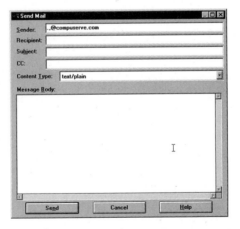

Using UseNet News with Your Web Browser

You can read UseNet newsgroup messages through your Web browser just as easily as you read Web pages. You can access newsgroups by entering the full name in the URL field preceded by **news:**. For example, you can read the Artificial Intelligence newsgroup by entering **news:comp.ai**. Once you have gotten a list of all the articles, just double-click the name of the article to read it.

To send messages to a newsgroup is as simple as clicking a hyperlink. Most news servers place a Post to Newsgroup hyperlink at the top of the news article lists. You need to make sure that you are looking at the articles list from the newsgroup you want to post to, and then just click the Post to Newsgroup link. You will be greeted with a Post News dialog box preconfigured with your name in the Sender field. Fill in the Subject line and type your article in the field provided, being sure to press the Enter key at the end of each line of text. Once your message is complete, click the Post button.

Searching Gopher Sites Through the Web

As mentioned earlier, you can easily look at Gopher sites through your Web browser. Gopher sites are simply text pages that are accessed through a menu system that generally appear in an outline format. The following steps allow you to go directly to a Gopher site.

1. In the Web Page field, type **gopher://domain.name**, where domain.name is the name of the computer running the Gopher server.

2. Press Enter. After the connection is made you will see a Gopher site appear with a long list of items that you can select from.

Accessing FTP Sites Through the Web

You do not have to use WinCIM to access Internet FTP sites, you can also use CompuServe Mosaic. FTP sites are basically computers that allow you to easily upload or download files. You can access an FTP site through the Web browser by following these steps.

1. In the Web Page field, type **ftp://domain.name**, where domain.name is the name of the computer running the FTP server.

2. Press Enter. Once the connection has been made you will see the FTP site appear. Generally you will see introductory text explaining what is and is not allowed on this server, and a short list of other places that you can go (mirror sites) to get the same files. You will also see a long list of file and directory names that you can select from in your search for information.

II

Gettting Connected

Further Reference: CompuServe's Internet Forums

CompuServe has many Internet Forums that are great places for swapping notes with other CompuServe members about the Internet and its resources. You can also download free and low-cost software to access the Internet through other services.

As shown in figure 10.20, there are forums that include information for new and old users on Internet Commerce, Publishing, Internet Resources, and the Internet World.

Fig. 10.20

CompuServe's many Internet forums let users swap notes and attend conferences on a wide variety of topics.

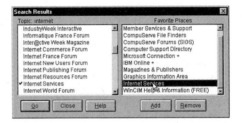

> **Note**
>
> Unlike America Online's Internet Center, CompuServe's Internet Forums do not provide a gateway to the Internet. To access Internet features such as e-mail, newsgroups, FTP sites, and the World Wide Web follow the instructions previously detailed.

To check it out, use the Find command and type **INTERNET.** If you know the name of the forum that you wish to enter, use the Go command and type the name of the forum that you wish to visit.

Looking Ahead: The Future According to CompuServe

For businesses, CompuServe plans to begin offering high-speed T-1 access, *firewall* security systems, and help in setting up Web-based cybermalls. CompuServe is in the process of designing a Windows 95 version of their popular WinCIM software, which should be available sometime during 1996.

Now that CompuServe is making the Internet a priority, it won't be long before CompuServe users enjoy access to all the tools and resources the Internet has to offer—for both businesses and the general public.

CHAPTER 11

Connecting Through America Online

If you've never surfed the Internet before, America Online is an excellent place to get your feet wet. America Online doesn't offer full Internet access—not yet, at least—but its point-and-click interface and colorful icons offer a fun, easy way to access Internet e-mail, newsgroups, Gopher and WAIS databases, file transfer protocol (FTP) sites, and the World Wide Web. America Online's Internet Connection offers a variety of resources—from a message board to an online version of Wired magazine—to help Internet novices tap into Net culture.

America Online isn't the only commercial online service to offer Internet access, of course. But its colorful icons and well-designed menus make its Internet gateway far easier to navigate than those provided by rivals Prodigy and Delphi. America Online's prices match those of its rivals. There's no extra charge to send or receive Internet e-mail; and access to newsgroups, databases, and FTP sites costs the same as the service's other features. This chapter shows you how to use America Online for Windows to access Internet e-mail, newsgroups, databases, files, and of course, the World Wide Web. You also get a glimpse of what America Online has in store for the future.

In this chapter, you learn the following:

- What sets America Online apart from other online services
- How America Online for Windows helps you navigate the Internet
- How to use America Online to send and retrieve Internet e-mail
- How to subscribe to (and unsubscribe from) a mailing list
- How to use America Online as a UseNet newsreader
- How to search Gopher and WAIS databases

■ How to use America Online to retrieve files from other Internet-connected computers (FTP)

■ How to use America Online to explore the World Wide Web

■ The future of America Online's Internet gateway

What Is America Online?

Arguably the hippest of the major online services, America Online also is the fastest growing—thanks, in part, to its easy-to-use graphical interface. Simply click an icon with your mouse to dash off an online message, join in a real-time chat session, drop in on a special-interest bulletin board, or download software or clip art from the service's library—all for $9.95 a month for five hours of online time, plus $2.95 an hour for any additional usage. America Online also has a new 30/30 plan that offers users 30 hours of access time for $29.95 a month. Any additional hours are still charged at the $2.95 rate.

America Online bulletin boards range from hardware and software support to subjects such as wine, aviation, investments, and small business. Its "chat" boards feature electronic "rooms" with names like "The Flirts Nook," "The Romance Connection," and "Red Dragon Inn." America Online also features the widest assortment of any online service of electronic magazines and newspapers, including online editions of *Time*, *The Atlantic Monthly*, *The Chicago Tribune*, and *Car and Driver* that allow members to swap notes with writers and editors.

◄ See "The Various Ways to Connect to the Internet: Which One Is Right for You?" p. 101

◄ See "Other Software for Connecting to the Internet," p. 157

Ranking in the top three with Prodigy and CompuServe, America Online is still coming on strong; it now boasts more than three million members, up from 300,000 only three years ago. Spurring its rapid growth have been strategic alliances with Tribune Co., Knight Ridder, CNN, Time, The New York Times, Reuters, NBC, ABC, The San Jose Mercury News, Apple, and Microsoft. America Online has also entered into co-marketing agreements with more than 30 companies, including modem manufacturers, magazines, affinity groups, and associations such as The National Education Association and SeniorNet, a non-profit, international organization for adults 55 and over interested in learning about computers.

Primarily a consumer-oriented service, America Online has long lacked many of the communications capabilities and information resources that make CompuServe attractive to businesses. But that's beginning to change. For example, America Online's new FlashSessions feature lets you go online—

immediately or at times you designate—to send mail that you have composed offline, retrieve mail that is waiting for you, and download software files that you have marked in previous online sessions, saving you time and money. America Online's Download Manager lets you select files from multiple forums, download them to your computer, and log off the service automatically when finished.

Caution

Warning to parents: America Online is not a G-rated service; some of the live chat boards feature discussions about adult topics, some of which are of a sexual or violent nature.

America Online for Windows

America Online's Windows version, initially released in January 1993, offers popular features such as pull-down menus, three-dimensional icons, tiling and cascading, multitasking, and resizing. The "flashbar" that runs across the top of the screen displays icons that provide instant access to news stories, stock quotes, chat rooms, online help, and departments such as Computing & Software. There's also a "mobile access" feature that lets subscribers who log on from out of town select and store multiple phone numbers for their most frequented destinations.

Windows users can also add sounds to real-time chat sessions and set up the software to let them know when a download is complete or a piece of mail arrives in their mailbox.

America Online recently updated the latest multimedia version of its Windows and Macintosh front-end programs. Version 2.5 features many improvements to the way the service looks and operates, including on-screen photos and a new "departments" structure that makes it easier for users to locate areas of interest, and a built-in World Wide Web browser. Each department has a new refreshing look that propagates AOL's reputation as the "hip" online service. Figure 11.1 shows the new look of America Online's Main menu.

II

Getting Connected

Fig. 11.1
America Online for Windows' Main menu showcasing the service's new, modern, multimedia look.

America Online's Internet Gateway

As one of the Big Three commercial online services, America Online provides a wide variety of Internet services and an intuitive interface. Through the service's Internet Connection, subscribers can access Internet e-mail, mailing lists, newsgroups, and Gopher and WAIS servers, not to mention FTP and the World Wide Web, which were newly added in the beginning of 1995. America Online also maintains a database of over 1,000 mailing lists and a storehouse of Gopher menus, both of which are available for searching.

The following is a rundown of America Online's current and future Internet offerings:

- *Internet Connection*—The starting point for America Online members seeking to explore the Internet, Internet Connection (see fig. 11.2) offers a gateway to e-mail, newsgroups, databases, and resources such as Zen and the Art of the Internet, The Electronic Frontier Foundation Forum, an online edition of Wired magazine, and a message board for discussing Internet-related topics.

  America Online's Internet Connection (see fig. 11.2) is a great place to swap notes with other America Online members about the Internet and its resources. You also can find out about America Online's upcoming Internet features, and problems other users are having with the service's Internet gateway and software.

- *E-mail*—America Online lets you swap messages and files with other America Online members, as well as with users of other online networks, such as CompuServe, MCI Mail, AT&TMail, and the Internet.

- *Mailing lists*—Through America Online, you can sign up for any of the thousands of mailing lists, or e-mail discussion groups, that the Internet has to offer.

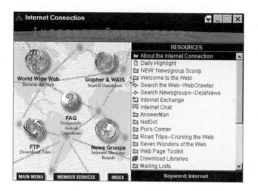

Fig. 11.2
America Online's
Internet Connec-
tion is the starting
point for members
who want to
explore the
Internet.

- *UseNet newsgroups*—America Online lets you access the full spectrum of 14,000 UseNet newsgroups through its graphical Windows interface.

- *Gopher and WAIS databases*—America Online offers a convenient front-end to a wide variety of Gopher and WAIS databases that the service believes merit the ranking, "Editor's Choices." Other databases are also available.

- *File-transfer protocol (FTP)*—FTP is America Online's newest Internet offering. FTP's graphical interface makes downloading files from remote computers as easy as clicking your mouse.

- *World Wide Web* —This popular Internet feature is now easily accessed with the 2.5 release of America Online for Windows. You can be surfing the Web with just a click of your mouse.

Note

If you already have an account with an Internet access provider but want to sample what America Online has to offer, you can use Trumpet WinSock or any other WinSock-compliant software to connect to the service via the Internet. America Online supports both an FTP site (**ftp.aol.com**) and a World Wide Web site (**www.aol.com**) that can provide you with as much information as you like. If either of these locations do not have the information you need, write to an America Online representative at **postmaster@aol.com**.

Using Internet E-Mail

Using America Online's e-mail gateway, you can quickly and easily send e-mail messages to friends, colleagues, and customers all over the world.

◀ See "How
the Internet
Works," p. 9

▶ See "How
Internet E-Mail
Works," p. 329

Using America Online to Send E-Mail Messages

Suppose you have an account on America Online, but your colleague in New York has an account with an Internet access provider—say, Pipeline.

To send your colleague a message, follow these steps:

1. Log on to America Online.

2. Open the Mail menu from the top of the screen and choose Compose Mail or press Ctrl+M. The Compose Mail dialog box appears (see fig. 11.3).

Fig. 11.3

Sending an e-mail message on America Online is as easy as filling in the on-screen message blank.

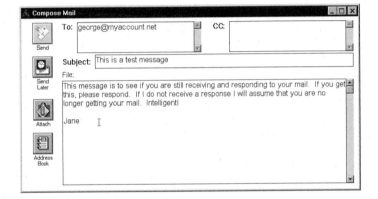

3. At the To: prompt, type your colleague's Internet address—for example, george@myaccount.net.

4. Tab past the CC: line to the Subject: prompt and type the subject of your message.

5. Tab to the message blank and type your message.

6. Click the Send icon to send the message.

Note

To prepare an America Online message before you log on, follow steps 2 through 5, and then click the Send Later icon on the left side of the Compose Mail window to queue that message to be sent the next time you log on to America Online. To send the message, log on to America Online, open the Outgoing Flashmail window and click the Send All button. You can also set up a FlashSession (Open the Mail menu and choose FlashSessions) to log on and send your mail automatically.

> **Note**
>
> The Attach File feature used to send files to other America Online members can also be used to send a file through the America Online Internet Mail Gateway. The message receiver must be able to receive MIME encoded messages, or the file will be received as a huge amount of garbage characters at the end of the message. You should limit your messages to 27K, or they will be sent as multiple messages.

Using America Online's Address Book to Store E-Mail Addresses

If you plan to send e-mail to a colleague on a regular basis, it's a good idea to enter his name in America Online's Address Book. That way, you won't have to search for his e-mail address every time you want to send him a note.

◀ See "The Various Parts of the Internet," p. 25

▶ See "How Internet E-Mail Works," p. 329

To enter a name in the address book, follow these steps:

1. Open the Mail menu and choose Edit Address Book.

2. Click the Create button. The Address Group dialog box appears (see fig. 11.4).

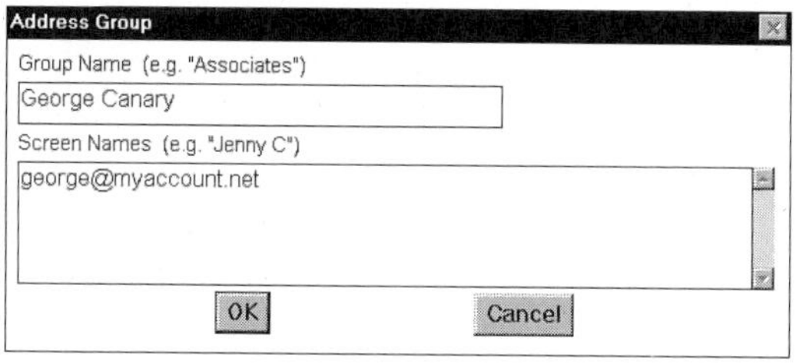

Fig. 11.4
America Online's Address Book lets you create and store Internet addresses for future reference.

3. At the Group Name prompt, type your colleague's first and last name (or company name, if your prefer); for example, George Canary.

4. Tab to the Screen Names prompt and type his e-mail address; for example, george@myaccount.net.

5. Click OK. You can use the Address Book's Modify feature to change the address if your colleague switches Internet accounts.

6. Click OK again to close the Address Book.

The next time you want to send Mr. Canary a message, simply open the Mail menu, choose Compose Mail or press Ctrl+M, and click the Address Book icon. Highlight George Canary and click the To: button, and then click OK. The program will fill in his e-mail address automatically.

II

Getting Connected

Joining Internet Mailing Lists

◀ See "The Various Parts of the Internet," p. 25

▶ See "Using Internet Mailing Lists," p. 417

With America Online, joining an Internet mailing list is no harder than using Internet e-mail. Suppose, for example, that you want to subscribe to MAGNET-L, a mailing list devoted to discussing the use of graphical UseNet clients, specifically the Magnet product. (Be aware, however, that sign-up instructions for mailing lists vary depending on what type of mailing list software the list uses.)

To find a list that interests you, click the icon labeled Internet Connection on the Main Menu. Double-click on the Mailing Lists option in the Resources list. From the Mailing List Directory screen, double-click the Search the Database icon. In the search window that appears, type one or more keywords that describe your interest and press Enter (see fig. 11.5). A list of database entries that match the search phrase will appear. Double-click a list title to view a description of the list and to find out how to join and leave the list.

Fig. 11.5
America Online lets you search for mailing lists of interest by typing in words and phrases.

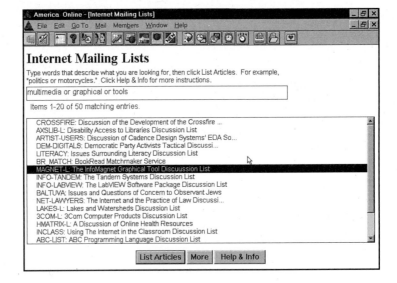

Subscribing to (and Unsubscribing from) a Mailing List

To use America Online to join the InfoMagnet Graphical Tool Discussion List, follow these steps:

> **Tip**
>
> You can see a copy of the instructions for subscribing to each list by double-clicking on the list name in the Internet Mailing Lists search dialog box.

1. Open the <u>M</u>ail menu and choose <u>C</u>ompose Mail.

2. At the To: prompt, type **listserv@earncc.earn.net**.

3. Tab to the Subject: prompt and type **Subscribe**.

> **Note**
>
> You can actually type anything you want in the Subject: field because Listserv ignores anything appearing in that field. Of course, if you don't fill in the Subject field, America Online will not send your message.

4. Tab to the message blank and type **SUBSCRIBE MAGNET-L** followed by your name; for example, SUBSCRIBE MAGNET-L GEORGE CANARY (see fig. 11.6).

5. Click the Send icon to send the message.

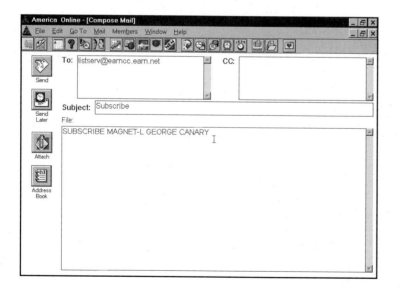

Fig. 11.6
America Online members can sign up for mailing lists on hundreds of topics.

II

Getting Connected

To quit the list, follow the same steps and send a message to the same address containing the command "unsubscribe" followed by your name—for example, unsubscribe George Canary.

> **Note**
>
> There are many different types of mailing list servers available, and not all of them use the unsubscribe command. Some of them use *signoff* or one of any number of possible commands. Because of this, you need to be sure to read and save any welcome messages that you get after you send your subscription messages. The welcome message will most likely tell you how to get information from the list and how to remove yourself from the list when you no longer wish to read it.

Some of the more active Internet mailing lists generate several hundred e-mail messages a day. Though America Online does not charge extra to receive those messages (as CompuServe does), you may miss out on some messages if you fail to clean out your mailbox every couple of days. That's because your America Online mailbox can hold only 550 e-mail messages at a time; additional messages are rejected. The sender of a message will get a notice stating that your mailbox is full and you can receive no more mail. This could make your LISTESERV members very upset, because they will get a copy of this for every message they send to that list. America Online also imposes size limitations on e-mail messages. Incoming messages can be no larger than 1 megabyte; messages over 27KB are split into several smaller messages.

Posting to a Mailing List

You also can use America Online to post a message on an Internet mailing list.

To post on the MAGNET-L list, follow these steps:

1. Open the <u>M</u>ail menu and choose <u>C</u>ompose Mail.
2. At the To: prompt, type **magnet-l@ earncc.earn.net**.
3. Type the subject of your message at the Subject: prompt.
4. Tab to the message blank and type your message.
5. Click the Send icon to send your message to the list. A copy is forwarded to every subscriber's e-mail box.

Participating in UseNet Newsgroups

▶ See "How UseNet Works," p. 749

America Online's newsreader interface, shown in figure 11.7, uses colorful navigational icons to make joining, browsing, and posting to newsgroups as easy as clicking your mouse. Want to join a newsgroup? Click the Add Newsgroups icon. Want to read the newsgroups to which you've subscribed?

Click the Read My Newsgroups icon. Unfortunately, you trade ease-of-use for lower performance. America Online's graphics slow things down quite a bit, making you wait up to a minute or longer to scroll through lists of newsgroup articles and zero in on the one you want. Another drawback is a lack of helpful features, such as the ability to quote from other users' articles in your own postings, create signature files to tack onto the end of your messages, filter out postings you'd rather not read, and see, at a glance, who posted the article and when he or she posted it. Some or all of these features are staples of other Internet newsreaders, such as those offered by CompuServe, Pipeline, WinNET Mail, and Internet in a Box.

Fig. 11.7
Once you reach the Newsgroups main window, you have instant access to any newsgroups that you want to read.

Like the rest of the service, America Online newsgroup access is priced at a low $2.95 an hour—although, depending on how much time you spend there, you might be better off opening an account with an Internet access provider that offers an "all-you-can-eat" plan.

Subscribing to Newsgroups
To subscribe to newsgroups through America Online, follow these steps:

1. Open the Go To menu and choose Keyword.

2. At the prompt, type **newsgroups** and click OK.

> **Note**
>
> You can also choose the Internet Connection icon on the Main Menu, and then select the News Groups icon on the Internet Connection screen.

3. Click the Add Newsgroups icon in the Newsgroups window.

4. Double-click the newsgroup category you want to browse; for example, Business and Commercial Newsgroups (see fig. 11.8).

> **Tip**
>
> Parents can control which newsgroups their children have access to. Simply choose the Parental Controls button and select your child's screen name from the list.

Fig. 11.8

America Online lets you browse newsgroup categories to find the group you want.

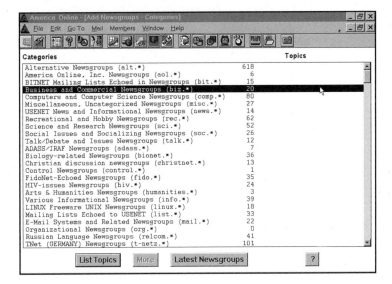

5. Double-click the newsgroup you want to join; for example, the Biz.General newsgroup.

6. Click the Add button.

7. Click the Windows 95 close button on each screen to close them.

You also can subscribe to newsgroups by name by clicking the Expert Add icon, typing the name of the newsgroup, and clicking Add. Of course, you'll need to know the newsgroup's name before you do that.

> **Note**
>
> To remove a newsgroup from your list, click the Read My Newsgroups icon to view your list. Highlight the newsgroup that you want to remove, and then click the Remove button. When prompted, confirm that you want to remove the selected newsgroup from your personal list. The newsgroup will not disappear from your personal list until you first close and then reopen the Read My Newsgroups window.

Reading Newsgroup Messages

Once you've subscribed to the newsgroups that interest you, you can begin reading the messages, or articles, that are posted to the groups by other Internet users.

To read messages, follow these steps:

1. Open the Go To menu and choose Keyword.

2. At the prompt, type **newsgroups** and click OK. Or you can choose the Internet Connection icon from the Main Menu, and then the News Groups icon from the Internet Connection screen.

3. Click the Read My Newsgroups icon.

4. Select a newsgroup; for example, biz.general.

5. To browse the newsgroup, double-click it.

6. To read an article posted to the newsgroup, double-click the subject line describing its contents. You can also click the Read button at the bottom of your screen (see fig. 11.9).

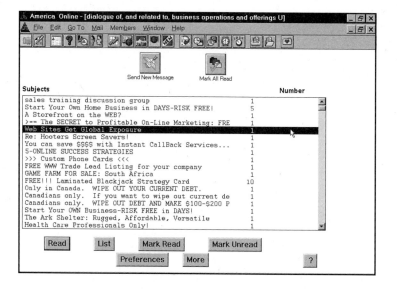

Fig. 11.9
Reading newsgroup articles on America Online is as simple as double-clicking the ones that interest you.

From the message screen shown in figure 11.10, you can perform many common mail tasks. To read the next article, click the Next button. To read the previous article, click the Previous button. The More button lets you read additional text of a lengthy newsgroup posting. The Reply to Group button allows you to reply to a posting.

II

Getting Connected

Fig. 11.10

The Read message screen allows you to continue reading new messages or send a response to the original poster or the entire newsgroup

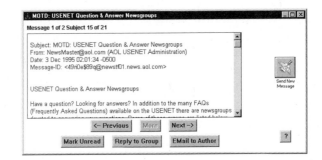

Note

America Online's Mark Read icon feature comes in handy if you go on vacation and don't want to have to dig your way out of a stack of unread messages when you return. Clicking this icon converts all the unread messages within the selected newsgroup to a "read" status, as if you had already read them. You can also save time by clicking the List Unread button, which displays only those articles you haven't read. Both of these icons are conveniently located on the Read My Newsgroups window, which is accessed by selecting the Read My Newsgroups icon from the main News Groups dialog box.

Tip

Are you tired of reading the same old newsgroups all the time? Click America Online's Latest Newsgroups icon on the Newsgroups screen.

Posting Newsgroup Articles

◀ See "How the Internet Works," p. 9

◀ See "The Various Parts of the Internet," p. 25

Once you've had a chance to read the articles posted by other newsgroup members, you'll probably want to try posting a few of your own.

To post an article to a newsgroup, follow these steps:

1. From the Main Menu, select the Internet Connection icon.

2. On the Internet Connection screen, choose the News Group icon.

3. Click the Read My Newsgroups icon.

4. Double-click the newsgroup to which you want to post—for example, biz.general.

5. Click the Send New Message icon.

6. At the Subject: prompt, type a few words describing your message.

7. Tab to the Message: prompt and type the text of your message.

8. Click the Send button.

Note

To create a signature file for your newsgroup postings, perform the following steps:

1. Use the keyword Newsgroups to go to the News Groups main screen.

2. Click the Set Preferences button.

3. Place your cursor in the Signature field and type the lines that you want to appear at the bottom of each of your newsgroup posts.

4. Click the OK button.

After you create your signature file, you need to select the Use Signature (Set in Global Preferences) checkbox for each message that you post to a newsgroup.

Responding to Newsgroup Articles

With America Online's newsreader, it's just as easy to respond to other users' postings as it is to post your own.

To respond to a newsgroup article, follow these steps:

1. From the Main Menu, select the Internet Connection icon.

2. On the Internet Connection screen, choose the News Group icon.

3. Click the Read My Newsgroups icon.

4. Double-click the newsgroup name you want to read.

5. Double-click the message to which you want to reply.

6. Select the Reply to Group button if you want to post your response to the entire newsgroup, or the E-Mail to Author button if you want to respond to the original post privately.

7. Type your response in the message blank that appears on your screen. Click the Send button when you are finished. The note is posted either to the newsgroup or to the original author, depending on the choice you made in step 6.

> **Tip**
>
> If you want to post your response to both the newsgroup and the original author, select a single checkbox on your message reply screen. If you have chosen the Reply to Group button when you started your response, you will see a checkbox allowing you to Copy Author of Original Message via Email. If you originally chose to send your reply to the original author, you will find a Copy to Newsgroup checkbox available.

> **Note**
>
> The Send to: field will automatically be filled in with the name of the newsgroup containing the posting to which you are responding. Likewise, the Subject: field will be filled with the title of the message to which you are responding.

Accessing Gopher and WAIS Databases

▶ See "Using Gopher and Popular Gopher Programs," p. 867

▶ See "Using WAIS," p. 897

America Online's Gopher service works somewhat differently than those usually found on the Internet. Instead of leaving novice Netsurfers to cruise from site to site sorting the wheat from the chaff, America Online has assembled a selection of interesting, useful, and reliable Gophers and labeled them as Editor's Choices. If you like, you can scroll through the list and visit popular sites such as The Electronic Newsstand, an online magazine rack. Or, if you want to venture beyond America Online's "Top 40," you can click the More "Other Gopher" Resources icon from the Other Gophers menu to access the rest of Gopherspace.

> **Troubleshooting**
>
> *I'm tired of slogging through menu after menu to access my favorite Gophers through America Online. Isn't there an easier way?*
>
> Unfortunately, America Online doesn't let you type Gopher addresses at a system prompt the way you can with a UNIX shell. Neither does it allow you to add a Gopher site to your list of favorite places—directly. However, if you just need to track down information from the Gopher rather than connect to the Gopher itself, a Veronica search (see "Using Veronica" later in this chapter) may give you what you're looking for more quickly. Another option is to use the Web browser to view the Gopher site. You can do this by typing **gopher://** before the address of the Gopher

> server that you are trying to reach. If you do this, you can save this Gopher address in your list of Favorite Places because America Online deals with the address as if it is a standard Web page.

America Online also makes Wide Area Information Servers (WAIS) databases available through its Gopher service. When you see the open book icon, a WAIS database or list of WAIS databases is most likely to be under it. Taken together, Gopher (the Internet equivalent of a table of contents) and WAIS (the equivalent of an index) complement one another to help you find the topics that interest you.

America Online's Gopher/WAIS interface was created by Pandora Systems of San Francisco. Pandora uses a program called Prospero, invented by the University of Southern California's Information Sciences Institute, to link Gopher sites to the America Online service. Pandora also selects the contents of the Editor's Choice menu and maintains contact with the site administrators responsible for maintaining these information resources.

Using Gopher

To use Gopher to search for the Career Guide to Industry published by the Bureau of Labor, follow these steps:

▶ See "Why Use Gopher?" p. 868

1. From the Main Menu, select the Internet Connection icon.

2. Choose the Gopher & WAIS button from the Internet Connection screen.

> **Tip**
>
> If you are currently buried in another area of America Online you can reach the Gopher and WAIS server by opening the Go To menu and choosing Keyword. At the prompt, type **gopher** and choose OK.

3. Scroll down the list of Gophers to Business and Employment. Double-click or highlight it and press Enter (see fig. 11.11).

4. Scroll down to Information Professionals List Gopher and double-click it.

5. Scroll down to The Legal Domain Network - Legal Information on the Internet and double-click it. You'll now be able to find information on the current laws that affect the Internet and read through a wide variety of discussions related to these issues.

Fig. 11.11
America Online lets you browse Gophers by scrolling down a list of topics such as Biology, Census, and Education.

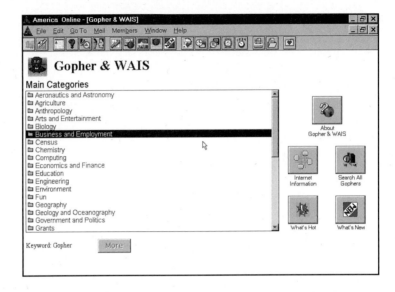

Using Veronica

▶ See "Using Gopher and Popular Gopher Programs," p. 867

▶ See "Searching on the Internet," p. 911

America Online also lets you use a tool called Veronica to search through Gopher menus. If you know the title of a Gopher menu or even the general topic you're looking for, Veronica can help you find it in the wilds of Gopherspace. Simply click the Search All Gophers button on the main Gopher and WAIS screen, and type the words or phrases that describe what you're looking for.

To use Veronica to ferret out information about stocks, follow these steps:

1. Open the Go To menu and choose Keyword.

2. At the prompt, type **gopher** and click OK.

> **Note**
>
> You can also use the Internet Connection screen to access Gopher and WAIS.

3. Click the Search All Gophers button.

4. Type the word or words that describe what you are looking for; for example, multimedia (see fig. 11.12). Click Search.

5. A list of all Gopher sites containing informational files with the word "multimedia" appears on your screen. To access those Gophers, double-click or highlight a listing and press Enter.

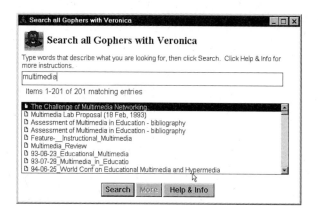

Fig. 11.12
America Online's
easy-to-use
Veronica feature
lets you search
the wilds of
Gopherspace for
the information
you need.

Using File Transfer Protocol (FTP)

America Online's file transfer protocol (FTP) interface became available to
members in late 1994; previously, it had been in "preview mode," one step
past beta test but without all the bugs worked out. Not only is the entire FTP
interface point-and-click, but the service has done a lot of little things to
make FTP easier for novices to use. For example, GIF files and other graphics
display automatically during the download, and, like America Online's
Gopher menu, a selection of popular FTP sites is available for users to browse.

▶ See "Using FTP
and Popular
FTP Programs,"
p. 837

> **Note**
>
> Clicking America Online's Search FTP Sites icon lets you search for FTP sites by typing
> a few words that describe what you're looking for, and then clicking the Search
> button. Unfortunately, there is currently no way to go directly to the FTP site you
> found through the search. For now, you'll need to write down the site location and
> type it in later.

The following steps show you how to use America Online's FTP feature:

1. Click the FTP icon from the Internet Connection menu.

2. Click the Enter FTP Area icon and then click the Go To FTP icon.
    A Favorite Sites menu appears on your screen (see fig. 11.13).

3. Double-click any of the entries on the menu or click the Other Site
    button to enter the site address for the host that you would like to
    access.

4. Click the Connect button to connect to the site you've chosen. America
    Online now attempts to establish a connection to the site address

specified. If the connection cannot be established, an alert box is displayed informing you of a problem.

Fig. 11.13
America Online's new FTP feature lets members browse files from popular sites.

5. Once connected, you'll see a menu stating the name of the site you are connected to and a list of directories and/or files. Each entry features a small icon indicating its type—directories (folder icons), text files (document icons), or graphics (picture icons)—followed by its name.

6. You can then choose from the following action buttons at the bottom of the screen:

   ■ *Open* displays the contents of the file on your screen.

   ■ *More* adds more list items if the window maximum has been exceeded.

   ■ *Download Now* opens a window and lets you choose the destination of the selected file and start the download process.

   ■ *Help (?)* displays a document that explains how America Online's FTP tools work.

Note

America Online recently added the capability to access FTP sites by supplying a login and password to access sites where you have an account, rather than just logging in anonymously. You also can use the Web browser to visit FTP sites. Simply type **ftp://** before the URL of the FTP site and the Web browser will take you there and get you logged in.

Caution

Unlike the files that are uploaded to America Online's forums, the FTP files it makes available are not checked for viruses. Just because you're using America Online, don't assume that these FTP files are safer than any others on the Internet!

Using the World Wide Web

America Online's World Wide Web interface was a new addition in 1995. Unlike many other online services that are providing Web access, the America Online browser is built in to version 2.5 of its software. You do not have to install a separate dialer or browser program, allowing you to easily jump from an internal America Online site to the Internet without having to make another phone call. America Online's World Wide Web browser can perform many of the same functions as the most popular Web browser available: Netscape Navigator. This includes the following:

- The ability to manually enter the URL that you want to visit
- Keep an organized list of your favorite sites to visit
- The opportunity to name the page at which you want to enter the World Wide Web
- Support for forms, which provide the ability to search the Web for information or answer online questionnaires
- Globally control how you see graphics on each World Wide Web page
- Page backwards through the sites that you have visited during the current online session
- Keep a copy of the sites that you have visited on your hard drive, so you can load them faster the next time you wish to visit them

Note

With the advent of a built-in World Wide Web browser, America Online also gave its members the ability to create their own Web pages. Of course, each member is required to use the same form, providing each page with a similar look and feel. All of these Web pages are accessible for any member of America Online and anyone who has access to the Internet. America Online has also included a search utility that allows individuals browsing the Web to search for a specific America Online member's Web page.

▶ See "How the World Wide Web Works," p. 457

▶ See "New Web Technologies," p. 723

The following steps show you how to enter the World Wide Web using America Online's browser:

1. Open the Main Menu and choose the Internet Connection icon.
2. From the Internet Connection screen, click the World Wide Web button.

3. This will take you to America Online's home page, shown in figure 11.14. From this page, you can jump to any other America Online site located on the Web. You can also jump to other members' personal home pages.

Fig. 11.14
The America Online home page makes it possible for all Web users to explore what America Online has to offer.

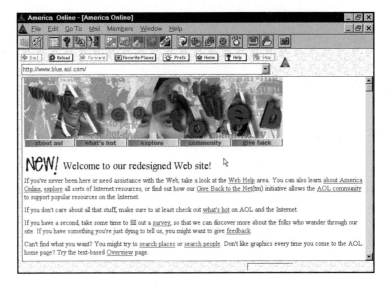

At this point, there are quite a few things that you can do with your America Online Web browser. You can select a link to jump to another page on the *America Online Web server,* enter the URL of another site that you want to visit, or edit your Web browser options. The following list details many of the options you will be presented with while cruising the Web:

- *Follow a link*—To follow a link on any page, click your left mouse button on any piece of highlighted text. Your status bar at the bottom of your Web browser will show you the address to which this link will take you.

- *Enter a URL*—To go directly to another Web site, you must know the address (URL) of that site. Once you know it, place your cursor in the URL field at the top of your Web browser screen and type the address preceded by **http://**. For example, if you want to go to the Web-Crawler Web searching utility, type: **http://www.webcrawler.com** and then press Enter.

- *Retrace your steps*—You can look at each of the sites you visited during the current online session by clicking the Back button. This button will take you back to the first site that you visited that day. There is no mechanism to travel forward through those sites again. You will have to click the links that you used the first time, or directly enter the URL of the site at which you wish to look.

■ *Go to a Favorite Place*—You can go directly to one of your favorite Web sites by clicking the Favorite Places tool, and then clicking the icon of the site to which you wish to go. You can add sites to this list automatically by clicking the heart-shaped icon in the upper-left corner of the Web browser window.

■ *Edit your browser preferences*—To edit the settings that your browser is currently using, you will need to choose the Preferences button, and then select the appropriate preferences section that you wish to change. You can change the default home page, the way your browser looks at graphical images, and how it deals with variations in baud rates.

Note

America Online's Web browser supports a handy right mouse click shortcut menu. This menu allows you to quickly save any image shown in your browser, cancel a file or page transfer, copy a URL to the Windows Clipboard, and a few other useful tools. If you spend a little time playing around with this menu, you may find that you will save time by getting where you want to be faster.

Looking Ahead: The Future According to America Online

America Online members now have access to the World Wide Web through a graphical browser. This addition has rounded out the set of Internet tools that the service offers its users. Plans also call for giving users the ability to automatically forward mail to Internet mailboxes and other addresses not on the same account. A new Search All Newsgroups icon will let users open a dialog box to search all newsgroup titles and descriptions by typing in words and phrases. Newsreader enhancements are also in the works. We must have patience while America Online makes these new features available.

For now, America Online provides an excellent on-ramp for Internet novices eager to surf the Net at an affordable price. However, novices don't stay novices for long—and users seeking broader Internet access and more sophisticated Internet tools might want to look elsewhere as they sharpen their skills.

Getting Connected

II

CHAPTER 12

Connecting Through Prodigy

Prodigy was the first to offer a full graphics-based online service. Eventually Prodigy gravitated from a proprietary graphics look to a Windows interface. The Internet services that Prodigy provides are available only with the Windows version of the Prodigy software.

This chapter describes the Internet services that are available on Prodigy, and how to use them. This includes the following:

- An overview of the Prodigy Internet services offered by Prodigy
- How to sign up and access the Internet through Prodigy
- How to use the Prodigy World Wide Web browser
- How to use FTP, Gopher, and other Internet services
- How to use the UseNet newsgroups provided on Prodigy
- How to use the Internet for e-mail

What Is Prodigy?

Prodigy is a full service online system that provides a complete range of news, sports, weather, member bulletin boards, and live chat. In addition, Prodigy has shopping services, an encyclopedia, and inservice e-mail to other Prodigy members. Prodigy also offers the full range of Internet services, including World Wide Web, UseNet News, and Internet e-mail. The FTP and Gopher services on the Internet are included within the World Wide Web browser.

You can access Prodigy only by using the Prodigy software. This special software is available for a nominal fee or often, even better, no fee. To access the Internet, you must have the Prodigy for Windows software. There is no special software for Windows 95, but the Windows 3.1 software runs fine, for the most part, under Windows 95. Prodigy discontinued plain-vanilla DOS-based software in early 1995.

When you are using the Windows version of Prodigy, use the point-and-click method with the normal Windows menu system at the top of the screen. In addition, Prodigy provides a toolbar at the bottom of the screen that you can customize to reflect how you want to use the service.

Prodigy is constantly revising the service. While many areas of the service have a true Windows interface, some areas still retain the old DOS-based look. With literally hundreds of different areas, it may take Prodigy a long time to convert to a true Windows look and feel over the entire service. For example, figure 12.1 shows a typical screen in the News & Weather area.

Fig. 12.1
Prodigy News.

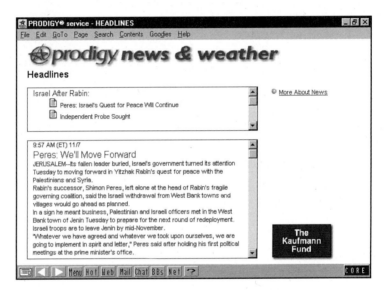

Notice how the headlines at the top and the story at the bottom of the screen reflect typical Windows with a vertical scrollbar for viewing the rest of the information.

Figure 12.2 is an example of the original Prodigy look.

This screen still uses the old Prodigy interface where there are no scrollbars for viewing the rest of the story. Instead, the left and right arrows on the toolbar are used to move up and down one page. Alternately, you could use the Page Up and Page Down keys to get to the previous or next page of the story. Unfortunately, the Page Up and Page Down keys do not work the same way when you are reading a Sports News story. If you are reading a Headline News story though, they do work. Prodigy is not consistent on the use of the keyboard across different areas of the service.

Fig. 12.2
Prodigy Weather.

What Services Are Offered?

In addition to Prodigy's wealth of internal information and services, you can also access almost every major part of the Internet, with one exception—you cannot Telnet from within Prodigy. Here's a quick look at what is available:

- *World Wide Web*. Prodigy now offers Netscape Navigator as its World Wide Web browser. This browser is the most popular in use on the Web and has enhancements that allow a variety of visual effects. Many WWW sites are "Netscape" enhanced and cannot be viewed without the special functions available only in the Netscape browser. The WWW browser also gives you access to FTP (File Transfer Protocol) and Gopher (a simple menu-based Internet access system).

- *E-mail*. You can send mail to other Prodigy members and anyone else in the world through Prodigy's Internet connection. Naturally, you can get mail from anyone on the Internet who knows your Prodigy ID. Prodigy members can look up your ID on the Member List, but this service is not available to those outside Prodigy.

- *UseNet Newsgroups*. Prodigy has a newsreader that allows you to read and download from thousands of Internet newsgroups. There is surely a newsgroup for your special interest.

Pricing

Prodigy offers several pricing plans, one of which will probably suit your needs. Be sure to read about the pricing plans when you sign up. Distinct areas and functions of the service are billed differently depending on which plan you choose. A small icon at the bottom right of the screen tells you whether you are in a Free, Core, Plus, or Fee area. In general terms, Free areas are just that, free with no time charge. Core areas are part of the basic monthly charge and may or may not be billed by time depending on the plan you choose. Plus areas are billed by time used. Fee areas involve an extra charge that are billed to your credit card before entering the area. You must agree to the charge for that area.

Connecting to Prodigy

In order to connect to Prodigy, you must first have the Prodigy software. Be sure to get the Windows version if you are using Windows 95 or Windows 3.1. Most new PCs come with Prodigy already installed, but if you need the software just call 1-800-PRODIGY and ask for it. The software is also sold in stores for a nominal fee.

Installing Prodigy

If you have a new computer with the software already installed, you are ahead of the game.

To install the Prodigy software, follow these steps:

1. Put the Prodigy disk in the drive, click Start and then Run.
2. Type **A:INSTALL.EXE** and click OK. Or, you can click Browse and navigate to the INSTALL.EXE program on the disk and then click OK.

The install program will transfer Prodigy from the disk to your hard disk and add the Prodigy program group to the File Manager. You may have to make your own shortcut to add Prodigy to the Start menu.

Starting Prodigy

To start Prodigy for the first time, press the Start button and navigate to the Prodigy icon in the Start menu. Then, click the Prodigy icon and you are on your way.

The program first dials an 800 number that lets you choose a local phone number based on your area code. Choose the highest speed that your modem will support. Prodigy has 14.4 kbps service available in most areas and is adding 28.8 kbps support in selected cities. If you are planning on using the World Wide Web, make sure you get the fastest speed possible.

Once you have chosen a local phone number and a backup number, Prodigy will hang up and dial the local number so you can sign on to the service. Signing on takes a few minutes. Your Prodigy software booklet contains a Prodigy ID that is four letters, two numbers, and the letter A. You can have up to six different IDs with one membership, letters A through F. The A account is the master account and is the only one that can grant access to certain areas of Prodigy to the other accounts. In addition to the ID, you also must supply a password. A temporary password is included with the Prodigy booklet to let you access the service the first time.

Once you are connected, type in your member ID and temporary password and begin the process of signing on to the service. Just follow the screen prompts. You have to tell Prodigy your name, address, and phone number. Have a credit card handy, too. This is how Prodigy Services bills you for your membership. Read the membership agreement and choose a billing plan. You also need to supply a personal password. Think about this carefully.

> **Caution**
>
> Don't choose a password that someone else can guess. Remember, anyone who knows your ID and password can sign on under your name and use your account incurring extra charges and invading your privacy.

Once you have filled in all the necessary forms (you can't call it paperwork, but that's what it is), you are a full member of Prodigy and can access all of the areas of the service. You can also sign up other members of your family using the same basic membership. Each additional member has the same basic four-letter, two-number ID with B through F at the end. In other words, Mom can be RKXV82A, Dad is RKXV82B, and the kids can hold RKXV82C through RKXV82F. If you have more than four kids you will need an additional membership.

Logging On

There are two ways for you to sign on to Prodigy once you are a member—regular logon and auto logon. The regular logon features a logon screen similar to the example in figure 12.3.

Enter your ID and password. Then you have the option of selecting the service area you want to use from the Select Destination drop-down list. Press the Sign On button and the software dials the service and connects.

Fig. 12.3

Prodigy logon
screen.

You can also use Prodigy's automatic logon feature, which Prodigy calls autologon. With autologon, you can access Prodigy without typing your ID and password. All you have to do is click the autologon icon and the software automatically dials the service and connects with your ID and password. While this is convenient, you run the risk of someone else using your Prodigy account from your computer. As an alternative, you can set autologon to prompt you for your password every time you sign on. If you want to use autologon, just use the jumpword autologon once you have signed on and follow the prompts for creating an autologon icon.

> ### Tip
> A Prodigy *jumpword* moves you from one area of the service to another without your having to use the menu structure. For example, if you are reading the news and want to go right to Sports, you can click the GoTo menu and type the jumpword **Sports**.

How Prodigy Is Organized

The main highlights screen gives you a hint as to how the service is organized. The left side of the screen usually presents six different areas that may be of special interest that day. You can find an index to other areas of the service in the two windows to the right. The upper-right window points you to a broad area of interest such as Highlights, Interest Groups, and Help. You can navigate by clicking any of the subjects in the lower-right window, such as Sports.

Each highlights screen is divided into three parts, just like the Sports highlights screen shown in figure 12.4.

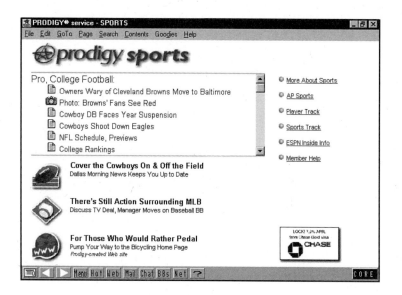

Fig. 12.4
Prodigy Sports
highlights.

The headlines are in the window at the upper-left. The lower-left shows some features that may be of interest and the upper-right gives you choices for navigating to specific features within the area.

If you click one of the headlines in the upper-left, you get the text of the story in a window directly below the headlines, as shown in figure 12.5.

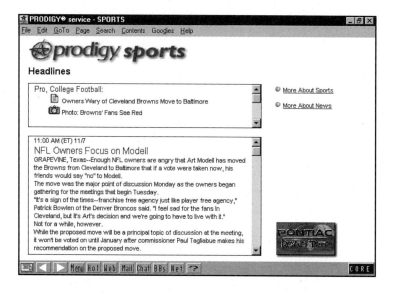

Fig. 12.5
Prodigy Sports
story.

Getting Connected

Prodigy is not yet consistent with the look and feel to all of its features, although they are rapidly moving in that direction. Some features do not use a typical Windows screen, as you can see in figure 12.6.

Fig. 12.6

Prodigy Sports scores.

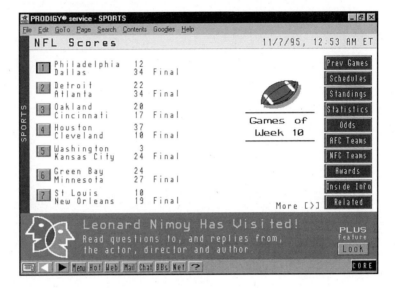

You can still use the point-and-click method for moving from one feature to another, but notice that the familiar Windows scrollbar is missing and that the buttons are different than the Windows buttons.

The Bottom Line

Across the bottom of the Prodigy screen is a series of buttons that Prodigy calls the toolbar. You can set the toolbar to reflect your personal preferences and the way you use Prodigy. Click the Goodies menu and then Tool Bar Setup to see a list of the buttons that are available. Figure 12.7 shows what is currently available, although new ones are occasionally added as Prodigy continues to expand its services.

Once you become familiar with how you use Prodigy, you can set up the toolbar so you can quickly navigate to your areas of interest.

GoTo

The GoTo menu choice is a quick way to get to most of Prodigy's features. You can enter a GoTo word or get a complete alphabetized list of all of Prodigy's features. How many features are there? Prodigy is constantly changing, but the last time I looked there were 269 pages in the A-Z Index with 10 entries per page from 14.4 kbps to Zurich Weather. That's 2,690.

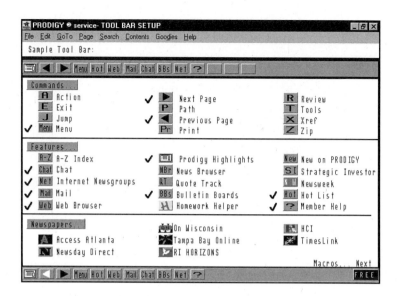

Fig. 12.7
Prodigy toolbar
options.

Note

Prodigy is moving away from the term *jumpword* and is now favoring the term *GoTo word*. You will still see both terms on the service, but they mean the same thing.

You can also build a personal hot list of your favorite features. With a hot list you can list a series of features that you use every time you sign on. You can press F3, see your list, and choose a feature. Or press the F4 key and jump immediately to the next feature on your hot list. The GoTo menu also lets you immediately add the feature you are viewing to your hot list.

Tip

You can build your own hot list by choosing Hot List from the GoTo menu or by pressing F3. The Hot List dialog box lists your current selections and gives you the option of adding more destinations or deleting one or more of the current destinations. To add a destination to your hot list, just press the Add GoTo Word button. If you are currently viewing a screen that you want to add to your hot list, press the Add To List button. You can also rearrange your hot list to suit your personal preferences.

Prodigy's Internet Services

There are several ways to access Prodigy's Internet services. The choice
Internet on the right of the main highlight screen will take you to the
Internet highlight screen shown in figure 12.8.

Fig. 12.8
Prodigy Internet
highlights.

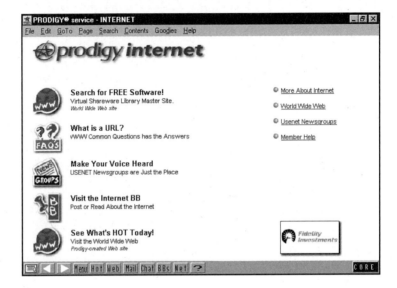

From here, you can access the World Wide Web or the UseNet newsgroups.
Internet e-mail is handled through the Prodigy Mail program.

How to Get to the Internet Area

There are several methods you can use to access the Prodigy Internet services.
If you want to send Internet mail, go to Prodigy Mail either by using the
jumpword "Mail" or by clicking Read mail in the GoTo menu. To get to the
World Wide Web, you can enter the GoTo word "WWW" or "Web." Many
times a Prodigy Headline will point to a World Wide Web site instead of an
internal Prodigy article. If you click a headline with the WWW symbol (a
world with a couple of satellites whirling around it) you can access that site
immediately.

The GoTo word "UseNet" takes you to the UseNet newsgroups. If you already
know the name of the newsgroup you want to read, you can type the name
into the jumpword dialog box and click the USENET Newsgroups button and
then OK.

Using the World Wide Web on Prodigy

Prodigy gives you complete access to the World Wide Web, or WWW as it is more commonly known. If your Prodigy software package does not already include the WWW browser, Prodigy will download it to your computer. Downloading the software takes only a few minutes; the browser is automatically configured and starts right away. From time to time Prodigy updates the browser software. When this happens, you see a dialog box telling you to wait while the update takes place.

Just before this book went to press, Prodigy announced that it will use the Netscape Navigator for accessing the World Wide Web. Netscape developed several enhancements to the standard HTML (HyperText Markup Language) used to transmit information over the WWW. Many WWW sites are "Netscape enhanced." With Prodigy and Netscape you get all the features of these sites.

Using Prodigy's World Wide Web Browser

Using Prodigy's Netscape browser is fairly simple. Most screens contain both text and graphics. As you read the information on the screen you will notice that certain words are highlighted. The words (and sometimes pictures) are links to other Web pages. When you move the mouse around the screen you see the pointer change into a hand when it reaches a link. Just click to follow that link.

▶ See "Using Netscape," p. 497

The World Wide Web browser has a standard Windows menu bar, a drop-down list that displays the current site, and a toolbar for shortcuts. You can access a site by typing the complete URL in the Netsite box or you can drop the box and click previous sites you have visited. The Back icon takes you back one site. The Reload icon is useful if your connection is interrupted and you want to reload the current page. If you get hopelessly lost (not uncommon) you can click the Home icon and return to your home page. There is also a Stop icon, which stops the incoming text or graphics.

Using the Options menu, you can customize the browser for your own personal tastes. If you find an interesting site, you can add that URL to your own personal list of Bookmarks so that you can easily return. It's a good idea to make a bookmark for an interesting site. As you cruise along the Web you will notice that the URLs are rather lengthy; trying to type a URL into the Netsite box can be frustrating because spelling and case both count.

Home Page

To help you begin your journey, Prodigy has its own home page that points you toward areas that might interest you. The Prodigy pages are only available from Prodigy itself and cannot be accessed by others on the Internet. Any time you access the World Wide Web browser you can always get back to the home page by clicking the Home button on the toolbar. Prodigy articles sometimes contain links to WWW sites so you do not always start your Web journey with your home page.

You do not have to use the Prodigy home page as your signon page. You can use the Options menu to set any URL as your personal signon page, such as the Netscape home page shown in figure 12.9.

Fig. 12.9

Netscape home page.

Your Own Home Page

If you have ever wanted to open the window and shout, "Hey, world, here I am!" you can now do it with a personal home page on Prodigy. Prodigy gives you the tools to make your own HTML file so that others on the WWW can see your message. Prodigy has a World Wide Web page that lets you include text and graphics and links to other pages. There is even a selection of artwork that you can include in your page.

Speed Limits on the Information Highway

Be warned that the World Wide Web is a graphic-intensive service. What you see on the screen is delivered to your computer as a text-based HyperText

Markup Language document. The browser takes the incoming information and formats it on the screen for you to view. If you want to see what is sent to your computer, choose Source from the View menu. What you see is the HTML document including all the instructions to the browser. This document tells the browser how to format the text on the screen and where to find the graphics that are associated with the text. Sometimes the browser has to access the original site several times to download all the text and graphics for one screen.

As the site sends information to your computer through Prodigy, you can see the progress at the bottom of the screen. Accessing any site is limited by the slowest link between the computers. Most of the time, the slowest link will be between your computer and Prodigy, but sometimes a Web site will be linked to Prodigy by an even slower link. Don't be surprised if it takes several minutes to download a graphic-intensive screen.

One option that you might want to consider while you are browsing is to turn graphics off. This will speed up your session considerably. Under the Options menu, uncheck Autoload Images. If you reach a site where you want to see the graphics, just check the Autoload Images (from the Options menu) and then reload the current URL by pressing the Reload button.

Using Gopher and FTP on Prodigy

Prodigy does not currently provide separate Gopher and FTP programs. However, the World Wide Web browser is capable of using both of these services.

Gopher

Gopher is a menu-based Internet program that was developed at the University of Minnesota. Like the World Wide Web, there are literally thousands of Gopher sites around the world. The Prodigy browser can access Gopher sites by beginning the URL with gopher://, followed by the Internet address of the Gopher site. For example, to get to the mother of all Gopher servers at the University of Minnesota, type **gopher://gopher.tc.umn.edu/** in the Netsite box and press Enter.

▶ See "Using Gopher and Popular Gopher Programs," p. 867

As you can see in figure 12.10, a Gopher site consists of a list of menu choices that direct you to the information you want.

Just point and click your way through the menu structure. As you travel from menu to menu you can always go back to the previous menu until you reach the main menu for that site. Most Gopher sites (but not all) have a menu choice that will connect you to other Gophers around the world.

Fig. 12.10

Gopher menu.

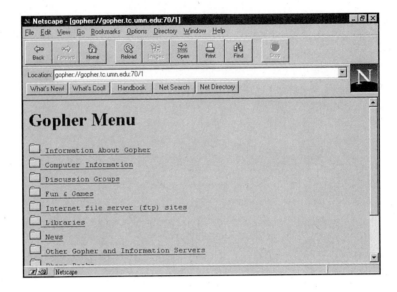

Gophers are not graphic-intensive like the World Wide Web, so getting from one place to another is much faster than with the WWW.

FTP

FTP is short for File Transfer Protocol and is just another way for computers to share information over the Internet. FTP is generally limited to transferring files from one computer to another. FTP sites consist of a directory list much like Windows File Manager. Figure 12.11 shows the directory structure for Microsoft's FTP site.

To get to an FTP site using the Prodigy browser, you have to use ftp:// followed by the address of the site. For example, to get to the Microsoft FTP site, type **ftp://ftp.microsoft.com/** in the Location box and press Enter.

Once you reach an FTP site, you can point and click just like you do for a Gopher site. Directory names are preceded by a folder icon and text files by a document icon. To download a file, just click the file name. If the file is a text file, the browser will display it on the screen. If it is any other type of file, the browser will prompt you for a file name and download the file to disk.

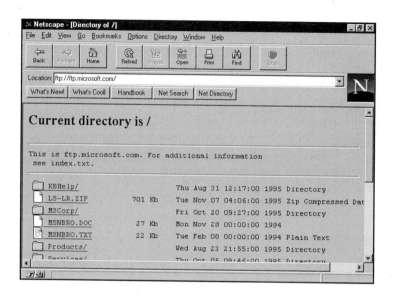

Fig. 12.11
Microsoft FTP site.

> **Note**
>
> Be aware that the Internet is not just for PC users. As a matter of fact, PC users are relative newcomers to the Net. Many of the files that are available through FTP are meant for UNIX or VMS operating systems and will be useless to a PC. Make sure you can use a file before you take the time to download it. The file name is usually an indication as to whether you can use the file or not. File names like WINDISK.EXE or WINDISK.ZIP are usually meant for PC users. A file name like README.TXT is usually a text file that can be used by almost any operating system. But file names like SZ.TAR.Z with several extensions are probably not usable on a PC.

UseNet News on Prodigy

Prodigy provides access to several thousand UseNet newsgroups. Surely there is one area that interests you. Newsgroups are similar to bulletin boards. You can read and post messages to the group. Some groups are *moderated* so your postings are screened before they become available to the general public. Most groups are *free form*—you see everything that is posted by others and everyone sees what you post.

Be forewarned that UseNet newsgroups are uncontrolled in the broadest sense of the term. There is no censorship and each group has a certain set of unwritten rules that participants are expected to follow. If you don't follow the proper "Netiquette" you may be "flamed," or worse yet, get hundreds of mail messages from outraged group users. Before posting to a newsgroup, take the time to read the Prodigy section on Netiquette. You can read a complete discussion of proper Netiquette by pressing the Netiquette button in the opening screen of the UseNet section of Prodigy.

Subscribing to UseNet Newsgroups

You can get to the UseNet newsgroups by pressing Internet on the Main Highlight screen and then UseNet Newsgroups on the Internet Highlight screen. You can also use the GoTo jumpword, "Usenet."

Prodigy lets you subscribe to as many newsgroups as you want. To subscribe, just follow these steps:

1. From the UseNet Newsgroups screen, click Newsgroups. You will see a list of the groups you're already reading.

2. Click the Find Newsgroup button.

3. Search for the group using one of the methods available in the dialog box, either the latest newsgroups added, all newsgroups, or selected newsgroups with a specific text pattern.

4. Click the Newsgroups button from the Internet area.

5. Select the name of the newsgroup from the list and then click the Add to Your Newsgroups button.

Once you have a list of newsgroups, you can either add it to your subscribed list, or go directly to that newsgroup by clicking the Go to Newsgroup button. This allows you to read and post to the group without subscribing. When you leave the newsgroup and return to the main menu, you can opt to subscribe to that newsgroup or not.

Reading Newsgroup Messages

Once you have selected a newsgroup that interests you, click the GoTo Newsgroup button. Prodigy takes a few seconds to "thread" the articles within the newsgroup and then displays a list of articles. *Threading* the articles lets you see the first posting and then any follow-up postings on the same subject in sequence. Each subject is preceded by the number of postings in that subject.

You can scroll through the list, select the subjects you want to see, then click the Go to Articles button to begin reading. As a shortcut, you can simply double-click the thread you want to read. When you finish reading the first article in the thread, click the Next Article button or the Previous Article button if you are not at the beginning of the thread. To see another thread, click the Next Thread button or the Previous Thread button.

While you are reading an article, you can respond to it by clicking the Respond button. There are several ways to send a response. You can post a public message to this or another newsgroup, or you can send a private message to the author. You can also forward the article to a third person via a private e-mail message.

You can save the article as a file, print it, or copy it to the Clipboard by pressing the Print/Save button.

Posting to Newsgroups

Once you have selected a newsgroup, you can post to it by clicking the Post New Article button. Prodigy provides a friendly little warning, shown in figure 12.12, before you can post.

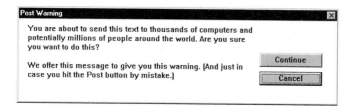

Fig. 12.12
Post Article warning.

Always think about what you are going to say and the possible responses before you post.

If you do decide to post an article, enter a subject and then the text of your message in the appropriate areas. Once you have written your article, press the Post button. You can always cancel before you post if you change your mind.

> ### Caution
>
> Remember that your posting has the potential of being read by millions of people all over the world. Every one of these people will get your e-mail address from the posting. If they don't like what you say, you could get thousands of mail messages in response to your posting. Be sure to read Part V of this book, "UseNet Newsgroups," before posting.

Unreadable Messages

Some articles may appear to be unreadable, as shown in figure 12.13.

Many people use the UseNet newsgroups to send non-text files over the Internet. These files could be programs, pictures, or binary files. Because some

Internet connections are only used for sending text, the person who posted the message has converted a binary file to text so that it may be sent over the Internet. If the author has used a special program to convert the file to text and you want to use it, you must convert it back to binary.

Fig. 12.13

Encoded article.

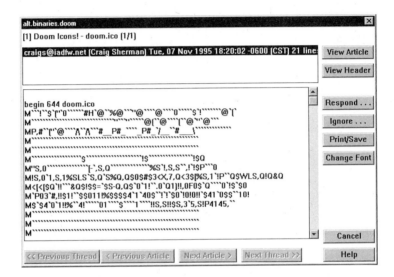

The most common form of converting binary to text and back is the UUEncode and UUDecode programs. Some newsreaders automatically encode and decode binary files, but the newsreader used with Prodigy does not. A publicly available program that does the conversion for Windows is WINCODE.EXE and is available on many FTP sites.

To use WINCODE.EXE with Prodigy UseNet newsgroups, you must first save the article to a file with the extension .UUE. Then run the WINCODE program to decode the file.

Even after the file has been decoded, some people send large programs over the Internet in a compressed format called ZIP. To uncompress a zipped file you need another widely available program called PKZIP. Like WINCODE, PKZIP is available on many FTP sites and is available in a Windows version. Both programs are shareware and can be downloaded and used on a trial basis. If you like and use the programs, you can register them with the author for a small fee.

Internet Mail

Prodigy mail is capable of both sending and receiving messages to and from anyone with an Internet connection. All you need to know is the address.

Getting Mail from the Internet

Getting mail from the Internet is the same as getting mail from another Prodigy member. The New Mail icon appears on the toolbar and you can get to Prodigy Mail by clicking this icon. Prodigy automatically runs the Mail program and displays a list of senders and subjects in the mail window as in figure 12.14.

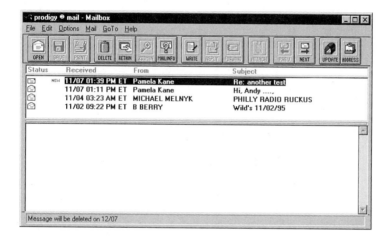

Fig. 12.14
Prodigy Mailbox.

Just double-click the message line or highlight the message and click the Open icon to read the mail. Once you have read the note, you can delete it, reply to it, or forward it to someone else. If the mail message has a file attached to it, you can download the file to your computer.

Sending Mail on the Internet

The only difference between sending mail to another Prodigy member and sending mail over the Internet to a non-member is how the mail is addressed.

To send this mail message, follow these steps:

1. Under the Mail menu, choose Write New Message, or click the Write icon on the toolbar.

2. In the To: box, type the full Internet address of the recipient.

3. Add a subject line and then write your message.

4. When finished, click the Send icon and your message is on its way.

You can attach a file to a mail message sent to another Prodigy member. Just press the Attach button and select the file. You cannot, however, attach a file to an Internet mail message.

Address Book

The Prodigy address book feature lets you keep important addresses readily at hand.

To add an address to your personal address book, follow these steps:

1. Click the Address icon on the toolbar.

2. Supply an easy-to-remember nickname.

3. Supply the mail address of that person.

   If you want to add an Internet address rather than a Prodigy address, click the Internet button so you get extra space for the address.

4. When finished, click OK.

To select an address from your address book when writing a message, follow these steps:

1. Click on the Address icon and then click the Select From button.

2. You can choose one or several names to receive the message, or send it to one person with a (computer) carbon copy (cc) to another.

3. When you have finished selecting the names, just press OK and return to writing your message.

How to Get More Information on the Internet Through Prodigy

The Internet Highlights page offers a wealth of information about the Internet. Just click the More About the Internet choice and then select from various Prodigy bulletin boards, World Wide Web sites, UseNet newsgroups, or Prodigy's own features about the Internet. You can even download a book about the Internet and Prodigy, as shown in figure 12.15.

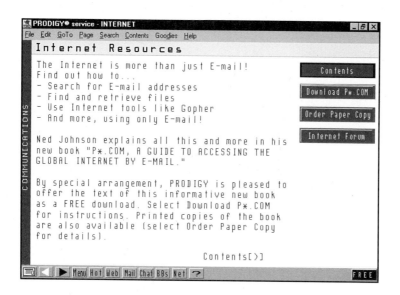

Fig. 12.15
More about the
Internet.

II

Getting Connected

CHAPTER 13

Connecting Through Microsoft Network

The Microsoft Network is perhaps the most exciting and controversial part of Windows 95. This completely new product component has sparked tremendous controversy in the communications industry, specifically among existing information service providers. In addition to offering the traditional online information service environment, Microsoft has designed MSN as the conduit to bring Windows 95 users to the general Internet, allowing fairly seamless integration of the communications tools that come with the new operating system and the resources of the emerging global network. In this chapter we look at

- What MSN is
- What MSN offers to the Internet user
- How to configure Windows 95 and MSN for Internet access
- How to start your MSN account
- How to use Windows 95 Internet (Internet Explorer and Exchange) applications with MSN

What Is the Microsoft Network?

MSN is the first foray that Mr. Gates & Company have made into territory generally deemed to belong to companies such as CompuServe, America Online, Prodigy, and others: the general *online information service*. Online information services provide a wealth of resources (software, databases, technical support) within a well-defined menu structure, available via a local call in most areas. But in recent months, even the venerable grandfathers of the online industry have begun to take advantage of the public's incredible hunger for general Internet access by first providing gateways for exchange of Internet mail, and then true access to FTP and the World Wide Web.

◄ See "The Various Ways to Connect to the Internet: Which One is Right for You?," p. 101

Microsoft Network is no different. Originally designed to compete directly with the existing services (with the added advantage of seamless integration with the Windows 95 desktop), Microsoft Network was soon expanded to allow access to the global Internet via its menus. While this indirect approach may seem inefficient to the "digerati," or Internet old-timers, for the millions exploring communications for the first time, it's probably ideal.

What MSN Isn't

One point of confusion, resulting from clever yet redundant naming of product components and capabilities, is especially nefarious in Windows 95. It's important to make a complete distinction between *a* Microsoft network system and *The* Microsoft Network proper.

With Windows for Workgroups 3.1 and Windows NT 3.1, Microsoft introduced its own true peer-to-peer networking using the NETBEUI protocol. This inexpensive networking system provides an extremely attractive alternative to more expensive network solutions for home and small business users, allowing any PC running these versions of Windows to connect and share resources with only simple network interface cards (other networking systems, such as Novell Netware, may cost thousands of dollars to license and require expensive server systems). Windows 95 also supports this same networking system. Any PC using one of these versions and connected thusly is said to be on "a Microsoft network."

This has nothing to do with being on The Microsoft Network information service, which serves a totally different purpose: sharing of information via a globally accessible menu structure, with access to the Internet if you desire. A Windows 95 PC can be using both, of course!

Basic Requirements for MSN

While there are some specific requirements for accessing the Internet using MSN, they're not onerous. Odds are you already have everything required. You'll need the following:

- A working installation of Windows 95
- An installed and fully operational modem (28.8 kbps preferred)
- Installed Microsoft Plus!
- Payment information (your credit card number and other vital financial statistics)

> **Note**
>
> While the basic Microsoft Network setup components come with your Windows 95 purchase, the specific Internet access tools you'll need come with the Plus! pack. You need both for complete Internet connectivity the "Microsoft way."

Setting Up Your Modem

Before you can begin using MSN, you'll need to set up your modem. This is greatly simplified under Windows 95 compared to previous versions. If you've already confirmed that your modem is working, skip ahead to "Installing Plus! and the Internet Jumpstart Kit," later in this chapter.

To set up your modem, follow these steps:

1. Make sure your modem is installed completely and all connections are secure. If it's an internal model, make sure the phone line is plugged into the modem at the back of your PC and at the wall socket. If it's an external model, also check that the modem cable is plugged into both the modem and the PC serial port, in addition to verifying that the modem is plugged into its power supply and is turned on.

2. Using the Windows 95 Start menu button, select Settings and click once on the Control Panel icon. The Control Panel window appears.

3. Double-click the Modems icon and Windows 95 displays the Install New Modem Wizard, as shown in figure 13.1.

Fig. 13.1
The Install New Modem Wizard walks you through configuration issues.

4. Click once on the Next> button to continue. Windows 95 automatically checks the serial ports on your PC to see whether a modem is attached, and attempts to identify what specific modem you are using. When it's finished, the Verify Modem dialog box appears.

II

Getting Connected

5. If the name of your modem is not displayed, you can click the Change button. Windows displays the Modem Properties dialog box, from which you can select the exact modem by manufacturer and model number. If your modem came with a driver disk specifically for Windows 95, you need to click the Have Disk button. Windows then prompts you for the location of the modem drivers. If you want to use the Windows 95 drivers for your modem, simply click the OK button to proceed.

◀ See "Connecting to a PPP or SLIP Account with Windows 95," p. 137

6. Windows returns you to the Verify Modem dialog box, which now displays the proper name for the modem you've selected. Click the Next> button to continue. Windows installs the driver for your modem, and displays the Modems Properties dialog box, as shown in figure 13.2. Click the OK button to close the Modems Properties dialog box and continue.

Fig. 13.2

When your modem installation is complete, Windows displays the properties for your new hardware device.

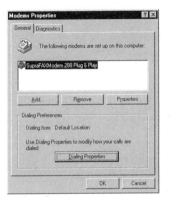

Troubleshooting

Windows 95 can't find my modem when I ask it to install it. What should I do?

If you have an external modem, check to make sure that it's connected properly to the communications port on your PC. Make sure the COM port is working. Right-click the My Computer icon on your desktop, and select the Properties menu item. Wait for the Properties dialog box to appear. Click the Devices tab once, and then select the Ports item from the list of devices that appears by double-clicking it. Select the COM port your modem is attached to by highlighting it with a single click. (If the port you've connected the modem to isn't in the list, then you know Windows hasn't even found the COM port, much less the modem attached to it.) Click the Properties button at the bottom of the dialog box, and the properties sheet for your port will appear. A message says whether the device is functioning properly. If it's not, check the hardware itself for a loose connection or duplicate COM ports. If Windows says the port is working, try turning the modem power off and then back on (sometimes modems will freeze and not respond to system queries).

If it's an internal modem, and it doesn't appear in the devices list (but the COM port number for it does), you may need to power down the entire computer system (there's no way to power down individual accessory cards). Internal modems have their own COM ports onboard, so they appear as both a COM port number and a modem entry to Windows 95.

Installing Plus! and the Internet Jumpstart Kit

As mentioned earlier in the chapter, while you can certainly get the basic MSN client program as an option with the basic installation of Windows 95, you really can't take advantage of Internet access via MSN without the full set of drivers and utilities that comes with the version of MSN in Microsoft Plus!.

You may not have installed any portion of Plus!; or you may have already installed Plus!, but not installed the Internet- or MSN-specific portions. Either way, follow these steps to add the necessary parts:

1. Follow the instructions packaged with Plus! to begin the installation. You may have purchased the CD-ROM version, which may start automatically when you insert it in your CD-ROM drive (if you have Auto-Run enabled). Or you may have the disk version, which requires you to run the SETUP.EXE program manually (using the Add/Remove Programs item in the Control Panel is an excellent way to begin this process, but using the Start menu Run command is fine).

Troubleshooting

My CD-ROMs don't open automatically when I put them in the drive. Why?

There are two requirements for the CD-ROM AutoRun feature of Windows 95 to function properly—it must be turned on, and the CD-ROM must support it. To verify that your installation of Windows 95 is set for AutoRun, right-click the My Computer icon on your desktop. Select the Properties menu item, and then wait for the Properties dialog box to appear. Click the Devices tab once, and then select your CD-ROM drive from the list of devices that appears by highlighting it with a single left-mouse click. Click the Properties button at the bottom of the dialog box, and the properties sheet for your CD-ROM drive will appear. Click the Settings tab, and make sure the Auto Insert Notification item is checked.

II

Getting Connected

2. When Plus! Setup starts, proceed until you see the screen. Click the Custom icon to proceed.

3. Windows displays the dialog box shown in figure 13.3. If you haven't installed Plus! before, you may want to select a combination or all of the options presented here. If you just need to add the Internet components, simply select the Internet Jumpstart Kit option.

Fig. 13.3
If you've installed Plus! before, you only need to select the Internet Jumpstart Kit option if that's all you want to add (make sure that selection is checked before you proceed).

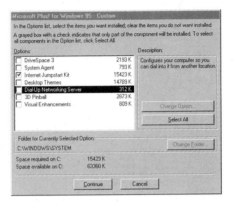

4. Click the Continue button to move on. Plus! Setup checks for necessary disk space, and then starts copying files as needed. When it's finished with the copy process, Windows displays the Internet Setup Wizard dialog box (if you selected other components, this may come before or after other Wizards as is appropriate).

5. Click the Next> button to proceed. The Microsoft Network dialog box appears. Click the OK button to proceed.

6. Plus! Setup displays the Installing Files dialog box. Click the Next> button and the copy process begins. When all files are copied, The Microsoft Network dialog box appears. Select the No; Sign Me Up option if that's appropriate, and proceed to the "Establishing Your MSN Account" section. If you're a member already from your previous Windows 95 installation, select Yes (and skip ahead to "Choosing an Access Method").

While you shouldn't shut down the Plus! Setup program at this point, it is a logical break in the installation process. In the next section, you'll start the procedure of setting up your MSN account, which is necessary before your Internet connection can be configured.

Establishing Your MSN Account

Before you can set up your Internet connection and configure your software, it's necessary to gain access to MSN. Continue by following these steps:

1. Microsoft Network Setup displays the dialog box, shown in figure 13.4, that explains all the benefits of MSN membership. Click the OK button to proceed.

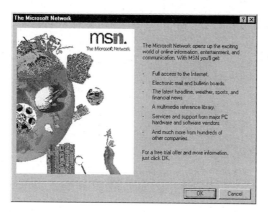

Fig. 13.4
MSN membership has many benefits, including simplified Internet access.

2. The next dialog box asks you to provide your area code and the first three digits of your phone number. Fill in these fields and click the OK button to proceed.

3. Microsoft Network Setup then displays a dialog box showing the toll-free MSN account startup number. Click Connect to proceed.

4. After Microsoft Network Setup concludes dialing, connection, and download, it displays a dialog box from which you can provide additional user information and review new information specific to your account.

5. Click the button with the envelope, and Microsoft Network Setup displays the dialog box shown in figure 13.5. Fill in the information requested and click OK. Setup returns you to the top level information dialog box. Click the checkbook icon to continue.

6. Microsoft Network Setup displays the payment plan dialog box. Select your preferred payment method and click OK to continue. Setup again displays the top level information dialog box. Select the bottom icon and read the rules for the MSN service.

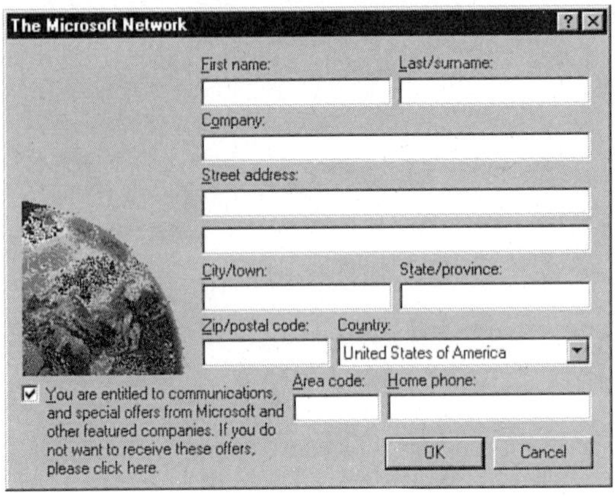

Fig. 13.5
Fill in the personal information that MSN needs to start your account.

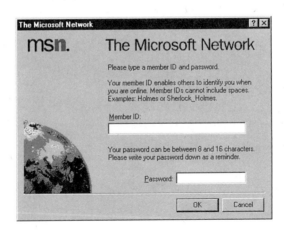

7. Be sure to read the system rules thoroughly. When you're finished, click OK and Microsoft Network Setup returns you to the top level information dialog box, but with a check mark beside every item you've reviewed.

8. Click the Join Now button to sign up. Microsoft Network Setup displays a dialog box to confirm the MSN connection number before your account information is sent. Click the Connect button to continue.

9. Microsoft Network Setup dials and connects to the MSN system. When it connects, you see the dialog box shown in figure 13.6. Fill in the fields with your preferred member ID and password.

Fig. 13.6
Be sure to provide a unique member ID for your account.

Selecting Member IDs and Passwords

Your MSN member ID must be unique, so be prepared to use something other than a variation of your name (especially if you happen to bear a common one such as Tom Smith or Mary Brown). If your member ID is already in use, MSN will prompt you for another one. Alter your first choice slightly, or think of something truly unique, unrelated to your name.

Passwords pose a challenge as well. While the likelihood of someone intercepting your MSN password is extremely minimal, it's a really good idea to follow the classic guidelines in selecting a password for MSN as well. Don't use the same password on more than one system. Don't choose something so obvious that your mother, a close friend, or anyone who's done a little research can guess it. One good way to construct a bulletproof password is to pick an easy-to-remember (but not obvious) phrase and insert a number in the middle of it that has special personal meaning for you (if you do that, you've mathematically increased the difficulty of someone guessing it because you now have two variables instead of one).

Whatever you choose, be sure to write it down so you have it later. If you are a member of several online services, this is especially critical because it is so very easy to confuse member IDs and passwords across systems (humans don't remember things as well as PCs!). Don't store a password list where it's easily found, and make a habit of changing your passwords with reasonable frequency.

10. If you're not lucky enough to live near a MSN POP (point of presence), you may get the dialog box shown in figure 13.7.

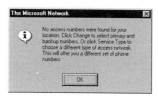

Fig. 13.7
Odds are it's going to be a long distance call to the MSN Internet connection, so you may see this dialog box asking you to pick the best MSN number.

Congratulations! You aren't through with MSN Internet setup entirely, but you have your MSN account; the rest is simply completion of configuration items on your system.

Choosing an Access Method

◀ See "The Various Ways to Connect to the Internet: Which One Is Right for You?," p. 101

◀ See "Connecting to a PPP or SLIP Account with Windows 95," p. 137

An important consideration when choosing an access number for using the Internet via MSN is the structure of MSN itself. Think of the Microsoft Network is to think of it as being composed of two primary networks: a classic dial-up network for the primary online information service (using simple asynchronous modem connections, much like any BBS), and a separate series of dial-up points-of-presence for a true TCP/IP or Internet network (using PPP).

To continue setting up your Internet connection via MSN, follow these steps (from the dialog box that appeared in step 10 of the last section):

1. Fortunately, Microsoft has kept this technical issue simple. Because your goal is to use MSN to connect to the Internet, you *must* select Internet and The Microsoft Network in the next dialog box, shown in figure 13.8.

Fig. 13.8

While you're offered two choices here, you really can't choose anything but the Internet and The Microsoft Network option.

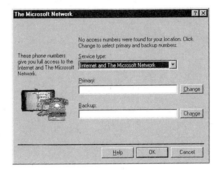

2. Click the Change button next to the Primary field. Setup displays the dialog box shown in figure 13.9. This dialog box gives you the options for choosing from lists of MSN POPs sorted by state. A little exploring may be in order here (bear in mind that it might actually be less expensive to call out of state than long distance *within* your state, so if there's no local number, do a little research and choose wisely).

3. When you've selected your primary connection, click OK, and Setup returns you to the dialog box first seen in figure 13.8. Click the Change button next to the Backup field, and Setup displays another dialog box very similar to that shown in figure 13.9. In this dialog box, you can choose your backup connection (to be used when the primary is busy

or otherwise unavailable). After you've chosen the backup connection, click OK again, and you return to the screen shown in figure 13.8, with your primary and secondary connections complete. Click OK and Setup displays a confirmation dialog box welcoming you to the service.

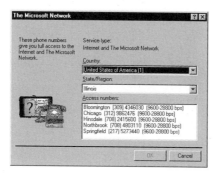

Fig. 13.9
Consider your phone tariffs carefully when choosing your connections.

4. Click the Finish button. Setup folds its tent and displays a dialog box asking you to restart Windows. Unless you have unfinished business running elsewhere, click the Restart Windows button. Setup closes all your applications, prompts you to save any open files, and restarts your PC.

Using the Internet with MSN

Now that you've worked through most of the configuration items required to use the Internet with MSN, let's look at all the really cool stuff Microsoft gives you as Internet tools with the Plus! pack, and the basics of using them with MSN.

After your machine restarts, your desktop sports new Inbox, Internet, and Microsoft Network icons.

Caution

Don't try to delete the MSN, Inbox, or Internet Explorer icons from your desktop. These are not real shortcuts like other Windows 95 icons, but unique registry entries that serve special functions beyond the capabilities of regular shortcuts. If you do succeed in removing them, they will not be simple to put back without a reinstallation.

II

Getting Connected

> **Note**
>
> MSN may update your software automatically, from time to time, when you first log in. Files may be transferred to your system if needed. This may take awhile, but it is usually totally automatic, and perfectly normal.

Getting On- and Offline with MSN

To test your MSN Internet connection, double-click The Microsoft Network icon. The MSN Sign In dialog box appears. Click the Connect button, and the MSN client connects to the service. Once connected, you see status messages signaling the process steps in logging you in, as shown in figure 13.10.

Fig. 13.10

After connecting to the network modem, the MSN client verifies your account status and your access privileges.

After the connection/logon process is complete, the MSN Central window appears, followed by the MSN Today window, as shown in figure 13.11.

Fig. 13.11

The MSN menus are totally graphically oriented and may take some time to load over a modem connection.

That's really all there is to starting up an MSN session. To get back offline, go to the MSN Central window (actually labeled The Microsoft Network) and choose File, Close, as shown in figure 13.12. A dialog box appears asking you to confirm your request to end the session. Click Yes and the MSN client shuts down the modem connection to MSN and closes all MSN windows.

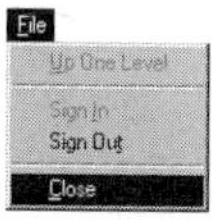

Fig. 13.12
You can shut down your MSN session quickly and easily from the MSN Central window menu.

> **Note**
>
> If you want to save time each time you log into MSN, you can turn off the MSN Today page by using the View, Options menu, selecting the General page, and then unselecting the Show MSN Today Title on Startup item.

Using the Internet Explorer with MSN

The Internet Explorer, Microsoft's World Wide Web browser, is designed with tight integration with MSN in mind. While you can use the Internet Explorer with other service providers, there are special links between it, the Dial-up Networking support in Windows 95, and the MSN client that offer real advantages.

For example, if you've followed the setup instructions in this chapter to configure Windows to use MSN as your Internet service provider, and you simply double-click the Internet Explorer icon on your desktop, Windows knows to use MSN to connect, as shown in figure 13.13.

▶ See "Using Microsoft Internet Explorer," p. 473

You'll need to type in your password and click the Connect button to start the connection process, but once it's started, the rest should be automatic (you can tell the MSN client to remember your password for future sessions by clicking the checkbox in the lower-left of the MSN Sign In window).

When the connection process is finished, Internet Explorer displays the MSN home page, as shown in figure 13.14.

Once you've connected and Internet Explorer displays the first page, you're live on the World Wide Web.

Getting Connected

II

Fig. 13.13
Starting Internet Explorer when you're not connected triggers the MSN connection process.

Fig. 13.14
Internet Explorer delivers the goods after it has the MSN connection.

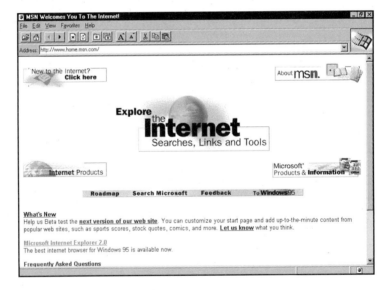

Using Internet Mail with MSN

▶ See "Using Microsoft Exchange," p. 349

After you've established your MSN account, you can take full advantage of electronic mail, both to other MSN members and to anyone on the Internet or other information services via the MSN Internet mail gateway. Once you have an Internet connection via MSN, you can fire up any Windows Internet mail program you want, or you can use the Microsoft Exchange client that comes with Windows 95 and the Microsoft Plus! Internet Jumpstart Kit. Because you have a live TCP/IP connection once you're online with MSN, any mail client that works with the Windows 95 Winsock stack will work with MSN.

Still, just as with the Internet Explorer, there are distinct advantages to using the Microsoft program. Using Exchange with MSN couldn't be simpler. If you're already online to MSN, simply double-click the Inbox icon on the Windows 95 desktop, and the Exchange program opens (see fig. 13.15).

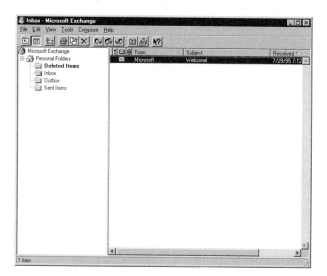

Fig. 13.15
Exchange provides a robust mail client for MSN and Internet mail.

You can also start Exchange first, and Windows will know to use MSN to connect to the Internet, just as it does with Internet Explorer.

▶ See "How Internet E-Mail Works," p. 329

▶ See "E-Mailing Outside the Internet and with Online Services," p. 401

▶ See "Using Internet Mailing Lists," p. 417

Troubleshooting

I'm able to get on The Microsoft Network fine, and really like using the Internet Explorer and Exchange. But after awhile, my modem suddenly disconnects. What gives?

Just as Windows 95 automatically connects you to the Internet when you open one of the Internet clients, it disconnects you automatically. By default, the MSN client program logs you off the Internet after 20 minutes (this is designed to save you excess phone charges). If you want to change this, open the Windows 95 Control Panel from the Start menu and double-click the Internet icon. Uncheck the box named Auto disconnect if you want this defeated, or leave it checked and adjust the time limit if desired.

II

Getting Connected

Using Internet UseNet Newsgroups with MSN

▶ See "How
UseNet
Works,"
p. 749

Using Internet news (otherwise known as UseNet news) with MSN is a little different from using other client programs with MSN. Microsoft hasn't provided a separate client program for news, choosing instead to rely upon the excellent interface of the MSN menu system and Exchange, to provide newsreader capability.

To access UseNet news with MSN, start at the main Microsoft Network window. Click the Categories portion of the menu, and the screen shown in figure 13.16 appears.

Fig. 13.16
The MSN menus guide you to UseNet news.

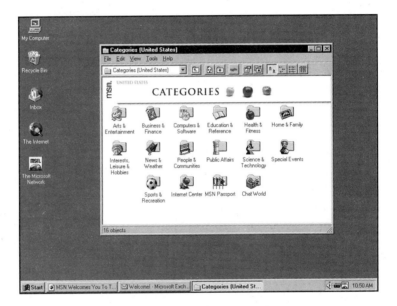

Double-click the Internet Center folder icon. MSN displays the Internet Center screen, shown in figure 13.17.

Fig. 13.17
MSN Internet Center provides a wealth of information opportunities, as well as the path to UseNet.

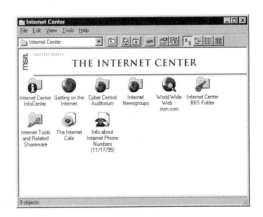

Double-click the Internet Newsgroups folder icon and MSN displays the Internet Newsgroups window.

Double-click the UseNet Newsgroups folder icon and MSN displays the groups. Double-click any group folder icon to see a list of groups, as shown in figure 13.18.

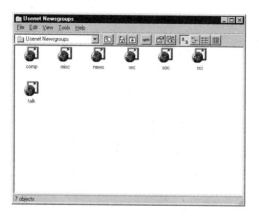

Fig. 13.18
The deeper you go in MSN UseNet groups, the more choices you'll find.

Keep traveling deeper through the news folders until you come to a screen with message headers, as shown in figure 13.19.

Tip

You can go directly to folders in MSN. Choose the Edit, Goto, Other Location menu item, and then enter the shortcut **go word** for the item (right-click the folder and view its Properties to see the go word).

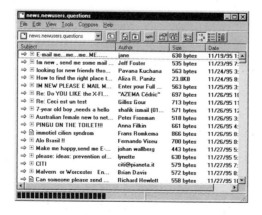

Fig. 13.19
At the final message list level, you'll see the headers for all messages in that group.

Getting Connected

II

▶ See "Using
Microsoft
Exchange,"
p. 349

It may take a while for the entire list of message headers to display. Once the list is complete, double-click any message to read it. MSN uses the Exchange message editor to display the message. You may respond or create a new news posting from the Exchange editor.

Caution

Please be aware that MSN won't be held responsible for content on the Internet. Newsgroups are notorious for containing material that will likely be found offensive by some people, so proceed with care if you harbor tender sensibilities.

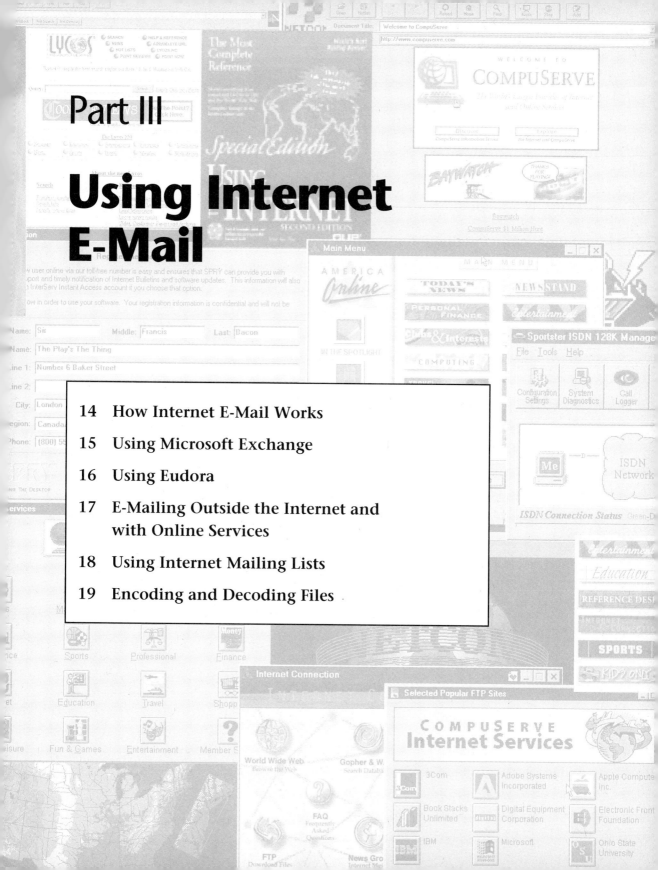

Part III

Using Internet E-Mail

14   How Internet E-Mail Works

15   Using Microsoft Exchange

16   Using Eudora

17   E-Mailing Outside the Internet and with Online Services

18   Using Internet Mailing Lists

19   Encoding and Decoding Files

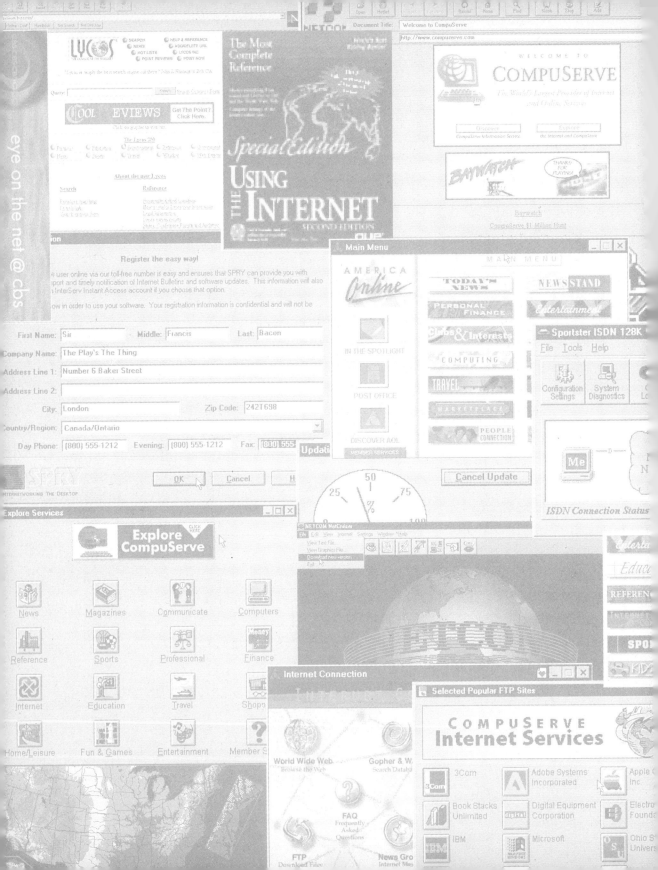

CHAPTER 14

How Internet E-Mail Works

Electronic mail (e-mail) is one of the widest used services on the Internet. E-mail is easy to send, read, reply to, manage, and is fast and convenient. For these reasons, it has grown from a simple service offered to researchers for communicating ideas and results to a complex, talented messaging system. This chapter looks at e-mail and its role on the Internet.

E-mail has many advantages over regular communications methods such as postal services or fax technology. It is much easier to write an e-mail message than to write a formal paper letter or note, for example. Many studies have shown that recipients are much more likely to reply to an e-mail message than a written request, primarily because of the ease of formulating the response.

E-mail can be read and written at any time, independent of time zones and business hours. This makes it easy for busy people to keep in touch with others on a daily basis, whenever they find some spare time. The ability to carefully formulate replies at leisure also helps prevent hasty comments. E-mail is also global, enabling messages to pass from Japan to the U.S. in minutes, regardless of the time they were sent.

E-mail is also economical and very fast. It is much cheaper to send an e-mail message than to send a letter, or to make a long-distance telephone call. Typically, e-mail messages can be delivered to a recipient within minutes of being sent, while replies are just as fast. E-mail doesn't require paper (ecologically sound) and it is easy to dispose of (no landfill problems). E-mail is simply an excellent choice for communications, which solves many problems without imposing many new ones.

In this chapter, we will look at several different aspects of e-mail, both in general and as they apply to the Internet. This chapter covers the following:

- Internet e-mail protocol
- Other e-mail protocols
- General rules for using e-mail
- Finding e-mail addresses
- Handling large files
- Handling binary files
- E-mail utilities
- E-mail etiquette

By the end of this chapter you should know enough about e-mail to allow you to use the Internet for sending and receiving e-mail. You'll also learn about transferring files through e-mail, and the rules of behavior generally accepted.

Simple Mail Transfer Protocol (SMTP)

The Internet uses a TCP/IP-family protocol called the Simple Mail Transfer Protocol (SMTP) as the standard method for transferring electronic mail over the Internet system. SMTP is also used in many local-area and wide-area networks, although there are many other competing e-mail protocols available for LANs. In many ways SMTP is similar to FTP. It is a simple protocol with basic operational capabilities.

SMTP is accessed by a system's electronic mail routing program. UNIX systems, for example, use a program called sendmail, which receives requests for e-mail transfers from the user's mail applications (such as the UNIX mail program, Lotus Notes, and so on). The actual source application of the mail doesn't matter, as long as it can communicate with the sendmail system (or equivalent routing program on other systems).

The sendmail utility implements SMTP and several other mail protocols simultaneously. Usually, this type of mail program runs all the time, especially in multi-user systems that support background processes. (Background programs that run all the time are known as *daemons* in the UNIX vocabulary.) On smaller systems, such as PCs, the mailing program must be run either as a Terminate-and-Stay-Resident (TSR) program (which runs in the background when activated by a trigger of some sort) or the mail program must be started up each time you want to transfer mail.

Companies that have large mail systems let the sendmail program run continuously so it can keep a constant watch for incoming and outgoing mail messages. System administrators set the program to check the Internet for incoming messages on a regular basis (usually at least hourly, often more frequently). The system's users do not interact with the sendmail program directly, instead using a front-end mail program (such as cc:Mail, Microsoft Mail, or Lotus Notes) for the composition and reading of mail messages.

SMTP handles messages in *queues* (also called spools). When a message is sent from a mail application to SMTP, it places it in an outgoing queue. SMTP attempts to forward the message from the queue whenever it connects to remote machines. Usually, if SMTP cannot forward the message within a predetermined amount of time (usually a day or two), the message is returned to the sender with an error message, or removed from the system.

When a connection is established between two computers that use SMTP, the two systems exchange authentication codes. After verifying each machine's status, one system sends a command to the other to identify the first mail message's sender and provides basic information about the message. The receiving SMTP system will return an acknowledgment, after which the message itself is transmitted. SMTP uses TCP/IP to handle the messages.

SMTP is smart enough to handle multiple destinations for the same message in an efficient manner. If more than one recipient of the same message is identified, the message is transmitted only once, but the receiving system will then make copies to each of the recipients. This reduces the amount of traffic between machines.

The sender and recipient address fields of an SMTP message use standard Internet formats, involving the user name and domain name. The technical details of SMTP are beyond the scope of this book and are unlikely to be pleasant reading for even the most technical person.

X.400 and X.500

The original dream for electronic mail was quite simple. Each message would have a standard header section with information about the sender, recipient, subject, and some status codes. The definition of the mail message format was agreed upon by the CCITT (International Consultative Committee on Telephones and Telegraphs), a United Nations sanctioned standards body. They called the mail standard X.400 (pronounced "X dot four hundred").

X.400 couldn't be used alone because some method of determining the routing to the recipient of each message was necessary. Enter another standard called X.500, which provides a mechanism for a master database of e-mail addresses. X.400 would create the package containing the message and X.500 would figure out who it was going to and how to get it there.

X.400 and X.500 are used by some systems, but have not achieved standard usage across all networks. The most common mail transfer method still remains SMTP.

Finding Someone's E-Mail Address

When you want to send mail to someone, you need the person's address (in this case, his or her e-mail address consisting of the username and machine they are using). There are several utilities available for determining someone's e-mail address, such as Finger, WHOIS, and Netfind.

These utilities do not guarantee being able to find e-mail addresses, because the majority of users are not on systems that enable these utilities to access their user lists (or they want to remain private). Current estimates are that only one or two percent of all Internet users can be located with one of these methods.

> **Note**
>
> Some large corporations and universities allow you to search for a user on their system. Some provide this search mechanism by finger and others by home pages. If you're having problems looking someone up at a particularly large institution with the tools in this chapter, you can also ask for help. Don't be afraid to send e-mail asking for help to the "postmaster" or "webmaster" of the site of the person you're trying to find. They might be able to point you to some special facility they have to help you find the person you're looking for.

> **Note**
>
> Web users can take advantage of two particularly good home pages to find other users. One is the Four11 information service, which can be accessed by going to **http://www.four11.com/**. You must join their database of users to be able to use it. But once you've signed on, you can search for anybody else in the Four11 listings. A good general directory of White Pages can be found at **http:// home.netscape.com/home/internet-white-pages.html**. Netscape users can simply select the White Pages menu item under the Directory menu heading. Simply follow the link of the particular White Pages you'd like to use.

In the near future, a global X.500 directory will exist that contains addresses for all users who want to be found (much like the telephone directory contains all numbers except those that have been specifically requested to remain unlisted). Such white pages are being created by various companies but none of them have come close to building a complete directory.

There are several direct methods of determining e-mail addresses, ranging from the obvious (telephoning a person and asking) to the more obscure (examining e-mail messages from a person for his or her address). Most people, though, rely on a set of standard utilities, covered in brief in the following sections.

Finger

Finger is a standard utility supplied with the TCP/IP protocol family that lets you determine who is a valid system user and who is logged into a system you have access to. It can be used to find out a person's username and if a mail recipient is logged in on the destination machine (if you are allowed to query the system). Not all sites will allow you to do a Finger, depending on how the system administrator has set up the system.

To determine if a user is on a machine, issue a command on the UNIX command line as follows:

> finger *username@domain.name*

where "username" is the user's login name and "domain.name" is the machine's domain. You must have the complete username and domain name. For example, the command:

> finger president@whitehouse.gov

would tell you if the President was a valid user and logged into the White House's network. It can also show other information about the user, if he has supplied it for general distribution. (This particular example won't actually work because of security restrictions at the White House, but you get the idea.)

If you happen to know the domain name of where a friend is located, but you don't know his username, you can also use Finger. You can see everybody who's currently logged into a particular system by simply specifying the "@domain.name". For example, the command:

> finger @whitehouse.gov

would tell you who's currently using the computer *whitehouse.gov*. You see the person's username in the left-hand column and his real name next to it.

III

Using Internet E-Mail

> **Note**
>
> There are a number of graphics-based finger programs for Windows 95. Each of them presents the same finger information, but formats it differently.

Finger can be used for purposes other than determining usernames and addresses. By Fingering some sites, you can get access to information such as Nielson television ratings, *Billboard Magazine* music charts, and details about recent earthquakes. Lists of Finger sites are available through UseNet. Here are a few Finger addresses for you to try:

> Earthquakes: **quake@geophys.washington.edu**
>
> Baseball scores: **jtchern@ocf.berkeley.edu**
>
> NASA press releases: **nasanews@space.mit.edu**
>
> Tropical Storm forecasts: **forecast@typhoon.atmos.colostate.edu**

To use these addresses, simply specify them in the Finger command. For the latest NASA press release, for example, you would issue the command:

> finger nasanews@space.mit.edu

and you will get a message returned with the information you need. You cannot use Finger through electronic mail, though, which poses a limitation for users with access to the Internet by e-mail only. For those users, one of the other search utilities must be used.

WHOIS

The *WHOIS* program and its accompanying database is maintained by Network Solutions, Inc., and AT&T. Contrary to popular belief, this isn't meant to be a complete database of all Internet users. The *WHOIS* database is a complete repository of everybody who is in charge of a part of the Internet—that is, the systems and network administrators for companies and organizations.

To use the WHOIS system, enter all or part of the proper name of the person you are trying to locate on a command line. If the WHOIS database has anything that matches the name, it is displayed or e-mailed to you.

There are several ways to use the WHOIS service. For most users who have full Internet access, the easiest way to use the WHOIS service is to Telnet into a WHOIS server and access the database directly. Alternatively (and for those without full Internet access), you can send an e-mail request to the WHOIS server and let it perform the search and mail back the results (a process that is not as time-consuming as it sounds). Users more comfortable with Gopher can also access WHOIS servers. Web users aren't left out because Internic has provided a home page for searching the WHOIS database.

Most users rely on the primary InterNIC server as their WHOIS site. A list of all WHOIS servers can be obtained through anonymous FTP to **sipb.mit.edu** as the file whois-servers.list in the pub/whois directory. Using an alternative server may reduce response time.

▶ See "Anonymous FTP," p. 838

Most UNIX systems, as well as some online services like Delphi, allow WHOIS commands to be entered directly on your command line. The syntax of the UNIX version of WHOIS (which is the same for most other versions) is:

```
whois [-h hostname] username
```

with the hostname optional. If a hostname is supplied, it needs to be preceded with a -h option to prevent the WHOIS server from thinking you are asking for a username. Examples of valid WHOIS queries are

```
whois -h tpci.com tparker
whois "doe, john"
```

When the WHOIS command displays its results, it will show all names that match with the corresponding NIC handle, a unique identification number, the e-mail address, and sometimes a telephone number if supplied by the user. Even more information can be displayed by querying with the NIC handle only. For example, if you queried for the name "John Doe" and found three matches, use the number of the user you want more complete details on, such as

```
whois NT123
```

where "NT123" was the unique number shown in the reply from the WHOIS server.

You can access the WHOIS system through e-mail, too. Address the message to one of the WHOIS servers (such as **mailserv@ds.internic.net**) with no subject specified. The body of the message should be the same as a WHOIS UNIX command, such as

```
whois tparker
```

One variant of the command that is commonly supported is to put a period in front of the person's username to identify to the WHOIS server that you are specifying a username and not an organization name (instead of relying on the -h option to show a host name). This would change the message body to

```
whois .tparker
```

III

Using Internet E-Mail

The problem with the WHOIS service is that it covers only a small percentage of the Internet's users (currently only about 80,000 of the over 20,000,000 Internet users). But then, that's not the intent of the database. The best use of WHOIS service is to find out e-mail address for network administrators in companies or organizations. If you receive junk e-mail from someone, you can simply use WHOIS is to find the network administrator for that user. You can then e-mail the offending user's network administrator and complain about the junk letter.

> **Note**
>
> You can use the InterNIC (the Network Solutions, Inc., database of addresses) system by Telneting to **ds.internic.net**, logging on as "guest", and selecting the option titled InterNIC Directory Services ("White Pages"). The software is still under development, but you will be able to see its capabilities. Information about InterNIC is available by sending e-mail to **info@internic.net**. Gopher users can access Internic by going to **rs.internic.net**. Web users can directly search the WHOIS server by pointing their browsers to **gopher://rs.internic.net/7waissrc%3A/rs/whois.src**.

Netfind

Netfind is a still-experimental service that approaches username location in a different manner than WHOIS. Instead of maintaining a database of users, Netfind goes out to different network gateways and queries them for the user names. Ideally, Netfind will be given an approximate geographical location to narrow its search.

When run, Netfind prompts you for two pieces of information (if you have them): the user's first and last names or a login name (only one of the two can be used), and a location for the user (which can be narrow, such as a specific site, or more general, such as a city or state).

You can access Netfind by logging into a Netfind server and query it for information. Unfortunately, it doesn't do a complete search as some systems will not allow queries of their user lists. Therefore, Netfind isn't much more comprehensive than Finger.

If you want to experiment with Netfind, Telnet to **bruno.cs.colorado.edu** and log in as "netfind". The master Netfind system will prompt you for your actions. There are several other Netfind servers available, mostly at universities and colleges.

> **Note**
>
> People with Web browsers have the added advantage of using some WHOIS home pages. Simply point your browser to **http://www.nova.edu/Inter-Links/netfind.html** and enter your Netfind keys.

Knowbot Information Service

The Knowbot Information Service (KIS) is an experimental service that tries to automate the address finding process. KIS doesn't maintain its own database but instead queries other address databases it knows about, including those mentioned previously. KIS uses, for example, the WHOIS server, the Finger utility, the X.500 directory, MCI Mail's directory, and several machine and country specific services.

By providing a front-end to several different addressing services, KIS lets you enter the search information only once, instead of having to retype names for each different service. It also lets you use a standard format, negating the need to keep track of syntax for three or four different address location utilities. Any information retrieved by KIS is reformatted and presented in a standard format, regardless of its origin.

You can use KIS by either Telneting to a KIS server or by addressing e-mail to the KIS server. There are several KIS servers available, which must be accessed through a specific port (usually port 185). If you have Telnet access, you can try the KIS system using this KIS server:

telnet nri.reston.va.us 185

> **Note**
>
> There are a number of home pages that have KIS search forms. One such Web page is at **http://info.cnri.reston.va.us/kis.html**. Simply enter the person's name that you're trying to find, select the information sources to search, and submit the query.

Other KIS servers are available. A current list is available from the **nri.reston.va.us** server. Note that the use of port 185 is mandatory and must be specified on the Telnet command line.

III

Using Internet E-Mail

E-mail requests for searches must follow a specific format. Response time from the KIS servers is usually very good. To send e-mail to the KIS server, address your query to:

netadress@nri.reston.va.us

The body of the message should have one or more of the following keywords in it, followed by the data to be used by the server:

- *Service* specifies any particular service you want to add to the default search list. Unless you have a lot of experience with KIS, don't use this parameter the first few times.

- *Org* is the organization to which the user belongs, usually specified as a full or partial domain name.

- *Identifier* uses the appended information for the search instead of a username. This is used when specifying a user ID number instead of a name (necessary for services like MCI Mail and CompuServe).

- *Query* is followed by the username you wish to locate.

An example of an e-mail query sent to the KIS server would have a message body of:

```
org tpci
query tparker
```

which would try to find the user tparker on any organization that has the letters tpci in the domain name.

UseNet User List

Users of UseNet unwittingly contribute to a user list (see chapter 30, "How UseNet Works"). As each newsgroup message passes through the Massachusetts Institute of Technology's servers, a program gathers all the user names and builds a database of UseNet users and their addresses.

You can query this list by e-mail, although few users seem to use it on a regular basis. To send a query to the UseNet User List, address a message to:

mail-server@pit-manager.mit.edu

No subject is required for the e-mail, but the contents of the message should be in the following format:

send *usenet-addresses/username*

For example, the following query will try to locate a UseNet user with the last name, Parker:

send *usenet-addresses*/parker

The response will include a list of the usernames that match your specified string, their full names (if it is supplied in the newsgroup postings), and the date of their last postings.

> **Note**
>
> If you want to make it easy for other users to track you down, send a couple of postings to a UseNet newsgroup so that you appear on the MIT list.

Files

Most e-mail systems do not impose limitations on the types of files that can be sent, as long as the network protocol can handle the characters. However, getting files into the proper format can require running the file through a utility. It is also common practice to compress large files for transmission.

ASCII Format Only

Most of the Internet relies on 7-bit ASCII characters, which are ideal for most text-based messages. Problems can occur with binary files and more complex icon-based languages (such as Chinese and Japanese), but there are solutions available for these files, too.

The Internet e-mail system handles binary files by converting them to 7-bit ASCII characters by using one of several different character-conversion programs. The most popular conversion utilities are UUEncode and UUDecode (see chapter 19, "Encoding and Decoding Files").

UUEncode converts 8-bit characters into a 7-bit representation that can be converted back to its original format with the UUDecode program. In some cases, UUEncoded files are tagged with the file extension .UU or .UUE, although this is not a widely used convention.

> **Caution**
>
> If your message is not 7-bit ASCII characters, it must be converted before being sent or the contents will be corrupted. Use UUEncode and UUDecode for binary files.

The Internet system is generally unable to handle binaries in their native form. Anything sent in this manner will be truncated to 7-bit ASCII, making it virtually impossible to reconstruct the original message. UseNet news and e-mail, in particular, face this restriction, so be sure to convert binary files to ASCII before sending.

Having issued that warning, the Internet doesn't care about the contents of the files you send. Assuming they have been properly converted to enable transmissions, you can send sound files, graphics, multimedia movies, and any other kind of application you want. The Internet ignores the contents of messages, concentrating only on the information in the message headers that are added by TCP/IP.

E-mail has a distinct advantage over the Internet when it comes to transferring files from a user application, as it allows disk formats to be completely ignored. A file written in Macintosh Word can be sent (UUEncoded, of course) to a user on a PC. The PC version of Microsoft Word will recognize the file's format as Macintosh Word and offer to perform a conversion for you. This type of conversion applies to most popular application formats, also making e-mail an efficient way to distribute files. This may not work well with graphics and sound files unless they are in a standard format (such as JPEG or MIDI).

Note

A new 8-bit to 7-bit converter that's gaining rapid use is the **MIME** encoding scheme. This method overcomes some of the technical shortcomings of UUEncode and UUDecode, and is well integrated into many newer programs. Its major shortcoming is that it's not as widely available for UNIX machines as UUEncode and UUDecode. Additionally, MIME is being incorporated into more and more newer applications, especially e-mail programs.

Note

The Macintosh has its own standard method of converting 8-bit files to 7-bit files, known as BinHex. BinHex essentially does everything that MIME and UUEncode/UUDecode do, but is Macintosh specific. There are a number of Windows 95 and UNIX programs available that will un-BinHex files.

File Compression

Large files are usually not transferred as they are, but are compressed by a utility to save on transmission time. There are several compression and expansion utilities in use, most of which are incompatible with each other.

DOS-based systems usually use one of two popular types of compression and expansion utilities, both from PKWare. PKZIP and PKARC are the utilities that compress files, enabling several files to be assembled into a single, larger library file for transmission. This is very useful when sending several small files to a single user. PKZIP and PKARC will create the archive file, then compress it to a smaller size than the original files. When the compressed archive file is received, the same utility can be used to first expand the file and then extract the contents.

These utilities are usually recognized by their file extensions in a DOS system. Files that have been compressed with PKZIP have the extension .ZIP, while PKARC files have the extension .ARC. ZIPped and ARCed files are not compatible because they use different algorithms. An .ARC file cannot be uncompressed with PKZIP.

Note

Windows 95 users can simplify the handling of ZIP files with a utility called WinZip. WinZip is a graphical front-end to PKZIP that offers some of the same functionality built in. You can get WinZip from anonymous FTP at **ftp.winzip.com**. The self-extracting executable can be found at winzip/winzip95.exe.

Macintosh users commonly use a compression utility called StuffIt, which produces files ending with .SIT. As with DOS utilities, StuffIt can handle multiple files and compresses all types of contents.

UNIX systems take a two-step approach to PKZIP and StuffIt by using different programs for different aspects. To collect several files into one large file, it's common to use the utility tar (tape archive). Tar accepts a number of command-line options for what operation to perform, the file to use, and which files to access. The most common syntax for it is:

    tar -cvf *filename*.tar files

Note

On some versions of UNIX, each command line option must be specified separately. So that instead of

    tar -cvf ...

You would need to type in

    tar -c -v -f ...

Another method in UNIX for collecting a lot of files together into one large file is *cpio* (copy in and out). It is a bit more complex to use than tar, so cpio is not generally used by casual users. Also cpio requires a file that contains a list of files to be collected and then the use of various file redirecting gymnastics. The most common syntax for using cpio is:

cpio -covB < [file with list] > filename.cpio

> **Note**
>
> When sending binaries or large files, first use a compression utility and then UUEncode the file.

Once a library file has been created, it can be compressed with a standard UNIX utility. Most UNIX systems support the commands compress and uncompress. A compressed file has the file extension .Z. Fortunately for Windows 95 users WinZip 6.0, a graphical front-end to PKZIP, can read in and extract compressed files.

> **Note**
>
> There is a much older set of UNIX compression and uncompression programs called *pack* and *unpack*. These programs are no longer used and are being phased out by all major UNIX operating systems manufacturers.

It is not unusual to receive files that have been put into a library, compressed, and then UUEncoded. File extensions are not usually sent through electronic mail, so make sure you clearly indicate in the Subject field of the message which utilities have been run on the file. For example, the following subjects tell the recipient how to treat the file when it is received:

Chapter 4 of Book (MS Word, ZIPped)

Graphics files (.arc)

Draft proposal (compressed)

By putting the details of the program used in parentheses, you save the recipient the trouble of trying to figure out which compression or conversion utilities you have employed. It is sometimes impossible to know which utility to use by looking at the ASCII characters in the file.

Legal Issues and E-Mail

There are several aspects of electronic mail that involve legal issues. These aspects are copyright, libel, and privacy.

Take care to avoid copyright issues when transferring files. It is illegal to distribute copyrighted information by any means, electronic or physical. This is not restricted to transferring binary versions of an application, although this is a primary source of litigation. Copyright regulations extend to cover published material, too. It is quite common to find graphics that have been scanned by a user for personal use distributed through the Internet. This is illegal, because the copyright owner has not granted the right to disseminate the material.

Some material is prohibited by federal laws (primarily certain types of pornography) and although e-mail may seem a simple way to send and receive this type of material, traffic monitoring and tracing is not a complicated matter. Even descriptions of some material may be illegal, depending on the country you are sending e-mail to or from. If you are sending mail out of the country, you may be placing your recipient in trouble.

Libel is as applicable within e-mail messages and newsgroups as in a published book. There have recently been several well-publicized cases of an Internet user suing another user for comments made in private correspondence and generally accessible messages in UseNet newsgroups. Again, prudence is important, because the legal definitions of libel may differ from country to country.

The right to privacy is not assured with electronic mail. Unlike mail sent through the postal service, there is no requirement for a company not to read your incoming and outgoing messages. This is especially applicable if you use your employer's equipment. In many cases, policies are not established for e-mail privacy, so assume all your e-mail is subject to scrutiny. Even on the networks, anyone with a gateway can read messages passing through. It has been suggested many times that several intelligence-gathering organizations routinely scan the high volumes of Internet traffic for items of interest.

Even though e-mail may be deleted from your mailbox, do not assume it has been completely destroyed. Backups are regularly made of system drives, especially in larger organizations. Company policies usually require regular backups that include incoming and outgoing mail messages. Subpoenas can be issued for your e-mail records.

Note

Another legal issue to deal with here in the United States: A couple of high-profile cases recently have involved someone sending threatening e-mail, in these cases to the President. The senders were arrested and are awaiting trial on federal charges. Penalties can include several years in prison and large fines. The general lesson to be learned from this is that behavior that is illegal in other forms (a threatening phone call or letter, for example) may be illegal in e-mail too, depending on your local or national laws.

Encryption

If you want to send a message with a degree of protection, you can use *encryption*. Encryption is not a guarantee that your message won't be read (anyone with the sophistication to tap an Internet gateway won't be bothered by a simple encryption scheme), but it may prevent casual browsing. Some compression software packages include a simple encryption process that can be turned on with a command line option.

Note

WinZip provides a means of password protecting ZIP archives. Before adding any files to an archive, select the Password menu selection under the Options menu heading. Type the password you want to use to encrypt your files and add as many files as you want.

Caution

WinZip does enable you to put in a password for ZIP files, but it can't do it alone. To use this feature, you must have the DOS-based version of PKZIP that WinZip can use.

There are many encryption schemes available, some commercial and some public domain. One of the most secure systems currently available uses the Data Encryption Standard (DES) public-key method. These systems are still breakable, but usually involve massive computer resources to be penetrated.

A popular DOS package for encrypting messages is PC-CODE, which performs a character transposition followed by a substitution, a process called *super encipherment*. This type of system requires the recipient to know a code word to decode messages.

One of the easiest code schemes available on many systems is called *ROT13*. The name derives from code wheels that had two sets of alphabets close together. One wheel was rotated to align with the second at some point in the alphabet, and the letters would be read from the two wheels. A ROT13, scheme would "rot"ate the wheels "13" positions (hence ROT13), so that the letter *A* would be *M*. This provides a simple code scheme.

Many mail systems and UseNet news readers have ROT13 built in, both for encryption and decryption. Consult your mail and newsreader documentation or help files for information on how to use this feature. This type of system is crude, but it doesn't require your recipient to have any secret codewords to break the message. In most cases, ROT13 is not used for security to protect from simple browsing. If a user sees a message that has ROT13 applied, he may be too lazy to decode it.

E-Mail Etiquette

The UseNet is governed by a code of conduct called *netiquette*. E-mail has a set of proposed rules for etiquette, both to protect the sender and recipient (see the earlier section "Legal Issues and E-Mail"), and to ensure proper behavior in electronic messages. Here are some of the more important guidelines:

- *Read your mail!* Many users let their e-mail back up, intending to read all the old messages when they have time. This is rude to the senders and may result in you missing something important. Keep it current. Also, if you find you are getting mail you shouldn't, inform senders that you should be taken off their distribution lists.

- *Specify a subject.* Always use a subject heading that identifies your message. This is necessary to allow the recipient to prioritize messages.

- *Clearly identify yourself.* Don't assume that your recipient knows who you are or can figure it out from the header information attached to your message. Give your name and any contact information that you want the recipient to have. To make this easy, copy a standard, short identification file into your messages.

- *Know and respect your recipient.* Even if you do not know the recipient, respect him. Do not use sarcasm or questionable humor unless you know the recipient will not take it personally. Also avoid the syndrome of assuming that e-mail is anonymous and hence allows you to say anything you want. E-mail can be easily traced back to the sender.

- *Avoid outbursts.* Do not get angry in your e-mail. It may come back to haunt you. Again, many users perceive e-mail as less formal than a

III

Using Internet E-Mail

written letter and hence they are freer to say what they want. If you want to blast someone, write your message offline and carefully consider the contents before sending it. Your e-mail could be printed out and used against you in the future.

- *Use proper English.* E-mail messages should be properly spelled, punctuated, and grammatically correct. A poorly written and misspelled letter reflects very badly on you.

- *Be brief.* There is a tendency to ramble when writing e-mail messages, as they often follow your train of thought. As with spelling and grammar, the succinctness with which you present your message reflects on you. Long, rambling messages with little real content tend to be ignored before the recipient has read the entire message.

- *Avoid copying messages to others.* For some reason, e-mail inspires users to send copies of a message to long lists of users, many of whom are uninterested in the contents. Only send copies to those who really should receive a copy, otherwise it can reflect badly on you.

- *Don't request replies or receipts unless necessary.* As with copies to many users, e-mail also inspires the "please reply" and "please confirm receipt" syndromes. A reply may not be appropriate, while confirmation notes can be a waste of time for the recipient. Use these requests only when absolutely necessary.

- *Avoid using Priority or Urgent tags.* Some mail systems let you tag the message as very important. Use these only when necessary, or your judgment may be questioned. It's the old "cry wolf" story.

- *If replying to a request, fully identify the original question.* Receiving e-mail with the sole contents "yes" or "no" without any indication of what was originally asked can be frustrating. It is sometimes best to copy portions of the original message into the reply.

- *Never assume your e-mail is private.* As mentioned earlier in this chapter, assume your e-mail is not private and can be read by others. If in doubt, carefully consider whether you want your e-mail contents to be made available to others to read.

Handling Unwanted E-Mail

Like it or not, eventually your e-mail address will be distributed to people you don't want to have it. In theory, e-mail addresses are private, but it is difficult to keep addresses this way unless you send mail only to a few discrete people. Your e-mail address will undoubtedly end up on a distribution list for someone who sends out junk e-mail. Junk mail includes get-rich-quick schemes, unsolicited business opportunities, requests for donations, newsletters that you never requested, and other types of promotional literature. How do you handle this type of mail?

Because the Internet is relatively unpoliced, there are only a few things you can do about unwanted mail. The most obvious is to simply delete the mail, which at times may not be prudent. However, downloading messages, scanning their contents, then deciding you don't want them can be both costly and time-consuming. Also, some users find themselves getting many messages of this type every day, so the simple weeding-out process of junk from important material can be tiresome.

Sometimes the direct approach will work. Send e-mail back to the originator (if they are identified) and request that your name be removed from the distribution list. In many cases, though, the sender uses an anonymous user ID or hides behind other user's names, especially if illegal or immoral schemes are involved.

You can send a message to the sender's system postmaster, informing him of the problem and requesting action be taken. To address mail to a postmaster, you need to know the originating domain. This is harder to hide in a message, so it can be usually determined by reading the e-mail header. Send your request to "postmaster@domain.name". The postmaster login is a special system administrator login. Hopefully, they can help control the offending user. If the postmaster of the system doesn't help, try the system administrator.

> **Note**
>
> While sending e-mail to the postmaster or system administrator is reasonable, they don't always read their e-mail. Why? Because the postmaster and system administrator's login names are used for other activities relating to their jobs. The system administrator gets e-mail about daily backups that completed, system problems, and the like. The postmaster receives similarly automated messages about e-mail and UseNet. If you really need to contact somebody in charge of a domain, use WHOIS to find the contact e-mail address.

Finally, if you receive harassing or threatening mail, consider calling a law enforcement organization. Getting threats on e-mail is the same as getting them by postal service mail or over the telephone, which is illegal. Unfortunately, not many law enforcement agencies have experience with electronic media, so be patient and explain the problem. Keep copies of all the mail messages.

III

Using Internet E-Mail

CHAPTER 15

Using Microsoft Exchange

Microsoft Exchange is likely to become the next big step in electronic mail on the Internet. In addition to seamless integration with most of the new Windows 95 features, Microsoft Exchange boasts a user interface that far exceeds the usability and configurability of most other e-mail clients.

As you'll quickly see, Microsoft Exchange takes a few days to get used to, but then immediately becomes one of your favorite and most valuable desktop tools.

With it, you can send and receive messages not only over the Microsoft Network (MSN), but also over the Internet, over Microsoft Mail, and even CompuServe. You'll be able to attach files of any kind to messages you send, and easily view and save attached files you receive.

Finally, Microsoft Exchange contains a set of features quite unique in the e-mail client world. You'll be excited to discover how they work.

In this chapter, you learn how to:

- Get and install Microsoft Exchange
- Send and receive messages
- Organize your messages
- Use Microsoft Exchange Information Services
- Use Internet Mail
- Configure and customize your copy of Microsoft Exchange

What Makes Microsoft Exchange Unique?

Microsoft Exchange represents a relatively new concept to the Windows world. Traditional e-mail programs under Windows, such as Pegasus or Eudora, are much more straightforward and simple than Microsoft Exchange. But don't worry, Microsoft Exchange is still easy to use.

As part of the job of being a killer e-mail client, Microsoft Exchange supports a number of things most e-mail clients don't bother with; it does much more. However, you must tell Exchange what you want it do.

Unlike traditional e-mail clients, Microsoft Exchange is just an interface; it really doesn't accomplish anything on it's own. Just like an operating system such as DOS or Windows won't do anything unless you buy software and install it first, Microsoft Exchange won't do anything unless you install Information Services.

This concept allows Microsoft Exchange to become an open architecture for accessing different kinds of information from one central location. With Microsoft Exchange, you can access Microsoft Mail post offices, CompuServe mail, Internet mail, Microsoft Network mail, faxes, and lots of other stuff. How handy to have all of your mail in one convenient place!

The following list describes three of the Information Services that make Microsoft Exchange unique:

- **The Personal Information Store**   The first and most important Information Service is the Personal Information Store. Microsoft Exchange uses the Personal Information Store to store all of your mail. This store (or storage place, as you might like to call it) is a collection of folders; each folder contains subfolders and messages.

  Later on, I'll show you how to organize your mail by creating folders in which to keep your messages.

- **The Personal Address Book**   Another important Information Service is the Personal Address Book. As you may know, Internet e-mail is relatively easy to understand, since even children have written notes to one another—the only difference here is there's no paper!

  Even though e-mail itself is quite simple, remembering those darned e-mail addresses can be a bit frustrating. This doesn't get to be too bad if your friends and colleagues have e-mail addresses like bob@acme.com or sue@aol.com—most of these are easy to remember. Unfortunately, it doesn't always work out that way. My brother's old e-mail address was something really crazy like

Mark_R_at_Millikin_Post_Office@postoffice.mail.millikin.edu

Even if I could remember it, I wouldn't want to type that out every time. No thanks.

Like most e-mail clients, Microsoft Exchange provides a place for you to keep an easy-to-use database of e-mail addresses of people you often write: the Personal Address Book.

I'll show you how to add addresses to your address book after I show you how to send a message.

■ Internet Mail   In order to use Microsoft Exchange with Internet Mail, we'll have to load in an Information Service called Internet Mail. With the Internet Mail support, you'll be able to access your POP3 mail account. To find out if your Internet service provider uses POP3, call them. They should be able to tell you. If they don't, you won't be able to use Internet Mail with Microsoft Exchange.

Installing Microsoft Exchange

Before you're able to do anything with Microsoft Exchange, you'll need to install it. Actually, you may have done this already. Windows 95 puts it on your machine (although not fully installed or configured) unless you specifically tell it not to.

In the next few sections, I'll show you how to figure out if you've installed Microsoft Exchange yet, and how to do it if you haven't.

Where to Find Microsoft Exchange

Microsoft Exchange is one of the easiest programs to get. Since a basic version of it comes bundled with Windows 95, you can install it when you install Windows 95. You can also install it after you've installed Windows 95.

Microsoft also has available a full-featured version of Microsoft Exchange. This version contains more features and customization options, although most people will not miss the extras. If you're a power user, you may want to check this out; otherwise, you'll likely be plenty pleased with the version that ships with Windows 95.

Since Microsoft Exchange is available from more than one place, you'll likely not need to read through this entire section. I'd suggest you read the next section, "Do I Need Microsoft Exchange?," if you're not sure whether or not you'll need (or want) to use Microsoft Exchange.

If, after reading this section, you decide you want to take the big Exchange plunge, I'll help you to get it installed and set up. To make the most efficient

III

Using Internet E-Mail

use of time, you can skim the headers until you reach the one that fits your situation, read it, then get started. I'm assuming that, although reading is fun, you'd rather get something done. So, without further ado...

Is Microsoft Exchange Installed Already?

It is quite possible that you've already installed Microsoft Exchange on your system. For the most part, you're probably aware that you've installed it, but, just in case, here's how to find out. First of all, look for the Inbox icon on your desktop.

> ### Tip
>
> If you don't see this icon, you probably told the Windows 95 Setup Wizard that you didn't want to install Microsoft Exchange. Don't worry, it's not too late. Skip ahead to the next section, "Installing from the Windows 95 Installation Disks or CD," and follow the directions there.

Double-click this icon. After a few moments of churning, you'll see one of the following two things:

■ The Microsoft Exchange main window (see fig. 15.1)

Fig. 15.1
The Microsoft Exchange main window. If you see this window, you're all set.

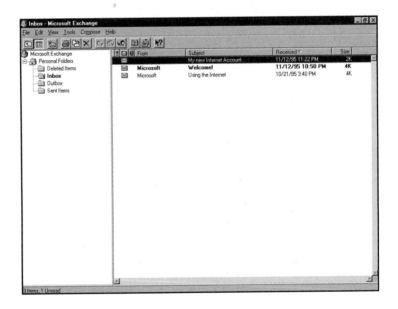

■ The Inbox Setup Wizard (see fig. 15.2)

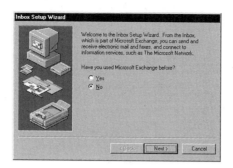

Fig. 15.2
The Inbox Setup Wizard. If you see this window, you haven't yet configured Microsoft Exchange.

If you see the Inbox Setup Wizard, you've installed Microsoft Exchange, but you haven't completed the installation process yet.

Installing from the Windows 95 Installation Disks or CD-ROM

In order to get started with this, you'll first need to be sure you have your Windows 95 installation disks handy. As a matter of fact, if you installed Windows 95 from a CD, you can put that CD in your CD-ROM drive now. Otherwise, keep the pack of disks next to your computer.

As you may know, Windows 95 has a cool auto-installation utility that allows you to install and uninstall different components of Windows 95 without a lot of hassle.

Tip

This section assumes you did not find the Inbox icon on your desktop. If you see the Inbox icon, you can skip this series of steps and move on to the next series.

To get started with the Microsoft Exchange installation, follow these steps:

1. Click the Start button on your taskbar.
2. Point to Settings and choose Control Panel. The Control Panel window appears.
3. In the Control Panel windows, double-click the Add/Remove Programs icon. The Add/Remove Programs Properties dialog box appears.
4. At the top of the dialog box, click the Windows Setup tab. You will see the Windows Setup properties, as shown in figure 15.3.
5. Be certain the Microsoft Exchange box is checked, then click OK. At this point, Windows 95 begins the Microsoft Exchange setup process.

III

Using Internet E-Mail

Fig. 15.3

To install Microsoft Exchange, select the Microsoft Exchange box and click OK.

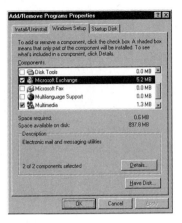

At this point, you should be looking at the Inbox Setup Wizard, as shown earlier in figure 15.2.

Although we're going to set up Exchange right now, there is another step involved—we'll also have to setup Internet Mail, which is available only with the Microsoft Plus! Companion for Windows 95 or the full-featured version of Exchange.

> **Tip**
>
> Although I'll provide a step-by-step guide to installing Microsoft Exchange, the Setup Wizard will ask questions that pertain to your specific machine. Therefore, what I mention here may not match what you see on your screen. If this happens, don't panic; just read each dialog box carefully and follow the directions.
>
> Also, if you've already set up an Information Service, you won't see any of this at all. You'll have to skip this section and read ahead to "Installing Internet Mail."

To complete the Microsoft Exchange installation, follow these steps:

1. The Setup Wizard asks you which services you'd like to use. Select which services you want to install, then click Next. The next dialog box appears.

2. This dialog box asks you to insert your Windows 95 Setup CD-ROM or floppy disk. Follow the instructions as appropriate for your system, then click Next. The Setup Wizard will copy a number of files from the CD-ROM or floppy disk. You may have to wait a few minutes or even change disks a few times.

3. Now, the Wizard would like to know if you've used Exchange before—in this case, you haven't, so click No. The next dialog box appears.

4. This dialog box confirms the Information Services you'd like to install. Again, you choose whichever services you'd like to install. If Internet Mail is present, be certain a check is in the box next to it—if not, you need to purchase the Microsoft Plus! Companion to get the Internet Mail support. To continue, click Next.

5. If you've selected any Information Services, the Setup Wizard will take you through them now.

If you selected Internet Mail in step 4, it's time to set it up. Leave the Setup Wizard where it is for right now—we'll come back to it in the section on installing Internet Mail.

Using Internet Mail

Internet Mail is the Information Service for Microsoft Exchange that gives you the power to send and receive Internet e-mail. Although it works with Microsoft Exchange, it doesn't come with it—you have to buy it separately as part of the Plus! Companion for Windows.

While I'm on the subject, let's go over what you need to use Internet Mail with Microsoft Exchange:

Internet Mail Requirements

To use the Internet Mail Information Service, you'll need:

- The Plus! Companion for Windows 95 or the commercially available full-featured version of Exchange.

- An Internet Service Provider. This is a company that provides you with access to the Internet.

- A modem or a network connection to the Internet.

- A POP3 mail account. If you're not sure about this one, call your service provider. Most people have one if they access the Internet over a modem.

- The IP address or domain name of your POP3 mail server. Your service provider can give you this information if you don't have it.

- The user ID and password you need to log in to the POP3 server.

Armed with this information, you're ready to begin.

III

Using Internet E-Mail

Installing Internet Mail

> **Tip**
>
> Before you begin the installation, close down any programs that may be running. If you have any software running that will conflict with the installation of the Plus! Companion, Setup will tell you. If so, simply close them down (use Alt+Tab to cycle through the running programs to close them down), then click OK in the error box.

To install Internet Mail, follow these steps:

1. If you're using the CD-ROM version of the Plus! Companion, put the CD in your CD-ROM drive. After a few moments, the Microsoft Plus! for Windows 95 window appears, as shown in figure 15.4. Click Install Plus! to continue.

> **Tip**
>
> Some CD-ROM drives do not support the Autoplay feature. If you have one of these, you will not see the Windows 95 window. To start the setup process in this case, you'll need to use the Add/Remove programs procedure described in the following step 2, using your D: drive (or whatever your CD-ROM drive letter happens to be) instead.

Fig. 15.4
From this window, you can install the Plus! Companion, look through a multimedia catalog of Microsoft products, or browse the contents of the CD-ROM.

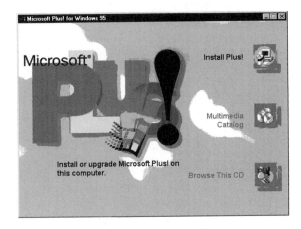

2. If you're using the floppy disk set, put the first disk in your floppy drive. Open the Start menu and choose Settings, Control Panel. Double-click Add/Remove Programs. The Add/Remove Programs Properties sheet appears. Click the Install button. The system will automatically find the setup program and display the path and file name in a box labeled Command Line for Installation Program. Check to be sure that the drive letter is correct, then choose Next. (At this point, whether you're using the CD-ROM or floppy disk, the rest of the installation process is the same.)

3. The Setup utility takes you through a number of screens. Read each dialog box carefully, and click Continue or Next until you see the screen shown in figure 15.5.

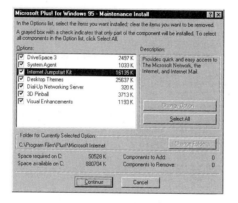

Fig. 15.5
In this window, indicate which elements of the Plus! Companion you wish to install. At a minimum, you need to install the Internet Jumpstart Kit to use Internet Mail with Microsoft Exchange.

4. Be certain that Internet Jumpstart Kit is checked. You may, if you wish, remove any of the other options you do not wish to install. To find out what an option is, highlight it, then read the descriptive text in the box to the right labeled Description.

5. After you've selected the components you wish to install, click Continue. Setup begins to copy files from the CD-ROM or floppy disk. Change disks as needed.

6. Depending on what other options you've installed, you may see other dialog boxes that ask you for different types of information. Eventually, however, you'll see the Internet Setup Wizard, as shown in figure 15.6. To continue, click Next. If you have file or printer sharing enabled on your machine, the Wizard asks if you want to disable it on the TCP/IP connection. In virtually every case, you should choose Yes here. The How to Connect dialog box appears.

Fig. 15.6

The Internet Setup
Wizard guides you
through the
Internet setup
process.

7. If you have an Internet service provider already, click the radio button labeled I Already Have an Account with a Different Service Provider. Otherwise, click the radio button labeled Use the Microsoft Network. To continue, click Next.

8. If you'll be using the Microsoft Network, Setup will need to install the Microsoft Network utility files. Be sure your Windows 95 floppy disks or CD-ROM are handy. If you're using a different provider, you'll have to answer a few questions about them in the next few dialog boxes.

9. In the next dialog box, type the name of your provider. This creates a Dial-Up Networking icon for that provider. If you've already created an icon for your provider, select it from the list. To continue, click Next.

10. Enter the telephone number information in the spaces provided. You'll also notice a box labeled Bring Up Terminal Window After Dialing. If you usually type your name and password, check this box. If the login process happens automatically, leave this unchecked. To continue, click Next.

11. Enter your userID and password information in the spaces provided. If, for some reason, you don't know what should go here, contact your Internet service provider. To continue, click Next.

12. An IP address is a special set of numbers that distinguishes you from every other machine on the Internet (for example, 231.32.42.214). In most cases, your provider assigns an IP address to you when you log in. If you don't know what your IP address is, your provider probably assigns you one. If you know your address, check the other box and type the address in. The subnet is nearly always 255.255.255.0. To continue, click Next.

13. This next dialog box deals with DNS information. DNS (Domain Name Service) is a complicated system of computers that makes it easier to use

the Internet. You'll need information for these boxes, but only your provider can give you the correct information. If you're unsure, contact your provider. To continue, click Next.

At this point, you need to configure Internet Mail itself. Since Internet Mail setup is a process separate from the installation of an Internet service provider, I'll cover it in a separate section. Also, if you create a new profile (I'll explain profiles later in this chapter), you'll only have to configure Internet Mail, not the stuff above.

Internet e-mail is quite a simple thing, but you'll need to know a few things to get it all working. Luckily, once you get it working, you'll never have to mess with it again. Also, if you add a new profile (profiles are discussed later in this chapter) to Microsoft Exchange, you'll want to refer back to this section if you want to use Internet Mail with that profile.

To configure Internet Mail, follow these steps:

1. This series of steps continues from where the previous series of steps left off. Now you are at Internet Mail. Be sure that the box labeled Use Internet Mail is checked. Enter your e-mail address and the address of your mail server. Again, if you don't have the information, your provider can get it for you. To continue, click Next.

2. In this dialog box, select which profile to use with Internet Mail. In most cases, you'll only have one profile (MS Exchange Settings). Use that one. If you'd like to create a separate profile for Internet Mail, click New. To continue, click Next.

The Quick Tour

In this section, I'll take you on a quick tour of Exchange, then teach you how to perform the basic e-mail tasks, like sending a message or saving a message you've received from a friend. If you already know how to do the basics, and you were looking for the good stuff, consider reviewing this section anyway. I'll point out a few tips and tricks to make your Exchange session more productive.

It's always important to take a good look around you, and get the feel of a program before you dig in. Kind of like the first time you drive a car other than your own. Look around, check out the controls, make sure you know where everything is. You'd be surprised how easy it is to learn a program if you take the time to give it a thorough once over first.

III

Using Internet E-Mail

Starting and Exiting Microsoft Exchange

Before we get into the different aspects of the user interface, let's review a few things. First let's cover the following two easiest ways to start Microsoft Exchange:

[Inbox]

- Double-click the Inbox icon on your desktop.
- Open the Start menu and choose Programs, Microsoft Exchange.

Although you're probably more than familiar with how to exit a Windows 95 application, Microsoft Exchange is a little different, so I thought I'd point out a couple of things.

Open the File menu. At the bottom of the menu you have the following two choices (see fig. 15.7):

- *Exit*—This item closes Microsoft Exchange but leaves all of your other messaging applications open. What other messaging applications? Well, in the background, you'll have several applications running to send and retrieve your mail and check for new mail in various different places. This is how Exchange runs so smoothly—it's only a front-end to the rest of the mail send/receive activities.

- *Exit and Log Off*—As you may suspect, this option closes any and all messaging applications on your system. Note that if you're running Microsoft Schedule+, it closes also.

Fig. 15.7
Choose Exit to leave the rest of your messaging applications (such as Schedule+) running. Choose Exit and Log Off to close all of your messaging applications.

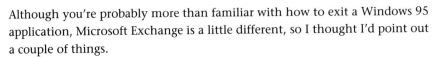

The Toolbars

Microsoft Exchange comes with a default set of buttons on a toolbar to help automate many of the tasks you'll perform on a daily basis. As with most Microsoft applications, you can customize or edit this toolbar to fit the way you use the program. Of course, it doesn't make much sense to worry about this until you've used the program for a couple of weeks.

To edit the toolbars, follow these steps:

1. Double-click the toolbar you wish to edit. Take care to double-click the background of the toolbar, and not a button. You will see the Customize Toolbar dialog box, as shown in figure 15.8.

Highlight the item here and click Add to add it to the toolbar

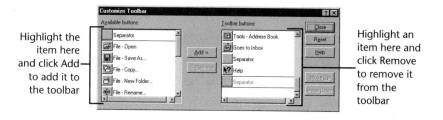

Highlight an item here and click Remove to remove it from the toolbar

Fig. 15.8
Use this window to customize the toolbar to your personal tastes. Use as many or as few buttons as you like, or simply change the order.

2. To add a button to the toolbar, drag it from the master list on the left to the toolbar list on the right.

3. To change the position of the button, highlight the button and use the Move Up and Move Down buttons to the right, or you can drag and drop the button to the new location.

4. When you've finished with your customizations, click Close.

Tip

Each window in Microsoft Exchange has a separate toolbar. Basically, there are three different windows: the main window, the send message window, and the received message window.

Each window type has a separate list of command buttons available, so a button you see in one window may not be offered in another.

The Mailbox Window

On the left, you'll notice the list of folders or mailboxes on your system. Keep in mind that your window may look different from the one in figure 15.9.

Fig. 15.9
The mailbox windows shows you a list of the personal folders you created for storing messages. It also shows you which folder you have open.

If a folder has other folders inside, you'll see a plus sign just to the left. To see the folders inside, either click the plus sign or double-click the name of the folder. The next level of folder appears.

Note that when you've selected a mailbox folder, it appears with an icon of an opened file folder.

The Message Window

On the right, you see a list of any messages or subfolders in the currently selected mailbox folder. At the top of this windows, you see a number of column headings, as well (see fig. 15.10). These columns give you brief, at-a-glance information about the item contained in the folder.

> **Tip**
>
> If you click a column header (such as From or Subject) the messages in the folder will be sorted based on that column. For example, clicking the Received column header will sort the messages in the order they were received.

Fig. 15.10

The message window contains a list of any message types in that folder.

> **Tip**
>
> Although, to stay within the scope of this book, I won't discuss them, Microsoft Exchange handles more types of information than e-mail. It will also organize and maintain all the faxes you've sent and received with Microsoft Fax, and, if you have the right software, will even store voice-mail messages. If you'd like more information about using these types of services, consider reading Que's *Special Edition Using Windows 95*.

For the most part, you'll use this window to read your incoming messages. If you have one there now, double-click it to bring up the Message Read window. I'll go into this in more detail in the next section.

Sending and Receiving Messages

Here's the meat and potatoes of the whole chapter. First let's cover a basic concept you should understand before you begin.

Microsoft Exchange doesn't actually send or receive mail. If this concept is confusing, consider that your mailbox outside doesn't send or receive mail, either. If you want to send a letter, you sit down at the table and write it out first. In Microsoft Exchange, this is represented by the New Message window. After you've written your letter, you put an address on it and place it in the mailbox, indicating you'd like it delivered. The address tells the deliverer where you want it to go.

When you compose a message with the New Message window, you need to tell the program to send it. However, as I said, Microsoft Exchange does *not* send the message. It simply places the message in your Outbox. With the U.S. Post Office, your Inbox and Outbox are the same box. In Microsoft Exchange, however, they are two different boxes. A messaging application running in the background "picks up" messages from the Outbox, delivers them, and places any incoming mail in your Inbox.

There are three different kinds of recipients in e-mail:

- *To:*—Any address in this field receives a copy of the message. The e-mail is addressed to the recipient. In most cases, this is the field you'll want to use.

- *Cc:*—This stands for Carbon Copy or Courtesy Copy. If the message is for John, but Bob should have a copy of it, put Bob in the Cc: field. A good example of this would be sending a report to another office and putting your supervisor in the Cc: field to let her know you sent the report.

- *Bcc:*—Similar to the Cc:, the Blind Cc: field sends a copy of the e-mail to any address in the field, but the other recipients are unaware that you also sent it to this address.

Tip

By default, the Bcc: field does not display in the New Message window. If you want to use it, open the View menu in the New Message window and choose Bcc box.

Sending a Message

Now that you understand the basic concept, let's get to the point. To send a message to someone, follow these steps:

1. Open the Compose menu and choose New Message. The New Message window appears, as shown in figure 15.11. Or, if you'd rather, you can use Ctrl+N or choose the New Message button on the toolbar.

Fig. 15.11

You can use the
New Message
window to create a
new message.

Cc: field—type
the address of
any person who
should have a
copy of the e-mail

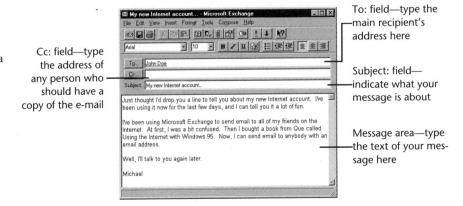

To: field—type the
main recipient's
address here

Subject: field—
indicate what your
message is about

Message area—type
the text of your mes-
sage here

2. Your text cursor should be in the To: field. If it's not, use the mouse to put it there. Type the address of the person to whom you'd like to send a message. When you're finished, press the Tab key. If you're just trying to get the hang of things, and you don't know anyone's e-mail address, just use your own.

> **Tip**
>
> Eventually, you'll create an alias in your address book instead of typing out the address each time. I'll show you how to do this in the next section.

3. If you'd like to courtesy copy another person (or persons), type the address(es) in the Cc: field. When you're finished, press the Tab key.

4. In the subject field, type a few words that indicate what your e-mail is about. When you're done, press the Tab key.

5. In the message area, type the text of your message. Be sure to end your message with an appropriate signature including your name.

6. If you're finished with your message, open the File menu and choose Send. Your message will be moved to the Outbox.

> **Tip**
>
> If you're using the Internet over a modem, the messaging service won't send your message right away. You'll have to wait until the next time the messaging service connects to the Internet.
>
> If, on the other hand, you need to send the message right away, open the Tools menu and choose Deliver Now.

Adding People to Your Address Book

Adding people's addresses to your Address Book makes it easier and faster to send mail; instead of typing out an entire address (that is, if you can remember it), you can simply type the person's name, and Exchange puts the address in for you. Although there are a number of different ways to accomplish the task of adding new addresses, I've learned that one method seems to be far and away the most effective.

I usually need to create a new address only when I'm ready to send an e-mail to that person. That way, I don't have to spend a lot of time adding addresses that I might not even use.

To add an address to your address book, follow these steps:

1. Open the Compose menu and select New Message. The New Message window appears.

2. Type the address in the To: field, then press Alt+K (this checks the format of the address). If you've typed it correctly, it will appear underlined.

3. Double-click the address to bring up the address Properties dialog box. The title of this dialog box contains the address you just typed (see fig. 15.12).

4. In the Display Name field, type the person's real name (or even a nickname you'd like to use).

5. To add this address to your Personal Address Book, click Add to Personal Address Book, then click OK.

Fig. 15.12
To add an address, type a name and click Add to Personal Address Book.

This returns you to your New Message window, where the To: field now displays the name you've typed in.

Using the Personal Address Book

Obviously, it doesn't make much sense to save all these names if you're not going to use them at some point.

When you create a new message, there are two ways to get to the names you've placed in your personal address book. First, open the Compose menu and choose New Message. At the top of the window, you'll see the edit box where you can type the address of a recipient. To use an entry from the Personal Address Book instead, you can

- Click the To: button
- Type the name instead of the address and then press Alt+K

Of course, it doesn't matter which method you use, as both will use the same address from the Personal Address Book.

To use the To: button, follow these steps:

1. Click the To: button next to the To: field. The Address Book window appears (see fig. 15.13).

Fig. 15.13

To add a name to the To: field of your new message, highlight the name and click To.

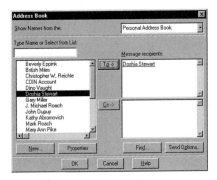

2. To put the person in the To: field of your new message, double-click the name or highlight the name and click the To button. The name appears in the Message recipients: box on the right.

3. When you've finished adding names, click OK.

This returns you to your new message with the names of the recipients you've selected. Continue with your new message as you normally would.

Although this process is quite straightforward, there is an even easier way to add names that isn't very obvious. Once you get the hang of it, though, you'll be addressing e-mail like a pro.

To add recipients to the To: field of your new message:

1. Open the Co<u>m</u>pose menu and select <u>N</u>ew Message. You will see a New Message window. Type the name in the To: field or at least the first few letters. For example, instead of typing **Juanita Martinez**, you can type **juan**.

2. Press Alt+K to check the names against the Personal Address Book.

3. If Microsoft Exchange finds the name, it appears underlined in the To: field; otherwise, it displays an error dialog box (see fig. 15.14).

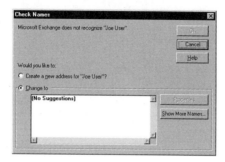

Fig. 15.14
You'll see this dialog box if Microsoft Exchange can't match what you typed to any names in the Personal Address Book.

Receiving Messages

Luckily, this one's really easy. When the Internet Mail service checks to see if you have any new mail, your new mail is automatically delivered to your Inbox. You don't need to do anything to receive your mail.

However, if you want to check for new mail right now, without waiting, open the <u>T</u>ools menu and choose <u>D</u>eliver Now Using and then choose the service you want to retrieve mail from. Incidentally, if you have new mail waiting to be delivered, this same menu option forces the immediate delivery of that mail.

Tip

If you have unread mail in your Inbox, you'll see a New Mail icon in the status area of your taskbar.

Viewing a Message

If you have new mail in your Inbox, you'll see the headers in the message window. To view a message, double-click on its header.

> **Tip**
>
> Note that Microsoft Exchange displays the header of any message you haven't yet read in **bold** type on the right hand side of the window. After you've read the message, the font returns to normal.
>
> Likewise, on the left, any folder that contains an unread message also appears in boldface.

> **Tip**
>
> If you'd like to see the full header of the e-mail, open the File menu and choose Properties. Then click the Internet tab in the dialog box that appears. Note that this will only work if the message is from the Internet. This will not work on messages from Microsoft Mail or other Information Services.

Replying to a Message

Often, you receive an e-mail and need to reply to the person who sent it. As with nearly all e-mail programs, Microsoft Exchange provides an automated method for accomplishing this task.

The following are the two different kinds of replies:

- *Reply*—This method automatically generates an e-mail to the sender only.
- *Reply to all*—This method automatically generates an e-mail to the sender and all recipients except yourself.

You can reply to a message that you've just read, while it is still open, or you can reply to a message that is not open; the menu options are the same in both the message window and the main Exchange window. To reply to a message, follow these steps:

1. If you don't have the message open already, click its header in the Inbox message area.
2. To reply to the sender, open the Compose menu and choose Reply to Sender or Reply to All (whichever you'd like to do). The New Message window appears with the sender's address in the To: field, the original header and body text indented, and a blank space for you put your reply.

Tip

The text of the message to which you're replying is indented by default, but the receiver won't see it that way. The indents are done with special formatting codes that only work with Microsoft Exchange. When you send mail over the Internet, Microsoft Exchange strips these special codes, so the reader won't see the indents.

3. Type your reply.

4. Open the File menu and choose Send. Your message disappears as Microsoft Exchange sends it to the Outbox to be delivered.

Forwarding a Message

A number of my friends are also on the Internet, and I like to share interesting or funny information with them. Even at work, I get an e-mail from time to time that someone else in my department may benefit from.

Forwarding mail is similar to replying, but you're not going to send anything back to the sender—in fact, when you forward, there is no address in the To: field; you need to supply your own.

To forward a message, follow these steps:

1. Open the message you want to forward.

2. Open the Compose menu and choose Forward. The New Message window appears with the subject in the title bar.

3. Use any of the methods you've learned so far to address the e-mail.

4. If you have any comments to add, add them at the top of the message.

5. To send the message, open the File menu and choose Send.

Saving and Organizing Messages

I've been using e-mail for quite some time now, and most of the time, I get junk. However, every once in a while, I'll get a piece of mail I'd like to keep. Even if you've just started in the world of e-mail and don't get very many messages, there will be a few you want to keep.

While it's certainly easy to just leave them in your Inbox after you've read them, this clutters it up considerably in a very short time. It's usually best to find a safe place for them.

III

Using Internet E-Mail

In order to save a message, you'll want to know how to do the following two things:

- Create folders in your Personal Information Store
- Move and copy mail messages from one folder to another

Creating Folders

Microsoft Exchange gives you four folders to start with (these are called *System Folders*) but you can create as many as you want.

The system folders are the following:

- Inbox
- Outbox
- Sent Items
- Deleted Items

Although these folders certainly cover the basics, most people might like a Saved Items folder, as well.

There are several different ways to create a folder, but I'll focus on the easiest way—the one you're most likely to use.

To create a folder, follow these steps:

1. Go to the main Microsoft Exchange window. You'll see your list of folders on the left.

2. Decide where in the tree you'd like to put your new folder. For example, do you want it to be a subfolder of the Inbox, or a top-level folder?

3. Using your mouse, open the folder (click it once) *above* where you want your folder to be. For example, if you want to create a folder under Inbox, open Inbox. If you want to create a top-level folder, open the Personal Information Store.

4. Open the File menu and choose New Folder. The New Folder dialog box appears (see fig. 15.15).

Fig. 15.15

Type a name for your new folder.

5. In the edit field, type a name for your new folder, such as **Saved Items**.

6. To create the folder, click OK.

Tip

If you should accidentally create the folder in the wrong place, don't panic. You can still move it. Just drag the folder to the new location, and Microsoft Exchange will move it for you, complete with any messages that may be in it.

Moving and Copying Messages

If you get a message you'd like to save in your Saved Items folder (or any-where else, for that matter), all you need to do is to move it to the new folder. If you'd like to keep a copy in the original folder, too, you can use copy in-stead, but the process is the same.

To move or copy a message to another folder, follow these steps:

1. In the message window, highlight the header of the message you'd like to move or copy.

2. Click the right mouse button and choose Mo<u>v</u>e or Cop<u>y</u> (whichever you'd like to do). The Move (or Copy) dialog box appears.

3. Click the folder in which you want to store the message (see fig. 15.16).

Fig. 15.16

Choose the folder where you want your message to go.

Tip

It's very tempting to double-click a folder to get to one underneath, but don't do that—you'll put the message in there, instead. If you want to open the next level of folders, click the plus sign once. The next level appears.

4. To move or copy the message, click OK.

III

Using Internet E-Mail

Tip

Notice that you can create new folders in the Move and Copy dialog boxes with the New button.

Tip

You can also move a message by dragging its header to the destination folder. If you'd rather copy the message, hold down the Ctrl key while you drag and drop.

Show Me the Really Cool Stuff!

I know, you've read enough. You've gotten a hang of the basic tasks, now you want to have some fun. After all, what good is a tool if isn't fun to use? Let's jump in...

Configuring Basic Options

Microsoft Exchange has a large number of options you can change to customize the way you use it.

To get started, open the Tools menu and choose Options. The Options dialog box appears with the General tab displayed. To change to a different set of options, click the appropriate tab at the top of the screen.

For more information on configuring, check out Que's *Using Microsoft Exchange*.

General Options

The General options cover most of the basic items you might like to change about Microsoft Exchange (see table 15.1).

Table 15.1 General Options

Option	What the Option Does
When New Mail Arrives	
Play a sound	When new mail arrives, Microsoft Exchange plays a sound, usually the default beep sound.
Briefly change the pointer	When new mail arrives, your mouse pointer briefly changes to an icon of an envelope. This way, you know what the beep means.
Display a notification	Microsoft Exchange puts a message dialog box on the screen informing you that new mail has arrived.

Option	What the Option Does
Deleting Items	
Warn before permanently deleting items	Normally, if you delete an item, it is simply moved to your Deleted Items folder. However, if you delete an item from the Deleted Items folder, it is gone forever. If this is checked, Microsoft Exchange prompts for confirmation before this happens.
Empty Deleted Items folder upon exiting	If this item is checked, Microsoft Exchange permanently deletes all the messages in the Deleted Items folder when you exit. If you'd like to keep them around, just in case, clear the check from this box.
When Starting Microsoft Exchange	
Prompt for a profile to be used	If this item is checked, Microsoft Exchange prompts you each time you start the program, asking you to choose a profile to use. This is handy if more than one person uses your computer. If not, it's usually a good idea to use.
Always use this profile	If you've selected this item, choose which profile you'd like to use when you start Microsoft Exchange. If you only have one profile, of course, this is the best one to use.
Other Options	
Show ToolTips on toolbars	If this item is checked, you'll see a brief description of each toolbar button whenever your mouse pointer is on it.
When selecting, automatically select entire word	This is a good item to have checked. When you select a sentence or phrase, Microsoft Exchange assumes you want to select the entire word at the beginning and at the end. This way, you don't have to be very accurate with the mouse—it saves a lot of frustration in most cases.

Tip

In the Control Panel, under Sounds, you can configure Microsoft Exchange to play a specific .WAV file when new mail arrives. I have a nice sound file of a telephone ringing. Of course, you must have a sound card for this to work.

Read Options

The Read options are a few things you can change that affect what happens when you perform tasks related to reading mail, such as replying to, forwarding, moving, or deleting new messages (see table 15.2).

III

Using Internet E-Mail

Table 15.2 Read Options

Option	What the Option Does
After Moving or Deleting an Open Item	
Open the item above it	If this item is selected, Microsoft Exchange displays the previous item in the current message folder whenever you move or delete an open message. If you start reading your mail at the bottom of the Inbox, you should select this option.
Open the item below it	If this item is selected, Microsoft Exchange displays the next item in the current message folder whenever you move or delete an open message. If you start reading your mail at the top of the Inbox, you should select this option.
Return to Microsoft Exchange	If you'd rather not move to another message when you move or delete an item, you should select this option.
When Replying To or Forwarding an Item	
Include the original text when replying	When you reply to a message, it's usually important to include some portion of the original message, so that the recipient understands your reply. If you'd like to do this (you can always delete the text if you don't need it for a specific reply), check this box.
Indent the original text when replying	Although this is a handy option, and works great when replying to another Microsoft Exchange user, it does not affect the appearance of your e-mail over the Internet.
Close the original item	If this option is checked, the current message closes if you forward it or reply to its sender. I, however, like to return to the message so that I can either save it (move it) or delete it.
Use this font for the reply text	Again, this is a cool option when replying to another Microsoft Exchange user, but it doesn't affect the final appearance of e-mail sent over the Internet. To change the font, click the Font button and choose the font you'd like to use.

Tip

I usually start reading my new mail at the top. After I've read an item, I either move it (to a Saved Items folder, if I want to save it), or delete it (if I don't care to keep it). At that point, I'd like to read the next message in the list—therefore, I use the Open Item Below It option.

Send Options

The Send options include the default settings for outgoing mail (see table 15.3).

Table 15.3   Send Options

Option	What the Option Does
Use this font	Microsoft Exchange uses this font whenever you compose a new message. This does not affect the appearance of outgoing Internet mail, only mail intended for another Microsoft Exchange user.
Request that a receipt be sent back when the item has been read	The Internet will send an e-mail to notify you that your message has been read.
The item has been delivered	The Internet will send an e-mail to notify you that your message has been delivered, but not necessarily read.

Tip

If you have either of the two previous items checked, you'll get an e-mail back every time you send one. If you send a lot of mail, your Inbox will be swamped with confirmations.

Set sensitivity	This option controls the default sensitivity of your outgoing e-mail. Choices are Normal, Personal, Private, and Confidential. In nearly all cases, leaving this to normal is fine.
Set importance	This option controls the default importance of your outgoing mail. Choices are High, Normal, and Low.
Save a copy of the item in the Sent Items folder	Place a check in this box if you'd like to save a copy of each message you send in the Sent Items folder. This option is most handy in a professional environment, where a paper trail can come in handy.

Delivery Options

For the most part, you'll not need to change any of the information in this tab. But, sometimes, this tab can cause some problems.

If you notice that your outgoing mail never seems to be delivered, be certain that Internet Mail is at the top of the list in the bottom window.

To change the position of Internet Mail, follow these steps:

1. Highlight Internet Mail.
2. Click the up arrow until Internet Mail is at the top.

Using Profiles

I have two roommates. You may have more than one person living with you, also—or sharing your computer at work. This makes collecting and organizing mail for more than one person rather difficult.

If you share your computer with someone else for any reason, you'll probably want to keep your e-mail separate. This allow for convenience as well as privacy.

Microsoft Exchange solves this problem with a technology called *profiles*. With profiles, each user can create a unique look and feel, folder set, user ID, password, and other settings that affect the way the program works.

Creating a New Profile

You may not realize it, but you've already created at least one profile. This profile (unless you'd decided to call it something different) is called MS Exchange Settings. If you have more than one person using the same computer for e-mail, you can create additional profiles.

To create a new profile, follow these steps:

1. Open the Start menu and choose Settings, Control Panel.
2. In the Control Panel window, double-click Mail and Fax. The profile Properties dialog box appears.
3. Click Show Profiles. The Microsoft Exchange Profiles dialog box appears.
4. Click Add. The Microsoft Exchange Setup Wizard appears.

At this point, you can create a custom profile for a particular user. The rest of the Setup Wizard is identical to the initial setup of Exchange. When prompted for the name of the profile, I'd recommend using the name of the person who will use the profile, if that's why you're creating the profile. That way, each user can select his or her own name from the list of profiles.

Using Microsoft Exchange with More Than One User

Now that you've created your new profile, you'll now want to choose which profile to use when you start Microsoft Exchange. To set this up, follow these steps:

1. Open the Tools menu and choose Options. The Options dialog box appears.
2. Be sure the General tab is selected.

3. Toward the bottom, under When starting Microsoft Exchange, select Prompt for a Profile To Be Used.

Each time you start Microsoft Exchange, a dialog box appears similar to the one shown in figure 15.17. From the list, choose the profile you want to use for that session, then click OK.

Fig. 15.17
Choose the profile you'd like to use and click OK.

Microsoft Exchange completes its startup procedure, and you are ready to go.

III

Using Internet E-Mail

CHAPTER 16

Using Eudora

Eudora is one of the most widely used e-mail programs on the Internet, partly because it's so good, and partly because it runs on multiple platforms. PC Eudora is the Windows 95 version. It's easy to set up, easy to use, and is intuitive. That is, most commands make sense and are linked in a logical way. For example, the Mailbox menu selection gives you the choice of In, Out, Trash, New, and a list of mailbox names. That sounds easy enough, doesn't it?

With Eudora, you can send mail, retrieve mail, file mail, resend mail, and save and edit mail—and not only text mail and binary mail, but video and audio mail as well. So far, however, I haven't seen too much multimedia e-mail, but things move quickly on the Internet.

You can create multiple versions of Eudora so that each user can have a different password. You can run PC Eudora from a shell or a SLIP account (see chapters 6 and 7). Because a SLIP account provides full GUI capabilities, that's what this chapter discusses.

In this chapter, you learn how to do the following:

- Set up Eudora
- Create, save, and edit Eudora mail
- Retrieve mail using folders and mailboxes
- Reroute mail along a specified path
- Send and retrieve multimedia and binary mail

Downloading and Installing PC Eudora

Eudora was written as a Mac program, and PC Eudora is adapted for Windows. You can get versions of both Windows and Macintosh from public sites, and you can also buy commercial programs. This chapter was written for the freeware version of Eudora, Eudora Light 1.5.2, which is available by anonymous FTP from **ftp.qualcomm.com** in the /quest/windows/eudora/ 1.5 directory. Download the executable EUDOR152.EXE and the README file. The commercial version 2.1.2 is available in the directory /quest/windows/eudora/2.1. Currently there is no Windows 95 specific version of Eudora Light. However, Eudora Pro is scheduled to be available for Windows 95 natively at the start of 1996. (See "Upgrading to Eudora 2.1.2" at the end of this chapter.)

NetCD95

Documentation for Eudora 1.5.2 is also available by anonymous FTP at **ftp.qualcomm.com** in the directory /quest/windows/eudora/documentation as 15MANUAL.EXE. It's a self-extracting archive that creates a Word for Windows 2.0 document. You'll also find that some features aren't supported in the freeware Windows 95 version. The documentation includes a table of contents, an index, and several useful appendixes, including extended information on character mapping, MIME, and UUCP. The documentation is complete with screen shots and diagrams to illustrate particular points.

> **Tip**
>
> To verify that you have the most current version, send mail to **listserv@vmd.cso.uiuc.edu**. Type **sub eudora *your first name-your last name*** in the message area. You will automatically be sent update announcements.

EUDOR152.EXE is a self-extracting file, so you can either run it or unzip it. If you don't have an unzip utility you can do the following:

1. Find a place on your hard drive for Eudora Light and create a directory for it.

2. Open the Start menu and choose Programs, MS-DOS Prompt.

3. Enter **cd *name***, where *name* is the name of the directory you want to install Eudora Light into.

4. Enter the full path name for the Eudora Light self-extracting executable.

If you do have an unzip utility, you can simply unzip the archive to whichever directory you like.

You can create a shortcut for the program on the desktop or in any Start program group. To create a shortcut for Eudora Light on the Windows 95 desktop, do the following:

1. Click the right mouse button somewhere on the desktop that isn't being used by an icon, a program, or the like.
2. From the context menu, choose Ne<u>w</u>, <u>S</u>hortcut.
3. Click the B<u>r</u>owse button in the Create Shortcut dialog box.
4. In the Browse dialog box, find the Eudora Light executable.
5. Click the Open button and then click the Next button.
6. Enter **Eudora Light** for the name of the shortcut.
7. Click the Finish button.

You can similarly create a shortcut for Eudora Light in the Start button groups. Simply perform the following:

1. Open the Start menu and choose <u>S</u>ettings, <u>T</u>askbar. The Taskbar Properties sheet appears.
2. Select the Start Menu Programs tab.
3. Click the Add button. The Create Shortcut dialog box appears.
4. Repeat steps 3 through 7 in the previous steps for adding a shortcut to the desktop.

The Eudora README file notes that Windows Eudora is a WinSock compliant program, and needs a WINSOCK.DLL file to run it. Windows 95 comes with Microsoft's own WINSOCK.DLL file, so Eudora will work fine.

> **Tip**
>
> If you install Eudora from NetCD95, it creates the Start button program icon for you.

As of this writing, version 1.5.2 is the current version. To update an older version, just transfer the new file, and run the executable through Windows Explorer. Press return when you're asked if you want to overwrite the old files. Your configuration, settings, existing mail, and nicknames will be transferred to the new version.

◀ See "A Brief Introduction to TCP/IP," p. 126

◀ See "Testing Your TCP/IP Connection," p. 135

III

Using Internet E-Mail

> **Note**
>
> You might find it easier to keep the icons for Trumpet WinSock, Eudora, Telnet, FTP, and WS-FTP in the same Start button program group. This will help you from fumbling around different directory windows while you're online. This is especially important if your access provider is a toll call.

Adapting Eudora for Several Users

If more than one person is using Eudora on the same PC, you can create as many versions as you want so that each is password-protected.

To create another Eudora folder, do the following:

1. Open the Start menu and choose Settings, Taskbar. The Taskbar Properties sheet appears.

2. Select the Start Menu Programs tab.

3. Click the Advanced button.

4. Choose File, New, Folder. Type in the name of the new Eudora folder and then select it.

5. Choose File, New, Shortcut.

6. Use the Browse button to find the Eudora executable.

Entering a Password

The first time you start up Eudora, you'll be asked for a password, which defaults to the POP server password (either the one your access provider gave you or what you changed it to). Once you've entered the password, you won't have to enter it again. If you happen to change the password on your POP account, you'll have to update your Eudora password. To do this, select the Special menu and choose Forget Password. The next time Eudora checks for mail, it will again ask you for your password.

To change the password, perform the following steps:

1. Choose Special, Change Password.

2. Enter the current password and click OK.

3. Enter the new password and click OK.

> **Note**
>
> If you're the only person using the program, you don't have to worry about your password being saved. If several people are going to use the same program, and security is an issue, you should have Eudora Forget Password every time you exit it.

Configuring Eudora

If you set Eudora to run minimized, when you double-click the Eudora icon, the program launches and a button appears for it on the taskbar. Clicking that item displays the Eudora window. If you don't run Eudora minimized, you'll run the program normally. Eudora automatically checks your POP server for messages every time it's started, which could mean a tedious wait if you're not really online. It also tries to connect when it starts up into the taskbar, but it realizes much sooner that you're not really connected to the POP server. You should run Eudora minimized unless you usually plan to create mail online.

> **Tip**
>
> To set the Eudora shortcut for running Eudora Light minimized, right-click the shortcut. From the context menu, choose Properties. The Properties sheet appears; click the shortcut tab. In the Run drop-down list box, choose Minimized. Click the OK or Apply button.

To personalize as much of Eudora as possible, you need to do the following:

1. Choose Special, Settings, which opens the Settings dialog box (see fig. 16.1), and select the Getting Started category.
2. The POP Account heading is your e-mail address, obtained from your Internet provider.
3. You can also fill in your real name, which will appear parenthetically after your address in the mail header.
4. Under the Personal Information category, you can leave Return Address blank if it will be the same as your mail address.
5. If you want the program to automatically check for mail, select the Checking Mail category. Enter a reasonable amount of time, 15 and 30 minutes is generally used. As long as you're connected to the Internet, Eudora will notify you if you have new mail, even if you're working in a non-Eudora application when it comes in.

Fig. 16.1
The Settings dialog box in PC Eudora provides information on how to manage your mail.

The information in the Display and Fonts category lets you change the way your messages look. You'll probably have a better idea of what suits you after you use the program for a while.

Customizing Eudora

The Settings dialog box, accessed from the Special menu, allows you to customize various Eudora settings (see fig. 16.2). Related settings are grouped together under various categories, listed on the left side of the dialog box. This section discusses some of the important (and fun) ones.

Fig. 16.2
You can customize your messages in the Settings dialog box.

A signature is usually used at the end of a message to indicate a full name, title, corporate affiliation, line of work, full address, or phone number, but it could be anything you want (if it's in good taste, of course). Creating a signature is covered later in the chapter. You can have Eudora Light automatically append your signature at the end of every letter you send out. Simply select the Sending Mail category and choose the Use Signature option.

The May Use Quoted-Printable option under the Sending Mail category refers to quoted-printable encoding, which Eudora supplies if needed for long messages or special characters. Quoted-printable is a way of encoding data to seven bits, which is used by most of the Internet (see chapter 19, "Encoding and Decoding Files"). It's suggested that this be left on.

The Attachments category is used for specifying a format for files transmitted along with e-mail. MIME (Multipurpose Internet Mail Extensions) allows you to send audio, video, and still images with or without text. BinHex converts non-text files to ASCII so you can exchange e-mail with people using different platforms.

If the Skip Big Messages option under the Checking Mail category is turned on, Eudora will download only the first few lines from very long messages. This is useful if you have a very slow connection. If you want to retrieve the entire message after you've read the beginning, you can do so by turning this option off.

When you have the option to Send On Check under the Sending Mail category, mail in the Out window will be sent every time the server is checked for new mail. You can also turn on Immediate Send, which is probably the choice for people working on a network. (See the "Sending Mail" section later in this chapter.)

The Unmodified Arrow Keys or Alt+Arrow Keys options under the Miscellaneous category lets you browse messages with greater ease. Enabling either of these options lets you navigate through e-mail messages with just the arrow keys, or requires you to hold down the Alt key. This is easier to use in that you don't have to keep opening and closing each message with the mouse.

The rest of the options in the various categories are self-explanatory and a matter of personal choice.

Creating Mail

Creating mail is a lot simpler than setting up all the bells and whistles. Eudora provides a message shell, and all you have to do is fill in your information.

To create mail, perform the following steps:

1. Click the New Message icon (or press Ctrl+N) to display the New Message dialog box shown in figure 16.3. This command works anywhere in the program.

2. The cursor immediately appears after the To field. Simply type in the recipient's address.

3. Fill in the S<u>u</u>bject line with something descriptive explaining what you're letter is about.

4. Fill in <u>C</u>c (carbon copy) or <u>B</u>cc (blind carbon copy), as you would with regular mail. Everybody in the <u>C</u>c field will see who else received your group e-mailing. The <u>B</u>cc field will hide who the other recipients are.

    You can't fill in Attachments. This line is to tell the recipient the names of any files sent with the message. When you tell Eudora to attach files, the program fills in the file name. See the section "Attaching Files to Mail" later in this chapter.

5. Fill in the text of the message.

Fig. 16.3

You can create a New Message at any time.

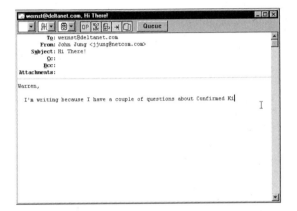

Making Nicknames

Eudora has a neat feature that lets you save Internet addresses as *nicknames*, so you don't have to remember long address strings.

To make a nickname, do the following steps:

1. Make sure you have a message open or highlighted.

2. Open the <u>S</u>pecial menu and choose Ma<u>k</u>e Nickname (or press Ctrl+K) to open the Nicknames dialog box (see fig. 16.4).

3. Choose <u>N</u>ew, and then specify a nickname.

4. Open the <u>W</u>indow menu and choose <u>N</u>icknames, or press Ctrl+L.

5. Find the N<u>i</u>ckname you just added, move the cursor to the <u>A</u>ddress box, and type in the corresponding address.

6. Choose <u>N</u>ew to add more nicknames. If you need to change an address, be sure the name you want is highlighted.

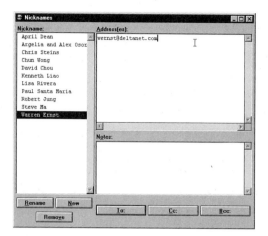

Fig. 16.4
The Nicknames feature means that you don't have to remember long addresses.

If you want to add a nickname after you've started a message, you can press Ctrl+K to get the New dialog box. Type in the name and click OK. That automatically saves the address in your current message to the chosen name.

You also can open the Window menu and choose Nicknames (or press Ctrl+L) to bring up the main Nicknames menu.

Using Nicknames

You can create a message with a nickname or use the entry to copy someone.

To create a message with a nickname, do the following steps:

1. Open the Window menu and choose Nicknames, or press Ctrl+L (see fig. 16.4).

2. Highlight a nickname by clicking it once.

3. Choose the To button to create a new message.

   Alternatively, you can begin a new message, press Ctrl+L, and then choose the To, Cc, or Bcc buttons.

Using the Quick Recipient List

In addition to creating a list of nicknames, Eudora provides a Quick Recipient List that lets you choose commonly used nicknames with a click of the mouse.

To add someone to the Quick Recipient List, choose one of the following:

■ With the current letter you're reading, highlight the address text in a message header. Next open the Special menu and choose Add as Recipient item.

■ Open the Special menu and choose Make Nickname item. Next type in a nickname and click Put it on the Recipient List.

■ For an existing nickname, open the Window menu and choose Nicknames, or press Ctrl+L. Put the cursor on the name you want to add and double-click. A checkmark to the left of the name indicates it's on the recipient list.

Removing a Recipient

To remove a recipient, choose one of the following:

■ Choose Special, Remove Recipient. While holding down the mouse button, drag the cursor over to the name you want to remove and then release the button (see fig. 16.5).

■ Choose Window, Nicknames. Double-click the name you want to remove.

Fig. 16.5
You can delete nicknames from your Quick Recipient List very easily.

Note

Don't worry when the address string doesn't appear in the message. Only the nickname appears in the message, but the corresponding address string will be used when you send the message.

Creating a Signature

You don't need a signature, but many people use one. It's a way of identifying yourself and your business or affiliation. Eudora lets you create a few lines of text and can automatically add it to every message you create. You also have the option of turning it off on select messages.

To create a signature, follow these steps:

1. Choose Window, Signature. The Signature window opens.

   You may get a very small Signature window like the one shown in figure 16.6. In that case, click the Maximize button at the far right of the window.

2. Type the signature you want to appear at the end of your messages. For example, if I was the president of Microsoft, I might have (see fig. 16.6):

> Bill Gates
> President
> Microsoft Inc.
> Serving Companies Worldwide

3. Open the <u>F</u>ile menu and choose <u>C</u>lose; then choose OK to save the changes.

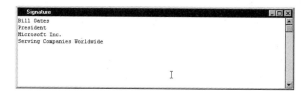

Fig. 16.6
Eudora gives you a window to type in your signature. Try to keep your signature small so as not to be obtrusive.

Saving Mail

After you've typed in your message, you can choose <u>S</u>ave, Save <u>A</u>s, or <u>C</u>lose, just like any other Windows program. But Eudora also has a friendly default, just in case you forget to save a message.

When you minimize a new message window, it automatically saves it in the Out window.

You can open the message again using standard Windows procedures, by highlighting the entry and pushing Enter, double-clicking the entry, or choosing <u>F</u>ile, <u>O</u>pen.

Choosing <u>F</u>ile, Save <u>A</u>s, and specifying a file name saves the mail to disk as a file.

Editing Mail

You can edit saved messages or lose changes since a message was last saved. Eudora also has a fail-safe feature that prompts you to save or discard changes if you try to close an edited message without saving it.

To edit your mail, do the following:

1. Make the changes.

2. Open the Control Box menu in the upper-left corner of the window and choose <u>C</u>lose, or press Ctrl+F4.

3. A warning dialog box appears asking if you want to save the changes.

4. Choose <u>Y</u>es or <u>N</u>o (see fig. 16.7).

III

Using Internet E-Mail

Fig. 16.7
You can save or discard changes to outgoing mail.

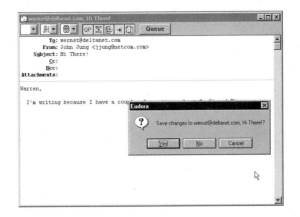

Eudora also sports some handy editing features, including cut and paste between messages, as well as find and sort.

> **Note**
>
> Eudora will only allow you to cut text in a message that you haven't already sent. And you can only copy text to an outgoing message. That includes replies to messages and messages you're sending again.

To cut and paste between messages, follow these steps:

1. Highlight the text, open the Edit menu, and choose either the Copy (Ctrl+C) or Cut (Ctrl+X) menu item.

2. Open the Mailbox menu and choose either In or Out.

3. Choose the message you want to copy to and place the cursor where you want the copy. Then select the Edit menu and the Paste (Ctrl+V) item.

You can also paste text as a quotation, which lets you include the text of a message you're responding to. Text can be pasted as a quotation with the menu item Paste as Quotation (Ctrl+'), under the Edit menu. This saves you from retyping the information, but also allows you to respond to several issues point-by-point. This should make you feel like a Net pro, since this is a time-honored tradition with e-mail.

Working with In, Out, Trash, and Transfer

There are three default mailboxes, working file windows—In, Out, and Trash. To call one up, open the Mailbox menu and then choose In, Out, or Trash, as shown in figure 16.8.

Fig. 16.8
Eudora comes with
three built-in
mailboxes.

When you minimize a new message, it defaults to Out, although you can send from any of the windows if you don't minimize it. It will appear to have no recipient and no subject in the directory listing until you close or save it, but it will always go to Out.

Choosing a mailbox only makes that the active window on your screen. It does not transfer messages there, even if they are highlighted when you choose it.

To transfer messages among the three mailboxes, choose one of the following:

- To use In, Out, or any mailbox, highlight a message, open the Transfer menu, and then choose any option that has a right arrow next to it. The right arrows help you remember the difference between Mailbox and Transfer.

- To put something in the trash, select the item, open the Transfer menu, and choose Trash. You can also select the item and click the Trash button, which is located in each mailbox window. Deleting messages will automatically transfer them to the Trash mailbox.

For more information about mailboxes, see "Creating Folders and Mailboxes" later in this chapter.

Sending Mail

There are two ways to send mail with Eudora—as you create each message, or all at once. As mentioned before, with the Sending Mail category in the Settings dialog box, you can check Immediate Send and/or Send On Check. If you choose both, they are available to you (Immediate Send only means you *can* send it immediately, but you don't have to). If Immediate Send is turned on, you click the Send button to send mail. If Send On Check is turned on, every time Eudora checks for mail your new messages will be sent.

Send On Check is a useful option for people who want to compose messages offline and send them all at once when you check for mail. This can save costs if your access provider is a toll call. And since some providers charge by the hour; this can help keep your time down online, too.

If you have selected the Keep Copies of Outgoing Mail option from the Settings dialog box and Sending Mail category, Eudora will leave mail that's been sent in Out and place an S in the left-hand column of the Out mailbox. This way, you can keep copies of your messages, and the S reminds you they've already been sent. If this option is turned off, it will place mailed messages into Trash.

Immediate Send is easy. Open the Message menu and choose Send Immediately, or press Ctrl+E. Eudora attempts to connect with the server, and send the message. This will work in the In, Out, or Trash windows.

Attaching Files to Mail

Sometimes you want to send files (text or program) along with a message. This option provides a quick and simple way to do that.

You can attach files to mail by doing the following:

1. Open the Message menu and choose Attach Document, or press Ctrl+H. You must have active mail open to attach a document.

2. Choose a document and click OK. The document's name and path will appear after Attachments in the header. You can highlight and delete it if you change your mind or if you choose the wrong file.

3. Specify a format for the file you're sending by clicking the BinHex/ MIME spinner, as shown in figure 16.9.

Fig. 16.9

You can choose the MIME or BinHex file format. MIME allows you to send video and audio, but the receiver has to have MIME capabilities as well.

BinHex files supply a standard way of transmitting binary files through e-mail services, even if they only accept text files. This means you can e-mail programs, pictures, and animation files.

MIME, or Multipurpose Internet Mail Extensions, is an Internet standard for audio, video, or still images by e-mail. This will necessarily become more popular, especially with multimedia resumes and presentations. The only catch is that you have to be sending to an e-mail program that accepts MIME. Thus, for ordinary mail, choose BinHex.

Caution

Some Windows 95 users might have problems decoding some BinHexed files. This is not a fault of BinHex. The problem is the compatibility of how files are stored on the Macintosh and Windows 95. The Mac can store files in a couple of ways, while Windows 95 can only store them one way. As a result, when you try to un-BinHex a Macintosh file under Windows 95, some files might become corrupted.

This compatibility problem can be overcome by simply using a Macintosh to un-BinHex the attachment. Once the attachment has been converted to a file on the Macintosh, you still have to get it to your PC. To this end, you must use either Apple File Exchange or PC Exchange to convert the file to a PC disk. These two utilities will correctly store the Macintosh data into a format readable by Windows 95.

Queuing Messages

To save money, you can compose messages offline and queue them so they're all sent at once. If you've turned on Send On Check, they'll be sent when Eudora checks for mail.

To queue messages, follow these steps:

1. Open the <u>M</u>essage menu and choose <u>C</u>hange Queuing. The Change Queuing dialog box appears (see fig. 16.10).

2. Click <u>R</u>ight Now or <u>N</u>ext Time Queued Messages Are Sent, or specify a time and day, as shown in figure 16.10.

Fig. 16.10
You have several options in the Change Queuing dialog box for sending mail.

Troubleshooting

After I queue a message, I get an error message saying there's an error connecting to my server.

If Immediate Send is turned on in the Settings dialog box and Sending Mail category, Eudora will try to send the message right away if you queue it. If you're not connected, it will try to connect anyway and then give you several error windows. Don't worry about it; the message will still be saved and sent the next time you're actually online.

When I try to send mail, I get a message error that says Error sending command to SMTP server. *What does this mean?*

It could mean you're not really online. Either your connection failed at the beginning, or else it went down some time afterwards. Just click OK, go back into your connect program, and log on. Or it could mean that the server is too busy to answer you. If you are logged on, try again in a few minutes.

Eudora doesn't keep copies of my mail messages. Can it do this?

You have to turn the Keep Copies of Outgoing Mail option on in the Sending Mail category of the Settings dialog box. Then the program will leave mail messages in the Out box. Otherwise, it will send them all to the trash.

You can choose Don't Send, which puts a kind of freeze on the file. If you're interrupted while composing a message, this is a good option to exercise. When it's turned on, a bullet appears on the far left side of the mail entry.

To change from Don't Send, simply open the Message menu, choose Change Queuing, and pick another option.

If you've queued several messages, you can open the File menu and choose Send Queued Messages (or press Ctrl+T) to send them. You have to be online at the time. While it may appear Eudora is trying to log on, it can't, and you get an error message.

Retrieving Mail

Unlike CompuServe and other online services, your mail is not waiting for you when you log onto the Internet. You have to get it.

To retrieve mail after you've logged on, open the File menu and choose Check Mail, or press Ctrl+M. Eudora attempts to connect with the server and retrieve your mail. If you have new mail, you are notified with a cheerful screen that says You have new mail (see fig. 16.11). Retrieved mail is filed in the In box.

Fig. 16.11
This dialog box appears when you have new mail.

Note

If you tell the program to poll for mail, it will try whenever the program is running, whether you're actually on the Internet or not. If you get an error message, don't worry about it. It won't affect anything.

Retrieving Mail with Attached Files

When you retrieve mail with attached files, Eudora presents you with a modified File Manager defaulted to the Eudora directory. You have to choose what to name the file, where to place it, and what format to save it in. It works the same way with MIME or BinHex files.

You can also have your attachments automatically decoded into a default directory. Simply choose Special, Settings. Find the Attachments category and click the long bar under the Attachment Directory heading. Use the modified Open File dialog box to specify a particular directory.

Now that you know the basics of how to get around in Eudora, you can consult table 16.1 for shortcuts.

Table 16.1   Eudora Shortcuts

Action	Shortcut Key Combination
Create a message	Ctrl+N
Check mail	Ctrl+M
Reply to a message	Ctrl+R
Send immediately	Ctrl+E
Attach documents	Ctrl+H
Send queued messages	Ctrl+T
Go to the In box	Ctrl+I
Open Nicknames window	Ctrl+L
Delete	Ctrl+D
Close	Ctrl+W
Quit Eudora	Ctrl+Q

Creating Folders and Mailboxes

Once you have new mail, you can read it and/or transfer it to other folders and mailboxes. (See the discussion of In, Out, and Trash in the "Working with In, Out, Trash, and Transfer" section earlier in the chapter.)

To create new folders, follow these steps:

1. Choose Transfer, New. The New Mailbox dialog box appears (see fig. 16.12).

2. Write the new name in the bar under the Name the New Mailbox instruction.

3. You can create a new folder by choosing the Make it a Folder box. By default, you can create multiple mailboxes within a folder.

Fig. 16.12

You can create any number of folders or mailboxes within a single folder.

Each mailbox and folder is represented in the Transfer, New menu. You can click and hold on any of the folder names, and get a pull-down menu of the mailboxes within that folder. If there are no mailboxes, you can still create folders and mailboxes from the New menu listed in each mailbox.

To get a more visual representation of your folders, open the Window menu and choose Mailboxes. The Mailboxes dialog box appears (see fig. 16.13).

Fig. 16.13

You can easily transfer mail among mailboxes and folders.

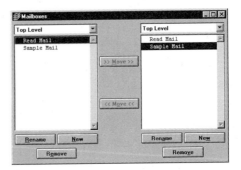

Moving mail around mailboxes and folders is as easy as pointing and clicking. Follow these steps:

1. Maximize a mailbox so that you get one-line listings of each message, as
   in figure 16.14.

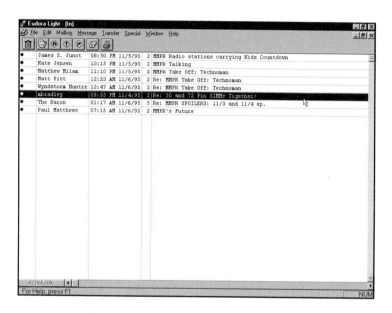

Fig. 16.14

Each line repre-
sents one message.

2. Highlight the message(s) you want to move.

3. Choose <u>T</u>ransfer and then select the name of the folder and mailbox
   you want the message moved to.

> **Caution**
>
> If you attempt to trash messages you haven't yet read, Eudora prompts you to make
> sure you know what you're doing.

Rerouting Mail

Eudora is pretty flexible when it comes to sending a message to other people,
replying to a message, or forwarding a message you received. Table 16.2 provides you with all the options for rerouting mail.

Table 16.2 Rerouting Mail

When You Want to...	Do This
Reply to a message	Open the Message menu and choose Reply, or press Ctrl+R, or click the Reply button. This puts the text of the original message into so-called quotations (see earlier discussion), creates a new message to the person you're replying to, and keeps the same subject.
Forward a message	Open the Message menu and choose Forward, or click the Forward button. This puts the text into quotations, keeps the subject the same, and leaves a blank space for the recipient.
Redirect a message	Open the Message menu and choose Redirect, or click the Redirect button. This puts the text in quotations, leaves the recipient blank and indicates the route that message has taken on the From line.
Send again	Open the Message menu and choose Send Again. The message will be sent to everyone it was sent to the first time and to the person who originated it.

Deleting Mail

You don't really delete mail, you put it in the trash. When it starts to build up, you empty it. Eudora sends mail to the trash from any mailbox. That means the message can be open, or its one-line entry can be highlighted. The following are two ways to trash mail from a one-line directory listing:

- Click the message you want to trash; then click the Trash button or press Ctrl+D. If you haven't yet read the message, and you have Require Confirmations for Deletes turned on in the Settings dialog box, Eudora prompts you with the message that appears in figure 16.15.

- Select the message you want to trash; then open the Transfer menu and choose Trash.

To trash an open message, open the Transfer menu and choose Trash.

Fig. 16.15
Eudora makes sure you really want to trash mail that you haven't read yet.

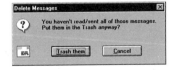

When you are ready to delete the trash, open the $\underline{S}$pecial menu and choose $\underline{E}$mpty Trash. If you specify $\underline{E}$mpty Trash on Quit in the Miscellaneous category in the Settings dialog box, Eudora will do this automatically. Deleting mail that's already in the trash will also empty the trash.

Upgrading to Eudora 2.1.2

Eudora 2.1.2 is the commercial version for the Macintosh or Windows 95, and offers several enhancements over the 1.5 freeware version, including extensive online help and a toll-free technical hotline. There are several features that make working with files easier, like a drag and drop capability for attaching files to messages. You're also given a message when there is no new mail.

Eudora 2.1.2 also allows you to direct-dial the Internet, without a SLIP connection. This would be best for someone who plans to use e-mail only. For more information, see chapter 14, "How Internet E-Mail Works," and chapter 18, "Using Internet Mailing Lists," for details about using e-mail to get other kinds of information.

You can get Eudora 2.1 by upgrading either Eudora 2.0 or 2.1. Both upgrades are available by anonymous FTP at **ftp.qualcomm.com** in the /quest/windows/eudora/2.1 directory. The executable 20TO212.EXE will upgrade Eudora 2.0 to 2.1.2, while 21TO212.EXE will upgrade Eudora 2.1 to 2.1.2.

At the start of 1996, a full Windows 95 version of Eudora Pro will be available. Eudora Pro 2.2 will be a native Windows 95 program, meaning it'll be a 32-bit application. If you can't wait, you can try out a beta version of Eudora Pro. Simply go to **ftp.qualcomm.com** and get the file EUD22B10.EXE from the /quest/windows/eudora/beta directory.

As of November 1995, the price for the Macintosh and PC versions ranged from $89 for one user, up to $45 per user for 250 users. You can also get a spell checker called Spellswell for an additional fee. You can reach the company at 1-800-2-EUDORA or **eudora-sales@qualcomm.com**.

III

Using Internet E-Mail

E-Mailing Outside the Internet and with Online Services

In chapter 14, "How Internet E-Mail Works," you saw how the Internet handles electronic mail. Not everyone is directly connected to the Internet, but instead rely on an online service provider such as CompuServe, America Online, or the Microsoft Network online service (MSN). These services make casual use of the Internet economically viable for a single user, as do many of the new independent Internet service providers. Neither online services nor Internet service providers require individuals to buy and operate complicated and expensive hardware and software, or a telephone line that supports high-speed transfers to an Internet gateway. The ability of online service providers to give their customers more ability to control access to Internet sites through parental controls, coupled with a true sense of having a community support system, may overshadow the often cheaper Internet service providers.

The recent connection of the more popular online services (including America Online, Delphi, CompuServe, and MSN) to the Internet has given many users better access to the Internet. The two primary Internet access services, CompuServe and America Online, account for a considerable portion of the users accessing UseNet newsgroups and sending electronic mail to other Internet users.

Special addressing is needed to send mail from within an online service out to other users on the Internet, and for an online service user to receive mail from somewhere else on the Internet. In this chapter you learn:

- The methods of sending and receiving mail from the most popular of these service providers (America Online, CompuServe, Delphi, GEnie, MCI Mail, MSN)

- General rules for sending files to and from online service users

- A source for determining the addresses of most online service providers

Direct and Indirect Service Providers

For convenience sake, it is useful to divide service providers into two types when it comes to e-mail handling—direct and indirect providers. The division is based on the manner in which mail is handled by each service provider.

Direct Service Providers

A *direct service provider* is transparent to the user. It provides the link to all the facets of the Internet, including e-mail, Internet Relay Chat, World Wide Web, FTP, and Gopher. Most direct service providers are invisible to the daily user. For example, UUNET Technologies is a popular Internet service provider that removes special addressing for the user's mailbox if the user has a registered domain name (for more information on domain names see chapter 5, "Connecting Through a LAN with Windows 95"). Direct service providers like UUNET Technologies are generally used by small companies and organizations that do not want to go to the trouble and expense of connecting directly into the Internet backbone, or who expect small quantities of traffic that make an Internet connection uneconomical.

> **Tip**
>
> Often your local library or your state's university system will provide low-cost Internet access to state or county residents.

◀ See "Connecting Through a LAN with Windows 95," p. 125

Someone sending mail to a user who accesses the Internet through a direct service provider does not have to make any special changes to the user's mail address. For example, a user's account may be jblow@abcdefg.com, even though abcdefg.com is not directly on the Internet backbone but uses UUNET Technologies to connect to it. The Network Information Center's mapping of the domain names knows to send all e-mail for users on abcdefg.com through UUNET's access point.

Even if the organization has not received its own registered domain name, e-mail can reach the organization through the direct service provider's network address. When an organization subscribes to the service provider, it receives a unique identifier within that provider's domain. Mail can reach the organization when addressed to the service provider, as seen later in this chapter in the section "Messages to UUNET Users."

Some special handling may be necessary for a user who wants to send mail out to the Internet through a direct service provider, but that is a limitation of the user's system, not the Internet. This limitation arises because some direct service providers use a different communications protocol to provide user-to-provider message transfers, then translate to TCP/IP for the Internet backbone.

In most cases, direct service providers cannot be used interactively. Messages are composed offline then the mail system connects and transfers information in the background. Typically, UNIX systems are used for these direct service provider operations, although there are several new Windows NT packages that are becoming popular.

Indirect Service Providers

An *indirect service provider* often requires special addressing to reach a user, or for the user to send e-mail to the Internet, as the users do not have a domain name dedicated to their personal computer. These indirect service providers are usually online services such as CompuServe, America Online, and MCI Mail, or one of the many independent Internet service providers appearing all over the country.

The Internet connection was really an afterthought for most of these systems, so their own internal mail systems (used for sending e-mail only to other users within that system) had to be modified to handle Internet e-mail. In most cases, mail to a user of such a system will be sent with the domain name of the recipient set to the service provider's, such as 12345.678@compuserve.com, where 12345.678 is the user's identification within CompuServe.

In most cases, access through an indirect service provider is chosen to reduce costs, especially when small amounts of mail are handled monthly. However, most of the indirect service providers have usage fees based on the number of characters handled or the amount of time you are connected, so the costs can become significant when a lot of time is spent on the service.

> **Tip**
>
> You can often find a local service provider by checking in your yellow pages. Often they will provide more flexibility and cost less than many of the large national providers.

> **Note**
>
> Many users find that the expense of using online service providers is considerable when spending more than an hour a day online. In most cases, it is less expensive to use a direct service provider, depending on the services required.

One problem with sending mail to an indirect service provider user is the identification of the user. Some systems (like CompuServe) have a unique number for each user. Addressing mail to a number invites errors, so undeliverable or incorrectly delivered mail can be a common problem with these systems. If the mail is incorrectly addressed and arrives at the wrong user's mailbox, chances are the user will simply delete the mail without letting the sender know it was incorrectly addressed.

Another problem with indirect service providers is that it is difficult to check user names online. Standard utilities (such as *whois*) that query a remote system for a user name do not work with many online service providers. There are very few directory services available for the majority of these services. America Online is one of the few indirect service providers that provide a directory of their users through the World Wide Web. You can reach their directory service at **http://home.aol.com**.

The indirect online service providers do have several advantages over the direct service provider. More importantly, they offer other features for users, including message bases, file transfers, online games, and search facilities for information. They also allow users to compose messages and replies offline, then send them automatically when connected through a modem, reducing expenses. Finally, most online services have attractive, easy-to-use graphical interfaces that many users prefer over the character-based systems offered by direct service providers.

Mail Message Contents

Most online service providers allow binary files to be transferred through their internal mail systems. CompuServe, for example, allows users to upload and download binary files with a common protocol, delivering the binary to the destination user without a problem. Internet e-mail, though, does not support binary files, which can pose some problems for users when they try to send or receive this type of file through an Internet mail system.

If you want to send binary files (executables, graphics, sound, or any other non-text-based file) using Internet e-mail, either to or from an online service provider, the file must be converted to a transferable format first. There are quite a few encoding methods that can be used for this purpose. The most common ones are MIME, UUEncode and UUDecode, and BinHex. When you are using UUEncode or UUDecode it is the user's responsibility to convert the file before it is sent. The mail system will not usually check the contents of the file, simply sending it as it is submitted unless it supports MIME. When you are using MIME, the characters will be encoded using the MIME standard, allowing you to send the binary file across the Internet error free.

> **Caution**
>
> Before sending a file over the Internet, make sure you are sending from a MIME compliant mail program, and the message recipient also uses a MIME compliant mail reader. Or you must use UUEncode on the file if you want it to be received uncorrupted.

▶ See "Encoding and Decoding Files," p. 439

To further complicate the problem of mailing binary files, not all online services provide the facilities for processing files converted to a MIME or similar format. In these cases, you must use UUEncode and UUDecode to properly convert your message before sending it. If you UUEncoded the file, you must make sure that the receiver of that message is able to UUDecode it, or your efforts are wasted. Downloading a file through FTP is a completely different process, so you do not have the same worries using that system.

All the service providers support standard text messages. However, there can be a problem with some systems that do not rely on ASCII characters (large IBM systems, for example, use EBCDIC). In most cases, ASCII to EBCDIC translation is performed automatically in the TCP/IP layers of the software and is transparent to the user.

Messages to UUNET Users

Earlier in this chapter it was mentioned that users of the UUNET Technologies service do not need special handling except when machine-specific addresses are not properly set. In some cases (notably, when the recipient of a message does not have his or her own registered domain name) it is necessary to specify the UUNET domain name as part of the address. This is usually only necessary if your mail is returned as undelivered and you know the destination is a UUNET user.

If the full address must be used, the domain name is written as UUNET.UU.NET. There is no regular domain name specified as part of the address (the .NET is actually the domain type specifier). The syntax for routing mail with this type of address is:

    username.domainname@UUNET.UU.NET

If there is a submachine that the message must be sent through, it too is specified as part of the address:

    username%machine.domainname@UUNET.UU.NET

For example, the address

tparker%beast%merlin.tpci@UUNET.UU.NET

would send mail to the primary machine, tpci, on the UUNET network, through the machines merlin and beast, to the user tparker. This type of addressing is usually needed when the hardware network is not properly set up to identify users and machines. Luckily, most systems don't need this type of addressing anymore, unless they use the UUCP mail system exclusively.

Notice that the format of this type of addressing requires the domain name to be separated by a period and not the "@" sign as usual.

Online Services

As a rule, each online service has its own domain name. Certainly the most popular services examined in this chapter do, although a few exceptions are shown in a table at the end of the chapter.

When sending mail to a user on one of these services with its own domain name, the format is usually simple:

username@domain.name

where "username" is the name or number of the user on the service and "domain.name" is the service's domain name. Case (upper- and lowercase), as with all Internet e-mail systems, is important, although some services have registered the most common variations to account for errors.

Sending mail out from these online services usually involves the same process, although some services require special handling to indicate the e-mail message is to be routed through an Internet gateway.

The most popular indirect service providers are mentioned in more detail in the following sections, indicating the system-dependent processes necessary to send and receive mail through the Internet. Any restrictions on the messages are also mentioned.

America Online

America Online was one of the first online services to provide full Internet access, including the newsgroups. The use of an attractive graphical interface makes America Online's Internet system easier to use than many other service's (see chapter 11, "Connecting Through America Online").

America Online offers all the major Internet services including e-mail, Gopher, the World Wide Web, WAIS, FTP, and UseNet access to their customers at no additional charge, over the standard monthly fee—with its five free hours—and a $2.95 per hour use charge.

◀ See "Connecting Through America Online," p. 263

To send mail from within America Online's e-mail system to the Internet, there is no special addressing required. The mail system can figure out where the mail is to go from the format of username@domain.name, so for example,

>   rmaclean@mig.com

is a valid entry for the Send To: field in the mail system. The rest of the mail message requires no special codes or identifiers.

Sending mail from the Internet to an America Online user requires the user's AOL user name and the domain name "aol.com". For example, mail addressed to

>   userID@aol.com

would find the person with the specified user ID. The domain name should be all lowercase.

> **Note**
>
> If you mail a message to a member of America Online, you may receive a message back stating that the AOL user's mailbox is full. America Online mailboxes cannot hold more than 550 pieces of mail from any source. You may have to wait a day and resend the message, or contact that individual in some other fashion.

America Online has recently added the ability to send MIME encoded files to anyone, anywhere on the Internet. Of course the recipient must also be using a service and mail reader that support the MIME format. They have also changed the way that they send messages. When you are sending long messages, either to other America Online members or to other Internet addresses the first 2K of each message will be sent as standard text. The rest of the message is sent as a MIME attachment.

> **Caution**
>
> America Online can only process one file attachment at a time. If someone mails an AOL user a message or an AOL member sends a file to an Internet user with multiple files attached, AOL's MIME encoder will encode all the files into one attachment. If this happens, you will have to have a third-party MIME decoder to separate the single attachment back into its original parts.

III

Using Internet E-Mail

CompuServe

CompuServe is the largest online service in the North American continent, but its Internet access is largely overlooked by its users because only e-mail support was available until recently (see chapter 10, "Connecting Through CompuServe").

◀ See "Connecting Through CompuServe," p. 231

CompuServe has a limit of approximately 2,000,000 ASCII seven-bit characters in a message. The system automatically converts eight-bit text to seven-bit. If you would like to send files to individuals on the Internet through CompuServe's mail system, you must use UUEncode and UUDecode on that file before sending it. If you do not, your file will be treated as a standard text file, resulting in the corruption of your data.

As with America Online, CompuServe does not charge any extra fees for Internet services like e-mail, UseNet, FTP, and the World Wide Web, in addition to the regular connect charges. CompuServe members receive five free hours with their monthly connect fee, and are charged $2.95 an hour for any time over the first five.

For a CompuServe user to send e-mail out to the Internet is relatively simple. The message is composed in the same manner as internal e-mail, but the address of the recipient is modified to provide the word "Internet" as part of the Send To line. For example:

> internet:president@whitehouse.gov
>
> and
>
> INTERNET: bozo@clowns_r_us.com

are valid e-mail addresses for sending mail outside the CompuServe system. Case is unimportant for the "internet" portion of the address. A space may follow the colon, or the address may follow immediately (the mail system will ignore any spaces that directly follow the colon).

To send mail to a user on CompuServe, you must know his or her CompuServe ID number, which usually is five numbers, a separator (which must be a period, commas are not supported, despite their frequent use in CompuServe ID numbers), and then three or four more numbers. The CompuServe domain name is compuserve.com.

> **Caution**
>
> When sending to a CompuServe user, make sure the user ID has a period, not a comma.

Addressing mail to a CompuServe user takes the usual Internet format. For example,

> 12345.678@compuserve.com

is a valid address (assuming the CompuServe ID is correct). If the CompuServe ID is invalid, the e-mail should be returned with an error message. Mistyping the CompuServe ID number is a common error, so it is worthwhile to ask for a confirmation of receipt message (although this incurs an additional expense).

Delphi

Delphi is still a very popular way to access the Internet because it offers all the Internet services. There is no Delphi-imposed limitation on message length. Delphi offers UseNet, e-mail, Telnet, and FTP services. Delphi also has a new Windows-based World Wide Web browser currently available. No additional charges are imposed for Internet e-mail.

Delphi members can send mail out to the Internet with a special format of address at the Send To: prompt. The format is

> internet"username@host.name"

where the normal Internet address is placed in quotation marks and preceded with "internet". For example, to send mail to the President from within the Delphi mail system, use the Send To: address:

> internet"president@whitehouse.gov"

Without the quotation marks, the Delphi system cannot properly parse the address and the mail will not be delivered properly.

To send mail to a Delphi user, the domain name delphi.com is used. The format uses the Delphi user name as part of the address:

> username@delphi.com

which is the usual Internet format.

GEnie

GEnie is General Electric's online service provider, a much smaller (in terms of users) service than the competition. To send mail to an Internet user from within the GEnie mail system, you must use a special address format. At the Send To: prompt, use the syntax

> username@host.name@INET#

Without appending the INET#, the mail parser will not direct the mail properly.

To send mail to a GEnie user, the domain name "genie.geis.com" must be used. For example, the address:

username@genie.geis.com

would be correct, assuming the user name is valid.

MCI Mail

MCI Mail was intended for user-to-user mail transfers, but Internet access has been added to provide better services for users. Many corporations use MCI Mail, and their employees must be reached through the MCI Mail Internet services instead of through a corporate domain.

Sending mail to an Internet user from within MCI Mail requires specifying several portions of the mail system's prompts in a special manner. When sending mail through MCI Mail, the system asks for the recipient's name in the TO: field. Use the recipient's real name (not the Internet addressee's user name) followed by (EMS). The (EMS) designation informs MCI that you are sending main to an external mail system. MCI Mail then asks for the EMS:; specify "internet". Finally, when the system asks for the MBX: give the full Internet address. To send mail to Santa Claus (using a mythical domain name) the process would be:

TO: Santa Claus (EMS)

EMS: internet

MBX: sclause@northpole.com

Sending mail to an MCI Mail user is complicated somewhat, by the naming scheme used by MCI. A user can have a user ID generally composed of either a 7 or 10 digit phone number, a user name made up of their first initial and full last name (such as tparker), or a full user name made up of their complete first and last names (such as tim_parker). The complication is that MCI Mail does not require unique user names of either form, so there may be more than one person with the names "tparker" or "tim_parker" on the system. The only unique identifier is the user ID number.

This lets you address mail to an MCI Mail user in one of three different ways:

userIDnumber@mcimail.com

shortname@mcimail.com

fullname@mcimail.com

Only the first format is guaranteed to reach the user you really want. Of course, the user names are much easier to use, so if you are going to send mail to an MCI Mail user frequently, you may want to check whether either of the name formats is unique. You can sometimes do this with test messages if the recipients are cooperative.

MCI Mail also offers group addresses to companies in the form of Remote Email System accounts. Addressing for Remote Email Systems works by including the name of the company in the address in the following format:

>   username%REMS ID@mcimail.com

The REMS ID field lets MCI Mail know which company should receive the message. The company's mail system then reads the user name to decide which specific individual in their company should receive that piece of mail.

For an example, if you wanted to send a message to Santa Clause at his toy factory with the MCI Mail ID number 9876543210, you would address the message to:

>   sclause%9876543210@mcimail.com

> **Note**
>
> If you do not know the MCI Mail user ID for the company, you can substitute the company's full name in the REM ID field. Remember to replace any spaces in the company's name with underscores.

Prodigy

Prodigy is simple to use as far as Internet access is concerned. A recent revision to the Prodigy mail system has expanded the mail service considerably, supporting all standard file types and addresses.

To send mail from within Prodigy to a user on the Internet, use the standard format of the recipient's address:

>   username@host.name

The mail system will parse the TO: entry and recognize it as an Internet address, routing it through Prodigy's gateway.

To send mail to a Prodigy user, use the domain name "prodigy.com" with the user's user ID on the system. For example,

TSR45AB@prodigy.com

◀ See "Connect-
ing Through
Prodigy,"
p. 287

would reach the user with the user ID TSR45AB. Prodigy imposes no limits on
the size of messages. For more information on the Prodigy services see chapter 12, "Connecting Through Prodigy."

The Microsoft Network

The Microsoft Network, or MSN as it is commonly referred to, is the new kid
on the block as far as service providers go. This service was started shortly after the release of the Windows 95 operating system. Since it has been available, the Microsoft Network has subscribed thousands of users, and is quickly
becoming one of the most popular new services to purchase Internet access
from.

Users of the Microsoft Network must use Microsoft Exchange when sending
and receiving messages. When MSN account holders need to send mail to
other users across the Internet they use the following standard addressing
system:

username@domain.name

So if an MSN user wanted to send mail to Santa Claus he would still enter
sclaus@northpole.com in the TO: field of the Exchange mail form.

> **Caution**
>
> At some times you may experience problems sending messages to a single address
> for no apparent reason. When this happens, change the address in the TO: field of
> the mail form to:
>
> [SMTP:usernam@domain.name]
>
> Assuming that the user name and domain name are correct, this will improve your
> chances of getting the message to its destination.

When sending mail to an MSN customer you simply need to address the message to:

MSNCustomerID@msn.com.

The Microsoft Network uses a series of numbers and letters for each
individual's member ID. Since each member ID must be unique you do not
have to worry about sending information to the wrong person. Generally
MSN member ID numbers are going to be some combination of their name,
nickname, or a reference to their favorite hobby.

List of Services

The following table presents a summary of the formats for addressing e-mail in and out of the most popular service providers.

Table 17.1 is based on the "Internet Mailing Guide" maintained by Ajay Shekhawat of the State University of New York, Buffalo. The complete guide may be obtained by anonymous FTP from **ftp.msstate.edu** in the directory /pub/docs. It is also available through some UseNet newsgroups. If you cannot find a copy of the Internet Mailing Guide, post a message to the newsgroup **news.answers** requesting either a mailed version or directions to its location.

As a rule, each online service has its own domain name. Certainly the most popular services examined in this chapter do, although a few exceptions are shown in table 17.1.

Table 17.1   How to Send Mail to and Receive Mail from Popular Services

Service	Send to a Service User	Send from within the Online Service
America Online	username@aol.com	username@host.name
AppleLink	username@ applelink.apple.com	username@host@ internet#
AT&T Mail	username@attmail.com	internet!host! username
BITNET	username%site. bitnet@gateway or username@site.bitnet Note: gateway must be both an Internet and BITNET gateway.	username@host@gateway username@domain.name Note: Varies between sites. Check with system administrator.
BIX	username@dcibix.das.net	
CGNET	username%CGNET@ Intermail.ISI.edu	Address mail to "intermail". The header of the message must have "Forward: Internet" on the first line, "To: username@host.name" on the second, and a blank third line.
CompuServe	nnnnn.nnn@ compuserve.com	internet:username@ host.name

(continues)

Table 17.1 Continued

Service	Send to a Service User	Send from within the Online Service
Delphi	username@delphi.com	internet"username@host.name"
EasyLink	username@eln.attmail.com	
EASYnet	VMS using NMAIL: nm%DECWRL::\"username@host\" Ultrix: username@host.name IP: \"username%host.name\"@decwrl.dec.com DECNET: DECWRL::\"username%host\"	
	Envoy (Canada)	att!attmail!mhs! envoy!username@ UUNET.UU.NET
	or	
	/C=CA/ADMD=TELECOM.CANADA/O=ENVOY/DD.ID =username@SPRINT.COM [RFC-822=\"username(a)host.name\] INTERNET/TELEMAIL/US	
FidoNet	firstname.lastname@ nnn.nnn.nnn.nnn.fidonet.org	First line of message is address:
	Note: replace four sets of nnn with FidoNet point, node, network, and zone numbers, respectively. Routes through UUCP.	username@host.name
GEnie	username@ genie.geis.com	username@host.name@ INET#
MCI Mail	username@mcimail.com	
	Note: users mail have more than one non-unique name (see MCI Mail above). Specify the recipient's name followed by (EMS) in the "To" section of the mail prompts, "internet" in the "EMS" section, and the full Internet address in the "MBX" prompt. See above for details.	
Microsoft Network (MSN)	usename@msn.com	username@host.name
NASA Mail	username@ nasamail.nasa.gov	Send mail to "POSTMAN" with the first line of the message set to "To: username@host.name"

Service	Send to a Service User	Send from within the Online Service
NSI-DECNET (Span)	username@host. SPAN.NASA.gov	AMES::\"username@ host.name\"
SINet	username@ node.SINet.SLB.COM or username%node@ node1.SINet.SLB.COM	M_MAILNOW::M_ INTERNET::"username@ host.name"
SprintMail	/G=firstname/S=lastname /O=organization/ADMD=	(C:USA,A:TELEMAIL,P INTERNET,"RFC-822":<user
THEnet	username%host.decnet@ utadnx.cc.utexas.edu	UTADNX::WINS%" username@host.name"

CHAPTER 18

Using Internet Mailing Lists

Once you have an e-mail account connected to the Internet, a wide range of activities opens up to you. Some are what you might expect, such as the capability to exchange messages with anyone in the world similarly connected. As you've seen earlier in this part of the book, you can exchange complex messages through the use of e-mail programs such as Eudora and Microsoft Exchange.

Now that you have your first foothold on the Internet, you have access to much more. The Internet has a wide range of services and resources that require varying levels of connection. Internet e-mail is usually the first level, and the most common level of access. There are many activities that you can access simply with an e-mail account.

In this chapter, you learn how to subscribe to and use Internet mailing lists to access, well, just about anything you can imagine!

In this chapter, you learn how to do the following tasks:

- Join and quit LISTSERV and Majordomo mailing lists
- Get descriptions of thousands of LISTSERV mailing lists
- Register by name with a LISTSERV mailing list
- Get files from LISTSERV and Majordomo mailing lists
- Learn guidelines for proper netiquette

What Are Internet Mailing Lists?

Every time I sign on to my e-mail account, I have a message waiting for me like the one shown in figure 18.1.

Fig. 18.1

My daily message from TFTD-L.

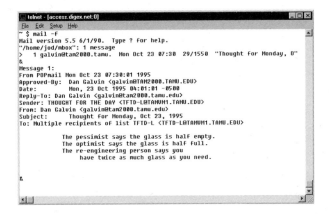

◀ See "Installing Microsoft Exchange," p. 351

◀ See "Downloading and Installing PC Eudora," p. 380

I get this message—well, a different one each weekday—because I have sub-scribed to an Internet mailing list called TFTD-L. ("TFTD" is an acronym for "Thought for the Day.")

There are several different varieties of Internet mailing lists available—you'll get an idea of just how many in a bit. Some are like TFTD-L, which has a spe-cific, limited function. It's essentially one-way, from the originator of the list to the recipients (although with TFTD-L, you can send comments and sugges-tions to the person who runs the list).

Other mailing lists function like magazines, periodically sending out long messages, each consisting of one or more articles concerning the list topic. Usually, these lists allow—even welcome and depend on—submissions from people like you who are members of the list. One of the more common types of lists, however, is one that functions as an e-mail *exploder*. Whenever any-one sends a message to the mailing list, a copy of the message is then sent out to each person on the list.

Internet mailing lists can serve a number of different activities, including the following:

■ The list administrator can use it to deliver information to the list subscribers.

■ Subscribers to the list can send out information to all the other subscribers.

■ You can post files to the list, or retrieve files of interest that other subscribers have posted.

Note that because of the restrictions that the Internet puts on files that are
sent through e-mail—mainly that they must be ASCII files—binary files such
as picture files, executables, and compressed file archives must be encoded
into ASCII first. This is discussed in chapter 19, "Encoding and Decoding
Files."

◀ See "ASCII
Format Only,"
p. 339

◀ See "Attaching
Files to Mail,"
p. 392

Regardless of how the list functions, however, each one has its own set of
rules, set by the list administrator. The following section discusses some of
these rules and some other distinctions about list types. You also learn how
to use mailing lists—including how to find what lists are out there and how
to subscribe to a list.

▶ See "Encoding
and Decoding
Files," p. 439

◀ See "Simple
Mail Transfer
Protocol
(SMTP)," p. 330

Mastering a Mailing List

To show you how easy it is to use a mailing list, it is best to simply show you
the steps needed to join one. To join TFTD-L, just send an e-mail message to
the e-mail address

LISTSERV@TAMVM1.TAMU.EDU

You can leave the Subject line blank, since it'll be ignored. The first line of
the body of the message has to be

SUBSCRIBE TFTD-L *Your Name*

For example, I'd use the following:

SUBSCRIBE TFTD-L Jim O'Donnell

(For step-by-step instructions on sending commands, see "Working with
LISTSERV Mailing Lists" and "Using Majordomo Mailing Lists," later in this
chapter.) You should get a response to that message in a couple of minutes,
so here's a little bit of background in the meantime. How to join and use any
given Internet mailing list is a function of how the list is administered. The
list may be as simple as someone doing everything manually, including
manually adding people to the list of recipients, reading all of the incoming
messages, and then using an alias list to send the message to everyone on the
list.

Usually, however, public mailing lists run automatically through software
systems on the host computer. There are several common list managers, the
biggest of which is LISTSERV. There is also a system called Majordomo, and
countless other less common or private systems. LISTSERV and Majordomo

and other systems will all perform the same basic function. However, each mailing list program runs a little differently, and has different features, advantages, and disadvantages. Next are some specific guidelines on subscribing to these systems.

Working with LISTSERV Mailing Lists

You already know a little bit about LISTSERV lists. You probably guessed that TFTD-L is one of them. LISTSERV is flexible and can perform many mailing-list options. It can be intimidating, especially because it tends to use very cryptic list names and commands. However, LISTSERV makes it easy to join and quit mailing lists, and to send messages to them.

There are two basic categories of actions you take with LISTSERV mailing lists. The first is sending commands, such as those to join or quit a list. The second is sending messages to the list itself. Since you have to join the list before you can use it, we'll discuss sending commands first.

Each time you want to send LISTSERV a command or commands, you must remember the following:

■ Commands are sent to LISTSERV through e-mail messages and the first part of the e-mail address—the part before the "@"—will always be "LISTSERV."

■ LISTSERV ignores the Subject line, so you can leave it blank.

■ LISTSERV doesn't care whether the commands are in uppercase, lowercase, or even mixed case.

With that information in mind, follow these steps to send one or more commands to a LISTSERV mailing list:

1. Use your Internet mail program to create a new mail message and send it to the LISTSERV address. The one for TFTD-L is **LISTSERV@TAMVM1.TAMU.EDU**. Depending on your mail program, you may type this address at the command line with the mail command:

   mail LISTSERV@TAMVM1.TAMU.EDU

   Or you may type **LISTSERV@TAMVM1.TAMU.EDU** on the To line of the e-mail message.

2. Leave the Subject line blank.

3. In the text area of the message, enter LISTSERV commands, one per line.

4. Send the e-mail message. The reply will usually come in a few minutes.

Subscribing to and Unsubscribing from LISTSERV Mailing Lists

By now, you should have received a reply from your subscription request (it normally takes a few minutes, but when dealing with the Internet, your individual results may vary) if you followed the example earlier in this chapter. When you subscribe to a LISTSERV list, you actually get two responses. The first shows the output of the commands you sent (in this case, only one command, the subscription request, was sent). It looks something like figure 18.2.

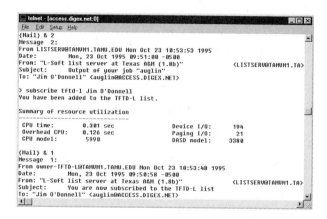

Fig. 18.2
The output message from the LISTSERV SUB-SCRIBE command.

The second message, usually resulting from a subscription command, is a welcoming message providing essential information about the list. Part of the welcome message from TFTD-L appears in figure 18.3.

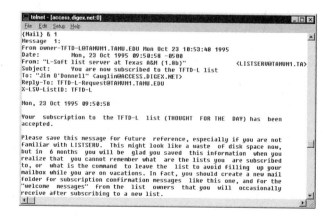

Fig. 18.3
The welcome message from TFTD-L.

III

Using Internet E-Mail

The important parts of the message are worth noting. As the welcoming message states in the first paragraph, it's probably a good idea to save a copy of it for future reference.

Probably the most important information is in the second paragraph, which is the difference between the list address, **TFTD-L@TAMVM1.TAMU.EDU**, and the corresponding LISTSERV address, **LISTSERV@TAMVM1.TAMU.EDU**. The first address is called the *mail exploder address;* anything sent to that address is (usually) sent to everybody on the list. The second address, as mentioned earlier, is the address to send commands.

> ### Tip
>
> To distinguish between LISTSERV addresses, remember that LISTSERV commands should go to the "LISTSERV" address and messages to a specific list, such as TFTD-L, should go to the "TFTD-L" address.

You're liable to feel a little foolish (and if you don't, a whole bunch of other people will probably send you e-mail to try to make you feel foolish) if you send a LISTSERV command to subscribe to the list to the wrong address.

Not only won't you be signed off, but a copy of your message is sent to everybody on the list! Fortunately, LISTSERV will sometimes recognize this mistake and save you some embarrassment by bouncing back your command with an explanation, as shown in figure 18.4.

Fig. 18.4
Oops! I used the wrong LISTSERV address!

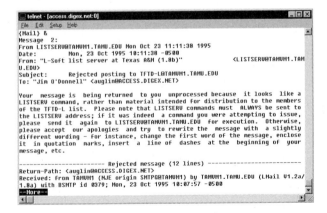

Similar to subscribing to a LISTSERV list, unsubscribing (or "signing off" to use the same terminology LISTSERV uses) is very straightforward. To unsubscribe, follow these steps:

1. Create an e-mail message to be sent to, for example

LISTSERV@TAMVM1.TAMU.EDU

2. Leave the Subject line blank.

3. In the message body, enter the command

SIGNOFF TFTD-L

4. Send the e-mail message.

Available Lists

Well, you know how to join TFTD-L now, but what other lists are available? Hopefully, LISTSERV can help. To get some help from LISTSERV, e-mail a command to the "LISTSERV" address, with the HELP command typed in the body text of the message. A few minutes after sending the help message, LISTSERV returns something like the reply shown in figure 18.5.

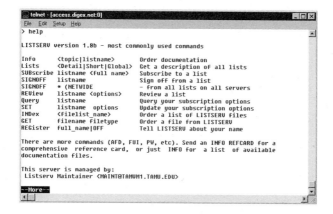

Fig. 18.5
The LISTSERV help message.

If you examine figure 18.5, you'll see a LIST command. Send an e-mail message to LISTSERV with this command:

LIST

Sending this command returns a list with the name and a short description of all the LISTSERV mailing lists that are administered at this computer (**TAMVM1.TAMU.EDU**, at Texas A&M). The beginning of the list looks like figure 18.6. Not all of the entries are shown (there are 113), but LISTSERV will send you the whole list. You can scroll through or treat it as any other e-mail message to view it.

Fig. 18.6

Local mailing lists at Texas A&M.

You might find something in these 113 groups of interest to you. It's also possible that you might not. One of the nice things about LISTSERV, however, is that not only does LISTSERV handle its own mailing lists, but a given LISTSERV site (at Texas A&M, for example) also knows about all (or many) of the other LISTSERV sites. To get this more complete listing, you need to issue a command to see the global list.

To display a global list, send an e-mail message to LISTSERV with the following command:

LIST GLOBAL

Figure 18.7 shows the reply after you request the global listing.

Fig. 18.7

Global mailing lists from Texas A&M.

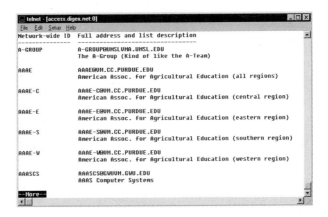

Again, most of the entries are not shown, but LISTSERV will send you an e-mail message with all of them. With well over 7,000 entries from which to choose, you should be able to find something to your liking.

Note

The fact that many LISTSERV systems are interconnected in this way allows you to send your commands to just about any of them, and LISTSERV will forward the command to the appropriate place. For example, even though the TFTD-L list resides on the LISTSERV at Texas A&M, I could subscribe to it by sending the SUBSCRIBE command to LISTSERV@UM.MARIST.EDU. The LISTSERV at Marist College will forward my request automatically to the one at Texas A&M, and I will be subscribed to the list.

If you want to narrow the search a little (or don't have the room on your computer or e-mail account to get the full global list; it's well over 100K long!), you can include search keywords in your command. For example, I'm a big hockey fan, so I might send the following e-mail message to LISTSERV:

LIST GLOBAL HOCKEY

Figure 18.8 shows the reply, which includes only lists dealing with hockey as a topic.

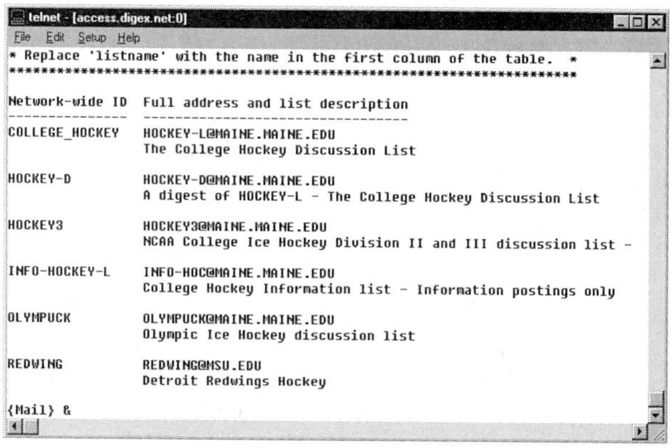

Fig. 18.8
Hockey-related lists that the Texas A&M LISTSERV knows about.

Notice in the global lists that the full address of each mailing list appears in the listing. If you want to join one of these lists, however, you can simply send your subscription request to the Texas A&M LISTSERV host, or to any others that you know about. Unless the name of the list is not unique (unlikely), the LISTSERV forwards the request appropriately. If the name isn't unique, LISTSERV is kind enough to send you a message to that effect, and to tell you what your options are.

▶ See "Anonymous FTP," p. 838

III

Using Internet E-Mail

NetCD95

> **Note**
>
> Probably the best way to find mailing lists that might be of interest to you is to request the global list and use your favorite editor to search through that list. You can also check out the list of lists on NetCD95 (the CD-ROM included with this book), under \docs\lists. Stephanie da Silva maintains this list of publicly available mailing lists; you can get a current copy of this list using anonymous FTP from **rtfm.mit.edu** in the directory /pub/usenet-by-group/news.lists. The list will be in 14 parts, named like
>
> Publicly_Accessible_Mailing_Lists,_Part_??_14
>
> As you might have guessed, this is also posted to the newgroup **news.lists** on a monthly basis, around the 19th of each month.

Using Other LISTSERV Commands

You now know everything you need to get started with LISTSERV, and, in fact, probably know everything you'll ever need to know. As you saw from the previous help message in figure 18.5, however, there are other things you can do in addition to subscribing, signing off, and requesting lists.

One of the things you had to do when subscribing was to list your name along with the subscription request. LISTSERV needs to have your full name (preferably your real one, although there usually isn't any way to verify this) before it will process subscription requests.

> **Note**
>
> One way to avoid having to specify your name each time you subscribe to a new mailing list is to register with the LISTSERV, using the REGISTER command:
>
> REGISTER James R. O'Donnell, Jr., Ph.D.
>
> This registers your name and e-mail address with this LISTSERV, so that you don't have to include your name on subscription requests.

After you send an e-mail message with this command, LISTSERV sends you a reply message similar to the one shown in figure 18.9.

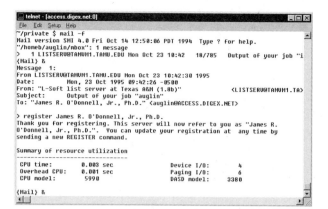

Fig. 18.9
LISTSERV response to the REGISTER command.

Note

The LISTSERV REVIEW command allows anyone to find out who the subscribers are on a given list. If you'd rather people not be able to tell if you are on a LISTSERV mailing list, you can do this with the LISTSERV REGISTER command. Send an e-mail message to LISTSERV with the command REGISTER OFF in the body of the message. Then, you won't be reported as a subscriber to any mailing lists that reside on that particular LISTSERV system.

If you're interested about learning more about LISTSERV, or about some of the less commonly used commands, you can send a message with the simple command, INFO, as the body of the message.

LISTSERV will send a reply message explaining what types of information it has available, as shown in figure 18.10.

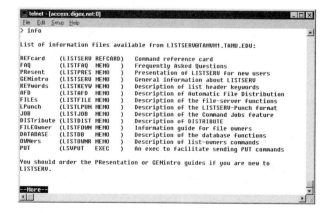

Fig. 18.10
LISTSERV information files.

III

Using Internet E-Mail

The last topic of general interest is how to retrieve files from LISTSERV. For example, each of the information files listed in figure 18.10 can be retrieved either through an INFO command, or by getting the appropriate file. So, to get the command reference card file REFcard (the first one on the list in figure 18.10), you can either e-mail the command INFO REFCARD or GET LISTSERV REFCARD.

In addition to the information files shown in figure 18.10, there are other files that a given LISTSERV will have. In order to get a list of those files, send the INDEX command to the LISTSERV server.

In response to the INDEX command, the Texas A&M LISTSERV sends you a list of files that looks something like the one shown in figure 18.11 (it's kind of messy, but, unfortunately, that's how it looks coming from the LISTSERV program).

Fig. 18.11
LISTSERV file index.

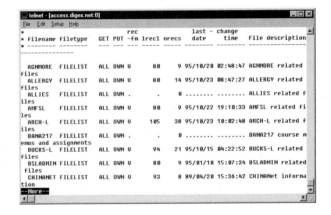

To get one of these files, send LISTSERV the GET command, followed by the file name and file type of the desired file, as in:

GET LISTSERV FILELIST

Sending Messages to a LISTSERV Mailing List

Once you are on a mailing list, depending on the nature of the list, you may want to send messages to the list, which will then get sent out to all the list subscribers. This process is very similar to sending a LISTSERV command, except that you use the list address, not LISTSERV. Follow these steps to send a message to the mailing list:

1. Use your Internet mail program to create a new mail message and send it to the mailing list address. For example, if I wanted to post a

comment to HOCKEY-L, I'd send a message to HOCKEY-L@TAMVM1. TAMU.EDU. (HOCKEY-L doesn't reside at Texas A&M, but remember that my request will get forwarded to the correct LISTSERV system.)

2. Put a meaningful subject in the Subject line. This is different than with LISTSERV commands, where the subject is ignored. When sending out a message to everyone on a list, you should make your subject as specific as possible so the other subscribers can tell at a glance whether or not they want to read your message.

3. Enter your message in the text area. You can post files to the mailing list by encoding the file and including it in your message.

◄ See "Attaching Files to Mail," p. 392

4. Send the e-mail message. You will usually receive a copy of your message back from the mailing list in a few minutes.

► See "File Encoding and Decoding with Microsoft Exchange and Eudora," p. 441

LISTSERV Miscellany

Although all of the procedures described so far have included only one command, you can place as many commands as you like in each message to LISTSERV. For example, if you want to change the name under which you are registered, subscribe to the HOCKEY3 mailing list, sign off the TFTD-L mailing list, and get the command reference card, you can send one message to:

LISTSERV@VM.MARIST.EDU

with the message body of

SUBSCRIBE HOCKEY3 Jim O'Donnell

REGISTER James R. O'Donnell, Jr.

SIGNOFF TFTD-L

info refcard

And everything you want will get done. To review what took place in this example, I first sent this message to a different LISTSERV site, this one at Marist College. As I mentioned, the list requests are forwarded; in the case of COMICS-L, to the University of Maine, and TFTD-L to Texas A&M. My name at the University of Maine will be "Jim O'Donnell," since that is what I included on the command line where I subscribed to HOCKEY3, but the Marist LISTSERV will register me as "James R. O'Donnell, Jr.". The last thing I wanted to again point out in this example is that you don't need to put all of your commands in capital letters; LISTSERV can't tell the difference.

III

Using Internet E-Mail

Using Majordomo Mailing Lists

Another type of program that you sometimes find running Internet mailing lists is a program called Majordomo. Majordomo tends to be used for smaller lists, and doesn't have the great connection of LISTSERV. A given Majordomo site is aware about the lists that it is running, but no others.

Sending Majordomo Commands

The procedure for sending commands to a Majordomo system is almost identical to that for LISTSERV commands, except the address is a little different.

1. Use your Internet mail program to create a new mail message and send it to the Majordomo address. The one I use is at **MAJORDOMO@VECTOR.CASTI.COM**. Depending on your mail program, you may type this address in at the command line with the mail command

   mail **MAJORDOMO@VECTOR.CASTI.COM**

   Or you may type **MAJORDOMO@VECTOR.CASTI.COM** on the To line of the e-mail message.

2. Leave the Subject line blank.

3. In the text area of the message, enter Majordomo commands, one per line, in uppercase, lowercase, or mixed case.

4. Send the e-mail message. The reply will usually come in a few minutes.

Getting Majordomo Help

Take a look at the Majordomo help message to get the lay of the land. Just as LISTSERV expects its command to be sent to the LISTSERV address, Majordomo expects commands to be sent to **Majordomo@VECTOR.CASTI.COM**. Send an e-mail message to the Majordomo address with the command in the body text of

   HELP

(Majordomo, like LISTSERV, also doesn't care about the letters being upper- or lowercase.) The response to a HELP command will look something like figure 18.12.

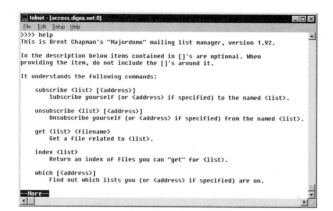

Fig. 18.12
A Majordomo help
message.

Subscribing to and Unsubscribing from Majordomo Lists

Subscribing to and unsubscribing from a Majordomo list is similar to the same operations for LISTSERV lists. In the case of Majordomo, however, UNSUBSCRIBE is used (rather than SIGNOFF) to quit a list. With Majordomo, you don't need to specify your name with the SUBSCRIBE command. The Majordomo server automatically recognizes the e-mail address and name from which you're sending the message.

> **Note**
>
> One feature of Majordomo that isn't in LISTSERV is that in the SUBSCRIBE or UNSUBSCRIBE command, you can optionally specify a different e-mail address. This is handy if you temporarily don't have access to the e-mail account you normally use, but want to issue a command as if it came from that address. Another time this comes in handy is if you need to unsubscribe from a list because the e-mail address from which you originally subscribed is no longer active.

Finding Majordomo Lists

In order to find out what mailing lists a given Majordomo supports, simply send an e-mail message to the Majordomo list with the LISTS command in the body of the message.

You receive a message like the one shown in figure 18.13.

Fig. 18.13

Majordomo lists message.

Majordomo Miscellany

Like LISTSERV, Majordomo allows multiple commands per e-mail message sent. And, you still have to be careful of where to send your messages. Commands are sent to

MAJORDOMO@VECTOR.CASTI.COM

If you want to send a message to all of the subscribers on the list, send the message to, for example:

DC-MOTSS@VECTOR.CASTI.COM

Like LISTSERV, Majordomo has the INDEX and GET commands for requesting an index of files, and retrieving one of those files, respectively. One convenient option that Majordomo has is the WHICH command; it tells you which lists you are a member of.

Accessing Private or Other Mailing Lists

It is likely, in your travels throughout the Internet, that you will run across other mailing lists that aren't LISTSERV or Majordomo lists. Not to worry, however. In almost all cases—except for truly private lists—these lists are run by people who welcome your participation, and they normally make it easy to figure out how to join, quit, and contribute to the list.

Understanding Different Mailing List Types

In addition to what software (or person) administers a mailing list, and what topic or topics the list covers, there are a few other distinctions between mailing lists that are important to understand.

Working with Moderated and Unmoderated Lists

A *moderated list* is one in which a person or persons reviews and approves all messages before they are posted to the list. These lists tend to have more formal discussions, and also, as you might expect, tend to stay on topic. In this type of list, all messages posted to the list first go to the list moderator for review. This type of list tends to be fairly informative, but usually has little *traffic* (messages flowing back and forth).

Most lists are *unmoderated*. If you want to reply or post a message to a list, you send it to the mailing list address and, after some small delay, your message is posted. These types of lists are more free-flowing than moderated lists, sometimes on topic, sometimes off. Quite often, several different discussions, or *threads*, are taking place at once. Usually, these different threads are distinguished by informative subject lines, although this isn't always the case. Traffic on an unmoderated list can be very heavy. Sometimes, however, the signal-to-noise ratio is low, and the possibility of a flame war always exists (see the "Using Netiquette" section later in this chapter).

Working with Digestified and Undigestified Lists

Sometimes, high traffic mailing lists are sent out as digests, rather than as individual messages. A *digest* is a collection of messages that the mailing list program or administrator accumulates and then sends out after a certain amount of time, or after a certain length is reached.

The advantage of a mailing list digest is that you are not receiving e-mail messages every couple of minutes. Having your computer beep or flash every time you get a message can be distracting. However, when you receive messages as a digest, it becomes harder to follow different conversation threads, because you can't identify a message by the subject line.

Using Netiquette

If you spend any amount of time on Internet mailing lists, in UseNet newsgroups, or on IRC (see chapter 38, "How IRC Works," and chapter 39, "Using mIRC and WebChat"), you quickly become familiar with *netiquette*, the term used to describe the proper way of behaving on the Net.

III

Using Internet E-Mail

As a newcomer, some of the people who have been around for a while may cut you some slack, but they are just as likely to get annoyed for any netiquette breaches on your part. There is certainly no enforcement mechanism on much of the Internet, but still, you don't want to get a bad reputation. On Internet mailing lists that are directly administered by someone, it is possible to get yourself thrown off the list.

But, as in most cases, good etiquette on the Internet is mostly a matter of common sense. If you keep a few things in mind, you shouldn't have any problems.

Understanding Bandwidth or Signal-to-Noise Ratio

Two terms that come up often in Internet discussions, of which mailing lists are an example, are *bandwidth* and *signal-to-noise ratio*.

Bandwidth refers to how much information can be transmitted over a mailing list (or whatever), whereas signal-to-noise ratio measures how relevant the discussion actually taking place is to the supposed topic of the discussion. There are quite a few ways that the relevant discussion (the signal) can be obscured by the irrelevant discussion (the noise). There are two more common ways to avoid noise: by reading the FAQ and by avoiding test messages.

Reading the FAQ!

Most Internet mailing lists that have been around for a while have a list of "Frequently Asked Questions," commonly referred to as a FAQ. This list of questions (and answers!) is usually posted frequently. Before you ask your own question on the list, it is usually a good idea to look through the FAQ to see whether the question has already been addressed.

If you have a hard time locating a FAQ, you might want to use the LISTSERV or Majodomo INDEX command to see whether you can retrieve the FAQ. If not, you can safely post a short little message asking whether there is a FAQ for this list.

Avoiding Test Messages

A common habit of people new to Internet mailing lists is the desire to send out a test message, "to see if it works." These messages usually have a subject of "Test message: do not read," and something like "This is a test, please ignore" in the body of the message.

Even with the "do not read" warning, this sort of message is liable to annoy a lot of people. Most of these mailing lists have been up and running a long time, and it's normally a safe bet to assume that they work as advertised. And in any case, sending a message to 10, 20, hundreds, or even thousands of people for a test is not good use of Internet bandwidth.

Replying to Questions

Many mailing lists exist to provide support for computer software or products from other users. In these sorts of lists, people frequently ask questions about how to perform a certain action, or ask for help fixing a problem that they might have. If you are able to help them with their problem, your first impulse might be to whip out a quick reply and post it to the list. That's not always the best way to do it.

Because of the way mailing lists work, being posted from a central machine far and wide across the Internet, there might be considerable delay between when a given message reaches different users. If the question asked was a relatively simple one, four or five or ten people might read it, solve it, and post a solution, before any of them have seen what other people have written.

If it's a fairly simple problem, it might be a better idea to e-mail your solution to the person who posted the original question, rather than to the whole list. Then, if it turns out that there is a lot of interest on the list in that topic, the original sender can summarize the solutions received and post the summary.

Avoiding Flame Wars

A fairly pernicious waste of Internet bandwidth deserves its own discussion, and that is the flame war. A *flame war* is what happens when someone (no blame here!) either gets a little too personal in a reply to someone else, or takes a comment from someone else a little too personally. Before you know it, the original topic of discussion is lost as the list becomes filled with passionate messages insulting different people. Very often, well-meaning souls who try to step in and moderate between two people are drawn in as well.

The best way to react if someone insults you—flames you—on an Internet mailing list is to take some time and decide whether it is really worth responding. Did you misread the intention of the mail? Are you taking it too personally? If you decide that you really need to respond, do everyone else on the list a favor, and take the discussion to private e-mail between you and the offending party. This will leave the mailing list open for the discussion it is intended for.

Changing Your E-Mail Address or Going on Vacation

One problem you might have after you have joined a mailing list is that you receive a lot more e-mail than you counted on. Even though TFTD-L sends out only one message a day (not including weekends), there are other lists that have much more traffic. Hopefully, you'll be able to check your e-mail often enough so that this isn't a problem, but what happens if your e-mail address changes or if you go on vacation?

When your e-mail address changes, that means your old account has probably gone away. But, the mailing list is still sending you e-mail. Even if your account has completely gone away, the computer system that the account was on still has to deal with all the messages the mailing list is sending out, probably by flagging them as undeliverable and sending them back. The computer that hosts the mailing list still has to send you out the message and deal with the undeliverable messages that get sent back.

Eventually, the mailing list will figure out that you have gone away, but you can save a lot of Internet bandwidth and resources by conscientiously quitting lists when your e-mail account changes.

A similar problem can happen when you are temporarily unable to access your e-mail account, usually when you go on vacation. In this case, your mailing lists continue to send you e-mail. If you belong to one or more high traffic mailing lists, you can potentially receive a huge amount of e-mail while you're on vacation. It is possible that the number of messages received might exceed the storage capabilities of your computer account or system. If this might be a problem, it's probably a good idea to temporarily quit your high traffic lists until you return.

To summarize, you can save yourself, the mailing list administrators of the lists to which you belong, the system administrators of your computer and the mailing list computer, and the whole Internet, a lot of time, effort, and otherwise wasted resources by doing the following:

- Quit all mailing lists when the e-mail address to which they are sent changes or is discontinued. If you forget to do this until after the address goes away, and thus can no longer use it to issue a command to quit, you must use a different address to send a message to the mailing list administrator asking him or her to remove your old address from the list.

- If you're going on vacation, or your e-mail will not be accessible for an extended period of time for some other reason, consider temporarily quitting any high volume mailing lists to which you belong. You probably won't be able to read all the messages you get while you're gone anyway, and so the messages are just going to tie up resources on the Internet and on your computer.

Anonymous Mailing Services

If you would like to be on a mailing list that is discussing a sensitive topic (one for adults who like Frosted Flakes, for instance), you can usually subscribe with a reasonable assurance that you can maintain your anonymity.

Most mailing list administrators respect the potential desire of their subscribers to remain anonymous.

Internet Mailing Lists and UseNet

There are many similarities between Internet mailing lists and UseNet (see chapter 30, "How UseNet Works"). Both allow many people with similar interests to have discussions and share information over the Internet. As we have seen, Internet mailing lists occur completely over e-mail; UseNet newsgroups use a different mechanism, and require a news reader at your computer. Because of this, Internet mailing lists are more widely available. In fact, there are some mailing lists that echo UseNet discussions, so that people who don't have access to a news reader can participate.

Regardless, the two share many of the same characteristics and limitations. Both are limited to ASCII information only, so binary files must be encoded before they can be sent. The same rules of netiquette apply to discussions. One advantage of UseNet, if you have access to a news reader on your computer, is that you don't have to worry about lots of messages piling up in your mailbox if your are away for an extended period of time.

III

Using Internet E-Mail

CHAPTER 19

Encoding and Decoding Files

In chapter 20, "How the World Wide Web Works," you learn about the hottest new way of using the Internet, the World Wide Web (WWW). As you've probably heard, the WWW allows you to easily surf around the Internet, viewing text, graphics, sounds, and movies—information in many different forms.

Long before the existence of the WWW, however, people were exchanging non-text information—graphics, sounds, and binary files, such as executables and zip archives—using other methods. Internet applications such as FTP (see chapter 34, "Using FTP") and Gopher (see chapter 35, "Using Gopher and Popular Gopher Programs") allow this binary information to be accessed and retrieved directly over the Internet. However, it's also possible to send and receive binary information through means that are normally restricted to text only, such as Internet e-mail and UseNet, by encoding and decoding files containing such information.

In this chapter, you learn how to do the following:

- Use Microsoft Exchange and Eudora to send encoded files through e-mail
- Recognize the most common forms of file encoding: MIME encoding, and UUEncoding
- Install and set up Wincode, a Windows 95 program for encoding and decoding files
- Use Wincode to encode and decode files
- Recognize the most common type of encoding used on the Macintosh platform, Mac BinHex

What Is File Encoding/Decoding, and Why Is It Needed?

Suppose that someone (finally!) took a decent picture of me playing hockey (as opposed to the pictures of me falling down that I usually get), and I want to send a copy of it home to my father. This being the computer age (and me being cheap), I decide to scan the picture and send a copy of the graphics file to him through e-mail. How do I send that graphics picture through e-mail (see fig. 19.1)?

Fig. 19.1
Look, Dad! I really can play hockey!

File *encoding* takes files with binary information, such as this graphics file, executable programs, or compressed file archives, and converts them to ASCII text files. *Decoding* converts them back. After a binary file has been encoded into an ASCII text file, it isn't in a very useful form. If it's a program, it can't be run; and if it's a picture, it can't be viewed. The file must be decoded back into its original binary form to be usable.

◀ See "ASCII Format Only," p. 339

As you probably figured out from the introduction to this chapter, there's a very important use for an encoded file: Unlike the binary file from which it is made, an encoded file can be more easily transmitted over the Internet. The original networks were never set up to carry anything but text, which generally uses only seven bits of information per byte. Because binary information uses all eight bits, the networks were not able to transmit it. There are ways of transmitting binary files over the Internet, particularly FTP and the World

Wide Web (WWW), but some Internet services are still limited to text. These are primarily Internet e-mail, including Internet mailing lists, and UseNet.

The process of encoding involves taking a binary file, in which eight bits per byte are used, and converting it into a text file that uses seven bits per byte. As you might guess, the encoded file is going to be bigger than the original file. It's common to compress a file before encoding it. Files meant to be used on a PC will generally be zipped (which can be unzipped using PKZIP and WinZip on the NetCD95).

NetCD95

◄ See "ASCII Format Only," p. 339

◄ See "What Are Internet Mailing Lists?" p. 418

▶ See "What Is FTP?" p. 837

What Types of Encoding and Decoding Are There?

The two most common types of encoding are MIME encoding and UUEncoding. *MIME* stands for *Multipurpose Internet Mail Extensions*, and was developed to provide a standard means of exchanging various types of binary information through the Internet. *UUEncoding* is an older "standard," originally developed for UNIX systems. Not all versions of UUEncode/UUDecode are compatible with one another, so when you have a choice, it's usually better to use MIME.

> **Note**
>
> You may be wondering why it's called *UU*Encoding and *UU*Decoding. In the fine tradition of many programs and commands that come from UNIX ("grep," "awk," "ls," and so on), the meaning of the command isn't immediately obvious. The clue comes from "UUCP," which comes from "UNIX-UNIX CoPy." So, UUEncoding and UUDecoding were originally meant to facilitate the transfer of binary files from one UNIX system to another UNIX system.

There is another kind of file encoding that's very popular in the Macintosh world called *BinHex*. Later in this chapter, you look at how to recognize files encoded with BinHex, but because it's not likely you'll find any Windows 95 files encoded this way, this chapter won't spend much time on it.

File Encoding and Decoding with Microsoft Exchange and Eudora

As discussed in their respective chapters (see chapter 15, "Using Microsoft Exchange," and chapter 16, "Using Eudora"), both Microsoft Exchange and

III

Using Internet E-Mail

Eudora are e-mail programs that run under Windows 95, and they both allow you to attach binary files to e-mail messages.

Sending Encoded Files Using Microsoft Exchange

Microsoft Exchange allows you to send encoded files using either MIME or UUEncode. To select between these two methods, follow these steps:

1. Start Microsoft Exchange by double-clicking the Inbox icon on your desktop, and open the Tools menu and choose the Services item.

2. Highlight the Internet Mail service entry and click the Properties button.

3. Click the Message Format button.

4. Select the Use MIME When Sending Messages check box to use MIME encoding and clear the check box to use UUEncode (see fig. 19.2).

Fig. 19.2

This check box in the Message Format dialog box controls whether it uses MIME or UUEncode encoding.

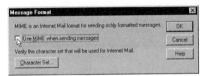

After you select the type of encoding, including an encoded file is fairly straightforward. From the Compose menu, choose the New Message item. This gives you the e-mail message composition window shown in figure 19.3, in which I have composed a quick message and am now ready to attach the binary graphics file.

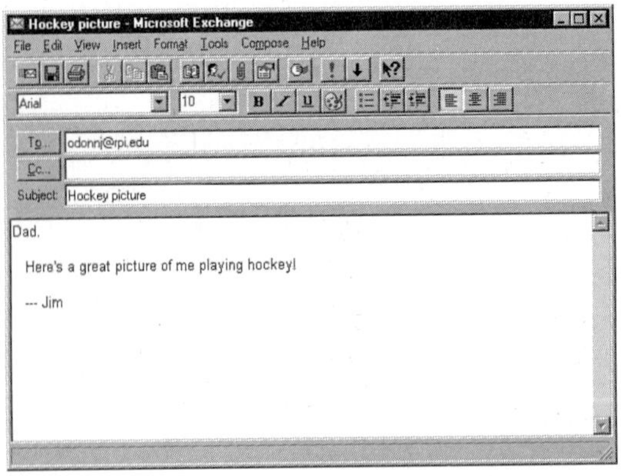

Fig. 19.3

When you want to send e-mail using Microsoft Exchange, this is the window it gives you in which to compose your message.

Figure 19.4 shows the menu bar in the Composition window. Files are attached to the message using the Paperclip button.

Click here to attach a file

Fig. 19.4
Click the Paperclip button of the menu bar to attach a file to your message.

In response to clicking the Paperclip button, the window shown in figure 19.5 appears. From here, you can select the file to be attached. If this is a binary file, such as the graphics file I am sending, make sure you click the radio button to insert the file as An Attachment. After you have made this selection, the composition window will appear (see fig. 19.6). From here, you can send the message normally, and the file that you attached will be encoded according to the method you selected.

Fig. 19.5
Select the file to attach to this e-mail message. If it's a binary file, make sure to click the radio button to insert it as An Attachment.

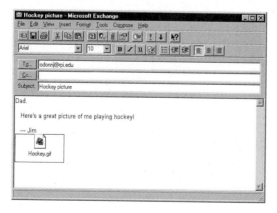

Fig. 19.6
After you have attached the file, it appears in the composition window as shown. The message is ready to be sent!

Using Internet E-Mail

III

Sending Encoded Files Using Eudora

Microsoft Exchange allows you to send encoded files using either MIME or BinHex. In the composition window for sending e-mail with Eudora, you can select between these two methods right from the menu bar, as shown in figure 19.7. Because you are using Windows 95, you will almost always want to choose MIME, unless you are sending the message to someone who is using a Mac. (Note that if both you and the recipient of the message are using Eudora, you can choose either method, as Eudora automatically detects the type of encoding. In general, however, unless the recipient is using a Mac, you will always want to use MIME.)

Fig. 19.7
Eudora allows you to select the encoding method right from the menu bar of each message; in general, you will want to use MIME encoding.

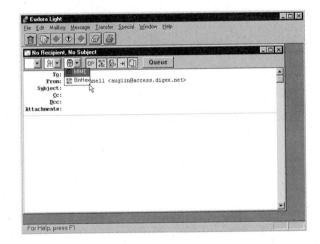

To attach a binary file to an e-mail message in Eudora, compose the message normally, and then choose the Attach File item from the Message menu (or type Ctrl+H), as shown in figure 19.8. You will be given a standard Windows 95 file selection dialog box from which you can select the file to include. Once that is done, the file name—or names, as more than one file can be attached—appear in the Attachments section of the message.

Fig. 19.8
Attach a file in Eudora by selecting this menu item, or typing Ctrl+H.

Recognizing Different Encoding Schemes

If you're using an e-mail program such as Microsoft Exchange or Eudora, the encoding and decoding method used will be pretty irrelevant. These programs encode outgoing files and decode incoming files automatically, and you'll never need to know exactly how. However, if you don't use these e-mail programs, or if you obtain an encoded file through some other means, it's important to know how to recognize what the encoded files look like—this makes it a lot easier to figure out how to decode them.

Figures 19.9 and 19.10 show the resulting e-mail messages with the attached hockey picture, using MIME encoding (from Eudora) and UUEncode encoding (from Microsoft Exchange).

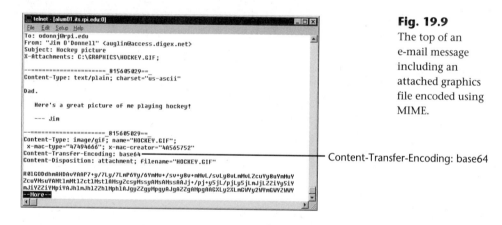

Fig. 19.9
The top of an e-mail message including an attached graphics file encoded using MIME.

Content-Transfer-Encoding: base64

Encoding: 6 TEXT, 2393 UUENCODE

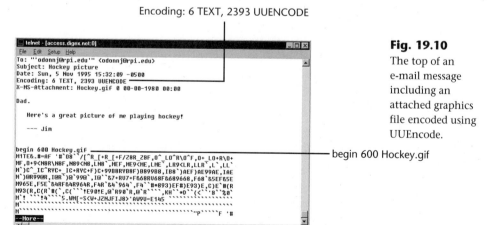

Fig. 19.10
The top of an e-mail message including an attached graphics file encoded using UUEncode.

begin 600 Hockey.gif

It's fairly easy to distinguish between files encoded with MIME and those encoded with UUEncode:

- MIME encoded files include a line, such as that shown in figure 19.9, that reads Content-Transfer-Encoding: base64.
- UUEncoded files begin with a line such as begin 600 Hockey.gif (the 600 is a UNIX file permission code that you don't really need to worry about), as shown in figure 19.10.
- UUEncoded files end with a line that reads end (not seen in fig. 19.10 because the file is longer than the screen).

At the end of this chapter, you'll take a look at what BinHex encoded files look like.

> **Caution**
>
> Whenever you look at an encoded file, either MIME or UUEncode encoding—by viewing it in an editor, for instance—be very careful not to change any of the characters inside the encoded file. If the file is a graphics or sound file, this can cause the decoded file to be distorted. If the encoded file is a zip file or executable program, changing any characters can render the decoded file useless.

Encoding and Decoding Files from Windows 95

As mentioned above, if the only encoded files you deal with go through Microsoft Exchange, Eudora, or some other e-mail program or UseNet newsreader that automatically encodes and decodes the files, there really isn't anything else you need to know. However, it is likely that you will run into an encoded file every once in a while that hasn't gone through your mailer, or you might need to encode a file that you aren't mailing right out. To do that, you need a program that allows you to encode and decode files from Windows 95. Wincode is such a program.

> **Note**
>
> The current version of Wincode, v2.6.1, is not a Windows 95, 32-bit application, and was written for Windows 3.1 and Windows for Workgroups. Thus, it references Windows 3.1 elements, such as the Program Manager. However, the program does work the same under Windows 95.

Installing Wincode

Assuming you're starting with a zip file containing the Wincode files
(I started with WNCOD261.ZIP), install Wincode as follows:

NetCD95

1. Unzip the file, preferably into its own subdirectory, such as c:\temp.
   Alternatively, you can install this directly from NetCD95 that accompanies this book.

2. From the Start button on the taskbar or from Windows Explorer, run
   c:\temp\install.exe. (If you're running the installation from a different
   directory or from NetCD, change the drive and/or directory as needed
   to match your system.)

   The first thing the installer will do is check for the free space available
   on your C: and D: drives and then display that information. You may
   get an error dialog box if you don't have a D: drive or if D: is a CD-ROM
   drive; if so, just press Cancel and the installation will continue. The
   installer then displays a dialog box like the one in figure 19.11, which
   shows the free space on your hard drives in order to give you an idea of
   where to install Wincode.

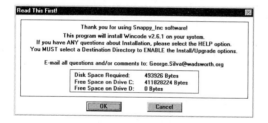

Fig. 19.11
After the Wincode
Installer checks
your C: and D:
drives, it shows
you how much
space you have
available on each
before asking you
where to install
Wincode.

This information allows you to answer the Installer's next question of
where to install Wincode, shown in figure 19.12.

Fig. 19.12
The Wincode
Installer gives you
the option of
selecting the
Destination
Directory in which
to install the
program.

3. Click OK to select the default directory or enter another directory in the
   place of the default, c:\wincode.

4. After you've chosen the destination for the installation of the program, you'll get the screen shown in figure 19.13, which gives you one more chance to review your options and continue with the installation (or decide not to). Note that unless you're still using the Program Manager, you should deselect the Add/Create Program Manager Group check box. Click Install to continue or Cancel to quit.

Fig. 19.13

The Wincode Installer screen when it's ready to commence with the installation. Review the options shown on this screen and click Install or Cancel.

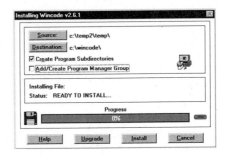

If you click Install at this point, the installation will commence and quickly finish (it's not that big of a program, really). You'll get a few other dialog boxes, mentioning that an installation log file was created and giving you an opportunity to view the README.TXT file (which tells you how, for a small fee, you can get full documentation for the program).

5. Because Wincode was written for Windows 3.1 and Windows for Workgroups, the installation process doesn't put an entry for the program in either the Start menu or a shortcut on the desktop. To give me easy access to the program, I created a standard Windows 95 shortcut to the program and put it on the desktop (see fig. 19.14). Note that, as will be shown later, Wincode supports drag-and-drop encoding and decoding of files.

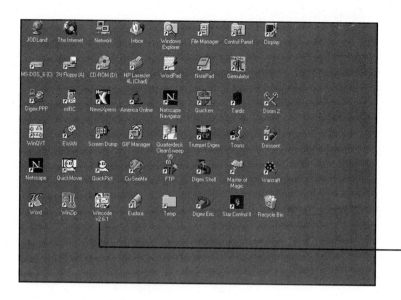

Fig. 19.14
This shows a
shortcut to the
Wincode program
on my Windows
95 desktop.

Shortcut to Wincode

Using Wincode to Encode a File

If you read through the README.TXT file for Wincode, you'll see that the author has an unusual method of marketing his program. The program itself is freeware; this means that the program is free, but it is copyrighted, and is, therefore, not public domain. The author charges $5 to receive the HELP file for the program. This $5 also entitles you to upgrades of the program and technical support via e-mail.

As the author states, however, using the program without the HELP file is relatively simple; you learn how to do that in the following sections. For the sophisticated parts of the program, however, and to support the author for producing a useful program, you might want to send him the $5 for the HELP file.

> **Note**
>
> You might be tempted to use the program without sending the author the $5 fee for the HELP file, especially if you don't need its more sophisticated features. Or, you might just never get around to sending in the money. As the author states, that's okay. If you get good use out of Wincode, however, you might want to send in the $5. It's a very reasonable price for such a slick program and you can support the author's further development of this and other Windows utilities.

When you start up Wincode, you see the screen shown in figure 19.15.

UUEncode button

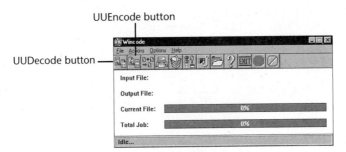

UUDecode button

Fig. 19.15

You can access Wincode's commands through the menus or by using the buttons along the top.

The first step is to select which encoding method you would like to use. This is done by choosing the Encode item from the Options menu, which results in the dialog box shown in figure 19.16. The encoding methods are shown in the Code Type drop-down list to the right; the two selections you are interested in are UUE (UUEncoding) or BASE64 (MIME encoding). Note that, in this version of Wincode, BinHex is not yet supported. Once you select one of these, you will be given the choice of a header type, as shown in figure 19.17. It's safe to select whatever the default value is here.

Fig. 19.16

Select either UUE for UUEncoding or BASE64 for MIME encoding.

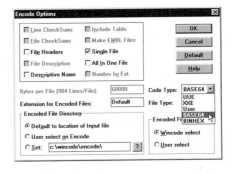

Fig. 19.17

You can go ahead and accept the default value of header type for your encoding selection.

To encode a file, either choose the Encode item from the File menu, click the Encode button, first button from the left in the toolbar on the top of the window, or simply drag a file from the Windows Explorer onto the Wincode shortcut icon on the desktop. In the first two cases, you'll get the dialog box shown in figure 19.18 in which you select the file(s) you'd like to decode.

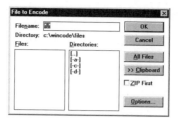

Fig. 19.18
This dialog box
allows you to
select file(s) to
encode.

As the file is encoded, the name of the input and output file appears in the appropriate places in the Wincode Window, and the status bars will move from left to right as the encoding occurs. If the process occurs without a problem, a dialog box appears telling you that the operation was a success.

Tip

If you encode a file and can't find the encoded file, you may need to check the Encoded File Directory section of the Encode Options dialog box (refer to fig. 19.18). You can select for the encoded file to be placed where the input file is, select a dedicated directory for encoded files (the default is c:\wincode\encode), or have Wincode ask you each time. There is also a similar section in the Decode Options and ZIP/UNZIP Options dialog boxes.

Using Wincode to Decode a File

Using Wincode to decode a file is as easy as using it to encode one. You simply choose the Decode item from the File menu, click the Decode button, the second button from the left, or drag the encoded file onto the Wincode desktop icon. For the first two methods a dialog box appears, allowing you to select the file to decode.

Note

You may be wondering how Wincode knows when to encode and when to decode a file if it is dragged and dropped onto the Wincode desktop icon. Because Wincode is a Windows 3.1/Windows for Workgroups application, it uses the file extension to detect encoded files, and will attempt to decode them. All other files are encoded. The Decode item in the Options menu (see fig. 19.19) allows you to enter a list of extensions by selecting the Extensions pushbutton, for Wincode to use to recognize encoded files (see fig. 19.20).

III

Using Internet E-Mail

Fig. 19.19
The Decode Options dialog box allows the selection of various decoding options.

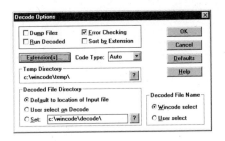

Fig. 19.20
This dialog box allows the user to specify the list of extensions Wincode will use to detect encoded files.

Other Features of Wincode

There are a couple more features of Wincode that I want to mention—a few of the more sophisticated features you can learn about by registering your copy of the program with the author and receiving the HELP file. Obviously, we've only discussed UUEncoding and UUDecoding one file. Wincode allows you to do much more. You can automatically concatenate split encoded files in an order that you specify, in order to join and then decode them. A very sophisticated feature is the ability to "hook" Wincode into a program like Eudora, which allows you to use Wincode's features directly from that other application.

◄ See "Using Eudora," p. 379

One thing you can do is set up Wincode to automatically zip a file or group of files before encoding, and/or unzip a zipped file archive after decoding. These options are enabled in the encode and decode dialog boxes (the encode dialog box is shown in fig. 19.16). To set this up, you need to choose the ZIP/UNZIP item from the Options menu. The ZIP/UNZIP Options dialog box appears, as shown in figure 19.21. The most important options you need to set are the locations of the zip and unzip program. After these are set, selecting the ZIP or UNZIP button in the encode or decode file selection dialog boxes allows this function to be done automatically.

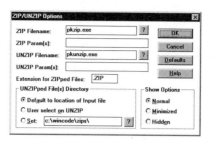

Fig. 19.21
Here you can tell
Wincode where to
find the programs
you use for
zipping and
unzipping files; it
can then do it for
you automatically.

File Encoding and Decoding on UseNet

As mentioned above, UseNet is similar to Internet e-mail in that only text
information can be exchanged. As will be discussed in later chapters, UseNet
is the Internet equivalent of the office bulletin board; in addition to text
messages that get posted, there is also the desire to post pictures and other
non-text information. Thus, the same need exists to be able to encode binary
information, and the same methods can be used. Currently, the standard on
UseNet groups is that BinHex is used in the Mac-specific groups, while
UUEncoding is used in most other cases. Just as with e-mail, if your
newsreader does not automatically decode such files, you'll need a program
like Wincode to do it.

▶ See "How
UseNet Works,"
p. 749

Recognizing Macintosh BINHEX

Sometimes on UseNet, or elsewhere on the Internet, you'll run into files that
have been encoded with something other than UUEncode or MIME encoding. Probably the most common of these files will be those encoded using the
Macintosh BINHEX program; a sample is shown in figure 19.22.

Fig. 19.22
This file looks a
little like a MIME
encoded file, but
it's a Macintosh
BINHEX file.

III

Using Internet E-Mail

Part IV

The World Wide Web

20   How the World Wide Web Works

21   Using Microsoft Internet Explorer

22   Using Netscape

23   Using Mosaic

24   Using Helper Apps

25   Planning Your Own WWW Home Pages

26   Using HTML to Build Your Home Page

27   Using Microsoft Internet Assistant to Build Web Pages

28   Using Netscape Navigator Gold and HotDog to Create Web Pages

29   New Web Technologies

CHAPTER 20

How the World Wide Web Works

The World Wide Web (WWW or Web) is one of the newest Internet services. The WWW allows you to combine text, audio, graphics, and even animation to make a document a learning experience. Links within WWW documents can take you quickly to other related documents. And the speed of the Internet makes it as easy to view a WWW document from halfway around the world as it is to view one from your hometown.

The various WWW browsers allow you to explore WWW Internet sites, giving you quick access to hypermedia documents provided at those sites. Not only does the WWW provide quick graphical access to hypermedia documents, it also allows you to use the same GUI to interface to other Internet services, such as FTP, Gopher, and UseNet newsgroups. The WWW is the closest the Internet has come to a comprehensive, user-friendly interface.

In this chapter, you learn the following:

- The history of the WWW
- Concepts important to understanding the WWW
- How to access the WWW

History of the WWW

The history of the WWW is fairly short. In 1989, some researchers at CERN (the European Laboratory for Particle Physics) wanted to develop a better way to give widely dispersed research groups access to shared information. Because research was conducted between distant sites, performing any simple activity (reading a document or viewing an image) often required finding the location of the desired item, making a remote connection to the machine where it resided, and then retrieving it to a local machine. In addition, each activity required running a number of different applications (such as Telnet,

FTP, and an image viewer). What the researchers wanted was a system that would enable them to quickly access all types of information with a common interface, removing the need to execute many steps to achieve the final goal.

Over the course of a year, the proposal for this project was refined, and work began on the implementation. By the end of 1990, the researchers at CERN had a text-mode (non-graphical) browser and a graphical browser for the NeXT computer. During 1991, the WWW was released for general usage at CERN. Initially, access was restricted to hypertext and UseNet news articles. As the project advanced, interfaces to other Internet services were added (WAIS, anonymous FTP, Telnet, and Gopher).

During 1992, CERN began publicizing the WWW project. People saw what a great idea it was, and began creating their own WWW servers to make their information available to the Internet. A few people also began working on WWW clients, designing easy-to-use interfaces to the WWW. By the end of 1993, browsers had been developed for many different computer systems, including X Windows, Apple Macintosh, and PC/Windows. By the summer of 1994, WWW had become one of the most popular ways to access Internet resources.

Important WWW Concepts

Like the word "Internet," which seems to imply a well-defined entity (which, of course, it isn't), "World Wide Web" seems to imply a fixed (or at least defined) set of sites that you can go to for information. In reality, the WWW is constantly changing as Internet sites add or delete access to their information. Learning about some of the basic concepts of the WWW will help you understand the nature of the Web.

Browsers

To access the WWW, it is necessary that you run a WWW browser on your computer. A *browser* is an application that knows how to interpret and display documents that it finds on the WWW. Documents on the WWW are hypertext documents (see the next section, "Hypertext (and Hypermedia)," for more information about hypertext). Hypertext documents are not plain text. They contain commands that structure the text by item (different headings, body paragraphs, and so on). This allows your browser to format each text type to best display it on-screen.

For example, if you connect to the Internet using a simple VT-100 compatible terminal, you have to run a text-based WWW browser like Lynx. This browser would format any documents that you receive so that they can be displayed in the fonts available on a terminal, and would let you move between key-words in the document by using the arrow keys. Lynx, however, will not display any graphic or multimedia objects in a Web document because it is designed to run on a text-only terminal that cannot display these objects. The graphics and multimedia objects cannot be displayed regardless of whether you are running Lynx on a terminal or in a terminal Window on your PC.

If you have a more sophisticated terminal like an X terminal, you can use a graphics-based browser like the X version of Mosaic. If you are running on a PC or Macintosh, you can use the PC or Macintosh version of the Mosaic browser, or one of the other WWW browsers that have been developed for these computers. These browsers are GUI applications that take advantage of the graphic capabilities of these terminals and computers, allowing you to use different sizes, fonts, and formatting for different text types.

In addition to displaying nicely formatted text, browsers can also give you the ability to access documents that contain other media besides text. For example, if you have a sound card in your PC, or a driver (a program that controls a piece of hardware) for your PC speaker, you can hear sound clips that are included in WWW documents. Some other media that can be accessed in WWW documents are still pictures and animations. Your browser may need helper applications to display different media files.

▶ See "Using Helper Apps," p. 577

Not only can you access different media in WWW documents, but some browsers can be set up so that appropriate applications will be started to display a document of a particular type. For example, if a WWW document contains a reference to a document that is in Microsoft Word for Windows format, you can set up your browser so that it automatically starts up Word for Windows to display that document when it is retrieved.

Some browsers also give you access to other Internet services. For example, you can access anonymous FTP servers, Gopher servers, WAIS servers, and UseNet news servers from many browsers. Many browsers also let you do remote logins using the Telnet protocol, although a helper application is usually required for this.

Hypertext (and Hypermedia)

When you use the WWW, the documents that you find will be hypertext documents. *Hypertext* is text that contains links to other text. This allows you to quickly access other related text from the text you are currently reading. The linked text might be within the document that you are currently reading, or it might be somewhere halfway around the world.

In addition to text, many of the documents you retrieve may contain pictures, graphs, sounds, or even animations. Documents that contain more than just text are called *hypermedia* documents, because they contain multiple media.

HTML

When you retrieve a document from the WWW, the text that you read on-screen is nicely formatted text. To do this, the documents that you read on the WWW cannot be plain text, or even text with specific formatting information in it (because the person who places a document on a WWW server doesn't know what type of computer or terminal is being used by the person reading the document).

To ensure that everyone sees documents displayed correctly on-screen, it was necessary to come up with a way to describe documents so that they are displayed in the best format for the viewing terminal or computer. The solution to this problem turned out to be HTML.

▶ See "HTML Basics," p. 622

HTML (hypertext markup language) is used when writing a document that is to be displayed through the WWW. HTML is a fairly simple set of commands that describes how a document is structured. This type of markup language allows you to define the parts of the document, but not the formatting, so the browser that you run when reading the document can format it to best suit your display.

▶ See "HTML Elements," p. 630

HTML commands are inserted around blocks of text in a document to describe what the text is. So, for example, within a document you have text that is marked as the various heading levels, simple paragraphs, page headings and footers, bulleted items, and so on. There are also commands that let you import other media (images, sounds, animations), and commands that let you specify the links to other documents (or text within the same document). Your browser gets the document and interprets the HTML commands, formatting each structure in the document (headings, bullets, plain paragraphs, and so on) in a way that looks best on your display. Figures 20.1 and 20.2 show the HTML code for the Mosaic welcome page and the corresponding file displayed in Mosaic for Windows.

> **Note**
>
> It's easy to learn HTML formatting commands. If you want to learn about them and create your own Web documents, see chapters 25–28.

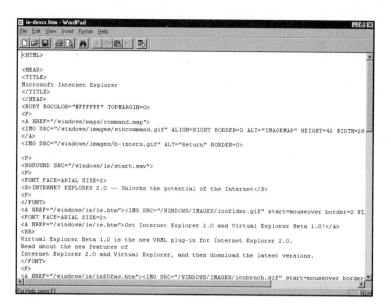

Fig. 20.1
The HTML code for a Microsoft Web page that discusses Microsoft Internet Explorer.

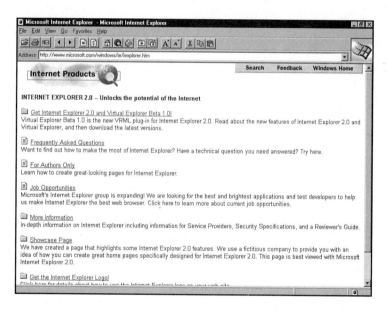

Fig. 20.2
The same Web page as it is displayed by Internet Explorer.

Links

One of the defining features of any hypertext documents is *links* (also known as *hyperlinks*). Links are simply references to other documents. But they aren't just stated references like "see page two for more information." They are actual live links, where you can activate the link and cause whatever it references to appear on-screen. When someone writes a hypertext document, he or she can insert links to other documents that have information relevant to the text in the document.

WWW documents are all hypertext documents. Besides its document description commands, HTML contains commands that allow links in a document. Many of them are hypermedia documents, containing links to pictures, sounds, or animations, in addition to document links.

There are two parts to a hypertext link. One part is the reference to the related item (be it a document, picture, movie, or sound). In the case of the WWW, the item being referenced could be within the current document, or it could be anywhere on the Internet.

The second part of a hypertext link is the anchor. The author of a document can define the anchor to be a word, a group of words, a picture, or any area of the reader's display. The reader may activate the anchor by pointing to it and clicking with a mouse (for a graphical-based browser) or by selecting it with arrow keys and pressing Enter (for a text-based browser).

> **Tip**
>
> One way of identifying an anchor on a graphical WWW interface is to watch the cursor. Your cursor may change to another shape when it passes over an anchor. For example, the cursor changes to a pointing hand in Mosaic.

> **Note**
>
> The terms link and anchor are often used interchangeably.

The anchor is indicated in different ways depending on the type of display you are using. If it is a color display, anchor words may be a special color, and anchor graphics may be surrounded by a colored box. If you have a black-and-white display, anchor words may be underlined, and anchor graphics may have a border drawn around them. On a simple terminal, anchor words may be in reverse video (and, of course, there would be no graphics!). See figure 20.3 for examples of anchors.

When you activate the anchor, your browser fetches the item referenced by the anchor. This may involve reading a document from your local disk, or going out on the Internet and requesting that a document be sent from a distant computer to yours. The reference indicates what type of item is being retrieved (HTML document, sound file, and so on), and your browser tries to present the material to you in the appropriate format.

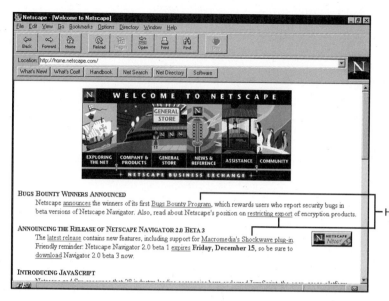

Fig. 20.3

An example of hypertext anchors in Netscape. (Anchor words are blue and underlined on-screen.)

— Hypertext anchors

Note

If you do not have the correct helper application for the type of item that is retrieved (a driver for sound files, for example), the item is still retrieved by your browser. Most browsers will offer you the option of saving the file to disk or defining a helper application for the file when you try to load a file of an unknown type.

URLs

One of the goals of the World Wide Web project was to have a standard way of referencing an item, no matter what the item's type (a document, sound file, and so on). To achieve this goal, a *Uniform Resource Locator (URL)* was developed.

A URL is a complete description of an item containing the location of the item that you want to retrieve. The location of the item can range from a file on your local disk to a file on an Internet site halfway around the world.

A URL reference can be set up to be absolute or relative. An *absolute reference* contains the complete address of the document that is being referenced, including the host name, directory path, and file name. A *relative reference* assumes that the previous machine and directory path are being used, and just the file name (or possibly a subdirectory and file name) are specified.

> **Note**
>
> If you save a document to your local disk, you should check to see if the references in the document are absolute or relative. If the document references other documents with relative addresses, you will not be able to view those documents unless you copy them to your local disk and set them up with the same directory structure as they had at the original site. Absolute references will always work unless your Internet connection fails or the referenced documents are moved.

The URL is not limited to describing the location of WWW files. Many browsers (including Mosaic) can access a number of different Internet services, including anonymous FTP, Gopher, WAIS, UseNet news, and Telnet.

A typical URL looks like this:

http://www.eit.com/web/www.guide

> **Note**
>
> The document **http://www.eit.com/web/www.guide** is an overview of the WWW.

> **Tip**
>
> Even if you are retrieving files from a server that is running on a PC, you must use a slash (/) to indicate a subdirectory, not a backslash (\).

The initial item in the URL (the part that ends with a colon) is the protocol that is being used to retrieve the item. A *protocol* is a set of instructions that defines how to use that particular Internet service. In this example, the protocol is HTTP, the Hypertext Transfer Protocol developed for the WWW project. The two slashes after the colon indicate that what follows is a valid Internet host address or symbolic location. It can be either the text as shown above, or the actual IP address of the site. In this URL, you want to find a file on that machine, what follows after the host name is a UNIX-style path for the file you want to retrieve.

The URL in the prior example tells a WWW browser to retrieve the file www.guide from the /web directory on the Internet host www.eit.com, using the HTTP protocol.

Other protocols that WWW browsers can use to retrieve documents are listed in the following table:

Protocol	Use
gopher	Starts a Gopher session.
ftp	Starts an FTP session.
file	Gets a file on your local disk if followed by ///c|; or, equivalent to FTP if followed by //. Any local disk may be specified, and it must be followed by the bar character rather than a colon, because the colon has a special significance in a URL.
wais	Accesses a WAIS server.
news	Reads UseNet newsgroups.
telnet	Starts a Telnet session.

HTTP

Another of the goals of the WWW project was to have documents that were easy to retrieve, no matter where they resided. After it was decided to use hypertext as the standard format for WWW documents, a protocol that allowed these hypertext documents to be retrieved quickly was developed. This protocol is HTTP, the Hypertext Transport Protocol. HTTP is a fairly simple communications protocol that takes advantage of the fact that the documents it retrieves contain information about future links the user may reference (unlike FTP or Gopher, where information about the next possible links must be transmitted via the protocol).

Although it is not necessary to know anything about the HTTP protocol to view documents on the WWW, if you are interested, you can find IEFT drafts that discuss the HTTP specification at the following URLs:

> **http://www.w3.org/hypertext/WWW/Protocols/HTTP/
> HTTP2.html**

> **http://www.ietf.cnri.reston.va.us/ids.by.wg/http.html**

Home Pages

All WWW users can set up their own home page to link to sites they use frequently. Home pages can also be developed for groups who use the same resources. For example, a project may need to set up a home page that gives links to all project-related items that exist.

> **Note**
>
> Many people refer to the primary welcome page of a site as the home page for that site. This is not really a home page because it is for general use and does not organize information that is of interest to one specific person or group.

Clients and Servers

Two terms heard frequently when the WWW is discussed are client and server. A WWW *client* is an account on an Internet site that requests a document from the WWW. The WWW *servers* are the collections of WWW documents at different sites on the Internet.

Client software is a program (like Mosaic) that you use to view WWW documents. Server software is a program that manages a particular collection of WWW documents on an Internet host.

Future Developments on the Web

As good as it currently is, people are working to make the WWW even better. Over the next few years, new developments will allow for display of more complicated documents and the addition of live communications in documents. Chapter 29, "New Web Technologies," discusses some of these emerging technologies in more detail.

VRML

▶ See "VRML: The WWW in Three Dimensions," p. 733

In an effort to add another demension to the Web, *VRML (Virtual Reality Modeling Language)* has been developed. VRML allows three-dimensional images to be displayed from the Web. This new capability will eventually allow for things like walk-throughs of buildings and environments, virtual examination of three-dimensional objects, etc.

Live Communications

▶ See "Audio Applications on the Web," p. 741

You can currently display audio and video on the Web, but you are limited to playing back previously created files. The next development will be incorporating live audio and video in Web documents. One of the products currently being developed will allow multiple users to connect to a Web sight and talk to each other as if they were in a room together.

Built-In Multimedia

Sun Microsystems has developed *Java*, a language based on C++ that allows you to load an object in a document without needing a special viewer for that object (the viewer is built in to the object, essentially). Not only does it eliminate the need for viewers, it also allows you to customize your viewer application. More information and demos of the HotJava browser can be found at **http://java.sun.com**. Netscape is also supporting the inclusion of Java objects in Web documents.

▶ See "Enhancing Your Web Browser On-the-Fly," p. 731

In addition to supporting Java, Netscape has developed a way to incorporate live objects directly into Web documents. Netscape has agreements with the developers of some helper applications to allows functions of the applications to be imported directly into Netscape. Instead of having to start a helper application in a separate window when you encounter a multimedia file, the relative pieces of the application appear directly in your document. The multimedia file is then played within the document.

Learning More about WWW

The WWW, like the Internet, changes constantly. New servers become available and old ones go away. Eventually, new protocols for accessing new Internet services will be available. New browsers will be written, and old ones will get new features. There is so much information changing rapidly that anything in hard print (like this book) will become out of date quickly. (Only somewhat out of date, though! Most of the information will be current.)

There are a number of ways that you can find out more information about what is current on the WWW. This section gives you pointers to some of the most useful sources of information.

UseNet Newsgroups

If you have access to UseNet newsgroups, a number of them are directly related to the WWW. The following table gives descriptions of them.

▶ See "Top UseNet Newsgroups," p. 1155

UseNet Newsgroup	Description
comp.infosystems.www.advocacy	Comments and arguments over the best and worst
comp.infosystems.www.announce	World-Wide Web announcements (Moderated)
comp.infosystems.www.authoring.cgi	Writing CGI scripts for the Web
comp.infosystems.www.authoring.html	Writing HTML for the Web

(continues)

IV

The World Wide Web

(continued)

UseNet Newsgroup	Description
comp.infosystems.www.authoring.images	Using images, imagemaps on the Web
comp.infosystems.www.authoring.misc	Miscellaneous Web authoring issues
comp.infosystems.www.browsers.mac	Web browsers for the Macintosh platform
comp.infosystems.www.browsers.misc	Web browsers for other platforms
comp.infosystems.www.browsers.ms-windows	Web browsers for MS Windows
comp.infosystems.www.browsers.x	Web browsers for the X-Window system
comp.infosystems.www.misc	Miscellaneous World Wide Web discussion
comp.infosystems.www.servers.mac	Web servers for the Macintosh platform
comp.infosystems.www.servers.misc	Web servers for other platforms
comp.infosystems.www.servers.ms-windows	Web servers for MS Windows and NT
comp.infosystems.www.servers.unix	Web servers for UNIX platforms
comp.os.os2.networking.www	World Wide Web (WWW) apps/utils under OS/2

Electronic Mailing Lists

Tip

These mailing lists tend to be of a more technical or administrative nature. (Post in newsgroups to ask questions about how to do something or where to find something on the WWW.)

▶ See "Top Internet Mailing Lists," p. 1073

There are several electronic mailing lists that are dedicated to the WWW. A number of them are run by the WWW Consortium (the following sections that contain no other subscribing information fall under this category). To subscribe to one of these groups, send e-mail to the address **listserv@w3.org** with the line:

subscribe *mailing_list_name your_name*

(Insert the name of the mailing list you want to join in place of *mailing_list_name* and your first and last name in place of *your_name*.)

www-lib

This mailing list contains discussions about architecture and new features, exchange of diffs, bug reports etc., for the W3C Reference Library. There is also a nice hypertext archive.

www-style

This mailing list contains a discussion of HTML style sheets to support standardization and implementations.

www-html

This mailing list is a technical discussion of the design and extension of the HTML language.

www-talk

This mailing list is for technical discussions among people who are interested in the development of WWW software.

www-security

This list discusses all aspects of security on the World-Wide Web.

To subscribe to the www-security mailing list, send an e-mail message to **www-security-request@nsmx.rutgers.edu** with the message body:

> subscribe www-security

This will subscribe the address that is in the mail header From field to the mailing list.

www-sites

This mailing list is for the discussing of issues of concern to commercial sites using World Wide Web technology.

To subscribe, send an e-mail message to **majordomo@qiclab.scn.rain.com** with the message body:

> subscribe www-sites Name *your_e-mail_address*

www-marketing

This list offers a discussion on how to use the web for sales and marketing.

To subscribe, send an e-mail message to **majordomo@xmission.com** with the message body:

> Subscribe www_marketing *your_e-mail_address*
>
> end

WWW Interactive Talk

WWW Interactive Talk (WIT) is a new type of discussion group that has been formed for the WWW. In some ways it is similar to UseNet newsgroups. The creators of this forum, however, have tried to overcome some of the limitations of the UseNet groups by structuring the discussion of a particular topic. Each topic is presented on a form that shows the topic and proposals for discussion about the topic. Under the proposals there are arguments for and against each proposal.

> **Note**
>
> The designers of WIT hope that this format allows readers to see if the topic has been adequately discussed before they submit their own comments. As a comparison, often in UseNet newsgroups, a point will be made over and over again, because readers respond before they see if someone else has already brought up the same point.

This is a new and somewhat experimental discussion format. Currently, there is a WIT discussion area set up at **http://www.w3.org/wit/hypertext/ WWW**. This area is not limited to WWW discussions (any topic can be introduced), but it is a place where you are likely to find some people to talk to you about the WWW.

The WWW Itself

Of course, one of the best places to find information about the WWW is on the WWW itself. Here are a few URLs that will take you places where you can find out more about the WWW and what can be found.

> **Note**
>
> When you view a document on the WWW, you are actually retrieving it from a computer somewhere on the Internet. When you do this, you are making demands on the Internet host that is providing the information, and also on the network itself. Please try to keep your document viewing to things that are of interest to you so that you don't make unnecessary demands on the network or individual Internet hosts.

World Wide Web Consortium
http://www.w3.org/hypertext/WWW/TheProject.html

This URL takes you to the World Wide Web Consortium. This document gives you pointers to WWW information. Some of the information you can find here includes: available client and server software; lists of WWW servers grouped by subject, by country, and by service; technical information about the WWW; and other background information.

NCSA Mosaic Demo Document
http://www.ncsa.uiuc.edu/demoweb/demo.html

Follow this URL to the NCSA Mosaic Demo Document. This document gives a brief description of Mosaic. Its main attraction, however, is a large list of interesting documents that can be found on the WWW.

InterNIC
http://ds.internic.net/cgi-bin/tochtml/0intro.dirofdirs/

This URL takes you to the InterNIC directory of directories at the main Internet Network Information Center. This resource is intended to help people locate information on specific topics. There are links from this document to many different lists of Internet resources. Many of these resources are in WWW format, or are accessible by one of the other Internet services (FTP, Gopher, and so on).

Entering the World Wide Web: A Guide to Cyberspace
http://www.eit.com/web/www.guide

This URL takes you to the document *Entering the World-Wide Web: A Guide to Cyberspace*. This document gives you a good overview of the World Wide Web, and points you to some interesting information repositories on the WWW.

Books

A number of books have been published recently to help you better understand and effectively use the WWW. Two books that you should reference are *Using the World Wide Web* and Special Edition *Using HTML*, both published by Que. Special Edition *Using HTML* gives you in-depth information on building exciting Web pages. *Using the World Wide Web* helps you understand what the WWW is and how to find the information you need most.

CHAPTER 21

Using Microsoft Internet Explorer

Until recently, there were only a few browsers available for the World Wide Web, but in the past year there has been an explosion of browsers. Many of these new browsers are based on the Mosaic browser (some look more like Mosaic than others), but these browsers have improved on the Mosaic interface to some degree.

One of the newest of these browsers is Microsoft's Internet Explorer, which comes bundled with the Microsoft Plus Pack for Windows 95 and is also available freely through Microsoft's WWW site. Internet Explorer is based on the Mosaic WWW browser, and the main improvement over Mosaic is the high level of integration with the Windows 95 operating system. This integration with Windows 95 allows you to use WWW Universal Resource Locators as shortcuts to WWW documents, and to place these shortcuts anywhere in your Windows 95 file system. Windows 95 treats these Internet shortcuts (as they are called by Microsoft) the same as any other shortcut.

In this chapter, you learn how to do the following:

- Set up Internet Explorer on your system
- Start up Internet Explorer and use its basic features
- Navigate the WWW with Internet Explorer
- Keep track of your favorite WWW documents

Setting Up Internet Explorer

Setting up Internet Explorer on a Windows 95 system is easy, especially if you have purchased the Plus! Pack for Windows 95. Microsoft has set up Internet Explorer to mesh easily with Windows 95; it can be installed and uninstalled through the Add/Remove Software control panel and takes advantage of Windows 95 networking to automatically start your network connection when you start Internet Explorer.

The basic system requirements for Internet Explorer are the same as those for Microsoft Windows 95 with the Plus! Pack installed; if your computer runs Windows 95 (and the Plus! Pack applications) satisfactorily, it should run Internet Explorer also.

Installing Internet Explorer from the Plus! Pack

If you have purchased the Microsoft Plus! Pack for Windows 95, you can install the Internet Explorer from the Plus! Pack installation disks. To install the Internet Explorer, open the Add/Remove Programs control panel, and select the Install button to install software. The Internet Explorer is part of the Internet Jumpstart kit, which includes the Internet Setup Wizard and the Dial-up Scripting tool (which is discussed in chapter 6, "Connecting to a PPP or SLIP Account with Windows 95").

Insert your Plus! Pack CD-ROM or floppy disk into your computer and select Next to select the installation media. Once the installation wizard has found the installation disk, you can select Finish to start the Plus! Pack setup program. Before Plus! proceeds with the installation, it first searches for Plus! components you have already installed.

When the Plus! Pack setup program starts, select the Add/Remove button to install Plus! Pack software. The setup program displays a list of the available software for the Plus! Pack. Select the Internet Jumpstart option and click the Continue button to start the installation. The setup program copies the necessary files onto your hard disk and sets up your system to use the Internet Explorer software.

Caution

If you uncheck one of the boxes for a component that is already installed on your system, the setup program will remove that component and you may lose the preferences or setup information for that component.

When the Internet Jumpstart software is installed, a new icon appears on your desktop. This icon (called The Internet) allows you to start Internet Explorer, as well as configure your connection to the Internet easily. In addition to the Internet Explorer software, the Internet Jumpstart includes the Internet Setup wizard which helps you easily set up your Internet connection.

By using the Properties option on the Internet icon, you can configure several very useful options for how Windows 95 operates with the Internet. For example, if you are using dial-up access to the Internet, you can configure Windows 95 to automatically start up your dial-up connection when you start a networking application (such as Internet Explorer). You can also configure a connection to automatically disconnect if you haven't used it for a while.

If you are directly connected to the Internet, the Internet Properties allows you to configure any proxy services that your network may have set up.

If you want to remove the Internet Explorer software, you can do so easily by starting the Plus! Pack setup program as above and unchecking the Internet Jumpstart software option. You can also use the Add/Remove Programs control panel to remove either the entire Plus! package or individual components.

Installing Internet Explorer without the Plus! Pack

If you have not purchased the Microsoft Plus! for Windows 95 package, you can still get the Internet Explorer (or you can get the latest version if you want to upgrade). Unfortunately, Microsoft has not yet made Internet Explorer available through their FTP server, but it is available through the Microsoft WWW page.

The current URL for downloading Internet Explorer is **http:// www.microsoft.com/windows/download/msie20.exe**. Save this executable on your local disk (preferably in a temporary directory).

To install Internet Explorer, double-click the filename from the Explorer. A dialog box is then displayed, informing you that Microsoft Internet Explorer version 2.0 will be installed. Click Yes to continue installing Internet Explorer. The installation application then displays the Internet Explorer license agreement. Click on the I Agree button to continue with the installation.

Next, the Internet Explorer files are installed onto your hard disk. The installation program tells you when the installation is complete, and advises you to restart your system to use Internet Explorer. Click OK to finish the installation.

Starting and Configuring Internet Explorer

Once you have installed Internet Explorer, you can start the program by double-clicking The Internet icon on your desktop. You can also start Internet Explorer through the Start Program menus, in the Internet Tools menu (which is in the Accessories menu).

The first time you start Internet Explorer, the Internet Setup Wizard starts and leads you through the setup process. The Wizard asks you whether you will connect to the Internet through a local network connection or through a dial-up connection. Then, the Wizard asks you to confirm the settings used for these connections. See chapter 5, "Connecting Through a LAN with Windows 95," for more information about these settings.

When you start Internet Explorer, the program automatically loads the Microsoft Network home page at the URL **http://www.msn.com**. (You can configure the program to start at any URL you like.) The Internet Explorer main window, showing the Microsoft Network home page, is shown in figure 21.1.

Fig. 21.1

The main Internet Explorer program window.

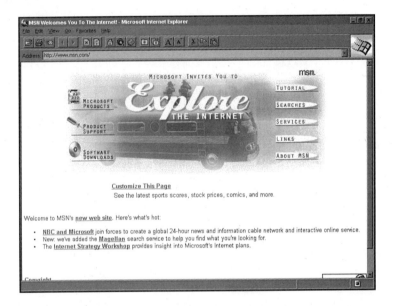

> **Note**
>
> If your connection to the Internet is not already active when you start Internet Explorer (and you have a dial-up connection defined on your system), you will be prompted whether you want to start up your Internet connection.

Understanding the Internet Explorer Display

The Internet Explorer window is made up of five main components (listed from the top of the display down to the bottom): the Menu bar, the toolbar, the address bar, the main page display window, and the status bar.

The toolbar contains 17 buttons that allow you to quickly perform most of the things you will do frequently when using the program. These toolbar buttons are shown in figure 21.2.

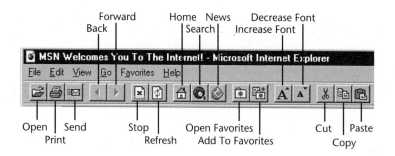

Fig. 21.2

The buttons on the Internet Explorer toolbar.

IV

The World Wide Web

The following list gives a basic description of what the buttons do:

- *Open* opens a URL, folder or local file.
- *Print* prints the current page.
- *Send* allows you to mail a shortcut to the current page to someone.
- *Back* moves to the previous page in the history list.
- *Forward* moves to the next page in the history list.
- *Stop* aborts the current operation in progress. You can also interrupt the current operation (if, for example, you discover that you don't really want to see the page you are downloading) by pressing the Esc key.
- *Refresh* reloads or refreshes the contents of the current document.
- *Home* opens the default Start page.
- *Search* opens the default Search page.
- *News* starts Internet Explorer's newsreading mode.
- *Open favorites* opens the folder with your favorite Internet shortcuts.
- *Add to favorites* adds the current page to your folder of favorite Internet shortcuts.
- *Increase font* displays the current document using a larger font.
- *Decrease font* displays the current document using a smaller font.
- *Cut* removes the current selection and copies it to the Clipboard.
- *Copy* copies the current selection to the Clipboard.
- *Paste* inserts the contents of the Clipboard to the current insertion point.

Right under the toolbar, Internet Explorer displays the address bar, which lists the current URL that is being displayed. As you move around the World Wide Web, it's fairly easy to lose track of where you are; the address bar allows you to keep track of your current URL or page location. You can also open a document by typing the URL or filename into the address bar. The drop-down menu on the address bar lists the files or URLs you have opened.

Tip

Selecting items from the URL/Internet shortcut list is sometimes difficult, since the entries are not very descriptive (most URLs don't tell you much about the document). The History list uses the document titles, which makes a better choice for revisiting documents.

Under the address bar is the main document display window. This window displays the current document.

At the bottom of the program is the status bar, which gives information about what Internet Explorer is currently doing. If, for example, Internet Explorer is in the process of loading a document, the status bar will indicate the document that is being loaded and the progress made in the loading process.

Configuring Internet Explorer

Internet Explorer can be configured in many ways, both in how the program displays documents and how it operates. Most of these options are set from the Options item found under the <u>V</u>iew menu. The exceptions are the options to display the toolbar, address bar and status bar, which are set directly from the <u>V</u>iew menu.

The Internet Explorer options page (open to the Appearance tab) is shown in figure 21.3.

Fig. 21.3
The Appearance tab of the Internet Explorer Options page.

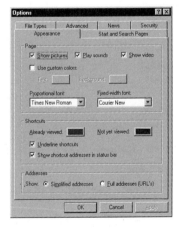

The Appearance tab allows you to set options that control how documents appear in the main display window. Options on this tab control whether images, sounds, and videos will be displayed automatically when the document is displayed. Options that control the fonts and colors of the text and links (called shortcuts in Internet Explorer) are also set on this page, as well as how addresses are shown in the address bar.

The Start and Search Page tab (shown in fig. 21.4) allows you to set the pages that are displayed when you click the Start and Search buttons on the toolbar. When you first install Internet Explorer, the "start" page is set to be **http://www.msn.com** and the "search" page is set to be **http://www.home.msn.com/access/allinone.htm**.

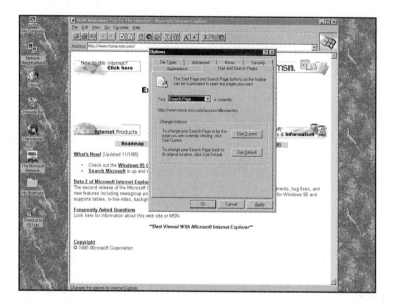

Fig. 21.4
Changing the start and search pages in Internet Explorer.

You can change the start or search page to be the document that is currently displayed by selecting the page you want to change from the drop-down menu and clicking the Use Current button. If you want to change the setting back to the default, click on the Use Default button.

The File Types tab (shown in fig. 21.5) allows you to change the programs that are started when a file is opened. This is the same operation as changing file associations through Windows 95 directly.

Fig. 21.5

Changing the file associations through Internet Explorer.

The Advanced tab (shown in fig. 21.6) allows you to change the history and document caching options. The History option tells Internet Explorer how many documents to remember in the history list. Since each document in the history list is a shortcut on your disk, you may want to reduce the number of documents in the history list if you are low on disk space.

Fig. 21.6

The Advanced tab sets the History and Cache options.

The Cache options control how Internet Explorer saves recent documents. To speed up redisplaying documents that you have recently visited, Internet Explorer saves (caches) recent documents on disk. The Cache controls allow you to set up the maximum amount of disk space that the cache can take up, and how often Internet Explorer checks to see if the cached files have changed.

The News tab sets the options for reading and posting UseNet news articles through Internet Explorer (see fig. 21.7). The tab has settings for the name of your UseNet news server (Internet Explorer uses the NNTP protocol to communicate with the server), and whether the server requires a login name and password to connect.

Fig. 21.7
Setting the UseNet
newsreading
options in Internet
Explorer.

The Posting options allow you to set the name and Internet e-mail addresses that are inserted in any UseNet posts you make. You should set these to be your real name and the e-mail address assigned by your Internet provider.

The Security tab allows you to control how often Internet Explorer will warn you about possible security problems when sending or receiving information over the Internet (see fig. 21.8). You can select whether you want Internet Explorer to warn you every time you send information to a WWW site, to warn you only if you send more than one field of information, or to never warn you about sending information.

Note

Sending information (such as a credit card number) over the Internet is a potential security problem because the information may be read by anyone who has a computer anywhere between your local Internet access provider and the remote Web site. While the possibility of this actually happening is small, it has happened and will probably continue to happen.

Some WWW browsers (such as Netscape) allow for more secure communication between your computer and Web sites.

The second part of the Security tab allows you to set up whether Internet Explorer will warn you when you enter and leave a secure site on the World Wide Web. These sites (generally running Netscape's secure Web server software) can keep track of the pages that you are viewing, so if you are concerned about the site knowing the pages you are downloading, you should leave this option set on High.

Fig. 21.8

Setting Security
options in Internet
Explorer.

Using the Internet Explorer Interface

◀ See "How the
World Wide
Web Works,"
p. 457

Internet Explorer is very similar in many ways to the Mosaic interface. Most
of the common tasks that you want to do when browsing the World Wide
Web with Internet Explorer can be done either by clicking links to URLs in
the main document display window or by clicking icons in the toolbar.

When Internet Explorer starts up, it displays the default home document as
defined on the Start and Search Page options tab. You can move between
documents on the World Wide Web in several different ways; you can click a
link in the document you are viewing, you can type in a URL to go directly
there, you can go to a URL that is saved in your history list (either by using
the back and forward buttons or selecting a URL directly from the history
list), or you can go to a document that is saved in your folder of favorite
URLs.

One of the main advantages of Internet Explorer over other Web browsers is
the high degree of integration between Internet Explorer and Windows 95.
Using Internet Explorer with Windows 95 allows you to copy a URL from
a document to your Windows 95 file system. These URLs become what
Microsoft calls Internet shortcuts, which act like file shortcuts in your file
system. By double-clicking an Internet shortcut, you can open the Web
document directly. You can also put Internet shortcuts into word processing
documents and even mail them to other people on the Internet.

When Internet Explorer is displaying a document, you can search for words
or phrases in the document by using the Find item on the Edit menu. This
brings up the regular Windows 95 Find text box, which will search the current document for the text you enter in the Find box. You have the option to
select whether the find is case-sensitive and whether the find starts at the top
of the page. Using Find is useful when the document you are displaying is
very large.

Using Links to Move Between Documents

The easiest way to move between documents is by clicking a link in the document that is being displayed. These links are usually shown in the document display by underlined text (or text that is in a different color). You can control how links are displayed by changing the options from the View, Options menu, on the Appearance options tab.

A link can be a word, group of words, or an image. When you move your cursor over a link, the cursor changes into the shape of a pointing hand. Looking at the page shown in figure 21.9, you can see several examples of links.

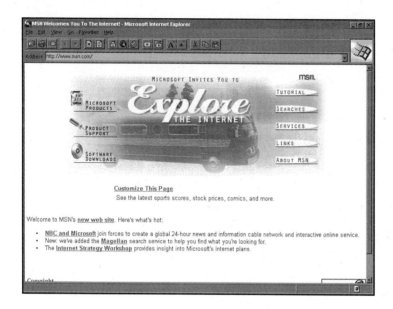

Fig. 21.9
Examples of hyperlinks in Internet Explorer.

Clicking a link causes Internet Explorer to load the document referred to in the link.

Opening URLs Directly

If you know the exact URL for a document, you can go directly to that document by opening the URL. This can be done in several ways. Clicking the Open icon on the toolbar brings up the Open Internet Address dialog box, shown in figure 21.10. This dialog box allows you to type in a URL into the Address box and open the document. The Address box has a drop-down list of the last documents you have opened, so you can quickly re-open them.

The Open Internet Address dialog box has the option to open the document in a new Internet Explorer window, and also allows you to open a file stored on your local disk (or local network) directly. Use the Open File button to bring up the standard Windows 95 file open dialog box.

Fig. 21.10

Opening a
document URL
through the Open
Internet Address
dialog box.

You can also open a URL document directly by typing the URL into the address box on the address bar. The address box also has a drop-down list of the last documents you have opened.

Note

If the address bar is not displayed on your Internet Explorer window, you can display it by selecting Address Bar from the View menu.

Using the History List

Internet Explorer, like most Web browsers, maintains a list of the documents that you have displayed during your exploration of the World Wide Web. This list, called the history list, allows you to backtrack through the documents you visit, without having to remember where you have been.

Unless you change the default history options, Internet Explorer keeps track of the last 300 documents you have displayed and stores these links (which are really just Internet shortcuts) in the folder C:\Program Files\Plus!\Microsoft Internet\history. You can, of course, change both the number of documents saved in the history folder and the folder they are placed in through the Advanced Options tab.

The past few documents in your history folder are quickly available through the File menu. This history list (shown in fig. 21.11) lists the most recent documents you have visited, sorted in alphabetic order. The document you are currently viewing is checked. You can display any of these documents by selecting the document name from the list.

You can, of course, move forwards and backwards through the history list by using the Back and Forwards buttons on the toolbar. These buttons will be active if you have documents before or after the current document in the history list.

If you want to show the entire list of documents in your history folder, you can select <u>M</u>ore history from the <u>F</u>ile menu. This opens the history folder (as shown in fig. 21.12), which contains the Internet shortcuts for the documents on your history list.

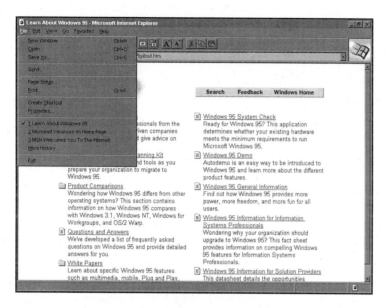

Fig. 21.11
The history list is shown on the <u>F</u>ile menu.

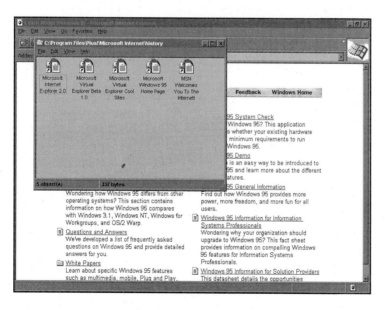

Fig. 21.12
The history folder holds Internet shortcuts for your history list.

You can use these shortcuts the same as any other shortcut in Windows 95. You can copy them to other folders, move them to your desktop, include them in documents, or mail them to other Windows 95 users. This feature, one of the most powerful in Internet Explorer, allows you to easily add links to WWW documents to your system and documents.

Unlike some other browsers, the history list remains intact after Internet Explorer is closed. When you start Internet Explorer the next time, the history list is still intact. While this allows you to keep track of documents you have seen between sessions, it can also present a potential problem with privacy, since anyone who has access to your computer can find the documents you have viewed. You can clear the history list by selecting the Empty button on View, Options menu, Advanced Options tab.

Using the Favorites List

Another way that Internet Explorer allows you to organize your documents is the Favorites list. This list, which is separate from the history list, allows you to add a document to the list of favorites, and to organize the favorites into folders.

The Favorites list is maintained by using options under the Favorites menu. Items on this menu allow you to Add the current document to the favorites folder, to Open the favorites folder, and to quickly move to the most recent additions to the favorites folder.

When you select Add to favorites from the Favorites menu, the standard Windows 95 File Save dialog box is displayed, allowing you to save the Internet shortcut into the favorites folder (or anywhere else in your file system, for that matter). You can create folders within your favorites folder, to group Internet shortcuts by categories that make sense to you.

When you select the Open favorites item from the Favorites menu, the favorites folder (shown in fig. 21.13) is displayed. This display is a standard Windows 95 Explorer window, which allows you to create new folders, and move or rename your Internet shortcuts as desired.

From the Favorites menu, you can also display the most recent additions to the favorites folder, by selecting one of the document URLs from the list.

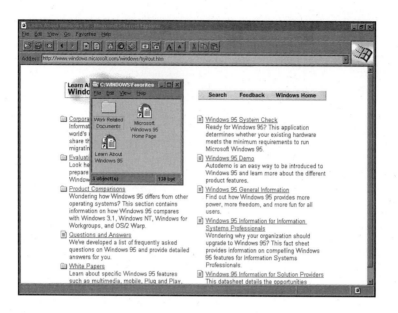

Fig. 21.13
The Favorites
folder is displayed,
showing several
shortcuts.

Mailing, Saving, and Printing Documents

Internet Explorer allows you to easily save and print the current document, and also to mail a shortcut to the document to someone else on the Internet.

The Save As option, found under the File menu, allows you to save the HTML source for the current document into a file on your local disk. The standard Windows 95 Save As dialog box is used.

You can also view the HTML source for the document you are currently viewing by selecting the Source option under the View menu. This brings up a new window displaying the HTML source for the current document. The HTML source is viewed using the Notepad editor, so you can save or edit the HTML source if you like.

The Print option, found under the File menu, allows you to print the current document on your printer. The standard Windows 95 printing dialog boxes are used. You can also use the Print button on the toolbar to print the current document.

You can send a shortcut to the current document to another Internet user by using the Send option, found under the File menu, or by clicking the Send button on the toolbar. This brings up a dialog box asking which of your Microsoft Exchange profiles you want to use to send the shortcut. Normally, you will use the Internet Mail profile, which brings up the mail page, as shown in figure 21.14.

Fig. 21.14

Mailing an Internet shortcut using Internet mail.

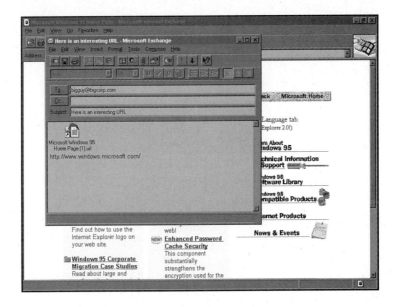

You must fill in the e-mail address you are sending the document shortcut to (in the To box), as well as an optional CC and Subject for the e-mail message. When you are finished composing the message, you can send the message by clicking the Send button (the button with the envelope).

Reading UseNet News with Internet Explorer

▶ See "Using NewsXpress," p. 775

▶ See "Using Agent," p. 791

While Internet Explorer is certainly not a full-featured UseNet newsreader, it does provide enough functionality that you can use it to read a fair amount of news. If you read more than a few newsgroups, or groups that have more than a few dozen messages a day, you will probably want to use a richer newsreader, such as Agent or NewsXpress.

Using Internet Explorer to read your news does provide the ability to automatically follow any URLs that are mentioned in news articles, and the ability to easily follow threads of articles, since articles with the same subject are linked together (using hypertext links).

▶ See "How UseNet Works," p. 749

To start reading news with Internet Explorer, select Read Newsgroups from the Go menu. The server that is used by Internet Explorer to read UseNet news is set on the News Options tab. When you first start reading UseNet news with Internet Explorer, the program downloads a list of the news groups that are available on the news server and displays this list (shown in fig. 21.15).

Tip

If you have problems reading news with Internet Explorer, check your settings for reading news (View, Options, News) to make sure that you have specified the news server correctly. If your server requires a username and password, make sure the values you have entered are correct. If the settings seem correct and you still have problems, check with the administrator of your news server to make sure you have permission to read news from the server.

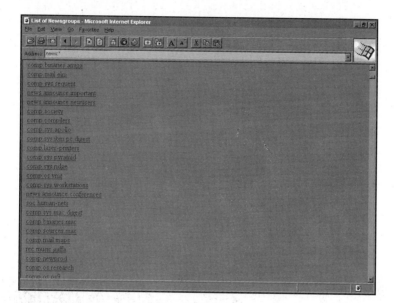

Fig. 21.15
The list of available UseNet newsgroups.

Note

Unfortunately, Internet Explorer presents the list of available newsgroups in the order that they are defined on the news server, not in alphabetic or any other order. You can use the Find option (located on the Edit menu) to look for a newsgroup you want.

Internet Explorer also does not indicate how many articles are available in the group before you start reading it.

You can start reading a UseNet group by clicking the group link. This opens the newsgroup and displays the 20 most recent articles in the group, giving the article number and subject of the article, along with the author of the article. In addition, the newsgroup display (shown in fig. 21.16) has links to display earlier articles and to post a new article in this newsgroup; it also indicates the number of articles in the group.

Fig. 21.16
The newsgroup display of the group **comp.infosystems. www.announce**.

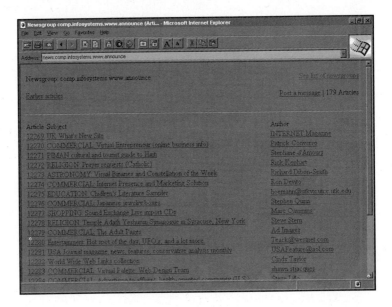

To read an article that is displayed on the list of articles, click anywhere in the listing for the article. Internet Explorer downloads the article and displays it (as shown in fig. 21.17). Any URLs that are listed in the article are shown as hypertext links, as are references to any other UseNet news articles. This makes it easy to locate any referenced documents or articles, by clicking the link.

Note that when you are reading an article, you have options (near the top of the display) to move to the next article or the previous article. You can also post a response to this article, or move back to the list of available articles.

Posting a response brings up the display shown in figure 21.18. This window allows you to edit the article you are posting. Note that the article you are responding to is included in the new article you are posting—you can (and should) edit the text to cut out any unnecessary information. When you are done editing your post, click the Post button to send your post to the news server.

Posting a new article in the newsgroup (which is done from the Newsgroup listing page) is similar to posting a response, except that the editing window is empty.

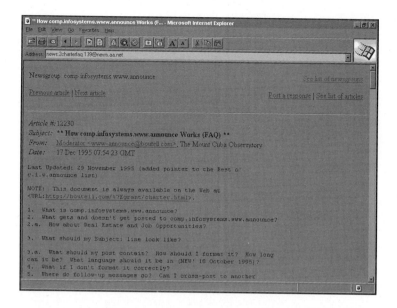

Fig. 21.17
Displaying an article in Internet Explorer.

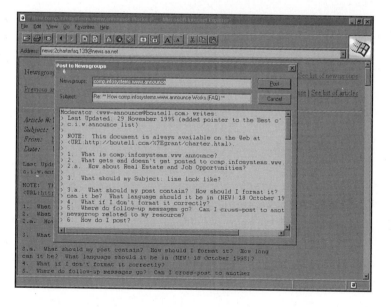

Fig. 21.18
Posting a response to a news article.

Viewing Multimedia Files with Internet Explorer

Along with most other Web browsers, Internet Explorer allows you to automatically process pictures, movies, and audio files when they are included in documents on the Internet. If you are connected to the Internet through a slow link (such as a modem running at less than 14.4 kbps) you can disable the automatic processing of these multimedia files by unchecking the options on the Appearance tab of the Options page.

Internet Explorer uses the content type of the multimedia file to determine how to display it on your system. Most WWW servers will tell the Web browser what type of file is being sent when the file is selected (for example, a picture in the Graphics Interchange Format is sent in image/gif format).

The viewer for the document types is defined on the File types tab of the Options page. Internet Explorer can display many file types automatically, but for some (such as images in Paintbrush format), an external viewer can be set. These file associations are the same as the normal Windows 95 file associations, so if you already have a viewer defined for a particular file type, Internet Explorer will use that viewer automatically.

Viewing Graphics Images with Internet Explorer

Internet Explorer eliminates the need for external viewers for the most common graphics formats by including built-in support for .GIF and .JPEG formats. Files in these formats are displayed inline if they are part of an HTML file, or on a new page if they are loaded separately.

Viewing Animations with Internet Explorer

One of the extensions that Microsoft has added to the Internet Explorer is the ability to display inline animations by including a viewer for files in the .AVI format. These can be displayed as part of a regular HTML page and shown just like a static image. No configuration is needed to display these inline animations; although if you are running over a slow link, you may want to disable these displays to cut down on the time needed to load pages.

In addition, Explorer allows the display of what Microsoft calls Marquee text, which is a line of text that scrolls horizontally across the page. This is useful for displaying items like a tip of the day, or for an item that you want to draw attention. Because these marquees are just text strings, loading them doesn't take much time, and allows for quick display.

You can view an example of inline animations, along with other Internet Explorer features, by viewing the URL **http://www.windows.microsoft.com/windows/ie/iedemo.htm**, a demonstration page for the features of Internet Explorer.

Playing Background Sounds with Internet Explorer

Another extension that Microsoft has added to Internet Explorer is the ability to load and play sounds along with the rest of the document you are displaying. These sounds, which can be in Windows .WAV, .MIDI, .AU, or .AIFF formats, are played either once or repeatedly (depending on how the document is set up).

No configuration needs to be done to set up the playing of background sounds (because this is built in to Internet Explorer), but if you are connecting to the Internet through a slow link, you might consider turning off the option to play sounds in the Options page of the View menu. Turning off sounds can greatly speed up loading of documents that have sounds in them, because sound files tend to be large.

Viewing VRML Sites with Internet Explorer

One of the most exciting (and newest) additions to Internet Explorer is the ability to view sites that use the Virtual Reality Modeling Language to display and manipulate VRML worlds. This ability is done through the Microsoft Virtual Explorer add-on, which is available through the WWW at the URL **http://www.windows.microsoft.com/windows/ie/vrml.htm**.

In order to use Virtual Explorer, you must be running Internet Explorer version 2.0. Installing Virtual Explorer is as simple as downloading the self-extracting executable with Internet Explorer, and confirming the installation through the dialog boxes.

Once Virtual Explorer is installed, you can explore the VRML features by starting at the URL **http://www.windows.microsoft.com/windows/ie/sites.html**, shown in figure 21.19. This document loads a demonstration virtual world and allows you to try out the VRML controls to move through this world. This document also lists several other sites that have virtual worlds for you to explore.

The VRML controls are shown under the main picture, and they allow you to slide your viewpoint (using the left control), move your viewpoint through the world (using the middle control), or tilt the view of the virtual world (using the right control). You simply click and hold the left mouse button on one of the controls, and move the mouse pointer in the direction you want to move your viewpoint.

The menu button on the left side of the control panel allows you to set up options that control how Virtual Explorer displays graphics. If the display of the virtual world seems slow, you can improve things by turning off the loading of textures and inlines.

Fig. 21.19

The Microsoft
Demonstration
Virtual World,
using Virtual
Explorer.

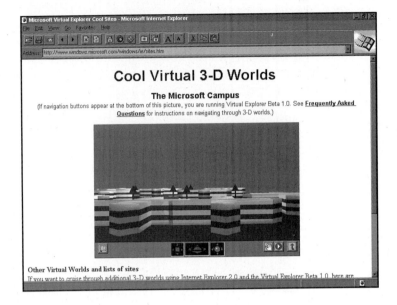

Virtual Explorer is still in an early beta, but it is a good demonstration of what may be the future of the World Wide Web and the Internet in general.

Other Internet Explorer Features

When Internet Explorer is loading a document, it will display a series of status messages in the status bar at the bottom of the display. Normally, these status messages are only briefly displayed, but if you are loading a large document or your Internet connection is particularly slow (or the WWW server you are connecting to is slow), these status messages can give you an idea of what is going on.

When you first open a URL, Internet Explorer displays the `looking up <host>` (where `<host>` is replaced by the host name of the URL). This is when Internet Explorer is checking to see if the host exists and what the IP address of the host is.

This is usually followed by the status message `contacting <host>`, where Internet Explorer tries to send the document request to the remote server.

Usually, if the remote server is up, Internet Explorer will start receiving the document requested and will display—through the percentage indicator at the right side of the status bar—an indication of the document being received and how much of the document has been received. This can be a valuable indication of how long the document will take to load. So if it appears that the reception process is going very slowly, you can abort the transfer.

> **Note**
>
> During the process of receiving a document, you will note that the Microsoft Windows 95 logo in the upper-right corner will have clouds moving behind it. This is a good visual indication that Internet Explorer is busy with an online task.

The status bar also indicates the URL of a link when you move your mouse cursor over the link. This is valuable when you want to know the exact URL of a link before loading it.

Another nice feature of Internet Explorer is the ability to increase or decrease the fonts used in the display of a document. Using the Fonts menu (which is found on the View menu), you can select a larger or smaller font for the current document. You can also use the Increase font and Decrease font buttons (on the toolbar) to do the same thing.

IV

The World Wide Web

CHAPTER 22

Using Netscape

Netscape is another popular Web browser that you can pick up on the Net. Although not free, Netscape is no more expensive than many of the commercial games that you might purchase—and it's a great deal more useful. Netscape has many nice features, including background image loading, secure data transmission, and multiple document windows.

In this chapter, you learn how to do the following:

- How to find and install Netscape 2.0
- How to use the Netscape interface
- How to navigate the Web with Netscape
- How to customize Netscape to your taste

Getting Netscape Up and Running

Trying the Netscape browser is easy. If you have an FTP program, you can retrieve the browser and evaluate it for 90 days for free (after that, you have to register and pay for it). Before you get the software, however, you should make sure that your system is properly set up to run Netscape. When you do get the Netscape software, you probably will want to get some external applications that allow you to automatically view movies, hear sounds, and experience all the multimedia documents that are available on the Web.

Will Your Computer Run Netscape?

Before you can run.Netscape for Windows on your personal computer, you must make sure that your computer system is capable of running the software. Although this requirement may seem to be fairly basic, it is disappointing (not to mention annoying) to spend several hours getting software and setting it up, only to discover that Netscape does not run under your operating system or that your modem is too slow to use Netscape effectively.

First, your computer system must be capable of running Microsoft Windows 95 (there are versions of Netscape for the 16-bit versions of Windows, but in this book, we are focusing on the use of Internet applications with Windows 95). If you do not already have Windows 95, you must purchase and install this software before you can run the 32-bit version of Netscape.

The basic Netscape for Windows configuration requires about 2.2MB of disk space for the Netscape software and documentation. You also need some temporary disk space (about 1M) to hold the compressed Netscape files while you are unpacking them. In addition to this basic disk space requirement, Netscape requires some disk space to hold temporary files while it is running; disk space for documents that you want to store locally; and disk space for any viewers that you need to display movies, image files, sound files, and so on.

◄ See "The Various Ways to Connect to the Internet: Which One Is Right for You?" p. 101

Needless to say, if you want to take full advantage of Netscape and use it to browse the WWW, you need an Internet account. If your PC is not directly connected to the Internet via Ethernet and you are using a SLIP or PPP connection, you need a relatively fast modem (14,400 bps is the minimum recommended speed, although the Netscape documentation says that 9,600 will work).

In addition to the system requirements, Netscape for Windows requires a direct connection to the Internet, through an Ethernet card in your system or through some kind of modem connection.

Where to Get Netscape

► See "What Is FTP?" p. 837

Although the Netscape software is not free, it is available through anonymous FTP. Netscape Communications Incorporated is allowing people to pick up the software from its FTP site, use the software for a 90-day trial period, and then pay for the software (a moderate $39 at the time this book went to press) if they decide to keep it. This section discusses how to get this software.

Note

Netscape Communications usually has available a released version of their software that you can purchase with or without documentation, for which they will provide support. They also often make available the next version of their software which is still under development (called a beta version). They do not charge a fee for use of the beta version, but the software does expire (becomes non-functional) after a certain date.

The basic Netscape software is available through anonymous FTP at the machine **ftp.netscape.com**. You can find either the latest released version of the software, or the latest beta version. The beta version can be found under the 2.0beta/windows directory. This directory has both a 16- and 32-bit version of the Netscape beta; be sure to pick up the 32-bit version to use with Windows 95, located in the file N32E20B3.EXE.

Note

In Windows 95, you store your files in *folders*. Many other operating systems use the term *directory*. Some FTP programs (like WS_FTP) simply show you the names of the directories on the remote host (and on your local machine), not using the iconic folder representation for the directories. For that reason, the term directory has been used when discussing the retrieval of files from FTP servers. If you use a graphical FTP client other than WS_FTP (or if you use a Web browser to retrieve files from the FTP server), you may see the directories represented as folders.

Tip

If you have an older version of Netscape (or another Web browser, such as Microsoft Internet Explorer), you can go to the Netscape home page (**http:// home.netscape.com**), follow the links to the latest version of Netscape, and download it from there.

If you have a Windows-based FTP program, such as WS_FTP (included on the NetCD95 that comes with this book), and you want to retrieve the Netscape software from the Internet, use the following procedure:

NetCD95

1. Connect to your Internet provider.

2. Start the FTP program.

3. Click Connect, and enter the address of the site that you are using. Enter **anonymous** as the user ID and your e-mail address as the password.

4. Navigate to the directory that contains the Netscape software on the Remote System.

5. When you reach the correct location, select the files to be transferred and initiate the transfer.

6. After transferring all the files you need, close your FTP connection; then exit FTP.

You may encounter one problem in obtaining the Netscape software; because this software is so popular, the Netscape site often is very busy. A limited number of users can connect to the site at the same time; at busy times, you may not be able to connect. Netscape communications has a number of different anonymous FTP machines available; try adding a number from 2 to 8 after "ftp" in the host name (for example, **ftp4.netscape.com**) to reach a less-busy machine. Or, there are a number of mirror sites where you can pick up the software, shown in table 22.1.

Table 22.1   Netscape Mirror Sites
http://mistral.enst.fr/netscape/
ftp://ftp.pu-toyama.ac.jp/pub/net/WWW/netscape
ftp://ftp.eos.hokudai.ac.jp/pub/WWW/Netscape
ftp://ftp.nc.nihon-u.ac.jp:/pub/network/WWW/client/netscape
ftp://ftp.leo.chubu.ac.jp/pub/WWW/netscape
ftp://ftp.tohoku.ac.jp/pub/network/www/Netscape
ftp://server.berkeley.edu/pub/netscape/

Another thing to keep in mind when you are looking for this software is that just as you move files around on your computer, the system administrators of the FTP sites occasionally move files or rename directories. If you can't find the files that you are looking for, look in another directory; they may be somewhere else.

Obtaining Auxiliary Software for Netscape

Although Netscape directly displays the text and inline graphics from HTML documents, you may want to obtain additional software to enable Netscape to handle pictures, sounds, and animations (movies). Chapter 24, "Using Helper Apps," discusses how to get and install viewers.

Installing Netscape on Your System

Since this version of Netscape is specifically for Windows 95, you should use the Programs Wizard to install the software. To set up the software, follow these steps:

1. Move the Netscape self-extracting file you retrieved from the FTP site to a temporary folder on your hard drive (for example, C:\install).

2. Run the self-extracting file by double-clicking it in the Windows Explorer, or by selecting Run from the Start button and typing in the path and name of the file (for example, C:\install\n32e20b3.exe).

   A DOS window appears, showing you the files that are being extracted from the self-extracting file. If any of the files being extracted currently exist, you are asked if it is OK to overwrite them. When all the files have been extracted, close the DOS window (if it hasn't closed by itself). The temporary folder now contains the original self-extracting file and several other files.

3. From the Start button select Settings, Control Panel.

4. Double-click the Add/Remove Programs icon.

5. Click Install.

6. Click Next.

7. Click Browse.

8. Find and open the folder containing the Netscape files (C:\install in this example).

9. Select the Setup.exe file and click Open.

10. Select Finish.

11. Follow the instructions in the Setup program. It suggests exiting all Windows programs while the installation is done, asks you where you would like to put your Netscape files, and performs the installation.

12. You will get a dialog box stating that your Netscape setup is complete. Click OK to close this dialog box. You then get a dialog box asking if you want to read the README file. Click Yes to read the file or No to exit to Windows.

13. When the setup finishes, it will leave an open window showing the contents of the Netscape/Program/Navigator folder, containing shortcuts to Netscape and its Readme file. Close this window.

14. The setup of the Netscape software is now complete. You can remove the files from the temporary folder; they are no longer needed.

IV

The World Wide Web

> **Note**
>
> You can easily add Netscape to your Start Menu/Programs item. Open the Program folder that is in the folder where you installed Netscape. Drag the Navigator folder from Program to your desktop. Open the Windows folder, then open the Start Menu folder (if multiple people have profiles on your PC, you'll need to open the Profiles folder under the Windows folder, then open the Start Menu under your personal folder). Drag the Navigator folder from the desktop to the Programs folder under the Start Menu folder.
>
> Now when you open the Start menu and select Programs from the taskbar, you will find an item called Navigator that will allow you to start Netscape Navigator.

Although you can customize the Netscape software to meet your needs, you can run the software without any further work. You will, of course, need to set up your Internet-connection software before using Netscape to access WWW documents.

Using the Netscape Interface

After you have installed all the software that you need to run Netscape, you can connect to your Internet provider and start Netscape. Netscape is a powerful application, but it is graphically oriented and not difficult to use after you are familiar with all of its features.

Starting Netscape

Before starting Netscape, you should be connected to the Internet. If your Internet connection is via your LAN, be sure that you are logged on to your network. If you are connected to the Internet through a modem, start your TCP/IP software, and log in to your account.

After you establish your Internet connection, open the Start menu and select Programs, Navigator, Netscape Navigator. Netscape starts up, and you are ready to explore the Internet with Netscape.

The Netscape Window

When Netscape starts, it loads the document that is specified as the home page in the Preferences dialog box (choose Options, General Preferences). Unless you have specified a personal home page, your window should look like the one shown in figure 22.1 (which shows the default Netscape welcome page).

Title bar   Menu bar   Toolbar   Location field   Directory buttons

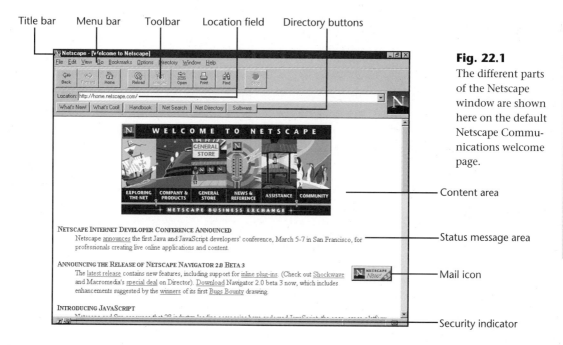

IV

The World Wide Web

Fig. 22.1
The different parts
of the Netscape
window are shown
here on the default
Netscape Commu-
nications welcome
page.

Content area

Status message area

Mail icon

Security indicator

The URL for the default home page is the following:

http://home.netscape.com

The following list briefly describes each window part. The remainder of this
chapter contains detailed discussion of Netscape's features.

- The *title bar* contains the usual window-function buttons (control
  menu, Maximize, Minimize, and Close buttons), as well as the name of
  the application (Netscape) and the name of the WWW document that
  you are viewing.

- The *menu bar* gives you access to all the functions that you need to use
  Netscape. You can retrieve documents to view, print documents, customize your Netscape window, navigate between documents, annotate
  documents, save files, and access Netscape's online help system.

- The *location field* shows the URL of the current document. When you
  open a document, its URL is displayed, and the Netscape logo (at the
  right end of the bar) blinks while the document is being retrieved.

- The *directory buttons* give you quick access to some items in the Directory menu.

- The *content area* is the area of the window in which you see the text of a
  document and any inline images that it may contain.

■ The *status bar* serves two functions. The first is to display host connection and document loading information. While Netscape is loading your document, it shows the progress of the different document elements (text and individual graphics) that are being loaded, using a counter to show the number of bytes loaded compared with the total size of the document or image that is being loaded.

When you are viewing a document, the status bar shows the URL of the hyperlink on which your cursor rests.

■ The *progress bar* to the right of the status bar is a bar graph showing what percentage of the entire document has been loaded.

■ The *security indicator* to the left of the status bar is key symbol that indicates the security status of your document. If the key is broken, the current document is not secure. If the key is unbroken on a blue background, the document is secure.

■ The *mail icon* to the right of the progress bar opens the Mail window and checks for new messages.

■ The *toolbar* gives you quick access to some of the most-used features in Netscape (see fig. 22.2). By default, the toolbar contains buttons labeled to describe the actions that they perform. You can configure the toolbar to show pictures that represent the actions or pictures with the descriptions printed below them.

Fig. 22.2
The buttons in the toolbar are found at the top of the screen.

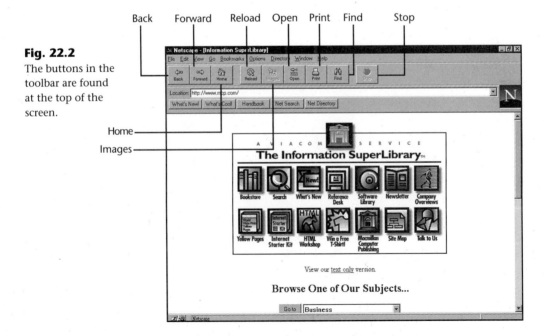

The following list provides basic descriptions of the toolbar buttons:

■ *Back* displays the preceding document in the history list.

■ *Forward* displays the following document in the history list.

■ *Home* goes to the default home page.

■ *Reload* reloads the current document.

■ *Images* loads the images in a document if you had image loading turned off.

■ *Open* enables you to open a URL.

■ *Print* sends the currently loaded document to your printer.

■ *Find* locates a text string in the current document.

■ *Stop* stops the loading process for the current document.

What Is a Home Page?

Your home page (or home document) is the document that you tell Netscape to display when it starts. This document should contain links to the documents and WWW sites that you use most frequently. Many people mistakenly use the term home page for the welcome page that you see when you connect to a WWW site. A home page gives you access to the WWW sites or documents that you use most. Your project or company may have its own home page to give members easy access to needed information. You can load someone else's home page or design your own.

When you start the Netscape software, it comes with the home page predefined as the Netscape Communications Corporation welcome page. You probably will want to change this page, because the Netscape page may not be very useful to you. In addition, retrieving a document causes a load on the machine on which the document is located. If everyone used the Netscape welcome page as his or her home page, the Netscape WWW server would become considerably slower.

Telling Netscape What Home Page to Load

Netscape allows you to set your home page in its Preferences dialog box. To use the Preferences dialog box, follow these steps:

1. Choose Options, General Preferences. The Preferences dialog box appears. The Appearance sheet should be displayed (see fig. 22.3).

Fig. 22.3

The Preferences dialog box lets you configure different Netscape features. You can set what home page to load (if any) on the Appearance sheet.

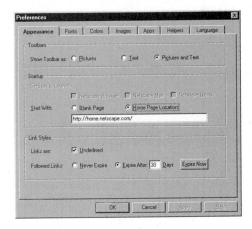

2. If you want a home page to be displayed, choose the Home Page Location radio button. (Choose the Blank Page radio button if you don't want to load a home page.)

3. Click the text box below the Home Page Location radio button.

4. Enter the URL of the document that you want to use as your home page.

5. Choose OK to save your home page setting and exit the Preferences dialog box.

> ### Tip
>
> You can click the Home button (the one that looks like a house, if you have pictures turned on) in the toolbar to reload your home page quickly.

Your home page can be a document on your computer or any document that you can access at a WWW site. (See chapter 25, "Planning Your Own WWW Home Pages," for details on creating your own home page or turning a file that's saved on your computer into a home page.)

When you start Netscape, the document that you defined as your home page will be displayed in the content area. After the home page loads, the URL for your home page appears in the location bar (if you have the location bar enabled). When your home page is loaded, you can click any of the links on your home page to load the documents that you use frequently.

If you want to return to your home page at any time, open the Go menu and choose Home. This command reloads your home-page document.

Moving Between Documents

After you start Netscape, you can move between WWW documents in several ways; you can click links in the document that you are viewing, or you can use Netscape's Open Location dialog box to enter a URL. You can also type a URL directly into the text box in the location field (press Enter at the end of the URL to load that document).

If you loaded a home page, that page probably includes links to other documents. After all, the purpose of the WWW is to enable you to move between related documents quickly without having to enter long path names. If a document contains no links, it's not a very useful WWW document. But even if your current document has no links, you can still move between documents by entering the URLs for the documents that you want to view.

> **Note**
>
> Netscape gives you a few other ways to move between documents. You can use Bookmarks that contain items with predefined URLs. Creating and using Bookmarks is covered in the section "Create Lists of Your Favorite URLs," later in this chapter.
>
> In addition, the Directory menu gives you access to some interesting, important Internet documents, and directory buttons enable you to load these documents quickly.

Using Links to Move Between Documents

A link can be a word, a group of words, or an image. Netscape can indicate the hypertext links in a document in several different ways. If you have a color monitor, the links can be displayed in blue and other text in black. (Graphics that contain links can be outlined in blue.) If you have a black-and-white monitor, the links can be underlined (the default).

◀ See "Hypertext (and Hypermedia)," p. 459

If you have a color display, Netscape enables you to keep track of the links that you've visited recently. After you load a document, the next time you come across a link to that document, the link is displayed in magenta rather than blue. You can set up Netscape so that the memory of your visit to a link expires after a certain period of time (or you can set it so that it never expires). You also can reset the expiration date of all links so that all links start out blue again.

IV

The World Wide Web

When you move your cursor over an area of the screen that contains an active link, your cursor changes from an arrow to a pointing hand. The URL associated with each link that you pass over appears in the status bar (if the status bar is enabled). To activate a link, click it. Netscape loads that document and displays the URL for the document in the location bar (if the location bar is enabled).

Look at the Netscape home page in figure 22.4. The phrases Java, Plug-ins, LiveScript, and WebFX's VRML plug-in, Netscape Bugs Bounty Program, Learn more, download now, Netscape Navigator Personal Edition, and lead position are links. When you run Netscape on a color display, you see the links in blue (they are underlined in the figure), which is the default hyperlink color. The URL of the active link (with the pointing-hand pointer over it) appears in the status bar.

Fig. 22.4
The Netscape home page shows the hyperlinks underlined.

Cursor over active link

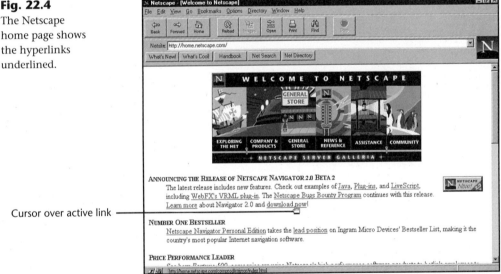

Customizing the Hyperlink Indicators

You can change the default appearance and color of the hyperlinks in the documents that Netscape loads. To customize Netscape's link attributes, follow these steps:

1. Choose Options, General Preferences. The Appearance sheet should be displayed in the Preferences dialog box.

2. To have links underlined in a document, select the Underlined checkbox.

3. You can set the number of days after which followed links (URLs that you've previously loaded) expire. Click the box next to the Expire After radio button, and enter the number of days. When the amount of time since you have accessed a link is longer than this time, the link becomes blue again.

   If you click the Never Expire radio button, any link that you follow will be shown in magenta until you clear all links.

4. Click Expire Now to clear the expiration information from all of your links immediately. A confirmation box appears, asking whether you definitely want to mark all of your links as not visited. If you choose Yes, all links will be displayed in blue, whether or not you have accessed them recently (until you access them again). Choose Cancel to leave the expiration information on your links as is.

5. When you have the options set to your satisfaction, choose OK.

You can also change the color of your new and followed links. To do so, see the section "Setting Netscape's Color Scheme," later in this chapter.

Moving Backward and Forward

Typing long URLs and scrolling through documents to look for the links you want can get rather tedious. If you're jumping between several documents, take advantage of three helpful navigating commands: Back, Forward, and Reload.

Netscape keeps information about what documents you have loaded (see the discussion of the history list in "How to Get Where You Were," later in this chapter) and allows you to move between these documents quickly by using the Back and Forward commands. The Back command takes you to the preceding document that you had open. To go back, choose Go, Back.

The next command is Forward. What you have to remember about Forward is that you can move forward only after moving back. (This concept is rather confusing, but it will make more sense after you read about history lists in "How to Get Where You Were," later in this chapter.) To move forward, choose Go, Forward.

The last command is Reload. This command redisplays the document that you are currently viewing. To reload the current document, choose Go, Reload.

Using URLs to Move Between Documents

◀ See "Using
Links to Move
between Docu-
ments," p. 483

If you don't want to go to any of the documents for which links are displayed
in the current document, or if you did not load a home page (you do not currently have a document displayed), you can load a new document by specifying its URL to Netscape. Refer to chapter 20, "How the World Wide Web
Works," for information on how to correctly format a URL. To enter a URL
directly, follow these steps:

1. Choose File, Open Location and the Open Location dialog box appears
(see fig. 22.5).

Fig. 22.5
The Open
Location dialog
box allows you to
directly enter the
URL for the next
document that
you want to view.

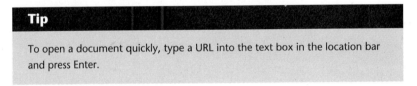

2. To open a new document, enter a new URL in the box.

> **Tip**
>
> To open a document quickly, type a URL into the text box in the location bar
> and press Enter.

3. Choose Open to load the URL that you entered, or click Cancel if you
do not want to load that document.

Opening Multiple Documents

A very useful feature of Netscape is its capability to display multiple documents at the same time. To open another document window, choose File,
New Web Browser. This window has the same history list as the window from
which it was opened, with the displayed document being the oldest document in the history list. You now can view any document you want in any of
the open Netscape document windows.

Caching Documents

When you are reading documents, you often move back and forth between
one document and others that are linked to that document. To keep from
having to load a document every time you view it, Netscape keeps copies of
the last few documents that you viewed on your local computer. Keeping
copies of previously viewed documents is called *caching*.

Caching keeps Netscape from making unnecessary demands on Internet resources. Caching does take up resources on your own computer, though, so you can cache only a limited number of documents. Netscape enables you to specify the amount of memory and disk that it can use for caching. Follow these steps:

1. Choose Options, Network Preferences. The Cache sheet should appear in the Preferences window (see fig. 22.6).

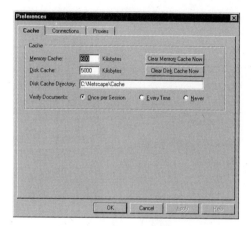

Fig. 22.6
Set the amount of memory and disk space to as much as you can spare to keep from reloading documents frequently.

2. The Cache sheet allows you to set up the amount of memory and disk space that Netscape can use for caching. The default settings are 600KB of memory and 5MB (5,000KB) of disk space. Change them if you want to use more or less of your system resources for cache.

3. You can set the folder that Netscape uses for disk caching. To do so, enter the path in the Disk Cache Directory text box.

4. If you want to clear the current contents of your memory or disk caches, click Clear Memory Cache Now or Clear Disk Cache Now. When you click either of these buttons, a confirmation box asks whether you definitely want to clear that cache. If you click Yes, the cache is cleared immediately. Click No if you decide not to clear the cache.

5. When you have the options set to your satisfaction, choose OK.

Setting Netscape's Color Scheme

You can set colors of parts of the Web pages displayed in Netscape. Some of the things you can set are:

IV

The World Wide Web

- The color that Netscape uses to display unexplored and followed links in a document.

- The colors that Netscape uses for document text, and the color or image that is used for the background.

- You can set Netscape so that it always uses your color specifications, regardless of the colors specified in a document.

To set your own color specifications, follow these steps:

1. Choose Options, General Preferences, then select the Colors tab (see fig. 22.7).

Fig. 22.7

Set up your link color, text color, and document background information from the Colors Preferences tab.

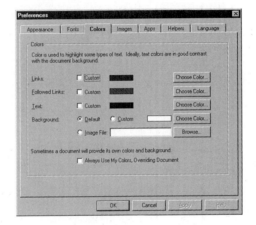

2. Select the color options you want.

3. Choose OK.

What You See When a Document Is Loaded

When you load a document, Netscape gives you a great deal of information about what is happening. Stars streak through the sky of the Netscape icon to the right of the location field, the Stop button in the toolbar turns red, and messages appear in the status area. All these signals help you follow the progress of a document load.

Status Bar Messages

Viewing a WWW document involves many different activities. Netscape needs to contact the server where the document lives, ask the server whether it has the document, and then ask the server to transfer that document to your computer. Through messages in the status area, Netscape tries to tell you what steps have been accomplished and what still needs to be done as it is loading the document. These messages can include the following:

- `Connect: Looking up Host:<hostname>`
- `Connect: Contacting Host:<hostname>`
- `Connect: Host Contacted: Waiting for reply…`
- `Document: Received <nnn> of <nnnn> bytes`
- `Transferring data`
- `Document: Done`

The Netscape icon is a useful indicator of the status of the document load. Stars streaking across the icon with no other activity can be the first (and sometimes, the only) indication that a problem exists—if, for example, your counter stops increasing, even though it hasn't reached the full load size.

It is nice to be able to watch the counter increase (and the bar graph) as the elements of the document are loaded. These features give you an idea of how far along you are and how much longer you can expect to wait before the document is loaded.

Stopping a Document Load

Occasionally, you may want to abort the loading of the current document. Perhaps you clicked a link inadvertently, or perhaps you discovered the document that you wanted to view contains huge graphics that you don't have time to download.

You can stop a document load in two ways. If your toolbar is displayed, click the Stop button to cancel the load. (The Stop button should be red while a document is loading.) You also can choose Go, Stop Loading to abort the load.

You will find that if you stop a load, you are likely to get a partial copy of the document that was loading. (A `Transfer interrupted!` message probably will appear at the end of the partial document.) Choose Go, Back to return to the preceding document, and continue your navigation from there.

Controlling the Loading of Graphics

Tip

The Images button in your toolbar becomes active when Auto Load Images is turned off.

Loading documents can take a few minutes, especially if the document contains many large graphics and your computer has a relatively slow (less than 9,600 bps) connection to the Internet. One thing you can do to speed the loading of the document is to tell Netscape not to load the inline graphics from the document. To do this Choose Options, Auto Load Images (the option is turned off when there is no checkmark next to it).

The next new document that you load will not have any graphics displayed; instead, placeholder icons will be displayed where the graphics should be (see fig. 22.8). To load the images that the placeholders represent, click the Images button in the toolbar, or choose View, Load Images.

Fig. 22.8

When you tell Netscape not to load inline graphics, it places icons where the graphics would be.

Image placeholders

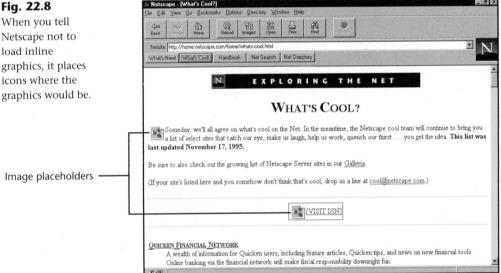

You can also load individual graphics from their placeholder icons. If you want to load a single graphic, right-click its placeholder and select Load this Image from the pop-up menu.

You can configure the following other image-related features of Netscape:

- By default, Netscape begins to display an image while it loads it. You can set Netscape so that it loads an entire image first and then displays it. This procedure may be faster if you have a good Internet connection.

- You also can set Netscape to dither colors so you can create the closest match to the color that is specified. It takes longer to do this, but it produces more accurate images.

■ You can set Netscape so that it displays the palette color closest to the one specified in the graphic. This method loads images faster, but the colors may be slightly off; however, it should be adequate for most graphics that you would be viewing online.

To set Netscape's image options, follow these steps:

1. Choose Options, General Preferences, then select the Images tab. The Images sheet enables you to specify how you want Netscape to load images and display colors (see fig. 22.9).

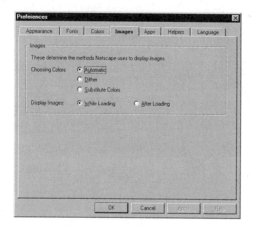

Fig. 22.9
The default image settings are Dither to Color Cube and Display Images While Loading.

2. Select the Display Images options you want.

3. Choose OK.

Looking for Information in a Document

If the WWW document that you are reading is short, you can scroll through the document (or press the Page Up and Page Down keys) to find information that interests you. If you have loaded a very long document, though, Netscape provides a quick way to look for information. Follow these steps:

1. Open the Edit menu Find dialog box (see fig. 22.10).

Fig. 22.10
The Find dialog box enables you to specify the search words and the direction of the search.

2. In the Find What text box, enter the word for which you want to search.

3. To specify the direction of the search, select U̱p (toward the beginning of the document) or Ḏown (toward the end).

4. Click Match c̱ase if you want Netscape to match the exact capitalization of the word that you entered.

5. Choose F̱ind Next to begin the search. If a match is found, Netscape scrolls the window to the section where the match appears and highlights the matching text. An alert box informs you if no match is found.

Saving Documents

In general, the purpose of the World Wide Web is to provide one copy of a document that many people can view. At times, however, you may want to save a copy of a document to your local computer. Netscape gives you several options for saving documents.

The first way to save a document is to choose F̱ile, S̱ave As. The Save As dialog box appears, enabling you to browse through your directories and store the file wherever you want. You can save the file as HTML, text, or the native format of the file.

> **Tip**
>
> Shift+click a link to save the document associated with that link to disk instead of displaying it.

You can save the document associated with a URL in your current document directly to disk rather than loading it into Netscape. To do so, right-click the link for that document and select Save this Link as from the pop-up menu that appears.

> **Note**
>
> When you save an HTML document to your local disk, remember that the document probably contains hyperlinks. These links can be relative or absolute. An *absolute reference* contains the complete address of the document that is being referenced, including the host name, directory path, and file name. A *relative reference* assumes that the preceding machine and directory path are being used; only the file name (or possibly a subdirectory and file name) is specified.
>
> If the document references other documents that have relative addresses, you cannot view those documents unless you copy them to your local disk and set them up with the same directory structure that they had at the original site. You may want to set

up a document and its linked documents on your local disk, if you want to be able to view the document without connecting to the Internet. One problem is that if the original document changes, you are not aware that you are viewing an outdated version of the document.

Absolute references always work unless your Internet connection fails or the referenced documents are moved.

Printing Documents

In addition to being able to save documents, you can print documents directly from Netscape. Choose File, Print to send a copy of the current document to your printer.

One of the nice features of Netscape is that you can preview the current document before printing it. Choose File, Print Preview. Netscape creates a preview of the document in a separate window (see fig. 22.11). This preview window enables you to look at each page of the document, zooming in and out wherever you want. When you are satisfied with the print preview, you can print the document directly from this window.

Fig. 22.11
The print preview window enables you to see what your document will look like before it is printed.

Customizing the Displayed Window Areas

Some of the window elements in Netscape are optional (not, however, the document viewing area; Netscape wouldn't be very useful without that!). The title bar and menu bar cannot be removed, but the toolbar, location field, and directory buttons can be turned off. Turning off these window elements gives you a bigger viewing area, but it also removes some time-saving and in-formational features. The following list describes how to turn these features off or back on (they are on if a checkmark appears next to them in the menu):

- To turn off the toolbar, choose Options, Show Toolbar.
- To turn off the location field, choose Options, Show Location.
- To turn off the directory buttons, choose Options, Show Directory Buttons.

Caution

If you remove either the location field or the directory buttons, the Netscape icon shrinks to a size that is more difficult to see. If you remove both of the areas, the icon disappears, causing you to lose one of the visual clues that gives you information about document loading.

If you remove the toolbar, you lose the ability to cancel document transfers quickly, because the Stop button in the toolbar has been removed from the window. (You can still cancel transfers by choosing Go, Stop Loading.)

Although these changes take effect immediately after you select the menu item, Netscape does not automatically save them as your default settings. To save the current settings as the default, open the Options menu and choose Save Options.

Working with Local Files

When you think of using Netscape, you think of retrieving documents from WWW servers on the Internet. Netscape can read documents from your local file system, as well as from halfway around the world. If you share documents among members of your organization, many of the documents that you view may be on a local file server or your local computer.

Netscape provides an option that makes loading a local file easy. If you want to load a local file, choose File, Open File. The Open dialog box appears (see fig. 22.12). This dialog box enables you to browse through all your local disks to find a file.

Fig. 22.12
The Open dialog box enables you to enter a local file name or browse your local file system to find the next document that you want to view.

You also can load a local file in the same manner that you load any URL. Choose File, Open Location to open the Open Location dialog box. To specify a local file, precede the location of the file with **file:///c|** (you can substitute any of your local disks for c). The three slashes tell Netscape that you are looking for a local file; the bar is used instead of a colon because the colon has a specific purpose in a URL. Use forward slashes between the folder names in the file location that you enter, even though you usually use the backslash to separate folder names in Windows 95. Netscape translates the slashes properly when it retrieves the file.

Local URLs can be used anywhere that URLs are used—as Bookmarks, links in documents, and so on.

◄ See "Using Links to Move Between Documents," p. 483

Effective Browsing Techniques

Navigating between WWW documents can be confusing. Documents often connect to documents that you have already read. You can't always remember which of several related documents contains the information that you really need.

Sometimes, you can't tell from the hyperlink whether the document is of interest to you, and loading documents uses valuable time. Often, you waste time loading documents that you dismiss immediately. This section helps you learn to reduce unnecessary document loading and circular navigating.

How to Keep Track of Where You've Been

Keeping track of where you are and where you were is one of the biggest challenges of using the WWW. Suppose that you're reading a document that deals with agriculture, and you click a hyperlink that takes you to Hay Field Seeding Suggestions. The document turns out to be one that you loaded earlier—when you found a hyperlink for Pasture Management Techniques. How can you avoid this frustrating repetition?

One suggestion is to have a home page that provides links to your most-visited WWW pages. This home page is useful, for example, if you work on a group project and frequently use documents with known locations. You can create your own home page, or someone can create a project home page for your group. In this scenario, you probably are already familiar with the servers, if not with the exact documents.

But what if you're navigating in uncharted waters on the WWW? Although it sounds difficult, you probably can learn to recognize the URLs of the sites that keep information that interests you. If the location field is displayed, the URL for the current document appears there. The status bar shows the URL of a hyperlink when you move the cursor over it (see fig. 22.13). As you move between documents, you begin to remember some of the URLs that you see frequently; when you put your cursor on a hyperlink, you recognize documents that you know.

Fig. 22.13

The status bar displays the URLs of hyperlinks when the cursor is on top of them.

How to Get Where You Were

Trying to navigate back to a document that you viewed in the current Netscape session also can be challenging. In general, to go to the document that you viewed before the current document, choose Go, Back (or click the Back button in the toolbar). Opening the menu and choosing the Go, Forward command (or clicking the Forward button) takes you to the last document that you viewed after the current document. This arrangement sounds rather confusing, but it is understandable if you examine how Netscape determines these links.

IV

Tip

If the History dialog box is open when you use the Forward and Back commands, you can see the highlighted item move in the list of URLs.

The Window menu contains an option called History, which displays a dialog box similar to the one shown in figure 22.14. Notice that a list of URLs appears in this dialog box; the URL for the current document is highlighted.

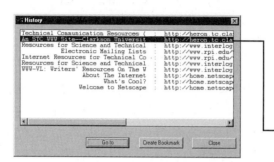

Fig. 22.14
The Netscape History dialog box shows a linear list of URLs that you visit.

Current URL is highlighted in history window

The history list shows you the URLs of the document chain that led you to this point, as well as any documents that you visited after the current document. If you use the Back command, you move up in the list; if you use the Forward command, you move down the list. Click any URL in the list and click Go To to jump to that document (and that point in the list).

Caution

You can use the Back and Forward commands to move between documents that you already visited (which are shown in the history list). If, however, you jump to a new document while you are in the middle of the list, you erase the links at the end of the list and cannot use the Forward command to return to those documents. The link for the document you just jumped to replaces all of the links past your current point in the list.

To move quickly between documents that you load, use the history list. If you want to add a new document to the list of documents that you're viewing, make sure that you're at the end of the list before you jump to that document. You don't have to use hyperlinks to add the document you load to the history list. Load the document from the Open Location dialog box (choose File, Open Location, or click the Open toolbar button), and it is added to the list.

You will notice when you open the Go menu that the last few documents that you visited (a maximum of 15) are displayed at the bottom of the menu (see fig. 22.15). The documents are shown in the order in which you opened them, with the most recent document appearing at the top of the list. The 10 newest documents are numbered so that you can access them quickly without using the mouse. A zero appears to the left of the most recently visited document; the nine documents following it are numbered sequentially.

Fig. 22.15
The Go menu enables you to quickly access the last few documents that you visited.

Create Lists of Your Favorite URLs

If you don't want to create a home page that contains all your favorite WWW documents, Netscape offers an alternative to keep track of these documents. To quickly access your favorite URLs, you can create Bookmark files. You can have any number of Bookmark files and can save any number of URLs to each file.

Setting Your Current Bookmark File

The default Bookmark file is BOOKMARK.HTM. You can have any number of Bookmark files, although only one can be set as the current Bookmark file. To set your current bookmark file, follow these steps:

1. Choose Bookmarks, Go to Bookmarks or Window, Bookmarks to open the Netscape Bookmarks window (see fig. 22.16).

2. Choose File, Open to get the Open Bookmarks File window (see fig. 22.17).

3. Use the browser to find the folder where you keep your Bookmark files. Click the file that you want to use as the current Bookmark file (the path is entered in the text box automatically when you click the file).

4. Choose Open to make the selections take effect, or click Cancel if you decide not to change the current Bookmark file.

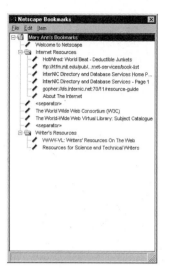

Fig. 22.16
The Netscape Bookmarks window lets you load and edit any of your bookmark files.

Fig. 22.17
The Open Bookmarks File window lets you browse your file system for the Bookmark file you want to load.

Creating and Editing Bookmarks

After you define your current Bookmark file, you can create Bookmarks in several ways. The simplest way is to choose Bookmarks, Add Bookmark. This command writes the title and URL of the current document as the last item in your Bookmark file. You do not need to visit a document, however, to add it to your Bookmark file. The Netscape Bookmarks window allows you to add and edit Bookmarks in the current Bookmark file.

To use the Bookmark List dialog box, follow these steps:

1. Choose Bookmarks, Go to Bookmarks or Window, Bookmarks to open the Netscape Bookmarks window.

2. To search for an item in your Bookmark list, enter the string of characters that you want to search for in the Find text box, and then click Find. Netscape finds all occurrences of the character string (regardless of capitalization), whether the string occurs as part of a word or as an entire word.

   The Find command searches from the current Bookmark down, and will find strings in the URLs associated with entries.

In addition to adding the current document, you can add any document to the list, edit the documents that currently appear in the list, group items onto submenus, and add separators in the lists.

If you want to edit one of the Bookmarks in the list, select it, then choose Item, Properties. Information about that Bookmark appears in the text boxes labeled Name, Location, Last Visited, Added On, and Description. You can edit the Name, Location, and Description entries. The name is the entry that appears in the Bookmark list. The location is the URL of the document. The description appears below the name when you view the Bookmark file as a document.

To add a new item to the list, select the item that you want the new item to follow. Then select one of the following from the Items menu:

- *Insert Separator* causes a line to be added below the selected item. This line appears when the Bookmarks are displayed in the Bookmarks menu.

- *Insert Folder* causes the words New Header to appear in the Bookmark list and the Name text box in the Bookmark Properties dialog box. Change the Name entry to whatever you want the header to be. Once you've created the folder, you can select current Bookmarks and drag them into the folder. The folder appears under your Bookmarks menu item, and Bookmarks within the folder appear as a submenu from that menu item.

- *Insert Bookmark* causes the words New Bookmark to appear in both the Bookmarks list and the Name text box in the Bookmark Properties dialog box, and enters the current time and date in the Added On field. Change the Name entry to whatever you want it to be. Then enter the URL of the document you are adding in the Location box. If you want to, you also can add a description of the document in the Description box.

To remove an item from the Bookmarks list, select the item, and then choose Edit, Delete. To copy an item, select it, and then choose Edit, Copy. To paste the item, select the item that you want the copied item to follow and choose Edit, Paste.

Using Bookmarks

Bookmarks enable you to access documents quickly. You simply open the Bookmarks menu and select any of the Bookmarks that appear at the end of the menu; Netscape loads the document associated with that Bookmark. If the Netscape Bookmarks window is open, you can select any item in the Bookmarks list and then choose Item, Go to Bookmark to load that document.

> **Note**
>
> Netscape has a feature that lets you quickly check to see whether the documents in your bookmarks list have changed recently. Choose Window, Bookmarks to open the Bookmarks window. From the Bookmarks window, select File, What's New. In the dialog box that appears, select either All bookmarks or Selected bookmarks, and then choose Start Checking. Netscape will go out and check the documents that you requested to see if they've changed since the last time you accessed them. When it is finished, you will get a dialog box telling you how many documents were checked, and how many have changed. The changed documents will be highlighted in your bookmarks list.

Sharing Bookmarks

Netscape makes it very easy for you to share your Bookmarks with other users. If you want to share entire Bookmark files, simply give the users a copy of your Bookmark files. Those people then can specify any of those files as their current Bookmark file, and they will be able to access the same documents that you can.

You also can save the current version of your Bookmarks list to a file from the Netscape Bookmarks window. Simply choose File, Save As, and use the Save Bookmarks File dialog box that appears to select the folder and file to which you want to write the Bookmarks. You then can give that file to other people.

If you get someone else's Bookmark files and you don't want to bother changing files all the time to use them, you can add the Bookmarks from those files to your main Bookmarks file. Open the Bookmarks file that you want to add the new Bookmarks to. In the Netscape Bookmarks window, choose File, Import. You get an Import Bookmarks File dialog box that allows you to select the file that you want to import from your file system. When you select the file that you want to import, all the Bookmarks from that file are added to the top of the current Bookmarks list, preserving any menu structure that was in the imported list.

Security

Many people seem to feel that because computers are machines, communications between computers is secure (no people are involved). Nothing could be further from the truth.

Communication on the Internet involves data being forwarded from the sending computer to the receiving computer through several intermediate computers. A possibility exists that someone could be looking at the information passing through the intermediate computers. He or she could even set up another computer to pretend to be the receiving computer, so that everything you send goes to someone who was not intended to see the information.

For this reason, sending sensitive information (such as your credit card number) over the Internet is not a good idea. Any information sent over the Internet is at risk—e-mail messages, file transfers, and particularly information from electronic forms that you may fill out with your WWW browser.

There is, however, a solution to this problem. Netscape Communications Corporation has built security features into its Web browser and server. A very secure encryption standard can be used for transmitting information between the Netscape browser and a Netscape server. This encryption prevents anyone who is observing the information at an intermediate point from making any sense of it. The Netscape browser shows the security status of the document that you are viewing in several ways as follows:

- If the key symbol to the left of the status bar is broken, the current document is not secure. If the key is unbroken on a blue background, the document is secure. If the unbroken key has 2 teeth, the encryption is high-grade; if it has 1 tooth, the encryption is medium grade. When you are viewing a secure document, a thin blue line will appear above the content area.

- Dialog boxes can warn you when you are entering or leaving a secure WWW server, and also warn you when you are going to submit information with an insecure form.

You can specify whether you want to see the alert dialog boxes for different security conditions. To do so, select Options, Security Preferences and then make sure the General tab is displayed (see fig. 22.18).

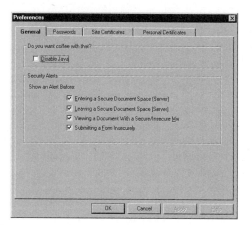

Fig. 22.18
You can specify how Netscape alerts you about the security status of the WWW servers and documents that you visit.

You also can get security information about the document that you are currently viewing from the Document Information dialog box (see fig. 22.19). Choose View, Document Info to display this dialog box.

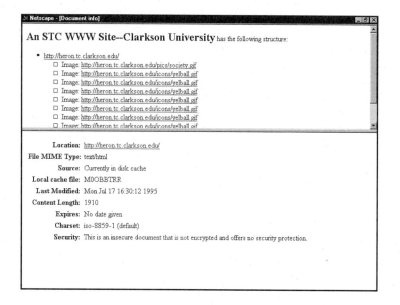

Fig. 22.19
The Document Information dialog box tells you the document title and location, and when it was last modified, in addition to information about the security of the document.

IV

The World Wide Web

Plug-In Applications

Before the Internet was commercialized, the standards for all Internet services were defined by the various Internet administrative committees, and all interfaces for a particular service (like FTP or Gopher) had the same features. Now that commercial companies are developing interfaces for the World Wide Web (the newest and least standardized Internet service). They are putting into their Web browsers proprietary features that other browsers do not have, attempting to become the standard rather than to follow it.

One of these proprietary features that Netscape has added is the *plug-in*, which adds the ability to embed pieces of helper applications directly into Web documents. With plug-ins, you don't need to start the helper application in a separate window when loading a multimedia file—you just use the piece of the helper application interface that appears in the document. Netscape has made agreements with a number vendors to incorporate plug-ins for their applications. Some of the plug-ins available at the time this book was published were:

- Adobe Acrobat Amber Reader
- Corel CMX Viewer for vector graphics
- Tumbleweed Software Envoy viewer
- Visual Components Formula One/NET Excel-compatible spreadsheet
- Progressive Networks RealAudio live audio player
- Macromedia Shockwave for Director for multimedia presentations
- VDOnet VDOLive for display of video images
- Paper Software WebFX for VRML environments

To see a list of the current plug-ins available for Netscape, open **http://home.netscape.com/comprod/products/navigator/version_2.0/plugins/index.html**. The remainder of this section discusses some of the more interesting and useful plug-ins.

RealAudio

Progressive Networks has made an agreement with Netscape Communications to develop a plug-in of their RealAudio product. RealAudio lets you listen to live audio broadcast over the Internet. To incorporate the RealAudio plug-in for Netscape, you must first load the RealAudio player onto your PC. To do this:

1. Go to the URL **http://www.realaudio.com/products/ra2.0/**.

2. Click Download 2.0 Beta Player.

3. Fill out the form that appears on this page.

4. Once the form is completed, select Go to download page and download the RealAudio player EXE file to a temporary directory on your PC, such as C:\Install.

5. From Windows Explorer, double-click the EXE file you loaded in the temporary directory to install RealAudio.

6. Enter the information requested by the setup program.

7. Choose the <u>E</u>xpress setup to install RealAudio with default setting.

8. During the installation, you will be asked if you want to install the Netscape plug-in. Click <u>Y</u>es.

After the RealAudio player is installed, the RealAudio will start up and play a message. You are now ready to use Netscape to view documents that include RealAudio plug-ins. You must first exit and restart Netscape after installing RealAudio in order to view RealAudio plug-ins in WWW documents.

For an example of a document that contains a RealAudio plug-in, open **http://www.realaudio.com/products/ra2.0/pn.htm**. Near the bottom of this page, you will see the control panel for the RealAudio player (see fig. 22.20). Click the Play/Pause button (the left-most button) to hear a message from the Vice President of Software Development at Progressive Networks.

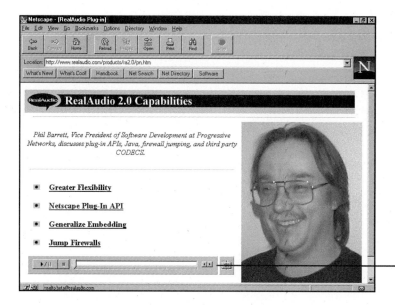

Fig. 22.20
The RealAudio control panel plug-in lets you start, stop and pause the audio, skip forward and back, and set the volume of the audio that is played.

RealAudio control panel

Shockwave

Macromedia has made an agreement with Netscape Communications to develop a plug-in (called Shockwave) of their Director product. Shockwave lets you view multimedia movies within your Web documents. To incorporate the Shockwave plug-in for Netscape you must first load the Shockwave player onto your PC. To do this:

1. Open the URL **http://www.macromedia.com/Tools/ Shockwave/sdc/Plugin/Win95Plg.htm**.

2. Under the Netscape 2.0 section, click one of the Shockwave for Director version 1.0b1 entries and download the Shockwave EXE file to a temporary directory on your PC, such as C:\Install.

3. From Windows Explorer, double-click the EXE file you loaded in the temporary directory. This unpacks the Shockwave files in a DOS window.

4. Close the DOS window and double-click the Setup.exe file from Windows Explorer.

5. Follow the installation instructions, making sure that the Install Shockwave for Director checkbox is selected.

6. Choose the directory where you want to keep Shockwave if it is other than the default C:\Netscape\Program.

7. When the installation is complete, close the Shockwave folder that appears open on your desktop.

You are now ready to use Netscape to view documents that include Shockwave plug-ins. You must first exit and restart Netscape after installing Shockwave in order to view Shockwave plug-ins in WWW documents.

For an example of a document that contains a Shockwave plug-in, open **http://www.macromedia.com/Tools/Shockwave/Vanguard/ index.html**. When the page is finished loading, you will see an animated graphic at the top of the page. From this page, you can view other examples of Shockwave plug-ins.

Acrobat Amber

Adobe has made an agreement with Netscape Communications to develop a plug-in (called Amber) of their Acrobat product. Amber lets you view Adobe PDF (Portable Document Format) files within your Web documents. To incorporate the Amber plug-in for Netscape you must first load the Amber viewer onto your PC. To do this:

1. Open the URL **http://www.adobe.com/Amber/Download.html**.

2. Click Download the Free Acrobat Amber Reader for Windows Now! and download the Amber EXE file to a temporary directory on your PC, such as C:\Install.

3. From Windows Explorer, double-click the EXE file you loaded in the temporary directory. This unpacks the Amber files in a DOS window.

4. Close the DOS window and double-click the SETUP.EXE file from Windows Explorer.

5. Follow the installation instructions. Choose the directory where you want to keep Amber if it is other than the default C:\Acroweb.

6. When the installation is complete, you can choose to read the readme.txt file or return to Windows 95. Close the Amber folder that appears open on your desktop.

You are now ready to use Netscape to view documents that include PDF files. You must first exit and restart Netscape after installing Amber to view Amber plug-ins in WWW documents.

To see how the Amber plug-in works, open **http://www.adobe.com/ Amber/amexamp.html**. From this page, you can load a number of PDF documents that can be displayed by the Amber plug-in. If you click the Acrobat Amber Overview link, you will load a document that tells you all about Amber and PDF (see fig. 22.21). Clicking the up and down arrows in the scroll bar will page up and down in the document.

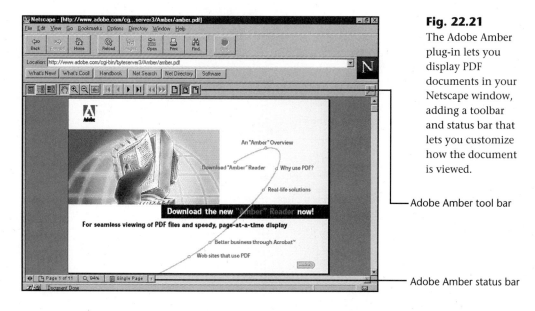

Fig. 22.21
The Adobe Amber plug-in lets you display PDF documents in your Netscape window, adding a toolbar and status bar that lets you customize how the document is viewed.

Adobe Amber tool bar

Adobe Amber status bar

WebFX

Paper Inc. has made an agreement with Netscape Communications to develop a plug-in of their WebFX product. WebFX lets you navigate through 3D virtual worlds within your Web documents. To incorporate the WebFX plug-in for Netscape you must first load the WebFX viewer onto your PC. To do this:

1. Open the URL **http://www.paperinc.com/wfxwin32.html**.

2. Click WebFX Plugin for Netscape 2.0, and choose one of the mirror sites shown on the page that appears.

3. From the mirror site page, choose Click Here to Receive the 32-Bit Windows Version. Download the WebFX EXE file to a temporary directory on your PC, such as C:\Install.

4. From Windows Explorer, double-click the EXE file you loaded in the temporary directory. This unpacks the WebFX files in a DOS window.

5. Close the DOS window and double-click the Setup.exe file from Windows Explorer.

6. Follow the installation instructions. Verify the location of your Netscape Program directory (the default is C:\Netscape\Program).

7. Choose the location where you want the WebFX files installed (the default is C:\Program Files\WebFX), and the Program Folder where you want the WebFX icons to appear.

8. When the installation is complete close the WebFX folder that appears open on your desktop.

You are now ready to use Netscape to view documents that include WebFX plug-ins. You must first exit and restart Netscape after installing WebFX in order to view WebFX plug-ins in WWW documents.

To see how the WebFX plug-in works, open **http://home.netscape.com/ comprod/products/navigator/version_2.0/plugins/vrml_sites. html**. From this page, you can load a number of VRML documents that can be displayed by the WebFX plug-in. If you click on any of the links on this page, you will load a 3D world that you can move through, using the command controls at the bottom of the window (see fig. 22.22).

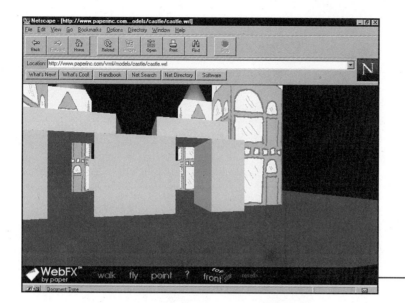

Fig. 22.22
The WebFX plug-in lets you display VRML documents in your Netscape window, adding a command bar that lets you move through the virtual world.

———— WebFX command bar

Other Internet-Related Features

Though the main function of Netscape is to allow you to view documents on the WWW, there are a number of other Internet-related services that you can access from Netscape.

Internet E-Mail

Netscape contains a complete Internet e-mail interface. You will need to tell Netscape your name, e-mail address, an outgoing mail (SMTP) server (an Internet host that can send e-mail), and an incoming mail (POP) server (an Internet host that collects your mail and holds it until you log in to read it). To set all these options, choose Options, Mail and New Preferences, and fill in the information on the Servers and Identity tabs in the Preferences window (see figs. 22.23 and 22.24).

> **Tip**
>
> You can send e-mail quickly by choosing File, New Mail Message from any Netscape document window.

Fig. 22.23
Fill in the incoming and outgoing mail server information, as well your mail account name and local mail folder on the Servers tab of the Preferences dialog box.

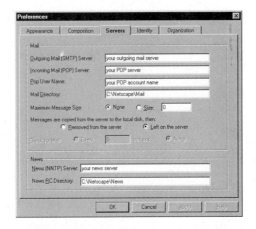

Fig. 22.24
Fill in your name and e-mail address (and any other personal information) on the Identity tab of the Preferences dialog box.

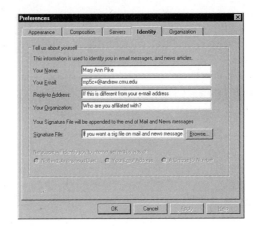

Once Netscape is configured correctly, to read your Internet mail choose Window, Netscape Mail (or click the mail icon to the right of the progress bar at the bottom of the Netscape window). You will be prompted for your Internet account password, and Netscape will log in to your account and transfer any mail that you have to your local disk. From the Netscape Mail window (see fig. 22.25) you can read your mail, organize your mail into folders, and send mail.

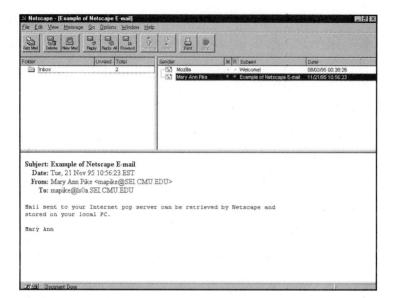

Fig. 22.25
The Netscape Mail
window has a
toolbar that allows
you to quickly read
and send mail.

IV

The World Wide Web

Caution

Be sure to choose File, Close when you want to close the Netscape Mail window. If
you choose File, Exit, it will exit all of your Netscape windows.

Reading UseNet Newsgroups

Netscape also provides an interface that lets you read and post to UseNet
newsgroups. In order to do this, you must choose Options, Mail and News
Preferences and enter an NNTP server (a machine that lets you read and post
to news groups) and the path to your News RC folder in the indicated text
boxes on the Servers tab of the Preferences dialog. Once you have entered a
valid server, you can open the News window by choosing Window, Netscape
News (see fig. 22.26). From this window you can subscribe to newsgroups,
load the messages headers from your subscribed groups, and read articles.

Caution

Be sure to choose File, Close when you want to close the Netscape News window.
If you choose File, Exit, it will exit all of your Netscape windows.

Fig. 22.26

The Netscape News window has a toolbar that lets you quickly read and post articles, reply to articles, and move between articles and newsgroups.

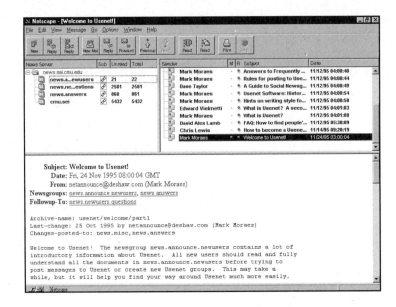

Click the newsgroup that you want to read. Netscape will load a list of the available articles. Click the article that you want to read and Netscape will load the article. When you read newsgroups, the toolbar in your Netscape News window lets you post new and followup articles, send a reply to the author of the article, and move back and forth between articles and newsgroups.

> **Caution**
>
> If you try to read a newsgroup that has several thousand unread articles, it could take a long time (over 30 minutes) to load the list of headers.

Java Compatibility

▶ See "What Is Java?" p. 731

Sun Microsystems has developed a new programming language based on C++ that allows Web pages to contain more than just pictures, sounds, and movies (which you need browser applications to view). With their Java language, when you download a Web page you can actually load a mini-application (called an *applet*) that can do almost anything the author of the applet wants it to do.

Netscape supports Web pages that contain Java applets. Some of the demo applications that you can find from the Netscape home page show how you can get live updates of information on your Web page, communicate live with other users, do expert graphics generation, and other activities not supported by the basic WWW concepts. These applets are designed to be very secure, with safeguards against viruses and tampering. This technology is in its infancy and not many Web browsers currently support it. But Netscape is among the leading Web browsers, and the flexibility that Java introduces to Web pages is so powerful that Java will probably take off in the next year.

To see some examples of what Java can do, load **http://home.netscape. com/comprod/products/navigator/version_2.0/java_applets/ index.html**, page down to the Java Applet Demos section of the document, and load any of the Web pages that are listed there. Following the demos section is the Java Resources section, which contains pointers to the Java home page and to other places where you can find out more about Java.

Note

Netscape provides a scripting language similar to Java (called *JavaScript*) that can be embedded in Web pages. This scripting language allows you to detect user events (like data input or mouse clicks) from the Web page, and to respond to those inputs immediately, rather than passing the information back to a server and having the server respond. It also lets you manipulate Java objects, giving you greater flexibility in designing your Web page. Both JavaScript and its documentation are currently under development. To get more information, open **http://home.netscape.com/ comprod/products/navigator/version_2.0/script/script_info/index.html**.

CHAPTER 23

Using Mosaic

The World Wide Web (WWW) is one of the best examples of *cyberspace*, the electronic world of interconnected computers. The Web is a system that links documents together so you can move among them with little effort. This lets you travel to many different places around the world, learning about any topic imaginable. Like any traveler in a new place, however, you can easily get lost.

Mosaic is an easy-to-use interface that lets you traverse the Web. The version 2.0 release of Mosaic has many convenient features that help you keep track of the places you have been and get back to those places quickly. The concepts discussed in chapter 20, "How the World Wide Web Works," are used throughout this chapter.

In this chapter, you learn to do the following:

- Set up Mosaic for Windows on your system
- Start up Mosaic and use its basic features
- Navigate effectively on the WWW
- Keep track of your favorite WWW documents
- Handle errors you may encounter

Getting Mosaic for Windows Running

Before you can try Mosaic for Windows on your personal computer, you have to obtain the software and set it up on your computer. Depending on how your system is set up, getting Mosaic for Windows to run can be as easy as just loading the software. If your system is not already connected to the Internet, however, getting Mosaic for Windows to run requires some extra work.

Can Your Computer System Run Mosaic for Windows?

First, you must make sure your computer system is capable of running the software. This section outlines what type of computer hardware and software you must have in order for Mosaic to run with reasonable performance.

Basic System Requirements

In this book, we are focusing on Mosaic running under Windows 95. Like Windows 95, Mosaic for Windows requires at least 4MB of free memory and an Intel 80386DX (20 MHz or higher) processor. Although these are the minimum system requirements, you may find that with this configuration your system runs very slowly. You may need to upgrade your processor or add additional memory to your system to improve performance.

The basic Mosaic for Windows configuration requires about 2.2MB of disk space for the Mosaic software and documentation. In addition to this basic disk space requirement, Mosaic needs disk space to hold temporary files while it is running. You also need disk space for any documents you want to store locally, and for any viewers that you need to display movies, image files, sound files, and so on.

Network Requirements

In addition to the system requirements previously mentioned, Mosaic for Windows requires a direct connection to the Internet, either through an Ethernet card in your system, or through a modem connection. The best configuration is with an Ethernet card, which is directly connected to a local Internet segment. This provides the best Mosaic performance and requires the least additional software.

If your system is not directly connected to an Internet segment, you have to get an account from an Internet provider. You have to obtain software that enables your system to run the Serial-Line Internet Protocol (SLIP) or Point-to-Point Protocol (PPP). This software allows you to connect to the Internet through a modem on your system.

Other Software Requirements

In addition to the basic system and network requirements, other software may be required to either set up Mosaic or enhance its capabilities. Because some supporting files for Mosaic for Windows and other files you find on the Internet may come packaged as zip files, you may need some software to unpack these archives. WinZIP (which is included on the NetCD95) is the software usually used for this; it can be found on many Internet FTP sites. See chapter 47, "Top FTP Sites," for information about FTP sites where you can find this software.

After Mosaic is running on your system, you can expand its capabilities by adding software that handles additional types of documents. Mosaic for Windows comes with software that lets you display some images, but you may want to get software to process sound files, animation files, and additional picture formats too. Obtaining and setting up these additional programs is discussed in more detail in chapter 24, "Using Helper Apps."

Where to Get Mosaic for Windows

One of the best features of Mosaic for Windows is that the basic software is free. The software, which is written and maintained at the National Center for Supercomputing Applications (NCSA) at the University of Illinois, is available through anonymous FTP.

▶ See "What Is FTP?" p. 837

Tip

When you download Mosaic, be sure to see whether there is a more recent version. If there is, it may run better and have fewer problems.

The basic Mosaic for Windows software is available through anonymous FTP at the site **ftp.ncsa.uiuc.edu**. This FTP site has versions of Mosaic for several different machine types, but you are interested in the Mosaic software for PC machines running Windows 95. The Windows 95 version of Mosaic can be found in the file MOSAIC20.EXE in the directory Web/Mosaic/Windows/Win95/. When you retrieve this self-extracting zip file, put the file in a temporary directory (for example, C:\install). The latest version of Mosaic for Windows (as of the writing of this book) is the final release of version 2.0.

Note

If you have an older version of Mosaic, you can also download the new Mosaic software by going to the NCSA Mosaic for Windows welcome page (there is a Mosaic hotlist entry for this page) and following the links for loading the latest version.

There is one problem you may encounter in obtaining the Mosaic software. Because this software is so popular, the NCSA site is often very busy. There are limits to the number of users that can connect to it at one time; at busy times, you may not be able to connect. If this happens, be patient and try again. If you still can't get connected, don't despair. Many other FTP sites have copies of the Mosaic files. Here are a couple alternative anonymous FTP sites and the directories in which to look for the software:

nic.switch.ch   /mirror/mosaic/windows

ftp.cac.psu.edu   /pub/access/test

There is one more thing to keep in mind. Just as you move files around on your computer, the system administrators of the FTP sites may occasionally move files or rename directories. If you can't find the files you are looking for, look in another directory. They may be somewhere else.

Installing the Mosaic for Windows 95 Software

Since this version of Mosaic is specifically for Windows 95, you should use the Add/Remove Programs in Control Panel to install the software. To set up the software, follow these steps:

1. Move the Mosaic for Windows self-extracting file you retrieved from the FTP site to a temporary directory on your hard drive (for example, C:\install).

2. Run the self-extracting file by double-clicking it in the Windows Explorer, or by selecting Run from the Start menu and typing in the path and name of the file (for example, C:\install\mosaic20.exe). The temporary directory now contains the original self-extracting file and several other files.

> **Note**
>
> After you have unpacked the Mosaic software, there is one file you should read before installing the software. The file README.WRI gives important installation and other information about the current version of Mosaic.

3. Click the Start button and select Settings, Control Panel.

4. Double-click the Add/Remove Programs icon.

5. Click Install.

6. Click Next.

7. Click Browse.

8. Find and open the folder containing the Mosaic files (C:\install in this example).

9. Select the Setup.exe file and click Open.

10. Select Finish.

11. Follow the instructions in the Setup program. It asks you a few questions about where you would like to put your Mosaic for Windows files, performs the installation, and then creates an entry for Mosaic in the Programs item on the Start button.

12. When the setup finishes, it will leave an open program group window showing the contents of the NCSA Mosaic v2.0 folder. Close this window.

13. The setup of the Mosaic for Windows software is now complete. You can remove the files from the temporary directory; they are no longer needed.

There are some customizations that can be done to the Mosaic for Windows software to personalize it to your needs (see "Customizing Your Mosaic Window" later in this chapter), but you can run the Mosaic software without any further work. You do need to set up your software to connect to the Internet before using Mosaic for Windows to access files on the Internet.

Using the Mosaic Interface

After you install the Mosaic software, you can connect to your Internet provider and start Mosaic. Mosaic is a powerful application, but it is graphically oriented and not difficult to use after you get familiar with its features.

Starting Mosaic

Before starting Mosaic, you first should be connected to the Internet (although you can start Mosaic and view local documents without connecting to the Internet). If your Internet connection is via your LAN, be sure you are logged on to your network. If you are connected to the Internet by a modem, start your TCP/IP software and log in to your account.

After you establish your Internet connection, start Mosaic by:

1. Clicking the Start button.

2. Selecting Programs from the Start menu.

3. Selecting NCSA Mosaic v2.0 from the list of programs.

4. Selecting NCSA Mosaic from the list of files.

When Mosaic starts the first time, it displays the Mosaic release notes document that is included with your installation. This document discusses the new features that were implemented in the final release, bugs that were fixed, and new HTML commands that are supported.

You are now ready to explore the Internet with Mosaic.

What Is a Home Page?

◀ See "Home
Pages," p. 465

Most people define a home page (or home document) as the document that
you tell your Web browser to display when it starts. This document should
contain links to the documents and WWW sites that you use most frequently. You can specify any document on the WWW to use as your home
page, or you can design your own. Your project or company may have its
own home page that you can use to get easy access to needed information.

Note

Many people also use the term home page for the welcome page that you get when
you connect to a WWW site. This is not technically correct, but it is a common usage.

When you start the Mosaic software, it comes with the home page predefined
as the NCSA Mosaic for Microsoft Windows welcome page. You probably
want to change this, because, for one thing, the NCSA Mosaic page is probably not very useful to you, unless you are involved in the installation and
maintenance of Mosaic at your site and you want to keep up with the latest
information from NCSA. In addition, retrieving a document causes a load on
the machine where the document is located. If everyone used the NCSA Mosaic home page as their home page, the NCSA WWW machine would become
considerably slower. The later section "Customizing Your Mosaic Window"
will show you how to specify your own home page.

The Mosaic Window

Mosaic's interface makes it easy for you to read and move between WWW
documents. A brief description of each window part (shown in fig. 23.1) is
given in this section. Each window function is discussed in more depth later
in this chapter.

■ The title bar contains the usual window function buttons (control
menu, Maximize, Minimize, and Close buttons). In addition, it has the
name of the application (NCSA Mosaic) and the name of the WWW
document you are viewing.

■ The menu bar gives you access to all the functions you need to use
Mosaic. You can retrieve documents to view, print documents, customize the look of your Mosaic window, navigate between documents, save
files, and access Mosaic's online help.

Title bar

Menu bar

Toolbar

Location bar

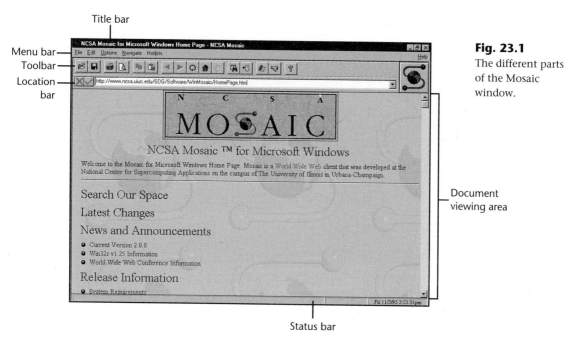

Fig. 23.1
The different parts of the Mosaic window.

Document viewing area

Status bar

- The toolbar gives you quick access to some of the most used features in Mosaic (see fig. 23.2).

- The Location bar shows the URL of the current document. When you open a document, its URL is displayed, and the Mosaic logo to the right of the Location bar and toolbar spins while the document is being retrieved.

- The document viewing area is the area of the window where you see the text of a document and any inline images it may contain.

- The status bar serves several functions. While a document is loading, the right-hand box shows a bar graph representing the percentage of the file that has been loaded. The middle box contains visual status indicators that tell you about the status of your document (whether a connection has been made to the WWW server or not, whether Mosaic is waiting to read data or currently reading it, the number of inline images that need to be loaded, and so on).

    When you are viewing a document, it shows the URL of the hyperlink that is under your cursor in the left-hand box. The current date and time are displayed in the right-hand box of the status bar.

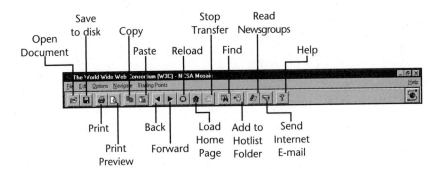

Fig. 23.2
The buttons on
the Mosaic
toolbar.

The following list gives basic descriptions of the toolbar buttons:

- *Open Document* opens a URL.
- *Save to disk* saves the current document to disk.
- *Print* prints the current document.
- *Print Preview* shows a print preview of the current document.
- *Copy* copies the current selection to the clipboard.
- *Paste* copies the contents of the clipboard to the current cursor location.
- *Back* displays the previous document in the history list.
- *Forward* displays the next document in the history list.
- *Reload* reloads the current document.
- *Load Home Page* goes to the default home page.
- *Stop Transfer* aborts the loading of a document.
- *Find* searches for a given string in the current document.
- *Add to Hotlist Folder* adds the URL of the current document to the end of your current hotlist.
- *Read Newsgroups* allows you to read UseNet newsgroups, if your copy of Mosaic and your network account are configured properly.
- *Send Internet E-mail* allows you to send Internet e-mail if your copy of Mosaic and your network account are configured properly.
- *Help* shows the About Windows Mosaic window.

IV

Are All Web Browsers Alike?

The World Wide Web has grown quickly over the last few years. At one time, when a new standard was being developed for the Internet, it went through many reviews by an Internet standards committee before it went into common use. Now, people are coming up with their own proprietary Web features and trying to make them the standard by distributing them widely and convincing people to use them.

Mosaic is HTML 2.0 compliant, which is the latest standard that has been approved by the Internet standards committees. Some browsers (like Netscape) support their own non-standard HTML commands. If someone has used one of these non-standard commands in their Web document, you will not be able to see the results of that command if you view the document with Mosaic.

Moving Between Documents

After you start Mosaic, you can move between WWW documents in two ways; you can click links in the document you are viewing or you can use Mosaic's Open Document dialog box to enter a URL. If you've loaded a document, it probably includes links to other documents. After all, the purpose of the WWW is to let you move quickly between related documents without having to enter long path names. If there are no links in the document, it's not a very useful WWW document. But, even if your current document has no links, you can still move between documents.

Note

A third way to move between documents is to use hotlists that contain items with predefined URLs. Creating and using hotlists is covered in the sections "Using Advanced Hotlist Manager to Track URLs" and "Quick Access to Your Favorite URLs," later in this chapter.

Moving Between Documents Using Links

Hypertext links in a document are indicated in the document viewing area. They may be indicated in a number of different ways. If your monitor is color, the links can be displayed in a different color than other text. If you have a black-and-white monitor, the links can be underlined. On all displays, when you move your cursor over an area of the screen that has an active link, your cursor changes from an arrow to a pointing hand.

◀ See "Hypertext (and Hypermedia)," p. 459

A link can be a word, a group of words, or an image. Look at the Windows Mosaic home page in figure 23.3. When you run Mosaic on a color display, you see a number of blue items. The words TM, World Wide Web, National Center for Supercomputing Applications, The University of Illinois, Urbana-Champaign, Search Our Space, Latest Changes, Current Version 2.0.0, Win32s v1.25 Information, and World Wide Web Conference Information are all in blue (the default hyperlink color, which you can change). Also, the large graphic at the top of the window is outlined in blue. For more information see the section "Customizing the Hyperlink Indicators in Windows," later in this chapter.

Fig. 23.3
The Windows Mosaic home page, with hyperlinks underlined and in blue.

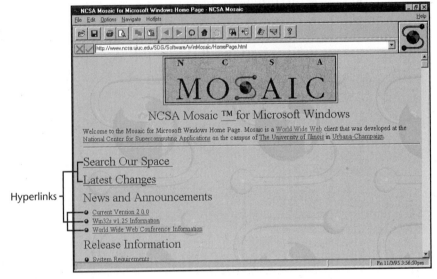

If you move your cursor over any of the blue words or over the graphic, the cursor changes to a pointing hand. The URL associated with each of the links that you pass over appears in the status bar (if it is enabled). To activate a link, place your cursor over the link and click. Mosaic loads that document and displays the URL for the document in the location bar (if it is enabled).

Moving Backward and Forward

> **Tip**
>
> The Mosiac toolbar has Back, Forward, and Reload buttons for quick access to these commands (refer to fig. 23.2).

Typing long URLs and scrolling through documents to look for the links you want can get rather tedious. If you're jumping between a number of documents, take advantage of three helpful navigating commands: Back, Forward, and Reload.

Mosaic keeps information about what documents you have loaded (see a discussion of the history list in the "How to Get Where You Were" section later in this chapter), and lets you move quickly between these documents using the Back and Forward commands. The Back command takes you to the previous document that you had open. To go back, open the Navigate menu and choose Back.

The next command is Forward. What you have to remember about Forward is that you can only move forward after moving back. (This concept is rather confusing, but makes more sense when you have read about history lists in the "How to Get Where You Were" section later in this chapter.) To move forward, open the Navigate menu and choose Forward.

The last command is Reload. This command redisplays the document that you are currently viewing. To reload the current document, open the Navigate menu and choose Reload.

What Is Caching?

When you are reading documents, you often move back and forth between one document and others that are linked to that document. To keep from having to load the main document from its URL every time you view it, Mosaic keeps copies of the last few documents you viewed on your local computer. This is called *caching*. Usually, several documents are kept in memory, which allows for very fast access of those documents. More documents can be cached on disk, where they can be loaded into memory quickly.

Caching is good because it keeps Mosaic from making unnecessary demands on Internet resources. It does take up resources on your own computer, though, so you can only cache a limited number of documents. You can set the number of documents that are cached and the location and size of your disk cache. To set up your caching options:

1. Open the Options menu and choose Preferences. The Windows Preferences dialog box appears.

2. Select the Cache tab.

3. Set the options to your liking. The default number of documents cached in memory is 2. You can change the location and size of your disk cache, along with a number of other options.

(continues)

(continued)

> **4.** Choose OK to set the preferences. If you don't want to make the changes, choose Cancel. You can also choose Apply to set the preferences without leaving the Preferences dialog box.

Moving Between Documents Using URLs

If you don't want to go to any of the documents whose links are displayed in the current document, you did not load a home page, or you do not currently have a document displayed, you can load a new document by specifying its URL to Mosaic. Refer to chapter 20 for information about how to correctly format a URL. To enter a URL directly, follow these steps:

1. Open the File menu and choose Open Document (or select Open Document from the toolbar). The Open Document dialog box shown in figure 23.4 appears.

Fig. 23.4
The Open Document dialog box lets you load any Web page into Mosaic.

2. `http://` appears highlighted in the box. If you are entering a URL for something other than a WWW document (an FTP URL, for example), simply begin typing to replace the highlighted text. If you are loading a WWW document, click in the field at the end of the text and type in the rest of the URL for the document you want to load.

3. Click the check box to load the URL that you entered. Mosaic loads that document and displays the URL for the document in the location bar (if you have it enabled). Click the X if you do not want to load that document.

What You See When a Document Is Loading

When you load a document, Mosaic gives you a lot of information about what is happening. The globe to the right of the location bar rotates, with its beacon flashing. A number of different messages appear in the status bar. These messages can include the following:

- ■ `Doing nameserver lookup on:<server>`
- ■ `Connecting to: <server>`
- ■ `Reading: <URL>`
- ■ `Waiting: <URL>`
- ■ `Transferring <URL>:<counter> bytes`
- ■ `Transferring inline image <filename.gif>:<counter> bytes`

It is nice to be able to watch the counter in the transfer messages increase as the document is loaded. The counter shows how many bytes have loaded for the current document or image, along with the total number of bytes. In addition, for each file that is loaded for the document (the main file and any associated inline graphics), a bar graph representing the percentage of the file that has been loaded appears in the right-hand box in the status bar. You will also see the icons in the center box of the status bar that give you information about the load.

Loading documents can take a few minutes, especially if the document has a lot of large graphics and your computer has a relatively slow (less than 9600 bps) connection to the Internet. You can speed up the loading of the document by telling Mosaic not to load the inline graphics from the document. To stop loading the inline images in Windows Mosaic, open the Options menu and choose Preferences. Choose the Document tab, then select the Display Inline Images check box. This feature is turned off if there is no check mark next to it.

If you turn off the loading of inline graphics, Mosaic displays placeholder icons in the document instead of the graphics. If you want to see one of the graphics that was not loaded, click the graphic icon and Mosaic loads that graphic.

Looking for Information in a Document

If the WWW document you are reading is short, it is easy to scroll through the document (or use Page Up and Page Down) to find information of interest to you. If you have loaded a very long document, though, Mosaic does provide a quick way to look for information. Follow these steps:

1. Open the Edit menu and choose Find, or click the Find toolbar icon, to bring up the Find dialog box.

2. Click the box next to Find What and enter the word or words for which you want to search.

3. Click Match <u>C</u>ase if you want Mosaic to match exactly the capitalization of the words you entered.

4. Choose <u>F</u>ind Next to begin the search. If a match is found, Mosaic scrolls the window to the section where the match is and highlights the matching words. An alert box informs you if no match is found.

If you have closed the Find dialog and want to search again for the last string you searched for, open the <u>E</u>dit menu and choose Find <u>N</u>ext.

Saving Documents

In general, the purpose of the World Wide Web is to be able to have one copy of a document that many people can view, although there are times when you might want to save a copy of a document to your local computer. Mosaic gives you several options for saving documents.

> **Tip**
>
> You can save a document as a text file. Open the <u>F</u>ile menu and choose Save As <u>T</u>ext. This brings up a Save As Text dialog box that lets you browse through your directories and store the current document as text only.

The first way to save a document is to open the <u>F</u>ile menu and choose Save <u>A</u>s. This brings up a Save As dialog box that lets you browse through your directories and store the HTML file wherever you like.

There is another way to save files. Right-click when your cursor is over the hyperlink of a document that you want to save and select Load Anchor to Disk. Instead of loading the document for viewing, Mosaic brings up a Save As dialog box. You then specify a file on your local disk where the document can be saved. You can save any format document in this manner—HTML file, image file, sound file, or unformatted text.

> **Tip**
>
> To load a hyperlink to disk, you can shift-click the hyperlink rather than select Load Anchor to Disk from the right-button menu.

Absolute and Relative Hyperlinks

When you save an HTML document to your local disk, remember that the document probably contains hyperlinks. These links can be relative or absolute. An absolute reference contains the complete address of the document that is being referenced, including the host name, directory path, and file name. A relative reference assumes that the previous machine and directory path are being used, and just the file name (or possibly a subdirectory and file name) is specified.

If the document references other documents with relative addresses, you can't view those documents unless you copy them to your local disk and set them up with the same directory structure they had at the original site. You might want to set up a document and its linked documents on your local disk if you want to be able to view the document without connecting to the Internet. One problem is that if the original document changes, you are not aware of it and are viewing an outdated version of the document.

Absolute references always work unless your Internet connection fails or the referenced documents are moved.

Printing Documents

In addition to being able to save documents, you can print documents directly from Mosaic. Open the File menu and choose Print to send a copy of the current document to your printer. The Print Preview item on the File menu allows you to preview the printed document, and Print Setup allows you to set up your printer.

You can also set up the format of the printed pages. Open the Options menu and choose Preferences. The Printing tab in the Preferences dialog box allows you to set up the margins and the document information that gets printed on each page.

Customizing Your Mosaic Window

This chapter has covered some of the features of Mosaic that let you move between documents. It is possible to customize a number of these features; you can set up Mosaic to behave in a way that is most comfortable for you. This section discusses how to set up Mosaic to your preferences. Most of the preferences you can set that are described in this section are reached by choosing Preferences from the Options menu. There are 13 types of preferences you can set (see fig. 23.5).

Fig. 23.5

Mosaic has Preferences pages that let you set up how documents are loaded and displayed, and Internet Services parameters, among other things.

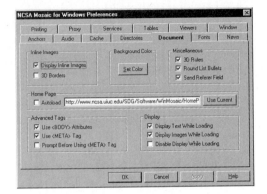

Customizing the Hyperlink Indicators in Windows

You can change the default appearance and color of the hyperlinks in the documents Mosaic loads. To do so, choose the Anchors tab from the Preferences dialog box and set the options you would like (see fig. 23.6).

Fig. 23.6

The Anchors tab in the Preferences dialog box allows you to define how hyperlinks are displayed within your Mosaic window.

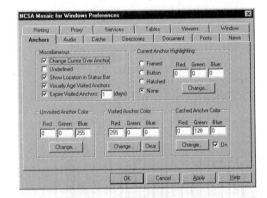

The following list describes the options on the Anchors tab:

- Checking Change Cursor Over Anchor causes Mosaic to change the cursor from a pointer to a hand when it's positioned over an anchor.

- The Underlined check box controls whether anchors are underlined.

- The settings for the different anchor colors (unvisited, visited, cached) take values from 0 to 255 for red, green, and blue components to create different identifying colors for the different anchor types.

- The Current Anchor Highlighting section of the window allows you to control how the current anchor is displayed. You can use the arrow keys to move between anchors if you have one of the highlighting types selected.

■ The other settings in this window allow you to control some other anchor display features and to decide how to treat visited anchors.

Document Customization

When you first select the Preferences menu item, the first set of preferences you can change are the Document preferences (see fig. 23.7). If you want to change something on this sheet and it is not currently displayed, open the Options menu, choose Preferences, then choose the Document tab. On this page are a series of options you have for selecting how your Mosaic window will look. Especially important here is the Home Page item, in the middle of the dialog box. You can specify the URL for your home page here (or none, if that is what you prefer). By checking the Autoload box, you can have this home page loaded automatically at startup. If you are viewing a document and decide that you want to use it as your home page, you can open this preference sheet and choose Use Current.

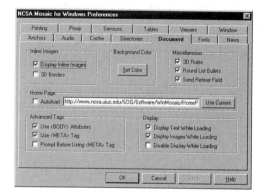

Fig. 23.7
The Document tab in the Preferences dialog box lets you define how Mosaic loads your documents, and allows you to specify your home page.

Other things you can do on this page are enable/disable the viewing of inline images, put 3D borders on inline images, change the background color of your documents, specify what is displayed while a document is loading, and enable the use of some advanced HTML tags.

Window Customization

Tip

You can also turn off the toolbar, location bar, and status bar for the current session directly from the Options menu.

The Preferences Window tab (shown in fig. 23.8) lets you set up your Mosaic window features. Many of the different window areas in Mosaic are optional (not, however, the document viewing area—Mosaic wouldn't be very useful without that!). The title bar and menu bar cannot be removed, but the toolbar, location bar, and status bar can all be turned off using this dialog box. Turning these window areas off gives you a bigger viewing area, but removes some time-saving and informational features.

Fig. 23.8

The Window tab in the Preferences dialog box lets you turn off some of the Mosaic Window areas, specify the display of the date and time, and set the placement of the Mosaic window when it starts up.

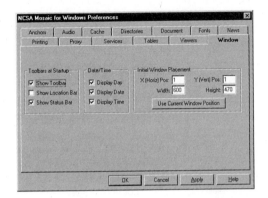

This sheet also lets you set what components (if any) of the date and time are displayed in the status bar, and the initial window placement.

Customizing the Displayed Fonts in Windows

You can customize the fonts that Mosaic uses when displaying documents. HTML documents use standard paragraph tags to describe each paragraph in the document. Mosaic lets you specify the font family, size, and style for each of the standard HTML paragraph tags.

1. Open the Options menu, select Preferences, and choose the Fonts tab (see fig. 23.9).

Fig. 23.9

The Fonts tab in the Preferences dialog box allows you to specify what fonts Mosaic uses to display different kinds of text.

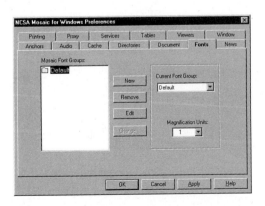

IV

The World Wide Web

2. From the Mosaic Font Groups list, double-click the Default folder, which contains the default fonts for all paragraph tags.

3. Select the paragraph tag of the font you want to change and choose Change (or, double-click the paragraph tag). When you select a paragraph tag, the Font dialog box appears, as shown in figure 23.10.

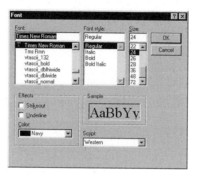

Fig. 23.10
The Font dialog box lets you define the font for the paragraph type you selected.

Even if you aren't familiar with HTML, you can guess what the different paragraph types are. For example, Normal is the regular text font, Heading1 is usually the large heading at the top of a document, and so on.

4. Scroll down through the Font list until you find the font you want and select it. You also can set the Font Style (bold, italic, and so on) and the Size.

5. Choose OK to make the selections take effect, or Cancel if you decide not to change the fonts.

The changes that you make take effect immediately and are used by Mosaic in future sessions.

Viewing Multimedia Files

One of Mosaic's best features is that it enables you to view documents of many different types. If you remember from earlier in the chapter, Mosaic is a multimedia application, which means that you can view files containing a number of different types of media: pictures, sound, and animation. Mosaic can display text and inline graphics directly (as well as some sound files), but to display other types of files, you must have viewers for these files installed on your machine.

After you have a viewer installed and Mosaic knows where to find it and what type of files it displays, you can load files of that type and Mosaic automatically starts the viewer to display them. Mosaic can recognize any of a number of standard image, sound, and animation formats. Some of the more common ones are shown in table 23.1.

Table 23.1 Multimedia File Types Recognized by Mosaic	
Media	**File Type**
Audio	WAV, MIDI
Image	JPEG, GIF
Video	MPEG, AVI
Formatted text	RTF

▶ See "Using Helper Apps," p. 577

If you find a file on a WWW server that is one of the types in table 23.1, set up an external viewer for that file type to work with Mosaic. You only need to click the hyperlink for the file, and Mosaic launches the viewer application with the file loaded. You now can use any of the features of the viewer application to examine, modify, or save the file you loaded.

Working with Local Files

When you think of using Mosaic to view documents, you probably think of retrieving documents from WWW servers on the Internet. Mosaic can read documents from your local file system, as well as from halfway around the world. If you share documents among members of your organization, many of the documents you view may be on a local file server, or possibly on your local computer.

Mosaic provides an option to make it easy to load a local file. If you want to load a local file, open the File menu and click Open Local File. This brings up the Open dialog box shown in figure 23.11; this dialog box lets you browse through all your local disks to find a file.

Fig. 23.11
You can use the Open dialog box to find HTML files on your local disks for Mosaic to display.

You also can load a local file in the same manner that you load any URL. Open the File menu and choose Open Document. To specify a local file in the URL box, precede the directory path of the file with file:///c| (you can substitute any of your local disks for c). The three slashes tell Mosaic that you are looking for a local file, and the bar is used instead of a colon because the colon has a specific purpose in a URL. Use slashes in the directory path you enter, even if you are describing a directory on a PC where the backslash is usually used. Mosaic properly translates the slashes when it retrieves the file.

Local URLs can be used just as all URLs are used—as items in hotlists, links in documents, and so on.

◀ See "URLs,"
p. 463

Effective Browsing Techniques

Navigating between WWW documents can be confusing. Documents often connect back to documents you already read. You may not know you're going to a document you've already seen because different words or pictures are used for the hyperlink than the ones used in the original document (although Mosaic does allow you to show previously visited hyperlinks in a different color).

Sometimes you can't tell from the hyperlink whether the document is of interest to you, and loading documents uses valuable time. Often, you waste time loading documents that you dismiss immediately. This section helps you learn to reduce unnecessary document loading and circular navigating.

How to Keep Track of Where You've Been

Keeping track of where you are and where you were is one of the biggest challenges of using Mosaic. For example, say you're reading a document that deals with agriculture and you click a hyperlink to take you to Hay Field Seeding Suggestions. The document turns out to be one you loaded earlier—when you found a hyperlink for Pasture Management Techniques. How can you avoid this frustrating repetition?

First, make sure that you have Mosaic set up to show previously visited hyperlinks in a different color. Another suggestion is to have a home page that provides links to your most-visited WWW pages. This home page is useful, for example, if you work on a group project and frequently use documents with known locations. You can create your own home page, or someone can create a project home page for your group. In this scenario, you probably are already familiar with the servers, if not the exact documents.

But what if you're navigating in uncharted waters on the WWW? Although it sounds difficult, you probably can learn to recognize the URLs of the sites that keep information of interest to you. If the URL bar is displayed, the URL for the current document is shown there. If you have the status bar displayed, it shows the URL of a hyperlink when you move the cursor over it (see fig. 23.12). As you move between documents, you begin to remember some of the URLs you see frequently—when you put your cursor over a hyperlink, you recognize documents you know.

Fig. 23.12
The status bar displays the URLs of hyperlinks.

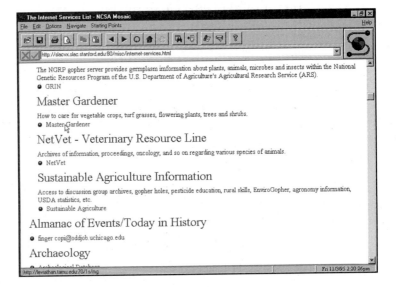

How to Get Where You Were

Trying to navigate back to a document you viewed in the current Mosaic session also can be challenging. In general, to go to the document you viewed prior to the current document, open the Navigate menu and choose the Back command (or choose the left arrow in the toolbar). Choosing the Forward command (or the right arrow) takes you to the last document you viewed after this document. This sounds rather confusing, but is understandable if you look at how Mosaic determines these links.

The Navigate menu has an item called Session History that brings up a window, similar to the one shown in figure 23.13. Notice, there is a list of URLs in this window—the URL for the current document is highlighted.

Fig. 23.13
The NCSA Mosaic History window shows a linear list of URLs you visit.

IV

The World Wide Web

Tip

If the History window is open when you use the Forward and Back commands, you can see the highlighted item move in the list of URLs.

The history list shows you the URLs of the document chain that led you to this point and any documents that you visited after the current document. If you use the Back navigation command, you move up in the list. If you use the Forward navigation command, you move down the list. Click any URL in the list and choose Load to jump to that document (and that point in the list).

Caution

If you move up to one of the higher level links and then jump to a new URL from that document, it wipes out all the URLs past the current document. So, while you can use the Back and Forward navigation commands to move between documents you already visited, if you jump to a new document while in the middle of the list, you erase the links from the current point to the end of the list.

To move quickly between documents that you load, use the history list. If you want to add a new document to the list of ones you're viewing, make sure you're at the end of the list before you jump to that document. You don't have to use hyperlinks to add the document you load to the history list. Load the document from the File menu's Open Document menu item or the Open Document toolbar button, and it is added to the history list.

Using Advanced Hotlist Manager to Track URLs

If you don't want to learn to use HTML commands to create a home page with all your favorite WWW documents, Mosaic has an alternative. To quickly access your favorite URLs, Mosaic lets you create *hotlists*, lists of URLs that you can access quickly.

As it is distributed, Mosaic has one preconfigured hotlist. The Starting Points hotlist lets you access a number of documents on the WWW that help you learn about the World Wide Web and the Internet, and gives you quick access to Internet Services and information repositories. You may want to create your own hotlists, though, to gain access to documents and services you use most. For example, you might want to have a hotlist for each project you work on, with each list giving you access to the documents and services you need for that project.

The Mosaic Advanced Hotlist Manager window allows you to add, delete, and edit Mosaic hotlists. To open the Advanced Hotlist Manager window, open the Navigate menu and choose Advanced Hotlist Manager (see fig. 23.14).

Fig. 23.14

The Mosaic Hotlist Manager window shows current folders and their items, and lets you create, delete, and edit these folders.

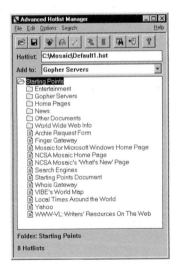

The address of the current hotlist and the current folder in the hotlist are shown in the Advanced Hotlist Manager window. The folders in the current hotlist are shown in the display area. If you double-click a folder in this list, the items from that folder are displayed below it.

Creating a New Folder

Tip

If you have a SuperVGA monitor, use Windows setup to choose a driver for a higher screen resolution (such as 1024 × 768) to get more menu items on-screen.

Folders let you group WWW documents that you use frequently. For example, you may want to have a folder for each project you work on. You can display the top-level folders in a hotlist as separate items on the menu bar, or as items under a single Hotlist menu item (see fig. 23.15 for an example of top-level folders displayed as menus). To display each folder as a menu, open the Options menu in the Advanced Hotlist Manager and select On Menu Bar. The folder names will be shown following the Navigate menu.

Fig. 23.15
The Internet Resources menu has been added to the menu bar.

To create a new folder in the current hotlist, follow these steps:

1. If the Advanced Hotlist Manager window is not already open, open the Navigate menu and choose Advanced Hotlist Manager.

2. Click the line below which you would like the new folder to appear.

3. Open the Edit menu and choose Insert New Folder. The Properties dialog box appears (see fig. 23.16).

Fig. 23.16
The Properties dialog box lets you enter the name of a new folder.

4. Click the box next to Title and enter the name of the folder you want to add.

5. Click OK. The new folder appears highlighted. You are now ready to add items to the folder.

Note

If you are going to show your folders as menu items, choose descriptive and short names for your folders. Mosaic displays these names in the menu bar, and there isn't much room! If the menu list becomes longer than one line, Mosaic expands the size of the menu bar as many lines as it needs to display all menu names. Another alternative is to select the One Root item from the Hotlist Manager Options menu. This will put all of your hotlists on the menu bar under the main heading of Hotlists.

Adding Items to a Folder

After you create a new folder, you can add items to the folder (you can also add items to any existing folder).

To add items to a folder, follow these steps:

1. To open the Advanced Hotlist Manager dialog box, open the Navigate menu and choose Advanced Hotlist Manager.

2. Click the folder that you want to add items to. If you want to place the items somewhere other than the end of the list of items in that folder, double-click the folder to display all of the items in it.

3. If there are existing items in that menu, you can place the new item anywhere in the list. If you click the name of an item in the Items section, the new item is added before the selected one. If you do not select one of the current items (or if you have just highlighted the folder rather than opening it), the new item is added to the end of the list.

4. When you have selected the menu and item position, open the Edit menu and choose Insert New Item to add a document to the menu. The Properties dialog box appears as in figure 23.17.

Fig. 23.17
In the Properties dialog box, enter the name of the document you are adding and the URL associated with it.

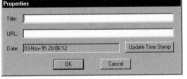

5. Enter the title and URL of the item you are adding in the appropriate boxes, and click OK. The item will be added to the folder.

Adding the Current Document to the Current Folder

The easiest way to add items to your hotlists is to add the title and URL of the current document to the current hotlist folder. To set the current hotlist folder:

1. To open the Advanced Hotlist Manager dialog box, open the Navigate menu and choose Advanced Hotlist Manager.

2. Click the Add to: listbox and select the folder that you want to add items to.

> **Tip**
>
> A quick way to add the current document to the end of your current hotlist folder is to choose the Add to Hotlist Folder button from the toolbar.

Now, to add the current document to the current hotlist folder, simply open the Navigate menu and choose Add Current to Hotlist.

If you are in the Advanced Hotlist Manager, you can add the current document to the selected folder. To do so, open the Edit menu and choose Add Current to Folder (or choose the Add to Hotlist Folder button from the Advanced Hotlist Manager toolbar). If you have an item selected in the folder, the current document will be placed in front of the selected item. If only a folder is selected, the current document will be placed at the end of the selected folder.

Adding the URLs from the Current Document to Your Hotlist

If you would like to add all of the URLs in the current document to your hotlist, from the Advanced Hotlist Manager open the File menu and choose Import Anchors From Current Document. All the URLs from the current document will be placed in a folder that is inserted at the end of the current hotlist. The folder's name will be the title of the current document. You can also add an individual URL from the current document to your hotlist by right-clicking the link and selecting Add Anchor to Hotlist from the pop-up menu.

Editing Hotlists

Once you've created your hotlist, you can rename folders, move or delete items, and change the names or URLs of items. You will need to open the Advanced Hotlist Manager to use any of these editing functions.

IV

The World Wide Web

Editing Hotlist Folders and Items

You can change the names of folders or items, or the URLs of items that are in your hotlist.

1. In the Advanced Hotlist Manager, select the folder or item you want to change.

2. Open the Edit menu and choose Properties (or choose the Properties button from the toolbar). The Properties dialog box shown in figure 23.18 appears, with the contents of the Title text box highlighted.

Fig. 23.18

Choosing Edit allows you to use the Properties dialog box to edit the title or URL of an existing menu item.

3. To replace the name of a folder or item, simply type in the new name. To edit the current name, click in the box and edit the name.

4. Edit the text in the URL box if you need to change the URL of an item.

5. Choose OK to make your changes take effect, or choose Cancel to ignore the changes.

Note

If you want to have a hotlist item that is the same or similar to an existing item, you can make a copy of the existing item. Select the item you want to copy by Ctrl-clicking the item with the left mouse button. Drag the cursor to where you would like the copy and release the button. You can now edit the copy as you would any other hotlist item.

Moving Hotlists Items

If you don't like the way items are ordered in your hotlist, you can move them around and regroup them. To move an item, simply select it and drag it to its new location. If you drag it to a folder, it will be placed at the end of the list of items in that folder. To place the item in front of an item in another list, drag the item and drop it on the second item. It will appear in front of the second item.

Caution

You cannot move an item in front of a folder. If you drop an item on a folder, it goes into the folder rather than in front of it in the list. Also, you cannot drag an item to a folder or part of the list that is off-screen. Try to resize the Advanced Hotlist Manager window so that both the item you are moving and the place where you want to move it appear in the window. If your list is too large for you to do this, you may need to move the item as far down as you can, scroll the window down, then move the item down again until you get it to the part of the list where you want it.

Deleting a Menu Item

Mosaic also lets you delete a menu item or an entire menu. To delete folders or items, click the name of the folder or item you want to delete, and choose Delete from the Edit menu or simply press the Delete key on your keyboard. You will get a confirmation dialog allowing you to cancel the deletion, or go ahead with it. Choose Yes to delete the item or folder.

Creating a New Hotlist

Hotlists are stored as files in your Mosaic directory. You can have multiple hotlist files that have any number of folders and items in them. If you want to create a completely new hotlist, simply open the File menu and choose New from the Advanced Hotlist Manager. You will have a blank hotlist with a single, empty, untitled folder in it. You can now add folders and items to your hotlist as described in the previous sections.

If you have a hotlist that you'd like to use as a basis for a new hotlist, you can modify your existing hotlist then save it in a new file.

Saving Your Hotlists

If you have modified an existing hotlist file, there is no need to save the changes you have made. The file is modified as you make the changes. If you are creating a hotlist file from scratch, or if you want to create a new hotlist by modifying an existing hotlist, you need to save the hotlist. To do so, from the Advanced Hotlist Manager, open the File menu and choose Save As. You will get the Save Hotlist dialog shown in figure 23.19. Enter the name of the hotlist file (if you leave off the .hot extension, Mosaic will add it automatically to your file name).

Fig. 23.19

You can save any number of hotlists to files on your local disk.

Quick Access to Your Favorite URLs

Now that you have all these hotlists set up, how do you use them? Simply select items directly from the Hotlist menu (or from the individual folder menus, if you've set up Mosaic to display them). Mosaic will load the document you select (as long as it can connect to the server and find the document). This saves you the trouble of having to remember and type in long URLs.

Loading a Hotlist

Since you can have any number of different hotlist files, the first thing you should do after starting Mosaic is load the hotlist file you want to use for this session. To load your hotlist file:

1. Open the Navigate Menu and choose Advanced Hotlist Manager.

2. From the Advanced Hotlist Manager, open the File menu and choose Open. The Open Hotlist dialog shown in figure 23.20 appears.

Fig. 23.20

You can load your current hotlist from a file on your local disk.

3. Select your hotlist file from the file browser and select Open.

Your hotlist file will be loaded into the Advanced Hotlist Manager, and will be displayed on the Mosaic menu bar.

Accessing Items in a Hotlist

Once your hotlist file is loaded, you can tell Mosaic how you want to access your hotlist folders. You can configure Mosaic to either display each of the top-level folders in your hotlist as a menu, or to display all of the top-level folders under one Hotlist menu item. Once you have your menus configured, you can easily access the items in your menu.

Setting Up the Hotlist Menus

You'll first need to configure Mosaic to display the hotlist menus. To do so:

1. Open the <u>N</u>avigate menu and choose Advanced Hotlist <u>M</u>anager. The Advanced Hotlist Manager window appears.

2. Open the Options menu and select On <u>M</u>enu Bar to display all the top-level folders as menus on the menu bar. They will appear between the Navigate and Help menus.

3. If you have too many menus defined to fit on the menu bar, select the One <u>R</u>oot item of the <u>O</u>ptions menu to display all of the top-level folder names beneath the Hotlists menu item.

4. Select <u>C</u>lose from the <u>F</u>ile menu to close the window.

When you select a folder from the hotlist menu, a menu containing the items in that folder appears. Select the item that you want to open.

Loading a Document from a Menu

Tip

Double-clicking an item in the Advanced Hotlist Manager causes Mosaic to load the URL for that item.

All documents in your hotlists are accessible from either the Hotlist menu or the top-level folder menus created from your hotlist. These menus appear between the Navigate and Help menus in the menu bar. To access a document in one of these menus, simply follow these steps:

1. Click the menu.

2. Choose an item from the menu. If the item you choose is also a menu, a submenu opens, and you choose an item from it (see fig. 23.21).

Fig. 23.21
The Starting Points folder and other top-level folders appear as submenus to the Hotlists menu.

When you release the mouse button after selecting an item, Mosaic loads the URL for that item.

Sharing Hotlists

Sharing hotlists is a good way to make co-workers and colleagues aware of information resources they would otherwise not know about. If you are sharing your hotlists with other Mosaic users, all you have to do is give them copies of your hotlist files. If, however, you would like to share your hotlists with users of other Web browsers you can still do this. Mosaic allows you to write out your hotlists as HTML files, and to read HTML files into your hotlist.

To save your hotlist as an HTML file:

1. From the Advanced Hotlist Manager, open the File menu and choose Export to HTML File.

2. Using the file browser, select the directory and enter a file name where you want the HTML file to be stored. When you select OK, your hotlist will be stored as an HTML file containing a list of links built from the items in your hotlist.

If your friends are using browsers that can save their hotlists as HTML files, they can share their hotlists with you. Mosaic allows you to read in the URLs contained in a local HTML file and incorporate them into your hotlists. To do so:

1. From the Advanced Hotlist Manager, open the File menu and choose Import HTML File.

2. Using the file browser, select the HTML file that you want to import. A folder will be added to the end of the current hotlist containing items that correspond to all of the links in the HTML file.

Using Built-In Hotlists

Mosaic, as distributed from NCSA, comes with one built-in hotlist folder—the Starting Points folder. You can edit this list to suit your particular needs, and you can delete the Starting Points hotlist just as you can delete any other user-configurable menu.

If you are new to the Internet and the World Wide Web, you may want to use the Starting Points hotlist to do some exploring and familiarize yourself with some of the most common Internet and WWW resources available. Some items in the Starting Points hotlist are:

■ The Starting Points Documents (at the end of the hotlist). These contain links to documents that provide access to Internet services, information about the Internet, and Mosaic reference pages.

- The NCSA Mosaic 'What's New' Page. This gives an overview of new WWW resources. There are links to previous months' announcements at the end of this document.

- World Wide Web Info menu. A menu containing links to documents that give background information about the WWW and have links to interesting WWW sites.

- Home Pages. A menu that links you to some of the more interesting home pages on the WWW.

- Gopher Servers. A connection to a number of different Gopher servers that also gives you access to Veronica searches.

- Other Documents. These contain links to some interesting WWW and Internet services, such as an online encyclopedia and Internet.

Other Internet-Related Features

Although the main function of Mosaic is to allow you to view documents on the WWW, there are a number of other Internet-related services that you can access from Mosaic.

Internet E-Mail

Mosaic allows you to send (but not read) Internet e-mail. The main purpose for this feature is to allow you to send WWW documents (or their URLs) to others who might be interested in them. You will need to enter your name, e-mail address, and an SMTP server (an Internet host that can send e-mail) on the Services tab of the Preferences dialog before you can send e-mail. Once Mosaic is configured correctly, simply open the File menu and choose Send Email. The dialog shown in figure 23.22 opens. Once you've composed your e-mail, choose Send to send it or Abort to cancel it.

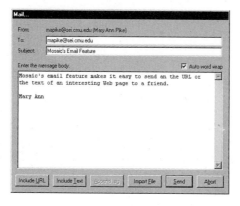

Fig. 23.22
You can enter the recipient, subject, and message in the Mail dialog box. Buttons let you include the URL of the current Mosaic document, text of the current document, or local file on your disk.

Collaborative Sessions

The current release of Mosaic incorporates a feature that allows you to send messages to other Mosaic users. To use the collaboration feature, open the File menu and choose Collaborate. You will see a dialog that asks you whether you want to join, host, or host and join a session. If you want to join a session that someone else is hosting, you will need to enter the name of their Internet host. Once you have done this, you will see the dialog shown in figure 23.23. In addition to sending messages to the other session users, you can send them the URLs of the documents you are loading, or you can actually control their Mosaic windows so that their Mosaic windows load the documents that you load.

Fig. 23.23

The Mosaic Collaborative Session window allows you to send messages to the other session participants.

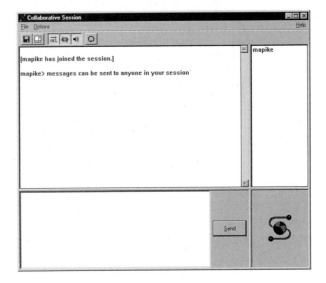

Reading UseNet Newsgroups

Although not as nice an interface as applications designed for the task, Mosaic does allow you to subscribe to and read UseNet newsgroups. In order to do this, you must enter an NNTP server (a machine that lets you read and post to newsgroups) on the News tab of the Preferences dialog. Once you have entered a valid server, you will need to choose Subscribe to pick the newsgroups that you want to read (see fig. 23.24).

Once you've subscribed to your newsgroups, you should close the Preferences dialog. To read your newsgroups, open the File menu and choose Newsgroups. Mosaic will display the newsgroups that you are subscribed to as shown in figure 23.25.

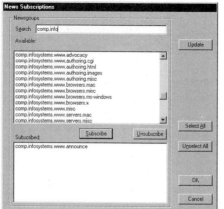

Fig. 23.24
The News
Subscriptions
dialog box lets you
search through a
list of all available
newsgroups and
select the ones that
you want to read
(you can also
subscribe to
newsgroups from
this dialog).

IV

The World Wide Web

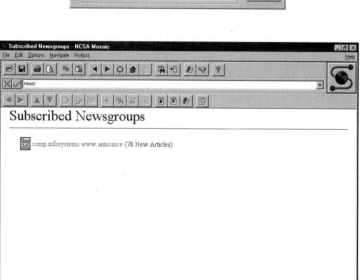

Fig. 23.25
When you read
newsgroups with
Mosaic, the first
thing that you will
see is a list of the
newsgroups that
you are sub-
scribed to.

Click on the hyperlink for the newsgroup that you want to read. Mosaic will
load a list of the available articles. Click on the article that you want to read.
Mosaic will load the article, as shown in figure 23.26. When you read
newsgroups, Mosaic puts an extra toolbar below the location bar. From this
toolbar, you can post new and followup articles, send a reply to the author of
the article, and move back and forth between articles and newsgroups.

Fig. 23.26

When you read an article, Mosaic shows you the author of the article, when it was posted, the title of the articles, and the news-groups it was posted to.

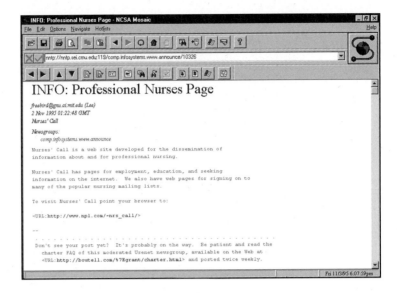

Problems that Occur While Navigating the WWW

The World Wide Web is really a concept still under development, and Mosaic is definitely an application still under development. With a complex application like Mosaic and a conceptually young Internet service like the WWW, there are bound to be problems occasionally.

Some problems that occur are related to limited resources on any particular Internet host (for example, the number of people who can connect to the host at one time may be limited). Traffic over the Internet is steadily growing and communications may be slow. Other problems may be actual bugs in Mosaic. Throughout this chapter, problems related to a certain topic are discussed when that topic is discussed. This section deals with problems that are common to many different Mosaic functions and not mentioned elsewhere.

User Errors

Sometimes you can inadvertently ask Mosaic to do something it can't do. You can make a mistake when typing in the URL, or try to fetch the right document from the wrong machine. Here are a few of the more common user errors and Mosaic's reaction to them.

- Enter an invalid protocol. Windows Mosaic gives you an `Access not available` error alert like the one shown in figure 23.27. Choose OK to make the alert disappear, and then try to load a valid URL.

Fig. 23.27
When Mosaic
encounters an
error, it usually
brings up an alert
box like this one
to let you know
what happened.

- Try to load a document that doesn't exist. You get a File/directory does not exist error alert. Choose OK to make the alert disappear, and then try to load a valid URL.

- Try to load from a site that doesn't exist. You get a Failed DNS Lookup error alert. Choose OK to make the alert disappear, and then try to load a valid URL.

Network Errors

A number of network-related errors can be caused by many problems. For example, a server being down, too much traffic on the network, too many people using a host's resources, or any number of other problems may occur. These types of problems are associated with having a large number of different types of machines and services on a large network.

The following list of error alerts is by no means all-inclusive, but it does show some of the most common errors. If you load the Bug List document from the Windows Mosaic Help menu and scroll down to the bottom, you see the link Common Error Messages in a section entitled Bug Like Features. This link loads a document (**http://www.ncsa.uiuc.edu/SDG/Software/ WinMosaic/errors.html**) that lists most of the errors that you can see—but it doesn't tell you what caused them or how to avoid them.

- SOCKET:Connection has been refused. This error usually occurs because the maximum number of people allowed to use the host's resources are currently online. Try again later.

- SOCKET:Connection timed out. This message comes up if Mosaic tries to communicate with a host and receives no answer in a specific time period. The host is too busy to answer or the machine is hung up.

- SOCKET:Host is down. The host that you tried to reach is down. Try to reach another host that provides the same service or try this one again later.

- Failed DNS Lookup. The host that you tried to reach does not exist. This may or may not be a real error. If you typed the name of the host incorrectly, it is an error. This error also seems to occur if Mosaic tries to look up the host and doesn't get a response from the name server in a specific period of time.

■ `Transfer canceled`. This error is not common, but seems to occur when there are communication problems. For example, if you connect to your Internet provider using the SLIP protocol, and the phone line that you use to dial in becomes noisy for some reason, it causes a transfer to abort.

CHAPTER 24

Using Helper Apps

Everyone has experienced multimedia. On any given day we exercise all our senses to process a variety of information. That information is packaged in different forms: text and pictures in the morning newspaper, highway billboards, the reports that we read at work, music and news on the radio, and video and graphics on the television set. The WWW offers access to a wealth of information, much of it stored as multimedia documents.

Most browsers, including Mosaic and Netscape, require that you download and install special helper applications (often called viewers or players) to see images or play movies and sounds. These external viewer programs allow you to display files in standard multimedia formats: JPEG image files, WAV audio files, and MPEG movie files, among others. When you have the different viewers installed on your PC, getting them to work with most browsers is a straightforward process.

In this chapter, you learn the following:

- What you can expect to find in multimedia documents
- Where to get different viewers
- How to install viewers on your PC
- How to set up browsers to use your installed viewers

After you read this chapter you should be able to set up viewers and configure your Web browser to use them.

Read, Listen, and Watch: Multimedia Is Here

Computer technology enhances the utility of multimedia. You can convert all kinds of information to digital data and then place that data on computer hard drives to be accessed from other files. This ancillary information allows the user to experience a topic, rather than just reading about it.

Graphics Galore: Images on the Web

If you enjoy thumbing through illustrated books or watching slide shows, you'll love the digital-image resources on the Web. For example, if you're a history buff, you can take a trip to the University of Georgia's library server to examine a collection of photographs that chronicle the various Works Progress Administration (WPA) projects that were built in Georgia, including streets, airports, and schools.

Two types of images are on the WWW. The first type are images that appear within Web documents. These inline images can be viewed in the documents when you open them in your browser. For example, the graphic icon or seal that is included at the top of a home page is an inline image. You can see them, but you can't manipulate them or store them on your computer.

Two image-file formats—GIF (Graphics Interchange Format) and XBM (X Bitmap)—can be displayed by most browsers as inline images. Recently, many browsers began supporting inline JPEG (Joint Photographic Experts Group) images also.

GIF and JPEG files are compressed to save space and transmission time. When you link to a Web page, the WWW document is retrieved and downloaded to your computer. You should be aware that your computer and the remote host don't have an exclusive, uninterrupted link. After all, it would waste valuable transmission-line time to have your computer linked to a remote host in Japan while your computer processes a graphic image. Normally, your computer (the client) and the remote server communicate several times before an entire Web page appears. If the page contains more than one inline GIF or XBM image, the images are downloaded to your PC individually and then displayed.

The second type of Web image is one that you ask to view or download. These images usually are in a graphic-file format that provides higher image resolution than GIF or XBM, such as JPEG (Joint Photographic Experts Group). (The latest versions of Mosaic and Netscape can display JPEG images inline.) The JPEG format is an industry standard for compressing 24-bit and 8-bit color, and gray-image files. GIF images take up less space than JPEG images, but they represent only 8-bit images and 256 colors, whereas JPEG supports 24-bit images and 16.7 million colors. Table 24.1 lists some of the most common image formats.

Table 24.1 Some Graphic File Formats	
File Type	**Description**
GIF	Graphics Interchange Format (bit-mapped)
JPEG	Joint Photographic Experts Group
PCX, BMP	Bit-mapped file format
PostScript	Intermediate print format
Encapsulated PostScript TIFF	Tagged image-file format
WRL	VRML 3-D object
XBM (X Windows Bitmap)	UNIX bitmap image

Web documents can contain links to graphic files that cannot be displayed inline (such as TIFF files). You can download these files, as if you were getting them from an FTP site, but you cannot view these files within your browser. You can, however, tell your browser to run a helper application to display these graphic files. There are at least 15 graphic-file formats, each of which requires the use of image-display software. (Table 24.1 lists some of the most common image formats.) Image-display software—known as viewer software—processes and presents images on your monitor.

> **Note**
>
> One advantage of using a viewer to look at the images is that you can change the image; magnify it, change the contrast, or even edit it.

You must, therefore, install and load a graphics viewer—either a commercial product or a shareware or freeware viewer—to see, manipulate, and store these images (table 24.2 lists some of the publicly available viewers). Once you've told your browser what viewer to use for a particular file type, it automatically launches the appropriate viewer application (such as LViewPro) when you download a file of that type (of course, you must have that viewer installed on your computer). Public-domain and shareware viewers, such as LViewPro for Windows 95, are available on the Net (and on the CD that accompanies this book). Commercial browsers, such as Internet In A Box, are bundled with viewers.

Table 24.2 Shareware and Freeware Image Viewers	
Medium Type	**Viewer**
GIF/JPEG/TIFF images	LViewPro, Paint Shop Pro, VuePrint, Poly View
PostScript files	GhostScript
Adobe PDF	Adobe Acrobat Reader

Let's Hear It—How to Enable Sound

The simplest way to listen to sounds (audio files) on the WWW is to purchase a computer that meets the standards for multimedia PCs. The Multimedia PC (MPC) Marketing Council (which consisted of Microsoft and other leading hardware and software companies) published a standard—the MPC Standard—for future developments in PC-based multimedia. The standard was founded on the Windows graphical user interface enhanced with multimedia software components and programming tools. Windows 95 is designed for multimedia, with a built-in application (Media Player) that handles video (.AVI files) and sound (.WAV and .MID files). Windows 95 also has built-in support for many CD players and video boards. Basic PCs typically have a single, small mono speaker that emits sound levels ranging from barely audible to adequate. The more recent 80486 and Pentium-based IBM-compatible computers go beyond these initial standards. Table 24.3 tells you what your system should have to be able to take full advantage of using sound in multimedia applications.

Sound cards play, record, or generate sounds of any kind, including speech, music, and sound effects. With an MPC-compatible PC and appropriate driver software, you can travel through the Web and listen to a jazz session, a volcanic eruption, or a debate on taxes. MPC computers require sound cards with specific requirements. Table 24.4 lists the common audio file formats that you are likely to come across. Table 24.5 shows some shareware audio players.

Table 24.3 MPC Sound-Card Requirements	
External Connections	**Input and Output**
Microphone	Built-in amplifier
Speakers/headphones	Synthesizer
Stereo system	Stereo channels
MIDI devices	8-bit DAC/ADC (16-bit recommended)
CD-ROM drive	22.05 KHz sampling rate (44.1 KHz recommended)

Table 24.4   Common Audio Formats

File Type	Description
UNIX AU	UNIX audio file
MID	MIME Midi file
RA	RealAudio file
WAV	Waveform audio

Table 24.5   Shareware and Freeware Audio Players

Medium Type	Player
WAV sounds	Media Player, WHAM
Midi sounds	Midi Gate
RA sounds	RealAudio AU sounds, WPLANY

> **Note**
>
> PCs that meet the MPC standard can play sound. Here is how to set up a PC that has a speaker but doesn't have a sound board. The PC speaker driver for basic PC speakers was developed by Microsoft and is available at no charge to licensed users of Windows. Download the file SPEAK.EXE from the URL address **http://www.ncsa.uiuc.edu/SDG/Software/WinMosaic/Viewers/Speak.htm** or FTP to **ftp.ncsa.uiuc.edu**, directory /Web/Mosaic/Windows/viewers, file SPEAK.EXE. You can use WWW or other search software to search other file archives for the file.
>
> The file SPEAK.EXE is a self-extracting file. Extraction will produce a SPEAKER.DRV file. Do not place that file in a separate directory from OEMSETUP.INF.

Lights, Camera, Action—How to Enable Movies

In the 1930s and 40s, audiences could watch the latest news events in movie theaters that played newsreels. In the 1950s, 60s, and 70s, television crews traveled all over the world to capture current events. In the 1980s, with the invention and wide distribution of video camcorders, individuals who captured interesting and newsworthy events could get their footage broadcast. Now, at the turn of the century, the Internet opens a vast avenue for video (news, entertainment, commercials, and so on) that people and companies record and place on the WWW.

By bypassing the traditional outlets for video—broadcast and cable companies—the Web promises to deliver a tremendous amount of specialized video information that we otherwise would not be able to access. In addition, because Web video is "on-demand," we can watch when our own schedule permits. One example of WWW video is a QuickTime movie that shows people hang-gliding from ridges and mountains in California (the video is on a server at Stanford University). Table 24.6 shows some of the video file formats that you may come across.

You can get digital movies through WWW browsers using MPEG (Motion Picture Experts Group) and QuickTime file formats. Download time, however, may be excessive if you are using SLIP/PPP dial-up connections. Regardless, expect a comparatively short playback time (for example, a 5-minute download at 14.4 kbps for a 10-second video clip). These frustrating time factors will become less of a problem as larger bandwidths and faster modems become available. Table 24.7 lists some of the video viewers that are available.

Table 24.6   Video Formats

Format	Description
AVI	Video for Windows
MPEG	(Motion Picture Standard for compressed video Experts Group)
QuickTime format	Apple Computer's cross-platform movie

Table 24.7   Some Freeware and Shareware Video Viewers

Medium Type	Player
AVI	Media Player
QuickTime movies	QuickTime Player
MPEG movies	MPEGPLAY

MIME—A Multimedia Standard

All the multimedia viewers that you come across handle MIME (Multipurpose Internet Mail Extensions) standard multimedia files. MIME was developed to extend the Internet e-mail standard (originally developed for text-only messages) to allow any type of data to be sent via e-mail. The WWW browsers use this same standard for identifying the type of multimedia files.

The basic MIME types identified by WWW browsers are text, audio, image, video, and application. (Application is a catch-all category that lets you associate almost any type of file with an application that will be able to display that file.) Browsers can be configured to use different viewers for different subtypes (video/avi and video/mpeg, for example).

Most Web browsers have a list of standard MIME types/subtypes in their helper application configuration section. Usually, you can add your own MIME types to these lists.

Finding and Installing Multimedia Viewers

You can run most Web browsers without installing any additional multimedia viewers. However, installing these viewers allows you to more fully experience Web documents. In general, to use a viewer, you load the viewer file on your local disk, unpack (and install if necessary) the viewer, then configure your browser to use the viewer for appropriate file types. This section tells you how to find and unpack/install viewers.

> **Note**
>
> If you are using a program that you already have installed as a viewer, skip ahead to the section on how to configure your particular browser to use viewers.

Retrieving Multimedia Viewers

A number of the helper applications discussed in this chapter can be found on NetCD95. If the viewer you want is not on the CD (or, if you want to check to see if there is a more recent version, you may be able to pick it up from one of the many software archives on the Internet. Both Mosaic (**http:// www.ncsa.uiuc.edu/SDG/Software/WinMosaic/viewers.htm**) and Netscape (**http://home.netscape.com/assist/helper_apps/ windowhelper.html**) have collections of helper applications at their sites. In addition, The Ultimate Collection of Winsock Software site (**http:// www.tucows.com**) is a great place to pick up a large variety of software.

NetCD95

To load a viewer that you find on a Web page, click the hyperlink for that viewer. Most browsers will automatically ask you if you want to save the file (since it is an executable file). When you say yes, you can fill in the information on where you want to put the file in the Save As dialog box that appears, and then choose OK. The viewer will be loaded to your disk, and you are ready to install it.

There are many viewer programs that can handle the different types of media files you find on the Web. Some of these are commercial software packages; others are shareware that you can find on the Internet. If you have more questions about viewers, or can't find the viewers you need, here are some additional sources of information:

- Use Gopher or FTP to go to some of the big software repositories on the Internet and look around for viewer programs. Chapter 47, "Top FTP Sites," and chapter 49, "Top Gopher Sites," list some of these servers.

- Chapter 50, "Installing and Using NetCD95," has a section that talks about the viewers that are included on NetCD95.

- If you have UseNet access, take a look at the newsgroup **comp.infosystems.www.browsers.ms-windows**. A discussion of viewers is an appropriate topic for this group.

Installing Multimedia Viewers

After you've found a viewer that you want to use and have downloaded the viewer file to your PC, you will most likely need to install the viewer. This may be as simple as unzipping the file you've retrieved, or it may involve going through a Windows setup procedure. In general, to install a multimedia viewer, follow these steps:

1. If you haven't already downloaded the files for the viewer that you need, consult the preceding section, "Retrieving Multimedia Viewers." Alternatively, find a viewer that interests you on NetCD95, and follow the installation instructions in chapter 50, "Installing and Using NetCD95." (Remember that the software included with the CD is shareware and must be registered and paid for if you use it.)

2. If the viewer comes as a ZIP file, create a directory for the viewer, move the ZIP file there, and unzip the file in the new directory. Look for a README file and follow any instructions that are in that file. This will probably be all you need to do for viewers that come as ZIP files.

3. If the viewer comes as a self-extracting archive (.EXE file), create a temporary directory and place the viewer file there.

4. Double-click the file to unpack it.

> **Tip**
>
> To execute a viewer's setup or installation file, double-click the file from Windows Explorer.

5. If the viewer has an install or setup program, open the Start menu, select Run, and enter the path to the install or setup file in the command line text box of the Run dialog box as follows:

```
c:\viewer\install.exe
```

To install the viewer, follow the directions on-screen.

Popular Multimedia Viewers

This section provides descriptions of applications that you can use to view graphics, photographs, and movies, and to listen to sounds that are available on the Web. The descriptions contain information about installing the applications, along with quick overviews of the main features of the applications.

LViewPro

Unzip the LViewPro file (LVIEWPRO.ZIP) into the directory where you want to keep the software. This is the 32-bit version of LviewPro, and must be registered ($30 fee) if you decide to keep using it. LviewPro lets you edit a number of different graphic file formats. In addition, you can do screen captures with LviewPro.

Midi Gate

Unzip the Midi Gate file (MIDIGATE.ZIP) into a temporary directory, then run the SETUP.EXE file. Select the directory where you want the application to be installed, and the setup program will proceed to install the application on your disk, and create an entry in your Start menu Programs item. You have a 30-day free-trial period before you have to pay the $10 registration fee. This application allows you to play midi sound files.

Mod4Win

Unzip the Mod4Win file (M4W230SL.ZIP) into the directory where you want to keep the application. After a 30-day trial period, you must pay the registration fee of $30 for this software. This application allows you to play sound files in a number of different formats.

MPEGPLAY

Unzip the MPEGPLAY file (MPEGW32H.ZIP) into a temporary directory, then run the SETUP.EXE FILE. Select the directory where you want the application to be installed, and the setup program will proceed to install the application on your disk, and create an entry in your Start menu Programs item.

If you are using an unregistered version of MPEGPLAY, you will get the About box every time you view a video with MPEGPLAY. In addition, the unregistered version of MPEGPLAY is limited to viewing MPEG files that are smaller than 1MB (which is not very big for an MPEG file). If you are going to be using MPEGPLAY a lot, you probably want to register it and get the better version (a $25 cost for individual users).

Paint Shop Pro

Unzip the Paint Shop Pro file (PSP311.ZIP) into a temporary directory, then run the SETUP.EXE file. Select the directory where you want the application installed, and the setup program proceeds to install the application on your disk. You have a 30-day free-trial period before you have to pay the $69 registration fee. In addition to allowing you to view and edit almost two dozen different graphic file formats, this application provides you with the capability to create your own graphic images.

PolyView

Unzip the PolyView file (POLYV220.ZIP) into the directory where you want to keep the application. The registration fee for this software is $20, which enables some of the more important features of the application (like being able to print your pictures). This application allows you to view and edit a number of different graphics file formats.

RealAudio

When you execute the RealAudio .EXE file (RA32_2B1.EXE), you have the option of doing an Express or Custom installation. If you do an express installation, the application is installed in the C:\raplayer directory. If you do a custom installation, you have the option of installing the application in a directory of your choice. When either installation option is complete, the Real Audio player starts, and a message thanking you for installing the software is played.

RealAudio gives you the ability to play real-time sound over the Internet. This application plays only .RA files. More information about RealAudio can be found at their Web site at **http://www.realaudio.com**. This application is freeware, and no registration is necessary.

VuePrint

When you execute the VuePrint exe file (VUEPRO42.EXE), it informs you that it will be installing its files in your Windows directory, and gives you no options for installing the files elsewhere. There are a number of alert boxes that inform you of some installation options you have. You get a 15-day trial period, after which you must pay the registration fee of $40.

This application is a graphic file viewer, a sound and movie file player, a screen saver, and decoder/encoder. If you pay the $40 application fee, it gives you the right to run the application on four computers with free technical support.

WHAM

Unzip the WHAM file (WHAM133.ZIP) into the directory where you want to keep the application. The registration fee suggested for this software is $25 to $30. This application allows you to play and record .WAV format sound files.

WPLANY

Unzip the WPLANY file (WPLNY12A.ZIP) into the directory where you want to keep the application. This application allows you to play about half-a-dozen different types of sound files (including .AU, .VOC, and .WAV). This software is freeware, with no registration fee required.

Viewing Multimedia Files from Internet Explorer

Along with most other Web browsers, Internet Explorer allows you to automatically process pictures, movies, and audio files when they are included in documents on the Internet. If you are connected to the Internet through a slow link (such as a modem running at less than 14.4 Kbps) you can disable the automatic processing of these multimedia files by unchecking the Show Pictures, Play Sounds, and Show Animations checkboxes on the Appearance tab of the Options dialog box, which you get by selecting View, Options.

Internet Explorer uses the content type of the multimedia file to determine how to display it on your system. Most WWW servers tell the Web browser what type of file is being sent when the file is selected (for example, a picture in the Graphics Interchange Format is sent in image/gif format).

The viewer for the document types is defined on the File Types tab of the Options dialog box. For many file types, Internet Explorer can display them directly, but for some (such as images in Paintbrush format), an external viewer can be set. These file associations are the same as the normal Windows 95 file associations, so if you already have a viewer defined for a particular file type, Internet Explorer uses that viewer automatically.

Viewing Multimedia Files from Netscape

Netscape can display text and inline graphics directly; to display other types of files, you must have viewers for these files installed.

After you have your viewers installed, and when Netscape knows where to find those viewers and what type of files they display, Netscape automatically starts the correct viewer when you click the hyperlink for a file of a recognized type. Netscape can recognize a number of standard image, sound, and animation formats, although you need to tell it what applications to use to view files of these formats.

Defining Helper Applications for Recognized MIME Types

Once you have installed viewers on your PC, you need to configure Netscape to use these viewers. The Preferences dialog box lets you easily specify which viewers you have and what file types they can handle. To specify a helper application for a particular file type, follow these steps:

1. Choose Options/General Preferences and select the Helpers tab (see fig. 24.1).

Fig. 24.1
The Helpers tab allows you to associate MIME types with helper applications, and to add new MIME types.

2. Scroll through the list of File types and associated files extensions until you find the file type that your viewer can handle, and select that file type.

3. If you need to add a new file extension to the list of extensions associated with that file type, enter them in the File Extensions field, separated by commas. Do not include the dot at the beginning of the file extension.

4. In the Action area, choose the radio button that describes what you want Netscape to do when it loads files associated with this MIME type.

   ■ Choose Save to Disk if you want to save the files directly to disk.

   ■ Choose View in Browser if you want Netscape to try to load and display the file itself. Netscape can only handle files that contain information formatted as text, HTML, JPEG, GIF, or XBM information.

   ■ Choose Launch the Application if you want to launch a viewer with the file loaded into it, enter the path to the application in the text box below the radio button. You can click Browse to bring up the Select an appropriate viewer dialog box in which you can look through your directories to find the viewer. Select the viewer in the dialog box and its path will be automatically entered in the text box.

   ■ You can also click the Unknown: Prompt User radio button if you want Netscape to bring up a dialog box that asks what you want to do with the file when it finds a file of that MIME type.

5. When all the information is entered correctly, click OK to close the Preferences dialog box and save the viewer information.

You can make additional changes to installed viewers at any time.

Note

Even though they are not specifically mentioned in the Helper Applications area of the Preferences dialog box, Netscape automatically launches many of the standard applications (like Word and Paintbrush) when it finds files whose extensions are associated with those applications.

Adding a New MIME Type

One of the nice features of the MIME standard is the MIME type application. The application MIME type lets you specify any subtype, so you can have a MIME type for any application that you run frequently. If you would like Netscape to be able to start an application when it tries to load a file of a particular type, add a new MIME type for that application. To do so:

1. Choose Options/General Preferences and select the Helpers tab.

2. Select Create New Type to bring up the Configure New Mime Type dialog box (see fig. 24.2).

Fig. 24.2

Enter the New MIME type and subtype in the Configure New Mime Type dialog box.

3. Enter *application* in the Mime Type text box. Then enter a word that describes the subtype in the Mime SubType text box. For example, if you want to start Word when you load a .DOC file, you could make the subtype x-word (an x is usually put in front of a user-defined subtype).

4. Click OK to add this new MIME type to the Helper Applications scroll list. The entry for this new type will be highlighted in the scroll list. You can continue with step three from the preceding section, "Defining Helper Applications for Recognized MIME Types," to finish configuring the file extension and viewer information for this new MIME type.

> ### Caution
>
> When you add a new MIME type, the type and subtype information should be entered correctly. Once you choose OK in this area of the Preferences dialog box and add that type, there does not appear to be a way of editing or removing the MIME type and subtype information from the scroll list.

Loading a File with an Unknown Viewer

If you selected the Unknown radio button as the action for a particular MIME type, Netscape brings up the dialog box shown in figure 24.3 when you try to load a file associated with that MIME type. Choose Save to Disk to bring up a Save As dialog box that lets you store the file anywhere on your local disk.

Fig. 24.3
If Netscape doesn't have a viewer configured for a file type, it will ask you what to do with the file when you try to load it.

Tip

To stop Netscape from starting the viewer you've defined for a file type, choose Options, General Preferences and change the Action on the Helpers tab to Unknown: Prompt User, or change the File Extensions to a non-existing value.

If you choose Configure a Viewer, you get the Configure External Viewer dialog box (see fig. 24.4). Netscape chooses the MIME type and subtype that it thinks is appropriate for this file. Enter the path of the viewer you want to use for this MIME type in the text box, or choose Browse to browse your local disk for the viewer application that you want (click the application and the path of the viewer will be entered in the text box). When the viewer information is correct, click OK. Netscape loads the file into the viewer. Netscape automatically starts this viewer anytime it loads a file of this MIME type.

Fig. 24.4
When Netscape tries to load a MIME type for which it has no viewer configured, it gives you the option of configuring a viewer for that MIME type.

Caution

Be careful if you configure a viewer from the Unknown File Type dialog box. Netscape may not choose an appropriate MIME type for the file type you've selected, and you may end up launching the application you've picked for other file types that it can't handle.

Specifying Netscape's Temporary Directory

When Netscape loads files into viewers, it first loads a copy of the file into a temporary directory, and then starts the viewer with a pointer to that temporary file. To tell Netscape where to put these temporary files in the Preferences dialog box, do the following:

1. Choose Options/General Preferences and select the Apps tab (see fig. 24.5).

Fig. 24.5

You can enter the directory where you want Netscape to store temporary files on the Apps tab of the Preferences dialog box.

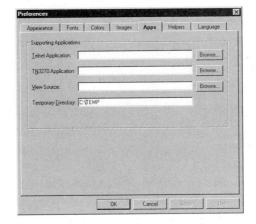

2. In the Temporary Directory field, enter the path to the directory where you want temporary files stored.

3. Click OK to close the Preferences dialog and save the temporary directory information.

Viewing Multimedia Files from Mosaic

Mosaic can display text and inline graphics directly, to display other types of files, you must have viewers for these files installed on your machine.

After you have a viewer installed and Mosaic knows where to find it and what type of files it displays, you can load files of that type, and Mosaic automatically starts the viewer to display them. Mosaic can recognize any of a number of standard image, sound, and animation formats. However, you have to tell Mosaic what helper applications to use to view those files.

Configuring Mosaic to Use Viewers

Once you have installed viewers on your PC, you need to configure Mosaic to use these viewers. Older versions of Mosaic required you to edit the MOSIAC.INI. However, there is now a sheet in the Preferences dialog box to let you easily specify which viewers you have and what file types they can handle. To configure Mosaic:

1. Choose Options/Preferences. In the Preferences dialog box, select the Viewers tab for a sheet that allows you to customize Mosaic to use viewers (see fig. 24.6).

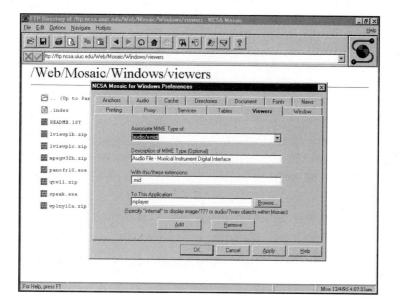

Fig. 24.6
The Viewers tab in the Mosaic Preferences dialog box lets you associate helper applications with any MIME type.

2. Click the arrow to the right of the Associate MIME Type of: text box. Scroll through the list until you find the MIME type for the viewer you are installing.

3. If you want, enter a description of the MIME type in the indicated text box (this is optional).

4. Enter the file extension(s) that are associated with this MIME type in the With this/these extensions text box. If you have multiple file extensions, separate them with a comma. Be sure to include the dot at the beginning of the file extension.

5. In the To This Application text box, enter the path to the viewer. You can click <u>B</u>rowse to bring up a Browse dialog box to let you look through your directories to find the viewer. If you click the viewer in the Browse dialog box, its path is automatically entered in the text box.

6. Once all the information on this sheet is entered correctly, click OK to close the Preferences dialog and save the viewer information.

You can make additional changes to installed viewers at any time by selecting the Associated MIME Type and making the changes. To remove a MIME type and its associated information, select the MIME type and choose <u>R</u>emove.

Configuring Application Viewers

One of the nice features of Mosaic is that you can define viewers for file types such as Word or ZIP, so that if Mosaic loads one of these file types, it automatically starts the correct application to display the file. You can add viewers like these by adding a new MIME type of application/<name>. For example, you can add a MIME type of application/word or application/zip. To add a new MIME type and its associated viewer, follow these steps:

1. Choose <u>O</u>ptions/<u>P</u>references. In the Preferences dialog box that appears, select the Viewers tab for a sheet that allows you to customize Mosaic to use viewers.

2. To add a completely new viewer, click <u>A</u>dd to get the Add Viewer dialog box (see fig. 24.7).

Fig. 24.7
Enter the information for a New MIME type and its associated file types and helper applications in the Add Viewer dialog box.

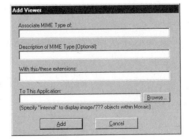

3. Enter the new MIME type in the Associate MIME Type of: text box (remember, it should be of the form application/<name>).

4. Fill in the remainder of the text boxes as described in steps 3, 4, and 5 of the preceding section, "Configuring Mosaic to Use Viewers."

5. Choose <u>A</u>dd to add that MIME type to the list (or Cancel to skip adding it).

6. Once all the information on this sheet is entered correctly, click OK to close the Preferences dialog box and save the viewer information.

Using Viewers

When you have viewers installed and have configured your browser to use the viewers, you're ready to go. If you're viewing a document that contains links to multimedia files, or if you're browsing an FTP or Gopher site, all you need to do is click the link to the multimedia document. Your browser loads the document, automatically starting the viewer that you defined for displaying that type of multimedia file.

Notice that because the image is loaded in an external application, you can continue to use your browser window while the helper application loads and displays the image.

Troubleshooting

I downloaded a picture and it opened fine in LView (or any other multimedia viewer). But I went back to view the picture later, and the file wasn't there. What happened?

The problem isn't with LView or any of the viewers. When your browser downloads multimedia files for viewing, it creates a temporary file, and that is what you view. If you want to save multimedia files that you download for later use, save them before you exit the viewer application—or load them to your local disk and then view them. If you decide that you'd like to keep a file after you exit the viewer, you may still be able to find the file in your browser's temporary directory if you haven't exited your browser.

CHAPTER 25

Planning Your Own WWW Home Pages

This chapter introduces you to concepts you will need to consider as you plan and develop your WWW home page. Some will be basic layout considerations as used in the print media. Other decisions, such as where you house your WWW home page, will be more complicated.

While following chapters outline how to create and enhance your pages, this chapter concentrates on how to plan your pages. Factors such as picking your audience, laying out your pages, finding a place to host your pages, and how to keep your visitors coming back for more are considered. The pricing structures used by WWW providers when charging you for your WWW pages are also examined.

In this chapter, you learn about the following:

- Who has home pages and why
- How to decide where to store your home page
- Mechanisms for storing and accessing HTML documents
- Designs for a good home page
- How to generate interest in your home page
- HTML editors and filters

Getting Started: Basic Decisions

Now that you've gotten an idea, from the previous chapters, of all the different things you can do on the World Wide Web, you are probably excited about putting up your own WWW home page.

Before you start planning your own home page, it might prove useful to look at who already has home pages. Figures 25.1 through 25.6 show some of the interesting people and organizations who have home pages.

Fig. 25.1
This figure shows the NASA Goddard Space Flight Center home page (**http://www.gsfc.nasa.gov/gsfc_homepage.html**).

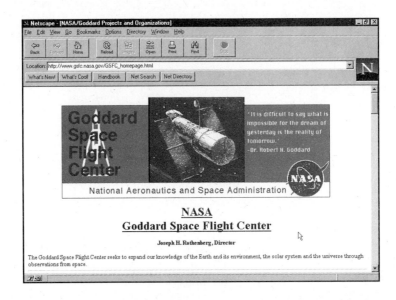

Fig. 25.2
This is Senator Kennedy's home page (**http://www.ai.mit.edu/projects/iiip/Kennedy/homepage.html**).

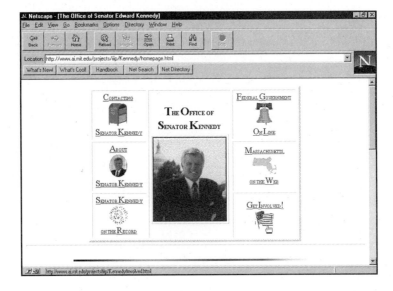

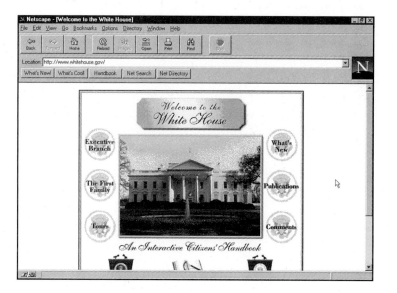

Fig. 25.3
The White House home page lists, among other things, the President's schedule (**http://www.whitehouse.gov/**).

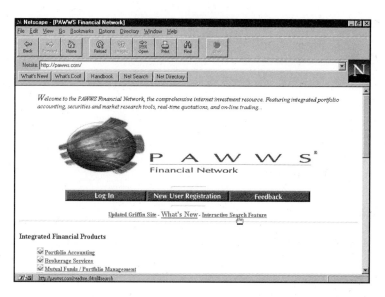

Fig. 25.4
The Pawws Financial Services home page allows you to view delayed stock quotes (**http://pawws.com/**).

Fig. 25.5
This figure shows the *USA Today* home page, which is updated daily (**http://www.usatoday.com/**).

Fig. 25.6
This figure shows the Czeslaw Milosz home page and allows you to listen to poetry snippets (**http://sunsite.unc.edu/ipa/milosz/milcov.html**).

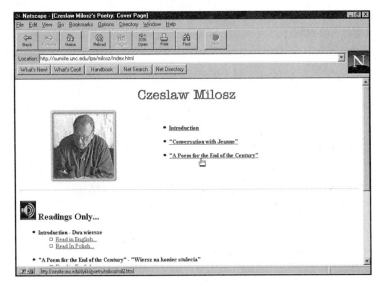

There are many reasons to have a home page, but they really narrow down to the following key points:

- You can reach an amazing number of people.
- It is relatively inexpensive compared to traditional advertising and information distribution methods.

Anyone who wants a presence on the World Wide Web can have one by simply creating a home page and posting it at a WWW site. If you can use a word processor, you can design an HTML document. Putting a home page on the WWW can be fun and rewarding.

The next three chapters will get you started on your way to establishing your presence on the World Wide Web.

Planning for Your Audience

With the release of Windows 95 and other network software products, we know that many more people will have access to the WWW than ever before. However, getting these millions of people to visit your home page is unlikely. This is mainly because of two factors. First, there are so many places to go and things to do on the Web, that people pick and choose where they spend their electronic time with some care. Secondly, unlike traditional advertising, which comes to the user, the Internet user must find your advertisement.

Your home page then should be targeted for a certain audience and should be designed to encourage them to visit your page. Who do you envision visiting your home page? Businesspeople? Casual users looking for something new and exciting? Special interest groups like a local Girl Scout troop or the Lion's Club? The wording of your home page, the graphics you decide to use, and where you decide to post announcements for your home page should all hinge on your anticipated audience. For instance, if a law firm was advertising its services, its choice of words and graphics would be conservative and lend an air of professionalism (see fig. 25.7).

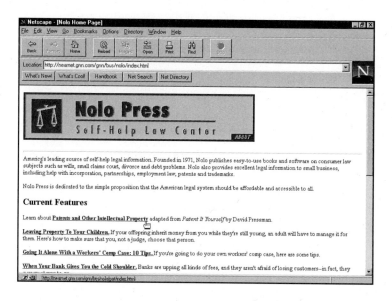

Fig. 25.7
The Nolo Press Self-Help Law Center.

However, a rock band could use wording and graphics that were more experimental, reflecting their style and statement (see fig. 25.8).

Fig. 25.8
The Rolling Stones home page reflects the style of their latest tour while allowing the user to listen to audio selections and order merchandise.

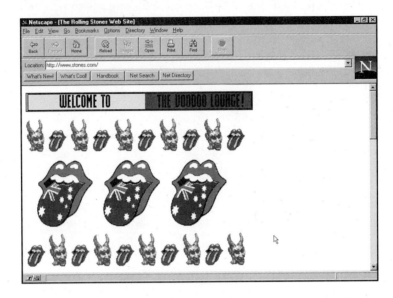

The law firm may wish to describe its company profile, its staff of dedicated employees, its hard-won cases, and happy clients. The rock band may give users information about upcoming concerts, and allow them to hear a cut from one of the group's CDs and order it right from their computer.

Remember, your home page, like your business card or résumé, says a lot about you. It is a reflection of the person or organization who created the page. A messy and hard-to-read page will not be as popular because it is not simple and engaging. Likewise, pages with huge quantities of text and many links often become tedious to users. Care must be made in creating a page that expresses all you want to say, while remaining desirable for users to access.

In many cases, repeat visitations are desirable. This is the case for anyone using the Web to market and/or sell a product or service. These types of pages especially must allow for ease of access and use.

The first *W* in WWW stands for *World*. This is important to keep in mind as you design and plan your pages. Whether or not you are interested in having a presence to the world when you put your page on the WWW, you *will* have a presence to the world. If your page has general access to one person on the Internet, it will have access to *all* persons on the Internet. This means you will get visits from people in other countries and other cultures. When designing your pages you may wish to keep this in mind. Slang or street phrases, which in one culture may be apparent, can be confusing for those to whom English is a second language. Likewise, content may be an issue as cultural, social, and political codes differ from country to country.

Even though the world has access to your pages, you need to be conscious of local laws and government guidelines. Just because a site in one country can offer encryption software for downloading does not mean that you can. Creating such a site in the United States is against the law.

This caution extends even to your page's content. For example, it may be completely legal for someone to post pornographic material to a site in one country, but completely illegal for you to do so in your country or city. The rule of thumb is to always go by the laws of the place you live in.

The bottom line with the Web is that it is currently unregulated and open territory. It is similar to the old West: anything and everything goes, and the laws are just beginning to be written. Indeed, this is one of its major attractions and one of the primary reasons that the Web is so popular—it offers something for everyone.

As the Web and Internet grow and mature you can expect to see changes in what is allowed and what is illegal. You should try to keep abreast of WWW developments. One method to do this is to keep current with the many Internet and Web magazines that are beginning to appear. Magazines such as *Boardwatch*, *Netguide*, *Wired*, *Mondo 2000*, and *Internet World* offer the latest breaking information on the politics of the Web and Internet.

Housing Your Home Page

One of the first questions you need to answer is, "Where am I going to store my home page?"

If your Internet provider allows users from the outside to FTP in, or is running a WWW server, you may be able to store your pages locally on your provider's computer.

If your provider does not allow FTP access from the outside and is not running a WWW server, you may need to find somewhere else to place your pages.

▶ See "Using FTP and Popular FTP Programs," p. 837

◀ See "Connecting Through CompuServe," p. 231

◀ See "Connecting Through America Online," p. 263

◀ See "Connecting Through Prodigy," p. 287

> **Note**
>
> Many companies that have Internet access allow their employees to create and maintain personal Web pages. Of course, this is a courtesy, but you can speak to your network administrator for company policies and to set up an account. Also, Internet access providers, like America Online and CompuServe, are now offering home page services.

▶ See "How UseNet Works," p. 749

Many commercial WWW providers exist. Finding them is a matter of reading the various Net newsgroups that discuss them. Some good newsgroups to read include the following:

> **comp.infosystem**
>
> **comp.infosystems.www**
>
> **comp.infosystems.www.announce**

Another good source is the What's New page at NCSA, or any of the many popular search engines. The following WWW URLs give you access to lists that allow you to see what's new on the WWW as well as search for information such as WWW providers and authors:

> **http://www.ncsa.uiuc.edu/SDG/Software/Mosaic/Docs/ whatsnew.htmlhttp://www.nexor.co.uk/**
>
> **http://cuiwww.unige.ch/**
>
> **http://www.lycos.com/lycosinc/index.html**

A Web Site Option for Your PC

If you have a networked PC, that is to say if your PC has a registered IP address and node name within a domain, you may want to investigate whether you can provide your own Web site. By simply adding Web server software to your PC, you can make your PC a Web site.

There are Windows 95 Web server applications available—Personal Web Server is part of Chameleon by NetManage, for example—that enable your PC to serve HTML documents back to requesting clients. If you choose to go this route, you can save quite a bit in provider costs and easily maintain your Web page.

One disadvantage may be that if your page becomes popular or is used to transmit large amounts of data, your local network traffic may increase and therefore decrease the throughput available for the rest of your networking needs. Electronic security and forms processing, cgi-bin, may be other issues to consider before moving to your own Web server. But if you have the necessary computer resources available—a 486 with 8M of RAM and a network card is recommended—then you can experiment with this approach until higher throughput capability or greater network security become necessary.

What Will It Cost?

There are many Internet providers and each has its own set of charges ranging from impossibly inexpensive to outrageously expensive. Services offered vary, but in general, price does not always mean quality. Many affordably priced services are very stable and have all the options you will need. Be wary of providers that have too many users and not enough hardware, as these systems are often so clogged that people cannot readily access your pages because of excess traffic.

Determining whether a particular provider can give you stable and quick service is not always easy. A good measure is to ask for a one- or two-week trial period. During that week, try out the service during different times of the day. Weekdays are busier than weekends with most of the local usage occurring in the morning (when people log in to start their day and read their e-mail), around dinner (just before leaving the office, or after classes), and throughout the evening (a free-for-all). If the system you are trying is sluggish more than 30 percent of the time, it is probably not meeting its users' demands. All systems display periods of sluggishness, as various high-priority programs and users do important transactions. But sustained sluggishness is a good indication of a weak system. If you find a performance problem, contact the sysop or administrator of the system and ask him about the problem. See what his immediate plans are for growth. If the sysop does not address your needs adequately, move on to a different provider.

> **Note**
>
> Many people who are used to free Internet access do not understand charging money for WWW services. There are many good reasons for charging for WWW space. The most compelling is the amount of resources it takes. Consider a Web server site getting several hundred requests per second for huge pictures, audio files, movies, and documents. The load requires large machines with the proper capabilities. By charging for the use of these machines, wasted bandwidth is kept to a minimum. Furthermore, as the Net increases in the number of users and the level of sophistication, more and more capable servers are required. Charging for service allows providers to meet the needs of the changing WWW population and technology.

If your access is free, you're lucky. Most people will need to pay for housing their WWW home page information. You will probably be charged either a simple monthly fixed fee, or by the amount of storage and throughput that your pages use on the Web server. If you are charged a fixed fee, the payment structure is simply like a cable TV charge. If you are charged by the amount you use, there are two charges, storage and throughput. In this respect, the WWW is kind of like a cellular phone, where you pay a basic fee every month to have the service *and* a variable fee depending on how much it is used. The following sections outline each of these charges in more detail.

Storage Charge

> **Tip**
>
> To avoid large monthly storage fees, limit the storage of large images, huge databases, and sound or movie libraries on services that charge fees. Store these items, instead, on anonymous FTP sites.

A *storage charge* is a monthly charge taken against the amount of disk space your pages and other data take to store. Rates go throughout the spectrum, but you can expect to pay between one and ten dollars per megabyte. A normal page, with 50 or so lines of text and a nice, but conservative, graphic takes about 20,000 bytes, and the charge is very inexpensive (on the order of pennies a month).

To calculate a monthly storage charge, simply take your total bytes used, divided by the number of megabytes per unit your provider is charging you, and take the result times the dollar amount they are charging you.

For example, if you are being charged $5 per megabyte, and you have a picture that is 17,285 bytes and a text file that is 4,892 bytes, your storage charge will be approximately 11 cents. The following detail the formula and steps that produce the result:

The formula:

$$Your\_Cost = (Total\_bytes\_used\ /\ Unit\_amount) * Cost\_per\_unit$$

The variables:

Total_bytes_used: 22,177 (17,285 + 4892)

Unit_amount: 1,048,576 bytes

Cost_per_unit: $5

Doing the calculation:

Your_Cost = (22,177 /1,048,576) * 5.00

Your_Cost = (0.021149635) * 5.00 Your_Cost = 0.1057 - or rounded up, 11 cents a month.

Note

Because of the cost of maintenance and user tracking, many providers ask for a minimum amount per month. For example, bills less than $25 might be rounded up to $25 to handle the administration of the account.

Throughput Charge

In many cases, you will be charged for the number of bytes transmitted to all the users visiting your pages. This is called a *throughput charge*. Prices again range from less than one dollar per megabyte to many dollars per megabyte. In general, take the size of your pages times the number of times they are accessed to figure out throughput charge. Most providers offer some type of logging capability to allow you to monitor your charges and some can even limit the number of users allowed to visit your site in order to keep charges at bay until you have a good idea of the popularity of your pages.

Tip

When choosing an Internet provider that imposes throughput charges, carefully consider the use of multiple, large graphic images within your page. Each time a user requests to visit your page through the Web server, all of the data from your page and its embedded inline graphics are transmitted over the network.

File versus HTTP Storage Mechanisms

There are two mechanisms for storing HTML documents: the FTP anonymous mechanism and HTTP.

Documents stored using the FTP anonymous method may be retrieved by using a ftp:// WWW prefix in the URL address. This method does not need a WWW server, as the browsers (such as Mosaic and Netscape Navigator) know intrinsically how to do an FTP. In this case, the user's browser contacts the machine containing your document via anonymous FTP, retrieves the document and its related information, and then displays it to the user. This method offers you the simplest way to create a Web page because so many sites offer inexpensive anonymous FTP.

The second mechanism for storage of WWW pages involves sites that run WWW servers (known as HTTP, or HTTPD servers). These sites offer the capability to have the server retrieve and transmit documents when requested by the user's browser. These types of documents may be retrieved by using an http:// prefix in the URL address.

There are basic differences in the capabilities between HTTP and FTP methods. Basically, HTTP does everything FTP does and more. The FTP method retrieves any document and satisfies links to other documents, images, and sounds. However, FTP does not allow you to access databases, forms, or participate in any kind of truly interactive activities. For these mechanisms you need the capabilities of an HTTP server.

It is possible to house your pages at an FTP site, while still making use of a Web server. A WWW browser, such as Mosaic, can load and view an HTML document stored locally or at a remote site. The remote site can be an FTP or an HTTP server. The same goes for files linked to the HTML document. However, for advanced capabilities such as forms processing, you must at least point the form to an HTTP server. This capability allows you to place documents on an FTP system, but have them point to a Web server for any complex needs you may have. This may save you money by allowing you to avoid bandwidth and storage costs on a commercial Web server.

Text versus Graphic Browsers

◀ See "Using Microsoft Internet Explorer," p. 473

◀ See "Using Netscape," p. 497

◀ See "Using Mosaic," p. 539

The question of how sophisticated you can get in designing your pages is hampered by the fact that not all users have the same browser with equal capabilities to access your information. Because some users are still using text-only browsers, such as Lynx, and others are on full graphic browsers, like Mosaic or Netscape Navigator, each views your information differently. Furthermore, there are many different versions of both text-only and graphic/text browsers and each version has its own flaws and strengths. Because of this, designing your pages to fit all people presents a problem.

One solution is to design multiple pages, and at the top of each page give the user the choice to switch to the other page, which supports a different type of browser. For example, at the top of the graphic page it could say

```
Click here to go to the text version of this page.
```

Likewise, at the top of the text page it could say

```
Click here to go to the graphic version of this page.
```

The obvious problem with this method is that it requires two versions of the same information. Furthermore, this does not fix the problem of some browsers' lack of support for certain HTML features.

The general solution is that while you design your pages to the audience you are trying to reach, try not to embody too much functionality in pictures. This way, if a user on a text-only system sees your page, it is still useful to them.

In general, feel free to include graphics in your documents, but realize that the more meaning you place in the graphics, the less text-only users will be able to glean from your page. However, as the Web progresses you will see fewer and fewer text-only browsers being used.

▶ See "Using HTML to Build Your Home Page," p. 621

Home Page Options

Chapter 26, "Using HTML to Build Your Home Page," details many of the formatting options available in home page design. However, before you begin to create your page, it is a good idea to review the kinds of data that can be incorporated into WWW documents.

Simple Text

Text for HTML documents can be entered through the use of any simple text editor, like Notepad, or a word processor. Simple commands embedded into the text instruct the browser how to format that text. Web pages are always simple ASCII documents. Notepad automatically saves your file as ASCII text. Specifically instructing your word processor to store the text in ASCII format is all it takes to create WWW pages.

Because most of the content of a page is usually text, formatting options are given that allow you to display the text in a pleasing manner. It is important to remember that each browser is different in that it is potentially running on different platforms. This means that each user may be seeing your page in a different size window, with different fonts and different color capability. The WWW browser takes care of making your information fit the user's window. To accomplish this, the browser changes the number of words on a line to fit the particular view. Because you may not always wish the browser to do this, special formatting commands exist that make it possible to override the browser's reformatting.

In addition to allowing you to control how text flows, the browser allows you to specify how text looks. This includes size, emphasis, and use of white space (areas with no text).

The following formatting command concepts can help you create effective home pages by allowing you to break text into more readable sections, and apply highlighting and emphasis to important words:

- *Variable font sizes* allows you to create titles and headings that allow the user to find information quickly.
- *Bulleting* allows lists to be made, and WWW browsers support multiple levels of bullets as well as numbered lists. Support for bulleting in your pages is made even easier by simple indentation commands, allowing bulleted items with multiple lines of text to flow and wrap correctly.
- *Horizontal Rulings* allow you to break areas by placing lines that stretch from left to right across the document.

Use of these simple formatting capabilities adds surprising life and professionalism to a document. It can often be the difference between a normal ho-hum page, and an outstanding page.

Links

Linking is what the Web is all about. Creating links, also known as *hyperlinks*, allows you to have objects on one page point to other pages. For example, a word, phrase, or picture in one document, when chosen by the user, can cause another document, sound, or picture to be retrieved. Even movies and binary files may be retrieved using links.

You can link any object to any document on your system or any other system on the Web. This capability allows you to have links in your document that take people to other locations.

You should place at least one link in each document. That link brings the user up a level in your document hierarchy. This is not mandatory, but is at least polite, as it gives the user somewhere to go from your page.

The simplest use of linking is to subdivide a long document into several small documents and use linking to move between them.

> **Tip**
>
> Don't place too many links on one page. An excessive number of links means the user won't be able to jump to them all and just makes extra work for you.

WWW browsers allow you to link to a tremendous number of services and ca-pabilities. You can link to an anonymous FTP, a WWW (HTTP) server, a Net news server, a mail handler, a Telnet session, or a Gopher service. Because of this, clicking on any hyperlinked object can cause any of a number of exciting things to happen, from retrieving binary files to logging into remote machines.

Inline Images

An inline image is a black-and-white, or limited-color, picture that is inserted directly into a document at the point the HTML command is issued. Color pictures may contain up to 256 colors, and may be dithered to simulate full-color pictures. The capability to use inline images allows you to create documents that include pictures. Text can be made to flow in and around the picture, with certain restrictions, much like a magazine layout.

WWW systems inherently know how to place GIF and XBM images inline with text. Depending on your browser, other image types may be externally viewed in a pop-up window, but may not be viewed inline in the browser.

Inline images can be used for the following reasons:

- To make a page appear more readable or entertaining
- To simulate a button that may be pushed
- To express information
- To create a map that may be pushed

The simplest use of inline images is just to increase the readability of a page. Inline images can be used to make fancy bullets, company logos, section separators, gothic lettering for paragraph starts, and other graphic elements. All the figures in this chapter show pages that use inline images to help com-municate their message. As you look at the various figures, you can see how each designer used the same inline image capability to produce a different look and feel.

One of the most interesting aspects of inline images is their ability to create custom buttons. In other words, by using the linking capability of the HTML document, you may create any type of graphic button and cause that button, when pushed, to access or hyperlink to other graphic images, sounds, or documents. This allows you to create very beautiful and creative interfaces, and add life to otherwise dull text pages. This *hyperlinking* is one of the rea-sons the WWW is so popular—simple point-and-click navigation (see figs. 25.5 and 25.9).

Fig. 25.9

The Yahoo! page combines hyperlinked text and forms. Selecting either the text or entering a search string brings you to the associated page.

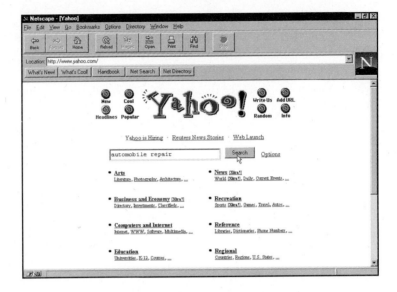

Inline images may be used to impart information that may be awkward in text format. Graphs, charts, formulas, scientific visualization, and statistical viewing are just some of the ways inline images can be used to express data.

It is also possible to create a picture where elements in the picture can be chosen. For example, a picture could show a scene of a desk, and touching different items on the desk with the mouse would cause different documents to be retrieved. This ISMAP capability offers many exciting design possibilities, but is often costly to implement in storage and throughput, and requires a server to work. ISMAP merely stands for "IS MAPped," indicating that the image is subdivided, or mapped, into multiple regions.

Figure 25.3, the White House page, shows an ISMAP. Each of the choices around the central picture can be selected, and when picked brings you to information about that choice.

> **Note**
>
> ISMAP capability is not discussed in this book, but information may be found online.

Tip

You don't need to store your inline images on the same system as your HTML documents. They may be pulled from anywhere in the world on-the-fly, and inserted in your document. However, be advised that the user will most likely have to wait longer while the server that houses the image to be inserted is contacted and the image is downloaded.

An important idea to remember is that the overuse of images leads to pages that are slow for modem users to retrieve and display. This also makes pages large and can increase your Web costs—something to consider if you are paying for your throughput. One advantage to WWW browsers is their ability to cache images. This means that if an image is used on more than one page, it only needs to be loaded once. This fact makes using images cheaper if you simply remember to reuse the same image file, as a page header, for instance, throughout your pages.

Sound

Sound may be linked in your documents and stored anywhere. Because sound files may be large (absolutely mammoth, in fact) you may want to store them where the price is cheapest and not on the same machine as your pages. Sounds are usually stored either in WAVE or AU format and require a *player* to be heard. Although most browsers support playing sounds using an external viewer, it is not a good idea to embody critical information in a sound format.

Unless you have unlimited free access, and storage and throughput, you are not going to offer a lot of sounds unless you are getting large commercial benefits from them. Because of their size, sounds have high storage and throughput costs. Although it should also be kept in mind that sounds also tend to be popular because there is a (surprisingly) large audience of users who have fast Internet access, and thus do not have to wait for a long download.

Creating sounds to place in your pages involves playing the sound from an external source and recording a sample of that sound onto your computer.

Many commercial and shareware programs exist that provide this capability for most of the popular platforms, including Windows 95. However, to input quality sound, most people end up investing in sound hardware for their computers. Most of the popular sound software supports WAVE or AU type format most commonly found on the WWW.

With the latest multimedia capabilities available on both home and office computers, providing pre-recorded sounds for a page has become much simpler. Most computers with CD-ROMs are provided with software to play music CDs and have the capability to *record* audio segments to disk. Once on disk, the sound recording can be precisely edited and special effects can be added. As in the case of commercial and shareware clip art, there are many places on the Internet that are repositories of sound clips. Also, there are more and more sound clip and special effects CDs available at a nominal cost.

Forms

Forms capabilities have opened up the Internet for major commercial possibilities. The use of form handling allows you to design documents that can accept information and decisions from the user. The form is then submitted to a Web server and a response is sent to the user. The response may be anything, from another form, a document, sound, or an image.

The use of forms requires that you have access to a Web server (HTTP). The document that contains the form may be housed anywhere, but the information submitted by the user *must* be sent to a Web server for processing. However, a single document may have many forms and each form may be sent to a different server if desired.

Forms may contain many different elements. Radio buttons allow you to pick one choice from many. Check boxes allow you to select many options from a list of choices. Text input lines and areas allow the user to enter free-form text. List and Option choosing allow users to select items from a list of choices. All of these may be combined to create useful forms for polling user input, gathering statistics, processing sales orders, controlling games and entertainment, or any other situation where user input is necessary or helpful.

Pictures, Movies, and Binaries

Besides allowing you to insert a GIF image inline in a document, the Web also allows you to retrieve, or download, GIF or JPEG images, MPEG movies, and other binaries and compressed files. In fact, support for many types of images and formats are possible. Most capable browsers will support GIF and JPEG, at least.

Any unknown file type encountered by a browser can be saved to the user's local disk as a binary file. Most browsers have a dialog window that pops up and asks the user what to do with the unknown file type just transferred. Netscape, for example, allows you to configure an external viewer or save the file to disk. This allows any data in any format to be transferred. Viewers exist that allow many formats to be viewed. Shareware and commercial PostScript viewers, MPEG movie viewers, and TIFF viewers, just to name a few, can be found on the Internet.

In general, if you offer a non-standard format, you should also offer the user the ability to download the viewer, or at least provide a link to the appropriate viewer.

Custom Options

One of the Web's most useful capabilities is that it can be modified to fit almost any need or application. Custom programs may be designed, using either a scripting language or a programming language, that can accept special links and forms, and produce a variety of interactive output.

Games, user tracking, session management, cash transaction processing, and order entry are just some of the applications for custom server code. Chapter 26, "Using HTML to Build Your Home Page," gives a brief overview of this custom code capability (called *CGI-bin*). This CGI-bin programming is usually written in C or PERL, scripting languages, and is used to process incoming information from a form and perform some manipulation on that data. One difficulty with using CGI-bin code is getting it designed. CGI-bin programming requires a bit of understanding and devotion to learn how it works. Furthermore it requires access to a server to test your program. However, if you lack the time or expertise, many organizations exist that will gladly custom design solutions to fit your needs. These companies can be found throughout the Web. Also offered on the Web are many sites that have pre-written CGI-bin software. This software can be used as a model, or as is often the case, as the solution itself, for custom capabilities.

▶ See "A Brief Look at CGI-bin," p. 665

What Goes into a Good Home Page

Even the most sophisticated computer user can be overwhelmed by an onslaught of data. And many of your users may not be all that savvy. You should make every effort—in the design of your home page—to keep it simple and to present your information in a logical way that leads the user in a orderly progression through your material.

▶ See "Using HTML to Build Your Home Page," p. 621

One way to make your information more accessible is to include ample *white space*. This is space that doesn't contain pictures or text. A full page of unparagraphed text will be intimidating to anyone. Try to present your information in lists or tables so that key points are easily identified. Also, don't put picture after picture. Try to frame them in the page, leaving some space around them. Use of white space (empty areas in your page) is important because it allows the components of your document to appear less crowded.

You should strive to present your information in easily assimilated portions. Pay attention to paragraph lengths. If they become too long, try to break them up into two or three shorter paragraphs. Figure 25.9 shows a good use of white space: each link stands by itself and does not crowd the other choices (refer to fig. 25.9).

If your document is very long, you might want to consider links that allow the user to jump around in the document. Or, instead of having one document that is five pages long, you might want to make a single page presenting key themes with links to other pages that describe in more detail, specific information the user might be interested in.

The use of graphics can add interest to your page. Even the most conservative page could use an inline picture in the title of the home page. Your choice of graphics depends on the type of image you are trying to present. The law firm used as an example earlier might use a simple square of granite or marble. The rock band might have a graffiti wall or some of their cover art.

Tip

If you are planning links to other pages from your home page, you might consider using the same graphic at the top of each page to create a sense of grouping or unity. As pointed out in the text, this also has the benefit of loading faster, as browsers cache images.

If you don't have pre-formatted graphics and textures in your computer, they are available for little or no cost at various sites around the Internet. Or you might try your local computer software stores for CD-ROM libraries of clip art and pre-created graphics.

It's not hard to create an attractive and dynamic HTML home page, but you should put some effort into the design to make sure that it has the suitable look and feel for your products and services.

Generating and Keeping Interest

The best way to create interest in your home page is to post it to the myriad of What's New groups on the Internet. If you've already been navigating on the Web, you probably have your favorite. Most everyone who is on the Web checks their favorite What's New groups weekly. Chapter 45, "Top Internet Mailing Lists," and Chapter 46, "Top World Wide Web Sites," cover many of the more popular lists and Web sites. Try subscribing to some of these lists or visiting some of the Web sites as starting points.

The method for posting to a list may be different for each list. If you have the URL for a list you would like to post to, go to it. Most lists contain the information for posting to it somewhere within the document. Posting to lists is generally very easy, requiring you to enter data into clearly labeled areas. Once you've created your HTML home page, you go to the lists appropriate for your field, and list your home page.

> **Note**
>
> Some What's New lists take a very long time to post additions. Sometimes these tend to be at universities, and if you post your notice during a break, there might not be anyone there to update the file.

> **Note**
>
> To get the best duration of promotion for your home page, post to pages that update immediately, and to lists that take a while. Then when the steam generated from the first list is waning, new users will be directed to you from the later posting lists.

The result of posting to these lists can be phenomenal. An art gallery that went online had *thousands* of people "walk through their virtual gallery" in the first week.

Unless you have a service or product that everyone just has to have, you need to figure out how you are going to get people back to your home page after their first visit. To keep interest in your home page, like anything else, you have to keep it in front of your audience. You could just re-post it to your favorite lists, but when people got to your page and found the same old stuff, they won't stay around. But if you were offering new features, then people would have a reason to visit you again. Offering new features allows you to re-post your announcement, each time talking about your newest addition. This helps to guide in the people who missed your advertising the first time around.

For example, the law firm might mention the addition of a new partner and invite users to check out the new partner's profile. The rock band could stagger their audio selections, changing it from time to time and announce the new selection in the appropriate lists.

> **Tip**
>
> When you plan your home page, also plan your future additions. An HTML home page can be a powerful sales and marketing tool. Use it to its full advantage!

Another way to get people to return again and again to your site is to offer free entertainment or information. Features such as the joke of the week will draw people to your site to see your "free service." Law firms and accountants can provide legal or tax tips that are updated on a periodic basis. Some sites have cartoonists who offer a daily or weekly chuckle.

Grouping yourself with other vendors in a Virtual Mall could help draw customers, just as malls in the real world do. But in general, a visible storefront in an online mall does not guarantee you any more business than simply advertising your wares on the popular lists. Paying extra for "prestigious" mall space is not always what it is worth.

HTML Editors and Filters

▶ See "Using Netscape Navigator Gold and HotDog to Create Web Pages," p. 699

The general method of building HTML pages is to create them in a standard text editor or word processor. This, however, requires that you become quite familiar with the HTML language. While HTML, in general, is fairly simple, if becoming an HTML guru is not on your agenda, you may want to investigate editors and filters. These systems allow you to create and view HTML pages in time-saving ways.

Editors

HTML editors are programs specially designed to allow you to create HTML documents interactively. These are usually point-and-click programs with nice user interfaces. These programs allow you to start with simple ASCII documents and create links, text formatting, and place images. There are many popular editors for Windows, including the following:

HotDog (Standard and Professional)

HoTMetaL

HTML assistant

HTMLed

HTML Writer

Each of these editors has different features, strengths, and weaknesses. Each also has different restrictions for use, and you should make sure to read any licensing or other agreements that come with the editor before using it.

Filters

Filters offer yet another method for creating HTML documents. By using a filter with your favorite text editor or word processor, you can extend its capabilities and create more complex HTML documents. This is often very useful because most popular editors already have bold and italic capability, and extending these to produce HTML code is generally easy.

Popular filters are available for the following software packages:

BibTeX

DECwrite

Framemaker

Interleaf

LaTex

MS Word

nroff

PowerPoint

QuarkXPress

Scribe

Texinfo

troff

VAXDocument

Word for Windows 2.0

Word for Windows 6.0

WordPerfect

Filters work by translating word-processor formats directly into HTML. Often, filters include extensions to the word processor that add the capability to create HTML links and drop inline images.

The World Wide Web

IV

Where to Find Editors

HTML editors may be found on the CD that is a part of this book. In addition, HTML editors may be found all over the Internet. Using WebCrawler to search for some of the editors produces many sites that provide the software. The Web has many sites that offer the editors, but most of the tools are concentrated on the following site that allows you to learn about many of them:

http://www.w3.org/hypertext/WWW/Tools/

Filters are also spread all over the Internet, but again, can be found concentrated in the following WWW site:

**http://www.w3.org/hypertext/WWW/Tools/
Word_proc_filters.html**

Download the software or filter and examine both the online documentation as well as any text files, readme files, or manuals that are included in the archive. Help can often be found in the WWW newsgroups as well as the IRC #www channel.

Pros and Cons

HTML editors and filters can provide a quick method for creating HTML documents. They are especially useful for the designer who lacks the time to handcraft HTML pages. Editors and filters are also useful for learning HTML. By using an editor or filter to create a page, and then looking at the resulting HTML document, you can learn how to create your own pages.

Nonetheless, there are numerous problems with using filters and editors. First is the fact that they are often limited or simply behind the times. This means that new capabilities in new browsers are often not found in the filter and editor. Second, filters and editors often produce messy HTML, code that is difficult to read and edit and is generally less efficient than HTML produced by hand.

By this I mean wasting bytes. Often, there are many ways to do the same thing in HTML, and sometimes editors often pick a less efficient method of producing a document. This results in an accumulation of unnecessary bytes in the document, which, while small in themselves, can compound into many dollars' worth of data when downloaded thousands of times a month.

The bottom line on editors and filters is, pick one that works for you and that you are happy with. Use it only if you find that it is truly a time-saving system.

CHAPTER 26

Using HTML to Build Your Home Page

This chapter familiarizes you with the HTML mark-up language and teaches you how to build your own WWW home page using HTML commands. You will also learn how to add form handling capabilities to your page. Anyone who can use a word processor should have no trouble mastering the techniques necessary to construct innovative and exciting WWW home pages.

While HTML contains many commands and capabilities, this chapter will focus on the commands most used to make simple pages and pages containing forms. In cases where more than one command will produce a similar output, this chapter will cover only the most popular command.

HTML 2+ and HTML 3 are extensions to HTML, and provide some advanced capabilities. Because HTML 2+ is used so frequently, this chapter will treat the three as the same and will refer to them as HTML. Keep in mind, though, that HTML 2+, which is widely referred to as Netscape extensions, and HTML 3, which is still in the draft stage, may not be implemented on all graphical Web browsers.

In this chapter, you learn:

- How to program in HTML
- URL naming conventions
- How to create and use HTML forms

Keep in mind that this chapter focuses on the techniques to create Web pages. To use the HTML codes presented in this chapter, you need to place them in a text file to be accessed by your Web provider's HTTP server. The next two chapters introduce you to a few methods of inputting the HTML elements.

HTML Basics

▶ See "Using Microsoft Internet Assistant to Build Web Pages," p. 667

▶ See "Using Netscape Navigator Gold and HotDog to Create Web Pages," p. 699

This section introduces you to the concepts necessary to understand how to create your own WWW pages. Included in this section are an overview of HTML functionality and a description of HTML formatting rules.

How HTML Works: An Overview

Hypertext Markup Language (HTML) is a language that allows users to embed simple commands within standard ASCII text documents to provide an integrated visual display. In other words, a document created in any word processor and stored in normal ASCII format can become a home page with the addition of a few HTML commands. The HTML commands allow the user to perform the following functions:

- Specify text size and flow
- Integrate inline pictures
- Create links
- Integrate audio and external pictures
- Create interactive forms

HTML has evolved since its inception, and currently supports many features, including full forms, movies, audio, and other capabilities.

The HTML Element

An HTML command is termed an *element*. HTML elements allow you to modify how a normal text document appears to the user when viewing it in a WWW browser. HTML elements are imbedded within the ASCII document and provide instructions to the browser concerning formatting and inclusion of outside elements, such as pictures and audio.

An HTML element always appears as a word or phrase placed between less-than and greater-than characters. For example, the following list shows some basic HTML elements:

```
<pre>

</a>

<b>

<img src="picture.gif">
```

Each of the commands in the preceding list share a common format in that they always begin with the less-than character (<) and always end with the greater-than character (>). The content between the two characters contains the HTML command itself.

HTML browsers ignore any element that does not make sense. That is, any element that is found, but doesn't contain a valid command, is skipped by the browser. This capability ensures that HTML documents can be understood by even the simplest of browsers by allowing them to skip over commands that they may not be able to handle.

Elements come in two basic types, non-empty and empty. To explain these two mechanisms, we need to examine how an HTML element is used to modify text.

Some text needs to be modified as a block. For example, if you wish to make a word or phrase bold, you need to specify both the START and END of the block of text that needs to be bold. In order to do this, an HTML element is placed at the BEGINNING of the word or phrase, and another HTML element is placed at the END of the word or phrase. The text that appears between the two elements are affected by the elements. This is known as a non-empty element.

Empty elements do not require an ending element to complete the command. Empty elements stand by themselves as complete commands. For example, if you wish to insert a picture into a text document, you only need specify a single element to do this. The concept of ending the picture does not make logical sense, thus no ending element is required.

Several elements exist that could be thought of as working as either empty or non-empty. For example, an element that specifies the beginning or ending of a paragraph could stand by itself as an empty element. There is no real necessity for marking both the start and end of a paragraph, only the start. However, a paragraph is a logical block, and thus, could be thought of as non-empty. In order to combat this problem, new releases of HTML support both empty and non-empty versions of some commands (in these cases, this chapter will fall back to the simplest use of the commands, the empty use).

When using non-empty elements, the decision of what to place for the ending element is simple. When a particular element is chosen for the beginning element, the SAME element is chosen for the ending element. The two elements are simply written slightly differently by causing the ending element to have a leading slash character (/) just before the element name. The following example shows this:

    `<b>` **This text will be bold** `</b>`

In this example, we desire to make text bold. The `<b>` element does this. Because we need to specify the SIZE of the area to be bold, this is obviously a non-empty element and will require a terminator. Because we choose the `<b>`

element, the terminator for this element is always `</b>`. This is a universal law in HTML. Elements that TERMINATE a block will be the SAME element that started the block, with the inclusion of the leading slash.

Elements are case independent, meaning that elements may be expressed in either uppercase, lowercase, or even mixed-case.

> **Tip**
>
> Making all your element commands uppercase can often save time when creating a document by allowing you to quickly separate commands from the text itself.

Many elements contain parameters that help describe what function the command is to perform. For example, an element that specifies that an image be placed inline in the document must specify the NAME of the image. This is considered a *parameter*, or argument. The following example shows just such a command:

```
<IMG SRC="flowers.gif">
```

This is an image (`<IMG>`) element and specifies that an image should be placed in the document. The `SRC=` portion of the element describes the name of the picture to be loaded. This is a parameter to the `<IMG>` element.

Parameters are always listed after the element name, and commands with more than one parameter may have the parameters listed in any order.

Notice that the data portion of the parameter (as in "flowers.gif" in the previous example) is placed in double quotes. In most cases HTML will honor data with or without quotes. However, use of quotes is required if you are embedding special characters or spaces within the data. In general, the best rule to follow is to always place the data portion of any parameter within quotation marks to ensure compatibility with all browsers.

How HTML Deals with Spaces and Carriage Returns

When you enter a document in your word processor, you may have added extra carriage returns and consecutive spaces for formatting purposes. However HTML ignores extra carriage returns and spaces, so when that document is displayed using HTML, carriage returns and consecutive spaces will not appear. This enables the browsers to make appropriate decisions as to how to display the document based on the user's window size and font size. You will undoubtedly find this to be a blessing because it decreases the amount of formatting you are required to do within your document. At the same time, you will find this to be an inconvenience because it is often difficult to get specific formatting that you do want.

The rules for space and carriage return are simple. More than one consecutive space is simply treated as a single space. Carriage returns are simply removed.

In order to overcome the limitations imposed by automatic formatting, HTML provides several elements for specialized formatting, such as <PRE>, <P>, and <BR>. These are described in the next section.

Reserved Words in HTML

Because of the use of the < and > characters to delimit an element, you may begin to suspect that using these characters inside your document may be a problem. In fact, the < and the & character, are characters that are reserved within HTML. As we already know, < is used to signify the start of an element. The & character is used to access characters that are not available on the keyboard (such as characters with accent marks, and so on). In order to correctly represent the <, >, and & symbols in a document, when you do not intend for them to be interpreted as HTML commands, you must replace them with alternate characters. The following is a partial list of the more frequently used special characters:

&lt	Replaces < less-than sign
&gt	Replaces > greater-than sign
&amp	Replaces & ampersand by itself
&quot	Replaces " double quote

For example, say you have the following text you need to place in HTML form:

The "A & B" new price is <$10.99>

The HTML version of this would be:

The &quot A &amp B &quot new price is &lt $10.99 &gt

While this seems awkward, this solves the problem of using the special characters without confusion and is not too difficult to remember or implement.

Note

Not all browsers support the entire set of special characters. Additionally, some browsers ignore the first space after a special character. If you experience trouble using a special character, revert back to the original character and check the results. To fix spacing problems try adding additional spaces around your special characters.

Many other special & strings exist for characters like ñ and Ü. Table 26.1 is a list of most of the special characters you can display by using &.

Table 26.1   Codes for Special Characters

Code	Character
&AElig	Æ
&Aacute	Á
&Acirc	Â
&Agrave	À
&Auml	Ä
&Ccedil	Ç
&Eacute	É
&Ecirc	Ê
&Egrave	È
&Euml	Ë
&Iacute	Í
&Icirc	Î
&Igrave	Ì
&Iuml	Ï
&Ntilde	Ñ
&Oacute	Ó
&Ocirc	Ô
&Ograve	Ò
&Ouml	Ö
&Otilde	Õ
&Oslash	Ø
&Uacute	Ú
&Ucirc	Û
&Ugrave	Ù
&Uuml	Ü

For lowercase letters, substitute the lowercase letter in the &string for the uppercase letter. For example ñ is displayed with &ntilde.

File Extensions and HTML

HTML automatically recognizes many types of files by their extension. The following is a list of extensions and their meanings to HTML. Extensions that are more than three letters should have the last letter removed (as in htm versus html) or should use the shortened version (as in .JPG versus .JPEG) when using them on platforms that do not allow longer extensions, such as DOS.

.HTML	An HTML document with text and elements
.GIF	A GIF formatted color image
.XBM	An X formatted black and white image
.XPM	An X formatted color image
.TXT	A text file, no changes are made
.TEXT	Same as .TXT
.JPEG	A JPEG compressed color image
.JPG	Same as .JPEG
.MPEG	An MPEG compressed series of images
.MPG	Same as .MPEG
.AU	An AIFF compressed audio file
.WAV	A WAVE compressed audio file

In addition to these formats, compression schemes such as .z and .gz extensions are supported. In some cases, files encountered with formats unknown to the Web browser are treated as .text files, and shown to the user without modification. Recently released browsers, however, prompt the user to save unrecognized formatted files to disk (for later use) or to configure a viewer on the fly. To get an idea of the file types and extensions recognized by Netscape Navigator 2.0, for example, click Options, General Preferences and select the Helpers tab. This displays a scrollable window of known file types and what action Netscape takes upon encountering each file you download.

URL Naming Convention

URL (often pronounced Earl) stands for Uniform Resource Locator, and is the mechanism used by the WWW to find a particular page, image, or sound. Basically, you can think of a URL as the address by which you find a page.

There are two types of URLs. The first is an *absolute URL*. This URL is a complete address, and nothing more is needed to find the information. The second type of URL is a *relative URL*. A relative URL is one that only contains the necessary address to find what you want from where you currently are.

For example, your street address might be:

1700 S. Stadium Dr.

Bontia, CT 47052

This would be an absolute address, as it is all that is necessary to find you. However, once I'm standing in your front lawn, the relative address of:

1800

would be all that is necessary for me to find a house on the next block. I no longer need the street, city, or state because I am already there.

HTML uses a similar mechanism when specifying addresses of where to find documents.

A typical absolute URL consists of the following items:

service://host:port/path/file.ext

"service://" indicates how the document is being accessed. Some of the more frequently used services include:

file://	Use FTP to retrieve a local file
ftp://	Use FTP to retrieve the file
http://	Use a WWW server to retrieve the file
gopher://	Use a Gopher mechanism
telnet://	Use Telnet to access a remote machine
news:	Read remote news

Notice that "news:" differs from the rest of the services in that it does not include the // characters. The // characters are not required on all the services, only on the ones shown with it.

"host" indicates in what machine the information you want to get resides (for example, your host might be www.somewhere.com).

":port" is optional, and needs only be included if the information is not available using the default port specified by the service, like in the case of a proxy server (for example, Gopher uses a default port of 70, HTTP uses 80).

"path" indicates the route from the URL home directory to the desired information (for example, the path to your home directory on machine www.somewhere.com might be usr/people/me).

"file.ext" indicates the actual name of the file you wish to retrieve.

Tip

While creating or editing your Web page, you should check it often to make sure of the accuracy of your HTML elements and that your text and graphics are positioned properly. One way to do this is to save your page, launch your Web browser, and use the file:// URL method to specify your page. Your browser will then display a preview of your page.

In many situations, a URL need not have the path and file.ext. In these cases, a default document will be provided from the requested system.

An example of an absolute URL would be:

> http://www.iquest.net/cw/cookware.html

This accesses the file cookware.html, which exists in the directory cw on the host www.iquest.net. The file will be accessed using the host's WWW server, as indicated by http://.

Relative URLs include only a piece of the full address. Relative URLs are only used inside an HTML document to find other information relative to that document and also stored on the same machine. For example, if the cookware.html file requires a p1.gif picture, the URL can be done one of the two following ways:

> ABSOLUTE: <img src="http://www.iquest.net/cw/new.gif">
>
> RELATIVE: <img src="new.gif">

The first syntax we understand, as it is absolute. The second relative syntax is a little more confusing. Because we had already retrieved the cookware.html file from the cw directory, the system will then look in the cw directory to satisfy any relative requests.

Troubleshooting

My URL command isn't working. It refuses to connect to the proper document.

Check the URL to see if any / separator characters were accidentally entered as \ characters. Users who are familiar with DOS frequently enter the incorrect slash out of habit.

Why do some of my URLs not work correctly with anchors?

Depending on your browser, you may find that relative URLs may not work correctly when using them with anchors (<A>). This may especially be true when using HTML files local to your computer. In cases where a relative URL fails, replace it with an absolute URL to fix the problem.

HTML Document Organization

The HTML standard specifies that a good HTML document should have elements that divide the document into descriptive and functional areas. In actual practice, however, many people choose to leave these elements out, or misuse the elements. Because of this fact, browsers basically ignore the formatting information, and you may as well. However, for the sake of completeness (and because you will encounter these elements), we will describe them.

The basic format for a good HTML document is as follows:

```
<HEAD>

            header information appears here

</HEAD>
<BODY>

            body information appears here

</BODY>
```

The actual commands <HEAD> and <BODY> will be described in the next section. However, the information placed between <HEAD> and </HEAD> is used to describe the document to the browser, and does not directly impact the user (usually). The information between the <BODY> and </BODY> elements includes your actual document information, and all formatting elements used to describe and display that information.

HTML Elements

This section describes the most frequently used HTML elements. These are the elements you will need to create any basic home pages.

Elements that Effect Text Size

The HTML creator has some control over the font size of the text that is displayed to the user. Obviously, this is highly browser dependent. Most browsers honor these commands, but some (mostly text-only) browsers ignore or change these commands.

The use of text size commands is for situations where you want to create titles that are larger than the rest of the text. This is used to call attention to, or delineate, text.

The text size commands are all non-empty, meaning that they require terminating elements. The basic format of the element is as follows:

```
<H?> The text to display </H?>
```

Where ? is a number one-through-six. <H1> specifies the largest heading size available, <H2> the second largest, and so forth, to <H6>, which is the smallest size (see fig. 26.1). The actual size of the font is dependent on user's browser. For example, a title and sub-title with regular text might appear like this:

<H1> The title </H1>

<H2> The sub-title </H2>

This is normal text that appears after the sub-title.

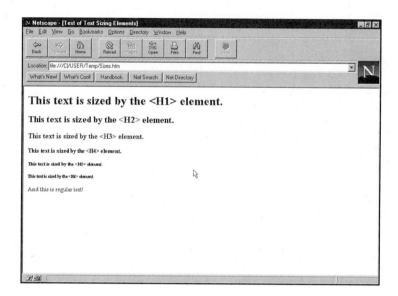

Fig. 26.1
This figure shows several different text sizes.

Notice that no text size was needed for the normal text, as the termination element </H6> simply changed the text size back to the default, normal, text size.

Elements that Affect Text Positioning

HTML tends to reorganize the positioning of text in your document, removing all carriage returns and extra spaces. If you want these extra carriage returns and spaces left in your document, how do you achieve it? Better yet, how do you keep HTML from playing with your document's format in the first place?

To achieve this capability, elements exist that force carriage returns and paragraph starts. In addition, formatting commands exist that instruct the HTML system not to modify the text in any way, allowing it to appear exactly as specified. The most common text formatting commands follow.

The World Wide Web

IV

Break Text Line

The <BR> command allows you to force a break (<BR>) into your document at the point of the <BR> command. This is a forced carriage return and will be absolutely honored by the browser. Because <BR> is an empty command, no terminating </BR> is required.

Example:

HTML:	This is an example
Result:	This is
	an example

Paragraph Break

The <P> command instructs the browser to begin a new paragraph. This is identical to the <BR> command with the exception that it places two carriage returns in the text. In general, all paragraphs should have a <P> at the beginning or end. This command is an empty command, with no </P> required. However, because paragraphs can be thought of as logical blocks, most HTML systems will honor </P> at the end of a paragraph for consistency.

Example:

HTML:	This is<P>an example
Result:	This is
	an example

Preformatted Text

The <PRE> command is useful when you want text to look exactly as you have it specified in the file. <PRE> is a non-empty element that requires a </PRE> to conclude the formatting of the text block. All text appearing between the <PRE> and </PRE> elements are displayed as is, including paragraphs, carriage returns, and spacing. This is the primary recommended method for forcing formatting to be exactly as you desire. However, when you use <PRE>, the text within the <PRE> is displayed in a non-proportional font and is restricted in sizing options.

For example:

HTML:	This is
	some text
	<PRE>
	This is
	some more text
	</PRE>

Result: This is some text
               This   is
               some more text

> **Tip**
>
> Avoid placing <BR> and <P> commands within a <PRE> </PRE> section as some
> Web browsers ignore them.

Horizontal Line

The <HR> command allows you to place a horizontal ruling at the position the
<HR> command is issued. On most browsers, this is accompanied by a blank
line above and below the ruling. The ruling appears as a horizontal line that
stretches across the page. This command is useful for delineating sections of
text from each other (see fig. 26.2).

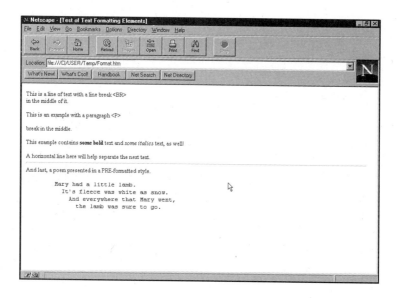

Fig. 26.2
This figure shows
elements that
affect text
formatting.

Elements that Effect Text Emphasis

Often, it is desirable to emphasize text by using **bold** or *italic* text. The following elements help create these types of effects.

Bold Text

The <B> command allows you to specify text that is bold. To use this, simply
put a <B> in front of the text you want bold, and a </B> terminator after the

text you wish bold. The text between the `<B>` and `</B>` will appear bold in the final display.

Example:

HTML:	This is `<B>`very bold`</B>` text
Result:	This is **very bold** text

Italicized Text

The `<I>` command allows you to specify text that is italic. To use this, simply put a `<I>` in front of the text you wish to be italic, and a `</I>` terminator after the text you wish to be italic. The text between the `<I>` and `</I>` will appear italic in the final display.

Example:

HTML:	This is `<I>`some italic`</I>` text
Result:	This is *some italic* text

Underlined Text

The `<U>` command allows you to specify text that is underlined. This is treated exactly as `<B>` and `<I>` are. However, only some of the browsers currently available honor this element. Some translate the element into bold or italic, while others simply ignore the element entirely.

Example:

HTML:	This is `<U>`underlined`</U>` text
Result:	This is <u>underlined</u> text

Elements that Insert Inline Images

One of the advantages of HTML is its ability to place images right into the document itself. This gives HTML documents a magazine look and feel, and greatly enhances the readability and enjoyment of a page.

The `<IMG>` command allows you to insert an image directly into the document at the point you issue the command. `<IMG>` is an empty command, and requires no closing `</IMG>` element.

The general form of the `<IMG>` command is as follows:

```
<IMG SRC="filename">
```

For example, `<IMG SRC="flower.gif">` would retrieve the image flower.gif from the CURRENT directory (because it is a relative URL) and will display it in the document. The SRC parameter is not optional, and should specify either an absolute or relative URL.

The <IMG> command has optional parameters that may be used to specify how the image is integrated with the document:

ALIGN

The ALIGN parameter specifies how the image is lined up with neighboring text on the left and right of the image. The three choices are: ALIGN=TOP, ALIGN=MIDDLE, and ALIGN=BOTTOM. Choosing one of these will cause the text to be aligned accordingly.

ALT

The ALT parameter specifies alternate text to be used to replace the image, in the event that the user's browser can not display images. This is a useful and important parameter because it solves the problem of creating a graphic page that can be used with a non-graphic browser.

The following figures show the IMG command, and how various parameters affect the display of the information.

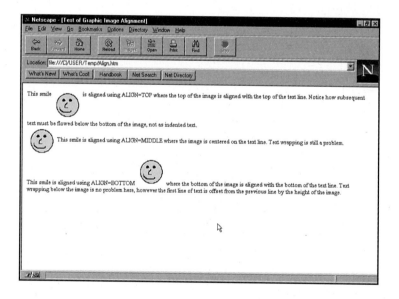

Fig. 26.3
This figure shows the IMG command with ALIGN set to TOP, MIDDLE, and BOTTOM.

You may display inline images with the .GIF, .XBM, and .XPM extensions. Current versions of the browsers do not allow .JPEG or .MPEG files to be displayed as inline images. (For information on other image formats, see the "Elements that Are Anchors and Links" section later in this chapter.)

Elements that Insert Lists and Indentation

HTML provides many mechanisms for achieving lists and indentation. However, the <UL> and <OL> elements are so useful that we will ignore the other methods and stick to these two.

The <UL> and <OL> elements, by themselves, provide indentation. When used with the <LI> element, they provide bulleted or numbered lists.

Indented Lists

The <UL> element specifies that all text beneath the <UL> element is to be moved to the right by one column. You may nest <UL> elements to make further indentations. Each </UL> restores the last section one column to the left. Using <LI> in conjunction with <UL> causes bulleted lists to be created. Figure 26.4 shows a few ways multiple indenting and listing can be used effectively.

Example:

This is an example of UL

<UL>This is indented one column

Same with this line

<UL>This is indented two columns

Same with this line

</UL>Now back to one column

</UL>Now back to no columns.

There is no difference between <UL> and <OL> when used in this manner.

Bulleted and Numbered Lists

Use the list item element, <LI>, to create bulleted lists with <UL> and to create numbered lists with <OL>. To use <LI>, place an <LI> at the beginning of each line to be bulleted or numbered.

Example:

This is a list of points

<UL>

<LI> This is the first point

<LI> This is the second point

If we are using <OL> instead, our example becomes:

Example:

This is a list of points

<OL>

\<LI\> This is the first point

\<LI\> This is the second point

\</OL\>That's all folks!

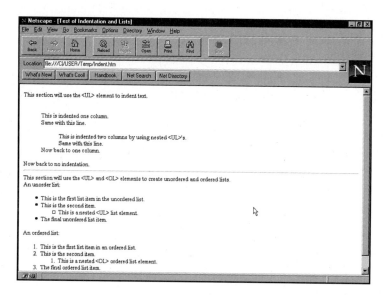

Fig. 26.4
This figure shows the multiple use of \<OL\> and \<UL\> list elements.

The automatic numbering includes the period and a space as part of the formatting.

The HTML system will automatically handle nesting the \<UL\> and \<OL\> elements, and will change the bullet style for each nested section (depending on the browser). Moreover, if a particular indented line runs past the width of the screen, it will automatically be wrapped correctly and will appear properly indented as it flows to the next line.

Elements that Are Anchors and Links

One of the most important aspects of HTML is its ability to point to other documents and pictures. This is termed an *anchor* by the HTML standard, but also is commonly called a link or hyperlink.

The basic concept of an anchor is to specify a reference to another object. HTML supports references to the following types of items:

- Any other HTML document
- Any non-HTML document (pictures, binary files, text, and so on)
- Any point within the current HTML document

The <A> and </A> anchor elements are used to create a link to another file or position within the current file.

To create an anchor, the <A> and </A> are placed around the item to be anchored. Either text or inline images may be anchored. For example, if the elements are placed around a text string, the string becomes a link. Then, by selecting that string, the link occurs. Likewise, if the anchor is placed around an image, touching the image causes the link to occur. If the link is to another document, the document is immediately retrieved and displayed. If the link is to a position within the current document, that portion of the document is jumped to and displayed. If the link is to a non-HTML file, the file is retrieved and displayed using the browser's external viewer capabilities or stored on the user's drive (as in linking to an executable).

There are no limits to the number of links, nor to where an anchor may be placed. Links may not be nested, of course, but beyond that, links may appear anywhere and point to anything.

To create a link to another document or file, you use the HREF parameter in the <A> command as follows:

```
<A HREF="file.html"> This text is linked </A>
```

In this example, the text "This text is linked" would appear chooseable to the user. Selecting it will cause the referenced file, file.html, to be retrieved and displayed to the user. In this case, the HTML parameter points to either an absolute or relative URL specifying the document to retrieve. By using an absolute URL, you can point to a local file in another directory on your server.

Another example of an anchor is as follows:

```
<A HREF="http://web.com/p.exe"><IMG SRC="p.gif"></A>
```

In this example, the image p.gif is anchored and selectable by the user. Upon the user selecting the image, the file p.exe is retrieved from the site web.com via that site's http:// Web server. In this case, because the file is not an HTML file, it will be sent to the user as a binary file to be stored on their local drive.

You also may anchor into a position within a document. This type of anchor is useful if you have a lengthy page that is broken into distinct text areas or subjects. The anchor essentially acts as an index to the document, allowing you to jump directly to any section that interests you.

To anchor a position, you start by specifying a label. The document you anchor to may be either the current document or any other document on any machine. To set up such a link, specify your anchor as follows:

```
<A HREF="#label1"> Select here to go there </A>
```

Now, to specify the place to jump to when the user selects the preceding string, GO TO that place in the document and insert a line like this:

```
<A NAME="label1"> This is the section to go to </A>
```

The #label1 in the HREF is used as a label within the current document. The word "label1" may be anything, with the # character specifying the label function (for example, #hello, #ok, and so on are valid as labels). The NAME= parameter specifies the label itself, which is given without the leading # sign. When the user selects the "Select here to go there" text, he will instantly be placed at the NAME= area of the document, which in this case would be "This is the section to go to". This capability allows you to create a table of contents and other indexes to use for jumping around within a document.

Troubleshooting

My label isn't working right. How can I fix it?

Make sure that you have spelled both the reference to the label, and the label itself, correctly. Since labels are case sensitive, make sure that capital and lowercase letters appear in the same places for all occurrences of the label.

To better illustrate this capability, here is a more concrete example:

```
<UL>
```
<LI> Pick `<A HREF="#l1">`here`</A>` for the News
<LI> Pick `<A HREF="#l2">`here`</A>` for the Weather
```
</UL>
```

    .

    .

    .

`<A NAME="l1">`The News`</A><P>`

Today's news is brought to you by those who care.`<P>`

Peace is everywhere, there is no news.`<P>`

.

.

.

```
<A NAME="12">The Weather</A><P>
```

If you lived in Hawaii, you would know what the weather was!<P>

In this example, a table of contents at the top allows the user to select "here" for News and Weather. The News and Weather items appear further in the file. Note that HREF is used at the source and NAME is used at the destination. The label you use should only appear once in the document, but may be referenced from as many locations as you want.

You may create links to within OTHER documents, by specifying the anchor as follows:

```
<A HREF="file.html#L1">Pick here</A>
```

In this example, the file file.html will be retrieved relative to the current URL, and the label L1 will be immediately jumped to within that document.

Browser Control Elements

Some of the elements exist to give the browser an easier time of understanding your HTML. We list these last because they are not necessary to make HTML work, but should be provided to adhere to the HTML standard.

Header Element

The <HEAD> element specifies the header of your document. This is used to place all items that are not part of the actual document contents. This includes the title and other descriptive items. You may completely ignore using <HEAD> elements, as they are not necessary to produce usable HTML. However, a good HTML programmer will include these. The <HEAD> element is always terminated with the </HEAD> element.

It is important to note that plain text that appears inside a <HEAD> </HEAD> element will appear in your document just as if the header elements were not present.

Title Element

The <TITLE> command is fairly useful. Most browsers have an area that shows the title of the current document to the user. This command allows you to specify that title for your document. The proper use of this command is to imbed it within a <HEAD> </HEAD> section, as shown in the following:

Example:

> <HEAD> <TITLE> Debi's Home Page </TITLE> </HEAD>

Body Element

The <BODY> element specifies the content of your document. This is the meat and potatoes of your page and contains the actual text itself, along with all formatting elements. The <BODY> element is always terminated with the </BODY> element.

A good HTML programmer will include these areas, but they are not necessary and may be ignored. Here is an example of a simple, full HTML document.

> <HEAD><TITLE>My first Page</TITLE></HEAD>
>
> <BODY>
>
> <H1>This is my first page</H1>
>
> <HR>
>
> Hello World!
>
> </BODY>

Combining Elements

Most of the HTML elements may be used together and in combinations. However, some combinations will not necessarily produce the expected result. Furthermore, in some situations, a result obtained in one browser may differ from the result obtained in another browser. The following list of items gives areas to be aware of in creating HTML pages and combining elements:

1. In general, browsers will not allow you to have text that is both bold and italic at the same time. Usually the inner-most set of elements is the one used for the effect. For example, <B><I>Hi</I></B> will produce an italic "Hi" instead of bold, or bold italic.

2. Multiple <P> or <BR> in a row are often treated as carriage returns, with duplicates ignored.

3. You may put text next to an image, with the ALIGN parameter allowing you to position the text. However, if the text runs past the end of the screen, it will wrap around to the next line, and will not lay nicely next to the image. Remember that people are using browsers in windows of different sizes.

4. You may put pictures next to pictures. To make the pictures have extra spacing between them, put a <PRE> and </PRE> around the entire set of pictures with the spacing you desire between each picture.

5. Pictures next to pictures may not necessarily look the same on all browsers. Some browsers will not load pictures larger than the screen. Other browsers will not honor <PRE> command before images, and will cause multiple images on a line to wrap to the next line if they extend past the end of the line. To avoid this situation it is a good idea to plan images so that they stand little chance of wrapping, or look good if they do wrap.

6. Placing large <H1> or other sized text next to a picture is possible if you include the picture within the element. For example, to put <H1> sized text next to a flower picture, use this syntax:

```
<H1><IMG SRC="flower.gif"> Flowers!</H1>
```

If you do not do this, the text will appear on the next line as <H?> elements, which imply blank lines before and after the element.

Creating a Simple Home Page

Now that you have the background and basic tools for creating HTML pages, it's time to write your own page. This section gives an example home page to use as a framework for creating your own page. A personal page has been chosen for this example, but it can easily be transformed into a commercial, educational, or entertainment page just by modifying the content and links.

The following listing shows the page in its entirety. Note that it uses pictures (.GIF) and links. You will obviously want to change the pictures to be your own (or omit them if you don't have pictures). The same applies to the links. Use your favorite text editor to enter the page. Then use the Open Local (or Load Local, or Open URL) feature of your particular browser to view your page (see fig. 26.5).

```
<HEAD><TITLE>My Home Page</TITLE></HEAD>

<BODY>

<H1><IMG SRC="p1.gif" ALIGN=MIDDLE>Welcome to my home page</H1><P>

<HR>
```

Welcome to my personal home page. This page is an example of a simple but powerful HTML document.<P>

Please pick one of the following choices:<P>

```
<UL>

<LI> <A HREF="#bio">A <b>brief</b> biography</A><BR>

<LI> <A HREF="me.gif">A picture of me</A><BR>
```

IV

```
<LI> <A HREF="http://web.nexor.co.uk/susi/susi.html">My favorite
searcher</A><BR>
```

```
<LI> <A HREF="http://www.iquest.net/">My providers homepage</A><BR>
```

```
<LI> <A HREF="file://martian.com/">Where I work</A><BR>
```

```
</UL>
```

```
<HR><HR>
```

```
<H2><A NAME="bio">My Biography</A></H2><P>
```

The following is a brief biography/resume. I currently work as a mission specialist for Martian Travel. Please feel free to contact me if you have use for an astro-engineer.<p>

```
<PRE>
```

Name: Webster Webmaster   Age: 36

Occupation: Engineer   Edu: PhD

Email: web001@webmaster.web

```
</PRE>
```

```
<hr>
```

```
<i>webmastered by web001@webmaster.web</i>
```

```
</BODY>
```

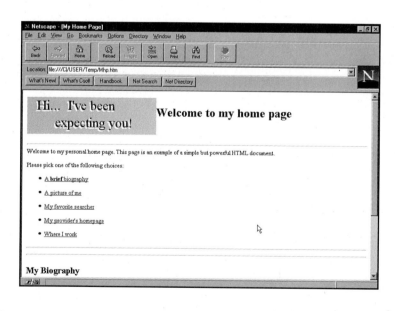

Fig. 26.5
An example of a complete WWW page.

> **Tip**
>
> By studying the HTML used to create "My Home Page," you can see there are many opportunities for typographical errors. Fixing typos, tuning and adjusting your page layout is done using a technique developed well before HTML... trial and error!

Notice that in designing the page, the general design concepts of not crowding too much information on the page and breaking-up the information into easily handled sections have been used. Experiment with various formatting techniques until you find the one that best fits your needs and style. For a thorough description of planning a home page, including planning the page's design, see chapter 25, "Planning Your Own WWW Home Page."

> **Tip**
>
> As you explore the WWW, you will see some interesting layouts and techniques on personal and commercial home pages. If you want to know the HTML codes used to produce the effects you see, take a look at the source code! Most graphic Web browsers allow you to "View Source," which opens your default text editor with the Web page's HTML text file shown.

Enhancing Your Page by Creating Interactive Forms

HTML's capability to handle forms allows interaction with the users in ways that simple links cannot manage. The following list offers just a few of the ways to use forms:

- User surveys and polls
- Search criteria for database retrieval
- Button and check box mechanisms for option selection
- Order entry
- Interactive message and newsgroup handling
- Game mechanisms

There are two basic steps to setting up a form system. The first involves creating your form in your HTML document. The second step is to determine the mechanism for retrieving the information. For this step, you can write the mechanism yourself, find an existing method, or have someone write it for you. In this chapter we will explore how to create the form in HTML.

How Forms Are Processed

Before you explore the elements used in the construction of forms, you need to have a basic understanding of how forms are processed.

Forms require the use of a World Wide Web server known as an HTTP daemon. HTTP (HyperText Transfer Protocol) is often referred to as HTTPD because it is a daemon (a background running process). The purpose of the HTTP server is to handle your form when it is submitted. Consider this—once a user has filled in a form, he or she submits it. To *whom* is it submitted? What *happens* to the information? And, *what* type of HTML response is returned to the user?

These questions indicate that there must be some intelligence handling the form information. This intelligence must be able to determine the type of form, be able to handle the incoming data, and produce some type of response to the user.

This is handled by a program or script running on an HTTP server. After a form is filled out, it is submitted to the server indicated in the form's URL. By analyzing the URL, the server hands the form to the appropriate program or script that deals with that form.

Basically, this all means that while forms are extremely useful, they cannot be used unless accompanied by software running on an HTTP server to process that form.

As you learn how to create forms, you will discover the mechanisms by which the server knows how to deal with a form and what options are available. You will also see what options exist for form builders who lack the expertise or time to create their own form handling systems.

The Basic Form Element

As previously discussed, a form is the mechanism for getting information back from a user. A document may contain more than one form, but forms never appear inside other forms. A form contains many elements that describe different aspects of the form. HTML form elements are:

- Radio buttons
- Check boxes
- Lists
- Text entry areas

A form contains one or more of these elements. There are no limits on the number of elements that may be used. However, there will certainly be a limit to the number of form elements a user will pay attention to, so plan your form with care.

The <FORM> element defines the beginning of a form. Because a form encompasses a block of other elements, the <FORM> element is obviously a non-empty element. Use </FORM> to define the end of the form.

The <FORM> element contains two parameters: the ACTION parameter and the METHOD parameter. An example of a <FORM> element is as follows:

```
<FORM ACTION="url" METHOD="technique">
```

The ACTION parameter specifies a valid relative or absolute URL. The form will be transmitted to the URL specified by ACTION when the form is submitted.

The METHOD specifies the technique used by the server to send the form data to the program specified by the ACTION. There are two basic types of METHODs—GET and POST.

The GET method is the oldest method. It is also the default. If you do not specify a method, GET will be used automatically. When a form using the GET method is received by an HTTP server, the form elements are converted into a command line statement and are passed to the program or script specified by the ACTION.

The POST method is newer and more powerful than GET. Because of the limitations of GET, it is recommended to use POST. In fact, most HTML documentation recommends that you change existing GETs into POSTs to remain compatible with future versions of the HTML language and HTTP servers. Instead of passing the form information to the ACTION via the command line, POST submits the form information via standard input (STDIN) on the HTTP server. While this may appear confusing, it does not need to be a crucial decision by you, the form designer. The software you are interfacing to will dictate whether or not the POST or the GET method should be used.

Look now at an example FORM element:

```
<FORM ACTION="http://www.com/cgi-bin/top" METHOD="POST">
```

In this FORM element, you can see that the form data will be sent to the ACTION specified as a server (http://) named www.com. The server will access the program or script named top, which appears in the server's cgi-bin directory. The METHOD indicates that the form will be submitted to the top program using the POST method.

Knowing what to use for an ACTION or METHOD consists of either talking to the staff at your server site or reading the documentation that accompanies your server's form handling software.

The INPUT Element

The `<INPUT>` element is the most often used form command because it lets you create many types of controls that allow the user to make choices. Controls include two types of buttons the user may turn on and off, as well as windows into which text can be typed. The INPUT element is an empty element, requiring no termination.

The INPUT element has many parameters. The most important one is TYPE. The TYPE parameter specifies what kind of INPUT to expect, and may be assigned any of the following values:

Checkbox	Implements a button that may be toggled either on or off.
Radio	Allows you to implement a group of buttons where only one of the group may be turned on at any one time.
Text	Allows the user to enter a line of text.
Password	Same as Text, but the characters entered by the user are shown as asterisks (or similar, concealing characters).
Reset	Causes a button to appear that, when selected, resets all the other form elements to their default values.
Submit	Causes a button to appear that will transmit the form to the URL (Action) when selected.

If no TYPE is specified in the INPUT element, TYPE=TEXT is assumed by default.

Here is an example of a simple `<INPUT>` command that implements a CHECKBOX style button (the NAME parameter is shown for completeness and is discussed next). Remember that this command may only appear between a `<FORM>` and `</FORM>` element:

```
<INPUT TYPE="CHECKBOX" NAME="test">
```

Each of the TYPE elements has its own parameters to help further define the element. The next sections show examples of each of the TYPE elements and explains their parameters. Almost all the elements discussed utilize the NAME parameter; therefore, these sections will begin by discussing the NAME parameter first.

> **Tip**
>
> Submit and Reset are the only two FORM elements that do not use the NAME parameter.

The NAME Parameter

NAME is a required parameter to all INPUT elements except the SUBMIT and RESET elements. Basically, the NAME parameter creates a label that will be associated with the user response. This allows the server that interprets the form to determine which response from the user goes to which form element.

The word you equate to NAME can be any word and never appears to the user in any form. Examples of the NAME parameter include the following:

```
NAME="user_text"
NAME="variable1"
NAME="variable2"
NAME="their_email_address"
NAME="a"
```

You will see NAME used in the examples of most of the other INPUT parameters. Please refer to these as working examples of the NAME parameter.

> **Tip**
>
> It's better to use names that are short but descriptive, as this reduces the amount of data transmitted. Descriptive names aid in locating the name when you need to modify the form.

Creating CHECKBOX TYPE Input Elements

```
<INPUT TYPE="checkbox" NAME="name" VALUE="value" CHECKED>
```

The CHECKBOX TYPE allows you to create a button that the user can turn on or off. It is like a toggle switch. This allows you to ask a simple question for which you get one of two possible responses. You may have any number of check boxes in your document. Each is independent of all the others. When a form is submitted, only the boxes that are checked by the user are actually submitted. The server always assumes all the other boxes are unchecked. If you want to have a check box checked by default (so that when the user initially sees it, it is already checked), place the parameter CHECKED in the element. The CHECKED parameter functions like a switch and requires no data or argument following the parameter

Checkbox elements may also contain a VALUE parameter. This allows you to set a string that is sent for the *on* state. If no VALUE parameter appears, the default of on is selected. VALUE is used in conjunction with NAME, which is set to a symbolic label equated to the VALUE. For example, if NAME="setting" and VALUE="on", then when the user selects that check box, the server will be sent "setting=on".

If more than one check box uses the same NAME, each one selected by the user will be sent to the server. For example, if one check box has NAME="pet" and VALUE="dog" and another check box has NAME="pet" and VALUE="cat" and both have been selected, both "pet=dog" and "pet=cat" will be sent to the server.

The following are some examples of check boxes (remember, this must appear within a <FORM> and </FORM> element. See "Creating a Complete Form" later in this chapter.

```
<INPUT TYPE="CHECKBOX" NAME="brochure" VALUE="yes" CHECKED> Would
you like a brochure?
```

This example will place a check box next to the string "Would you like a brochure?".

By default, the check box will be checked (CHECKED). When the information is sent to the server, it will be sent "brochure=yes" (because of NAME and VALUE).

The following is a more complex example:

```
Select the type of pet you have:<P>
<INPUT TYPE="checkbox" NAME="pet" VALUE="dog" > Dog<P>
<INPUT TYPE="checkbox" NAME="pet" VALUE="cat" > Cat<P>
<INPUT TYPE="checkbox" NAME="pet" VALUE="fish" > Fish<P>
<INPUT TYPE="checkbox" NAME="pet" VALUE="horse" > Horse<P>
<INPUT TYPE="checkbox" NAME="pet" VALUE="bird" > Bird<P>
<INPUT TYPE="checkbox" NAME="pet" VALUE="snake" > Snake<P>
```

This set would produce output as shown in figure 26.6.

As you can see, following the text "Select the type of pet you have:," six check boxes are displayed. Each box is labeled by a type of pet, allowing users to indicate whether or not they have that type of pet. Any of the boxes may be marked by a user. For each box that is marked, a string consisting of the NAME and the VALUE will be sent to the server. For example, if the user selected Dog and Horse, "pet=dog" and "pet=horse" will be sent to the server.

Fig. 26.6
Any or all of these
check boxes may
be checked by the
user.

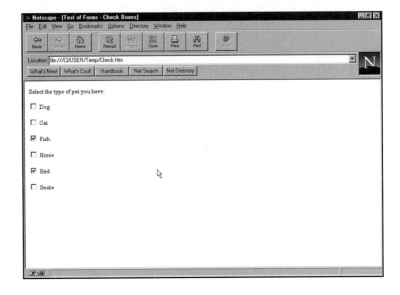

Because each check box is unique, you should never have two check boxes
with the same NAME and VALUE parameter. It is okay to have check boxes
with the same NAME and different VALUEs, or the same VALUE and different
NAMEs.

Creating RADIO TYPE Input Elements

```
<INPUT TYPE="radio" NAME="name" VALUE="value" CHECKED>
```

The RADIO TYPE allows you to create a button that acts just like CHECKBOX
in that you can turn it on and off. However, radio buttons differ in that,
within a group of buttons, only one may be selected at a given time. Selecting
a button in a group will de-select the button that is currently picked and turn
on the newly selected button. This is useful when you want the user to select
only one choice from a series of choices.

> **Note**
>
> To allow the user to make more than one selection from a group of choices, use the
> CHECKBOX parameter. To force the user to only select one option, use the RADIO
> parameter.

Like CHECKBOX, RADIO buttons have a NAME field that allows you to label
the box for the server. Each RADIO button that has the same NAME is in the
same group. Out of that group, only one button may be activated at any
time.

The VALUE field acts just as it does for CHECKBOX and specifies a unique word that is sent with the form when that particular button is activated.

If one of the buttons in a group has the CHECKED parameter, it is automatically depressed when the form is first displayed to the user. This allows you to select a default button in a group.

The following are examples of radio buttons (this must appear within a <FORM> and </FORM> element).

```
What type of credit card are you using?<P>
<INPUT TYPE="radio" NAME="credit" VALUE="visa" CHECKED> Visa<P>
<INPUT TYPE="radio" NAME="credit" VALUE="mc" > Mastercard<P>
<INPUT TYPE="radio" NAME="credit" VALUE="discover" > Discover<P>
<INPUT TYPE="radio" NAME="credit" VALUE="diners" > Diners Club<P>
<INPUT TYPE="radio" NAME="credit" VALUE="ae" > American Express<P>
```

This set would produce output as shown in figure 26.7.

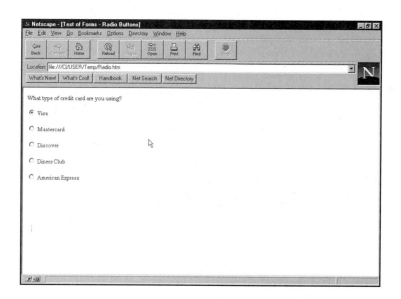

Fig. 26.7
An example of HTML radio buttons. Only one radio button may be selected at any time.

This example will display five radio buttons below the string "What type of credit card are you using?". Each of the radio buttons belongs to the group "credit."

The first button, Visa, is selected by default (CHECKED). If the user were to select the Discover choice, as an example, when the form is submitted the server will receive "credit=discover" (NAME=VALUE) for this group of buttons.

Tip

Radio buttons that are in the same group do not necessarily need to be grouped together on the screen as well.

Creating TEXT TYPE Input Elements

```
<INPUT TYPE="type" NAME="name" VALUE="value" SIZE=40 MAXLENGTH=100>
```

It is frequently useful to accept single lines of free-form input from a user. This can be used to take e-mail addresses, phone numbers, credit card numbers, comments, or any other simple typed information.

Like most of the other INPUT elements, TEXT regions have a NAME field that allows you to label it for the server. Place a symbolic name for this text box in the NAME parameter. For example, setting NAME="email" will send the server "email=", followed by whatever text the user enters in that field.

The VALUE parameter will set a default string to appear in the box when it is first displayed. If no VALUE parameter is encountered, the box will be empty when first displayed.

A SIZE parameter allows you to set the size of the displayed text box. Setting SIZE="40", for example, will set a text window 40 characters wide. If text is typed that is longer than 40 characters, it will scroll correctly. Many browsers support multiple lines of text and allow you to set SIZE=width,height to specify more than one line. For example, setting SIZE="40,10" sets a text window 40 characters wide by 10 lines high. Because HTML also supports a multiple line TEXTAREA command, it is recommended that you do not use this feature within TEXT itself.

If you do not include the SIZE parameter, the TEXT window will automatically be set to 20 characters.

Troubleshooting

I created a text area of a specific SIZE, but my characters don't fit.

Different browsers handle SIZE differently. Some equate it to number of characters, others to different width rules. As a good practice, do not make SIZE too large as it may not fit on all users' screens. A normal size of between 10 and 40 characters will work fine in most cases.

Tip

Only the physical size of the window on-screen is affected by SIZE, not the amount of text that can be typed into the window by the user.

A MAXLENGTH parameter is included to set a maximum number of characters that may be entered for text fields. If no MAXLENGTH parameter appears, the text field is of an unlimited length. For example, if `MAXLENGTH="100"`, only 100 characters may be typed per line.

The following are some examples of text windows. (As mentioned in "Creating a Complete Form" later in this chapter, this must appear within a `<FORM>` and `</FORM>` element.)

```
Please enter your E-MAIL address: <INPUT TYPE="text" NAME="email">
```

This line will place a text entry window next to the string "Please enter your E-MAIL address:".

Whatever the user enters will be transmitted to the server as "email=" followed by his or her typed text.

For example, if the user types **debi@high.tech.com**, the server will receive "email=debi@high.tech.com."

The following is another example:

```
Enter your first name: <INPUT TYPE="text" NAME="first"
MAXLENGTH=20> <P>
Enter your last name: <INPUT TYPE="text" NAME="last"
MAXLENGTH=20><P>
Enter your address: <INPUT TYPE="text" NAME="address" SIZE=80><P>
Comments: <INPUT TYPE="text" NAME="comments" VALUE="Please send
info" SIZE=80><P>
```

This set would produce output as shown in figure 26.8.

This example displays four lines. The first line allows the user to enter his or her first name. The first name is limited to 20 characters of typed text (MAXLENGTH). When the user submits the form, "first=" will be sent to the server immediately followed by the information he or she typed.

The second line repeats the actions of the first line, but for the last name of the user. Again, the use is limited to entering a maximum of 20 characters.

The third line allows the user to enter an address. The address window is 80 characters wide (SIZE=80), but the user may type unlimited amounts of information into that window (by the lack of a MAXLENGTH statement).

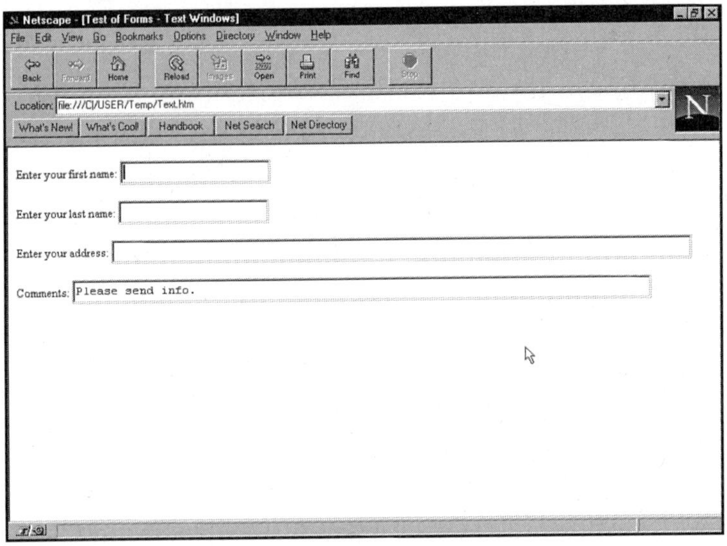

Fig. 26.8
A single line text area in an HTML form can be typed in by the user.

The final line allows the user to enter a comment. The size of the window is again set to 80 (SIZE=80). The window will initially display to the user with the string "Please send info" already in it as a default string (VALUE=). The user may change the string by typing in the window.

Tip

MAXLENGTH is useful when using forms with databases, to ensure that the information typed by the user is not longer than the maximum size allowed by your particular database.

Creating PASSWORD TYPE Input Elements

```
<INPUT TYPE="password" NAME="name" VALUE="value" SIZE=40
MAXLENGTH=100>
```

You may want to accept information from a user, but not have it appear on the user's screen. This allows you to collect passwords, credit-card numbers, and other personal data while keeping the user assured that prying eyes will not see what is entered. The PASSWORD type allows this action. While it does not encrypt the data in any way, it does keep the data from appearing physically on the user's screen as it is typed.

The NAME, VALUE, SIZE, and MAXLENGTH parameters all work exactly as they do for TEXT.

The following is an example of a password window (it must appear within a <FORM> and </FORM> element):

```
Please enter your account password: <INPUT TYPE="password"
NAME="pass" SIZE=10>
```

This line will display a text window after the string "Please enter your account password."

The window will be sized to display only 10 characters (SIZE=10), but will accept any length string entered (by the lack of a MAXLENGTH statement). When the typed information is sent to the server, "pass=" is transmitted followed by the user's typed text (NAME=). The user will only see asterisks, or a similar character (depending on the browser) regardless of what they type.

Tip

PASSWORD is not a secure mechanism for transmitting data. The typed information is only inhibited from being displayed on the user's screen. No encryption of the data is done while it is transmitted by the server.

Creating a Button to RESET a Form

```
<INPUT TYPE="reset" VALUE="value">
```

HTML has the capability to define a single button that can reset a form. The form is reset to all its default values as specified by the various parameters of each of the form's elements.

The RESET type button does not have a corresponding NAME= parameter, because it is never transmitted to the server. RESET is handled in the user's browser, automatically, as the user depresses the button.

The only parameter used by RESET is the VALUE= parameter. Whatever you set VALUE= to will be used as the label for that button.

The following is an example of the RESET button (this must appear within a <FORM> and </FORM> element).

```
<INPUT TYPE="reset" VALUE=" Push here to reset this form ">
```

This line will result in a button being created that has the string "Push here to reset this form" in it. When the user pushes the button, all text fields will be set to their default values. Text fields with no default value specified will be cleared. Check boxes and radio buttons with CHECKED set in their definitions will be automatically turned on, with the non-CHECKED definitions automatically turned off. TEXT and PASSWORD areas with VALUE= statements will be set to the string specified by VALUE=, or will be blanked if no VALUE= statement appears.

> **Tip**
>
> Remember that RESET sets forms to their default values. If a particular form element has no default value, it will be turned off if it is a button, or will be set to a blank if it is a text region.

Creating a Button to SEND a Form

```
<INPUT TYPE="submit" VALUE="value">
```

The INPUT element TYPE="submit" is used to create the button that submits the form to the server.

> **Note**
>
> Every form you create **must** have a SUBMIT button definition or the data will never be processed!

When this button is selected, the form and its current contents will be sent to the server specified by the ACTION of the <FORM> line, using the <FORM> line's METHOD.

The SUBMIT type button does not have a corresponding NAME= parameter, because the button itself is never transmitted to the server. Instead, SUBMIT causes the entire form to be transmitted when the user depresses the button.

The only parameter used by SUBMIT is the VALUE= parameter. Whatever you set VALUE= to will be used as the label for that button.

The following is an example of the SUBMIT button (it must appear within a <FORM> and </FORM> element as mentioned in "Creating a Complete Form" later in this chapter):

```
<INPUT TYPE="submit" VALUE=" Push here to send this form ">
```

This line will result in a button being created that has the string "Push here to send this form" in it. When the user pushes the button, all filled in fields will be sent to the server specified in the <FORM> statement. Fields and buttons that are not set to anything will not be transmitted.

Using the TEXTAREA Element

```
<TEXTAREA NAME="NAME" ROWS=10 COLS=40> </TEXTAREA>
```

Often, it is useful to be able to accept a block of text from the user. Having this ability allows users to cut and paste entire documents into HTML pages.

This, in turn, allows large quantities of information to be passed back and forth. It can save both HTML-page room, as well as database room, by combining what would be many TEXT elements into a single TEXTAREA.

The TEXTAREA element is not a TYPE of the INPUT command, but instead it is its own element just as INPUT is.

Like most of the other INPUT elements, TEXT regions have a NAME field that allows you to label it for the server. Place a symbolic name for this text box in the NAME parameter. For example, setting NAME="body" will send the server "body=," followed by whatever the user types in for that TEXTAREA.

The TEXTAREA element also has ROWS and COLS parameters. These are used to specify the size of the TEXTAREA window that is displayed to the user. This does not limit the user in how much he or she can type, but merely limits the size of the window displayed to the user. As the user types and overfills the window, the window should automatically grow sliders to aid in moving the view for the user.

To use ROWS and COLS, simply set them equal to the number of rows and columns you want in your TEXTAREA. For example, setting ROWS=10 and COLUMNS=80 sets a field 10 characters high and 80 lines wide.

The TEXTAREA element is a NON-EMPTY element. This means that it must have a </TEXTAREA> terminator. Anything between the <TEXTAREA> and </TEXTAREA> elements will appear as default information inside the text area. If nothing appears between the two elements, no default information will be placed in the text area when it appears to the user.

The following is an example of the TEXTAREA element (remember, this must appear within a <FORM> and </FORM> element; see "Creating a Complete Form" later in this chapter):

```
<TEXTAREA NAME="resume" ROWS=8 COLS=80></TEXTAREA>
```

In this example, a text area is created that is eight lines high by 80 characters wide. The user may type any amount of information into this area. The area contains no default information.

The following is another example:

```
Please enter any special instructions:<P>
<TEXTAREA NAME="instructions" ROWS=5 COLS=40>No special instruc-
tions</TEXTAREA>
```

This set would produce output as shown in figure 26.9.

Fig. 26.9
As shown here,
the TEXTAREA
form element
accepts more than
one line of typed
text.

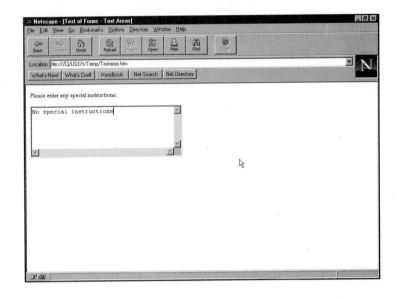

Troubleshooting

Some browsers will not deal with the default text specified between the <TEXTAREA> and
<TEXTAREA> elements. When displayed by these browsers, the text will appear outside of
the text area.

One solution is to try the VALUE= parameter within the <TEXTAREA> element. Some
browsers recognize this as an alternative mechanism for specification of default text.
It is possible that your browser may not accept either mechanism, in which case
there is no way to have default text.

This example places a text window 5 lines high by 40 characters wide. It is
named 'instructions' and will be passed to the server as 'instructions=' followed by whatever text the user enters. The first time the field is presented to
the user, it has the default contents of "No special instructions."

Using the SELECT Element to Create a List

```
<SELECT NAME="LIST">    </SELECT>
```

HTML form handling allows you to create several types of lists. Each list presents one or more items to the user and may have a single item or several
items selected from the list.

When lists are displayed, they appear either in an inset window, or in a pop-
up window. Inset windows that contain a list larger than the window itself

will have a slider on the side that allows you to access other items in the list. Where check boxes are useful for small lists, the <SELECT> element allows lists of any size to be created.

Lists are bounded by the <SELECT> and </SELECT> elements. Only two things may appear between these two elements. The first is any free-form text; and the second is the <OPTION> element. No other HTML elements may appear between the <SELECT> and </SELECT> elements.

The <SELECT> element starts a list. The NAME parameter must be associated with the <SELECT> element and allows you to label the list for the server. Place a symbolic name for this text box in the NAME parameter. For example, setting <SELECT NAME="list1"> will send the server "list1=" followed by the name, for each item selected in the list. For example, if the list contains "Dog", "Cat" and "Mouse", and "Dog" and "Cat" are selected, both "list=Dog" and "list=Cat" will be sent to the server. The specification of "Dog", "Cat", and "Mouse" are done using the <OPTION> element that is discussed later in this section.

The <SELECT> element has an optional SIZE parameter. If the SIZE parameter is missing, it is assumed to be equated to the value 1. When size is set to 1, the list is as a pop-up window where you may select only one of the items in the list. This use is similar to radio-buttons, where only one of a group may be selected.

When the SIZE parameter is larger than 1, it is presented as an inset window containing a list of selectable items. The number that is assigned to SIZE sets the maximum number of items that are in the inset window at one time. For example, if the list is set to SIZE=5, five items from the list are visible at one time. Items not visible in the list may be accessed by using the slider that appears to the right of the list.

Another optional parameter of the <SELECT> element is the MULTIPLE parameter. MULTIPLE has no value associated with it. Using MULTIPLE forces the list to be displayed in an inset, scrollable window. Additionally, when MULTIPLE is present, the user may select more than one item from the list. This is done by holding down the Ctrl key while selecting additional items in the list.

The <OPTION> element appears between the <SELECT> and </SELECT> elements. There is one <OPTION> for every item that may be picked in the list. <OPTION> has one parameter associated with it—SELECTED.

If SELECTED is set, the item associated with that <OPTION> is automatically selected by default. If MULTIPLE is specified in the <SELECT> element, more than one SELECTED parameter may appear.

The following is an example of the SELECT element (this must appear within a <FORM> and </FORM> element):

```
Please select your favorite ice cream toppings:<P>
<SELECT NAME="list1" SIZE=3 MULTIPLE>
<OPTION SELECTED> Chocolate
<OPTION> Fruit Preserves
<OPTION> Nuts
<OPTION> Butterscotch
<OPTION> Candy sprinkles
</SELECT>
```

This set would produce output as shown in figure 26.10.

Fig. 26.10

The inset list window shows three items; the slider allows the user to select the options that are hidden.

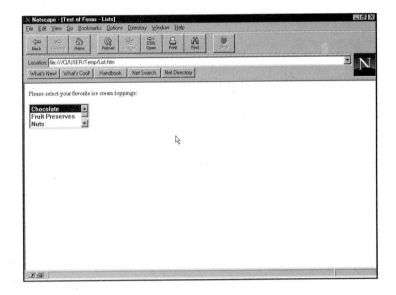

In this example, a select box is created that is large enough for three items. The rest of the items will be accessible by scrolling (SIZE=3). The select area will allow the user to select more than one item (MULTIPLE), and each item selected will be transmitted to the server using "list1=," followed by the item that was selected. The select box in this example has five items in it that may be chosen by the user.

Chocolate is selected by default (as almost everybody loves chocolate), but may be de-selected by the user if desired.

> **Note**
>
> Remember that no HTML element should appear between the <SELECT> and
> </SELECT> elements except the <OPTION> element.

Creating a Complete Form

Now that you have examined the fundamental elements necessary to complete a form, let's put them all together and see how a form actually looks.

For this example, you will create an order form that allows the user to purchase a new car (see fig. 26.11). The order form will begin by accepting free format text from the user, for a name, phone number and address. The form displays a series of radio buttons that allow the user to pick the color of the car. Beneath the radio buttons is an inset list of options for the car. The user may pick one option from the list, or hold down the CTRL key while picking from the list to select multiple options. After the inset box, a series of checkboxes allows the user to select how they want to be responded to. Finally, the SUBMIT button is displayed, which allows the user to actually send the form to the HTTP server.

```
<FORM ACTION="http://www.car.com/cgi-bin/sellcar" METHOD=POST>
Enter your name:  <INPUT TYPE="text" NAME="name" SIZE=40> and
➥phone:  <INPUT TYPE="text" NAME="phone" SIZE=20><P>
Enter your address: <TEXTAREA NAME="address" ROWS=5 COLS=50>Put
➥your address here</TEXTAREA><P>
Choose a color for your car<P>
<INPUT TYPE="radio" NAME="color" VALUE="red" CHECKED> Red
<INPUT TYPE="radio" NAME="color" VALUE="white" > White
<INPUT TYPE="radio" NAME="color" VALUE="blue" > Blue
<INPUT TYPE="radio" NAME="color" VALUE="black" > Black
<INPUT TYPE="radio" NAME="color" VALUE="cream" > Cream<P>
Select your car options:
<SELECT NAME="options" MULTIPLE SIZE=4>
<OPTION> Bucket Seats
<OPTION> Sport Styling
<OPTION> AM/FM Radio
<OPTION> CD Player
<OPTION> Turbo charged engine
<OPTION> Tinted Windows
</SELECT> <P>
Select what you want us to do now:<P>
<INPUT TYPE="checkbox" NAME="dispose" VALUE="mail"> Send informa
➥tion about my choices<BR>
<INPUT TYPE="checkbox" NAME="dispose" VALUE="sale"> Have a sales
➥person call<BR>
<INPUT TYPE="checkbox" NAME="dispose" VALUE="make"> Make me a car
➥and call me when it's done<P>
<INPUT TYPE="submit" VALUE=" Press this button to submit your form
➥">
</FORM>
```

Troubleshooting

I created my forms, but everything appears to be a text area, even my radio buttons and check boxes.

Some browsers are not case independent in the button type. Therefore, make sure to use "radio," "checkbox," and "text" when defining these buttons. Use of uppercase may not work in many browsers for these words.

Fig. 26.11
The new car order form combines most of the FORM elements.

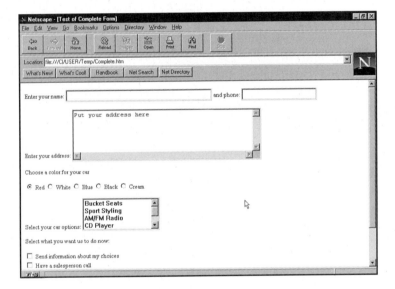

This example begins by opening the form with a <FORM> statement. In this statement, you specify that the form is to use the POST method of transferring data and that it is to send any filled out form to the URL http://www.car.com/cgi-bin/sell car as specified by the ACTION statement.

Next, you accept the user's name, address, and phone number using TEXT windows. The address is entered into a multiple-line TEXTAREA, while the phone numbers and user's name are each single-line text windows.

Next, the user is allowed to select the color of his or her car as one of five possible choices. Note that you have defaulted the color to Red, and that only one color can be picked from the list because it is a RADIO type group of buttons.

Beneath the car color choices is a select box with various options for the car. The user may select any number of these options because the <SELECT> element has the MULTIPLE parameter within it.

Toward the end of the form, the user can select up to three METHODs of follow-up. They may check any or all of the three CHECKBOX elements.

Finally, the last button allows the user to send the form to the server specified (car.com) by the ACTION parameter of the <FORM> element.

Understanding How Forms Are Submitted

Anybody can design a form. The resulting form will be usable, in that it can be filled out and submitted. However, at this point you must ask, "submitted where?". For a form to be useful, it must be submitted to some place that will know what to do with the data in the form. Because each and every form is different, this often requires custom solutions.

There are two problems associated with determining how a form is handled. The first problem is where to send the form data. In other words, what to set the ACTION parameter of the <FORM> element to.

Second, you must determine what you want to do with the data. You may want the data to be e-mailed to you. Or, you may want the data appended to a file or integrated into a database. The database can be designed to provide instant feedback to the user so that immediately after the user submits the form, the entire HTML system is modified to incorporate the user's information. There are an infinite amount of things you can do with form data depending on your needs.

Interestingly enough, both of these problems have the same solutions. If you can write a shell script, in PERL perhaps, or a fairly simple program in C or similar language, you probably have enough skill to write your own form-handling software. For people who do not have the programming or script skills, or simply lack the time, off-the-shelf solutions already exist for many form needs.

Before you see how a solution can be implemented, you need a better under-standing of exactly how a server deals with a form. To do this, let's examine a simple example. In this example, you will play the role of the user. You have just filled out a form and you hit the SUBMIT button. At that moment, the user's browser software accumulates the information contained in the form and transmits it to the URL pointed to by the ACTION parameter of the <FORM> element.

So far so good. Your information is somewhere between you and the server that is going to handle it. When the information reaches the server, it is examined by the server. The URL must direct the server where to find a program that will handle your form data. For example, the following may have been your ACTION URL:

```
<FORM ACTION="http://www.com/cgi-bin/remailer?bob@www.com"
METHOD="POST">
```

In this FORM element, you see a valid URL for the ACTION that points to a server (http://) named www.com. The server finds a program named remailer in the cgi-bin directory (more on cgi-bin later). The METHOD is POST so the server will communicate with the remailer program using that method. If there is information to be passed to the remailer program on the command line, it is separated by the question mark character (?) from the program name itself.

So, back to your data. As your data enters the server (www.com), the server examines the URL information and (in this example) invokes the remailer program. It hands the string bob@www.com on the command line to the remailer program and also transmits the contents of your filled-out form to the remailer program. The transmission occurs on the command line for GET methods and through standard input for POST methods.

The server's software (remailer, in this case) examines and handles the form information and formats a response for you, the user. The response is sent back to you via the server and arrives on your screen.

So, we can again see the two basic problems. First, where do you send your data? Second, what to do with it?

The simplest way to handle a form is to have all the submitted forms e-mailed to a single destination where they can be examined at will. This is known as *form remailing*, and many server sites already provide some type of form remailing services. Commercial form remailers typically involve a small monthly charge to pay for the service of forwarding your e-mailed forms. Form remailers require you to provide a single e-mail address to send the contents of all forms. Remailers then take all incoming forms, format them into readable responses, and send the forms to you. This method is easiest because it is usable even if you don't have access to a server site. This means that you can run pages out of a directory using file://, and still take advantage of form handling capabilities.

If you have access to a server site and can design your own software or scripts, you can easily implement your own form handling program. It is beyond the scope of this chapter to provide details on how to construct server form-handling software, as that subject would be a book in itself. However, the methods are simple enough that anyone with about a moderate level of experience in writing scripts should be able to implement simple form-handling programs.

Another solution involves finding archives of existing software. Many form-handling systems have been placed in the public domain on the Internet. These often may be used outright or modified slightly to accommodate any special needs. However, use of pre-existing software again requires that you have access to a server on which to implement it.

Finally, many consultants and service bureaus exist that are more than happy to implement custom-designed form solutions. These groups will write your software as well as help you find a cost-effective server site on which to place it.

A Brief Look at CGI-bin

At the end of the last section, you saw an example of the use of CGI-bin in what appeared to be a path. Here is the line again, for your reference:

```
<FORM ACTION="http://www.com/cgi-bin/remailer?bob@www.com"
METHOD="POST">
```

While the CGI-bin looks like a path, in effect it is a special word recognized by the server (in this example, www.com). CGI (Common Gateway Interface) is a special mechanism for interfacing Web servers with programs, allowing them to handle form and other input. CGI-bin programs may be pointed to from any link or form. Links pass all information to the form on the command line, as if a GET were issued. Forms pass information by GET or POST METHOD.

When a server sees a URL coming across that contains the CGI-bin directory, it knows to call the program referenced by the URL and hand it the data in the URL and form (if a form is present). It also knows to expect a response from the CGI-bin program that it sends back to the user.

Anytime a browser submits a form to a server, it expects a valid HTML response from the server. If no response is received in a reasonable period of time (two to three minutes in most browsers), the browser returns an error. All CGI-bin programs must return some form of HTML response to the user via the server. This is accomplished by the CGI-bin program's writing the desired response, as valid HTML, to standard output (STDOUT). The server receives the output and sends it back to the user's browser (in the form of valid HTML).

Conclusion

As you can see, HTML provides both simple and complex methods of providing information to and receiving data from the user. If you want to "get the message out," then text sizing, formatting, and anchors may be all you need to tell the world about yourself or your organization.

HTML forms provide a quick-and-easy method for the document user to transmit data back to the document's originator. HTML documents and their forms will undoubtedly prove to be popular mechanisms for individuals, groups, and companies to provide information to the Internet community in an exciting and attractive manner. In the future, companies will consider HTML documents for advertising and HTML forms for product ordering as common marketing tools.

If, while designing your page, you run into questions not answered in this chapter, feel free to make use of the experts who abound on the Internet. WWW help is available 24-hours a day from live people via the #WWW group on IRC (Internet Relay Chat). Likewise, non-real-time help may be found on the Net News group **comp.infosystems.www**. Finally, many documents exist on the Internet and WWW concerning the WWW and authoring your own pages. Use WebCrawler to search for HTML, WWW, HTTP for starters. See chapter 38, "How IRC Works," for more information about the IRC.

CHAPTER 27

Using Microsoft Internet Assistant to Build Web Pages

The World Wide Web is a large collection of documents stored on the Internet. Each of the documents can link to other documents through a technology called hypertext.

As you've seen the World Wide Web before and, doubtless used it, you know how the process works. The magic lies in these mystical documents.

Although we traditionally refer to the World Wide Web as interactive, it becomes truly interactive when we can publish our own documents on the Web and allow others to view them and communicate with us.

To capture that true interactivity within the Office suite, Microsoft has released an add-on application for Microsoft Word that gives Word the power to help you create Web documents.

In this chapter, you learn:

- Where to find Internet Assistant and how to install it
- How to use Internet Assistant to browse the Web
- How to create Web pages with Internet Assistant
- How to convert Word documents into Web pages

What Is Internet Assistant?

Internet Assistant is an add-on for Microsoft Word for Windows. An add-on is a program, utility, or software package feature that doesn't ship with the product. Add-ons are usually produced after the software is finished. Although Internet Assistant is provided at no additional charge to registered users of Microsoft Word, most add-ons are available for a small licensing fee.

The main purpose of Internet Assistant is to enable Word users to easily share information via the World Wide Web.

Internet Assistant enables you to do two new things with Word:

- Create and edit HTML Documents
- Browse the World Wide Web

If you've ever spent any time writing HTML with a text editor before, you know that it can be painstaking and time consuming. The main advantage to Internet Assistant is that it incorporates all the advantages of a full-featured word processor into your HTML editor.

When Internet Assistant was first written, it was one of the better HTML editors. Although it didn't provide support for the more advanced features of HTML, it did provide the user with a graphical representation of the HTML document.

Since that time, other graphical editors have sprung up, some better than others. Most offer more HTML support than Internet Assistant, but few offer the spell-checking and grammar-checking and Auto Text type features.

If you're looking to create a small, simple Web page (like a Web page for yourself), Internet Assistant is a good choice for you. If you're with a large company that wants to create a major Web site, you'll be better off with Live Markup.

Internet Assistant Requirements

Most software has that fun little list of requirements that you must adhere to in order for the product to work properly. Of course, Internet Assistant is no exception.

In order for Internet Assistant to work properly, you'll need a system with the following:

- A PC with a 386DX or higher processor (486 recommended)
- Microsoft Windows 95 operating system or Microsoft Windows NT Workstation operating system version 3.51 or later (will not run on earlier versions of Windows)
- English, French, German, or Italian language versions of Microsoft Word for Windows 95 or Microsoft Word 6.0 for Windows NT
- 6 MB of memory (8 MB recommended)
- 4 MB of free hard disk space

- Microsoft Mouse or compatible pointing device
- VGA or higher-resolution video adapter (SVGA 256-color recommended)

The Correct Version of Word

Internet Assistant is designed to work with Microsoft Word—however, it's quite picky about which version of Word you're using. Internet Assistant comes in two versions:

- 1.0—for Word 6.0 for Windows
- 2.0z—a beta version for Word 6.0 for Windows NT or Word 7.0 for Windows 95

This chapter covers only Word for Windows 95. If you have Word 6.0, but you're running it under Windows 95, you'll need to get the other version.

Tip

To find out which version of Word you're using, open the Help menu and choose About Microsoft Word.

If you'd like to use the version for Word 95, you'll need to use the English, French, German, or Italian version Word 7.0 for Windows 95. If not, Internet Assistant will not work.

Future versions of Internet Assistant may support other versions of Word, depending upon customer demand. If you have any questions about the availability of versions of Internet Assistant after the printing of this book, call the Microsoft Customer Service line.

Downloading and Installing Internet Assistant

Because Internet Assistant is an add-on available for no charge, you'll have to get it yourself. Fortunately, the World Wide Web makes the whole process quite simple.

Where to Find Internet Assistant

Microsoft keeps an updated copy of Internet Assistant as well as documents about current bugs, current versions, and current support issues on its Web

IV

The World Wide Web

site. The Web site contains a compressed file you can download into a temporary directory (such as C:\TEMP or C:\INCOMING and execute from there.

To download Internet Assistant from the Microsoft World Wide Web site:

1. Start your Web browser.

2. Browse to **http://www.microsoft.com/msoffice/freestuf/ msword/download/ia/ia95/default.htm**. You will see the Internet Assistant page (see fig. 27.1).

Fig. 27.1
Since Microsoft regularly updates its Web site, this page may look a bit different than this when you view it.

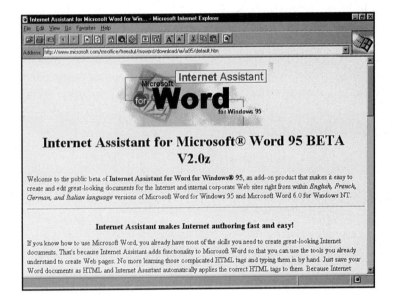

3. Look for the link called Download Internet Assistant NOW. Click the link to see the next page.

4. Read over the information on this page. This information may change from time to time, so you'll want to be sure you're up to date before reading on.

5. When you're finished, click the Download Internet Assistant NOW link.

6. Depending upon which browser you're using, you may see a window that asks you what you want to do with this file. Click Save As or something that looks like I want to save this file. Specify a temporary directory (C:\TEMP or C:\INCOMING will work) and click OK to save the file.

After a few moments (it may take as long as 15 minutes depending upon the speed of your connection), you'll have the archived file saved on your hard disk. I'll show you what to do with it in the next section.

Installing Internet Assistant

As you may know, the file you've just downloaded is a self-extracting archive of compressed files. Unlike other self-extracting archives, this one runs the setup program automatically, extracts the files, automatically, and deletes the setup files when you're done, leaving only the original archive. A handy feature, indeed.

Therefore, once you've downloaded the file, all you need to do is to double-click it in Explorer to start. Here's how to fully install Internet Assistant on your machine:

1. Double-click WORDIA2B to start the installation process. A dialog will appear asking if you want to install Internet Assistant (see fig. 27.2). Click Yes to continue.

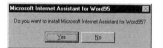

Fig. 27.2
Click Yes to
continue.

2. The Setup program will extract the setup files automatically and start the Setup process. Setup will display a disclaimer dialog.

3. After you've read the disclaimer dialog, click Continue. Setup will search for components you've already installed on your machine, and check to see how much disk space you have, then display the Internet Assistant License Agreement.

4. Read this agreement. If you agree, click Accept to continue with the installation. After a few moments, you'll see the Microsoft Internet Assistant for Word Setup dialog box (see fig. 27.3).

5. By default, Internet Assistant will be installed in your Program Files directory. Normally, you won't need to change this. If you do, however, click the Change Folder button and specify a new directory.

6. To continue the installation process, click the Complete icon button on the left-hand side of the dialog. A gauge dialog indicating installation progress will appear.

Fig. 27.3
Click the Complete button to begin the installation.

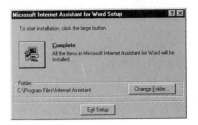

7. When the installation process is finished, you'll see a dialog offering you two choices. You can either Launch Word (which you'll probably do) or Exit the Setup process (if you want to wait awhile, first).

8. To continue, click Launch Word. After Word starts, a dialog will appear indicating that the Setup process is done.

You've completed the Setup process. Now you're ready to be productive.

Using Internet Assistant to Browse the Web

Internet Assistant provides two major functions: Web browsing and Web page publishing. With that dual functionality comes the most powerful reason to use Internet Assistant.

Since Internet Assistant can be a Web browser *and* an HTML editor, you can browse the Web for pages you like or ones that look like something you'd like to design and then use that material (with a bit of editing, of course) to create your own pages.

To learn to browse the Web with Internet Assistant is to tap into the huge world of online documents and become a part of the greatest innovation of computer communications, but more than that, Internet Assistant allows you to participate in that world, as well.

With Internet Assistant, Word can download Web pages from the Internet. After you've downloaded the Web page, you can:

- Save the Web page as a Word document
- Use a portion of that Web page in one of your own Web pages

> **Tip**
>
> Don't try to use Internet Assistant as your normal browser. It's much too slow, and doesn't support many of the new formatting features you'll find in Netscape, Mosaic, and Internet Explorer.

Opening a Web Document

With Internet Assistant, there are several ways to open a Web document. The easiest is to use the Open URL command:

1. Open the File menu and choose the Open URL command. You will see the Open URL dialog box.

2. Type in the URL of the document you wish to view (see fig. 27.4).

3. Click OK to view the document.

IV

The World Wide Web

Fig. 27.4
Type the URL of the document and click OK.

Note

Internet Assistant is not the best Web browser on the planet—in fact, it's rather poor. The fundamental purpose of Word is that of a word processor, and the fundamental purpose of Internet Assistant is to enable you to create HTML documents (Web pages) with Word.

Downloading a page will take a long time, and may be frustrating. Also, newer HTML documents won't look right in Internet Assistant. This is intentional, as Internet Assistant assumes you'll want to save these Web pages as Word documents.

After a few moments, the Web page will appear on the display. Note, though, that each graphic in the document will load separately, creating a long wait.

With each page or graphic within the page, Internet Assistant will display a small dialog box indicating the progress of the current transfer. To abort the current transfer, click Cancel. If, after you've already downloaded part of a document, you'd like to reload it, open the File menu and choose the Reload command.

Surfing the Net

As with most browsers, Internet Assistant has a few features that make your Web browsing experience a bit easier. Keep in mind, though, that the feature set is (at least relative to other full-blown browsers) quite limited.

To assist with browsing the Web, Internet Assistant has two toolbars, each loosely based on the original toolbars for Word.

The Standard toolbar contains tools for opening, printing, and saving Web documents, as well as a few others; the formatting toolbar contains tools for browsing the Web.

The following table introduces each button in detail:

Button	Description
Standard Toolbar	
Tool01	Creates a new, blank document
Tool02	Opens an existing document
Tool03	Saves the current document
Tool04	Prints the current document
Tool05	Switches to Print Preview
Tool06	Find text within the current document
Tool07	Copy hyperlink (URL) to Clipboard
Tool08	Show/Hide paragraph codes
Tool09	Show/Hide HTML codes
Tool10	Zoom control
Tool11	Tip Wizard
Tool12	Help
Formatting Toolbar	
Tool13	Switch to HTML Edit view
Tool14	Go Back
Tool15	Go Forward
Tool16	Open URL
Tool17	View History
Tool18	Open Favorite Places
Tool19	Add current page to Favorite Places
Tool20	Open Home Page
Tool21	Cancel/Stop

Obviously, the first thing you'll want to do is follow a hypertext link to another page.

> **Tip**
>
> In keeping with the standard Windows 95 terminology, Microsoft often refers to a hyperlink as a *shortcut*.

To browse through the various hyperlinks, or shortcuts on a page, click it (just like you would in any other browser).

> **Tip**
>
> In some cases, when the hyperlink points to a different part of the same document (known as a bookmark), you'll have to double-click the link instead of single-click. Generally, try the single-click first. If that doesn't work, use a double-click.

If you've clicked a hyperlink that brings up a page you don't want to see, use the Go Back button on the Formatting toolbar to go back to the previous page, where you can choose a different link.

If you've gone back too many pages, use the Go Forward button to undo your last Go Back. Because the Go Forward button really acts as an undo button for the Go Back button, it will only work after you've gone back a page. Also, if, after you've gone back, you choose a new hyperlink, the Go Forward function will not work.

The History Folder

The History Folder contains a list of the last 50 pages you've viewed. To view the History:

1. Open the Window menu and choose History List. The History List will appear. If you don't see this option, you are not in Web browse view. To switch to Web browse view, open the View menu and choose Web Browse.

2. The History List dialog box contains a list of the last 50 pages you've viewed (see fig. 27.5). To review one of the pages, highlight the title in the list, then click Go To.

Fig. 27.5
To review a page
you've already
seen, double-click
its name in the
History List dialog
box.

3. If you want simply to copy the URL of the document to the clipboard, highlight the title in the list (note the URL is indicated toward the bottom of the window) then click Copy HyperLink.

The Favorites Document

With the Favorites Document, you can keep track of the Web pages you visit most often. Although it doesn't provide a nice menu structure, it's quite handy for keeping track of pages you visit frequently, and when you add a page to your Favorites document, you can simple click its name to get it back again.

To add a Web page to your Favorites document:

1. If you haven't opened the Web page yet, open the File menu and choose the Open URL command. Type the URL in the Open URL dialog box, and click OK. After a few moments, your page will appear.

2. With your page displayed, open the Tools menu and choose Add to Favorite Places. Word will churn for a few minutes while it adds your document to the list.

To see a Web page you've saved in your Favorite Places document:

1. Open the Tools menu and choose Open Favorite Places. After a few moments, you'll see your Favorite Places document with a list of all the pages you've added (see fig. 27.6).

2. To visit one of the pages in the list, simply click its name. After a few minutes, you'll see that Web page on your display.

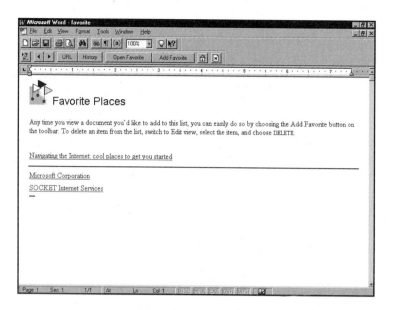

Fig. 27.6
The Favorite Places document is a list of documents you visit most often.

Tip

If the Web page you're trying to view has changed, moved, or been deleted, or its file name has changed, you may get an error message saying that Internet Assistant cannot download the page.

In rare cases, the machine with the page on it may be off or temporarily down. Before giving up, try again the next day and see if it works.

Using Internet Assistant to Build Web Pages

So far, you've spent most of the time in the Web browse view. Internet Assistant includes an additional view that allows you to create and edit HTML documents: HTML Edit view.

When you're in Web browse view, you can't type any text or make any changes to the current document; you'll need to switch to HTML Edit view. To do this, open the View menu and select the HTML Edit command, or click the Switch to Edit view button on the Formatting toolbar.

This button switches the active view to HTML Edit view where you can edit and revise Web documents. However, if no document is present in Web view, this button will return you to Normal view.

If you want to create an HTML document from scratch:

1. Open the File menu and choose New. The New dialog appears. This dialog contains a collection of templates that you can use to create a new document.

2. The HTML template is in the General collection; click the General tab.

3. Double-click the HTML icon in the list of templates (see fig. 27.7). A new, blank document window will appear in Word.

Fig. 27.7
The New dialog box contains a collection of document templates.

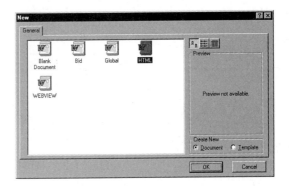

Again, the toolbars will change, giving you convenient access to the features you use when composing HTML documents.

A Review of HTML

To get a good grasp of exactly what Internet Assistant can do for you, it is important to have at least a passing knowledge of HTML. Throughout this section, I will assume that you have some experience with HTML. If you don't, feel free to browse through chapters 25, "Planning Your Own WWW Home Pages," and 26, "Using HTML to Build Web Pages," for more detailed information on HTML and how it works.

To get started on a new HTML document:

1. Open the File menu and choose New. You'll see a dialog with a collection of templates for new documents you can create.

2. Under the General tab, double-click HTML. In a few minutes, you'll see a blank document entitled Document1 on your screen.

> **Tip**
>
> To ensure that any relative links you create will keep the path of your document, you should save and title your document before creating any new links.

3. Open the File menu and choose Save. You'll see the Save As dialog box.

4. In the Save File As Type box, select HTML Document (*.htm). This will save your document in HTML source file format.

5. In the File Name box, type a name for your file, and then click OK. Word returns you to your blank document.

6. Open the File menu and choose HTML Document Info. You will see the HTML Document Head Information dialog. In the Title box, type a title for your document, then click OK.

7. In the document window, type the text of your document as you would any other document.

Using the Word Styles to Create HTML Formatting Codes

If you've ever created an HTML document before, you may be tempted to insert HTML code at this point. However, you won't want to do that.

Internet Assistant creates the HTML code when you save your document based on the style you've applied to each section.

Here's a brief list of the common HTML codes and the Word styles you should use with Internet Assistant:

- Base Paragraphs—Normal,P
- Headings—Heading 1,H1; Heading 2,H2; etc.
- Bulleted Lists—List Bullet,UL
- Numbered List—List Number,OL

> **Tip**
>
> For more detailed information about HTML styles and their equivalent in Word, open the Help menu and choose Internet Assistant for Word Help, click the Index tab, and type style and press Enter. In the Topics Found dialog, double-click HTML Tags and Equivalent Word Commands.

Format your document by applying styles from the Style box or using buttons on the Formatting toolbar. For a list of the formatting elements available to you, click HTML Tags and Equivalent Word Commands.

Create links to other documents by clicking the Hyperlink button. You can link to documents that are already on the Web, or you can create links among a set of documents that you have authored and want to publish on the Web. For tips on structuring your HTML documents, click Guidelines for Publishing Web Documents.

Inserting a Hyperlink

There are three different types of hyperlinks that you can create with Internet Assistant:

- A link to a local document
- A link to an URL
- A link to a different place within the same document

Since there are several differences in the way in which you'll approach each type, each one is covered separately—if you're not familiar with the differences, read all three.

Link to a Local Document

This type assumes that you are writing the document on the hard drive on which it will reside. This is most often the case, but even if it's not, one will usually keep the same basic directory structure if the Web documents are moved to another machine.

To insert a hyperlink to a local document:

1. If you want to make a hyperlink out of existing text, highlight the text. If not, place the text cursor where you want the hyperlink to be.

> **Tip**
>
> If you'd like to use a graphic for your link instead of text, you can do that with the Image button. That is covered later in this chapter in the "Adding Graphics" section.

2. Open the Insert menu and choose Hyperlink. You'll see the Hyperlink <A> dialog box (see fig. 27.8). At the top of this dialog, select the to Local Document tab. If you've highlighted text to be the link, that text will appear in the Text to display box. If not, type an appropriate word or phrase in this box.

Fig. 27.8
Use the HyperLink
<A> dialog box to
create a link to a
local document.

3. In the Directories window, indicate the path to the local document. If the document is not a Word document or HTML, indicate the file type in the List Files of Type list at the bottom of the window (if the correct file type is not listed, choose All Files). In the file list window, highlight the file you wish to use as your hyperlink.

4. To create the hyperlink, click OK. The dialog will disappear and you'll be returned to your document. The text of the hyperlink will appear in a blue underlined font.

Link to a URL

If you'd like to create a link to one of your favorite Web pages, or perhaps there is another page that contains information that will add to the information you've presented in yours, you can create a link to that page.

To insert a hyperlink to another document on the Web:

1. If you want to make a hyperlink out of existing text, highlight the text. If not, place the text cursor where you want the hyperlink to be. If not, type an appropriate word or phrase in this box.

> **Tip**
>
> If you'd like to use a graphic for your link instead of text, you can do that with the Image button. This is covered later in the "Adding Graphics" section.

2. Open the Insert menu and choose Hyperlink. You'll see the Hyperlink <A> dialog box (see fig. 27.9). At the top of this dialog box, select the to URL tab. If you've highlighted text to be the link, that text will appear in the Text to display box.

Fig. 27.9
Use the HyperLink
<A> dialog box
to create a link
to a document
elsewhere on the
Internet.

3. Toward the bottom of the dialog you'll see a field, and a list (most likely, this list will be empty, unless you've added a link before). If the list contains URLs, you can click one of them to have your link point to that URL.

4. To create the hyperlink, click OK. The dialog will disappear and you'll be returned to your document. The text of the hyperlink will appear in a blue underlined font.

Link to a Bookmark

In HTML documents, as with Word documents, you can label a place in a document with a specific name—this is called a *bookmark*. You can also create a link to a bookmark. This link is often found in the same document.

For example, let's say you've created a document that contains several sections. At the top, you could create a list of the various sections, linking each section name to the section itself.

To create a link to a bookmark, you must first create the bookmark. To create the bookmark:

1. Move your text cursor to the place in the document you'd like to label with a document. If you're creating a bookmark for sections, for example, move the text cursor to the beginning of the line that contains the title of that section.

2. Open the Edit menu and choose Bookmark. You'll see the Bookmark dialog box (see fig. 27.10).

3. In the Bookmark Name box, type a name for the bookmark. Use something that indicates the location so you'll remember it later. The bookmark name must not contain any spaces.

4. To create the bookmark, click Add.

Fig. 27.10
Use the Bookmark
dialog box to
create a new
bookmark in the
current document.

Tip

If the Add button is grayed out, check to be sure your bookmark name starts with a
letter or number, and doesn't contain any spaces or punctuation marks.

Once you've created the bookmark, you can create a link to it. To create a
link to the bookmark:

1. If you want to make a hyperlink out of existing text, highlight the text.
   If not, place the text cursor where you want the hyperlink to be. If not,
   type an appropriate word or phrase in this box.

Tip

If you'd like to use a graphic for your link instead of text, you can do so with
the *Image* button. This is covered in the section "Adding Graphics."

---

2. Open the Insert menu and choose Hyperlink. You'll see the Hyperlink
   <A> dialog box (see fig. 27.11). At the top of this dialog box, select the
   to Bookmark tab. If you've highlighted text to be the link, that text will
   appear in the Text to display box.

Fig. 27.11
Use the HyperLink
<A> dialog box to
create a link to a
different section
of the current
document.

3. On the left side of the dialog box you'll see a list of bookmarks in the current document. If this list is empty, you'll need to create the bookmark first. Highlight the bookmark you want to link to.

4. To create the hyperlink, click OK. The dialog will disappear and you'll be returned to your document. The text of the hyperlink will appear in a blue underlined font.

Adding Graphics

What would the World Wide Web be without graphics? Well, kind of boring, actually. To spice up your pages, insert a graphic or two.

Many HTML authors, though, will take that advice a bit too far. If you've spent a fair amount of time on the Web, you'll have run across the pages that contain so many graphics that it takes way too long to retrieve the entire page; by the time the page is in, the reader is no longer interested. If you're creating pages for commercial purposes, it's important to capture the eye of your reader and draw her in, not turn her away.

Another major issue when dealing with graphics is size. It's very easy to create graphics that are fairly large to create a nice-looking page; however, the same problems arise. The reader will move on to another, faster page.

Generally, when I design graphics for my company's Web pages, I try to keep the total size of the page under 50 or 75 KB.

> **Tip**
>
> To find out how big your pages are, add up the size of the HTML text file, plus any graphics files you've included in the page.

Another important consideration is graphics type. The two most common types of graphics are GIFs and JPEGs. Although the arguments over which is better are age-old (just like the arguments over the PC versus the Macintosh), both have distinct advantages.

The GIF (Graphics Interchange File) format, developed by CompuServe, uses a 256-color palette drawn from a total of 16.7 million colors. The color palette is an index of which 256 colors are used in that particular graphic. In the days of DOS when only one picture was traditionally on the screen at a time and most graphics adapters support 8-bit color resolution (256 colors), this worked very well.

However, on the Web, a page will typically have more than one graphic. This can create a problem, since each graphic will have its own palette, which could result in a total of more than 256 colors on the page. When this happens on a 24-bit display, there's no problem; however, on an 8-bit display, the graphics may turn colors that you don't want. To avoid this problem, I typically decrease the number of colors in the graphic to 64 or even 32 (depending upon the complexity of the image). This decreases the likelihood of my graphics becoming distorted.

The JPEG (Joint Photography Experts Group) format utilizes all 16.7 million colors. Since they require a 24-bit color resolution for proper rendering, they tend to look grainy on 8-bit displays. Also, the same problem occurs as with GIFs when more than one is displayed on an 8-bit display. On a 24-bit display, they look dynamite; the color depth is remarkable, and the images are clear and pure.

While Internet Assistant doesn't give you the ability to create graphics, you can use it to add graphics to your page.

To add a graphic to your page:

1. Place your text cursor where you want the graphic to be.

2. Open the Insert menu and choose Picture. You will see the Insert Picture dialog box (see fig. 27.12).

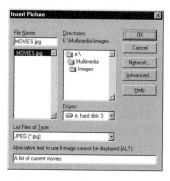

Fig. 27.12
Use the Insert Picture dialog box to add a graphic to your document.

3. In the List Files of Type list, select which type of graphic you'd like to place in your document. In the Directories window, indicate the path to the image file. In the file list window, highlight the file you wish to use as your hyperlink.

4. In the ALT field at the bottom, type a short description for the graphic. This text will be displayed on any browser that doesn't display images.

5. To complete the process, click OK.

In addition to adding hyperlinks and adding graphics, you can also add a graphic that acts like a hyperlink—when you click the graphics, it brings up a new document, just like regular hypertext.

To use a graphic as a hyperlink:

1. Place your text cursor where you want the graphical hyperlink to be.

2. Open the Insert menu and choose the HyperLink command. You'll see the Hyperlink <A> dialog.

3. Select the tab for the type of link you want to create. Follow the steps listed in the previous sections for establishing the destination of the link.

4. Click the Image button. You will see the Insert Picture dialog.

5. In the List Files of Type list, select which type of graphic you'd like to place in your document. In the Directories window, indicate the path to the image file. In the file list window, highlight the file you wish to use as your hyperlink.

6. In the ALT field at the bottom, type a short description for the graphic. This text will be displayed on any browser that doesn't display images.

Creating Rules

In typography, the term *rule* refers to a dark line used to separate different types of information. Rules are used quite often on the World Wide Web—even the first Web browsers had support for automatic rules.

The Horizontal Rule command creates a solid line across the display. To create a horizontal rule:

1. Place your text cursor where you'd like the rule to be located. It's usually best to put the cursor at the beginning of a line instead of the end of a line.

2. Open the Insert menu and choose Horizontal Rule. You will see a thin black line through your document (see fig. 27.13).

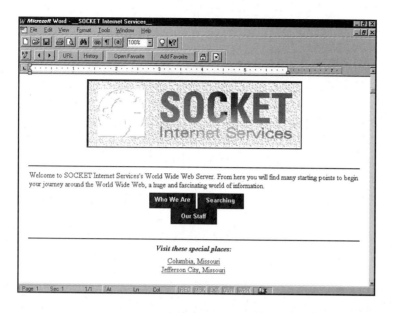

Fig. 27.13
Use horizontal rules to separate major areas of your document.

Tip

With newer browsers, you can change the characteristics of horizontal rules (such as thickness, alignment, and percentage width). Internet Assistant, however, does not allow for this flexibility. If you know how to add these commands, you can add them to your HTML document with a text editor after you've saved it in Word and closed it.

Inserting Unsupported HTML Code

To insert HTML code that Internet Assistant doesn't support:

1. Place your text cursor where you want the HTML code to be.

2. Open the Insert menu and choose HTML Markup. You will see the Insert HTML Markup dialog box. At the bottom of the dialog box is an edit field you use to type in direct HTML code (see fig. 28.14). Anything you type in this field will be added to your document as HTML code without translation of any kind.

Fig. 27.14
Type in the exact
HTML code you
want to use.

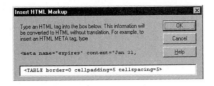

3. Type in the HTML code you want to add.

4. To add the new code, click OK.

When you return to your document, the new HTML source will appear as blue underlined text. Don't get this confused with HyperLink text, though; a HyperLink will usually not have <> pairs on either side.

If you wish to edit the HTML code later on, double-click the code to bring up the dialog again.

Creating Forms

A spectacular feature of the World Wide Web is its interactive properties. With a technology called *forms*, a user can communicate information to the remote computer.

Most forms look like Windows dialog boxes. They have different types of controls for allowing the user to enter different types of information.

In most cases, a form is used to get some sort of information from the user, for example, signing in to the Web server (to keep track of users who see your Web pages) or registering a product (such as software).

Some companies have been quite creative with fill out forms. Pizza Hut now maintains a site (**http://www.pizzahut.com**) that allows a user to order pizza over the Internet (see fig. 27.15). Sorry, this service is only available in a limited area, but you can still get a demo of how it works.

Most forms work in a simple manner. The Web document itself contains code that tells the Web browser to insert text boxes, check boxes, and drop-down list boxes in the document. The user types text into a text box, checks or unchecks a check box, and selects an item from a drop-down list box.

After the user has "filled out" the form, he or she clicks on the Submit button. This causes Internet Assistant (or any other browser) to send the form data to a remote system. The remote system has a program running on it that looks for incoming forms and processes them.

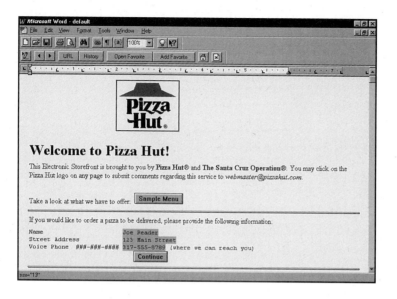

Fig. 27.15
The Pizza Hut site was one of the first commercial sites to support online ordering.

Creating Form Fields

Internet Assistant uses Word's Form command capabilities to create HTML forms. However, there are some areas that do not overlap. Creating simple HTML forms is explained in this section. If you want to create more complex forms, you'll need to understand how Internet Assistant handles certain form elements and attributes. To get this information, consider reading *Running a Perfect Web Site*, by Que Corporation.

With the Internet Assistant Forms toolbar, you can create simple forms to submit information and to perform Web searches.

To create a form field in your Web document:

1. Open the Insert menu and choose Form Field.

2. A message will appear reminding you that you are creating a new form (see fig. 27.16).

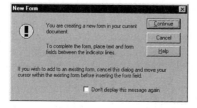

Fig. 27.16
Click the check box at the bottom if you don't want to see this message box each time you create a new form field.

3. Click Continue.

4. Two boundaries will appear in your document: Top Of Form and Bottom Of Form.

5. The Forms toolbar will appear.

6. The Form Field dialog box will appear.

At this point, things can get a little complicated. Let's go through the options available to you from here:

- If you're ready to insert a form field in your form, choose the Form Field Type and then choose OK.

- If you're not quite ready to insert form fields into your form, choose Cancel. You can always go back and add them later.

I would recommend the second option. This allows you to simply create the boundaries for your form, then type in the text for your form, and finally insert the form fields. For example:

1. Type in the rest of your document, so you'll know where your form is going to be in relation to the rest of the document.

2. Place your cursor where you want your form to be.

3. Follow steps 1 through 6 for creating your form boundaries.

4. Click the Cancel button on the Form Field dialog box.

You should now have a blank and empty form area. At this point, you may begin to create a layout for the form itself:

1. Type in any text that will appear in the form. For example, **Enter your name:**.

2. After all the text is in place, you should see your form as you want it to appear.

3. For each field (Name, Address, or whatever), place your cursor where you want the user to type in the information (or check a box, or select an option).

4. Click the buttons on the Forms toolbar that correspond to the form field you want to put in place.

> **Tip**
>
> In Internet Assistant, you use the Insert Form Field command to create an entire HTML form. The Insert Form Field command behaves differently in Word, where it inserts a single form field at a time.

To understand how to use the form fields, I'll give a brief explanation of each one and explain how to use it.

The Text Box

Use a text box any time you want the user to type information (see fig. 27.17). If the user can use either of the following, it's best to use them. Leave the text box for things like names, addresses, and the like.

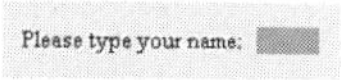

Please type your name:

Fig. 27.17
Use the text box when you want the user to type information.

To insert a Text Box in your form:

1. Place your cursor where you want a text box to appear.

2. Click the Text Box button in the Forms toolbar.

3. You should notice a rectangular gray area in your form.

> **Tip**
>
> When working with forms in Internet Assistant, remember that they don't look as nice as in Netscape or Internet Explorer. When you save the form and view it with the more popular browsers, though, they will look fine.

The Check Box

Use a check box any time you want the user to indicate Yes or No to a question (see fig. 27.18). For example, if your form is used to register a piece of software, you might use a check box to ask the customer if he or she already has a previous version: I have a previous version already installed.

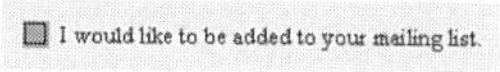

☐ I would like to be added to your mailing list.

Fig. 27.18
Use a check box when the user should indicate Yes or No.

To insert a check box in your form:

1. Place your cursor where you want a check box to appear.

2. Click the Check Box button in the Forms toolbar.

3. You should notice a small black square in your form.

The Drop-Down List Box

Use a drop-down list box any time a question will have a certain number of answers, and the user can simply choose one—for example, "How did you hear about our product?". For this question, you could create a list box with Friend, Relative, Coworker, Advertisement, and Salesperson in it. The user could select the appropriate answer from the list.

Fig. 27.19
Use the drop-down list box whenever the user should choose from a list of options.

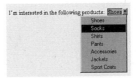

To insert a drop-down list box in your form:

1. Place your cursor where you want a drop-down list box to appear.

2. Click the Drop Down Form Field button in the Forms toolbar.

3. You should notice a rectangular gray area in your form.

The Submit Button

After your form is complete, you'll need to give the user a way to submit the form for processing:

1. Click the Submit button in the Forms toolbar.

2. In the Form Submit Button dialog box, type the submission information for the form. If this doesn't make sense, see chapter xx on CGI-BIN programming.

Fig. 27.20
Provide a Submit button for user to click when the form is complete.

Tip

You can also use this dialog box to customize the appearance of the Submit button. To insert text to the left of the Submit button, use the cursor keys to move the insertion point. It's important to include a Reset button so that after your form is filled out and submitted, a user can restore all form-field values back to their defaults. From the Forms toolbar, choose the Reset button.

When you have finished creating your form, choose Protect Form from the Forms toolbar. Before you can test your form to make sure it will behave as you expect, you must save the form first, and then switch to Web Browse view.

Since forms are not visually differentiated from the rest of a document, I recommend using a Hard Rule before and after a form to clearly separate it from the rest of the document.

Using CGI Programs

Creating forms with Internet Assistant is only half of the process necessary to fully implement forms on your system. You must also use CGI programs to act upon data submitted by a form document. To fully implement your forms on a Web server, you must work with your system administrator. If you are the system administrator and you are not familiar with how forms work with the World Wide Web, read the next section.

It is important to realize that forms must be handled by external programs written to receive the incoming data and act upon it. Internet Assistant does not contain any features for actually using forms, but instead contains the necessary tools to create the form. Forms are a two part process, and Internet Assistant provides a solution for only one of those parts.

If you'd like more information on how to set up CGI executables to use forms in your Web presence, browse to the following URL:

http://www.ncsa.uiuc.edu/SDG/Software/Mosaic/Docs/fill-out-forms/overview.html

This link contains vast resources to answer almost all your questions about implementing form support for your Web presence.

Web Pages and Word Documents

Finally, we reach the point where HTML and Word come together. Use Internet Assistant to make Web pages out of Word documents, or Word documents out of Web pages.

Building a Web Page from an Existing Page

Many times I find myself browsing through the Internet, and I discover a page that has a nice look to it. I'd like to do something similar. Or, perhaps, that page contains some interesting information I'd like to include in one of my own pages.

With Internet Assistant, I can download the page, then save it as my own, making any edits necessary. Editing a Web page? Yes, since Internet Assistant does both, it's extremely easy.

To edit an existing Web page and save it on your hard disk:

1. Open the File menu and choose Open URL. You will see the Open URL dialog.

2. Type the URL of the page you wish to download, and press Enter. After a few minutes the page will appear on your display.

3. Open the View menu and choose HTML Edit. The page may change slightly, or even dramatically in appearance. Any HTML code that Internet Assistant doesn't recognize will appear in blue underlined text. This can be quite confusing, since the hyperlinks look the same.

Fig. 27.21
A sample HTML document with non-supported HTML source in it.

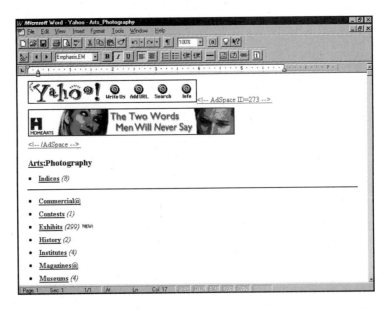

IV

4. Open the File menu and choose Save As. You will see the Save As dialog. If the HTML document was given a title by its author, that title will appear in this box. If you'd like to change it, type a new title now.

5. To save the file, click OK. The Save As dialog will disappear.

6. Make any edits or changes as per the instructions I have given you so far. When you're finished, save the document and final time, then close it.

> ### Tip
>
> When you've finished with an HTML document, especially if you've added HTML code not supported by Internet Assistant, it is wise to check your file with a full-fledged browser. Indeed, it's good to check the file with several. Most Web page creators will test with Netscape and Mosaic at the least.

Building Web Pages from Word Documents

This is perhaps my favorite feature of Internet Assistant. With it, you can convert virtually any Word document to a Web page in minutes, even seconds.

However, you will have to watch out for a few things—HTML doesn't support all the fancy formatting features that Word has. Some of that will get lost or change slightly from its appearance.

Word Formatting that Won't Convert to HTML

If you're converting an existing Word document to a Web page, you'll notice that some of your original formatting is lost. If this is the case, consult the following list of Word formatting features not supported in HTML by Internet Assistant:

- Annotations
- Borders and shading
- Captions
- Character formatting (for example, superscript)
- Drawing layer elements
- Embedded objects, or "cut and pasted" objects, such as equations, clip art, Word Art, and MS Draw objects
- Fields—only the field result is converted
- Footnotes and endnotes
- Frames

- Graphics embedded via the Clipboard
- Headers and footers
- Indented paragraphs in any paragraph style other than OL or UL
- Index entries
- Page breaks and section breaks
- Revision marks
- Tabs in any paragraph style other than PRE and DL
- TOC entries

In many cases, if you're familiar with HTML, you can make minor changes to the look of your document to make it fit with the HTML support in Internet Assistant.

Redesigning Your Document for HTML

Since the stylistic features listed in the previous section will not be included in your HTML document, it is important to get a good idea of what your document will look like without them. There are two ways to do this:

1. Remove the formatting and features listed previously from your Word document.

2. Load the Word document, then save it as HTML, then reopen the HTML document. Anything not converted will, of course, not appear.

The second method is much easier to use, of course. Remember, however, to select HTML in the Save File as Type drop-down list box in the Save As dialog box. When I create a new HTML document, I use this method. It allows me to be as certain as possible as to the final appearance of my document. Remember, each Web browser will display your document differently. With a little experience and bit of experimentation, you'll begin to create great looking HTML documents with very little effort.

You can try this process with any existing Word document. It's actually kind of fun. It's especially fun if you have a copy of Netscape or Mosaic to view your final document with. Let's walk through one quickly:

1. Open any existing Word document (preferably not too long).

2. After your document is finished loading, open the File menu and choose Save As.

3. Select HTML Document from the Save as Type drop-down list box (see fig. 27.22). Click Save to save the document.

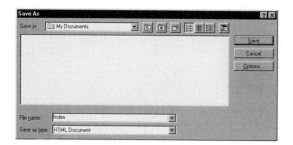

Fig. 27.22
Set the Save as
Type list box to
HTML Document.

4. Open the File menu and choose Close. Don't worry, your original document is still intact.

5. Open the File menu and choose Open.

6. Select HTML Document from the Files of Type drop-down list box.

7. Highlight the name of your document in the dialog box.

8. Click Open. You will see the saved version of your HTML document.

If you notice anything different about your document from when you saved it, those formatting features are not supported by Internet Assistant.

Creating a Word Document from a Web Page

You'll also want to be able to save documents you find on the Web. In most cases, you'll want to save them as Word documents. This gives you the ability to change them, edit them, add tables, or whatever else you'd like to do.

Here are the instructions for converting a Web document to Word document.

1. Enter Web browse view.

2. Open the document you want to convert (use the Open URL button).

3. After the document is fully downloaded, select File/Save As from the menu bar.

4. Type a name for the file in the File Name: edit box.

5. Choose Word Document from the Save File as Type: drop-down list box.

6. Click OK.

Your document now resides on your hard disk as a Word document.

CHAPTER 28

Using Netscape Navigator Gold and HotDog to Create Web Pages

In this chapter, we explore the process of creating Web pages using two excellent page-editing packages: Netscape Navigator Gold and HotDog. Netscape Navigator Gold is a recently announced product that couples Web browsing with Web editing. HotDog is a very capable shareware HTML editor that is available on the Web and on the CD-ROM included with this Special Edition. With it, you'll see just how easy it is to implement the most up-to-date HTML elements into stylish Web pages.

In this chapter, you learn:

- The basic capabilities of Navigator Gold and HotDog
- How to configure HotDog and Navigator Gold
- How to use Navigator Gold and HotDog to create a simple page
- How to use HotDog to create a page containing forms and tables
- How to preview and publish your page

Getting to Know Netscape Navigator Gold

Navigator Gold is the latest Web page editor to hit the scene. What sets Navigator Gold apart from the rest of the pack is the built-in WYSIWYG page-editing capability. With Navigator 2.0 Gold, there's no ambiguity about what your page layout will resemble when you're done authoring. The key to Navigator Gold's text features lies in the WYSIWYG concept. *From the start*, all HTML codes are hidden from you but are interpreted and displayed the way they eventually will be when viewed by a Web browser. The technique is identical to the way most high-cost WYSIWYG word processing programs operate.

Designing a Web page using a non-WYSIWYG editor forces you to completely consider the page layout before starting the basic structure of the page. This means that you need to consider the number, types, and sizes of graphics, text, links to other URLs, and forms before you begin because moving HTML codes around your page isn't the easiest thing to do. With Navigator Gold, however, it's no problem because what's displayed in the editing window is exactly what shows up on any visitor's Web browser. In the course of creating or editing your page, if something needs to be moved, you point, click, and move it. It's that simple. Also, if you want to add something such as another horizontal rule, a graphic, and some text with an anchor to an external URL, just drag the appropriate icons from the toolbars, and you're on your way. One of the neat aspects of Navigator Gold is that you can browse and edit without ever leaving Navigator. This is done the way the previous Navigator version allowed browsing, mail, and news to be accessed through the same program but in different independent windows. This also means that you can preview your page by simply clicking an icon. The page you're currently editing is pulled into the browser's window to be previewed.

Some of the most interesting pages on the Web employ advanced graphic techniques. Navigator Gold does its best to add these capabilities to your desktop.

A couple of the greatest advantages to using Navigator Gold involve its support for embedded graphics. The author can drop in QuickTime and MacroMedia movies, as well as Adobe Acrobat formatted files. When a visitor's browser accesses the graphic on the page, the images are downloaded and automatically launched.

Finally, frames—a new Web page concept to be implemented—allow the author to set up certain areas of the page to be fixed or scrollable, independent of what's going on in the other page frames. If you want to design a page with several sections that group information by topic, for example, this feature allows you to set up an area with an overall scrollable index to your page that remains visible to the visitor, even while he browses different page sections. His Web browser displays the information from the chosen page section in a scrollable window and simultaneously displays the index in another scrollable window. You can even submit form data in one frame and receive results in another frame (see fig. 28.1).

Other graphics features that should be mentioned are the capabilities to automatically convert input graphics to the standard GIF format and to create transparent and interlaced GIF images within the page.

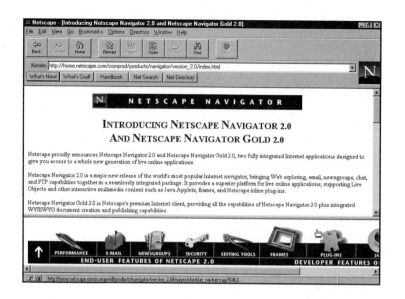

Fig. 28.1
Netscape 2.0
supports separate,
scrollable frames.

Another useful capability of Navigator Gold is that you can configure your
own toolbars—like the big word processors let you do. Therefore, the tools
you use most often can be made available without cluttering up your desktop
with lots of specialized tools you don't need very often. Figures 28.2 and 28.3
both show you the Navigator Gold Editor window with the Format and Edit
Toolbar functions identified.

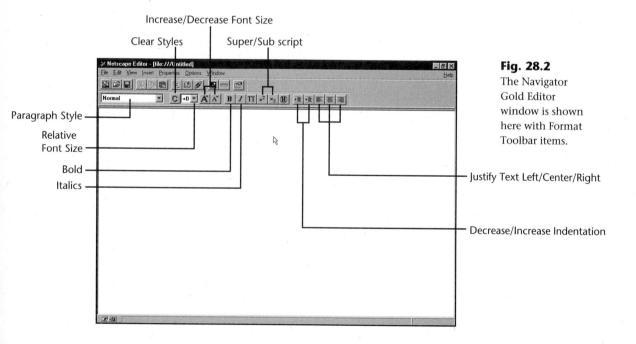

Fig. 28.2
The Navigator
Gold Editor
window is shown
here with Format
Toolbar items.

Fig. 28.3

The Navigator Gold Editor window is shown in this figure with File/Edit Toolbar items (the Format toolbar is not shown).

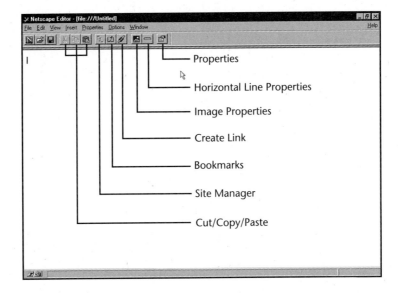

> **Note**
>
> The pasteboard is another good idea whose time has come. Frequently used elements such as page header logos, index ISMAPS, copyright notices, and "go back to calling page" icons can be stored in the pasteboard and dragged-and-dropped to a new location on demand. You can set up a set of special elements you want at your fingertips this way and conveniently access them whenever you want.

Downloading and Installing Netscape Navigator Gold

To ensure that you get the latest copy of Navigator Gold, the first step of installing the software is downloading the program from Netscape. To do this, follow these simple steps:

1. Launch your current Web browser.

2. Enter the following URL to access the Netscape home page:

   http://home.netscape.com/comprod/mirror/index.html

3. Click the Windows 95 or NT link.

4. Click the Netscape Navigator Gold link.

5. If requested, click either on your map location or on your listed continent to choose the closest download site.

6. Click any listed site to initiate an FTP download of the software.

The self-extracting file will then be transferred to your PC. Your Web browser may sense that a file in octet stream format is being transferred and not know what to do with it. If asked by your browser, specify that the file should be saved to disk. The file name that will be downloaded will vary, depending on the exact release version of Navigator Gold.

When you have the executable file on your hard drive, launch the WINZIP application, which has been included on the CD-ROM. Open the Navigator Gold archive file that you just downloaded and extract it into an empty folder, C:\GOLDTEMP, for instance. Once the file is UNZIPPED, launch Windows Explorer, change to C:\GOLDTEMP, and run the SETUP application (SETUP.EXE). SETUP will suggest a destination folder in which Navigator Gold will be installed. Select the default folder or enter your own, and SETUP will install the software and create a Windows Program Group and a Start button program entry.

To launch Navigator Gold, click Start and Netscape to pop up the Netscape Program Group, and then double-click the Netscape program icon.

Getting to Know HotDog

HotDog is a recently introduced HTML editor developed by Sausage Software. Like most HTML editors, HotDog is *not* WYSIWYG. Rather, HotDog displays the HTML elements on-screen, like a simple text editor.

An HTML editor is generally better to use than expensive word processors for creating and editing a Web page. One reason for this is that you don't have to consciously save the file as an ASCII text file each time you end an editing session. Because all HTML files are ASCII files, HotDog saves them that way. Another reason HotDog is better than a word processor for editing Web pages is that HotDog *knows* HTML. HotDog can prepare the HTML text in the proper format and context for immediate use on the Internet!

In addition, most graphical Web browsers widely available today support HTML 2, but HotDog supports HTML 2+ (commonly called Netscape Extensions), which is a nearly finalized standard. Furthermore, HotDog supports some of the proposed HTML 3 standard, which is still in the draft stage.

> **Note**
>
> Keep in mind that the HTML 3 features included in this release of HotDog have been implemented in the most recent beta versions of Mosaic 2.0 and Netscape 2.0. Not all users have Web browsers that support *all* these elements.

It has been the philosophy of the authors of HotDog to include only the HTML 3 features that are currently supported by browsers. As more HTML 3 features are supported, these capabilities will be added to HotDog. Although you can search the Web for a copy of the HTML 3 specification, you won't see the unsupported features in the HotDog Help files.

Remember, though, that you don't need to have all the HTML elements memorized to create a good Web page. Just as in the expensive word processors, HotDog uses pull-down menus with step-by-step templates for complex elements and toolbars with icons for text formatting and positioning. As long as you have these tools handy, you're only a point-and-click away from producing the desired HTML effect.

HotDog comes in standard and professional versions. All the features of the standard version are available in the professional version, with additional productivity enhancements.

The HotDog Standard editor is currently version 1.3.1. Its basic capabilities are numerous; I'll go over the key features so that you can start creating a page as soon as possible. First, there are point-and-click effects—just select the text to change with your mouse and click the tool of your choice. This is a great way to simply create different effects, such as header text and boldface. Second, there's a URL template—each time you want to add an anchor, graphic, or target, HotDog remembers all your previous URL entries so you don't have to retype long references. This is especially useful if you're using the same graphic as a headline on multiple pages or as a separator. Additionally, you can drag and drop a file from Windows Explorer or the HotDog file manager to instantly create an anchor.

Other standard features include form and table editing, context-sensitive Help, and the incorporation of background page colors or graphic backdrops. To assist in the editing of a page containing extended characters, there's an auto-extended character translation capability. HotDog allows you to launch a Web browser—if you have one installed on your system—to preview your page layout. Finally, you can take advantage of the Publish feature that prepares your page for installation on your HTTP server with a minimum of fuss.

> **Note**
>
> For those intent on being serious Web page authors, consider HotDog Professional. The Pro version has the same features as the standard version with several enhancements, including customizable toolbar configurations, shortcut keys, user-defined HTML templates, and multi-language spell check modules. For more information on HotDog Pro, contact the author's Web page at **http://www.sausage.com/** for software mirror sites, how to get product upgrades, and technical support.

Installing HotDog

HotDog is distributed on the included CD as a self-extracting archival file, and it requires approximately 2MB of disk space. There are also minimum recommended hardware requirements specified by the authors as being a 486 with 8MB of RAM. I have found that HotDog runs satisfactorily on less, but to paraphrase the authors, it "runs more like a dog than hot."

NetCD95

The procedure to install HotDog is essentially the same as the Navigator Gold installation. First, click Start and Run from the taskbar. Click Browse and select HOTDOG10.EXE from the CD-ROM or from your hard disk. Click Open, and then click OK.

The Setup program now asks you to accept the default folder or specify one to install HotDog in. Select a folder, and when asked if replaced system files should be backed up, choose Yes. Accept the default backup folder and HotDog installation will continue. Finally, you are asked whether you want to create a new program folder for HotDog or add it to an existing folder. When you make your selection, HotDog installation is complete.

HotDog does require the Microsoft Visual Basic library VBRUN300.DLL to run. The VBRUN300.DLL file is already installed in Windows 95, but if it has been lost or corrupted, you can download it from Sausage Software's Web site and many other locations.

If you were to use the default folder, C:\HOTDOG, to install the program in, the automatic setup program would create four subfolders to store HotDog files. The purpose of each subfolder should be self-explanatory:

- AUTOSAVE (empty after installation)
- BACKUP (empty after installation)
- PUBLISH (empty after installation)
- TEMPLATE (contains one basic template file)

HotDog installs certain files necessary for proper operation in your WINDOWS\SYSTEM folder. Those files are CMDIALOG.VBX, CTL3D.DLL, TRUEGRID.VBX, VSVBX.VBX, and VSVIEW.VBX. Additionally, HotDog adds a HOTDOG.INI file to your WINDOWS folder. The good thing is that you really don't have to keep track of these files because HotDog has an uninstall utility.

When you launch HotDog for the first time, you are presented with the main window with a welcome screen superimposed. (It can be disabled at any time by selecting the Don't Show This Screen Again check box at the bottom.) This screen contains some quick access to HotDog's Help file for general help and HTML references. The HotDog startup screen is shown in figure 28.4.

Fig. 28.4
The welcome screen introduces you to HotDog.

If you select Use HotDog Now, the welcome screen vanishes, and you are now ready to begin an editing session. Before you begin, notice how the standard template has been called up for you to start off with. All the necessary HTML elements required to produce proper HTML grammar are there for you to begin with, as shown in figure 28.4.

Before beginning an editing session, take a moment to go over the features you'll find on the opening screen. Basically, there are two toolbars and several pull-down menus for you to access all of HotDog's capabilities. Figure 28.5 highlights the toolbar, button bar, and pull-down menus. All these features are discussed in greater detail in the sections "Reviewing HTML Basics" and "Creating Advanced Pages" later in this chapter.

Now that you've gotten past the basic HotDog start-up window, it's a good time to begin creating your page. Start by selecting the text Type_Document_Title_Here and replace it with the title you want to have on your page. Notice that the text you replaced is within the <HEAD> and <TITLE> elements.

Editing window

Button bar

Pull-down menus

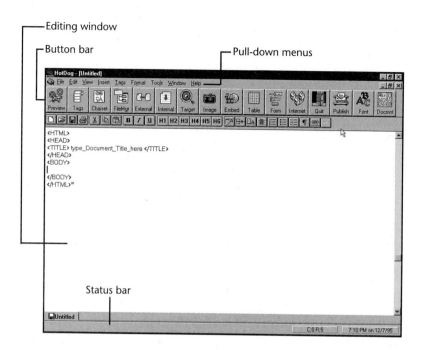

Fig. 28.5
Notice the toolbar and menus in the HotDog editing window.

Status bar

Before creating a new Web page in HotDog, let's first look at some of the tools you need to be familiar with. The first ten icons on the Elements (lower) toolbar are standards that you should be familiar with because they can be found on many other types of word processors, editors, and spreadsheet programs. In order, from left to right, you'll find icons to:

- Start a new document
- Open an existing document
- Save/Save as a document
- Print
- Cut a selection
- Copy a selection
- Paste selection
- Bold
- Italicize
- Underline

The next six icons are the tools for creating the HTML elements for the start and end of a heading level or for modifying selected text to the specified heading level. The next three icons are for image alignment, followed by an icon to set the text formatting mode to centered. The following three icons are for creating ordered, unordered, and definition lists, while the final three icons insert paragraph (<P>), line break (<BR>), and horizontal ruling (<HR>) elements into your document body. Again, refer to figure 28.5 for toolbar element locations.

The button bar (above the toolbar) is available for more complex HTML editing, which benefits more from a pop-up menu approach. While the first icon is a convenient location for accessing the Preview feature (which is discussed in "Testing Your Page"), the following icons are more significant for editing:

- *Tags*—Arranged alphabetically, this pop-up menu contains direct access to every available HTML element in HotDog.

- *Charset*—Allows direct selection and insertion of extended characters and reserve words.

- *FileMgr*—A Windows 3.11 File Manager look-alike that allows you to select a file for direct insertion as a hypertext link, image, or preformatted text.

- *External*—Allows quick creation of external hypertext links. This pop-up menu remembers your previous external links.

- *Internal*—Allows quick insertion of an HTML target jump within the current document. This pop-up keeps track of all defined target labels.

- *Target*—Creates an author-defined target label at the cursor position in the document.

- *Image*—Allows the creation of an anchor using an inline image—when the user clicks the image, another URL document (external or even remote) is launched.

- *Embed*—Allows the embedding of files that can then be viewed by users, assuming they have the proper application. This is similar to OLE object capability in Windows—the user just clicks the file to launch the application (an example of this is clicking an embedded Excel spreadsheet to launch Excel on the user's PC).

- *Table*—Allows the quick creation and formatting of a blank table at the current cursor position—includes options for header rows and columns, borders, cell padding, cell spacing, and caption text entry.

- *Form*—Allows quick definition of form elements. Selecting the form element type on the left portion of the pop-up menu causes the appropriate element's properties text-entry boxes to be shown on the right portion of the menu.

- *Internet*—Allows quick creation of external file, mail, or newsgroup links. The author can choose to create HTML, FTP, Gopher, Telnet, or UseNet news links.

- *Quit*—Allows you to leave HotDog with an option to save any new editing.

- *Publish*—Allows instant document publishing (discussed later in this chapter).

- *Font*—Gives access to a few more text formatting elements that are not readily available on the toolbar.

- *Document*—Allows quick access to overall document formatting parameters such as background colors, background graphics, and banners.

- *Options*—Allows access to set up user preferences for general configuration, editing, display, file locations, publishing, saving, and start-up options. (Note that with screen resolutions less than 800 × 600, the Options button does not appear.)

Reviewing HTML Basics

In this section, I'll try to quickly revisit some basic HTML elements and show how to access them to produce valid HTML. Use of most of the HTML elements covered in the following sections follow one of these two approaches, using either Navigator Gold or HotDog.

- Select the HTML element you want to apply. For instance, if you want the next text you type to be bold, click the Bold icon on the toolbar and then type the text you want to be bold when the user displays your page. The <B> and </B> elements are automatically placed on either side of the current cursor position.

- Select the already-present document text and choose one or more of the icons from the toolbar. As in the first example, select the text you want to be bold, and then click the Bold icon. The <B> and </B> elements are automatically placed around the text you selected.

Again, because there's more than one way to produce the same result, to save time and confusion, I'll only use the first method in the following examples. (The remainder of this section assumes that you have planned your page before beginning to create it!)

In the following sections, I'll tell you whether the methods shown to demonstrate an editor's capabilities apply to either or both of the two editors. Because Navigator Gold is WYSIWYG and HotDog isn't, I'll concentrate on

IV

The World Wide Web

demonstrating "how to" with HotDog. In general, the editing concepts apply equally to either, the only difference being the style of how the editors implement the action.

> **Tip**
>
> Regardless of the editing software you decide to use, creating or editing your Web page will go much smoother if you have some idea of what you want the page to look like when you're done! You'll save lots of work and re-work by planning ahead.

HEAD, TITLE, and BODY Elements

◀ See "Planning Your Own WWW Home Page," p. 597

HotDog places the <Head>, <Title>, and <Body> elements in the editing window when the program starts. All the opening and closing forms of the elements are in the correct relationship, so you just have to replace the title string, as previously explained, and then move your cursor into the *body* of the document.

Heading Levels

You'll probably want to start your page with at least one major heading level. To do this, place your cursor in the correct position in the editing window and click any heading icon on the toolbar. This places the <H#> </H#> elements on either side of the cursor (where the # sign represents a header level one through six). Now, simply type the heading. If you want to align the heading to the left, center, or right, your code would look like one of these lines:

```
<H1 ALIGN=LEFT>This is the heading.</H1>
<H1 ALIGN=CENTER>This is the heading.</H1>
<H1 ALIGN=RIGHT>This is the heading.</H1>
```

Left alignment is the HTML default for all text in the document, so the ALIGN=LEFT is not required.

Text Entry and Formatting

To make your Web page readable, it's important to remember the concept of white space and text breaks, as discussed earlier. Because each user's Web browser windows are set to different sizes and the browsers format the flow of text to fit the window, your document should use many paragraph breaks and line breaks to separate text into proper sections.

When typing the text for your page, each time you come to the logical end of a paragraph, hit the Enter key and place a paragraph break (<P>) by itself on a line. This is done by clicking the paragraph icon (¶) on the toolbar. This makes the breaks easy to find later—if you want to modify them.

Paragraph alignment is available in HTML 3. If you want to have a centered or right-justified paragraph to follow, your code would look like one of these lines:

```
<P ALIGN=CENTER> …paragraph text… </P>
<P ALIGN=RIGHT> …paragraph text… </P>
```

Because left justification is the default, there is no need for `<P ALIGN=LEFT>`. Notice that the HTML 3 usage of the `<P>` element *can be non-empty*.

To break lines using the `<BR>` element, merely click the `<BR>` icon on the toolbar. It doesn't get any more straightforward than that!

Centering text is just as easy. Click the Center Text icon on the toolbar and begin typing the text to be centered. HotDog places the `<CENTER>` and `</CENTER>` elements around your cursor.

Entering text with Navigator Gold is even simpler. Merely type (or paste) the text where you want it. Carriage returns are automatically converted to an equal number of `<P>` elements. The process for creating centered or left/right-justified text is identical to HotDog's method.

Text Attributes

Some of the most often and most easily used Web page elements involve text attributes. The bold, italic, and underline attributes are the most common. You assign these attributes by clicking the Bold, Italic, and Underline icons on the toolbar. Other text formatting attributes such as blinking and pre-formatted text are available from the pull-down menus—choose Format, Blinking, and Tags, Content, Pre-Formatted Text.

Separators and Graphics

Another way to separate text and areas in the Web browser window is to use horizontal rules. To do this in either Navigator Gold or HotDog, simply hit the Enter key to get to a new line in the editing window, and then click the horizontal rule icon (`<HR>`) on the toolbar (see fig. 28.6).

Another slick way of placing a horizontal rule is by using graphics. There are many icon libraries that you can find by searching the Web. These libraries typically contain a number of colored lines, which have been created using paint programs and saved as GIF files. To place a graphic line, click the Image icon on the button bar. Fill in the name of the GIF file that contains the line image and leave the Document to Launch field empty. To place any type of graphic image in your page (such as a GIF of a product, scenery, or people), follow this procedure. To use a graphic as an anchor, simply fill in the Document to Launch field with a valid URL, and HTTP control will be handed over to that document when the user selects the graphic.

Fig. 28.6

Horizontal lines, shown in Navigator Gold, help separate text.

When creating inline graphics to be displayed when a page is loaded, you should keep in mind the alignment of the image with respect to the line of text that sits with it—unless the graphic sits alone, perhaps separated from the text with the <P> element. Using HotDog, place the cursor within the <IMG> element between two fields, type a space, and click one of the alignment icons on the toolbar. This action automatically enters the appropriate ALIGN= parameter in the <IMG> element. When using Navigator Gold, click the Image tool and you will be offered alignment elements within the Image edit window, as shown in figure 28.7.

Fig. 28.7

You can set your image source and properties with this screen in Navigator Gold.

Troubleshooting

Why won't my inline images display properly in my browser?

If your inline images are not appearing, and your <IMG SRC=> line appears instead, there's probably a typo in your document's <IMG> element. Make sure all your <IMG> parameters are spelled correctly and, if you used the toolbar to align the image, make sure that there is a space separating the ALIGN=parameter text from the rest of the text.

> *Why do I get a small error icon where my inline image should be?*
>
> There are three reasons why your browser would display an error icon instead of your inline image. One reason could be that your browser "timed out" before the image could be supplied by a remote server. This happens if your network is very slow. Another reason you could be receiving an error icon is that your browser has requested a graphic that cannot be found on the server. In this case, make sure the inline graphic file names are correct and that they are where you're telling your browser to look for them! The third reason could be that you have confused the browser with inconsistent usage of absolute or relative URLs. When in doubt, use the absolute URL to your inline image and, again, make sure the directory path and file name are correct.

If you want to place an ISMAP graphic into your document using HotDog, open the Insert menu and choose the Image (Advanced) command. You can then specify an ISMAP by selecting the Image Map check box. Image border width and alignment are also available from this menu.

Indented Text and Lists

In HotDog, to create an ordered or unordered list at the cursor position, click the Ordered (numbered) icon or the Unordered (bulleted) icon on the toolbar. HotDog inserts the appropriate `<UL>... </UL>` or `<OL>...</OL>` element pairs in the document. Your cursor is positioned between the list heading elements (`<LH>` and `</LH>`), which have previously gone unmentioned because they are not necessary in HTML. Placing text within this non-empty element is equivalent to typing text into a list in order to produce indented text. By manually typing in the `<LI>` element or by clicking the Tags icon on the button bar, and then selecting `<LI>`, you are ready to begin entering your list items.

Definition lists are another useful way to format text pairs. Clicking the Definition List icon (the one with the horizontal lines and colons) creates the basis for you list. HotDog automatically places the `<DL>  </DL>` elements in your document, along with the list heading (`<LH>`) element pair. HotDog fails to provide you with the HTML elements to define the term and definition portions of the list, however. To define the term, or left-hand portion of the list, use the definition list term (`<DT>`) element. The text of the `<DT>` element is completed when the definition list definition (`<DD>`) is encountered.

The default format for the definition list is to place the term on one line and to place the definition indented on the next line. If you want the term and definition on the same line, use the form <DL COMPACT> when creating the definition list. Remember that when you use the COMPACT parameter in a definition list, if the definition wraps around to the next line in the Web browser's window, the wrapped text will be indented as well. This is true, of course, whether or not you use the COMPACT parameter.

In Navigator Gold, click the Ordered List or Unordered List icons on the toolbar, if you've configured the toolbar that way, and begin typing. Pressing the Enter key automatically produces the next list item (<LI>) element.

Anchors

As you read in chapter 26, anchors, also known as hypertext links, can be embedded in your page to refer to a variety of graphic or sound files, external or remote Web pages, and labels within your document (or other documents). HotDog allows you to insert all types of links through the use of these three icons on the button bar:

- External
- Internal
- Target

As discussed in the section "Getting to Know HotDog" previously in this chapter, these pop-up menus allow you to quickly create external links (such as to other HTML documents on your HTTP server or HTML documents on other servers), create labels to jump to within your HTML document, and create internal links that cause the user's Web browser to jump to those labels within your document. See figures 28.8 and 28.9.

> ### Tip
>
> If you create all the labels in your document before entering the internal links that cause the jumps to those labels, **HotDog** lists all your predefined labels when you click the Internal icon. Being able to select from predefined labels eliminates the possibility of typographical errors that would confuse the Web browser and cause it *not* to jump to the mistyped label.

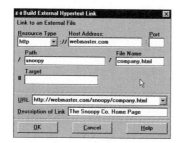

Fig. 28.8
This is a HotDog
pop-up menu that
builds external
hypertext links.

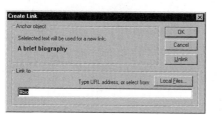

Fig. 28.9
This is the
Navigator Gold
screen showing
internal link
creation.

Creating Advanced Pages

In this section, you learn how add and put to use some forms and table elements using HotDog. You also try spicing up the page by adding background graphics, changing the Web browser's screen color, and adding a mail link.

Adding Tables

The HotDog Table icon on the button bar has just about everything you need to quickly create sophisticated-looking tables in your document. Simply fill in the text box for the caption text and select whether you want the caption to be above or below the table. Then type the total number of rows and columns for the table, including header rows or columns. Figure 28.10 shows an example of a four-row by five-column table with one-heading row and one-heading column. You can specify the absolute table size (in pixels) or relative table size (as a percentage of screen width). Also, you can set the amount of space between each table cell and the amount of padding between the cell outline and contents.

When you're done with the table setup, HotDog places the table element codes in your document. The code for the table in figure 28.10 is:

```
<TABLE COLSPEC="L20 L20 L20 L20 L20" BORDER=2 CELLPADDING=8
➥ CELLSPACING=6>
<CAPTION ALIGN=top>Paper Carrier Totals by Quarter</CAPTION>
<TR><TH></TH><TH>Q1</TH><TH>Q2</TH><TH>Q3</TH><TH>Q4</TH></TR>
<TR><TH>John</TH><TD>5000</TD><TD>5500</TD><TD>6400</TD>
➥<TD>5300</TD></TR>
```

```
<TR><TH>Mary</TH><TD>6500</TD><TD>6400</TD><TD>6500</TD>
➡<TD>6700</TD></TR>
<TR><TH>Gus</TH><TD>7100</TD><TD>6800</TD><TD>6400</TD>
➡<TD>6500</TD></TR>
</TABLE>
```

Fig. 28.10
An example of a table shown in a Netscape browser.

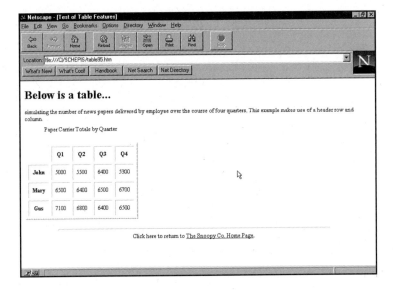

HotDog now leaves you in the middle of this code to begin entering your table text! Notice that the first line sets up the table and column definitions. Also, notice that the `<TABLE>` element is non-empty and is terminated with `</TABLE>`. The second line defines the caption and its placement. The remainder of the code defines the start of each table row, with `<TR>` and `</TR>`, the table headers, `<TH>` and `</TH>`, and the table data, `<TD>` and `</TD>`.

Now comes the hard part because all these elements blend together when you're trying to enter text! One at a time, carefully place your cursor between each of the `<TH></TH>` pairs and enter your table headings. Note that HTML does not differentiate between the column or row table headers, so remember that all the `<TH></TH>` pairs in the top line are for your column headers and all the `<TH></TH>` pairs in the first column are your row headers. After you've entered all your headers, carefully place your cursor between each of the `<TD></TD>` pairs to enter the body of the table data.

Tip

To at least partially avoid the complexity of adding text to a newly created **HotDog** table, as described in this chapter, place the cursor in the Sample Table provided by the Create Table pop-up menu. Type the text and data directly into the sample table. When you're done, click OK, and the text is automatically placed between the proper HTML table elements. Figure 28.11 shows the table information used to create the example.

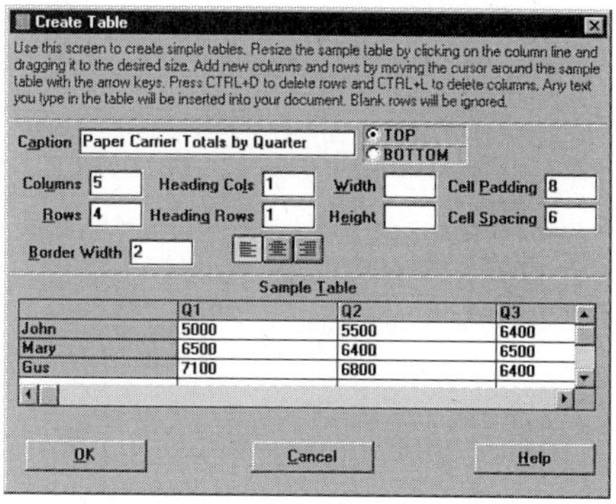

Fig. 28.11
Using HotDog's Table toolbar icon to create a filled-in table.

If you want, you can add an anchor in a table. To do so, properly place the cursor between two HTML elements, say between <TD> and </TD>, for example, and follow the same procedure you would for inserting any other anchor. Your anchor is highlighted in the Web browser (the same way any other anchor is highlighted) and the action you specified will be initiated when the user clicks it.

Adding Forms

Adding forms capabilities to your page is even easier than adding tables. As you can see in figure 28.12 and as discussed earlier, all the form tools you need are immediately available by clicking the Form icon on the button bar.

◀ See "Enhancing Your Page by Creating Inter-active Forms," p. 644

The first time you enter a form element, HotDog prompts you for a POST *method* and *action*. This refers to the *cgi-bin* program or script on the HTTP server that processes the posted form information and returns some data to the user. Once the method and action values are entered, HotDog inserts the <FORM ...> and </FORM> elements in the document. By keeping the cursor position between the <FORM> elements, more form features can be added.

Fig. 28.12
Creating form
elements using
HotDog.

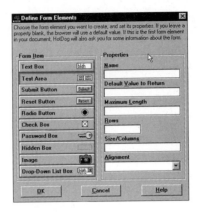

As you continue to add form fields, it is a good idea to test the layout of your document often. This allows you to double-check the length of your text fields and the contents of your drop-down lists. You should also make sure your radio buttons are grouped properly.

As you test your form, keep in mind that no valid action will be taken when you click the SUBMIT button. In order to make the form work when you test it, you'll have to have access to the HTTP server where a CGI-bin program resides to handle the submit request. Remember, when you submit, you are asking a server to do something with your submitted data. If your CGI-bin program does not exist, you will receive a browser error from your server.

Setting Page Colors and Adding Background Graphics

Setting your Web page screen background color is an easy way to invoke just a little more interest out of your visiting audience. The parameter to set the background color, BGCOLOR=, is used as part of the <BODY> element, as shown below:

```
<BODY BGCOLOR="#FFFFFF">
```

The text following the # sign and between double quotes represents the chosen color. The color coding is defined as the hexidecimal value of the RGB components of color. In the example, above, the color white is defined as R=FF, G=FF, and B=FF. To set the background color to purple, which uses equal parts of red and blue, define the parameter BGCOLOR="#C100C1".

To set the background color in HotDog, select the Document icon from the button bar, and then select the Graphics/Colors tab. Click the RGB Code pull-down menu at the lower right, select a color, and click OK. If you want to change the selected color, adjust the color scroll bars.

Tip

To check out a wide range of background colors and to see the corresponding hex color codes, access the following page with your browser:

http://www.epas.utoronto.ca:8080/cgi-bin/epas/coloredit

Adding background graphics to your page may be less complex than adding background colors because all you have to do is select the graphic to use as the background. The background graphic must be downloaded to the user's browser before any text or anchors can be displayed, so keep the graphic file size small. The browser will tile the graphic to fill the window.

Tip

To add interest to your page without adding a complex, large background graphic, try a texture as a background. Texture graphics are usually small files that load quickly and don't take much emphasis away from the document text itself.

To set up a background graphic, select the Document icon from the button bar, as before, and select the Graphics/Colors tab. Enter the name of the graphic in the background graphic text box.

Mailto Links

Adding a *mailto* link in your document allows users to "mail to" any valid, specific e-mail address. This is useful if you want to receive personal feedback, comments, or questions about your document. At the bottom of many Web pages, you'll see the author's (or curator's) name, address, or business affiliation, and occasionally, the author's e-mail address. This address can be mere text, or if you want, you can make it a *mailto* link.

A *mailto* link looks like any other type of anchor and has the following form:

```
Click here to <A HREF="mailto:webauthor@webmagic.com">mail to the
author.</A>
```

Simply enter the proper user mailing address in place of "webauthor@web magic.com" used in the example, above.

Testing and Publishing Your Page in HotDog

It takes quite a lot of work before you feel sure that your page is ready for action. Rather than waiting to complete your editing and creating, it's helpful to peek at the page as you're going along. If you have a Web browser installed on the PC that you're working on, HotDog gives you the opportunity to "visit" your page, just as if it was on the Web, before you even finish it! As mentioned before, Navigator Gold allows instant previewing within Netscape. In this section, you'll see how to use HotDog to preview your work by selecting a viewer and testing the page, and then how to publish your work.

Configuring a Viewer and Previewing Your Page

Once you've made enough edits or have attempted to format your document in a new way, you'll want to preview your page. The first time you click the Preview icon on the button bar, HotDog asks you to configure a browser by providing a pop-up window (see fig. 28.13).

Fig. 28.13
Configuring HotDog's browser for previewing.

Once you've configured the browser, merely click the Preview icon on the button bar to launch the browser. HotDog remains idle behind the browser, awaiting your return to editing. While you're in the browser, all the inline graphics, text formatting, anchors, tables, and forms are displayed just as they are over the network through your HTTP server. Selecting anchors or links while previewing produces the same effect as selecting the link once the page is published.

Tip

If your local Web browser is too old to be compliant with HTML 3, some of the text formatting, tables, and forms may not display properly for you. Download an HTML 3-compliant release of a browser and reconfigure HotDog for the new viewer.

If you download a more recent browser, or a browser from a different provider, you'll want to re-configure HotDog to recognize this. To configure a new browser, click the Options icon on the button bar, or click Tools, Options from the menu bar. When the Tools pop-up menu appears, select the File Locations tab. Enter the new browser in the appropriate text box and click Save Options.

Publishing the Page

HotDog provides a publish feature that allows you to perform certain author-specified automatic document changes. Most of these changes involve configuring the document text for use on a UNIX HTTP server. Shown below are the options available to you when you select the Options icon from the button bar and click the Publishing tab:

- *Remove All Carriage Returns*—Removes carriage return characters—line feed pairs (CRLF)—that are useful to lay out your page but do not have any effect on formatting within a browser. Some browsers have problems with spurious carriage returns.

- *Publish as UNIX Text File*—Removes the carriage return portion of a CRLF to provide compatibility with UNIX text file conventions that only use the line feed character.

- *Convert Extended Characters to HTML Code*—Translates extended characters, such as umlauts and acute accents, into proper HTML codes. Most browsers cannot handle extended characters directly.

- *Replace \ with / in File Names*—Allows you to convert from the standard PC directory separator to the standard UNIX directory separator.

- *Extension for Published Documents*—Allows you to select the three-character file extension for published files.

- *Replace Text List*—Allows you to replace any specified text anywhere in the document with the specified replacement text. This is quite useful if you're using abbreviations for URLs, replacing one URL for another, and replacing anchor file extensions from, typically, .HTM to .HTML.

Simply select the options you want to use, type any replacement text fields, and click Save Options. Finally, publish the document by selecting the Publish icon on the button bar.

CHAPTER 29

New Web Technologies

Two years ago, almost no one had heard of the World Wide Web. UseNet, e-mail and Internet mailing lists, Telnet, and FTP were the tools of choice for exchanging ideas and information through the Internet. The establishment of the World Wide Web and the release of browsers for "surfing the Web" allowed people to view and exchange text, graphics, and other information interactively for the first time. The use of hypertext links allowed related information through the world to be linked together.

Just as the development of the World Wide Web has been faster than anyone could have imagined two years ago, the new developments appearing on the horizon will extend the capabilities of the Internet and the World Wide Web in ways that can scarcely be imagined today. Adding to the text, graphics, sound, and other information currently available on the Web, new developments will add increased capabilities, three-dimensional graphics, real-time audio and video, and who knows what else!

In this chapter, we look at the developments on the horizon that give us a glimpse into the future of the World Wide Web. In particular, we discuss the following:

- *SGML*—the Standard Generalized Markup Language; a means of producing documents for multiple uses, including HTML.
- Modular enhancements to Web browsers available by sending applets in real-time with WWW documents.
- *VRML*—the Virtual Reality Modeling Language; a way to develop three-dimensional VRML worlds on the Web.
- Multimedia video and audio applications for the Web.
- Some hints on how you can keep up with new WWW developments yourself.

SGML on the Web

Information is transmitted on the World Wide Web through documents using markup tags that identify the structure and type of information content in a standard way—these standards allow others to write software (Web browsers) to present the information. Separating the process of identifying the information structure from the way it will be presented gives Web publishers the ability to take advantage of technological advances to display captured information content in increasingly new and fresh ways without always having to go back and revise the source text.

What Are SGML and HTML?

Standard Generalized Markup Language (SGML) is an international standard designed to facilitate the exchange of information across systems, devices, languages, and applications. *HTML is HyperText Markup Language*, an implementation of SGML markup for distributing knowledge on the World Wide Web. The use of disciplined markup added to content enables authors all over the world to prepare information for Internet distribution, knowing that people using Web browser software on various platforms will be able to view it.

Although the development of HTML and SGML proceeded on separate intersecting paths, the paths have converged with the standardization of HTML 2.0 (and soon HTML 3.0) as conforming SGML. While SGML purists would assert that HTML, in particular early HTML, does not rigorously implement all of the SGML principles—for example, hierarchical structure and elimination of presentation-specific markup from a document instance—documents which conform to the HTML 2.0 (and later) DTD rules now meet the SGML criteria.

SGML and HTML were created to solve a problem: people using different computer systems and document processing tools had difficulty passing information to one another. Although the difficulty of passing information between proprietary applications has improved somewhat with import filters, it is still a problem for those who pass documents between more than one proprietary application. The benefits of using standard markup designed to cross proprietary boundaries is well illustrated by the growth of the Web and successful SGML implementations. The problems that can occur when proprietary extensions are added to some but not all browsers are also illustrated by the current dilemmas that Web publishers encounter.

SGML defines a way to write and implement markup rules. The markup rules are called a *Document Type Definition (DTD)*. The HTML DTD is one set of SGML rules.

What Is a DTD?

An SGML *Document Type Definition (DTD)* is the specification of the rules for a set or class of documents with the same structure. The rule specification includes the definition of what elements can appear, the name or tag that will be used to identify them, where the elements can be used (you might not want to allow a list to appear in a footnote), what attributes can be used to provide additional information (for example, security level), and external entities that may be used in conjunction with the content to provide components stored elsewhere (for example, graphic image files).

HTML is defined by its DTD, a defined set of markup rules for a particular, widely applicable type of hyperlinked information that includes several levels of headings, paragraphs, lists, and so on—most of the early information distributed via the World Wide Web.

Contrary to rumor, SGML is not necessarily more complex than HTML. The structure of the information itself and the owner's decision about what elements need to be identified determine the complexity of an SGML implementation, not the inherent characteristics of SGML. An SGML memo DTD is simpler than HTML; the DTD for the Department of Defense's CALS project is much more complex.

The Benefits of SGML

The major benefits of using full SGML as well as HTML are as follows:

- The ability to define your own markup rules to fit special needs that HTML does not handle well.

- A Style Editor that allows the publisher to set Paragraph Styles (font family, size, color), Content Formatting (justification, indentation, spacing), before or after text (and style), and miscellaneous features such as table formatting, background color, or page breaks for a print style sheet.

- A Navigator feature that generates an expanding table of contents when the publisher right-clicks an element type and then selects the Add button. Additional Navigators for figures or experts can also be provided.

- The use of entities, which allow a safe, easy way to include boilerplate components into an SGML document

SGML Viewer: Panorama FREE and Panorama Pro

SoftQuad's Panorama is the first SGML viewer (helper application) to enter the Web scene that can display SGML information from any set of rules (any

DTD) without first converting it to HTML. Because Panorama is already available, we have used it to illustrate points in this section and will tell you how to obtain and use it. SoftQuad Panorama, developed for SoftQuad by Synex Information AB in Sweden, is available in two versions: a freeware version commonly called Panorama FREE and the commercial, supported version, Panorama Pro. When just the term Panorama is used, I am referring to generic capabilities available in both versions.

Panorama and Panorama Pro are viewers/helper applications. They work in conjunction with a compatible Web browser such as NCSA Mosaic, Netscape Navigator, and most browsers based on Spyglass Mosaic. The browser sends the request to download the information and delivers it to Panorama for display. Both versions of Panorama allow you the same, full capabilities to access and view SGML files on the Web. You may select among Styles and choose any Navigator (expanding Table of Contents) that the information provider makes available. For the curious, the abilities to show tags and navigate the SGML tree are also available.

However, some features are available only in Panorama Pro that may make it desirable, even mandatory, and worth the $199 suggested retail price. Features available only in Panorama Pro include the following:

- The ability to Print, Save, and Open (local) files
- The ability to create your own Styles and Navigators
- The ability to create and manage Webs (a new facility for creating your own links among documents, bookmarks, and annotations)
- Technical support (the freeware version has none)

> **Tip**
>
> Some users may need the capabilities that the additional features provide; others may purchase it just because the features are fun to use. If you are preparing SGML information for the Web, you will need the Pro version to prepare the style sheets and Navigators to deliver with your information.

The fact that the less full-featured version is freeware makes the need to decide painless. You can try the free version first, then upgrade later.

Installing Panorama FREE

If you already have NCSA Mosaic or a Spyglass Browser installed, the configuration step for SoftQuad's Panorama FREE is easy because the Panorama setup

IV

The World Wide Web

includes configuration of the browser(s) to use Panorama as a helper app for SGML documents. To install Panorama FREE, perform the following steps:

1. Copy the file panofr10.exe from the NetCD into a temporary folder on your hard drive.

2. Execute panofr10.exe, which is a self-extracting compressed file, in Windows or DOS. For example, from the Windows 95 Explorer, double-click the panofr10.exe file name in the temporary folder.

3. Run the program setup.exe, and answer the questions it gives you. It is safe to accept the default selections for most questions.

   For each NCSA Mosaic, Spyglass Mosaic, and Netscape Navigator you have installed on your system, you should be asked if you would like to configure the browser to work with Panorama FREE. If you answer yes to this question, the browser will be set up to use Panorama FREE as a helper app for SGML documents.

> **Note**
>
> If Panorama FREE does not give you the option of being installed with one of your browsers—this will happen with some versions of Netscape Navigator— or if you add a browser after Panorama FREE is installed, you can perform this step manually. In your browser, choose Options, General and select the Helpers tab. Add a helper application for MIME types text/sgml and text/x-sgml using the following information, which is the same for both except for the MIME subtype:
>
> ```
> MIME type: text
> MIME Subtype: sgml for one, x-sgml for the other
> Suffixes (or extensions): .sgml, .sgm
> Program: xxx/panorama.exe (where xxx is the path to the
> folder where you installed Panorama)
> ```

4. You will then be asked which of the compatible browsers to set up for the initial execution from Panorama FREE. Select your favorite browser. You can change this selection through the Options menu in Panorama FREE.

◄ See "Using Helper Apps," p. 577

5. When the Setup program completes, you are ready to access SGML files on the Web. Connect to the Internet, bring up Netscape, and look for "SGML on the Web" resources.

That's it. You're ready to go. Access NCSA/SoftQuad SGML on the Web at the URL **http://www.ncsa.uiuc.edu/SDG/Software/Mosaic/Web/ SGML.sgml** to find SGML information on the Web. As you access an SGML file, your browser will recognize the SGML MIME type and automatically bring up Panorama to display it.

SGML Example versus HTML Example

Let's take a look at a site that has both SGML and HTML versions to try to get some idea of how they differ. You won't see any dramatic differences between these two for this site, but there are some important differences that will be discussed.

Fig. 29.1

The HTML version of JPL's Magellan Image Data document.

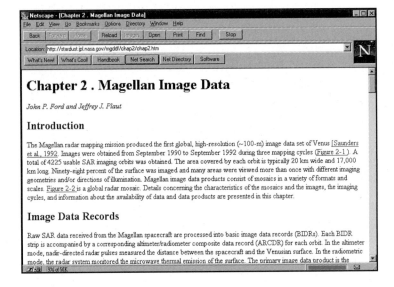

First, take a look at figure 29.1 and figure 29.2. They show some information from the Jet Propulsion Laboratory on Magellan Image Data. Figure 29.1 shows the hypertext link that enables you to view figure 29.2. To navigate through the chapter, you need to scroll up and down through the document.

Figures 29.3 and 29.4 show the same document in their SGML versions. The information is the same, and the presentation is not dramatically different. The important differences are the following:

■ The SGML Navigator shown at the left of the browser window allows easy navigation throughout the document. It's possible to use tags to accomplish a similar effect in HTML, but SGML does this automatically from the SGML source.

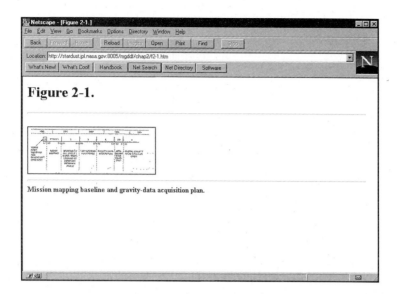

Fig. 29.2
You can view the document's figures by clicking hypertext links.

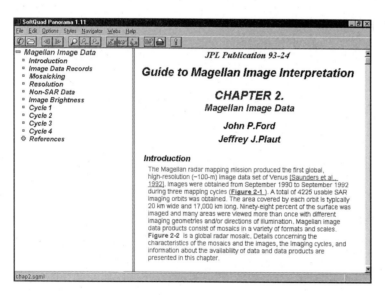

Fig. 29.3
The SGML version of the Magellan Image Data document includes a Navigator to allow easy movement through the document.

■ Incorporating graphics information naturally within the document is easier with SGML.

■ A greater variety of presentation styles are available with SGML documents.

Fig. 29.4

Graphics can be easily incorporated into SGML documents.

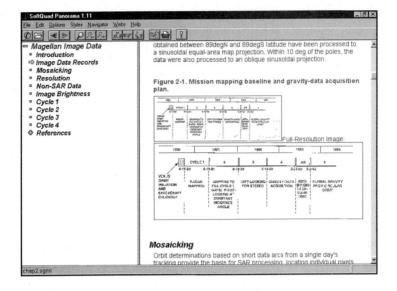

Other SGML Applications

"An add-on that will handle any SGML DTD?"—yes, it appears to be almost here. It will use Java to bootstrap itself and will handle arbitrary language semantics including SGML. Waterloo's MetaClient is an example of the overlapping nature of new Web technologies. SGML and Java are combined in an applied generic Modular approach to provide an SGML plug-in mega-applet.

The goals of the MetaMedia Project at the University of Waterloo are "the creation and analysis of *structured networked executable media*. Rather than monolithic downloadable applications, we are building a system that will support the dynamic definition of the syntax and semantics of arbitrary *executable content languages*." In more simplistic terms, their project is to produce a MetaClient that can understand arbitrary SGML. The approach is intended to produce not single-purpose plug-in applications, but rather a mega-applet approach that can receive language syntax rules with the content and deliver the information in an appropriate fashion. Language includes but is not limited to SGML. The grammar-driven front end is designed to handle not only arbitrary SGML markup but also any arbitrary grammar-driven language. I'm speculating that sooner or later this approach could handle dynamic translations between English, French, German, Russian, Chinese, and the like.

I will be eager to see how successful it is. For further detail and information see The MetaMedia Project at the URL **http://www.cgl.uwaterloo.ca/ ~mmccool/Meta/index.html**.

Enhancing Your Web Browser On-the-Fly

By design, Web browsers have provided basic capabilities to view text and, in the case of GUI browsers, simple graphics. Additional capabilities for special- ized multimedia features have been provided by viewers or helper apps. Although new versions and new browsers continuously deliver enhanced functionality, there is a limit to what they can incorporate and still be practical.

Sun's new Java and JavaScript languages have begun an exciting new wave of plug-in techniques for adding functionality to the Web. Hyper-G applies this modular approach to the handling of Internet information.

What Is Java?

In the spring of 1995, news of Java, a new language Sun had been researching for several years, began to come out—a language to deliver applets, small pro- grams along with content, to the client machine. By delivering these applica- tions with the information, it's possible to add unlimited functionality to Web browsers that support it.

The Java approach includes the following characteristics:

- Object-oriented—modular components, safe, reusable
- Simple—designed to be easy to use
- Distributed programs and processing—automatic update of just the components you need that execute on the user's machine
- Architecture neutral and portable—interoperable code that runs on any platform without additional steps to prepare it
- Interactive with users and other components—plug-and-play compo- nents to isolate and add functions

We will show an example of a Java document using Netscape Navigator 2.0, which includes Java support. There are other browsers with Java support— and many more to come—including, of course, Sun's own HotJava browser.

HotJava is a WWW browser developed by Sun that is written in Alpha 3 Java. HotJava was created to demonstrate the use of the language rather than to be, at this point, a full-featured browser. It supports downloaded Alpha 3 Java applets, and is available in versions for SPARC/Solaris and for 32-bit Windows (NT and 95).

To obtain the HotJava browser, go to The HotJava Browser at the URL **http:/ /java.sun.com/hotjava.html**.

A Java Example

The central site for well-organized Java information with easy-to-follow links is Java™ Programming for the Internet at the URL **http://java.sun.com/**.

There are also many Java applets that can be obtained from the URL **http://www.gamelin.com/**.

It is through that URL using Netscape Navigator 2.0 that I found and loaded a simple game of hangman, called Hang Duke at the URL **http://www/javasoft.com/JDK-prebeta1/applets/Hangman/index.html**.

This game allows you to try to save Duke from an unfortunate fate by guessing the word represented by the line of dashes. Correct guesses, entered by hitting the letter you want to guess, result in the letters being filled in (and also give appropriate audio feedback). Incorrect guesses result in the incorrect letter being displayed, a piece of Duke being shown on the gallows, and an unfortunate scream. If you get the word, as shown in figure 29.5, Duke is set free and dances a little jig for you. If you fail, shown in figure 29.6, poor Duke....

Fig. 29.5

Save poor Duke by guessing the word. If you get it, a grateful Duke will dance a little jig for you.

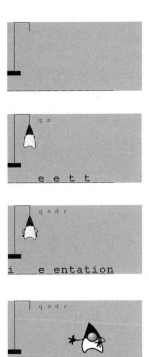

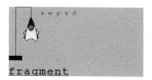

Fig. 29.6
If you can't get the word...poor Duke.

This may seem like a silly little example, but by being able to deliver small applications to your browser, its functionality can be infinitely increased, when necessary. Ticker tapes and animations, interactive forms data checking, revolving chemical components that educate, games for relaxation—these are just a few of the current uses.

What Is Hyper-G?

Hyper-G, with client browsers Amadeus for Windows and Harmony for UNIX, offers a "modular" approach to handling storage and delivery of Internet information, especially with hyperlinks, which it stores in a separate database. The technology is being developed by IICM, the Institute for Information Processing and Computer Supported New Media at Graz University of Technology, Austria. From what I read about the technology, this "real hypermedia" technology guarantees automatic hyperlink consistency which would solve the problem of broken links and provide other benefits.

The volume of information is increasing so fast both within sites and across the Web that managing content files and links becomes increasingly difficult, much less reworking information to take advantage of new improvements. The Hyper-G is designed to address this problem. Hyper-G is a server technology, designed to support most if not all of the current methods of delivering Web information, including Gopher, HTML, FTP, and Hyper-G.

For more information on Hyper-G and links to instructions for downloading the software, see IICM at the URL **http://hyperg.iicm.tu-graz.ac.at**.

VRML: The WWW in Three Dimensions

Virtual reality and 3-D technology developments have brought excitement to our lives—to game players with Doom, to remodelers designing improvements to homes, to forensic scientists, researchers, and to anyone who can benefit from information presented in three dimensions. VRML brings this technology to the Web by allowing the creation and viewing of 3-D VRML worlds.

What Is VRML?

VRML, the Virtual Reality Modeling Language, is an authoring standard, currently defined at version 1.0, for creating 3-D documents on the Web. These documents create VRML worlds that a user can navigate in and around using the capabilities of a VRML compatible browser. The current standard is file-based, involving the transfer of 3-D scenes to the local computer—VRML source files usually have a WRL extension—after which all navigating through the scene is done there. Like HTML documents, VRML worlds can contain links to other documents, graphics, text, HTML documents, or other VRML worlds.

VRML has its roots in the OpenInventor 3-D standard developed by Silicon Graphics, which is still very active in developing VRML and tools for its use. The VRML standard is currently defined at version 1.0, with a committee of VRML users and developers continuing its development. Freeware, shareware, and commercial VRML tools are becoming widely available. In the next section there are VRML examples using WebFX, a VRML plug-in module for Netscape Navigator 2.0

Installing WebFX, a VRML Plug-In for Netscape

To get a little better feel for what using a VRML browser is like, we will install and try out one of them, WebFX by Paper Software. The version of WebFX used here is designed to work as a plug-in module for Netscape Navigator 2.0. The instructions for installation are as follows:

1. Download the program npwfx32d.exe by going to the URL **http://www.paperinc.com/wfxstep1.html**, and following the steps shown there, and putting the program into a temporary directory on your hard drive.

2. Run npwfx32d.exe—this is a self-extracting file that will unpack itself into the temporary directory.

3. Run setup.exe. If you installed Netscape Navigator 2.0 in the default location and wish to do the same for WebFX, you may select the defaults for each entry in the WebFX setup process.

4. You should get a message. WebFX is now installed as a Netscape Navigator plug-in module and will automatically run when you encounter a VRML source file when using Netscape.

Configuring WebFX

WebFX allows you to customize its behavior in several different ways. This customization is achieved using a pop-up menu and submenus that first appear by a right-click.

Each of the six entries shown in the main pop-up window gives you different options for customizing WebFX. The most important submenus are as follows, but feel free to experiment with these and the others to get a feeling for what you can do with WebFX:

- *ViewPoints*—It's pretty easy to get lost in a VRML world, especially when you're just learning your way around. The Entry View selection in this submenu enables you to quickly move back to the point at which you entered the VRML world.

- *Detail*—After a VRML world has been downloaded to your computer, the navigation through that world is handled locally. Because VRML worlds can be quite complex, this process can be slow, particularly on older computers. If you find this to be the case on your computer, you can adjust the level of detail by use of this submenu. By switching from Solid to Wireframe or Point Cloud, you decrease the complexity of the image and may improve the response time.

- *Heads up Display*—The entries in this submenu dictate what information is shown on the WebFX heads up display when it is enabled.

Example VRML World on the World Wide Web

Here is an example VRML world that gives a good example of what can be achieved with VRML worlds that might not be as effective with a standard HTML Web page. It also demonstrates how these two types of documents and ways of presenting information can be very effectively used in tandem.

Using Netscape Navigator 2.0 with the WebFX plug-in installed, connect to the URL **http://esewww.essex.ac.uk/campus-model.wrl**.

Note the WRL extension denoting a VRML world source document. After the connection is made by Netscape, the WebFX plug-in is called, the VRML world source is downloaded, and the image shown in figure 29.7 is shown. While it isn't readily obvious, this the University of Essex campus, as seen from a long way off.

Fig. 29.7

The entry point to
the University of
Essex VRML
world.

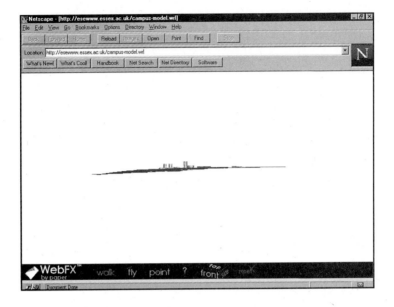

To get a closer look, put WebFX in fly mode and fly in toward the VRML
world. Give yourself a little bit of height to be able to see more of the campus
buildings. As you get closer, you will see the campus layout shown in figure
29.8.

Fig. 29.8

Fly in closer to the
university and see
a view of the
campus.

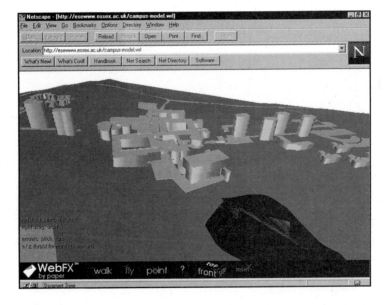

As we learned earlier, VRML worlds and HTML documents can call one another interchangeably. The University of Essex site uses this ability to not

only convey the three-dimensional layout of their campus, but to allow visitors to learn more about the different campus facilities. In figure 29.9 , a cursor has been placed over a building which has a hypertext link, indicated by the presence of the hand cursor and the URL label in the upper left-hand corner of the screen. This building is the library. By double-clicking, an HTML Web page is called that gives information about the library (see fig. 29.10).

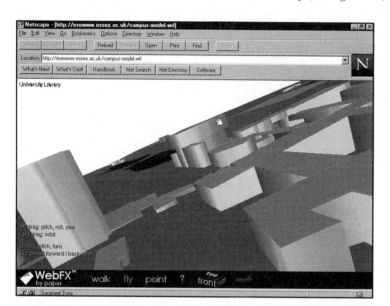

Fig. 29.9
By placing the pointer over a given building and clicking...

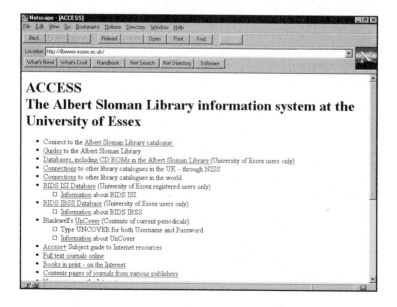

Fig. 29.10
...you can jump to an HTML document with information about it.

Because the VRML world is a 3-D model, you can look at it from any angle, including from below (which isn't very helpful) and from above, as shown in fig. 29.11—giving you a useful map of the University of Essex campus!

Fig. 29.11
We can even fly up high enough and look down to get an aerial map of the campus.

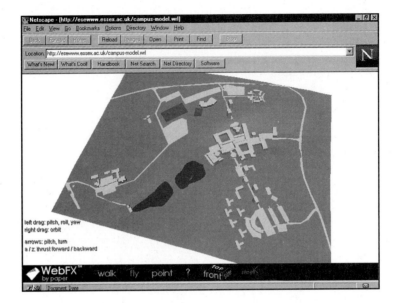

VRML Resources on the Internet

After you have your system setup to view VRML documents, you'll want to start cruising the Internet and the Web to see what VRML resources and worlds are there. The list is growing every day. Following are a few of the bigger sites that will direct you to many other VRML resources—browsers, authoring tools, worlds, and object libraries:

- The makers of WebFX maintain a directory of many VRML worlds located at **http://home.netscape.com/comprod/products/ navigator/version_2.0/plugins/vrml_sites.html**.

- A group called Mesh Mart maintains a Web site of many VRML resources, including browsing and authoring tools and VRML worlds at **http://cedar.cic.net/~rtilmann/mm/vrml.htm**.

- NCSA, the authors of NCSA Mosaic, have a VRML Web page at **http:// www.ncsa.uiuc.edu/General/VRML/VRMLHome.html** (VRML at NCSA).

- A repository of VRML information is maintained at **http://rosebud.sdsc.edu/vrml/**.

- *Wired* has a VRML forum at **http://vrml.wired.com/**.

- As discussed previously, Silicon Graphics is very active in VRML development. A site with information about its WebSpace products is located at **http://webspace.sgi.com/**.

Video Applications on the Web

In addition to the text, graphics, and simple sounds that are accessible through the World Wide Web, there are continuing efforts to enhance the multimedia capabilities of the Web. Several video applications are being introduced that give you this ability—two examples are StreamWorks, by Xing Technology Corporation, and Shockwave, by Macromedia. We will use Shockwave as an example to demonstrate some of these capabilities. You can get more information about StreamWorks from the Xing Technology at URL **http://www.xingtech.com/**.

Installing Shockwave

The Macromedia Shockwave for Director plug-in application is a cross-platform integration tool for multimedia designers to combine animation, sound, and digital video, along with graphics, text, and who knows what else to create truly dynamic presentations of information on the Web. This product will make the popular Macromedia Director technology available on the Web, and from reports it is a robust plug-in implementation that is available now. Partnerships with Sun, Microsoft, Netscape, Silicon Graphics, Navisort, and others are quickly bringing technology integrated with popular browsers to the Web that provide the ability to produce interactive media content such as product demos and press kits for the entertainment and advertising industries.

The words integrated, cross-platform, compressed, and interactive, associated with the implementation of this popular software on the Web make it a likely candidate to increase even further the power of the Web.

Information about Shockwave begins at the Welcome to Macromedia! page at URL **http://www.macromedia.com/**.

You can choose to read information, or if you want to obtain and install the plug-in, you can do the following:

- Click the hotspot, Get the Shockwave Plug-In Now, which takes you to Shockwave: Plug-In Center at URL **http://www.macromedia.com/ Tools/Shockwave/sdc/Plugin/** or go to Macromedia: Director— "Shockwave Technology" for the Shockwave Quick Start at URL **http:/ /www.macromedia.com/Tools/Shockwave/shock.html**.

- Choose the link to obtain the Shockwave plug-in for the platform you desire, for example, Shockwave for Windows 95 at URL **http:// www.macromedia.com/Tools/Shockwave/sdc/Plugin/ Win95Plg.htm**.

- Select one of the sites that corresponds to the version for your browser, and click to download the plug-in. Be sure to read the section on what the system requirements are to run Shockwave.

- Download sw10b132.exe into a temporary directory.

- Double-click sw10b132.exe. It will unzip and leave several files including setup.exe.

- Double-click setup.exe to install the Shockwave plug-in.

You are now ready to run Shockwave examples!

Using Shockwave

Links to examples demonstrating the software may be found at Macromedia Shockwave Vanguard at URL **http://www.macromedia.com/Tools/ Shockwave/Vanguard/**.

Caution
As you might imagine, video information can get quite large. Keep this in mind, and keep an eye on the status bar of your browser when you download Shockwave examples, especially if you have a slow connection to the Internet.

Other examples can be found through **http://www.teleport.com/ ~arcana/shockwave/**.

This site, in particular, features a brief video animation that shows a little bit of what Shockwave can do (and has the benefit of being small, allowing for quick download time). They have animated their Shockwave Web Sites banners, as shown in figure 29.12.

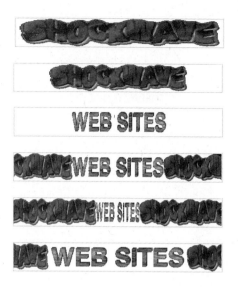

Fig. 29.12
The Shockwave
Web Sites list
includes a video
animation of their
welcome banner.

IV

The World Wide Web

Audio Applications on the Web

In addition to the video multimedia Web applications discussed in the previous section, there are dedicated audio applications also becoming available. Some of these, such as WebPhone, by the Internet Telephone Company, specialize in point-to-point uses—in essence, offering low-cost telephony over the Internet. Other applications, such as TrueSpeech, by the DSP Group, Inc., and RealAudio, by Progressive Networks, are a bit more general, offering live, point-to-point capability, as well as on-demand audio from stored sources.

The RealAudio application will be used to demonstrate some of the audio capabilities you can get through the Net. To find out more about WebPhone, see the Internet Telephone Company at URL **http://www.itelco.com/**.

▶ See
"WebPhone,"
p. 988

For more information about TrueSpeech, see the DSP Group, Inc., at URL **http://www.dspg.com/**.

Installing RealAudio

You can listen to other audio with the RealAudio add-in from Progressive Networks. The RealAudio home page is at URL **http://www.realaudio*.com**.

Note
A version of the RealAudio software is already built into Microsoft's Internet Explorer.

NetCD95

1. Copy the file ra32_2b1.exe from the NetCD95 into a temporary folder on your hard drive.

2. Execute ra32_2b1.exe, which is a self-extracting compressed file, in Windows or DOS. For example, from the Windows 95 Explorer, double-click the ra32_2b1.exe file name in the temporary folder. After extracting its files, the RealAudio setup program will automatically be executed.

3. It is safe to accept the default selections for the RealAudio questions. RealAudio will configure itself as a plug-in application for Netscape Navigator 2.0. For other browsers, you may need to manually set it up as a helper app. In your browser, choose Options, General and select the Helpers tab. Add a helper application for MIME types text/sgml and text/x-sgml using the following information, which is the same for both except for the MIME subtype:

```
MIME type: audio
MIME Subtype: x-pn-realaudio for the other
Suffixes (or extensions): .ra, .ram
Program: xxx/raplayer.exe (where xxx is the path to the
folder where you installed RealAudio)
```

That's it. You're ready to go.

Using RealAudio

A list of RealAudio locations is kept at URL **http://www.prognet.com/contentp/hotcoolnew.html** (see fig. 29.13).

Fig. 29.13
You can access an extensive list of RealAudio sites at this URL.

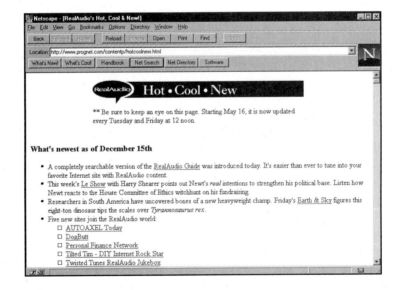

You can jump to WBN's Personal Finance Network (see fig. 29.14) and listen to the personal finance tips—this starts up the RealAudio player, establishes a connection to the RealAudio sound file, and starts playing it (see fig. 29.15).

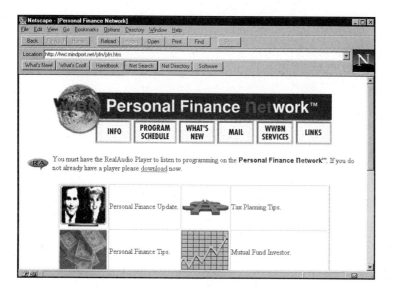

Fig. 29.14
WBN maintains a Personal Finance Network Web site that features RealAudio programming.

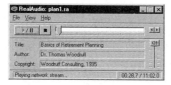

Fig. 29.15
Sit back and listen to WBN's personal finance tips.

Keeping Up with New Technology

When you talk about the future of the Web, you are talking about the cutting edge of technology where significant changes occur rapidly. If you want to keep up with the latest and greatest you need to check major sites every week to see if there are new versions and products. Web sites that provide primary information about a new technology one week tend to be reorganized relatively frequently so you need to be flexible and persistent to find good information.

Those who work with Web futures work with prerelease beta software that sometimes has many bugs still in it. The software changes rapidly; last week's bugs may be fixed, but new features may completely change how one accesses a feature—for example, bookmark management—and new problems may occur with features that worked fine before. Accessing the latest and greatest on the Web is not a venture for the faint of heart. It is hairy but it is also fun to see what's coming.

> **Tip**
>
> While it's always a good idea to make frequent backups of your computer files, it's particularly a good idea if you're going to be spending a lot of time working with beta-release software.

These factors make it difficult to provide correct information in a book such as this one. The information will change before the publication process can be completed; this is true about the Internet in general, and it is even more true when you are talking about new technologies. However, we can tell you some good ways to keep up with new developments. In general, if you want to stay out on the cutting edge, try to do the following:

- Keep your eyes and ears open. Keep your notepad handy. Record addresses wherever they appear.

- Use the search sites to see if the Web indexes list the new sites where information can be found. If you do not already have a couple of good search sites such as Lycos, Infoseek, OpenText, or WebCrawler in your bookmark list, click the Net Search button in Netscape or go to W3 Search Engines at URL **http://cuiwww.unige.ch/meta-index.html**, which contains pointers to a variety of search sites.

- Go to the sites found in your search and read the information. Pay attention to license and hardware requirements. You'll need sufficient disk space and sometimes special hardware, such as a sound card, to experiment with some of the new technologies.

- You will usually find information about downloading the latest software needed to access a feature. You may need to follow a few links to find it. Follow the instructions that are provided. This is likely to be the best and latest information and, in general, it will tell you what you need to know.

- For most of the latest software, you are instructed to download the software into a temporary folder (sometimes stated as a directory) and execute the self-extracting compressed file. In Windows 95, the Save to Disk dialog box allows you to set up a new folder before you download the file, and I recommend that you do so.

- You can execute the self-extracting file in several ways. I usually double-click it in the Explorer; sometimes I click Start on the taskbar, then choose Run, Browse to locate the file, and then OK to execute it.

- Next, check for a readme file to look for the installation instructions. Sometimes these are located on the Web, on or near the page where you downloaded the software. Sometimes the instructions will have another name with a .TXT or a .DOC extension. Use Word Pad or your favorite editor to read them. Frequently they contain important information, so do read them.

- Usually, after any special instructions, they will tell you to run setup.exe or install.exe. Before you actually do this, decide what you want to name the folder you will install the components in. Especially when you want to preserve more than one version—this is important. Then run the setup or installation program.

- Follow any instructions to configure the software.

- Test away and let the developers know if you encounter problems. You'll normally find the address on the same page you find the download link.

Frequently, beta versions are freely available for testing. However, unless you have the patience to put up with a few problems and the time to inform the developers when you find them, you might be better off to wait until the software is stable.

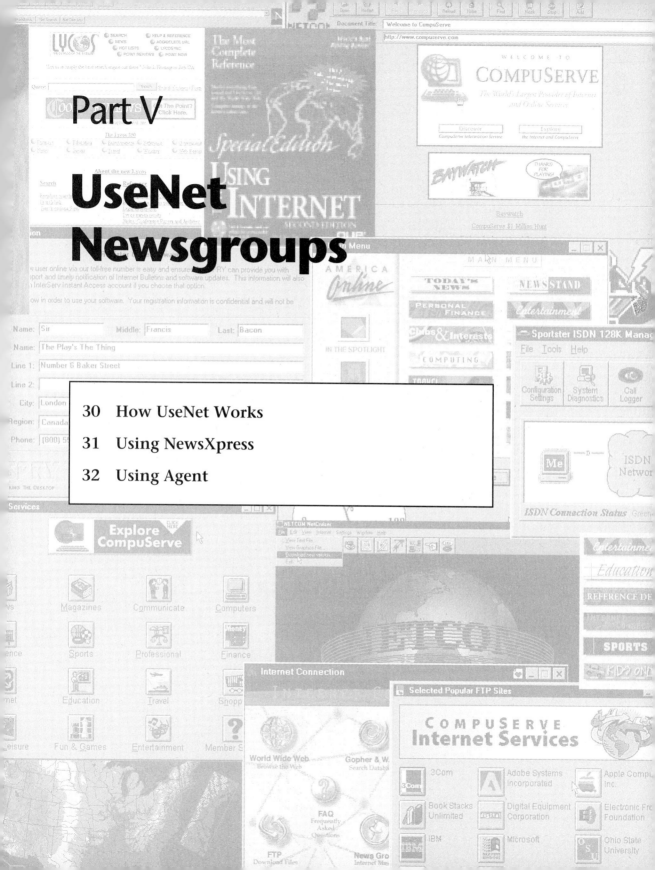

Part V

UseNet Newsgroups

30   How UseNet Works

31   Using NewsXpress

32   Using Agent

How UseNet Works

For many users, UseNet is the Internet. Even with the explosive growth of the World Wide Web (see "How the World Wide Web Works," chapter 20), the UseNet is still one of the most popular parts of the Internet's many services, with millions of users accessing it daily. Like all Internet services, no special hardware is required to access UseNet.

The term UseNet refers to a mechanism that supports discussion groups—called *newsgroups* in the UseNet vocabulary—that allow users from anywhere on the Internet to participate. Originally conceived for the exchange of technical information, the UseNet soon became much more. Newsgroups were developed for non-technical subjects such as hobbies, news items, and social subjects.

With UseNet, you can access anywhere from 8,000 to more than 15,000 newsgroups (depending on the capabilities of your news server) covering an incredible variety of subjects. Looking for details on programming with the latest C++ language compiler for Microsoft? There's a newsgroup for it. Your aquarium has a growth of brown algae on the glass? Check the aquaria newsgroups. You're trying to decide which suspension fork to add to your mountain bike? The thousands of enthusiastic cyclists in newsgroups specializing in bikes can help. You want a sound clip of a shuttle take-off to rattle your PC's new sound card and speakers? There are many places to look. Any subject you can think of probably has a newsgroup for support.

This chapter teaches you the following:

- What UseNet is
- How UseNet is organized
- How you can best use UseNet

- How to find newsgroups
- How to post your own comments
- Surfing and lurking—terms you will encounter
- How to use news filtering and search services
- Netiquette: Your behavior on UseNet

This chapter discusses general UseNet information, most of which will apply to every operating system. In the next chapter, we will discuss NewsXpress, a popular newsreader that works under Windows 95.

What Is UseNet?

UseNet is not a network, but a service carried over the Internet. In many ways, you can think of UseNet as an organized electronic mail (e-mail) system, except there is no single user that mail is sent to. Instead, the messages you and everyone else using UseNet write are sent to a newsgroup section, available for anyone who accesses that newsgroup.

Some of the e-mail terminology applies to UseNet. You write something that you want to let others read—a message or article—and send it (post it) to the newsgroup. You can use a special piece of software called a *reader* to look at newsgroup contents. Also, just about all Web browsers can also read news, as shown in figure 30.1 with Internet Explorer.

Fig. 30.1

Most Web browsers, such as Microsoft's Internet Explorer shown here, are capable of reading UseNet news.

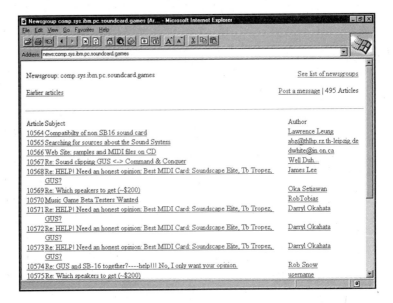

The sending and receiving of UseNet newsgroups is handled by software that knows how to download the articles, as well as how to post them to the network. In addition to the capabilities available through your Web browser, if you have one, a wide variety of public domain, shareware, and commercial software exists that gives you access to UseNet newsgroups. Two excellent freeware programs, NewsXpress and Free Agent, are discussed in chapters 31 and 32, respectively.

◀ See "Reading UseNet News with Internet Explorer," p. 488

◀ See "Reading UseNet Newsgroups," p. 572

The UseNet is not managed or controlled by anyone specifically, but is more a matter of communal control. Once a newsgroup has been created, anything can be sent to the newsgroup and made accessible to everyone else on the Internet (unless a group is specifically created to prevent this, as you will see shortly in the section "Moderated Newsgroups").

There are no formal rules about the language you can use in an article, or about your behavior on UseNet. There are generally accepted principles that have been adopted by the UseNet community as a whole, but there is no real enforcement other than other users' force of opinion. If you are accessing UseNet through a company or organization, the system administrators may impose some rules on you, but these are locally decided and not set by UseNet.

A Very Brief History of UseNet

The origins of UseNet lie with the UNIX operating system in a release called V7. V7 offered a program called UUCP (UNIX to UNIX Copy), which allowed two machines to transfer files easily. In 1979, UUCP was used by two Duke University graduate students, Jim Ellis and Tom Truscott, to exchange messages between their two servers.

Other users got in on the act and used UUCP to provide messaging between their machines. University of North Carolina's Steve Bellovin went as far as writing a set of shell scripts to provide simple news software between UNC and Duke. These routines transferred and managed messages and news between the two sites. In 1980, the system was described to a wide audience at the annual Usenix conference. (Usenix is a UNIX user group.)

The shell scripts led to a version written in the C programming language, which was widely distributed and led to many new machines joining the informal news network. This software was modified several times more with many new features added at each step, resulting in the main routines for handling uploading and downloading newsgroups, and managing the articles with newsreaders.

Apart from the software for handling the articles within a newsgroup, several newsreaders have been developed over the years to allow users to access the newsgroups through a friendly front end. Naturally, all the newsreaders were developed with different features and capabilities. Most of the popular newsreaders are freeware or shareware, and are readily accessible to anyone who wants them. There are newsreaders available for just about every operating system.

UseNet Behavior

What limits are there on your behavior on UseNet? As mentioned earlier, UseNet doesn't have formal rules. Instead, the network users and your local system administrator impose limits, although in some cases they cannot be enforced.

This has one of two outcomes. If someone complains about your behavior on a UseNet newsgroup (or newsgroups) to your system administrator and he or she agrees, you may get warned about your network access or have your account taken away. If the system administrator doesn't care (or you don't have one), then there is nothing the UseNet community can do other than continue to post articles against you. That's one of the double-edged swords of UseNet. In theory, you can say anything you want, regardless of how many people you hurt or insult. On the other hand, as a newsgroup reader, you have to put up with this behavior. Luckily, there are some steps you can take to eliminate this type of posting.

There are a few individuals who continue their personal attacks on the UseNet, unhindered by system administrators or coworkers. On the whole, though, UseNet users are a well-behaved group who follow a set of mutually agreed-upon guidelines for network behavior, often called *netiquette*. You learn about it later in this chapter in the section called "Netiquette."

Newsgroup Names

With thousands of newsgroups available, a naming system is necessary to allow you to find the groups that are of interest to you. The UseNet user community tries to create newsgroups that are tightly focused on a subject, so you don't get messages about a car for sale in the middle of a newsgroup devoted to automotive technical advice.

> **Tip**
>
> UseNet newsgroups are named to allow users to rapidly identify a newsgroup's subject matter. Most newsreaders allow you to search for strings within newsgroup names, to help you find newsgroups you are interested in.

To help differentiate groups, there are several levels of newsgroup names used. The first level of hierarchy is a generic identifier that lets you know whether the newsgroup is technical, social, recreational, or some other general category. There are a few such identifiers in use:

Identifier	Category
biz	Business
comp	Computers
news	General news and topical items
rec	Recreational (hobbies and arts)
sci	Scientific
soc	Social
talk	Debate-oriented
misc	Newsgroups that don't readily fall into one of the other categories

These groups are usually circulated worldwide. There is another group category called "alt" (for alternative) that, while very popular, is not as widely distributed and tends to be less formal than the other groups. The alt groups are usually where stronger language and behavior is tolerated, almost like an underground newspaper tends to be more radical than the mainstream versions.

> **Note**
>
> Some system administrators don't download the alt groups, both to cut down the amount of material that must be transferred and to filter out some of the more adult-oriented material that is in the alt newsgroups at times. Given the looser nature of the alt groups as far as behavior is concerned, though, the alt groups can be the source of some interesting conversations and information.

Following the main newsgroup identifier is the next level, which tends to give the primary subject area. For example, **rec.audio** and its subgroups talks about audio systems, **sci.biology** is biology-oriented, and **alt.tasteless** has some very bizarre material in it. In most cases, there is a further division below this level, breaking the subject into even more specialized areas. These third-level areas are usually used when a newsgroup gets too many messages covering a wide variety of subjects to sustain a casual reader.

For example, **rec.autos.driving** is about the driving experience and how to better handle a car. The newsgroup **rec.autos.antique** is for aficionados of older cars. The **rec.autos.tech** group is where discussions of manifolds, gasoline, and rack-and-pinion steering are found. In many cases, there can be a half dozen special classes underneath the general category. That's not always the case, of course, as less popular newsgroups may have only one title.

> **Note**
>
> You may find some variety in sites and what they carry. For example, some sites don't carry certain groups, while some newsgroups seem to show up with different names depending on where you access them from.

There can be even further specification of a newsgroup name, although this is unusual. A common place to find long newsgroup names is the computer section. For example, there is a newsgroup called comp.os.ms-windows.apps. word-proc, obviously about word processors for the Windows operating system. Newsgroups with five or six name layers are the exception in all but the comp and sci groups.

The names are similar in the alt newsgroups. In many cases there are identical groups, differing only in the first part of the name. For example, there is both a **rec.autos.antique** and **alt.autos.antique** newsgroup. The same subjects are discussed in both, although the alt groups are not as widely distributed. This duplication can happen when the readership of an alt group grows large enough to justify the creation of a group in an "established" hierarchy. So, **alt.autos.antique** might "graduate" to become **rec.autos.antique**; however, the original alt group will often continue on, with a gradually decreasing readership as people move over to the rec version.

Often, though, alt newsgroups have no equivalent mainstream group because of the contentious issues involved or because of the smaller circulation of the newsgroup. For example, a newsgroup devoted to the highlights of the social season in Kansas City will be of little interest to a reader in Australia, so an alt group with limited distribution is ideal.

New and Bogus Newsgroups

New newsgroups are usually created by popular assent, with enough users wanting the group to sustain its continued use. However, it is possible for anyone to create a new newsgroup if they know the procedure. Unfortunately, new newsgroups that are created as a joke—known as *bogus newsgroups*—are common, usually to be removed a day or two later when no traffic is experienced in the newsgroup. The adding and removing of bogus newsgroups can take a bit of time as well as annoy users. An example of a bogus newsgroup is **swedish.chef.bork.bork.bork**, based on a character from Jim Henson's *Muppet Show*.

New newsgroups are often proposed in a special newsgroup called **news.announce.newusers** where support for the new group is determined, a process called a "call for votes" or CFV. New groups can be created unilaterally by an existing group, but netiquette demands a call for votes first in all but the alt hierarchy.

Moderated Newsgroups

Not all newsgroups are open and free for any type of posting. There is the moderated newsgroup, in which one or more users determine whether each message posted to the group is sent for distribution or deleted. The moderator is usually a volunteer who tries to ensure the newsgroup remains on-topic and cuts out any obnoxious or overly insulting articles. He or she also can edit articles to keep users from rambling too much.

Moderated newsgroups are not widespread, but most are popular because they deal specifically with a single subject. For example, the moderated newsgroup **rec.audio.high-end** is devoted to discussions and information about the high-end audio market, meaning the best in sound reproduction possible. By having the newsgroup moderated, readers can avoid the "I need a $100 amplifier" type of message.

Moderating a newsgroup is a lot of work and tends to be thankless. It is not unusual for the role of moderator to change as the load in the group becomes overwhelming for a single person. In some cases, newsgroups can revert from moderated status to open, allowing any posting. One problem with moderated newsgroups is that postings tend to take longer to appear because they must first be screened by the moderator.

When posting to a moderated newsgroup, you don't have to do anything special. The UseNet software will route the message to the moderator's e-mail address automatically.

A list of moderated newsgroups and the moderator's name and e-mail address is available from the newsgroup **news.announce.newuser**. The header of articles in a moderated newsgroup usually makes it clear that the group is moderated and by whom.

Threads

Usually an article will inspire replies. These replies build themselves into a series. This is called a *thread*. Some newsreaders are designed to allow you to follow threads conveniently, keying on the subject of all articles in the thread.

Unfortunately for users who like to follow threads, the subject tends to change in the space of a posting or two, without the subject title changing. This results in a posting in **rec.bicycles.tech** starting out dealing with brake pads and ending up with more than half the postings talking about hair-raising falls down a steep cliff when brakes failed. Threads, for this reason, should be treated as a guideline only.

One advantage to threads is that it allows a user to collect all articles about a particular subject and post them for others to access in a convenient manner. For example, **rec.pets.cats** may have a thread about combing long-haired pets that can grow to several hundreds of articles. These may be gathered and edited by a newsgroup reader and reposted as a summary of the subject.

What Do I Need to Know?

When you first get involved with UseNet, it can be overwhelming. There is a little intimidation about the number of people your postings can get to, as well as an overwhelming sense from the sheer amount of information you have access to. Just finding out how to use UseNet properly can be confusing. For that reason, a number of files have been created to help you get started, and there is a newsgroup dedicated to helping first-timers, who are called *newbies* in the UseNet lexicon. A friendly word of advice, don't leap into UseNet and start posting articles without knowing what the rules are. You don't want to incur the wrath of thousands of users!

Most newsgroups that you will want to investigate as a first-time user have the word "newuser" in the newsgroup title. Most newsreaders can scan newsgroup titles, so this is an easy way to get started.

The best newsgroup to try is one we've mentioned already, called **news.announce.newusers**. This is where proposals for new newsgroups are posted. Part of the **news.announce.newusers** newsgroup is the regular posting of a set of articles on UseNet, netiquette, and postings. When you find an article that contains valuable information for new users, use your newsreader to save the article to a file so you can read it at your leisure.

Five of the important articles that appear on **news.announce** **.newusers** are:

- Rules for Posting to UseNet
- A Primer on How to Work with the UseNet Community
- Answers to Frequently Asked Questions about UseNet
- Emily Postnews Answers Your Questions on Netiquette
- Hints for Writing Style for UseNet

Note

If you check the **news.announce.newusers** newsgroup and can't find the guides mentioned, wait a few days. They are usually posted weekly or bimonthly, and your news service may have deleted them if the postings are older than the system's preset expire time.

The **news.announce.newusers** newsgroup also has a complete list of all active newsgroups and their general subject, a list of moderated newsgroups, and guides to information about each newsgroup.

Another important newsgroup for new users is **news.answers**, which as its name implies, gets you answers to your questions (specifically about UseNet). This group has many veteran users who try to help new users as much as possible, all in the spirit of the UseNet community.

The **news.answers** newsgroup has one other important role. When any newsgroup has a list of Frequently Asked Questions (FAQs) that explain the basics about the newsgroup's subject, it is usually cross-posted to **news.answers**. *Cross-posting* means it is posted to two or more newsgroups at the same time.

Getting Started in a Newsgroup

When you first start reading a newsgroup, it is advisable to avoid posting unless you are really determined to let your opinion be heard. Monitor the newsgroup for a little while to find out who the regulars are, what the overall tone of the newsgroup is (is it lighthearted or serious, academic or sarcastic), and whether your messages are worth posting.

▶ See "Top UseNet Newsgroups," p. 1155

Tip

It's a good idea to monitor newsgroups for a while until you feel confident about your own postings.

Before you start asking questions that are considered basic and silly, look for a FAQs (frequently asked questions) file. These are usually posted on a regular basis varying from every couple of weeks to monthly, depending on the newsgroup. Alternatively, check in the **news.answers** newsgroup. The reason for this advice is simple. Nothing is more annoying for frequent users of, say, **rec.aquaria** to receive a posting asking how big of a fish tank should be bought. Usually, the basic information questions are fully answered in the FAQs. Asking this kind of trivial question will either get you a polite note to check the FAQs or a roughly worded reprimand for wasting the newsgroup's time.

Posting Articles

When you read through a newsgroup, there are bound to be many things you want to comment on. That's what the UseNet is all about—inspiring and supporting communications between users. You may notice the most effective postings are well-reasoned, logical, properly laid out, have good grammar and spelling, and don't ramble. Try to follow the same pattern.

Many users have to pay a fee (either through a service provider or download time charges) to receive their newsgroups and nothing will annoy them more than receiving long and pointless postings. Keep this simple fact in mind when you write. Some subjects need many lines to fully explain your ideas, but don't use up valuable space for nothing.

Good grammar and spelling are sometimes difficult to maintain when typing quickly, but do try your best to keep your sentences properly constructed. The odd spelling mistake is easily tolerated, but a message full of them will invite disdain. When you are first getting started with posting messages, it is advisable to write your replies offline and make sure they are properly structured before sending them over the network. A few minutes of effort will enhance your status in the newsgroup considerably. Also avoid long, rambling paragraphs. Some users don't seem to know when a paragraph break should be made. Many UseNet users will delete an article immediately if they don't see some structure to the posting.

> **Tip**
>
> If you are using a Windows newsreader and it doesn't have a spelling checker (and most don't), use a word processor to compose and check your article then copy and paste it into the newsreader.

Not everyone has a fancy message reader that reformats messages to fit on-screen. When you write a message, make sure you use a reasonable line length. UseNet newsgroups are ASCII-based with no formatting characters embedded. Use a 60-65 character line length, and don't forget to remove any special codes your word processor may add (that is, save as a text file).

Another important no-no: Avoid uploading sizable files such as graphics to a newsgroup that is text-based. A typical graphics file will take up hundreds of kilobytes of space. If you're paying by the line, downloading this file can cost a considerable amount and then it will be something you probably won't want. There are dedicated newsgroups for graphics, or post a message asking if anyone wants your long file first.

> **Note**
>
> If you post a long file, be considerate and put the phrase "(long)" in the subject area to warn other users. A better alternative is to check for a dedicated subgroup for binaries, pictures, or music files. They exist for many of the newsgroups that regularly involve these lengthy items.

When you gather enough courage to participate in the newsgroups by posting your own articles, there are a few things you have to take care of. First (and most important) is making sure your postings get to their target newsgroup and are not returned to you as undeliverable. Many newbies try sending a message to their favorite newsgroup reading something like this: "This is a test. Don't read it!" When they see the message in the newsgroup, they know they are okay. Unfortunately, millions of other users have down-loaded the message (costing money and time) and thousands have probably read it (wasting their time). The normal newsgroups are not the place to test your postings!

There is an easy way to test whether your postings are going to the newsgroups properly: Use one of the newsgroups specifically designed for testing. The most commonly used newsgroups for this purpose are **misc.test** and **alt.test**. When they receive a posting from a user, they send an auto-matic reply to indicate success (this kind of automatic reply is called a "ro-bot" in the UseNet lexicon). You don't have to read the test newsgroups di-rectly, as the reply signifies success. Still, many users like to scan the test newsgroups to see their first posting online.

V

UseNet Newsgroups

Signatures

The other important aspect of sending articles is to design your own signature file. Most new users expect to sign their articles with a simple name and sometimes an e-mail address. That's not the way it's usually done on UseNet. Instead, most postings have a several-line block at the end of the article that has the poster's name, e-mail address, and a saying of some sort. Sometimes, there is an ASCII character-based doodle of some sort. Having a witty or clever signature block is a source of prestige on the network.

> **Tip**
>
> Keep your signature blocks short! Few things are more annoying than scrolling through pages of fancy signature files when the message was not worth the effort.

It would be awkward to have to type in the entire signature block every time you post, so most newsreaders have a feature that allows you to read a file from the hard disk and tack it on at the end of your article. These are called sig files. The name of the file varies with the operating system and newsreader.

It is easy to create a sig file. Use a text editor and restrict yourself to the primary ASCII characters. Design a three or four line block that gives all the information about contacting you that you want to send to the newsgroups. Some users put their address and telephone number, while others prefer not to. At a minimum, the signature should have your name and your e-mail address. Phony names are strongly discouraged. You can usually tell young UseNet users by their "Dr. Avenger" or "MegaDeath" name types. Reprobations usually follow, or the user's postings are ignored.

A good signature file is brief. Having a 10 line signature block may look really fancy, but most readers hate wasting the download time. Forget about having huge graphics of your Firebird's Screaming Eagle, or an eight line representation of your favorite rock band's logo. Stick with the minimum. Preferably avoiding graphics entirely until you are much more proficient and respected on the UseNet.

A common addition to a signature block is a quotation or saying that you like. These tend to be short and most often humorous. They are fine in signature blocks, as long as they are not obnoxious or too lengthy, because they add a little individualism to your postings. If you scan a few newsgroups for a while, you will see some excellent examples of good signature blocks.

An archive of good and very bad signature blocks is maintained in the newsgroup **alt.fan.warlord**. If you receive the alt newsgroups, it may be worth a few minutes to look at some of the examples. The sig file I use for my e-mail is shown in figure 30.2. However, because it is a little long, I use the abbreviated version shown in figure 30.3 for my postings to UseNet.

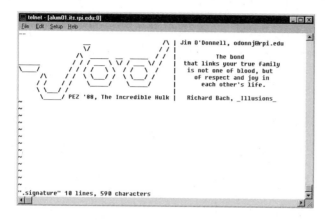

Fig. 30.2
The normal sig file I use for my e-mail—this is a little long for UseNet postings.

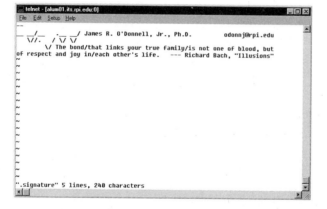

Fig. 30.3
This is the abbreviated version that I use for UseNet.

Tip

Did you notice that the first line of the sig files shown in both figure 30.2 and 30.3 consists of a line containing two dashes? Many newsreaders and e-mail programs recognize that this denotes that the rest of the message is a signature block; it's a good idea to start your sig file off this way, too.

> **Note**
>
> Want to see what a bad signature file looks like? Check out **alt.fan.warlord**.

Anonymous postings are not welcome on the UseNet and because most newsreaders put your Internet address in the header block anyway, they aren't really anonymous. Make sure you sign your messages. If you don't want to use a signature block, at least add a line with your name.

Anonymous Postings

Some service providers allow you to post articles to newsgroups anonymously. On many newsgroups, this is considered very bad behavior: if you don't have the honesty to sign your name, you shouldn't be posting. Many veteran UseNet users set up their system to automatically remove any anonymous postings.

As a general rule, if you have the ability to post anonymously, don't. You may feel you can say things anonymously that you wouldn't say if your name was attached to it, but those sentiments are probably best left unsaid. Besides, many "anonymous" services aren't really anonymous because they maintain a record of who posted what article. These records can, in theory, be used against you.

Note that there are some newsgroups, particularly some of those in the alt hierarchy, in which anonymous postings are considered acceptable. You should be extra careful, if posting anonymously to such a newsgroup, not to abuse the privilege. Also, note that no communication on the Internet is completely secure or anonymous, so be careful not to say or post anything that might come back to haunt you.

> **Note**
>
> To find out more about one anonymous posting service, send an e-mail message (it doesn't matter what you include in the message) to **anon@anon.penet.fi**. The service will assign you an anonymous mail ID (used for e-mail going through that service only) and send you some information about what you need to do to use the service. You can also get this information by sending e-mail (again, it doesn't matter what) to **help@anon.penet.fi**.

Cross-Posting

Occasionally, you will see a message that is posted on more than one newsgroup. This is called cross-posting and is discouraged. It is also called *spamming* in UseNet jargon. The only time cross-posting is really approved is when the subject fits properly into more than one newsgroup. An example may be about a plant that is toxic to dogs. Cross-postings to the pets and plants newsgroups would be appropriate.

If you want to cross-post, make sure the article belongs in the newsgroups you choose. A common problem is a new user listing 10 or more newsgroups; some of which are hardly applicable, but they happen to be the user's favorites. If you are replying to an article that is cross-posted, make sure the reply belongs in all the groups, too.

If a posting should be in a subgroup of a large newsgroup, you may want to post a note to the main group informing readers of the more detailed posting in the subgroup. For example, if you have a binary you want to upload to a programming group, place it in the binaries subgroup with a note to the readers of the parent newsgroup that you have placed the binary on the system. This avoids having to page through the binary in both places.

A common and hated example of cross-posting is the "get rich quick" or pyramid scheme article, which inevitably appears many times a year in dozens of newsgroups simultaneously, all thanks to a single user who didn't use common sense. Not only is this kind of message inappropriate in the first place, cross-posting makes it even more annoying. If you see such a post, rather than posting an angry reply yourself—thus creating even more of a waste—you should either ignore it, or jot off a quick e-mail note to the postmaster of the offender letting him know that there is a user abusing Internet privileges.

> **Tip**
>
> To send a note to the postmaster of a user such as
> **johndoe@internet.domain.name**, you can usually use the address
> **postmaster@internet.domain.name**.

Who Gets Your Article?—Distribution

It doesn't make much sense to have a UseNet user in Japan read your query about good restaurants in Paris. One of the things you have to think of when posting an article on UseNet is who gets to read it. The article's distribution is an important aspect of your postings.

Most news programs let you specify the distribution with a single word. In most cases, you want the entire UseNet to read your message so you use the "world" setting, which means everywhere on the Internet. In many cases, this is the default value for a posting, but you should get into the habit of checking this regularly to make sure it applies.

Other settings that may be available to your news program include your organization only, your geographic area (city, state, province, and so on), or your country or continent.

If you do post a local-oriented message to the inappropriate distribution ("There's a great Chinese food restaurant next to Algonquin Park" doesn't have much meaning to anyone who doesn't live in the area), you should expect some nasty notes, and rightly so. Don't waste other people's time and money with posts that they can't use.

Replying to an Article

All newsreaders let you reply to a posted article with a simple command. Replying is the same as composing a new message, except the heading information is pre-filled for you (taken from the original message). There are two kinds of replies, usually. The first is an e-mail reply to the original poster. The second is to post another article to the same newsgroup. In general, you should reply through e-mail if your reply will only be of interest to the original poster. If it will be of general interest to the whole newsgroup, then reply through a follow-up post.

Most newsreaders will let you choose to include the message you are replying to in your article, sometimes indented. It's fine to include relevant portions of the original, but if you are replying back to the newsgroup, don't keep the entire message unless it is short. Judiciously cut the original down to the salient parts that your reply is addressing. This saves not only download time but also other users' reading time.

Copyrights

Don't post something to the network that is protected by copyright. This includes text, graphics, music, and many other forms of electronic files. Some users adopt an "I don't care. What can they do?" attitude. It's dangerous, as many users have found out when they wound up charged with a copyright violation. Be careful about posting material other than your own words. If in doubt, don't.

The same warning applies for items you capture off UseNet. Just because someone posted a file, don't assume it's free of copyright. There have been several highly-publicized cases of pictures scanned into a file and distributed on UseNet that have led to copyright violation charges against the user who unknowingly downloaded and used them. Again the same warning applies: if you're not sure the file is free of copyright, don't use it.

> **Tip**
>
> If you want to post copyrighted material, very often you can send a quick e-mail message to the copyright holder and get his or her permission. You should probably save your request and the reply, and if you get permission, you can go ahead and post the material.

Posting Files

You know how to write articles and how to reply to them, but how do you upload the binary, graphics, or other large files you have on your system's hard drive? UseNet, like all of the Internet, is based on 7-bit ASCII characters, hence it won't handle 8-bit binaries. Instead, they will be converted to 7-bit, ruining their contents.

A couple of utilities are available for loading binary files onto the UseNet. UUEncode and UUDecode are the most popular. See chapter 19, "Encoding and Decoding Files," for more information.

> **Note**
>
> You can't send binary files to UseNet newsgroups. They must be converted to 7-bit format first.

Filtering and Searching for News

A common problem for many users is the sheer volume of articles that are interesting and should be read on a daily basis. Another common problem occurs when you are looking for articles on a particular subject. It can take a considerable amount of time to page through the subject lists alone of the newsgroups that deal with programming, for example, to find information you need. Even with threaded newsreaders that help a little, finding articles on a specific subject can be difficult because the "subject" line of the article doesn't always reflect the contents.

The structure of UseNet doesn't allow you to perform search functions through all the newsgroups unless you do a full newsgroup download and run a utility over each article for some keywords. That process can take hours alone. Luckily, there is a solution—news filtering and searching systems.

News Filtering

The most popular news filtering service is provided by the Database Group or Stanford University's Department of Computer Science. You can send a profile of the articles you are interested in to the service, which will return news articles to you on a regular basis that pertain exactly to your profile. The summaries provide the first fifteen lines of the article, along with the date, posting person, and subject lines. All communication with the filtering service is through e-mail.

To use the news filtering service, compose an e-mail message to **netnews@db.stanford.edu** with the following two lines in the message:

        subscribe <keywords>

        period <frequency>

where the keywords are the subjects you are interested in the filter finding for you and the period is how often you want the summaries e-mailed to you. The subject line of the message you send to the service is ignored. Each line in the message must have no leading whitespace characters (spaces or tabs). Case doesn't matter with the keywords. For example, the message:

        subscribe pascal programming

        period 2

will result in you receiving mail every two days with all the articles that have to do with Pascal programming.

The filtering service scans your keywords and uses them to assess the relevance of each article. It does this by assigning a score from 0 to 100 for the article's relevance to your keyword list. You can tell the service to send only articles that have a high correlation by using the keyword THRESHOLD in a message:

        subscribe guppies breeding aquaria

        period 5

        threshold 80

This will return any articles that meet the minimum score of 80 when the service matches articles. The default value for the threshold (unless you specify otherwise) is 60.

You can set a time limit for the filtering service, if you want. Suppose you are writing a term paper on the Bill of Rights and want the filtering service to perform for the next 30 days. You add the keyword "expire" and the number of days the search is to be active:

> subscribe bill of rights
>
> period 1
>
> threshold 80
>
> expire 30

which will give you daily updates on all articles on your subject (with a score of 80 or higher on the matching scale) for the next 30 days only. After the timer has expired, your searches are deleted from the filtering service's database.

There are more features available through the Stanford News Filtering Service, but you should contact the group for a copy of their information sheet. You can get a copy from the **news.answers** newsgroup or from many of the online services.

News Searching

A relatively new service on the World Wide Web is now available for searching for topics through UseNet called *DejaNews*. Its URL is **http:// www.dejanews.com/dnhome.html**, and its home page is shown in figure 30.4.

V

UseNet Newsgroups

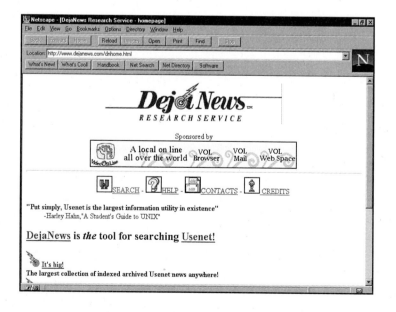

Fig. 30.4
The DejaNews Research Service allows you to search throughout the UseNet hierarchy for topics of interest.

When you click the SEARCH hypertext link shown in figure 30.4, you can search for articles throughout the UseNet hierarchy on whatever topic interests you. DejaNews is not all inclusive, because it doesn't cover any of the alt.*, soc.*, talk.*, or *.binaries newsgroups. That still leaves plenty of ground that it does cover. I did my best to stump DejaNews by looking for articles about the Pittsburgh Condors, a basketball team that I vaguely remember used to play in Pittsburgh when I was growing up. As shown in figure 30.5, I perform this search by asking for a search on Pittsburgh & Condors—the ampersand indicates that you want articles that contain both words, otherwise if will find articles containing one or the other.

Fig. 30.5

Hmmm... Can I find anything on the Pittsburgh Condors?

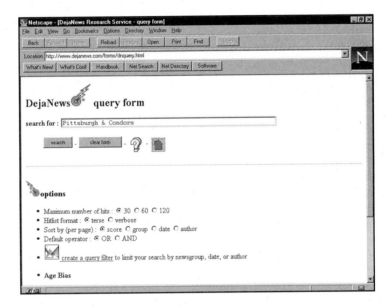

As a result of this search, DejaNews was able to find five articles. Lo and behold, there was some information about the old Pittsburgh Condors (see fig. 30.6). Of course, things weren't perfect, I got a couple of articles like that shown in figure 30.7, which weren't quite what I had in mind. (I could have eliminated those articles by searching for "Pittsburgh Condors," with the quotes, which would have looked for articles with that phrase, rather than just the individual words.)

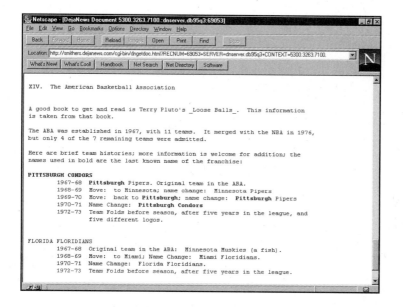

Fig. 30.6
DejaNews was able to find some truly obscure information for me by scouring the UseNet hierarchy.

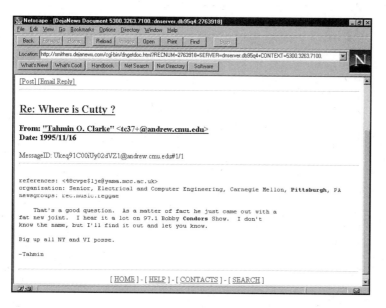

Fig. 30.7
Of course, if you aren't careful how you specify your search, not all the articles will be quite what you expect!

Netiquette

As mentioned earlier, users of the UseNet are expected to follow a set of guidelines for their behavior called *netiquette*. The complete guide to netiquette is available for you to read in the newsgroup **news. announce.newusers**. It is called "Emily Postnews Answers Your Questions on Netiquette." Before you write your first posting, capture this article and read it thoroughly.

One overwhelming rule on the UseNet is that insulting, degrading, or racist comments are totally out (unless you are in one of the wackier newsgroups such as **alt.tasteless**). Reputations are widespread on the UseNet and if you continue with your silly comments, other users will automatically exclude any posting you send.

It has been mentioned before, but it's important to keep your postings clear and succinct. Edit long articles to make them more readable. Repeat posters of long, wordy articles tend to be ignored. If you are excerpting or quoting someone else's article in yours (a common practice), keep the excerpt short and directly relevant. Don't copy the entire message.

Avoid personal messages. UseNet is not a private e·mail service for small groups to communicate; use e-mail for that function. Millions of systems will download your comments (at considerable cost in some cases), so don't be cavalier with their time and money.

Finally, the big one. Despite what the newspapers and some PR companies say, UseNet is not for business items, advertisements, get-rich-quick schemes, or similar postings. Blatant postings to many newsgroups to solicit customers have been tried several times with universal condemnation. It's okay to mention a service you provide, a local store that did good work, or a company that handled something properly for you when it is in context with the rest of the articles in a newsgroup, but direct soliciting should be considered forbidden. One exception to this rule is that there are groups where bartering, swapping, and selling personal items is permissible. For instance, many of the comp.sys groups allow folks to use the newsgroup to sell computer hardware and software they no longer need. If you're in doubt as to whether this is acceptable in a given newsgroup, read the newsgroup FAQs or ask the group first.

Pyramid schemes, form letters, and the poor child who is trying to get the world's largest collection of stamps, business cards, credit cards, and so on are either bogus, illegal, or a major breach of netiquette. The user groups may not have control over what you post (unless they convince your system administrator), but the network is very quick to condemn this kind of behavior.

Abbreviations

To save typing time and make postings shorter, many users employ a set of abbreviations that are commonly known to represent phrases. These are usually typed in capital letters.

Common abbreviations are "IMHO" (in my humble opinion), "BTW" (by the way), and "OTOH" (on the other hand). You will encounter some abbreviations that you can't figure out quickly, because they are used by small groups of users or veterans who are reluctant to type out phrases. One, for example, which had many UseNet users scratching their heads for a while is "ROTFL," which was eventually disclosed as standing for "rolling on the floor laughing." After that, it began showing up all over the place.

Not all abbreviations actually represent a phrase. For example, you will see "<G>" or "<g>" often used. This means "grin" and is meant as a moderator of the tone of the sentence, or to show the poster was making a point with tongue in cheek.

> **Note**
>
> It's a good idea to use abbreviations sparingly, because they make some postings difficult to read. Excessive use of abbreviations also is a hallmark of a newbie.

Flames

You won't be reading messages on the UseNet long before you see the word *flame*. This has nothing to do with fire, at least in the literal sense. It has its origins in the aeronautical term "flame out" which means to either have your engines quit or your plane catch fire. UseNet uses the term to mean a sharp retort or criticism—sometimes even an insult. There are even newsgroups devoted to flaming.

A user will flame someone when he or she gets mad, by sending a sarcastic or insulting rejoinder to the person who posted the offending article. Usually, flames are inspired by a particularly stupid comment, a stupid response to another article, or a major breach of netiquette.

For the most part, new users are recognized as such and are treated with a little more tolerance than veteran users, although there are some users with no patience at all. You will often see the comment "Don't flame me" in a message, obviously from a user who knows the article may inspire a reply (called *flame-bait*) or who is trying to plead innocence or newbie status.

V

UseNet Newsgroups

It is not unusual for a newsgroup to degenerate into a flame war or flame fest for a little while. In such a case, one flame leads to another until a good percentage of the newsgroup's articles are flames. While this can be moderately amusing for a while, it can wear thin quickly. Still, the UseNet community as a whole admires a well thought out and presented flame. The best flames don't appear outright insulting, with subtlety a characteristic of a real flame master.

Shouting

The UseNet is based on simple characters typed on a screen, so there must be some mechanism to emphasize certain words in a message. Users have developed several methods to accomplish this. For example, light emphasis is usually indicated by an underline character before and after a word, as in "this is a _very_ important point," or asterisks in the same manner, such as "make *sure* you save the file first."

The extreme is shouting, which is indicated with uppercase letters, such as "this is a VERY important point." The trick with emphasis is to use it subtly and not to excess. Typing long sentences or paragraphs in uppercase is considered bad manners. Make sure you don't use the Shift-lock key on your keyboard when typing. Excessive shouting is sure to get you flamed.

If you are prone to swearing, get used to typing random characters to replace the offensive (to some) words. For example, "the @#$*&^ company lost the &%^@# key to the car" is a lot less offensive and manages to get the point across. Leave the filling in to the reader. Because some words have different meanings in other countries, this is probably the best way to communicate the feelings.

Surfing and Lurking

The UseNet has many terms that you will encounter as you spend more time in the newsgroups. A couple of terms you will eventually see are *lurking* and *surfing*.

Lurkers are users who read newsgroups but don't post. There's nothing wrong with being a lurker (and no one will know you are doing it), but many UseNet veterans feel that lurkers miss out on the really interesting parts of the UseNet—interaction and participation. That doesn't mean you have to post all the time, but you should post when you feel you have something to say.

Lurking is useful when you want to watch how a discussion on a newsgroup proceeds before committing yourself to it, or when you want to check out a newsgroup for general interest. Most UseNet veterans will advise newcomers to the network to lurk for at least six months before posting, because this gives time to assimilate the overall behavior of the UseNet and the tone of each newsgroup.

Surfers are people who cover a lot of newsgroups, essentially moving from one to the other in the way a wave surfer covers water. Again, there's nothing derogatory about surfing, and it is a term you will see often. In some ways, frequent UseNet users are slightly envious of those with the time to spend surfing across many newsgroups.

Smileys

Smileys (sometimes called *emoticons*) are those little symbols in a message that are made up of a few characters meant to be viewed sideways. The most famous smiley is :), which when viewed from the side has a smiling mouth under two eyes. This is a very simple smiley. There are now entire books devoted to the different and wonderfully complex smileys.

When using smileys in your postings, use them with moderation. Excessive smiley use tends to make your article look silly. A smiley can be very effectively used to modify the tone of a posting, such as "that was really dumb :)" which is intended to mean you are grinning as you say it, essentially having a smile over the subject.

Some of the more popular smileys are:

Smiley	Meaning
:-) or :)	happy
:-(	sad
:-< or :-c	mad or really sad
:-o	wow! or surprise
:-@	screaming or yelling
:-}	grin
'-) or ;-)	wink

Writing Postings: A Checklist

After all the information and rules mentioned in this chapter, you may be feeling a little overwhelmed (and perhaps leery) about posting. You shouldn't. On the whole, the UseNet is populated with considerate, interesting users who tolerate a few goofs along the way. However, a few guidelines will help cut down on the number of flames headed your way:

■ Use the proper newsgroup. Don't waste users' time by sending the message to the wrong place. Also, avoid cross-posting unless your article is very relevant to the other groups.

■ Make sure the distribution is correct. Sending a local message to a group who can't use it is inviting a sharp response.

■ Make sure your posting has something to say. Sending a reply that reads "I agree" is a waste. Only post if you have something to add to the discussion.

■ Don't ramble. Keep your postings to the point. Remember, many users pay to download your messages and resent getting and reading a 100-line article that is a waste of their time.

■ Proper presentation is important. Try to use proper grammar and spelling at all times.

■ Use a short, inoffensive signature block. Consider the user who has to pay to download your wonderful 45-line picture of the Mona Lisa rendered with "@" characters.

■ Use sarcasm and insults carefully. You may look like a fool if you don't. It's more fun to send than receive, and your inappropriate comments are sure to get you blasted.

■ Unless you are really sure of yourself and ready to receive double the amount back, don't flame anyone. A gentle comment is better. If you do flame with abandon, make sure you wear your asbestos underwear.

CHAPTER 31

Using NewsXpress

In chapter 30, "How UseNet Works," you learn about UseNet, the Internet collection of newsgroups used for discussion and dissemination of information on literally thousands of different topics. Chances are, if you're interested in it, you can find a group on UseNet that is discussing it.

Traditionally, though, many of the newsreaders available on Internet access systems—shell accounts running the UNIX operating system—reflect their UNIX heritage. They tend to be very powerful, but they are based on command-line prompts and command codes and are extremely difficult to become proficient at. For many PC-based systems, a new generation of newsreaders is being developed with a much more intuitive, graphical interface. The NewsXpress program for Windows is just such a program.

In this chapter, you learn how to do the following:

- Install the NewsXpress program
- Set up NewsXpress to connect to and access your Internet provider's news server
- Subscribe and unsubscribe from UseNet newsgroups
- Select and read UseNet articles
- Save and reply to UseNet articles, and post articles of your own
- Access encoded binary files included in UseNet articles

Why Use NewsXpress?

UseNet has been around for a long time and is still one of the most used areas of the Internet. UNIX system newsreaders that allow you to read UseNet articles and post articles of your own have been around for a long time, as well.

These newsreaders provide you with powerful tools for doing their respective function, but they're not very easy or a lot of fun to use. Take a look at figure 31.1, which shows a typical help screen from a UNIX newsreader, giving you some of the command options you can execute while reading UseNet news. Sure, everything you might want to do is somewhere in there, but it'll take forever to learn how to do it all.

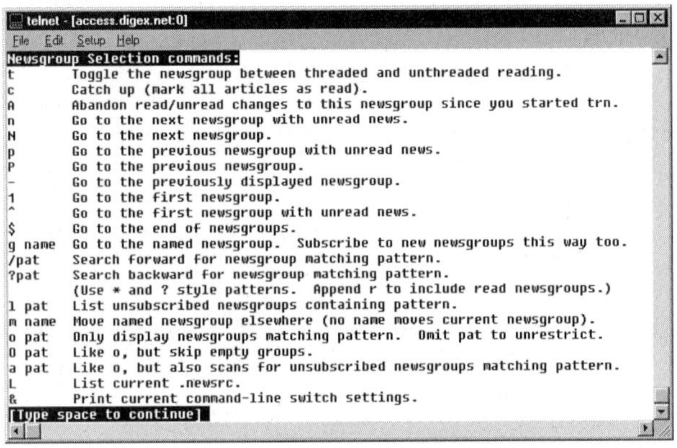

Fig. 31.1

Accessing UseNet through a command-line newsreader can be very confusing.

NewsXpress takes all of the command-line drudgery out of accessing UseNet, giving an easy, intuitive Windows interface to the process of searching for, reading, and responding to UseNet news.

Setting Up

The version of NewsXpress used herein is NewsXpress version 1.0. This program was developed for Windows 3.1 and Windows for Workgroups but works well under Windows 95. This version of NewsXpress does not have an automated installation procedure, but manually installing is not very difficult.

Installing the Software

To install NewsXpress, follow these steps:

1. Create a directory in which to install NewsXpress—I used C:\NX—and copy the file NX10B4-P.ZIP from the NetCD into that directory.

2. Unzip NX10B4-P.ZIP. This will give the following files (if you have your Windows Explorer set up to hide MS-DOS file extensions for registered file types, this list might look a little different, but the files will still be there):

> NX.EXE
>
> CTL3DV2.DLL
>
> MIME.EXT
>
> NEWSXPRS.FAQ
>
> NX.HLP
>
> READ.ME

3. If you don't have CTL3DV2.DLL in your Windows 95 system directory (probably C:\WINDOWS\SYSTEM), move it there; otherwise, delete it.

4. Move MIME.EXT into your NX working directory. This will probably be the same as the installation directory, so you should be able to leave it there.

5. Create an entry for NewsXpress in the Start menu of your taskbar, or create a shortcut to it on your desktop (or both). If you create a shortcut desktop icon for it, it'll look like the one shown in figure 31.2.

That's it! Your installation is complete! You might want to take this opportunity to take a quick look at the READ.ME file, which gives some history for the program and gives the e-mail address of its author if you want to send him e-mail with questions, suggestions, or bug reports.

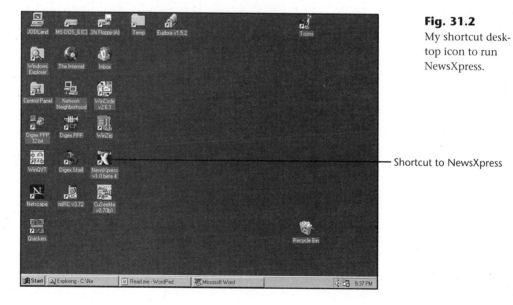

Fig. 31.2
My shortcut desktop icon to run NewsXpress.

— Shortcut to NewsXpress

UseNet Newsgroups

V

Connecting to the News Server

◀ See "Simple
Mail Transfer
Protocol
(SMTP),"
p. 330

The first time you run NewsXpress, you will be given the Setup dialog shown in figure 31.3 (you can get at this dialog at any other time by opening the Config menu and choosing Setup). You must fill in the information for NNTP server and a valid e-mail address in order to use NewsXpress. Additionally, in order to be able to send e-mail from within the program, you must also supply the information for SMTP server. This information should be provided to you by your Internet access provider.

Note that the Authorization Information is only needed if your Internet provider's news (NNTP) server requires authorization. If it does, this information will probably be the login ID and password of your account.

Caution

If your Internet provider's news server does not require authorization, then don't put anything in the Username and Password boxes. In this case, even if you put your correct login ID and password, the news server will not let you connect.

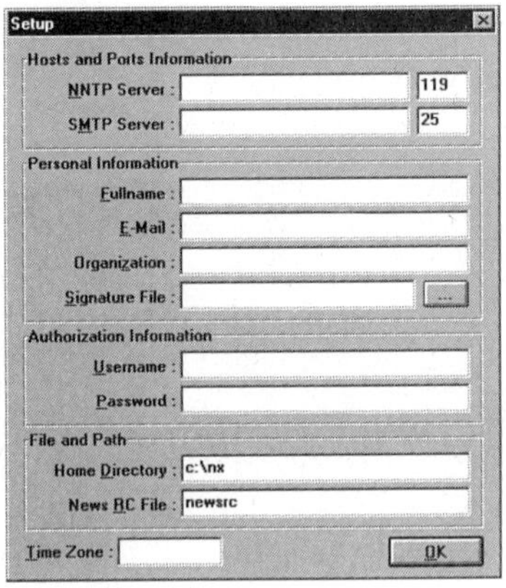

Fig. 31.3
When you first
start NewsXpress,
you will get this
Setup dialog box.
At a minimum,
you must specify
your NNTP server
and e-mail
address.

Configuring NewsXpress

Once you have correctly filled in the setup information, you should probably take a look at the preferences information before you connect to the news server for the first time. Most of the default options are acceptable, but there are a few you should be aware of, and you might want to take a look at the rest. Open the Config menu and choose Preferences, and you'll get something like what is shown in figure 31.4.

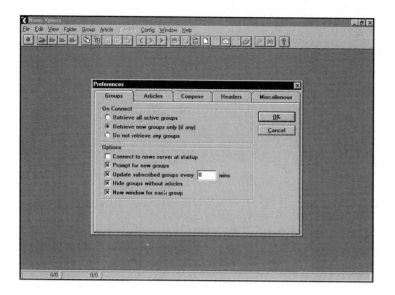

Fig. 31.4
Selecting the
Preferences item
under the Config
menu gives you
this dialog box for
customizing
NewsXpress.

There are a couple of options under the Groups tab shown that you might want to change. First, once you have established that you have all of your setup information correct, you might want to deselect the Connect to News Server at Startup box. Then when you run NewsXpress, it will connect you immediately (provided that your Internet connection is either active or set up to start automatically). Also, I've found that I like to uncheck the Hide Groups without Articles box; if checked, this will cause NewsXpress to not list newsgroups with zero new articles in them. I find this a little confusing and would rather see all of the newsgroups I am subscribed to, even if they don't have anything new in them.

The rest of the default preferences are pretty reasonable. You might want to take this opportunity to look around the four other tabs in this window, but you shouldn't need to make changes in any of them.

Connecting to UseNet

Once you have gotten your setup and preferences information the way you like it, you are ready to connect. Open the File menu and choose Connect, and you're off and running (see fig. 31.5)!

Fig. 31.5
Once you have
setup NewsXpress,
you're ready to
connect to
UseNet!

Retrieving Newsgroup Names

The first thing NewsXpress does every time you connect to the news server is
to check for new newsgroups to give you the opportunity to subscribe to
them. Now, the first time you connect, *every* newsgroup is new, so it might
take as long as five or 10 minutes for NewsXpress to download all of the
newsgroup names—there are over 15,000 of them! Once you have gotten by
your first connect, on each succeeding connect it will only take a few seconds
to list the new newsgroups for you. And you can even avoid that delay if you
want by unchecking the Retrieve New Groups Only (if Any) box in the
Groups tab of the Preferences dialog.

Subscribing to and Unsubscribing from Newsgroups

Once NewsXpress has retrieved the names of all of the new newsgroups, it
will display them for you and give you the chance to subscribe to the ones
you find of interest. The dialog that gives you this choice will look something
like the one shown in figure 31.6. Now, with over 13,000 groups to choose
from, you might be wondering how you can ever look through all of the
groups to find the ones you want to read.

Fig. 31.6
Each time you
start NewsXpress,
you'll be given the
opportunity to
subscribe to new
newsgroups. The
first time you start
it up, they're all
new!

The answer to that question lies in two facts. First, as we found out in chapter 30, "How UseNet Works," UseNet newsgroups are hierarchical, with newsgroup names going from the general to the specific as you read them left to right. For instance, one of the groups I read is **alt.sports.hockey.nhl.pit-penguins**. That means it's in the alt group, which means it has a more limited distribution and appeal, is about sports, hockey, the NHL, and lastly, about my favorite team, the Pittsburgh Penguins. The way NewsXpress allows you to take advantage of this hierarchical structure is through the Filter box shown near the bottom of figure 31.6. Similar groups will have similar words in their names, and NewsXpress uses the Filter box to only list those newsgroups that contain that text. So I can narrow my search for newsgroups to those concerning hockey by typing that into the Filter box (see fig. 31.7).

◀ See "Newsgroup Names," p. 752

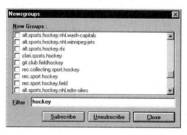

Fig. 31.7
Overwhelmed by your choices? NewsXpress can filter the list of groups to a more manageable size.

So I can select a few of my hockey related newsgroups (or whatever strikes my fancy). Subscribing to the groups is done by either highlighting the newsgroup name and pressing the Subscribe button or by using the mouse pointer to put a check in the check box to the left of the newsgroup. When finished, choose the Close button, and you will be subscribed to the selected groups.

Figure 31.8 shows the resulting Newsgroups dialog after I have subscribed to a few hockey newsgroups. Note that, as with most UseNet newsreaders, NewsXpress will automatically subscribe you, as a new UseNet user, to the three groups, **news.announce.newgroups**, **news.announce.newusers**, and **news.newsusers.questions**. These groups contain articles helpful to new users, so if you haven't used UseNet before, you might want to check them out.

V

UseNet Newsgroups

Caution

If you are accessing the Internet and UseNet over a dial-up connection, don't look at any of these newsgroups yet! See below to find out some things about newsgroups with a lot of unread articles in them.

Fig. 31.8
Once you have selected some newsgroups to join, you are ready to begin.

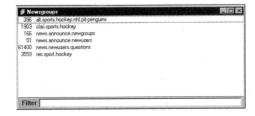

Before we leave the subject of subscribing and unsubscribing from newsgroups, let me say a couple more things. Anytime you want to check out the list of newsgroups again, with an eye towards joining a few more, you can do so by choosing the Show All Groups On/Off menu bar button (see fig. 31.9). This will list all of the newsgroups and allow you to subscribe and unsubscribe from them, either by using the Subscribe and Unsubscribe menu bar buttons or by checking and unchecking the box to the left of each newsgroup name. The Filter box still works in this window, as well.

Fig. 31.9
Anytime you want to look at the list of all the newsgroups, click the Show All Groups On/Off button.

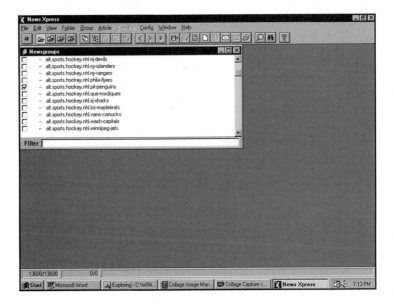

There's one more important thing you need to know before we start reading articles. Referring back to the newsgroup list in figure 31.8, we see there is a number listed to the left of each newsgroup name. This number is the number of unread articles in that newsgroup. As you can see, this number can get quite large—for the **news.newusers.questions** newsgroup it is listed as 61,400 unread articles. This is important to consider when you want to read one of these newsgroups, particularly over a dial-up connection to the Internet because of the way NewsXpress works.

When you select a newsgroup to read, NewsXpress contacts the news server and retrieves just the header information—such as the sender, date, and subject—of each message. Normally, this is a fairly quick process, but you probably don't want to sit around and wait for it to download 61,400 articles worth of information!

Tip

If there's a group you want to read, such as news.newusers.questions, but there are too many new messages, you can use the Catch up button shown in figure 31.9 to mark all of those messages as read, thus "catching up" with that group. For a group like **news.newusers.questions**, this is okay because the important information for new users is periodically reposted.

Selecting and Reading Articles

Well, we're ready to start reading news. Selecting a newsgroup to read is as simple as double-clicking the newsgroup name in the Newsgroups dialog. When you do this, NewsXpress will contact the news server to get the header information and present you with a summary list similar to that shown in figure 31.10.

Here again we see one of the valuable features of NewsXpress. As discussed in chapter 30, "How UseNet Works," most newsgroups in UseNet have "threaded" conversation. This means that, within a newsgroup, different conversations can be going on at once, the articles for each separate conversation lead from one to another and usually have the same subject. We'll see in the "Saving and Replying to Articles and Posting Your Own" section following how to keep conversation threads going by posting "follow-up" articles. Note in figure 31.10 how NewsXpress distinguished between separate articles, shown with a document icon, and conversation threads, shown with a folder

◀ See "Threads,"
p. 756

icon. You can read a separate article by double-clicking the document icon. By double-clicking a folder icon, you see the separate articles listed—or even other folders—that make up that conversation thread.

Fig. 31.10
Here are the article headers from the newsgroup **alt.sports.hockey. pit-penguins**.

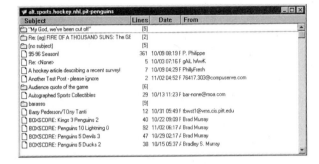

As mentioned, to read an article, you just need to double-click the appropriate document icon, and NewsXpress will retrieve the article and display it, as shown in figure 31.11.

Fig. 31.11
By double-clicking an article, I can retrieve and read the entire thing.

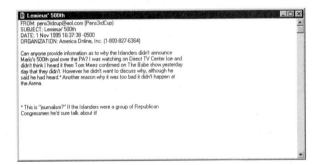

Once you have started to read articles from a given newsgroup, you don't need to go back to the summary list every time. You can follow articles through the threads of different conversations using the Previous Article, Next Article, and Next Unread Article buttons. The first time you read through a newsgroup, the Next Article and Next Unread Article buttons are equivalent. It's only if you jump around within a newsgroup that they become different. In any case, unless you need to review an article you have already read (and didn't save), you should probably use the Next Unread Article button.

Saving and Replying to Articles and Posting Your Own

There are a variety of different actions you might want to take while reading UseNet articles, usually concerned with saving articles you find of interest or replying and continuing on the conversation, either through e-mail or within the UseNet newsgroup. Most of these actions can be performed within NewsXpress by using the menu bar buttons shown in figure 31.12.

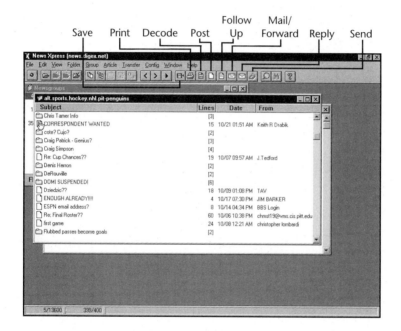

Fig. 31.12
The menu bar buttons allow you to perform the most-used functions in NewsXpress.

Saving Articles

Periodically while reading UseNet news, you will find an article that you want to keep. This may happen quite often if you are reading a newsgroup that is set up to distribute binary files—graphics or executables, for instance. When reading an article, you can save a copy of it by clicking the Save menu bar button. You will be given a dialog to enter a file name, and the article will be saved.

Fig. 31.13
If you want to keep a copy of an article, click the Save button while reading it.

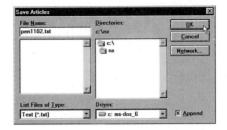

Note

Remember that this version of NewsXpress is a Windows 3.1/Windows for Workgroups application. Though it runs fine under Windows 95, you need to re-member that you are restricted to the normal Windows 3.1 file name, no more than eight characters and a three character extension.

E-Mail Options

Quite often, you will want to reply to an article that someone has posted to UseNet. There are many reasons that you might want to do this: to answer a question that someone has asked, to correct a mistake someone has made, or perhaps to defend your favorite hockey team against someone's slanderous assault. You have basically two options for making such a reply, either by sending the original sender e-mail or by posting a follow-up article to the UseNet newsgroup.

The rule of thumb to use when choosing between these two options is, "Is my post going to be of general interest to the newsgroup?" If the answer is no—perhaps because the original sender asked a very narrow question—then it is best to reply through e-mail. However, if your post will be of general in-terest or if you are continuing a conversation thread that is ongoing in the newsgroup, then you should post a follow-up article to the newsgroup.

In NewsXpress, each of these options, along with a few more e-mail and UseNet options, are very straightforward. To send an e-mail reply to an article you are viewing, click the Reply menu bar button (refer to fig. 31.12). You will be given a window such as that shown in figure 31.14. Note that the ar-ticle to which you are replying has been included in the message, set off with the ">" character (this is known as *quoting*). After you have included your re-ply, you can send the message by clicking the Send menu bar button.

Fig. 31.14
If you want to reply to someone who posted an article, usually the best way to do it is to reply through e-mail.

Two other e-mail options are available using the menu bar Mail/Forward button. If you are reading a UseNet article and you click this button, you will be given the dialog shown in figure 31.15. This enables you to forward the article to someone else through e-mail. You might think a friend of yours, who doesn't have access to UseNet, might be interested in the article, so you can e-mail it to him or her.

If you choose Mail/Forward when you aren't reading an article, you can send a regular e-mail message to someone. In this case, you get the same window that shows up in the Reply case shown previously (refer to fig. 31.14) but without the To: information filled in and without any quoted text. Once you have completed the message, you send it the same way by clicking the Send menu bar button.

Fig. 31.15
You can forward a UseNet article to someone through e-mail, too.

UseNet Options

Your two options for sending articles to UseNet are analogous to the Reply button and the mail part of the Mail/Forward button for e-mail. They are accessed with the Follow Up and Post menu bar buttons shown in figure 31.12. As you can probably figure out, a follow up is a reply sent to UseNet to a given article; newsreaders such as NewsXpress which can thread articles will group this reply together with the other articles in the same thread and make it easier for everyone to read them. In the same way, you can post an article to the newsgroup, which will start a new thread. In either case, you will get a window similar to that shown in figure 31.16; the one shown, as indicated, is for a follow up. For a new post, the same window appears, without the subject filled in and without any quoted text.

V

UseNet Newsgroups

Fig. 31.16
If you want to reply to a UseNet article and you think your post will be of general interest to the group, you can post a follow up article to the newsgroup.

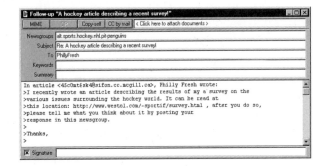

Posting and Retrieving Non-Text Information

As discussed in chapter 19, "Encoding and Decoding Files," and chapter 30, "How UseNet Works," articles posted to UseNet are restricted to text only information. It is possible, however, to exchange binary files through UseNet, by encoding the information before posting it. In order to make use of the information, then, you must be able to decode it when you read the article.

NewsXpress supports encoding of binary information in UseNet articles and e-mail messages using either MIME or UUEncode encoding. For outgoing articles or e-mail, the appropriate method is chosen when the binary file is attached to the message. See figure 31.16: near the upper-right part of the window is a box labeled <Click here to attach documents>. If you do this, you get a dialog with a file selector that allows you to select the file or files to attach. Another option given in this dialog is the encoding method. Here the choice is made of whether or not to use UUEncode encoding. If you elect not to use UUEncode encoding, you can select MIME encoding by clicking the MIME button shown in figure 31.16.

> **Note**
>
> As a general rule of thumb, UUEncode encoding is more widely used in UseNet postings, and MIME encoding is more widely used for e-mail. You might want to look around a given newsgroup to see which method is more common before posting an article including an encoded binary file.

> **Caution**
>
> Before posting an article to UseNet with a (possibly lengthy) encoded binary file,
> make sure that the article is appropriate for that newsgroup. There are newsgroups
> set up for the exchange of binary picture or executable files, but posting a long
> encoded message to a discussion newsgroup is considered a no-no.

Retrieving articles with encoded files is a little easier in NewsXpress. For
MIME encoded files, it is automatic. The encoded file attachment will be detected, decoded, and saved to the directory specified in the Miscalleneous
[sic] tab of the Preferences dialog.

◄ See "What
Types of Encod-
ing and Decod-
ing Are There?"
p. 441

For UUEncoded files, there's just one more step involved. NewsXpress is not
able to automatically detect articles with UUEncoded attachments, so you
need to tell NewsXpress to decode the attachment in such an article.

◄ See "Recogniz-
ing Different
Encoding
Schemes,"
p. 445

> **Note**
>
> Note that when retrieving and reading especially long articles from UseNet, as can
> often happen for files including encoded attachments, you might get the warning
> shown in figure 31.17. Even though NewsXpress is not able to display the entire file
> in this case, it has retrieved it all, and it can be successfully decoded.

V

UseNet Newsgroups

Once you are viewing an article with a UUEncoded attachment, such as that
shown in figure 31.18 (see chapter 19, "Encoding and Decoding Files," for
tips on recognizing the different types of encoding), you can decode the attachment by clicking the Decode menu bar button. This will give you the dialog shown in figure 31.19, allowing you to select where to save the decoded
file. Once this is done, you can then use the decoded file, such as the graphics file I retrieved and decoded, as shown in figure 31.20.

Fig. 31.17
It's possible when
viewing an article,
particularly one
with an encoded
attachment, that
it'll be too big to
view all at once.
Don't worry, it'll
still decode
successfully.

Fig. 31.18

If you are viewing an article with a UUEncoded file included, you can decode the file.

Fig. 31.19

When you decode the article, you'll be given a dialog to select where NewsXpress should put the decoded file.

Fig. 31.20

Here's the graphics file I got from that article, none the worse for its time spent hiding as a text file.

CHAPTER 32

Using Agent

As the number of UseNet newsgroups has increased, and the number of articles posted in these groups has skyrocketed, efficient newsreading software has become a necessity. It has become increasingly important for newsreading software to have the ability to sort groups of articles that relate to the same topic (called threading), to kill (or ignore) articles that are not interesting, and to allow the reader to only retrieve articles that are wanted.

Two newsreaders that meet these criteria (and more) are the products from Forté—Free Agent and Agent. Free Agent is a full-featured newsreader that is available at no charge for personal use at home, to students or staff at educational institutions, and to non-profit organizations. Agent is a complete newsreading package available commercially that includes all the features of Free Agent, plus e-mail, folders for saving your news articles, and increased article sorting and filtering.

This chapter discusses both the Free Agent and Agent newsreaders (since some readers may not qualify for the licensing of the Free Agent newsreader). The versions covered in this chapter are Free Agent 1.0 and Agent .99.

In this chapter you learn how to:

- Obtain, install, and configure both newsreaders
- Subscribe and unsubscribe from newsgroups
- Read articles and navigate in newsgroups
- Follow an article thread
- Post new articles
- Extract files from articles
- Manage e-mail

Getting and Installing Agent

Information about obtaining the different Forté products can be found at the World Wide Web URL **http://www.forteinc.com/forte**. This site also includes a summary of the features of the two newsreaders, answers to common questions about the readers, and licensing information.

You can download a copy of the Free Agent newsreader to the site **ftp.forteinc.com** through an anonymous FTP. You can find a copy of the Free Agent reader in the directory /PUB/FORTE/FREE_AGENT in the file FAGENT10.ZIP (for version 1.0 of Free Agent).

The Agent newsreader can be purchased in several different ways. Probably the easiest is to call Forté at the contact information listed at the end of this chapter. You can order Agent over the phone and download the actual software from **ftp.forteinc.com**. Forté gives you a license key that allows the software to function.

In either case, the software you receive will be a ZIP archive that you should unpack into an installation directory. The files in the zip archive are the entire distribution of the newsreader; no separate setup program is needed.

Starting and Configuring Agent

When you start Free Agent (by double-clicking the Free Agent icon), the program first asks you to accept the licensing agreement, stating that you are qualified to run the Free Agent reader. If you are not eligible to run the Free Agent reader, you must purchase the Agent newsreader. After the license agreement, the Free Agent program prompts for the configuration information shown in figure 32.1.

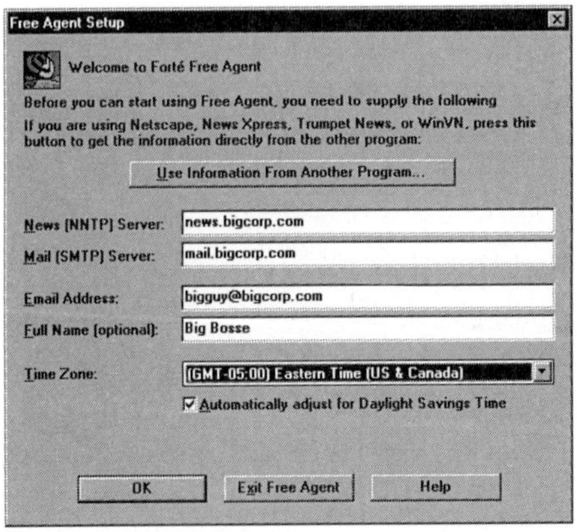

Fig. 32.1
Setting up the initial configuration information for Free Agent.

The configuration page asks you to set up the NNTP server that will be used to read news, the host that serves as your mail server, and your e-mail address and full name (to be used in your posts and outgoing mail). Free Agent also asks you to set the time zone you are in and whether your location observes daylight savings time.

> **Note**
>
> Note that if you have already set up another newsreader on your system, you may be able to use the information for that reader to configure Free Agent. Click Use information from another program to tell Free Agent what newsreader you have already configured. Free Agent can get information from Netscape, NewsXpress, Trumpet News, and WinVN.
>
> In addition to the basic configuration information, Free Agent can import the list of newsgroups you have read from these other programs.

After you have filled in the configuration information, click OK to continue. At this point, Free Agent goes online to your news server to retrieve a list of the newsgroups that are available. If you don't want Free Agent to do this now, click No to abort this step.

> **Note**
>
> If your news server carries lots of groups or is heavily loaded, downloading the list of newsgroups can take awhile. A server that carries all possible UseNet groups can have well over 10,000 groups available.

While Free Agent is downloading the list of available groups, it keeps a running status report of the number of groups it has downloaded in the status bar at the bottom of the screen. Once Free Agent has completed downloading the list of available groups, it allows you to begin subscribing to and reading newsgroups.

If you are installing the Agent newsreader, the program asks for a license key when it first starts up to enable the news program. Enter the license key given to you by Forté. (If you have received the key via e-mail, you can copy it to your Clipboard and press Ctrl+V to copy the license key from the Clipboard.) Once you have entered your license key, click OK to continue.

You are presented with the same configuration screen as in figure 32.1—except an additional option to select the spelling dictionary is added. Fill in the requested information as previously described.

After you have entered the initial configuration information, enter the main program where you have many additional configuration options. These program options are set from the Options menu where there are several different groups of options that can be set.

Setting Agent Preferences

The Preferences dialog box allows you to set the parameters that Agent uses when retrieving articles, posting articles, and interacting with the user. The first page allows you to set up your user profile information (see fig. 32.2).

Fig. 32.2

Information about the user is set on the User Profile page.

On this page you can set your E-Mail Address, Full Name, Organization, and Reply To address (if it is different from your regular e-mail address). These fields are used when you post new articles to groups or reply to a post via e-mail. In addition, if your news server requires you to supply a user name and password when you connect, this page allows you to enter this information.

The next page is the System Profile page, which includes exactly the same information you entered when you first started Agent. If you entered incorrect information at that time, re-enter your news server, e-mail server, and time-zone information here.

The third page is the Online Operation page that allows you to define how Agent interacts with the news server when it is connected to the server (see fig. 32.3). The two main types of operation are online and offline operation. You can select the defaults for these modes of operation by clicking the Use Offline Defaults or Use Online Defaults buttons. These buttons set up the common defaults for the two modes of operation.

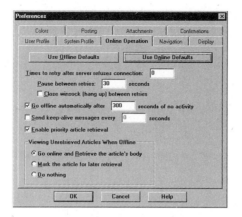

Fig. 32.3
Online and offline modes are set on this page.

If you pay by the hour for your Internet connection, you should probably pick the offline mode of operation. In this mode, when you ask Agent to retrieve new articles in your subscribed groups, it will open a connection to your news server, retrieve just the headers for the new articles in your selected groups, and then go offline immediately.

This allows you to look through the headers of the articles and select the articles you are interested in reading. Once you have picked the articles, you then ask Agent to retrieve the articles from the server. Agent again connects to your server, downloads the article bodies you want, and goes offline. You can then read the articles without being connected to your Internet provider (which can save you a significant amount of money).

On the other hand, if you don't pay by the hour for your Internet connection or you are directly connected to the Internet (at work or school, for example), you would probably pick the online mode of operation. In this mode, when you ask Agent to get the new articles in your subscribed groups, it connects to your server and gets the article headers. When you select an article to read, Agent immediately gets the article from your server and presents it to you.

The options that can be set on this page are as follows:

- *Times to Retry After Server Refuses Connection* controls how many times Agent will try to connect to your news server if the first connection fails.

- *Pause between Retries* controls how long Agent waits between connection attempts. The amount of time is specified in seconds.

- *Close Winsock (Hang Up) between retries* controls whether Agent hangs up your Internet connection between attempts to contact your news server. You probably don't want to check this unless you set up a significant delay between connection attempts.

- *Go Offline Automatically* allows you to let Agent close the connection to your news server after a period of inactivity. (Activity is defined as sending or retrieving something from the news server, not reading articles or headers on your local computer). The inactivity time is specified in seconds.

- *Send Keep-Alive Messages* controls whether (and how often) Agent sends a command to your news server to keep the connection active. This is used when dealing with Internet connections that automatically time out when no activity is detected for a period of time. Normally, unless your Internet service provider closes your connection after inactivity, you should not check this option because it needlessly increases your network traffic.

- *Enable Priority Article Retrieval* allows you to enable a feature of Agent where you can request that an article be retrieved from the server while Agent is busy downloading other article headers or bodies. Agent will, in this case, open a second connection to your news server to immediately try to get the requested article for you.

- The three options under *Viewing Unretrieved Articles When Offline* allow you to control what Agent does if you double-click an article that has not been retrieved when Agent is not connected to your news server. If you select *Go Online and Retrieve the Article's Body*, Agent does exactly that. If you select *Mark the Article for Later Retrieval*, Agent will not go online, but just mark that article for the next batch of retrievals. *Do Nothing*, tells Agent to ignore double-clicks to an article when offline.

The next page is the Navigation page (see fig. 32.4). This page allows you to enable or disable different options that control how Agent displays and navigates between articles. These options are self-explanatory, so the information on the page will not be duplicated here.

The Display page allows you to control how Agent displays articles (see fig. 32.5). The first options here let you pick whether the tool and status bars are displayed in the main window. The Articles settings let you control how many spaces are equivalent to a tab character and what characters are treated as quoting included material when they appear at the beginning of a line.

Fig. 32.4
The Navigation page controls how Agent displays articles.

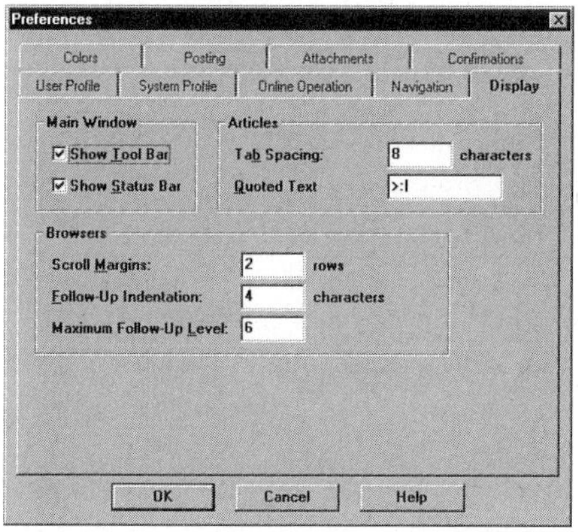

Fig. 32.5
Many article options are set on the Display page.

Tip

It is a usual practice when quoting UseNet articles to put a quote character (most usually a right angle bracket, >) at the beginning of each line of quoted material. Agent displays these quoted lines in a different color than the regular lines of an article.

The Browsers settings allow you to control how much each follow-up line is indented from the original article, the margins allowed when scrolling articles and the maximum number of levels of follow-up articles that will be displayed.

The Colors page allows you to set up the colors to be used when displaying different items (see fig. 32.6).

Fig. 32.6
Setting up the
colors Agent will
use.

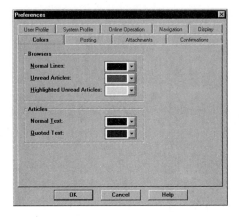

The Posting page sets up the different options used when posting new articles
(see fig. 32.7). The only really non-obvious options are the various "introduction" settings near the bottom of the page. These control what text will be
used at the beginning of follow-up articles, e-mail replies, and forwarded
e-mail messages. This introductory text helps people remember the article
you are referring to.

In the Agent newsreader, there are additional options that allow you to
specify introductory when replying to e-mail because Agent can receive as
well as send e-mail.

Fig. 32.7
The Posting page
controls how
Agent posts new
articles.

The Attachments page allows you to control how Agent handles binary file
attachments when posting articles (see fig. 32.8). The Message Partitioning
options control whether attachments are sent in one large message or if the
attachment is broken up into smaller chunks of a specified number of lines.

> **Tip**
>
> Some news servers have a limit on the size of articles they will accept. It is probably a good idea to limit the size of your articles to 900 lines or so.

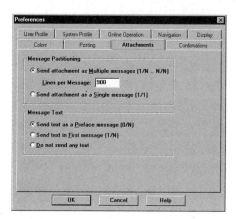

Fig. 32.8
Setting up options that control attachments.

The Message Text options control how the text of an article with an attachment is sent. Options are to send the article text as a separate message (before the attachment is posted), send the text in the same message as the attachment, or not to send text when sending an attachment.

The Confirmations page controls when Agent will ask you to confirm an action (see fig. 32.9). These are pretty much self-explanatory.

Fig. 32.9
Configuring when Agent asks for confirmation.

The Agent newsreader has an additional page (see fig. 32.10). The Spelling page allows you to set up the options that control the built-in spelling checker in Agent (Free Agent does not have the spelling checker option).

Fig. 32.10
The spelling checker is configured on the Spelling page.

Options to control the spelling checker include settings for the default language dictionary and whether the checker will always suggest a new spelling when a mistake is discovered. The spelling checker also has the capability to detect repeated words in an article.

The Agent spelling checker can also be set to ignore words in all uppercase (which are often acronyms), words in quotes, and words with numbers in them. These settings help to reduce the number of false spelling mistakes that are detected. Finally, you can include a custom dictionary that includes words you often use that are not in the regular dictionary.

Setting Up Signatures in Agent

One thing that you will soon notice when reading UseNet news articles is that people often include standard text at the bottom of their articles. This text is called a signature, and it usually includes information about the person posting the article (their e-mail address, for example) and sometimes a witty or amusing statement. These signatures should be brief (four lines is customary).

Using the Signatures dialog box (choose Options, Signatures), Agent allows you to define signatures that you can add to your postings. The Signatures dialog box, shown in figure 32.11, lets you set up any number of possible signatures and allows you to specify one of them as being the default signature. When you post an article, you are prompted for the signature to use; you might have one signature for posting to a serious, work-related group, and another for a more light-hearted group that you read for fun.

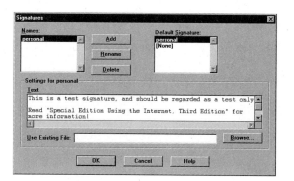

Fig. 32.11
Create your
signature with
this box.

Signature files are controlled from the Signatures dialog box. To add a new
signature, click the Add button and type in a name for the new signature
("personal" in the example). Then type in the text for the signature in the
Text box. If you have the text of your signature stored in a file, fill in the file
name in the Use Existing File box. Click OK to add the signature to the list of
available signatures. You can also select one of your signatures to be the default signature. If you have a default signature, it will be used automatically
whenever you post.

Setting Up Inbound E-Mail

The Agent newsreader (as opposed to the Free Agent version) can receive
e-mail as well as send it. You can configure the Agent newsreader to receive
e-mail by using the Inbound Email dialog box (choose Options, Inbound
Email).

When you first bring up the Inbound Email dialog box, Agent asks you to define the folder to be used to receive incoming e-mail messages. Setting up the
incoming e-mail folder is done on the New Folder dialog box (see fig. 32.12).
The default name for this incoming folder is Inbox. Type the name you want
to use for the incoming folder into the Folder Name box and click OK to create the folder.

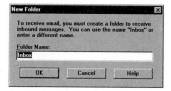

Fig. 32.12
You must create
the incoming
e-mail folder
before you can
receive mail.

You will note that the incoming mail folder shows up in your list of subscribed newsgroups.

V

UseNet Newsgroups

After the incoming mail folder is created, you can configure your e-mail options. The System Profile page of the Inbound Email dialog box, shown in figure 32.13, allows you to configure how to receive mail. Agent has two methods of receiving mail messages, POP and SMTP. With the POP (Post Office Protocol) method, Agent will periodically connect to your POP mail server and retrieve any waiting messages. With the SMTP method, Agent will start an SMTP server on your machine, which can receive incoming mail messages at any time.

Fig. 32.13

Your e-mail options are set on this page.

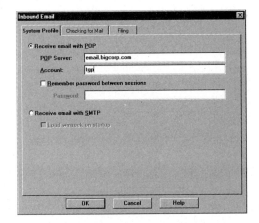

> ### Tip
>
> If you are paying by the hour for your Internet connect time, you should probably use the POP method to receive mail. Agent only has your Internet connection open long enough to receive your e-mail and then closes it, saving you connect time.

If you are using POP, Agent gives you the option to type in your POP account password (along with the POP server and account name information) and to remember the POP password so you don't have to type it in each time. If you are using SMTP, Agent allows you to specify whether your Winsock library is loaded when Agent starts up.

The Checking for Mail page, shown in figure 32.14, allows you to specify how often Agent will check for mail on your POP server (there are no options for this if you use SMTP because the SMTP server is always waiting for incoming mail). In addition, you can control whether your mail is deleted from the POP server when you read it and whether large messages should be automatically retrieved.

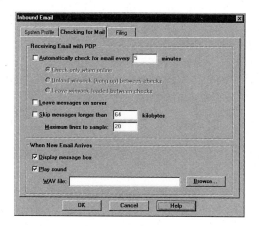

Fig. 32.14
Setting up your
mail retrieval
options.

In addition, you can set up options to display a message and/or play a sound when new mail arrives. You can specify a particular .WAV file for the sound played.

One advanced e-mail feature in Agent is set up with the Filing page. This page lets you to set up mail filters that allow you to automatically file a message into a folder if it meets certain criteria. For example, you could set up a filter to refile all messages from "Fred Rogers" into a folder called "neighbors." Mail filters are an advanced (and very powerful) option and won't be further described here.

Setting Up Your Fonts

The Fonts dialog box (choose Options, Fonts) allow you to set up the fonts that will be used to display groups, folders, and messages (the Browser font). Also, fonts used in message subjects and fixed and variable text in message bodies can also be set.

Setting Up Your Window Layout

One of the nicest features of the Agent newsreaders is the ability to change the window layout to suit your needs. By default, the layout has two small windows on the top half of the main display, and a large window on the bottom half. The top left window displays the groups available, the top right window shows the articles that are available, and the bottom window displays messages in the group.

While this layout is OK for many readers, some will want to change it. For example, I prefer to have a narrower (but longer) window for the message text because many articles are long but not wide. Agent allows you to configure your window layout by choosing Options, Window Layout. This brings up the Window Layout dialog box shown in figure 32.15.

Fig. 32.15
Configuring the way Agent displays your windows.

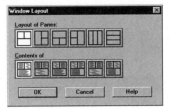

The Window Layout dialog box allows you to configure the layout of the different display windows as well as the contents of those windows. The Layout of Panes option lets you pick the different styles for the three panes. For example, you can have the large window on the left of the screen and the two smaller windows on the right.

In addition, the Contents Of option lets you decide what is displayed in each pane. In this option, the box with the red text in it represents the pane that will display the list of available messages. The box with the black text is for the pane that displays the list of available newsgroups. The box with the blue text represents the pane where the body of the article or message is displayed. By selecting one of these layouts, you can put the information you want where you want it.

Also, once you have picked a general window layout, you can change the size of each of the panes by dragging one of the borders between the panes to the desired size. Using these controls, you can make the screen look exactly the way you like.

After you have decided on a window layout, you can save this configuration as the default by selecting the Save as Default Window Layout item on the Options menu.

Setting Group Options

In addition to the preferences that control Agent's behavior in general, there are options that you can set for each UseNet group. These options control:

- When to mark messages as being read
- What messages are eligible to be removed from the local disk
- When to remove articles from the local disk

- When to retrieve articles from the news server
- What fields to include when posting articles
- Where to store binary attachments to postings when they are extracted

You can set these options for all groups and also override these settings for individual groups. These options are set through the De_f_ault Properties and _P_roperties choices found under the _G_roup menu.

Subscribing to and Unsubscribing from Newsgroups

When you first started Agent, the program retrieved a list of the available newsgroups from your news server. This list of all available groups can be displayed by choosing _G_roup, S_h_ow, _A_ll Groups and Folders.

> **Tip**
>
> To get the list of available newsgroups from the server at any time, select _R_efresh Group List from the _O_nline menu. To update your list of groups by getting just the newsgroups that have been recently created, select Get New _G_roups from the _O_nline menu. You can then display just these newly created groups by choosing _G_roup, S_h_ow, _N_ew Groups.

To subscribe to a newsgroup, select the group name and click the subscribe button (or press Ctrl+S). This marks the group as being subscribed. You can display just the groups you are subscribed to by choosing _G_roup, S_h_ow, _S_ubscribed Groups and Folders.

> **Tip**
>
> Because some news servers carry thousands of groups, you can use the Find and Find Next buttons to search for a group name that contains a text string.

If you aren't sure what a group is about, you can sample some articles from the group before you subscribe to it. Double-click the group name in the list of available groups and Agent will ask you what you want to do, whether to sample a few article headers from the group (50 article headers is the default), get all article headers for the group, or subscribe to the group. Before you subscribe, you might want to get the sample headers and see what topics are being discussed.

To unsubscribe from a newsgroup, click the group name in the list of groups, and click the Unsubscribe button on the tool bar (or Ctrl+S). The group will be removed from the list of subscribed groups.

Reading Articles in Newsgroups

Once you have selected the groups that you are interested in, you can begin the actual process of receiving news articles for these groups. There are several ways to retrieve the article headers for your subscribed groups:

- Click the Get Headers in Subscribed Groups button, or select Get New Headers in Subscribed Groups under the Online menu. This retrieves all the headers in all of your subscribed groups.

- Select a group (or multiple groups) and click the Get Headers in Selected Group button, or select Get New Headers in Selected Groups under the Online menu. This retrieves all the new headers only in the group you selected.

- Select a group (or multiple groups), and select Get All Headers in Selected Groups under the Online menu. This retrieves all headers (including articles that you have already read or purged from your local disk) for the selected groups.

- Select a group (or multiple groups), and select Sample 50 Headers from Selected Groups from the Online menu. This retrieves the article headers from the 50 most recently posted articles in the selected groups.

No matter how you retrieve the article headers, you will be presented with the screen as shown in figure 32.16. If you are working in offline mode (that is, you have configured Agent to read the article headers only and wait for you to select which articles you want to read), you will be presented with the headers for the articles. The first article in the newsgroup has not been retrieved yet, so Agent tells you that you can press Enter to retrieve the article now, or type **M** to mark the article for later retrieval.

When you mark an article for retrieval, the download icon is shown next to the article (see fig. 32.17). Also, when an article has been retrieved from the server, there is a text page icon next to the article.

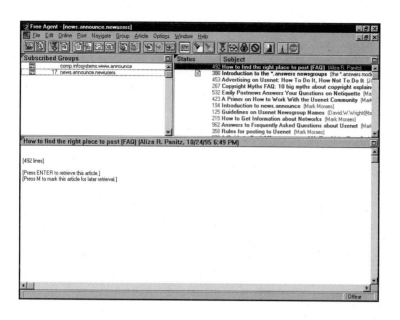

Fig. 32.16
Selecting articles for retrieval.

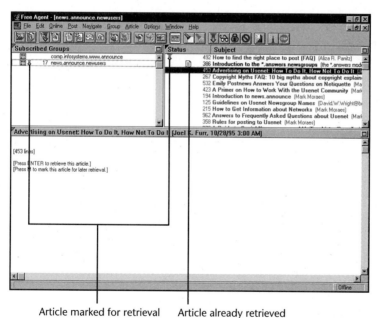

Fig. 32.17
Articles marked for retrieval or already retrieved are marked with special icons.

Article marked for retrieval   Article already retrieved

To actually retrieve the article bodies, select Get Marked Article Bodies from the Online menu. You can also select articles with the mouse and select Get Selected Article Bodies from the Online menu without having to go through the steps of marking the articles individually.

Once you have retrieved the articles that are interesting to you, you can begin the process of reading the articles. There are several ways of moving between articles:

- Double-clicking the article header displays that article's body.

- Selecting an article and pressing Enter displays that article.

- Clicking the Next Article button moves to the next retrieved article in the group.

- Using the arrow keys on your keyboard moves between articles and displays them.

- Typing **N** moves to the next article in the group and displays it.

There are also several features that deal with all the articles in the group you are currently reading:

- Click the Skip to Next Unread Group button or select Skip to Next Unread Group from the Navigate menu to mark all the articles in this group as being read and move to the next group that contains unread articles. You can also type **S** to perform this function.

- Mark the current article as being read (or unread) or all the articles in the current group as being read (or unread) by using the appropriate items under the Article menu.

- Delete the current article or just the article body by selecting the Delete article or Delete article body items under the Article menu.

In Agent and Free Agent there are usually several ways to do common tasks; you can click one of the toolbar buttons, use one of the regular menu commands, or type a keyboard shortcut if you prefer to use the keyboard.

Following Article Threads

When you read a newsgroup that has many different people posting articles about a common subject, using a newsreader that allows you to automatically follow these article *threads* (articles that share a common subject) can make it much easier to read the group. Being able to follow article threads allows you to ignore conversations that do not interest you and to keep track of who has said what in a thread.

When you retrieve the article headers for a group, Agent displays the headers in the group window. As shown in figure 32.18, Agent displays the articles that are responses to an article by indenting these headers below the original article.

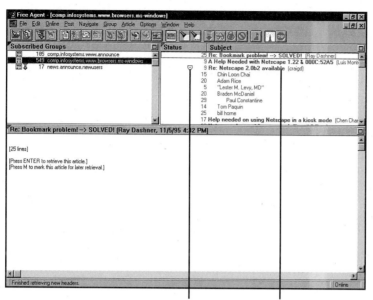

Fig. 32.18
The article
headers, showing
an article thread.

Open/closed icon   Original article header

You also see an open/closed indicator to the left of the header for the original article, indicating that the thread is being displayed either expanded or collapsed. When the thread is displayed expanded, all the articles in the thread are shown. On the other hand, if you display the thread collapsed, only the first header in the thread is displayed, with an indication of how many articles are in the thread. Switching between expanded and collapsed mode is done by clicking the open/closed icon.

Displaying article threads in collapsed mode allows you to see more article headers in a group. This is especially important in groups where there are only a few threads active at a time; you can easily ignore or read the threads you are interested in.

There are several Agent commands specifically used to read articles in threads. These commands are:

- Click View Next Article in Thread or Skip to Next Article in Thread moves to the next article in the thread. If you are at the end of the thread, it moves to the next article in the group.

- Use the analogous commands under the Navigate menu to move to the next article in the thread.

- Ctrl+T views the next article in the thread.

- The T command skips to the next article in the thread.

Agent also has several commands to either ignore or automatically retrieve an article thread. You can use the Ignore Thread button to prevent Agent from retrieving or displaying any articles in the current thread. On a busy newsgroup, this command can significantly reduce the amount of time you spend reading the group. You can also use the Ignore thread item under the Article menu or the I command.

You can also use the Watch Thread button to direct Agent to always retrieve articles in the thread. The Watch Thread item under the Article menu also does this, or you can use the W command from the keyboard.

Posting Articles

Agent allows you to post new articles to newsgroups and to post follow-up articles to articles that you read. You can post a new article to a group by clicking the Post New Article button, selecting New Article from the Post menu, or using the P keyboard command. Posting a new article brings up the window shown in figure 32.19.

Fig. 32.19
Posting a new article.

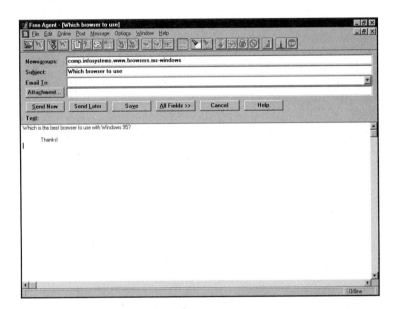

When you post a new article, you should fill in the subject and the text of the article, as well as an optional list of e-mail addresses you want to send copies of the article to.

When you have filled in the fields, select the options to send the article. You can send the article immediately by using the Send Now button, later, or save the article into a file. If you choose to send the article later, you can use the Post Articles and Emails item from the Online menu to actually send the article. This is useful if you want to save up several posts or e-mail messages and send them all at once.

To post a follow-up article to the article you are reading, click the Post Follow-Up Article button, select the Follow Up Article item from the Post menu, or use the F keyboard command (type the letter **F**).

Posting a follow-up article fills in the subject of the article for you and inserts a copy of the article you were reading. The inserted article is quoted and inserted at the beginning of each line.

> **Tip**
>
> When you are quoting an article, cut out any unnecessary text from the quoted article, leaving only the text necessary to provide context to your reply.

Extracting Files from Articles

Some articles posted to UseNet groups actually contain binary information that is encoded to allow it to pass through the UseNet news systems. This information is usually encoded in either UNIX UUEncode form or the MIME Internet standard. Agent allows you to automatically decode these binary files.

To decode the information in encoded articles, select the article (or multiple articles if the binary attachment is split across articles) and select one of the following options:

- Click the Launch Binary Attachment button (or select Launch Binary Attachments from the File menu). This decodes the attachment in the articles and automatically starts the viewer for the attachment. Agent uses the Windows 95 file associations to determine which viewer to launch to display the attachment.

- Select Save Binary Attachment from the File menu to decode the attachment from the articles and save it into a file on your disk.

- Select Delete Binary Attachment from the File menu to delete the attachment from the articles on your disk.

When you attempt to decode a multi-part binary attachment, Agent searches the subject lines of the articles to put the articles in the correct order to decode them properly. If an article in the sequence is missing, the article will not decode properly.

Managing E-Mail

As with most newsreaders, Agent and Free Agent have the ability to send e-mail messages, both in response to an article or a new message. In addition, the Agent newsreader can receive e-mail messages and has facilities to manage these messages.

When you set up the e-mail facilities in Agent (as described in the earlier "Starting and Configuring Agent" section), you specified the default folder for receiving new mail. This folder was created and appears in your list of subscribed groups. You can also view your mail folders by selecting Show, Folders under the Group menu.

Sending New E-Mail Messages

You can send a new e-mail message by clicking the Post New Email Message button (or by selecting New Email Message from the Post menu). This brings up the window shown in figure 32.20. On this screen, fill in the e-mail addresses to send the message to, the subject of the message, and the text body of the message.

Fig. 32.20

Sending a new e-mail message with the Agent newsreader.

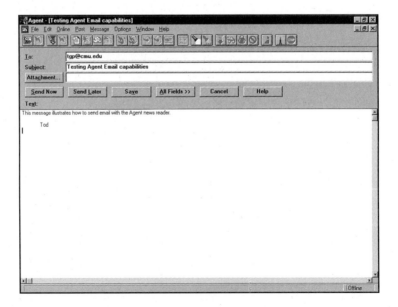

You have the option to attach a file to the message (by clicking the Attach-ment button), and to send the message now, later, or to save the message in a file on your disk.

To reply to an existing e-mail message, click the Post Reply via Email button (or select Reply via Email from the Post menu). This brings up the window to send the e-mail message but presets the subject of the message and includes the text of the message you are replying to.

You also have the option to forward an e-mail message to other people; select Forward via Email from the Post menu. This is similar to the Reply via Email option because it includes the text of the e-mail you are forwarding but the introductory text at the top of the message is slightly different.

Reading E-Mail Messages

The Agent newsreader has the ability to receive new e-mail messages (the Free Agent newsreader does not have this feature). While you might not want to use Agent as your primary e-mail reader, it is quite serviceable as a home mail reader (or if you do not receive much e-mail).

Depending on how you configured your e-mail options, you will receive e-mail into your Inbox folder at different times when Agent is running. If you configured your Agent reader to use the SMTP mode for receiving e-mail, Agent can receive new e-mail messages any time that the reader is in Online mode. If you are using the POP method of receiving e-mail, Agent will check for new e-mail on your POP server periodically.

In either case, when you have received new e-mail, Agent will display a dialog box letting you know that new e-mail has arrived (see fig. 32.21). You can configure Agent to display this box, play a sound, or both when new mail shows up. Close the box by clicking OK.

Fig. 32.21
You are notified that new e-mail has arrived with this dialog box.

You can read your e-mail messages by clicking the Inbox folder, which dis-plays the mail reading screen as shown in figure 32.22. This screen is very similar to the display used when reading news articles and uses the same win-dow layout as the news display.

Fig. 32.22

Reading e-mail messages with Agent.

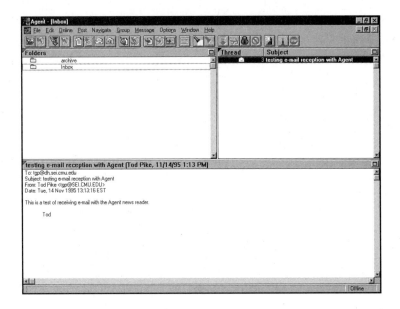

Selecting an e-mail message and typing Enter (or double-clicking the message) displays the e-mail message. In a manner similar to reading news articles, buttons are available for skipping to the next message and skipping to the next message in a thread. The same options for collapsing and expanding threads of e-mail messages also exist in reading e-mail, giving you a lot of flexibility in dealing with your e-mail.

Agent also gives you the ability to copy or move your e-mail messages between folders. You can create a new folder by selecting New Folder from the Group menu. (You can rename a folder by selecting the folder and selecting Rename Folder from the Group menu.) To move a message to a folder, select the message header in the header window and drag the message header to the folder you want the message in.

> **Tip**
>
> By default, Agent moves the message to the folder when you drag the message. You can copy the message to a folder by holding down the Ctrl key on your keyboard while dragging the message.

You can also copy or move messages between folders by selecting either Copy to Folder or Move to Folder from the Message menu. These menu selections bring up a list of available folders; select a folder and click OK to move (or copy) the message.

For people who receive a lot of e-mail, or for those who want to automatically organize their mail, Agent offers e-mail filters. These filters allow you to select incoming mail messages according to information in the mail headers (the subject of the message, for example) and automatically file the message into a folder.

For example, if you subscribe to an Internet mailing list on horses, you might file all messages coming from this mailing list into a folder called HORSES. This allows you to separate incoming mail into different interests and lets you read important messages faster.

Agent's e-mail filters are maintained through the Filing tab on the Inbound Email dialog box, shown in figure 32.23.

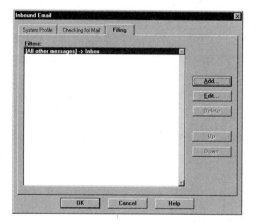

Fig. 32.23
Configuring e-mail filters.

You can add a new filter by clicking the Add button, which brings up the screen shown in figure 32.24. This screen lets you select the field you are using to control the filter (the from field in this example), the text to search for (horse-list in our example) and the folder to file the message into.

Once you have added a filter, it will function automatically until you remove it. You can edit the filter at any time by selecting the filter and clicking the Edit button in the Filing page of the Inbound Email dialog box.

Fig. 32.24
Adding a new
e-mail filter.

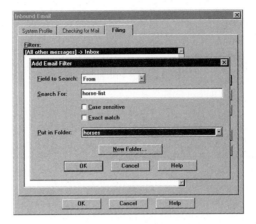

Tip

Since filters are executed from the top of the list down, be careful how your filters are organized. You might, for example, have a filter to file all messages from John Smith into a folder called SMITH. You may have a filter to file all messages with a subject of eating into a folder called FOOD. If John Smith sends a message with a subject of eating, it may be filed into either the SMITH or FOOD folder, depending on which is higher on the list. You can change the order of filter execution by clicking the Up or Down buttons.

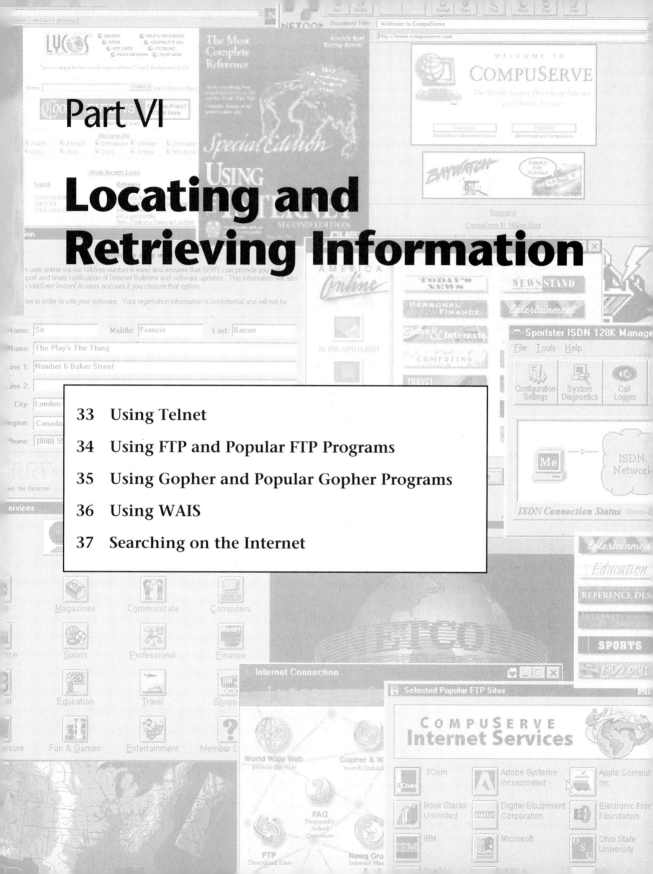

Part VI

Locating and Retrieving Information

33   Using Telnet

34   Using FTP and Popular FTP Programs

35   Using Gopher and Popular Gopher Programs

36   Using WAIS

37   Searching on the Internet

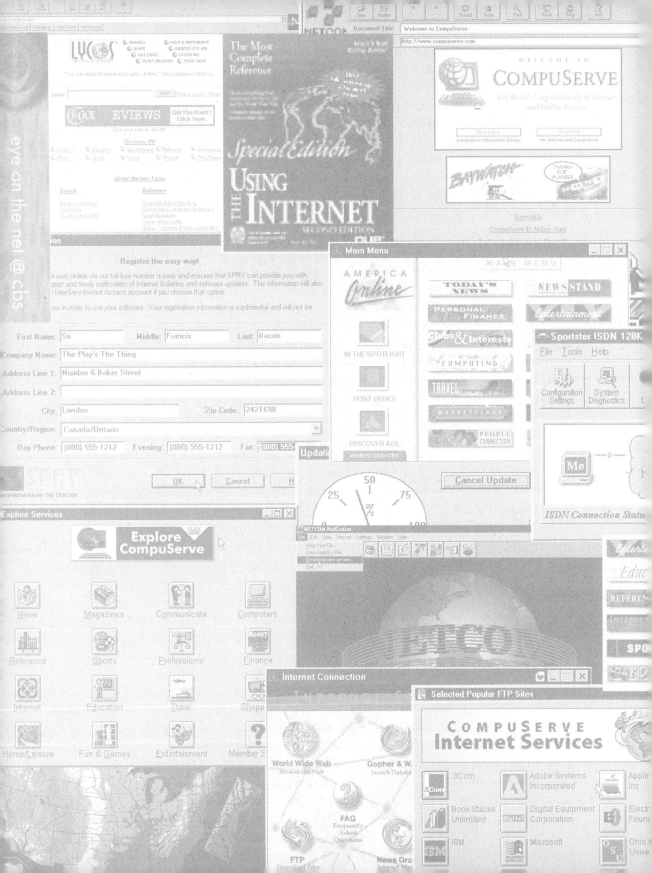

CHAPTER 33

Using Telnet

Now you've got your connection to the Internet up and running. In chapter 14, "How Internet E-Mail Works," you learned about e-mail and you may have already used the Net to send messages quickly and simply anywhere in the world. Hopefully, you also have had a chance to peek around in a couple of newsgroups on UseNet. By now, you should be getting a feel for the amount of power and potential that's available on the Internet.

Now it's time to broaden your horizons. I hope you've got your bags packed, because we're taking this show on the road!

In this chapter, you learn the following:

- How to use Telnet to connect to your account on a remote computer
- How to run Telnet on a command-line account
- Ways to get, set up, and use Windows-based Telnet programs

What Is Telnet?

Telnet is a program that lets you log in to a remote computer directly through the Internet. Telnet takes advantage of the way computers are linked on the Net by passing your commands from the computer where you're located, onto another computer, which sends it to a third computer, and so on until it reaches the computer you want to access. If you have a direct network connection to the Internet, using Telnet can save you the cost of long-distance bills and also won't tie up phone lines. Even if you have to use a dial-up SLIP or PPP connection to the Internet, telnetting still saves you the long-distance phone call, if your SLIP/PPP number is a local call.

Technically, Telnet is a *protocol*. A protocol is a set of instructions that is used by computers to explain how they'll share information. The proper noun,

◀ See "Connect-
ing to Host
Resources
Using Telnet,"
p. 34

Telnet, is usually meant to describe an application that uses the Telnet protocol. The gerund, telnetting, is used to describe using an application that uses
the protocol, to connect to a remote computer system, as in, "I telnetted to
the MUD."

Protocols work something like this: Let's say you agree to buy a book from
a friend in France for 10,000. The value 10,000, while a definite number,
means different things depending on whether we're talking about Francs,
Dollars, Marks, Pounds, or Lire. When you and your friend agree to negotiate
a price in a specific type of currency, you suddenly have a frame of reference
from which you can determine value. When two computers agree that they'll
share information using a specific protocol, the packages of information that
they share with each other suddenly make sense.

You may have heard of protocols if you've ever uploaded or downloaded a
file. When uploading or downloading a file, the computer you are connected
to will usually give you a list of options for transferring the file that includes
names like Xmodem, Zmodem, or Kermit. Xmodem, Zmodem, and Kermit
are also protocols—they're sets of standards that tell the receiving computer how the sending computer will be packaging the information that it's
sending.

◀ See "A Brief
Introduction to
TCP/IP," p. 126

The Telnet protocol does the same sort of thing as an upload or download
protocol, only it's telling the remote computer how to transfer commands
from the local computer, on which you're working, to another computer in a
remote location. This makes it possible for a user in New York to work on a
computer in San Francisco (or Berlin, or Alice Springs, or wherever).

Why Use Telnet?

Let's say you're on a business trip and you'd like to be able to get in touch
with your Internet account to pick up your e-mail and read up on the latest
UseNet news. Or perhaps you were just talking to friends who said they have
programs set up on their computers that perform the type of analysis that
your company needs.

In either case, you could use a modem to dial in to the remote system and do
what you need to do. Depending on where you're located, where the other
computer is located, and how long you need to be connected, you could tie
up a lot of long-distance time.

Fortunately, you can take advantage of the unique linking of computers
through the Internet, which enables you to connect to a remote computer

much easier and cheaper than dialing direct. And it's surprisingly easy to use, considering it's a tool that can interact with so many different types of machines to do so many things.

The Telnet protocol is usually contained within a small piece of software that is used while accessing the Internet. Because the Telnet protocol is a standard that is used almost universally throughout the Internet, the mechanics of running Telnet are pretty much the same practically everywhere, regardless of how it's packaged.

Some Quick Background Information

Many people aren't familiar with some of the terminology related to the big computers that comprise quite a bit of the Internet. Some knowledge about how these computers work can help you understand how the Telnet program works, and can help explain some of the choices that various Telnet programs offer you.

What's a VT100? Or an ANSI? Or a TTY?

Once upon a time, most of the automated computing in the world was done on big machines each of which had a huge central processing unit—often big enough to fill up a whole room. These machines could be used by lots of people, but they couldn't always fit in the same room as the computer (and you probably wouldn't want them all there, anyway).

Users accessed these machines through individual workstations called *terminals*. Terminals are basically keyboards and screens used for entering data. Unlike a PC, a terminal has no processor of its own. It has to be connected to a main computer in order to work.

Manufacturers made terminals fairly standard so they could be used in connection with a variety of computer types. Digital Equipment Corporation (otherwise known as Digital or DEC) manufactured a line of terminals that were fairly common for use with larger computers called the VT series. The VT100 and the VT102 (a slight variation) were probably the most common types of terminal, though you may have also heard of other variations, such as the VT52 or the VT220. (Generally, the higher the number a VT series terminal had, the more sophisticated it was.)

When "regular folks" (not just government scientists or computer science majors) first started using the Internet, most of the big computers on the Net were set up to send and receive information through terminals like the then common VT100. If you wanted to contact one of the big computers through your PC, you needed a program that would "dumb-down" your PC, making it act like a terminal and enabling you to enter and retrieve data from the big machines. Programs like the HyperTerminal program included with Windows 95 are intended to make a PC look like or *emulate* these earlier terminals. For example, HyperTerminal can auto-detect and emulate the VT52 and VT100 terminals, in addition to TTY and ANSI. However, HyperTerminal isn't designed to connect via the Internet; its primary purpose is to connect to systems via an asynchronous serial connection, using a modem, or null-modem cable. Windows 95 comes with a basic Telnet program for use with a Winsock Internet connection. We'll take a close look at it later in the chapter.

Remember, while a PC is hooked up to a remote computer, it acts much like those earlier terminals. The PC is basically being used to display information while the computing actually takes place at a remote machine.

> **Tip**
>
> If you have a choice, choose VT100 or TTY (unless the folks at the computer to which you're trying to connect have specifically told you to use another type of terminal). VT100 is probably the most common terminal type and TTY is probably the most basic.

Simply put, ANSI and TTY are other standards for entering data and displaying information. Computers that support ANSI terminals can usually display some text in color. TTY is an extremely plain **tele*type*** style terminal, which probably depends entirely on the remote computer for how the information is displayed on-screen. (A teletype is one of those machines you'd see in newsrooms in old movies that is basically an automated typewriter that types out input from an external source; a TTY terminal is simply an electronic version of the classic news teletype.)

What to Expect When You Connect

If you're used to using a command-line account, you're probably already accustomed to dealing with the Internet through a text-based environment. Telnet doesn't provide a lot of flash; after all, a program has to keep things somewhat simple in order to allow any two random computers to work with each other, despite obvious differences in hardware and software. Telnet will only provide you with command-line access to remote machines.

You may want to go back and read some of the earlier information on interacting with the Internet through a command-line account. Regardless of the service that you access through Telnet (be it an individual account, an automatic BBS on a remote machine, an interactive role-playing game, or a weather server) you will need to follow the same general procedures that are used for accessing a command-line account.

If you're completely unfamiliar with executing commands through a command-line prompt (and are not particularly willing to give it a try), consider using a World Wide Web browser (such as Microsoft Internet Explorer, Mosaic, or Netscape) instead. World Wide Web browsers don't provide you with the same ability to send direct commands to the remote computer that Telnet does, but a browser provides the graphical interface to which you've become accustomed. Even though browsers do connect to a "remote host" (the Web server), it's not designed for direct command-line user input the way a Telnet host is.

◀ See "How the World Wide Web Works," p. 457

◀ See "Using Microsoft Internet Explorer," p. 473

◀ See "Using Netscape," p. 497

◀ See "Using Mosaic," p. 539

A Brief Word about Addresses

In order to run Telnet, you need to know the address of the computer that you want to reach. The important information is the *host name* of the computer. Telnet uses this host name to contact the remote computer, much like you use telephone numbers to call your friends.

Some corporate network systems may require you to use a *proxy* server to telnet through the local area network security firewall (a *firewall* is the network component that keeps intruders outside your network from getting in). A proxy Telnet server lets you telnet to it, and then it handles the actual transaction to the outside Internet. See your system administrator for specific information if you need to know more about your system's security procedures.

Figuring Out a Host Name from an E-Mail Address

In chapter 14, "How Internet E-Mail Works," you learned about addresses for e-mail on the Internet. An e-mail address might look something like the following:

```
bk@access.digex.net
```

bk is the user you want to contact, who is located at access.digex.net.

The phrase access.digex.net points to a specific computer, and is called a *host name*. In order to use Telnet, you must know the host name of the computer that you want to telnet to. If someone wants you to be able to telnet to his or her system, they'll give you their computer's address in the form of a host name.

VI

Locating and Retrieving

> **Note**
>
> You will come across host names for specific computers in a lot of places as you're surfing the Net. If you use a Gopher server (described later in chapter 35, "Using Gopher and Popular Gopher Programs") to connect to remote locations, the Gopher will often give you a message stating the name of the host that it's trying to reach. You may want to write this address down, so that you can telnet directly to that site instead of having to cut through the Gopher to get there.

If, for some reason, you need to guess what a particular computer's host name is, you can often get it by looking at the e-mail address of someone who works on that system. From the previous example, you could guess that **access.digex.net** is the remote computer's host name.

But it's not always that simple to determine the e-mail address. If Mary Beth works on her computer at Loyola College, her e-mail address might appear to me as **Mary_Beth@grey.loyola.edu**. It might also appear as **Mary_Beth@green.loyola.edu**. But if you tried to telnet either **green.loyola.edu** or **grey.loyola.edu**, you would probably get an unknown host error message from your computer.

So what does that mean?

Most likely, the distinction between the green node and the gray node is local. This is important at Loyola, where they've got to direct the mail and generally handle a bunch of users. The Internet doesn't have to worry about such a fine distinction—it just needs to connect to **loyola.edu** and the local computers handle it from there.

So if you need to guess a node name from an address and the full address doesn't work, try lopping off the first word to the right of the @ symbol, and try again. (In other words, **mary_beth@grey.loyola.edu** would yield a host name of **loyola.edu**.) If that doesn't work, call or e-mail the other person and ask her to give you the Telnet address.

Names and Numbers that Mean the Same Thing

In addition to its host name, each computer has a numerical name that means the same thing as its host name. Let's use a fictitious example, say a computer whose host name is **hal.jupiter.net** with a numerical address of 11.16.19.94 (you'll recognize this set of numbers as an IP address).

When you're using Telnet and you have to enter a computer's address, you can either use its host name (**hal.jupiter.net**) or its numerical address (11.16.19.94). Sometimes, however, it's helpful to know the number address, even though it may not be quite as easy to remember as its host name.

> **Tip**
>
> Some people think words are easier to remember than numbers (but they're sometimes harder to spell). The Net identifies computers by numbers, so try the numerical address if the host name doesn't work.

Think of it this way: If your name is Mary Elizabeth Jones, you may be called Mary, Mary Beth, Mary Elizabeth, MEJ, or any other combination of things. Regardless of your name style, your Social Security number remains constant.

Likewise, computer operators sometimes change the names of the machines they operate. If a business adds computers or a school reconfigures its system, the system operators may alter names. Generally, the computer retains its numerical name, even though the host name has changed. Knowing the numerical name, therefore, makes it easier to find the computer that you're trying to reach.

> **Note**
>
> Sometimes you can reach a computer through its numerical address when you can't reach it through its host name. There are Name Server computers throughout the Internet that turn the host names into their numerical equivalents. Occasionally a Name Server crashes and it becomes difficult—if not impossible—to telnet another computer by using its host name. If, however, you know the numerical address, you don't need the service that the Name Server provides; instead, you can dial direct.

Running the Telnet Program from a Command-Line Account

> **Note**
>
> Experienced users often refer to connecting to a remote computer as telnetting. For example, "I telnetted to my account back at my college to pick up my e-mail."

Let's use another fictitious example. Say you're in California and you would like to reach your account at your local service provider in Washington, D.C., at **hal.jupiter.net**. For now, let's assume that you're borrowing a few minutes on a friend's command-line account in California to access your computer in Washington. Regardless of whether you're using a command-line account or a TCP/IP connection, the basics of telnetting a remote site are roughly the same.

Connecting to a Remote Computer Using Telnet

If you're connecting to the Internet through a command-line account, you're basically dialing in to another computer that holds all of the programs you need in order to access the Internet. One of these programs is Telnet.

Let's say you want to run the Telnet program and connect to your account at **hal.jupiter.net**. To do this, use the following steps:

1. Log in to the local account.

2. After you've logged in and gotten the command-line prompt, type **telnet hal.jupiter.net**. (Please remember this is only an example address, this system really doesn't exist!)

   The next steps are the same as if you were dialing directly into the service provider that gives you your command-line account.

3. Once Telnet has connected to the remote computer, the Username: prompt appears.

4. Enter your username.

5. After you have entered your username, the remote computer sends a prompt for your password.

6. Type your password.

7. You should now be logged in to your remote account.

Once you type the password, you're logged in to your account and you can use it whether you're at a terminal plugged in to the machine itself or logged on through a friend's account on the other side of the country. Telnet disappears, settling in to the background where it handles processing your commands to the remote computer. Telnet will automatically close when you log out of the remote account.

Note

Telnet is almost completely transparent. That means that once it's running, it disappears and you don't even know that it's there.

It's important to remember that when you log in to another computer through Telnet, you're connecting through several other computers. Sometimes, if there's a lot of activity on the Net, the connection may seem sluggish or it may take a while for the remote computer to respond to your commands.

For those accustomed to using Windows, it may seem like their system has locked up. This phenomenon is generally referred to as *netlag*. It can sometimes be annoying, but it doesn't necessarily mean that there's something wrong with your system.

Troubleshooting

When I try to use Telnet, I get a Trying... *message, but nothing else happens. What's wrong?*

If the remote computer that you're trying to call is extremely busy or is down for some reason, Telnet still tries to put you through. The Trying... message stays on-screen, but you won't get connected. In this case, you should probably break out of the connection by pressing Ctrl+], which interrupts Telnet and gives you the following prompt:

```
telnet>
```

At this prompt, you can either type a new address that you want to telnet, or you can type **quit** or **q** to go back to your original connection.

If you have tried to telnet a nonexistent system (or if you just used the wrong name), Telnet responds with a message that says unknown host. If you get this message, double-check the name of the system that you're trying to reach and then try again.

A Second Way of Starting Telnet from a Command-Line Account

Many of the Internet access providers are actually providing what's called a shell account on a computer that is running the UNIX operating system. If you are telnetting from a computer that's running UNIX, there are several commands you can use to increase the utility of the very simple Telnet program.

Generally, you start Telnet by entering **Telnet** and then the address of a particular computer. In the earlier fictitious example, telnet **hal.jupiter.net** was entered. This line turns on Telnet and tells it where to connect. Telnet takes it from there.

There is a second way of starting Telnet from a UNIX-based system.

1. At the command prompt, type **telnet**. This prompts the following command line from the Telnet program:

   ```
   telnet>
   ```

2. At the Telnet prompt, type **open** *Hostname*, where *Hostname* is the address of a specific computer. For example, if I wanted to connect to **hal.jupiter.net**, I would type **open hal.jupiter.net** (some systems may use "connect" instead of "open").

3. When prompted, give your username and password. You should now be connected to the remote computer.

This second method is equivalent to typing telnet hostname, and, frankly, I think it's easier to just type the whole thing as one command. Nevertheless, it's helpful to know about the Telnet prompt because there are a few more commands that can be useful, particularly if you're trying to do a bunch of things at the same time.

Using UNIX to Do Two (or More) Things at Once

Say that you and your friend Juan are working together on a project, and he has written you a note asking you to take some information you've gathered and run it through a program on his account. Telnet makes this easy by letting you directly log on to his account.

Since you know Juan's e-mail address is **juanm@hal.jupiter.net**, you can guess that the address of the computer to which you're trying to connect is the part of the address to the right of the @, or **hal.jupiter.net**.

Tip

Remember, for purposes of telnetting, the host name of a computer may include more or less information than the host name on the right side of an e-mail address. Use the e-mail host name only in situations in which you need to guess the host name.

To access Juan's account, you would follow these steps:

1. Type **telnet hal.jupiter.net**. (Again, this is a fictitious example, this system doesn't really exist.)

2. When your computer connects to the remote computer, enter Juan's username and password when prompted.

Let's say that when you tried to do this, you forgot the password that you needed in order to access the account. Fortunately, you knew it was in an e-mail message that Juan had sent to you earlier in the day. If, for some reason, you didn't want to log off Clarknet and try to connect again after getting the password, you could use a few UNIX tricks to keep you logged on the remote computer while you open up your e-mail and get the necessary password. You can keep your Telnet session running, open your mail program (or other application), and return to Telnet by following these steps:

1. Press Ctrl+]. This will bring up the Telnet prompt.

2. Type **z**. This puts Telnet in the background.

3. You should now see a command-line prompt. Enter your mail program (or other application) and get the information that you need.

4. When you're ready to return to Telnet, type **fg**. This brings Telnet back to the foreground.

Using this routine can be helpful if you need to get information from a mail message, check the name of a file, or otherwise use your local host computer to perform some function while logged on to a remote site.

Closing a Connection to a Remote Computer

If you're running Telnet from a command-line account, Telnet usually shuts itself off when you log off of the remote computer.

You may reach a point where the netlag is positively unbearable because another computer bogs down or, for some reason, you need to shut down your Telnet connection to another computer. To shut down, follow these steps:

1. Press Ctrl+] to display the Telnet command-line prompt.

2. Type **close**, which shuts off your remote connection and turns off Telnet.

Running Out of Time

When you log on to a remote computer, that computer often keeps track of how active you are on the system. Telnetting a computer ties up part of its ability to serve other users, and system operators want to ensure their machines are as accessible as possible. Therefore, if you log on to a remote computer and are inactive (not typing anything) for about 15 minutes, the remote computer may log you off. If you send a Telnet connection into the background and forget about it, or if you fail to get back to it in time, the remote computer might log you off and you will have to log on again.

Connecting to a Telnet Address with a Port

You may see an occasional Telnet address that lists a "port," such as **hal.jupiter.net** port 2001. Telnetting a particular port enables you to log onto a remote system for a particular purpose, such as a multiuser game or retrieving weather information.

The whole concept of ports goes all the way back to those days when computing was generally done from a large central machine. If you remember the information about terminals from earlier in this chapter, terminals were plugged into ports (actual sockets on the back or side of the machine) on the big machines to serve as input/output devices. On the back of your PC, you

VI

Locating and Retrieving

probably have a printer port and a serial port, as well as ports for your keyboard and your mouse (and maybe a few others).

Just like your keyboard port is specially designed to get information from a keyboard (or a mouse port from a mouse or mouse-like device), ports on Internet Hosts are set up to do specific functions. Multiuser games (like MUDs, MUSHes, DikuMUDs, and the like) are usually found on port 4201. World Wide Web Servers are normally found on port 80. Telnet access is also provided through a specific port (23), which the Telnet protocol assumes unless you specifically tell it otherwise.

All ports numbered 80 will usually have Web sites (even if not all Web sites are active on port 80); likewise, most Port 23s will be used for Telnet, and multiuser games will normally be found on 4201. This is because, believe it or not, there is an Internet organization that actually assigns port numbers to specific Internet uses. These port assignments are, in turn, used in a standard fashion by most hosts throughout the Net. It's possible that specific system administrators may use other ports, but these are the most common ones.

Telnetting a Port

Telnetting a port is remarkably simple. To telnet the previous fictional example, hal.jupiter.net port 2001, you would type the following:

> **telnet hal.jupiter.net 2001**

Telnet automatically logs you on to whatever system is running on port 2001.

Some users with command-line accounts (particularly at colleges and universities) work on a machine called a *VAX*. A VAX is a computer made by DEC, the same company that came up with all those different types of terminals. VAX computers usually don't use UNIX, the operating system used by many machines on the Internet. Consequently, there are occasionally some added steps that you have to take while using a VAX that you don't need when running a machine with UNIX. One of these involves telnetting to a specific port.

If you're operating out of a command-line account on a VAX system, you'll need to use the statement /port= before the port number when you give the Telnet address of the remote computer that you're trying to reach. To telnet to hal.jupiter.net 4201, on a VAX you would type:

> **telnet hal.jupiter.net /port=4201**

Telnetting for Fun

Multi-User Dimensions (MUDs) and their cousins (MOOs, MUSHes, etc.) are multi-player games that work because lots of users can all telnet the same machine to play at the same time.

Generally, when you telnet to a MUD, you take the part of a character in a game with hundreds, if not thousands of characters. Games are not resolved immediately; rather, the fun is that a plot can develop over months. A premium is placed on originality, inventiveness, and one's ability to stay in character.

As an example, let's say you wanted to telnet to DUNE II, a MUSH loosely based on the universe created by Frank Herbert in his series of Dune Books. At the time of this writing, DUNE II was located at mindport.net, port 4201. To join the fun on DUNE II, you would do the following:

1. At the command-line prompt, type **telnet mindport.net 4201**.

2. When you connect to DUNE II, the credits screen will appear, and you will notice that you have three options. To just take a look around, type **connect guest guest**.

   In this case, you'll be a character named "guest"; the password for this character is also "guest."

3. The game from here is a text-based adventure. Feel free to talk to people (preface your comments with a quotation mark (") to say something to someone else) and wander around. Press buttons. "Read" things. "Look" at things. You'll get the hang of it soon enough. You may want to venture into the Newbie room, where all sorts of helpful stuff will be available.

4. When you decide you want to create a character, telnet to the MUSH, and then type the following:

   create your_new_character's_name your_personal_password

5. From then on, when you want to log on to the MUSH, you'll type the following:

   connect your_character's_name your_password

Using Telnet on a SLIP/PPP Account

The difficult aspect of using Telnet on a SLIP or PPP account involves setting up your TCP/IP connection. After you've got your SLIP or PPP account running, starting a Windows-based Telnet program is just like starting any other Windows Winsock application. (See chapter 6, "Connecting to a PPP or SLIP Account with Windows 95," for more information.)

Using Windows 95 Telnet

The simplest approach to using Telnet under Windows 95 is to use the version that comes free with the operating system. Windows 95 Telnet is nothing fancy to look at, but is fairly simple to use and is very reliable.

VI

Locating and Retrieving

Setting Up Windows 95 Telnet

You can start using Windows 95 Telnet this easily:

1. Click the Windows 95 Start button. When the Start menu pops up, select the Run menu item. Windows 95 will display the Run dialog box as shown in figure 33.1. (If you've used the Run dialog box before, there will be another command already there.)

Fig. 33.1

Running Windows 95 Telnet is very simple.

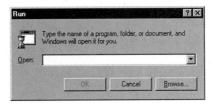

2. Type **telnet**, and click once on the OK button (any previous command will automatically be erased when you start typing). The Telnet window will appear as shown in figure 33.2.

Fig. 33.2

The Windows 95 Telnet client window is clean and straightforward in design.

You can also run the Windows 95 Telnet client from the MS-DOS prompt from within Windows 95 (just like any other Windows application). Telnet can be started from the MS-DOS window command line in this version of Windows.

Adding Telnet to the Windows 95 Start Menu

If you find you're using the Windows 95 Telnet frequently, you may want to set up an icon for it in the Windows 95 Start menu (there's not one by default). To set up an icon, follow these steps:

1. Right-click an empty space on the Windows 95 taskbar. A pop-up menu displays several items; select Properties with a click of the left mouse button.

2. The Taskbar Properties dialog box will appear. Select the Start Menu Properties tab.

3. Select the Add button. The Create Shortcut dialog box will appear.

4. Click Browse, and choose the TELNET.EXE file from your Windows directory. Click the next button, and the Select Program Folder dialog box will display your group options. Pick the group you want the icon in and click the Next> button.

Windows 95 will display the Select a Title for the Program dialog box. Type the name you want the menu entry to have, and click the Finish button.

> **Tip**
>
> You can also use Windows Explorer to set up an icon quickly. Just use Explorer to view the directory where Telnet is (your Windows 95 directory, usually C:\WINDOWS), click the TELNET.EXE file, and drag it to your desktop. Windows 95 will create a shortcut icon automatically.

Connecting with Windows 95 Telnet

Connecting to a remote system with Windows 95 Telnet is also simple. To telnet to a system:

1. Select the Remote System menu item from the Connect menu. The Connect dialog box shown in figure 33.3 will appear (you can select from the history list at the bottom of the pop-up menu if the connection you want is listed).

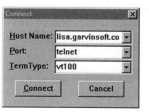

Fig. 33.3
Enter the name of the Telnet host in the Host Name edit box.

2. Enter the host name you want to connect to and select the port and terminal emulation you need, if different from the defaults (these settings will probably work for the great majority of hosts).

3. Click the Connect button to complete the connection. The login prompt for the host system will appear in your Telnet screen.

Note

You can log your complete Telnet session using the Terminal, Start Logging command from the Windows 95 Telnet main menu. This is very useful for capturing commands and other host specific functions to print out later.

Using Telnet Through a Local Area Network (LAN)

Using Telnet through a Local Area Network depends on the amount of flexibility that the LAN administrators have granted to the users. Generally, LAN administrators will set up access to the Internet through one point on the LAN. The computers connected to the LAN all gain access to the Net through this one point of access. The LAN administrators can then determine how much access the users of the LAN can get from this one source.

On some LANs, individual workstations are set up with their own individual IP address. If you can run TCP/IP at your workstation, then you should be able to run software such as the NCSA WINTel software or the Chameleon Telnet for Windows program the same way as you would through a SLIP or PPP connection.

If TCP/IP isn't available at your individual workstation, your LAN administrator may have created a special mechanism for using Telnet and other Internet utilities. How will you know if TCP is available at your station? You'll probably have to ask your LAN administrator, but if your workstation is set up with programs like Telnet, Mosaic, and FTP, you probably have your own IP address.

If you don't have your own IP address, some Internet access may still be available. Network administrators will sometimes provide access to special versions of Internet utilities that can be used without having to give users their own IP address. All Telnet utilities are going to ask for the same types of information, regardless of how they look. Telnet will always require a host name and, when applicable, a relevant port number. If you have this information, you should be able to use Telnet regardless of the way your LAN administrators have packaged it.

Don't Be Afraid to Ask for Help

When you log on to a new system, ask for help if you need it. Most systems that allow Telnet access also have extensive help files for users. These can usually be reached by typing **HELP** at a command-line prompt. (If HELP doesn't work in all capitals, try it in all lowercase, or try entering a question mark. One of them should eventually work. For some systems, the command MAN followed by a command may also produce help on that command although this help is generally limited to help about the operating system, not help files about their services accessible by Telnet.) No one keeps track of whether you've ever read the help files or how many times you went back to check the same thing. If you don't understand something, read the help file and read any other help files that seem like they might have something to do with your problem.

Telnetting to remote systems may sometimes require that you learn the language that those systems use. Remember, these remote systems have a lot of computing power that you can use to your advantage if you take the time to figure out what makes them tick.

Tip

A standard abbreviation among computer users is RTFM—Read The Fine Manual. When connecting to remote computers, be sure to check out their manuals (the system's Help files).

CHAPTER 34

Using FTP and Popular FTP Programs

The Internet and its predecessors have always been intended as a means for information exchange. The oldest services on the Internet were developed for this purpose. One of these services is *FTP*, which allows you to examine the files of remote hosts on the Internet, and transfer files between your host and those hosts.

FTP, like many early Internet services, was developed by computer scientists to be used by computer scientists. Computers were pretty primitive, most lacking the graphic capabilities that are taken for granted today. The people who used the computers expected them to be complicated, so the developers made no effort to make the interface to the service easy to use. And, unless you knew where to find the files you wanted, you'd never know the information was out there because there was no way to search the FTP sites.

Although new Internet services are always being developed, the old services are still useful. So, today's Internet users (some of whom are computer scientists who appreciate a good interface) have designed a new look for old services, including FTP.

In this chapter, you learn about the following topics:

- How FTP works
- How to use the Windows 95 FTP client
- How to use WS_FTP, a popular Windows FTP client

What Is FTP?

You already have seen how you can use e-mail to send a message over the Internet. Now that most e-mail programs support MIME or some type of automatic encoding/decoding mechanism, you can send any type of file through e-mail (although there is a limit to the size of the files you can send through e-mail). Suppose, however, that you want to make a collection of files available to anyone who wants to get them. It would be very inconvenient (for you and everyone else) if the people who wanted the files had to contact you and find out what was available, and then request that you send them the files they wanted through e-mail. A much better method of making the files available exists—the *file transfer protocol* (FTP) service. This service is designed to allow you to connect to a computer on the Internet (using an FTP program on your local machine), browse through the files available on that computer, and then download or upload files.

> **Note**
>
> Unlike Internet e-mail, FTP allows you to directly transfer both text and binary (program, graphics, and so on) files. (You can send binary files through e-mail, but you must encode them as text first.) You must explicitly tell FTP that you are transferring binary files, however.

What Are Client/Server Services?

▶ See "What Is Gopher?" p. 867

◀ See "Important WWW Concepts," p. 458

The FTP service is an example of a client-server system. In this kind of system, you use a program on your local computer (called a client) to request a service from a program on a remote computer (called a server). In the case of FTP, the server on the remote computer is designed to let you download and upload files, but many other services are available on the Internet. Some of these, such as Gopher and the World Wide Web (WWW), are discussed in other chapters.

For a computer system to let you connect to it using an FTP program, the system must have an FTP server running on it. The administrators of the machine must set up this machine and decide which files and information will be made available on the FTP server.

Anonymous FTP

> **Tip**
>
> You can (and in rare cases must) use FTP instead of anonymous to log in to an anonymous FTP server.

One common type of FTP server is an anonymous FTP server. With this kind of server, you can connect and download or upload files without having an account on the machine. If the FTP server isn't anonymous, you must provide a user name and password, when you connect to the server, just as though you were logging in to the machine. On an anonymous FTP server, you use the special user name anonymous when you connect. This anonymous user name lets you log in by providing any password you want (often, the server asks you to enter your Internet mailing address as your password).

> **Note**
>
> If you want to retrieve files from a machine that does not have anonymous FTP service, you must have an account on that machine that you can log in to.

Anonymous FTP servers are one of the major means of distributing software and information across the Internet. A large amount of software—often provided free of charge—is available on anonymous FTP servers. Software is available for many different types of computer systems, such as UNIX, IBM PC, and Macintosh systems.

Using FTP from the Command Line

A number of Windows-based FTP clients are now available (one of them, WS_FTP, is described in detail later in this chapter). Originally, FTP was developed to be used from a command-line prompt. The FTP client that comes with Windows 95 is a DOS command-line client.

> **Note**
>
> To start the Windows 95 FTP client, open the Start Menu and select <u>R</u>un. In the Run dialog, enter **ftp** in the <u>O</u>pen field, and then click OK. A DOS window running a command-line FTP client will appear.

> **Tip**
>
> If you've selected Use AutoDial in your Internet Properties box dialog, the connection to your Internet service provider will start automatically when you try to open a connection to an FTP server.

The exact method you use to connect to an FTP server depends on the software available from your Internet service provider. In general, once you have started the command-line version of FTP, you use the open command on your local machine and give the machine to which you want to connect. For example, from the DOS FTP client, if you want to FTP to the machine **rs.internic.net** (a site that has many documents related to the Internet), use the command **open rs.internic.net**.

When you connect to the FTP server, you are prompted for a login name. If you have an account on the FTP server machine, you can use your account name; if this is an anonymous FTP site, use the login name anonymous. After the account name, you are prompted for a password. Naturally, if you logged in using your account name, you will use your account's password here. If this is an anonymous FTP site, you can use anything for the password, but by convention you should use your e-mail address for the password. This way, the FTP site maintainer can keep track of who has been using the server and contact people who have downloaded files.

Most FTP programs have similar commands. Some of the most useful ones follow:

Command	Purpose
ls	Lists files in the current directory on the FTP server
dir	Lists files, with more information
get *file*	Downloads *file* to your machine
put *file*	Uploads *file* from your machine
cd	Changes directory on the FTP account
lcd	Changes directory on your local computer
bye	Logs out from the FTP server
help	Displays a help message showing a list of available commands
binary	Tells the FTP server that you will be downloading a binary file

Your FTP program may have other commands available or may use different names for these commands.

Windows-Based FTP Clients

Because more and more PCs are being used as Internet hosts, a number of Windows-based interfaces to standard Internet services have been developed. Most commercial PC TCP/IP packages include interfaces to a number of Internet services, including FTP. The NetCD95 that comes with this book contains several commercial and shareware FTP interfaces. After your PC is connected to the Internet, you need only install the FTP interfaces to begin your exploration of one of the Internet's oldest (and greatest) sources of programs and documents.

Most commercial TCP/IP packages provide an automated setup program to install the different applications (or, they will at least provide detailed installation instructions). If you get one of the shareware TCP/IP applications packages (like those included on the NetCD95 that comes with this book), it is usually just a matter of placing the ZIP file for the application in a directory and unpacking it. As an example, you see how to install and use the WS_FTP32 application later in this chapter.

Locating Files

One of the most frustrating problems with the Internet is the difficulty of finding information such as FTP sites, host resources, sources of information, and so forth. Imagine that you went into your local public library and found that instead of the books being arranged on shelves according to a book classification scheme, the books were in piles all over the floor. Rather than use a central card catalog, the librarians placed notes on some of the piles stating what people had found in that pile. This scenario is how the Internet has been for most of its existence; many resources are available, but no way to easily locate them exists.

Most FTP sites don't have a listing of all their available files, although some do. Generally, the only way to locate a file or find interesting files is to move around in the directories on the FTP server and look at the files in those directories.

Because the file and directory names are in whatever form is used by the machine the FTP server is on, what you see when doing a directory listing varies depending on the type of system you connect to. If the server is running on a UNIX system, for example, the file names appear in upper- or lowercase and can be of any length. If you want to download a file, you must be sure to type the file name exactly as it appears when you do a directory listing.

> **Note**
>
> It also is important to use the exact case when changing directories while using FTP from the command line.

On some machines (especially the very large archive sites), the site maintainers keep an index of available files with brief descriptions of what they are. These indexes are very useful and make finding useful files much easier. When you enter a directory, you should look for a file called INDEX (in upper- or lowercase letters). You also should look for a file called README (readme, read.me, or something similar). These README files are generally descriptions of the contents of the directories, or information about the server system. You should always download the README files and read the contents—the files are put there for a reason. You might also find a file called ls-lR that gives a detailed listing of the directory structure on the site.

If you have a question about an FTP server or about the contents of the files there, send an e-mail message to the postmaster of the FTP machine. For example, if you connect to the machine **rs.internic.net**, send e-mail to the address **postmaster@rs.internic.net**. Some FTP servers have a different person to contact; in this case, the name of the contact person appears when you connect to the machine or is in a README file in the first directory you see when you connect.

▶ See "Archie,"
p. 927

There is an Internet service called Archie that allows you to search a database containing a list of the files on a number of anonymous FTP servers. The Archie servers connect to FTP sites that register with them and update their database information on a regular basis. For more information about Archie and how to use it, see chapter 37, "Searching on the Internet."

Downloading and Uploading Files

After you find a file you are interested in, you can download the file to your service provider account or your local PC if your provider allows you to do so automatically. Be aware of several things before you download the file, however. First, use the dir command on the file (or a long directory listing, if your Windows-based FTP client can do it) and make a note of the size of the file you want to download. Make sure that the system you are downloading to has enough space to store the file; you may have to leave the FTP program and remove some files before you can download the file.

Also check whether the file you are interested in downloading is a binary file. A binary file is one that contains characters that can't be printed or displayed. Generally, executable programs, compressed files (files made smaller with a program such as PKZIP or the UNIX compress program), and picture or sound files are binary data. If you want to download a binary file, you must tell the FTP program. Most programs have a binary command to do so. If you aren't sure whether the file is binary, tell your server that it is; in most cases (unless the hosts specify end-of-line differently), you can transfer non-binary files in binary mode without problems.

If the file is very large and the FTP server is slow or the Internet connection is slow (the machine is in Europe or Asia, for example), transferring the file may take several minutes. If the Internet connection is very slow, the download may stop and you will be logged out; in this case, you should try again. In general, transferring large files after normal work hours is a good idea because the system and network load is lighter.

In general, you probably won't upload many files to Internet FTP sites. Unless you are doing development of a useful utility program that you want to make available to others, you won't find much of an opportunity to do uploads. On most anonymous FTP sites that allow uploads, you will see a directory called incoming, which is set up to be a place where uploads should be put. If you place a file in the area for uploads, you should upload a short description of what the file is, or send an e-mail message to the site maintainers to tell them what you uploaded.

Troubleshooting

I can't execute a binary file that I transferred.

If you try to execute a program, or view a graphic or some other binary file that you have retrieved from an FTP site, and the file appears to be corrupted, check to make sure that you transferred the file using binary mode. If you transfer a binary file in ASCII mode, the file will be corrupted.

Installing WS_FTP32

The original version of WS_FTP was a 16-bit application designed to run un-der Windows 3.1. WS_FTP32 is a 32-bit application primarily designed for use with Windows NT and the Windows 95 operating system. The application it-self is very similar to the 16-bit version, with only a few minor differences in the appearance of the main window.

VI

Locating and Retrieving

The WS_FTP32 program can be found on the NetCD95 accompanying this book. You must be running Windows 95 to use WS_FTP32. You can install WS_FTP32 by running the NetCD95 installation as described in chapter 50, "Installing and Using NetCD95." Alternatively, you can copy the file from NetCD95 to a directory of your choosing on your hard drive and unzip the file into the directory where you want to keep the application.

If you can't use the CD to load WS_FTP (or if you would like to check to see if a newer version exists), you can use the Windows 95 FTP client discussed earlier in this chapter to get the WS_FTP32 ZIP file (currently ws_ftp32.zip) from **ftp.usma.edu** in the directory /pub/msdos/winsock.files. You should also be able to find it at **ftp.winsite.com** (formerly **ftp.cica.indiana.edu**) in the directory /pub/pc/win95/netutil, or at any of the WinSite mirror sites, including **wuarchive.wustl.edu**, **ftp.cdrom.com**, **ftp.monash.edu.au**, **ftp.uni-stuttgart.de**, **nic.switch.ch**. WinSite gives you a complete list of mirror sites if your connection fails because all of the anonymous FTP slots are taken. If you download this application instead of using it from NetCD95, you must unzip the files to the directory of your choice.

Tip

Once you've unzipped WS_FTP32, you can create a Windows 95 shortcut to it. Simply right click the ws_ftp32.exe file and select Create Shortcut. Drag the shortcut that appears to someplace that's easy for you to access—a folder that appears under Programs on your Start menu, for example.

Using WS_FTP

WS_FTP32 (hereafter referred to as WS_FTP) is a Windows 95 FTP client. It allows you to connect to hosts on the Internet using the FTP protocol. After you are connected, you can examine the directories on the host and send and receive files to the host (if you have read and write privileges).

Connecting to a Host

Tip

To reopen the Session Profile dialog after WS_FTP is started, choose Connect from the command buttons at the bottom of the window.

When you want to use WS_FTP to retrieve or upload a file, the first thing you must do is establish your connection to the Internet (if your host is not permanently connected to the Internet). When your host is on the Internet, follow these steps to connect to the remote host:

1. Open the Start menu and select Programs. To start WS_FTP, select WS_FTP from whatever Program item you put it under. By default, you get the WS_FTP window and a Session Profile dialog box (see figure 34.1). You must fill in the information in the Session Profile dialog box to make a connection with a remote host.

> **Note**
>
> WS_FTP comes with preconfigured profiles for several of the most popular FTP sites. See "Defining Host Profiles" later in this chapter for more information about selecting preconfigured profiles.

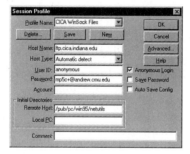

Fig. 34.1
The WS_FTP window and Session Profile dialog box both appear when you start WS_FTP.

2. Click in the text box next to Host Name and enter the name of the Internet host you want to connect to.

3. Unless there is a problem reading the directories on the remote host, leave the Host Type set to Automatic detect.

> **Troubleshooting**
>
> *No remote directories are shown after I connect.*
>
> If you connect to your FTP server correctly, but no directories or files are shown for the server, it may be that WS_FTP does not know how to handle the directory information that the server is returning. Try changing the WS_FTP host type from auto detect to whatever the machine you are connecting to actually is.

VI

Locating and Retrieving

4. Click in the text box next to <u>U</u>ser ID. If you are going to be connecting to an anonymous FTP server, click the Anonymous <u>L</u>ogin check box, and the value is automatically set to anonymous. If you are going to log in to a personal account on the remote machine, enter your user ID here.

5. Click in the text box next to Pass<u>w</u>ord. If you have clicked the Anonymous <u>L</u>ogin check box and you have previously set up your e-mail address, your e-mail address is automatically entered here. If it is not, and you are doing an anonymous login, enter your full Internet e-mail address.

   If you are logging in to a personal account, first make sure that the Anonymous <u>L</u>ogin check box is off. Then enter the password for your account (the password will not be shown).

6. If you are connecting to a machine that needs an account name as well as a user ID, click in the A<u>c</u>count box and enter the account name.

7. Click in the Remote H<u>o</u>st box under Initial Directories and enter the path of the directory you want to examine, if you know it. If you leave this blank, you are shown the top level directory for the host you specified.

8. Click in the Local <u>P</u>C box under Initial Directories and enter the path on your local file system where you want to store files that you retrieve.

9. Choose OK to establish the connection.

The Session Profile dialog box disappears, and WS_FTP attempts to connect to the account that you specified. You see the actual FTP commands in the log area at the bottom of the WS_FTP window. As long as everything is going well, you don't have to worry about these messages. If a problem occurs, you will be notified of it.

If your connection is made, your WS_FTP window shows the name of the remote machine in the title bar (see figure 34.2), and the Connect button will change to <u>C</u>lose. The left side of the window is entitled Local System, and the right side is entitled Remote System. Both sides contain a split viewing area where the top half of the viewing area shows the directories under the current one, and the bottom half shows the files in the current directory.

Remote directories

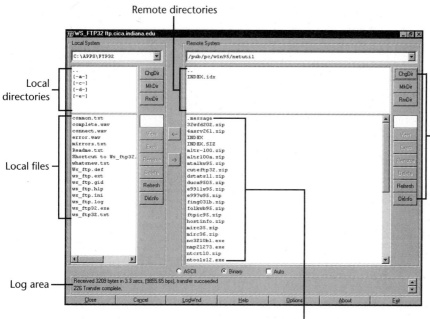

Local directories

Local files

Log area

Fig. 34.2
The WS_FTP
window shows
you the local
and remote file
systems, and lets
you manipulate
files and directo-
ries on both
systems.

Directory
and file
command
buttons

Remote files

Troubleshooting

I can't connect to the FTP server.

You may get one of several different error messages in the log area. One message
may be that the remote host was not found. This usually means that you entered the
name of the server incorrectly. Check the name and try it again.

Another message you may get is that your connection is refused. This usually occurs
when a machine is already at its maximum capacity for FTP connections (many
servers only allow a limited number of anonymous FTP connections). If you get a
connection refused message, try to make the connection again (people are always
disconnecting from the FTP servers). If you try a few times and still cannot connect,
try to connect at a later time, or try another machine that has the same information.
A number of sites, called mirrors, have copies of the files that are on popular servers.
Many popular servers will show you a list of mirror sites if they refuse your
connection.

Working in Directories

> **Tip**
>
> If you want to see more of your directory and file lists without maximizing the window, stretch the window so that it goes from the top of the screen to the bottom.

After you establish a connection to your FTP host, you can manipulate the files on both your local and remote machine. You can upload files from your computer to the remote host, download files from the remote host, move between directories, and delete files and directories (if you have these privileges).

Setting Your Directories

After you establish your FTP connection, the WS_FTP window shows you the local directory you specified on the left side of the window and the remote directory you specified on the right side of the window. Buttons to the right of each directory area let you manipulate your directories if you have privileges (see fig. 34.3).

Fig. 34.3
The directories on the remote and local machines are shown. Buttons to the right of each directory area allow you to change, create, and delete directories as needed.

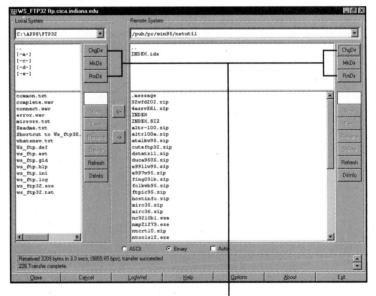

Directory operations

Tip

You can double-click a directory to change to that directory.

To manipulate your directories, follow these steps:

1. If your local and remote directories are not set correctly, use scroll bars in the directory areas to find the directory you want; select the directory and click the ChgDir button to move to that directory. If you click the ChgDir button without selecting a directory, you get the Input dialog box shown in figure 34.4.

Fig. 34.4
When you click the ChgDir or MkDir buttons, the Input dialog box asks for the name of the directory.

2. If you want to make a new directory under the current directory on either the local or remote file system, click the MkDir button. You see the Input dialog box asking for the name of the directory you want to create. You must have write privileges to be able to create a new directory.

3. If you want to remove a directory, you must first select the directory. When it is selected, click the RmDir button. You see the Verify Deletion dialog box shown in figure 34.5 asking if you are sure that you want to delete the directory. Click Yes if you want to delete the directory, or No if you don't. You must have write privileges to be able to remove a directory.

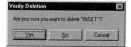

Fig. 34.5
WS_FTP prompts you for confirmation before deleting a directory.

VI

Locating and Retrieving

> **Tip**
>
> Some directory listings may be too large to be edited with Notepad. If you want to set a different editor as your default, see "Customizing Your Window" later in this chapter. (WordPad is a good alternative.)

Fig. 34.6

Clicking the DirInfo button brings up Notepad with a file list showing the modification dates and sizes of the files in the current directory.

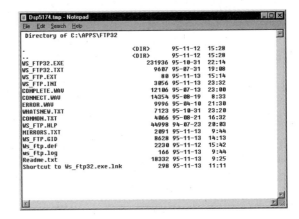

4. If you want to see more information about the files in a directory, click the DirInfo button. Notepad is started and shows a long directory listing (file modification dates and sizes shown) of the current directory (see fig. 34.6). You can save this information as you would any Notepad file.

5. If the directory you are examining is changed outside of WS_FTP, WS_FTP does not show you the changes unless you rescan the directory. Click the Refresh button to get the most recent directory information.

Working with Files

The local and remote files for the current directories are shown below the directories. Buttons to the right of each file area let you manipulate your files if you have privileges (see fig. 34.7).

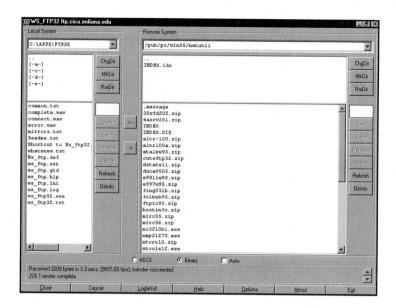

Fig. 34.7
WS_FTP lets you view, execute, rename, and delete files in your local and remote directories. You can also rescan the directory and edit a copy of the directory listing.

To manipulate your files, follow these steps:

1. If you want to view one of the text files in the directory, use the scroll bars in the file areas and select the file. Click the View button to view the file (see fig. 34.8). The viewer that you set up in the Options dialog is used to view the file.

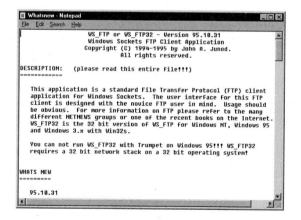

Fig. 34.8
When you view a file, your specified viewer is started (the default is Notepad) with the file loaded.

VI

Locating and Retrieving

> **Tip**
>
> To associate a file extension with an application, see "Defining Executable File Associations" later in this chapter.

2. If the operating system knows what type of application to run for a particular file extension, WS_FTP lets you automatically open that application with a file loaded, similar to the way you can double-click a file in the file manager, WS_FTP calls this executing a file. If you want to execute one of the files in your local or remote directory, use the scroll bars to find the file in the file areas and select the file. Click the Exec button to execute the file. If the file is on the remote system, WS_FTP first downloads the file to the Windows temporary directory and then executes the file.

▶ See "Protecting Your Computer," p. 1066

> **Caution**
>
> Do not use the Exec button on an executable file, unless you are absolutely sure of what it will do and you are sure you have it in the right location. You could introduce a virus to your PC by executing a questionable EXE file. It's always a good idea to run a virus checker on files that you get from an anonymous FTP site.

> **Tip**
>
> On some file systems, you can use the Rename command to move a file by specifying the complete path name in the new name.

3. If you want to rename a file on the local or remote directory, use the scroll bars to find the file in the file areas and select the file. Click the Rename button to change the name of the file. You must have write permission to be able to rename the file.

4. If you want to delete a file on the local or remote directory, use the scroll bars to find the file in the file areas and select the file. Click Delete to remove the file. You must have write permission to be able to delete the file.

Troubleshooting

I'm looking for a file on an FTP server, but it appears in the list of directories.

FTP servers (particularly UNIX-based servers) occasionally have directories that are actually links to other directories, and files that are links to other files. The linked directories don't have any files in them, but they point to directories that do contain the files. By the same token, linked files do not have anything in them, but they point to the actual files.

Unfortunately, you have to choose whether WS_FTP interprets links as links to files or links to directories (see "Setting up Default Session Options" later in the chapter for information on how to do this). If you tell WS_FTP to interpret links as files, it doesn't understand what the linked directories are and shows them as files. Then when you try to examine the linked directory, you get the error Not a plain file. If you tell WS_FTP to interpret links as directories, it shows linked files as directories, and you get the error No such file or directory when you double-click one.

If you have WS_FTP set to show links as directories, you can still download a linked file. To do so, make sure no files are selected (click Refresh to clear any previously selected files). Click the left transfer arrow, and enter the name of the file in the input box that appears. Click OK and WS_FTP will begin downloading the file.

Retrieving Files

The main thing you will probably use WS_FTP for is retrieving files (especially if you are limited to connecting to anonymous FTP sites). After you establish your FTP connection, the WS_FTP window shows you the local directory you specified on the left side of the window, and the remote directory you specified on the right side of the window. To retrieve a file from the remote machine, follow these steps:

1. If your local and remote directories are not set correctly, use the directory commands described in the preceding section to navigate to the appropriate directories.

Caution

When you transfer a file, if the receiving machine already has a file by that name, the file on the receiving machine will be overwritten with no warning. To prevent this, see the Send Unique and Receive Unique options described in "Setting Up Default Session Options" later in this chapter.

2. To download a file, select the file in the remote file area and click the arrow that's pointing to the local directory. Or double-click the file name if you have double-click set up to do transfers (see "Customizing Your Window" later in this chapter for information on setting up the double-click behavior). The Transfer Status dialog box appears to show you the progress of the transfer (see fig. 34.9). You can abort the transfer by clicking Cancel in the Transfer Status box, or by choosing Cancel from the command buttons at the bottom of the window.

Fig. 34.9

The Transfer Status dialog box shows you what percentage of your file transfer is completed and lets you abort the transfer.

> ### Caution
>
> If you abort a download or upload, the receiving machine will have a partial file created. Be sure to delete this partial file.

3. To upload a file, select the file in your local directory and click the arrow pointing to the remote directory. Or double-click the file name if you have double-click set up to do transfers. (See "Customizing Your Window" later in this chapter for information on setting up the double-click behavior.) The Transfer Status dialog box appears to show you the progress of the transfer. You can abort the transfer by clicking Cancel in the Transfer Status box, or by choosing Cancel from the command buttons at the bottom of the window.

> ### Note
>
> You can see the actual FTP commands executed for any remote file operation in the log area at the bottom of the WS_FTP window. If you double-click the log area, or if you choose LogWnd from the command buttons at the bottom of the screen, you will get a window that shows a complete history of all the FTP commands WS_FTP has executed in this session. The only time you should need to look at this is if an error occurs while trying to connect to a machine or transfer a file or if you are interested in information such as how long it takes files to transfer and average transfer rate (which are also kept in the log area). If your connection to an FTP server was refused, the FTP server will often send you a message referring you to mirror sites; you can read that message in the log window.

Troubleshooting

I can't do anything with the remote directories or files.

If you try to do directory or file operations and WS_FTP seems to be busy for a long time without doing anything, or returns a "send" error in your log area, your connection to the FTP server may have timed out. Most servers will disconnect you after a period of inactivity—if you stop changing directories or transferring files—in order to free up the connection for others to use. (Sometimes, WS_FTP does not seem to recognize that the server has disconnected and will stay busy, requiring you to click the Cancel button.) Whenever your connection times out, you must click the Close button in order to reset WS_FTP so that you can make a new connection.

Customizing WS_FTP

You can set up a number of features of WS_FTP to make the application more convenient for you to use. You can define profiles of the sites you use frequently, customize your window, and set default values for some of the transfer options. This section tells you about all the different customizations.

Customizing Your Window

You can change the arrangement of the buttons and viewing areas in your WS_FTP window. To change the layout of the window, follow these steps:

1. Choose Options from the row of buttons at the bottom of the window. You should see the Options dialog box shown in figure 34.10.

Fig. 34.10
The Options dialog box allows you to customize the look and operation of WS_FTP.

VI

2. Click Program Options to open the Program Options dialog box, in which you can customize the look of your WS_FTP window (see fig. 34.11).

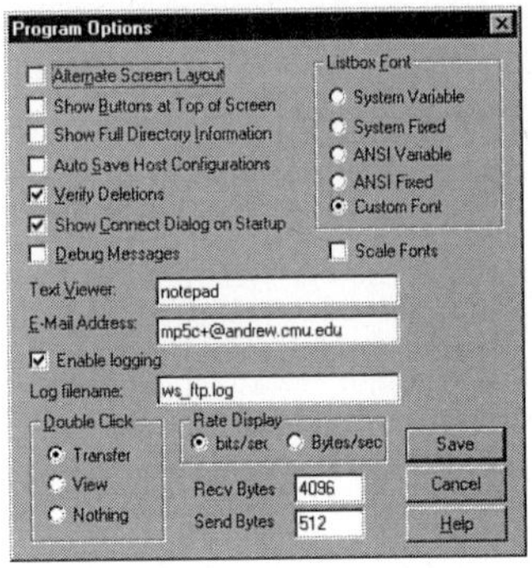

Fig. 34.11

The Program
Options dialog
box allows you to
customize the look
of WS_FTP.

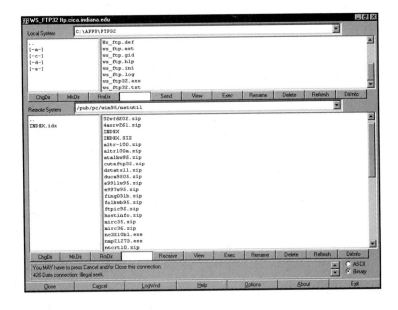

3. Click the Alternate Screen Layout check box to reformat the WS_FTP
   window so that the local directory is on the top, and the remote directory is on the bottom, with the directory list on the left, and the file list
   on the right (see fig. 34.12). This places your buttons along the bottom
   of each directory area.

Fig. 34.12

Setting the
Alternate Screen
Layout puts the
local directory
information at
the top of the
window, and the
remote directory
information at the
bottom of the
window.

4. Click the Show Buttons at the Top of Screen check box to move the row
   of command buttons from the bottom of the window to the top of the
   window (see fig. 34.13).

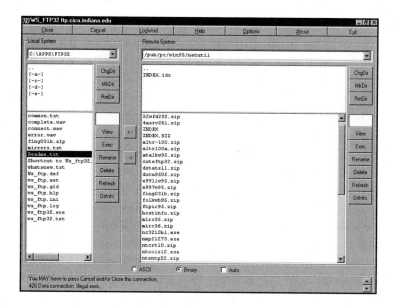

5. Click the Show Full Directory Information check box to display additional file information if available.

6. Click the Auto Save Host Configurations check box to set the Auto Save Config option in the Session Profile to default to on.

7. Click the Verify Deletions check box if you want to be asked for confirmation when you delete a file (this is the default).

8. Click the Show Connect Dialog on Startup check box if you want the Session Profile dialog box to be displayed when you first start WS_FTP (this is the default).

> **Note**
>
> There is a Debug Messages option that causes additional debug messages to be displayed in the log area. However, the author of WS_FTP does not recommend turning this on because all valid error messages are already displayed in the log area.

9. Click in the text box next to Text Viewer to set the default application to be used when you view an ASCII file from one of the directories (this will default to Notepad).

10. Click in the text box next to E-Mail Address to set the default e-mail address to be used when logging in to an anonymous FTP server.

11. Click the Enable Logging checkbox if you want to create a log file for each file transfer. Enter the name you want to use for the log file in the text box next to Log filename. A file of that name will appear in the same directory as the file you are uploading/downloading.

12. In the Listbox Font area, click the radio button for the font that you want to use in the directory and file list areas. If you don't want to use one of the standard fixed or variable width fonts, you can click the Custom Font button. This brings up the Font dialog box shown in figure 34.14. This window allows you to scroll through and select one of the fonts available on your system.

Fig. 34.14
The Font dialog box allows you to select the font family, style, and size of the font for the WS_FTP directory and file areas (a sample of the font you select is shown).

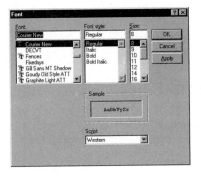

13. Click the Scale Fonts check box to set WS_FTP so that the fonts outside of the directory and file list areas will shrink if the window size is reduced.

14. Click one of the radio buttons under Double Click box to set the action that double-clicking on a file will have:

   ■ Transfer causes the file to be transferred to the other system (uploaded or downloaded) when you double-click it.

   ■ Execute tries to execute the file in the same manner as the Exec button.

   ■ Nothing sets it so that nothing happens (surprise!).

15. In the Rate Display box, click the radio button to set the format used to show your data transfer speed (either bits or bytes per second).

16. Click in the text box next to Recv Bytes to set the size of data chunks read during file transfers. Try using 4096.

17. Click in the text box next to Send Bytes to set the size of the data packets written during file transfers. If you are directly connected to the
Internet, use 4096; otherwise, the value depends on your TCP/IP stack
implementation.

18. Choose Save when you have finished setting up the options. (Choose
Cancel if you want to abort these changes.)

You also can customize the size and location of your WS_FTP window. To do
this, open the Options dialog box and choose Save Win Loc. The next time
you start WS_FTP, your window will appear the same size and in the same
place as it was when you chose that button.

Defining Host Profiles

If you connect to some Internet hosts on a regular basis, you will probably
want to set up automatic connections to those hosts to save you the trouble
of filling in the box each time you connect. To set up a host profile, follow
these steps:

1. Choose Connect from the row of command buttons. You should see
the Session Profile dialog box shown in figure 34.15.

Fig. 34.15
The Session Profile
dialog box allows
you to set up the
parameters for a
connection and
save them to use
in a later session.

2. To modify an existing session, select it from the drop-down list next to
Profile Name. To clear the fields for a new session, click New.

3. In the text box next to Profile Name, enter the name for this session.
Good choices for names are the name of the site (if it is well known) or
the type of files that can be found on the site (such as "PC games").

4. In the text box next to Host Name, enter the name of the Internet host
you want to connect to.

VI

Locating and Retrieving

> **Tip**
>
> If your e-mail address is not entered in the Program Options dialog box, you will be prompted for it after you click Anonymous Login.

5. If you are connecting to a personal account, enter the name of the User ID you are going to connect to. Otherwise, click the Anonymous Login check box, which fills in this field with **anonymous** and the Password field with your Internet e-mail address. To save the password with the profile, click the Save Password check box.

> **Caution**
>
> Do not enter your password and save the session information if you are connecting to a personal account because it would be possible for someone to find your password stored on the hard disk and decrypt it, or simply use the stored password to connect to your personal account and access your files.

> **Tip**
>
> Open the Options dialog box and choose Save Dir Name to quickly save the local and remote directory names as the defaults for the profile of the current session.

6. If you want to enter values for the Remote Host and Local PC Initial Directories, fill in these fields.

7. If you want to save this session information, choose Save. Otherwise, choose Cancel to close the window.

You also can configure a number of advanced features for a profile. If you click Advanced, you see the dialog box shown in figure 34.16.

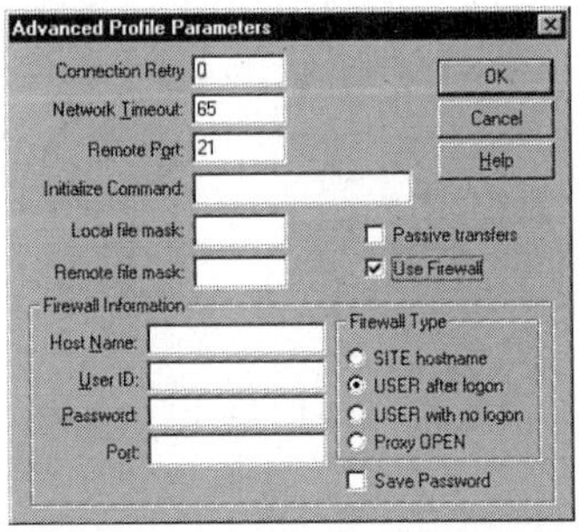

Fig. 34.16
The Advanced Profile Parameters dialog box allows you to set up advanced connection features for your profiles.

- The Connection Retry field lets you specify the number of times a connection will be tried before failing.

- Network Timeout specifies the amount of time (in seconds) that WS_FTP waits for a response from the remote host before failing (note that your initial connection timeout is set by your WinSock DLL).

- Remote Port is normally set to 21 for FTP transactions, but may need to be set to something else if you are going through a firewall (ask your Internet system administrator).

- If you always upload or download the same type of files, enter the mask for those file types in the Local file mask or Remote file mask text boxes (*.zip, for example). Once WS_FTP has made the connection, click Refresh to activate the mask so that you view only those file types.

- Click the Passive transfers check box if you need to use PASV Transfer Mode (specifies that the FTP client initiates the data transfer connections rather than the server). This may be needed if your host is behind a firewall.

- Click the Use Firewall check box if your computer is behind a firewall. Check with your system administrator for the type of firewall you are using and click the appropriate radio button under Firewall Type. Fill in the entries under the Firewall Information section (your system administrator should be able to tell you what needs to go in these boxes, also).

Deleting Host Profiles

WS_FTP comes with a number of predefined session profiles that allow you to get to Internet hosts that contain popular programs. You will probably want to delete these entries if you have no need to connect to those hosts. To delete a profile, select it from the drop-down list next to Profile Name in the Session Profile dialog, and then choose Delete.... Contrary to the three dots at the end of Delete..., the profile you select will be deleted immediately with no confirmation.

Setting Up Default Session Options

You can set up the default values for some of the fields in the connection Session Profile window. To set these defaults, follow these steps:

1. Choose Options from the row of buttons at the bottom of the window.

2. Click Session Options to open the Session Options dialog box in which you can customize your default session settings (see fig. 34.17).

VI

Locating and Retrieving

Fig. 34.17
The Session
Options dialog
box allows you to
set defaults for
some of the
parameters in your
Session Profile.

3. If you know the type of host you will usually connect to, select the host type from the Host Type drop-down list. The default value of Automatic detect will work for most host types.

4. Click the Auto Update Remote Directories check box if you want the remote directory to be refreshed after a file operation (this is the default).

5. Click Show Transfer Dialog if you want WS_FTP to display the Transfer dialog box that shows the percentage complete and allows you to abort the transfer (this is the default).

6. Click Use PASV Transfer Mode if you need to specify that the FTP client initiates the data transfer connections rather than the server.

> **Note**
>
> You may need to use PASV transfer mode if your machine is on a network that has a firewall.

7. Click Sort Remote File Listbox if you want the remote file area to be sorted alphabetically (otherwise, the files are shown in the order transmitted from the remote host).

8. Click Use Firewall if your system is on a network behind a firewall. You must make sure that the firewall information in the Advanced section of the Session Profile window is properly filled out for each connection session.

9. Click Send Unique (host assigns name) if you want the remote host to make sure that no conflict in file names exists between the remote and local host.

10. Click Receive Unique (PC assigns name) if you want the local host to make sure that no conflict in file names exists between the remote and local host. Any files received that would conflict with an existing file will have the sixth through eighth characters replaced with an incremental number between 000 and 999.

11. Click Prompt for Destination File Names if you want to be shown the destination file name for every file transferred. You can change the destination by entering a full path if you want.

12. Click one of the radio buttons under Sounds to control how WS_FTP indicates events with sound. Your options are:

    - None eliminates all sound indicators.

    - Beeps causes a single beep to be sounded for all events.

    - Wave causes the files Complete.wav, Connect.wav, and Error.wav to be used for, respectively, transfer completions, successful connections, and errors.

13. Click one of the radio buttons under Transfer Mode to set the default mode that FTP should use to transfer files. The options are:

    - ASCII transfers the file as text, properly translating the end-of-line character between the remote and local system.

    - Binary must be used for any type of executable or encoded file (like a file from a word processor, a graphic file, or a sound file). This option can be used for text files if the remote and local systems are of the same type.

    - L8 must be used for VMS non-text file transfers.

    - Auto Detect transfers files in binary unless the file extensions have been predefined as ASCII using the Extension setup option described in the next section, "Defining ASCII File Extensions."

14. Click one of the radio buttons under View Links to specify how you want links to be shown. As Files shows all links as files; As Directories shows all links as directories.

15. When you have completed setting up the session profile defaults, click Save to save these values for the current session. To save them as defaults for all future sessions, click Save as Default.

VI

Locating and Retrieving

Defining ASCII File Extensions

If you have your file transfer mode set to Auto Detect, your files will be transferred in binary mode, except for those that have file extensions that you have defined as ASCII. To define ASCII file extensions, follow these steps:

1. Choose Options from the row of command buttons at the bottom of the WS_FTP window.

2. Click Extensions to open the Auto Detect Extensions dialog box, in which you can define the extensions of ASCII files (see fig. 34.18).

Fig. 34.18

The Auto Detect Extensions dialog box allows you to create a list of file extensions that identifies files as ASCII.

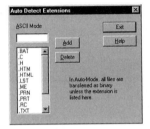

3. Click in the text field under ASCII Mode and enter the file extension. It can be up to ten characters long and should contain any punctuation that would normally precede it or be a part of it.

4. Choose Add to add the extension to the list. Files with this extension will now be transferred in ASCII mode if the mode is set to Auto Detect.

If you would like to delete an extension from the list, select the extension and choose Delete. The extension will be immediately deleted. Choose Exit to close this window.

Defining Executable File Associations

You can execute any file in the remote or local directory list. If the file is a non-executable file, you need to specify the application that is started when you execute the file (for example, you might want to start Lview when a GIF file is executed to view the picture in the GIF file). To associate file extensions with applications, follow these steps:

1. Choose Options from the row of command buttons at the bottom of the WS_FTP window.

2. Click Associations to open the Associate window (see fig. 34.19).

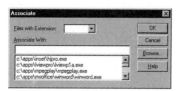

Fig. 34.19
The Associate
window allows
you to specify the
application that
should be started
when you try to
execute a file.

3. Click in the box next to Files with Extension: and enter the three letter extension (do not enter the initial period). If you want to modify an extension, click the arrow to the right of the list to get a drop-down list of the currently defined extensions.

4. Click in the box under Associate With and enter the path to the application you want to start. You can scroll through the list of applications below the box and click the one you want to enter in the box. If the application you want is not in that list, you can choose Browse to bring up a file browser that lets you select the application from your local file system.

5. Choose OK to add the extension to the list.

> **Caution**
>
> Any file association that you enter will be saved in the WIN.INI file and will also work from the file manager of your machine. You cannot delete associations that you create in this window without editing your WIN.INI file.

Exiting WS_FTP

When you have finished transferring files, close the FTP connection by choosing Close from the command buttons at the bottom of the window. At this point, you can make another FTP connection by choosing Connect from the command buttons at the bottom of the window. If you are finished using WS_FTP, choose Exit from the command buttons.

CHAPTER 35

Using Gopher and Popular Gopher Programs

This chapter introduces you to the most popular rodent in cyberspace: Gopher. In this chapter you look at the history of the Gopher protocol and how you use it to make information location and retrieval breathtakingly simple. You also look at several popular Gopher client programs, and you learn how to start them quickly and easily.

In this chapter, you learn the following:

- What the Gopher protocol does
- How Gopher servers store information
- How to set up and use a Gopher client program
- How to locate and retrieve information using Gopher
- How to use the Veronica system to search "Gopherspace"

What Is Gopher?

The term *Gopher* refers to a network protocol, a server type, and one of many Gopher client applications used to access information. When you use a Gopher system, you're really using all three entities. The name Gopher comes from the team mascot of the University of Minnesota, who developed Gopher. It's also a clever twist on that old rhubarb, "I'm a Gofer, I go fer this, I go fer that!"

As you've seen in earlier chapters, there are many different ways to send and receive information via the Internet. Most of the protocols are for point-to-point connections with servers or systems known in advance (such as File Transfer Protocol or a Telnet session); e-mail requires an exact address, and UseNet newsreaders must have a specific server to connect to.

◀ See "Using Telnet," p. 819

◀ See "Using FTP and Popular FTP Programs," p. 837

Gopher is different in design and execution from all of these systems. The Gopher protocol and software allow you to "browse" information systems, so you don't necessarily need to know exactly where something is stored before you look for it. Although you need to know the address of a Gopher server to get started, after you're there, the Gopher server software presents information in a clear, structured, hierarchical list—much like a table of contents in a book. This familiar mode of presentation makes even the most complex information easy to access and retrieve. Most Gopher sites have links to others, so after you hook up to one site, it's pretty easy to jump to another.

There are many excellent Gopher client programs available from commercial software vendors, and there are some incredible shareware and freeware Gophers. This chapter discusses a very popular freeware client program, *HGopher*, in detail.

> **Note**
>
> Most Web browsers also support Gopher very well. Simply use the *gopher://* prefix when composing URLs to Gopher sites in your browser.

The sum total of all Gopher resources on the Internet is known as *Gopherspace*, a simple abstraction that describes a constantly growing, always changing system.

Why Use Gopher?

Gopher is incredibly simple to use. If you can use the table of contents in a book or magazine and click a mouse, you can use Gopher. There's also an incredible amount of information awaiting you in Gopherspace, from the latest article in your favorite magazine to the guitar tablature and lyrics for those golden oldies you haven't heard for years.

Gopher is primarily designed as a document retrieval system; however, you can find many types of information on Gopher servers, from simple text to sound and video files.

Although Gopher resources are plentiful and it's easy to use, there are other excellent reasons to use it instead of other systems. Gopher is a "stateless" protocol, in the sense that no connection to the remote server site stays open. When you make a request for information using Gopher, the client application on your system connects to the server site, gets the data, and closes the connection, all in real time. Other protocols (FTP, Telnet) tie up a logical port on the host system, preventing other users from getting in. Using Gopher makes you a better "netizen" by maximizing resources.

Understanding Gopher Terminology

Just as with every other Internet technology, Gopher has its own associated jargon or argot. Some of the basics include the following:

- *Item.* A directory, text document, image, or search (basically anything you can retrieve, or any process you can activate). Items are usually represented by specific icon types.

- *Document.* The actual information associated with an item (usually text, but this term refers to almost any form of organized information or media). Like items, specific icon types represent documents.

- *Bookmark.* A menu entry linked to a description of how to retrieve an item.

- *Server.* The system that provides the Gopher menus and stores the documents.

You may encounter other terms specific to particular Gopher clients; however, if you can grasp these, you can master navigating Gopherspace without much additional information.

What Is Gopher+?

The original Gopher protocol was a great advance in ease-of-use for network information retrieval. Even so, it soon became obvious that there were limits to the capabilities of the first generation of Gopher servers. One major limitation was the inability to provide detailed information about the resources stored on the server.

That's where Gopher+ comes in. This set of extensions allows servers to deliver more detailed information about Gopher resources *before* transfer, making Gopher an even more efficient method of distributing information. So the user can choose to retrieve a simple document in plain ASCII or a complex one in PostScript.

In addition, this identifies graphics file types, so Gopher clients can automatically call the proper viewers. Also, Gopher+ servers can provide multiple views of information (the remote user might select from English or French text, for example). Version information is available for documents at some sites. Information about server administration also is commonly available, so if you have a problem, you can contact the parties in charge via direct mail.

Using HGopher

One of the most popular Gopher client applications for Microsoft Windows is *HGopher*, a public domain version written by Martyn Hampson. Hampson bases HGopher on an earlier program written for UNIX systems but has elegantly transformed it for the Windows environment. It is easily the equal of many commercial attempts at a Gopher client.

> **Note**
>
> HGopher uses external applications for viewer support, so you may need other applications or utilities to take full advantage of its potential. If you spend any time at all on the Internet, this will not be a major obstacle. You probably have some, if not all, of these programs already. You find them listed later in the chapter, explaining where to get them (see "Setting Up Viewers" later in this chapter).

Installing HGopher

The first place to start when exploring the Internet with Gopher is to get your client software up and running. You can obtain a very good client, HGopher, from most FTP sites. The main FTP site to find this at is **lister.cc.ic.ac.uk** in the directory /PUB/WINGOPHER. The file name there is HGOPHER24.ZIP. In addition, check out **dewey.tis.inel.gov** in the directory /PUB/WINDOWS/ARCHIVES/NETWORKING. You'll also find HGopher on most of the other major Windows Winsock shareware sites on the World Wide Web.

To install HGopher, follow these steps:

1. Create a directory for HGopher (for example, C:\HGOPHER).
2. Copy the HGopher ZIP file to the directory created in step 1.
3. Using an archive utility such as PKUNZIP or WinZip, decompress the HGopher archive.

NetCD95

> **Note**
>
> Don't forget to practice safe computing! Please use a virus checker on downloaded files, preferably after decompression.

If you want to add an icon for HGopher to the Windows 95 Start menu, follow these steps:

1. To create an icon for HGgopher in the Windows Start menu, right-click an empty space on the Windows 95 task bar. A pop-up menu will display several items; select Properties with a click of the left mouse button.

2. The Task Bar Properties dialog box appears. Select the Start Menu Programs tab.

3. Select the Add button. The Create Shortcut dialog box appears.

4. Click Browse, and choose the HGOPHER.EXE file from the directory where HGopher was decompressed. Click the Next> button, and the Select Program Folder dialog box will display your group options. Pick the group you want the icon in and click the Next> button.

Tip

You can also use Windows Explorer to set up an icon quickly. Just use Explorer to view the directory where HGopher was decompressed, click the HGOPHER.EXE file, and drag it to your desktop. Windows 95 will create a shortcut icon automatically.

Note

You can use the installer from NetCD95 to save the time of finding and downloading the HGopher ZIP file.

Tip

Niko Mak Computing's WinZip 6.0 is an excellent 32-bit shareware file compression/decompression utility designed specifically for Windows 95. It's available on the NetCD95 CD-ROM accompanying this book.

To start HGopher, follow these steps:

1. Connect to the Internet via your server or provider.

2. After you're connected, start HGopher by clicking the HGopher icon in your Start menu program group you set up earlier or double-clicking the HGopher icon on your desktop.

3. The HGopher main program window appears with the default bookmarks loaded (as shown in fig. 35.1).

Fig. 35.1

The main
HGopher program
window shows
the default
bookmarks.

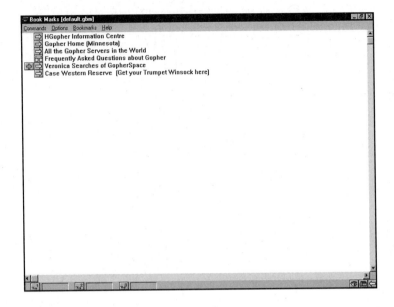

Configuring HGopher

Now that HGopher is on your system and running, it's time to configure it.
HGopher needs some basic information about your network and your computer to function optimally.

To configure HGopher, follow these steps:

1. With HGopher running, choose Options from the HGopher main
   menu.

2. Choose Gopher Set Up from the menu. The Gopher Set Up Options
   dialog box appears (see fig. 35.2).

Fig. 35.2

You can specify
your default server
in the Gopher Set
Up Options dialog
box.

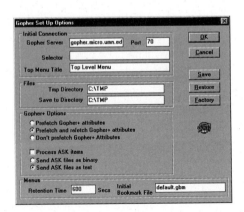

3. If the cursor is not in the Gopher Server field, click the Gopher Server field at the top left in the Initial Connection area of the dialog box with the mouse or move to it using the Tab key.

4. Type **gopher.micro.umn.edu** in the field (you may want to enter a different Home Gopher server later).

5. Using the mouse, click the Tmp Directory field.

6. Enter the complete directory path name for HGopher to store temporary information in (make sure the directory exists).

7. Using the mouse, click the Save to Directory field.

8. Enter the complete directory path name you want to use for storing information retrieved during your Gopher sessions (again, make sure the directory exists).

9. Choose <u>S</u>ave. This action saves your settings to the HGOPHER.INI file (HGopher recalls them automatically when you start each session).

10. Choose OK to return to the main HGopher window.

That's it! Now you're ready to start burrowing your way into new worlds of online information.

Navigating with HGopher

Now that you have completed the installation and basic configuration of HGopher, you can browse at will. Select Go Home from the Commands menu and your HGopher installation will take you to the home of all Gophers, the University of Minnesota (see fig. 35.3).

▶ See "Top Go-
pher Sites,"
p. 1175

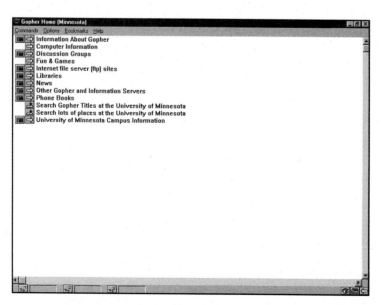

Fig. 35.3
The top page of the University of Minnesota Gopher server is a great place to start your investigation of Gopherspace.

VI

Locating and Retrieving

Why arrange the HGopher window this way? It's really quite simple. From the top down, the HGopher program is designed for ease-of-use and simple navigating. At the top left, you have the standard Windows application devices, from the system icon, the window title (HGopher shows the current Book Mark page title) to the window zoom controls. Next is a standard Windows menu, some of which you have already used in setting up HGopher. At the bottom of the window is the status bar, which tells the status of current connections. It also has several other icon controls, which are discussed a little later.

The remaining real estate is where all the real fun takes place. The main window displays the menu information during the browsing session. This area shows all Gopher resources, with different icon types representing various data types or different ways to access the information.

What do all of these icons mean? Remember, Gopher information is in a structured hierarchy. Every graphic element of a Gopher menu, therefore, tells us something about that resource or represents some means of navigating that ordered list. The following are icon descriptions:

- *Right arrow.* Signifies another directory or additional information (perhaps many documents) at a lower level in the storage order. This is functionally the same as a subdirectory in DOS.
- *Left arrow.* A higher level or "back." This is functionally the same as a parent directory in DOS.
- *Glasses symbol.* A simple text document.
- *Binary symbol (1111).* A binary file.
- *Music symbol.* A sound file.
- *Book symbol.* An index.
- *Film symbol.* A movie.
- *Big H.* An HTML hypertext document.
- *Terminal symbol.* A Telnet resource.
- *IBM Terminal symbol.* A TN3270 resource.
- *Plus symbol.* Gopher+ resource (attributes unknown).
- *Bullet symbol.* Information line, not a resource.
- *Red and Blue Screens symbol.* Multiple views of resource.

As I mentioned earlier, there are also a number of icon indicators or controls on the HGopher status line. They include the following:

- *Lightning symbol.* Connection status.

- *World symbol.* Location status (you're not at home). A click flips you to the default Bookmarks page.

- *Bookshelf symbol.* Location status (you're on the default Bookmarks page). A click flips you to the current site page.

- *Eye symbol.* View mode. This icon changes, depending on if your are copying a single file or a directory.

- *Closed folder symbol.* Copy to File mode; only appears when you are on a file and you click the eye icon.

- *Open folder symbol.* Copy to Directory mode; only appears when you are on a file and you click the eye icon.

- *Right arrow.* Signifies another directory or additional information (perhaps many documents) at a lower level in the storage order (same as in the main window).

- *Left arrow.* A higher level or "back" (same as in the main window).

All these controls serve the purpose of making it easier for you to identify the type of information you're dealing with and to get back and forth more easily. Even with all this, you may find you use only two or three controls to burrow your way around.

Use these steps to see just how easy navigating with HGopher is:

1. With Windows 95 running and connected to the Internet, click the Start menu button and find the program icon you created for HGopher, or the icon you created on the desktop.

2. Select HGopher and open it by clicking the program icon (or double-clicking the icon on the desktop).

3. After HGopher opens to the University of Minnesota Gopher site page, move the mouse cursor to the Information About Gopher line and select it by clicking once on the type. HGopher displays the Information About Gopher page (see fig. 35.4).

> **Note**
>
> To move to a resource, always double-click the description. Don't click the symbols next to the description line (that performs another function covered shortly).

4. Move the mouse cursor to the Previous Menu (Top Level Menu) line and double-click. HGopher takes you back to the page you started from.

VI

Locating and Retrieving

Fig. 35.4

The University
of Minnesota
Information About
Gopher page.

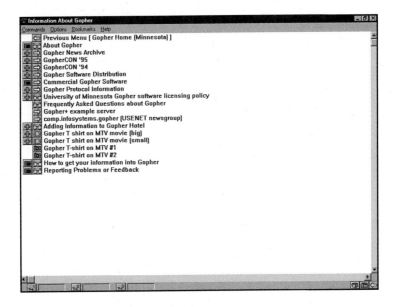

Transferring Files with HGopher

While Gopher is great for cruising for document retrieval, don't be afraid to
use it to get other data formats as well. In fact, using HGopher is a very easy
way to perform FTP transfers.

Follow these steps to transfer a file using HGopher:

1. Return to the University of Minnesota site (see fig. 35.5). Highlight the
   Other Gopher and Information Servers entry and double-click to travel
   to it.

2. Using the techniques you mastered earlier, navigate to the Oakland
   University OAK Software Repository (hint: because you're dealing with
   hierarchical information, start with the most general, such as North
   America, then USA, then California), as shown in fig. 35.6. You may
   have to scroll down the HGopher display page to find the OAK Repository at Oakland U. entry.

3. Select the SimTel item and move to that area.

4. Select the Win95 item and move to that area.

5. Select the graphics item and move to that area. HGopher displays a list
   of files.

6. Scroll down the page and select a file by double-clicking it. HGopher
   displays the standard Save As dialog box (see fig. 35.7).

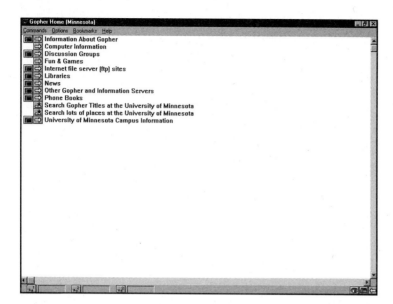

Fig. 35.5

The University of Minnesota Gopher server main page contains links to many other sites.

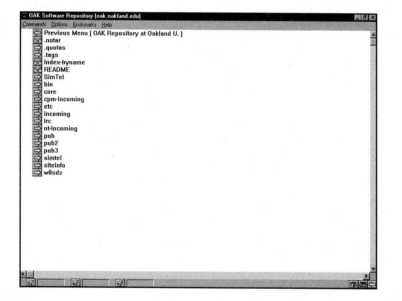

Fig. 35.6

The OAK Software Repository FTP server menu displays the many "goodies" at this site.

7. Choose OK to confirm the download directory (where you want the file stored on your local system).

8. Select the Backward arrow button at the lower right corner of the HGopher window. The HGopher display moves back to the previous page while the download proceeds. Note that the session progress indicators at the lower left of the HGopher window display the status of both the FTP transfer and the page move (see fig. 35.8).

Fig. 35.7
Use the Save As
dialog box to tell
HGopher where to
save files on your
local drive.

Fig. 35.8
HGopher uses
progress indicators
to tell you the
status of your
retrieval request.

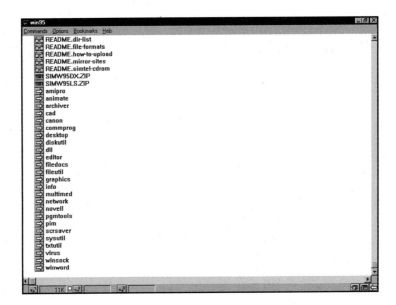

Marking the Gopher Trail with Bookmarks

As you burrow merrily through Gopherspace, you'll probably want to visit
certain sites again and again. Wouldn't it be nice to mark your trail, so that
it's easy to return to your favorite spots quickly and easily?

Most Internet programs have a "bookmark" or "hot list" feature to aid in
navigation, so you don't have to endlessly retrace your steps or memorize or
otherwise record endless lists of server addresses. HGopher makes it easy to
return to any location by using its Bookmarks feature.

Here's how easy it is to set up a HGopher bookmark:

1. Navigate to the University of Minnesota site again. Highlight the Other Gopher and Information Servers entry and double-click to travel to it.

2. Using the techniques you mastered earlier, navigate to the Cambridge University Press Gopher in the United Kingdom (again, start with the highest level in the hierarchy, for example, Europe, and move "downward" to your goal. When you arrive, your screen should look like figure 35.9.

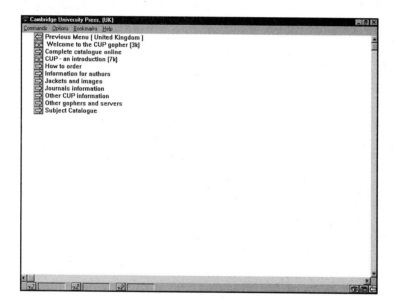

Fig. 35.9
The Cambridge University Press server offers many types of information regarding university publications, all easily accessible from the Gopher menu.

3. Select the Jackets and images entry with a single click.

4. Choose Bookmarks from the HGopher main menu. When the menu appears, choose Mark Menu.

5. Choose Bookmarks from the HGopher main menu. When the menu appears, choose Show Bookmarks. Your screen now appears as in figure 35.10.

Fig. 35.10

You can use the Show Bookmarks command to jump to the current Bookmarks menu without losing your current server menu.

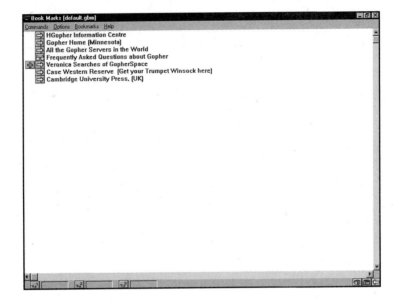

Notice that the Cambridge University Press (UK) Gopher now appears in the default bookmark list. Any page marked this way, from any server you visit, will appear there as well. You can now return to any site on the bookmark list with two simple clicks!

It's important that you save your changes to the HGopher Bookmarks menu. Although HGopher is a very stable client program and certainly prompts you to save changes when you exit the program, it's always best to play it safe and save any change as soon as possible (computers do crash unexpectedly for a wide variety of reasons; power fluctuations alone account for many a tale of digital woe).

To save your HGopher bookmark settings, follow these steps:

1. Choose Bookmarks from the main HGopher menu.

2. If you want to update the current bookmark list, when the list drops down, choose Save Bookmarks on the Bookmarks menu. HGopher updates the current bookmark file with your changes.

3. If you want to save a special set of bookmarks, choose Save Bookmarks As. HGopher displays a standard Save As dialog box, as shown in figure 35.11.

4. Enter the name you want to give the new bookmark file. You may click one of the grayed-out names in the file list, but be aware that you replace that file when you save (HGopher asks you to confirm the replacement at that time with the message This file already exists. Do you want to replace it?).

5. Choose OK to save your changes.

If you make an error when adding bookmarks or you want to start with the default bookmarks file but delete some entries, you can do this easily from the HGopher Bookmarks menu. Follow these steps:

1. Choose Bookmarks from the main HGopher menu.

2. Choose Show Bookmarks from the Bookmarks menu. HGopher then displays the current bookmarks menu page.

3. If you want to edit a bookmarks file other than this, choose Bookmarks from the main HGopher menu again, then choose Load Bookmarks. HGopher displays the standard Open dialog box, and you can select the desired file. Otherwise, proceed to step 4.

4. Highlight the entry you want to delete with a single mouse-click. Then choose Bookmarks, Remove Bookmark from the main HGopher menu.

5. Save your changes as described in the preceding procedure.

You can also edit a bookmark listing's details to change the description, server specification, port setting, data type, and so on by following these steps:

1. Choose Bookmarks from the main HGopher menu.

2. Choose Show Bookmarks from the Bookmarks menu. HGopher then displays the current bookmarks menu page (if you're already there, go directly to step 3).

3. Highlight the entry you want to delete with a single mouse-click. Then choose Bookmarks, Edit Bookmark from the main HGopher menu. HGopher displays the Create/Edit Bookmark dialog box (as shown in fig. 35.12).

4. Edit the bookmark information as needed. (Be sure not to alter any information with which you are unfamiliar. If you need assistance with the specifics, use the excellent HGopher Help system).

VI

Locating and Retrieving

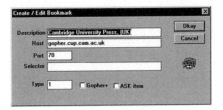

Fig. 35.12
Use the Create/
Edit Bookmark
dialog box to
update or alter
bookmarks if
needed.

You may also create bookmarks if you have the necessary information. Follow
these steps:

1. Choose Bookmarks from the main HGopher menu.

2. Choose Show Bookmarks from the Bookmarks menu. HGopher then
   displays the current bookmarks menu page (if you're already there, go
   directly to step 3).

3. Choose Bookmarks, Create Bookmark from the main HGopher menu.
   HGopher displays the Create/Edit Bookmark dialog box, as shown in
   figure 35.13. (Note that there is no information in the dialog box fields;
   you must provide all necessary information if you create a bookmark
   entry "from scratch.")

Fig. 35.13
HGopher lets you
set up a bookmark
from scratch, but
you need to know
all the specifics for
the bookmark
before you begin.

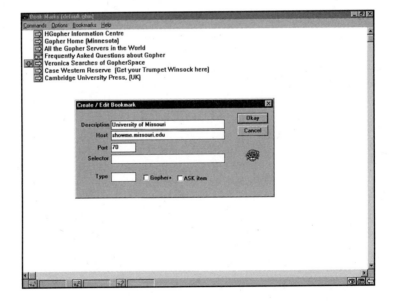

Using Other HGopher Features

Although HGopher is very easy to use, it also has other feature options that can give you a lot of power over how it operates. Control over the page cache (the memory and drive space used to store recently displayed pages for quick redisplay), network setup, language preferences, fonts, and other program variables give the user a tremendous amount of power over the interface and operation of the program.

Resetting HGopher's Page Display Storage

HGopher gives you several levels of menu pages in normal operation. As you travel through Gopherspace, you can easily move forward and backward through the menus, without reloading them every time—this is because HGopher stores the menus locally for quick and easy retrieval. Although this is a great idea, it doesn't always work perfectly.

If you ever find your page cache filled with the same menus (you click the Forward and Backward symbols at the lower right of the HGopher window, but you see the same set of menus as you move), you can do a cache flush to reset the system. Follow these steps:

1. Choose Options from the main HGopher menu.
2. When the menu list drops, choose Flush Cache.

That's all there is to it!

Choosing the Copy Mode

You can choose the manner in which HGopher handles information when you retrieve it from a Gopher. Usually you want to truly browse, reading text on your display. But what if you want the information in a file for later retrieval, distribution, or review? HGopher gives you options for each of these cases.

You can save documents to either a specific file in a particular location once, or tell HGopher to place all documents in a specific directory when you save them. Normally HGopher places documents in the specified temporary directory and simply asks you to verify the file name when you save. If you change the Copy Mode setting under the Options menu by choosing Copy to Directory, HGopher lets you specify a new default directory for documents. This can be really useful if you want to save multiple documents organized by location or topic.

Altering the Default Gopher Set Up Options

Although you've already performed the basic configurations to get HGopher up and running on your system, you may find that you want to alter some of these later. For example, you may want to alter the default home Gopher site that HGopher goes to when it first loads.

To alter the default server and other options, follow these steps:

1. With HGopher running, choose Options from the HGopher main menu. Choose Gopher Set Up from the menu. The Gopher Set Up Options dialog box appears (see fig. 35.14).

Fig. 35.14

When using the Gopher Set Up Options dialog box, be sure to confirm any information before you enter it here, or it may affect your capability to connect to Gopher sites.

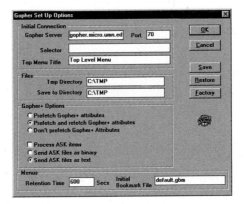

In this dialog box, you can edit any of the program defaults as necessary. Again, don't alter any item you don't understand or have tested alternative specifications for (see HGopher Help for more information).

Altering Network Set Up Options

If you've been able to connect to Gopher sites without fail, you probably don't need to change any of the network specifications. If you find you can connect to most but not all servers and resources, you may need to enter alternative domain name server addresses to correct the problem.

To change the network settings, follow these steps:

1. Choose Options from the main HGopher menu and then choose Network Set Up. The Network Setup dialog box appears, as shown in figure 35.15.

Fig. 35.15
The Network Setup
dialog box allows
you to specify
alternate domain
name servers. Be
sure to confirm
any information
before you enter it.

2. The Use Vendor Provided check box should already be selected. If you have had no trouble finding information, don't change this. If you're experiencing trouble, proceed to step 3.

3. If your service provider, network, or TCP/IP dial-up utility doesn't provide reliable domain name search service, you can specify alternate servers by selecting the Use DNS check box. If you do this, you must have verified Domain Name Server addresses ready for use in step 4.

4. Enter the DNS addressed in dotted quad (numeric form) in the DNS fields. These must be entered in numeric format, for example, as 128.206.2.252, not dns.ic.ac.uk.

> **Note**
>
> Don't make any changes in this dialog box that you don't understand, haven't tested, or have not been provided by qualified personnel. Your computer won't burst into flames if this stuff is wrong, but you won't have much luck doing Gopher searches.

5. The Local Domain usually is not required; however, you need to enter your local system here, if any entry is made at all (for example, if your machine address is clark.superman.na.earth, you enter **superman.na.earth** in this field).

Setting Up Viewers

HGopher can display almost any type of information found on a Gopher site, as long as you have the proper helper application set up and linked to HGopher's system. For example, if you want to view JPEG-compressed files, you need a compatible viewer, and you need to tell HGopher where to find it.

Some example Windows applications archives are the following:

- LVIEW31.ZIP (for JPEG and other images)
- MPEGV11D.ZIP (for MPEG movies)

■ MPEGW32G.ZIP (for MPEG movies)

■ AVIPRO2.EXE (for Video for Windows)

■ WHAM131.ZIP (for audio files)

You can find these viewers at most popular FTP or Web sites, such as the following:

■ **ftp.cica.indiana.edu**

■ **gatekeeper.dec.com/pub/micro/msdos/win3/**

■ **ftp.gatekeeper.dec.com/pub/micro/msdos/win3/sounds/**

■ **ftp.papa.indstate.edu/winsock-l/Windows95/**

■ **http://www.tucows.com/**

■ **http://cwsapps.texas.net/**

You also can find these and other utilities on the NetCD95 CD-ROM that accompanies this book. See the "Multimedia Editors and Viewers" section of chapter 50, "Installing and Using NetCD95," for additional details. For information on setting up these viewers, see chapter 24, "Using Helper Apps."

To set up HGopher for a viewer, follow these steps:

1. Choose <u>O</u>ptions from the main HGopher menu and then choose <u>V</u>iewer Set Up. The Viewers dialog box appears, as shown in figure 35.16.

Fig. 35.16
You can specify custom viewers for a wide variety of information formats in the HGopher Viewers dialog box.

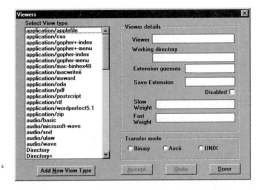

Tip

If you don't have viewers for a data type, see the Viewers section of chapter 50, "Installing and Using NetCD95," and chapter 24, "Using Helper Apps."

2. Select image/jpeg from the Select View type scroll list. When you click it, the fields in the right half of the dialog box display the current settings for this data type.

3. Enter the information for your viewer utility in the fields provided. See HGopher Help for detailed information regarding the proper specifications.

Caution

Be sure to choose Accept before clicking Done to save your changes for each viewer type. This dialog box does not save all changes at exit, so Accept all changes for each viewer type as you go.

To test the viewer with an HGopher session, follow these steps:

1. Connect to the Internet via your server or provider.

2. After you're connected, start HGopher by clicking the HGopher icon in your Start menu program group you set up earlier or by double-clicking the HGopher icon on your desktop.

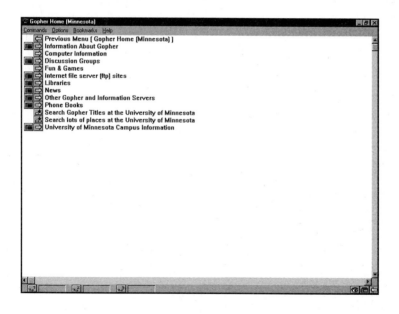

Fig. 35.17
HGopher will open to the University of Minnesota Gopher menu.

VI

Locating and Retrieving

3. Using the techniques you learned earlier, set up a bookmark for NASA Space Images at the host **gopher.earth.nwu.edu** (use the selector specification **ftp:explorer.arc.nasa.bov@pub/SPACE/JPEG**) as shown in figure 35.18.

Fig. 35.18
The NASA Space Images archive contains many opportunities to test viewer support with HGopher.

4. Load the bookmark by selecting Show Bookmarks from the Bookmark menu. Select any of the JPEG files and double-click to retrieve. The viewer decodes and displays the image when the transfer is completed.

Searching Gopherspace with Veronica

So far in this chapter, you've looked at the basics of navigating the vast burrows of Gopherspace by using two typical Gopher programs, or clients. While this is pretty simple (and actually a lot of fun), there are other tools you can use to speed up your burrowing and increase your awareness of this rich Internet resource.

What Is Veronica?

One of the cooler things about the Net is that even in such a hive of technobabble, geekdom, and cyberspeak people retain their sense of humor. Some of the nicest touches are the names given different software packages and services. C'mon, who doesn't crack a smile when you think of "using" a Gopher?

Another classic running joke on the Net is the use of puns on cartoon character names. This trend started with the use of the term "Archie" for server software that searches FTP archives. Not to be outdone, the developers of a search application for Gopherspace concocted the following gem:

Very **E**asy **R**odent-**O**riented **N**et-wide **I**ndex to **C**omputerized **A**rchives

otherwise known as *Veronica* (while I'm not aware of a Betty application, I'm sure somewhere, someone is working feverishly to wrap that name around an acronym, too).

Veronica is a service that keeps an index of the titles of all articles in Gopherspace (a daunting task, to be sure). Veronica only searches for words in directory or document titles (it doesn't do a full-text search of the contents of Gopher resources). A "title" is the title of the Gopher resource as shown by the server it's on. You can access Veronica through most Gopher clients and servers; there is no "Veronica client," per se. The result of a Veronica search is a list of Gopher items, displayed in the form of a Gopher menu.

Many Veronica menus display a list of multiple Gopher servers offering Veronica. It theoretically shouldn't matter which server you choose, as they should all provide the same information, but practically you may find one to be better than another on a specific topic (the servers update the index periodically, but the schedule is different from system to system). There's also network traffic to consider, as some servers are more popular than others.

Other Veronica systems simply offer a single menu item and select the server for you after you enter the search specification.

Using Veronica to Search Gopherspace

If your default Gopher server doesn't offer a Veronica service, you can always fall back to the one at the University of Minnesota. It's available at **gopher.micro.umn.edu**. While the following general example uses HGopher to demonstrate a Veronica search, you can use any Gopher client to do so—Veronica is a service provided by the server, not the client.

To use Veronica with HGopher, follow these steps:

1. Connect to the Internet via your server or provider.

2. Open HGopher by clicking the HGopher icon in the Windows Start menu or by double-clicking the HGopher icon on your desktop.

3. After HGopher opens to the University of Minnesota Gopher site page, select the Other Gopher and Information Servers item. HGopher displays the menu after a few seconds.

4. Select the Search Titles in Gopherspace Using Veronica item. HGopher displays the menu for that item, as shown in figure 35.19.

Fig. 35.19
You can select from a wide variety of search types and areas from the Veronica item menu.

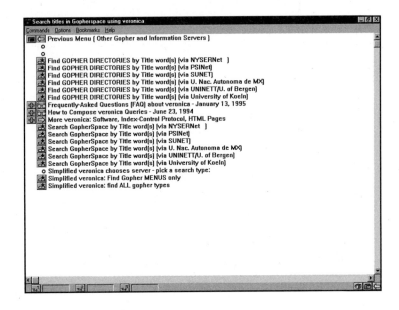

5. Select one of the Search Gopherspace items and double-click. HGopher displays the Index Search dialog box, as shown in figure 35.20.

Fig. 35.20
Make your search string as specific as possible.

6. Enter the search specification in the Search Strings field.

7. Choose OK, and HGopher displays the menu of items found relating to that specification.

Tip

If you get a message such as ***Too many connections Try again soon*** during a Veronica search, don't despair. Pick another server, or do try again soon. Many servers are busy, and there are certain peak traffic periods for each locality.

Tailoring Your Veronica Queries

How you construct and enter your Veronica query will make as much of a difference as which server you work with. When entering your queries, follow these guidelines:

- Use multi-word queries to narrow your search more quickly. Veronica supports Boolean operators (AND, NOT, OR).

- Think creatively about information. There may not be a document or directory titled "Boston Red Sox," but there may be document containing information on that team under "baseball AND losers."

- Use wildcards in your queries. Like MS-DOS, Veronica will support the asterisk (*), but only at the end of words.

- Use the -t flag to narrow your searches for specific document types. Official Gopher document types, from the Gopher Protocol Document, are:

0	Text file
1	Directory
2	CSO name server
4	Mac HQX file
5	PC binary
7	Full text index (Gopher menu)
8	Telnet session
9	Binary file
s	Sound
e	Event (not in 2.06)
I	Image (other than GIF)
M	MIME multipart/mixed message
T	TN3270 session
c	Calendar (not in 2.06)
g	GIF image
h	HTML (HyperText Markup Language)

What Is Jughead?

Another type of Gopherspace directory search is named after yet another cartoon character, Archie and Veronica's friend, Jughead. Developed at the University of Utah by Rhett "Jonzy" Jones, this search tool acronym stands for (cue drum roll, prepare to groan):

Jonzy's **U**niversal **G**opher **H**ierarchy **E**xcavation **A**nd **D**isplay

Jughead is similar to Veronica in that it offers a means to search Gopherspace, but it differs in important ways. Jughead, like Veronica, runs as a server on

VI

Locating and Retrieving

the Gopher site and provides a pre-built table of directory information that can be searched. Unlike Veronica, Jughead is usually implemented for a particular Gopher site, allowing more complete searches of that site versus an overview of the totality of Gopherspace. Think of Veronica as a good general Gopherspace search tool, and Jughead as the tool of choice for deep burrowing of a local system.

Jughead also offers Boolean search specifications and supports some special commands we look at later in this section.

Searching with Jughead

A good place to start using Jughead is the University of Utah. While this example uses this specific Gopher site and Jughead server, you can use these techniques at any site that supports this server type.

To use the Jughead server at the University of Utah:

1. Connect to the Internet via your server or provider.

2. Open HGopher by clicking the HGopher icon in the Windows Start menu or by double-clicking the HGopher icon on your desktop.

3. After your HGopher client opens, move to the University of Utah Gopher site as shown in figure 35.21.

Fig. 35.21
The University of Utah Gopher is a great place to start working with Jughead.

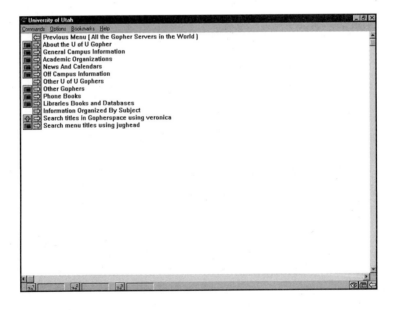

4. Select the Search Menu Titles Using Jughead item. The University of Utah server displays the Jughead menu (see fig. 35.22).

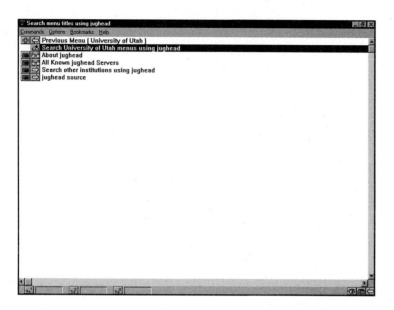

Fig. 35.22
The University of Utah Gopher Jughead menu offers local searching, plus references for other Jughead servers around the world.

5. Select the Search the University of Utah Menus Using Jughead Item. The Jughead server will display the Index Search dialog box as shown in figure 35.23.

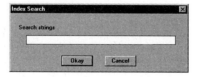

Fig. 35.23
The sparse appearance of the Jughead page hides the power this search engine offers.

6. Using the mouse, place the cursor in the search specification entry field and click once. Type your search specification in the field as shown in figure 35.24.

7. Select the Okay button, and Jughead will display the results of your search as shown in figure 35.25.

VI

Locating and Retrieving

Fig. 35.24
Make your search
string as specific as
possible.

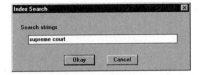

Fig. 35.25
Jughead delivers
the goods, fast.

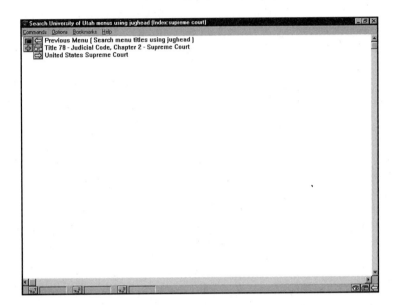

Tip

You can get a great list of Jughead servers from the University of Utah Jughead menu.
Select All Known Jughead Servers for a great reference. Be sure to make a bookmark!

Tailoring Your Jughead Queries

How you construct and enter your Jughead query makes a big difference in
the level of success you achieve in your searches. When entering your queries, follow the same general guidelines for Boolean searches as outlined in
the previous section about Veronica.

In addition to the common Boolean search techniques, Jughead supports
some special commands. The general format for these commands is:

    ?command what

Each special Jughead command must be prefixed by the question mark, followed by the command, a space, and then the command search string. Jughead supports the following special commands:

- `?all what`—returns all matches on search string `what`
- `?help [what]`—returns help document and any optional matches for search string `what`
- `?limit=n what`—returns the quantity *n* items matching search string `what`
- `?range=n1-n2 what`—returns matches from *n1*-*n2* for search string `what`

While these special commands allow great flexibility in narrowing your searches, you can only use one special command per query. If you happen to make an error with any of these commands, Jughead will return a help document with the type of error included in the document title.

Jughead also reserves special characters for itself. If you use any of the following in a query, it will be interpreted as a space:

> !"#$%&'()+,-./:;?@[\]^'{|}~

In other words, if you enter **supreme.court**, Jughead will see it as "supreme court," which under Boolean logic reads as "supreme AND court," which may limit your search in ways you may not anticipate.

Sites of Interest: The Best of Gopher

There's such an incredible variety of information available via Gopherspace that it's difficult to recommend any specific place to start. For a great general reference of Gopher sites, begin with the Other Gopher and Information Servers item at the University of Minnesota server and proceed from there. For additional specific references, be sure to see chapter 49, "Top Gopher Sites."

CHAPTER 36

Using WAIS

WAIS stands for *Wide Area Information Servers* and is pronounced "ways." WAIS searches for words in documents. To do a WAIS search, you supply a keyword for the information you want and the WAIS servers search their databases for text or multimedia matches.

Suppose you want to find details about how the NAFTA agreement is effecting your industry. Use a WAIS client, select the servers, and enter the keyword NAFTA, your industry, and any other words to narrow down a search. WAIS comes up with a list of documents ranked according to how many times the keywords are mentioned.

For example, if you search to see how the NAFTA agreement effects the apparel industry in Mexico, you search for the keywords NAFTA, Mexico, and apparel. In response, you might get a list of documents detailing the process of the trade talks, the agreement itself, lists of companies planning to expand trade with Mexico, and documents about U.S. firms moving operations to Mexico.

You can then tell WAIS to look for more documents similar to the ones you indicate as closest to what you want. WAIS takes your documents as examples and tries to find matches based on those documents. This relevance feedback search is one of the most useful features WAIS has.

WAIS goes beyond Gopher, FTP, and Archie searches, because all kinds of information can be indexed on a WAIS server. You'll find still and moving pictures, sound files, and programs, as well as documents.

◀ See "Using FTP
and Popular
FTP Programs,"
p. 837

WAIS was originally developed by Thinking Machines, Apple Computer, Dow
Jones, and KPMG Peat Marwick, but the freeware WAIS is no longer supported by those companies. CNIDR (Clearinghouse for Networked Information Discovery and Retrieval) now maintains freeware WAIS.

Tip

A FAQ (frequently asked questions) list for WAIS can be retrieved by an anonymous
FTP at **rtfm.mit.edu** under the directory /pub/usenet/news.answers/wais-faq. The
document, about eight pages long, also lists some WAIS mailing lists and WAIS client
software sites for most platforms.

There are different ways to conduct a WAIS search. Until the Windows-based
client software was written, you had to log on to a public WAIS server and
use UNIX commands. You still can, but WAIS software for Windows makes
WAISing a breeze. There are also other accessible, but limited, ways to conduct a WAIS search using e-mail and Gopher.

In this chapter, you learn how to do the following:

■ Look at searching WAIS servers with the WAIS client programs
   WinWAIS and WAIS Manager

■ Search WAIS space with HGopher

■ Use e-mail to conduct a WAIS search and retrieve documents

Using WinWAIS

NetCD95

WinWAIS was developed by the Information Systems Division of the United
States Geological Survey. That's why WinWAIS includes a map and the ability
to use location on earth as a search criteria, but we'll leave that to the
geologists.

The executable file for WinWAIS is wwais24.exe, available by anonymous
FTP from **ridgisd.er.usgs.gov** in the directory /software/wais. You can also
obtain it from **http://tucows.com**, an excellent general repository of
Winsock software. Version 2.4 contains bug fixes. The instructions for loading in the following section pertain only to this version. Previous versions
need to be set up differently.

Installing WinWAIS

After you retrieve the necessary file to install WinWAIS on your system, all you have to do is extract the program files, run the setup program, and create the icons. To create the icons for WinWAIS, follow these steps:

1. To create a Start menu shortcut icon for WinWAIS, right-click an empty space on the Windows 95 taskbar. A pop-up menu displays several items; click Properties.

2. The Taskbar Properties dialog box appears. Select the Start Menu Properties tab.

3. Click the Add button. The Create Shortcut dialog box appears.

4. Click Browse, and choose the wais.exe file from the directory you created for WinWAIS. Click the Next button, and the Select Program Folder dialog box displays your group options. Pick the group you want the icon in and click the Next> button.

> **Note**
>
> You can also put a shortcut icon for WinWAIS on your desktop very quickly and easily. Just use Windows Explorer to open the directory where wais.exe is located, click once to select it, and then drag it to the desktop. Windows will automatically create a shortcut icon for you there.

WinWAIS comes with Dialler (that's the way it's spelled—the programmer is Australian), a SLIP communications program. You already have a SLIP or PPP dialer that comes with Windows 95 to connect you to the Internet. If you want to use the WinWAIS Dialler, you may want to create a Start menu or desktop shortcut icon for it too. To create the Dialler icon, follow the same basic procedure as above, just select the waisdial.exe file instead of winwais.exe. If you do choose to use the WinWAIS Dialler, be aware of its shortcomings: it won't support 28.8 modems, and can be a real pain to set up.

◄ See "Connecting to a PPP or SLIP Account with Windows 95," p. 137

> **Note**
>
> Ignore the readme.txt file. The sections in the file that deal with installation problems are inaccurate; they haven't been updated to include the latest bug fixes for version 2.4.

VI

Locating and Retrieving

Searching for WAIS Information

After you have WinWAIS installed and set up, you can search for information. First, you have to choose which source to search. WinWAIS comes with two source options, WAIS and ALLSRC. WAIS is the Directory of Sources, a handy place to look if you don't know where to begin. ALLSRC contains hundreds of popular source sites, identified in the list by a descriptive name (such as Whitehse.src, a source for White House files).

To set up a search session, follow these steps:

1. With Windows running and an active Internet connection established, open WinWAIS by selecting the WinWAIS 2.4 icon in the Windows 95 Start menu or from your desktop (whichever you created earlier).

2. Choose File, Select Sources.

3. Click the Source Group list box arrow control. Choose WAIS or ALLSRC.

4. If you choose Directory of Sources, click Done or press F3 to go back to the search window.

5. If you choose ALLSRC, go through the list and double-click each source you want to add. You can also choose Add All, as shown in figure 36.1. (To remove a source, double-click it.) Click Done to go back to the search window.

Fig. 36.1

You can choose the Directory of Servers to start.

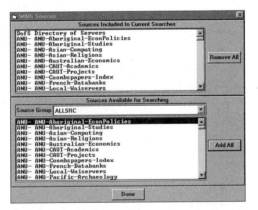

Tip

The fewer sources you include, the quicker your search can be.

6. Type the words you want to match in the Tell Me About box.

7. Click Search. The Status line (at the bottom of the screen) should soon say Querying Directory-Of-Servers and an IP address of the server.

Tip

If you get a WinSock Error dialog box, it just means WinWAIS couldn't reach that server. If you selected multiple servers, WinWAIS will continue the search with the next server in your list after you click the OK button in the error dialog box.

When the search is complete, the Status line will indicate the number of sources found. They'll be indexed in the Resulting Documents window on the bottom half of the screen, as shown in figure 36.2.

Fig. 36.2
Be patient; it may take a few moments for WinWAIS to check all the servers you've asked it to, especially over a SLIP or PPP connection.

WAIS searches are ranked according to how many times the specified words appear in a document. WinWAIS lists these rankings with asterisks under Score. The more asterisks, the higher up the document, the more times your search words appeared in the document.

> ### Tip
> Remember, this isn't artificial intelligence. WAIS can only respond to exact word matches, and bases a rank on the number of citations.

To retrieve a document, follow these steps:

1. Double-click an entry in the Resulting Documents window. WinWAIS will display the document shown in figure 36.3.

Fig. 36.3

When you double-click a document title, WinWAIS displays it complete with highlights showing your search reference.

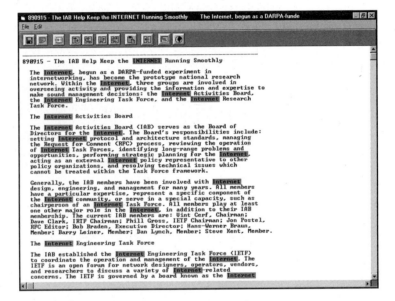

2. To get back to the search window, open the File menu and choose File, Done (or press F3).

Using Relevance Feedback

A WAIS search is powerful because it can use what's called *relevance feedback,* which means it can take any resulting document and search for more documents similar to it.

To search using relevance feedback, follow these steps:

1. Perform a search.

2. In the Resulting Documents list, click the document(s) that are most like the one(s) you're looking for.

3. Choose Add Doc. The document appears in the Similar To box (see fig. 36.4). Choose Delete Doc to delete it from the same box.

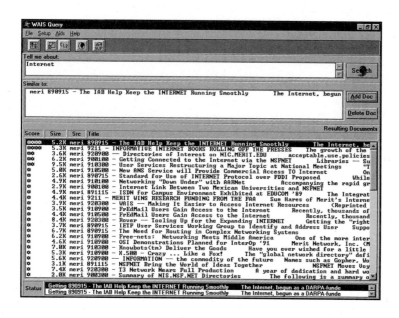

Fig. 36.4
A relevance feedback search with WinWAIS.

4. Click the Search button (a globe icon) to search for more documents.

Saving Information to the Clipboard

To copy the information to the Clipboard, follow these steps:

1. Click at the beginning of the text, drag the mouse to the end and let go.

2. Open the Edit menu and choose Copy, or press Shift+F6, or click the Clipboard icon.

3. Open Windows Notepad and choose Paste to copy the Clipboard information.

What the WAIS Finds Tell You

WAIS supplies you with a document that tells you details about what information is available at a particular sources, and how to get it. In many cases, you can get the document itself. Some sites, however, are available only by another retrieval method, such as FTP. The retrieved document will say so.

◀ See "Using FTP and Popular FTP Programs," p. 837

For example, if you query the Directory of Servers for the OSHA Technical Manual, WAIS initially comes up 46 documents. Double-clicking the OSHA Technical Manual entry retrieves the information. It's not a text file but a document that tells you where to get the text file. To retrieve the file, you need to use a different tool.

▶ See "Searching on the Internet," p. 911

VI

Locating and Retrieving

Troubleshooting

All of a sudden I can't do a search with WinWAIS. I keep getting Connect error messages.

Did you add a new TCP/IP stack, or move .DLL files around? Check to make sure you're using the right version of files for the TCP/IP stack program.

The only source I can access is the Directory of Servers. What happened to the other sources?

Make sure the file Allsrc.src is in your WinWAIS directory. If not, copy it from the unzipped file. If you already deleted the unzipped files, retrieve WinWAIS again, put it in a temporary directory, unzip it, and copy Allsrc.src to your WinWAIS directory.

No matter what I do, I can't conduct a search. What's the problem?

The name server could be down, which means nobody can get through. Or the source server could be down. Try FTPing or pinging the server to see if it's down. If you get no response, it's probably not you and you'll have to wait until it's up.

Using WAIS Manager 3.1

Overall, WAIS Manager is easier to use than WinWAIS, although neither is very difficult. Earlier versions of WinWAIS were riddled with setup bugs, but that's been fixed. Now, you need to go through a few more steps to install WAIS Manager.

The simplest way to get the latest version of WAIS Manager is to visit the Ultimate Collection of Winsock Software at **http://www.tucows.com/softwais.html** using your favorite Web browser.

Installing WAIS Manager 3.1

It's a little tricky to set up WAIS Manager 3.1 because it was written with a utility called Toolbook. To unzip and install WAIS Manager 3.1, follow these steps:

1. Extract waisman3.zip to a new directory (we'll call it \WAISMAN, but you don't have to). The program will create two directories, \WAISMAN3 and \WAIS_SRC. The file programs are in \WAISMAN3, and the sources are in \WAIS_SRC.

2. To create an icon for WinWAIS, right-click an empty space on the Windows 95 Taskbar. A pop-up menu displays several items; select Properties with a click of the left mouse button.

3. The Taskbar Properties dialog box appears. Select the Start Menu Properties tab.

4. Click the Add button. The Create Shortcut dialog box appears.

5. Click Browse, and choose the WAISMAN3.TBK file from the directory you created for WAISMAN. Click the next button, and the Select Program Folder dialog box displays your group options. Pick the group you want the icon in and click the Next> button.

Tip

Windows 95 won't have a file association for .TBK Toolbook files by default. Use Windows Explorer's View, Options, File Types dialog to set up support for Toolbook applications.

Searching with WAIS Manager 3.1

Although this section comes after the instructions on WinWAIS, we're going to assume you haven't done a WAIS search before—on the theory that you will choose one WAIS client or the other, but not both.

The first thing you need to do is define your search terms. WAIS Manager 3.1 is so friendly it even comes with a list of searches, to give you an idea of what kind of information is available.

To use a pre-defined search, do the following:

1. Using the Windows 95 Start menu button, locate the icon you created for WAIS Manager. Click the icon to launch the program.

2. Choose Query, Select Query to get the list shown in figure 36.5, or press the large yellow question mark icon.

Fig. 36.5
Choosing a stored query with WAIS Manager 3.1.

3. Double-click a query. You will go back to the main menu, the appropriate source will be listed in the Database section, and some keywords will be listed under Keywords.

4. If the keywords aren't what you were looking for, you can change them or go back and select another query.

5. Specify a maximum number of documents WAIS Manager should look for.

6. Open the Search menu and choose Search Selection or press the button showing a magnifying glass above a stack of papers.

7. WAIS Manager returns a list of possible hits. To retrieve a document, double-click the entry. WAIS Manager displays the document in WordPad.

8. To save the document, choose File, Save As and specify a name.

To create your own search terms, follow these steps:

1. Using the Windows 95 Start menu button, locate the icon you created for WAIS Manager. Click the icon to launch the program.

2. Choose Query, Select, Query or press the large yellow question mark icon to get a list of sources.

3. Choose one or more sources.

4. Click OK.

5. Choose Keywords, but remember, this is more of a natural language search, not a Boolean search strictly using and/or.

6. Choose a maximum number of documents you want retrieved (the higher the number, the longer the search will take).

7. Open the Search menu and choose Search Selection or press the icon displaying a magnifying glass over a globe.

8. WAIS Manager returns a list of possible hits. To retrieve a document, double-click the entry.

Using Relevance Feedback

When you use relevance feedback, you show WAIS the kind of documents you're looking for and it attempts to get more. To use relevance feedback, conduct a search according to the previous guidelines. Then follow these steps:

1. Click the document you want to use as a model for other documents.

2. Click the icon showing a magnifying glass over two connected documents.

That's it. You can keep going this way for a long time, either narrowing your original search or getting further away from it—whatever you're looking for.

Saving WAIS Information

After you find related documents, you can save the information, print it, or return to the search results by using one of the following:

- Open the File menu and choose Save As to save the information to a disk file.
- Open the File menu and choose Print, to print the file.
- Open the File menu and choose Done, or press F3 to go back to the search results menu.

Saving Queries for Future Use

You can save queries that you plan on using again. To save queries, do the following:

1. Choose the Keywords and a source.

2. Open the File menu and choose Save Queries. The query is saved under the keywords (for example, a query to find "Degas paintings" is listed under "Degas paintings" in the saved query list).

The next time you look in the list of saved queries, the query will be there.

Using Viewers

WAIS Manager can retrieve nearly any kind of files, but it needs viewers to show them to you. You'll need to have the program it assigns to a file type in order to see it. To change assignments, follow these steps:

1. Open the Options menu and choose Default Viewers.

2. Click a type of file to see what program WAIS Manager can view it with:

   Choose WAIS Type, Delete WAIS Type to delete a format. Choose WAIS Type, Edit WAIS Type to change the program. Choose WAIS Type, New WAIS Type to add a file format.

3. Click OK.

4. Click the entry you just created.

5. Click in the View With box and type the name of the viewer file.

6. Choose OK.

VI

Locating and Retrieving

WAIS Searches with E-Mail

You also can search WAIS servers with an e-mail request. The beauty of that is, once you've made the request, you can let the software do the work for you. The down side is it takes longer, and you can't do relevance feedback.

You use your regular mail client program. To e-mail a search to WAIS space, you must do the following:

■ Address the mail to **waismail@quake.think.com**.

■ Format the request exactly this way, substituting the words in italics with your own parameters:

search *sourcename keywords*

The source name is the database you want to search, and the keywords are what you're looking for (see fig. 36.6).

Fig. 36.6

Performing a WAIS search with e-mail.

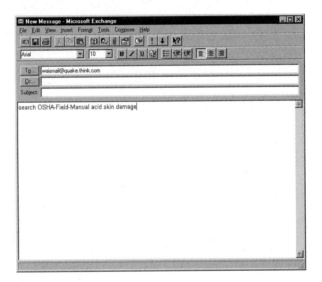

When you get the results back, you can choose which documents to retrieve. Again address e-mail to **waismail@quake.think.com**, and type the word **retrieve** followed by the *DocID*.

Troubleshooting

WAIS Manager sometimes gets hung up on "Retrieving document from remote server," for long periods of time. What does this mean?

It could mean that the server is down, and the program won't give up trying to get to it. Or it could mean the application has quit. Press Ctrl+Alt+Del once to see if you get a message saying the application has stopped responding to the system. This will bring up the Close Program dialog box, the user interface for the Windows 95 task manager. Don't press Ctrl+Alt+Del again, or Windows 95 will reboot the computer, and you'll lose any unsaved work. The Close Program dialog box offers you the choice of ending the hung task, shutting down, canceling, or using Ctrl+Alt+Del to reboot (not always the safest choice, but sometimes it's the only way to free up the system).

CHAPTER 37

Searching on the Internet

The best way to learn how to search for information on the Internet is to forget what you know about searching for information. There's information, and lots of it. There are software programs, graphics, magazine articles, job postings, government reports, weather maps, and thousands and thousands of documents. The hardest part about searching on the Internet is understanding that the chicken came before the egg, so to speak. That is, the information existed before the programs to find the information.

Unlike commercial databases, no one planned how everyone was going to access the information. And before the advent of very fast, 486- and Pentium-based PCs, most people didn't have enough raw power to operate more than a bare-bones search tool like Archie or Telnet.

Now, with the World Wide Web, you can apply the easy-to-use browser interface to the task of searching the Net. There are a wide variety of Web sites that specialize in helping you find your way in the maze of Internet information.

In this chapter you learn the following:

- The many kinds of information available on the Internet
- The different tools needed to access information
- How to decide which tool to use
- Some sample searches using different tools

Available Information

There is probably every kind of information you can want floating around somewhere on the Internet. That's not to say that you will always be able to get to it. However, if it exists in a computer somewhere, you probably can get to it through the Internet.

▶ See "Privacy and Security on the Net," p. 1033

Not that you should be able to get anything that exists (some things should remain private—corporate strategy, for example). Internet security will become a bigger issue in the next few years as more people become adept at searching for and retrieving information.

Because you're at the beginning of an Internet information revolution, it's not always easy to find what you want—or to even know how to find it.

While the majority of information is still free on the Internet, commercial services are popping up. In this chapter, you're going to look at free information (because once somebody wants to sell you something, they will make sure you know how to find them). You'll begin with the simple and go on to the sublime (in Internet terms, anyway).

What Are Search Engines?

The Internet is such a large conglomerate of systems and resources that any attempt to create a comprehensive catalog is doomed to failure. The rate of growth of information currently exceeds any technology's ability to keep pace. Fortunately, the World Wide Web, as a subset of the total Internet, is a bit more manageable in this respect.

The HTTP protocol that drives Webspace offers tools that allow the design of automated search and indexing *engines*, programs that gather data and present it to the Web user in a searchable format. There are several examples of this type of utility on the Web. These programs run on server systems as separate tasks from other server types, perhaps sharing processor resources with the other servers (HTTP, FTP, etc.) in use at that site. Several of the engines have developed from information management research projects in the graduate departments of major universities and have rather beefy hardware to support them; some of these have been developed even further as commercial entities.

Web search engines provide many valuable services:

- Automated search of Webspace for new sites
- Indexing of available sites by URL
- Indexing of site by page titles, text content, quality of content, and "freshness" of content

While early examples of search engines were restricted to simple indexes of Web sites by URL and home page title, most Web search engines now extend their reach beyond Webspace into UseNet News archives, WAIS, Gopher sites, and even Telnet resources. As the commercialization of Web search engines continues, expect to see not only indexing of content itself but reviews and commentary regarding the indexed sites and material. Competition in this niche service area will only benefit the Web user with a more rich and robust set of tools for research and recreation.

> **Note**
>
> Don't mistake a site that simply lists new or interesting sites as a true search engine. The "Pick of the Day" type of site is fun and even useful but rarely has any real software muscle behind it for true searching.

Popular Web Search Engines

Some of the older, venerable Web search sites are still available, and some have been transformed into totally commercial entities (you may even see a spot of advertising here and there, helping pay for some of the processor horsepower needed to keep the indexes current). Table 37.1 lists some of the most popular sites presently available at press time (be aware that the Web changes daily, so don't be surprised if a site moves or disappears altogether):

Table 37.1 Popular Web Search Sites

Site	Address
555-1212.Com Business Search	**http://www.555-1212.com**
Aliweb	**http://web.nexor.co.uk/ public/aliweb/aliweb.html**
City Net	**http://www.city.net/**
Commercial Advertising Server	**http://www.comcomsystems. com/**

(continues)

VI

Locating and Retreiving

Table 37.1   Continued

Site	Address
CUI World Wide Web Catalog	http://cuiwww.unige.ch/cgi-bin/w3catalog
EINet Galaxy	http://www.einet.net/
Excite NetSearch	http://www.excite.com
Harvest Search	http://harvest.cs.colorado.edu/harvest/demobrokers.html
HTML555-1212.Com Area Code Search	http://www.555-1212.com/ACLOOKUP
IBM InfoMarket	http://www.infomkt.ibm.com
Infoseek	http://www2.infoseek.com
Inktomi's Search Engine	http://inktomi.berkeley.edu/query.html
Lycos Search	http://www.lycos.com
Maple Square-Canada	http://www.canadas.net/Maple-Square/
New Rider's Yellow Pages	http://www.mcp.com/nrp/wwwyp
Nikos Search	http://www.rns.com/nikos/nikos.html
Open Market	http://www.directory.net/
Open Text Search	http://www.opentext.com
PointCom Reviews	http://www.pointcom.com/
Power Link Search	http://www.powerlink.com/
Savvy Search	http://rampal.cs.colostate.edu:2000
Tribal Voice Search	http://www.tribal.com
UK WWW Catalogue	http://www.scit.wlv.ac.uk/wwlib
Virtual Yellow Pages	http://www.vyp.com
W3C	http://www.w3.org/
Wandex	http://www.netgen.com/cgi/wandex
WebCrawler Search	http://www.webcrawler.com
What's New Too	http://newtoo.manifest.com

Site	Address
WWW Virtual Library	**http://www.w3.org/hypertext/ DataSources/bySubject/ Overview.html**
Yahoo Search	**http://www.yahoo.com**
Yellow Pages	**http://www.yellow.com**

That's enough references to provide an idea of the richness and variety of sites available and even keep you busy for a few minutes, at least. If you want to cut through the crowd and get down to the best of the best, check out the next three sections and see what the most popular engines on the Net have to offer.

Using Lycos

The Lycos search engine was first developed at Carnegie Mellon University and later commercialized by a company incorporated as Lycos, Inc., for licensing to other institutions and commercial concerns. The Lycos catalog contains over 10 million pages of Internet content that is available for your perusal (Lycos, Inc., claims this accounts for over 91% of the Web).

To use the Lycos catalog, follow these steps:

1. With Windows running and your Internet connection established, open your Web browser (we use Microsoft Internet Explorer for this example).

2. Enter **http://www.lycos.com** into your browser's address line to activate the page request. Your browser will display the Lycos home page (see fig. 37.1).

3. Click once in the Query: field near the top of the Lycos page. Enter the term you want to search for—for example, **virtual reality** (see fig. 37.2).

4. Click the Search button, and Lycos will process your search. Note that the URL in the browser Address field will have changed to reflect your query as well. Don't be surprised if the search takes several seconds (or even minutes) as the Lycos site is very, very popular. When the search is completed, Lycos will return a page similar to the one shown in figure 37.3.

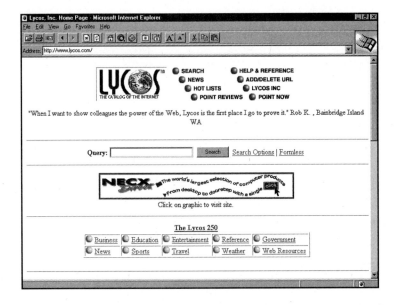

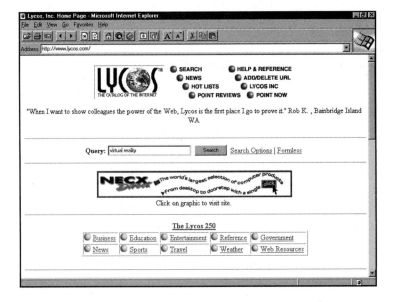

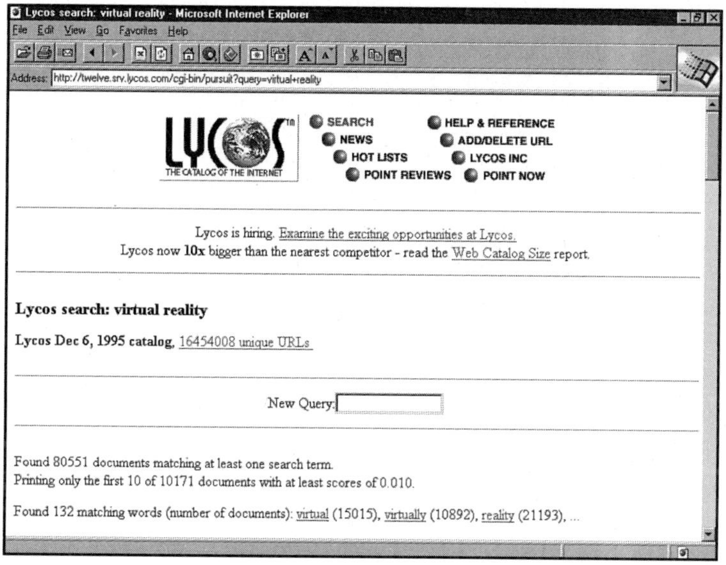

Fig. 37.3
Lycos will return a
search results page
that contains
statistical informa-
tion regarding
your query.

5. You need to page or scroll down to see the actual search results. The
Lycos engine will only format text for the first 10 documents that
match your search criteria. Each entry is formatted with a main reference title (actually a live anchor to the site) and an excerpt from the
document. You may want to go directly to the site from this page or
simply add the URL to your hot list directly from here for later reference
(see fig. 37.4).

Beyond such powerful yet rudimentary searches, Lycos offers other rich resources. One is the Help & Reference section of Lycos, available from the
main Lycos menu. Another is The Lycos 250, a table of anchor references to
pre-indexed areas of the catalog organized by popular search areas (see fig.
37.5). This appears mid-page on the Lycos home page, but with some systems
you may have to scroll down to view it. The Lycos 250 allows you to peruse
the catalog by broad topic with greater speed since the topic areas are pre-
indexed.

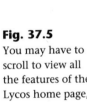

Fig. 37.4

Many browsers will let you add a link to your hot list directly from the cursor position. For example, a right-mouse click in Internet Explorer displays a menu for adding to the Favorites list.

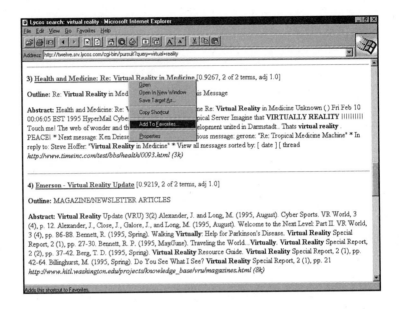

Fig. 37.5

You may have to scroll to view all the features of the Lycos home page, depending upon the resolution and size of your monitor.

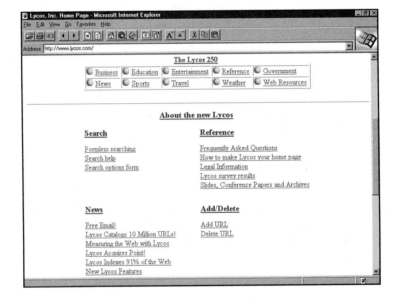

You can also take advantage of a variety of tools to fine-tune your searches on Lycos. There's a Search Form that gives you more complete control over the database engine using a simple HTML form that you fill out on-screen. To access the form, simply click the Search Options link on the Lycos home page to the immediate right of the Search button where you entered your first Lycos query. Lycos displays the Lycos Search page (see fig. 37.6).

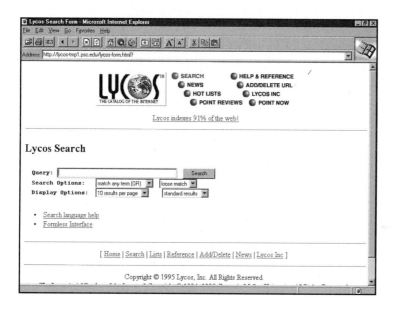

Fig. 37.6
The Lycos Search form gives you control over how tight a search to perform and how you want the results displayed.

There are also links that provide help on the WebCrawler search language and assistance with the Formless interface.

Lycos has also recently moved into the field of providing commentary on Web content through the acquisition of Point Communications, who reviews Web sites and publishes its views at **http://www.pointcom.com**. You can reach the Point site via the POINT NOW link in the main Lycos banner menu map as well.

Using WebCrawler

Another search engine is the WebCrawler, now owned by America Online, Inc. WebCrawler's a bit flashier than some other sites, but still delivers a decent search. To use WebCrawler:

1. With Windows running and your Internet connection established, open your Web browser (we'll use Microsoft Internet Explorer again).

2. Enter **http://www.webcrawler.com** into your browser's address line to activate the page request. Your browser will display the WebCrawler home page (see fig. 37.7).

Fig. 37.7
WebCrawler has a very straight-forward form interface.

3. Click once in the field near the top of the WebCrawler page. Enter the term you want to search for. Click the Search button, and WebCrawler processes your search. When it's finished, it displays a list similar to the one shown in figure 37.8.

4. Since WebCrawler isn't formatting text for each entry, it tends to be pretty fast. You'll also get 25 entries on your first page, with a button at the bottom of the page to return the next 25 (see fig. 37.9). Don't click the button unless you mean it because you won't be able to use the Back button in your browser to re-create the first 25 list (since the server sees a "next 25" request at this location as updating the same page, moving back will take you back to the initial query page).

5. Click any link to travel to the page or site referenced.

Fig. 37.8
WebCrawler
reports results in a
straight list format.

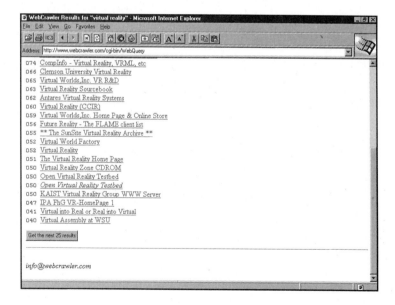

Fig. 37.9
Twenty-five
responses not
enough?
WebCrawler has
more ready to go.

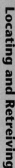

While WebCrawler attempts to deliver page references in a prioritized list, you may need to adjust your search criteria slightly to narrow your search to get what you need or add another criteria point (for example, instead of "virtual reality" try a search on "virtual reality browser"). To do this, return to the main WebCrawler home page and adjust the search criteria as needed using the controls in the home page form (see fig. 37.10).

Fig. 37.10
WebCrawler exposes its search controls on the main home page, making it simpler to refine your search.

Using Yahoo!

Another great Web search resource is Yahoo!, originally created by David Filo and Jerry Yang while still students in the electrical engineering program at Stanford University. Netscape Communications made this site famous by including a reference to it in the Netscape browser. Simply clicking the Net Search button brought up the Yahoo! home page search form (later versions of Netscape include several other search links as well). It's estimated that over 200,000 users per day visit Yahoo!, totaling over two million search requests per day. The San Jose *Mercury News* has compared Yahoo! to "Linnaeus, the 18th century botanist whose classification system organized the natural world."

1. With Windows running and your Internet connection established, open your Web browser (we'll use Netscape for this example).

2. Enter **http://www.yahoo.com** into your browser's address line to activate the page request. Your browser displays the Yahoo! home page (see fig. 37.11).

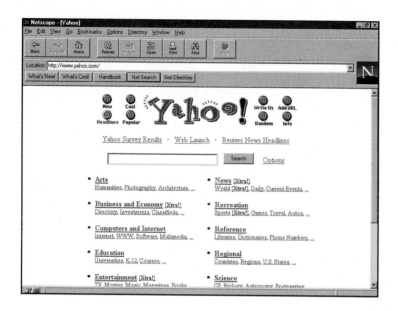

Fig. 37.11
Yahoo! offers a clean, well-designed home page with many broad topics organized for rapid display.

3. Click once in the field near the top of the page. Enter the term you want to search for—for example, **internet phone**. Click the Search button to start your search. Yahoo! returns the results (see fig. 37.12).

Note that Yahoo! displays a header link for each search hit in addition to the reference itself. This allows you to jump to related information that doesn't necessarily tightly match your search criteria. Sometimes it's useful to have a broader context in which to consider your research—that's part of the charm of the Web that the staff of Yahoo! obviously respects and works to preserve, without letting it interfere with the business of finding specific information.

Yahoo! has added yet another nice touch with the inclusion of the Reuters News Service to the search engine. From the main Yahoo! page, you can directly access the news service with a single click, resulting in the main news page (see fig. 37.13).

VI

Locating and Retrieving

Fig. 37.12
Yahoo! reports
your search results,
complete with
statistics and
information about
what classification
areas your search
results were drawn
from.

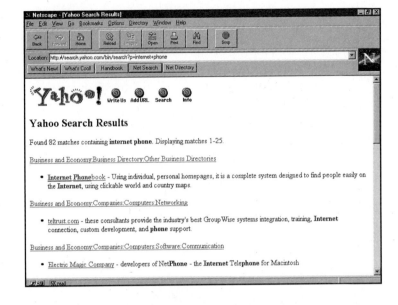

Fig. 37.13
Yahoo! offers a
rich headline
service in addition
to the traditional
search engine.

In addition to the Reuters link at the top of the page, any of the main categories on the Yahoo! home page may have the word Xtra! in the title link to that area. This indicates additional Reuters news headlines organized by category, available directly from these links.

Gathering Information with Telnet

The Internet is a vast ocean of information. What if you're not sure exactly what information exists, but you're certain of the subject you want to find?

Literally hundreds of government agencies, corporations, and universities maintain Telnet sites crammed with current information like magazine articles, consumer warnings, and advisories. Telnet won't search for subjects or anything else, but it's a good way to retrieve files. One of the easiest things you can do on the Internet is Telnet to a remote site and tap its resources.

◀ See "Using Windows 95 Telnet," p. 831

The Telnet program that comes with Windows 95 is very simple to use. It's limited, but sometimes that can be good. When you use Telnet, you know where you're going, even if you don't know what you're going to find. Telneting takes you to a specific place and lets you explore that place only.

You can get a listing of Telnet sites from books and Internet discussion groups on several of the commercial online services.

Suppose you want to read the Food and Drug Administration's monthly magazine, *FDA Consumer,* but don't feel like going to a major library. You wonder, does the FDA keep a BBS where I can read the magazine online?

You bet they do, and you bet you can. You can find out from an Internet resource listing that the address is **fdabbs.fda.gov** and the login is **bbs** (the password is **bbs**, also). That's all you need to know.

> **Note**
>
> Rules and procedures will differ from Telnet system to system, from host to host. Please expect some differences in procedures as you explore different systems.

> **Note**
>
> The InterNIC Directory maintains lists of freely available information resources, products, and services. To access InterNIC, use a gopher client and choose these directories successively:
>
> InterNIC: Internet Network Information Center
>
> Information About the InterNIC
>
> InterNIC Directory and Database Servers
>
> Information About the Directory of Directories or Information on Accessing our Services

Using the Windows 95 Telnet program, log in and register as a new user. Follow the system prompts to get to the **Topics** list shown in figure 37.14.

Fig. 37.14
The FDA's BBS is accessible by Telnet.

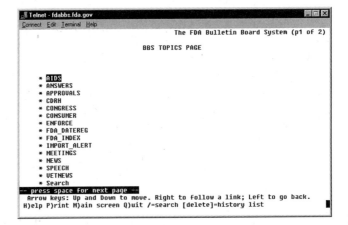

The topic "Consumers" contains the FDA Consumer magazine index and selected articles. Type **?** to get a listing of commands (see fig. 37.15).

You'll notice that the FDA BBS is set up using the Lynx interface, a character-only version of an HTTP server—an alternative way to access World Wide Web documents for those without a Web browser (or the equipment to run one). This means you have access to the FDA Web site via Telnet. The only thing you're missing is the graphics; in fact, you're gaining tremendous speed by not having to download them.

Follow the menus at the bottom of the screen for further navigation instructions.

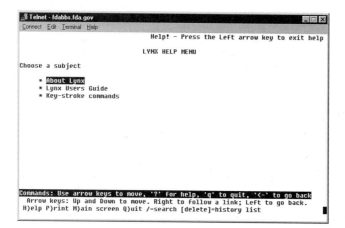

Fig. 37.15
The Lynx help
menu in the FDA
BBS tells you how
to get around.

That's all there is to Telneting. Once you know a site you are interested in, come back month after month (or whenever). Telnet isn't fancy, but it's a lot easier than trying to find out where else on the Internet there is an article about new FDA labeling.

Using WSArchie

WSArchie is an Archie client. It enables you to do searches on registered anonymous FTP sites using a simple form to fill in the information you want to search for. The host address and directory paths of the files that are found are returned to you.

Archie

Archie, a derivative of archive, lets you search for file names that are stored at public sites. You don't need to know the exact name, just a part of the name.

Archie was the first of the information retrieval systems developed on the Internet. The purpose of Archie is simple: to create a central index of files available on anonymous FTP sites around the Internet. To do so, the Archie servers connect to anonymous FTP sites that agree to participate and download lists of all the files on these sites. These lists of files are merged into a database, which users can then search.

You can access the Archie databases in several different ways (for ease of access on the Internet, several different sites have Archie databases; they all contain the same information). If your host has an Archie client (WSArchie, a Windows-based Archie client is discussed later in this chapter), it makes the database search simple. If your host does not have an Archie client, you can use the Telnet program to connect to one of the Archie machines and search the database there. You can also do an Archie search by e-mail, although this can be a little time consuming. Send e-mail to **archie@archie.internic.net** with the word *help* in the message body for instructions on how to do an e-mail Archie search.

When you have connected to one of the Archie database machines (through a client program or through Telnet), you can search the database for a program or file. Because the database only knows about the names of the files, you must know at least part of the file name you are looking for. For example, if you are looking for a program that compresses files (makes them smaller), you can search the database for the word *compress*. You can tell the Archie program to return the location of all the files named compress, or that have compress as part of their name, by specifying either an exact match or substring search. You can also specify whether the case of the file names has to match the case of your search string.

The Archie server returns to you the machine name and location of the files that match the string you are searching for (if any). This allows you to use the FTP program to connect to the machine and download the file to your local machine. The main limitation of Archie is that you must know at least something about the name of the file to search for it; if you don't have any idea what the file is called (for example, you want a program that searches for viruses on your machine and don't know that it is called scanv) you may have to try several searches using different strings before you find something that looks useful.

> **Note**
>
> Running an Archie search is a bit like using a spell-checker or doing a find-and-replace in your word processor. Bear in mind that the search server programs can only work with what you give them and will try for as exact a match as possible—so be sure to spell carefully.

Another limitation of Archie is that not all sites on the Internet that have anonymous FTP participate in the Archie database. So if there is a file that you would be interested in, but it is at a site that does not participate in the Archie database, you would not be able to find that file with Archie. Even given these limitations, Archie is a very useful tool for locating files for downloading through FTP.

The WSArchie program can be found on the NetCD95 accompanying this book. You can install WSArchie by running the NetCD95 installation as described in chapter 50, "Installing and Using NetCD95."

If you can't use the CD to load WSArchie, or want to check to see if a newer version exists, you can use FTP to get the WSArchie ZIP file (currently WSARCH08.ZIP) from **ftp.winsite.com** in the directory **/pub/pc/win3/ winsock**.

> **Note**
>
> If you download WSArchie instead of using it from NetCD95, you must unzip the files to the directory of your choice.

Setting Up WSArchie to Work with WS_FTP

WSArchie uses the Internet Archie service to search for files at anonymous FTP sites. If you have WS_FTP installed on your system, you can retrieve the files found directly from WSArchie. First, you must tell WSArchie where to find the WS_FTP program and what parameters it should use. To set up the FTP parameters, follow these steps:

1. Start the WSArchie application. Choose Options, FTP setup. You see the FTP Setup dialog box shown in figure 37.16.

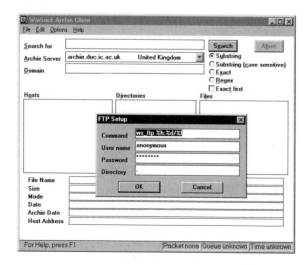

Fig. 37.16
You can set up WSArchie to automatically retrieve files resulting from your search using WS FTP.

2. Click in the text box next to Command and enter the complete path to the WS_FTP file on your hard disk. Do not delete the ws_ftp %h:%d/%f; simply add the path information to the front of it.

3. Click in the text box next to User Name and enter the name of the account you are going to log in to. This will default to "anonymous," and you should not change it unless you have a personal account you can log in to.

4. Click in the text box next to Password and enter the password you will use to log in to the account. Many anonymous accounts allow you to log in with any password; however, many ask that you use your e-mail address, and some require it, so you should enter your Internet e-mail address here (your password will not be displayed on the screen).

5. Click in the box next to Directory and enter the path to the directory where you want the retrieved file to be placed.

6. Choose OK to complete the setup.

Doing a Search

When you want to use WSArchie to look for a file at an anonymous FTP site, the first thing you must do is establish your connection to the Internet (if your host is not permanently connected to the Internet). To use WSArchie to do an Archie search, follow these steps:

1. Double-click the WSArchie icon to open the WinSock Archie Client window (see fig. 37.17).

Fig. 37.17

Don't be intimidated by all the text fields in the WSArchie interface. It's really quite simple to use.

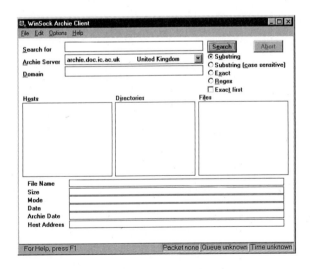

2. Click the radio button next to the type of search you want to do. The following table describes the different types of searches. If you check the Exact first box, WSArchie tries to perform an Exact search first. If it doesn't find a match, it does the search specified by the radio button.

Search Type	Description
S̲ubstring	WSArchie returns any files it finds whose names contain the search string (upper- and lowercase letters are ignored).
Substring [c̲ase sensitive]	WSArchie returns any files it finds whose names contain the search string with the case of the letters matching exactly.
Ex̲act	WSArchie returns any files it finds whose names exactly match the search string that was entered (including case).
R̲egex	WSArchie returns any files it finds that match the regular expression specified.

> **Note**
>
> A regular expression is a way of specifying the possible values for a search string without specifying the exact letters. For each letter position, you can specify ranges of letters to find, ranges of letters to exclude (precede the letters with ^), any number of occurrences of a specific character (follow the character by a *), or any number of characters to ignore (use .*). For example, [0-9] would match any number; [^a-zA-Z] would match any non-letter; [0-9]* would match any number of numbers; win.*[0-9] would match any file name that started with "win" and ended in a digit, with any number of other characters in between. If you want to search for a special character (like a period) you can precede it with a backslash (\).

3. Click in the text box next to Search For and enter the name of the file (or part of the name) that you want to search for.

4. If you want to use a server other than the default one, select a different server from the drop-down list next to the words A̲rchie Server (see fig. 37.18). You might want to scroll through the list and pick one geographically close to you.

> **Note**
>
> It's generally considered good netiquette to choose the site nearest you when transferring files (this lowers overall network traffic and improves performance for everyone). However, if sites close to you are clogged with traffic, it's okay to visit a geographically remote one—just don't start a bad habit.

Fig. 37.18

Choosing a server near you may yield quicker response time. If the server is extremely popular, however, it may pay to choose one less geographically close.

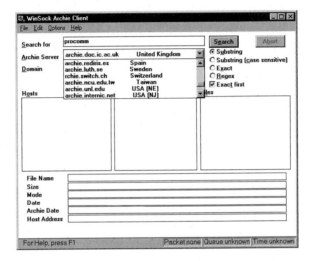

5. If you want to limit your search to a specific domain (such as "edu" for educational hosts), or site (such as "umn.edu"), or even to a specific machine (ftp.umn.edu), click in the text box next to <u>D</u>omain and enter the information. This can be useful if you know that a file is located at a site, but can't remember the location, or if you only remember part of the site name.

6. When you have all the search parameters set, click the S<u>e</u>arch button. After the search has begun, you can abort it by clicking the A<u>b</u>ort button. You might want to do this if you realize that you started an incorrect search, or if the status bar (discussed in the next section, "Getting the Results") indicates that your search will take a very long time to finish.

Getting the Results

WSArchie begins your search by attempting to connect to the Archie server you have specified. Your title bar shows the server you have selected and the timeout period for connection attempts. The timeout period specifies how long WSArchie will wait for the server to respond before it decides that the request has failed. WSArchie will try to connect to the Archie server three or four times before it gives up. When WSArchie connects to the Archie server, you will be assigned a place in the server's queue depending on the number of other pending requests.

Troubleshooting

I can't connect to the Archie server.

If you try to do an Archie search and get a message saying that you can't connect to the server you have chosen, the server may be down or may no longer exist. Try selecting a different server and doing the search again.

In the status bar at the bottom of the window, WSArchie gives you information about the progress of your request, including your place in the queue and the number of seconds that it expects to elapse before your request is serviced (this information will not be updated after you have been placed in the queue). When WSArchie makes a connection to the Archie server, it increments the packet count (the number of transmitted data units) in the status bar as it receives information from the Archie server.

Note

You may see timeout errors in the status bar as the information from the search is returned to WSArchie. This is usually OK because the communications protocol will try again if the transmission fails occasionally. As long as your packet count is increasing in the status bar, your connection should be OK. If the connections should for some reason be broken (the Archie server goes down, or serious noise develops on the communications line), you should get an alert box informing you of a timeout failure.

If the Archie search was successful, WSArchie shows you the results. In the Hosts area of the window, you see a list of hosts that had files that matched your search string (see fig. 37.19). The Directories area shows you the directory paths to the files, and the Files area shows you the names of the files that matched in the selected directory.

VI

Locating and Retrieving

Fig. 37.19

WSArchie gives you fairly complete information regarding the results of your search. Note that the result of this search is a directory. To view the contents of the directory, click twice on the name, and WSArchie will retrieve the file listing.

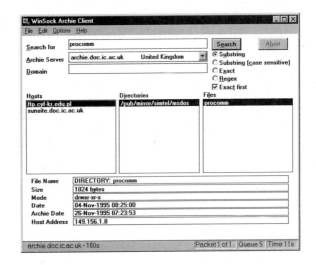

To examine the information about the files that were found, follow these steps:

1. Click the host you want to look at. The Directories area shows you the directories on that host that contain matching files.

2. Click the directories you want to examine. The files that match your search are listed in the Files area.

3. When you click each file, WSArchie shows you information about that file, including the following:

   - The name of the file
   - The size of the file, in bytes
   - The protection of the file
   - The date the file was last modified
   - The date the Archie server last checked the file's existence
   - The IP address of the host where the file resides

If any of the results shown in the Files area are directories, you can retrieve the contents of those directories. Click a directory item and choose File, Retrieve (or just double-click the directory item). The files in that directory are shown in the Files area.

You can save the results of a search in a text file. Choose File, Save. Use the file browser in the Save As window to specify the file where you want to write the results. The information is saved as a list of hosts. Each directory that contains matching files is listed under its host name, with the names of the matching files shown under each directory.

> **Note**
>
> The protection of each matching file is shown using the representation of the file system where it resides. If the file is a UNIX file (the most common anonymous FTP hosts), the protection will be shown as read, write, execute (rwx) for each of three classes of users (for example, rwxr-xr-). If any of the three access modes is not permitted for a particular user group, a hyphen (-) is in that position instead of the letter. The first protection shown is for the owner of the file. The second is for users in the owner's group. The third is for all other users. Any file you want to retrieve must have read protection set for all other users.

Retrieving Files

Now that you have the results of your WSArchie search, you can retrieve any files that interest you. To do this, you could always write down the name of the host and the directory path of the file that interests you; then use any FTP program to connect to the host's anonymous FTP account and retrieve the file. If you have WS_FTP, however, retrieving the file is a much simpler process.

After you have set up your WS_FTP information, you can automatically retrieve a file from WSArchie. To do so, follow these steps:

1. Select the file that you want to retrieve in the Files area of the WinSock Archie Client window.

2. Choose File, Retrieve (or double-click the file you want to retrieve).

3. The FTP Command dialog box confirming the location of the file and the program you've specified to retrieve it appears (see fig. 37.20). Choose OK to start the file retrieve, or Cancel if you don't want to go ahead with the transfer.

Fig. 37.20
The FTP Command dialog box displays the complete specification for retrieving the file. If you set up your FTP program correctly, the rest is automatic.

VI

Locating and Retreiving

WS_FTP is started iconified. If the connection to the host is made successfully and the file is found, a Transfer Status dialog box is available to show you the progress of the transfer if you maximize the WS_FTP program (see fig. 37.21).

Fig. 37.21
WS_FTP's Transfer Status dialog box gives you the low-down on your file retrieval request.

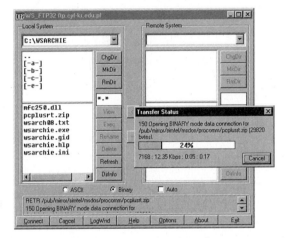

When the transfer is complete, the WS_FTP icon disappears. You can check the incoming directory you specified to see if the file was transferred successfully.

> **Caution**
>
> WS_FTP does not check to see if you already have a file in the incoming directory with the same name as the one you are transferring (unless you have activated the Receive Unique feature in the Session Options dialog box). If you transfer a file with the same name as one already in the directory, the one in the directory is overwritten.

Setting Your Default Search Parameters

You can set default values for the search parameters so that every time you start WSArchie, these values are set to the ones most useful to you. To set your default search parameters, follow these steps:

1. Choose Options, User preferences. The User Preferences dialog box appears (see fig. 37.22).

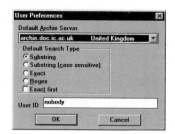

Fig. 37.22
If you use a
particular set of
settings repeatedly,
set them as the
program defaults
using the User
Preferences dialog
box.

2. Select your default Archie server from the Default Archie Server drop-down list.

3. Select the radio button that corresponds to the type of search you do most frequently (Substring, Substring [case sensitive], Exact, or Regex).

4. If you want to try exact matches first, click the Exact first check box.

It is not necessary to change the User ID field.

Exiting WSArchie

When you have all your Archie searches, choose File, Exit to close WSArchie.

Gopher

Gophering is a big part of searching the Internet. Gopher searches are menu-based, and therefore highly structured according to someone else's sense of logic. You don't have the direct simplicity of FTP and Telnet.

What you do have is access to lots of servers loaded with information, and you have to do very little work to get to it. Underneath the smooth Gopher interface is a constant switching of sites, computers, and remote logins. When you cruise Gopherspace, you're cruising the Internet, with the hard part hidden. Veronica and Jughead are just another two ways to extend the power of Gopher searches. Most Web browsers will also handle Gopher and these search tools as well.

◀ See "Connect-
ing with
Windows 95
Telnet," p. 833

◀ See "Why Use
Gopher?"
p. 868

◀ See "Searching
Gopherspace
with Veronica,"
p. 888

◀ See "What Is
Jughead?"
p. 891

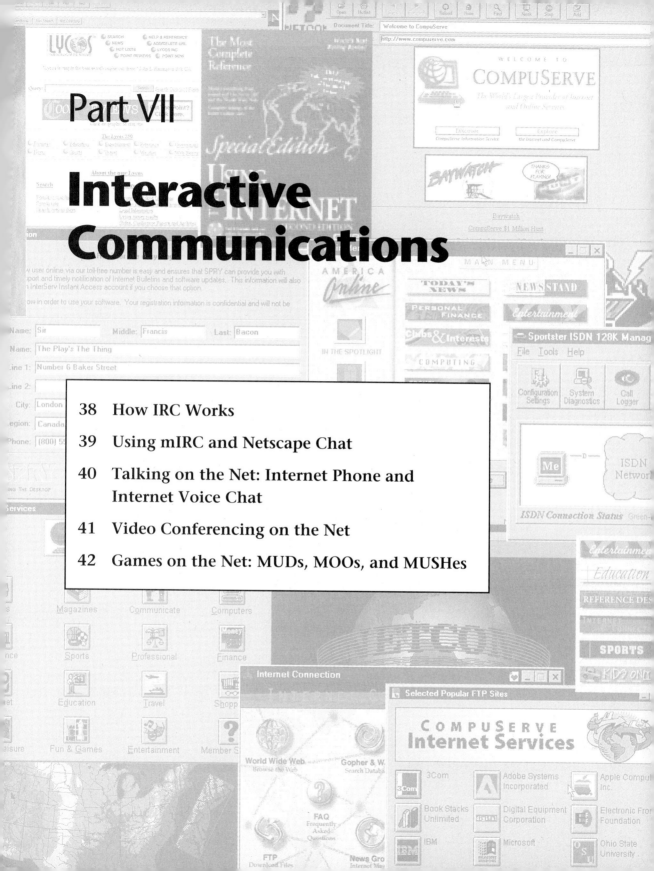

Part VII

Interactive Communications

38   How IRC Works

39   Using mIRC and Netscape Chat

40   Talking on the Net: Internet Phone and
      Internet Voice Chat

41   Video Conferencing on the Net

42   Games on the Net: MUDs, MOOs, and MUSHes

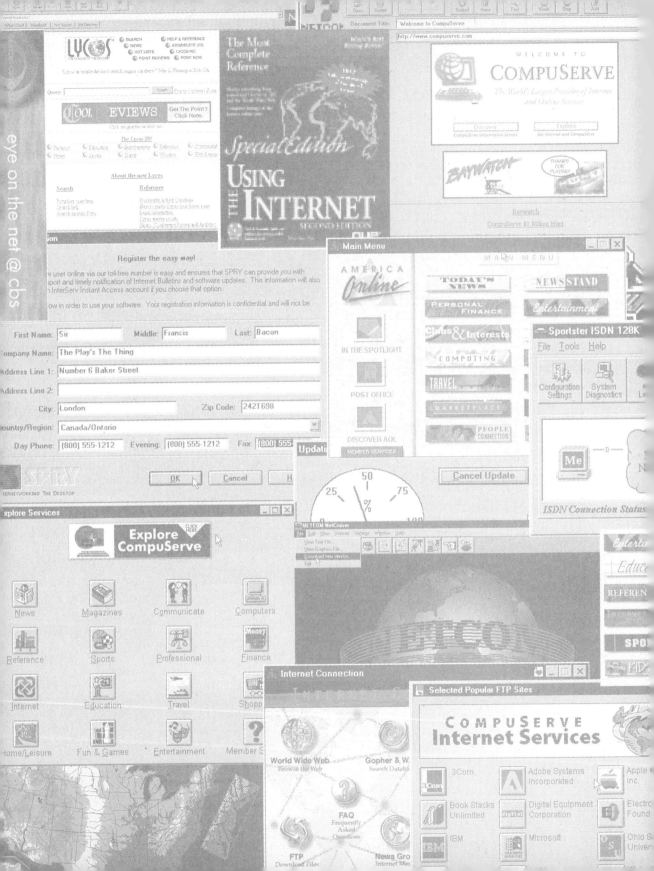

CHAPTER 38

How IRC Works

This chapter introduces Internet Relay Chat (IRC) and explains what it is and how it works. If you have a basic understanding of IRC and want to get connected right away, skip ahead to chapter 39, "Using mIRC and WebChat."

Internet Relay Chat provides the electronic equivalent of a telephone party line. Instead of dialing up with your telephone, you use your computer's Internet connection to access the IRC system. Because the IRC uses the Internet, you can talk to people all over the world about hundreds of different subjects at any time. The usual style of IRC is more like a friendly gathering than a business or organizational meeting. However, IRC allows the use of private one-on-one or multiparty conversations, which can be a lot more in-depth and controlled. Usually, though, IRC is much more social than any other part of the Internet.

In this chapter, you learn the following:

- The basics of IRC
- What you can do with IRC
- How IRC works
- The importance of clients and servers

The Basics of IRC

Internet Relay Chat might become one of the most useful and enjoyable parts of the Internet for you. It allows you to talk to people from all over the world about a wide variety of topics. At its core, IRC was made for you to meet people and have some fun. But before getting into the details of how to use IRC, you need to know how IRC started and what its major uses are.

What Is the Purpose of IRC?

IRC is used mostly as a recreational communication system. It allows you to communicate with people all over the world about thousands of different topics and subjects. Because of its interactive nature, an IRC conversation is much more chaotic than the one-at-a-time, debate-style conversations you might see on UseNet newsgroups. It is possible with IRC, though, to create private, invitation-only conversations that can be as controlled and in-depth as anything that can be done over the phone—even more so, in some cases, as IRC also allows the transfer of files and other information.

> **Note**
>
> Although most uses of IRC are currently recreational, there is nothing stopping business from using this form of communication for conducting business meetings, seminars, and other activities.

Many college students use IRC as a substitute for making long distance telephone calls because once you have an Internet connection, using IRC is free. There is no limit to how many people can be on IRC, or how many topics of conversation may be active simultaneously.

Some recreational and educational organizations hold meetings online at specified times. There are writing and philosophy groups and even an acting group that performs online. There are some business organizations that take advantage of the long distance conferencing ability IRC provides. However, as with any other communication on the Internet, information is not necessarily secure and some companies prefer to interact within a more controlled medium.

> **Note**
>
> Any information sent across the Internet gets passed through many intermediate computer sites on its way to its destination. There is no way to be sure that someone is not looking at the information as it is passed along. IRC does provide some means for adding privacy to your conversations. For information about securing general Internet activity, see chapter 43, "Privacy and Security on the Net."

History of IRC

IRC was developed in the late 1980s by a Finnish college student looking to improve the quality of interactive communication on his computer bulletin board. The project eventually moved in focus from private bulletin board systems to the Internet. The initial versions of IRC allowed for only simple communication among users. As time passed, more features were added and improvements in performance were made. Today's IRC offers many interesting features, is programmable, and gives access to users all over the world.

Internet Relay Chat has grown steadily with the Internet. The activity on the hundreds of IRC channels has increased greatly over the last few years. Initially, you needed to be on a UNIX workstation to use IRC, because the Internet has its roots in the UNIX operating system. Over the last few years, the amount of software available for PCs and Macintoshes that provides access to IRC services has grown significantly.

To get connected to IRC, you need to have at least some way of connecting to the Internet. The quality of service you get is dependent on the quality of your Internet connection. For more information about the types of Internet connections you can get, see chapter 4, "The Various Ways to Connect to the Internet: Which One Is Right for You?"

How Internet Relay Chat Works

Internet Relay Chat relies on TCP/IP, the networking protocol that the Internet is based on. IRC uses two of the basic components of a TCP/IP based network—servers and clients. The only part of the system you deal with directly is the client.

IRC Clients

The "client" is just a fancy name for the software you run on your computer to connect to IRC. The client software allows you to connect to the IRC server, which accepts connections from many IRC clients at the same time. The various IRC servers across the Internet are interconnected—from an IRC server you can access the conferences and users connected to many other IRC servers.

◀ See "What Are FTP Servers?," p. 26

IRC clients provide varying levels of control over how much you can customize your IRC sessions. In the next chapter, you learn about an IRC client that runs under Microsoft Windows. In all cases, the client you use greatly effects your perception of IRC. The best clients are very flexible and still remain simple to use. Some IRC clients restrict you from performing certain functions that IRC servers provide.

> **Note**
>
> To learn about what kind of Internet connection you currently have, see chapter 4, "The Various Ways to Connect to the Internet: Which One Is Right for You?"

IRC Servers

The servers are the core of the IRC system. IRC servers provide all of the supporting structure that allows Internet Relay Chat to work. The servers maintain information on the current available channels. Every time a new channel is added, the information about it has to be passed to every other IRC server. Servers also administrate which users are currently connected, and what options and features they have set up. All of this information is exchanged between servers as it changes, and the technical details of how this is accomplished are quite complicated.

IRC servers are maintained by people called IRCops, short for IRC operators. These individuals run the servers and keep everything on IRC running properly.

There are more than 100 IRC servers running on the Internet. When you first start your IRC client, you will probably be asked to enter the Internet address of the server you want to connect to. If your Internet service provider maintains an IRC server of its own, it's generally a good idea to try that one first. Otherwise, you should pick an Internet server that exists geographically close to where you are. The reason for this is that the farther away the IRC server is from your connection, the farther messages between your client and server have to travel. The following is a short listing of some IRC servers. (There should be one in the general region you are located.)

Server Address	Location
irc.netsys.com	California
irc.caltech.edu	Cal-Tech University
irc.indiana.edu	Indiana University
csa.bu.edu	Boston University
wpi.wpi.edu	Massachusetts
irc.tc.umn.edu	University of Minnesota
mothra.syr.edu	Syracuse, New York
irc.nada.kth.se	Sweden

> **Note**
>
> When you connect to an IRC server, you will usually be asked for a port number in addition to the Internet address. This port number specifies additional information that might be needed by the IRC server. Most of the time, the port number will be 6667. So unless it is specified to be something else, you should use this number as the default. Some clients will assume this value for the port number if you do not enter one.

There are listings available on the Net of current IRC servers. For various reasons, IRC servers are sometimes shut down. Many of the IRC servers are set up by universities and colleges. When computing resources are scarce, these organizations take the least necessary systems offline first. This usually includes IRC, network games, and other recreational programs.

Telneting to IRC

If you do not have full access to the Internet, but do have access to the Internet program Telnet, you still can use IRC. There are systems that allow you to Telnet in to them to access IRC (see fig. 38.1). However, using Telnet access to IRC is fairly limited. There are only a handful of IRC Telnet sites available. The ones that do exist can only handle a certain number of users at a time. You can't customize your interaction with IRC, and will get fairly poor performance when compared to more direct IRC access. It is definitely advisable to pursue other means of accessing IRC before using Telnet. However, if you can't get better access, here is a short listing of some Telnet IRC sites with the IRC port number:

Site Address	Port Number
skyhawk.ecn.uoknor.edu	6677
vinson.ecn.uoknor.edu	6677
sci.dixie.edu	6677
caen.fr.eu.undernet.org	6677
obelix.wu-wien.ac.at	6677

Fig. 38.1
Telnet IRC access
can be slow and
very restrictive,
and you some-
times end up in
an IRC backwater,
such as the
dungeon shown
here!

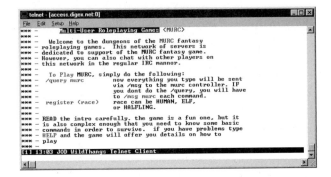

Net Splits

Sometimes, while using IRC, there will suddenly be no activity on any of the channels. If the connection to your server is still running, you may see a message explaining that a Net split has occurred. As you might have guessed, a Net split refers to a discontinuation of Internet service from one site to another.

The IRC system uses mostly direct links from one server to another. For example, say there are two servers, X and Y. Each has a direct link on the IRC system. Each of these servers supports three other servers on their respective side of the link between them. If the connection between X and Y goes down, the servers on each side of the X to Y connection are cut off from each other (see fig. 38.2).

Fig. 38.2
The effect of a Net
split is to isolate
part of the IRC
network.

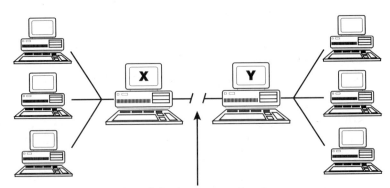

A break in the connection here
cuts off all four servers on the right side
from all four servers on the left

The best indicator of a Net split is the sudden disappearance of everyone in the channel or conversation group that you were talking in. Unfortunately, as a user of IRC, there is no way to speed up the recovery from a Net split.

Often it is a physical problem with parts of the Internet and must be serviced by whomever maintains that part of the Internet.

> **Note**
>
> The Internet was designed to minimize the effects of a Net split, allowing connections to be rerouted through different pathways. However, IRC does not take advantage of these capabilities.

Talking on IRC

Getting adjusted to conversations on IRC might take some time. Because everything is typed in instead of spoken, the use of language and expression of opinion is different than normal conversation. Using the IRC system is often referred to as IRCing (pronounced urk-ing). You will learn about the details of communicating on IRC in the next chapter.

The format that IRC is based on is topic specific channels. When you connect to IRC, you will be able to see a listing of the current active channels and the topics being discussed on them. The channel names cannot be changed once they are created. However, the topic of each channel is changed fairly frequently, and gives a better indicator of what is being discussed there.

Nicknames

IRC provides a mechanism for identifying yourself by a nickname. Nicknames are extremely encouraged and help to add color to the text-based world of IRC. Nicknames are limited to nine characters, but you will be surprised at how creative people are with so few. Many people use animal and food names in combination with their own. In chapter 39, "Using mIRC and WebChat," you learn how to pick and set your nickname. If you don't pick a nickname, IRC will usually use your computer account name instead.

IRC Channels

Channels are a lot like local pubs or night clubs. Depending on the time of day you stop by, the number and type of people who are there will be different. On many of the popular channels, most of the users know each other and tend to connect to IRC at the same time of day. Some channels are more friendly to new users than others. In chapter 39, "Using mIRC and WebChat," you learn about some of the more well-known channels as well as good places to get started.

The Undernet

The Undernet is a term often used to describe the entire IRC system. However, the Undernet is actually an IRC system separate from a standard IRC system. A few years ago, several IRC operators started to feel that the major IRC system (sometimes referred to as EFNet) was becoming overloaded with users and needed some significant improvements. There were too many IRC servers that were not interested in making major changes, so they went off and improved the system on their own. The result is a separate, and arguably better, IRC system called the Undernet.

To connect to the Undernet, all you have to do differently is connect to an Undernet server instead of an EFNet server. All of the Undernet IRC servers have the word Undernet in their Internet address. Here is a listing of several Undernet IRC servers:

Undernet Internet Address	Location
caen.fr.eu.undernet.org	Europe
ca.undernet.org	Canada
au.undernet.org	Australia
us.undernet.org	USA
pasadena.ca.us.undernet.org	West-USA
boston.ma.us.undernet.org	East-USA

The designers of the Undernet rebuilt several parts of the networking communication system that IRC is based on. They have fixed many of the annoying bugs that the EFNet IRC currently has, and have made an effort to make the Undernet a friendlier place. The Undernet is currently much smaller than the EFNet, but it is still large enough to carry a variety of topics of conversation.

Other Sources of Information on IRC

With the growth of the World Wide Web, there are now several Web sites with great information about Internet Relay Chat. For starters, take a look at take a look at the Web site **http://www.yahoo.com/ Computers_and_Internet/Internet/Chatting/IRC/**. This site provides an index of World Wide Web sites that have information and frequently asked questions about IRC. For information about how to connect to a Web site, see chapter 20, "How the World Wide Web Works."

CHAPTER 39

Using mIRC and Netscape Chat

In chapter 38, "How IRC Works," you learned about Internet Relay Chat, the Internet equivalent of CompuServe's CB or America Online's chat rooms—a place to chat with other folks about a particular topic of interest. IRC has a collection of discussions, called *channels*, for discussion of information on literally thousands of different topics. Chances are, if you're interested in it, you can find a group on IRC that is discussing it.

Traditionally, though, many of the programs for accessing IRC, called IRC clients, that are available on Internet access systems reflect their UNIX heritage—shell accounts running the UNIX operating system. They tend to be very powerful, but are based on command-line prompts and command codes, and are extremely difficult to become proficient at. For many PC-based systems, a new generation of IRC clients is being developed with a much more intuitive, graphical interface. The mIRC program for Windows 95 is just such a program.

In this chapter, you learn how to do the following:

- Install the mIRC program
- Set up mIRC to connect to and access an IRC server
- Join IRC channels and have private discussions
- Exchange files with other IRC users
- Customize mIRC options, fonts, and actions
- Install and use Netscape Chat

Why Use mIRC or Netscape Chat?

As we discussed in chapter 38, "How IRC Works," Internet Relay Chat has been around for a long time, and is a very popular place for people on the Internet to hang out. At any given time, there may be as many as eight or nine thousand people from all over the world connected with IRC. UNIX system IRC clients have been around for a long time as well. So, why do you need mIRC or Netscape Chat, a relative newcomer that allows you to connect to IRC from Windows 95?

The answer to this question is the same as the answer to the question of why use Windows 95 when you can use MS-DOS, which has been around for a long time as well. Both MS-DOS and UNIX IRC clients can provide you with powerful tools for doing their respective function...but they're not very easy or fun to use. Sure, everything you might want to do is somewhere in there, but it'll take forever to learn how to do it all.

mIRC and Netscape Chat take all the command-line drudgery out of accessing IRC, giving an easy, intuitive Windows interface to the process of joining discussions, having private conversations, and exchanging files over IRC.

Installing mIRC

The version of mIRC used herein is mIRC version 3.8. The archive that mIRC is distributed in includes both 16- and 32-bit versions. With Windows 95 you'll want to use the 32-bit version. This version of mIRC does not have an automated installation procedure, but doing the steps manually is not very difficult.

To install mIRC, follow these steps:

1. Download the file MIRC38.ZIP from one of the following locations and put the following into the directory from which you want to run mIRC (for example, C:\Mirc\):

   ```
   ftp://ftp.undernet.org/pub/irc/clients/windows/mirc38.zip
   ftp://ftp.onramp.net/pub/ibm/IRC/mirc38.zip
   ftp://ftp.demon.co.uk/pub/ibmpc/win3/winsock/apps/mirc/
   ➥mirc38.zip
   ```

2. Unzip MIRC38.ZIP. This will give the following files (if you have your Windows Explorer set up to hide MS-DOS file extensions for registered file types, this list might look a little different, but the files will still be there):

MIRC.EXE (16-bit version)
MIRC32.EXE (32-bit version)
MIRC.HLP
ALIASES.INI
MIRC.INI
POPUPS.INI
REMOTE.INI
README.TXT
UPDATE38.TXT
VERSIONS.TXT

3. Add an entry for mIRC in the Start or Programs menu, or create a short-cut to it on your desktop (or any combination of the three). Since mIRC tends to get pretty involved with lots of windows, you might want to set it up to always start up maximized (see fig. 39.1).

That's it! Your installation is complete! You might want to take a quick look at the README.TXT and VERSIONS.TXT file, which gives some history for the program and other information.

Fig. 39.1
Because you will want to use the whole screen when running mIRC, set up your shortcut to run the program maximized.

Setting Up mIRC

When you first start mIRC, there's some setup information that you will need to fill in in order to connect. To access this screen, hit the Setup Information toolbar button or select the Setup item under the File menu. You will get the setup screen shown in figure 39.2.

Fig. 39.2
This is the setup
screen after I have
filled in all of
the necessary
information.

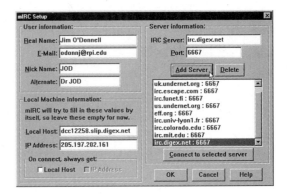

On this screen, fill in the real name you want to appear in IRC, along with
your e-mail address, and a main and alternate choice of nickname. The
nickname is what you will be identified by on IRC. If you have a dedicated local host name and IP number, click the Local Info button and fill in that information (see fig. 39.3). If your Internet service provider furnishes
you an IP number upon connection, click one of the choices in the On
connect, always get:. The list of IRC servers is accessed by clicking Add Server,
as shown in figure 39.4—you can choose from the ones shown, or
one that may be provided by your Internet service provider.

> ## Tip
>
> The IRC servers shown are publicly available servers and tend to be pretty busy. If
> your Internet service provider has an IRC server of its own (see fig. 39.4; my provider
> gives me access to its server, **irc.digex.net**), you should add it to the mIRC server
> list and use it.

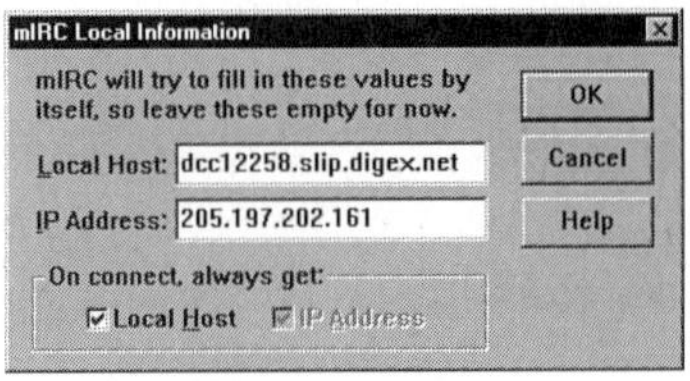

Fig. 39.3
You can enter your
local info into this
dialog box.

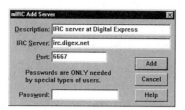

Fig. 39.4
If your Internet service provider has its own IRC server, make sure you add it to the list!

Accessing the IRC Using mIRC

Once you have set up mIRC, you are ready to connect. After you have closed the setup window (and any time you start mIRC), you will see the mIRC Status window, which will remain empty until you connect to IRC.

Connecting to IRC

To connect to IRC, click the Connect to IRC server toolbar button, or select the Connect item from the File menu. If you have filled out the setup information correctly, you will be connected to IRC. You will see a screen similar to that shown in figure 39.5—the mIRC status window. This is the IRC server's Message Of The Day (MOTD).

Joining the Discussion

Once you have connected to an IRC server, you are ready to join the conversation. But which one? Often, IRC has thousands of channels—the IRC term for discussion groups—how can you find out which group you want to join?

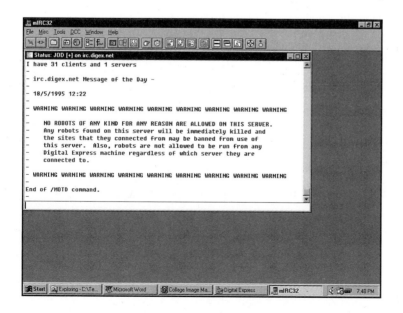

Fig. 39.5
Once you have connected to an IRC server, you will get a Message Of The Day (MOTD) similar to the one shown here.

If you are completely new to IRC (and mIRC), there are a few places you can start. By clicking the Channels folder button you get the window shown in figure 39.6. By default, mIRC comes with a list of channels listed in this window that are good places for new IRC users to join in order to get a feel for the system. Once you have found other channels to join, you can add them to this list to have easy access to them in the future.

Fig. 39.6
Clicking the Channels folder toolbar button gives you this list of IRC channels to choose from, or you can add your own.

But how do you find other groups to join? mIRC allows you to get a list of the names of all of the available public channels by clicking the List channels button. Because there may be thousands of channels, it might take a few minutes for mIRC to list them all in the list window that pops up. You should wait until all of them are listed before trying to browse through this list—mIRC continuously sorts the groups alphabetically as it adds them to the list, so it will be impossible to scroll through the list until they are all there.

Note

To narrow down your list of groups, you can type a phrase into the window shown in figure 39.7. For example, by typing **irc** in that window, mIRC will only list those channels with irc in their names. If you want to narrow your search to the more (or less) popular groups, you can specify a minimum and/or maximum number of users for the listed groups.

Tip

You can join a channel by double-clicking its name in the List Channels window.

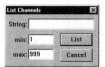

Fig. 39.7
mIRC can give
you a list of the
channels that
are available via
the List Channels
toolbar button.

What if you can't find a channel for what you want to discuss? You can just start your own channel! The procedure for this is the same as for joining an existing channel. If you join a channel that doesn't exist, IRC creates the channel, with you as its only member. If your topic is pretty obscure, you might have to wait awhile before anyone else joins your channel.

Once you have joined a channel through any of the methods mentioned above, you see a window for that channel similar to figure 39.8. The left side of the window is the main part where everything everyone in the channel says (including you) will appear. The right side shows a list of the nicknames of everyone in the channel. The input line on the bottom of this (and most mIRC windows) is the area where you type the things you want to send.

Private Conversations

Once you have joined a channel and entered a discussion, or after you have been on IRC for a while and have gotten to know other folks, you might want to have a one-on-one discussion with someone. There are two ways of doing this in IRC, and mIRC allows you to access them both. The first is to use private messages via the IRC /msg or /query commands. The second is to use the Direct Client-to-Client protocol, which is described in the next section.

If you want to send a message to your friend Phan, instead of just typing a message, preface it with **/msg Phan** in the input line of any window. This sends a message only to the IRC user whose nickname is Phan. You also can type the command **/query Phan** with no message to open an mIRC Query window (see fig. 39.9). Everything you type in this window will be sent to Phan only.

> ### Note
>
> If you send a message using /msg Phan <message>, a query window will not be created, but the message will be sent to only Phan. If Phan replies to your message by sending a private message back, mIRC will then automatically create a query window.

Fig. 39.8
Once you're in
a channel, you
can join the
conversation!

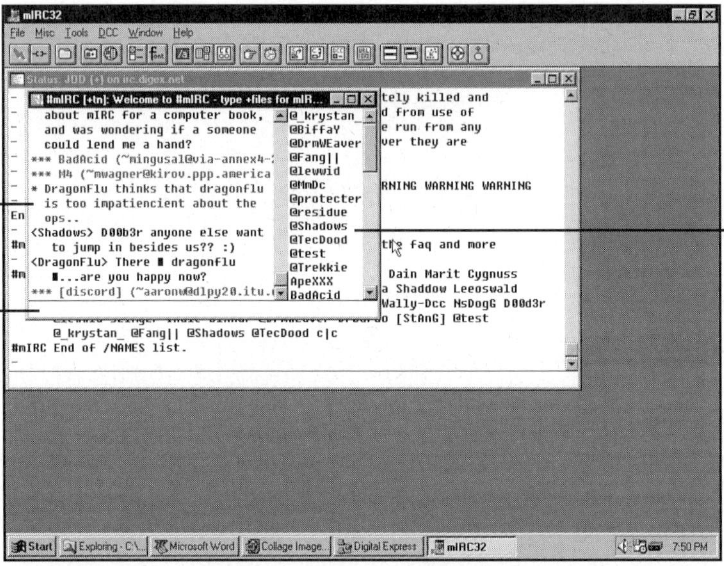

Main window

Nicknames
list

Input line

Fig. 39.9
If you want to
have a private
conversation with
someone, mIRC
allows you to do
that with a Query
window.

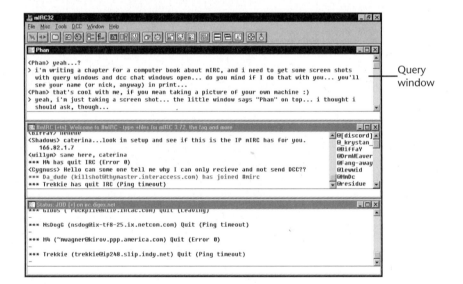

Query
window

> **Caution**
>
> Be careful about having private conversations on IRC. Normally, when having a one-on-one conversation with someone on IRC you can assume it will be private—just between the two of you. However, because of the nature of IRC, there is no guarantee. Using DCC Chat (see next section) is *more* secure, but is not a guarantee of privacy. Don't say anything you might regret (particularly if you expect to be a Supreme Court nominee someday)!

A Little More Privacy Using DCC

As mentioned in the previous section, IRC offers a way to have a one-on-one conversation with someone else using something known as a Direct Client-to-Client (DCC) connection. To have a conversation with someone, you can use DCC Chat. You can also send and receive files from someone over IRC using DCC Send and DCC Receive.

To initiate a DCC Chat with someone, either click the DCC Chat toolbar button, or select the Chat item in the DCC menu. mIRC gives you a dialog box in which to select the nickname of the person you want to talk to. Then, you will get a screen similar to that shown in figure 39.10. You'll notice that the chat window has the message Waiting for acknowledgment because a DCC connection can only be initiated with the agreement of both IRC clients.

Once the DCC Chat is accepted, the chat window behaves the same way as the query window discussed in the previous section. Everything you type in the input line will be sent only to the other person. However, because this is a direct connection between your IRC client (mIRC) and theirs, bypassing any IRC servers, it should be quicker and more secure (though not completely secure!).

As mentioned above, a DCC connection can also be used to send and receive files from another user on IRC. To send a file to someone, click the DCC Send a File to Someone toolbar button, or select the Send item in the DCC menu. You will be given a dialog box similar to that shown in figure 39.11, allowing you to select the IRC user and file (or files) that you want to send. Once you have selected the files, an mIRC pop-up window informs you of the progress of your DCC Send.

Fig. 39.10

A Direct Client-to-Client (DCC) Chat with someone is usually a faster, more private way to communicate one-on-one.

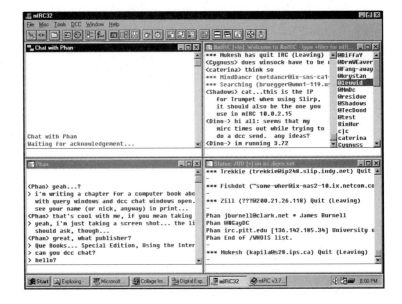

What about receiving files? Didn't I mention something called DCC Get? You may have noticed that there isn't a DCC Get a File from Someone toolbar button, or a Get item in the DCC menu. The reason for this is that when someone uses DCC Send to try to send you a file, mIRC recognizes this and automatically asks you if you wish to receive the file (see fig. 39.12)—click Get to do so. If you do, a DCC Get window pops up to show you the progress.

Fig. 39.11

You can send a file to someone else on IRC using DCC Send.

> **Note**
>
> When you receive a file via DCC Get, the file will be given the name it had on the sending computer, and it will be put in the mIRC directory (for example, C:\Mirc). You can change this default location (along with other aspects of mIRC's DCC behavior), by hitting the DCC Options toolbar button, or by selecting the Options item in the DCC menu.

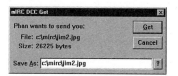

Fig. 39.12
If someone else on IRC wishes to send you a file, mIRC asks if you wish to accept it. If you do, mIRC retrieves it with DCC Get.

Setting mIRC Options

There are a series of ways to customize the behavior and look of mIRC by setting the different IRC options. The mIRC options can be set up by clicking the appropriate toolbar button (see fig. 39.13).

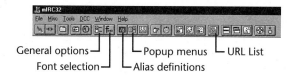

General options—
Font selection—
—Popup menus
—Alias definitions
—URL List

Fig. 39.13
You can access and change mIRC options by using these toolbar buttons or choosing an option under the Misc menu.

General Options

The bulk of the options that you can set to customize mIRC's settings are accessed by clicking the General Options toolbar button, or selecting the Options item from the Misc menu. Within the general options window, there are several categories of options that you can access and change by selecting the appropriate tab.

IRC Switches

The first mIRC general options window is known as IRC Switches (see fig. 39.14). The default settings for most of these options are good, and you can feel free to experiment with them to see what you like. There are a few in particular that you might want to change. The two options in the upper-left have to do with mIRC's connection with an IRC server. Checking the top box will have mIRC automatically connect with its default IRC server upon startup of the program—if you always use the same server, you might want to check this box. If you have or are using an IRC server that frequently disconnects you, check the second box, which will have mIRC attempt to reconnect with the server if it is disconnected.

Two other options that you might want to change are also on the left side, and have to do with mIRC's response to private messages from other users. The top box in this group of options, Iconify query window, starts a private message window as an icon in mIRC. I usually like to see these messages right away, so I uncheck this option. The last option in this group, Whois on query, displays the nickname, address, and server in the status window of any user who sends you a private message.

Fig. 39.14

IRC options allow you to change some of mIRC's general settings.

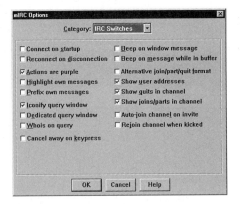

Feel free to experiment with the other options in this window to see if you like the way they change mIRC's behavior.

Action Lists

The Action Lists general option window allows you to define actions that you would like mIRC to take in response to certain events (see fig. 39.15). These events are as follows:

- *Perform*—You can type IRC commands into this window, which executes upon connecting to an IRC server.

- *Highlight*—If you type a series of words into this window, separated by spaces, any time these words appear in any mIRC window they will be highlighted. This is a good way to highlight messages from certain people, or about certain topics.

- *Notify*—This is a very handy list. A list of IRC nicknames entered here, separated by spaces, will cause mIRC to notify you, by displaying a message in the status window, whenever one of the users named is on IRC. This is a great way to keep an eye out for friends on IRC with whom you want to chat (or, not-so-good-friends whom you want to avoid).

- *Auto-Op*—Any IRC user nicknames entered into this box cause mIRC to automatically make those users operators in an IRC channel in which you are an operator.

- *Protect*—If you are an operator in an IRC channel, putting user names in this box allows you to protect these users. If another user de-ops (removes operator status) or kicks (kicks off the channel) someone on your protected list, mIRC will automatically do the same to him or her.

- *Ignore*—Any IRC user nicknames in this box cause mIRC to ignore anything those users say—you will not even see messages from them.

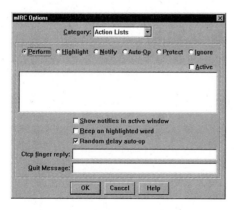

Fig. 39.15
Action Lists allow you to define actions that mIRC takes in response to a variety of IRC events.

VII

Interactive Communication

> **Note**
>
> In addition to entering information into the appropriate box for the Action Lists options discussed previously, you must also check the <u>A</u>ctive box for the options to be activated.

URL Catcher

◀ See "Important WWW Con-cepts," p. 458

◀ See "Using Netscape," p. 497

A very handy feature of mIRC is its URL Catcher (see fig. 39.16). If the <u>E</u>nable URL catcher box is checked, mIRC scans all incoming messages to see if they contain World Wide Web (WWW) URLs and Internet FTP and Gopher ad-dresses. For instance, if my friend Phan sends me the URL of his WWW home page, as shown in figure 39.17, mIRC grabs it and puts it in its URL list, which is accessed by clicking the URL List toolbar button. Also, by filling in the Location and name of WWW browser: field with a supported browser (currently only Netscape Navigator), mIRC can be used to automatically view a URL from the URL list.

Fig. 39.16
The URL Catcher scans all incoming text for Internet and WWW addresses, and saves them to your URL list.

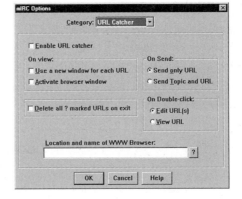

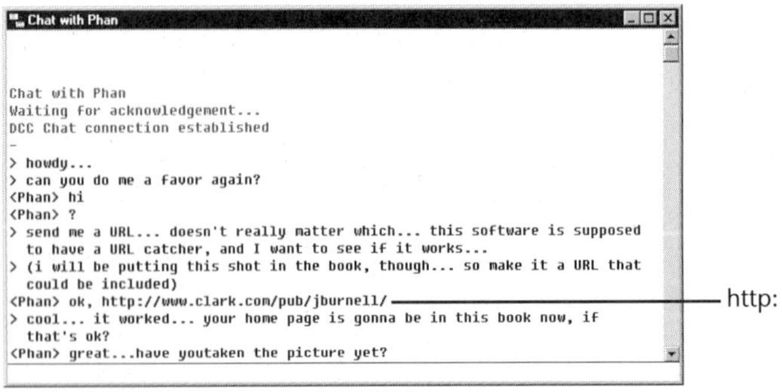

Fig. 39.17
Whenever someone sends you a WWW URL or FTP address, the mIRC URL Catcher sees it and puts it in your URL list.

Other General Options

The other general option windows allow you to control the following aspects of mIRC's operation:

- *Event Beeps*—Controls what events mIRC notifies you of using audible beeps.

- *Logging*—Allows you to have mIRC automatically log channel or one-on-one (Query or DCC Chat) discussions to files on your computer, as well as specify the path where the log files will be put.

- *Sound Requests*—Specifies how mIRC handles incoming and outgoing sound requests—basically allowing mIRC to send, receive, and play .WAV sound files.

- *Servers*—Setting this up allows mIRC to act as an ident server and sends the specified User ID and System as identification. The default values mIRC puts in this box are usually fine, and you should never need to look at it.

- *Double-click*—Allows you to set up actions mIRC will take when you double-click in its different windows.

- *Extras*—Miscellaneous extra mIRC options. These are pretty self-explanatory—go ahead and experiment with them if you'd like.

Fonts

By default, mIRC displays text in all of its windows using the fixed system font. Clicking the Font selection toolbar button or selecting the Fonts item in the Misc menu allows you to specify different fonts for the different mIRC windows. You can choose one of the preselected fonts, or select Other, which allows you to pick any font you currently have on your system (see fig. 39.18).

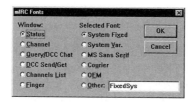

Fig. 39.18

mIRC allows you to select what font to use for its different types of windows. If you select Other:, you will be asked to select from any available font.

VII

Interactive Communication

Popup Menus

mIRC has a very powerful and useful feature called Popup Menus. These are user-defined menus that appear when you right-click the mouse in different mIRC windows. While you can define each of these menus by clicking the Popup menus toolbar button or selecting the Popups item in the Tools menu, the default menus provided with mIRC are very useful. The best way to modify these menus would be to use the defaults as a starting point.

Figure 39.19 shows a sampling of how one of the popup menus is defined. The one shown appears when you right-click in either the main part of a channel or in the status window. While this definition looks kind of complicated, it is pretty easy to figure out by comparing the definition with the actual menus (see fig. 39.20).

Fig. 39.19

mIRC allows you to define popup menus that appear with a right-click in the different windows. They allow you to perform mIRC actions easily.

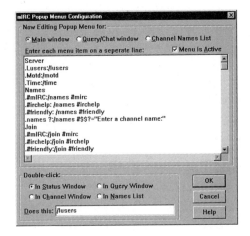

Fig. 39.20

Once the popup menus are defined, they can be accessed in mIRC. The default popup menu for the main window is shown here.

Netscape Chat and IRC

The Netscape Chat program also allows you to connect up to IRC from Windows 95. In addition to being able to connect to Netscape's Chat server, Chat is also able to connect up to IRC servers. These two systems, Chat server and IRC servers, offer similar capabilities, though we will see that Netscape Chat doesn't work as well with IRC as a dedicated program such as mIRC.

Installing Chat

Netscape Chat can be installed on your Windows 95 system by following these steps:

1. Download the file NC32105.EXE by requesting Netscape Chat from the following URL (see fig. 39.21), and saving it to a temporary directory:

   http://home.netscape.com/comprod/mirror/index.html

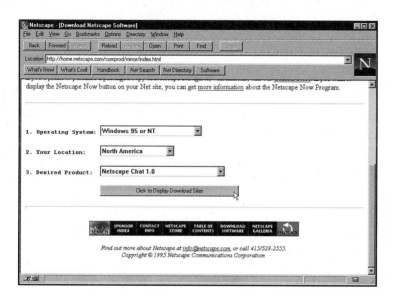

Fig. 39.21
The Netscape Chat software can be requested from this Netscape Web page.

2. Run the self-extracting file NC32105.EXE, and run the resulting program, SETUP.EXE. The default setup options will put the program in the C:\NSCHAT directory.

3. Add an entry for Netscape Chat in the Start or Programs menu, or create a shortcut to it on your desktop (or any combination of the three).

Connecting to IRC Using Chat

As mentioned above, Netscape Chat can be used with either a Netscape Chat server or IRC servers. Before being used with either, however, there is some setup information that must be entered. Netscape Chat is designed to work closely with Netscape Navigator, so when it is run it will also launch Navigator. So, the location of Netscape Navigator must be entered into Chat's Preferences dialog box (see fig. 39.22).

Fig. 39.22
Netscape Chat is designed to work alongside Netscape Navigator, so you must enter Navigator's location into the Chat Preferences dialog box.

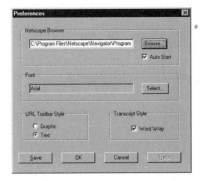

Netscape Chat comes loaded with the default location of a Netscape Chat server at **iapp.netscape.com**. To connect to an IRC server, you need to enter the information for the server into the Chat Server Connection dialog box shown in figure 39.23, which comes up when you click the Connect toolbar button (the one on the left that looks like a light bulb).

Fig. 39.23
You can connect Netscape Chat to IRC by entering your IRC server information into the Server Connection dialog box.

Group Conversation

To join an IRC channel, select the Group Conversation item under the File menu. Netscape Chat will put up the Conversation Channels window, as shown in figure 39.24. You can scroll through the list to find a channel you are interested in, click it, and then click the Join button. For example, figure 39.25 shows the window, after I have connected to the #irchelp channel.

Fig. 39.24
The Netscape Chat Conversation Channels dialog box shows you what IRC channels are available for you to join.

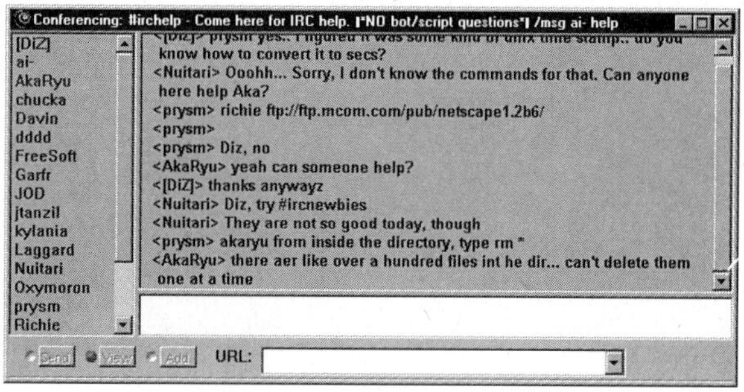

Fig. 39.25
Here I am connected to the #irchelp channel.

Note

When the Conversation Channels window pops up, Netscape Chat loads in the names of all the channels into the window. Because there may be thousands of channels, this can take a couple of minutes. Since the list is alphabetized as entries are loaded in, you won't be able to scroll through the list to find a channel of interest until the list has been fully loaded.

Personal Conversation

Just as private conversations are possible with mIRC, you can also have them with Netscape Chat. By selecting the Personal Conversation item under the File menu, the Show People window is shown (see fig. 39.26). By entering a filter in the lower-right (where * is a wildcard) and clicking Refresh, you can list the names of users with certain groups of letters in their name. For instance, if I am looking for my friend Damone, I can use the string Dam* in the filter. As shown in figure 39.27, if he is listed, I can initiate a personal conversation with him by clicking his name and then the Talk button. If he accepts my invitation to a personal conversation, we can then talk one-on-one (see fig. 39.27).

Fig. 39.26

I can use Netscape Chat's Show People dialog box to look for folks on IRC. Here I am looking for my friend Damone.

Fig. 39.27

Netscape Chat allows you to have personal, one-on-one conversations.

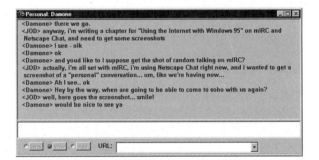

Caution

Just as with mIRC and all current IRC programs, you should assume that even private, one-on-one IRC conversations are not completely secure.

Netscape Chat versus mIRC

Though Netscape Chat works with IRC, it was designed to work with the Netscape Chat server, where its ability to work closely with Netscape Navigator can be used to full advantage. Some of the advantages of a dedicated program such as mIRC over Netscape Chat are as follows:

- IRC can have thousands of channels at any one time. mIRC allows you to list channels containing a given phrase or group of letters (such as irc), while Netscape Chat can only list all of them.

- When you are looking for a person on IRC, Netscape Chat does allow you to list all of the users with a given group of letters in their name (for example, Dam* to look for Damone). mIRC, on the other hand, allows you to use the IRC "notify" system that automatically tells you whenever any of a list of other users are on IRC.

- Private conversations are possible through both mIRC and Netscape Chat. mIRC gives you a couple of different ways of doing this, using either the IRC Query or more secure DCC Chat methods. Netscape Chat's method is to create a private, invite-only channel and then issue an invitation to the other person to join that channel. If the other person is not using Netscape Chat as well, this method can be a little confusing.

In short, while both are good programs, mIRC is a more versatile program for IRC use. Netscape Chat, on the other hand, is better suited for use with the Netscape Chat server, where some of its capabilities to work closely with Netscape Navigator can be exploited.

CHAPTER 40

Talking on the Net: Internet Phone and Internet Voice Chat

The Internet is about communication. Every improvement made in the Net relates to increasing speed, improving capabilities, or aiding communication in some other way. The Information in Information Superhighway is the stuff of communications. People still need to communicate often, even in this technological world in which we now live. So it should come as no surprise that the Internet is being increasingly used for just that—interpersonal communication.

It is interesting that it has taken so long for the Internet to employ the oldest form of human communication, speech. But many new applications apply the data transfer power of the Internet to let people actually hear and speak to one another in real time. It's a far cry from e-mail, which seems impersonal in comparison.

In this chapter, you will learn the following:

- Whether or not it's realistic to use the Internet for voice communications
- The hardware requirements for setting up your computer to talk on the Internet
- How to get and configure the applications that you need for using the Internet for "phone" conversations
- How to choose which Internet voice application is best for you

Using the Internet as a "Phone"

The science behind using the Internet as a vocal communication platform is not very complicated. Computers don't know what kind of data they're handling, and the Internet is certainly not aware of what kind of data is being transferred across it. It doesn't matter if the data being uploaded is a program file, image, digitized movie, or voice. Data is nothing more than data, zeros and ones. The Internet simply moves this data from one point to another, then back again. If that data is voice, then you have the ability to make a "call" thousands of miles away—and escape the highly unpleasant long-distance tolls of the phone company!

All you really need is a way to digitize your speech for transmission across the Net, a way to convert the digitized speech you receive back into sound, and software to handle all the details in between.

This is how people can speak to each other via the Internet: On one end, a user speaks into a microphone. The sound card in his computer converts the analog signal of the speaker's voice into digital data. This data is stored for a very short time in the computer's memory, where it is broken down by a voice communications program into chunks of data called *packets*. From the local computer, the data is transferred through a modem out to the Internet. The Internet is designed to get data packets from point A to point B, so the packets show up where they are supposed to. Once the data enters the remote computer via its modem, the data is put back together in memory. It is then fed through that computer's sound card, where the data is converted back into an audio signal, which is output through the speakers. This whole process happens very fast, and there is nothing really extra special about it. Most computer programs do exactly the same thing: change information into digital data, process it, transfer it, then convert it back into information again.

System Requirements

There are two obvious hardware requirements for engaging in voice communications over the Internet: a sound card and a modem (or a direct connection to the Internet). We'll discuss each in a moment. But there are some other hardware and software requirements and considerations to keep in mind. The following lists what you need to run a phone emulator on the Internet:

- A fast processor (50 MHz, minimum).
- A fair amount of RAM (12-16M is best).
- A good set of speakers with a built-in amplifier and volume, bass, and treble controls.
- A microphone with an on/off switch and a long cord.
- A TCP/IP connection to the Internet.

If you don't have a direct TCP/IP Internet connection, you'll also need a Winsock compatible SLIP or PPP dial-up connection.

> **Caution**
>
> Chatting in real-time on the Internet uses a lot of system resources. Many applications, such as Netscape, use near-continuous disk access, which can use enough system resources to "break up" your voice communications. When using any of the Internet voice applications discussed in this chapter, avoid using Netscape or other "disk hogs" at the same time.

Your Sound Card

Since a voice conversation involves both speaking and listening, you have to have a way to get sound into your computer and a way to get it back out again. Fortunately, most computers these days already come with a device built specifically for this purpose: a sound card.

All sound cards are capable of converting digital data to audible audio, and most can digitize audio in real time from a microphone input. Any card that can do both is capable of being used for voice communications over the Internet.

A 16-bit stereo sound card is best. Though an 8-bit card may work with some of the programs mentioned in this chapter, a 16-bit card will work with all of them. Creative Labs' Sound Blaster 16 is the industry standard; if you have a Sound Blaster card (or compatible) hooked up to a compatible microphone and a set of speakers or headphones, you're all set for holding conversations on the Internet.

> **Caution**
>
> Windows 95 gives you great multitasking capabilities, but you still can't do two things that access the same hardware device at the same time. For example, you can't listen to a music CD while chatting on the Internet, since both use your audio card.

Unfortunately, most of the sound cards in the world today operate in *half duplex* mode; that is, you can record audio or play audio, but you can't do both simultaneously. This means that your Internet conversations will be limited to a one-way-at-a-time mode. Most people have experienced this type of conversation when using a CB radio or speakerphone; while one person is talking, the other listens. Participants in a conversation must take turns.

There are very few sound cards on the market that support *full duplex* mode; that is, that can record and play sound simultaneously. With such cards, some of the programs mentioned in this chapter support full telephone-style two-way conversations. Unfortunately, full duplex sound cards are relatively rare and expensive. Three that are currently on the market are the Gravis UltraSound Max, the ASB 16 Audio System, and the Spectrum Office F/X (which is an all-in-one fax, modem, and sound card). As DSP (Digital Sound Processor) chip technology becomes more prevalent in the PC marketplace, we're bound to see more, less expensive, full duplex sound cards. (As a side benefit, most will double as modems, since DSP chips are capable of handling both tasks equally well—even simultaneously.)

You can easily test your sound card to see if it supports full duplex operation by using Sound Recorder, an application included with all versions of Windows. To test your sound card, follow these steps:

1. Open a copy of Sound Recorder, which is located in your Windows directory. Then load in a .WAV file using <u>F</u>ile, <u>O</u>pen.

2. Open a second copy of Sound Recorder, and press the record button on the toolbar of this second copy.

3. Now press the play button on the toolbar of the first copy of Sound Recorder, the one that you loaded the .WAV file into in step 1.

4. If you get the warning dialog box shown in figure 40.1, you've got a half duplex sound card, like most of us. Sorry. However, if the .WAV file plays okay, you're one of the lucky ones—your card is working in full duplex mode!

Fig. 40.1

Run two copies of Windows Sound Recorder to test whether you have a full duplex audio card. If you see this warning dialog box, your card is only half duplex.

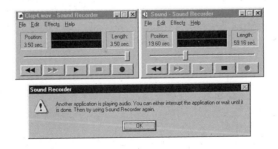

> **Note**
>
> Some of the programs discussed in this chapter support using two half duplex sound cards to simulate full duplex operation. However, unless you are a real whiz at setting up PC cards, with a complete understanding of IRQs, and such, don't even think about trying it.

Your Modem

If you're lucky enough to have a direct TCP/IP connection to the Internet from work or school, voice communications will be a joy. If not, don't despair—you can still communicate over a SLIP or PPP dial-up connection via modem. You'll find that voice doesn't use nearly the bandwidth that graphics and video do, so chatting over the Internet on a dial-up connection is not only realistic, but is usually indistinguishable from communicating over a direct connection.

The term "modem" is a portmanteau for "modulator-demodulator"; it's a device that converts digital data from the computer to analog signals (audio beeps) the phone lines can handle. If you have ever listened to your modem as it is working, you've gotten an earful of annoying screeches from your phone. That sound is the converted data being sent along the phone lines.

The most common modem now in use is the 14.4 modem. The number refers to how fast it is; that's a rate of 14.4 kilobits per second, which simply means that a 14.4 modem can transmit a little over 14,000 pieces of information (bits) over the phone lines each second. The 28.8 modem is becoming very popular and will soon be the king of modems. Older modems of 9600 baud (9.6 kbps) or less are too slow to use on the Internet.

Most modern modems are actually capable of sending data much faster than their rated speed by using built-in data compression techniques. When a 14.4 modem uses compression, it can transfer nearly 57.6KB of information per second. However, if you have noisy phone lines (hissing and the like) compression becomes less useful. Noises on the phone line are confusing to modems; line noise can be misinterpreted as data, resulting in erroneous information. That's why most modems have built-in error correction capabilities, too.

A normal phone conversation turned into digital data requires five to eight times the data transmission bandwidth of the original conversation. Without software data compression techniques, real-time voice communication via the Internet would be unfeasible.

> **Note**
>
> Here's a "Mr. Wizard" explanation of how data compression works: Imagine a series of little sponge balls. If those balls (representing data) have to move through a plastic tube (representing the phone line) via the efforts of gravity alone, they will line up just barely touching and flow slowly out the other end. But if you take a ramrod and push quite hard and fast, the rate that the sponge balls come out increases rather dramatically. The sponge balls compress, but retain their original shape when they pop out the other end.

Internet Telephone Software

Voice communications is one of the fastest-developing application areas on the Internet. Why? The reason is simple, and familiar: money. Long-distance phone conversations are costly when they are handled by AT&T, MCI, or Sprint; they're free when placed over the Internet.

Though the technology is only a few short years old, there are already several good Internet voice communications programs available. We'll cover a couple of the most popular, then take a quick look at some of the up-and-comers. Most work very similarly, differing in only a few details and features, and to some degree in their look and feel.

> **Tip**
>
> Most of the Internet voice applications discussed in this chapter can be downloaded from the Consummate Winsock Applications List site at **http://cwsapps.texas.net**.

> **Internet Voice Chat**
>
> Internet Voice Chat (see fig. 40.2) was one of the very first programs to use the Internet for voice communications. Written by a student at the University of Pennsylvania named Richard Ahrens, IVC was fairly easy to use and simple to install. There was even a very primitive answering machine embedded in the program.
>
> It had its problems; IVC compressed audio data in blocks instead of on the fly, so while it was compressing audio, a remote listener heard nothing. But considering this was the work of a college student, and considering Ahrens asked a meager $25 for each registration, it was still one of the best deals on the Internet—especially since it had no competition at the time.

Today, IVC suffers one very important problem that makes using it difficult at best. Ahrens was bought out by a Canadian company that is developing its own version of his software. (Now, however, they'll run into some stiff competition from other companies.)

When IVC was bought, Ahrens was prohibited from further developing or supporting the shareware version. Literally overnight, people who were using it suddenly could not get support or register their software. Since you can't use IVC until you register it, this made it impossible for new users to get set up with the program. Though it can still be downloaded from the Consummate Winsock Applications List page at **http:/ /cwsapps.texas.net** and a few other places on the Net, it's impossible for new users to run it, since they can't register it.

The sudden disappearance of IVC annoyed many Internet users. Now in certain UseNet newsgroups, there are "crack codes" floating around to unlock the program for general use. The legality of this behavior is, to say the least, questionable.

It seems a sad ending for a pioneering program.

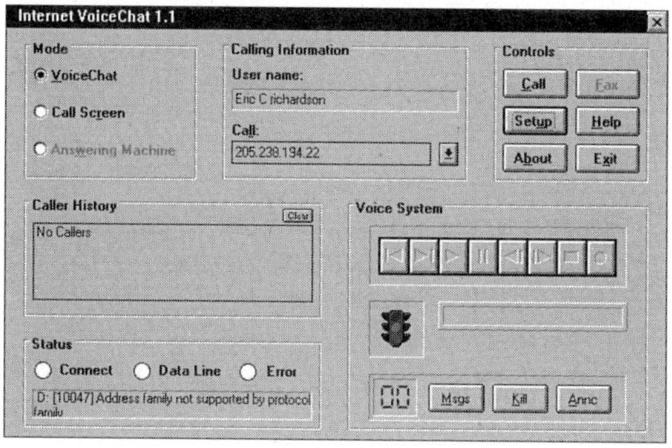

Fig. 40.2
Internet Voice Chat, an early Internet voice program, shows a high degree of sophistication considering its age.

The Internet Phone

The Internet Phone by VocalTec was one of the first large scale marketed software packages to use the Internet. With the right hardware, the I-phone allows full duplex voice conversations.

Note

VocalTec is now also working on a new audio software project, I-Wave, which promises to use audio on the Web in new and different ways. Watch this company; they are on the right track for your ears.

The Internet Phone is shareware. Though it does not expire after a trial period, you are limited to just 60 seconds of chatting before you get unceremoniously kicked out of a conversation. However, one minute is enough to see just how useful this product is. The $30 registration fee isn't much for what it does.

Installation and Configuration

Anyone with FTP or Web access can download the Internet Phone from a wide variety of Internet sites, including VocalTec's home page at **http:// www.vocaltec.com/**.

To install it, follow these steps:

1. The program you downloaded is a self-extracting zip archive; in its current incarnation, it's called Iphone17.exe.

2. Using Windows Explorer, create a new folder on your C: drive called Iphone.

3. Drag the icon for the Internet Phone program archive file into this new folder.

4. Double-click the icon. A DOS box appears and asks you if you want to extract the archived files. Type **y** for yes. The files extract. Close the DOS box window when the process is done.

5. Double-click the new icon for Setup.exe. The Internet Phone is installed on your system, and a program group is created for it.

How Internet Phone Works

The I-phone piggybacks on the Internet's pre-existing IRC (Internet Relay Chat) servers. Unbeknownst to many IRC users, their IRC host computers are thus pulling double duty. VocalTec enables the user to choose from a number of servers that already exist, so they don't have to charge you to use a special server of their own. The I-phone uses on-the-fly compression, so you don't really notice any lag when online, no matter which IRC server you're connected through. IRC servers simply receive and retransmit I-phone data; at this time the servers lack the capability to discriminate between voice transfer or text. As long as IRC servers continue to house Internet Phone transfers, VocalTec has a sure winner. However, the Internet Phone's use of IRC servers puts VocalTec in the position of looking for friendly IRC servers to keep up with the growth of the I-phone.

Although using IRC servers for Internet phone traffic is a truly inspired idea, there could eventually be a problem with usage of the I-phone bogging down IRC servers. Although I-phone comes preprogrammed to use several friendly IRC servers, there is nothing to stop users from deciding to meet via a particular IRC server. In cases such as this, the organization that owns the server may not want to act as an I-Phone host. This is understandable, as hosting I-phone sessions is not what IRC servers were designed for.

After the I-phone is installed on your system, you can be online in seconds.

If you're not connected to the Internet via a "land-line" TCP/IP connection, the first thing you need to do is establish a SLIP or PPP TCP/IP dial-up connection. Once online, you can fire up the Internet Phone program.

From here, establishing a conversation is as easy as choosing the CALL icon (the little face icon) from the menu bar (see fig. 40.3). I-phone will automatically connect to an IRC server and let you start chatting.

Fig. 40.3
The layout of the Internet Phone has all the controls the user needs accessed from one screen. The ten "tiles" keep track of the last ten people accessed. With one touch, you can automatically connect to them if they are online.

Of course, it is best to take a few minutes to configure the I-phone first to get optimum results.

Configuration involves the following few steps:

1. Under <u>P</u>hone, choose the <u>C</u>all option. You'll get the list of phone servers shown in figure 40.4.

2. Using the default IRC server is fine, or pick any other from the list. Make sure that the Auto-connect on startup checkbox is checked. Now just by starting the application, you will be connected.

Fig. 40.4
The Internet
Phone lets you set
up one of many
IRC servers as your
default phone
connection.

3. Under Options, choose Preferences (see fig. 40.5). Confirm that the audio in and out settings are what you want. (Sometimes you won't have a choice.)

Fig. 40.5
The Preferences
dialog box lets you
configure audio
options.

4. Under the same Option menu, go to User Information. Fill out your personal information. After all, everyone is just as curious about who they are speaking to as you are (see fig. 40.6).

Fig. 40.6
From the Options,
User Information
menu option, you
can enter a little
information that
you would like
other Internet
Phone users to see.

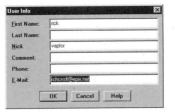

5. Choosing Set Voice Activation (VOX) Level from the Options menu enables you to set the threshold where your mike kicks on and off as you speak. (This is also done via the little button to the left of your readout—bottom right of the main I-phone box.)

6. It's a good idea to choose Test System Configuration from the Options menu, too, to make sure everything is working together properly.

Making a Call

Now you are ready to talk to someone online. Connecting is super easy. When you start the application, you'll see the main program window. The I-phone will automatically connect to the IRC server you chose in step 2 of the configuration procedure listed in the previous section. You will see connection progress as a small line of dots across the connect screen. This usually takes less than 15 seconds. Once you are online with the IRC server, a message in the scroll box will say `IRC Connected`.

Finding someone to chat with is very easy, too. By clicking the call icon (the telephone in the upper-left corner of the I-phone window), you will see a list of people and topics that is just like a list of IRC (Internet Relay Chat) channels (see fig. 40.7). You can join several topics at once. General is the best topic to join; it's also the default topic. To get a list of topics, click the Topics button. Be prepared for some wild topic names out there. As you highlight each person, a little bit of information about that person will be displayed at the bottom of the call window.

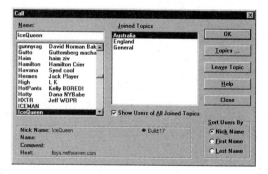

Fig. 40.7
The Call box shows people and groups you can chat with.

To initiate a call, double-click the person you are interested in chatting with. You'll hear a tone signifying that an attempt to connect is being made. If the target of your conversation is already talking to someone, you'll get a traditional busy signal along with a message saying that they are busy.

When you find someone to talk to, you'll find that the voice quality is quite similar to a speaker phone. The only lag that you'll really notice is from distance. Just as a transatlantic phone call experiences a bit of lag, the same lag exists with the Internet. After all, it's the same cable (or satellite link).

> ### Tip
>
> When speaking to people from different countries, remember to avoid odd slang or excessive contractions. Also remember to speak slowly and very clearly— accents are magnified when you can't see the person speaking.

The main display keeps a list of the last ten people that you either spoke to or tried to call on little one-click call buttons. With this feature, a single click of the button (which VocalTec calls a *tile*) you can be connected to a cyber-friend that you chat with often. I would like to see a way to store the last 50 or so people you chatted with. The ten tiles are so easy to use, I think something like an audio hotlist would be a good idea, too.

> ### Note
>
> The I-Phone has some nice extras that you will find very useful. You can use the View Statistics option under the Options menu to display some very useful information. The stat sheet shows incoming and outgoing packets, but what I really find useful are the lost packet indicators and the average round-trip delay display (see fig. 40.8). The higher the percentage becomes on the lost packet indicator, the worse the quality. I have found the most loss you can handle without the conversation becoming nearly impossible is around 30 to 35 percent. After 35 percent, incoming audio is in short bursts with long gaps separating them. The round-trip delay number is in milliseconds, so if the statistic window shows a delay of 684, the round trip is .684 seconds. That may seem like a long time for computers, but it is subjectively very fast.

Fig. 40.8

When speaking with someone using the Internet Phone, you can pull up a display on the remote user you are speaking to and information on the quality of the connection.

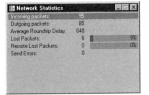

When you call and chat with a friend, you will notice that the tile with his name changes along with the words in the message display.

While you are trying to call a friend, the tile shows a hand knocking at a door, with the message display telling you the name of the person you are calling. If you accidentally chose the wrong person, you will know almost immediately.

When you are actually talking to a friend, his tile changes to a little microphone and the message display states you are speaking. I find this useful if I set my VOX (voice activation) level to be too touchy. It is possible to set your VOX so that the slightest sound (like clearing your throat, or even breathing) causes your mike to lock open.

As you listen to your distant friend, his tile becomes a little speaker while your message indicator informs you that you are listening.

You can bring up the View Info menu button (the second from the left) while chatting with someone to see his nickname and the comment he wrote while setting up. Other information that can be displayed includes a phone number and Net address. The last piece of information that can be seen is his local time, so you can get a feeling of just how early it may be for a friend of yours in Europe (see fig. 40.9)! The information in this window will partially disappear if you disconnect from a friend, but it will keep the nickname and contact information if you wish to chat again.

Digiphone

Another major Internet phone application is Obicom's Digiphone (see fig. 40.9), distributed by Third Planet Publishing. Where the I-phone uses IRC servers, Digiphone uses direct point-to-point connections to other users with Digiphone software.

Fig. 40.9
To begin contacting users, type in the remote person's e-mail name in the Remote Site box. From this box, Digiphone resolves the individual's IP address.

Without having to go through a central server of any kind, Digiphone is immune to server problems. When you use a server of any kind, your transmissions have to be received and retransmitted by the server computer. Though problems at the server end do not happen very often, they can. It's just one more thing to worry about.

Digiphone is a commercial application without any freely downloadable demo available for it. The Digiphone Web site at **http://www.planeteers.com/** tells you where you can buy it, but that's it. This is the only software I have for Internet access that I had to purchase before I could try it out. At $59 dollars, the price is reasonable, but it does make it difficult for potential users to get a good feel for the program before buying.

> **Tip**
>
> Don't be fooled into trying the Web address **http://www.digiphone.com** for Digiphone information. That's a different, totally unrelated company. The Digiphone program is from Obicom International Telecommunications.

Installation and Configuration

When you get Digiphone on CD-ROM, installation is easy. The install program runs very quickly because the vast majority of information on the CD-ROM is extra (wave files) and is not really needed. The actual Digiphone program fits on just one 1.44M diskette.

Digiphone features a compact user interface (see fig. 40.5). Each option is actually launched via the taskbar.

Digiphone automatically registers each user the first time it is used.

To set up Digiphone, select Settings from the menu, then enter your e-mail name and mail server. Digiphone automatically resolves the IP addresses involved. Keep in mind that you need to enter the e-mail address of the ISP you are going to use Digiphone with. For the mail server address, you can enter the IP address or name of the mail server. If you don't know either, you will have to contact your ISP (Internet Service Provider) and obtain this information. Remember that mail servers have a unique name associated with them (such as mailserver.domain.com). Simply entering your domain name will not be enough for Digiphone to work with.

> **Note**
>
> If your ISP assigns you an IP address each time you log on, that means you have a dynamic IP address, not a static IP address. With a dynamic IP address, you will not know what address the rest of the Internet knows your computer by until you log on. To find out if you have a static or dynamic IP, contact your Internet Service Provider.

The Provider Settings window allows users with dynamic IP addresses to use Digiphone. This is done by entering a range that your IP address will fall under. Internet Service Providers set aside a block of IP addresses to be used over and over as people log on to the Internet via their server. Contact your ISP to find out what range they use for dynamic IP addresses. To enter the range of dynamic IP addresses, use Advanced Direct Dial Configuration from the Provider Settings window.

When Digiphone is launched, your taskbar shows the main Digiphone minimized along with a TCP/IP connected indicator. To do anything with the Digiphone, you need to right-click the minimized Digiphone to get a list of actions you can take. From here, you can configure the Digiphone. Right-click the minimized Digiphone, and choose the Connection settings. A nice feature allows the user to choose to employ compression, encryption, or both (see fig. 40.10). On this same screen there is a sampling rate, which shows how much data is used per second as you send data. Using the default sampling rate is good if you feel you can squeeze higher fidelity; increase the number by blocks of one thousand. The higher the number, the better the quality, but the performance will begin to suffer. This is something that needs to be set for each computer, as no two systems are the same.

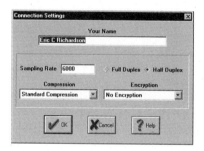

Fig. 40.10
Each user of the Digiphone can set compression or encryption. As encryption and security are becoming important issues, this is a very nice feature.

If you have a Sound Blaster card, Digiphone will work in full duplex, which is really nice. If you don't have a 100 percent Sound Blaster compatible, you are stuck with half duplex.

Caution

Be careful not to select Full Duplex mode if you don't have a Sound Blaster (or 100 percent compatible) when installing Digiphone. I accidentally knocked out my sound driver by testing this. The program won't auto-seek your soundcard type. It would be nice to see it do so and automatically adjust the settings on Digiphone. If you are not sure what card you have and cannot find any supporting literature, select Half Duplex.

From the minimized Digiphone on the taskbar, choosing VOX settings will bring up the VOX box. The VOX level sets the threshold to activate the mike. If you set the number higher, you will have to make quite a bit of noise for your mike to begin transmitting; if it is set very low, you will have to whisper to avoid your mike locking open. Setting the VOX to be less sensitive is better; many people find it useful to keep background noise to a minimum and the microphone from transmitting when it really shouldn't. If the person you are speaking to says that the first syllable of speech always seems to be cut off, that is an indicator that you need to make the microphone a bit more sensitive. The alternative to that is to make a noise right before you begin to speak; any very short grunt will actually work quite well.

Included on the Digiphone CD-ROM is a nice collection of .WAV sounds. Open Explorer and move to the CD-ROM; from there move to the ringers folder where you will find many interesting files to copy into your main sound files folder.

The Digiphone CD came with two accessory diskettes. These disks hold what may be some of the best reasons to go out and buy Digiphone. They contain a high quality suite of Internet access applications which are designed to get anyone up and running on the Internet (see fig. 40.11). The cornerstone of this collection is the DigiSock TCP/IP dial-up stack, which can get you set up with a SLIP or PPP Internet connection. If you are looking for some new connection software to access the Internet, look no further.

Fig. 40.11
The additional undocumented applications that come with Digiphone make up a substantial addition to your purchase.

Making a Call

If you know the e-mail address of a friend with whom you wish to chat, enter her name in the Remote Site field on the main Digiphone control panel. Then enter her domain name and hope she is online. By entering the domain name, a general search is made of people within that domain. If people are online with Digiphone, you see their e-mail addresses displayed on a list; from that list you can choose the names of those you'd like to chat with. If you don't already know whether a friend is online, there is no simple way to check in advance.

When I tested the Digiphone, I didn't know anyone specific to try to speak with. The manual suggested that I download a list of users from their Web site. While exiting to a second application to retrieve a list of information isn't my idea of ease of use, it did get me up and running. Digiphone does let you search a list of users from the Directories menu option. Choosing Global let's you get information about a specific name, country, state, or time zone.

Receiving a call is a lot easier than making one. A question box pops up indicating the person who wishes to speak to you and an Accept or Reject button. One feature I find neat is the ringing sound file that comes with Digiphone is actually a phone bell ringing. Odd how a program that is so modern would use a traditional ringing phone sound that has not existed for most people for the past 15 years.

Internet Global Phone

Internet Global Phone is strictly for those who are interested in becoming skilled programmers. The IGP is nowhere near ready to run when you download it—in fact, you have to finish it to suit your own needs.

In real estate, they have what they call "fixer uppers." This pretty much describes IGP. Written in Microsoft Visual C++, IGP requires that you build your own user interface. On the other hand, it is totally free. You can get the software by starting an FTP session to **ftp.cica.indiana.edu/win3/demos/ IGP**. If you want the source code, FTP to **ftp.cs.tu-berlin.de/pub/local/ kbs/tubmik/gsm/ddj**. This is a good example of college students doing a lot of work on their own and subsequently developing something on the Internet for all to use. In its current state, Internet Global Phone is really more of a learning tool.

Speak Freely

Speak Freely supports three forms of data compression as well as secure communications using data encryption with DES, IDEA, and/or a key file (see fig. 40.12). If the PGP (Pretty Good Protection) program is available on your system, it can be invoked automatically.

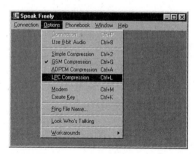

Fig. 40.12
Though it looks plain, Speak Freely packs a lot of power under the hood, including built-in data encryption and several compression options.

There are Windows and UNIX versions of Speak Freely. Users of the program for both platforms can find one another by communicating with a phone book server.

Multicasting is also implemented, which allows you to create multi-party discussion groups that users can subscribe to or drop at their discretion. For those without access to multicasting, a broadcast capability allows transmission of audio to multiple hosts (at least, it does on a fast local network).

Speak Freely was written by John Walker, the founder of Autodesk and the programmer who created AutoCAD. The latest version of Speak Freely can be downloaded from his home page at **http://www.fourmilab.ch/**.

WebTalk

WebTalk is the first Internet voice communications program to come from a major, established player in the software industry: Quarterdeck, the publishers of the QMosaic WWW browser. Intended as an add-on to QMosaic, WebTalk is still in beta testing as this is written, but promises to be a major force in defining the future of voice communications on the Internet, if for no other reason than the marketing muscle behind it.

For the latest on WebTalk, including a downloadable demo version of the program, check out Quarterdeck's home page at **http://www.quarterdeck.com/**.

WebPhone

If there were an award for "Flashiest User Interface Design for an Internet Voice Communications Program," WebPhone would win it hands down. This program is configured to look and work like a high-tech cellular telephone (see fig. 40.13).

Fig. 40.13
If looks were everything, WebPhone would have it all. The user help is just as classy looking, and is complete and genuinely helpful, as well.

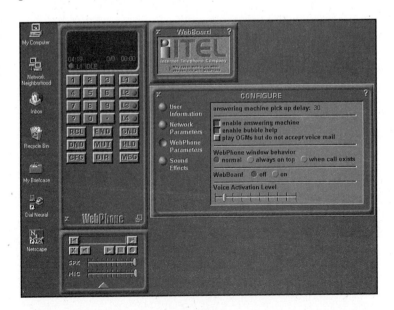

Because its user interface is based on a common, everyday item, WebPhone is uncommonly easy to use. What you can't figure out right away is clearly explained in WebPhone's truly helpful (and downright fun to use) online help pages.

WebPhone (from the Internet Telephone Company—honest!) gives you a plethora of user options, plus four phone lines. It offers full duplex operation with the right sound card and half duplex for the rest of us.

ITEL's Directory Assistance Server connects you to other WebPhone users worldwide, and you also have a local phone book. Voice mail is promised for the final release.

You can try out the latest version of this program for free by downloading it from ITEL's home page at **http://www.itelco.com**. WebPhone's one-time "activation fee" is $49.95.

PowWow

"Unique" is an overused word, but PowWow (see fig. 40.14) really is a unique personal communications program for the Internet. Besides voice chat (our topic at hand), PowWow lets you chat with up to seven people by keyboard (as well as voice), send and receive files, play .WAV format sound files, and browse the World Wide Web together as a group. It is probably the most sociable Internet application I have ever seen.

Fig. 40.14
PowWow is optimized for friendly use by small groups.

Perhaps it comes as no surprise that this program is of Native American origin (a very social people). It was created through the auspices of Tribal Voice, an organization run by Native Americans from many tribes, which is dedicated to providing a Native American presence in the high-tech industry through free and low-cost computer software and services. All Tribal Voice products are "Native American in concept, architecture, and implementation."

PowWow connects to users through their e-mail addresses. All that's necessary is that they be running PowWow, too.

PowWow is tremendously personalizable. You can send the URL of your home page to the people you're chatting with, and they can click the link to view it. You can set it up to send a JPEG image of yourself along to those who want to view it. You can chat with one or many, using voice or text. You can ask others to tag along with you as you browse the Internet as a group—a really neat feature that I haven't seen in any other software, anywhere.

There's even an Answering Machine mode where you can enter a message (up to 255 characters) that you would like displayed to those who try to connect to you when you have the Answering Machine mode turned on.

This program is well worth a look, if only to check out its truly unique features. The latest version can be found at **http://www.tribal.com/**. This site also includes a comprehensive phone book of PowWow users.

Cyberphone

Cyberphone (see fig. 40.15) is an Internet phone application that supports both full and half duplex operation. It even comes with a set of drivers that purport to give you full duplex operation with a Sound Blaster compatible sound card, which usually only supports half duplex operation.

Fig. 40.15
Cyberphone sports a user-friendly interface window with big, colorful, clearly labeled, easy-to-understand buttons.

With versions available for Windows, Linux, and Solaris, Cyberphone can claim to be one of the few cross-platform compatible Internet voice communication applications. It also supports multiple users, and saves different user information files (including passwords) for each. Cyberphone is server-based, which means that e-mail addresses and IP addresses are not required to initiate conversations—you just click the recipient's name in your phone book.

(You can manually dial to an IP address if you want to, though.) One of the program's more dubious features is the ad at the bottom of the Cyberphone window—there's a menu item to download new ads, each of which provides a direct link to the advertiser.

Cyberphone can be downloaded from the Cyberphone home page at **http://magenta.com/cyberphone/**.

TS Intercom

Telescape's TS Intercom (see fig. 40.16) not only allows people to talk over the Internet, it also lets them view images and transfer files while they talk.

Fig. 40.16
The TS Intercom program window displays two images, one specified by you, and one by the person you're chatting with.

In beta testing as this is written, the most finely-tuned part of TS Intercom so far seems to be the installation file, which has a slick interface and nice graphics. It makes unzip-and-install-it-yourself style shareware programs look anemic by comparison.

On the techie side of things, TS Intercom lets you set Word Length and Fidelity options, both of which affect audio transmission quality, which can improve performance over a slow connection.

One slick feature of TS Intercom is its ability to let you set up a signature image file in .GIF, .JPEG, or .BMP format. While this picture can be of you (if you're of the type who wants everyone to know what you look like), it can also be an image of a project, design, or other topic under discussion.

Setting up a chat session is pretty easy. You can e-mail your intended recipient using a built-in link to your favorite mail program before starting up. TS Intercom maintains a phone book of people you've chatted with in the past.

Perhaps TS Intercom's most useful feature is its capability to send and receive files during a chat session. This has its fun aspects (sending picture and sound files, and so on) but it can also be very useful when you need to exchange documents, CAD files, or spreadsheets in a business environment.

The latest version of TS Intercom can be downloaded from **http://www.telescape.com/**.

Real-Time Audio Player Programs

What if you have no desire to talk to someone else over the Web? What if all you want to do is listen—in real time?

Real-time audio is an emerging technology on the Internet, and there are a couple of relatively new programs that will get you involved and show you what the excitement is all about. The two top contenders right now are Progressive Networks' RealAudio and DSP Group's TrueSpeech. RealAudio is covered in chapter 29, "New Web Technologies."

TrueSpeech

Any sound can be digitized, including speech. But sounds digitized in the proprietary TrueSpeech format by DSP Group, Inc., can be compressed and still retain excellent quality. DSP says that its technology can compress one minute of digitized speech to a file only 64K in size. It licenses this technology to developers (for a fee), but provides a free real-time player called TSPlay32 (see fig. 40.17) to users who want to play them. It can be downloaded from **http://www.dspg.com/**.

Fig. 40.17
The TrueSpeech Internet Player plays wave files, and is optimized for playing digitized speech.

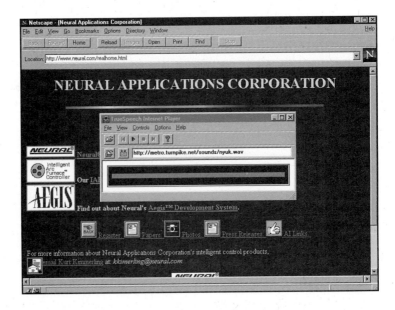

TSPlay32 is a Win95 program (there's also a Windows 3.1 version) that plays TrueSpeech files and regular wave files to boot. (This program can also easily be configured as a Web browser helper application for playing all the waves that come its way over the Web.)

One of its best features is that it can play sound files in real time, as they are downloading; you don't have to wait for a file to download first. If you don't like what you hear, you'll know right away and can cancel the transfer in mid-stream. This can save you lots of expensive connect time if you're pre-viewing many sound files, but keeping only a few. Of course, nothing is per-fect—TrueSpeech sometimes gets ahead of a download and has to pause and wait for it to catch up, but you can always hit the Play button to start the file playing over again from the beginning.

TrueSpeech is unique in that it is on the forefront of a new World Wide Web technology: programs that can access the Web independently of a browser. You can run TSPlay32 all by itself and choose to load and play a file from your disk or network; but you can also tell it to load a URL and it will con-nect to the Web and play a file directly from the site where it is stored, all without the aid of Netscape or any other browser. This kind of independent program is going to open up the Web and make it seem more like a wide-area network than a communications service. Look for more programs like TSPlay32 in the near future.

Changes Voice Communication Is Making on the Net

Speaking by way of the Internet is still in its infancy, but there is a tremen-dous amount of potential in such technology.

Just as the telephone revolutionized conversation early in this century, Internet talk software could initiate another revolution in the way we con-verse. Voice communications on the Internet is still in its "hobbyist" stage, much as radio was in the '20s. Though it is currently not practical to make initial contact with people in the business world with Internet phone utili-ties, that day may come sooner rather than later.

For personal communications, where price is a major factor in limiting long distance calls, Internet voice chat utilities are already unmatched in economy, if not usefulness.

Long distance phone companies have already indicated that they are not amused with this emerging technology. Expect to see it challenged in the courts, especially when the money to be made becomes substantial and the money lost by the phone companies makes it worth their while.

The Future

In the near future, we'll see fiber optic data lines in every home. One fiber optic cable running into your house could handle phone, live video feeds, cable TV, and Internet WAN (Wide Area Network) connections, and still be ready to accommodate lots more data. Until we see widespread fiber optic data distribution, however, there is still much more that can be done with existing technology. Refinements are being made to the electronic hardware we are all using now. In conjunction with the hardware improvements, programmers are always making better and better software.

The future of audio on the Internet includes the following possibilities:

- Conference calling in full duplex
- The Internet answering machine ("Sorry, I'm not online now")
- Talk forwarding to other terminals
- Sending files to each other as you talk about something
- Remote talking, so you don't have to be sitting in front of your computer

What will happen in the future is still just speculation. The many different voice utility applications will probably settle into one standard (or a very few).

Voice communications on the Internet has the potential of becoming as popular as the World Wide Web. It is very possible that on business cards, people will someday have Internet voice contact information right under their e-mail address.

Note

For more information on the topic of voice communications on the Internet, check out the Internet Phone FAQ (Frequently Asked Questions) file on UseNet. This file is posted on the 5th and 19th of each month to the UseNet newsgroups **alt.internet.services**, **alt.bbs.internet**, **alt.culture.internet**, **alt.winsock.voice**, **alt.winsock.ivc**, **comp.sys.mac.comm**, **comp.os.ms-windows.apps.comm**, **alt.answers**, **comp.answers**, and **news.answers**. The latest version of the FAQ is also available on the World Wide Web at **http://www.northcoast.com/~savetz/voice-faq.html** and **http://rpcp.mit.edu/~sears/voice-faq.html**.

Video Conferencing on the Net

41

The Internet is, in its raw form, communication. It should come as no surprise, then, that those of us who use the Internet have pushed progress in the direction of better and faster ways to transmit data.

Previous chapters have shown you that there's a move to make communicating via the Internet more natural. Voice communications have made great strides in that direction, and real-time video conferencing—which was fiction just a few years ago—is quickly becoming a reality on the Internet.

In this chapter, you learn:

- The history of video conferencing
- The advantages of video conferencing
- How to acquire and set up a popular video conferencing utility, CU-SeeMe
- What the future holds for video conferencing

Communications and Video Conferencing

The Internet has recently become quite popular with the business community; this interest has spawned a large amount of capital investment in the Internet and is beginning to reap rewards. The commercial community is now busily working to develop ways of information exchange that duplicate face-to-face conversation.

The private market (including colleges and universities) has been the major driving force behind the Internet in the past. However, as both the business and private sectors see advantages to video conferencing via the Internet, the world can expect this technology to grow rapidly.

We are now poised on the verge of finally making Dick Tracy-like gadgetry available to anyone on the Internet. With the strong multitasking power of Windows 95, simply downloading software may be all that is needed to implement useful video conferencing capabilities via the Internet. Many previous attempts to bring video conferencing into the mainstream have failed due to the extreme cost of the hardware involved. Purchasing such equipment is still beyond the budget of most companies. An approach that uses inexpensive off-the-shelf consumer hardware in combination with innovative new software is much more practical and affordable.

The History of Video Conferencing

Twenty years ago, AT&T made an attempt to create a device that would allow two-way communication that went beyond the telephone. It was called the Picturephone. Although it worked, it never made it beyond the "odd new developments" segment of the evening news. At that point, the technology simply was not in place to create a worldwide network of Picturephone terminals—which would have been very large and impossibly expensive to manage, anyway. However, the Picturephone did start many people thinking about how to better transmit data and voice in a real-time environment. It is interesting to note that although the Internet did exist in the form of ARPANET at that time, it would still be quite a few years before serious work would go into merging it with video conferencing.

In the latter part of the 1970s, satellites offered the next chance of real-time video conferencing. There have been communications satellites orbiting the Earth since the very early days of orbital launches, but until the '70s it was nearly impossible for anyone to use a satellite communications *transponder* due to the extreme costs. (Most people over 30 can still remember how novel it was to watch a live broadcast from the other side of the world for something such as the 1972 Winter Olympic Games.) Unless you happened to be a television network or government, you simply couldn't afford it. In the late '70s and early '80s, with so many new satellites going up, renting a transponder became much less expensive. Video conferencing then became practical for larger companies; in most ways, it was no different than setting up a closed circuit television system with a camera at each end.

> **Note**
>
> A *transponder* is analogous to a modem, but it communicates over a channel on a satellite rather than a telephone line. Most modern satellites used for TV have 24 transponders each for video, with a large and variable number of audio channels.

Video conferencing is still expensive when using the older technology, though high-speed phone lines or fiber-optic links are now used in lieu of satellites.

What may very well make long distance audio-visual communication commonplace on the Internet is modern digital technology—the same technology that was used in large part to create the computers that make up the Internet.

The Advantages of Video Conferencing

Companies worldwide share one common mantra: "Save Money." If anything pushes the development of video conferencing on the Internet, it will be this concept.

Many Kinko's and other copy stores nationwide have video conferencing suites available for rent. It is far less expensive to rent one of these suites for between $150-$200 an hour and have people out of the office for a part of a day than it is to send a delegation to the other side of the world. This saves times as well as money, and time is still the most important commodity in business.

Video conferencing is able to foster better feelings in the people taking part in a long-distance conference than mere phone conferences can. Simply simulating a face-to-face meeting puts people at ease, even though everyone involved is aware of the distances being spanned. As with e-mail, IRC, or even the telephone, there exists a natural curiosity about what someone looks like.

Besides satisfying curiosity, video conferencing lets people convey meanings beyond what is being verbalized. All the speakers (and non-speakers) in a meeting are constantly giving visual cues as to what they may be feeling or thinking. Simply put, body language has always been important, and observing body language is a superb way to get "gut feelings" about situations. Ask any long-time salesperson about body language—you may be surprised what they can tell just by reading a person for hidden signs.

Then, too, when group effort becomes important and colleagues are scattered over a great distance, video conferencing shines. When talking about physical objects, such as when architects need to confer on a three-dimensional model of a proposed building, seeing something is far better than trying to describe it. Data sharing can also be integrated into some video conferencing schemes, which lets people remotely work on the same spreadsheet, program code, document, or design. The old adage says that a picture is worth a thousand words, but a three-minute video conference can be worth a day of discussion when everyone can see and manipulate the same data.

> **Tip**
>
> A good way to keep up to date on what is going on with video conferencing is to use IRC. There are many useful channels for video-conferencing information. Try contacting the CU-bot for up-to-date information—just send the bot a private message (**/msg cu-bot help**).

For more information on the topic of video conferencing, you might want to check out links to this topic on the CU-SeeMe Web site at **http://cu-seeme.cornell.edu**. (see fig. 41.1).

Fig. 41.1
The CU-SeeMe home page on the Web is a wonderful source of information on video conferencing on the Internet.

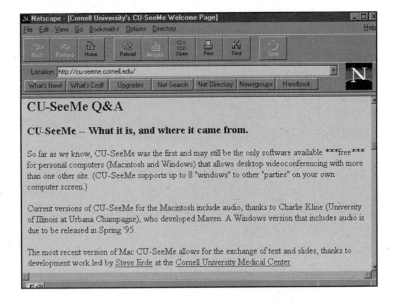

The Problem of Bandwidth

To understand how the Internet can be capable of transmitting and receiving the volumes of data that are involved in video conferencing, you need to comprehend the concept of *bandwidth*. Most people think bandwidth is the amount of data that can be transferred. While this is essentially correct, the true definition is a bit more complicated than the popular view.

My father, an electrical engineer, told me a good analogy that exists between current (amps) and voltage (volts). It's like the relationship between a hose and the water that flows through it. It is possible to have a hose with a huge diameter but just a moderate amount of water moving through it—the water trickles out of the hose. On the other hand, if you have a hose with a small diameter and the same flow of water, you get a high-pressure jet. If you connect a bunch of hoses of different diameters end to end, the water can only flow through the whole length at the speed allowed by the thinnest hose in the system.

I've found that this same concept pretty much applies to digital bandwidth. Keeping with this analogy, the water flow rate (meters/second) is equivalent to data rate (bits/second). (Bits per second is the basis for rating of the speed of modems.) The data line (hose) limits how much data (water) can pass. The more constricted the data line is, the less data can flow in a given time period.

The Internet as a whole is made up of very dissimilar data lines; some are as slow as regular phone lines while others are very fast. The Achilles heel of transfer speed on the Internet is wherever a step down in the speed of the data lines takes place. This is a "choke point," where the data traffic jam piles up. From the choke point all the way down to the end-user, data transmission is slowed to the speed of the choke point. This is why someone working on a computer directly connected to the Internet (such as an Internet service provider) has tremendous transfer rates. With a fast connection and no choke points, data flows better than water over Niagara Falls.

When you attempt to send both video and sound over the Internet, you are sending a huge amount of data down your data line. When this raw data is fired out into the Internet, the first choke point hit disrupts the flow of data. The result is slow data reception and choppy video and audio at the receiving end.

Hardware for Video Conferencing

The hardware needed for setting up desktop video conferencing is widely available. For high-end equipment, it is possible to spend in excess of $1,000, but a budget under $500 will do nicely (assuming you already have the computer).

◀ See "Other Software for Connecting to the Internet," p. 157

Your Computer

The first and most important piece of equipment you should already have: your computer. If it is running Windows 95 relatively quickly and with no

problems, you should have smooth sailing. Usually, Windows 95 likes to reside in a fairly fast PC with a good amount of memory. Those general parameters also match up to the requirements of video conferencing.

Video Capture Board

The only piece of equipment you have to buy for two-way video
conferencing is a video capture board (VCB). A VCB allows your computer to
take an image from a video source (like a video camera) and translate it to
digital data. It's how you'll get a live video image of you into your machine
and onto the Internet. You need one that handles live video in real-time, not
just single images.

VCBs are easy to install, but *first read the instructions*. (It's amazing how many
people think instructions are to be read only as a last resort.) Usually a VCB
can be installed in just a few minutes by taking the cover off your computer,
locating an empty expansion slot, and placing the board in it. Sometimes the
VCB replaces your video card, so be aware of that.

Using Windows 95 does not necessarily excuse you from having to install any
driver software that comes with a video capture board. After the board is installed, power up your computer. If Windows 95 does not automatically detect anything new, go to My Computer and open the Control Panel. You see
a screen that says "To begin installing your new hardware, click Next." Try to
click Next and let Windows 95 try to find the changes you made. I have had
pretty good luck with letting Windows 95 tell me about the changes I made.
If your computer cannot find the new device (sometimes it thinks it is just a
video card), install the drivers. Keep the number of the manufacturer's tech
support line nearby in case you get into a bind.

Camera

The next piece of equipment is not as vital as you may think. The camera for
your computer simply plugs into the video capture board you just installed.
Here again, after reading over the literature that comes with your camera, try
to get Windows 95 to see if a new piece equipment has been added to the system. Don't be surprised if it does not, as VCBs and cameras are not standardized for computers.

One point to look for when you purchase your camera is how physically
stable the thing is. If it has double-sided tape on its feet, don't buy it. It
should be stable and preferably bottom heavy so it won't tip over if you
bump into your desk. (Think about how many times you whack your knees
into your desk during the average day!) The camera should have some nice
options, such as letting you control the zoom and aperture setting. There are

really nice cameras out there that come with a remote to let the sender sit back and control the zoom and pan so viewers won't end up with a tight shot of someone's nose looking back at them. The camera should also be somewhat portable.

A camcorder is an alternative to using a special camera to video conference. With virtually no effort, a camcorder can be attached to a video capture board. If you purchased a VCB that has an audio and video input, you can probably just hook the camcorder into it. To get an idea of just what audio and video connectors are, look at the back of your VCR. The little circular connectors labeled "Audio" and "Video," in and out, are the very same. If your camcorder has an audio and video connector, just go to any electronics store and buy a length of VCR dubbing cable. More than likely it will be color coded. The two popular schemes are a combination of red and black or white and yellow. Using a camcorder is great if you don't want to purchase a special one-use-only camera. The video quality you will end up transmitting is quite similar to a tape recorded on the camcorder.

Sound Card

The sound card is something you probably already have. Cards that seem to work well are the higher end 16-bit cards. Cards that employ 32-bit sound are really great, but if you have an older computer, odds are you won't have VESA or PCI slots (high bit slots, 32 and 64 respectively) anyway, so just make sure you have a good 16-bit sound card.

There are many good sound cards on the market today. Finding a sound card with good bundled software makes the audio portion of video conferencing much more manageable. A software package that has a mixer incorporated into it allows the end user to better control the audio environment.

A microphone is used in conjunction with the sound card to transmit audio with the video. Microphones are not very expensive; good ones are usually less than $25.

Monitor

A monitor is the interface to your eyes when you are video conferencing on the Internet. For the purpose of video conferencing, a killer monitor doesn't really bring you any great advantages as technology stands now. Most applications used by Windows 95 require a good monitor, anyway. As the technology driving the Internet is growing quickly, a good monitor will probably be needed in the near future! If you are buying a new monitor, go for a 15-inch or larger monitor capable of displaying a resolution of 1024×768. A monitor with a non-glare screen is less fatiguing to look at for long stretches of time.

You can see that the hardware needed for video conferencing is nothing rare or unusual. Setting up your system is as easy as putting in your video capture card, connecting your camera or camcorder, and loading any special drivers that Windows 95 may need.

CU-SeeMe: A "Free" Video Conferencing Program

With video conferencing for the Internet still in its infancy, there are very few software packages available via the Internet to connect people to each other. One of the best and most widely available programs currently available is CU-SeeMe (see fig. 41.2). It's a free video conferencing program that is available from the CU-SeeMe Web site at **http://cu-seeme.cornell.edu**.

Fig. 41.2
The CU-SeeMe main program title bar. As soon as the program starts, CU-SeeMe begins waiting for a connection to be made.

Besides the version for Windows 95/ Windows 3.1, there is also a version of CU-SeeMe available for the Macintosh and UNIX. This way, almost anyone accessing the Internet from home, school, or the office can video conference with each other.

Besides the hardware requirements, a PPP/SLIP account is a must. As for modems, 14,400 bps is the slowest you can get away with, as long as the modem is using compression to "fake" a 57,600 connection. A 9600 modem or slower simply does not get the job done (but no one really has 9600 modems anymore, do they?).

A good quick way to judge if you are able to run CU-SeeMe well is to check how well you can access the Web. Using your Web browser as a diagnostic tool is actually a pretty good idea. If you are waiting eons for your browser to download complex files, you'll also have problems with CU-SeeMe.

Not much video equipment has been fully tested to work with CU-SeeMe. A list of tested hardware is available on the CU-SeeMe Web server.

But you already have a video capture board and camera hooked up, right? Sure you do, because you want to try CU-SeeMe yourself.

Reflectors

Just as IRC (Internet Relay Chat) uses one computer to host many individual users, CU-SeeMe uses the one-to-many concept. CU-SeeMe employs very powerful UNIX computers to handle the job of actually connecting individual users together. UNIX is just an operating system, but it is far more powerful than Windows 95 and a whole lot less user-friendly to those without lots of UNIX experience.

The centralized CU-SeeMe server computers are called *reflectors*. A reflector keeps track of who is connected to it, what data is coming in from people sending video, and what data is going out. Reflectors are like the air traffic controllers of the Internet, except they don't take coffee breaks. When connected to a reflector site, you can view up to eight different people sending video at once. (Of course, the more you are trying to watch, the more likely you are to bog your system down.)

When using a reflector, you can choose to either transmit data and become a sender or simply sit back and watch what is going on and become a *lurker*, just like those who read but never type on IRC (Internet Relay Chat).

Many colleges have their own reflectors. Usually when there is a NASA mission, you can connect to a college reflector and view what is going on at NASA. Having a cable TV system that is still in the dark ages, I am very happy to link to a CU-SeeMe site during a shuttle mission to watch and listen to what is going on. (The other alternative is to drive to someone's house with a better cable provider, which I have also done in the past!)

When there is a constant feed, such as during a NASA mission, most colleges ask people not to transmit data. This is done so only the NASA information is going out, allowing more people to lurk. Lurking at times like this is not only acceptable but preferable.

It is possible to use CU-SeeMe without a reflector—if both participants have a stable IP address, private conferencing is possible. Each user just needs to type the other's address in. Of course, as this is not encrypted at all, it is not secure, but it is still better than chatting via a reflector.

Installation

CU-SeeMe is not a very difficult program to use or obtain. The version I have was downloaded from the CU-SeeMe Web home page (**http://cu-seeme.cornell.edu**).

> **Note**
>
> There is also a commercial version of CU-SeeMe. Check out White Pine Software's site at **http://www.wpine.com/cuseeme.html** for information.

The file is zipped, so unzip it in its own folder. Remember, you can pretty much name the folder anything you want (some of us still have to break the habit of keeping folder and filenames to eight or less characters).

Once it is unzipped, bring up Windows Explorer and drag the icon into the folder you have all your Internet utilities in. (If you bought this book, it's more than likely that you spend a lot of time using the Internet, so just keep a folder on your desktop with your Net goodies inside.) Once you start CU-SeeMe, you see the main program window. In just a few minutes, you will be able to set it up and start receiving information from people. If you decided against getting the camera and capture board, all you can do is watch, but that's okay, too.

Configuration

Configuring CU-SeeMe is fast—just open the Edit menu, choose Preferences, and type your name or handle into the Preferences dialog box (see fig. 41.3).

Fig. 41.3

The Preferences box, which is an option under the Edit menu, shows everything you need to configure CU-SeeMe.

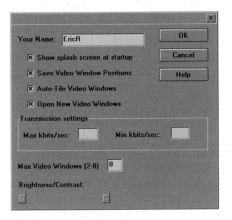

The Show Splash Screen at Startup option tells you which reflector you are connected to. Save Video Window Positions keeps your daughter windows where you want them next time. Auto Tile Video Windows spaces them at a nice distance every time a new window is opened or started. Open New Video Windows does not ask your permission to pop open a display as soon as someone on the reflector begins transmitting from his camera.

Operation

When pulling up the Connect window from the <u>C</u>onference menu option (see fig. 41.4), you see the Connect box. Just type the IP address of a reflector there, and you're off and running. The drop-down box has a list of IP addresses in it if you don't know any.

Fig. 41.4
The Connect box is the most-used option in CU-SeeMe. From here, you enter the IP address of the site or reflector you want to connect to. If you have a camera, you can select to send video or not; you should always leave the I Will Receive Video check box enabled.

Once you connect to a reflector, anyone who is already set up to transmit data does so automatically. As soon as a new sender connects, the standard video startup screen appears. The square with "CU-SeeMe for Windows" displayed is where the image of the participant with a camera appears (see fig. 41.5). The eye indicates if they have the receive video option turned on: "yes" if the eye is open (and you have a camera), "no" if the eye is closed. The speaker tells the status of the person's audio panel. If there is an "X" through the speaker, he has all sounds muted. If the microphone is depressed, it means you can chat verbally with that person in private mode. This is not as good as the Internet Phone program, but you can still communicate verbally, albeit not as clearly as with the Internet voice utilities. It is also possible to speak to someone who is sending video even if you do not have a camera set up. The last two buttons are to display information such as bytes transmitted and the IP address of the sender. The bottom numbers display frames per second (fps) and kilobytes per second (kps).

Fig. 41.5
This is a good example of the features incorporated into an incoming video window. The window usually ends up being roughly two inches by two inches.

A few seconds after the new video window pops into existence, an image of the sender appears. Besides verbal and video, those sending video have an option of typing messages at the same time they send video. These appear across the bottom of their video window (see fig. 41.6). Sometimes when data is missing or there is a bottleneck somewhere, partial information comes across.

As is pretty obvious from the figures, the picture quality isn't astounding. The images are about 120×120 pixels in size and are not updated very often. In fact, if you achieve a transfer rate of over 15 fps, consider yourself blessed by the gods of the Internet. I have tested CU-SeeMe on a Pentium 100 with a direct connection to a server off a T1; I did not get much above 15 fps myself in those situations.

The images are rather low resolution. Not only do the images need to be small, but keeping the resolution down keeps the data outbound to a minimum. CU-SeeMe does use compression, but when sending even low-end audio and images there is still a large amount of information being compressed. Until compression on the fly gets a little better, we have to be satisfied with these resolution and audio limitations. (Figure 41.6 shows the difference between receiving complete data and incomplete data during a CU-SeeMe video conference.)

Fig. 41.6

These windows show the range between normal data flow and interrupted flow. The window on the upper-left shows a normal user window. The user on the right is having trouble. The unreliable data flow has caused a breakup.

Audio is controlled by choosing the Conference option on the main menu and selecting Show Audio Panel. The audio panel has only a few options, but this option is all you really need.

Figure 41.7 shows the basic audio panel. The line through the microphone button mutes outgoing audio. Lurkers can speak to each other; if you don't want to hear them, just uncheck that option. When listening to someone, the intensity shows on the bar.

Fig. 41.7
CU-SeeMe's basic audio panel lets you choose who— and who not—to listen to. Uncheck the Hear Lurkers box to cut off audio from Lurkers.

The audio has a bad habit of popping and hissing a lot. Sometimes 30-50 percent of the audio is distorted to the point of being impossible to understand. Although this can get annoying, one needs to remember this is still new software in a totally new field of the Internet.

Pulling up the Participants menu allows you to choose the Show All command to view all the senders and lurkers. From here, you can get a good idea what is going on. If you want to chat with just one lurker, press the microphone button on his line. If you want to know a bit more about him, click the information buttons (see fig. 41.8).

Fig. 41.8
This figure shows a full site, with NASA sending and many lurkers watching.

Limitations

Reflectors can't handle very many people at once; it is somewhat common to get an error about too many lurkers being connected. When this happens, there is no recourse but to wait and try again later.

Lag time is also something that we all deal with on the Internet. As it is caused by many independent variables, it is a sure bet that Internet lag will continue to haunt us for generations.

> **Note**
>
> One subtle but ubiquitous annoyance with video conferencing is the human element. Until the day we embed a small camera in the middle of all monitors, people in video conferences will either appear to be looking away from the person they are speaking to or will have that weird look of staring directly into the camera. When exposed to cameras, most people tend to act different—not necessarily goofy like when we were kids with uncontrollable desires to mug for the camera—just a bit stiff.

The Future of Video Conferencing

The problems inherent in transmitting real-time video and audio on the Internet won't slow the growth that video conferencing on the Net is beginning to experience. In fact, video conferencing looks to be a bright star of the Net for years to come.

The MBONE

The *Multicast Backbone*, commonly called the *MBONE*, is the newest gun in the arsenal of video conferencing. The MBONE has existed for a few years but is still not very well known yet. The MBONE is able to multicast video and audio, which lets one person video conference with just one person or many people with great ease. The MBONE supports multi-person conferencing at the same time, and it is being used for live Internet video broadcasts of events like rock concerts and conferences, as well. The MBONE is basically a combination of improved equipment and tweaking of the current technology in use. You will undoubtedly hear more about the MBONE in the future.

> **Note**
>
> The MBONE is a more-or-less permanent arrangement, and it requires a commitment at the network administration level. If you would like your workstation-based LAN to become part of the MBONE, the IP multicast software is available by anonymous FTP.

To find out how to download and set up the MBONE software, get the document called "mbone-connect" from **ftp://genome-ftp.stanford.edu/pub/mbone/.** But first, read the MBONE FAQ (Frequently Asked Questions) list at **http://www.best.com/~prince/techinfo/** for more details about how MBONE works.

The Virtual Meeting Room

AT&T is back at it, from the Picturephone a few decades ago to the virtual meeting room today. The virtual meeting room's purpose is to try to fool our senses into thinking we are in a real meeting, interacting with other people. The theory is that even when the mind knows something is not real, if the five senses say otherwise the mind just might allow itself to be fooled. Virtual reality is the driving force behind this, as it is in many innovative Internet applications. Many futurists think the two will end up being the same thing.

Holographic Video Conferencing

Holography is a very exciting area of science. When we are able to project realistic holograms, the virtual meeting room will be outdone. The hardware and software for *Star-Trek: The Next Generation* holodeck-type three-dimensional holography like this is quite awhile off, but we are making rapid strides in that direction. Maybe someday we will just plug into the Net and stay there. Video conferencing then will be our best way of communicating over distance. In fact, it might be almost indistinguishable from meeting in the flesh.

What to Do

Video conferencing is currently being used as a toy for the technologically curious and as a legitimate tool for business. Many software manufacturers are looking into writing more commercial software such as CU-SeeMe. The history of software and applications for the Internet has shown that usually college students and hackers start working on something, and then it becomes popular; a company eventually gets involved because there is profit to be made.

Keep on the prowl for new and potentially interesting software as it comes out. However, with the complexity of video conferencing software, even an early beta version of a new program without a lot of nice extras still takes up a large amount of hard drive space. Having a hard drive of one gigabyte or larger is generally a prerequisite for video conferencing exploration. Windows 95 can help, with good compression software built right into it via the

DriveSpace utility. I download lots of software, play around with it, and then archive it on a pile of floppies.

> **Tip**
>
> For my archiving purposes, I use all those nice free disks mailed to me by America Online, CompuServe, and PRODIGY. I get about 70 free disks a year. Just slap a new label on and erase the disk via Explorer to make it ready for useful service.

Whenever you are importing lots of new software, it is imperative that you do regular backups of your data and check for virus problems. With that said, go out of your way to try to find great repositories of software that are updated often. Once you find yourself downloading every new piece of video conferencing software just to see what new goodies have been incorporated, you will know there is no going back to being satisfied with the telephone.

CHAPTER 42

Games on the Net: MUDs, MOOs, and MUSHes

This chapter discusses Internet-based gaming and describes some of the most popular online games. There are far too many games on the Internet for us to cover in one chapter. This chapter discusses how Windows 95 fits in with traditional Internet games, and describes some of the PC games that are now taking advantage of the Internet. Most of the games discussed here require that you have TCP/IP access to the Internet—either via SLIP or PPP accounts or through your online service.

Traditional Internet games were first developed on UNIX systems, where they were very popular, but have only recently been seen on personal computers. The most popular games on the Internet have always been *multiuser dungeons*, *multiuser dimensions*, or *multiuser dialogues*, depending on who you talk to (MUDs)—virtual worlds ranging from social fantasies to high adventure. MUD players create a character who interacts with the world and other player-controlled characters. Another popular game on the Internet is Netrek, a real-time, multi-player arcade, and strategy game with a theme loosely based on *Star Trek*. Netrek players command starships and travel the galaxy conquering planets and blowing up their friends.

Personal computer game publishers are now responding to the popularity of the Internet, and many new games are being released with Internet-based, multi-player support. We're going to take a quick look at Stars!, a Windows-based strategy game, and also discuss how popular games such as DOOM are moving on to the Internet. You can also look forward to many new games that take advantage of the new multimedia and networking features of Windows 95. If the popularity of interactive, multi-player games on UNIX computers is any sign, online games will become a major force in the gaming industry.

In this chapter you will learn:

- How MUDs work
- The basics of finding, connecting to, and using MUDs
- How Netrek works
- The basics of playing Netrek
- Details about PC-based games making their way onto the Internet, including DOOM, Quake, and Stars!

> **Caution**
>
> Experience has shown that the interactive nature of Internet games can be highly addictive. Internet gamers are frequently known to log several hundred hours of game play per year.

What Are MUDs?

MUDs are possibly the oldest and most popular multi-player games on the Internet. Simply put, MUDs are virtual worlds where players control characters who interact with other players' characters. There are many forms of MUDs, and it is practically impossible to create a description that applies to all MUDs. Most MUDs present a fantasy or science fiction setting; others provide no theme, or serve as virtual meeting places for business or educational users. Some MUDs concentrate on adventure and combat, while others are designed for socializing. Most MUDs are text-based, but work is being done on graphical MUDs.

People familiar with classic, text-based adventure games such as Adventure or Zork should feel right at home in a MUD. Similarly, IRC users might feel quite comfortable in a MUD.

> **Note**
>
> Many descendants of the MUD now go by different names. In this chapter, I use "MUD" to describe all members of the family of MUD-related game—including MUD, MUCK, MUSE, MUSH, MOO, and so on. In instances where I refer to a specific form of MUD, I will refer to it by more precise name.

A History of MUDs

The first MUD was written in the late 1970s by two Essex University students. After several rewrites and ports to more powerful computers (the original version ran on a DEC microcomputer and used 50k of RAM) the system was hooked up to an experimental ARPANET gateway and began serving users from around the world.

MUD development progressed slowly until the late 1980s when several people began development of new MUD servers for use with UNIX-based systems. Most of the MUD servers in use today owe at least part of their design to the MUDs designed in the late 1980s.

Types of MUDs

Most of the MUDs in use today fall into one of two categories:

- *AberMUD, LPMUD, DikuMUD*—These MUDs are the most "lightweight" of the MUDs, with less support for "world building" than their more full-featured cousins. AberMUDs are among the oldest MUDs in use today, and the simplest. LPMUDs are more powerful, and are among the most popular MUDs around. LPMUDs are often used for combat-oriented games.
- *TinyMUD (and variants)*—TinyMUD and its descendants (most specifically, TinyMUSH) have rich world-building capabilities, allowing players to extend the MUD beyond the original design. TinyMUDs are often used for socially oriented systems.

There are also several other MUD systems in use today. One of the more interesting systems out there is *MOO*—a MUD based on an object-oriented programming system. MOO is very powerful, though slower than other (simpler) MUD systems.

How MUDs Work

MUDs are based on a client/server architecture running over the Internet. MUD administrators set up the MUD "server"—the Internet host to which players connect. Players run the MUD "client"—the program used to connect to and play on the MUD. All the action on the MUD is calculated on the server, and players use the client program to control their characters. Note that when people talk about connecting to the MUD, they generally are referring to the MUD server.

MUD Clients

Most MUDs are based on simple commands such as "go north" or "kill bob," so players can use a MUD almost as easily from a UNIX terminal as from a graphical client for Windows 95. In general, any MUD client (such as GMud32 or TinyFugue) will work with any MUD server, but some clients have special features that work only with some types of MUDs (for example, some clients are provide special combat features that only work on LP MUDs).

MUD Servers

MUD servers run on large computer platforms and consume large amounts of resources. Most of these resources are devoted to the MUD's database, which describes the world, its inhabitants, contents, and more.

Most MUDs fall into one of the types previously discussed and generally have custom modifications (the "world" is what makes the MUD succeed or fail, so most MUD administrators put a lot of work into describing and expanding the database before the MUD is opened to the public). Customizing the database allows the MUD's creators to set the tone for the MUD and determine what characters can do there.

MUD servers are accessible via a standard Internet address, with the addition of a port number. The port number is generally four digits, and tells the client where to find the MUD on the server machine. For instance, the former ZenMOO was located at **cheshire.oxy.edu** and the port number is **7777**.

Telneting to MUDs

If you don't have access to a MUD client, you can use Windows 95's built-in Telnet application to connect to the MUD server. Open the Start menu and choose Run. Enter **telnet**. Once Telnet has launched, choose Connect, Remote System, and fill in the fields for Host Name and Port (you can ignore the TermType field). Press Enter and you should be connected to the MUD within a few seconds. An example of this is shown in figure 42.1.

Users with shell accounts can also access a MUD. On a UNIX system you would typically do this by typing:

> **telnet *host port***

Replace *host* and *port* with the hostname and port number of the MUD server—don't type *host* or *port*.

For example, ZenMOO users would type:

> **telnet cheshire.oxy.edu 7777**

The UNIX-based MUD client TinyFugue is also becoming fairly popular. The command to access TinyFugue is generally **tf** or **tinyfugue**. Thus, by following the previous example, you would type either:

> **tf cheshire.oxy.edu 7777**

or

> **tinyfugue cheshire.oxy.edu 7777**

If neither command works, you might want to ask your system administrator about installing TinyFugue.

Fig. 42.1
Connecting to a MUD with Windows 95's Telnet.

MUD Culture

MUDs represent virtual worlds, with fictional characters and plots, so it should come as no surprise that MUDs have developed a culture of their own. It is important to be aware of MUD traditions and jargon. Conversely, people who ignore MUD etiquette will often get a bad reputation.

MUD Jargon

Over the years, MUDs have developed a jargon of their own. Some important terms include the following:

- *Bot*—A bot is a character that is controlled by a computer program rather than by a human being.
- *Furry*—This is anything cute and fuzzy. Generally this means a human/animal crossover character, but it has other implications as well.
- *God*—This is the owner of the MUD; the person who set it up.

- *Lag*—This is the elapsed time between when you enter a command and when it's actually executed. Lag can come from heavy usage of the server, or heavy usage of network bandwidth.

- *Tiny*—This is a prefix indicating that something is related to MUDs, or based in MUD-life rather than real life. Many MUD dwellers have been known to have TinyFriends, and perhaps a TinyGirlfriend or TinyBoyfriend.

- *Spam*—a Spam occurs when someone (or something) suddenly outputs large amounts of material to the screen, thereby messing up everyone's terminals. Spams are highly frowned upon.

- *Wizard*—Wizards are the leaders of the MUD, though their roles vary from MUD to MUD. In general, Wizards are responsible for building the world appropriately, and keeping the game enjoyable while keeping the regular players from getting out of line. The Wizards generally report to the God of the MUD.

MUD Etiquette

The first thing to realize about MUD culture is that it isn't uniform. What might annoy one group of people might amuse yet another. However, there are some general guidelines:

- Many people take MUDding very seriously. Always keep this in mind while playing.

- It is considered bad form to speak out of character without explicitly stating that you are indeed speaking out of character. Don't ask other players about their real lives.

- Don't do anything you wouldn't do in real life, unless it's something appropriately in character. In particular, unwarranted obnoxious behavior and flames will get you a reputation as a jerk.

- Always read the appropriate "help" and "news" files on the MUD to get an idea of the theme and current status of the MUD. Ask Wizards and experienced players for help when you need it, but otherwise try to stay out of their hair.

- Don't be a dork. Trite as this might seem, this advice is necessary because many of the problems that people have with MUDs could be solved easily if one person wasn't being silly or stubborn about something he or she has no business being involved with in the first place. If something seems like it will cause trouble, it probably will.

MUDs and Real Life

With MUDding, the line between real life and fantasy can get blurred fairly quickly. While we won't suggest that dragons really could jump out of your computer and eat you, it's quite possible for you to find your personal emotions and life get entangled with your character's virtual emotions and life. For this reason, many MUDders feel very strongly about how much they do and do not mix up real life and online life. It is important to respect other people's desires in this manner—while some MUD users are very friendly and eager to meet other MUD users in person, other MUD users have no interest in meeting other players "off-line," and will get *very* annoyed if you press the issue.

MUD Clients for Windows 95

There are several MUD clients for Windows and Windows 95. These clients make it easier to store lists of frequently visited MUDs, and allow you to record macros for complex commands. Many clients also allow you to enter multiple MUDs simultaneously, so you can "lurk" on one while chatting or moving around on another. My favorite client is Gmud (available from the MUD section of the Papa Winsock archive at **ftp://papa.indstate.edu/ winsock-l/mud/**). Figure 42.2 shows Gmud in action.

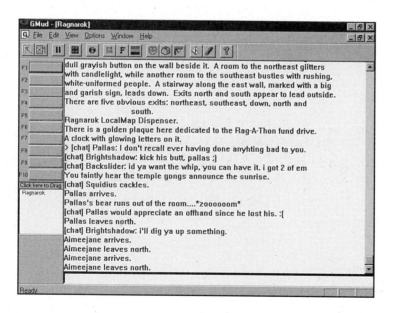

Fig. 42.2
The Gmud MUD client.

Joining a MUD

Before joining a MUD, you'll have to find one you are interested in. UseNet users can check out **rec.games.mud.announce** for posts detailing the latest and greatest MUDs. You can also find lists of MUDs at one of several Web sites. World Wide Web users can also check out a listing of sample MUD sites at **gopher://spinaltap.micro.umn.edu/11/fun/Games/MUDs/ Links/all/**. If this site is inaccessible, try using a Web search engine (such as Lycos—**http://www.lycos.com/**) to find the type of MUD you are looking for—many MUDs now have home pages devoted to them.

Connecting to the MUD

When you have a site in mind, launch your MUD client and open a connection. Most MUD clients will then give you a dialog box listing possible worlds to connect to and allow you to enter new ones.

To connect with Gmud, click the Connect button, which brings up the Connect to a Mud Server dialog box. Click the Add button, then enter the appropriate information for the server you want to connect to. Once the information is entered, the MUD appears in the list and you can double-click the name to connect. Figure 42.3 shows this Gmud connection screen.

Fig. 42.3
Connecting to a
MUD with Gmud.

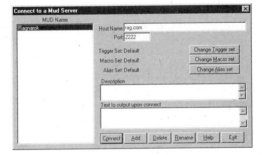

After you successfully connect to the MUD, you should see some form of login banner or list of possible commands. At this point you will be directed to enter your name and a password. This process varies depending on the type of MUD and whether you have a character there already. On an LPMUD, you are commonly asked for your character name, then your password. If your character name is new, you might also be asked some supplementary information for the administration's sake. On a MUSH and some other TinyMUD variants, you will need to type different commands, depending on whether or not you already have a character.

If you wanted to create a new character, you would type

> **create *character password***

If you wanted to connect to an existing character, you would type

> **connect *character password***

Note

Replace the italic words as appropriate (in this case, with the character name and password).

For example, to create ElfBane with the password BuzzCut!, you would type

> **create ElfBane BuzzCut!**

You would then be able to access this character by typing:

> **connect ElfBane BuzzCut!**

Note

If you do not have access to a Windows client such as Gmud, or if you are accessing the Internet via a shell account, remember that you can always connect to a MUD via Telnet or TinyFugue, as previously described in the section "Telneting to MUDs."

Choosing a Character Name

Your character's name provides a way to identify you. In general, you should pick one character name and stick with it. On the other hand, don't be afraid to change your name if it becomes necessary. There are several issues to consider in picking a name:

- Many people use the same name character name across multiple MUDs, especially in the case of social MUDs. You might find that your name conflicts with the name of someone who is well known, which can lead to all sorts of problems.

- In heavily themed MUDs, character names usually have something to do with MUD background. "ElfBane" makes sense in "Enraged Goblins MUD" but doesn't fit so well in *BattleStar Galactica*. Likewise, "Starbuck" doesn't fit so well in "Enraged Goblins MUD."

- Don't pick a name that is obnoxious or that may annoy others.

Pre-Registration

Some MUDs require you to register your character before you begin playing. This ensures that only serious players are involved in the MUD. Information on how to register will usually be displayed when you first connect to the MUD. Send your registration information to the contact person once and wait a week or two for a response—MUD administrators are often quite busy, and they don't like impatience.

Getting Help

The first thing to do after connecting to a MUD and getting a character is to find local help. The best place to start is the MUD's own online help system, which lists the administrators and how to get in touch with them. The help files also describe how a particular MUD is set up, what the theme is, and what rules of behavior are in effect. Once you are familiar with the files, you can begin asking questions of other MUD users.

Help Files

Getting help is easy, but the commands often vary by system. The most common command is **help** or **help** *topic*.

If **help** doesn't work, try substituting **@help**. On some systems you might also want to try **.help** and **+help** to view help files on advanced commands.

Other Users

More experienced MUD users are an excellent source of information—many are friendly and willing to help out a new player. In general, the nicer you are toward experienced players, the nicer they will be to you. The less you ask of an experienced player, the more help they will give you when you need it. See the section "Dealing With Other Users" later in this chapter for more information on interacting with other users.

MUD Administrators

The MUD administrators can give you some help, but keep in mind that they are very busy. Further, while MUD administrators are more willing to put up with "newbie" questions, they also have the ability to kick you out if you annoy them. Administrators are best at answering technical questions and solving problems with the MUD, so it might be best to ask those questions of the administrators and save the rest for your fellow players.

Exploring the MUD

Much of the MUD fun comes from exploring new and unfamiliar parts of the world. Navigating the MUD is extremely simple, but there are a few points that are worth remembering, in case you ever get in a jam.

Basic Directions

MUDs are generally made of rooms that are connected by *exits*. Exits, in turn, point to other rooms. Common exits are north, south, east, and west. To access an exit, you need only type the name of the exit (on some systems you might need to type **go** before the name of the exit).

Conventionally, most rooms have exits in the cardinal directions (north, south, east, west), and they are often abbreviated (n, s, e, w) as well. There are six other common exits: northeast (ne), southeast (se), northwest (nw), southwest (sw), up (u), and down (d). While few rooms will have all of these exits, most rooms will have at least one.

It is sometimes hard to determine what all the exits from a room are. On many MUDs you can enter the command **exits** to see a list of all the exits from the current room.

Teleporting

Some MUDs support a concept of *teleporting*, which allows you to jump to another room without navigating there by hand. This technique is mostly a tool for Wizards, but some MUDs also leave the option open to players in some circumstances. The most common variant of this is the **home** command, which takes you to your starting room.

Dealing with Other Users

Another important aspect of many MUDs (especially social MUDs) is the interaction between players' characters. MUDs offer many different ways for characters to interact, and this chapter barely scratches the surface. A good place to start is to determine who is on the MUD. The command for this is system-dependent, but is generally either **WHO**, **who**, or **@who**.

Examining Other Users

One of the first things to do on meeting another character is to see what he looks like. Easy enough:

> **look *player name***

For example:

> **look ElfBane**

will return the description of ElfBane. Some systems use different syntax—**look at ElfBane** and **ElfBane** are both common variants. For more detailed information, some systems have additional commands, such as **examine** and **@examine**.

Setting Your Description

Now you know how to view other players, but what about when they look at you? Use **look** to view your own character, and you'll probably find that you need a description. Again, this varies from system to system. Common variants include

> **describe me as "This is a description of me"**
>
> **@desc me="This is a description of me"**

Read the online help for "description" and "gender" for more help on this matter.

Talking with Other Users

The next step is to have a conversation with another user. You should automatically hear everything said in the same room as you, so you need to worry only about what you say to others. The syntax

> **say *sentence***

works on most systems. For example:

> **say "Hi, I'm Bob!"**

would cause everyone else in the room to see

> **Bob says, "Hi, I'm Bob!"**

Private Conversations

Sometimes you don't want everyone in the room to hear what you're saying. Many systems support the **whisper** command, allowing you to talk in the room without being overheard. Unfortunately, other players can sometimes tell that you are whispering to each other. If that is the case, or if you want to hold a conversation with someone who isn't in the room, consider the **page** command, which will send a message to anyone on the MUD. Unfortunately, pages cost "money" (see the next section, "Objects, Possessions, and Money") on some servers. Please see your server's help files for more information on paging and whispering.

Objects, Possessions, and Money

What would a virtual world and virtual characters be like without virtual possessions? MUDs support all sorts of activity with objects, and many of the commands you might expect work for objects as well. Simple examples include:

> **get keys**
>
> **examine keys**

give keys to Sean

drop mug

give 35 coins to Sean

If you entered the above commands in order, you would pick up the keys, look at them in detail, give them to a character named Sean (assuming Sean was in the same room), put down your mug, and give 35 of your coins to Sean.

The funds and objects you start with are usually at the discretion of your site administrator. You'll have to beg, borrow, steal, or earn the rest.

Combat

Combat-oriented MUDs are populated with monsters (and occasionally other players) that will try to kill you, unless you kill them first—use the **kill** command to attack a monster or another character. After eliminating enough opponents, you might rise in level and become more powerful. Combat-oriented MUDs generally use **kill** in the form of

kill *target*

Kill also works in some social MUDs, though the results vary. A common example is the MUSH, which requires you to spend a number of coins equal to the desired percentage chance of actually killing the target. For example, if you wanted to have a 50 percent chance of killing Sean, you would have to spend 50 coins to try it:

kill Sean = 50

To up your odds to 75 percent, you'd have to spend 75 coins. 100 coins buys Sean a certain death.

> **Note**
>
> Player character "death" means different things in different places. Some MUDs treat it lightly, while others treat it very seriously. As always, know the local conventions before you go around killing people.

Leaving the MUD

When you are ready to leave the MUD, take care to clear up any short-term business with other players, and be sure to return home. Then sign off of the MUD, generally using the **QUIT** command (though it might be **logout**, **quit**, or **@quit**, depending on the system).

Advanced Concepts

There's too much development and history behind MUDs to cover every-thing here—even if we had an entire book with which to work. We hope that you'll learn more about MUDs via the online help system. Eventually you might want to become a builder (covered in the next section, "Building and Programming"), and maybe even a Wizard.

Building and Programming

Most TinyMUDs, TinyMUD variants, MUSHes, and MOOs support *building* to some extent. This allows MUD users to extend the world to their own tastes, creating new objects to use and areas to explore. Generally, building requires approval from a Wizard, and you are generally given a task area in which to build. Building is both a privilege and a responsibility, but some people find it to be one of the most rewarding parts of MUDding. Experienced builders are often in demand to work with MUDs that are in development, but even they need work before they can go online.

Becoming a Wizard

Being a Wizard means different things on different MUDs. In combat MUDs, players with the most combat experience become Wizards and serve some-where between the administrator and high-powered players. On social MUDs, Wizards are needed to help maintain the MUD and oversee the building of new areas. Wizards on social MUDs behave as social caretakers rather than military leaders.

More Information on MUDs

Not surprisingly, there is a lot of online information regarding MUDs. The **rec.games.mud** newsgroups on UseNet cover many aspects of MUDding. There are also several Web sites devoted to MUDding, including the following:

The MUD FAQ:

> **http://www.math.okstate.edu/~jds/mudfaq-p1.html**

MUD Information and resources:

> **http://www.cis.upenn.edu/~lwl/mudinfo.html**

Netrek

Netrek is a client/server, real-time, interactive, multi-player action and strat-egy game with a theme loosely based around the *Star Trek* universe. Players control starships and fly around the galaxy conquering planets and blowing up each other. The object is for one team to conquer all the opposition's planets. Netrek has a large following in the academic community, and is now making its way into the home with software versions written for Windows 95.

How Netrek Works

Netrek uses an extended version of the client/server architecture:

- You start your Netrek client by connecting to a specific server or by connecting to the *MetaServer*—an Internet site that lets you pick from currently available games in progress.

- The client and server use encryption to verify that all the players are humans. This measure was added because people started using lightning-fast computer-controlled "bots" to beat slower human opponents, which was no fun for the human players.

Once connected to the server, you authenticate your character and begin playing. Each Netrek server keeps track of the players who use the server regularly, including running tallies of time spent online as well as combat statistics.

Netrek on Windows 95

Most development of Netrek clients has been on UNIX platforms, but ports for Win32 and Windows 95 have begun to appear. As of this writing, the ports are still in a development stage, though we've found them to be fairly stable and quite playable. One word of warning: these clients are designed to fit on a monitor with at least 1024×768 resolution, and things will be cramped if your graphics card can't handle it. Further, these clients expect you to have your display set for "small fonts," and they get very confused if you have set "large fonts" or a custom font size.

There are three Netrek clients available for Windows 95, and all are ports from the UNIX versions of Swine, Cow, and Cow-Lite. All three versions have similar interfaces and they start in similar ways, so our instructions here should apply to all three. At the time of this writing, all three versions were still in development, and they still bore much of the legacy of their UNIX roots. In particular, they all need to be started from the command line, and they all have peculiar problems with the mouse (they expect a three-button mouse, and they accept only key presses when the mouse is in the active window).

You can find Swine, Cow, Cow-Lite, and lots of helpful Netrek material at the Netrek home page: **http://www.cycor.ca/TCave/netrek.html**.

Joining a Game

Open an MS-DOS shell (unfortunately, Netrek sometimes has trouble with the Start menu's Run command—this situation should improve with future versions of the Netrek software that are more suited to Windows 95) and change the directory to the location of the Netrek client. If you have a specific server in mind, type the following:

netrek –h *hostname*

Or type **netrek –m** to use the MetaServer. The MetaServer allows you to pick from a list of open games and identifies the current number of players in each game. Figure 42.4 shows the MetaServer display.

Fig. 42.4
Using the Netrek MetaServer to find an open game.

When you're connected to the server, the full Netrek window will come up. If you have a 1024×768 resolution monitor, this window covers most of the screen. If you have less resolution, the window extends beyond the screen boundary (you can still play the game, but you won't get the full effect).

As in MUDs, you must first enter your character name and password. After you have signed on, you will see four colored boxes for various races at the bottom of the top-left quadrant of the window. Center the mouse over a race and type the letter of the ship type you want:

S for Scout

D for Destroyer

C for Cruiser

B for Battleship

A for Assault Ship

Once you've selected your ship type, the window will change to the game display. The local area is displayed on the upper left, with the entire galaxy displayed on the upper right. The lower right contains a message box for talking with other players, while the lower left contains statistics on the game. Figure 42.5 shows the Netrek main window during a game.

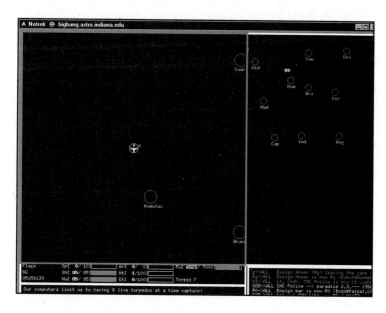

Fig. 42.5
Netrek: boldly game where no one has gamed before.

Getting Killed

Unless you're lucky and very nimble, you're probably going to get thoroughly beaten when you first start playing Netrek. Unlike traditional arcade games in which you begin with easy opponents before graduating to the difficult challenges, Netrek drops you right into the middle of things and you'll often be facing opponents with years of practice.

With this said, we encourage you to practice and get used to things, gaining skill and watching how other ships maneuver. Use the right mouse button to change direction and use the number keys to set your speed. The left button fires photon torpedoes, while clicking both the left and right buttons at once (or clicking the middle button, if you have a three-button mouse) fires a phaser blast. Notice how your speed affects your turns, and just about everything affects your energy display in the lower left. Try attacking a few enemies (races are easily distinguishable by color) to see how they react and to see what types of maneuvers they perform.

Pressing **h** brings up a window that lists all the key commands. You can modify the key settings by editing the netrekrc file, which is located in the same directory as the Netrek client.

When you die, you'll go back to the startup screen to pick another ship.

When you're ready to quit, press **q** to self-destruct. Then press the quit box on the startup screen.

More Information on Netrek

You can find more information on Netrek on the UseNet **rec.games.netrek.*** newsgroups. You can also find more information at the Netrek home page on the Web (at the time of this writing, it was **http://www.cycor.ca/TCave/ netrek.html**).

DOOM and Beyond

PC games are now starting to get hooked up over the Internet, whether the game designers intended it or not. While iD Software's DOOM shipped without built-in Internet access, several users have managed to coerce the game to play over the Internet. The setup of the system is fairly difficult, but interested hackers can set up Internet DOOM via the instructions listed in the DOOM FAQ, located (at the time of this writing) at **http://doomgate. cs.buffalo.edu/docs/FAQ/doomfaq/**. Meanwhile, iD Software (the creator of DOOM) is working on Quake, a new client/server game designed especially for Internet-based games. Also, Microsoft is preparing to release WinDOOM, a Windows 95-specific version of DOOM that might incorporate direct Internet play via Windows 95.

Stars!

Another good example of a PC game that takes advantage of the net is Stars!, a strategic conquest game that uses Internet e-mail to communicate between players. Stars! is a shareware program, available from **http:// beast.webmap.com/stars!/**. To give you a taste of what the full version is like, Stars! lets you run a small, multi-player game with the unregistered version. Figure 42.6 shows the game play of Stars!.

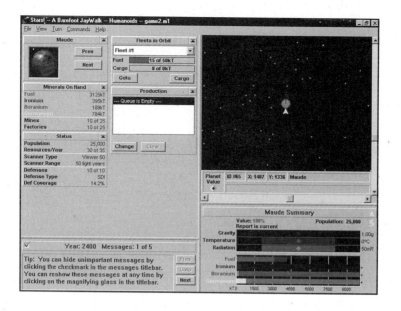

Fig. 42.6
Conquer the
Galaxy in Stars!.

To run a multi-player game, open Stars! and select a new game. Choose the advanced options, which allow you to add more players. The advanced options also allow you to pick races and configure the style of the game. The registered version also allows for customizable alien races in your Stars! game. Figure 42.7 shows some of the advanced setup options in Stars!.

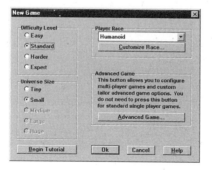

Fig. 42.7
Preparing to
challenge your
friends in Stars!.

Once you've added the players you want, you can begin the game as normal. You will see a multi-player game hosting window, entitled Stars! Host Mode, which lets you run the game and generate new turns. Figure 42.8 shows this screen.

Fig. 42.8

Hosting a multi-player game in Stars!

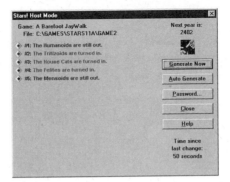

More Information on Online Games

There is a lot of information about online gaming on the Internet. A favored site for game players looking for the latest and greatest is **http://happypuppy.com/**, which has several games for major platforms. Another good site to watch is Microsoft's home page at **http://www.microsoft.com/**. Microsoft has been working with developers to develop all new games that take advantage of Windows 95 and the Internet.

Last, but not least, we have Zarf's List of Interactive Games on the Web, a site with links to all sorts of World Wide Web-based games. Most of these games aren't really multi-player, and certainly none are real-time, but many are very interesting. They highlight up-and-coming developments in the World Wide Web system. The site is at:

http://www-cgi.cs.cmu.edu/afs/andrew/org/kgb/www/zarf/games.html

Part VIII

Internet Security

43   Privacy and Security on the Net

44   Protecting Yourself from Viruses

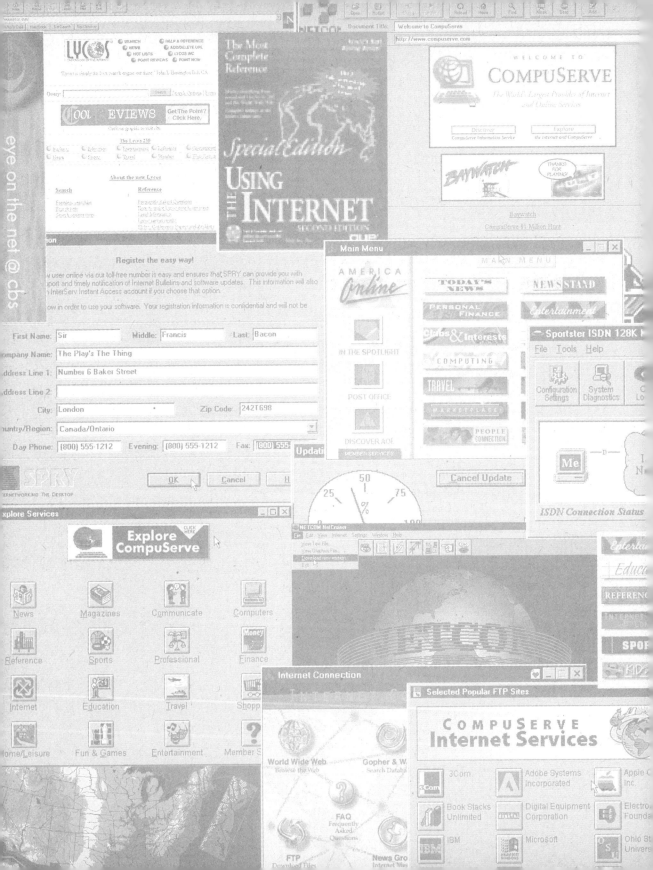

CHAPTER 43

Privacy and Security on the Net

The Internet continues to grow exponentially. Where once only large computer facilities—universities, the government, and Fortune 500 corporations—were interconnected, today any individual with a personal computer can hook into the Internet. With the introduction of Windows 95, all a computer owner has to do is subscribe to the Microsoft Network or any other commercial online service and *voilà,* another member of the Internet community. With this growth comes security and privacy risks that were only of concern to larger facilities a few years back.

This chapter discusses the risks that you, as an individual computer user, face when you travel the electronic superhighway. We will also give you tips on how you can protect your computer and yourself against unauthorized intrusion into your right to privacy.

In this chapter, you learn the following:

- What risks your Internet host faces
- How the host's risks affect you
- Methods of protecting your computer
- Methods of protecting your privacy

Internet Security Overview

The moment you connect your computer to any other computer, whether by local area network with coworkers or by a dial-up connection to an Internet provider, you subject yourself to some risk that your data could be compromised. Your data could be stolen or destroyed. Your communications could be intercepted or misdirected.

The security of Internet host sites is nebulous at best. Eventually all of them will face some sort of break-in. It might be a hacker trying to prove that he or she can gain unauthorized access to an Internet site, or it might be a malicious attempt to destroy data. Being forewarned is your best defense against your data being corrupted or used in an unauthorized fashion.

Classic Hacking Methods

Almost every computer that supports multiple users is protected to some degree by the use of a login name and password. This serves two functions. First, users can be restricted to using only certain functions on the host. For example, each user can be restricted from accessing another user's files. Even if one user is allowed to read some common files, that user can be restricted to changing or replacing those files. The second function of the login name and password is to make sure that whoever uses the computer is authorized to do so.

Password Attacks

Passwords are the main point of security for most Internet sites against unauthorized access. Unfortunately, most users don't realize the importance of passwords and choose easily guessed combinations of letters. A proper password should contain letters, numbers, punctuation marks, and symbols. An intruder counts on the fact that users often choose passwords that are combinations of their name, common names, or even just the word "password."

How does an intruder obtain a login name and a password? Obtaining a login name is easy. Every post to a UseNet newsgroup contains the name and Internet address of the person who posted it. Guessing a password may be just that, a guess. A hacker can even use the power of his own computer to run through a list of common passwords in the hope that one of them works.

Note

On operating systems used by hosts on the Internet there is a root or supervisor account that can access every file and program on the system. This "super account" is the target of most hackers who want to do something more than read someone's files. New computers have a default name and password that is the same for every installation. Some administrators never get around to changing the default password, making it easy for someone to gain access with supervisor status.

Any system that allows access through the use of passwords has to store the passwords somewhere. The password file is usually encrypted by a one-way encryption routine. This means that your password is encrypted in such a manner that it cannot be decrypted. When you log on, the password that you enter is encrypted and compared with the password stored in the file. This method is more secure than decrypting the stored password and comparing it to the one you type at log on. Hackers rely on the fact that the password file, since it is encrypted, is easily obtained. They can then use a crypt-and-compare program to try various combinations of passwords until they find one that matches. There are programs available that can crypt-and-compare every word in the dictionary in an amazingly short period of time.

Another method commonly used by hackers is simply being aware that the more difficult a password is to guess, the more likely the user is to write it down. If you can't remember that your password to your Internet host is "BLxtj63JRB," you might be tempted to write it on a "yellow stickie" and attach it to you monitor. All a visitor has to do is look, no guesswork involved.

You might get a phone call from a purported representative of your Internet host. "We have had a serious break-in by a group of hackers and have to check all our accounts. Would you give me your current password so we can see if anyone has cracked your account." You might be tempted to give it, but don't! Instead, get a name, not just a number, hang up and call the company back. You are probably the victim of a hacker attack known as social engineering.

Data Interception

As you have seen in previous chapters, the data you send to someone else on the Internet, or even on a local network, is placed in data packets with the address of both the recipient and the sender. On the local network, all machines get all the packets but usually only read the ones intended for them. On the Internet, a packet is routed from one Internet site to another until the final destination is reached.

Just because a packet is addressed to another site or network node does not prevent someone along the way from examining the contents of that data packet. You have no way of knowing if the data packet you sent was even received by the intended recipient. You also have no way of knowing that a data packet your computer receives is the same one that was sent to you. Somewhere along the way, someone may be intercepting your communications and reading your messages.

Keyboard Logging

Windows 95 is a multitasking operating system. The task bar shows you what programs are running, but a program can hide that icon so you can't be sure which programs are running at any one time. Every time you move or click the mouse, press or release a key, get a packet of data from the modem or network, or use a file, Windows 95 records that *event*. The event is then placed in a message queue and sent to the running programs. Just as Windows 95 watches these events, so could a hacker's program. There might be a program running in the background that monitors keystrokes and places them in a hidden file. All the hacker has to do is get access to this file and read everything you typed.

Logging programs are not restricted to programs. There might be a program that intercepts the communications stream to the modem and logs all incoming and outgoing calls. Maybe the entire communication is written to a hidden file as it is being sent to the modem.

Firewalls

In order to increase security, many network administrators have installed firewalls on their systems. In a building, a firewall prevents the spread of a fire from one part of a building to another. In computer terms, a *firewall* can be thought of as a way of isolating different parts of a system. A firewall can limit access to and from the network or between computers on the same network. Some systems have a dedicated gateway computer that routes all incoming and outgoing packets between the network and the Internet. Other firewalls consist of routers that filter out unwanted packets.

The most common firewall blocks all incoming TCP traffic with the exception of mail and FTP. Both of these services are routed to a dedicated host rather than every host on the network. Other filters block RIP, BGP, and other routing information except from trusted sources. ICMP redirects are blocked from all sources.

Routers have all the tools necessary for a network administrator to implement security measures if configured properly. Unfortunately, many administrators configure the router improperly, leaving holes in the firewall. For example, a router may be set to block all incoming connections to the range of privileged ports (0-1023) allowing an intruder access to all the ports from 1024 and higher. This particular "backdoor" implementation allows an intruder to add another Telnet daemon at one of the higher ports and reinitialize the Internet services managed by *inetd*.

One of the disadvantages of installing firewalls is the cost. Firewall implementations can consist of a combination of hardware and software costing hundreds of thousands of dollars just to install. Administration cost of firewalls can also be considerable. Yet even the best firewall money can buy is no guarantee that an intruder can't gain access. The only way to make a system truly safe from intrusion is by turning the Internet connection off.

Password Security

The best and most expensive firewall in the world may not stop an intruder who possesses a valid ID and password. Just because a user has a password does not mean that the password is secure. A would-be intruder can guess a password or try a list of frequently used passwords until he or she hits the proper one. The key to security is choosing and guarding a proper password.

Password Guidelines

It's generally easier to say what a proper password is not rather than what it is. Passwords should not be one of the following:

- Any word that can be found in the dictionary
- Less than 6 characters long
- A name
- Related to the user in any way

Some systems have programs to help the user choose a password. These programs tend to enforce some or all of the above rules. In general, a password should be as meaningless as possible, yet easy to remember so that you don't have to write it down.

One-Time Passwords

Passwords are often the weakest link to security. Although they may be encoded at the destination, they are rarely encoded at the source. Any time a password is transmitted in plain text, the potential exists for interception. One-time dynamic passwords are only good for one login, and then expire. Even if they are intercepted, they are no longer valid and of little use to a would-be intruder. One-time dynamic password schemes can be accomplished by hardware, software, or a combination of both.

Hardware Security. Devices from vendors such as Security Dynamics, Digital Pathways, and Enigma Logic can provide almost the ultimate security for a host. Each user possesses a device about the size of a credit card that has an LED display. When a user logs in to the host, he or she must enter a Personal Identification Number (PIN) and the number displayed on the LED. The number displayed on the LED changes over time, so once a user logs in, the password is never used again. Even if the security card is lost or stolen, the thief needs the user's PIN in addition to the number displayed on the security card.

Software. Several different software schemes are available to implement a type of dynamic one-time passwording. One of these systems is the S-Key program. When a user logs in to the host system, the host issues a challenge in the form of a string of letters or numbers. The user then enters this string into the S-Key client and the program displays an answer to the challenge in the form of a string that the user can send back to the host. If the challenge is not answered properly, the host terminates the connection.

Your Risk

You might think that a break-in on an Internet host does not affect you. Don't hackers break into government, university, or businesses computers? If you merely use your computer to browse the World Wide Web over a dial-up connection you might suppose that a break-in would have no consequences for you. In most cases you would be right. But there is a risk, although small, that you might be compromised, too. Figure 43.1 shows a message sent to all users by an Internet host advising them that a hacker has attempted to penetrate the mail system.

Fig. 43.1
Security informa-
tion from an
Internet provider.

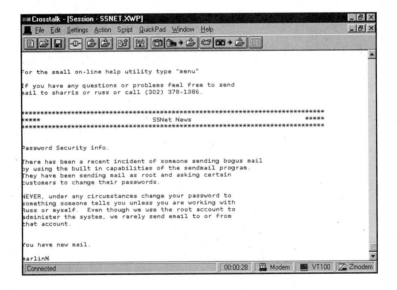

If you pay for your Internet services by the hour and a hacker obtains your ID and password, you could wind up paying for the hacker's computer time. If a hacker has gained access to an Internet site that relays your messages, he or she might be able to read those messages and use the information. Suppose you ordered a left-handed sprocket bevel from the International House of

Hardware using your Internet connection and you sent them your Visa card number over the computer so they could send you the merchandise by next day air. You always run the risk that an employee of the International House of Hardware will send his mother-in-law on a vacation to Hong Kong using your Visa number. But, you also face the risk of having Harry the Hacker intercept your Visa number from an intermediate Internet site.

Your communication over the Internet can also be subject to what is known as the "man in the middle." Harry the Hacker may not be satisfied with just intercepting and reading your communication with the International House of Hardware. He could just stop your data packets and pretend he was the International House of Hardware. He ends up with your Visa number and you don't get anything in the next FedEx delivery. Or he gets a left-handed sprocket bevel by next day air, and you get a Visa bill in next month's mail.

Rest assured that most hosts on the Internet go to extraordinary lengths to prevent unauthorized usage. But it seems that every time one security hole is discovered and fixed, the hackers come up with yet another method for obtaining access.

Risks from Common Internet Utilities

When you sign up for Microsoft Network, available to all Windows 95 users, you are in touch with the wonderful and risky world of the Internet. Almost any Internet host can give you access to the World Wide Web, FTP, Gopher, Mail, and Telnet. These are the most common utilities used for surfing the Net. Other services include Archie, UseNet newsreaders, and IRC (Internet Relay Chat). How to use these utilities is covered in other chapters; let's discuss what risks are involved with using them.

You might be tempted to think of these services as one-way streets. Unless you have an Internet node set up on your computer and allow others to use one of these services to access your computer, it would seem that you are in control. You request data from someone else, but no one can get data from you that you do not send. This is not always the case. If you use one of the TCP/IP daemon programs provided on the CD in the back of this book, be aware that you are opening up your computer to almost everyone in the world.

World Wide Web

This graphics-based utility is quickly becoming the method of Net cruising most favored by PC users. The flashy graphics and point-and-click links make it easy to visit Internet sites around the world. However, the program that produces all of these wonders also makes it the most risky for your computer and your data.

The Hypertext Markup Language (HTML) that makes your World Wide Web browser work also places your computer at serious risk. Windows 95 browsers are able to read and write files, launch applications, and even run a DOS session in the background. The very functions that make the World Wide Web so versatile, make it vulnerable.

The browser included with Windows 95 is the Microsoft Internet Explorer. There are no security options available with this browser, and the help file makes no mention of any security problems with the World Wide Web.

One of the most popular World Wide Web browers is the Netscape Navigator. Netscape is more aware of security than other browsers and includes several options for alerting you to possible security risks. Netscape tries to establish a secure link using encrypted packets between the two linked sites. A small key icon, shown in figure 43.2, is the indication of whether the link is secure. If the key is broken, then text is being sent in the clear, but if the key icon is connected, the link has been encoded and only the two machines can understand what is happening between them.

Fig. 43.2
The Netscape
security key.

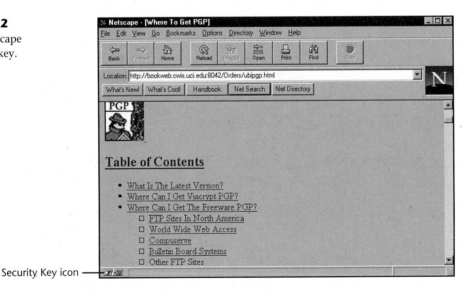

Security Key icon ——

Netscape includes a whole package of security options that you can set by clicking on Options and Security menu choices. Many times there is nothing the browser can do to make a connection secure. In this case, the Netscape

Navigator displays a warning before you submit information that might be compromised and gives you a chance to cancel before the data is sent as shown in figure 43.3.

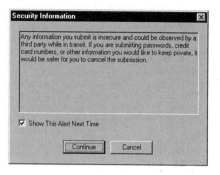

Fig. 43.3
A Netscape security warning.

FTP

If you use FTP to access files from another site, there are certain risks you take. The program you obtain from the FTP site might contain a virus or be a Trojan horse. Although most reputable site managers make sure the programs they offer for downloading are free from viruses, if you don't personally know how the site is screened, you risk getting a program that contains a virus. See chapter 44 for a discussion of viruses and how to protect yourself from them.

Certainly the FTP site is more at risk than a user who merely downloads a file from the site. The security holes in the FTP site itself may place you at risk when you download a file. If a hacker has penetrated the FTP site, the file that is logged on the site's index may not be the file you download.

There is also the possibility of a "man in the middle" intercepting your FTP request and furnishing a program that is nothing like the one you are trying to download from the FTP site. This risk is small, but it does exist.

Gopher

Like FTP sites, Gopher sites can contain files that are available for downloading. Unlike FTP and World Wide Web, some Gopher programs give you no indication as to which site you are connecting to. If you use a World Wide Web browser to connect to a Gopher, at least you can see the URL in the address window. The Microsoft Internet Explorer, as well as other World Wide Web browers, shows the site in the lower-left corner of the screen before a connection is made. The Microsoft Internet Explorer says Shortcut to... and then lists the document name followed by the site name. Other Internet browsers show the complete URL that lists the type of connection, site name, and document path. After the connection is made, Microsoft Internet Explorer shows the URL in the window near the top of the screen labeled `Connected to:`.

Downloading a document or program from a Gopher site carries the same risk as with FTP sites. The only difference is the potential break-in methods that a hacker might employ when compromising the site.

Telnet

The biggest risk with Telnet is if you allow Telnet access to your computer. Telnet allows a remote user access to the site just as if he or she were at a console at the site itself. This is the method used by hackers to log in to a remote computer. If you don't allow Telnet sessions on your computer, you can rest assured that a hacker can't log in to your system by that method.

If you use Telnet to contact a remote computer on which you have an account, you can be at risk from a keystroke logging program running on your computer, or an interception of your Internet packets by a third party. Of special interest to a hacker would be your log on sequence because you send your login ID and password in the clear over the Internet. If this communication were intercepted somehow, there is nothing to prevent a hacker from subsequently logging on to that computer as you.

Mail

One of the most tempting targets of an intruder is e-mail. Your e-mail may contain credit card information, passwords, or maybe even intimate personal information. Your e-mail is delivered to your host and stored in a file until you retrieve it. There is a certain level of security on most host computers so that only you can read what is in your e-mail file—actually, you and the system administrator, who has access to all files on the system. If an intruder has your account ID and password or the administrator's password, he or she could also read your mail.

Keeping Your Communications Private

I'm sure you are aware that your telephone conversations may be overheard by someone listening in. If not, you should be. Law enforcement agencies can tap phone conversations with the approval of a judge, but there are strict laws governing when and how an agency of the government can tap a phone line. If you are not engaged in any illegal activities, the risk is minimal that the government is listening in. Anyone with a portable phone and a set of alligator clips can tap the phone line between you and the local switching office. Yes, it's illegal, but it's easy to do.

The increased use of cellular phones has made the task of listening even easier and less risky for the perpetrator. Cellular phones are transmitted by radio, and anyone with a radio receiver set to the correct frequency can listen in—and it's not even illegal if the contents of the conversation are not divulged.

So, too, can the communications between computers be tapped. We have already discussed how the packets sent over the Internet can be intercepted, but there are other ways that someone could listen in on your computer conversations.

A phone tap can work just as well with a modem as with voice. A modem is merely a device that modulates and demodulates a digital signal on a carrier tone. With the proper equipment to demodulate the carrier tone, computer communications can be tapped just like voice conversations. Likewise any digital information sent over a cellular phone equipped with a modem can be intercepted. In fact, intercepting cellular calls is even easier since the call is broadcast by radio.

As a matter of fact, if someone were really interested in what you were doing with your computer, they could intercept radio frequency signals emitted from your computer even when you are not connected to the outside world. Your keyboard controller emits a certain frequency as does your video monitor. These radio frequency emissions can be picked up and analyzed by someone equipped with sophisticated detection gear. It may sound like grist for a James Bond spy movie, but it can and does happen—but probably not to you.

For the Truly Paranoid

Is a person paranoid if people are really out to get him or her? That is an interesting question. There is a high probability that no one has planted a keyboard logger in your computer, or is intercepting your e-mail. You probably don't see anyone lugging equipment up the nearest telephone pole, or mysterious vans with a roof full of antennas parked in front of your house. Still, there are some people for whom even the possibility of someone intercepting what is thought to be a private message is anathema. For you there is hope.

VIII

Internet Security

Encryption Programs

One of the ways in which you can ensure the privacy of your data is by encryption. Encryption is as old as government and armies; with computer technology it's now available to everyone. As a matter of fact, encryption has become important enough that the government has gotten into the act and developed a standard called *Data Encryption Standard,* or *DES.* In fact, the U.S. government thinks that DES is so good that it has prohibited the export of programs that use RSA algorithms.

Phil Zimmerman may have started out paranoid when he brought military-grade encryption to the general public when he created Pretty Good Privacy (PGP). Certain governmental agencies blanched at the thought that average citizens could now encrypt messages using methods that take years of supercomputer time to crack. This and the fact that PGP was distributed free over the Internet took Phil Zimmerman out of the realm of the paranoid. People were out to get him, especially the U.S. Government. The government has accused Zimmerman of distributing a government-approved encryption standard outside of the U.S., which is a violation of federal statutes.

Phil's legal troubles aside, his program is more than pretty good. It is an easy way for anyone to encrypt data into an almost unbreakable form. Additionally, PGP uses the concept of Private Key/Public Key encryption—something that can only be done by computers.

Cypher Keys

The basis of any encryption scheme is to change a message into a form that is meaningless to anyone who does not have the key to change it back. Simple substitution of one letter for another, something we all see in newspaper cryptograms, is the easiest form of key to crack. Once you know that every occurrence of the letter "E" in the original message is replaced by the letter "Y," decoding the message is easy. Another method would be to change the words in the original message into numbers. These numbers could signify the page, line, and word counts in a book. If you know the code and have the book, you just go to the page and line, and count the number of words in that line until you get to the substituted word. The key is the book. If you don't know which book to use, you can't decode the message.

With the advent of computers, elaborate algorithms can be developed to substitute one letter for another. These algorithms are so sophisticated that reversing the process without the key becomes almost impossible. If you have the key, the message can be decoded almost instantaneously.

Public Key

The problem with a public key is that anyone who has it can not only decode the message, but can also encode a message using that key. If everyone has the key, then encoding is worthless. The concept of Public Key encoding solves the problem. There are two keys for every encryption, a public key and a private key. You can send your public key to anyone who wants to send a message to you. They encrypt the message using your public key, but the only way to decode the message is to use your private key. Even if everyone in the world has your public key, they cannot decode a message to you that was built using that key.

There are a few caveats associated with public key encoding. You must be sure that the public key you get is the public key of the person to whom the message is intended. Key exchange is, if you pardon the expression, the key to secure communications. Once a public key exchange has been made and verified, further communication between the two parties is for all intents and purposes *absolutely* private. There are even methods built into the exchange to verify the public and private keys of the originator and sender of the message.

PGP

A testament to the popularity of PGP encoding is the fact that the Internet world took to it rather rapidly. Check almost any UseNet newsgroup and you will see many messages signed with "PGP public key..." followed by the public key for that person. If you are paranoid, or if people are out to get you, you too can use PGP. Unfortunately, while PGP is available for almost any operating system—and Phil Zimmerman has even published the source code—it is not available for Windows 95. However, it is available for MS-DOS, and several Windows interfaces are available to help the DOS dysfunctional.

The PGP program for DOS is available free of charge from an FTP site maintained by MIT. You can reach this site by World Wide Web at:

http://bs.mit.edu/network/pgp.html

Once you answer a series of questions, you can download the ZIP file that contains the software and documentation. The file we downloaded was named PGP262.ZIP. This represents PGP version 2.6.2. Always get the latest version.

The first thing you must do is unzip the file. If you don't have an unzip program, you should also download PKZIP. This program is available world-wide and is usually distributed as a self-extracting archive with an .EXE extension. The PKZIP program is also included on the CD in the back of this book.

VIII

Internet Security

The PGP262.ZIP file contains two other zipped files, plus a text file called SETUP.DOC. The text file tells you how to install PGP for almost any type of computer. Scroll through the text until you find the set up instructions for MS-DOS. Some of the DOS terms are slightly different than the Windows 95 terms. For instance a directory is a folder in the Win95 world. You can run an MS-DOS session in Windows 95 and follow the instructions in the PGP setup file, or point and click your way around "My Computer" until you create the appropriate folders.

Now comes the fun part if you have never worked from the DOS prompt. You have to change your AUTOEXEC.BAT file and add a few lines. After you change the file, you have to restart your computer so that the lines you added to your AUTOEXEC.BAT file will take effect. The documentation that comes with the program tells you what to do, but remember that it was written for a DOS user and not a Windows 95 user. You can use the Notepad to edit the AUTOEXEC.BAT without having to use the DOS prompt. Add the lines indicated in the PGP documentation SETUP.DOC and restart the computer. Click Start and choose Shut Down from the menu. Click Restart Windows and wait while Windows 95 closes and restarts.

Unzip the file PGP262I.ZIP, which contains the actual PGP program. Remember that this is a DOS program and will only work in the MS-DOS session that is a part of Windows 95.

Don't neglect the documentation that comes with PGP, especially the first part where Phil Zimmerman discusses why your file should be encrypted. The next part of the documentation tells you how to set up and use the software—written from a DOS point of view. If your entire knowledge of PCs is with Windows or Windows 95, you should print the documentation if you want to use PGP from the MS-DOS command line. If you don't do DOS, there is help.

WINPGP4

There are some Windows programs that form an interface with the DOS version of PGP. Basically, the Windows interface merely sends the proper DOS commands to PGP depending on what options you choose from the Windows program. When this chapter was written, only one program was designed to work with Windows 95 and that was WINPGP4. The archive file is WINPGP4.ZIP and is available from:

**ftp://ftp.oakland.oak.edu/simtel/win95/security/
winpgp4.zip**

If that URL does not work with the World Wide Web browser, try:

ftp://ftp.oakland.oak.edu/

Work your way down the FTP menu structure until you find the correct directory. There are several programs available that are Windows overlays for PGP.

After you have downloaded the archive file, WINPGP4.ZIP, extract the executable file by using PKUNZIP. The extracted files include the setup program WINPGP4.EXE. Click Start, Run. Either browse to WINPGP4 or enter the name and press OK.

The setup program will install the program in a new folder (or an old one if you so choose). Choose a program group for the program in the start menu.

Once WINPGP4 is up and running, you never have to use the PGP DOS command line again; it is done for you. Just choose the operation you want from the menu or buttons shown in figure 43.4. WINPGP4 will run the PGP program in a DOS window. When PGP is finished with an operation, you will have to press a key to exit the DOS window. Clicking the mouse will not work.

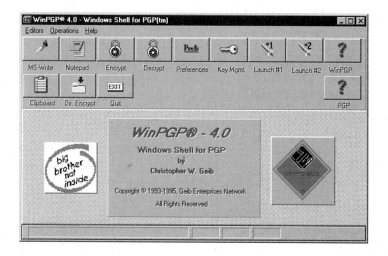

Fig. 43.4
The main screen for WINPGP4.

Your first task is to generate your private and public keys. Click the Key Management button and then choose Create Keys from the dialog box. WinPGP4 runs PGP with the proper parameters in a DOS box. Just read and follow the instructions.

VIII

Internet Security

Caution

You need to supply a key phrase (password) in order to generate your key. This phrase should be kept absolutely private. You will not see the phrase as you type, so choose a phrase that reflects your typing skills. Make it easy to remember, easy to type, and difficult to guess.

Once you have generated your own key, you should save your key to a file so you can send it to others. Click the Key Management button again and choose Extract a key from your key ring from the dialog box. Then pick the key you want to extract and the name of a file for the key. The default extension is .PGP.

When someone sends you their key, add it to the public key ring by pressing the Key management button and choosing Add key (public or private) to key[ring]. Note that the dialog box is not big enough for the entire phrase. Enter (or browse for) the name of the file containing the key, and then choose a key ring. The default key ring is Public.

Sending encoded messages is a multi-step process. First, compose a message using your favorite word processor. WINPGP4 has buttons that will launch Windows Write or Windows Notepad. Write your message, and save it with a .TXT extension.

Click the Encrypt button and choose the type of encryption. See the documentation for the differences in types. Enter the name of the document in the box. You can browse for the document if you can't remember the file name. Then enter the recipient's name in the box. You can browse a list of keys on your public key ring and click the recipient's name if that is easier for you.

After you click OK, WINPGP4 launches PGP in a DOS box. PGP asks for your pass phrase and then encrypts the message to a file with the extension PGP. Once this message is encrypted, it can only be decrypted by the recipient using his or her private key. *You* can't even decrypt the message, even though you were the one who encrypted it in the first place.

Tip

If you are worried about the security of your own computer, be sure you erase the clear text file after you encrypt the message. Even erasing the file is not enough to ensure privacy unless you reuse the space. Remember, deleted file are not overwritten and can be recovered. WINPGP4 has an option to overwrite and then delete the original file once the encryption is complete. The truly paranoid will want to make sure the clear text has also been removed from memory, and Windows 95 virtual memory.

If you receive an encrypted message, reverse the process. Save the message to disk with the extension PGP. Launch WINPGP4 and click the Decrypt button. Enter or browse for the name of the file (usually with a PGP extension). You can also name the output file for the clear text file. It's a good idea to use this option since PGP writes the clear text to a file with the same basic name as the PGP file, but with no extension. If you choose a file name with a TXT extension, you can read the clear text directly from WinPGP4 by launching the MS-Write or Notepad buttons. Once you have entered the file names, WINPGP4 launches PGP with the proper parameters and switches in a DOS box. Enter your pass phrase, and PGP decrypts the message and writes the clear text to a file. Press a key to close the DOS box and return to WINPGP4.

There are many other features offered by WINPGP4. Be sure to read the help files before you choose an option. Figure 43.5 shows a PGP encrypted message in the Windows 95 word processor before decryption. Care to try your hand at decryption?

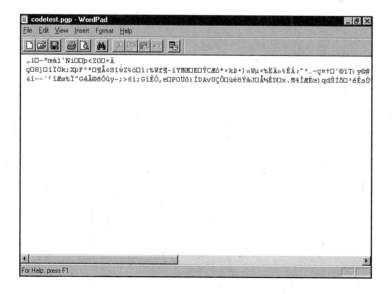

Fig. 43.5
A PGP encrypted message.

VIII

Internet Security

> **Note**
>
> WinPGP4 is shareware meaning you can use it before you buy it. However, until you register your copy, you will often see a message box that reminds you that you are only trying it. Once you register your copy, these annoying messages disappear.

Network Security

If your computer is connected to a local area network, you can restrict access to your resources. Windows 95 and Windows for Workgroups have built-in networking capabilities. Your Windows 95 computer probably has a Network Neighborhood icon on the desktop if you are connected to a network.

You can decide which of your computer's resources you want to share with others on the network. Click Network Neighborhood, then select your own computer from the list of people on the Net. A typical example of the resources available on a small network is shown in figure 43.6.

Fig. 43.6
Windows 95 network resources for a typical small network.

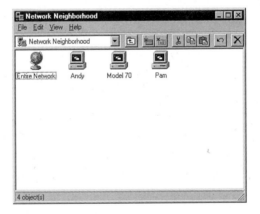

To select the computer resources you want to share, click the My Computer icon on the desktop. As you click each item in the list, you can select File, Properties. When the properties dialog box appears, click the Sharing tab and see how sharing is enabled for that item. You can choose to share the resource with everyone on the network, as shown in figure 43.7, or set up a password so only some of the people on the network have access to the resource. You can grant either full or read-only privilege to the network users. You always have the option of not sharing with others on the network.

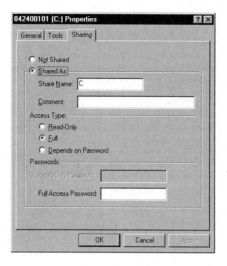

Fig. 43.7
Sharing network
resources through
Windows 95.

Remember the tree-like structure of the file system when you let others on
the network share your files. If you share your C drive, others on the network
can access every folder on your disk. However, when you choose File, Properties for one of your folders, you will notice that sharing is not enabled (see
fig. 43.8). This does not mean that others cannot access that folder, it only
means that the folder is not available on the network as a separate resource.
Notice that the dialog box in figure 43.8 does indicate that the folder is included in the shared resource C:\.

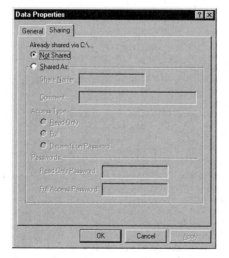

Fig. 43.8
Folder Not
Shared. Or Is It?

NetWare

If your LAN is part of a NetWare LAN, there are individual protections you can place on your files. Each NetWare folder and file can be set with Read, Write, Create, Modify, Erase, File Scan, Access Control, and Supervisory attributes. Files and folders can have any or all of these attributes. Since the rights attributes vary among different versions of NetWare, check your documentation or with your network administrator to find out how to set them up on your situation.

CHAPTER 44

Protecting Yourself from Viruses

A funny thing happened on the way to Windows 95. There is no anti-virus software included with the operating system. Given the publicity surrounding the development of Microsoft AntiVirus (MSAV)—a frail clone of Central Point Software's Anti-Virus product (CPAV)—and its inclusion with DOS 6+, it's a curiosity.

Could it be that Windows 95 is such a secure operating system that no virus could ever get through? No. The people at Microsoft, when asked, responded that they didn't want to be in the anti-virus business any longer. It's no wonder. MSAV was the perennial last horse in the anti-virus product testing races. It's also not too unlikely that Central Point wasn't up to the challenge of dealing with the changes that Windows 95 requires for full anti-virus protection using a scanning technique.

One of the charms of the Internet is the availability not just of information, but of thousands of programs you can run on your own PC without paying a dime up front. The downside is that you don't know whether you're getting a little extra something—a computer virus—along with what might be a very useful program.

In the entire pantheon of routine PC use, no single subject is more arcane—or more misunderstood—than computer viruses. Almost the entire body of knowledge is owned by a very few: those who write viruses and those who find them.

In this chapter, you learn the basics of computer viruses and virus protection:

- What a virus is
- What a virus isn't
- How viruses spread

- How to protect yourself
- When you're at risk
- How to choose an anti-virus product for Windows 95

What Is a Virus?

Even the best virus-busters haven't been able to agree on the perfect definition of a virus. Two words—program and replicate—are key. In order to get from place to place (computer to computer, disk to disk) or *replicate*, some *program* must operate to make that happen. There are two other elements that are present in some but not all viruses, a *trigger* and a *payload*. A trigger is a section of program that looks for a certain event such as a date, a particular number of disk accesses, or a set number of duplications. The trigger can be used to activate the payload section of the virus. The payloads of some viruses are relatively benign. The "stoned" virus, for example, simply announces that your computer is "stoned." Others carry more dangerous payloads such as erasing all data on a drive, scrambling the file allocation table (FAT), or rendering a drive unreadable. A virus does not need a payload and trigger to be classed as a virus, but it must replicate.

In the simplest terms, a virus is a *program* that *replicates*. It doesn't have to do any damage, it just has to spread. In order to spread, a virus must somehow get the user to run it. This is easily accomplished by appending the virus programming code to another program that the user is certain to run. Because almost all PC programs are stored on hard or floppy disks, all a virus has to do is change the file that contains the program without the user being aware of what is being done.

Program Infectors

This class of virus is the simplest to write and the easiest to find. Under DOS (and, if you look deep enough, under Windows 95), all executable programs have a file name that ends with either .EXE or .COM. Most people have become so accustomed to clicking on a colorful screen icon that they don't remember—or never knew—that there are some strict parameters for what goes on behind the scenes and screens.

A *program infector* is passed when an infected program is run and appends the virus code to another .EXE or .COM file. When the second program is run, it appends the virus code to a third program, and so on until every program stored on the disk is infected. As a general rule, each time an infected program is run, it will infect another one. However, general rules are often broken. Some viruses will infect multiple programs when they are run. So, the general rule with viruses is that there are no rules.

Boot Sector Infectors

Every hard disk and diskette contains what is known as a *boot sector*. This is the first physical sector on the disk. It stores a small program designed to get a PC up and running. Every time you reboot your computer, this small program runs. A boot sector infector (BSI) can only be "caught" by booting up your PC with an infected disk (see note). If you never have a disk in drive A or set your computer to always boot from the hard disk, you cannot be infected with a boot sector virus.

Boot sector viruses are hard to catch, but easy to spread. Once a PC is infected, any disk access—even a simple folder check—can pass a BSI from a hard disk to a floppy. If that floppy is used to boot another computer, the virus spreads.

Remarkable as it may seem, 90 percent of reported virus "hits" in mid-1995 were BSI viruses. Even computers using Windows 95 begin by reading the first sector on the disk to start the operating system loading. BSIs may be the most prevalent form of virus attacks in the Windows 95 environment for the next several years.

Protecting against BSI viruses is simple. Tell your computer *never* to boot from a floppy drive. Most computers can be set to boot from the hard drive by changing the boot configuration stored in ROM. Check your computer's manual to see if the configuration can be changed on your model.

> **Note**
>
> Remember the rule that there are no rules when it comes to computer viruses. A type of virus, called a *dropper*, exists that places a virus in the boot sector. These programs can infect a boot sector even if the computer is never started from an infected floppy.

Macro Viruses

Another now broken rule of computer viruses is that only programs, not data, can contain a computer virus. A *macro* is data that affects the way a program operates. In a way, a macro is a program within a program. Usually macros are a way to save keystrokes when using a program such as a word processor, database, or spreadsheet. Several programs have within their macro language the capability to perform many of the functions of a virus—replication and possibly destruction. Some programs even have the macro equivalent of the AUTOEXEC.BAT file, a macro that runs whenever the program is started.

Macros are now being favored by some virus writers. If you use sophisticated programs with a rich macro language, such as Microsoft Word, you should be aware of the existence of macro viruses. Microsoft Word has the capability of embedding a macro right in the file. As the PC operating systems get more diverse with DOS, OS/2, and Windows 95, macro viruses may become more of a problem than program viruses.

What a Virus Is Not

It often seems that there are more myths associated with computer viruses than truth. The problem is that with the exception of those who develop viruses, few people really know how they work. Most of these are the anti-virus researchers who develop programs to combat viruses. For those who market anti-virus products, the worse the scare, the better the sales, so there is a built-in prejudice in hyping the problem.

The media get most of their information from people who sell anti-virus products. Seldom does a person who writes viruses come forward and tell the media why and what they are doing. Users who have no concept of what a computer virus is and does often blame a virus for anything that makes them lose data. Legends are grown from the fruit of ignorance.

The truth is that most computer viruses (there are thousands of different ones) do not destroy a computer or its data. Most viruses do nothing more than replicate and waste space and time. But there are several widespread viruses that do have a destructive phase known as a *payload*. The payload can vary from erasing files to formatting a hard disk and destroying all the data on it. Often the payload, if present, will be triggered on a certain date or by certain actions. Payloads and triggers vary from one virus to another.

If you get a computer virus, the odds are that you won't lose all of your data. Of the thousands of viruses that have been written, only a few become successful in replicating throughout the computing community. Most are spotted quickly and eliminated before becoming widespread. The most successful (if that's the right term) viruses are those with no payload. They merely replicate themselves and go relatively unnoticed. A virus with a payload announces its presence in dramatic fashion and can be eliminated once spotted.

Many myths about computer viruses have built up since the first ones were discovered in the late '80s. There have been stories of burning monitors and viruses transmitted by the control signals of modems. Recently, the Internet community was hit by the pseudo "Good Times" virus. Supposedly, mail and newsgroup messages that contained the words "good times" would release a virus and destroy the files of anyone who read the message. The virus itself was a myth, but Internet users replicated the warning message in virus-like proportions.

My favorite virus myth came from a tongue-in-cheek story written in *PC World* on April 1, 1991, shortly after the Gulf War. The story told of an American manufacturer of printers who, at the behest of the military, sent a shipment of printers to Iraq with a computer virus embedded in the read only memory. The Coalition forces delayed the invasion of Iraq until the virus took hold in the Iraqi air defense system. When the air war began, the Iraqis could not shoot down the U.S. planes. True? Not a bit. Funny? Very.

A year later, a reputable national news magazine reported the exact same story. The magazine reported the story almost verbatim, but as absolute truth from an unnamed source deep within the Pentagon. When confronted by those who had read the original story in *PC World*, the magazine refused to admit that the story was an April Fool's joke and never printed a retraction or correction. In fact, they printed a confirmation. Because that particular magazine has a much wider distribution than *PC World*, many more people think the story is true than know it's a hoax.

Now that you know the basics of what a virus is and isn't, let's see how these little beasts came into being and how the public has been led and misled by the media.

A History Lesson—The Virus Wars

The opening salvos were fired in the fall of 1987 when the (c)Brain virus was found at the University of Delaware in October, the Lehigh virus at the university of the same name the following month and, in December, the Jerusalem virus was discovered at Hebrew University. In early 1988, the Stoned virus popped up. In October of 1988, the first computer virus conference was held. The virus writers and virus "experts" were at war.

But it was pretty much kid stuff until 1989 when the so-called "Dark Avenger" came on the scene with the first fast-infecting virus. Hot on Dark's heels came *polymorphic* viruses—viruses whose code changed with every iteration so standard techniques couldn't find them. Then along came *multipartite* viruses, *stealth technique* viruses and, in 1995, macro viruses that break all of the existing rules.

> **Note**
>
> Most viruses attempt to hide their actions from the user. The most common technique is for the virus to intercept error messages such as the write protect error and not report it to the user. Other viruses adjust the memory size of the computer so that the memory space it uses is hidden from other programs. Advanced stealth techniques include intercepting all queries about file size and reporting the uninfected size instead of the real size. Even more advanced viruses can set the processor into single step mode and monitor each and every processor instruction and memory access. The virus is written this way to protect itself from discovery and removal.

> **Note**
>
> Most anti-virus software looks for a virus in a file or on the boot sector by comparing the bytes in the file with a known sample of the virus. To counter this technique, some viruses change form from one replication to another. The virus part of the file is encrypted differently each time the virus replicates to another file. A small portion of the code remains unencrypted and is used to decrypt the virus as it is loaded into memory. This unencrypted portion of the virus is often interspersed with random do-nothing instructions. The program operates in the same way each time it is run, but even this portion of the file contains an almost infinite variation of bytes.

War Games

In the late '80s, newly-minted "virus experts" began to pump out anti-virus products as fast as the virus writers could get new viruses into distribution. The careful, generic approaches of some of the first anti-virus products were pushed aside by "scanners," most of which purported to "find all known viruses." There was speculation that some of the less honorable anti-virus types were writing their own viruses and distributing them so *only* their products would find the newest addition to the virus army.

The stakes were high, particularly for those who hoped to amass a fortune from selling their products. The virus writers had little more at stake except tweaking the most outrageous vendors with yet another variant of an "old standard" that the latest scanner couldn't find.

Apocalypse Now

The date was set for Friday, October 13th, 1989. On that date, the relatively benign Jerusalem virus and the heavily payloaded Columbus Day virus were scheduled to bring a halt to the world of computing as we knew it. Or that's what the media, fed by dis- and misinformation would have had us believe.

The show, as the old saying goes, didn't live up to its advance reviews. The Jerusalem virus has a payload that will erase any program run on any Friday the 13th. The Columbus Day virus will erase all data on a hard disk on any date after Columbus Day, October 12. Friday, October 13, 1989 came and went and computers kept on working. Few had been infected with those viruses.

The really big media show was two and a half years later.

Armageddon

The so-called Michelangelo virus, a BSI virus with a payload that destroys all the data on a hard disk on March 6 of any year was discovered in 1991. Fifty million—that's right, 50,000,000—PCs were predicted to roll over and succumb to data death on March 6, 1992, 517 years after the birth of Michelangelo. With one notable exception, the Associated Press who "considered the source" of the information, the media fell back in love with the concept of imminent destruction. Perhaps as a result of the extensive publicity and the almost overnight production of anti-Michelangelo products, there were very few reported "hits."

> **Note**
>
> Naming computer viruses began as soon as the first one was discovered. Often the name associated has nothing to do with the virus itself. A case in point is the Michelangelo virus. It's doubtful that the person who devised the virus had the Italian Renaissance painter Michelangelo, born in 1475, in mind when he or she chose the trigger date of March 6. The Michelangelo virus was named by a European anti-virus researcher who was not familiar with the history of Texas—"Remember the Alamo," March 6, 1835.

Hype or Help?

It's unlikely that the media, twice-burned by hyping an empty fear, will ever cover computer viruses with quite the intensity of the Jerusalem/Columbus Day and Michelangelo scares. Nevertheless, the list of known viruses, both lab viruses and those "in the wild," continues to grow and virus incursions are almost commonplace today. The war is by no means over, but it's being fought in a quieter fashion.

Representing the Defense

There are three basic ways to combat the most common viruses.

- Known virus scanners
- Validity checkers
- Behavior blockers

Of the three, known virus scanning has developed into the most prevalent form of virus protection for the PC. Why? When asked at an international virus conference, one well known speaker uttered one simple word: "Marketing."

Known Virus Scanning

The principle of *virus scanning* is simple. Viruses are program code, which is nothing more than a set of numeric values that tells the computer what to do. Each and every virus has a specific *signature*, a set of numbers in a particular order unique to the virus. A scanner can examine a program file or boot sector and determine if there is a signature of any one of the known viruses present. If there is, the scanner identifies the virus and notifies the user.

While it sounds simple enough, there are some drawbacks. First, the operative word is "known." The person who programs the scanner must know the signature of a particular virus. This is not always easy. To obtain a signature, the programmer must have a sample of the virus and select a series of program instructions that occur only in that virus. If the programmer does not have a sample of the virus, he or she cannot write a scanner that identifies that particular virus. With the geometric increase in the number of viruses being released, the work involved can rapidly overcome the energy of even the most avid anti-virus programmer. Every time a new virus is discovered, the anti-virus program must be updated to reflect the additional knowledge.

Another problem faced by scanners is the proliferation of a type of virus known as the *polymorphic* viruses. These are viruses that, while doing the same thing, change the programming code from generation to generation. No two samples of the same virus contain the same series of programming instructions. It then becomes very difficult for a scanner to identify the virus from a series of programming instructions.

Validity Checks

Because the computer stores programs as files on a disk, any change in the file can be noted. This is the principle that guides the anti-virus technique of *validity checking*. A mathematical formula calculates a valid signature for the program file and stores the number in a separate data file. If a virus changes the contents of the program file, the calculated signature will no longer match the stored signature.

An advantage of validity checks over scanners is that the virus does not have to be known by the anti-virus program. The fact that the file has changed can be used to alert the user to the presence of a virus. This means that even mutating viruses and new viruses can be easily noted by a validity checking anti-virus program.

The disadvantage is that you don't know the name of the virus that is present in the system or how it got there. Also a validity check requires that the program file be uninfected with a virus when the signature is first calculated. If the file is already infected, a validity check will show no change.

Behavior Blockers

The third class of anti-virus software are programs that prohibit any virus-like activity. For example, there is seldom, if ever, a need to change the boot sector of a disk. A *behavior blocker* prevents this particular sector from being changed. Once a program has been installed, the basic executable file should never need changing. A behavior blocker can monitor this type of activity too.

Behavior blockers quickly fell into disfavor as a means of preventing viruses simply because they are subject to many false alarms. Because there are legitimate programs that may appear to have virus-like activity, a behavior blocker usually displays a warning and allows the user to either proceed with the questioned activity or not. An unsophisticated user may often choose to proceed where he or she should stop, or stop a perfectly legitimate function.

When You're at Risk

Every personal computer is equipped with a piece of hardware that will guarantee that no computer virus will infect your machine. It's called a plug. Remove it from the wall socket and you will never get a computer virus. If you choose to use your computer, you run the risk of computer viruses.

Your risk depends on *how* you use your computer. If you never place a disk in the A drive, never add new programs, and are not connected to a network, you should worry more about lightning strikes than about computer viruses. This is safe computing. A virus is a social disease. Only contact with a program from an outside source can infect your computer. This program could be on the boot sector of a disk or contained in a new program added to your mix.

Any new program adds to the computer virus risk, no matter where it comes from. There have been cases where brand new computers with bundled software have been shipped with a computer virus. Even shrink-wrapped new software packages have been known to contain viruses. Computer stores often accept returns from unhappy customers, take the software package into the back room, redo the shrink wrap, and place it back on the shelves for another customer.

Software programs that you download from a bulletin board or obtain from an Internet FTP site can also be infected with a computer virus. Most reputable sites check and double-check the program before offering it for downloading, but sometimes a virus is a new one that is not trapped by their scanner. Some sites couldn't care less if you are infected by one of their programs. There are even some sites that deliberately distribute viruses. Your best defense is to know the site's reputation before downloading.

The highest risk is from your friendly computer repair person. That's right. The person who is supposed to fix your computer is the one that is most likely to infect you. When something goes wrong and you call the repair person, they bring with them a whole package of utility programs to try to repair any data damage. They place the disk in drive A, reboot the computer, and run a set of diagnostic programs. These utility disks travel from one sick computer to another. It is highly probable that one of the problems has been a computer virus. If the technician's diagnostic disk has become infected by one of these computers, that disk could introduce the virus to your system.

What to Do When the Worst Happens

Most computer users will spend a happy life of computing without ever being hit by a computer virus. For this reason, only a small percentage are prepared when a computer virus does hit. The three most important steps you can take to prevent disaster in the event of a computer virus hit are:

1. Back up
2. Back up
3. Back up

Back Up!

The roving mouse pointer may be a far worse enemy than the most dreaded computer virus. A click of the big "X" delete icon on the toolbar $^3/_4$, not the "x" close button on the title bar $^3/_4$, means delete. That click can cause your precious document to disappear. You even get a chance to confirm that you want your document to go away, and you just might do it. I know. It happened to this chapter. Back up.

Back Up!!

That 1.5GB hard disk can be a disaster waiting to happen. Mechanical things can break down in use and a hard disk is a *very* delicate instrument mounted in a shock-proof sealed case. How sturdy is that hard disk when confronted by earthquakes in California, hurricanes in Florida, or tornadoes in Kansas? Could your data survive a fire? Probably not. Back up.

Back Up!!!

In the rare event of a computer virus, your only hope may be a backup. If it is one of the viruses that has a destructive payload, your backup could be the only way to restore your data. The programs on your backup may be infected, but at least your data files will be safe. It's far easier to re-install the software from the original disks and restore the backed up data files than it is to recreate all the data from scratch. Back up.

Restoring a Virus-Infected Computer

There are many programs that can attempt to repair a virus-infected file or boot sector. Because some viruses overwrite the original information in the host, repair is not always possible. Still, a good number of viruses retain all the information of the host and a repair program can remove the virus code from the file and restore it to the original condition.

Sometimes, the repair can be worse than the virus. Most boot sector viruses replace the original boot sector with a virus sector and move the original to another sector on the disk. After the virus run its own code, it loads the original boot sector into memory and lets the computer complete the boot process as usual. To effect a repair, all you have to do is move the original boot sector back into the proper place. Repair programs must know where the original boot sector is located or they might move the wrong sector. Then the computer won't work at all. You can't even use another repair program that will do it right.

Some file-infecting viruses destroy a portion of the original program and cannot be removed. In this case, the only option is to delete the file and re-install the program from the original disks. Even if a virus can be removed from a program, your best choice is to re-install the program from the original disk. Only use a repair program if you are unable to locate a disk version of the program.

Windows 95 and Computer Viruses

Don't be fooled by the sales pitch. Under all the icons, Start buttons, and long file names, Windows 95 is MS-DOS. If you know the technical aspects of MS-DOS, you will see that the hard disk still contains a Master Boot Record in sector 1, and a DOS boot record on the first sector of the second side. The familiar IO.SYS and MSDOS.SYS files are still present in the root directory as hidden system files, although they are not the same as the MS-DOS files of the same name. The disk directory structure and File Allocation Table are still in the same place on the drive as under MS-DOS. The CONFIG.SYS and AUTOEXEC.BAT files still begin the process of starting the computer.

The difference with Windows 95 and MS-DOS lies in the IO.SYS program, which contains the basic function calls for the disk operating system. Without getting too technical, MS-DOS is an unprotected operating system that allows any program to have access to all areas of memory. A true protected operating system will isolate the memory allocated for programs from the memory used by the operating system. Windows 95 is a hybrid of the two.

Unfortunately, as this chapter went to press, it has only been two and a half months since the release of Windows 95. Anti-virus researchers have not been able to study the effects of every virus on Windows 95, but of those that have been studied, a few pleasant surprises have developed.

Boot Sector Self Check

Windows 95 has a built-in integrity check for the boot sector. When Windows 95 detects a change in the boot sector, it displays a window and informs you that you may have a virus. The scheme that Windows 95 employs is not foolproof. Technically, a hard disk has two boot sectors, the Master Boot Record (MBR), which is the first sector of the disk, and the DOS Boot Sector (DBS), which is the first sector of the partition. Windows 95 displays the warning message if either of these sectors is infected, but always identifies it as the Master Boot Record.

Windows 95 misses some viruses that definitely change the Master Boot Record. Apparently, Windows 95 does not perform an integrity check of the entire sector, but only checks the vector (address) of interrupt 13h, the disk I/O vector. Windows 95 issues no warning for a virus such as "Jumper B," which does not change the vector of interrupt 13h. At this time, most boot sector viruses change the vector of interrupt 13h, but as Windows 95 becomes more popular, more viruses are likely to appear that circumvent the built-in check.

File Viruses under Windows 95

First the good news. In November of 1995, there were no Windows 95 specific viruses. But with apologies to "Field of Dreams," build it, and they will
come. Surely, the Windows 95 system requires more programming knowledge than MS-DOS, so maybe the 13-year-olds won't be writing Windows 95
specific viruses. But in analyzing many existing virus, the programming involved shows that some of the virus authors have a very extensive knowledge
of MS-DOS systems programming. Maybe they should work for Microsoft instead of against it.

Now the bad news. Most of the MS-DOS viruses work under Windows 95.
When you run one of your old MS-DOS programs under Windows 95, you
run it in a DOS box. Windows 95 sets up a separate DOS environment for the
program and runs it just like it would under the old MS-DOS system. When
you look at the technical aspects of a DOS program running under Windows
95, you find that Windows 95 tries to manage the DOS interrupts. DOS programs that use undocumented interrupt functions may fail (crash) under
Windows 95. Although Microsoft tried to make all older DOS and Windows
3.1 programs compatible with Windows 95, not all will operate properly. A
side effect of the miscompatibility is that not all viruses will work properly either. This is good.

While you are working in the DOS box with older DOS programs, any virus
infection will spread just as it did under the older DOS system. When you
exit the DOS box, however, if you have inadvertently introduced a *resident
virus* (a virus that acts like a Terminate-and-Stay-Resident program), Windows
95 assumes that you have run a pop-up utility and refuses to close the DOS
session until you disable the pop-up. Even though this feature is not designed
as a virus behavior blocker, it acts as one. When you exit the DOS box, the
resident virus is disabled.

Just as in the previous version of Windows, every Windows 95 program has a
DOS stub program. If you try to run a Windows program from DOS, the stub
program runs and informs you that the program must be run under Windows. If you have a virus active in the DOS session when you run a Windows
stub, the stub can become infected. The DOS program is not Windows aware
and the virus could overwrite a portion of the file that contains the Windows
program. The next time you run the program from Windows, you will find
that the file is corrupted and either will not operate or will crash the system.

Windows 95 treats the DOS stub program a bit differently than the previous
versions of Windows. In the older versions, if attempted to run a Windows
program from the DOS box, the stub would run instead. When Windows 95

specific programs are started from the DOS box, the stub is bypassed and the Windows 95 program runs normally. Because Windows 95 does not load and run the DOS stub, many viruses, even if memory resident, will not infect the program.

Protecting Your Computer

When considering virus protection for your computer, you first must ask yourself, do you want a fancy Windows 95 GUI interface or protection from viruses? Because almost all computer viruses are DOS based, it makes sense to have a virus protection program that is also DOS based. As was stated above, marketing is the driving force behind anti-virus programs. Almost all of the better anti-virus programs are scanners that check for the signature of known viruses in the program files stored on the disk. There are only a few anti-virus programs that are written specifically for the Windows 95 system, and these are not necessarily the best, only the first to have the proper interface. Remember that even though Windows has been in the market for a long time and has a large user base, most of the best anti-virus packages are still DOS based.

There are several reasons why anti-virus developers choose to use DOS for their programs as opposed to Windows or Windows 95. From a technical point of view, DOS gives the anti-virus programmer full access to the system and files where Windows and, especially, Windows 95 attempts to hide some of the more technical aspects of the system from the program. Hiding the more technical concepts makes sense for most user programs and allows them to operate in an almost endless variety of configurations, but it also makes the identification of viruses much more difficult for the anti-virus program.

If you want to be safe from viruses, you should always start your computer in MS-DOS instead of Windows 95 before running an anti-virus program. You can make a DOS bootable disk by running the File Manager program and choosing the Make System Disk in the Disk menu. To start MS-DOS from the disk:

1. Choose Shut Down from the Start menu and close Windows 95.

2. Place the disk in drive A and then restart your computer.

3. Turn your computer off for several seconds or press the reset button if you have one. Do not use the Ctrl+Alt+Del restart since this method may leave a resident virus active in memory.

Which Anti-Virus Programs Are Best?

Unfortunately, no one has yet to agree on how to test anti-virus programs. Scanners can reliably test for 100 percent of the viruses programmed into their database. The only question is what virus signatures are in the database. Testing organizations run various anti-virus scanners against the viruses that the testing organization has obtained. If the virus sets are not the same, then the scanner might fail to notice some of the viruses in the testing suite. There might also be viruses that are not included in the testing suite that the anti-virus scanner will find.

The only thing that is reliable in anti-virus testing is that the major computer magazine's testing procedures will always rate anti-virus programs in the order of the advertising expenditures of the various commercial packages. Programs that are distributed free or as shareware seldom rate highly in the major computer publications.

There has been a large shake-out in the anti-virus business since the early '90s. Many companies with great products but poor marketing have been adsorbed by companies with poor products and great marketing. Unfortunately, the larger companies kept their own products in distribution and only bought the good products to keep them off the market. Users are more impressed by full-page four-color ads and flashy graphics than in products that work. Because most users will never get a computer virus anyway, they are usually satisfied with the anti-virus product they have.

When choosing an anti-virus program, the first problem you run into is determining whether the product is any good. When you purchase a word processor, you can read the box, check the documentation, or even try the features yourself and decide if the program meets your needs. But, chances are, you don't possess a full set of computer viruses that you can use to test the capabilities of the problem. The box or ad might state that the program finds 5,632 different viruses, but if you're hit with the 5,633rd, the product has been a waste of money and time.

Nor can you rely on the popularity of a particular anti-virus package. Popularity often reflects on the marketing ability of the company and not the product's capabilities. In fact, popularity may jeopardize the program by making it a target for virus writers who are out to prove that they can write a virus that the most popular anti-virus product will not detect. When Microsoft chose to include Central Point Anti-Virus (CPAV) as Microsoft Anti Virus (MSAV) in the release of DOS 6, virus writers figured out how to get around the protection before DOS 6 was on the market.

VII

Internet Security

Getting Reliable Virus Information

One of the more reliable sources of anti-virus information has been the UseNet newsgroup **comp.virus** and its e-mail newsletter Virus-l. The group was moderated by Ken Van Wyck at Carnegie Mellon University and contained a frank discussion of virus and anti-virus products by professionals all over the world. Unfortunately, the newsgroup and newsletter have been temporarily suspended because of the work load involved. The group may be reactivated at some time (maybe even now), and the archives of old postings are available by FTP from many sites. Check for a directory called "virus" on an FPT site or search the World Wide Web for "Virus-l." Other Internet sources of information are the **alt.com.virus** newsgroup and **http://www.yahoo.com/Computer** and Internet/Security and Encryption/ Viruses.

Most of the major online services have sections where you can check for virus information. Let me restate that. Most of the major online services have sections where you can check for virus *misinformation*. There are many people who profess to be experts in the field, but there are only a few who really are. In years of watching the bulletin board postings to virus topics, the amount of misinformation is so overwhelming that one tires of trying to correct the postings of the self-appointed "experts."

A Couple of Recommendations

Surprisingly enough, some of the best anti-virus products are free. If you feel more comfortable with a commercial product, there are several good ones on the market. Most of the better anti-virus programs originate in Europe because the virus problem is greater there than in the U.S. By reading the **comp.virus** newsgroup over the years, two products stand out as the best of the lot, Doctor Solomon's Anti-Virus Toolkit, a commercial product from England, and F-Prot by Frisk Software International of Iceland, which is free to individual users and also offers a commercial version.

Dr. Solomon's Anti-Virus Toolkit

Because the term "virus" is disease related, it's no wonder that many of the anti-virus products are doctor related. But Dr. Alan Solomon is a real doctor, a Ph.D., anyway. He began producing anti-virus products in England when the threat was new, and has continued producing one of the best commercial anti-virus products ever since. Dr. Solomon is one of the foremost computer virus researchers in the world today.

Dr. Solomon's Anti-Virus Toolkit can both find and repair viruses. The scanner, FINDVIRU.EXE, is one of the fastest and best in the business. The latest version of the Toolkit has a Windows interface that lets you select features from menus and buttons.

Dr. Solomon's Toolkit contains several features that aren't found on other scanners. It can scan a file that's in compressed format, such as .ZIP and .AJR. When you download programs from an Internet site or from a BBS, it is most likely in some compressed format. With the Toolkit, you can look inside these files without going through the process of decompression first. If you find a virus, you can delete the compressed file and never expose your computer to danger.

Some computers use a compression program for program files. Programs such as PKLite and LZExe make a program file smaller by compressing it and adding a small program to the beginning of the file that decompresses it at run time. Dr. Solomon's Anti-Virus Toolkit can scan inside compressed programs.

Dr. Solomon takes particular care when it comes to the repair of virus-infected files. The program must be 100 percent sure that the virus is the *exact* same virus for which the repair is made. The Toolkit does not rely on just a virus signature. A Cyclical Redundancy Check or CRC determines if the virus is the same as the one for which the repair routine is written.

Dr. Solomon's Anti-Virus Toolkit is a commercial product and is available in many computer outlets. It is distributed by S&S International. The address is:

> S&S International PLC
> Alton House
> Gatehouse Way
> Aylesbury, Buckinghamshire HP19 3XU
> United Kingdom

The telephone number is:

> Voice: +44 (01)296 318700
> Fax: +44 (01)296 318777

S&S International maintains a World Wide Web site at:

> **http://www.sands.com**

F-PROT

If you like the idea of getting something for nothing, then F-PROT is the program for you. Frisk International distributes one of the best anti-virus programs free to non-commercial individual users. They also have a professional version that's available for a reasonable fee to individuals, companies, and educational institutions.

The free version of F-PROT is DOS based, but has a nice user interface with a point-and-press menu system. The professional version comes with a Windows interface. A Windows 95 specific version may be in the works.

The scanner is fast and accurate and consistently ranks among the best in identifying viruses, even when the tests are performed by competing companies. F-PROT includes a repair module, as well as a fairly complete description of most common viruses.

F-PROT is widely distributed on the Internet. The official distribution is by FTP through Simtel Mirror sites, although many online services carry the program too. Rather than reading about it, download it and try it for yourself. It costs you nothing more than connect time.

F-PROT comes in a zipped file named FP-*nnn*.ZIP, where *nnn* is the latest version number. An official Simtel mirror site is:

ftp://oak.oakland.edu/SimTel/msdos/virus

Check in the directory /pub/msdos/virus for the program. If you need to find another site, you can FTP Frisk International at:

ftp://complex.is/pub/README

for a list of official sites. Frisk International does not distribute the program from its FTP site.

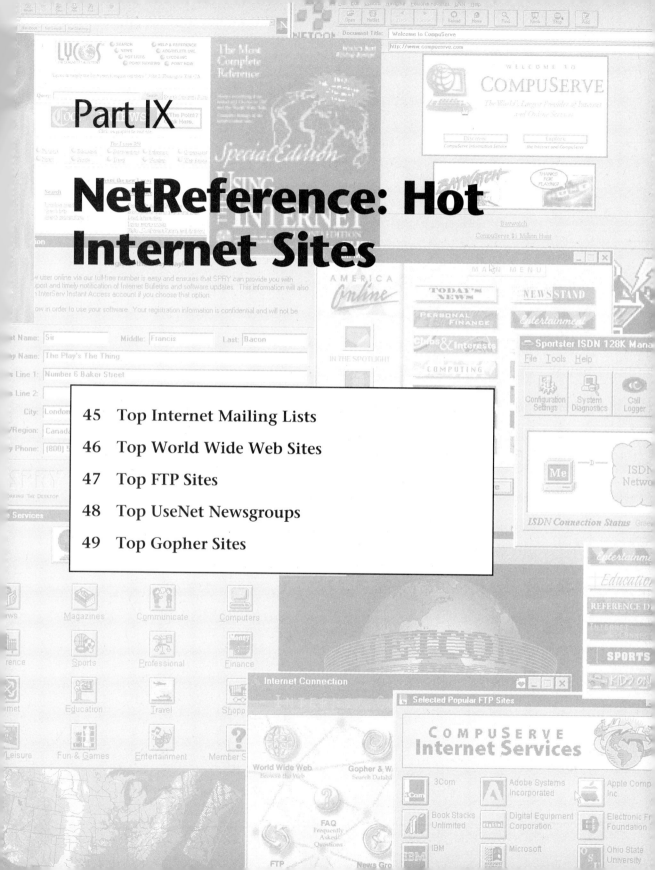

Part IX

NetReference: Hot Internet Sites

45   Top Internet Mailing Lists

46   Top World Wide Web Sites

47   Top FTP Sites

48   Top UseNet Newsgroups

49   Top Gopher Sites

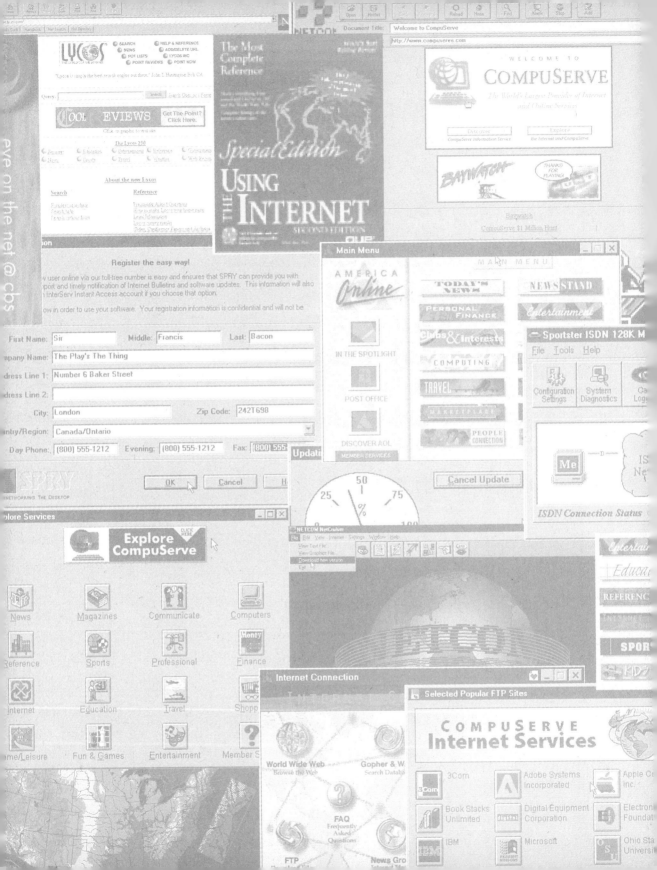

CHAPTER 45

Top Internet Mailing Lists

Mailing lists are a great no-frills way to keep up with news on your favorite software, participate in discussions about the Internet, and ask questions (or provide answers) about practically any computing topic. While there are thousands of lists on a huge variety of topics from religion to entertainment to politics to math, we've limited the discussion in this chapter to lists that are related to computing topics.

Before subscribing to any of the lists described here, be sure to review chapter 18, "Using Internet Mailing Lists." That chapter presents a discussion of how to use mailing lists, mailing list rules and protocol, and other things you should know before diving in. Failure to know what you are doing before joining a mailing list can result in considerable embarrassment.

You should also be sure to read the welcome message you get from the list when you first subscribe. In most cases, you'll get a message explaining the purpose of the list, where to send requests to unsubscribe, and other important information. It's always a good idea to save a copy of this message. This will save you the embarrassment of sending an unsubscribe message to the list instead of the administrative address.

Tip

When subscribing to lists, or sending any requests to the automated list processing addresses, turn off the signature feature in your mail program. Signatures cause some automated e-mail processors to spew a long reply with many error messages.

Each list described in this chapter has two lines following the list name. The first line gives the e-mail address to send your subscription request to. The second line tells you the format the subscription request should be in.

Remember from chapter 18 that subscription requests should be in the body of the message, not the subject. If the subscription line includes <firstname> <lastname> at the end, this means to include your first name and last name (without the <> angle brackets).

With all of that said, what will you find in this chapter? The chapter is broken down into these three parts:

- Mailing lists about the Internet, Internet software, and services that are part of the Internet
- Discussions of computer hardware and software
- Where to find more Internet mailing lists

Mailing Lists about the Internet

In this first section, we list mailing lists that discuss topics about the Internet. These lists include general Internet topics and Internet-related software. It also looks at lists that have to do with a particular segment of the Internet, like the Web and mailing lists.

Advanced HTML
LISTSERV@UA1VM.UA.EDU
subscribe adv-html

This discussion group mailing list is a place where you can pose questions about creation of Web pages using some of the advanced features of HTML such as tables, HTML 3.0, scripts, and so on. This list is designed for experienced Webmasters, sysops, Internet trainers, and advanced Web page authors.

Bestweb
listserv@vm.ege.edu.tr
subscribe bestweb

Bestweb is used to announce Web sites that the participants find interesting and worth visiting.

Communications/Modems/BBSs
LISTSERV@SAKAAU03.BITNET
subscribe COMM-L

Questions and discussions on this list range from beginners asking about the advantages of various brands of modems to advanced issues about modem and communication configuration.

Country Codes
listserver@ic.ac.uk

subscribe country-codes <firstname> <lastname>

This is a low volume list (one message per month) that exists to distribute the country codes used for Internet domain names around the world. There's also some information in the messages about e-mailing to foreign countries.

Cruising the Internet
listserv@unlvm.unl.edu

subscribe cruise-l

This list features questions (mostly from new users) regarding cruising the Internet. E-mail, UseNet, WWW, FTP, IRC, and other Internet services are fair game for discussion.

Cybermind
majordomo@jefferson.village.virginia.edu

subscribe cybermind

According to the official description, this list is for the discussion of "philosophy and psychology of cyberspace." However, this high volume list routinely strays far off topic. In addition to the stated topic, you'll find frequent discussions of philosophy, sexuality, sociology, and psychological issues that have little or nothing to do with computing or cyberspace.

Firewalls
Majordomo@GreatCircle.COM

subscribe firewalls

This list discusses Internet firewall security systems and related issues.

Free World Dialup
Majordomo@enterprise.pulver.com

subscribe free-world-dialup

This discussion group is talking about how to patch the Internet Phone software to allow it to communicate with regular phones, not just Internet phone users. The idea is to come up with a global phone system that would bypass the phone companies.

Help-Net
listserv@vm.temple.edu

subscribe help-net

Help-Net is a forum where new Internet users can ask questions about the Internet and Internet software.

Hyper-G
listproc@iicm.tu-graz.ac.at

subscribe hyper-g

This mailing list is for questions and answers regarding the Hyper-G information system. Hyper-G is an enhanced hypertext system that offers many improvements compared to HTTP and the Web.

Internet Basics
listserv@listserv.syr.edu

subscribe ibasics

Internet Basics is a newsletter that distributes lessons about the Internet. The lessons are aimed at introducing novice users to the Internet and are designed for school library media specialists. However, new Internet users in any profession will find the information here useful.

IBM PC TCP/IP
listserv@vm.marist.edu

subscribe IBMTCP-L

This list is for technical questions and answers regarding the IBM MVS TCP/IP software. This is not a general TCP/IP discussion.

Internet Phone
Majordomo@enterprise.pulver.com

subscribe iphone

This list can be used for questions and answers relating to the use of Internet Phone software. Discussions of other software that transmits audio and voice on the Internet are also welcome.

Internet SIG
majordomo@netf.org

subscribe isig

This list serves as a question and answer forum for new and intermediate users on the Internet.

Internet Service Providers
listserv@listserv.aol.com

subscribe ISP-ADMIN-LIST <firstname> <lastname>

Internet Service Providers (ISPs) administrators use this list to discuss issues pertaining to their businesses. This can include dealing with spammers, privacy and security topics, and legal aspects of operating an ISP.

Java Announce

java-announce-request@java.sun.com

subscribe

This list distributes official announcements from Sun regarding the Java language.

Java Interest

java-interest-request@java.sun.com

subscribe

This list is for programmers interested in programming applets with the Java language.

HotJava Interest

hotjava-interest-request@java.sun.com

subscribe

This list is used by those interested in Sun's HotJava WWW browser.

List Managers

Majordomo@GreatCircle.COM

subscribe list-managers

This list discusses issues that Internet mailing list managers deal with. The questions here should be of a general nature about things like mailing list policies, techniques, and software. Technical questions about specific mailing list software should not be discussed here. This list is intended for people running the mailing list servers, not managers or owners of individual mailing lists.

Listserv for Windows 95

listserv@win95.dc.lsoft.com

subscribe LISTSERV95-L

This list is the official technical support list for LSoft's Listserv for Windows 95. Any questions about setup or operation of the software can be sent to this list.

IX

Hot Internet Sites

List Owners

> **listserv@searn.sunet.se**
>
> **subscribe LSTOWN-L**

The List Owners list is a forum for questions and answers about managing a mailing list. The list is intended for questions from owners of mailing lists as opposed to those running list software (which is the topic of List Managers at **Majordomo@GreatCircle.COM**).

Majordomo Announcements

> **Majordomo@GreatCircle.COM**
>
> **subscribe majordomo-announce**

This list is used to distribute official announcements about the Majordomo mailing list software.

Majordomo Users

> **Majordomo@GreatCircle.COM**
>
> **subscribe majordomo-users**

The Majordomo users list is a forum for questions, answers, tips, and bug reports related to the Majordomo mailing list software.

Mediaweb

> **LISTSERV@vm.temple.edu**
>
> **subscribe mediaweb**

Mediaweb is a discussion group for Webmasters running sites related to radio, television, movies, and other media-related enterprises.

Netscape

> **LISTSERV@IRLEARN.UCD.IE**
>
> **subscribe netscape**

This discussion group is a forum for any questions and answers you may have regarding the Netscape Web browser.

NetTrain

> **LISTSERV@UBVM.cc.buffalo.edu**
>
> **subscribe nettrain**

This list is for discussion of issues relevant to training other users on the Internet. Participants can be professional Internet trainers or anyone with an interest in training Internet users. This is not a forum for new user questions.

Net Watch

> **Majordomo@enterprise.pulver.com**
>
> **subscribe netwatch**

This is a discussion group for those interested in new Internet developments and their applications to business.

New Lists

> **LISTSERV@vm1.nodak.edu**
>
> **subscribe new-list**

This list is used to post announcements of new Internet e-mail mailing lists.

TCP/IP for PCs

> **listserv@list.nih.gov**
>
> **subscribe pcip**

This list is a discussion of technical questions regarding the TCP/IP protocol for PCs. This includes questions about TCP/IP for DOS and Windows. The questions can be about the TCP/IP protocol in general or about specific TCP/IP packages. The questions generally run toward intermediate and advanced issues rather than beginning-level starter questions.

Pegasus Mail for Windows

> **listserv@ua1vm.ua.edu**
>
> **subscribe pm-win**

This discussion group is a forum where Pegasus Mail for Windows users can ask questions and get answers regarding this Internet e-mail program.

Spam

> **spam-request@zorch.sf-bay.org**
>
> **subscribe**

This is a forum for discussing anti-spamming issues. Cancelbots, killfiles, mail filters, and other technology based solutions are discussed here. Participants also discuss "social" solutions, such as convincing an offender's service provider to discontinue service and educating users about proper use of the Internet.

Voice on the Net

> **Majordomo@enterprise.pulver.com**
>
> **subscribe von**

IX

Hot Internet Sites

This list discusses voice on the Internet technologies in general and the many voice on the Net products. Discussions about RealAudio, StreamWorks, DigiPhone, and any other Internet voice products are appropriate.

WinVN

> **Majordomo@news.ksc.nasa.gov**
>
> **subscribe winvn**

Here's the place to ask questions and get answers about WinVN, the popular UseNet newsreader for Windows.

WWW BuyInfo

> **www-buyinfo-request@allegra.att.com**
>
> **subscribe www-buyinfo**

The purpose of this list is to discuss ways to conduct financial transactions on the Web. Technical issues (such as protocols, clients/servers, and authentication) as well as the effects and desirability of these capabilities are discussed.

WWW HTML

> **www-html-request@w3.org**
>
> **subscribe**

This is a group for a technical discussion of HTML, development of HTML systems, software, protocols, and other developments of interest to the HTML community. This list is not a forum for users with questions about how to use HTML to create Web pages.

WWW Security

> **Majordomo@ns2.rutgers.edu**
>
> **subscribe www-security**

This list is for discussion of issues related to security on the Web, enhancements to current security, and security proposals.

WWW Talk

> **www-talk-request@w3.org**
>
> **subscribe**

This group is a forum for technical discussions among WWW software developers. This is not a forum for users to ask questions about Web browsers.

WWW VRML

> **info-rama@wired.com**
>
> **subscribe www-vrml**

This list is the definitive source for technical discussions among those developing VRML specifications and VRML software for the Web.

WWW Marketing
> **majordomo@xmission.com**
>
> **subscribe www_marketing**

This list looks at how to market goods and services on the Web, how to attract customers to your site without spamming, designing Web pages that successfully sell your product, and other similar issues.

Mailing Lists about Computers and Software

In this section, we look at mailing lists that have to do with computers, computer hardware, and computer software. Discussion groups range from topics for new users to lists for experienced professionals.

Microsoft Access
> **listserv@peach.ease.lsoft.com**
>
> **subscribe access-l**

This discussion list is open for any issues relating to the Microsoft Access database. Questions range from novice level to professional developers.

Agents
> **listproc@sunlabs.sun.com**
>
> **subscribe agents**

This list is devoted to discussions related to software agents. This can include discussions of agent programming, what agents do, how agents interface with other software, and the capabilities of software.

BIG-LAN
> **listserv@listserv.syr.edu**
>
> **subscribe big-lan <firstname> <lastname>**

This list is for discussions of issues related to big LANs (whole building or multiple building "campus" LANs qualify as big). Routers, bridges, backbones, multiple protocols, and related issues are all appropriate.

cc:Mail
> **listserv@vm1.ucc.okstate.edu**
>
> **subscribe ccmail-l**

IX

Hot Internet Sites

Lotus's cc:Mail e-mail program is discussed here. The issues are mostly relevant to cc:Mail site administrators.

CD-ROM Publishing

Mail-Server@knex.via.mind.ORG

subscribe cdpub <firstname> <lastname>

The CD-ROM Publishing list discusses software and hardware for creating and mastering CD-ROMs. Of particular focus here are desktop recording systems for desktop systems. Discussions of systems for all platforms and related hardware appropriate.

CD-ROMs

listserv@listserv.ucop.edu

subscribe cdrom-l

This list features discussions of CD-ROMs, mostly for end users. Announcements of new CD-ROM hardware and software products, help requests, and items for sale are all appropriate as long as they relate to CD-ROMs.

CD-ROM LAN

listserv@idbsu.idbsu.edu

subscribe cdromlan

CD-ROM usage in networked settings is discussed here.

Cisco

cisco-request@spot.Colorado.EDU

subscribe

This discussion list features new product announcements, questions and answers, features, and other issues related to Cisco networking hardware. Gateways, ATM switches, and other hardware are discussed in this high-volume list.

Computer Law

listserv@nervm.nerdc.ufl.edu

subscribe cmplaw-l

This list is the place for questions and answers about laws related to computing. Legal issues for software and hardware vendors as well as end users are appropriate here.

CompuNotes

> **majordomo@rust.net**
>
> **subscribe components**

CompuNotes is a weekly newsletter distributed in the form of a mailing list. Topics in the newsletter include news related to computing, software reviews, and commentary about the PC industry.

Macromedia Authorware

> **listserv@cc1.kuleuven.ac.be**
>
> **subscribe aware**

The Authorware discussion list is for topics related to Macromedia's Authorware software. Issues discussed can be specific to either Mac or Windows development or cross-platform issues. Discussion of third-party software related to Authorware development is also common.

Macromedia Director

> **listserv@uafsysb.uark.edu**
>
> **subscribe direct-l**

Join this list to take part in discussions about Macromedia Director for Windows and Macintosh. Third-party software and multimedia file formats used with Director are also suitable topics here.

DVI

> **listserv@calvin.dgbt.doc.ca**
>
> **subscribe dvi-list <firstname> <lastname>**

This list is for discussions of programming and applications for Intel's DVI system.

EDI

> **listserv@uccvma.ucop.edu**
>
> **subscribe edi-l**

This list discusses Electronic Data Interchange (EDI). Discussions can be about general EDI principles or specific software or systems for EDI.

Edupage

> **listproc@elanor.oit.unc.edu**
>
> **subscribe edupage**

Edupage is a newsletter that contains a summary of news items about information technology. There are usually two or three issues per week.

Effector Online
listmaster@eff.org
subscribe effector-online

This is a newsletter from the Electronic Frontier Foundation. Most of the topics in the newsletter are related to protecting first amendment freedoms of computer users, particularly those using online services, BBSs, and the Internet. This can include reports on pending legislation, actions by major service providers, and suggestions for what you can do to get involved.

Excel-G
listserv@peach.ease.lsoft.com
subscribe excel-g <firstname> <lastname>

This list is for questions and answers of a general or end user nature relating to Microsoft Excel.

Excel-L
listserv@peach.ease.lsoft.com
subscribe excel-l <firstname> <lastname>

This Excel list is designed as a forum for developer issues about Excel. Undocumented tips and tricks are welcome here. New users are welcome to read the list but entry-level questions should be discussed on the Excel-G list.

Gateway 2000
gateway2000-request@sei.cmu.edu
subscribe

This is for questions and answers for users of Gateway 2000 computers. Technical questions about the system, components, upgrades, and anything else related to Gateway 2000 PC systems is acceptable.

IBM PC
listserv@vmd.cso.uiuc.edu
subscribe I-IBMPC

The name of this list is a bit deceiving. The list can be used for questions and answers regarding PC hardware of all types (not just IBM models). Software issues related to hardware are also welcome.

IN-TOUCH: WIN95
> **intouch-request@islandnet.com**
> **subscribe**

This is a weekly newsletter that contains brief reviews and descriptions of selected new shareware for Windows 95.

Lotus Notes
> **listserv@vm1.ucc.okstate.edu**
> **subscribe notes-l**

This list discusses issues related to Lotus Notes, primarily from a Notes system administrator point of view.

Microsoft Windows NT Server Lan Manager
> **listserv@list.nih.gov**
> **subscribe lanman-l**

This list is a discussion of the MS Windows NT server Lan Manager software.

Modems
> **listserv@vm.its.rpi.edu**
> **subscribe MODEMS-L**

This high-volume list is a good forum for discussions at all levels regarding modems. Technical questions and answers, setup and configuration, and modem related software problems are all appropriate. General modem questions as well as questions specific to individual brands and models are discussed here.

MS-DOS Software Announcements
> **listserv@SimTel.Coast.NET**
> **subscribe msdos-ann**

This list has a broader scope than the title would imply. This is a one-way announcement list from the maintainers of the Simtel Coast to Coast Software archive. The list announces and describes new additions to the MS-DOS archive as well as Windows 3.x and Windows 95 software.

Microsoft Mail
> **listserv@yalevm.cis.yale.edu**
> **subscribe msmail-l**

IX

Hot Internet Sites

This list is for questions and answers for MSMail users and administrators. Subscribers are also using the list for issues related to Microsoft Exchange, the successor to MSMail.

Novell GroupWise

listproc@tribble.uvsc.edu

subscribe ngw

This list is for questions and answers from GroupWise users and administrators.

Novell LAN

listserv@listserv.syr.edu

subscribe novell

This list discusses all Novell products. The primary focus here is Novell networking products but discussions of business applications come up here, too.

Pagemaker

listserv@indycms.iupui.edu

subscribe pagemakr

Questions and answers about Pagemaker for Windows and Mac are the topic here. Questions typically range from beginning level to experienced pros sharing tips.

PC Building

listserv@tscvm.trenton.edu

subscribe pcbuild

This discussion list is for issues related to building (or upgrading) PC systems. Questions about components as well as systems in general are appropriate.

PCI SIG

pci-sig-request@znyx.com

subscribe

This list is for technical discussions related to the PCI bus. The issues here should be general in nature and not about specific details related to a particular product.

PC Technical Support

listserv@vm.ege.edu.tr

subscribe pctech-l

This list is a forum for discussing technical questions about PCs. Most of the issues here are hardware-related support issues but general operating systems questions are also acceptable, if they have some connection to hardware.

PhotoCD

> **listserv@info.kodak.com**
>
> **subscribe photo-cd**

This list is Kodak's official mailing list for discussion of the PhotoCD technology and products.

Remote Work

> **Majordomo@unify.com**
>
> **subscribe remote-work**

This list discusses telecommuting issues. Questions and answers may be related to telecommuting in general or software packages used for remote work connectivity.

Software Entrepreneurs

> **softdist-request@toolz.atl.ga.us**
>
> **subscribe**

This is a forum for software entrepreneurs to discuss the software they have developed, successful marketing techniques, and anything else related to developing and selling a new software product.

Windows for Workgroups

> **listserv@umdd.umd.edu**
>
> **subscribe wfw-l**

Questions and answers about Microsoft's Windows for Workgroups are discussed here. Most of the topics are specific to Windows for Workgroups (like 32-bit disk access and WFW networking), although some generic Windows questions crop up here.

Windows 95

> **listserv@peach.ease.lsoft.com**
>
> **subscribe win95-l**

This high-volume (several hundred messages per day) list is the place for just about any question or discussion on Windows 95. Applications, the Windows 95 desktop, communications, installation, hardware, networking, and more are all acceptable topics here.

Windows
listserv@vm1.mcgill.ca

subscribe windows

This group is for general discussions and technical questions and answers about Microsoft Windows.

Windows Help Compiler
listserv@admin.humberc.on.ca

subscribe winhlp-1

This discussion group is a question and answer forum for issues related to compiling Windows help systems.

Microsoft Windows News
enews@microsoft.nwnet.com

subscribe winnews

Microsoft distributes this mailing list as the official newsletter for those interested in Windows 95 and related issues. News of future product enhancements, bug fixes, new online resources, and other Windows 95 topics are presented here.

Microsoft Windows NT
listserv@peach.ease.lsoft.com

subscribe winnt-1

Questions and answers about Windows NT Workstation and Server are the topic of this group.

WordPerfect Corporation
LISTSERV@UBVM.cc.buffalo.edu

subscribe wpcorp-1 <firstname> <lastname>

Even though WP Corp. is no longer a distinct entity, this group still exists as a question and answer forum about their products and the company. Most of the questions here relate to the WordPerfect word processor.

WordPerfect for Windows
listserv@ubvm.cc.buffalo.edu

subscribe wpwin-1

This group is for discussion of all WordPerfect products for Windows. These include WordPerfect for Windows, WordPerfect Presentations for Windows, and Novell GroupWise.

Where to Find More Mailing Lists

The 100 or so lists described in this chapter are not all of the Internet and computing lists on the Internet by any stretch of the imagination. And there are thousands of lists about non-computing topics that may be of interest to you. To find these additional lists, here are a few sources.

If you have Web access, there is a terrific searchable database of over 20,000 mailing lists at **http://www.liszt.com/**. This database includes listserv, listproc, majordomo, and independently managed lists from over 500 sites. It is the most comprehensive resource for mailing lists I have seen.

There is also a similar, but smaller, database of lists at **http://scwww.ucs.indiana.edu/mlarchive**. The database at **http://www.nova.edu/Inter-Links/cgi-bin/news-lists.pl** indexes mailing lists as well as UseNet newsgroups.

For a list of all known lists run by listserv, send a message to **listserv@listserv.net**. The body of the message should be:

> **lists global**

This will return a long list of known lists. The list will include a subscription address and the first line of the official description of the list. If you want to limit the response to lists about a specific topic, add / followed by the topic to the end of the command, like this:

> **lists global /business**

Another source of lists is the monthly list of lists published by Stephanie da Silva. This list is posted on the **news.lists** and **news.answers** newsgroups on the 29th of each month. It is a multipart posting (currently 17 parts and growing). The list is also archived at the FTP site **rtfm.mit.edu** in /pub/usenet-by-group/news.answers/mail/mailing-lists. You can get the list on the Web at **http://www.NeoSoft.com:80/internet/paml/**.

You may also want to consider subscribing to the New Lists mailing list described earlier in this chapter.

If you are looking for a mailing list related to a product of service, you may want to look for a related Web site. Often times a company will include a page listing mailing lists related to their products (or mailing lists they use to support their products).

IX

Hot Internet Sites

One final note on how *not* to find mailing lists. It's a bad idea to send a message like, "I'm looking for a mailing list about dogs," to a totally unrelated mailing list such as a list about Windows 95. If you have exhausted all of the methods listed here to find a list, it's okay to send a message to one of the new user question lists (such as Cruising the Internet or Help Net). But this shouldn't be the first method you try.

CHAPTER 46

Top World Wide Web Sites

With the explosive growth of the Web, there are Web pages about every imaginable topic. The number of pages on the Web is growing faster than can be accurately measured. With so many pages out there, it's hard to know where to start looking for anything.

As with the other listing chapters in this book, we're going to concentrate on sites related to computers and the Internet. There are thousands of companies and organizations in the computing and Internet industries with Web sites. You'll use these sites to get product information, technical support, and even download software.

In this chapter, you find Web sites for:

- Computer hardware manufacturers
- Software for business and productivity
- Sites for computer games and fun
- Computer hardware and software stores on the Web
- Web browsers
- The latest in Web technology with Java, VRML, interactive chatting, radio broadcasts, and more
- Software for connecting to the Internet, reading e-mail, and other Internet activities
- Web searches and directories

Computer Systems

The Web is an excellent resource to help you prepare for a shopping trip for a new computer. You can comparison shop to see what models and features all these companies offer. Once you have all this information, you'll be ready to buy the right system, with or without the help of the retail sales world.

And after you buy your new computer, how can you get the inevitable product support questions answered? Using the Web to get tech support sure beats waiting on hold on the phone. And the Web is always there, 24 hours a day, seven days a week, unlike most tech support phone staffs. And while the tech support staff can give you more personalized answers to any problems you have, most common problems can be quickly solved with a trip to tech support on the Web.

Here are some Web sites for some of the more popular brands of computers on the market today.

IBM
http://www.ibm.com

It seems appropriate to begin a discussion about computer resources on the Web with IBM. After all, IBM's products dominated the world of mainframe computers in the early days of computers. In fact, its personal computers helped usher in the whole personal computer trend. So this is where we start our look at Web resources for computer aficionados.

The IBM Web site includes news about IBM and the computer industry, information and news about the many computer systems IBM sells, and a searchable software library with many software files for IBM products. The software includes utilities and diagnostics for IBM hardware, upgrades and fixes for IBM software, and even some free software.

Fig. 46.1
Look for news and information about PCs from IBM as well as the rest of the PC industry here.

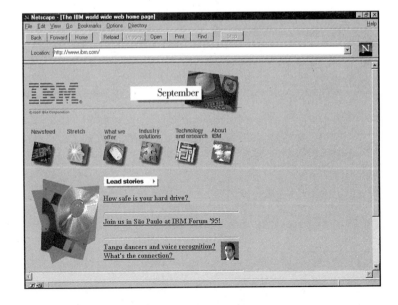

Acer America
http://www.acer.com

Acer makes low-cost computers that are popular sellers in many of the leading discount retailers. Its Web site offers information for U.S. customers as
well as for customers living in the many other countries Acer serves. There's a
typical mix here of product information, support (such as a special section
with information Acer users need to update their computers for Windows
95), and downloadable files.

Compaq Computer Corp.
http://www.compaq.com

Compaq is one of the leading manufacturers of PCs for Windows and DOS,
and it is also Microsoft's leading "systems partner" for Windows 95.
Compaq's Web site describes its efforts in this role to work with Microsoft on
Plug and Play, Hot Dockable Notebooks, and some other technology advances. Additional areas of information at the Web site include product descriptions, a separate area for the new Compaq Presario, and special ordering
and pricing information for government, education, and medical customers.

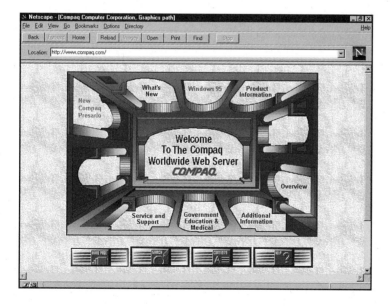

Fig. 46.2
Compaq delivers
information about
its popular
hardware with
special sections
for customers in
the government,
educational,
and medical
communities.

IX

Hot Internet Sites

Dell Computer Corp.
http://www.dell.com

Dell was one of the first major computer manufacturers in the mail order business. Its Web site includes information about its products (which are mainly desktop and laptop PCs), employment opportunities, and a user survey.

Packard Bell
http://www.packardbell.com

This basic support page has file updates and product information for Packard Bell's popular line of low-cost computers.

Component and Peripheral Hardware

Many computer users buy computers that they can take out of the box and use as is. They never need to add new hardware, upgrade existing equipment, or replace anything when it breaks down.

But for the rest of us, there's always a faster CD-ROM drive, a bigger hard drive, a better video card, or a new toy like a scanner to add. For those of you who enjoy a couple of hours of browsing at the computer store, browsing at hardware manufacturers' Web sites listed here provides a similar thrill.

And, like the computer systems sites listed earlier in this chapter, most of these sites offer more than just information about their products. You can get technical support, fixes, driver updates, links to online stores that sell their products, and more.

Intel
http://www.intel.com

Here's the home page of the company that makes the processors that power most of the personal computers in use today. This Web site offers easy to read information about the many types of processors available (486s, Pentiums, and the new Pentium Pro). Depending on the technical level of information you need, you can get simple comparisons of the speeds and features of the various processors or detailed specifications for how the processor is built and how it works. (A lot of the technical documentation here is in either Adobe Acrobat's Portable Document Format or PostScript.)

Fig. 46.3
Intel's site focuses on their proces-sors, especially the newer Pentiums and Pentium Pros.

If you've been considering upgrading the processor in your PC, Intel makes upgrade processors (called OverDrive) that you can use. Figuring out which OverDrive processor is right for your computer and your needs can be diffi-cult, but you can read all about them here. With the information you get here, you should be able to walk right in to your local computer retailer (or go to one of the Web-based computer stores listed later in this chapter) and buy the OverDrive chip that's right for you.

Intel makes more than just processors; they also make modems, network cards, and video conferencing hardware. Information about all these products is available here, too.

Ascend Communications
http://www.ascend.com/

There comes a time in every Web surfer's life when the modem is just too slow. If you decide it's time to replace your modem with a high-speed, state-of-the-art ISDN device, Ascend is one of the leading manufacturers. Ascend's Web site includes information about its ISDN products as well as links to information you need to know to order ISDN service from your phone company.

IX

Hot Internet Sites

Diamond Multimedia
http://www.diamondmm.com

Diamond makes a variety of multimedia products, including video cards, CD-ROM drives, and even some modem and telephone products. The Web site contains product announcements and descriptions, links to software fixes for video drivers, and information about support for Windows 95 with Diamond products.

U.S. Robotics
http://www.usr.com

U.S. Robotics is a leader in the modem industry. It manufactures a variety of modems for PCs, including the well-known brands Courier and Sportster. Look at this Web site to get product specifications on each of these brands. You can also download support files.

Hayes
http://www.hayes.com/

This modem manufacturer makes a variety of products for PCs and servers. In addition to standard information about its products and technical support at the Web site, Hayes has a nice section called "Tech Tips." Tech Tips answer commonly asked questions that Hayes' tech support team answers about its products and about modems in general, such as how to install a modem on a PC and select the right comm port or IRQ or how to troubleshoot lost data. Also available for download are technical documents such as the Hayes Technical Reference Manual. This manual includes a list of the entire Hayes AT command set, which is the industry standard used by software to communicate with modems.

NEC Corp.
http://www.nec.com

NEC makes so many computers and peripherals (including a very popular line of high-quality, high-speed CD-ROM drives) that it's difficult to decide where to list them. When you look closely at NEC's product information at the Web site, you'll see that most of the links there describe its many peripherals. You can get information on a wide variety of products, some of which aren't tied to PCs (such as PBX phone systems and Satellite Earth Station Systems).

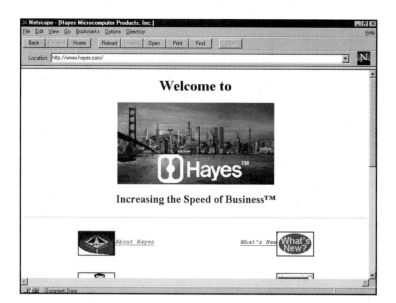

Fig. 46.4
Hayes modems
and information
about modems in
general are found
here.

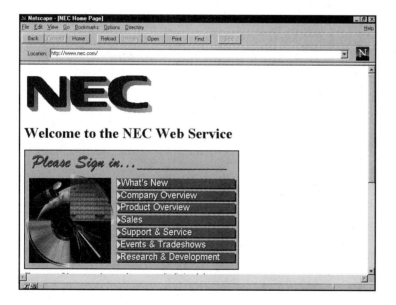

Fig. 46.5
NEC has a variety
of computer and
other high-tech
equipment on
display here.

IX

Hot Internet Sites

Creative Labs
http://www.creaf.com/

Creative Labs makes the industry's leading line of sound cards, the Sound
Blaster. Other related products include CD-ROM drives, video capture and
playback cards, multimedia kits, and new sound cards that include a modem.

In addition to product information and support, there are links to background information on Sound Blaster compatibility. There is also a Web interface to all the files on its FTP site.

Hewlett Packard
http://www.hp.com/

This company makes many computer products including systems, scanners, and specialized components, but you're probably most familiar with its printers. The Web site has scores of documents with product information and specifications for all HP printers. You can download new versions of printer drivers and find out what HP products are Windows 95 compatible. HP is also making a push to sell themselves in the Internet community and they are adding Internet information here such as an Internet primer, case studies, and the like to their Internet business partners.

Fig. 46.6

HP printers are the most familiar products you will see here.

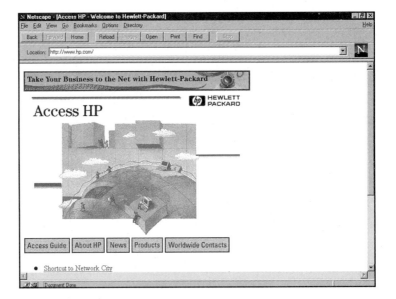

Western Digital
http://www.wdc.com

If you've ever bought a new hard drive for a PC, there's a good chance you've seen a Western Digital drive, probably one of the respected Caviar models. Western Digital drives are very popular in mail order, as well as in retail computer and electronics outlets. The Web site contains detailed specifications for all its current drives, including a nice table that compares all the drives feature by feature. There's also information about Western Digital multimedia and input/output cards.

Conner Peripherals
http://www.conner.com/

Conner is well known for its hard drives and tape drives. The drives are included as standard equipment in many brands of PCs and are sold as add-ons in retail outlets. Conner's site includes information about its products as well as links for service and support. If you're considering moving to Windows 95, you can download a free program called Storage Detective that will advise you on your hard drive needs when you move to Windows 95. It also includes information about the data back ups you need to make before upgrading to Windows 95.

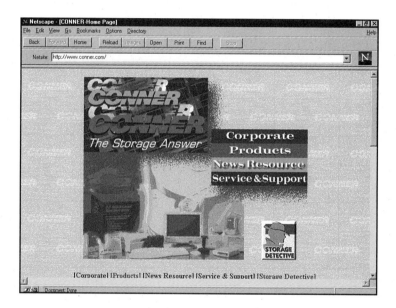

Fig. 46.7
If you plan to upgrade your hard drive or add a tape backup drive, visit Conner.

ATI Technologies
http://www.atitech.ca

ATI manufactures high-performance video cards for PCs. The Web site has links to updated drivers and information for ATI PC video products.

STB Systems
http://www.stb.com

STB makes a variety of fast video accelerators for PCs. Its Web site includes information about STB Systems products. There are links to an e-mail address for technical support and to an FTP site where you can download drivers.

IX

Hot Internet Sites

Fig. 46.8
ATI video cards can speed up your PC or give you the capability to capture and playback video on your PC.

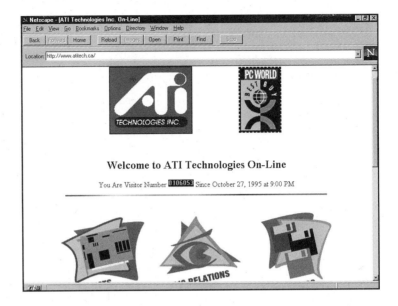

Thrustmaster
http://www.thrustmaster.com/

This company makes realistic flight simulator joysticks (and a few other types of joysticks). The Web site includes product information, technical support, and special troubleshooting and configuration information for using Thrustmaster products with Windows 95.

Motorola
http://www.motorola.com/

The Information Systems group at Motorola is responsible for their modems, PCMCIA cards, ISDN terminal adapters, and other communications and networking hardware. Look to their part of the Web site at (**http://www.motorola.com/MIMS/ISG/**) for product information, announcements, software, support, lists of retailers that sell Motorola devices, and more.

Computer Productivity Software

The real reason you invest a couple of thousand dollars (or more) in your computer is usually to do something productive. It might be to type a memo, to calculate the profit for your company's yearly widget sales, or to create a graphic logo for a new company.

Whatever it is that you do with your computer, you probably have a substantial investment in software. You spent several hundred dollars on the operating system and applications you use every day, and you spent weeks or even months perfecting the use of them.

So take a few minutes to investigate the Web sites for the major applications you use most. You may find some new information about how to use your software that will make your job easier. Maybe you're considering switching word processors. The Web is a great source for comparing the features of the software. And, of course, it's a great place to find answers to common questions and to learn about patches or fixes for any bugs.

Microsoft
http://www.microsoft.com

You have heard of Microsoft, right? The Internet community has been the source of endless humor at the expense of the world's largest software company, but don't expect to find Microsoft's plans to buy the Catholic Church or the Justice Department here.

So what can you find at Microsoft's Web site? It has descriptions and sales pitches for all its desktop application products, like Word, Excel, and PowerPoint. Windows (NT, 95, 3.1) gets the coverage it deserves here, too. You can also find out about Microsoft's new online service, The Microsoft Network. There's a massive file download area where you can get some of Microsoft's free products and upgrades, including the Microsoft Internet Explorer, Microsoft Internet Assistant for Word, and Microsoft Word viewer. Updated Windows 3.1 and NT files are there now and as soon as updates for Windows 95 are available, I'm sure they'll be posted on the site. Microsoft has recently introduced a search feature to help you find information on this large site.

Tip

If you're having problems saving documents from Word 6, check out the information here about macro viruses. The Web site tells how to determine if Word is infected and includes a small program to fix it and prevent future virus infections.

IX

Hot Internet Sites

Fig. 46.9
The world's largest software company tells you about its products and services here.

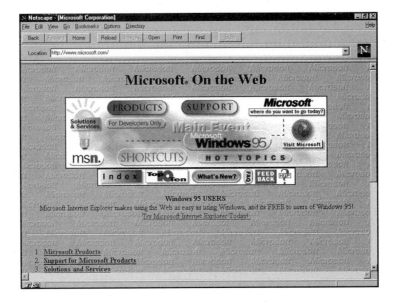

Lotus
http://www.lotus.com

A pioneer in the PC software industry, Lotus continues to make popular software for business applications. Although Lotus was recently acquired by IBM, it still maintains its own Web site. This site offers extensive information about 1-2-3 and the other SmartSuite products.

Fig. 46.10
Personal productivity tools such as 1-2-3 and group products such as Notes are all part of the solutions at Lotus.

Macromedia
http://www.macromedia.com

Many game and edutainment software developers use Macromedia software to create multimedia products. Macromedia's Web page has information about these products as well as about its new products that deliver better multimedia and video on the Web.

Quarterdeck
http://www.qdeck.com

Quarterdeck made its name in the PC business by making software that makes DOS and Windows run better, such as memory managers. This Web site describes these products as well as its new Web and Internet software, which you can currently download for free and use on a trial basis.

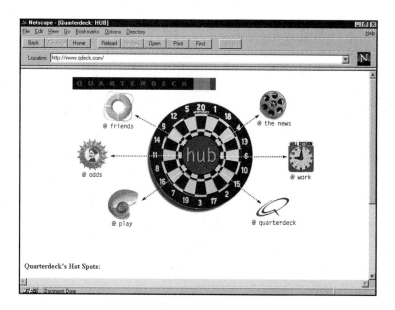

Fig. 46.11
Quarterdeck's products can make your PC run faster and better.

Novell Inc.
http://www.novell.com

This Web site has information about the Novell Perfect Office products (including WordPerfect, at least for the time being) and about the many Novell networking products. There are neat virtual "tours" here, too.

Borland
http://www.borland.com

This is the Web site for the maker of the popular dBASE database software and compilers such as the Delphi programming environment.

Corel Corp.
http://www.corel.ca/

Corel is the maker of the popular CorelDRAW! program for Windows. Corel's home page links to information about the latest, greatest version of the software. Product support is linked here too.

Adobe
http://www.adobe.com

In addition to many other products, Adobe makes Acrobat. Acrobat files (in a format called PDF) are being used by many Web sites to create Web pages that have complicated layout that HTML can't produce. The Adobe site includes directions for downloading and using the free Acrobat reader, which lets you view these Acrobat files on the Web.

WinZip
http://www.winzip.com

NetCD95

WinZip is a popular software used for file compression on PCs. WinZip is shareware and you can download and try versions for both Windows 3.1 and Windows 95 from this Web site.

> **Tip**
>
> You can configure your Web browser to use WinZip as a helper application to unzip files when it encounters zipped files on the Web.

NetCD95

◀ See "Windows 95 and Computer Viruses," p. 1064

Mcafee Antivirus
http://www.mcafee.com

If you cruise the Internet and the Web, you're taking some risk if you don't protect yourself from computer viruses. Mcafee is best known for its antivirus software, which you can download from this site. Their latest versions include protection against viruses in Word for Windows macros as well as traditional types of viruses.

Symantec Corporation
http://www.symantec.com/

Symantec makes a popular line of utilities software, including the Norton utilities. Its Web site contains plenty of product information about these. As a public service, Symantec also includes a Virus Information Center. Here you can learn about any new computer viruses that may be running rampant, and download new signature updates for Central Point AntiVirus, Norton AntiVirus, and other anti-virus products.

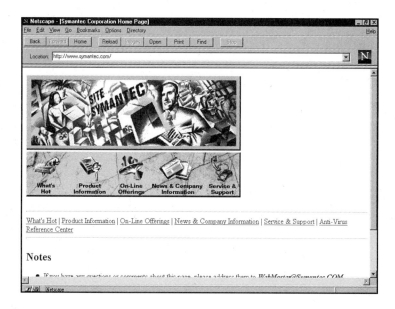

Fig. 46.12
Symantec has software to protect your computer from dangerous viruses.

PC Software Links
http://alfred.uib.no/People/wolf/daniel/pc-eng.html

This site isn't a software site but rather a page with links to many major software vendors' pages and to pages related to vendor software.

Fun and Games

You justify dropping a few hundred dollars on a new video card or CD-ROM drive by explaining how much time it will save you and how much more productive you'll be. But if it happens to make your favorite computer game run faster or better, you won't complain.

Computer game makers have made really good use of the Web. Some of the sites listed in this section are the most interesting ones in the chapter. Most of the sites offer demos of games, hints and tips, information on new games, and tech support. Many of the sites hold frequent contests and give away all sorts of cool or useful stuff.

Burn:Cycle
http://www.burncycle.com/

This ever-changing Web site makes good use of animation. New "episodes" of Burn:Cycle are added on a weekly basis. The site itself is rather surreal because you're introduced to the game through parts of the game itself. You can also download screen shots and movie clips that are scattered throughout the Web pages.

Maxis
http://www.maxis.com/

Maxis is best known for its SimCity game. You can get hints and tips on software (avoid diagonal roads and rail lines in SimCity), download free software and demos, or visit the Teacher's Lounge. The Teacher's Lounge is a collection of Web resources for teachers using simulation in education. Finally, don't miss the links to online user groups.

7th Level
http://www.7thlevel.com

This game maker is one of the first companies I've seen use Internet Relay Chat (IRC) on the Web to host Web conference rooms. Here, you can discuss a variety of topics in real time with other users who share an interest in gaming and 7th Level games. In addition, you'll find a good assortment of free demo software (I got a demo of Monty Python's Complete Waste of Time the last time I visited), product support, information, and chances to enter contests.

Electronic Arts
http://www.ea.com

Electronic Arts makes games for video-game systems such as 3DO as well as for PCs. Check out its Web pages to see demos of hot new games and get product support for existing games. You can even submit an application to beta test new games. Some of the popular EA games you may be familiar with are BioForge and College Football USA.

Simon and Schuster Interactive
http://www.mcp.com/musoft/ssint/

This Web site has links to popular interactive multimedia *Star Trek* products including the *Star Trek Omnipedia* and *Star Trek Next Generation Interactive Technical Manual*. Other non-Trek products featured here include educational products such as *Total Amazon* and *American Heritage History of the Civil War*.

Berkeley Systems
http://www.berksys.com

Who hasn't seen the Flying Toaster screen saver? Often imitated and spoofed, Berkeley is a leader in this not-so-necessary-but-still-fun category of software. The Web site includes samples of its screen savers and other goodies.

Activision
http://www.activision.com

Cool games from these folks include MechWarrior 2 and Pitfall. You can download sample video clips or images from these popular games and even participate in ongoing contests for little prizes such as hats and t-shirts.

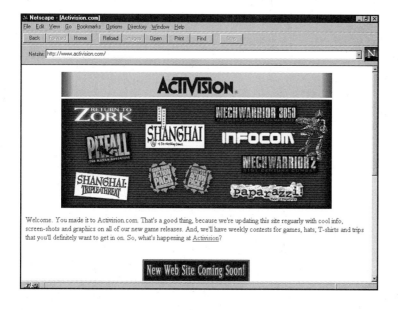

Fig. 46.13
Get a feel of what it's like to pilot a multi-ton mechanical fighter with this MechWarrior demo.

Epic MegaGames
http://www.epicgames.com/

Epic has a variety of games in many genres. Its more popular titles include One Must Fall, Epic Pinball, and Jill of the Jungle.

IX

Hot Internet Sites

Id Software
http://www.idsoftware.com/

No discussion of computer game software would be complete without a mention of DOOM. Here's the Web page for the company that started it all. There's not much here, but if you don't already have a copy, this site is the place where you can download various shareware versions.

Note

If you can't get enough of DOOM, here are a few more sites (not affiliated with Id) where you can get additional levels, DOOM editors, lists of people to play against over a modem, and much more.

DOOMgate: **http://doomgate.cs.buffalo.edu/**

Dwango MultiPlayer Network: **http://www.dwango.com/**

"Official" DOOM FAQ: **http://happypuppy.com/hleukart**

List of DOOM Sites: **http://www.msilink.com/~solso/doom.html**

For even more sites than this, see Yahoo's DOOM index at **http://www.yahoo.com/Recreation/Games/Computer_Games/Doom/**.

InterPlay
http://www.interplay.com

InterPlay is one of the bigger and better known game publishers in the computer software world. At its Web site, you'll find information on many of its titles, including Star Trek: 25 Anniversary and Star Trek: Judgment Rites, Virtual Pool, Descent, Cyberia, and dozens of others. InterPlay takes a very thorough approach to technical support on the Web; its entire customer support database is online, organized by game. So if you are having a problem with a game, Cyberia for example, choose Cyberia from the list and then search for your particular problem. There's also a good variety of product announcements, downloadable upgrades and patches, and hints for game playing.

LucasArts Entertainment Company
http://www.lucasarts.com

From the same creative genius that brought us the *Star Wars* and *Indiana Jones* movies, LucasArts now offers a great collection of entertainment CD-ROMs, including several based on the *Star Wars* and *Indiana Jones* movies. The Web site has demos and screen shots from popular games such as Dark Forces and The DIG, an online magazine called The Adventurer, and special online offers.

Sierra Online
http://www.sierra.com

Sierra is a major game developer with titles including King's Quest, Space Quest, and Ultra Pinball. Online they have a stock market challenge where you pit your stock trading skills against other online players. You need to register to use this (registering is free) but this gives you access to your own customizable Web page on the Sierra site.

Where to Buy Computer Stuff Online

Many of the software, hardware, and game sites listed throughout the rest of this chapter have online stores where you can order their products. That's one way to shop, but what if you're looking for several products from different vendors?

In that case, you need to go to one of the big online retail sites that functions like a computer superstore. These sites usually carry the same wide selection you find in a "real" store or a major mail-order outlet. Many of these sites offer special offers for online shoppers. You can get prices that are more up-to-date than magazine ads and search the products at your leisure.

Egghead Software
http://www.egghead.com/

If you're not familiar with Egghead, you may not know that this software retailer has some of the best deals around on selected hardware. The Web site has special sections for corporate, government, and business users. Most of the site is arranged around a "store" theme. You can browse the store by product category or use a search field to search for products by name. You can order products online (with a discount if you join the CUE club) or use another search page to find the store closest to you.

ElekTek Inc.
http://www.elektek.com/

This hardware and software reseller carries a variety of PC systems, as well as peripherals and software. To help you find products you may like, ElekTek includes lists of best selling products in several categories on the premise that the best sellers have more and better features, are easier to use, and are more reliable.

IX

Hot Internet Sites

Fig. 46.14

Save money shopping for software and hardware online at Egghead.

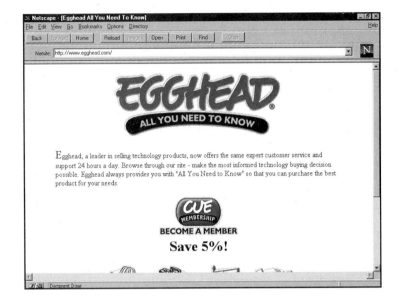

Ingram Micro
http://www.ingram.com/

Ingram Micro is a large computer products distributor that sells software and hardware to retail outlets. Its Web site includes best-seller lists (although they were several months out-of-date when I visited last), lots of industry news, and information about the products it carries and the vendors who make them. You can't order anything here, but you can get a lot of product information on over 30,000 products from hundreds of companies.

Insight Direct
http://www.insight.com/

You can order online from this large mail-order vendor, but you have to set up an account first. Insight carries hardware and software for the PC, and its Web site offers the latest pricing information, including specials for Web customers. The Tech Talk section includes answers to frequently asked questions, driver updates and documentation, and links to manufacturers' Web pages.

Fig. 46.15
You'll find just about any imaginable computer software and hardware product at Insight.

Computer Price Cruncher
http://www.killerapp.com

Here's a useful page if you're looking for a new computer or new parts for an existing computer. Through this page, you can comparison shop online. You narrow your search to the type of equipment you're looking for (such as sound card or CD-ROM drive), or you can narrow it further to just a particular vendor; the Cruncher returns a table with specifications for all matching products. From this table, you can proceed to a list of resellers selling each product. This list is complete with the selling price, address, phone number, and a link to the seller's Web site if they have one. The number of sellers was still small when I looked at this, but it will certainly grow and get even better over time.

NECX Direct
https://necxdirect.necx.com/docroot/index.html

This online superstore boasts an inventory of over 20,000 computer items. NECX encourages you to buy a membership, which entitles you to discount prices, but you can still browse the site and shop as a guest without a membership. This site offers daily "Super Deals" and it does have some very good prices. The site is organized by product category with categories such as notebooks, multimedia hardware, RAM, modems, and printers.

IX

Hot Internet Sites

Fig. 46.16
Comparison shop
for the best deals
on PCs and
peripherals with
the Price
Cruncher.

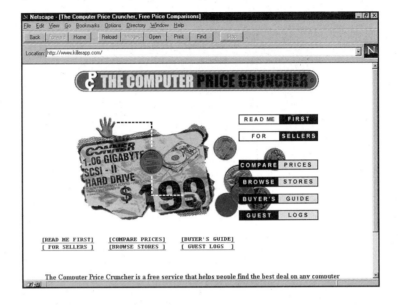

Fig. 46.16
Comparison shop
for the best deals
on PCs and
peripherals with
the Price
Cruncher.

> **Tip**
>
> The "s" at the end of *https* in this Web address indicates that this server is secure.

Lots of Free (or Really Inexpensive) Software

The Internet and the Web just wouldn't be what they are today without the hundreds of thousands of programs you can download and try for free. It's hard to find a Web site that doesn't have at least one link to some software that you can download for free.

But there are a few major sites whose sole reason for being here is as a storehouse for shareware, freeware, and public domain software. These are usually divided into several categories such as word processing, utilities, or Internet tools. Some of these sites have links to tens of thousands of files with gigabytes of drive space. It's a sure thing that you'll find something of interest at one of these sites.

Software Creations BBS
http://www.swcbbs.com

This site is a new type of Web site, a BBS on the Web. All the usual BBS features are here, including a large file area (they claim to get 70–100 new files every day), message areas, and reviews of software. In addition to software that you can download for free, several companies and authors have software that you can purchase and download from the site. To use this site, you have to fill in a rather lengthy registration, but registration is free. However, parts of the site aren't free, including many of the file areas. You have to pay to get access to those.

TUCOWS
http://www.tucows.com

The Ultimate Collection of Winsock Software is a must visit site for any Windows user who likes to tinker with all of the latest Internet software. You will find links to every category of Internet software and helper applications here.

Fig. 46.17
This is a huge collection—the ultimate collection—of Internet software for Windows on the Internet.

Note

While many of the shareware sites listed in this section contain some Windows 95 software, it can be difficult to find them among the thousands of Windows and DOS programs. Here are a few sites that specialize in software for Windows 95. You'll also find information about Windows 95 and links to other, non-software items here.

The Windows 95 Page: **http://biology.queensu.ca/~jonesp/**

Windows 95 Resource Center: **http://www.cris.com/~randybrg/win95.html**

One Stop Windows 95 Site: **http://www.win95.com/**

Stroud's Consummate Winsock List
http://cwsapps.texas.net/

Stroud's list rates hundreds of programs related to using the Internet. The
site has lists categorized by type of application, such as Web browsers, e-mail
clients, newsreaders, and so on. There are also categories devoted to lists
of top-rated software, starter kits recommended for new users, links to new
programs, and more. The links for each program include descriptions of the
software, the maker's Web page if available, a description, and a link to a
download site if the software can be downloaded. The download links
connect to the main site for each program so the copy you get will always
be up to date.

Winsite
http://www.winsite.com

▶ See "WinSite
(formerly
CICA)" p. 1139

This Web page links you to the FTP site for one of the biggest and best-known
sites for Windows software. This site was formerly known as CICA and has
recently turned commercial and adopted a new name. The files here are
grouped in directories for Windows 3.x, Windows 95, and Windows NT.
Within these groupings, you'll find directories for applications (such as Access, Word, and Excel), games, network utilities, drivers, and Internet software. There are about two dozen categories in all.

California State University Windows World
http://coyote.csusm.edu:80/cwis/winworld/winworld.html

This Web server keeps a list of the 50 most popular downloads and lists of all
new software with descriptions. There is also a good search page to help you
find the software you are looking for. The site is divided into more than 50
categories from address books to image-morphing software to Word macros
and add-ons.

World File Project
http://filepile.com

This site claims to be the largest collection of shareware and freeware on the
Internet, and I haven't seen anything that would disprove that claim. They
have over 500,000 programs for DOS, Windows, OS/2, and other systems.
They charge a small monthly fee to access the full collection (currently $15
for 3 months, with a 15MB per week download limit) but there is a small
sampling of about 1,300 programs available for free access.

Jumbo
http://www.jumbo.com/

This Jumbo site has more than 23,000 programs available for download. Windows, DOS, OS/2, and UNIX platforms are all represented here. The site is searchable and divided into about half a dozen categories.

SimTel
http://www.coast.net/SimTel/

This site gained fame for being one of the best places to find DOS software available on the Net. It has added extensive collections of Windows 3.x and Windows 95 software as well, and they have an OS/2 repository.

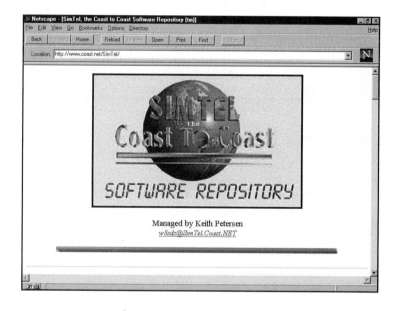

Fig. 46.18
This DOS and Windows software site is one of the major collections on the Net. Many shareware and freeware authors post their software here first.

PGP
http://web.mit.edu/network/pgp.html

PGP (Pretty Good Privacy) is a program for encrypting messages on the Internet. It's free, it works on a variety of programs, and it's the standard that most people use. So if you need to send private e-mail that you don't want to be read by anyone except the intended recipient, see this Web page for some background, downloading, and configuration directions. If you need PGP for commercial purposes, you need to contact ViaCrypt at **http://gn2.getnet.com:80/viacrypt/**.

Harris Semiconductor
http://mtmis1.mis.semi.harris.com/ftp.html

This Web page is an index of links to FTP sites with software for DOS, Windows, UNIX, OS/2, and X Windows.

Tile.Net/FTP
http://tile.net/ftp-list/

This is another index of FTP sites sorted by contents, country, site name, and domain name.

Web Browsers, Servers, and Add-Ons

The Web is an excellent source of information about browsers, servers, and related software. You'll find extensive online help, FAQs, installation instructions, troubleshooting, and more on the Web.

Netscape Communications
http://www.netscape.com

◀ See "Getting
Netscape Up
and Running,"
p. 497

If there is one company whose name has become synonymous with the Internet and the Web, it is Netscape. This is without a doubt one of the most frequently visited sites on the Web. This company makes the popular Web browsing software bearing its name. Netscape Navigator is currently the most widely used Web browsing software. Netscape also makes other related products including Web server software, an Internet Relay Chat client program, and software for developing online applications. A new version of Netscape Navigator called Netscape Navigator Gold has added features for creating Web pages.

◀ " The Basics of
IRC," p. 941

Netscape's large Web site includes links to download their software (which you can try for free), helpful information for learning your way around the Web, and links to many directories and search pages. You'll also find press releases and information about the many companies involved in developing products in conjunction with Netscape.

NCSA Mosaic
http://www.ncsa.uiuc.edu

This is the home of the original "killer app" Web browser—Mosaic. There's much more here than just Mosaic though. The NCSA has multimedia exhibits, information about their high performance computing systems, and links to some of the technical publications. Other software they develop relates to scientific, modeling, data analysis, and file transfer and sharing.

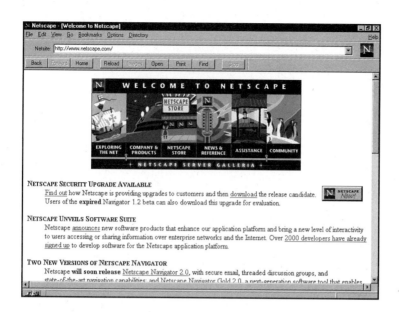

Fig. 46.19
Read about
Netscape's market
leading products
and innovative
technologies.

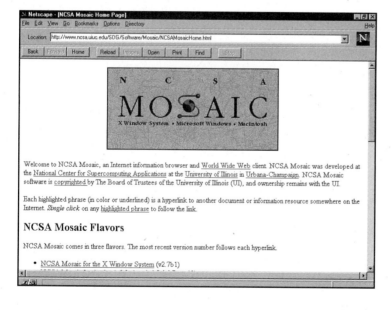

Fig. 46.20
NCSA's original
graphical Mosaic
browser opened
the floodgates
of interest and
development on
the Web.

If you follow the Mosaic link, you'll be able to read about and download Mosaic for Windows, Mac, and X Windows. NCSA maintains a popular "What's New" page, tutorials about the Internet and the Web, and links to information on VRML and SGML.

IX

Hot Internet Sites

Microsoft Internet Explorer
http://www.microsoft.com/windows/ie/iexplorer.htm

◀ See "Setting Up Internet Explorer," p. 473

This popular Web browser is distributed as part of Microsoft Plus! for Windows 95. It is also available for free download. Check the Web site for the most recent version of the browser and announcements about new features. Watch for Microsoft to update and improve this browser regularly to keep up with and keep ahead of competing browser products.

> **Tip**
>
> Microsoft's site is infamous for changing addresses of individual pages frequently. If this address doesn't work, try starting at **http://www.microsoft.com** and following the links to Internet Explorer.

SlipKnot
http://plaza.interport.net/slipknot/slipknot.html

Many people think that if you only have a shell (command line) account with your Internet service provider, you have to suffer through a text based Web interface. SlipKnot is a clever product that gets around this limitation for Windows users. It gives you a Windows-based graphical WWW browser that you can use without having a SLIP or PPP account.

NCompass
http://www.excite.sfu.ca/NCompass

This Web browser for Windows 95 and NT is especially designed to make the most of inline movies and interactive 3D.

BrowserWatch
http://www.ski.mskcc.org:80/browserwatch/index.html

With the dozens of Web browsers available, most people don't have the time it takes to keep up with the constant flood of new versions, new features, and new products. This page collects all of that information in one place so that you only need to check one Web page to get all of this information. It also keeps track of what browsers people use to access it, in case you are interested in which browsers are most popular.

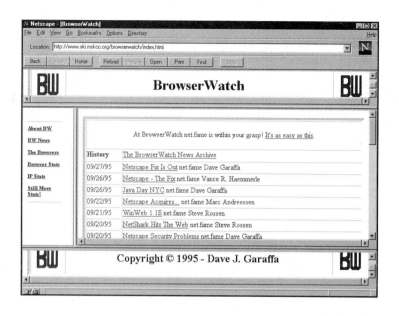

Fig. 46.21
BrowserWatch will
help you keep up
to date on the
latest and greatest
Web software.

First Floor Software
http://www.firstfloor.com

This company makes a product called Smart Bookmarks that allows you to
monitor Web sites for changes. You can learn more about the product here or
download a copy.

CGI Programmer's Reference
http://www.best.com/~hedlund/cgi-faq/

This site provides a reference to the Common Gateway Interface (CGI). There
is a CGI FAQ and links to sites with example CGI scripts and more CGI information.

The Internet Factory
http://www.aristosoft.com/

This company makes Web server software that runs in Windows 95 and NT.
You can download a trial version from their site. The software comes in two
versions, the Commerce Builder and the Communications Builder. Read
about both here and see which one best fits your needs. And if you have
some free time, check out the chat rooms.

IX

Hot Internet Sites

Questar
http://www.questar.com/

This company makes a Web server called WebQuest that runs in Windows 95 and NT. The primary distinguishing features of the software are that it allows database queries without any use of CGI and allows for creation of multiple domains. Check out their site to download a trial copy or read more about it.

HTML Creation

In chapters 26, 27, and 28, we looked at the language used to create Web pages, HTML, and some software that makes creating Web pages easier. In this section we'll explore some Web sites where you can find the best software and information for creating Web pages.

HTML Assistant
http://fox.nstn.ca/~harawitz/index.html

This HTML editor for Windows has earned lavish praise from some of the leading computer magazines. There is a free version of this you can download from the site as well as a Pro version available to buy. Other related products here include a utility for "grabbing" Web addresses from any document and a graphics editor specially designed for creating backgrounds for Web pages.

Ken Nesbitt's WebEdit
http://nesbitt.com/

This is the home page for the popular WebEdit HTML editor. You can download and use WebEdit for free. If you register it, you get additional features like a table editor and toolbar.

Sausage Software
http://www.sausage.com

Sausage Software has a uniquely named HTML editor—Hot Dog—for Windows. Download a free copy or read about the differences in the new professional version.

SoftQuad
http://www.sq.com

SoftQuad is a leading maker of software for creating Web pages. Their HoTMetaL product for creating Web pages in HTML has won prestigious awards. They also have products for creating more complex Web pages in the SGML language.

NaviSoft
http://www.navisoft.com

NaviSoft makes Web server software (NaviServer) and an HTML editing program (NaviPress). You can download free trial versions of both of these from their Web site. They also have a Web page hosting service. This lets you put your Web pages on their server for a small fee. This charge varies depending on whether the Web pages are personal or commercial and based on the size and number of visitors to your pages.

Internet Assistant for Word
http://www.microsoft.com/msoffice/freestuf/msword/
download/ia/default.htm

This HTML editor from Microsoft works in Microsoft Word for Windows and comes in versions for Word 6 and Word for Windows 95. Anyone familiar with Word will find this editor easy to pick up.

Excel to HTML Converter
http://rs712b.gsfc.nasa.gov/704/dgd/xl2html.html

Here's a special purpose macro for converting a range of cells in an Excel spreadsheet into an HTML table.

HTML
http://www.w3.org/pub/WWW/MarkUp/MarkUp.html

If you are looking for information about HTML straight from the horse's mouth, this is the correct end of the horse to examine. This is the official home of all of the official specifications for HTML.

Java, VRML, and RealAudio Heat Up the Net

It's easy to get lost in all of the new technology on the Web. Just when you think you are doing well because you got your computer set up to play movies from the Web, along come VRML and Java and you feel lost again. This section will look at all of the latest ways to exchange information and add value to the Web.

Java
http://java.sun.com

There's a picture of a steaming cup of Joe on this page but the site has nothing to do with beans, cappuccino, espresso, or any other variation of this all purpose beverage.

The Java site has more information about Java (including technical information for developers who want to create Java applications) and links to browsers that support Java (Sun has a browser named HotJava that demonstrates the technology and Netscape has built Java support into Netscape 2). There are also links to many example pages that include Java applications.

Fig. 46.22

This hot cup of Joe is your introduction to the hot worlds of Java and HotJava. (Who would want it cold?)

VRML
http://vrml.wired.com

Wired magazine runs this site and has become the "official" home of VRML information on the Web. Mostly what you will find here are transcripts and papers from the folks who designed and shaped VRML.

This isn't the only VRML site around. You may also want to see **http://sdsc.edu/vrml/**.

WebSpace
http://www.sgi.com/Products/WebFORCE/WebSpace/

Silicon Graphics has developed this VRML browser and several related VRML tools. The browser is available for several different platforms including Windows 95.

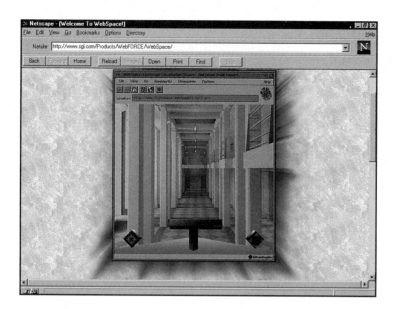

Fig. 46.23
Visit virtual worlds
with WebSpace
software from SGI.

Worlds Inc.
http://www.worlds.net

Worlds Inc. makes what they call "social computing" applications. Their
Worlds Chat software is used to communicate and interact with other users
in a 3D virtual world on the Web. Download the chat software from their
site, visit the Internet World's Fair (their "theme park" online), and get information about VRML+—the technology behind World's Chat.

WebChat
http://www.irsociety.com/webchat.html

WebChat is a multimedia chatting system that runs in most popular Web
browsers. This multimedia aspect means that as you are "chatting" by exchanging words via typed text, you can also exchange audio, pictures, and
video. You don't need any additional software to participate in chat with
this. You simply enter your comments in a form and watch the comments of
others appear on screen. There are links to many different servers running
"channels" for hundreds of different chat topics.

Prospero Systems
http://www.prospero.com/globalstage

This is a Web-based chatting system that uses a small separate chat program
in addition to your Web browser. You can download the software for free.
The software will connect to IRC chat channels as well as new servers using
their GlobalStage server.

WorldView
http://www.intervista.com

This VRML Web browser is available for Windows 95 and NT. It runs either by itself or in conjunction with another browser like Netscape.

PaperSoftware
http://www.paperinc.com

Here's one final VRML site that's worth a look. This company makes a VRML browser called WebFX that works directly within Netscape.

RealAudio
http://www.RealAudio.com

This program enables your Web browser to play "radio"-like audio in real time on your Windows PC. Several of the early uses of RealAudio broadcasts have included live sporting events, O. J. Simpson Trial Updates, music clips, and talk shows. The RealAudio software you use to listen to these broadcasts is available for free download. If you want to broadcast RealAudio events on your Web server, you can download a free trial version of the server software.

RealAudio Sampler	
Santa Monica Bank:	**http://www.smbank.com**
WSKU:	**http://www.wksu.kent.edu**
Batman Forever:	**http://batmanforever.com**
A little bit of everything:	**http://town.hall.org/radio**

Internet Phone
http://www.vocaltec.com

The Internet Phone is an inventive little application that lets you use your computer and the Internet to simulate telephone calls. Visit this site to learn more and download a free trial version.

CU-SeeMe
http://www.wpine.com/cu-seeme.html

CU-SeeMe (pronounced "See You See Me") is a video and audio conferencing program for the Internet. You can transmit and receive audio and video with your computer over the Internet. The software comes in versions for Windows. You can download a free trial version from this site. There is also a short list of sites using CU-SeeMe that you can visit.

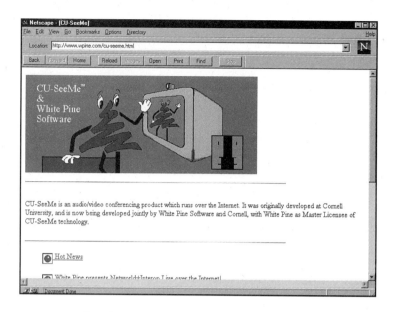

CU-SeeMe is an audio/video conferencing product which runs over the Internet. It was originally developed at Cornell University, and is now being developed jointly by White Pine Software and Cornell, with White Pine as Master Licensee of CU-SeeMe technology.

Fig. 46.24
Cu-SeeMe is another application that started at a university and is now being licensed for commercial development.

Xing
http://www.xingtech.com

This company makes a product called Streamworks that is used to broadcast audio or video on the Net. (I am watching NBC's NBC Pro, an Internet broadcast of the NBC Evening News, as I write this.)

Combo Deals: Web Browsers, E-Mail Readers, and the Kitchen Sink Rolled into One

If you are looking for a suite of Internet programs that includes all of the software you need for any Internet task, several companies make these all in one combos. You'll find these sold through retail software stores and sometimes available for free download for a trial version on the Net.

NetManage
http://www.netmanage.com

NetManage makes two of the most popular software packages for connecting to the Internet. Their "Chameleon Sampler" was used for several years by many publishers and service providers with books and as a starter kit. Many people still use this. This sampler is a smaller version of their full retail Chameleon product, which comes in different varieties for dial-up and network use. Read all about the different versions of the product to see which one is

NetCD95

IX

Hot Internet Sites

right for your needs. You can download trial versions of some products and order online. Special information about configuring Windows 95 and the Chameleon software to work well together is also available along with technical support.

Fig. 46.25
NetManage's Chameleon software has long been popular in wide area networks and they have leveraged that popularity into the Internet market.

Internet in a Box
http://www.compuserve.com/prod_services/consumer/ consumer.html

CompuServe bought Spry, the company that makes Internet in a Box, in 1995. While they've done a good job upgrading this software, they've made it next to impossible to find the Web pages about it. But now that you know where it is, you can read all about this Internet suite. This is a very popular program and is a real leader in retail sales. They also have a related product, Mosaic in a Box.

InterAp
http://www.stac.com/Homepages/Software/intcont.html

If you want more than just a Web browser and basic connectivity software, InterAp is a powerful Internet software package. This software includes all of the usual clients (Web browser, e-mail, news, FTP, etc.), but it also includes a scripting tool and scheduler. With these, you can automate Internet tasks that you perform frequently and schedule them to run at any convenient time. These act like "Intelligent Agents," gathering and sorting information for you from the Web, newsgroups, e-mail, or any other Internet source. InterAp also is OLE 2 compliant so it works well with Windows applications like Microsoft Office. Some of the sample scripts that come with InterAp show how to automatically publish Internet information in Word and Excel. Use this Web page to learn more about the features and download a free trial copy.

Frontier Technologies
http://www.frontiertech.com

Frontier's SuperHighway Access and SuperTCP are two of the most comprehensive Internet access packages available. The SuperHighway Access product is geared more toward individuals (or businesses) who just need to connect to the Net. SuperTCP has many additional tools that would be used for networking and connecting to mainframes in a corporate network setting. They also have a CD-ROM product that includes the Lycos search database (see the description of Lycos later in this chapter) along with the Frontier browser. With this, you can search for sites of interest offline; then when you find a page you want to load, the Web browser fires up and off you go.

Emissary
http://www.twg.com

Here's another all in one package for Windows. Check their site for the availability of a free trial version. The strength of this package is that all of the services are integrated.

Other Internet Software

Most of the emphasis on Net software these days is about the Web. While Web browsers are perfect for viewing Web pages, they aren't always the best at other Internet tasks. Some Web browsers include, for example, the ability to read e-mail and news, but there are other programs designed specifically for e-mail and news that do a much better job. We'll take a quick look at the cream of the crop here.

Eudora
http://www.qualcomm.com/ProdTech/quest/

This is the home of the popular Eudora e-mail software for Windows and Macs. Read all about the free ("Light") and retail ("Pro") versions of the software, download the free version, and download other related software.

NetCD95

IX

Hot Internet Sites

NewsXpress
http://www.malch.com/nxfaq.html

NewsXpress is still my favorite newsreader. I may be out of sync with the times as so many other people tell me Forté's Agent (and Free Agent) is the best, but I find NewsXpress easier to use. There is a FAQ and a link to the latest version here. (You can find Agent at **http://www.forteinc.com/ forte/agent**.)

SurfWatch Software
http://www.surfwatch.com

You've heard all about the amount of explicit material on the Web. If you are looking for a way to block access from your computer to this (maybe your kids use the Internet and there are certain things you don't want them learning there), this software allows you to screen out objectionable material. Read about all of the software's features, how you can get it, and what online services are integrating it at their Web site.

NetNanny
http://www.netnanny.com/netnanny

This is another program that prevents access to objectionable material on the Net. Parents can decide which words, phrases, and sites they want NetNanny to watch for and configure it to monitor activity and keep track of what happens or to shut down when one of the screen sites or phrases is detected.

Fig. 46.26
While there is no real substitute for parental involvement and supervision on the Net, NetNanny will help you protect your kids when you can't.

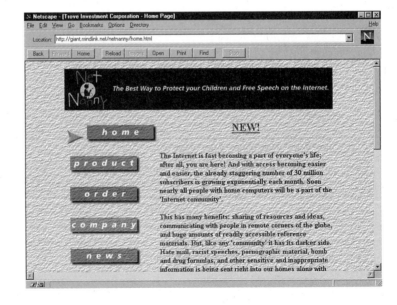

L-Soft International
http://www.lsoft.com/

If you are interested in running your own mailing list, this is an excellent place to start. L-Soft is the premier company in the mailing list software business. It has recently released a version of its popular LISTSERV for Windows 95. The software is available for free download and trial. Paying and registering allows you to run more lists with additional subscribers.

Internet Service Providers

Unless you are connecting to the Internet through a LAN connection at work or through a university, you will need to have an Internet account. In this section we will look at companies that specialize in Internet access. (The next section will look at online services that also offer access to the Internet.)

MCI
http://www.mci.com

If you didn't discover this from the InternetMCI commercials on television, MCI sells Internet access. You can also find out about their other telecommunication services here.

UUNET Technologies
http://www.uu.net

UUNET is one of the largest Internet Services Providers. Many other service providers connect to the Internet through UUNET. They offer connections from dial-up service for individuals through their AlterDial service to T1 and T3 lines used for high-speed connections by corporations and other service providers. See their Web page to find out more about these services including pricing, availability, and options.

PSI
http://www.psi.net

This company is a large nationwide Internet service provider. For new customers it offers a complete startup kit including software called Instant Interramp. PSI also owns another service provider named Pipeline USA. Pipeline offers internet connectivity for individuals and includes award-winning software to connect easily.

IX

Hot Internet Sites

IQuest
http://www.iquest.net

I had to mention this company because I get my Internet service through them. They're a small provider in Indianapolis with local numbers throughout Indiana.

Portal
http://www.portal.com

This Internet service provider boasts connections in over 1,000 cities with 200,000 modems. They have services for individuals as well as corporations looking to connect.

Demon Internet
http://www.demon.co.uk

This is the home of the U.K.'s largest service provider. They offer low priced, one-fee dial-up accounts and leased line accounts.

WinNet
http://www.win.net/

NetCD95

This Internet service provider has a special front end program for e-mail and news reading offline. With this service and software, most users will find they spend only a few minutes connected to the Internet for mail and news each day instead of hours.

The List (of Internet Service Providers)
http://thelist.com

This site, which is a service of *Internet World Magazine*, is a large online listing of Internet service providers. You can search for a service provider by name or domain name, look through lists that are organized by states in the U. S. as well as foreign country listings, and a list organized by area code. The information provided about each service provider includes the name, servies offered, and rates, as well as phone, e-mail, and Web addresses, where available.

Online Services

These services all offer a way to get connected to the Internet. In addition, they all have special services that their subscribers have access to that other Internet users can't access through them. These include special forums for discussion of common topics, chat areas, up-to-date news and weather services, travel planning, and financial management services to name just a few.

CompuServe
http://www.compuserve.com

Read about the products and services from this major online service provider at their Web site. This service has a typical mix of services but they are best known amongst experienced computer users for their good technical support areas sponsored by hundreds of computer hardware and software companies. Business users are also apt to find the mix of services here to be of interest.

◀ See "An Introduction to CompuServe," p. 232

Prodigy
http://www.prodigy.com

Once the ugly duckling of online services, Prodigy has blossomed and is rapidly gaining in popularity. They were the first of the major online services to offer a Web browser and have made a real effort to make a better interface to their whole service. They offer the usual mix of services like news, sports, chat, and file areas with more of an emphasis for non-technical and non-business related use.

Microsoft Network
http://www.msn.com

Microsoft plans to use this extensively for providing support on Microsoft software products. They are also lining up many major content providers to fill the services with news, entertainment, and more.

◀ See "What Is the Microsoft Network?" p. 309

America Online
http://www.aol.com

This online service appeals mostly to users connecting from the home or small business. They have a very large and growing subscriber base and easy to use software for Windows.

◀ See "What Is America Online?" p. 264

Searches and Directories

If you need to find something on the Web, you may want to use one of the Web pages that indexes or lists pages on the Web. With one of these pages, you can search for a category of pages or a specific page.

Lycos
http://www.lycos.com

Lycos has the biggest database of Web pages that I have seen on the Web. From their search page, you can initiate a search of over ten million Web pages, a number that is constantly growing. The good news is, if it's on the

IX

Hot Internet Sites

Web, chances are you can find it from Lycos. I have never found a topic that existed on the Web that I couldn't find in Lycos. They've recently upgraded the hardware that runs this search and it is now very fast.

One downside of this search engine is the number of "hits" returned. I searched on "Macmillan" and got over 1,400 matches. Luckily, the first one was the one I wanted (Macmillan Information Superlibrary, Home of Que on the Web). Hits are ranked in order with the ones most likely to be what you are looking for first.

Another downside is the repetition of pages. For example, the Macmillan search lists the Macmillan Information Superlibrary no less than six different times with six different (but equally functional) addresses (**http:// www.mcp.com**; **http://mcp.com**; **http://www.mcp.com:80**, and so on). So, to make the best use of this resource, try to make your search specific by using more than one keyword, go to the search page with options (click the Search Options link on the home page) and choose Match All Terms (AND) in the search options box and still be prepared to wade through some long lists of results.

Yahoo!
http://www.yahoo.com

This is one of the most popular directory services on the Web. It has over 40,000 sites indexed into 14 top level categories. These categories include Art, Computers and Internet, News, and Recreation to name just a few. There is also a simple search feature. A couple of popular items here are the listings of new and cool pages and the random link.

WebCrawler
http://webcrawler.com/

This searcher was recently bought by America Online, but it remains available and free for use to all Internet users. This was one of the first major Web search pages and is very well known. The WebCrawler database has about 200,000 Web pages that it has visited and indexed. There are also another two million documents in the database that it has addresses for but hasn't visited and indexed yet. So the database is big enough to give you some lengthy results but still small enough that it shouldn't overwhelm you. You'll also find a list of the 25 most popular pages on the Web here.

World Wide Web Worm
http://www.cs.colorado.edu/home/mcbryan/WWWW.html

This is a powerful but simple to use search index. All of the typically used options here can be set by choosing them from menus on the search form.

World Wide Web Yellow Pages
http://www.mcp.com/nrp/wwwyp

This is the online version of New Rider's best selling *World Wide Web Yellow Pages.* You can search it by keyword or category. If you submit a page to be added and it is added to the index, it will also be added in the next printed edition of the book.

InfoSeek Corp.
http://www.infoseek.com

This is a commercial Web search service that allows users to sample the search database for free. In addition to the search, there are categorized lists of cool sites. By joining as a paying customer, you can extend your searches to UseNet newsgroup articles and special electronic publications for business, health, and other industries on the Net.

Interactive Age Hot 1000
http://techweb.cmp.com/techweb/ia/hot1000/hot1.html

This special little directory focuses on the Web sites for the top 1,000 North American companies (ranked by U.S. sales in dollars). There are links to all of the top 1,000 that have Web pages and phone numbers for all companies.

CUI Search Catalog
http://cuiwww.unige.ch/w3catalog

This is a small searchable database of Web pages.

ElNet Galaxy
http://galaxy.einet.net/search.html

This directory is a combined search page and index. The index is divided into about a dozen major categories. The search page (at the preceding main address) allows you to search on all links in their "Galaxy" (the database of entries), just Web pages, just the Web links, or other subparts of the list. The index is at **http://galaxy.einet.net/galaxy.html**.

NCSA What's New
http://www.ncsa.uiuc.edu/SDG/Software/Mosaic/Docs/archive-whats-new.html

This was one of the earliest attempts to keep track of new additions to the Web. This page was started by the same fine folks that developed Mosaic. When it started, it was a good place to keep track of the few dozen new Web page announcements each month. At this point, the site gets hundreds of new entries every day. There's no real organization to this except by day (and old announcements are archived by month). This might be useful if you are looking specifically for new sites or if you have the time to scan the entire up-date on a daily basis.

World Wide Web Virtual Library
http://www.w3.org/hypertext/DataSources/bySubject/Overview.html

This is a large directory organized by subject area. The top level topics in the directory are very specific, such as Aboriginal Studies and Vision Science. There are over 100 top level categories here.

McKinley Internet Directory
http://www.mckinley.com/

This is another combination of a directory style index and search engine. The real draw of this site is that many of the Web pages in their directory are rated. In fact, they have rated over 30,000 sites with a four-star rating system. The more stars there are, the better the site is. Sites are graded on the basis of completeness, "up-to-dateness," organization, and how easy the site is to access.

In addition to the database of graded sites, there are another 500,000 sites in a separate database waiting to be graded, but you can still search this database as well.

Another interesting feature here is what they call a "concept" search. This takes the key word (or words) that you enter and generates a list of similar or related words and searches for them as well. So a search for "books" might turn up a publisher's Web site, even if the Web site didn't specifically use the word "book."

Point Communications's Best of the Web
http://www.pointcom.com/

This is another site that isn't interested in indexing and cataloging every page on the Web. Instead, the focus is on just the best sites. They have reviews of the sites they see as best divided into 15 categories. You can browse by cat-egory or search the database. Sites are judged on content, presentation, and "experience" (a very subjective measure of whether or not the site is fun and worth going to). All three categories are scored from 0–49, with higher scores being better.

NetFind
http://www.nova.edu/Inter-Links/netfind.html

This search page is used to find e-mail addresses.

Four11 White Page Directory
http://www.four11.com/

This service is used to find people and their e-mail address from the Web. In order to use this, you have to fill in a form giving your name and e-mail address. They use this registration to build the database you can search. So everyone who does a search gets added.

Submit It!
http://www.submit-it.com

Wouldn't it be nice if there were a way to submit an announcement about your new Web page to all of the major directories at once instead of filling out a form for each one? That is exactly what Submit It! does. Simply select the check boxes for each directory that you want your page submitted to, fill in all of the requested information in the form, and before you know it, you'll have more visitors at your Web page than you can handle.

Stanford Net News Filtering—SIFT
http://sift.stanford.edu/

This site is home to a search mechanism of a different sort. SIFT searches UseNet news messages on a daily basis to find topics that you specify and creates a Web page of UseNet articles for you. The service is free (thanks to the Stanford Digital Library Project) and is one of the best ways to cut through the UseNet news clutter.

> **Note**
>
> DejaNews has a service similar to SIFT. The address for that page is **http://www.dejanews.com**.

Snoopie Internet File Finder
http://www.snoopie.com

Snoopie is a search page for FTP sites. This is a new service and it is currently available for free but it will become a commercial service. This site has indexed a few million files on over 400 FTP sites. It works somewhat like Archie (discussed in chapter 34, "Using FTP") but is much faster. In some cases it also finds more files than Archie.

The Best of the Rest

It's time for that final catch all category. The sites listed in this last section don't really fit in anywhere else but they are all worth mentioning.

Walnut Creek CD-ROM
http://www.cdrom.com/

Walnut Creek makes a wide variety of low-cost CD-ROMs. Most of its products are compilations of software or information that is freely available. The value to you is the convenience of having it all together on one CD and not having to spend hours (or days) downloading it all. The Web site tells you about all its current and new CD-ROM titles, as well as upcoming new products, all of which can be ordered online. Sample files from CD-ROMs and multilingual catalogs are available. You can also find information about getting your own CD-ROM projects published.

Windows 95 Internetworking Headquarters
http://www.windows95.com/

This is a great place to get answers about networking, especially networking through the Internet with Windows 95. There is also a large collection of related software.

Fig. 46.27

Explore your Internet connectivity and tools for Windows 95 at the Windows 95 InteNetworking Headquarters.

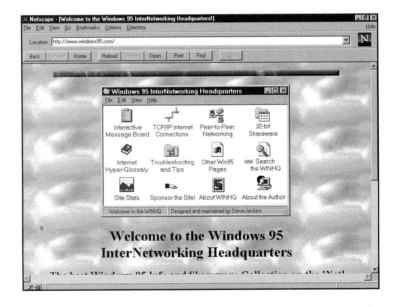

Electronic Frontier Foundation
http://www.eff.org

I consider this to be one of the most important sites on the Web. This group is actively involved with protecting the constitutional rights of "Netizens." They work to protect freedom of the electronic press. They encourage thought and debate on the proper role of government involvement in the Net and look for solutions that balance freedom and responsibility.

The Alerts link here takes you to current events that affect online freedom. These include pending legislation as well as court decisions and proceedings. When the matter is legislation, there is usually information explaining who you can contact to voice your opinion.

You'll also find links to their newsletter (the current issue as well as an archive of back issues) and other sites with related content. Whatever your opinion on the state of the Net, I'd encourage you to get involved here.

Intergraph
http://www.intergraph.com

If your company needs an Internet server but you have no interest in the technical details of installing and configuring one, you may be interested in the complete Web server from this company. It comes with the computer and all of the software needed to run the server preinstalled. See the Web page for more information and about this and related products and services.

The WELL
http://www.well.com

The WELL (Whole Earth 'lectronic Link) was one of the first Internet service providers. In addition to Internet service, they have a number of special conferences and information sources for their customers, much like a commercial online service like CompuServe or AOL would provide through forums or special interest groups. You can check out a sampling of the services available to their customers, register for their service, and download a software toolkit for use with their service from the home page.

Mecklerweb
http://www.mecklerweb.com

MecklerMedia publishes several magazines, in print and on the Web, about the Internet and the Web. They also sponsor Internet World, one of the largest conventions for Internet users and vendors. You can get highlights from

IX

Hot Internet Sites

the printed magazines as well as updates and extras that aren't in the magazine. The Net Day page gives you a daily update on late breaking Internet news online. The site includes an online chat area for discussion of a variety of topics.

ISDN
http://www.pacbell.com/isdn/isdn_home.html

This is a good source of ISDN information. PacBell has been a leader in implementing ISDN for their customers. While some of the information here will be useful only to customers in the PacBell area, most of it will be useful to anyone considering ISDN.

Internet Society
http://info.isoc.org/home.html

The Internet Society is an organization for coordination of the Internet. Individuals, corporations, and government agencies can join and participate in the development of the Internet. To learn more or find out how to join, check out their page.

CPSR
http://www.cpsr.org/home

The Computer Professionals for Social Responsibility (CPSR) is devoted to focusing public attention and policy on information technology. The impact of technology on society, the workplace, and privacy are some of the issues discussed here. Visit their page to see how to become a member and get involved.

CHAPTER 47

Top FTP Sites

Anonymous FTP sites are a great way for Net users to find software and computer-related information. In this chapter, I've collected a list of some of the best FTP sites that relate to software, the Internet, and computer hardware. From the few dozen sites, most FTP users will find just about any file they could ever need. Specifically, the list includes:

- Sites with large collections of free software
- Sites with software for accessing the Internet and information about the Net
- Computer hardware and software vendors with sites
- A few other important sites
- Some suggestions for finding more sites of interest

Collections of Free Software

One of the most popular uses of anonymous FTP sites is to provide large collections of freeware, shareware, and public domain software. The best sites of this type have several gigabytes or more of software that you can download. This section will look at the biggest and best.

WinSite (formerly CICA)
ftp.winsite.com (formerly **ftp.cica.indiana.edu**)

CICA was long known in the Internet community as one of the best sources of PC software for Windows. They've recently gone commercial and changed their name (the old address will cease to function soon too, so use the **ftp.winsite.com** address). The site is now much faster and allows many more connections than before. The files at the site are organized into directories for Win 3.1, NT, and 95. These are all in the \pub\pc directories. Under \pub\pc\win95 you'll find the directories listed in table 47.1.

Table 47.1 Windows 95 Directories at WinSite	
access	patches
demo	pdoxwin
desktop	pim
drivers	programr
dskutil	sounds
excel	sysutil
games	txtutil
icons	uploads
misc	winword
miscutil	wpwin
netutil	

Although WinSite is easier to connect to than the old CICA, there are still mirror sites. If you find the main site busy or slow, try one of these mirrors. (There are other mirrors but I've only listed the ones that are relatively easy to connect to and fast.)

Table 47.2 WinSite Mirrors	
Address	**Directory**
uiarchive.cso.uiuc.edu	/pub/systems/pc/winsite/
ftp.agt.net	/pub/cica-win3/
wuarchive.wustl.edu	/systems/ibmpc/win3
	/systems/ibmpc/win95
	/systems/ibmpc/winnt
ftp.cdrom.com	/pub/cica
ftp.gatekeeper.com	/pub/micro/msdos/win3
ftp.agt.net	/pub/cica-win3
uiarchive.cso.uiuc.edu	/pub/systems/pc/winsite
ftp.pht.com	/pub/cica
archive.orst.edu	/pub/mirrors/ftp.winsite.com/

> **Tip**
>
> When you try to connect to Winsite, you'll get a message with a list of current mirrors. If you are using WS_FTP to connect, use the LogWnd feature to look back and see the current list.

Washington University at St. Louis
wuarchive.wustl.edu

This is a *big* site with over 45 gigabytes of disk space of files to download. Look in the /systems/ibmpc directory for archives related to Windows and DOS. The subdirectories here include mirrors of some major PC archives including Winsite and SimTel. Other highlights here include the /packages/ www directory with mirrors of Netscape and Mosaic, /multimedia with a large collection of graphics and multimedia, and /usenet with archives of many UseNet newsgroups.

This is a busy site and is usually very difficult to connect to. Try connecting to one of the mirror sites listed in table 47.3.

Table 47.3   WUArchive Mirrors

Address	Directory
archive.orst.edu	/pub/mirrors/wuarchive.wustl.edu/
ftp.sterling.com	/wuarchive

Oregon State University
archive.orst.edu

This site is one of the largest mirror sites on the Net. It has partial mirrors for about three dozen major FTP sites. They primarily mirror the directories from a site that the site is best known for. The mirrors are all in the /pub/mirrors directory. The subdirectory names here are the mirrored sites name. Some of the major sites mirrored that should be of interest are:

ftp.cdrom.com	ftp.winsite.com
ftp.mcom.com	prep.ai.mit.edu
ftp.novell.com	rtfm.mit.edu
ftp.tsoft.net	simtel
ftp.uu.net	wuarchive.wustl.edu

IX

Hot Internet Sites

Walnut Creek CD-ROM
ftp.cdrom.com

This site has over 50 gigabytes of files online for download. Walnut Creek distributes several dozen CD-ROM collections of software from this site. These CD-ROMs are a convenient way to collect much more software than you could conveniently download. Some of the CD-ROMs are a CICA collection, the official Slackware Linux, a couple of Doom collections, and more. Some directories of interest are:

/pub/cica

/pub/doom and /pub/doom2

/pub/games

/pub/gutenberg

/pub/internet

/pub/simtel

/pub/win95

Tip

You can order Walnut Creek CD-ROMs by calling 1-800-786-9907 or e-mailing **orders@cdrom.com.**

InfoMagic
ftp.infomagic.com

Infomagic publishes several popular CD-ROMs containing collections of freeware and shareware. One of the best known collections is the 4-CD Linux set. Look in the /pub/mirrors directory for files that they publish on CD. Look in the directory pub/cds for a catalog of CDs and ordering info.

Winsock-L FTP Archive
papa.indstate.edu

This is the most comprehensive collection of Internet software for Windows anywhere on the Net. The /winsock-l directory contains all of the software of interest here. For Windows 95 software, look in /winsock-l/Windows95. This is a busy site with a relatively low limit on the number of users so you may want to try one of the mirror sites listed in table 47.4.

Tip

Stroud's Consummate Winsock list at **http://cwsapps.texas.net/** on the Web is a partner to the Winsock-L FTP site.

Table 47.4 Winsock-L FTP Mirrors	
Address	**Directory**
ftp.iquest.com	/pub/windows/papa
ftp.enterprise.net	/pub/mirror/winsock-l/
ftp.adeptcom.com/mirrors	/papa-winsock/
ftp.infomagic.com	/pub/mirrors/PC-Networking/WinSock-l

There is also a CD-ROM version of the site available.

Simtel
ftp.coast.net

This is another well-known site for PC files. They have large collections here for Windows 95 and NT as well as MS-DOS, OS/2, and Windows 3.1. Look for all of the directories related to this in /pub/systems/pc/simtel. There's a major mirror for this site at **oak.oakland.edu** in the /SimTel directory.

Digital Equipment Corporation
gatekeeper.dec.com

This large FTP site has a collection of shareware and freeware for many different types of computers. There isn't a Windows 95 directory here yet but based on the quality of the other archives (and mirrors) expect to find some Win 95 files here soon. They would probably be in a subdirectory of /pub/micro.

Exec-PC
ftp.execpc.com

This site is the FTP home of the Exec-PC BBS, one of the most popular BBSs in the world. In addition to general freeware and shareware areas, many software companies use Exec-PC as the main distribution site for their software. To get the most of this service, you'll need to buy an account.

OC Games Archive at University of Massachusetts Lowell
ftp.uwp.edu

This site has a large collection of PC games, mostly that run in DOS. It is an official site for *Apogee*, *Epic MegaGames*, and *GameBytes* magazines. There are action and arcade games, games that run as BBS doors, flight simulators, patches for commercial games, and more. Look for all of this in the /msdos/ games directory.

Internet Software and Information

This section looks at sites that have one or more Internet programs that are of special interest. Keep in mind that many of the sites listed in "Collections of Free Software" have directories devoted to Internet software. The section also lists sites with documentation and information about the Net.

RTFM
rtfm.mit.edu

"Read the (friendly) manual" at this site. This site has a large collection of FAQs from UseNet and other Net sources. This is the best place to start looking if you need information about the Net or any of the thousands of topics that are dear to Net users' hearts. Look in the /pub directory in any of the /usenet... subdirectories.

NCSA
ftp.ncsa.uiuc.edu

This is the home FTP site for Mosaic, the Web browser that really started the Web revolution. The files relevant to Mosaic and the Web are in the /Web directory. The subdirectories of /Web are:

> /Mosaic
>
> /html
>
> /httpd
>
> /tools

Also of interest here is the /Hyper-G directory. This is a mirror of the ftp.iicm.tu-graz.ac.at/pub/Hyper-G directory. (Hyper-G is discussed later in this chapter.)

Netscape
ftp.netscape.com

Here's the FTP home of the Netscape Navigator Web browser and server software. The current officially released version of the Web browser is found in
the /netscape directory. If there is a beta version available to the public for
anonymous download, it will be in a different directory. (For example, when
the new 2.0 version was being beta tested, it was in the /2.0beta directory.)
The various versions of the Web server software are in the /server directory.

> **Note**
>
> There are other alias names for this server such as **ftp.mcom.com**. Some of these
> names are old and based on the old name of the company so they may not work in
> the future. Use the **ftp.netscape.com** address for best luck connecting.
>
> Also, if you have trouble connecting to **ftp.netscape.com**, try
> **ftp2.netscape.com**. If this doesn't work, replace the 2 with either 3, 4, 5, 6, 7, or
> 8. These alternate names provide additional connections when the server is busy.

Qualcomm
ftp.qualcomm.com

This is the home site for Eudora. You'll find the latest free versions, upgrades
for commercial versions, and documentation in the /Eudora directory and its
subdirectories.

InterNIC
ds.internic.net

The InterNIC site maintains a collection of many documents about the
Internet. Look in the /rfc, /fyi, and /std directories. RFCs are "Requests for
Comments," the working notes of the committees that develop the protocols
and standards for the Internet. A fully accepted RFC becomes a STD, an
Internet Activities Board Stardard. FYIs are a subset of RFCs and tend to be
more informational and less technical

◀ See "Internet
Administra-
tion," p. 11

UUNet
ftp.uu.net

UUNet is one of the main distribution centers for UseNet news. They are also
a major Internet service provider. Look in the /index directory for many files
to help you find your way around here. Most of the documents about the
Internet are in /inet.

IX

Hot Internet Sites

Stardust
ftp.stardust.com

This site has information about the Windows Sockets specification and the Windows Telephony application programming interface (TAPI).

Hyper-G Archive
ftp.utdallas.edu

This site has information and software relating to Hyper-G. Look for this in the /pub/Hyper-G directory. Hyper-G is a Web-like information system that is growing in popularity. Look in the /Amadeus directory for a Windows based client to Hyper-G. (This site is a mirror of the /pub/Hyper-G directory of **iicm.tu-graz.ac.at**. It's also mirrored at **ftp.ncsa.uiuc.edu** under /Hyper-G.)

Java
java.sun.com

The /pub directory here has the latest version of the HotJava browser for Windows. (There's more useful information if you access through the Web at **http://java.sun.com**.)

Electronic Frontier Foundation
ftp.eff.org

This group is actively involved with protecting the constitutional rights of "Netizens." Look in the /pub directory for the files of interest here. From there, the /alerts subdirectory has announcements of a critical time sensitive nature such as impending votes on legislation. The /EFF subdirectory contains information about EFF and newsletters. /Net_info and /Privacy should also be of interest to many Internet users. There are many other directories here that will be of interest if you are involved or interested in political activism of any sort.

CPSR
cpsr.org

The Computer Professionals for Social Responsibility site has information about congressional reform, taxes, and a mirror of the Berkeley Cypherpunks site.

Cypherpunks
ftp.csua.berkeley.edu

Among other things, you'll find the home site of the Cypherpunks archive here in the /pub/cypherpunks directory. This directory has much information and some software for cryptography and anonymous services on computers and the Net.

Trumpet Software
ftp.trumpet.com.au

This site is the home of the famous Trumpet Winsock, which many Windows 3.1 users used to connect to the Net. If you've got the dial-up networking in Windows 95 configured correctly, you don't need this with Windows 95 but there are other shareware and freeware Internet programs here. There's an IRC client, a newsreader, and other software.

WS_FTP
ftp.usma.edu

The /pub/msdos directory here is the main site for the WS_FTP client. Other related programs are here as well. This site is rather slow and most of the major archives carry these programs but this is where you'll be sure to find the most recent version. (The author of WS_FTP requests that users from commercial domains get his programs from the Web at **http://www.csra.net/ junodj/**.)

Vocaltec
ftp.vocaltec.com

You can pick up crippled trial copies of Vocaltec's Internet Voice Phone software in the /pub directory here.

Computer Privacy Digest
ftp.cs.uwm.edu

Look in /pub/comp-privacy/ for the archives of the Computer Privacy Digest.

GreatCircle
ftp.greatcircle.com

This site has many informational files related to Internet security and firewalls.

Trusted Information Systems
ftp.tis.com

This site has information and software for cryptography, computer and Internet security, and privacy enhanced mail (PEM). Look in the /pub directory for all of these topics and more.

Commercial Software and Computer Hardware

The sites listed in this section support software products from major software vendors. Many computer hardware manufacturers are using FTP to provide drivers, utilities, and information related to their products. This section also looks at some of the more important sites from major vendors.

Microsoft
ftp.microsoft.com

The Microsoft site has two primary components. First, there are many directories with information about various Microsoft products. These are divided into categories like desktop applications and operating systems and the files are organized into directories according to these categories. For instance, /deskapps/word contains directories with information about Microsoft Word, which is classified as a desktop application. In addition to information, these directories contain available driver updates and software related to the product. To find where something is on this site, start by reading the dirmap.txt file in the root directory.

The other component of the site takes all the files and information and categorizes them by type instead of by application. So, the /Softlib directory has all of the software at this FTP site, regardless of which application it relates to. Likewise, the /KBHelp directory has a collection of all of the Knowledge Base files for all applications. (The Microsoft Knowledge Base collects information about technical support problems and solutions for various MS products.)

Adobe Systems
ftp.adobe.com

Of most interest to most Windows Internet users will be the /pub/adobe/Applications/Acrobat/Windows directory where you will find the current version of the Adobe Acrobat Reader. Users of other Adobe software will want to look in /pub/adobe/Applications and /pub/adobe/Support.

ATI
ftp.atitech.ca

Look in the /pub directory here for drivers, utilities, and technical documentation for ATI video hardware.

Cirrus Logic Inc.
cirrus.com

Look in the /pub/support directory here for drivers, utilities, and technical documentation for Cirrus video chipsets, modems, PCMCIA devices, and other hardware.

Cabletron Systems
ctron.com

This site has information, drivers, and demo software related to Cabletron networking hardware.

3Com
ftp.3com.com

This site supports network cards and hardware from 3Com. Look in the /pub directory here for drivers, software, and information for use with 3Com networking products. The /pub/adapters/drivers directory contains up-to-date drivers for 3Com network adapters. The /pub/docs directory contains bug lists and technical tips.

Adaptec
ftp.adaptec.com

This site provides support for many Adaptec networking products. Look in the /pub/BBS directory to find drivers and utilities for these products. Some subdirectories here are arranged according to product line, such as the /adaptec and /FutureDomain subdirectories. Others are by operating system, such as the /os2, /win95, and /winnt directories.

Autodesk
ftp.autodesk.com

Look here in the /pub directory for support and update files for Autodesk software including AutoCad.

Lotus
ftp.ccmail.com

Look in the /pub/comm directory for files and information relating to the cc:mail e-mail program and Notes groupware.

Creative Labs
ftp.creaf.com

You'll find drivers and utilities for Creative Labs Sound Blaster and related products in the /pub/creative/files directories. There are some patches for software products from other companies that have problems working with Creative Labs products in the /pub/patches.

Digi International
ftp.digibd.com

The /drivers directory has driver software for Digi International LAN products including LAN to LAN modem connectivity and ISDN devices.

Kodak
ftp.kodak.com

This site has files and information related to digital photography and computer images.

Novell
ftp.novell.com

This site has software and information for Novell's networking products as well as their business applications. Look in /pub/updates/busapps for files related to WordPerfect and other Novell business software. Novel LAN product files are in /pub/updates/mgt, /pub/updates/msg, pub/updates/napi, and /pub/updates/nwos directories.

Quarterdeck
ftp.qdeck.com

Information and updates for Quarterdeck products including CleanSweep, Web Author, and Internet Suite are included here.

Spry
ftp.spry.com

This site has information and helper files for the Spry (now CompuServe) Internet In a Box products.

Sparco
ftp.sparco.com

This site has a catalog for ordering from this computer hardware reseller's 42,000 products.

Supra
ftp.supra.com

This site has utilities, Flash ROM updates, configuration profiles, and drivers for Supra modems.

Telebit
ftp.telebit.com

This site has software support and information for Telebit Netblazer (in the /pub/netblazer directory) and modem products.

US Robotics
ftp.usr.com

USR's modems and communications products are supported here. When you log in as anonymous, you'll be dumped into the /SYS/PCB directory. The site is a little bit difficult to navigate because the subdirectory names are all numbers. (The site has been copied from their BBS, maybe they'll take the time to clean this up some time in the future.) These numbers are explained in the index file in this directory. A couple of subdirectories of interest are:

> Communications: /dl02
>
> DOS/Windows Utilities: /dl03
>
> Internet: /dl24
>
> FAQs and Setup Docs: /DOCS/ASCII

In the /DOCS/ASCII directory, many of the filenames are numbers so you'll need to get the index file to find any documentation relating to the modem you have.

Western Digital Corporation
ftp.wdc.com

There is documentation here for Western Digital drives and related software. The documentation includes drive parameter tables and troubleshooting information. There are also drivers for WDC drive controller cards and their line of Paradise Video cards.

McAfee
mcafee.com

The area of highest interest here should be the /pub/antivirus directory. This contains the McAfee antivirus software and some related antivirus programs and information.

WinZip
ftp.winzip.com

The /winzip directory is the main site for the popular WinZip file compression/decompression software. The new software for creating self-extracting WinZip files is also here.

Other Sites of Interest

Not every important FTP site fits neatly into one of the other categories in this chapter. This section takes a look at a few important sites that may be of interest that fall outside of the other categories.

Ziff
ftp.zdbop.ziff.com

This site has files from Ziff's many magazines and ZDLabs benchmark programs. The magazine files include shareware and freeware discussed in the magazines. Some of the magazines include the text of feature articles, hardware reviews, comparative benchmarks, and other editorial content. In order to find anything, you need to know which issue of the magazine it was in as the directories are arranged by year and month of the issue.

The ZDLabs benchmarks programs are all in the /zdbop directory.

Que and Macmillan Computer Publishing
ftp.mcp.com

Macmillan uses this site to support the books it publishes. You'll find software related to its books and updates for software on disk and CD with books.

Internet Wiretap
wiretap.spies.com

This site has a collection of information about government activities. Look for these in the /Gov directory. There are also collections of electronic books and other online texts and an archive about arcade video games.

American Civil Liberties Union
aclu.org

Look in the /aclu directory for a collection of information relating to ACLU activities.

Book Stacks Inc.
ftp.books.com

This site has electronic copies of hundreds of books available for download. See the file DIR.TXT for an explanation of the directory structure here. This will help you find books and authors of interest.

Etext
ftp.etext.org

This FTP site provides a public file server for anyone to post electronic texts that they would like to disseminate (and that are not copyright violations). The site serves to allow users to freely express and spread information about a variety of political, social, religious, literary, and other topics. As the site encourages discussion of controversial topics, the administrator warns that you may find some of the texts objectionable or offensive.

FTP Lists and Directories

This chapter can't list every anonymous FTP site. In fact FTP sites change so often, it's impossible for any one source to keep track of all sites. So, if you need to find a site that isn't listed in this chapter, here are a few places to look to help you find it.

First, Perry Rovers maintains a large list of FTP sites. The list is updated monthly. He posts it to several newsgroups including:

> news.newusers.questions
>
> alt.sources.wanted
>
> comp.archives
>
> comp.archives.admin
>
> comp.sources.wanted
>
> alt.answers
>
> comp.answers
>
> news.answers

The list is also available by FTP in at **oak.oakland.edu** in /SimTel/msdos/info/ftp-list.zip.

Another way to find FTP sites is through the Web site at **http://tile.net/ftp-list/**. This site has an FTP list that is categorized by site name content. The site is searchable but it is really just as useful to find pages through the categories.

You can also search for FTP sites through the Web at **http://www.snoopie.com/**. This is a new service and is currently available for free but it will become a commercial service. This site has indexed a few million files on over 400 FTP sites. It works somewhat like Archie (discussed in chapter 34, "Using FTP") but much faster. In some cases it also finds more files than Archie.

Beyond these sources, if you are looking for FTP sites with content related to a particular topic, look for a newsgroup or FAQ related to that topic. For example, the **comp.sys.ibm.pc.hardware.*** FAQ has a long list of PC hardware vendors with FTP sites.

CERT Coordination Center
info.cert.org

CERT (Computer Emergency Response Team) is involved in facilitating Internet security, preventing the spread of computer viruses and worms, and providing patches for software with security problems. System administrators should look in the /pub/cert_advisories for information about how to obtain a patch or work around for a known security problem. /pub/virus-l contains archives of two virus mailing lists.

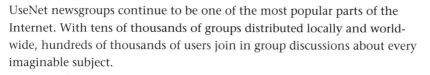

CHAPTER 48

Top UseNet Newsgroups

UseNet newsgroups continue to be one of the most popular parts of the Internet. With tens of thousands of groups distributed locally and world-wide, hundreds of thousands of users join in group discussions about every imaginable subject.

One of the biggest uses of UseNet is to discuss computing and Internet topics with newsgroups. It makes sense that computer and Internet users would have an interest in discussing these topics on UseNet. There are hundreds of groups devoted to specific topics such as answering questions about individual computer programs and pieces of computer hardware. Other groups take on broader topics such as the role of the Internet and computing in society.

This chapter presents descriptions and a few lists of some of the best and most useful UseNet groups related to computing and Internet issues. Some of the major categories of groups you will find in this chapter are:

- The best groups for information about UseNet and newsreading software
- Where to find information about general computing issues
- Groups discussing Internet services and software not related to UseNet
- Information about computer hardware, mostly related to hardware that runs the MS-DOS and Microsoft Windows operating systems
- Groups discussing computer software, mostly related to applications that run under MS-DOS and Microsoft Windows operating systems

A Look at Some Popular Groups

Before presenting the descriptions and lists of specific groups, there are two interesting lists of the most popular newsgroups to look at. The first of these two tables lists the most popular groups in order of how many people read them. The second table lists the groups that generate the most megabytes of messages across UseNet.

Before presenting the first table, you may note that the estimate of the number of total readers in the most popular groups has dropped since the previous edition of this book (if you've seen that edition, too). This is a little misleading because total UseNet readership is actually growing, but these lists are based on a small statistical sample of readers at selected news sites. The person who maintains these lists found that some of the sites were misrepresenting their readership last year and has implemented some new statistical procedures to ensure the accuracy of the data. The net result is that the estimates are now lower because the old data presented an inaccurately high number of readers. The data for both of these tables is from July 1995.

Table 48.1   Top 40 Most Popular Newsgroups by Number of Readers

Rank	Name	Number of Readers	Sites	Articles	Megabytes
1	news.announce.newusers	510,000	91%	39	0.6
2	alt.sex	260,000	57%	11,408	11.5
3	rec.humor.funny	240,000	80%	78	0.3
4	alt.sex.stories	220,000	51%	8,307	58.7
5	news.answers	200,000	88%	2,451	0.5
6	news.announce.important	180,000	87%	1	0
7	alt.binaries.pictures.erotica	170,000	47%	18,619	829.6
8	misc.jobs.offered	170000	80%	34,342	51.9
9	news.newusers.questions	160,000	87%	8,296	14
10	comp.lang.c	150,000	83%	5,161	7
11	comp.unix.questions	150,000	84%	1,718	2.9
12	rec.arts.erotica	140,000	65%	39	0.4

Rank	Name	Number of Readers	Sites	Articles	Megabytes
13	rec.humor	140,000	78%	4,752	7.1
14	rec.arts.movies. reviews	120,000	74%	146	0.7
15	comp.risks	120,000	81%	3	0.1
16	news.groups	120,000	87%	5,998	10.6
17	alt.tv.simpsons	110,000	57%	5,158	6.7
18	rec.food.recipes	110,000	74%	399	1.3
19	news.announce. newgroups	110,000	89%	184	1.5
20	comp.lang.c++	100,000	82%	5,875	8.3
21	alt.sex.bondage	99,000	54%	6,499	13.6
22	rec.arts.startrek. info	98,000	72%	48	0.2
23	misc.jobs.misc	95,000	78%	1,928	2.4
24	rec.video	93,000	74%	2,056	2.2
25	rec.arts.startrek. current	92,000	71%	5,738	7.4
26	misc.jobs. contract	90,000	76%	15,736	20.3
27	alt.sex.movies	89,000	50%	5,543	10
28	alt.bbs	89,000	63%	1,687	3.2
29	comp.os.linux. announce	89,000	76%	166	0.6
30	alt.binaries. pictures. erotica.female	88,000	40%	11,218	375.9
31	misc.education	87,000	72%	1,423	2.4
32	comp.dcom. telecom	87,000	81%	245	1.1
33	news.lists	86,000	88%	66	1.8
34	rec.nude	84,000	71%	4,582	7.3
35	alt.sex.stories.d	82,000	48%	814	0.9
36	rec.food.cooking	82,000	75%	9,137	13.7
37	rec.sport.baseball	81,000	71%	4,400	8.9
38	comp.graphics	79,000	78%	1,863	3.1
39	comp.dcom. modems	79,000	84%	5,027	8
40	alt.personals	78,000	57%	5,952	7.3

The rank and group name are self-explanatory. After that, the columns are as follows:

- *Number of readers* is the estimated total number of people reading the group worldwide.

- *Sites* is the percentage of UseNet sites that carry this group. (Recall from chapter 30, "How UseNet Works," that not all sites carry all groups.)

- *Articles* is the number of articles posted to the group in the survey month.

- *Megabytes* is the number of megabytes of posted articles in the survey month.

Table 48.2   Top 40 Most Popular Newsgroups by Number of Megabytes of Postings

Rank	Name	Megabytes	Articles	Readers	Sites
1	alt.binaries.warez.ibm-pc	1364.4	19,565	4,600	19%
2	alt.binaries.multimedia.erotica	868.5	8,666	16,000	22%
3	alt.binaries.pictures.erotica	829.6	18,619	170,000	47%
4	alt.binaries.pictures.erotica.orientals	386.8	6,346	57,000	35%
5	alt.binaries.pictures.erotica.female	375.9	11,218	88,000	40%
6	alt.binaries.pictures.erotica.male	293.6	8,433	33,000	40%
7	alt.binaries.multimedia	271.9	2,990	42,000	50%
8	alt.binaries.sounds.music	266.8	5,217	22,000	43%
9	alt.binaries.pictures.erotica.bondage	255.9	4,644	14,000	22%
10	alt.binaries.pictures.erotica.breasts	198.9	5,113	11,000	18%
11	alt.binaries.nude.celebrities	186.8	8,153	10,000	19%
12	alt.binaries.sounds.tv	182.3	3,667	14,000	36%
13	alt.binaries.pictures.supermodels	177.1	9,762	74,000	42%
14	alt.binaries.pictures.erotica.teen	170.8	6,252	14,000	18%
15	alt.binaries.pictures.erotica.amateur.female	162.9	6,042	20,000	23%

Rank	Name	Megabytes	Articles	Readers	Sites
16	alt.sex.pictures	162	9,910	53,000	40%
17	alt.binaries.pictures.erotica.pornstar	161.5	3,977	4,900	11%
18	alt.binaries.pictures.misc	159.2	4,240	66,000	51%
19	alt.binaries.pictures.boys	138.2	2,462	2,700	17%
20	alt.binaries.pictures.erotica.cartoons	137.7	3,347	21,000	26%
21	alt.binaries.pictures.erotica.anime	133	2,940	11,000	21%
22	rec.games.trading-cards.marketplace	131.5	25,644	15,000	50%
23	alt.binaries.sounds.movies	128.4	3,221	17,000	35%
24	alt.sex.pictures.female	117.5	7,795	36,000	33%
25	alt.binaries.pictures.cartoons	114.2	2,392	27,000	41%
26	alt.test	102.3	19,227	27,000	61%
27	alt.binaries.pictures.erotica.teen.male	101.3	2,582	1,500	10%
28	alt.binaries.pictures.erotica.fetish	100.4	3,697	13,000	21%
29	alt.binaries.pictures.erotica.blondes	90.1	5,066	73,000	38%
30	alt.binaries.pictures.teen-idols	84.9	2,236	3,000	15%
31	alt.binaries.pictures.celebrities	79.3	5,299	22,000	31%
32	alt.binaries.sounds.mods	75.9	2,327	15,000	35%
33	alt.binaries.games	75.6	1,773	2,700	14%
34	alt.binaries.sounds.cartoons	72.5	1,549	5,400	25%
35	alt.binaries.sounds.misc	62.9	1,395	39,000	48%
36	alt.binaries.pictures.erotica.teen.female	62.3	3,189	3,700	9%
37	alt.binaries.pictures.utilities	61.6	2,251	54,000	50%
38	alt.binaries.misc	61.6	1,361	9,600	32%
39	alt.sex.stories	58.7	8,307	220,000	51%
40	alt.sex.fetish.feet	56.6	2,704	25,000	41%

You'll notice that this table paints a markedly different picture of UseNet. Almost all of the groups that have the most megabytes of postings have to do with posting binary files, most of them of a pornographic nature. And the number one group is a place for software pirates to trade illegal software. So even though the number of people reading some of these groups is low, you can see how easy it is for the media to portray the Internet and UseNet as a cesspool.

> **Note**
>
> The data in both of these tables was compiled by Brian Reid. He occasionally gathers new data and posts it to **news.lists** and **news.groups**.

UseNet News and Software Groups

If you are reading this chapter, you must have some interest in UseNet. Here are some important newsgroups that will help you find more information about UseNet itself, specific newsgroups, and software for reading and posting news.

alt.answers

This group is for postings of FAQs about newsgroups in the alt hierarchy.

alt.culture.usenet

Read here for discussions about UseNet as a community and its related culture.

alt.test

Use this group to prove to the rest of the UseNet community that you aren't a newbie. Post your test messages here rather than in other newsgroups. Then, check this group to see if your post works. Other groups where testing is okay are **news.test** and **misc.test**. Most local hierarchies also have test groups for users at their local sites.

alt.usenet.offline-reader

Questions and answers about offline newsreaders (software that downloads all of the messages you want quickly while you are connected to UseNet and then allows you to read posts and compose replies while disconnected, saving you money on connection costs) are discussed here. Also look at **alt.usenet.offline-reader.forte-agent** for discussions specific to the Agent and Free Agent newsreaders, which have offline capabilities.

comp.answers

This moderated group contains FAQs about newsgroups in the comp hierarchy.

news.announce.newgroups

This moderated group is for posting announcements about newly approved groups (remember that in the "big seven" newsgroup hierarchies, new groups must be approved) and calls for new groups.

news.announce.newusers

This is a moderated newsgroup with informative articles about UseNet procedures, etiquette, and other essential issues that new UseNet readers should read.

news.answers

This moderated group is the home for posting FAQs and other regularly posted information.

news.groups

This group is for general discussions about newsgroups.

news.groups.questions

If you are looking for a group that discusses a topic and don't know where to look, ask where to look here.

news.groups.reviews

Moderated postings describing the content of various newsgroups.

news.lists

This moderated group is where to find up-to-date lists of available newsgroups, new news sites, top groups, and more. Other lists include FTP sites, mailing lists, and so on.

news.newusers.questions

If you have any questions about UseNet that aren't answered in any of the other information groups, here is the place to post.

news.software.nntp

Mainly of interest to persons running a news server, this group discusses Network News Transport Protocol (NNTP), which is the software protocol that runs UseNet.

news.software.readers

This group is the place for questions, answers, and announcements about news reading software.

General Computing Issues

Many groups discuss general issues about computing. These can include issues such as the role of computers and the Internet in society, uses of the Internet, and rights and responsibilities in the computing world, to name just a few.

alt.censorship

While this group is not specifically about computing issues, censorship as it relates to online services and the Internet is often debated here.

alt.culture.internet

Here are discussions of the Internet as a whole, as a community, and its related culture.

alt.cyberspace

This group hosts discussions about all aspects of the online computing community including the Internet, BBSs, special online services, and the industry that has grown up around them. The history, future, and purpose of cyberspace are all fair game here.

alt.privacy

Most of the posts in this group are about privacy as it relates to computing and the Internet. The Communications Decency Act, Clipper, and PGP have been topics of much attention here. Other related groups of interest would be **alt.privacy.anon-server**, **alt.privacy.clipper** (although posts here have dwindled since the Clinton administration backed off on this ill-fated idea), and **alt.security.pgp**.

comp.org.eff.news.talk

The Electronic Frontier Foundation (EFF) is devoted to issues that affect the basic rights of computer users. This group is used for news and discussion about issues that affect rights and freedoms of computer users. Of related interest are **comp.org.cpsr.announce** and **comp.org.cpsr.talk**. (CPSR is an acronym for Computer Professionals for Social Responsibility.)

Internet Services and Software

In addition to hundreds of groups that discuss the Internet as a whole, and various parts of the Internet, there are many groups discussing related topics. We'll look at groups about online services, BBSs, and other forms of networked computing as well as many groups related to the Internet.

alt.bbs

This group is for general discussions about bulletin board systems. As many online computing mavens are involved in BBSs and the Internet, there are a lot of UseNet users with BBS interests. So, there are many other UseNet groups that discuss more specific BBS topics. Look at table 48.3 to see if there are any groups discussing a specific topic you are interested in.

Table 48.3 Bulletin Board System (BBS) Groups	
alt.bbs.ads	alt.bbs.ra
alt.bbs.allsysop	alt.bbs.renegade
alt.bbs.citadel	alt.bbs.school
alt.bbs.doors	alt.bbs.searchlight
alt.bbs.doors.binaries	alt.bbs.tribbs
alt.bbs.drealmbbs	alt.bbs.unixbbs
alt.bbs.first-class	alt.bbs.uupcb
alt.bbs.gigo-gateway	alt.bbs.waffle
alt.bbs.internet	alt.bbs.watergate
alt.bbs.lists	alt.bbs.wildcat
alt.bbs.lists.d	alt.bbs.wme
alt.bbs.majorbbs	alt.binaries.bbs.pcboard
alt.bbs.metal	alt.binaries.bbs.renegade
alt.bbs.pcboard	comp.bbs.majorbbs
alt.bbs.pcbuucp	comp.bbs.misc
alt.bbs.powerboard	comp.bbs.tbbs
alt.bbs.public-address	comp.bbs.waffle

alt.irc

Many people enjoy using Internet Relay Chat (IRC) for real time "conversations" with many people on the Internet. This general group is a place to ask questions about how IRC works, IRC software, and IRC etiquette. Look to the following list for some more specific IRC related groups.

◀ See "What Is the Purpose of IRC?" p. 942

IX

Hot Internet Sites

alt.irc.announce

alt.irc.games

alt.irc.hottub

alt.irc.ircii

alt.irc.questions

alt.irc.undernet

alt.irc.undernet.chatzone

alt.lang.vrml

◀ See "What Is VRML?" p. 734
VRML (Virtual Reality Modeling Language) creates 3-D virtual worlds on the World Wide Web. This group discusses the coding used to create these worlds.

alt.mud

MUDs (MultiUser Dungeons) are popular forums for online gaming. This group discusses general topics applicable to any type of MUD. For discussions of specific MUD topics, see the following groups.

rec.games.mud.admin

rec.games.mud.announce

rec.games.mud.diku

rec.games.mud.lp

rec.games.mud.misc

rec.games.mud.tiny

alt.online-service

This group is for general discussions about online services, such as CompuServe, America Online, or the Microsoft Network. For discussions specific to any of the major online services, see the groups in the following list:

alt.america.online

alt.online-service.america-online

alt.online-service.compuserve

alt.online-service.delphi

alt.online-service.freenet

alt.online-service.imagination

alt.online-service.microsoft

alt.online-service.prodigy

alt.online-service.well

alt.online-service.winnet

alt.winsock

This group is the premier group for questions, answers, and announcements about any Windows Internet software that uses the WinSock protocol. This includes software for connecting to the Internet like Trumpet WinSock, NetManage Chameleon, and Windows 95's built-in SLIP/PPP connections as-well-as applications that use the WinSock connection like Netscape, Eudora, WS_FTP, and so on. The following are some related groups you may want to see:

◀ See "Installing TCP/IP Support in Windows 95," p. 127

alt.winsock.trumpet

comp.os.ms-windows.apps.winsock.misc

comp.os.ms-windows.apps.winsock.mail

alt.winsock.programming

alt.winsock.ivc

comp.os.ms-windows.apps.winsock.news

alt.www.hotjava

The Java language and the related HotJava Web browser are two of the hottest new developments on the Internet. Discussions of the Java language and coding, Java applets, and the HotJava browser are all appropriate here.

◀ See "What Is Java? " p. 731

comp.infosystems

This information systems group is a place to discuss systems and software used to exchange information. Examples of information systems include gopher, WAIS, and the Web, all of which have specific groups devoted to them. See the following list for the names of some related groups. (The Web groups are discussed later in this section.)

comp.infosystems.gopher

comp.infosystems.interpedia

comp.infosystems.wais

comp.infosystems.www.authoring.html

If you are writing your own Web pages using HTML (Hypertext Markup Language), this group is a good source for expert advice and information. Another group that may be of interest is **alt.hypertext**. If you're using SGML for Web authoring, you may want to see **comp.text.sgml**.

◀ See "How HTML Works: An Overview," p. 622

IX

Hot Internet Sites

comp.infosystems.www.browsers.ms-windows

◀ See "Important WWW Concepts," p. 458

This is a good group for World Wide Web (WWW) discussions that involve end user software and problems. Appropriate topics here would include Netscape, Mosaic, and Microsoft Internet Explorer. The following are other specific Web groups:

bit.listserv.www-vm

comp.infosystems.www.advocacy

comp.infosystems.www.announce

comp.infosystems.www.authoring.cgi

comp.infosystems.www.authoring.images

comp.infosystems.www.authoring.misc

comp.infosystems.www.browsers.mac

comp.infosystems.www.browsers.misc

comp.infosystems.www.browsers.x

comp.infosystems.www.misc

comp.infosystems.www.servers.mac

comp.infosystems.www.servers.misc

comp.infosystems.www.servers.ms-windows

comp.infosystems.www.servers.unix

comp.infosystems.www.users

comp.internet.net-happenings

This moderated group announces Internet events. Postings are organized by type, such as software or WWW. Events can be new versions of software, new Web sites, and so on.

comp.os.ms-windows.networking.ras

This group discusses RAS, which is the Remote Access Server in Windows NT and Windows 95. RAS allows you to have remote dialup access to a computer via a modem.

comp.protocols.*

> **Note**
>
> Here we are using the * as a wildcard. There is no group with the name **comp.protocols** but several groups begin with that as part of their names.

Several groups here discuss various computer protocols. The following are some groups of interest, mostly related to the Internet:

> **comp.protocols.ppp**
>
> **comp.protocols.snmp**
>
> **comp.protocols.tcp-ip**
>
> **comp.protocols.tcp-ip.domains**
>
> **comp.protocols.tcp-ip.ibmpc**

comp.security.firewalls

Firewalls are a form of protection for networks on the Internet. Discussion of firewall hardware and software are appropriate here.

Computer Hardware

This section will look at many groups where you can buy and sell computer hardware and get answers to questions about computer hardware.

alt.sys.pc-clone.*

There are several groups here where you can ask questions about several popular brands of PCs. Other users of the same brand of computer are often good sources of unofficial technical support. And if you're considering buying one of these brands, you may want to see what kind of questions and problems other users have.

> **alt.sys.pc-clone.acer**
>
> **alt.sys.pc-clone.dell**
>
> **alt.sys.pc-clone.gateway2000**
>
> **alt.sys.pc-clone.micron**
>
> **alt.sys.pc-clone.zeos**

biz.comp.hardware

You'll find ads here for buying and selling computer hardware. In addition to individual pieces of hardware, resellers can post catalogs and lists of hardware. There are also a lot of cross postings for software and services that don't belong here. A similar group is **biz.marketplace.computers.pc-clone**. There is a lot of cross posting between these groups.

comp.sys.ibm.pc.hardware

Although this group has IBM in the name, discussions of all PC hardware built around the IBM standard are appropriate. Several groups for specific hardware components follow:

comp.sys.ibm.pc.hardware.cd-rom

comp.sys.ibm.pc.hardware.chips

comp.sys.ibm.pc.hardware.comm

comp.sys.ibm.pc.hardware.misc

comp.sys.ibm.pc.hardware.networking

comp.sys.ibm.pc.hardware.storage

comp.sys.ibm.pc.hardware.systems

comp.sys.ibm.pc.hardware.video

comp.sys.ibm.pc.soundcard.advocacy

comp.sys.ibm.pc.soundcard.games

comp.sys.ibm.pc.soundcard.misc

comp.sys.ibm.pc.soundcard.music

comp.sys.ibm.pc.soundcard.tech

misc.forsale.computers

This is home to the world's largest computer garage sale. Whether you are looking to buy or sell computer hardware, this is the place to post and read. There are also many groups for specific hardware, many of which have many more posts than this main general group. Table 48.4 lists these groups.

Table 48.4   Computer Hardware for Sale Groups
misc.forsale.computers.d
misc.forsale.computers.discussion
misc.forsale.computers.memory
misc.forsale.computers.modems
misc.forsale.computers.monitors
misc.forsale.computers.net-hardware
misc.forsale.computers.other
misc.forsale.computers.other.misc
misc.forsale.computers.other.systems
misc.forsale.computers.pc-clone
misc.forsale.computers.pc-specific.audio
misc.forsale.computers.pc-specific.cards.misc
misc.forsale.computers.pc-specific.cards.video
misc.forsale.computers.pc-specific.misc
misc.forsale.computers.pc-specific.motherboards

misc.forsale.computers.pc-specific.portables

misc.forsale.computers.pc-specific.systems

misc.forsale.computers.printers

misc.forsale.computers.storage

Computer Software

The computer software groups cover a wide range of interests. Many of them provide forums to get answers about various software programs (there were thousands of messages a day in the Windows 95 groups when Windows 95 was first released) when you can't get answers from the company's official technical support. There are also places to trade tips and tricks about topics like programming and playing computer games.

alt.games

This group discusses games in general. Most of the discussions are about computer game software. There are also many groups for discussions of individual popular games. The following groups listed in table 48.5 include some binary groups where game add-ons for popular games like Doom and Descent are posted.

Table 48.5 Computer Gaming Groups	
alt.binaries.descent	**comp.sys.ibm.pc.games.action**
alt.binaries.doom	**comp.sys.ibm.pc.games.adventure**
alt.binaries.games	**comp.sys.ibm.pc.games.announce**
alt.binaries.games.discussion	**comp.sys.ibm.pc.games.flight-sim**
alt.games.dark-forces	**comp.sys.ibm.pc.games.marketplace**
alt.games.descent	**comp.sys.ibm.pc.games.misc**
alt.games.doom	**comp.sys.ibm.pc.games.rpg**
alt.games.doom.announce	**comp.sys.ibm.pc.games.strategic**
alt.games.doom.ii	**rec.games.computer.doom.announce**
alt.games.doom.newplayers	**rec.games.computer.doom.editing**
alt.games.dune-ii.virgin-games	**rec.games.computer.doom.help**
alt.games.mechwarrior2	**rec.games.computer.doom.misc**
alt.games.wing-commander	**rec.games.computer.doom.playing**
alt.mechwarrior2	**rec.games.computer.puzzle**
alt.net.and.modem.games	**rec.games.computer.xpilot**

alt.news.microsoft

This group is used for general questions and answers about any Microsoft products.

biz.comp.software

You'll find ads here for buying and selling computer software. In addition to individual programs, resellers can post catalogs and lists of software. There are also a lot of cross postings for hardware and services that don't belong here.

comp.os.ms-windows.*

There are many groups that discuss the Microsoft Windows software. In the list of groups in table 48.6, you will find groups that discuss all versions of Windows (3.x, 95, and NT). There are groups for users, system administrators, new users, and experts. (Programmers should see the coverage of programming groups later in this section.)

Table 48.6   Microsoft Windows Groups
comp.os.ms-windows.advocacy
comp.os.ms-windows.announce
comp.os.ms-windows.misc
comp.os.ms-windows.networking.misc
comp.os.ms-windows.nt.admin.misc
comp.os.ms-windows.nt.admin.networking
comp.os.ms-windows.nt.advocacy
comp.os.ms-windows.nt.misc
comp.os.ms-windows.nt.pre-release
comp.os.ms-windows.nt.setup
comp.os.ms-windows.nt.setup.hardware
comp.os.ms-windows.nt.setup.misc
comp.os.ms-windows.nt.software.backoffice
comp.os.ms-windows.nt.software.compatibility
comp.os.ms-windows.setup
comp.os.ms-windows.win95.misc
comp.os.ms-windows.win95.setup
comp.os.ms-windows.networking.tcp-ip
comp.os.ms-windows.networking.windows
comp.os.ms-windows.nt.admin.misc

comp.os.ms-windows.nt.software.services

comp.os.ms-windows.pre-release

comp.os.ms-windows.video

comp.os.ms-windows.apps

This group discusses general issues about applications software that runs in Microsoft Windows. Several groups that discuss specific types of software follow:

comp.databases.ms-access

comp.os.ms-windows.apps.comm

comp.os.ms-windows.apps.financial

comp.os.ms-windows.apps.misc

comp.apps.spreadsheets

comp.os.ms-windows.apps.utilities

comp.os.ms-windows.apps.word-proc

comp.os.ms-windows.programmer

Programmers writing software for use in any version of Windows will find this and the following related groups to be good for discussion of general Windows programming issues. Table 48.7 is a list of some specific groups of interest.

Table 48.7 Microsoft Windows Programming Groups
comp.os.ms-windows.programmer.controls
comp.os.ms-windows.programmer.drivers
comp.os.ms-windows.programmer.graphics
comp.os.ms-windows.programmer.memory
comp.os.ms-windows.programmer.misc
comp.os.ms-windows.programmer.multimedia
comp.os.ms-windows.programmer.networks
comp.os.ms-windows.programmer.nt.kernel-mode
comp.os.ms-windows.programmer.ole
comp.os.ms-windows.programmer.tools
comp.os.ms-windows.programmer.tools.mfc
comp.os.ms-windows.programmer.tools.misc
comp.os.ms-windows.programmer.tools.owl

(continues)

Table 48.7   Continued
comp.os.ms-windows.programmer.tools.winsock
comp.os.ms-windows.programmer.vxd
comp.os.ms-windows.programmer.win32
comp.os.ms-windows.programmer.winhelp

Miscellaneous Computing Topics

Here are a few remaining computing groups that don't fit neatly into any of the other categories in this chapter.

alt.binaries.sounds.d

Who doesn't like to add a few sounds to their computer to spice up Windows events or just to listen to for fun? This group is for discussion of sound files. Sounds and useful sound software are posted in the following groups:

alt.binaries.sounds.cartoons

alt.binaries.sounds.midi

alt.binaries.sounds.misc

alt.binaries.sounds.mods

alt.binaries.sounds.movies

alt.binaries.sounds.music

alt.binaries.sounds.samples.music

alt.binaries.sounds.tv

alt.binaries.sounds.utilities

alt.cd-rom

This group discusses a range of CD-ROM hardware and software topics. New product announcements, hardware and software for sale, and questions and answers about CD-ROM setup and use are common topics here.

alt.zines

This group is for announcements about new zines, new issues, calls for contributors, and discussions about popular zines.

biz.comp.services

Announcements and advertisements about computing services are here. These include legitimate services but beware of chain letters, pyramid schemes, and other low-life offers designed only to separate you from your money. A similar group is **biz.marketplace.services.computers**. There is a lot of cross posting between these groups.

comp.publish.cdrom.multimedia
Multimedia software creators can use this group. Other related groups of interest include **comp.publish.cdrom.hardware** and **comp.publish.cdrom.software**.

Where to Find More Groups

This chapter just scratches the surface of the groups available in UseNet. We've concentrated on computing and Internet related groups in this chapter, as these will have the most relevance to most of the people reading this book. But we know that you have some interests outside of computing and would like to find some groups of special interest to you. Here are a couple of ways to find more groups.

Use Your Newsreader Group List

If you are using any of the popular newsreaders such as Agent (or the free version Free Agent) or NewsXpress, you have a complete list of the groups available at your news site handy in the newsreader. See chapters 30 and 31 for discussions of how to search for newsgroups within each of these news programs. Use this feature to search for a key word that is part of the topic you are looking for. Since the names of most groups are fairy self-explanatory, you can probably find what you are looking for.

Look at David Lawrence's Lists of Groups

David Lawrence keeps a list of newsgroups called the List of Active Newsgroups. The list includes names and one-line descriptions of all the active groups (groups that still have messages posted to them and that haven't been replaced or deleted from official use) in the major hierarchies. This list is posted in two parts on a regular basis to the **news.lists**, **news.groups**, **news.announce.newgroups**, and **news.answers** groups. Check any of these for the most recent copy of the list. If it isn't there when you check (since it may have been expired from your news server), you can always get a recent copy by FTP from **rtfm.mit.edu**. There, it's in the directory /pub/usenet-by-group/news.lists. From there, change to one of the subdirectories with the name of one of the groups listed previously. If you are looking for groups in the alt hierarchy or one of the other alternative hierarchies, David Lawrence's list of groups in the Alternative Newsgroup Hierarchies is posted in three parts to these same newsgroups and FTP sites.

IX

Hot Internet Sites

> **Note**
>
> Remember that your news site may not carry all of the groups in these lists. After you find a group in this list, you'll have to check your newsreader to see if it's available on your site. If it isn't there, contact your site's administrator directly if you want to request that they carry it.

If All Else Fails...

You've read this chapter, looked through the list of groups in your newsreader, and searched all through Lawrence's lists and still can't find a group discussing a topic you need. Is there any way left to find a group?

Sure. Ask someone that knows. The best places to ask these questions are **news.newusers.questions** and **news.groups.questions**. Post a short message to one of these groups plainly stating the topic you are looking for. If a group exists, someone will probably respond to you by following up your post or e-mailing you an answer. Don't post your question to dozens of groups all over the Net, that will only make many enemies for you. Be sure the subject explains the post (such as "Looking for an Iguana group") as this will make it easier for someone to help you. (The answer to this post would be **rec.pets.herp** or **sci.bio.herp**, depending on whether your iguana interests are scientific or recreational.)

CHAPTER 49

Top Gopher Sites

There was a time when Gopher servers were popping up all over the Internet and Gopher was heralded as the future of the Internet. But, times have changed and most organizations that are putting new servers on the Internet are putting up Web servers (and FTP sites to supplement them). Gopher has been relegated to second class citizen by many users.

But there are still many good Gopher servers on the Internet. In fact, some of the best Web sites began their existence as Gopher sites. Likewise, many of the best FTP sites are also accessible by Gopher.

With these factors in mind, we have not included an extensive list of Gopher sites in this book. We've focused our energy on the more popular Web and FTP sites. But, we have included a listing of essential sites here broken down into these two categories:

■ Web and FTP sites listed in chapters 46 and 47 of this book that are accessible by Gopher

■ Some key Gopher servers of interest that don't have equivalent servers in other chapters

Gopher Sites that Correspond to Servers in Other Chapters

Most of the best Gopher sites on the Internet have added a Web or FTP server. Many of these sites were good enough or important enough in the world of the Internet and computing that they have been listed in one of the other chapters. Rather than repeat those descriptions here, the following table is a list of selected good sites from chapters 46 and 47 that have Gopher servers with the same (or related) information. Each entry in the table includes the site name, the address to use for Gopher access, and the chapter where you will find a description of the WWW or FTP server.

Users with Web browsers or an FTP client will probably find it better and easier to use these sites through their WWW or FTP address.

Site Name	Address	Chapter with Detailed Coverage
InterNIC	**gopher.internic.net**	47
Merit Network Information Center	**nic.merit.edu**	46
Electronic Frontier Foundation	**gopher.eff.org**	46, 47
Microsoft	**gopher.microsoft.com**	46, 47
Creative Labs	**gopher.creaf.com**	46, 47
Novell	**gopher.novell.com**	46, 47
PSI	**gopher.psi.net**	46
CPSR	**gopher.cpsr.org**	46, 47
Winsite	**gopher.winsite.com**	46, 47
Papa WinSock-L	**papa.indstate.edu**	47
WUArchive	**wuarchive.wustl.edu**	47
Internet Wiretap	**wiretap.spies.com**	47
Internet Engineering Task Force	**ietf.cnri.reston.va.us**	46

Other Gophers

Just because the WWW is much more popular than Gopher, it doesn't mean there's nothing of value in gopherspace. This section looks at a few selected Gopher servers with Internet and computing information that may be of interest. Some of these only exist as Gopher sites while a few of them have WWW or FTP servers that weren't listed elsewhere in this book.

University of Minnesota
gopher.tc.umn.edu

This is the best place on the Net to get information about Gopher. This site is often referred to as the Mother Gopher. The University of Minnesota is the home of the Gopher system and you'll find expert information about Gopher server and client software here. The main menu item to check out here is "Information About Gopher," which has several submenus about Gopher. Another menu choice that will be of real use is "Other Gopher and Information Servers." This menu has several lists of Gopher servers arranged and categorized. The phone books at this site can be useful, especially for someone who's at a particular educational institution.

NSTN
gopher.nstn.ca

This site has an option called Internet Public Library. Choose the "NSTN CYBRARY" option from the main menu to get to this and look at these menu choices:

> Beginner's Corner (Internet Guides)
>
> Library Catalogs Worldwide (Hytelnet)
>
> Internet Information by SUBJECT
>
> Internet SEARCH Facilities

Software Tool and Die: The World
obi.std.com

Some of the information here is available only to the subscribers of this Internet service provider. But, the following publicly accessible menu choices should be of interest:

> Internet and USENET Phone Books
>
> Bulletin Boards via the Internet
>
> FTP
>
> Internet Information and Resources

University of Southern California Gopher Jewels
cwis.usc.edu

This site is home to a listing of Gopher servers known as Gopher Jewels. To get to this, choose Other Gophers and Information Servers from the main menu then choose Gopher Jewels. The main menu here has a listing of menu choices explaining how Gopher Jewels is organized. The menu option Jump to Gopher Jewels Main Menu takes you to the menu for Gopher servers arranged by subject category. Subject categories include education, business, government, Internet and computing, law, and many other topics.

Counterpoint Publishing's Internet Services
gopher.counterpoint.com

This server hosts some otherwise hard to find information about the U.S. federal and state governments. Information here includes the United States Federal Register, United States Commerce Business Daily, Code of Federal Regulations, and State Environmental Regulations.

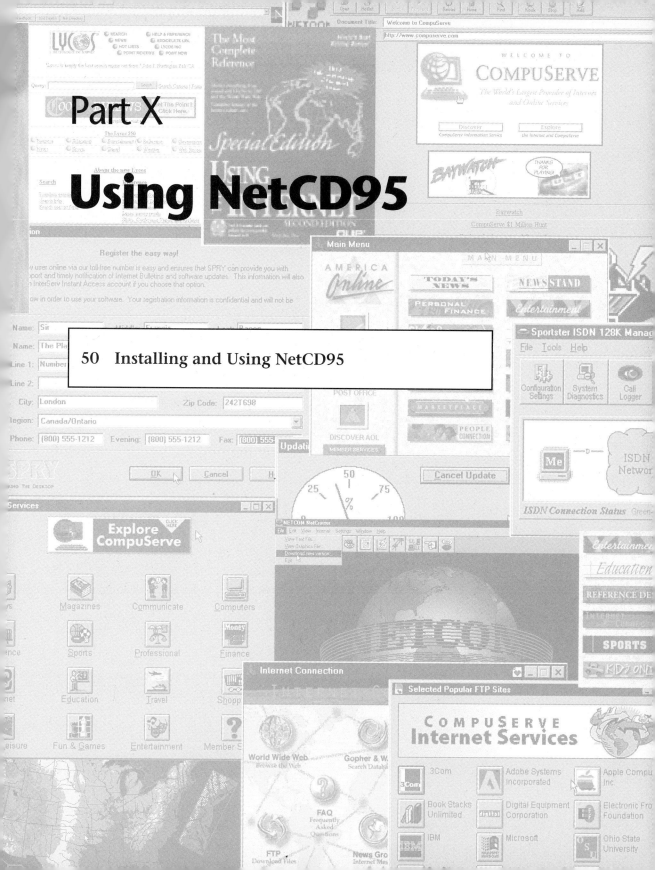

Part X

Using NetCD95

50 Installing and Using NetCD95

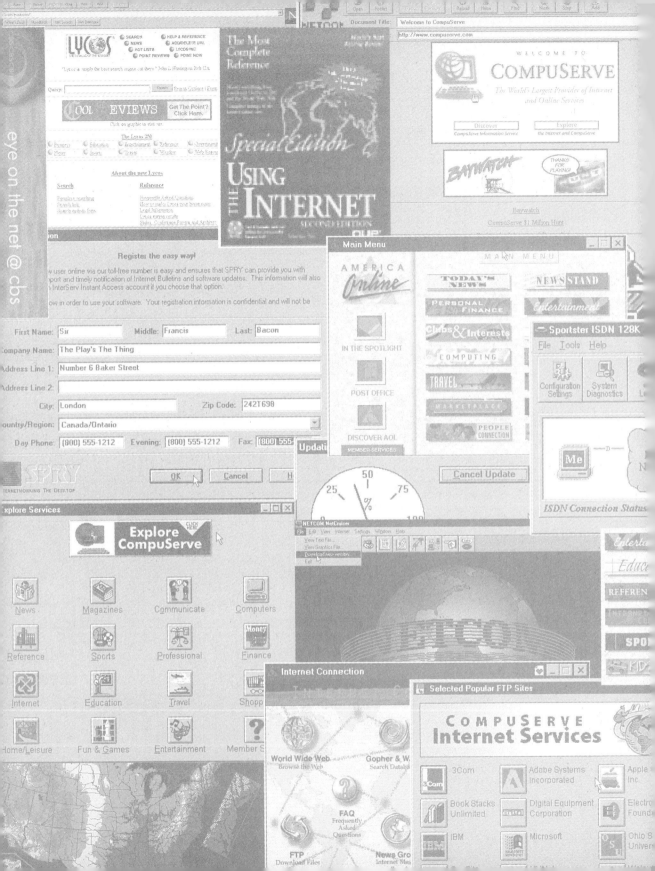

CHAPTER 50

Installing and Using NetCD95

If you've read the other chapters in this book, you may be turning to this to find a list of software to use with one of the areas of the Internet you've read about. Or if you're like me, this may be the first chapter you turn to when you buy the book (or even before you buy it). Regardless of which order you read the book, this chapter is here to present a complete list of the software on the enclosed NetCD95.

There is a huge variety of software on NetCD95. We've spent hundreds of hours online over the last few months looking for new and useful programs to include here.

If you want to learn more about all the contents of NetCD95, load the file net1.htm from NetCD95 (see fig. 50.1). This hypertext HTML document includes links to descriptions of all the software on NetCD95.

The files for most of the programs are in either ZIP or self-extracting format. These files can be extracted from the CD-ROM to your hard drive using WinZip or any other ZIP utility.

From the NetCD95 page, click the Files link button to move to the page listing all the categories of files (see fig. 50.2).

To see the software on NetCD95 in any of these categories, click the category in the table. This opens a page listing all the software in that category. The list includes the name of each program, a link to copy the software from the CD to your hard drive, and a link to information about the program. (This information may be on NetCD95 or at the Web site for the program.)

At the bottom of each page in the category lists, the Files link takes you back to the main page with the table listing all the categories.

Fig. 50.1

The Main NetCD95 page is shown here in Netscape. At the bottom of the page, you'll find a link to Que's home page on the Web and an e-mail link to our technical support department.

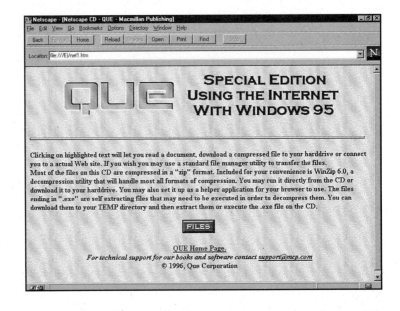

Fig. 50.2

The table on this page has links to all the categories of software on the CD-ROM. The Sites link below the table provides a list of links to valuable online sources of software and information.

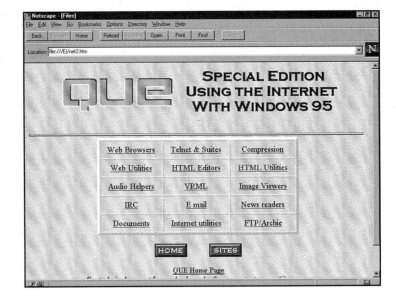

> **Note**
>
> Much of the software on NetCD95 is *shareware*. Shareware is software you can try before you buy. It is not free, but it is a neat idea.
>
> Shareware software is written by talented and creative individuals. Quite often their software provides the same power and options found in retail software. However, with shareware you have the advantage of being able to try and evaluate the product before paying for it.
>
> All the shareware on NetCD95 includes a text file (or instructions within the program itself) explaining the license and registration procedure for the program. After reading the license, you are obligated to pay for the software if you use it beyond the trial period explained in the license. Paying the registration fee often (but not always) can give you additional benefits such as technical support from the author, a printed manual, or a registration code that unlocks additional features in the software. Consult the documents with the individual programs to see what registration will get you. Registering will often put you on the program author's mailing list so that you receive information about updates, bug fixes, and new versions.
>
> Some of the other software on NetCD95 falls into 2 other categories: *freeware* and *public domain*. Freeware software is like shareware except that there is no fee to use it. For both shareware and freeware, the author has registered and maintained the copyright on the software, meaning that the author controls the rights to sell, redistribute, or modify the software. Public domain software differs in that the author has freely given up all claim to the copyright so that anyone can do anything they please with it.
>
> Please read the documentation with each program carefully to determine which category it falls into. If you are interested in using the software or redistributing it and can't determine from the documentation if there are any restrictions, there is usually an e-mail address for the author so you can make contact and determine for sure what is and isn't allowed.

All-in-One-Suites

- Instant Interramp for Windows 95
- Internet Chameleon Websurfer
- NetCruiser
- NetShark Lite
- Pipeline

- PSINet
- Turnpike
- WinNet

E-Mail

- Eudora
- Pegasus
- WinBiff

UseNet News

- NewsXpress
- Trumpet NewsReader
- WinVN

FTP and Archie

- Cute FTP
- FTP Serv-U
- FTP Internet Connection
- Trumpet Archie
- Trumpet FTP
- Windows FTP Daemon
- WS_FTP
- WSArchie

World Wide Web

- AmberGL
- Hot Java
- I-Comm
- Indexer
- Fountain

- HomeSpace Builder
- Microsoft Internet Explorer
- NavFlyer
- NetShark Lite
- Panorama
- SlipKnot
- Microsoft Virtual Explorer
- VRScout
- VRWeb
- Web Space
- WebFX
- WebWatch
- WorldView

HTML Editors

- Color Wizard
- Color Manipulator
- EasyHelp
- HotDog
- HTML Assistant for Windows
- HTML Author
- HTML Easy Pro
- HTML Notepad
- HTML Writer
- HTMLed
- Kenn Nesbitt's WebEdit
- Live MarkUp
- Microsoft Internet Assistant
- SoftQuad Hotmetal
- Web Spinner
- Web Wizard: The Duke of URL
- Webber

- WebEdit
- WebForms
- WebWebMania

Multimedia Editors and Viewers

- Adobe's Acrobat Reader
- ACDSee
- CoolEdit
- Drag and View
- GraphX Viewer
- LView Pro for Windows 95
- MapThis
- Midi Gate
- Mod4Win
- MPEGPLAY
- Paint Shop Pro
- PolyView
- Quicktime Player
- QuickTime VR Player
- Real Audio
- Streamworks
- VuePrint
- Web Image
- Wham
- WinJpeg
- WinECJ
- WPLANY

IRC

- IRC 4 Windows
- Trumpet Chat
- Visual IRC
- WS-IRC

Utilities and Other Software

- Anzio Lite
- ARJ
- CommNet For Windows
- CRT
- Drag and Zip
- Drag and File
- F-Prot
- Finger
- Finger Daemon
- Here
- Internet Control Center
- Internet Tele Cafe
- IP Manager
- NetTerm
- NetTools
- PC BinHex
- PowWow
- Pueblo 3d Mud
- Stilleto
- Surfer Central
- Trumpet Telnet
- UUCode
- WinCode
- WinWAIS
- WinZip
- WSChat

Internet Documents

- Internet Service Provider Lists
- List of FTP Sites
- RFCs
- STDs
- FYIs

Part XI

Appendixes

A   Country Codes

B   Time Zone Code Table

C   Vendor Contacts for Selected Internet Software and Services

D   Glossary

APPENDIX A
Country Codes

Most organizations in countries outside of the U.S. have two-letter codes appended to the end of their Internet addresses to indicate the countries they are in. The following is a list of country codes you might encounter in your journeys around the Internet.

Code	Country
AD	Andorra
AE	United Arab Emirates
AF	Afghanistan
AG	Antigua and Barbuda
AI	Anguilla
AL	Albania
AM	Armenia
AN	Netherlands Antilles
AO	Angola
AQ	Antarctica
AR	Argentina
AS	American Samoa
AT	Austria
AU	Australia
AW	Aruba
AZ	Azerbaijan
BA	Bosnia and Herzegovina
BB	Barbados
BD	Bangladesh

(continues)

Code	Country
BE	Belgium
BF	Burkina Faso
BG	Bulgaria
BH	Bahrain
BI	Burundi
BJ	Benin
BM	Bermuda
BN	Brunei Darussalam
BO	Bolivia
BR	Brazil
BS	Bahamas
BT	Bhutan
BV	Bouvet Island
BW	Botswana
BY	Belarus
BZ	Belize
CA	Canada
CC	Cocos (Keeling) Islands
CF	Central African Republic
CG	Congo
CH	Switzerland
CI	Cote D'Ivoire (Ivory Coast)
CK	Cook Islands
CL	Chile
CM	Cameroon
CN	China
CO	Colombia
CR	Costa Rica
CS	Czechoslovakia (former)
CU	Cuba
CV	Cape Verde
CX	Christmas Island
CY	Cyprus
CZ	Czech Republic
DE	Germany

Code	Country
DJ	Djibouti
DK	Denmark
DM	Dominica
DO	Dominican Republic
DZ	Algeria
EC	Ecuador
EE	Estonia
EG	Egypt
EH	Western Sahara
ER	Eritrea
ES	Spain
ET	Ethiopia
FI	Finland
FJ	Fiji
FK	Falkland Islands (Malvinas)
FM	Micronesia
FO	Faroe Islands
FR	France
FX	France, Metropolitan
GA	Gabon
GB	Great Britain (UK)
GD	Grenada
GE	Georgia
GF	French Guiana
GH	Ghana
GI	Gibraltar
GL	Greenland
GM	Gambia
GN	Guinea
GP	Guadeloupe
GQ	Equatorial Guinea
GR	Greece
GS	South Georgia and South Sandwich Islands
GT	Guatemala

(continues)

XI

Appendixes

Code	Country
GU	Guam
GW	Guinea-Bissau
GY	Guyana
HK	Hong Kong
HM	Heard and McDonald Islands
HN	Honduras
HR	Croatia (Hrvatska)
HT	Haiti
HU	Hungary
ID	Indonesia
IE	Ireland
IL	Israel
IN	India
IO	British Indian Ocean Territory
IQ	Iraq
IR	Iran
IS	Iceland
IT	Italy
JM	Jamaica
JO	Jordan
JP	Japan
KE	Kenya
KG	Kyrgyzstan
KH	Cambodia
KI	Kiribati
KM	Comoros
KN	Saint Kitts and Nevis
KP	Korea (North)
KR	Korea (South)
KW	Kuwait
KY	Cayman Islands
KZ	Kazakhstan
LA	Laos
LB	Lebanon
LC	Saint Lucia

Code	Country
LI	Liechtenstein
LK	Sri Lanka
LR	Liberia
LS	Lesotho
LT	Lithuania
LU	Luxembourg
LV	Latvia
LY	Libya
MA	Morocco
MC	Monaco
MD	Moldova
MG	Madagascar
MH	Marshall Islands
MK	Macedonia
ML	Mali
MM	Myanmar
MN	Mongolia
MO	Macau
MP	Northern Mariana Islands
MQ	Martinique
MR	Mauritania
MS	Montserrat
MT	Malta
MU	Mauritius
MV	Maldives
MW	Malawi
MX	Mexico
MY	Malaysia
MZ	Mozambique
NA	Namibia
NC	New Caledonia
NE	Niger
NF	Norfolk Island
NG	Nigeria

XI

Appendixes

(continues)

Code	Country
NI	Nicaragua
NL	Netherlands
NO	Norway
NP	Nepal
NR	Nauru
NT	Neutral Zone
NU	Niue
NZ	New Zealand (Aotearoa)
OM	Oman
PA	Panama
PE	Peru
PF	French Polynesia
PG	Papua New Guinea
PH	Philippines
PK	Pakistan
PL	Poland
PM	St. Pierre and Miquelon
PN	Pitcairn
PR	Puerto Rico
PT	Portugal
PW	Palau
PY	Paraguay
QA	Qatar
RE	Reunion
RO	Romania
RU	Russian Federation
RW	Rwanda
SA	Saudi Arabia
Sb	Solomon Islands
SC	Seychelles
SD	Sudan
SE	Sweden
SG	Singapore
SH	St. Helena
SI	Slovenia

Code	Country
SJ	Svalbard and Jan Mayen Islands
SK	Slovak Republic
SL	Sierra Leone
SM	San Marino
SN	Senegal
SO	Somalia
SR	Suriname
ST	Sao Tome and Principe
SU	USSR (former)
SV	El Salvador
SY	Syria
SZ	Swaziland
TC	Turks and Caicos Islands
TD	Chad
TF	French Southern Territories
TG	Togo
TH	Thailand
TJ	Tajikistan
TK	Tokelau
TM	Turkmenistan
TN	Tunisia
TO	Tonga
TP	East Timor
TR	Turkey
TT	Trinidad and Tobago
TV	Tuvalu
TW	Taiwan
TZ	Tanzania
UA	Ukraine
UG	Uganda
UK	United Kingdom
UM	U.S. Minor Outlying Islands
US	United States
UY	Uruguay

(continues)

XI

Appendixes

Code	Country
UZ	Uzbekistan
VA	Vatican City State (Holy See)
VC	Saint Vincent and the Grenadines
VE	Venezuela
VG	Virgin Islands (British)
VI	Virgin Islands (U.S.)
VN	Vietnam
VU	Vanuatu
WF	Wallis and Futuna Islands
WS	Samoa
YE	Yemen
YT	Mayotte
YU	Yugoslavia
ZA	South Africa
ZM	Zambia
ZR	Zaire
ZW	Zimbabwe

Time Zone Code Table

Talking to people and connecting to sites on the Internet is so easy that you may forget that the people you're talking to may be ending their day while you're just starting yours. When you send mail to someone, you might want do it when you know that person is likely to be using his or her Internet account. Or, you may want to try to connect to machines in the middle of the night—when the machines are less busy.

An easy way to find out what time it is to use the time zone property sheet of the Windows 95 clock utility. If the clock is not displayed in your taskbar, turn it on. To do so:

1. Choose Settings, Taskbar from the Start button.
2. Select the Show Clock check box.
3. Choose OK to close the Taskbar Properties Window and enable the clock.

You should see a digital clock on the far right of your taskbar. To open the Date/Time Properties window and view time zone information:

1. Right click the clock and select Adjust Date/Time. The Date/Time Properties window opens.
2. Choose the Time Zone tab. You should see the time zone map shown in figure B.1.
3. Click the area of the world where the machine or person you want to contact lives. The list box above the map shows you the name of the time zone and the time there relative to Greenwich Mean Time.
4. You can also click the list box above the map and get a list of major cities around the world (see fig. B.2). The list is organized relative to Greenwich Mean Time, not alphabetically, so you may have to look through the list a little before you find the city you're looking for (or one close to it).

Fig. B.1
The Date/Time
Properties window
of the taskbar
clock lets you view
time zones from
around the world.

Fig. B.2
The Time Zone list
box contains
entries for all of
the world time
zones with major
cities in the time
zones shown.

> **Note**
>
> Greenwich Mean Time (GMT) is the current time in Greenwich, England. All time zone times are given relative to GMT. For example, the Eastern Standard time zone in the U.S. and Canada is GMT -05:00. This means that when it's noon in Greenwich, England, it's 7:00 a.m. in the Eastern Standard time zone. If you know your local time and how it's related to GMT, you can figure out the current time in Greenwich and in any other time zone.

To make it a little easier to find the time in some of the major cities of the world, an alphabetized list is given in table B.1.

Table B.1   Major Cities, Territories, and Islands, and Their GMT Time

Adelaide, Australia GMT+09:30

Adis Abeba, Ethiopia GMT+03:00

Alaska, USA GMT-09:00

Amsterdam, Holland GMT+01:00

Aukland, New Zealand GMT+12:00

Athens, Greece GMT+02:00

Baghdad, Iraq GMT +03:00

Bangkok, Thailand GMT+07:00

Beijing, China GMT+08:00

Beirut, Lebanon GMT+02:00

Berlin, Germany GMT+01:00

Bern, Switzerland GMT+01:00

Bogota, Columbia GMT-05:00

Bombay, India GMT+05:30

Brasillia, Brazil GMT-03:00

Brisbane, Australia GMT+10:00

Brussels, Belguim GMT+01:00

Budapest, Hungary GMT+01:00

Buenos Aires, Argentina GMT-03:00

Cairo, Egypt GMT+02:00

Calcutta, India GMT+5:30

Calgary, Alberta, Canada GMT-07:00

Canberra, Australia GMT+10:00

Caracas, Venezuala GMT-04:00

Casablanca, Morroco GMT

Chicago, Illinois, USA GMT-06:00

Copenhagen, Denmark GMT+01:00

Dakar, Senegal GMT

Dallas, Texas, USA GMT-06:00

Damascus, Syria GMT+02:00

Dar es Salaam, Tanzania GMT+03:00

Denver, Colorado, USA GMT-07:00

Dublin, Ireland GMT

Edinburgh, Scotland GMT

Guam (US territory) GMT+10:00

Hanoi, Vietnam GMT+07:00

Honolulu, Hawaii, USA GMT-10:00

Helsinki, Finland GMT+02:00

Hong Kong (British colony) GMT+08:00

XI

Appendixes

(continues)

Table B.1 Continued

Istanbul, Turkey GMT+02:00

Java Island (Indonesia) GMT+07:00

Jerusalem, Israel GMT +02:00

Johannesburg, South Africa GMT+02:00

Juneau, Alaska, USA GMT-09:00

Kabul, Afghanistan GMT+04:30

Kampala, Uganda GMT+03:00

Khartoum, Sudan GMT+02:00

Kiev, Ukraine GMT+02:00

Kigali, Rwanda GMT+02:00

Kinshasha, Zaire GMT+01:00

Kuala Lumpur, Malaysia GMT+8:00

Kuwait, Kuwait GMT +03:00

La Paz, Bolivia GMT-04:00

Lima, Peru GMT-05:00

Lisbon, Portugal GMT+01:00

London, England GMT

Los Angeles, California, USA GMT-08:00

Madras, India GMT+05:30

Madrid, Spain GMT+01:00

Manila, Philippines GMT+08:00

Melbourne, Australia GMT+10:00

Mexico City, Mexico GMT-06:00

Mogadishu, Somalia GMT+03:00

Montreal, Quebec, Canada GMT-05:00

Moscow, Russia GMT+03:00

Nairobi, Kenya GMT +03:00

New Delhi, India GMT+05:30

New York, New York, USA GMT-05:00

Nicosia, Cyprus GMT+02:00

Osaka, Japan GMT+09:00

Oslo, Norway GMT+01:00

Paris, France GMT+01:00

Papua, New Guinea GMT+10:00

Perth, Australia GMT+08:00

Phnom Penh, Cambodia GMT+07:00

Prague, Czech Republic GMT+01:00

Reykjavik, Iceland GMT

Riyadh, Saudi Arabia GMT+03:00

Rome, Italy GMT+01:00

St. Johns, Newfoundland, Canada GMT-03:00

St. Petersburg, Russia GMT+03:00

Santiago, Chile GMT-04:00

Sapporo, Japan GMT+09:00

Sarajevo, Bosnia-Herzegovina GMT+01:00

Saskatoon, Saskatchewan, Canada GMT-06:00

Seoul, South Korea GMT+09:00

Singapore GMT+08:00

Stockholm, Sweden GMT+01:00

Sumatra Island (Indonesia) GMT+0700

Sydney, Australia GMT+10:00

Tahiti (French Polynesia) GMT-09:30

Taipei, Taiwan GMT+08:00

Tehran, Iran GMT+03:30

Tijuana, Mexico GMT-08:00

Tokyo, Japan GMT+09:00

Toronto, Ontario, Canada GMT-05:00

Tripoli, Libya GMT+01:00

Vancouver, British Columbia, Canada GMT-08:00

Vienna, Austria GMT+01:00

Vilnius, Lithuania GMT+02:00

Warsaw, Poland GMT+01:00

Winnipeg, Manitoba, Canada GMT-06:00

Zagreb, Croatia GMT+01:00

Zurich, Switzerland GMT+01:00

XI

Appendixes

Vendor Contacts for Selected Internet Software and Services

There are many different software products you can choose from to access Internet services. We've talked about a number of them in this book, and many of them are included on NetCD95.

Some of the software is freeware, and you don't have to worry about paying any registration fees (however, sometimes there is a commercial version of freeware available). Much of the software is shareware, and if you use it on a regular basis you should pay the registration fee to the author. A few Internet services are so new (or so unusual) that only commercial software for using those services is available.

This chapter lists vendor contact information for shareware and commercial Internet software. Vendors of freeware are also listed when there is a commercial version of the software available. In addition, major Internet service providers are listed, as well as vendors that provide Internet connection hardware and software.

Internet Applications

Agent
Agent
c/o Forte
2141 Palomar Airport Road, Suite 100
Carlsbad, CA 92009
(619)431-6496
(619)431-6497 Fax
Web: **http://www.forteinc.com/forte/**

Electronic version of Agent and manuals is $29. Shrink-wrapped version of Agent (disks and printed manuals) is $40 + $5 shipping ($8 to Canada, $16 elsewhere). There is also a freeware version of this software.

Digiphone
Third Planet Publishing Inc.
P.O. Box 797728
Dallas, TX 75379
(214)713-2630
(214)713-7613 Fax
E-mail: **3pp@planeteers.com**

Eudora Light
QUEST
Qualcomm, Inc.
6455 Lusk Boulevard
San Diego, CA 92121-2779
(619)658-1291
(619)658-1500 Fax
(800)2-EUDORA Ordering Information for Eudora Pro
Product Literature E-mail: **eudora-lit@qualcomm.com**
Web: **http://www.qualcomm.com**

Cost of Eudora Pro is $89 for a single user. Eudora Light is freeware.

Gmud32
Dan Kelly
1136 Mellon Street, Apt. #1
Pittsburgh, PA 15206-1526
E-mail: **entropy@infobahn.icubed.com**

Shareware registration fee is $20.

HotDog
Sausage Software
Level 1
10 Stutt Avenue
Doncaster 3108
Australia
+61 3 9816 3922 Fax
E-mail: **sales@sausage.com**
Web: **http://www.sausage.com/howorder.htm**

HotDog is shareware. Cost for the standard version is US $29.95, Pro is
$99.95. Payment form is credit card (Bankcard, Mastercard, Visa), interna-
tional money order, or check. Credit card payment by fax, secure online registration (when working), e-mail, or post. Money order or check (payable to
Sausage Software) can be mailed to this address.

Internet Phone

Vocaltec, Inc.

157 Veteran's Drive

Northvale, NJ 07640

(201)768-9400

(201)768-8893 Fax

E-mail: **info@vocaltec.com**

Web: **http://www.vocaltec.com**

$69 registration fee. To have media shipped to you, add $10 for shipping and handling.

LView Pro

MMedia Research

LView Pro Registration

1501 East Hallandale Beach Boulevard, #254

Hallandale, FL 33009

(305)458-9698 Fax

E-mail: **mmedia@world.std.com**

Web: **http://mirror.wwa.com/mirror/busdir/lview/lview.htm**

$30 registration fee. To have media shipped to you, add $5 for shipping and handling.

Microsoft Products (Internet Explorer, Internet Assistant)

Microsoft Sales Information Center

One Microsoft Way

Redmond, WA 98052-6399

(206)882-8080

(800)426-9400 Sales

(206)936-7329 Fax

(206)936-6735 BBS

Web: **http://www.microsoft.com**

Midi Gate

Pierre R. Schwob, President

PRS—Program Research & Software Corporation

502 Kinwick Centre

32 Hollywood Road

Hong Kong

(+852) 2543-7773

(+852) 2541-9843 Fax

E-mail: **prs@prs.com**

Web: **http://www.prs.net/**

There is a $10 registration fee.

Mod4Win
Jens Puchert
JSInc.
P.O. Box 6173
Syracuse, NY 13217-6173
(315)451-8150
E-mail: **jpuchert@mailbox.syr.edu**
Web: **http://scuzzy.fmmo.ca/mediatrix/mod4win.htm**

$30 registration fee. To have media shipped to you, add $5 shipping and handling fee.

MPEGPLAY

Michael Simmons
P.O. Box 506
Nedlands WA 6009
Australia
(Int)+ 61 9 344 1998
E-mail: **michael@ecel.uwa.edu.au**

$25 registration fee. To have media shipped to you, add $5 shipping and handling fee.

Netscape
Netscape Communications Corporation
501 East Middlefield Road
Mountain View, CA 94043
(800)NETSITE
E-mail: **info@mcom.com**
Web: **http://merchant.netscape.com/netstore/index.html**

Netscape is free for educational or not-for-profit use. Commercial users are allowed a 90-day evaluation period, after which a license fee must be paid to Netscape Communications Corporation. There are several different purchase options ranging from $39 for a copy of the software to $59 for a copy of the software and hardcopy documentation.

Paint Shop Pro

JASC, Inc.
P.O. Box 44997
Eden Prairie, MN 55344

(800)622-2793
(612)930-9171 Voice
(612)930-9172 Fax

$69 registration fee. To have media shipped to you in the U.S., add $5 shipping and handling fee. (See order form included with product for information on other products and shipping fees.)

Panorama Pro
SoftQuad, Inc.
56 Alberfoyle Crescent, Suite 810
Toronto, Ontario, Canada M8X 2W4
(416)239-4801
(416)239-7105 Fax
E-mail: **mail@sq.com**
Web: **http://www.sq.com**

PolyView
PolyBytes
3427 Bever Avenue S.E.
Cedar Rapids, Iowa 52403
E-mail: **polybytes@kagi.com**
Web: **http://198.207.242.3/authors/polybytes/default.html**

Single license cost is $20.

Stars!
Star Crossed Software
38451 Harrington Road
Lebanon, OR 97355
E-mail: **stars@webmap.com**
Web: **http://www.webmap.com/stars!**

Single license cost, $30; $95 for eight licenses.

Wham
Andrew Bulhak
21 The Crescent
Ferntree Gully Vic 3156
AUSTRALIA
E-mail: **acb@yoyo.cc.monash.edu.au**

$25-$30 registration fee requested by the author.

WinPGP

Christopher W. Geib
c/o Geib Enterprises Network
7605 Mt. Hood
P.O. Box 24353
Dayton, OH 45424
Web: **http://www.firstnet.net/~cwgeib/welcome.html**

WinZIP

Nico Mak Computing, Inc.
P.O. Box 919
Bristol, CT 06011-0919
E-mail: **70056,241@compuserve.com**

VuePrint

Hamrick Software
4025 E. Chandler Blvd.
Suite 70-F16
Phoenix, AZ 85044
E-mail: **handysoft@aol.com**
Web: **http://www.primenet.com/~hamrick/**

Registration fee of $40.

Internet Service Providers

America Online

America Online, Inc.
8619 Westwood Center Drive
Vienna, VA 22182
(703)448-8700
(800)827-6364
E-mail: **fulfill2@aol.com**
Web: **http://www.aol.com**

CompuServe

CompuServe
5000 Arlington Centre Blvd
P.O. Box 20961
Columbus, OH 43220
(800)848-8990
Web: **http://www.compuserve.com**

Microsoft Network
Microsoft Corp.
One Microsoft Way
Redmond, WA 98052-6399
(206)882-8080
(800)426-9400 Sales
(206)936-7329 Fax
(206)936-6735 BBS
Web: **http://www.microsoft.com**

NETCOM
3031 Tisch Way
San Jose, CA 95128
(408)983-5950
(408)983-1537 Fax
Web: **http://www.netcom.com**

Prodigy
Prodigy Services Company
445 Hamilton Avenue
White Plains, NY 10601
(914)448-8000
(800)PRODIGY
Web: **http://www.prodigy.com**

Internet Connections Hardware and Software

Adtran
901 Explorer Blvd.
Huntsville, AL 35806
(800)827-0807
(205)971-8699 Fax
E-mail: **infor@adtran.com**
Web: **http://www.adtran.com**

Adtran's ISU Express for ISDN is in chapter 8, "Setting Up an ISDN Connection."

Alpha Telecom Inc.

7501 South Memorial, Ste 212
Huntsville, AL 35802
(205)881-8743
(205)880-9720 Fax
E-mail: **ati_usa@iquest.com**
Web: **http://iquest.com/~ati_usa/**

Alpha Telecom makes ISDN rack-mounted NT1s. In addition, they have stand-alone NT1s and a newly introduced NT1 with POTS ports. They are mentioned in the NT1 discussion of chapter 8, "Setting Up an ISDN Connection."

Artisoft, Inc

2202 North Forbes Blvd.
Tucson, AZ 85745
Web: **http://www.artisoft.com**

Lantastic includes Internet utilities in 6.1 Suite.

Ascend Communications

1275 Harbor Bay Pkwy.
Alameda, CA 94502
(800)621-9578
(510)769-6001
(510)814-2300 Fax
Web: **http://www.ascend.com**

Ascend's routers for ISDN are used by many ISPs.

AVM Computersysteme Vertriebs GMBH

Voltastraße 5, D-13355
Berlin, Germany
+49(0)30/46707-0
+49(0)30/46707-299 Fax

AVM of America, Inc.

80 E. Sir Francis Drake Blvd.
Larkspur, CA 94939
(415)464-4710
(415)464-4701 Fax

AVM has a very broad line of ISDN products including ISA terminal adapters and PCMCIA terminal adapters and NetWare ISDN router software.

Chase Research, Inc.

545 Marriott Drive, Suite 100
Nashville, TN 37214
(615)872-0770
(615)872-0771 Fax
Web: **http://www.chase.com**

Chase has a number of ISDN products.

Cisco Systems

170 West Tasman Dr.
San Jose, CA 95134-1706
(800)553-6387
(408)526-4000
(408)526-4100 Fax
Web: **http://www.cisco.com**

Cisco has a line of ISDN routers and cards.

Digi International

6400 Flying Cloud Dr.
Eden Prairie, MN 55344
(800)344-4273
(612)943-9020
Web: **http://www.digibd.com**

Digi International makes a number of ISDN boards.

Frontier Technologies Corporation

10201 N. Port Washington Rd.
Mequon, Wisconsin 53092
(414)241-4555
(414)241-7084 Fax
E-mail: **tcp@frontiertech.com**
Web: **http://www.frontiertech.com**

Frontier makes an excellent TCP/IP stack for Internet and other use,
SuperTCP Pro. They just introduced a CD research tool, "Cybersearch," that
combines an extensive listing of Web sites with a search tool that allows you
to check the Internet without connecting. Once you've done your search using the CD, you can connect and your browser goes automatically to the
sites. They have added WinISDN support to their product.

XI

Appendixes

FTP Software, Inc.

2 High Street
North Andover, MA 01845
(508)685-4000
(508)659-6557 Fax
Web: **http://www.ftp.com**

FTP makes TCP/IP software and is planning to integrate ISDN
features such as WinISDN.

Gandalf Technologies

130 Colonnade Rd. South
Nepean, Ontario
Canada K2E-7M4
(800)426-3253
(613)723-6500
(613)226-1717 Fax

Gandalf makes ISDN routers that can be configured with a graphical user
interface.

IBM Corporation

One Old Orchard Rd.
Armonk, NY 10504
(800)426-2255
(800)426-3395 IBM Info
(800)426-3333
(914)765-1900
(914)765-7640 Fax
Web: **http://www.ibm.com**

IBM's WaveRunner is an ISDN card also available in PCMCIA form. IBM also
makes a very flexible NT1.

ISDN Systems Corporation

8320 Old Courthouse Rd.
Vienna, VA 22182
(800)566-9472
(703)883-0933
(703)883-8043 Fax
Web: **http://www.cisco.com**

ISDN Systems Corporation's Secure Link II and the entire company were
merged into Cisco. The card features Win95 graphical user interface.

IDSN*tek

P.O. Box 3000
San Gregorio, CA 94074
(415)712-3000
(415)712-3003 Fax
Web: **http://www.isdntek.com**

ISDN*tek's Internet Card is a simple, inexpensive product.

Lion Communications Industries

117 Isabella Drive
Farnborough, Orpington, Kent
BR6 7UF, UK
44 1689 861208
E-mail: **lion@electranet.com**

The Lion Datapump is a flexible ISDN product not yet available in the U.S.

Microsoft Corp.

One Microsoft Way
Redmond, WA 98052-6399
(206)882-8080
(800)426-9400 Sales
(206)936-7329 Fax
(206)936-6735 BBS
FTP: **ftp.microsoft.com**
Web: **http://www.microsoft.com**

Microsoft's TAPI and TCP/IP stack will grow in importance. MSN is a means
of Internet connection.

Motorola ISG

5000 Bradford Dr., S.E.
Huntsville, AL 35805
(800)451-2369
(205)430-8000
(205)830-5657 Fax
Web: **http://www.motorola.com**

Motorola's BitSURFR is discussed in chapter 8, "Setting Up an ISDN
Connection."

NetManage, Inc.
10725 N. De Anza Boulevard
Cupertino, CA 95014
(408)973-7171
(408)257-6405 Fax
E-mail: **sales@netmanage.com**
Web: **http:////www.netmanage.com:80**

Their Chameleon line of TCP/IP software is delivered with WinISDN, which
they co-wrote.

Spry Incorporated
316 Occidental Avenue South
Seattle, WA 98104
(206)447-0300
Web: **http://www.spry.com**

Now a part of CompuServe, Spry makes Internet in a Box. WinISDN is being
integrated into the package.

Teles
GmbH Dovestraße 2-4
D-10587 Berlin, Germany
+49(0) 30/39928-00
+49(0)30/39928-01 Fax

Teles Corp.
1818 Gilbreth Road # 211
Burlingame, CA 94010
(415)652-9191
(415)652-9192 Fax

Teles makes a broad line of ISDN products including adapter boards and
all-in-one software packages for PCs, video telephones and teleconferencing
systems, PBX boards, and software.

Tone Commander Systems, Inc.
11609 49th Place West
Mukilteo, WA 98275
(800)524-0024
(206)349-1010 Fax
E-mail: **tcs@halcyon.com**

Tone Commander makes a broad line of stand-alone and rack-mounted
NT-1s, plus ISDN attendant consoles.

3Com Corporation

5400 Bayfront Plaza
Santa Clara, CA 95052
(800)638-3266 Product Info
(408)764-5000
(408)764-5001 Fax

(Accessworks)
670 North Beers St., Bldg. One
Holmdel, NJ 07733
(908)721-1337
(908)888-4456 Fax

3Com makes a number of ISDN products.

US Robotics

Consumer Services Division
7770 N. Frontage Rd.
Skokie, IL 60077
(800)342-5877
(708)676-7314 Fax
(708)982-5092 BBS
E-mail: **support@usr.com**
Web: **http://www.usr.com**

Corporate Services Division
9100 N. McCormick Blvd.
Skokie, IL 60076
(708)982-5010
(708)982-5151
(708)982-5092 BBS
E-mail: **support@usr.com**
Web: **http:///www.usr.com**

US Robotics has introduced a serial port ISDN device with POTS connections.
USR has a very broad selection for ISDN.

Xylogics

53rd. Ave.
Burlington, MA 01803
(800)892-6639
(617)272-8140
(617)273-5392 Fax
(617)273-1499 BBS

XI

Appendixes

An extensive line of ISDN products.

Xyplex
295 Foster St.
Littleton, MA 01460
(800)338-5316
(508)952-4700
(508)952-4702 Fax
Web: **http://www.xyplex.com**

ISDN products.

ZyXEL
4920 E. La Palma Ave.
Anaheim, CA 92807
(800)255-4101
(714)693-0808
(714)693-0705 Fax
Web: **http://www.zyxel.com**

ZyXEL recently introduced a parallel port ISDN device.

APPENDIX D
Glossary

The Internet can be rather confusing to new users. It has its own jargon, just as many professions or hobbies do. Learning the jargon can make the Internet less foreign to you. As the Internet has grown over the years, a whole vocabulary has developed to describe Internet features and related activities. As you read documents and participate in conversations on the Internet, you may come across terms that you are unfamiliar with. This section explains some of the most common terms you may encounter.

account A user ID and disk area restricted for the use of a particular person. Usually password protected.

ACM Association for Computing Machinery, a professional society for people connected with the computer industry.

address See *e-mail address* and *host address*.

Agent The commercial version of the Free Agent newsreader.

alias A short name used to represent a more complicated one. Often used for mail addresses or host domain names.

America Online (AOL) A commercial online service that gives its subscribers access to the Internet in addition to its other features.

analog A form of electronic communication using a continuous electromagnetic wave, such as television or radio. Any continuous wave form, as opposed to digital on/off transmissions.

anonymous FTP An Internet service that allows you to access a public collection of files on a host without having to log in to a personal account on the host. Usually, you can log in as user anonymous, using your e-mail address as the password.

applet   A small application written in the Java language that can be downloaded with your Web document to add programmable features to Web pages. See also *Java*.

Archie   An application that allows you to search easily for information at anonymous FTP sites on the Internet.

archive   A repository of files available for access at an Internet site. Also, a collection of files—often a backup of a disk, or files saved to tape to allow them to be transferred.

ARPA   Advanced Research Projects Agency, a government agency that originally funded the research on the ARPANET (became DARPA in the mid 1970s).

ARPANET   An experimental communications network funded by the government that eventually developed into the Internet.

article   Message submitted to a UseNet newsgroup. Unlike an e-mail message that goes to a specific person or group of persons, a newsgroup message goes to directories (on many machines) that can be read by any number of people.

ASCII (American Standard Code for Information Interchange)   Data that is limited to letters, numbers, and punctuation. A standard exists that defines how the letters, punctuation, and numbers are stored in the lower seven-bits of a byte (each character is represented by a unique number).

ATM (Asynchronous Transfer Mode)   A developing technological advance in communications switching. This technology uses hardware switches to create a temporary direct path between two destinations so data can be exchanged at a higher rate.

AUP (Acceptable Use Policy)   The restrictions that a network segment places on the traffic it carries. (These policies used to be more prevalent when the government was running the Internet backbone.)

backbone   The major communications lines of a network. Usually refers to the central high-speed line of a WAN. The Internet backbone was funded by the National Science Foundation before the Internet became commercial.

bandwidth   The maximum volume of data that can be sent over a communications network.

bang   A slang term for an exclamation point.

bang address   A type of e-mail address that separates host names in the address with exclamation points. Used for mail sent to the UUCP network, where specifying the exact path of the mail (including all hosts that pass on the message) is necessary. The address is in the form of *machine!machine!userID,* where the number of machines listed depends on the connections needed to reach the machine where the account userID is.

BBS (Bulletin Board System)   A system that allows you to connect to a computer to upload and download files and leave messages for other users.

binary file   File whose data contains nonprintable characters, including graphics files, programs, and sound files.

BinHex   A program that is used to encode binary files as ASCII so they can be sent through e-mail.

bit   The basic unit of digital communications. There are 8 bits in a byte.

BITNET (Because It's Time Network)   A non-TCP/IP network for small universities without Internet access.

bookmarks   Term used by some World Wide Web browsers for shortcuts to URLs you access frequently. Other Internet clients (such as Gopher) also use bookmarks.

bot (IRC)   A program that watches an IRC channel and automatically responds when certain messages are entered.

bounce   An e-mail message you receive that tells you that an e-mail message you sent wasn't delivered. Usually contains an error code and the contents of the message that wasn't delivered.

bps (bits per second)   Units of measure that express the speed at which data is transferred between computers.

bridge   A device that connects one physical section of a network to another, often providing isolation.

browser   A utility that lets you look through collections of things. For example, a file browser lets you look through a file system. Applications that let you access the World Wide Web are called Web browsers.

BTW (by the way)   An abbreviation often used in online conversations.

XI

Appendixes

byte A digital storage unit large enough to contain one ASCII character. Compare to *bit.*

CERN The European Laboratory for Particle Physics, where the World Wide Web was first conceived of and implemented.

CGI (Common Gateway Interface) A method for interfacing Web servers with programs to allow input from users on Web pages.

channel An Internet Relay Chat term that refers to a group of people discussing a particular topic.

chat A real-time conversation with other Internet users. IRC provides a text-based client, while Web-based chat clients let you use pictures and audio.

CIX (Commercial Internet Exchange) A consortium of commercial providers of Internet service.

client User of a service. Also often refers to a piece of software that gets information from a server.

CNRI (Corporation for National Research Initiatives) An organization formed to foster research into a national data highway.

coaxial A type of wiring where the signal wire is in the center of a shielded cable. Compare to *twisted pair.*

command line Line on a terminal-based interface where you enter commands to the operating system. Some Internet accounts are command-line based.

compress A program that compacts a file so it fits into a smaller space. Also can refer to the technique of reducing the amount of space a file takes up.

CompuServe A commercial online service that gives its subscribers access to the Internet in addition to its other features.

CPSR (Computer Professionals for Social Responsibility) An organization that encourages socially responsible use of computers.

CREN (Corporation for Research and Educational Networking) An organization formed by the joining of two different educational networks to enhance the capabilities of the two networks.

CWIS (Campus Wide Information Service) A hypertext-based system that provides information about people and services on a campus.

cyberspace   A term used to refer to the entire collection of sites accessible electronically. If your computer is attached to the Internet or another large network, it exists in cyberspace.

daemon   A program that runs automatically on a computer to perform a service for the operating system.

DARPA (Defense Advanced Research Projects Agency, originally ARPA)   The government agency that funded the research that developed the ARPANET.

decode   Transform a file from an encoded format to its original format. For example, to use binary files sent through e-mail, you must decode the files from ASCII to binary data.

dedicated line   See *leased line*.

DES (Data Encryption Standard)   An algorithm developed by the U.S. government to provide security for data transmitted over a network.

dialup   A type of connection where you use a modem to connect to another computer or an Internet provider via phone lines.

Dialup Networking   Built-in Windows 95 support for networking over modems. Eliminates the need for third-party SLIP or PPP software to connect to dial-in Internet accounts.

digest   A form of mailing list where a number of messages are concatenated (linked) and sent out as a single message.

digital   Type of communications used by computers, consisting of individual on and off pulses.

DNS   See *Domain Name System*.

DOD (Department of Defense)   A U.S. government agency that originally sponsored the ARPANET research.

domain   Highest subdivision of the Internet, for the most part by country (except in the U.S., where it's by type of organization, such as educational, commercial, and government). Usually the last part of a host name—for example, the domain part of ibm.com is .com, which represents the domain of commercial sites in the U.S.

Domain Name System (DNS)   The system that translates between Internet IP address and Internet host names.

XI

Appendixes

dot address   See *host address*.

download   Move a file from a remote computer to your local computer.

ECPA (Electronic Communications Privacy Act)   A law that governs the use and restrictions of electronic communications.

EDUCOM   A nonprofit consortium of educational institutions that help introduce electronic information access and management into educational organizations.

EFF (Electronic Frontier Foundation)   An organization concerned with the legal rights and responsibilities of computer usage.

e-mail   An electronic message delivered from one computer user to another. Short for *electronic mail*.

e-mail address   An address used to send e-mail to a user on the Internet, consisting of the user name and host name (and any other necessary information, such as a gateway machine). An Internet e-mail address is usually of the form *username@hostname*.

emoticon   See *smiley face*.

encode   Transform a file from one format to another. For example, to send binary files through e-mail, you must encode the files from binary to ASCII data.

encryption   The process of scrambling a message so it can be read only by someone who knows how to unscramble it.

EtherNet   A type of local area network hardware. Many TCP/IP networks are EtherNet-based.

EUDORA   A popular PC e-mail application.

expire   Remove an article from a UseNet newsgroup after a specified interval.

FAQ (Frequently Asked Question document, often pronounced "fak")   Contains a list of commonly asked questions on a topic. Most UseNet newsgroups have a FAQ to introduce new readers to popular topics in the newsgroup.

FARNET   A group of networks interested in promoting research and education networking.

feed   Send UseNet newsgroups from your site to another site that wants to read them.

finger   A program that provides information about users on an Internet host (possibly may include a user's personal information, such as project affiliation and schedule).

firewall   A device placed on a network to prevent unauthorized traffic from entering the network.

flame   Communicate in an abusive or absurd manner. Often occurs in newsgroup posts and e-mail messages.

forms   Online data entry sheets supported by some World Wide Web browsers.

frame relay   A type of digital data communications protocol.

Free Agent   A popular shareware newsreader.

freenet   A publicly accessible Internet site (for example, in a library) that does not charge users for limited accounts.

freeware   Software that is made available by the author at no cost to anyone who wants it (although the author retains rights to the software).

FTP (File Transfer Protocol)   An Internet communications protocol that allows you to transfer files between hosts on the Internet. See also *anonymous FTP*.

FWIW (For What It's Worth)   An abbreviation often used in online conversations.

FYI (For Your Information)   An abbreviation used often in online conversations. An FYI is also a type of Internet reference document that contains answers to basic questions about the Internet.

gateway   A device that interfaces two networks that use different protocols.

GIF (Graphics Interchange Format)   A compressed graphic file format. GIF files can be displayed without helper applications by WWW browsers.

gigabit   Very high-speed (1 billion bits per second) data communications transfer rate.

gigabyte   A unit of data storage approximately equal to 1 billion bytes of data.

Gopher A menu-driven system/application that lets you access archives of information on Internet hosts that provide Gopher service.

Gopherbook An application that uses an interface resembling a book to access Gopher servers.

GUI (Graphical User Interface) A computer interface based on graphical symbols rather than text. Windowing environments and Macintosh environments are GUIs.

gzip A file compression program originally designed to replace the UNIX compress utility.

hacking Originally referred to playing around with computer systems; now often used to indicate destructive computer activity.

headers Lines at the beginning of an e-mail message or newsgroup post that contain information about the message—its source, destination, subject, and route it took to get there, among other things.

Hgopher (Hampson's Gopher) A Windows Gopher interface.

home page The document that your World Wide Web browser loads when it starts up. It should have links to other documents that you use frequently.

hop-check A utility that allows you to find out how many routers are between your host and another Internet host. See also *traceroute*.

host address A unique number assigned to identify a host on the Internet (also called *IP address* or *dot address*). This address is usually represented as four numbers between 1 and 254 and separated by periods—for example, 192.58.107.230.

host name A unique name for a host that corresponds to the host address. A host name contains the name of the machine and the subdomain of the organization the host belongs to. For example, **indigo.cmu.edu** would be a machine named *indigo* in the *cmu.edu* subdomain. See also *domain, subdomain,* and *Domain Name System (DNS)*.

hosts Individual computers connected to the Internet; see also *nodes*.

HotDog A popular shareware HTML editor.

hotlist A list of your favorite World Wide Web sites that can be accessed quickly by your WWW browser. See also *bookmarks*.

HTML (Hypertext mark-up language)   The formatting language that is used to create World Wide Web documents.

HTTP (Hypertext Transport Protocol)   The communications protocol that allows WWW hypertext documents to be retrieved quickly.

hyperlinks   See *links*.

hypermedia   An online document that can contain a mixture of media, including text, graphics, sound, and animation. Most WWW documents are hypermedia documents.

HyperTerminal   A terminal emulator that comes with Windows 95. See also *terminal emulation*.

hypertext   An online document that has words or graphics containing links to other documents. Usually, selecting the link area on-screen (with a mouse or keyboard command) activates these links.

IAB (Internet Architecture Board)   A group of volunteers who work to maintain the Internet.

IEEE (Institute of Electrical and Electronics Engineers)   The professional society for electrical and computer engineers.

IETF (Internet Engineering Task Force)   A group of volunteers that helps develop Internet standards.

IMHO (In My Humble—or Honest—Opinion)   An abbreviation often used in online conversations.

Internet   The term used to describe all the worldwide interconnected TCP/IP networks.

Internet Explorer   A Microsoft Windows 95 Web browser.

Internet Assistant   A Microsoft application that allows you to develop HTML documents in Microsoft Word.

Internet Society   See *ISOC (Internet Society)*.

InterNIC   The NSFNET manager sites on the Internet that provide information about the Internet.

IP (Internet Protocol)   The communications protocol used by computers connected to the Internet. Used to get information from one Internet host to another, while TCP provides a protocol for keeping track of the data transferred and checking for errors. See also *TCP (Transmission Control Protocol)*.

IP address   See *host address*.

IRC (Internet Relay Chat)   A live conference facility available on the Internet.

ISDN (Integrated Services Digital Network)   An emerging digital communications standard, allowing faster speeds than are possible using modems over analog phone lines.

ISO (International Standards Organization)   An organization that sets worldwide standards in many different areas. For example, the organization has been working on a network protocol to replace TCP/IP (this isn't widely supported, however).

ISOC (Internet Society)   An educational organization dedicated to encouraging use of the Internet.

ISP (Internet Service Provider)   Any commercial provider of Internet accounts and high-speed connections.

Java   A language developed by Sun MicroSystems, Inc. that allows small applications to be downloaded with a Web document to add programmable features to Web pages. See also *applet*.

JPEG (Joint Photographic Experts Group)   A compressed graphic file format. JPEG files can be displayed without helper applications by many WWW browsers.

kill file   A file used by some newsreader software that allows you to automatically skip posts with certain attributes (specific subject, author, and so on).

knowbots (Knowledge robots)   Programs that automatically search through a network for specified information.

labels   The different components of an Internet host name.

LAN (Local Area Network)   A network of computers that is limited to a (usually) small physical area, like a building.

leased line   A dedicated phone line used for network communications.

links   The areas (words or graphics) in a hypertext document that cause another document to be loaded when you activate them.

listproc   Software that automates the management of electronic mailing lists. See also *LISTSERV, majordomo, SmartList*.

LISTSERV   Software that automates the management of electronic mailing lists. See also *listproc, majordomo, SmartList.*

local   Pertaining to the computer you are now using.

local host   The computer you are currently using.

login   Provide a user-ID and password to allow you to use the resources of a computer.

lurking   Observing, but not participating in an activity, usually a UseNet newsgroup.

LYCOS   A popular Web search tool.

mailers   Applications that let you read and send e-mail messages.

mailing list   A service that forwards an e-mail message sent to it to everyone on a list, allowing a group of people to discuss a particular topic.

mail reflector   Software that automatically distributes all submitted messages to the members of a mailing list.

majordomo   Software that automates the management of electronic mailing lists. See also *listproc, LISTSERV, SmartList.*

man   A UNIX command that provides information about UNIX commands. (man is short for manual entry.)

MBONE (Multicast backbone)   An experimental network that allows live video to be sent over the Internet.

Merit (Michigan Educational Research Information Triad)   The organization that initially managed NSFNET.

MILNET   DOD's (Department of Defense) network.

MIME (Multi-purpose Internet Mail Extensions)   An extension to Internet mail that allows for the inclusion of non-textual data such as video and audio in e-mail.

modem   An electronic device that allows digital computer data to be transmitted via analog phone lines.

moderator   A person who examines all submissions to a newsgroup or mailing list and allows only those that meet certain criteria to be posted. Usually, the moderator makes sure that the topic is pertinent to the group and that the submissions aren't flames.

XI

Appendixes

Mosaic   A graphical interface to the World Wide Web (WWW).

MOTD (Message of the day)   A message posted on some computer systems to let people know about problems or new developments.

MPEG (Motion Picture Experts Group)   A popular video file format. MPEG files must be displayed with helper applications by most WWW browsers.

MSN (Microsoft Network)   A commercial online service run by Microsoft that allows access to the Internet in addition to its other features.

MUDs (Multi-User Dungeons)   Interactive real-time, text-based games accessible to anyone on the Internet.

multimedia   Presenting information using more than one type of media; for example, sound, text, and graphics.

NETCOM NetCruiser   A complete Internet service package.

Netfind   A service that allows you to look up an Internet user's address.

netiquette   Network etiquette conventions used in written communications, usually referring to UseNet newsgroup postings, but also applicable to e-mail.

NetManage   The producer of Chameleon, a popular TCP/IP package that provides interfaces to a number of Internet services for Windows.

netnews   A collective way of referring to the UseNet newsgroups.

NetScape   A popular commercial World Wide Web browser.

network   A number of computers physically connected to enable communication with one another.

newbie   Someone who is new to the Internet and unfamiliar with its services and social protocols. See also *netiquette*.

NewsXpress   A popular shareware newsreader.

newsgroups   The electronic discussion groups of UseNet.

newsreaders   Applications that let you read (and usually post) articles in UseNet newsgroups.

NFS   (Network File System)   A file system developed by Sun Microsystems that is now widely used on many different networks.

NIC (Network Information Center)   A service that provides administrative information about a network.

NII (National Information Infrastructure)   The government's vision of a high-speed network giving everyone in the country access to advanced computer capabilities.

NNTP (Network News Transport Protocol)   The communications protocol that is used to send UseNet news on the Internet.

nodes   Individual computers connected to a network. See also *hosts*.

NREN (National Research and Education Network)   A proposed nationwide high-speed data network to be used for educational and research purposes.

NSF (National Science Foundation)   Funder of the main Internet backbone in the U.S. during the late 1980s and early 1990s.

NSFNET   A Network funded by the National Science Foundation; the backbone of the Internet during the late 1980s and early 1990s.

OC3 (Optical Carrier 3)   A protocol for communications over a high-speed optical network.

online   Existing in electronic form (for example, an online documentation). Also, connected to a network.

OTOH (On The Other Hand)   An abbreviation often used in online conversations.

packet   The unit of data transmission on the Internet. A packet consists of the data being transferred with additional overhead information, such as the transmitting and receiving of addresses.

packet switching   The communications technology that the Internet is based on, where data being sent between computers is transmitted in packets.

parallel   Means of communication in which digital data is sent multiple bits at a time, with each simultaneous bit being sent over a separate line.

PDIAL   A list of mailing lists maintained by Stephanie da Silva **(arielle@taronga.com)**, periodically posted to the **news.answers**, **news.announce.newusers**, and **news.lists** UseNet newsgroups.

PDN (Public data network)   A service such as SprintNet that gives access to a nationwide data network through a local phone call.

peer-to-peer   Internet services that can be offered and accessed by anyone, without requiring a special server.

PEM (Privacy Enhanced Mail)   A standard for automatically encrypting and decrypting mail messages to provide more secure message transmission.

PGP (Pretty Good Privacy)   An application that allows you to send and receive encrypted e-mail.

ping   A utility that sends out a packet to an Internet host and waits for a response (used to check if a host is up).

PSI Pipeline USA   A complete Internet service package.

POP (Point of Presence)   Indicates availability of a local access number to a public data network.

port (hardware)   A physical channel on a computer that allows you to communicate with other devices (printers, modems, disk drives, etc.).

port (network)   An address to which incoming data packets are sent. Special ports can be assigned to send the data directly to a server (FTP, Gopher, WWW, Telnet, e-mail) or other specific program.

post   Send a message to a UseNet newsgroup.

postmaster   An address to which you can send questions about a site (asking if a user has an account there or if they sell a particular product, for example).

PPP (Point-to-Point Protocol)   A driver that allows you to use a network communications protocol over a phone line, used with TCP/IP to allow you to have a dial-in Internet host.

Prodigy   A commercial online service that gives its subscribers access to the Internet in addition to its other features.

protocol   The standard that defines how computers on a network communicate with one another.

provider   Someone who sells—or gives away, in some cases—access to the Internet.

PSI Pipeline USA A complete Internet service package.

public domain software   Software that is made available by the author to anyone who wants it. (In this case, the author gives up all rights to the software.)

QuickTime   A popular video file format. QuickTime files must be displayed with helper applications by most WWW browsers.

RAS (Remote Access Service)   A service that allows other computers to remotely connect to a Microsoft NT computer.

repeater   Device that allows you to extend the length of your network by amplifying and repeating the information it receives.

remote   Pertaining to a host on the network other than the computer you now are using.

remote host   A host on the network other than the computer you currently are using.

rlogin   A UNIX command that allows you to log in to a remote computer.

RFC (Request For Comments)   A document submitted to the Internet governing board to propose Internet standards or to document information about the Internet.

router   Equipment that receives an Internet packet and sends it to the next machine in the destination path.

serial   Means of communication in which digital data is sent one bit at a time over a single physical line.

server   Provider of a service. Also often refers to a piece of hardware or software that provides access to information requested from it. See also *client*.

SGML (Standard General Markup Language)   A powerful markup language that allows you to structure documents so they can be displayed on any type of computer.

shareware   Software that is made available by the author to anyone who wants it, with a request to send the author a nominal fee if the software is used on a regular basis.

signature   A personal sign-off used in e-mail and newsgroup posts, often contained in a file and automatically appended to the mail or post. Often contains organization affiliation and pertinent personal information.

site   A group of computers under a single administrative control.

SLIP (Serial Line Internet Protocol)   A way of running TCP/IP via the phone lines to allow you to have a dial-in Internet host.

SmartList   Software that automates the management of electronic mailing lists. See also *listproc, LISTSERV, majordomo.*

SMDS (Switched Multimegabit Data Service)   A type of high-speed digital communications protocol.

smiley face   An ASCII drawing such as :-) (look at it sideways) used to help indicate an emotion in a message. Also called *emoticon.*

SMTP (Simple Mail Transport Protocol)   The accepted communications protocol standard for exchange of e-mail between Internet hosts.

SNMP (Simple Network Management Protocol)   A communications protocol used to control and monitor devices on a network.

socket   Abstraction in the file system used for Internet connections (lets you read and write to an Internet service as if it were a file).

SONET (Synchronous Optical Network)   A high-speed fiber optics network.

store and forward   A type of system that collects information (like e-mail) for a user, then forwards the information when the user connects to the system.

subdomain   Any subdivision of the major Internet domains. For example, *cmu.edu* is a subdomain assigned to Carnegie-Mellon University, and *cs.cmu.edu* is a subdomain assigned to the Computer Science department of Carnegie-Mellon. See also *domain.*

subscribe   Become a member of a mailing list or newsgroup; also refers to obtaining Internet provider services.

surfing   Jumping from host to host on the Internet, to get an idea of what can be found. Also used to refer to briefly examining a number of different UseNet newsgroups.

T1   Communications lines operating at 1.544M per second.

T3   Communications lines operating at 45M per second.

TAR (Tape Archive program)   A UNIX-based program that creates packages of directory structures.

TCP (Transmission control protocol)   The network protocol used by hosts on the Internet. TCP controls data transfer (keeps track of what has been transferred and whether there were any errors), while IP takes care of actually sending the data between the hosts. See also *IP*.

Telnet   A program that allows remote login to another computer.

terminal emulation   Running an application that lets you use your computer to interface with a command-line account on a remote computer, as if you were connected to the computer with a terminal.

thread   All messages in a newsgroup or mailing list pertaining to a particular topic.

toggle   Alternate between two possible values.

traceroute   A utility that allows you to find out how many routers are between your host and another Internet host. See also *hop-check*.

traffic   The information flowing through a network.

Trumpet Winsock   A popular shareware implementation of sockets for Windows, along with some basic Internet clients. See also *sockets*.

twisted pair   A type of wiring where pairs of communications wires are twisted together to minimize interference. Compare to *coaxial*.

UNIX   An operating system used on many Internet hosts.

upload   Move a file from your local computer to a remote computer.

URL (Universal Resource Locator)   Used to specify the location and name of a World Wide Web document. Can also specify other Internet services available from WWW browsers. For example, http://www.nsf.gov or gopher://gopher2.tc.umn.edu.

UseNet   A collection of computer discussion groups that are read all over the world.

user name   The ID used to log in to a computer.

UUCP (UNIX to UNIX Copy Protocol)   An early transfer protocol for UNIX machines that required having one machine call the other one on the phone.

UUDecode   A program that lets you construct binary data that was UUEncoded.

XI

Appendixes

UUEncode   A program that lets you send binary data through e-mail.

Veronica   An Internet service that allows you to search the directories and files on Gopher servers for information of interest to you.

viewers   Applications that are used to display non-text files, such as graphics, sound, and animation.

virus   A computer program that covertly enters a system by means of a legitimate program, usually doing damage to the system; compare to *worm*.

VMS (Virtual Memory System)   An operating system used on hosts made by Digital Equipment Corporation.

VRML   (Virtual Reality Modeling Language) An experimental language that lets you display 3-D objects in Web documents.

WAIS (Wide Area Information Servers)   A system for searching and retrieving documents from participating sites.

WAN (Wide Area Network)   A network of computers that are geographically dispersed.

Web Chat   An application that allows you to carry on live conversations over the World Wide Web.

Web Crawler   A Web search tool.

WELL (Whole Earth 'Lectric Link)   One of the first Internet public access sites.

WHOIS   A service that lets you look up information about Internet hosts and users.

WinZip   A Windows interface for creating archives of compressed files.

worm   A computer program that invades other computers over a network, usually non-destructively; compare to *virus*.

WS_FTP   A Windows FTP client that lets you easily transfer files between hosts on the Internet.

WSGopher   A Windows Gopher client that lets you easily browse Internet Gopher servers.

WWW, Web (World Wide Web)   The newest Internet service, originally developed to allow viewing of linked hypermedia documents containing graphics, sounds, and video. WWW clients can also interface (although on a limited basis) to other Internet services like FTP, Gopher, UseNet newsgroups, and e-mail. See also *browser*.

X-modem   A communication protocol that lets you transfer files over a serial line. See also *Y-modem, Z-modem*.

Y-modem   A communication protocol that lets you transfer files over a serial line. See also *X-modem, Z-modem*.

YAHOO   A Web site that contains lists of many topics to be found on the Web and includes a search tool to find sites you are interested in.

Z-modem   A communication protocol that lets you transfer files over a serial line. See also *X-modem, Y-modem*.

zip   Probably the singular most popular file compression and archive program for PCs.

XI

Appendixes

Index

Symbols–A

7th Level Web site, 1106

<A> HTML element, 638-640
abbreviations (country codes), 1191-1198
abbreviations for phrases in newsgroups, 771
AberMUDs, 1013
aborting
  files
    downloading, 854
    uploading, 854
  Web page loading
    in Mosaic, 551
    in Netscape, 513
absolute hypertext links, 553
absolute URLs, 463, 627-629
Acceptable Use Policies (AUPs), networks, 1220
access methods (service providers), 122-123
accessing
  accounts with Telnet, 828
  Archie, 927
  FTP sites
    with America Online, 281-282
    with CompuServe, 261
    with Prodigy, 300-301
    with WinCIM, 252-253
  Gopher sites
    with America Online, 279
    with CompuServe, 261
    with Prodigy, 299-300
    with Veronica, 280
  IRCs
    with mIRC, 953-959
    with Telnet, 945
  mailing lists, 432, 1089-1090
  Mosaic Hotlists items, 568-569
  MSN, 315-317
  MUDs via Telnet, 1014-1015

newsgroups
  with CompuServe, 260
  with NewsXpress, 779
  with Prodigy, 296
software from FTP sites, 28
Telnet sites with WinCIM, 253-254
WAIS databases with Veronica, 280
Web sites
  from CompuServe hotlists, 260
  from Mosaic hotlists, 568-571
  with America Online, 283-285
  with bookmarks, 525
  with Internet Assistant, 673
  with Prodigy, 297
accounts, 1219
  hacking, 1038
  MSN
    establishing, 315-317
    IDs, 317
    passwords, 317
  personal accounts (host profiles), 860
  PPP, 20
  Remote Email System accounts (MCI Mail), 411
  SLIP, 20
  Telnet, accessing, 828
Acer America Web site, 1093
ACM (Association for Computing Machinery), 1219
acquiring
  Exchange, 351-352
  Internet Mail, 355
  viruses, 1061-1062
  WinWAIS, 898
Action Lists (mIRC), 961-962

ACTION parameter, <FORM> HTML element, 646
activating hypertext links, 462, 507-508
Activision Web site, 1107
Adaptec FTP site, 1149
adapters
  dial-up
    installation on Windows 95, 138
    TCP/IP support, 140
  networks (Windows 95 support), 139
Add as Recipient command (Special menu), 387
Add New Interface dialog box (Chameleon Internet software), 169
add-on utilities
  Internet Assistant, 667-669
    downloading, 669-672
    installation, 669-672
  MetaClient (SGML), 730
  Web sites, 1116-1120
Add/Remove Programs control panel, 138
Add/Remove Programs Properties dialog box, 353
adding
  domains to LANs, 134
  e-mail addresses to Personal Address Book, 365
  gateways from LANs, 132
  icons (Explorer), 833
  keys, 1048
  recipients (e-mail), 367
  Telnet to Windows 95 Start menu, 833
  viewer applications to Mosaic, 594
  Web sites to CompuServe Hotlists, 259

address books, 350
addresses, adding, 365
America Online, 269
ECCO (Chameleon Internet software), 170
Prodigy, storing e-mail addresses, 306
WinCIM, storing e-mail addresses, 237-238
addresses
3Com Corporation, 1217
Adtran, 1211
Agent, 1205
Alpha Telecom Inc., 1212
America Online, 1210
Artisoft, Inc, 1212
Ascend Communications, 1212
AVM Computersysteme Vertriebs GMBH, 1212
AVM of America, Inc., 1212
Chase Research, Inc., 1213
Cisco Systems, 1213
CompuServe, 1210
Digi International, 1213
e-mail, 1224
attaching to Web pages, 719
bang addresses, 1221
changing, 435-436
finding, 332-333
Internet Mail, 351-352
InterNIC, 127
KIS, 337-338
Netfind, 336-337
Personal Address Book, 350-351, 365
storing in America Online address book, 269
storing in Prodigy address book, 306
storing in WinCIM (CompuServe) address book, 237-238
UseNet user list, 338-339
WHOIS database, 334-336
Eudora Light, 1206
Frontier Technologies Corporation, 1213
FTP Software, Inc., 1214
Gandalf Technologies, 1214-1218
Gmud32, 1206
host addresses, 1226

HotDog, 1206
IBM Corporation, 1214
IDSN*tek, 1215
Internet Phone, 1207
InterNIC server, 336
IP addresses, 12, 24, 126, 130
ISDN Systems Corporation, 1214
Lion Communications Industries, 1215
LISTSERV mailing lists, 422-423
LView Pro, 1207-1218
Microsoft Corp., 1215
Microsoft Products, 1207
Midi Gate, 1207-1208
Mod4Win, 1208
Motorola ISG, 1215-1218
MPEGPLAY, 1208
MSN, 1211
NETCOM, 1211
NetManage, Inc., 1216
Netscape, 1208-1218
numerical, 824-825
Paint Shop Pro, 1208-1209
Panorama Pro, 1209
PolyView, 1209
Prodigy, 1211
Spry Incorporated, 1216
Stars!, 1209
Teles, 1216-1218
Telnet, 823
host names, 823-824
ports, 829-830
Tone Commander Systems, Inc., 1216
US Robotics, 1217
UUNET Technologies, 405-406
VuePrint, 1210
Wham, 1209
WinPGP, 1210
WinZIP, 1210
Xylogics, 1217-1218
Xyplex, 1218
ZyXEL, 1218
administrators (MUDs), 1020
Adobe Systems
Amber helper application, 530-531
FTP site, 1148
Web site, 1104
ADSLs (asymmetric digital subscriber lines), 227
Adtran
addresses, 1211
telephone numbers, 1211
Web site, 1211

Advanced HTML mailing list, 1074
Advanced Research Projects Agency (ARPA), 10, 1220
Agent newsreader, 1219
addresses, 1205
configurations, 792-805
downloading binary files from newsgroups, 811-812
e-mail capabilities, 801-803, 812-816
filtering e-mail messages, 815
following newsgroup message threads, 808-810
font preferences, 803
FTP site, 792
installation, 793
newsgroup option settings, 804-805
posting newsgroup messages, 810-811
preferences, setting, 794-800
reading e-mail messages, 813-816
reading newsgroup messages, 806-808
responding to newsgroup messages, 811
sending e-mail messages, 812-813
signature file attachments, 800-801
spell checking capablities, 800
starting, 792-805
storing e-mail messages, 814
subscribing/unsubscribing to newsgroups, 805-806
telephone numbers, 1205
Web site, 792, 1205
window layout preferences, 803-804
Agents mailing list, 1081
aggregating B channels (narrowband ISDN), 203
Air Mosaic Web browser, 168
aliases, 1219
ALIGN parameter, <IMG> HTML element, 635
alignment
inline images, 635
text in Web pages, 631-633
allocation (host names), 132
Alpha Telecom Inc., 1212
ALT parameter, <IMG> HTML element, 635

alt.answers newsgroup, 1160
alt.bbs newsgroup, 1163
alt.binaries.sounds.d
    newsgroup, 1172
alt.cd-rom newsgroup,
    1172-1174
alt.censorship newsgroup,
    1162
alt.com.virus newsgroup, 1068
alt.culture.internet
    newsgroup, 1162
alt.culture.usenet newsgroup,
    1160
alt.cyberspace newsgroup,
    1162
alt.games newsgroup, 1169
alt.irc newsgroup, 1163-1164
alt.lang.vrml newsgroup, 1164
alt.mud newsgroup, 1164
alt.news.microsoft newsgroup,
    1170
alt.online-service newsgroup,
    1164-1165
alt.privacy newsgroup, 1162
alt.sys.pc-clon .* newsgroup,
    1167
alt.test newsgroup, 1160
alt.usenet.offline-reader
    newsgroup, 1160
alt.WinSock newsgroup, 1165
alt.www.hotjava newsgroup,
    1165
alt.zines newsgroup, 1172
Amber helper application,
    530-531
America Online (AOL), 117,
    263-285, 406-407, 1219
    accessing Gopher sites, 279
    accessing WAIS databases,
        279
    accessing Web sites, 283-285
    addresses, 1210
    BBSs, 264
    cost, 264
    e-mail
        address book, 269
        capabilities, 266-269
        sending, 407
    Favorite Places utility, 285
    FTP capabilities, 267,
        281-282
    future developments, 285
    Gopher capabilities, 267-280
    Internet gateway, 266-267
    mailboxes (full), 407
    mailing list capabilities, 266,
        270-272

MIME encoded files, 407
newsgroup capabilities, 267,
    272-278
posting to mailing lists, 272
posting newsgroup articles,
    276-277
reading newsgroup
    messages, 275-276
responding to newsgroup
    messages, 277-278
sampling with WinSock, 267
sending e-mail messages,
    268-269
storing e-mail addresses, 269
subscriber growth, 264
subscriber orientation, 264
subscribing/unsubscribing
        to mailing lists, 270-272
        to newsgroups, 273-274
    telephone numbers, 1210
    WAIS capabilities, 267-280
    Web browser preferences,
        285
    Web site, 1131, 1210
    Windows features, 265
    WWW capabilities, 267,
        283-285
American Civil Liberties
    Union FTP site, 1152
American Standard Code for
    Information Interchange,
    see ASCII
amplifiers, 181
analog devices, integrating
    with ISDN, 193
analog in-band signaling, 190
analog port options (external
    ISDN terminal adapters), 207
analog signaling, 177-182,
    1219
anchors (hypertext links),
    462-463, 637-640, 714, 717
animation files, viewing with
    Internet Explorer, 492
anonymous FTP, 11, 27-28,
    839, 1219
anonymous mailing lists, 436
ANSI, 822
answering errors (modems),
    troubleshooting, 155
anti-virus software, 1058,
    1066-1067
    behavior blockers, 1061
    CPAV (Central Point Anti-
        Virus), 1067
    Dr. Solomon's Anti-Virus
        Toolkit, 1068-1069

F-PROT, 1069-1070
    MSAV (Microsoft Anti Virus),
        1067
    scanning, 1060
    validity checks, 1060-1061
    Web sites, 97
APIs (application program
    interfaces), 113
applets (Java), 536, 732, 1220
Archie, 842, 927-929, 1184,
    1220
    accessing, 927
    connecting, 927
    exiting, 937
    expressions, 931
    finding files with, 29-31
    limiting, 932
    NetCD95, 929
    parameters, setting, 936-937
    retrieving files, 935-936
    running, 928
    searches, 930-935
    searching databases, 928
    troubleshooting, 933
    WS_FTP, 929-930
archives, 1220
ARPA (Advanced Research
    Projects Agency), 10, 1220
ARPANET, 10, 1220
articles (newsgroups), 43, 1220
    anonymous posting, 762
    cross-posting, 763
    decoding with
        WINCODE.EXE in Prodigy,
        303-304
    downloading with WinCIM,
        243
    marking with America
        Online, 276
    posting, 758-759, 1232
        by geographic region,
            763-764
        guidelines, 773-774
        in terminal emulation
            mode, 249-250
        reader distribution,
            763-764
        with Agent/Free Agent
            newsreaders, 810-811
        with America Online,
            276-277
        with CompuServe Web
            browser, 261
        with Internet Explorer,
            490
        with Prodigy, 303
        with WinCIM, 244

reading
  in terminal emulation
    mode, 248-249
  reading with Agent/Free
    Agent newsreaders,
    806-808
  with America Online,
    275-276
  with CompuServe Web
    browser, 260
  with Internet Explorer,
    488-490
  with Mosaic, 572-573
  with MSN, 326
  with Netscape, 535-536
  with NewsXpress,
    783-784
  with Prodigy, 302-303
  with WinCIM, 242-243
responding to
  via e-mail with
    NewsXpress, 786-787
  with Agent/Free Agent
    newsreaders, 811
  with America Online,
    277-278
  with NewsXpress, 787
saving
  with NewsXpress,
    785-786
  with WinCIM, 243
selecting with NewsXpress,
  783-784
threads, 756, 808-810, 1235
uncompressing with PKZIP,
  304
see also messages,
  newsgroups
Artisoft, Inc, 1212
Ascend Communications
  addresses, 1212
  telephone numbers, 1212
  Web site, 1095, 1212
**ASCII (American Standard
  Code for Information
  Interchange)**, 1220
  defining file extensions, 864
  files (e-mail), 339-340
  newsreader (CompuServe),
    246-251
**assigning IP addresses to
  Windows 95 workstations,**
  130
**Association for Computing
  Machinery (ACM)**, 1219
**asymmetric digital subscriber
  lines (ADSLs)**, 227

**Asynchronous Transfer Mode
  (ATM)**, 227-228, 1220
**AT command set, integrating
  with external ISDN terminal
  adapters**, 201
ATI Technologies
  FTP site, 1149
  Web site, 1099
**ATM (Asynchronous Transfer
  Mode)**, 227-228, 1220
**Attach Document command
  (Message menu), Eudora**, 392
attaching
  e-mail addresses to Web
    pages, 719
  files to e-mail messages
    with America Online, 269
    with Eudora, 392-393
    with Prodigy, 306
    with WinCim, 237
  signature files to newsgroup
    postings, 760-762
    with Agent newsreader,
      800-801
    with America Online, 277
    with terminal emulation
      mode, 250
    with WinCIM, 245
attenuation (signaling),
  180-182
attributes (Web page text),
  711
audio files, see **sound files**
audio players, 581
**AUPs (Acceptable Use
  Policies), networks**, 1220
**Auto Detect Extensions dialog
  box**, 864
Autodesk FTP site, 1149
**AUTOEXEC.BAT files,
  changing**, 1046
**.AVI files, viewing with
  Internet Explorer**, 492
AVM of America, Inc., 1212

B

<B> HTML element, 633-634
**B channels (narrowband
  ISDN)**, 188, 193-194, 203
Back command
  Mosaic, 548-550
  Netscape, 509
backbones, 10, 1220

**backdoor options to Internet
  access**, 116
**background colors (Web
  pages), setting**, 718-719
**background graphics (Web
  pages)**, 718-719
**background textures (Web
  pages)**, 719
backing up viruses, 1062-1063
**band signaling, DTMF (dual
  tone multiple frequency)**,
  188
bandwidth, 1220
  estimating usage, 229-230
  mailing lists, 434
  video conferencing
    complications, 998-999
bang e-mail addresses, 1221
**Basic Rate Interface (BRI),
  narrowband ISDN**, 187
batching e-mail, 108
baud rates (modems), 142, 215
BBSs (Bulletin Board Systems),
  1163, 1221
  America Online, 264
  Internet access, 120
**Bcc box command (View
  menu)**, 363
**behavior blockers (anti-virus
  software)**, 1061
Berkeley Systems Web site,
  1107
Bestweb mailing list, 1074
BIG-LAN mailing list, 1081
binary files, 1221
  downloading
    from newsgroups with
      Agent/Free Agent
      newsreaders, 811-812
    from newsgroups with
      NewsXpress, 788-789
  e-mail, 339-340
  encoding, 404
  FTP, 843
  sending, 404
  service providers, 404-405
  uploading to newsgroups,
    765, 788-789
  Web pages, design
    considerations, 614-615
BinHex files, 393, 453
BinHex program, 1221
BITNET, 1221
bits, 1221
bits per second (bps), 1221

BitSURFR external ISDN terminal adapter, 199, 202-207
biz.comp.hardware newsgroup, 1167-1174
biz.comp.services newsgroup, 1172-1173
biz.comp.software newsgroup, 1170
blockers (behavior blockers), anti-virus software, 1061
<BODY> HTML element, 641
body content (Web pages), 641
bogus newsgroups, 755
bold text (Web pages), 623, 633-634
Book Stacks Inc. FTP site, 1153-1154
bookmarks (Web pages), 1221
    creating, 523-525, 682, 882
    deleting in Netscape, 525
    editing, 523-525, 881
    errors, 881
    Gopher, 869, 878-882
    linking to with Internet Assistant, 682-684
    mailing with Internet Explorer, 487-488
    Mosaic, 562-567
    Prodigy interface, 297
    saving as files, 525
    setting in Netscape, 522
    sharing, 525-526
    using in Netscape, 525
    see also Favorite Places utility; hotlists
Bookmarks menu commands (HGopher), 879
    Create Bookmark, 882
    Edit Bookmarks, 881
    Load Bookmarks, 881
    Mark Menu, 879
    Remove Bookmark, 881
    Save Bookmarks, 880
    Save Bookmarks As, 880
    Show Bookmarks, 879
Boot Sector Infectors, see BSI
boot sectors
    DBS (DOS Boot Sector), 1064
    MBR (Master Boot Record), 1064
    Windows 95, checking, 1064
Borland Web site, 1104
bots (MUDs), 1015, 1221
bouncing e-mail messages, 1221

bps (bits per second), 1221

 HTML element, 632, 711
BRI (Basic Rate Interface), narrowband ISDN, 187
bridges (networks), 1221
broadcasts, 130
Browse dialog box, 381
browsers, 1221
    character-based, 119
    security, 1040-1041
    VRML browsers (WebFX), 532
        configurations, 735
        downloading, 734
        installation, 734
    Web browsers, 458-459
        Air Mosaic, 168
        America Online, 283-285
        configuring to preview HotDog Web pages, 720
        home page design considerations, 608-609
        HotJava, 467, 731
        Hyper-G utility, 733
        Internet Assistant, 672-677
        Internet Explorer (MSN), 321, 473-495, 1227
        Internet services, 459, 465
        Lynx, 459
        Mosaic, 257-259, 459, 540-542, 1230
        NetLauncher, 255-257
        Netscape, 497-518, 1040, 1230
        Prodigy, 297-299
        text-based, 458
        text-only viewing options, 217
    Web sites, 1116-1120
BrowserWatch Web site, 1118
browsing newsgroups with WinCIM, 241
BSI (Boot Sector Infectors), 1055
    droppers, 1055
    Michelangelo virus, 1059
    protecting, 1055
built-in analog fax/modems, external ISDN terminal adapters, 208
built-in Mosaic hotlists, 570-571
bulleted lists (Web pages), 636
bulletin board systems, see BBSs

Burn:Cycle Web site, 1106
business dealings on the Internet, 82
button bars (HotDog), 708
buying
    Exchange, 351
    Internet Mail, 355
bytes, 1222

C

Cabletron Systems FTP site, 1149
cabling
    coaxial, 1222
    fiber optic, 184
    twisted pair, 184, 1235
caching (Web pages)
    with Mosaic, 549
    with Netscape, 510-511
California State University Windows World Web site, 1114
call for votes (CFV), newsgroups, 755
call preferences (dial-up networking software), 143
call waiting, 190
cameras (video conferencing), 1000-1001
Campus Wide Information Service (CWIS), 1222
canceling file downloads/uploads, 854
carriage returns (HTML recognition), 624-625
catalogs (Lycos), 915
categories (newsgroups), 752-756
cc:Mail mailing list, 1081-1082
CD-ROM LAN mailing list, 1082
CD-ROM Publishing mailing list, 1082
CD-ROMs mailing list, 1082
censorship-related Web sites, 51
Center For Democracy & Technology Web site, 68
centering text in Web pages, 711
Central Point Anti-Virus, see CPAV
CERN, 1222

CERT (Computer Emergency Response Team), 1154
CFV (call for votes), newsgroups, 755
CGI (Common Gateway Interface), 1222
 CGI-bin programs, 666
  Web page forms, 693
 Web page design considerations, 615
 Web sites, 693
 Programmer's Reference Web site, 1119
Challenge Authentication Protocol (CHAP), 147
Chameleon Internet software, 168-172
 components, 171-172
 configurations, 168-172
 ECCO Internet address book, 170
 installation, 168-172
 NEWTShooter utility, 170
Change Password command (Special menu), Eudora, 382
Change Queuing command (Message menu), Eudora, 393-394
changing e-mail addresses, 435-436
channels (IRCs), 947, 1222
 selecting with mIRC, 953-955
 selecting with Netscape Chat, 966
CHAP (Challenge Authentication Protocol), 147
character-based browsers, 119
characters (MUDs)
 descriptions, 1022
 naming, 1019
 registering, 1020
Chase Research, Inc., 1213
chats, see IRCs
check box controls (Web page forms), 648-650, 691-692
Check Mail command (File menu), 394
checks (validity checks), viruses, 1060-1061
child pornography limitations, 63
Church of Scientology legal case, 81-82
Cirrus Logic Inc. FTP site, 1149

Cisco Systems
 addresses, 1213
 mailing list, 1082
 telephone numbers, 1213
 Web site, 1213
city time zones, 1200-1203
CIX (Commercial Internet Exchange), 1222
client/server computing
 FTP, 26-27, 838
  anonymous, 839
  connecting to, 840
  files, 841-842
  windows-based, 841
 Gopher, 31-33
 MUD architecture, 1013-1015
 Telnet, 34-35
 WAIS, 33-34
 WWW architecture, 35-38, 466
clients, 1222
 e-mail, 350
 FTP, 26
 HGopher, 870-871
 IRCs, 943-944
 MUDs, 1014, 1017
 networks (TCP/IP configurations), 134
 Windows 95 FTP client, 839
 WS_FTP, 1236
 WSGopher, 1236
Clipboard, saving to, 903
clipper chip, 72
Close command (Control Box menu), Eudora, 389
Close command (File menu), Eudora, 389
Close Program dialog box, 909
closing
 Archie sessions, 937
 Telnet sessions, 829
 WS_FTP, 865
 see also quitting
CNRI (Corporation for National Research Initiatives), 14, 1222
coaxial cabling, 1222
coded messages, 71
codes (countries), 1191-1198
color
 background color (Web pages), setting, 718-719
 hypertext links, Netscape settings, 508
 Web pages, Netscape settings, 511-512

Columbus Day virus, 1058-1059
3Com Corporation
 addresses, 1217
 FTP site, 1149
 telephone numbers, 1217
 Web site, 1217
combat-oriented MUDs, 1023
combining HTML elements, 641-642
command line, 1222
command-line accounts
 FTP, 839-840
 Telnet, 826-827
  disconnecting, 829
  starting, 827-828
commands
 Bookmarks menu (HGopher)
  Create Bookmark, 882
  Edit Bookmarks, 881
  Load Bookmarks, 881
  Mark Menu, 879
  Remove Bookmark, 881
  Save Bookmarks, 880
  Save Bookmarks As, 880
  Show Bookmarks, 879
 Commands menu (HGopher), 873
 Compose menu (Exchange)
  Forward, 369
  New Message, 363, 442
  Reply to All, 368
  Reply to Sender, 368
 Control Box menu (Eudora), 389
 dial-up scripting software, 149-151
 Edit menu (Eudora), 390
 File menu (Eudora)
  Check Mail, 394
  Close, 389
  New Folder, 370
  Open, 389
  Properties, 368
  Save As, 389
  Send, 364, 369
 File menu (Exchange), 360
 FTP, 840
 HGopher menu
  Bookmarks, 879
  Gopher Set Up, 872
  Options, 872
 HTML commands, 460
 Jughead, 895
 LISTSERV mailing lists, 422-423, 426-428

GET command, 428
INDEX command, 428
INFO command, 427
INFO REFCARD
  command, 428
LIST command, 423
REGISTER command, 426
REVIEW command, 427
Mailbox menu (Eudora)
  In, 390
  Out, 390
  Trash, 390
Majordomo mailing lists
  HELP command, 430
  sending, 430
  SUBSCRIBE command,
    431
  UNSUBSCRIBE
    command, 431
Message menu (Eudora)
  Attach Document, 392
  Change Queuing, 393,
    394
  Forward, 398
  Redirect, 398
  Reply, 398
  Send Again, 398
  Send Immediately, 392
Options menu (HGopher),
  884
Special menu (Eudora)
  Add as Recipient, 387
  Change Password, 382
  Empty Trash, 399
  Forget Password, 382
  Make Nickname, 386
  Remove Recipient, 388
  Settings, 383
Transfer menu (Eudora)
  New, 396
  Trash, 391, 398
UNIX
  man, 1229
  rlogin, 1233
View menu (Exchange), 363
WHOIS database, 335
Window menu (Eudora)
  Nicknames, 386
  Signature, 388
Windows 95 Telnet menu,
  834
**Commands menu commands
  (HGopher), 873**
**commercial activity on the
  Internet, 82**
**Commercial Internet
  Exchange (CIX), 1222**

**commercial service providers,
  117**
  America Online, 263-285,
    406-407, 1219
  CompuServe, 231-234,
    408-409, 1222
  Delphi, 409
  e-mail
    receiving, 413-415
    sending, 413-415
  GEnie, 409-410
  MCI Mail, 410-411
  MSN, 309-326, 476, 1230
  newsgroups, 604
  Prodigy, 287-306, 411-412,
    1232
communications
  digital, 1223
  video conferencing, 995-996
    advantages of, 997-998
    bandwidth
      complications, 998-999
    cameras, 1000-1001
    commercial availability,
      997
    CU-SeeMe program,
      1002-1008
    future developments,
      1008-1009
    guidelines to keeping
      updated, 1009-1010
    hardware requirements,
      999-1002
    history of, 996-997
    holographic, 1009
    integration with virtual
      reality, 1009
    limitations, 1008
    monitor requirements,
      1001-1002
    PC requirements,
      999-1000
    reflectors, 1003
    sound card requirements,
      1001
    video capture boards,
      1000
  voice communications on
    the Net, 971-972
    future developments, 994
    impact on Internet
      technology, 993-994
    modem requirements,
      975-976
    sound card requirements,
      973-975

    system requirements,
      972-976
    TrueSpeech helper
      application, 992-993
    via Cyberphone, 990-991
    via Digiphone software,
      983-987
    via Internet Global Phone
      software, 987
    via Internet Phone
      software, 977-983
    via Internet Voice Chat
      software, 976-977
    via PowWow, 989-990
    via Speak Freely, 987-988
    via TS Intercom, 991-992
    via WebPhone, 988-989
    via WebTalk, 988
**Communications Decency
  Act, 67**
**Communications/Modems/
  BBSs mailing list, 1074**
**comp.answers newsgroup,
  1161**
**comp.infosystems newsgroup,
  1165**
**comp.infosystms.www.authoring.
  htmle newsgroup, 1165**
**comp.infosystems.www.browsers.
  ms-windows newsgroup,
  1166**
**comp.internet.net-happenings
  newsgroup, 1166**
**comp.org.eff.news.talk
  newsgroup, 1162-1163**
**comp.os.ms-windows .*
  newsgroup, 1170-1171**
**comp.os.ms-windows.
  programmer newsgroup,
  1171-1172**
**comp.os.ms-windows.apps
  newsgroup, 1171-1174**
**comp.os.ms-windows.
  networking.ras newsgroup,
  1166**
**comp.protocols .* newsgroup,
  1166-1167**
**comp.publish.cdrom.multimedia
  newsgroup, 1173-1174**
**comp.security.firewalls
  newsgroup, 1167**
**comp.sys.ibm.pc.harware
  newsgroup, 1167-1174**
comp.virus newsgroup, 1068
**company-wide access to
  Internet, 103**
**Compaq Computer Corp. Web
  site, 1093**

Compose menu commands (Exchange)
Forward, 369
New Message, 363
Reply to All, 368
Reply to Sender, 368
compression (files), 1222
e-mail, 340-342
extensions, 341
packing, 342
StuffIt, 341
unpacking, 342
WinZip, 341, 871
CompuNotes mailing list, 1083
CompuServe, 117, 231-234, 408-409, 1222
addresses, 1210
ASCII newsreader, 246-251
cost, 232-233
database access, 232
e-mail capabilities, 235
forums, 232, 262
FTP capabilities, 235
future developments, 262
hotlists (Web sites), 259-260
Internet gateway, 234-235
mailing lists, 235
Mosaic Web browser, 257-259
sending e-mail messages, 408-409
subscriber orientation, 232
telephone numbers, 1210
Telnet capabilities, 235, 253-254
terminal emulation mode, subscribing to newsgroups, 247
UseNet newsgroup accessibility, 235
Web site, 255, 1131, 1210
WWW capabilities, 235, 254-261
see also WinCIM
CompuServe Information Manager for Windows, *see* **WinCIM**
computer crime laws, 91
Computer Emergency Response Team, *see* **CERT**
Computer Fraud and Abuse Act, 93
Computer Law mailing list, 1082
Computer Price Cruncher Web site, 1111

Computer Privacy Digest FTP site, 1147
Computer Professionals for Social Responsibility (CPSR), 14, 1222
computers
anti-virus products, 1058
linking via Telnet, 820-821
mailing lists, 1081-1088
network security, 1050-1051
newsgroups, 1162, 1167-1169
protecting, 1066
radio frequency, tapping into, 1043
software newsgroups, 1169-1172
Telnet
connecting, 826-827
disconnecting, 829
terminals
ANSI, 822
defined, 821
HyperTerminal, 822
TTY, 822
VT series, 821
VAX computers, 830
viruses, 95, 1056-1057
acquiring, 1061-1062
anti-virus products, 1067
changing, 1058
defined, 1054
macros, 1055-1056
naming, 1059
restoring, 1063
scanning, 1058, 1060
Windows 95, 1064
Web sites, 1091-1094, 1109-1112
see also PCs
configurations
Agent newsreader, 792-805
Chameleon Internet software, 168-172
CU-SeeMe video conferencing program, 1004
dial-up networking software connections, 145-146
Digiphone, 984-986
DNS addresses for LANs, 133-134
Eudora, 383-384
Free Agent newsreader, 792-805
gateways for LANs, 132

helper applications for Netscape, 588-591
HGopher, 872-873
Internet Explorer Web browser, 474-475, 478-481
Internet in a Box software, 160-167
Internet Mail, 359
Internet Phone software, 978-981
Mosaic for use with viewer applications, 593-594
NewsXpress newsreader, 778-779
PCs as Web servers, 604
service providers for Internet in a Box software, 163
TCP/IP
for network clients, 134
for Windows 95, 129-134
viewer applications
for Mosaic, 594-595
for Netscape, 588-589
Web browsers to preview HotDog Web pages, 720
Web pages for UNIX servers, 721
WebFX VRML browser, 735
WINS for Windows 95 workstations, 131
conflicts (TCP/IP stacks) with Internet software, 158, 158-159
Connect dialog box, 833
connecting
Archie, 927, 933
FTP
servers, 840
troubleshooting, 847
Telnet, 822-823, 826
ports, 829-830
remote computers, 826-827
Windows 95, 833-834
to IRCs
with mIRC, 953
with Netscape Chat, 965-968
to MUDs, 1018-1019
to NewsXpress newsreader, 778
to service providers with dial-up networking software, 141-148
WS_FTP, 844-846
connection failure (modems), troubleshooting, 156

Connection Timer Settings dialog box (Internet in a Box software), 164
connections
dial-up networking software
configurations, 145-146
troubleshooting, 155-156
host servers with domain
suffixes, 134
Internet, 19-21, 102
high-speed, 215-218
via America Online,
263-285
via BBSs, 120
via Chameleon software,
168-172
via corporate systems,
103-104
via dedicated gateways,
104-105, 109
via Dedicated-56 lines,
219-220
via dial-up networking
software, 137-156
via direct gateways, 102
via Internet in a Box
software, 160-168
via ISDN lines, 182-194
via LANs, 125-135
via MSN, 309-326
via NetCruiser Internet
software, 172-175
via Prodigy, 287-306
via professional
organizations, 120
via public libraries, 120
via service providers, 102,
105, 110-117
via Switched-56 lines,
219-220
via T1/T3 lines, 224-225
via third-party gateways,
103, 110
via WinSock, 151-153
wiring technologies,
selecting, 229
TCP/IP, testing, 135
Conner Peripherals Web site,
1099
Constitution of the United
states Web site, 48
content area
Mosaic, 545
Netscape, 503
contractual agreements on
the Internet, 83

Control Box menu commands
(Eudora), 389
control panels
Add/Remove Programs, 138
Network, opening, 127
converters
MIME, 340
UUDecode, 339
UUEncode, 339
converting
host names to IP addresses,
131
Macintosh files, 340
Web pages to Word
documents, 697
Word documents to Web
pages, 695-697
see also decoding
Copy command (Edit menu),
390, 903
Copy dialog box, 371
copy modes (HGopher), 883
copying
e-mail messages, 371-372,
390
Internet material (implied
consent considerations), 75
URLs to Windows 95
workstations with Internet
Exchange, 482
Copyright Web site, 77
copyrights
e-mail, 343
Internet concerns, 72
clearances, 78
fair use doctrine, 79
registration of works,
77-79
newsgroup considerations,
764-765
Corel Corp. Web site, 1104
corporate domain names, 103
Corporation for National
Research Initiatives (CNRI),
14, 1222
Corporation for Research and
Educational Networking
(CREN), 1222
cost (service providers), 122
Counterpoint Publishing's
Internet Services Gopher
site, 1178
country codes
abbreviations, 1191-1198
Internet hosts, 23
mailing list, 1075

CPAV (Central Point Anti-
Virus), 1067
CPSR (Computer Professionals
for Social Responsibility), 14,
1222
FTP site, 1146
Web site, 1138
crackers, 90
Create Bookmark command
(Bookmarks menu),
HGopher, 882
Create/Edit Bookmark dialog
box, 881
Create Shortcut dialog box,
381, 833, 871, 899
Creative Labs
FTP site, 1150
Web site, 1097-1098
CREN (Corporation for
Research and Educational
Networking), 1222
crime on the Internet, 90
cross-posting newsgroup
messages, 763
Cruising the Internet mailing
list, 1075
cryptology software, 71
CU-SeeMe (video conferencing
program), 1002-1008
audio controls, 1007
configurations, 1004
downloading, 1003-1004
installation, 1003-1004
limitations, 1008
operating, 1005-1007
system requirements, 1002
Web site, 1002, 1004, 1124
CUI Search Catalog Web site,
1133-1138
cursors, identifying hypertext
links, 462
Customize Toolbar dialog box,
361
customizing
directories, 849-850
Eudora, 384-385
Exchange, 372-373
FTP files, 850-853
Gopher
defaults, 884
networks, 884-885
HGopher, 872-873
hypertext links
with Mosaic, 554-555
with Netscape, 508-509
profiles, 860-861

Sessions Profile window, 861-863

WS_FTP windows, 855-859

Cut command (Edit menu), 390

cutting
e-mail messages with Eudora, 390

CWIS (Campus Wide Information Service), 1222

cyber-crimes, 91-95

Cybermind mailing list, 1075

Cyberphone Internet telephony software, 990-991

cyberspace, 1223

cypher keys, 1044

Cypherpunks FTP site, 1147

D

D channels (narrowband ISDN), 188-192

daemons, 1223

DARPA, 1223

data (Web page tables), 716

data bits (modem settings), 142

Data Encryption Standard (DES), 1223

data entry (Web page forms), 647-656

data interceptions (security), 1035

databases
CompuServe access, 232
searching with Archie, 842, 928
WAIS, 279-280, 1236
WHOIS database, 334-336

David Lawrences's newsgroup list, 1173-1174

DBS (DOS Boot Sector), 1064

DCC (Direct Client-to-Client) chats with mIRC, 957-959

debugging messages (WS_FTP window), 857

Decode command (File menu), HGopher, 451

Decode command (Options menu), HGopher, 451

decoding
files, 1223
defined, 440-441
UseNet, 453
Wincode, 451
Windows 95, 446

newsgroup messages with WINCODE.EXE in Prodigy, 303-304

UUDecoding, 441

decompressing files with WinZip, 871

dedicated connections, 111

dedicated gateways, 109

dedicated lines, 1228

Dedicated-56 Internet connections, 219-220

Default Hosts dialog box (Internet in a Box software), 167

Default Viewers command (Options menu), 907

defaults (Gopher), changing, 884

defining
ASCII file extensions, 864
executable files, 864-865
host profiles, 859-861

definition lists (Web pages), 713

DejaNews newsgroup search utility, 767-768

delay command (dial-up scripting software), 150

deleting
bookmarks in Netscape, 525
documents, 1062
domains from LANs, 134
e-mail messages, 343, 398-399
gateways from LANs, 132
host profiles, 861
Mosaic Hotlists folder items, 567
recipients (Eudora), 388
Web sites from CompuServe hotlists, 259

delineating text in Web pages, 633

Deliver Now command (Tools menu), 364, 367

delivery options (Exchange), 375

Dell Computer Corp. Web site, 1094

Delphi, 409

Demon Internet Web site, 1130

Department of Defense (DOD), 1223

DES (Data Encryption Standard), 344, 1044, 1223

designing
bookmarks, 882
folders in Eudora, 382
profiles, 376

DHCP, 132

dial-up adapters
installation on Windows 95 workstations, 138
TCP/IP support, 140

dial-up networking software
call preferences, 143
connecting to service providers, 141-144
connections
configurations, 145-146
troubleshooting, 155-156
disconnect preferences, 143
installation, 138-139
manual/operator assisted calling options, 143
password encryption options, 146
phone number settings, 144
protocol settings, 146
server connection settings, 146
TCP/IP
settings, 146
stack conflicts, 159
terminal window options, 143
timeout feature, disabling for large downloads, 143

dial-up scripting software, 148-151
commands, 149-151
downloading, 149
installation, 149
on Windows 95 workstations, 140-141
RoboDUN, 153-154
setup for Internet connections, 149
uninstalling support for, 141

Dialer Setup dialog box (Internet in a Box software), 162

dialing errors (modems), troubleshooting, 155

Dialler (WinWAIS), 899

dialog boxes
Add New Interface (Chameleon Internet software), 169
Add/Remove Programs Properties, 353

Auto Detect Extensions, 864
Browse, 381
Close Program, 909
Connect, 833
Connection Timer Settings (Internet in a Box software), 164
Copy, 371
Create Shortcut, 381, 833, 871, 899
Create/Edit Bookmark, 881
Customize Toolbar, 361
Default Hosts (Internet in a Box software), 167
Dialer Setup (Internet in a Box software), 162
Encode Options, 451
FTP Command, 935
FTP Setup, 929
Gopher Set Up Options, 872, 884
How to Connect, 357
Index Search, 890
Input, 849
Internet Properties, 839
Mailboxes, 396
Move, 371
NetCruiser Login, 172
Network Interface (Internet in a Box software), 164
Network Protocol, 128
Network Setup, 884
New, 387
New Key Request (Internet in a Box software), 168
New Mailbox, 396
New Message, 385
Open File, 395
Options, 372, 855
PPP Settings (Internet in a Box software), 165
Program, 833
Program Folder, 833
Program Options, 855, 860
Properties, 365, 376
Run, 832
Save As, 876
Select a Pricing and Access Option (Internet in a Box software), 161
Select Program Folder, 871, 899
Session Options, 861
Session Profile, 844-845, 857
Settings, 383

SLIP Settings (Internet in a Box software), 165
Task Bar Properties, 871
Taskbar Properties, 833, 899
Transfer Status, 854
User Preferences, 936
Verify Deletion, 849
Viewers, 886
WinSock Error, 901
ZIP/UNZIP Options, 452
dialup connections, 111
dialup networking services, 1223
Diamond Multimedia Web site, 1096
digestifying/undigestifying mailing lists, 433
digests (mailing lists), 1223
Digi International
    addresses, 1213
    DataFire internal card ISDN terminal adapter, 209-211
    FTP site, 1150
    telephone numbers, 1213
    Web site, 1213
Digiphone (Internet telephony software), 983-987
    addresses, 1206
    configurations, 984-986
    connecting to other parties, 986-987
    e-mail, 1206
    installation, 984-986
    telephone numbers, 1206
    Web site, 983
digital communications, 1223
Digital Equipment Corporation FTP site, 1143
digital service units (DSUs), 225
digital signaling
    sampling, 181
    versus analog signaling, 177-182
DikuMUDs, 1013
direct connections to Internet, 109
direct gateways, 102
direct service providers, 402-406
directories
    customizing, 849-850
    double-clicking, 849
    FTP sites, 1153-1154
    indexes (FTP), 842
    InterNIC, 926

linking (WS_FTP), 853
naming, 860
temporary directories (Netscape), specifying, 592
troubleshooting, 853, 855
Web sites, 1131-1135
directory buttons (Netscape), 503
directory numbers (DNs), narrowband ISDN B channels, 194
disconnect preferences (dial-up networking software), 143
disconnecting from Telnet, 829
disks (Boot Sector Infectors), 1055
display preferences
    graphics files in Mosaic, 551
    Internet Explorer Web browser, 479
    Mosaic, 555-556
    Netscape, 517-518
    Web pages with Mosaic, 555
displaying
    directories, 849-850
    MIME types for multimedia files in Netscape, 590-591
    modem status indicators for dial-up networking software, 144
    Telnet, 828-829
    time zones, 1199-1200
distortion, 181
distributing newsgroup postings by geographic region, 763
distributors of information (legal concerns), 56
<DL> HTML element, 713
DNs (directory numbers), narrowband ISDN B channels, 194
DNS (Domain Name System), 106, 126, 1223
    Internet Mail, 358
    LAN configurations, 133-134
Document Type Definition (DTD), 725
documents
    deleting, 1062
    Gopher, 869
    Internet, 1187

searches
  relevance feedback, 906-907
  terms, 906
  WAIS Manager 3.1, 905-906
WAIS
  relevance feedback, 902-903
  results, 903-904
  retrieving, 902-903
DOD (Department of Defense), 1223
domain identifiers, 106
Domain Name System (DNS), 106
domain names, 22-24, 88, 105-110, 114, 126
  corporate, 103
  fingering, 333
  service providers, 406
  UUNET Technologies, 405-406
domains (LANs), 1223
  adding, 134
  deleting, 134
Done command (File menu), 902
DOOM MUD, 1028
DOS
  launching, 1066
  Windows 95 viruses, 1065-1066
DOS Boot Sector, *see* DBS
double-clicking directories, 849
downloading, 1224
  Acrobat Amber helper application, 530-531
  binary files from newsgroups
    with Agent/Free Agent newsreaders, 811-812
    with NewsXpress, 788-789
  CU-SeeMe video conferencing program, 1003-1004
  dial-up scripting software, 149
  Eudora, 380-382
  files, 854
    canceling, 854
    disabling timeout feature for dial-up networking software, 143
    with FTP, 26-31

FTP files, 252, 842-843
Internet Assistant, 669-672
Internet Explorer Web browser, 475-476
Mosaic software, 541-542
Navigator Gold, 702-703
NetLauncher Web browser, 255
Netscape, 498-500
newsgroup messages with WinCIM, 243
PC speaker drivers, 581
PGP (Pretty Good Privacy), 1045
RealAudio helper application, 528-529
Shockwave helper application, 530
viewer applications, 583-584
Virtual Explorer add-on utility, 493
viruses, 1062
Web pages to edit with Internet Assistant, 694-695
WebFX VRML browser, 734
WINPGP4, 1047
WinSock, 152, 160
Dr. Solomon's Anti-Virus Toolkit, 1068-1069
drop-down list box controls (Web page forms), inserting with Internet Assistant, 692
droppers, 1055
DSUs (digital service units), 225
DTD (Document Type Definition), 725
DTMF (dual tone multiple frequency), band signaling, 188
DUNE II, 831
duplex sound cards, 974
DVI mailing list, 1083

E

e-mail, 21, 38-41, 114, 1183, 1224
  addresses, 1224
    attaching to Web pages, 719
    bang addresses, 1221
    changing, 435-436
    finding, 332-333

Internet Mail client software, 351-352
    InterNIC, 127
    KIS, 337-338
    Netfind, 336-337
    numerical, 824-825
    Personal Address Book, 350-351
    storing in America Online address book, 269
    storing in Prodigy address book, 306
    storing in WinCIM address book, 237-238
    Telnet, 823-824
    UseNet user list, 338-339
  Agent newsreader capabilities, 801-803, 812-816
  America Online capabilities, 266-269
  batching, 108
  binary files
    encoding, 404
    sending, 404
  coded messages, 71
  CompuServe capabilities, 235
  converters
    MIME, 340
    UUDecode, 339
    UUEncode, 339
  copyrights, 343
  defined, 329-330
  deleting, 343
  Digiphone, 1206
  encryption, 344-345
    DES (Data Encryption Standard), 344
    ROT13, 345
  etiquette, 345-346
  Eudora client application
    attaching files, 392-393
    copying, 390
    creating, 385-386
    cutting, 390
    deleting, 398-399
    editing, 389-390
    MIME, 392
    pasting, 390
    queuing messages, 393-394
    saving, 389
    sending, 391-392

Exchange client application, 350-378
federal laws, 343
files
    ASCII, 339-340
    binary files, 339-340
    compressing, 340-342
fingering, 333-334
    domain names, 333
    usernames, 333
folders, creating, 370-371
FTP, passwords, 840
gateways, 40
Gmud32, 1206
KIS, keywords, 338
libel issues, 343
locating users from home pages, 332
mailers, 1229
MCI Mail client software, 411
messages
    attaching files to, with America Online, 269
    attaching files to, with Prodigy, 306
    attaching files to, with WinCim, 237
    bouncing, 1221
    copying, 371-372
    filtering with Agent newsreader, 815
    forwarding, 369
    moving, 371-372
    organizing, 369-370
    reading with Agent newsreader, 813-816
    reading with Prodigy, 305
    receiving, 367
    replying, 368-369
    saving, 369-370
    sending from Web pages, 719
    sending with Agent/Free Agent newsreaders, 812-813
    sending with America Online, 268-269
    sending with CompuServe Web browser, 260
    sending with Prodigy, 305-306
    sending with WinCIM, 236-237
    service providers, 404-405

    storing in Agent newsreader folders, 814
    unwanted, 346-347
Mosaic capabilities, 571
MPEGPLAY, 1208
MSN capabilities, 322-323
Netscape capabilities, 504, 533-535
Paint Shop Pro, 1208-1209
Personal Address Book, 366
PGP program, 1232
President of the United States, 344
Privacy Enhanced Mail, 1232
privacy issues, 68
Prodigy capabilities, 289, 305-306
receiving via service providers, 413-415
recipients, 363, 367
retrieving with Eudora, 394-395, 395
right to privacy, 343
routing with Eudora, 397-398
security, 1042
sending
    CompuServe, 408-409
    Delphi, 409
    GEnie, 409-410
    KIS, 338
    MCI Mail, 410-411
    postmasters, 347
    Prodigy, 411
    service providers, 404, 413-415
    system administrators, 347
service providers
    availability, 108
    direct, 402-403
    indirect, 403-404
SMTP, 330-331
standards, 40-41
store and forward systems, 1234
subpoenas, 343
TSR program, 330
UUNET Technologies, 405-406
vacations, 436
WAIS searches, 908-909
Wham, 1209
WHOIS database, 334-336
WinCIM services, 234
X.400, 331-332
X.500, 331-332

ECCO Internet address book (Chameleon Internet software), 170
ECPA (Electronic Communications Privacy Act), 1224
EDI mailing list, 1083
Edit Bookmarks command (Bookmarks menu), 881
Edit menu commands (Eudora)
    Copy, 390
    Cut, 390
    Paste, 390
    Paste as Quotation, 390
editing
    bookmarks, 881
        in Netscape, 523-525
    downloaded Web pages, 694
    e-mail messages with Eudora, 389-390
    Mosaic Hotlists, 565-567
    toolbars (Exchange), 361-363
    Web pages with Internet Assistant, 678
editors
    HTML editors, 618-619, 1184-1185
        HotDog, 703-709, 1226
        Internet Assistant, 667-672, 1227
        Navigator Gold, 699-703
        pros and cons, 620
        Web sites, 620
    multimedia, 1185
EDUCOM, 1224
Edupage mailing list, 1083
EFF (Electronic Frontier Foundation), 14-15, 1224
    FTP site, 1146
    Web site, 68, 1137
Effector Online mailing list, 1084
Egghead Software Web site, 1109
EINet Galaxy Web site, 1133
Electronic Arts Web site, 1106
Electronic Communications and Transactional Records Act, 70
Electronic Communications Privacy Act (ECPA), 69, 1224
Electronic Frontier Foundation (EFF), 14-15, 1224
    FTP site, 1146
    Web site, 68, 1137

Electronic Privacy
  Information Center Web
  site, 71
electronic signatures, business
  dealings on the Internet, 85
ElekTek, Inc. Web site, 1109
elements (HTML), 622-624,
  709-714
    <A>, 638-640
    <B>, 633-634
    <BODY>, 641

, 632, 711
    combining, 641-642
    <DL>, 713
    empty, 623
    <FORM>, 646-647
    <HEAD>, 640
    <HR>, 633
    <I>, 634
    <IMG>, 634
    <INPUT>, 647-656
    inserting in Web pages
      created with Internet
      Assistant, 687-688
    <LI>, 636-637
    non-empty, 623
    <OL>, 636-637
    <P>, 632, 710
    parameters, 624
    <PRE>, 632-633
    <SELECT>, 658-661
    <TABLE>, 716-717
    <TD>, 716
    <TEXTAREA>, 656-658
    <TH>, 716
    <TITLE>, 640-641
    <TR>, 716
    <U>, 634
    <UL>, 636
Emissary Web site, 1127
emoticons (newsgroups), 773,
  1224
empty HTML elements, 623
Empty Trash command
  (Special menu), Eudora, 399
Encapsulated PostScript TIFF
  files, 579
Encode command (File menu),
  HGopher, 450
Encode command (Options
  menu), HGopher, 450
Encode Options dialog box,
  451
encoding
    binary files, 404
    files, 445-446, 1224

defined, 440-441
    MIME, 407
    sending, 442-443, 444
    UseNet, 453
    Wincode, 449-451
    Windows 95, 446
  MIME, 441
  quoted-printable encoding,
    384
  UUEncoding, 441
encryption, 1044, 1224
  passwords for dial-up
    networking software, 146
  PGP (Pretty Good Privacy),
    1044
  software, 71
  e-mail, 344-345
    DES (Data Encryption
      Standard), 344, 1044
    ROT13, 345
endproc command, dial-up
  scripting software, 150
Entering the World Wide
  Web: A Guide to Cyberspace
  Web site, 471
Epic MegaGames Web site,
  1107
errors
  bookmarks, 881
  inline images,
    troubleshooting, 712
  modem answering,
    troubleshooting, 155
  modem dialing,
    troubleshooting, 155
  Mosaic
    network errors, 575-576
    user errors, 574-575
  queuing messages, 394
  Telnet, 827
  WS_FTP, 854
establishing MSN accounts,
  315-317
Etext FTP site, 1153
EtherNet, 1224
etiquette
  e-mail, 345-346
  Internet, 16-17
  MUDs, 1016
  see also netiquette
EUDOR152.EXE, running, 380
Eudora e-mail client
  application, 1224
    configuring, 383-384
    customizing, 384-385
    downloading, 380-382

e-mail operations
    attaching files, 392-393
    copying, 390
    creating, 385-386
    cutting, 390
    deleting, 398-399
    editing, 389-390
    MIME, 392
    pasting, 390
    queuing messages,
      393-394
    retrieving, 394-395
    routing, 397-398
    saving, 389
    sending, 391-392
  encoded files, sending, 444
  EUDOR152.EXE, running,
    380
  folders, creating, 382,
    396-397
  installing, 380-382
  mailboxes, creating, 396-397
  nicknames, 386-387
  passwords, 382-383
  Quick Recipient list, 387
  quoted-printable encoding,
    384
  recipients, deleting, 388
  shortcuts, 395
  signatures, 384, 388-389
  upgrading, 399
  Web site, 1127
Eudora Light Corporation,
  contact sources, 1206
Excel to HTML Converter Web
  site, 1121
Excel-G mailing list, 1084
Excel-L mailing list, 1084
Exchange e-mail client
  software
    customizing, 372-373
    defined, 350-351
    delivery options, 375
    e-mail, 350
    Information Services
      Internet Mail, 351-352,
        356-360
      Personal Address Book,
        350-351
      Personal Information
        Store, 350
    installing from Windows 95
      disks/CD-ROM, 353-355
    profiles, creating, 376
    purchasing, 351-352
    read options, 374

receiving e-mail messages, 363
send options, 375
sending
e-mail messages, 363-364
encoded files, 442-443
starting, 360
toolbars, 360-363
windows
Mailbox Window, 361
Message Window, 362
Exec-PC FTP site, 1143
executable files
defining, 864-865
EUDOR152.EXE, running, 380
Exit and Log Off command (File menu; Exchange), 360
exiting
Archie, 937
Telnet, 829
WS_FTP, 865
see also quitting
expiration dates (hypertext links), setting with Netscape, 509
Explorer icons
adding, 833
creating, 871
expressions (Archie), 931
extensions
ASCII, defining, 864
filenames, compressing files, 341
external ISDN terminal adapters, 199-208
analog port options, 207
built-in analog fax/modems, 208
Internal NT1 support, 208
multilink PPP support, 207

F

F-PROT, 1069-1070
fair use doctrine, 79
FAQs (Frequently Asked Questions), 1224
DOOM, 1028
mailing lists, 434
newsgroups, 757-758
MUDs, 1024
WAIS, 898
FARNET, 1224

Favorite Places utility
America Online, 285
Internet Assistant, 676-677
Internet Explorer Web browser, 486-492
see also bookmarks
federal laws
computer privacy, 69
e-mail, 343
feeding newsgroups, 1225
fiber optic cabling, 184
fields (Web page forms), inserting with Internet Assistant, 689-693
File menu commands (Eudora)
Check Mail, 394
Close, 389
New Folder, 370
Open, 389
Properties, 368
Save As, 389
Send, 369
File menu commands (Exchange)
Exit, 360
Exit and Log Off, 360
file transfer protocol, *see* FTP
filenames (extensions), 341
files
ASCII extensions, defining, 864
attaching e-mail messages to
with America Online, 269
with Prodigy, 306
with WinCim, 237
AUTOEXEC.BAT files, changing, 1046
binary files, 1221
downloading, 788-789, 811-812
e-mail, 339-340
encoding, 404
FTP, 843
sending, 404
service providers, 404-405
uploading to newsgroups, 765, 788-789
Web pages, design considerations, 614-615
BinHex files, 393
compression, 1222
e-mail, 340-342
extensions, 341
packing, 342
StuffIt, 341

unpacking, 342
WinZip, 341, 871
decoding, 1223
defined, 440-441
UseNet, 453
Wincode, 451
Windows 95, 446
decompressing with WinZip, 871
downloading, 854
canceling, 854
disabling timeout feature for dial-up networking services, 143
with FTP, 26-31, 27
e-mail
ASCII, 339-340
attaching, 392-393
binary files, 339-340
copyrights, 343
encoding, 445-446, 1224
defined, 440-441
MIME, 407
UseNet, 453
Wincode, 449-451
Windows 95, 446
EUDOR152.EXE, running, 380
executable files, defining, 864-865
extensions (HTML recognition), 627
finding, 28-29
with Archie, 29-31
with Gopher, 31
with Telnet, 34-35
with Veronica, 32-33
with WAIS, 33-34
FTP
customizing, 850-853
downloading, 842-843
downloading with WinCIM, 252
finding, 28-29
indexes, 842
locating, 841-842
transferring, 838
uploading, 842-843
virus precautions, 253
indexes (FTP sites), 29
linking with WS_FTP, 853
Macintosh, converting, 340
names, searching with Archie, 927

retrieving
    with Archie, 935-936
    with WS_FTP, 853-855
    searches (WAIS Manager
        3.1), 905-906
    transferring, 853, 876-877
    troubleshooting, 855
    uploading
        canceling, 854
        to newsgroups, 765
        to newsgroups with
            WinCIM, 244
        with FTP, 26, 27
        with WS_FTP, 854
    viruses (Windows 95),
        1065-1066
filtering
    e-mail messages with Agent
        newsreader, 815
    newsgroups, 766-767, 781
filters (HTML), 619
    pros and cons, 620
    Web sites, 620
finding
    e-mail users, 332-333
    Exchange, 351-352
    files
        FTP files, 28-29, 841-842
        with Archie, 29-31
        with Gopher, 31
        with Telnet, 34-35
        with Veronica, 32-33
        with WAIS, 33-34
    mailing lists, 431, 1089-1090
    MUDs with Web search
        engines, 1018
    newsgroups with Internet
        Explorer, 489
    viewer applications, 583-584
    Web sites, 37-38
finger utility, 1225
finding
    e-mail users, 333-334
    sites, 334
firewalls, 115, 1036-1037,
    1225
Firewalls mailing list, 1075
First Amendment Cyber-
    Tribune Web site, 49
First Amendment issues
    applicable to the Internet,
    48-51
First Amendment-related web
    sites, 50
First Floor Software Web site,

1119
flame wars (mailing lists), 435
flaming, 771-772, 1225
folders
    creating, 370-371, 396-397
    e-mail messages
        copying, 371-372
        moving, 371-372
    Eudora, creating, 382
    Mosaic hotlists
        adding URLs to, 564-565
        creating, 563-564
        deleting items, 567
        editing, 566
        moving items, 566-567
fonts (display preferences)
    in Agent newsreader, 803
    in Internet Explorer, 495
    in mIRC, 963
    in Mosaic, 556-557
forgery, 85
Forget Password command
    (Special menu), Eudora, 382
<FORM> HTML element,
    646-647
formats
    graphics files, 578-580, 684
    movie files, 581-582
    sound files, 580-581
formatting
    directories, 849-850
    Eudora, 384-385
    Exchange, 372-373
    HGopher, 872-873
    profiles, 860-861
    Sessions Profile window,
        861-863
    text in Web pages, 610,
        622-624, 710-711
    Web pages with Internet
        Assistant, 679-680
    WS_FTP windows, 855-859
forms (Web pages), 644-663,
    1225
        CGI-bin programs, 693
        check box controls,
            inserting with Internet
            Assistant, 691-692
        checkbox controls, 648-
            650
        creating, 662-663
        creating with HotDog,
            717-718
        creating with Internet
            Assistant, 688-693
        design considerations,

614
    drop-down list box
        controls, inserting with
        Internet Assistant, 692
    fields, inserting with
        Internet Assistant,
        689-693
    lists, 658-661
    password encoding,
        654-655
    processing, 645
    radio button controls,
        650-652
    reset buttons, 655-656
    send buttons, 656
    sending data to Web
        servers, 646
    submit buttons, inserting
        with Internet Assistant,
        692-693
    submitting, 664-665
    text areas, 656-658
    text box controls,
        652-654, 691
    troubleshooting, 663
    user input, 647-656
forums (CompuServe),
    232, 262
Forward command
    Compose menu (Exchange),
        369
    Message menu (Eudora), 398
    Mosaic, 548-550
    Netscape, 509
forwarding e-mail messages,
    369
Four11 White Page Directory
    Web site, 1135
frame relay (packet
    switching), 220-224, 1225
Free Agent newsreader,
    791-816, 1225
    configurations, 792-805
    downloading binary files
        from newsgroups, 811-812
    following newsgroup
        message threads, 808-810
    font preferences, 803
    FTP site, 792
    newsgroup option settings,
        804-805
    posting newsgroup
        messages, 810-811
    reading newsgroup
        messages, 806-808
    responding to newsgroup

messages, 811
sending e-mail messages,
812-813
starting, 792-805
subscribing/unsubscribing to
newsgroups, 805-806
Web site, 792
window layout preferences,
803-804
see also Agent newsreader
free speech on the Net, 48-51
**Free World Dialup mailing
list, 1075**
freenet, 1225
freeware, 28, 1225
audio players, 581
NetCD95, 1183
video players, 582
viewer applications, 580
**frequency selective
attenuation (bandwidth),
180**
Frequently Asked Questions,
see FAQs
**frontdoor options (service
providers), 116**
**Frontier Technologies
Corporation**
addresses, 1213
Frontier Internet software,
175
telephone numbers, 1213
Web site, 1127, 1213
**FTP (file transfer protocol), 26,
1184, 1225**
America Online capabilities,
267, 281-282
anonymous FTP, 1219
anonymous servers, 27-28
CERT (Computer Emergency
Response Team), 1154
client/server architecture,
838-839
clients, 26, 841
command-line accounts,
839-840
commands, 840
CompuServe capabilities,
235
defined, 837-838
directories, customizing,
849-850
files
binary files, 843
customizing, 850-853
downloading, 842-843
downloading with

WinCIM, 252
indexes, 842
locating, 841-842
transferring, 838
uploading, 842-843
virus precautions, 253
interfaces, installing, 841
logging on/off, 846
passwords, 840
Prodigy capabilities, 300-301
security, 1041
servers, 26-27
connecting to, 840
postmasters, 842
troubleshooting, 847, 853
sites
3Com, 1149
accessing with America
Online, 281-282
accessing with
CompuServe, 261
accessing with Prodigy,
300-301
accessing with WinCIM,
252-253
Adaptec, 1149
Adobe Systems, 1148
Agent/Free Agent
newsreaders, 792
America Online, 267
American Civil Liberties
Union, 1152
ATI, 1149
Autodesk, 1149
Book Stacks Inc.,
1153-1154
Cabletron Systems, 1149
Cirrus Logic Inc., 1149
Computer Privacy Digest,
1147
CPSR, 1146
Creative Labs, 1150
Cypherpunks, 1147
Digi International, 1150
Digital Equipment
Corporation, 1143
directories, 1153-1154
Electronic Frontier
Foundation, 1146
Etext, 1153
Exec-PC, 1143
file indexes, 29
finding files, 28-29
Gmud client software,
1017
GreatCircle, 1147
hardware-related,
1148-1152

Hyper-G Archive, 1146
InfoMagic, 1142
Internet Global Phone,
987
Internet Wiretap, 1152
InterNIC, 1145
Internic, 11
Java, 1146
Kodak, 1150
lists, 1153-1154
Lotus, 1149
Lynx, 119
MBONE video
conferencing program,
1009
McAfee, 1151
Microsoft, 1148
mIRC, 950
Macmillan Computer
Publishing, (Que), 1152
Mosaic, 541-542
Navigator Gold, 703
NCSA, 1144
Netscape, 499-500, 1145
Novell, 1150
OC Games Archive at
University of
Massachusetts Lo, 1144
Oregon State University,
1141
PC speaker drivers, 581
postmasters, 29
Qualcomm, 1145
Quarterdeck, 1150
Que, (and Macmillan
Computer Publishing),
1152
README files, 28
RTFM, 1144
Simtel, 1143
SLIP/dial-up scripting
support, 140
software, 1139-1148
software-related,
1148-1152
Sparco, 1150
Spry, 1150
Stardust, 1146
Supra, 1151
Telebit, 1151
Trumpet Software, 1147
Trusted Information
Systems, 1148
US Robotics, 1151
UUNet, 1145
Vocaltec, 1147
Walnut Creek CD-ROM,
1142-1154

Washington University at
St. Louis, 1141
Western Digital
Corporation, 1151-1154
WinSite, 1139
WinSock, 114, 152, 160
WinSock-L FTP Archive,
1142-1143
WinZip, 1152
WS_FTP, 1147
Ziff, 1152
storing home pages with,
607-608
versus Telnet, 35
WinCIM capabilities,
251-253
Windows 95 FTP client, 839
see also WS_FTP
**FTP Command dialog box,
935**
FTP Setup dialog box, 929
FTP Software, Inc., 1214
Furry (MUDs), 1015
**FYI (For Your Information)
documents, 11**

G

games
interactive, 42
MUDs, 1011-1015, 1230
administrators, 1020
building worlds, 1024
categories of, 1013
characters, descriptions,
1022
characters, naming, 1019
characters, registering,
1020
client/server architecture,
1013-1015
clients, 1014, 1017
combat-oriented, 1023
connecting to, 1018-1019
DOOM, 1028
etiquette, 1016
FAQs, 1024
finding with Web search
engines, 1018
Gopher sites, 1018
Help, 1020
history of, 1013
Internet resources, 1024
joining, 1018

navigating, 1020-1021
Netrek, 1024-1028
private conversations,
1022
quitting, 1023
real-life implications,
1017
servers, 1014
Stars!, 1028-1029
teleporting, 1021
telnetting to, 1014-1015
terminology, 1015-1017
user interaction,
1021-1022
virtual possessions,
1022-1023
Web sites, 1024
Wizards, 1024
telnetting, 830-831
DUNE II, 831
WWW sites, 1105-1109
**Gandalf Technologies, contact
sources, 1214-1218**
**Gateway 2000 mailing list,
1084**
**gateways (Internet), 109, 127,
1225**
America Online support,
266-267
CompuServe support,
234-235
direct, 102
e-mail, 40
LANs, 132
**GEnie commercial service
provider, 409-410**
**GET command (LISTSERV
mailing lists), 428**
**GET method, <FORM> HTML
element, 646**
**getip command (dial-up
scripting software), 150**
**GIF (Graphics Interchange
Format) files, 578, 684, 1225**
gigabits, 1225
gigabytes, 1225
**GMT (Greenwich Mean Time),
1200**
Gmud client software, 1017
**Gmud32, contact sources,
1206**
**Go Home command
(Commands menu;
HGopher), 873**
Gods (MUDs), 1015

Gopher, 937, 1226
advantages, 868-869
America Online capabilities,
267, 278-280
bookmarks, 869, 878-882
creating, 882
editing, 881
errors, 881
defaults, changing, 884
defined, 867-868
documents, 869
finding files with, 31
Gopher +, 869
Gopherspace, 868
HGopher client software
copy modes, 883
customizing, 872-873
defined, 870
files, transferring,
876-877
icons, 870-871
installing, 870-871
navigating, 873-875
page display storage, 883
starting, 871
viewers, 885-888
icons, 874-875
items, 869
Jughead client application,
891-892
commands, 895
queries, 894-895
networks, changing, 884-885
Prodigy capabilities, 299-300
searching with Jughead,
892-894
security, 1041-1042
servers, 32, 869
sites, 32, 1176
accessing with America
Online, 279
accessing with
CompuServe Web
browser, 261
accessing with Prodigy,
299-300
accessing with Veronica,
280
Counterpoint
Publishing's Internet
Services, 1178
MUDs, 1018
NSTN, 1177
Software Tool and Die:
The World, 1177

University of Minnesota, 1176-1177
University of Southern California Gopher Jewels, 1177
Veronica client application
defined, 888-889
indexes, 889
queries, 890-891
searching, 889-890
troubleshooting, 890
Web browsers, 868
Gopher Set Up command (HGopher menu), 872
Gopher Set Up command (Options menu; HGopher), 884
Gopher Set Up Options dialog box, 872, 884
Gopherbook, 1226
Gopherspace, 32
GoTo menu (Prodigy), 294
government regulation of material on the Internet, 67-68
graphics files
as image maps, 686
as Web page backgrounds, 718-719
design considerations, 616
formats, 578-580, 684
storing, 613
Web pages
adding with Internet Assistant, 684-686
design considerations, 611-615, 684
display preferences in Mosaic, 551
loading preferences for Netscape, 513-515
placeholders, 514
viewing with Internet Explorer, 492
see also inline images
Graphics Interchange Format, see GIF files
GreatCircle FTP site, 1147
guide articles (newsgroups), 757
guidelines for passwords, 1037
GUIs (Graphical User Interfaces), 1226
gzip utility (file compression), 1226

H

hacking, 1034, 1226
accounts, 1038
keyboard logging, 1036
passwords, 1035
Hang Duke (Java-created game), 732
hard disks (Boot Sector Infectors), 1055
hardware
FTP sites, 1148-1152
ISDN, 199-214
newsgroups, 1167-1169
security, 1037
video conferencing requirements, 999-1002
Web sites, 1094-1100
Harris Semiconductor Web site, 1116
Hayes
AT command set, integrating with external ISDN terminal adapters, 201
Web site, 1096
HDSLs (high bit-rate digital subscriber lines), 227
<HEAD> HTML element, 640
headers (Web pages), 640, 1226
headings (Web pages)
tables, 716
text, 710
Help
MUDs, 1020
Telnet, 835
HELP command (Majordomo mailing lists), 430
Help-Net mailing list, 1075-1076
helper applications
Adobe Amber, 530-531
built-in with Java, 467
configurations for Netscape, 588-589
Mosaic, 583
Netscape, 528-532, 583
configurations, 590-591
MIME type configurations, 590
Panorama (SGML), 725-728
RealAudio, 528-529, 586, 741-742
Shockwave, 530, 739-740
TrueSpeech, 741, 992-993
using with Netscape, 500
VuePrint, 587
WebFX, 532
WHAM, 587
WPLANY, 587
see also audio players; viewer applications
Hewlett Packard Web site, 1098
HGopher client application, 1226
bookmarks, 878-882
creating, 882
editing, 881
errors, 881
copy modes, 883
customizing, 872-873
defaults, changing, 884
defined, 870
files, transferring, 876-877
HGopher menu commands
Bookmarks, 879
Gopher Set Up, 872
Options, 872
icons, 870-871, 874-875
installing, 870-871
Jughead, 891-892, 894-895
navigating, 873-875
NetCD95, 871
networks, changing, 884-885
page display storage, setting, 883
searching
with Jughead, 892-894
with Veronica, 889-891
starting, 871
Veronica, 889-890
queries, 890-891
troubleshooting, 890
viewers, 885-888
hiding
Telnet, 828-829
viruses, 1058
high bit-rate digital subscriber lines (HDSLs), 227
high-speed Internet connections, 215-218, 226-227
history lists
Internet Assistant, 675-676
Internet Explorer, 484-486
Mosaic, 561
Netscape, 521
holographic video conferencing, 1009

home pages, 465-466, 505, 520, 544, 1226
  binary files, 614-615
  body content, 641
  browser considerations, 608-609
  CGI-bin programs, 615, 666
  content considerations, 603
  creating
    with HTML, 621, 642-644
    with Prodigy, 298-299
  designing, 597-605, 615-616
  e-mail addresses, finding, 332
  forms, 644-663, 1225
    checkbox controls, 648-650
    creating, 661-663
    creating with Internet Assistant, 688-693
    design considerations, 614
    fields, inserting with Internet Assistant, 689-693
    lists, 658-661
    password encoding, 654-655
    processing, 645
    radio button controls, 650-652
    reset buttons, 655-656
    send buttons, 656
    sending data to Web servers, 646
    submitting, 664-665
    text areas, 656-658
    text box controls, 652-654
    troubleshooting, 663
    user input, 647-656
  generating interest in, 617-618
  graphics files, 611-616
  headers, 640
  horizontal rules, inserting, 633
  HTML editors, 618-619
    pros and cons, 620
    Web sites, 620
  HTML filters, 619-620
  hypertext links, 637-640
    anchors, 637-640
    design considerations, 610-611
  indexing contents with anchors, 638

lists
  bulleted, 636
  indented, 636
  numbered, 636-637
  ordered, 636-637
  unordered, 636
Mosaic defaults, 544
movie files, 614-615
Netscape preferences, 505-506
posting to mailing lists, 617-618
Prodigy preferences, 298
promoting, 617-618
related WWW sites, 604
service provider charges, 605-607
service provider support for, 603-605
sound files, 613-614
standardized format, 630
storage charges from service providers, 606-607
storing
  with FTP, 607-608
  with HTTP, 607-608
target audiences, 601-603
text
  bold, 623, 633-634
  delineating, 633
  formatting, 610
  formatting with HTML tags, 622-624
  inserting with simple text editors, 609-610
  italicizing, 634
  line breaks, 632
  paragraph breaks, 632
  preformatted, 632-633
  underlining, 634
throughput charges for service providers, 607
titles, 640-641
see also Web pages
hop-check utility, 1226
horizontal rules (Web pages), 711
  creating with Internet Assistant, 686-687
  inserting, 633
host names, 23-24, 126, 1226
  allocation, 132
  nodes, 824
  numerical addresses, 824-825
  Telnet, 823-824
  translating to IP addresses, 131

host profiles
  defining, 859-861
  deleting, 861
  personal accounts, 860
hosts, 1226
  addresses, 1226
  connecting to with domain suffixes, 134
  Internet, 21
    country codes, 23
    domain names, 23
    growth, 19
    IP addresses, 24
    recent population, 10
  remote hosts, 1233
HotDog (HTML editor), 703-705, 1226
  addresses, 1206
  button bar, 708
  creating Web pages, 709-714
    forms, 717-718
    tables, 715-717
  installation, 705-709
  previewing Web pages, 720-721
  starting, 706
  system requirements, 705
  telephone numbers, 1206
  toolbar, 707
  Web site, 705, 1206
HotJava Interest mailing list, 1077
HotJava Web browser, 467, 731
hotlists, 1226
  CompuServe, 259-260
  Mosaic, 562-567
    accessing items from, 568-569
    adding URLs to folders, 564-565
    built-in, 570-571
    creating, 567
    editing, 565-567
    folders, creating, 563-564
    folders, deleting items, 567
    folders, editing items, 566
    folders, moving items, 566-567
    loading, 568
    loading Web pages from, 569
    menus, setup, 569
    saving, 567

saving as HTML files, 570
sharing, 570
Prodigy, 295
see also bookmarks
**How to Connect dialog box,
357**
<HR> HTML element, 633
**HTML (HyperText Markup
Language), 36, 460, 622, 724,
1227**
carriage return recognition,
624-625
commands, 460
creating Web pages, 621,
642-644
documents, *see* home pages;
Web pages
editors, 618-619, 1184-1185
HotDog, 703-709, 1226
Internet Assistant,
667-672, 1227
Navigator Gold, 699-703
pros and cons, 620
Web sites, 620
elements, 622-624, 709-714
<A>, 638-640
<B>, 633-634
<BODY>, 641

, 632, 711
combining, 641-642
<DL>, 713
empty, 623
<FORM>, 646-647
<HEAD>, 640
<HR>, 633
<I>, 634
<IMG>, 634
<INPUT>, 647-656
inserting in Web pages
created w/ Internet
Assistant, 687-688
<LI>, 636-637
non-empty, 623
<OL>, 636-637
<P>, 632, 710
parameters, 624
<PRE>, 632-633
<SELECT>, 658-661
<TABLE>, 716-717
<TD>, 716
<TEXTAREA>, 656-658
<TH>, 716
<TITLE>, 640-641
<TR>, 716
<U>, 634
<UL>, 636

file extension recognition,
627
filters, 619
pros and cons, 620
Web sites, 620
security, 1040-1041
space recognition, 624-625
special character support,
625-626
tags, 36
utilities, 1184-1185
versus SGML, 728-729
Web sites, 1120-1121
**HTML Assistant Web site,
1120**
**HTTP (Hypertext Transfer
Protocol), 464-465, 1227**
storing home pages with,
607-608
**HTTPD (HyperText Transfer
Protocol Daemon), 645**
**human rights related Web
sites, 51**
Hyper-G browser utility, 733
FTP site, 1146
mailing list, 1076
hypermedia, 1227
**HyperTerminal terminal
emulator, 822, 1227**
**hypertext documents,
see Web pages**
**hypertext links, 36, 459-463,
637-640, 1227-1228**
absolute, 553
activating, 462, 507-508
anchors, 462-463, 637-640,
714-717
color, changing with
Netscape, 508
customizing
with Mosaic, 554-555
with Netscape, 508-509
expiration dates, setting with
Netscape, 509
identifying, 462
image maps, 612, 686, 713
inserting in Web pages with
Internet Assistant, 680-684
moving between Web pages
in Mosaic, 547-548
references, 462
relative, 553
to bookmarks with Internet
Assistant, 682-684
to local files with Internet
Assistant, 680-681

to URLS with Internet
Assistant, 681-682
underlining with Netscape,
508
Web page design
considerations, 610-611
**HyperText Markup Language,
see HTML**
**Hypertext Transfer Protocol,
see HTTP**

I

<I> HTML element, 634
**IAB (Internet Architecture
Board), 11, 1227**
IBM Corporation
addresses, 1214
PC mailing list, 1084
PC TCP/IP mailing list, 1076
telephone numbers, 1214
Web site, 1092, 1214
icons
creating, 899, 904
Explorer
adding, 833
creating, 871
Gopher, 874-875
HGopher, creating, 870-871
**Id Software Web site,
1108-1138**
**identifiers (newsgroups),
752-756**
**identifying hypertext links,
462**
IDs
hacking, 1038
MSN accounts, 317
**IDSN*tek, contact sources,
1215**
**IEEE (Institute of Electrical
and Electronics Engineers),
1227**
**IETF (Internet Engineering
Task Force), 11, 1227**
**image maps (hypertext links),
612, 686, 713**
<IMG> HTML element, 634
**implied consent
considerations for copying
material, 74**
**In command (Mailbox menu),
390**
**IN-TOUCH: WIN95 mailing
list, 1085**

Inbox Setup Wizard, 352
indecency on the Internet, 67
indented lists (Web pages), 636
indenting text in Web pages, 713-714
   see also lists
INDEX command (LISTSERV mailing lists), 428
Index Search dialog box, 890
indexes
   FTP files, 29, 842
   Gopher, 889
indexing Web page contents with anchors, 638
indirect service providers, 403-404
   economics of, 403
   sending e-mail messages with, 404
infectors (program infectors), 1054-1055
inflammatory speech concerns, 51
INFO command (LISTSERV mailing lists), 427
INFO REFCARD command (LISTSERV mailing lists), 428
InfoMagic FTP site, 1142
Information Law Web site, 76
Information Services (Exchange)
   Internet Mail, 351-352, 356-360
   Personal Address Book, 350-351
   Personal Information Store, 350
InfoSeek Corp. Web site, 1133
Ingram Micro Web site, 1110
inline images
   alignment, 635
   inserting in Web pages, 634-635, 712
   storing, 613
   text-only browser alternatives, 635
   troubleshooting, 712
   Web page design considerations, 611-613
   see also graphics files
<INPUT> HTML element, 647-656
Input dialog box, 849

inserting
   anchors in Web page tables, 717
   check box controls in Web page forms with Internet Assistant, 691-692
   drop-down list box controls in Web page forms with Internet Assistant, 692
   horizontal rules in Web pages, 633
   HTML elements in Web pages created with Internet Assistant, 687-688
   hypertext links in Web pages with Internet Assistant, 680-684
   inline images in Web pages, 634-635, 712
   mailto links in Web pages, 719
   submit buttons in Web page forms with Internet Assistant, 692-693
   tables in Web pages with HotDog, 715-717
   text
      in Web pages, 711
      in Web pages with simple text editors, 609-610
   text box controls in Web page forms with Internet Assistant, 691
Insight Direct Web site, 1110
inspecting networks for obscenity, 65
Install New Modem Wizard, 311
installation
   Agent newsreader, 793
   BitSURFR external ISDN terminal adapter, 202
   Chameleon Internet software, 168-172
   CU-SeeMe video conferencing program, 1003-1004
   dial-up adapters on Windows 95 workstations, 138
   dial-up networking software, 138-139
   dial-up scripting software, 140-141, 149
   Digi International DataFire internal card ISDN terminal adapter, 210

Digiphone, 984-986
Eudora e-mail client application, 380-382
Exchange e-mail client application, 353-355
FTP interfaces, 841
HGopher, 870-871
HotDog, 705-709
Internet Assistant, 671-672
Internet Explorer
   Web browser
      from Microsoft Web site, 475
      from Plus!, 474-475
Internet in a Box software, 160-167
Internet Mail client application, 356-359
Internet Phone software, 978-981
mIRC, 950-951
modems, troubleshooting, 312
Mosaic, 542-543
Navigator Gold, 702-703
NetCD95, 1181-1183
NetCruiser Internet software, 172
NetLauncher Web browser, 256-257
Netscape Chat, 965
Netscape Web browser, 500-502
NewsXpress newsreader, 776-777
Panorama, 726-728
Plus! (MSN), 313-314
Prodigy software, 290
RealAudio helper application, 529, 741-742
Shockwave, 739-740
SLIP for Windows 95 workstations, 140-141
TCP/IP, 127-129, 139-140
viewer applications, 584-585
Virtual Explorer add-on utility, 493
WAIS Manager 3.1, 904-905
WebFX VRML browser, 734
Wincode, 447-448
WinWAIS, 899
WS_FTP, 844
Institute of Electrical and Electronics Engineers (IEEE), 1227
Integrated Services Digital Network, *see* ISDN

Intel Web site, 1094-1095
Intellectual Property lawyers, 75
Interactive Age Hot 1000 Web site, 1133
interactive gaming, 42
InterAp Web site, 1126-1127
intercepting e-mail messages, 1035
interfaces
  Chameleon Internet software settings, 169
  FTP, installing, 841
  Internet Explorer Web browser, 476-478, 482
  Mosaic, 543-547
  Netscape, 502-506
  Prodigy, 288
    GoTo menu, 294
    hotlists, 295
    organization, 292-295
    toolbar, 294
Intergraph Web site, 1137
internal card ISDN terminal adapters, 208-212
internal NT1 support (external ISDN terminal adapters), 208
International Standards Organization (ISO), 1228
Internet
  addresses (country codes), 1191-1198
  administration, 11
  applications, troubleshooting, 156
  ASCII files, 339-340
  connections, 19-21, 102-107
    high-speed, 215-218
    via America Online, 263-285
    via BBSs, 120
    via Chameleon software, 168-172
    via corporate systems, 103-104
    via dedicated gateways, 104-105, 109
    via Dedicated-56 lines, 219-220
    via dial-up networking software, 137-156
    via direct gateways, 102
    via Internet in a Box software, 160-168
    via ISDN lines, 182-194
    via LANs, 125-135

    via MSN, 309-326
    via NetCrusier Internet software, 172-175
    via Prodigy, 287-306
    via professional organizations, 120
    via public libraries, 120
    via service providers, 102, 105, 110-117
    via Switched-56 lines, 219-220
    via T1/T3 lines, 224-225
    via third-party gateways, 103, 110
    via WinSock, 151-153
    wiring technologies, selecting, 229
  culture, 15-17
  dedicated gateways, 109
  documents, 1187
  finger utility, 333-334
  First Amendment issues, 48-51
  future developments, 13
  FYI documents, 11
  gateways
    America Online support, 266-267
    CompuServe support, 234-235
    direct, 102
    e-mail, 40
    LANs, 132
  growth, 17-19
  history, 9-15
  host sites, 21
    country codes, 23
    domain names, 23
    growth, 19
    IP addresses, 24
    recent population, 10
  legal issues, 47
  mailing lists, 418-420, 1074-1081
    accessing, 432
    bandwidths, 434
    FAQ (Frequently Asked Questions), 434
    flame wars, 435
    LISTSERV, 420, 429
    Majordomo, 430-432
    netiquette, 433
    signal-to-noise ratios, 434
  newsgroups, 1163-1167
  non-profit organizations, 13-15

    online access, 101
    RFCs, 11
    security, 22, 526-527
      firewalls, 1036-1037
      hardware, 1037
      intercepting messages, 1035
      keyboards, 1036
      login names, 1034-1035
      passwords, 1034-1038
      PIN (Personal Identification Number), 1037
      routers, 1036-1037
      software, 1038
    services available, 107
    student access, 110
    Windows 95 built-in support, 125
Internet Architecture Board (IAB), 11, 1227
Internet Assistant (HTML editor/Web browser), 667-669, 1227
  adding graphics files to Web pages, 684-686
  converting Web pages to Word documents, 697
  converting Word documents to Web pages, 695-697
  creating horizontal rules for Web pages, 686-687
  creating Web page forms, 688-693
  creating Web pages, 677-688
  downloading, 669-672
  Favorite Places list, 676-677
  formatting Web pages, 679-680
  history list, 675-676
  inserting hypertext links in Web pages, 680-684
  inserting unsupported HTML code in Web pages, 687-688
  inserting Web page form fields, 689-693
  installation, 671-672
  software requirements (Microsoft Word), 669
  system requirements, 668-669
  toolbars, 673-674
  Web browsing functions, 672-677
  Web site, 670, 1121

Internet Basics mailing list, 1076
Internet domain names, 88
Internet Engineering Task Force (IETF), 11, 109, 1227
Internet Explorer (MSN Web browser), 321, 1227
  advantages to using with Windows 95, 482
  configurations, 474-475, 478-481
  display preferences, 479
  downloading from Microsoft Web site, 475-476
  Favorites list utility, 486-492
  font preferences, 495
  history list, 484-486
  history/document caching preferences, 480
  installation
    from Microsoft Web site, 475
    from Plus!, 474-475
  interface, 476-478, 482
  newsreader preferences, 480
  posting newsgroup messages, 490
  printing Web pages, 487-488
  reading newsgroup messages, 488-490
  saving Web pages, 487-488
  search page preferences, 479
  security preferences, 481
  setup, 473-475
  start page preferences, 479
  starting, 475-481
  status messages, 494
  toolbar, 477
  viewing graphics files in Web pages, 492
  viewing multimedia files, 587-588
Internet Factory Web site, 1119
Internet Freedom and Family Empowerment Act, 58, 66
Internet Global Phone software, 987
Internet in a Box software, 160-168
  components, 167-168
  configurations, 160-167
  installation, 160-167
  ISDN support, 166
  registering, 162
  Web site, 1126

Internet International Directory, 176
Internet Mail client software, 351-352
  configuring, 359
  DNS (Domain Name Service), 358
  installing, 356-359
  purchasing, 355
  requirements, 355
Internet Network Information Center (InterNIC), 12
Internet Phone communication software, 977-983
  addresses, 1207
  configurations, 978-981
  connecting to other parties, 981-983
  installation, 978-981
  mailing list, 1076
  telephone numbers, 1207
  Web site, 1124, 1207
Internet Properties dialog box, 839
Internet Relay Chats, *see* IRCs
Internet service providers, *see* ISPs
Internet Setup Wizard, 314
Internet SIG mailing list, 1076
Internet Society (ISOC), 14, 1138, 1228
Internet Voice Chat software, 976
Internet Wiretap FTP site, 1152
Internet worm, 93
InterNIC (Internet Network Information Center), 12, 127
  direct access systems, 109
  directories, 926
  FTP site, 1145
  Web site, 471
InterNIC server, 335-336
InterPlay Web site, 1108
InterServ service provider (Internet in a Box software), 161
IP (Internet Protocol), 1227
  addresses, 12, 24, 126, 130
  packets, sending, 135
IPCP (Internet Protocol Control Protocol), 113
IPXCP (Internet Packet Exchange Control Protocol), 113

IQuest Web site, 1130
IRCs (Internet Relay Chats), 41-42, 941-943, 1186, 1228
  accessing
    with mIRC, 953-959
    with Telnet, 945
  bots, 1221
  channels, 947, 1222
    selecting with mIRC, 953-955
    selecting with Netscape Chat, 966
  clients, 943-944
  connecting to
    with mIRC, 953
    with Netscape Chat, 965-968
  DCC chats with mIRC, 957-959
  history of, 942-943
  mIRC, 950
    Action Lists, 961-962
    font display preferences, 963
    installation, 950-951
    options, 959
    popup menus, 964
    setup, 951-952
    switches, 960
    URL Catcher, 962
  Net splits, 946-947
  Netscape Chat, 950, 964-969
  private sessions
    with mIRC, 955-957
    with Netscape Chat, 967-968
  purpose of, 942
  servers, 944-945, 948
  switches (mIRC), 960
  talking on, 947
  telnetting to, 945
  Undernet, 948
  user nicknames, 947
  Web sites, 948
ISDN (Integrated Services Digital Network), 111, 177, 1228
  backward capability with analog devices, 186
  connections, 111
  hardware, 199-214
  integrating analog devices, 193
  Internet connections, 182-194
  Internet in a Box support, 166

narrowband ISDN, 187-194
  B channels, 188, 193-194
  D channels, 188-192
  Signaling System #7, 192
NT1 boxes, 192
options, 196
ordering codes, 196
ordering service, 194-196
PRI, 218
requirements for operation, 187
routers, 213-214
S/T interfaces, 192
standards, 195
terminal adapters
  built-in with routers, 213-214
  external, 199-208
  internal card, 208-212
U interfaces, 192
Web sites, 199, 1138
wiring, 196-198
ISDN Systems Corporation, contact sources, 1214
ISO (International Standards Organization), 1228
ISOC (Internet Society), 14, 1138, 1228
ISPs (Internet service providers), 13, 20, 44-45, 102, 105, 110-117, 1228, 1232
  access availability, 121
  access methods, 122-123
  backdoor options, 116
  commercial
    America Online, 263-285, 406-407, 1219
    CompuServe, 231-234, 408-409, 1222
    Delphi, 409
    GEnie, 409-410
    MCI Mail, 410-411
    MSN, 309-326, 476, 1230
    newsgroups, 604
    Prodigy, 287-306, 411-412, 1232
    receiving e-mail from, 413-415
    sending e-mail to, 413-415
  configurations for Internet in a Box software, 163
  connecting to with dial-up networking software, 141-144, 147-148

cost, 122
cost for home page support, 605-607
Demon Internet, 1130
frontdoor options, 116
InterServ (Internet in a Box software), 161
IQuest, 1130
The List, 1130
logins with dial-up scripting software, 150
mailing list, 1076-1077
MCI, 1129
NetCom Internet Service, 172
personal access, 104
Portal, 1130
protocol options, 112-114
PSI, 1129-1138
security, 123
selecting, 121-124
service options, 114-115
services, 121
software requirements, 123
support for Web pages, 603-605
technical support, 124
telephone line connections, 110
throughput charges for home pages, 607
UNIX-based, 147
UUNET Technologies, 1129
Web sites, 1129-1130
WinNet, 1130
italic text (Web pages), 634
items (Gopher), 869
IVC (Internet Voice Chat), 976

J

Java, 731, 1228
  applets, 536, 732, 1220
  FTP site, 1146
  mailing lists, 1077
  Netscape compatibility, 536-537
  Web sites, 537, 732, 1121-1125
  WWW enhancements, 467
JavaScript
  Netscape compatibility, 537
  Web sites, 537
Jerusalem virus, 1058-1059
joining MUDs, 1018

JPEG (Joint Photographic Experts Group) files, 578, 685, 1228
Jughead (Jonzy's Universal Gopher Hierarchy Excavation & Display), 891-892
  commands, 895
  queries, 894-895
  searching Gopher sites, 892-894
Jumbo Web site, 1115

K

Ken Nesbitt's WebEdit Web site, 1120
keyboards, logging, 1036
keys
  adding, 1048
  cypher keys (security), 1044
  public keys
    PGP (Pretty Good Privacy), 1045-1046
    security, 1045
keywords
  KIS, 338
  mailing lists (LISTSERV), 425
kill files (newsreaders), 1228
KIS (Knowbot Information Service), 337-338
  keywords, 338
  sending e-mail, 338
  telneting, 337
  WWW sites, 337
knowbots, 1228
Kodak FTP site, 1150

L

L-Soft International Web site, 1129
labels, 1228
Lag (MUDs), 1016
LANs (local area networks), 1228
  DNS configurations, 133-134
  domains
    adding, 134
    deleting, 134
  gateways
    adding, 132
    configurations, 132
    deleting, 132

subnet masks, 130
subnets, 126
Telnet, 834
launching
    DOS, 1066
    Exchange, 360
    FTP command-line accounts,
        839-840
    HGopher, 871
    Telnet
        command-line accounts,
            827-828
        Windows 95, 832
    WebCrawler, 919-920
    WinWAIS, 900
    Yahoo!, 922
Law Jokes Web site, 50
law-related Web sites, 48
laws
    computer crimes, 91
    curbing obscenity on the
        Internet, 67
    federal laws (e-mail-related),
        343
LCP (Link Control Protocol),
    113
leased lines, 1228
legal issues, 47
legislation to curb obscenity
    on the Internet, 67
<LI> HTML element, 636-637
libel issues (e-mail), 343
libelous Net behavior, 53-54
libraries (Internet access
    from), 120
limiting searches, 932
line breaks (Web page text),
    632, 711
Link Control Protocol (LCP),
    113
linking
    computers via Telnet,
        820-821
    WS_FTP, 853
links, see hypertext links
Lion Communications
    Industries, contact sources,
    1215
The List Web site, 1130
LIST command (LISTSERV
    mailing lists), 423
List Managers mailing list,
    1077
List Owners mailing list, 1078
listing new newsgroups with
    NewsXpress, 780

listproc software, 1228
lists
    FTP sites, 1153-1154
    mailing lists, 418-420
    Web pages, 713-714
        bulleted, 636
        definition lists, 713
        forms, 658-661
        indented, 636
        numbered, 636-637
        ordered, 636-637,
            713-714
        unordered, 636, 713-714
Listserv for Windows 95
    mailing list, 1077
LISTSERV mailing lists, 420,
    423-426, 429, 1229
    addresses, 422-423
    commands, 422-423,
        426-428
        GET command, 428
        INDEX command, 428
        INFO command, 427
        INFO REFCARD
            command, 428
        LIST command, 423
        REGISTER command, 426
        REVIEW command, 427
    keywords, 425
    messages, sending, 420,
        428-429
    subscribing/unsubscribing,
        421-423
live voice on the Net, 42
Load Bookmarks command
    (Bookmarks menu), 881
loading
    graphics files (Web pages),
        Netscape preferences,
        513-515
    local Web pages
        with Mosaic, 558-559
        with Netscape, 518-519
    Mosaic hotlists, 568
    URLs in Netscape, 510
    Web pages
        aborting with Mosaic,
            551
        aborting with Netscape,
            513
        from Mosaic hotlists, 569
        status bar messages in
            Mosaic, 550-551
local area networks, see LANs
local hosts, 1229
local loops (twisted pair
    cabling), 184

local Web pages, loading
    with Mosaic, 558-559
    with Netscape, 518-519
locating FTP files, 841-842
logging (security), 1036
logging on/off
    FTP, 846
    MSN, 320-321
    Prodigy, 291-292
    service providers, with dial-
        up scripting software, 150,
        1229
    Telnet, 829
login names, 1034-1035
Lotus
    FTP site, 1149
    mailing list, 1085
    Web site, 1102
LPMUDs, 1013
LucasArts Entertainment
    Company Web site, 1108
lurking (newsgroups),
    772-773, 1229
LViewPro viewer application,
    585
    addresses, 1207-1218
    telephone numbers,
        1207-1218
    Web site, 1207-1218
Lycos (Web search engine),
    915-919, 1018, 1229
    catalogs, accessing, 915
    Help & Reference, 917
    Web site, 1131-1132
Lynx Web browser, 119, 459

M

Macintosh files, converting,
    340
Macmillan Computer
    Publishing Web site, 175
Macromedia Web site, 1103
Macromedia Authorware
    mailing list, 1083
Macromedia Director mailing
    list, 1083
macros (viruses), 1055-1056
Mailbox menu commands
    (Eudora)
    In, 390
    Out, 390
    Trash, 390
Mailbox Window (Exchange),
    361

mailboxes
America Online, 407
creating, 396-397
out (minimizing messages),
391
transferring messages, 391
Mailboxes dialog box, 396
mailers, 1229
mailing bookmarks with
Internet Explorer, 487-488
mailing lists, 39-40, 418-420,
1229
accessing, 432
Advanced HTML, 1074
Agents, 1081
America Online capabilities,
266, 270-272
anonymous, 436
bandwidth, 434
Bestweb, 1074
BIG-LAN, 1081
cc:Mail, 1081-1082
CD-ROM LAN, 1082
CD-ROM Publishing, 1082
CD-ROMs, 1082
Cisco, 1082
Communications/Modems/
BBSs, 1074
CompuNotes, 1083
CompuServe, 235
Computer Law, 1082
computers, 1081-1088
Country Codes, 1075
Cruising the Internet, 1075
Cybermind, 1075
digestifying/undigestifying,
433
digests, 1223
DVI, 1083
e-mail
addresses, 435-436
vacations, 436
EDI, 1083
Edupage, 1083
Effector Online, 1084
Excel-G, 1084
Excel-L, 1084
FAQs, 434
finding, 1089-1090
Firewalls, 1075
flame wars, 435
Free World Dialup, 1075
Gateway 2000, 1084
Help-Net, 1075-1076
HotJava Interest, 1077
Hyper-G, 1076

IBM PC, 1084
IBM PC TCP/IP, 1076
IN-TOUCH: WIN95, 1085
Internet Basics, 1076
Internet Phone, 1076
Internet related, 1074-1081
Internet Service Providers,
1076-1077
Internet SIG, 1076
Java Announce, 1077
Java Interest, 1077
List Managers, 1077
List Owners, 1078
listproc software, 1228
LISTSERV, 420, 423-426, 429
addresses, 422-423
commands, 422-423,
426-428
GET command, 428
INDEX command, 428
INFO command, 427
INFO REFCARD
command, 428
keywords, 425
LIST command, 423
REGISTER command, 426
REVIEW command, 427
sending messages,
428-429
subscribing/
unsubscribing, 421-423
Listserv for Windows 95,
1077
Lotus Notes, 1085
Macromedia Authorware,
1083
Macromedia Director, 1083
Majordomo software, 432,
1229
finding, 431
HELP command, 430
Majordomo
Announcements, 1078
Majordomo Users, 1078
sending commands, 430
SUBSCRIBE command,
431
subscribing/
unsubscribing, 431
UNSUBSCRIBE
command, 431
Mediaweb, 1078
Microsoft Access, 1081
Microsoft Mail, 1085-1086
Microsoft Windows
News, 1088

Microsoft Windows NT,
1088
Microsoft Windows NT
Server LAN Manager, 1085
Modems, 1085
moderated, 39
moderating, 433
MS-DOS Software
Announcements, 1085
Net Watch, 1079
netiquette, 433
Netscape, 1078
NetTrain, 1078
New Lists, 1079
Novell GroupWise, 1086
Novell LAN, 1086
Pagemaker, 1086
PC Building, 1086
PC Technical Support,
1086-1087
PCI SIG, 1086
PDIAL, 1231
Pegasus Mail for Windows,
1079
PhotoCD, 1087
posting to
with America Online, 272
with WinCIM, 240
questions, replying to, 435
reflectors, 1229
Remote Work, 1087
signal-to-noise ratios, 434
SmartList software, 1234
software, 1081-1088
Software Entrepreneurs,
1087
Spam, 1079
subscribing, 1234
with America Online,
270-272
with WinCIM, 238-240
TCP/IP for PCs, 1079
test messages, avoiding, 434
TFTD-L (Thought for the
Day), 418
threads, 1235
unmoderated lists, 433
unsubscribing
with America Online,
270-272
with WinCIM, 238-240
UseNet, 437
Voice on the Net, 1079-1080
Windows, 1088
Windows 95, 1087

Windows for Workgroups, 1087
Windows Help Compiler, 1088
WinVN, 1080
WordPerfect Corporation, 1088
WordPerfect for Windows, 1088
WWW BuyInfo, 1080
WWW HTML, 1080
WWW Marketing, 1081
WWW-related, 468-469
WWW Security, 1080
WWW Talk, 1080
WWW VRML, 1080-1081
mailto links, inserting in Web pages, 719
Majordomo software, 432, 1229
    finding, 431
    HELP command, 430
    Majordomo Announcements, 1078
    Majordomo Users, 1078
    sending commands, 430
    SUBSCRIBE command, 431
    subscribing/unsubscribing, 431
    UNSUBSCRIBE command, 431
Make New Connection wizard, 141
Make Nickname command (Special menu), 386
man UNIX command, 1229
manual/operator assisted calling options (dial-up networking software), 143
Mark Menu command (Bookmarks menu), 879
marking
    Gopher bookmarks, 878-882
    newsgroup messages with America Online, 276
Master Boot Record, *see* MBR
maximum receive units (MRUs), 166
maximum transmission units (MTUs), 165
Maxis Web site, 1106
MBONE (Multicast Backbone) video conferencing program, 1008-1009, 1229
    FTP site, 1009
    Web site, 1009

MBR (Master Boot Record), 1064
Mcafee Antivirus Web site, 1104, 1151
MCI Web site, 1129
MCI Mail, 410-411
McKinley Internet Directory Web site, 1134
Mecklerweb Web site, 1137-1138
Mediaweb mailing list, 1078
menu bars
    Mosaic, 544
    Netscape, 503
menus (Mosaic hotlists), setup, 569
Merit (Michigan Educational Research Information Triad), 12, 1229
Message menu commands (Eudora)
    Attach Document, 392
    Change Queuing, 393, 394
    Forward, 398
    Redirect, 398
    Reply, 398
    Send Again, 398
    Send Immediately, 392
Message Window (Exchange), 362
messages
    debugging (WS_FTP window), 857
    e-mail
        attaching files to, with America Online, 269
        attaching files to, with Prodigy, 306
        attaching files to, with WinCim, 237
        bouncing, 1221
        copying, 371-372
        deleting, 343
        filtering with Agent newsreader, 815
        forwarding, 369
        moving, 371-372
        organizing, 369-370
        queuing, 393-394
        reading with Agent newsreader, 813-816
        reading with Prodigy, 305
        receiving, 363, 367
        replying, 368-369
        saving, 369-370
        sending from Web pages, 719

    sending through indirect service providers, 404
    sending with Agent/Free Agent newsreaders, 812-813
    sending with America Online, 268-269
    sending with CompuServe Web browser, 260
    sending with Exchange, 363-364
    sending with Prodigy, 305-306
    sending with WinCIM, 236-237
    service providers, 404-405
    storing in Agent newsreader folders, 814
    transferring from mailboxes, 391
    unwanted, 346-347
encrypting, 1044
mailing lists
    avoiding, 434
    posting to with America Online, 272
    minimizing in out mailboxes, 391
newsgroups
    anonymous posting, 762
    cross-posting, 763
    decoding with WINCODE.EXE in Prodigy, 303-304
    downloading with WinCIM, 243
    marking with America Online, 276
    posting, 758-759, 1232
    posting by geographic region, 763-764
    posting, guidelines, 773-774
    posting in terminal emulation mode, 249-250
    posting with Agent/Free Agent newsreaders, 810-811
    posting with America Online, 276-277
    posting with CompuServe Web browser, 261
    posting with Internet Explorer, 490

posting with Prodigy, 303
posting with WinCIM,
244
reader distribution of
postings, 763-764
reading in terminal
emulation mode,
248-249
reading with Agent/Free
Agent newsreaders,
806-808
reading with America
Online, 275-276
reading with
CompuServe Web
browser, 260
reading with Internet
Explorer, 488-490
reading with Mosaic,
572-573
reading with MSN, 326
reading with Netscape,
535-536
reading with NewsXpress,
783-784
reading with Prodigy,
302-303
reading with WinCIM,
242-243
responding to via e-mail
with NewsXpress,
786-787
responding to with
Agent/Free Agent
newsreaders, 811
responding to with
America Online,
277-278
responding to with
NewsXpress, 787
saving as new with
WinCIM, 243
saving with NewsXpress,
785-786
selecting with
NewsXpress, 783-784
threads, 756, 1235
threads, following with
Agent/Free Agent
newsreaders, 808-810
uncompressing with
PKZIP, 304
sending to LISTSERV mailing
lists, 420, 428-429
MetaClient add-on utility
(SGML), 730

MetaMedia Project (SGML)
Web site, 730
METHOD parameter, <FORM>
HTML element, 646
Michelangelo virus, 1059
Michigan Educational
Research Information Triad
(Merit), 1229
Microsoft
addresses, 1215
FTP site, 1148
telephone numbers, 1215
Web site, 1101, 1215
Microsoft Access mailing list,
1081
Microsoft Anti-Virus,
see MSAV
Microsoft Internet Explorer
Web site, 1118
see also Internet Explorer
Microsoft Mail mailing list,
1085-1086
Microsoft Network, see MSN
Microsoft Products, contact
sources, 1207
Microsoft Windows News
mailing list, 1088
Microsoft Windows NT
mailing list, 1088
Microsoft Windows NT Server
Lan Manager mailing list,
1085
Microsoft Word
documents
converting to/from Web
pages, 695-697
redesigning for
conversion to Web
pages, 696-697
Internet Assistant
requirements, 669
MID (MIME Midi) files, 581
Midi Gate
contact sources, 1207-1208
viewer application, 585
MIME (Multipurpose Internet
Mail Extensions) file types,
340, 582, 1229
America Online, 407
encoding, 441
Eudora e-mail, 392
helper application
configurations for
Netscape, 590
minimizing messages in out
mailboxes, 391

mIRC, 950
accessing IRCs with, 953-959
Action Lists, 961-962
connecting to IRCs, 953
DCC chats, 957-959
font display preferences, 963
FTP sites, 950
installation, 950-951
IRC switches, 960
options, 959
popup menus, 964
private IRC sessions, 955-957
selecting IRC channels,
953-955
setup, 951-952
URL Catcher, 962
versus Netscape Chat, 969
misc.forsale.computers
newsgroup, 1168-1169
Mod4Win viewer application,
585, 1208
modems, 1229
answering errors,
troubleshooting, 155
baud rates, 215
service provider support,
123
setting for Windows 95
workstations, 142
configuring dial-up
neworking connections to
service providers, 142
connection failure,
troubleshooting, 156
data bit settings, 142
data compression settings,
146
dialing errors,
troubleshooting, 155
installation,
troubleshooting, 312
parity settings, 142
requirements for voice
communications on the
Net, 975-976
security, 1043
setup for use with MSN,
311-313
speaker volume, setting, 142
status indicators, displaying
for dial-up networking
software, 144
stop bit settings, 142
universal drivers, 200
Modems mailing list, 1085
moderated mailing lists, 39

moderated newsgroups,
755-756, 1229
moderating mailing lists, 433
modes (HGopher), 883
monetary charges for Web site
areas, 86
monitoring newsgroups
before posting to, 757-758
monitors (video conferencing
requirements), 1001-1002
Mosaic (Web browser), 459,
1230
  Back command, 548-550
  caching Web pages, 549
  collaborative sessions with
    other users, 572
  CompuServe support for,
    257-259
  configuring for use with
    viewer applications,
    593-594
  content area, 545
  customizing hypertext links,
    554-555
  default home page settings,
    544
  display preferences, 555-556
  e-mail capabilities, 571
  errors
    network errors, 575-576
    user errors, 574-575
  font preferences, 556-557
  Forward command, 548-550
  FTP sites, 541-542
  graphics file display
    preferences, 551
  helper applications, 583
  history list, 561
  hotlists, 562-567
    accessing items from,
      568-569
    adding URLs to folders,
      564, 565
    built-in, 570-571
    creating, 567
    editing, 565-567
    folders, creating, 563-564
    folders, deleting items,
      567
    folders, editing items, 566
    folders, moving items,
      566-567
    loading, 568
    loading Web pages from,
      569

  menus, setup, 569
  saving, 567
  saving as HTML files, 570
  sharing, 570
  installation, 542-543
  interface, 543-547
  menu bar, 544
  multimedia file capabilities,
    558
  navigating Web sites,
    547-553, 559-562
  network requirements, 540
  printing Web pages, 553
  reading newsgroup
    messages, 572-573
  Reload command, 548-550
  returning to Web pages,
    560-562
  saving Web pages, 552-553
  searching Web pages,
    551-552
  software
    downloading, 541-542
    requirements, 540-541
  sound file compatibility, 558
  starting, 543
  status bar, 545
  status bar messages, 550-551
  system requirements,
    540-541
  title bar, 544
  toolbar, 545, 546
  tracking sessions, 559-560
  URL location display, 545
  video file compatibility, 558
  viewer applications
    adding, 594
    configurations, 594-595
Motion Picture Experts Group,
  see MPEG files
Motorola ISG
  addresses, 1215-1218
  telephone numbers,
    1215-1218
  Web site, 1100, 1215-1218
Move dialog box, 371
movie files
  formats, 581-582
  Shockwave helper
    application, 530
  viewer applications, 582
  Web page design
    considerations, 614-615

moving
  between Web pages
    with hypertext links in
      Mosaic, 547-548
    with Mosaic commands,
      548-550
    with Netscape
      commands, 509
    with URLs in Mosaic, 550
    with URLs in Netscape,
      510
  e-mail messages, 371-372
  see also navigating
MPC (Multimedia PC)
  Council, 580
MPEG (Motion Picture Experts
  Group) files, 582
MPEGPLAY viewer
  application, 586, 1208
MRUs (maximum receive
  units), 166
MS-DOS Software
  Announcements mailing list,
  1085
MSAV (Microsoft Anti Virus),
  1067
MSN (Microsoft Network), 45,
  309-326, 1230
  access methods, 315-319
  accounts
    establishing, 315-317
    IDs, 317
    passwords, 317
  addresses, 1211
  developments, 309-310
  e-mail capabilities, 322-323
  logoffs, 320-321
  logons, 320-321
  modem setup, 311-313
  newsgroup capabilities,
    324-326
  Plus!, installation from,
    313-314
  system requirements,
    310-313
  telephone numbers, 1211
  troubleshooting, 323
  Web site, 1131, 1211
  WWW capabilities, 321
MTUs (maximum
  transmission units), 165
MUDs (Multi-User
  Dimensions/Dungeons), 121,
  830, 1011-1015, 1230
  administrators, 1020
  building worlds, 1024

categories of, 1013
characters
 descriptions, 1022
 naming, 1019
 registering, 1020
client/server architecture,
 1013-1015
clients, 1014, 1017
combat-oriented, 1023
connecting to, 1018-1019
DOOM, 1028
etiquette, 1016
FAQs, 1024
finding with Web search
 engines, 1018
Gopher sites, 1018
Help, 1020
history of, 1013
Internet resources, 1024
joining, 1018
navigating, 1020-1021
Netrek, 1024-1028
private conversations, 1022
quitting, 1023
real-life implications, 1017
servers, 1014
Stars!, 1028-1029
teleporting, 1021
telnetting to, 1014-1015
terminology, 1015-1017
user interaction, 1021-1022
virtual possessions,
 1022-1023
Web sites, 1024
Wizards, 1024
**Multicast Backbone (MBONE)
 video conferencing program,
 1008-1009**
**multilink PPP (external ISDN
 terminal adapter support),
 207**
**multimedia files, 578-583,
 739-740, 1230**
 displaying MIME types for in
 Netscape, 590-591
 editors, 1185
 MIME types, 582-583
 Mosaic capabilities, 558
 processing with Internet
 Explorer, 491-494
 viewer applications, 1185
 downloading, 583-584
 finding, 583-584
 installation, 584-585

viewing
 with Internet Explorer,
 587-588
 with Mosaic, 592-595
 with Netscape, 588-592
**Multimedia PC Marketing
 Council,** *see* **MPC Council**
**Multipurpose Internet Mail
 Extensions,** *see* **MIME file
 types, 582**

N

**NAME parameter, <INPUT>
 HTML element, 648**
naming
 characters in MUDs, 1019
 directories, saving, 860
 viruses, 1059
narrowband ISDN, 187-194
 B channels, 188, 193-194,
 203
 D channels, 188-192
 Signaling System #7, 192
**National Information
 Infrastructure (NII), 13, 1231**
**National Research and
 Education Network (NREN),
 1231**
**National Science Foundation
 (NSF), 11, 1231**
navigating
 HGopher, 873-875
 MUDs, 1020-1021
 Web sites
 with Internet Assistant,
 673-677
 with Internet Explorer,
 477, 482-483
 with Mosaic, 547-553,
 559-562
 with Netscape, 507-522
 with NEWTShooter
 utility (Chameleon),
 170
**Navigator Gold HTML editor,
 699-702**
 creating Web pages, 709-714
 downloading, 702-703
 installation, 702-703
 starting, 703
NaviSoft Web site, 1121
**NBF CP (NetBIOS Frames
 Control Protocol), 113**

NCompass Web site, 1118
NCSA FTP site, 1144
NCSA Mosaic, *see* **Mosaic**
**NCSA What's New Web site,
 1133-1134**
NEC Corp. Web site, 1096
**NECX Direct Web site,
 1111-1112**
Net splits (IRCs), 53, 946-947
Net Watch mailing list, 1079
NetCD95
 Eudora, 381
 freeware, 1183
 HGopher, 871
 installing, 1181-1183
 public domain software,
 1183
 shareware, 1183
 WinZip, 871
 WS_FTP, 844
 WSArchie, 929
NETCOM
 addresses, 1211
 Internet Service, 172
 NetCruiser, 172, 1230
 telephone numbers, 1211
 Web site, 1211
**NetCruiser Internet software,
 172-175**
Netfind, 336-337, 1135, 1230
**netiquette, 16-17, 53, 302,
 1230**
 e-mail, 345-346
 mailing lists, 433
 newsgroups, 752, 770-773
NetLauncher Web browser
 downloading, 255
 installation, 256-257
NetManage, Inc.
 Chameleon Internet
 software, 168-172,
 1125-1138, 1230
 contact sources, 1216
NetNanny Web site, 1128
netnews, 1230
Netrek MUD, 1024-1028
Netscape (Web browser), 1230
 aborting Web page loading,
 513
 activating hypertext links,
 507-508
 addresses, 1208-1218
 Back command, 509

bookmarks
  creating, 523-525
  deleting, 525
  editing, 523-525
  saving as files, 525
  setting, 522
  sharing, 525-526
  using, 525
caching Web pages, 510-511
content area, 503
customizing hypertext links,
  508-509
directory buttons, 503
display preferences, 517-518
downloading, 498-500
e-mail capabilities, 504,
  533-535
Forward command, 509
FTP sites, 499-500, 1145
graphics files loading
  preferences, 513-515
helper applications, 500,
  528-532, 583, 588-591
history list, 521
home page preferences,
  505-506
installation, 500-502
interface, 502-506
Java compatibility, 536-537
JavaScript compatibility, 537
loading local Web pages,
  518-519
menu bar, 503
navigating Web sites,
  507-522
opening multiple Web
  pages, 510
plug-in applications,
  528-532
printing Web pages, 517
progress bar, 504
reading newsgroup
  messages, 535-536
Reload command, 509
saving Web pages, 516-517
searching Web pages,
  515-516
security, 526-527
security indicator, 504
starting, 502
status bar, 504
status bar messages, 512-513
status displays, 512-515
system requirements,
  497-498

telephone numbers,
  1208-1218
temporary directories,
  specifying, 592
title bar, 503
toolbar, 504-505
tracking sessions, 519-520
URL location field, 503
viewing multimedia files,
  588-592
Web page color scheme
  settings, 511-512
Web sites, 499, 503, 702,
  1208-1218
Netscape Chat, 950, 964-969
  connecting to IRCs, 965-968
  installation, 965
  private IRC sessions, 967-968
  selecting IRC channels, 966
  versus mIRC, 969
  Web site, 965
**Netscape Communications
  Web site, 1116**
Netscape mailing list, 1078
**Netscape Navigator Gold
  HTML editor, 699-703, 1040**
NetTrain mailing list, 1078
NetWare LANs, 1052
**Network control panel,
  opening, 127**
**network errors (Mosaic),
  575-576**
**Network File System (NFS),
  1230**
**Network Information Center
  (NIC), 1231**
**Network Interface dialog box
  (Internet in a Box software),
  164**
**Network News Transport
  Protocol (NNTP), 1231**
**Network Protocol dialog box,
  128**
**Network Setup dialog box,
  884**
networks, 1230
  Acceptable Use Policies
    (AUPs), 1220
  adapters (Windows 95
    support), 139
  backbones, 10, 1220
  bridges, 1221
  broadcasts, 130
  clients (TCP/IP
    configurations), 134
  evolution of, 191

gateways, 127
Gopher, changing, 884-885
inspecting for obscenity, 65
LANs, 126, 1228
legal concerns, 54
libel concerns, 57
nodes, 1231
packets, 1231
  routers, 1233
  sending, 135
  switching, 1231
PDNs, 1232
POP (Point of Presence),
  1232
ports, 1232
protocols (Gopher), 867-868
repeaters, 1233
security, 1050-1051
TCP/IP connections, testing,
  135
traffic, 1235
user agreements, 85
WANs, 1236
**New command (Transfer
  menu), Eudora, 396**
New dialog box, 387
**New Folder command (File
  menu), Eudora, 370**
**New Key Request dialog box
  (Internet in a Box software),
  168**
New Lists mailing list, 1079
New Mailbox dialog box, 396
**New Message command
  (Compose menu), 363, 442**
New Message dialog box, 385
new newsgroups, 755
  listing with NewsXpress, 780
"newbies" (newsgroups),
  756-757, 1230
news services, 115
news.announce
  newsgroup.newgroups,
  1161-1174
news.announce
  newsgroup.newusers, 1161
news.answers newsgroup,
  1161
news.groups newsgroup, 1161
news.groups.questions
  newsgroup, 1161
news.groups.reviews
  newsgroup, 1161
news.lists newsgroup, 1161
news.newuser
  newsgroups.questions, 1161

news.software
  newsgroup.nntp, 1161
news.software
  newsgroup.readers, 1162
newsgroups, *see* UseNet
  newsgroups
newsreaders, 752, 1230
  Agent
    configurations, 792-805
    downloading binary files
      from newsgroups,
      811-812
    e-mail capabilities,
      801-803, 812-816
    filtering e-mail messages,
      815
    following newsgroup
      message threads,
      808-810
    font preferences, 803
    FTP site, 792
    installation, 793
    newsgroup option
      settings, 804-805
    posting newsgroup
      messages, 810-811
    preferences, setting,
      794-800
    reading e-mail messages,
      813-816
    reading newsgroup
      messages, 806-808
    responding to newsgroup
      messages, 811
    sending e-mail messages,
      812-813
    signature file
      attachments, 800-801
    spell-checking capablities,
      800
    starting, 792-805
    storing e-mail messages,
      814
    subscribing/
      unsubscribing to
      newsgroups, 805-806
    Web site, 792
    window layout
      preferences, 803-804
  Free Agent, 791-816, 1225
    configurations, 792-805
    downloading binary files
      from newsgroups,
      811-812
    following newsgroup
      message threads,
      808-810

    font preferences, 803
    FTP site, 792
    newsgroup option
      settings, 804-805
    posting newsgroup
      messages, 810-811
    reading newsgroup
      messages, 806-808
    responding to newsgroup
      messages, 811
    sending e-mail messages,
      812-813
    starting, 792-805
    subscribing/
      unsubscribing to
      newsgroups, 805-806
    Web site, 792
    window layout
      preferences, 803-804
  kill files, 1228
  NewsXpress, 776, 1230
    accessing newsgroups,
      779
    configurations, 778-779
    connecting to, 778
    filtering newsgroups, 781
    installation, 776-777
    reading newsgroup
      messages, 783-784
    responding to newsgroup
      messages, 787
    responding to newsgroup
      messages via e-mail,
      786-787
    saving newsgroup
      messages, 785-786
    selecting newsgroup
      messages, 783-784
    selecting newsgroups,
      783-784
    setup, 776-779
    subscribing/
      unsubscribing to
      newsgroups, 780-783
    uploading/downloading
      binary files in
      newsgroups, 788-789
  WinCIM (CompuServe),
    241-246
  NewsXpress newsreader, 776,
    1230
    accessing newsgroups, 779
    configurations, 778-779
    connecting to, 778
    filtering newsgroups, 781
    installation, 776-777

    reading newsgroup
      messages, 783-784
    responding to newsgroup
      messages, 787
    responding to newsgroup
      messages via e-mail,
      786-787
    saving newsgroup messages,
      785-786
    selecting newsgroup
      messages, 783-784
    selecting newsgroups,
      783-784
    setup, 776-779
    subscribing/unsubscribing to
      newsgroups, 780-783
    uploading/downloading
      binary files in newsgroups,
      788-789
    Web site, 1128
NEWTSHooter utility
  (Chameleon Internet
  software), 170
NFS (Network File System),
  1230
NIC (Network Information
  Center), 1231
nicknames
  Eudora, 386-387
  IRC users, 947
Nicknames command
  (Window menu), Eudora,
  386
NII (National Information
  Infrastructure), 13, 1231
NIUF (North American ISDN
  Users' Forum), 198
NNTP (Network News
  Transport Protocol), 1231
nodes (networks), 1231
  host names, 824
  see also hosts
noise (signaling), 179
non-empty HTML elements,
  623
North American ISDN Users'
  Forum (NIUF), 198
Novell, Inc.
  FTP site, 1150
  GroupWise mailing list,
    1086
  LAN mailing list, 1086
  Web site, 1103
NREN (National Research and
  Education Network), 1231

NSF (National Science Foundation), 11, 1231
NSFNET, 11, 1231
NSTN Gopher site, 1177
NT1 boxes (ISDN), 192
numbered lists (Web pages), 636-637
numerical addresses, 824-825

O

obscenity concerns, 61-67
obscenity limitations, 59
obtaining WinWAIS, 898
OC Games Archive at University of Massachusetts FTP site, 1144
OC3 (Optical Carrier 3) protocol, 1231
<OL> HTML element, 636-637
one-time passwords, 1037-1038
online, 1231
online access to the Internet, 101
    via America Online, 263-285
    via BBSs, 120
    via Chameleon software, 168-172
    via corporate systems, 103-104
    via dedicated gateways, 104-105, 109
    via Dedicated-56 lines, 219-220
    via dial-up networking software, 137-156
    via direct gateways, 102
    via high-speed connections, 215-218
    via Internet in a Box software, 160-168
    via ISDN lines, 182-194
    via LANs, 125-135
    via MSN, 309-326
    via NetCruiser Internet software, 172-175
    via Prodigy, 287-306
    via professional organizations, 120
    via public libraries, 120
    via service providers, 102, 105, 110-117
    via Switched-56 lines, 219-220

via third-party gateways, 103, 110
via WinSock, 151-153
online bars and cafes, 120
online gaming
    DOOM, 1028
    Internet resources, 1030
    Netrek, 1024-1028
    Stars!, 1028-1029
online services, *see* service providers
Open command (File menu), Eudora, 389
Open File dialog box, 395
opening
    HGopher, 871
    multiple Web pages with Netscape, 510
    Network control panel, 127
    WebCrawler, 919-920
    WinWAIS, 900
    Yahoo!, 922
Optical Carrier 3 (OC3) protocol, 1231
Options command (HGopher menu), 872
Options command (Tools menu), Eudora, 372, 376
Options dialog box, 372, 855
Options menu commands
    Decode, 451
    Default Viewers, 907
    Encode, 450
    ZIP/UNZIP, 452
Options menu commands (HGopher), 884
ordered lists (Web pages), 636-637, 713-714
ordering ISDN service, 194-196
ordering codes (ISDN), 196
Oregon State University FTP site, 1141
organizing e-mail messages, 369-370
Out command (Mailbox menu), 390
out mailboxes, 391
overwriting files, 853

P

<P> HTML element, 632, 710
Packard Bell Web site, 1094
packet-switched networks, 119

packets, 1231
    IP packets, sending, 135
    routers, 1233
    switching, 220-224, 1231
packing files (compression), 342
Pagemaker mailing list, 1086
Paint Shop Pro viewer application, 586, 1208-1209
Panorama viewer application, 725-728
Panorama Pro viewer application, contact sources, 1209
PAP (Password Authentication Protocol), 147
PaperSoftware Web site, 1124
paragraph breaks (Web page text), 632
parameters
    Archie, 936-937
    HTML elements, 624
parity (modem settings), 142
passing passwords to PPP servers, 147
$PASSWORD variable (dial-up scripting software), 150
Password Authentication Protocol (PAP), 147
passwords, 1034-1035
    encryption options for dial-up networking software, 146
    Eudora, 382-383
    FTP, 840
    guidelines, 1037
    hacking, 1035, 1038
    MSN accounts, 317
    passing to PPP servers, 147
    PIN (Personal Identification Number), 1037
    Prodigy accounts, 291
    public/private keys, 1048
    security, 1037-1038
    software, 1038
    Web page forms, 654-655
    WinZip, 344
Paste as Quotation command (Edit menu), Eudora, 390
Paste command (Edit menu), Eudora, 390
pasting e-mail messages with Eudora, 390
patent law, 76
payloads
    Michelangelo virus, 1059
    viruses, 1054, 1056-1057

PC Building mailing list, 1086
PC Eudora, *see* Eudora e-mail client software
PC Software Links Web site, 1105
PC Technical Support mailing list, 1086-1087
PCI SIG mailing list, 1086
PCM (Pulse Code Modulation), 225
PCs
    anti-virus products, 1058
    configuring as Web servers, 604
    linking via Telnet, 820-821
    mailing lists, 1081-1088
    network security, 1050-1051
    newsgroups, 1162, 1167-1169
    protecting, 1066
    radio frequency, tapping into, 1043
    software newsgroups, 1169-1172
    speaker drivers, 581
    Telnet
        connecting, 826-827
        disconnecting, 829
    terminals
        ANSI, 822
        defined, 821
        HyperTerminal, 822
        TTY, 822
        VT series, 821
    VAX computers, 830
    video conferencing requirements, 999-1000
    viruses, 95, 1056-1057
        acquiring, 1061-1062
        anti-virus products, 1067
        changing, 1058
        defined, 1054
        macros, 1055-1056
        naming, 1059
        restoring, 1063
        scanning, 1058, 1060
        Windows 95, 1064
    Web sites, 1091-1094, 1109-1112
PDF (Portable Document Format) files, 530-531
PDIAL mailing lists, 1231
PDNs (Public data networks), 1232
peer-to-peer Internet services, 1232

Pegasus Mail for Windows mailing list, 1079
PEM (Privacy Enhanced Mail), 1232
performing Archie searches, 930-932
personal access to Internet, 104
personal accounts (host profiles), 860
Personal Address Book, 350-351, 365-366
Personal Identification Number, *see* PIN
Personal Information Store, 350
PGP (Pretty Good Privacy) encryption program, 1044-1046, 1232
    AUTOEXEC.BAT files, changing, 1046
    downloading, 1045
    Private Key/Public Key encryption, 1044
    public keys, 1045-1046
    Web site, 1115
    WINPGP4, 1046-1050
Phoenix Project, 95
phone by net, 42
phone number settings (dial-up networking software), 144
PhotoCD mailing list, 1087
photographs, copyright concerns, 80
Picturephones, 996
PIN (Personal Identification Number), 1037
PING program, 135
ping utility, 1232
PKZIP utility, uncompressing newsgroup messages, 304
placeholders (Web page graphics files), 514
Playboy Web site, 81
playing sound files with Internet Explorer, 493
plug-in applications
    Netscape, 528-532
    see also helper applications
Plus! Internet software package, 313-314
Point Communications's Best of the Web Web site, 1134
Point of Presence (POP) networks, 1232

Point to Point Protocol, *see* PPP
polymorphic viruses, scanning, 1060
PolyView viewer application, 586, 1209
POP (Point of Presence) networks, 1232
popup menus (mIRC), 964
pornography
    censorship concerns, 60
    child pornography limitations, 63
    legal issues, 61-67
Portal Web site, 1130
ports, 1232
    telnetting, 829-830
positioning text in Web pages, 631-633
POST method, <FORM> HTML element, 646
posting
    newsgroup messages, 758-759, 1232
        anonymously, 762
        by geographic region, 763
        cross-posting, 763
        guidelines, 773-774
        in terminal emulation mode, 249-250
        with Agent/Free Agent newsreaders, 810-811
        with America Online, 276-277
        with CompuServe Web browser, 261
        with Internet Explorer, 490
        with Prodigy, 303
        with WinCIM, 244
    to mailing lists
        with America Online, 272
        with WinCIM, 240
postmasters (e)-mail, 29, 347, 842, 1232
PostScript files, 579
POTS (plain old telephone service), Internet access, 111
PowWow Internet telephony software, 989-990
PPP (Point to Point Protocol), 112, 140, 1232
    accounts, 20
    connections, 112
    servers, passing passwords to, 147
    settings for Internet in a Box software, 165

PPP Settings dialog box
(Internet in a Box software),
165
<PRE> HTML element,
632-633
pre-defined searches (WAIS
Manager 3.1), 905-906
preferences
    Agent newsreader, setting,
    794-800
    fonts in Mosaic, 556-557
    see also display preferences
preformatted text (Web
pages), 632-633
President of the United States
e-mail address, 344
Pretty Good Privacy (PGP)
encryption program, 72,
1232
    AUTOEXEC.BAT files,
    changing, 1046
    downloading, 1045
    Private Key/Public Key
    encryption, 1044
    public keys, 1045-1046
    Web site, 1115
    WINPGP4, 1046-1050
previewing Web pages with
HotDog, 720-721
PRI (Primary Rate Interface)
    ISDN, 218
    narrowband ISDN, 187
printing Web pages
    with Internet Explorer,
    487-488
    with Mosaic, 553
    with Netscape, 517
Privacy Enhanced Mail (PEM),
1232
privacy issues and e-mail, 68
Private Key/Public Key
encryptions, 1044
private sessions (IRCs)
    with mIRC, 955-957
    with Netscape Chat, 967-968
proc command (dial-up
scripting software), 149
procedures (Telnet), 925
processing Web page forms,
645
Prodigy, 117, 287-306,
411-412, 1232
    accessing newsgroups, 296
    account passwords, 291
    addresses, 1211
    attaching files to e-mail
    messages, 306

billing methods, 291
connecting to, 290-292
cost, 289-290
e-mail capabilities, 289,
    305-306, 411
FTP capabilities, 300-301
Gopher capabilities, 299-300
home pages
    creation utilities, 298-299
    preferences, 298
installing software, 290
interface, 288
    GoTo menu, 294
    hotlists, 295
    organization, 292-295
    toolbar, 294
Internet information, 306
Internet services, 296-297
logons, 291-292
newsgroup capabilities, 289,
    301-304
posting newsgroup
    messages, 303
reading e-mail messages, 305
reading newsgroup
    messages, 302-303
sending e-mail messages,
    305-306, 411
software, 287, 290
starting, 290-291
storing e-mail addresses in
    address books, 306
subscribing to newsgroups,
    302
telephone numbers, 1211
Web browser, 297-299
Web site, 1131, 1211
WINCODE.EXE, decoding
    newsgroup messages,
    303-304
WWW capabilities, 289,
    297-299
profiles
creating, 376
customizing, 860-861
host profiles
    defining, 859-861
    deleting, 861
Session Profile window,
    customizing, 861-863
WS_FTP, 845
Program command (Start
menu), Exchange, 360
Program dialog box, 833
Program Folder dialog box,
833

Program Options dialog box,
855, 860
program infectors, 1054-1055
Programs command (Start
menu), 380, 845
progress bars (Netscape), 504
promoting home pages,
617-618
properties (TCP/IP), 129
Properties command (File
menu), 368, 1050
Properties dialog box,
365, 376
Prospero Systems Web site,
1123
protecting
    against viruses, 1062-1063
    BSI (Boot Sector Infectors),
    1055
    computers, 1066
protocols, 464, 1232
    CHAP, 147
    defined, 819
    dial-up networking software
    settings, 146
    frame relay, 220-224
    FTP, 837, 1225
    Gopher, 867-868
    HTTP, 464-465, 1227
    IP, 1227
    NNTP, 1231
    OC3, 1231
    PAP, 147
    PPP, 20, 140, 1232
    service provider options, 112
    SLIP, 20, 1234
        installation for Windows
        95 workstations,
        140-141
        uninstalling support for,
        141
    SMDS, 1234
    SMTP, 330-331, 1234
    SNMP, 1234
    TCP, 1235
    TCP/IP, 126-127
        configurations for
        Windows 95, 129-134
        dial-up networking
        software settings, 146
        installation on
        Windows 95
        workstations,
        127-129, 139-140
        properties, 129
        stacks, software conflicts,
        158-159

Telnet
  addresses, 823
  defined, 819-820
UUCP, 1235
X-modem, 1237
Y-modem, 1237
Z-modem, 1237
providers, *see* ISPs; service
  providers
PSI Pipeline USA, 1129, 1232
Public data networks (PDNs),
  1232
public domain issues, 77
public domain software, 1183,
  1233
public figures and libel on the
  Internet, 54
public keys/private keys (PGP
  encryption), 1045-1046
  passwords, 1048
  security, 1045
  WINPGP4, 1047
publishers (legal concerns), 55
publishing Web pages with
  HotDog, 721
Pulse Code Modulation
  (PCM), 225
purchasing
  Exchange, 351-352
  Internet Mail, 355
  WinWAIS, 898

Q

Qualcomm FTP site, 1145
Quarterdeck
  FTP site, 1150
  Web site, 1103
Que and Macmillan Computer
  Publishing FTP site, 1152
queries
  Jughead, 894-895
  saving, 907
  Veronica, 890-891
  WHOIS database, 335
  wildcards, 891
Query menu commands, 905
Questar Web site, 1120
questions (mailing lists),
  replying to, 435
queues (SMTP), 331
queuing e-mail messages
  Eudora, 393-394
  troubleshooting, 394
Quick Recipient list (Eudora),
  387

QuickTime movie files, 582,
  1233
quitting
  Archie, 937
  MUDs, 1023
  WS_FTP, 865
quoted-printable encoding,
  384

R

RA (RealAudio) files, 581
radio button controls (Web
  page forms), 650-652
radio frequencies, tapping
  into, 1042-1043
RAS (Remote Access Service),
  1233
read options (Exchange), 374
reader distribution
  (newsgroup postings),
  763-764
reading
  e-mail messages
    with Agent newsreader,
      813-816
    with Prodigy, 305
  newsgroup messages
    in terminal emulation
      mode, 248-249
    RFCs, 11
    with Agent/Free Agent
      newsreaders, 806-808
    with America Online,
      275-276
    with CompuServe Web
      browser, 260
    with Internet Explorer,
      488-490
    with Mosaic, 572-573
    with MSN, 326
    with Netscape, 535-536
    with NewsXpress,
      783-784
    with Prodigy, 302-303
    with WinCIM, 242-243
README files, 28
real-time audio, 42
RealAudio
  helper application, 528-529,
    586
  installation, 741-742
  Web sites, 108, 741-742,
    1121-1125

receiving e-mail messages,
  363, 367, 413-415
recipients (e-mail), 363, 367,
  388
Redirect command (Message
  menu), 398
references (hypertext links),
  462
reflectors
  mailing lists, 1229
  video conferencing, 1003
regenerators, 181
REGISTER command
  (LISTSERV mailing lists), 426
registering
  characters in MUDs, 1020
  copyrights, 77
  Internet in a Box software,
    162
relative hypertext links, 553
relative URLs, 463, 627-629
relevance feedback (WAIS),
  902-903, 906-907
Reload command
  Mosaic, 548-550
  Netscape, 509
reloading Web pages, 509
  with Mosaic, 549
  with Netscape, 509
Remote Access Service (RAS),
  1233
remote computers (Telnet),
  connecting, 826-827
Remote Email System
  accounts (MCI Mail), 411
remote hosts, 1233
Remote Work mailing list,
  1087
Remove Bookmark command
  (Bookmarks menu), 881
Remove Recipient command
  (Special menu), 388
removing e-mail recipients
  (Eudora), 388
repairing virus-infected
  computers, 1063
repeaters (networks), 182,
  1233
replicates (viruses), 1054-1057
Reply command (Message
  menu), 398
Reply to All command
  (Compose menu), Exchange,
  368

Reply to Sender command (Compose menu), Exchange, 368
replying
  to e-mail messages, 368-369
  to mailing list questions, 435
Request for Comments, *see* RFCs
reset buttons (Web page forms), 655-656
responding to newsgroup messages, 764
  via e-mail with NewsXpress, 786-787
  with Agent/Free Agent newsreaders, 811
  with America Online, 277-278
  with NewsXpress, 787
restoring PCs after virus infection, 1063
Retrieve command (File menu), 934
retrieving
  e-mail file attachments, 394-395
  files
    Archie, 935-936
    WS_FTP, 853-855
  WAIS documents, 902-903
returning to Web pages
  with Mosaic, 560-562
  with Netscape, 520-522
REVIEW command (LISTSERV mailing lists), 427
RFCs (Request for Comments), 11, 1233
right to privacy
  e-mail, 343
  Internet, 68-72
rlogin UNIX command, 1233
RoboDUN dial-up scripting software, 153-154
ROT13, 345
routers, 1036-1037, 1233
  DSUs, 225
  ISDN, 213-214
routing e-mail with Eudora, 397-398
rows (Web page tables), 716
Run command (Start menu), 832, 839
Run dialog box, 832
running
  Archie, 928
  EUDOR152.EXE, 380

FTP command-line accounts, 839-840
HGopher, 871
Telnet, 832
WebCrawler, 919-920
WinWAIS, 900
Yahoo!, 922

S

S/T interfaces (ISDN), 192
sampling
  America Online with WinSock, 267
  digital recording, 181
Sausage Software
  Web site, 1120
Save As command (File menu), 389, 906
Save As dialog box, 876
Save Bookmarks As command (Bookmarks menu), 880
Save Bookmarks command (Bookmarks menu), 880
Save Queries command (File menu), 907
saving
  bookmarks as files, 525
  clipboards, 903
  directory names, 860
  e-mail messages, 369-370, 389
  Mosaic hotlists, 567
    as HTML files, 570
  newsgroup messages
    as new with WinCIM, 243
    with NewsXpress, 785-786
  queries, 907
  WAIS searches, 907
  Web pages
    with Internet Explorer, 487-488
    with Mosaic, 552-553
    with Netscape, 516-517
scanning viruses, 1058, 1060
Scientology, Church of, legal case, 81-82
Scope IDs (Windows 95 workstations), 131
scripting (dial-up), 140-141
scripting languages (JavaScript), Netscape compatibility, 537

SDSLs (symmetric digital subscriber lines), 227
search engines, 37, 913-915
  Archie, 927-929
    accessing, 927
    expressions, 931
    limiting, 932
    parameters, 936-937
    results, 932-935
    retrieving files, 935-936
    running, 928
    searches, 930-932
    WS_FTP, 929-930
  defined, 912-913
  Gopher, 937
  knowbots, 1228
  Lycos, 915-919, 1018, 1229
    catalog, accessing, 915
    Help & Reference, 917
  WebCrawler, 259, 919-922, 1236
  Yahoo!, 922-925, 1237
Search menu commands, 906
Search Selection command (Search menu), 906
searches
  Archie, 930-932
    limiting, 932
    results, 932-935
    running, 928
  databases with Archie, 928
  file names with Archie, 927
  pre-defined searches (WAIS Manager 3.1), 905-906
  relevance feedback, 906-907
  results, viewing, 934
  Telnet, 925-927
  terms, creating, 906
  viewers, 907
  WAIS, 900-902
    e-mail, 908-909
    relevance feedback, 902-903
    results, 903-904
    saving, 907
  WAIS Manager 3.1, 905-906
  WinWAIS, troubleshooting, 904
searching
  databases with Archie, 842
  Gopher
    Jughead, 891-894
    queries, 890-891
    Veronica, 888-890
  Web sites, 1131-1135
    with Mosaic, 551-552
    with Netscape, 515-516

security
  cypher keys, 1044
  data interceptions, 1035
  e-mail, 1042
    DES (Date Encryption
      Standard), 344
    encryption, 344-345
    ROT13, 345
  encryption, 1044
    DES (Data Encryption
      Standard), 1044
    PGP (Pretty Good
      Privacy), 1044
  firewalls, 1036-1037
  FTP, 1041
  Gopher, 1041-1042
  hacking, 1034
  hardware, 1037
  HTML, 1040-1041
  intercepting messages, 1035
  Internet, 22, 526-527
  Internet Explorer
    preferences, 481
  Internet service providers,
    123
  keyboards, logging, 1036
  logging, 1036
  login names, 1034-1035
  modems, 1043
  Netscape, 504, 526-527
  networks, 1050-1051
  passwords, 1034-1038
    guidelines, 1037
    hacking, 1035
    one-time passwords,
      1037-1038
  PGP encryption program,
    1045-1046
  PIN (Personal Identification
    Number), 1037
  public keys, 1045
  routers, 1036-1037
  software, 1038
  tapping telephone lines,
    1042-1043
  Telnet, 1042
  warnings, 1038-1039
  Web pages, 527
  WINPGP4, 1046-1050
security issue Web sites, 91
<SELECT> HTML element,
  658-661
Select a Pricing and Access
  Option dialog box (Internet
  in a Box software), 161

Select Program Folder dialog
  box, 871, 899
Select Query command (Query
  menu), 905
Select Sources command (File
  menu), 900
Send Again command
  (Message menu), 398
send buttons (Web page
  forms), 656
Send command (File menu),
  364, 369
Send Immediately command
  (Message menu), 392
send options (e-mail),
  Exchange, 375
sending
  binary files, 404
  commands (Majordomo
    mailing lists), 430
  e-mail messages
    from Web pages, 719
    GEnie, 409-410
    KIS, 338
    MCI Mail, 410-411
    postmasters, 347
    through service
      providers, 413-415
    system administrators,
      347
    with Agent/Free Agent
      newsreaders, 812-813
    with America Online,
      268-269, 407
    with CompuServe Web
      browser, 260, 408-409
    with Delphi, 409
    with Eudora, 391-392
    with Exchange, 363-364
    with Prodigy, 411
    with Prodigy, 305-306
    with WinCIM, 236-237
  encoded files
    with Eudora, 444
    with Exchange, 442-443
  IP packets, 135
  LISTSERV mailing list
    messages, 420, 428-429
  Web page form data to Web
    servers, 646, 656
Serial Line Internet Protocol,
  see SLIP
serial ports
  external ISDN terminal
    adapter issues , 200-201
  third-party drivers, 200

servers, 1233
  anonymous FTP servers,
    27-28
  Archie, troubleshooting, 933
  connection settings for dial-
    up networking software,
    146
  FTP, 26-27, 838-839
    connecting to, 840
    files, 841-842
    passwords, 840
    postmasters, 842
    troubleshooting, 847, 853
  Gopher, 32, 869
  InterNIC server, 335-336
  IRCs, 944-945, 948
  Jughead, 892-894
  MUDs, 1014
  PPP servers, 147
  WAIS servers, 33
  Web servers, 37, 466, 604
  WINS servers, 131
  WWW sites, 1116-1120
Service command (Tools
  menu), 442
service profile identifiers
  (SPIDs), narrowband ISDN B
  channels, 194
service providers, 13, 20,
  44-45, 102, 105, 110-117,
  1232
  access availability, 121
  access methods, 122-123
  backdoor options, 116
  binary files, 404-405
  commercial, 117
    America Online, 263-285,
      406-407, 1131, 1219
    CompuServe, 231-234,
      408-409, 1131, 1222
    Delphi, 409
    GEnie, 409-410
    MCI Mail, 410-411
    MSN, 309-326, 476, 1131,
      1230
    Prodigy, 287-306,
      411-412, 1131, 1232
  configurations for Internet
    in a Box software, 163
  connecting to with dial-up
    networking software,
    141-144, 147-148
  cost, 122
  cost for home page support,
    605-607
  direct, 402-406

domain names, 406
e-mail
    receiving, 413-415
    sending, 413-415
frontdoor options, 116
indirect, 403-404
InterServ (Internet in a Box
    software), 161
logins with dial-up scripting
    software, 150
NetCom Internet Service,
    172
personal access, 104
protocol options, 112-114
security, 123
selecting, 121-124
service options, 114-115
services, 121
software requirements, 123
support for Web pages,
    603-605
technical support, 124
telephone line connections,
    110
throughput charges for
    home pages, 607
UNIX-based, 147
usernames, 406
Web sites, 1130-1131
**Session Options dialog box,
861**
**Session Profile dialog box,
844-845, 857**
**Sessions Profile window,
customizing, 861-863**
**Settings command (Special
menu), 383**
**Settings command (Start
menu), 357, 376**
Settings dialog box, 383
**Settings menu commands
(Taskbar), 1199**
setup
    connecting to service
        providers with dial-up
        networking software,
        141-144, 149
    Internet Explorer Web
        browser, 473-475
    mIRC, 951-952
    modems for use with MSN,
        311-313
    Mosaic hotlists menus, 569
    NewsXpress newsreader,
        776-779
Setup Wizard, 354

**SGML (Standard Generalized
Markup Language), 724-730,
1233**
    benefits of, 725
    Document Type Definition,
        725
    MetaClient add-on utility,
        730
    versus HTML, 728-729
    viewer applications, 725-726
shareware, 28, 87, 1233
    audio players, 581
    NetCD95, 1183
    video players, 582
    viewer applications, 580
sharing
    bookmarks in Netscape,
        525-526
    Mosaic hotlists, 570
shell protocols, 112
Shockwave helper application
    installation, 739-740
    using with Netscape, 530
    Web site, 739
shortcut icons, *see* **icons**
shortcuts, *see* **hypertext links**
shouting (newsgroups), 772
**Show Bookmarks command
(Bookmarks menu), 879**
**Shut Down command (Start
menu), 1046, 1066**
shutting down Archie, 937
Sierra Online Web site, 1109
**signal-to-noise ratios (mailing
lists), 434**
signaling
    analog in-band signaling,
        190
    attenuation, 180-182
    digital versus analog,
        177-182
    noise, 179
    switching, 179, 185-187
    transmission, 179, 184-185
**Signaling System #7
(narrowband ISDN), 192**
**Signature command (Window
menu), 388**
signature files, 384, 1233
    attaching
        to newsgroup messages
            with Agent newsreader,
            800-801
        to newsgroup postings,
            760-762

    to newsgroup postings
        with America Online,
        277
    to newsgroup postings
        with terminal
        emulation mode, 250
    to newsgroup postings
        with WinCIM, 245
    creating, 388-389
**Simon and Schuster
Interactive Web site, 1107**
**Simple Mail Transport
Protocol (SMTP), 1234**
**Simple Network Management
Protocol (SNMP), 1234**
SimTel
    FTP site, 1143
    Web site, 1115
sites, 1234
    fingering, 334
    FTP sites
        accessing with America
            Online, 281-282
        accessing with
            CompuServe Web
            browser, 261
        accessing with Prodigy,
            300-301
        accessing with WinCIM,
            252-253
        Adaptec, 1149
        Adobe Systems, 1148
        Agent/Free Agent
            newsreaders, 792
        America Online, 267
        American Civil Liberties
            Union, 1152
        ATI, 1149
        Autodesk, 1149
        Book Stacks, Inc.,
            1153-1154
        Cabletron Systems, 1149
        Cirrus Logic, Inc., 1149
        3Com, 1149
        Computer Privacy Digest,
            1147
        CPSR, 1146
        Creative Labs, 1150
        Cypherpunks, 1147
        Digi International, 1150
        Digital Equipment
            Corporation, 1143
        directories, 1153-1154
        Electronic Frontier
            Foundation, 1146
        Etext, 1153

Exec-PC, 1143
file indexes, 29
finding files, 28-29
Gmud client software, 1017
GreatCircle, 1147
hardware-related, 1148-1152
Hyper-G Archive, 1146
InfoMagic, 1142
Internet Global Phone, 987
Internet Wiretap, 1152
InterNIC, 1145
Internic, 11
Java, 1146
Kodak, 1150
lists, 1153-1154
Lotus, 1149
Lynx, 119
MBONE video conferencing program, 1009
McAfee, 1151
Microsoft, 1148
mIRC, 950
Mosaic, 541-542
Navigator Gold, 703
NCSA, 1144
Netscape, 499-500, 1145
Novell, 1150
OC Games Archive at University of Massachusetts, 1144
Oregon State University, 1141
passwords, 840
PC speaker drivers, 581
postmasters, 29
Qualcomm, 1145
Quarterdeck, 1150
Que and Macmillan Computer Publishing, 1152
README files, 28
RTFM, 1144
Simtel, 1143
SLIP/dial-up scripting support, 140
software, 1139-1148
software-related, 1148-1152
Sparco, 1150
Spry, 1150
Stardust, 1146
Supra, 1151

Telebit, 1151
Trumpet Software, 1147
Trusted Information Systems, 1148
US Robotics, 1151
UUNet, 1145
Vocaltec, 1147
Walnut Creek CD-ROM, 1142-1154
Washington University at St. Louis, 1141
Western Digital Corporation, 1151-1154
WinSite, 1139-1141
WinSock, 114, 152, 160
WinSock-L FTP Archive, 1142-1143
WinZip, 1152
WS_FTP, 1147
Ziff, 1152
Gopher sites, 32, 1176
accessing with America Online, 279
accessing with CompuServe, 261
accessing with Prodigy, 299-300
accessing with Veronica, 280
Counterpoint Publishing's Internet Services, 1178
MUDs, 1018
NSTN, 1177
Software Tool and Die: The World, 1177
University of Minnesota, 1176-1177
University of Southern California Gopher Jewels, 1177
legal concerns, 54
Telnet sites
accessing with WinCIM, 253-254
IRCs, 945
VRML sites, 735, 738-739
WWW sites
7th Level, 1106
accessing from Favorites list in Internet Explorer, 486-492
accessing from history list in Internet Explorer, 484-486
accessing from Mosaic hotlists, 568-571

accessing with America Online, 283-285
accessing with bookmarks, 525
accessing with Internet Assistant, 673
accessing with Prodigy, 297
Acer America, 1093
Activision, 1107
add-on utilities, 1116-1120
Adobe, 1104
Adobe Amber helper application, 530-531
Adtran, 1211
Agent/Free Agent newsreaders, 792, 1205
Alpha Telecom, Inc., 1212
America Online, 267, 1131, 1210
anti-virus, 97
Artisoft, Inc, 1212
Ascend Communications, 1095, 1212
ATI Technologies, 1099
AVM of America, Inc., 1212
Berkeley Systems, 1107
bookmarks, 297, 682, 1221
Borland, 1104
browser-related, 1116-1120
BrowserWatch, 1118
Burn:Cycle, 1106
California State University Windows World, 1114
censorship-related, 51
Center For Democracy & Technology, 68
CGI Programmer's Reference, 1119
CGI-bin program-related, 693
Chase Research, Inc., 1213
Cisco Systems, 1213
clipper chip-related, 72
3Com Corporation, 1217
Compaq Computer Corp., 1093
CompuServe, 255, 259-260, 1131, 1210
computer crime laws, 91

Computer Price
   Cruncher, 1111
computer-related,
   1109-1112, 1091-1094
Conner Peripherals, 1099
Constitution of the
   United states, 48
Copyright Web site, 77
Corel Corp., 1104
CPSR, 1138
Creative Labs, 1097-1098
CU-SeeMe video
   conferencing program,
   1002, 1004, 1124
CUI Search Catalog,
   1133-1138
Cyberphone Internet
   telephony software, 991
DejaNews newsgroup
   search utility, 767
Dell Computer Corp.,
   1094
Demon Internet, 1130
dial-up scripting software,
   149
Diamond Multimedia,
   1096
Digi International, 1213
Digiphone, 983
digital subscriber lines,
   227
direct access with
   Internet Explorer,
   483-484
directories, 1131-1135
DOOM MUD, 1028
Egghead Software, 1109
EINet Galaxy, 1133
Electronic Arts, 1106
Electronic Frontier
   Foundation, 68, 1137
Electronic Privacy
   Information Center, 71
ElekTek, Inc., 1109
Emissary, 1127
Entering the World Wide
   Web: A Guide to
   Cyberspace, 471
Epic MegaGames, 1107
Eudora, 1127, 1206
Excel to HTML
   Converter, 1121
fair use doctrine
   (copyright law), 79
finding, 37-38
firewalls, 115

First Amendment Cyber-
   Tribune, 49
First Amendment-related,
   50
First Floor Software, 1119
Four11 White Page
   Directory, 1135
frame relay, 220
Frontier Technologies
   Corporation,
   1127-1138, 1213
FTP Software, Inc., 1214
game-related, 1105-1109
Gandalf Technologies,
   1214-1218
Hang Duke (Java-created
   game), 732
hardware-related,
   1094-1100
Harris Semiconductor,
   1116
Hayes, 1096
Hewlett Packard, 1098
HotDog, 705, 1206
HotJava Web browser,
   467, 731
HTML Assistant, 1120
HTML editors, 620
HTML filters, 620
HTML-related, 1120-1121
HTTP specifications, 465
human rights related
   Web sites, 51
Hyper-G browser utility,
   733
IBM, 1092
IBM Corporation, 1214
Id Software, 1108-1138
IDSN*tek, 1215
Information Law Web
   site, 76
InfoSeek Corp., 1133
Ingram Micro, 1110
Insight Direct, 1110
Intel, 1094-1095
Interactive Age Hot 1000,
   1133
InterAp, 1126-1127
Intergraph, 1137
Internet Assistant, 670,
   1121
Internet Engineering Task
   Force, 109
Internet Explorer, 475
Internet Factory, 1119

Internet Freedom and
   Family Empowerment
   Act, 58
Internet in a Box, 1126
Internet Phone, 978,
   1124, 1207
Internet Service
   Providers, 1129-1130
Internet Society, 1138
Internet standards, 113
Internet telephone
   software, 976
Internet telephony-
   related, 994
InterNIC, 11, 127, 471
InterPlay, 1108
IQuest, 1130
IRC-related, 948
ISDN routers, 213
ISDN standards, 195
ISDN Systems
   Corporation, 1214
ISDN-related, 199, 1138
Java applets, 732
Java-related, 537, 732,
   1121-1125
JavaScript, 537
Jumbo, 1115
Ken Nesbitt's WebEdit,
   1120
L-Soft International, 1129
Law Jokes Web site, 50
law-related, 48
libel on the Internet, 54
Lion Communications
   Industries, 1215
local loop data rates, 187
Lotus, 1102
LucasArts Entertainment
   Company, 1108
LView Pro, 1207-1218
Lycos, 1131-1132
Macmillan Computer
   Publishing, 175
Macromedia, 1103
Maxis, 1106
MBONE video
   conferencing program,
   1009
Mcafee Antivirus, 1104
MCI, 1129
McKinley Internet
   Directory, 1134
Mecklerweb, 1137-1138
MetaMedia Project
   (SGML), 730

Microsoft Corp., 1101, 1215
Microsoft Internet Explorer, 1118
Microsoft Network, 1131, 1211
Microsoft Products, 1207
Midi Gate, 1207-1208
Mod4Win, 1208
Mosaic helper applications, 583
Motorola, 1100
Motorola ISG, 1215-1218
moving between with Netscape commands, 509
moving between with URLs in Netscape, 510
MSN, 476
MUD-related, 1024
multimedia files, processing with Internet Explore, 491-494
navigating with Internet Assistant, 673-677
navigating with Internet Explorer, 477, 482-483
navigating with Mosaic, 547-553, 559-562
navigating with Netscape, 507-522
navigating with NEWTShooter utility (Chameleon), 170
NaviSoft, 1121
NCompass, 1118
NCSA Mosaic, 471, 1116-1117
NCSA What's New, 1133-1134
NEC Corp., 1096
NECX Direct, 1111-1112
NETCOM, 1211
NetFind, 1135
NetManage, Inc., 1125-1138, 1216
NetNanny, 1128
Netrek MUD, 1026
Netscape, 499, 503, 702, 1208-1218
Netscape Chat, 965
Netscape Communications, 1116
Netscape helper applications, 583

Netscape plug-in applications, 528
NewsXpress, 1128
NIUF (North American ISDN Users' Forum), 198
Novell, Inc., 1103
online gaming, 1030
opening multiple pages with Netscape, 510
Packard Bell, 1094
Panorama Pro, 1209
PaperSoftware, 1124
PC Software Links, 1105
PC speaker drivers, 581
PGP, 1115
Pizza Hut, 688
Playboy, 81
Point Communications's Best of the Web, 1134
PolyView, 1209
Portal, 1130
PowWow Internet telephony software, 990
Pretty Good Privacy encryption software, 72
Prodigy, 1131, 1211
Prospero Systems, 1123
PSI, 1129
public domain works, 77
Quarterdeck, 1103
Questar, 1120
RealAudio, 108, 528, 586, 741-742, 1121-1125
Sausage Software, 1120
searching, 1131-1135
security issues, 91
server-related, 1116-1120
service providers, 1130-1131
Shockwave, 739
Shockwave helper application, 530
Sierra Online, 1109
Simon and Schuster Interactive, 1107
SimTel, 1115
SlipKnot, 1118
Snoopie Internet File Finder, 1135
SoftQuad, 1120
Software Creations BBS, 1112-1113
software licensing, 86
software-related, 1100-1105, 1112-1116, 1125-1129

Spry Incorporated, 1216
Stanford Net News Filtering, 1135
Stars!, 1209
STB Systems, 1099
Stroud's Consummate WinSock List, 1114
Submit It!, 1135
SurfWatch Software, 1128
Symantec Corporation, 1105
Teles, 1216-1218
The List, 1130
The WELL, 1137
Thrustmaster, 1100
Tile.Net/FTP, 1116
Tone Commander Systems, Inc., 1216
Total Clearance, Inc., 78
trademark laws, 87
TrueSpeech, 992
TrueSpeech helper application, 741
TS Intercom Internet telephony software, 992
TUCOWS, 1113
U.S. Robotics, 1096
URLs, 463-465
US Robotics, 1217
USB-related, 201
UUNET Technologies, 1129
video, 108
video conferencing-related, 998
Virtual Explorer add-on utility, 493
VRML-related, 1121-1125
VuePrint, 1210
Walnut Creek CD-ROM, 1136
Web copyright issues, 76
Web page background colors, 719
Web page-related, 604
WebChat, 1123
WebCrawler, 259, 1132
WebFX VRML browser, 532, 734
WebPhone Internet telephony software, 989
WebSpace, 1122
Western Digital, 1098
Windows 95 Internetworking Headquarters, 1136

Windows 95 ISDN
support, 201
WinNet, 1130
WinPGP, 1210
Winsite, 1114
WinSock, 114, 152
WinZIP, 1210
WinZip, 1104
WIT (WWW Interactive
Talk), 470
World File Project, 1114
World Wide Web
Consortium, 470-471
World Wide Web Virtual
Library, 1134-1138
World Wide Web Worm,
1132
World Wide Web Yellow
Pages, 1133
Worlds, Inc., 1123
WorldView, 1124
Xing, 1125
Xylogics, 1217-1218
Xyplex, 1218
YAHOO, 1237
Yahoo, 1132
ZyXEL, 1218
sizing
text in Web pages, 630-631
WS_FTP windows, 859
slander on the Internet, 53
SLIP (Serial Line Internet
Protocol), 112, 1234
accounts, 20
connections, 112
installation for Windows 95
workstations, 140-141
settings for Internet in a Box
software, 165
uninstalling support for, 141
WinWAIS Dialler, 899
SLIP Settings dialog box
(Internet in a Box software),
165
SlipKnot Web site, 1118
SmartList software mailing
lists, 1234
SMDS (Switched Multimegabit
Data Service), 1234
smileys (newsgroups), 773,
1234
SMTP (Simple Mail Transfer
Protocol), 330-331, 1234
SNMP (Simple Network
Management Protocol), 1234

Snoopie Internet File Finder
Web site, 1135
sockets, 1234
SoftQuad Web site, 1120
software, 1160-1162,
1186-1187
accessing from FTP sites, 28
cryptology, 71
developments on the Web,
743-745
freeware, 1183
FTP sites, 1139-1152
Internet telephony, 976-977
Cyberphone, 990-991
Digiphone, 983-987
Internet Phone, 977-983
Internet Voice Chat, 976
PowWow, 989-990
Speak Freely, 987-988
TS Intercom, 991-992
via Internet Global Phone
software, 987
WebPhone, 988-989
WebTalk, 988
licensing agreements, 86
mailing lists, 1081-1088
Mosaic requirements,
540-541
newsgroups, 1163-1172
Prodigy, 287, 290
public domain, 1183, 1233
security, 1038
service providers, 123
shareware, 1183
Web sites, 1100-1105,
1112-1116, 1125-1129
Software Creations BBS Web
site, 1112-1113
Software Entrepreneurs
mailing list, 1087
Software Tool and Die: The
World Gopher site, 1177
SONET (Synchronous Optical
Network), 227-228, 1234
sound cards
duplex, 974
requirements
for MPC, 580
for video conferencing,
1001
testing for voice
communications on the
Net, 974
voice communications on
the Net, 973-975

sound files, 741-743
formats, 580-581
Internet support, 42
Mosaic compatibility, 558
player applications, 581
playing with Internet
Explorer, 493
RealAudio helper
application, 586
Web page design
considerations, 613-614
WHAM helper application,
587
WPLANY helper application,
587
spaces (HTML recognition),
624-625
Spam
mailing list, 1079
MUDs, 1016
spamming, 83
Sparco FTP site, 1150
Speak Freely Internet
telephony software, 987-988
speaker drivers, 581
speaker volume (modems),
setting, 142
special characters (HTML
support), 625-626
Special menu commands
(Eudora)
Add as Recipient, 387
Change Password, 382
Empty Trash, 399
Forget Password, 382
Make Nickname, 386
Remove Recipient, 388
Settings, 383
spell checking utilities, Agent
newsreader capablities, 800
SPIDs (service profile
identifiers), narrowband
ISDN B channels, 194
spools (SMTP), 331
spreading viruses, 1054
Spry, Incorporated
addresses, 1216
FTP site, 1150
telephone numbers, 1216
Web site, 1216
stacks (TCP/IP), software
conflicts, 158-159
Standard Generalized Markup
Language, see SGML
Stanford Net News Filtering
Web site, 1135

Stardust FTP site, 1146
Stars! MUD, 1028-1029, 1209
Start menu commands
    Program, 360
    Programs, 380, 845
    Run, 832, 839
    Settings, 357, 376
    Shut Down, 1046, 1066
starting
    Agent newsreader, 792-805
    DOS, 1066
    Exchange, 360
    Free Agent newsreader,
        792-805
    FTP command-line accounts,
        839-840
    HGopher, 871
    HotDog, 706
    Internet Explorer Web
        browser, 475-481
    Mosaic, 543
    Navigator Gold, 703
    Netscape, 502
    Prodigy, 290-291
    Telnet
        command-line accounts,
            827-828
        Windows 95, 832
    WebCrawler, 919-920
    WinSock, 153
    WinWAIS, 900
    Yahoo!, 922
status bar messages
    Mosaic, 550-551
    Netscape, 512-513
status bars
    Mosaic, 545
    Netscape, 504
status displays (Netscape),
    512-515
status indicators (modems),
    displaying for dial-up
    networking software, 144
status messages (Internet
    Explorer Web browser), 494
STB Systems Web site, 1099
stop bits (modem settings),
    142
storage charges (home pages)
    from service providers,
    606-607
store and forward e-mail
    systems, 1234
Stored Wire and Electronic
    Communications and
    Transactional Records
    Act, 69

storing
    e-mail addresses
        in America Online
            address books, 269
        in Prodigy address books,
            306
        in WinCIM address
            books, 237-238
    e-mail messages in Agent
        newsreader folders, 814
    home pages
        with FTP, 607-608
        with HTTP, 607-608
    inline images for Web pages,
        613
    URLs in Mosaic Hotlists,
        562-567
Stroud's Consummate
    WinSock List Web site, 1114
students, Internet access, 110
StuffIt, 341
subdomains, 1234
submit buttons (Web page
    forms), inserting with
    Internet Assistant, 692-693
Submit It! Web site, 1135
submitting Web page forms,
    664-665
subnet masks (LANs), 130
subnets (LANs), 126
subpoenas (e-mail), 343
SUBSCRIBE command
    (Majordomo mailing lists),
    431
subscribing
    mailing lists, 1234
        LISTSERV mailing lists,
            421-423
        Majordomo mailing lists,
            431
        with America Online,
            270-272
        with WinCIM, 238-240
    newsgroups, 1234
        with Agent/Free Agent
            newsreaders, 805-806
        with America Online,
            273-274
        with NewsXpress,
            780-783
        with Prodigy, 302
        with terminal emulation
            mode in CompuServe,
            247
        with WinCIM, 241-242
Super TCP Internet
    software, 175

Supra FTP site, 1151
surfing, 772-773, 1234
SurfWatch Software Web site,
    1128
Switched Multimegabit Data
    Service (SMDS), 1234
Switched-56 Internet
    connections, 219-220
switching
    packets, 220-224, 1231
    signaling, 179, 185-187
Symantec Corporation Web
    site, 1105
symmetric digital subscriber
    lines (SDSLs), 227
Synchronous Optical Network
    (SONET), 227-228, 1234
system administrators
    (e-mail), 347

T

T1 lines, 224-226, 1234
T3 lines, 224-225, 1234
<TABLE> HTML element,
    716-717
tables (Web pages)
    adding anchors to, 717
    inserting with HotDog,
        715-717
tags (HTML), see elements
talking on IRCs, 947
TAPI (Telephony API), 201
TAR (Tape Archive) programs,
    1234
Task Bar Properties dialog
    box, 871
Taskbar command (Settings
    menu), 1199
Taskbar Properties dialog box,
    833, 899
TCP, 1235
TCP/IP (Transmission Control
    Protocol/Internet Protocol),
    126-127
    configurations
        for network clients, 134
        for Windows 95, 129-134
    connections, testing, 135
    dial-up networking software
        settings, 146
    installation on Windows 95
        workstations, 127-129,
        139-140
    properties, 129

SMTP (Simple Mail Transfer Protocol), 330-331
stacks, software conflicts, 158-159
Telnet (LANs), 834
TCP/IP for PCs mailing list, 1079
<TD> HTML element, 716
TDM (Time Division Multiplexing), 224
technical support (service providers), 124
TEIs (terminal endpoint identifiers), narrowband ISDN B channels, 194
Telebit FTP site, 1151
telephone line connections to service providers, 110
telephone numbers
Adtran, 1211
Agent, 1205
Alpha Telecom, Inc., 1212
America Online, 1210
Artisoft, Inc, 1212
Ascend Communications, 1212
AVM Computersysteme Vertriebs GMBH, 1212
AVM of America, Inc., 1212
Chase Research, Inc., 1213
Cisco Systems, 1213
3Com Corporation, 1217
CompuServe, 1210
Digi International, 1213
Digiphone, 1206
Eudora Light, 1206
Frontier Technologies Corporation, 1213
FTP Software, Inc., 1214
Gandalf Technologies, 1214-1218
Gmud32, 1206
HotDog, 1206
IBM Corporation, 1214
IDSN*tek, 1215
Internet Phone, 1207
ISDN Systems Corporation, 1214
Lion Communications Industries, 1215
LView Pro, 1207-1218
Microsoft Corp., 1215
Microsoft Network, 1211
Microsoft Products, 1207
Midi Gate, 1207-1208
Mod4Win, 1208

Motorola ISG, 1215-1218
MPEGPLAY, 1208
NETCOM, 1211
NetManage, Inc., 1216
Netscape, 1208-1218
Paint Shop Pro, 1208-1209
Panorama Pro, 1209
PolyView, 1209
Prodigy, 1211
Spry, Incorporated, 1216
Stars!, 1209
Teles, 1216-1218
Tone Commander Systems, Inc., 1216
US Robotics, 1217
VuePrint, 1210
Wham, 1209
WinPGP, 1210
WinZIP, 1210
Xylogics, 1217-1218
Xyplex, 1218
ZyXEL, 1218
telephones (Internet software), 976-977
Cyberphone, 990-991
Digiphone, 983-987
Internet Global Phone software, 987
Internet Phone, 977-983
Internet Voice Chat, 976
PowWow, 989-990
Speak Freely, 987-988
TS Intercom, 991-992
WebPhone, 988-989
WebTalk, 988
Telephony API (TAPI), 201
teleporting in MUDs, 1021
Teles, contact sources 1216-1218
Telnet, 1235
accessing MUDs, 1014-1015
accounts
accessing, 828
command-line accounts, starting, 827-828
addresses, 823
host names, 823-824
numerical, 824-825
CompuServe capabilities, 235, 253-254
connecting, 822-823, 826
ports, 829-830
remote computers, 826-827
defined, 819-820
disconnecting, 829

displaying, 828-829
finding files with, 34-35
help, 835
hiding, 828-829
host names, 824
LANs, 834
linking computers, 820-821
procedures, 925
RTFM
searches, 925-927
security, 1042
sites
accessing with WinCIM, 253-254
IRCs, 945
time limits, 829
troubleshooting, 827
Trying...message, 827
UNIX, 828-829
versus FTP, 35
Windows 95
adding to Start menu, 833
connecting, 833-834
starting, 832
telnetting, 830-831
DUNE II, 831
KIS, 337
ports, 830
to IRCs, 945
to MUDs, 830, 1014-1015
templates (Web pages), 678
temporary directories (Netscape), specifying, 592
terminal adapters (ISDN)
built-in with routers, 213-214
external, 199-208
analog port options, 207
built-in analog fax/ modems, 208
Internal NT1 support, 208
multilink PPP support, 207
internal card, 208-212
Terminal command (Windows 95 Telnet menu), 834
terminal emulation, 247, 1235
terminal endpoint identifiers (TEIs), narrowband ISDN B channels, 194
terminal windows (dial-up networking software options), 143

terminals
ANSI, 822
defined, 821
HyperTerminal, 822
ports, 829-830
TTY, 822
VT series, 821
Terminate-and-Stay Resident
programs, *see* TSRs
terms, searching for, 906
test messages (mailing lists),
avoiding, 434
testing
newsgroup postings, 759
sound cards for voice
communications on the
Net, 974
TCP/IP connections, 135
text (Web pages)
attributes, 711
bold, 623, 633-634
centering, 711
delineating, 633
formatting, 610, 622-624,
710-711
headings, 710
indenting, 713-714
inserting, 609-610, 711
italicizing, 634
line breaks, 632, 711
paragraph breaks, 632
positioning, 631-633
preformatted, 632-633
sizing, 630-631
underlining, 634
text areas (Web page forms),
656-658
text box controls (Web page
forms), 652-654, 691
text-based Web browsers, 458
<TEXTAREA> HTML element,
656-658
TFTD-L (Thought for the Day),
418
<TH> HTML element, 716
third-party serial port drivers,
200
threads
mailing lists, 1235
newsgroup messages, 756,
808-810, 1235
throughput charges (service
providers) for home pages,
607
Thrustmaster Web site, 1100
TIFF (Tagged image file
format) files, 579

Tile.Net/FTP Web site, 1116
Time Division Multiplexing
(TDM), 224
time zones
displaying, 1199-1200
GMT (Greenwich Mean
Time), 1200
table of, 1200-1203
timeout feature (dial-up
networking software),
disabling for large
downloads, 143
TinyMUDs, 1013, 1016
<TITLE> HTML element,
640-641
title bars
Mosaic, 544
Netscape, 503
titles (Web pages), 640-641
To: button (e-mail Personal
Address Book), 366
Tone Commander Systems,
Inc., contact sources, 1216
toolbars
Exchange, 360-363
HotDog, 707
Internet Assistant, 673-674
Internet Explorer Web
browser, 477
Mosaic, 545-546
Netscape interface, 504-505
Prodigy interface, 294
WinCIM, 234
toolkits (anti-virus),
1068-1069
Tools menu commands
Deliver Now, 364, 367
Options, 372, 376
Service, 442
Total Clearance, Inc. Web site,
78
<TR> HTML element, 716
traceroute utility, 1235
tracking
Mosaic sessions, 559-560
Netscape sessions, 519-520
trade libel on the Internet, 53
trademarks, 87
traffic (networks), 1235
Transfer Status dialog box,
854
transferring
files
FTP, 838
HGopher, 876-877
overwriting, 853
messages from mail-
boxes, 391

translating host names to IP
addresses, 131
transmission (signaling), 179,
184-185
Transmission Control
Protocol/Internet Protocol,
see TCP/IP
transmit command (dial-up
scripting software), 150
transponders (video
conferencing), 996
triggers (viruses), 1054
troubleshooting
Archie, 933
dial-up networking software
connections, 155-156
directories, 853-855
files, 855
FTP
binary files, 843
connecting to, 847
inline images, 712
Internet applications, 156
modems
answering errors, 155
connection failure, 156
dialing errors, 155
installation, 312
MSN, 323
queuing messages, 394
security, 1038-1039
service providers, 404
TCP/IP stack conflicts with
software, 158-159
Telnet, 827
Veronica, 890
WAIS Manager 3.1, 909
Web page forms, 663
WinWAIS, 904
WS_FTP, 845
TrueSpeech helper
application, 741, 992-993
Trumpet Software FTP site,
1147
Trumpet WinSock,
see WinSock
Trusted Information Systems
FTP site, 1148
TS Intercom Internet
telephony software, 991-992
TSRs (Terminate-and-Stay
Resident) programs, 330
TTY, 822
TUCOWS Web site, 1113
twisted pair cabling, 184, 1235
TYPE parameter, <INPUT>
HTML element, 647

U

<U> HTML element, 634
U interfaces (ISDN), 192
U.S. Robotics Web site,
  1096
<UL> HTML element, 636
uncompressing newsgroup
  messages with PKZIP, 304
underlining
  hypertext links with
    Netscape, 508
  Web page text, 634
Undernet (IRCs), 948
undigestifying mailing lists,
  433
Uniform Resource Locators,
  see URLs
UNIMODEM, 200
uninstalling
  dial-up scripting support,
    141
  SLIP support, 141
universal modem drivers, 200
Universal Serial Bus (USB),
  201
University of Minnesota
  Gopher site, 1176-1177
University of Southern
  California Gopher Jewels
  Gopher site, 1177
UNIX, 1235
  commands
    man, 1229
    rlogin, 1233
    Telnet, 828-829
UNIX to UNIX Copy Protocol
  (UUCP), 1235
UNIX-based service providers,
  147
unmoderated mailing lists,
  433
unordered lists (Web pages),
  636, 713-714
unpacking compressed files,
  342
UNSUBSCRIBE command
  (Majordomo mailing lists),
  431
unsubscribing
  mailing lists
    with America Online,
      270-272
    with WinCIM, 238-240

newsgroups
  with Agent/Free Agent
    newsreaders, 805-806
  with America Online, 274
  with NewsXpress,
    780-783
unzipping files with WS_FTP,
  844
upgrading
  Eudora, 399
  WinSock to Windows 95,
    152-153
uploading, 1235
  binary files to newsgroups
    with NewsXpress, 788-789
  files
    canceling, 854
    to newsgroups, 244, 765
    with FTP, 26-27
    with WS_FTP, 854
  FTP files, 842-843
URL Catcher (mIRC), 962
URL location display
  Mosaic, 545
  Netscape, 503
URLs (Uniform Resource
  Locators), 463-465, 1235
  absolute, 463, 627-629
  accessing from Favorites list
    in Internet Explorer,
    486-492
  accessing from history list in
    Internet Explorer, 484-486
  adding to Mosaic hotlist
    folders, 564-565
  copying to Windows 95
    workstations with Internet
    Explorer, 482
  direct access with Internet
    Explorer, 483-484
  linking to with Internet
    Assistant, 681-682
  loading in Netscape, 510
  relative, 463, 627-629
  storing in Mosaic hotlists,
    562-567
US Robotics,
  contact sources, 1151, 1217
  Sportster internal card ISDN
    terminal adapter, 208
USB (Universal Serial Bus),
  201

UseNet newsgroups, 40, 43-44,
  119, 749-751, 1230, 1235
  abbreviations for phrases,
    771
  accessing
    with CompuServe Web
      browser, 260
    with NewsXpress, 779
    with Prodigy, 296
  alt.answers, 1160
  alt.bbs, 1163
  alt.binaries.sounds, 1172
  alt.cd-rom, 1172-1174
  alt.censorship, 1162
  alt.com.virus newsgroup,
    1068
  alt.culture.internet, 1162
  alt.culture.usenet, 1160
  alt.cyberspace, 1162
  alt.games, 1169
  alt.irc, 1163-1164
  alt.lang.vrml, 1164
  alt.mud, 1164
  alt.news.microsoft, 1170
  alt.online-service, 1164-1165
  alt.privacy, 1162
  alt.sys.pc-clone.*, 1167
  alt.test, 1160
  alt.usenet.offline-reader,
    1160
  alt.WinSock, 1165
  alt.www.hotjava, 1165
  alt.zines, 1172
  America Online capabilities,
    267, 272-278
  articles, 43
  BBS, 1163
  binary files
    downloading with Agent/
      Free Agent newsreaders,
      811-812
    downloading with
      NewsXpress, 788-789
    uploading with
      NewsXpress, 788-789
    uploading with WinCIM,
      244
  biz.comp.hardware,
    1167-1174
  biz.comp.services, 1172-1173
  biz.comp.software, 1170
  bogus, 755
  browsing with WinCIM, 241
  categories, 752-754
  CFV, 755

comp.answers, 1161
comp.infosystems, 1165
comp.infosystems.www.
  authoring.html, 1165
comp.infosystems.www.
  browsers.ms-windows,
  1166
comp.internet.net-
  happenings, 1166
comp.org.eff.news.talk,
  1162-1163
comp.os.ms-windows.*,
  1170-1171
comp.os.ms-windows.apps,
  1171-1174
comp.os.ms-
  windows.networking.ras,
  1166
comp.os.ms-
  windows.programmer,
  1171-1172
comp.protocols.*, 1166-1167
comp.publish.cdrom.
  multimedia, 1173-1174
comp.security.firewalls, 1167
comp.sys.ibm.pc.hardware,
  1167-1174
comp.virus newsgroup, 1068
CompuServe accessibility,
  235
computer-related, 1162,
  1167-1169
copyright considerations
  when posting to, 764-765
David Lawrence's list,
  1173-1174
DejaNews search utility,
  767-768
FAQs, 757-758
feeding, 1225
files, decoding/encoding,
  453
filtering, 766-767, 781
finding with Internet
  Explorer, 489
flaming, 771-772
guide articles, 757
history of, 751-752
identifiers, 752-756
improper signature files, 761
Internet-related, 1163-1167
lists, 1173
lurking, 772-773, 1229
mailing lists, 437
messages
  anonymous posting, 762
  cross-posting, 763

decoding with
  WINCODE.EXE in
  Prodigy, 303-304
downloading with
  WinCIM, 243
marking with America
  Online, 276
posting, 758-759, 1232
posting by geographic
  region, 763-764
posting, guidelines,
  773-774
posting in terminal
  emulation mode,
  249-250
posting with Agent/Free
  Agent newsreaders,
  810-811
posting with America
  Online, 276-277
posting with CompuServe
  Web browser, 261
posting with Internet
  Explorer, 490
posting with Prodigy, 303
posting with WinCIM,
  244
reader distribution of
  postings, 763-764
reading in terminal
  emulation mode,
  248-249
reading with Agent/Free
  Agent newsreaders,
  806-808
reading with America
  Online, 275-276
reading with
  CompuServe Web
  browser, 260
reading with Internet
  Explorer, 488-490
reading with Mosaic,
  572-573
reading with MSN, 326
reading with Netscape,
  535-536
reading with NewsXpress,
  783-784
reading with Prodigy,
  302-303
reading with WinCIM,
  242-243
responding to via e-mail
  with NewsXpress,
  786-787

responding to with
  Agent/Free Agent
  newsreaders, 811
responding to with
  America Online,
  277-278
responding to with
  NewsXpress, 787
saving as new with
  WinCIM, 243
saving with NewsXpress,
  785-786
selecting with
  NewsXpress, 783-784
threads, 756, 808-810,
  1235
uncompressing with
  PKZIP, 304
misc.forsale.computers,
  1168-1169
moderated, 755-756, 1229
monitoring before posting
  to, 757-758
MSN capabilities, 324-326
Netiquette, 302, 752,
  770-773
Netrek MUD, 1028
new, 755, 780
"newbies", 756-757
News, 1184
news.announce.newgroups,
  1161-1174
news.announce.newusers,
  1161
news.answers, 1161
news.groups, 1161
news.groups.questions, 1161
news.groups.reviews, 1161
news.lists, 1161
news.newusers.questions,
  1161
news.software.nntp, 1161
news.software.readers, 1162
option settings in Agent/Free
  Agent newsreaders,
  804-805
Prodigy capabilities, 289,
  301-304
responding to, 764
selecting with NewsXpress,
  783-784
shouting, 772
signature files, attaching to
  postings, 760-762
smileys, 773

software-related, 1160-1167, 1169-1172
subscribing, 1234
  with Agent/Free Agent newsreaders, 805-806
  with America Online, 273-274
  with NewsXpress, 780-783
  with Prodigy, 302
  with WinCIM, 241-242
surfing, 772-773
table of, 1156-1160
testing postings, 759
topics, 43-44
unsubscribing
  with Agent/Free Agent newsreaders, 805-806
  with America Online, 274
  with NewsXpress, 780-783
users, 338-339
viewer application-related, 584
WinCIM options, 245
WWW-related, 467-468
user agreements for networks, 85
user errors (Mosaic), 574-575
user input (Web page forms), 647-656
user names, 1235
User Preferences dialog box, 936
$USERID variable (dial-up scripting software), 150
usernames
fingering, 333
service providers, 406
users
e-mail
  finding, 332-333
  UseNet user list, 338-339
  WHOIS database, 334-336
security, 1038-1039
utilities, 1186-1187
HTML, 1184-1185
NEWTShooter (Chameleon Internet software), 170
ping, 1232
PKZIP, uncompressing newsgroup messages, 304
traceroute, 1235
see also add-on utilities

UUCP (UNIX to UNIX Copy Protocol), 1235
UUDecode, 339, 441, 1235
UUEncode, 339, 441, 788, 1236
UUNET Technologies, 402
addresses, 405-406
FTP site, 1145
Web site, 1129

V

validity checks (anti-virus products), 1060-1061
VAX computers, 830
VCBs (video capture boards), requirements for video conferencing, 1000
Verify Deletion dialog box, 849
Veronica (Very Easy Rodent-Oriented Net-wide Index to Computerized Archives), 888-889, 1236
defined, 888-889
finding files with, 32-33
Gopher searches, 889-890
indexes, 889
integration with America Online, 280
queries, 890-891
troubleshooting, 890
video capture boards, *see* VCBs
video conferencing, 42, 995-996
advantages of, 997-998
bandwidth complications, 998-999
cameras, 1000-1001
commercial availability, 997
CU-SeeMe program, 1002-1008
future developments, 1008-1009
guidelines to keeping updated, 1009-1010
hardware requirements, 999-1002
history of, 996-997
holographic, 1009
integration with virtual reality, 1009
limitations, 1008

monitor requirements, 1001-1002
PC requirements, 999-1000
reflectors, 1003
sound card requirements, 1001
video capture boards, 1000
video files
Mosaic compatibility, 558
QuickTime, 1233
Web sites, 108
video players, 582
viewer applications, 1236
advantages, 579
configuring for use with Netscape, 588-589
downloading, 583-584
finding, 583-584
freeware, 580
HGopher, 885-888
installation, 584-585
LViewPro, 585
Midi Gate, 585
Mod4Win, 585
Mosaic
  adding, 594
  configurations, 594-595
movie files, 582
MPEGPLAY, 586
multimedia, 1185
Netscape, configurations, 590-591
newsgroups, 584
operating, 595
Paint Shop Pro, 586
Panorama (SGML), 725-728
PolyView, 586
shareware, 580
Shockwave, installation, 739-740
testing, 887-888
WAIS Manager 3.1, 907
Viewers dialog box, 886
viewing
.AVI files with Internet Explorer, 492
graphics files in Web pages with Internet Explorer, 492
HTML source code for Web pages with Internet Explorer, 487
multimedia files
  with Internet Explorer, 587-588
  with Mosaic, 592-595
  with Netscape, 588-592

search results, 934
VRML worlds with Internet
Explorer, 493-494
**Virtual Explorer add-on
utility, 493**
**Virtual Memory System
(VMS), 1236**
**virtual possessions (MUDs),
1022-1023**
**virtual reality, integration
with video conferencing,
1009**
**Virtual Reality Modeling
Language,** *see* VRML
viruses, 95, 1236
acquiring, 1061-1062
alt.com.virus newsgroup,
1068
anti-virus products, 1058,
1067
CPAV (Central Point
Anti-Virus), 1067
Dr. Solomon's Anti-Virus
Toolkit, 1068-1069
F-PROT, 1069-1070
MSAV (Microsoft Anti-
Virus), 1067
anti-virus Web sites, 97
backing up, 1062-1063
behavior blockers, 1061
BSI (Boot Sector Infectors),
1055
changing, 1058
Columbus Day virus,
1058-1059
comp.virus newsgroup, 1068
defined, 1054, 1056-1057
downloading, 1062
droppers, 1055
FTP file precautions, 253
hiding, 1058
history of, 1057-1058
Internet worm, 93
Jerusalem virus, 1058-1059
macros, 1055-1056
Michelangelo virus, 1059
naming, 1059
payloads, 1054-1057
polymorphic viruses, 1060
program infectors,
1054-1055
protecting, 1066
replicates, 1054-1057
restoring, 1063
scanning, 1058, 1060

spreading, 1054
triggers, 1054
validity checks, 1060-1061
Windows 95, 1064
boot sectors, checking,
1064
files, 1065-1066
**VMS (Virtual Memory
System), 1236**
Vocaltec FTP site, 1147
**voice communications on the
Net, 971-972**
future developments, 994
impact on Internet
technology, 993-994
modem requirements,
975-976
sound card requirements,
973-975
system requirements,
972-976
testing sound cards for, 974
TrueSpeech helper
application, 992-993
via Cyberphone, 990-991
via Digiphone software,
983-987
via Internet Global Phone
software, 987
via Internet Phone software,
977-983
via Internet Voice Chat
software, 976-977
via PowWow, 989-990
via Speak Freely, 987-988
via TS Intercom, 991-992
via WebPhone, 988-989
via WebTalk, 988
**Voice on the Net mailing list,
1079-1080**
**VRML (Virtual Reality
Modeling Language), 466,
733-739, 1186, 1236**
browsers (WebFX), 532
configurations, 735
downloading, 734
installation, 734
Internet resources, 738-739
Web sites, 735, 738-739,
1121-1125
worlds, 493-494, 735-738
VT series terminals, 821
**VuePrint helper application,
587, 1210**

W

**WAIS (Wide Area Information
Servers), 33, 897, 1236**
accessing with Veronica, 280
America Online capabilities,
267, 278-280
Clipboards, saving to, 903
defined, 897-898
documents, retrieving,
902-903
FAQs, 898
queries, saving, 907
relevance feedback, 902-903
results, 903-904
searches, 900-902
e-mail, 908-909
saving, 907
servers, 33
troubleshooting, 904
viewers, 907
WAIS Manager 3.1
defined, 904
icons, creating, 904
installing, 904-905
pre-defined searches,
905-906
relevance feedback,
906-907
searches, 905-906
troubleshooting, 909
viewers, 907
**waitfor command (dial-up
scripting software), 149**
Walnut Creek CD-ROM
FTP site, 1142-1154
Web site, 1136
**WANs (Wide Area Networks),
1236**
**warnings (security),
1038-1039**
**Washington University at
St. Louis FTP site, 1141**
**WAV (Waveform) audio files,
581**
Web Chat, 1236
Web pages, 36
accessing from Mosaic
Hotlists, 568-571
.AVI files, viewing with
Internet Explorer, 492
background colors, setting,
718-719
background textures, 719

binary files, design
considerations, 614-615
body content, 641
bookmarks, 523-526, 1221
browser considerations,
608-609
caching
with Mosaic, 549
with Netscape, 510-511
CGI-bin programs, 615, 666
color schemes, Netscape
settings, 511-512
configuring for UNIX
servers, 721
content considerations, 603
converting to Word
documents, 697
creating
from existing Web pages
with Internet Assistant,
694-695
from Word documents,
695-697
with HotDog, 703-714
with HTML, 621, 642-644
with Internet Assistant,
677-688
with Navigator Gold,
699-702, 709-714
designing, 597-605, 615-616
display preferences with
Mosaic, 555
downloading to edit with
Internet Assistant, 694-695
editing with Internet
Assistant, 678
font preferences in Mosaic,
556-557
formatting with Internet
Assistant, 679-680
forms, 644-663, 1225
CGI-bin programs, 693
checkbox controls,
648-650, 691-692
creating, 662-663
creating with HotDog,
717-718
creating with Internet
Assistant, 688-693
design considerations,
614
drop-down list box
controls, inserting with
Internet Assistant, 692
fields, inserting with
Internet Assistant,
689-693

lists, 658-661
password encoding,
654-655
processing, 645
radio button controls,
650-652
reset buttons, 655-656
send buttons, 656
sending data to Web
servers, 646
submit buttons, inserting
with Internet Assistant,
692-693
submitting, 664-665
text areas, 656-658
text box controls,
652-654, 691
troubleshooting, 663
user input, 647-656
generating interest in,
617-618
graphics files
adding with Internet
Assistant, 684-686
as backgrounds, 718-719
design considerations,
611-616, 684
display preferences in
Mosaic, 551
formats, 578-580, 684
image maps, 686
loading preferences for
Netscape, 513-515
placeholders, 514
storing, 613
viewing with Internet
Explorer, 492
headers, 640
horizontal rules, 711
creating with Internet
Assistant, 686-687
inserting, 633
HTML editors, 618-620
HTML filters, 619-620
HTML source code, viewing
with Internet Explorer, 487
hypertext links, 459-463,
637-640, 1227-1228
absolute, 553
activating, 462
activating with Netscape,
507-508
anchors, 637-640, 714
color, changing with
Netscape, 508
customizing with Mosaic,
554-555

customizing with
Netscape, 508-509
design considerations,
610-611
expiration dates, setting
with Netscape, 509
identifying, 462
image maps, 612, 686,
713
inserting with Internet
Assistant, 680-684
relative, 553
to bookmarks with
Internet Assistant,
682-684
to local files with Internet
Assistant, 680-681
to URLS with Internet
Assistant, 681-682
underlining with
Netscape, 508
indexing contents with
anchors, 638
inline images
alignment, 635
inserting, 634-635, 712
text-only browser
alternatives, 635
troubleshooting, 712
Java applet support, 536
lists, 713-714
bulleted, 636
definition lists, 713
indented, 636
numbered, 636-637
ordered, 636-637,
713-714
unordered, 636, 713-714
loading
aborting in Mosaic, 551
aborting with Netscape,
513
from Mosaic hotlists, 569
status bar messages in
Mosaic, 550-551
local
loading with Mosaic,
558-559
loading with Netscape,
518-519
mailto links, inserting, 719
Mosaic Hotlists, 562-567
movie files
design considerations,
614-615
formats, 581-582
Shockwave helper
application, 530

moving between
  with hypertext links in
    Mosaic, 547-548
  with Mosaic commands,
    548-550
  with URLs in Mosaic, 550
multimedia files, 578-583,
  739-740
  displaying MIME types in
    Netscape, 590-591
  MIME types, 582-583
  viewer applications,
    downloading, 583-585
  viewing with Internet
    Explorer, 587-588
  viewing with Mosaic,
    592-595
  viewing with Netscape,
    588-592
opening multiple with
  Netscape, 510
posting to mailing lists,
  617-618
previewing with HotDog,
  720-721
printing
  with Internet Explorer,
    487-488
  with Mosaic, 553
  with Netscape, 517
promoting, 617-618
publishing with HotDog,
  721
related WWW sites, 604
reloading, 509, 549
returning to
  with Mosaic, 560-562
  with Netscape, 520-522
saving
  as local files in Mosaic,
    552
  as text files in Mosaic,
    552
  with Internet Explorer,
    487-488
  with Mosaic, 552-553
  with Netscape, 516-517
searching
  with Mosaic, 551-552
  with Netscape, 515-516
security, 527
service providers
  charges, 605-607
  support for, 603-605

sound files
  design considerations,
    613-614
  formats, 580-581
  Mosaic compatibility, 558
  playing with Internet
    Explorer, 493
standardized format, 630
storage charges from service
  providers, 606-607
storing
  with FTP, 607-608
  with HTTP, 607-608
tables
  adding anchors to, 717
  inserting with HotDog,
    715-717
target audiences, 601-603
templates (Internet
  Assistant), 678
text
  attributes, 711
  bold, 623, 633-634
  centering, 711
  delineating, 633
  formatting, 610, 622-624,
    710-711
  headings, 710
  indenting, 713-714
  inserting, 609-610, 711
  italicizing, 634
  line breaks, 632, 711
  paragraph breaks, 632
  positioning, 631-633
  preformatted, 632-633
  sizing, 630-631
  underlining, 634
throughput charges for
  service providers, 607
titles, 640-641
URLs, 463-465
video files (Mosaic
  compatibility), 558
see also home pages; WWW
  sites
Web servers, 37, 466, 604
WebChat Web site, 1123
**WebCrawler search engine,
  259, 919-922, 1236**
  starting, 919-920
  Web site, 1132
WebFX VRML browser, 532
  configurations, 735
  downloading, 734
  installation, 734

**WebPhone Internet telephony
  software, 988-989**
WebSpace Web site, 1122
**WebTalk Internet telephony
  software, 988**
The WELL Web site, 1137
Western Digital Corporation
  FTP site, 1151-1154
  Web site, 1098
**WHAM helper application,
  587, 1209**
White Pages, 332
**WHOIS database, 334-336,
  1236**
**Wide Area Information Server
  (WAIS), 33**
wildcards (queries), 891
**WinCIM (CompuServe
  Information Manager for
  Windows), 233-234**
  address book, storing e-mail
    addresses in, 237-238
  downloading newsgroup
    messages, 243
  FTP capabilities, 251-253
  newsreader features, 246
  posting newsgroup articles,
    244
  posting to mailing lists, 240
  reading newsgroup
    messages, 242-243
  sending e-mail messages,
    236-237
  subscribing/unsubscribing
    to mailing lists, 238-240
    to newsgroups, 241-242
  toolbars, 234
  UseNet newsgroup options,
    245
Wincode, 452
  decoding files, 451
  encoding files, 449-451
  installing, 447-448
**WINCODE.EXE (Prodigy),
  decoding newsgroup
  messages, 303-304**
windows
  layout preferences for Agent/
    Free Agent newsreaders,
    803-804
  Mailbox Window, 361
  Message Window, 362
  Sessions Profile window,
    customizing, 861-863

WS_FTP
customizing, 855-859
debugging messages, 857
sizing, 859
Windows 95
boot sectors, checking, 1064
built-in Internet support, 125
files, decoding/encoding, 446
FTP clients, 839
Internetworking Headquarters Web site, 1136
mailing list, 1087
Setup Wizard, 352
Start menu icons, creating, 870-871
Telnet
adding to Start menu, 833
connecting, 833-834
menu commands, 834
starting, 832
viruses, 1064-1066
Windows for Workgroups mailing list, 1087
Windows Help Compiler mailing list, 1088
Windows Internet Naming Standard, see WINS
Windows mailing list, 1088
WinISDN API (Chameleon Internet software support), 169
WinNet Web site, 1130
WINPGP4
addresses, 1210
files, downloading, 1047
public/private keys, creating, 1047
security, 1046-1050
telephone numbers, 1210
Web site, 1210
WINS (Windows Internet Naming Standard), configurations for Windows 95 workstations, 131
WinSite
FTP site, 1139-1141
Web site, 1114
WinSock, 113, 1235
connecting to the Internet, 151-153
downloading, 152, 160
sampling America Online, 267

starting, 153
upgrading to Windows 95, 152-153
WinSock Error dialog box, 901
WinSock-L FTP Archive FTP site, 1142-1143
WinVN mailing list, 1080
WinWAIS
defined, 898
Dialler, 899
icons, creating, 899
installing, 899
obtaining, 898
starting, 900
troubleshooting, 904
WAIS searches, 900-902
WAIS Manager 3.1
searches, 905-906
troubleshooting, 909
WinZip, 341
addresses, 1210
e-mail, 1210
FTP site, 1152
interface, 1236
NetCD95, 871
passwords, 344
telephone numbers, 1210
Web site, 1104
wiretap laws, 69
wiring (ISDN), 196-198
wiring technologies (Internet connectivity), selecting, 229
WIT (WWW Interactive Talk), 470
wizards
Inbox Setup Wizard, 352
Install New Modem, 311
Internet Setup, 314
Make New Connection, 141
Setup Wizard, 354
Windows 95 Setup Wizard, 352
Wizards (MUDs), 1016, 1024
Word
documents
converting to Web pages, 695-697
creating from Web pages, 697
redesigning for conversion to Web pages, 696-697
Internet Assistant requirements, 669
WordPerfect Corporation mailing list, 1088

WordPerfect for Windows mailing list, 1088
World File Project Web site, 1114
World Wide Web Consortium Web site, 470-471
World Wide Web, see WWW
World Wide Web Virtual Library Web site, 1134-1138
World Wide Web Worm Web site, 1132
World Wide Web Yellow Pages Web site, 1133
worlds (VRML), 493-494, 735-738
Worlds, Inc. Web site, 1123
WorldView Web site, 1124
worms, 1236
WOSA (Windows Open Systems Architecture), 114
WPLANY helper application, 587
WRL (VRML) files, 579
WS_FTP client, 1236
Archie, 929-930, 935-936
connecting to, 844-846
errors, 854
executable files, defining, 864-865
exiting, 865
files
downloading, 854
retrieving, 853-855
uploading, 854
FTP site, 1147
host profiles, 859-861
installing, 844
links, 853
NetCD95, 844
profiles, 845
Session Profile window, customizing, 861-863
troubleshooting, 845
windows
customizing, 855-859
debugging messages, 857
sizing, 859
zipping/unzipping, 844
see also FTP
WSGopher client, 1236
WWW (World Wide Web), 21, 35-38, 457, 1184, 1237
America Online capabilities, 267, 283-285
books on, 471

browsers, 458-459
  Air Mosaic, 168
  America Online, 283-285
  America Online,
    preferences, 285
  configuring to preview
    HotDog Web pages, 720
  Gopher, 868
  home page design
    considerations, 608-609
  HotJava, 467, 731
  Hyper-G utility, 733
  Internet Assistant,
    672-677
  Internet Explorer (MSN),
    321, 473-496, 1227
  Internet services, 459,
    465
  Lynx, 459
  Mosaic, 459, 540-542,
    1230
  Mosaic for CompuServe,
    257-259
  NetLauncher, 255-257
  NetScape, 497-518, 1230
  Prodigy, 297-299
  text-based, 458
  text-only viewing
    options, 217
built-in media via Java, 467
client/server architecture,
  466
CompuServe capabilities,
  235, 254-261
development, 35
future developments, 38,
  466-467
history of, 457-458
HTML security, 1040-1041
live audio/video support,
  future developments, 466
mailing lists, 468-469
MSN capabilities, 321
newsgroups, 467-468
Prodigy capabilities, 289,
  297-299
search engines, 37
  Archie, 927-929
  defined, 912-913
  Gopher, 937
  knowbots, 1228
  Lycos, 915-919, 1018,
    1229
  table of, 913-915
  WebCrawler, 259,
    919-922, 1236
  Yahoo!, 922-925, 1237

service provider options, 115
sites
  7th Level, 1106
  accessing from Favorites
    list in Internet Explorer,
    486-492
  accessing from history list
    in Internet Explorer,
    484-486
  accessing from Mosaic
    Hotlists, 568-571
  accessing with America
    Online, 283-285
  accessing with
    bookmarks, 525
  accessing with Internet
    Assistant, 673
  accessing with Prodigy,
    297
  Acer America, 1093
  Activision, 1107
  add-ons, 1116-1120
  Adobe, 1104
  Adobe Amber helper
    application, 530-531
  Adtran, 1211
  Agent, 1205
  Agent/Free Agent
    newsreaders, 792
  Alpha Telecom, Inc.,
    1212
  America Online, 267,
    1131, 1210
  anti-virus, 97
  Artisoft, Inc, 1212
  Ascend Communications,
    1095, 1212
  ATI Technologies, 1099
  AVM Computersysteme
    Vertriebs GMBH, 1212
  AVM of America, Inc.,
    1212
  Berkeley Systems, 1107
  bookmarks, 297, 682,
    1221
  Borland, 1104
  browser-related,
    1116-1120
  BrowserWatch, 1118
  Burn:Cycle, 1106
  California State
    University Windows
    World, 1114
  censorship-related, 51
  Center For Democracy &
    Technology, 68

  CGI Programmer's
    Reference, 1119
  CGI-bin program-related,
    693
  Chase Research, Inc.,
    1213
  Cisco Systems, 1213
  clipper chip-related, 72
  3Com Corporation, 1217
  Compaq Computer
    Corp., 1093
  CompuServe, 255,
    259-260, 1131, 1210
  computer crime laws, 91
  Computer Price
    Cruncher, 1111
  computer-related,
    1091-1094, 1109-1112
  Conner Peripherals, 1099
  copying URLs to
    Windows 95
    workstations with
    Internet Explorer, 482
  Copyright Web site, 77
  Corel Corp., 1104
  CPSR, 1138
  Creative Labs, 1097-1098
  CU-SeeMe video
    conferencing program,
    1002, 1124
  CUI Search Catalog,
    1133-1138
  Cyberphone Internet
    telephony software, 991
  DejaNews newsgroup
    search utility, 767
  Dell Computer Corp.,
    1094
  Demon Internet, 1130
  dial-up scripting software,
    149
  Diamond Multimedia,
    1096
  Digi International, 1213
  Digiphone, 983
  digital subscriber lines,
    227
  direct access with
    Internet Explorer,
    483-484
  directories, 1131-1135
  DOOM MUD, 1028
  Egghead Software, 1109
  EINet Galaxy, 1133
  Electronic Arts, 1106
  Electronic Frontier
    Foundation, 68, 1137

Electronic Privacy Information Center, 71
ElekTek, Inc., 1109
Emissary, 1127
Entering the World Wide Web: A Guide to Cyberspace, 471
Epic MegaGames, 1107
Eudora, 1127, 1206
Excel to HTML Converter, 1121
fair use doctrine (copyright law), 79
finding, 37-38
firewalls, 115
First Amendment Cyber-Tribune, 49
First Amendment-related, 50
First Floor Software, 1119
Four11 White Page Directory, 1135
frame relay, 220
Frontier Technologies Corporation, 1127-1138, 1213
FTP Software, Inc., 1214
game-related, 1105-1109
Gandalf Technologies, 1214-1218
Hang Duke (Java-created game), 732
hardware-related, 1094-1100
Harris Semiconductor, 1116
Hayes, 1096
Hewlett Packard, 1098
HotDog, 705, 1206
HotJava Web browser, 467, 731
HTML-related, 620, 1120-1121
HTTP specifications, 465
human rights related Web sites, 51
Hyper-G browser utility, 733
IBM Corporation, 1092, 1214
Id Software, 1108-1138
IDSN*tek, 1215
Information Law Web site, 76
InfoSeek Corp., 1133
Ingram Micro, 1110

Insight Direct, 1110
Intel, 1094-1095
Interactive Age Hot 1000, 1133
InterAp, 1126-1127
Intergraph, 1137
Internet Assistant, 670, 1121
Internet Engineering Task Force, 109
Internet Explorer, 475
Internet Factory, 1119
Internet Freedom and Family Empowerment Act, 58
Internet in a Box, 1126
Internet Phone software, 978, 1124, 1207
Internet Service Providers, 1129-1130
Internet Society, 1138
Internet standards, 113
Internet telephone software, 976, 994
InterNIC, 11, 127, 471
InterPlay, 1108
IQuest, 1130
IRC-related, 948
ISDN-related, 195, 199, 213, 1138, 1214
Java-related, 537, 732, 1121-1125
JavaScript, 537
Jumbo, 1115
Ken Nesbitt's WebEdit, 1120
KIS (Knowbot Information Service), 337
L-Soft International, 1129
Law Jokes Web site, 50
law-related, 48
legal concerns, 54
libel on the Internet, 54
Lion Communications Industries, 1215
The List, 1130
local loop data rates, 187
Lotus, 1102
LucasArts Entertainment Company, 1108
LView Pro, 1207-1218
Lycos, 1131-1132
Macmillan Computer Publishing, 175
Macromedia, 1103

Maxis, 1106
MBONE video conferencing program, 1009
Mcafee Antivirus, 1104
MCI, 1129
McKinley Internet Directory, 1134
Mecklerweb, 1137-1138
MetaMedia Project (SGML), 730
Microsoft Corp., 1101, 1215
Microsoft Internet Explorer, 1118
Microsoft Network, 1131, 1211
Microsoft Products, 1207
Midi Gate, 1207-1208
Mod4Win, 1208
Mosaic helper applications, 583
Motorola, 1100
Motorola ISG, 1215-1218
moving between with Netscape, 509-510
MSN, 476
MUD-related, 1024
multimedia files, processing with Internet Explorer, 491-494
navigating with Internet Assistant, 673-677
navigating with Internet Explorer, 477, 482-483
navigating with Mosaic, 547-553, 559-562
navigating with Netscape, 507-522
navigating with NEWTShooter utility (Chameleon), 170
NaviSoft, 1121
NCompass, 1118
NCSA Mosaic, 1116-1117
NCSA Mosaic Demo Document, 471
NCSA What's New, 1133-1134
NEC Corp., 1096
NECX Direct, 1111-1112
NETCOM, 1211
NetFind, 1135
NetManage, Inc., 1125-1138, 1216
NetNanny, 1128

Netrek MUD, 1026
Netscape, 499, 503, 702, 1208-1218
Netscape Chat, 965
Netscape Communications, 1116
Netscape helper applications, 583
Netscape plug-in applications, 528
NewsXpress, 1128
NIUF (North American ISDN Users' Forum), 198
Novell, Inc., 1103
online gaming, 1030
opening multiple pages with Netscape, 510
Packard Bell, 1094
Panorama Pro, 1209
PaperSoftware, 1124
PC Software Links, 1105
PC speaker drivers, 581
PGP, 1115
Pizza Hut, 688
Playboy, 81
Point Communications's Best of the Web, 1134
PolyView, 1209
Portal, 1130
PowWow Internet telephony software, 990
Pretty Good Privacy encryption software, 72
Prodigy, 1131, 1211
Prospero Systems, 1123
PSI, 1129
public domain works, 77
Quarterdeck, 1103
Questar, 1120
RealAudio-related, 108, 528, 586, 741-742, 1121-1125
Sausage Software, 1120
searching, 1131-1135
security issues, 91
server-related, 1116-1120
service providers, 1130-1131
Shockwave, 530, 739
Sierra Online, 1109
Simon and Schuster Interactive, 1107
SimTel, 1115
SlipKnot, 1118

Snoopie Internet File Finder, 1135
SoftQuad, 1120
Software Creations BBS, 1112-1113
software licensing, 86
software-related, 1100-1105, 1112-1116, 1125-1129
Spry Incorporated, 1216
Stanford Net News Filtering, 1135
Stars!, 1209
STB Systems, 1099
Stroud's Consummate WinSock List, 1114
Submit It!, 1135
SurfWatch Software, 1128
Symantec Corporation, 1105
Teles, 1216-1218
Thrustmaster, 1100
Tile.Net/FTP, 1116
Tone Commander Systems, Inc., 1216
Total Clearance, Inc., 78
trademark laws, 87
TrueSpeech, 992
TrueSpeech helper application, 741
TS Intercom Internet telephony software, 992
TUCOWS, 1113
U.S. Robotics, 1096-1138, 1217
URLs, 463-465
USB-related, 201
UUNET Technologies, 1129
video, 108
video conferencing-related, 998
Virtual Explorer add-on utility, 493
VRML, 1122
VRML-related, 1121-1125
VuePrint, 1210
Walnut Creek CD-ROM, 1136
Web copyright issues, 76
Web page background colors, 719
Web page-related, 604
WebChat, 1123
WebCrawler search engine, 259, 1132

WebFX VRML browser, 532, 734
WebPhone Internet telephony software, 989
WebSpace, 1122
The WELL, 1137
Western Digital, 1098
Windows 95 Internetworking Headquarters, 1136
Windows 95 ISDN support, 201
WinNet, 1130
WinPGP, 1210
Winsite, 1114
WinSock, 114, 152
WinZip, 1104
WIT (WWW Interactive Talk), 470
World File Project, 1114
World Wide Web Consortium, 470-471
World Wide Web Virtual Library, 1134-1138
World Wide Web Worm, 1132
World Wide Web Yellow Pages, 1133
Worlds, Inc., 1123
WorldView, 1124
Xing, 1125
Xylogics, 1217-1218
Xyplex, 1218
YAHOO, 1237
Yahoo, 1132
ZyXEL, 1218
see also Web pages
software developments, 743-745
WWW BuyInfo mailing list, 1080
WWW HTML mailing list, 1080
WWW Interactive Talk (WIT), 470
WWW Marketing mailing list, 1081
WWW Security mailing list, 1080
WWW Talk mailing list, 1080
WWW VRML mailing list, 1080-1081
www-html mailing list, 469
www-lib mailing list, 469
www-marketing mailing list, 469

www-security mailing list, 469
www-sites mailing list, 469
www-style mailing list, 469
www-talk mailing list, 469

X

X-modem protocol, 1237
X.400 protocol (e-mail),
   331-332
X.500 protocol (e-mail),
   331-332
XBM (X Bitmap) files, 578
Xing Web site, 1125
Xylogics, contact sources,
   1217-1218
Xyplex, contact sources, 1218

Y–Z

Y-modem protocol, 1237
Yahoo!, 922-925, 1132, 1237

Z-modem protocol, 1237
Ziff FTP site, 1152
zip (file compression), 1237
ZIP/UNZIP command
   (Options menu), 452
zipping/unzipping
   (WS_FTP32), 844
zones (time zones)
      displaying, 1199-1200
      GMT (Greenwich Mean
         Time), 1200
      table of, 1200-1203
ZyXEL, contact sources, 1218

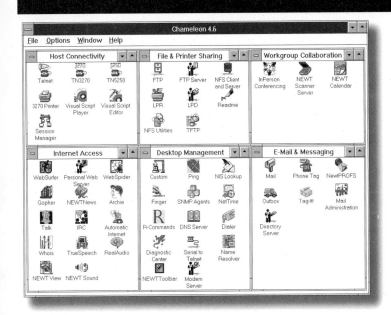

Complete and Return this Card
for a *FREE* Computer Book Catalog

Thank you for purchasing this book! You have purchased a superior computer book written expressly for your needs. To continue to provide the kind of up-to-date, pertinent coverage you've come to expect from us, we need to hear from you. Please take a minute to complete and return this self-addressed, postage-paid form. In return, we'll send you a free catalog of all our computer books on topics ranging from word processing to programming and the internet.

Mr. ☐   Mrs. ☐   Ms. ☐   Dr. ☐

Name (first) ☐☐☐☐☐☐☐☐☐☐☐☐   (M.I.) ☐   (last) ☐☐☐☐☐☐☐☐☐☐☐☐☐☐☐☐☐

Address ☐☐☐☐☐☐☐☐☐☐☐☐☐☐☐☐☐☐☐☐☐☐☐☐☐☐☐☐☐☐☐☐☐☐

City ☐☐☐☐☐☐☐☐☐☐☐☐☐☐☐☐   State ☐☐   Zip ☐☐☐☐☐ ☐☐☐☐

Phone ☐☐☐ ☐☐☐ ☐☐☐☐   Fax ☐☐☐ ☐☐☐ ☐☐☐☐

Company Name ☐☐☐☐☐☐☐☐☐☐☐☐☐☐☐☐☐☐☐☐☐☐☐☐☐☐

E-mail address ☐☐☐☐☐☐☐☐☐☐☐☐☐☐☐☐☐☐☐☐☐☐☐☐☐☐

1. Please check at least (3) influencing factors for purchasing this book.

Front or back cover information on book .... ☐
Special approach to the content .... ☐
Completeness of content .... ☐
Author's reputation .... ☐
Publisher's reputation .... ☐
Book cover design or layout .... ☐
Index or table of contents of book .... ☐
Price of book .... ☐
Special effects, graphics, illustrations .... ☐
Other (Please specify): _____ ☐

2. How did you first learn about this book?

Saw in Macmillan Computer Publishing catalog .... ☐
Recommended by store personnel .... ☐
Saw the book on bookshelf at store .... ☐
Recommended by a friend .... ☐
Received advertisement in the mail .... ☐
Saw an advertisement in: _____ ☐
Read book review in: _____ ☐
Other (Please specify): _____ ☐

3. How many computer books have you purchased in the last six months?

This book only .... ☐   3 to 5 books .... ☐
2 books .... ☐   More than 5 .... ☐

4. Where did you purchase this book?

Bookstore .... ☐
Computer Store .... ☐
Consumer Electronics Store .... ☐
Department Store .... ☐
Office Club .... ☐
Warehouse Club .... ☐
Mail Order .... ☐
Direct from Publisher .... ☐
Internet site .... ☐
Other (Please specify): _____ ☐

5. How long have you been using a computer?

☐ Less than 6 months   ☐ 6 months to a year
☐ 1 to 3 years   ☐ More than 3 years

6. What is your level of experience with personal computers and with the subject of this book?

	With PCs	With subject of book
New	☐	☐
Casual	☐	☐
Accomplished	☐	☐
Expert	☐	☐

Source Code ISBN: 0-7897-0646-6

7. Which of the following best describes your job title?

Administrative Assistant ☐
Coordinator ☐
Manager/Supervisor ☐
Director ☐
Vice President ☐
President/CEO/COO ☐
Lawyer/Doctor/Medical Professional ☐
Teacher/Educator/Trainer ☐
Engineer/Technician ☐
Consultant ☐
Not employed/Student/Retired ☐
Other (Please specify): _____ ☐

8. Which of the following best describes the area of the company your job title falls under?

Accounting ☐
Engineering ☐
Manufacturing ☐
Operations ☐
Marketing ☐
Sales ☐
Other (Please specify): _____ ☐

9. What is your age?

Under 20 ☐
21-29 ☐
30-39 ☐
40-49 ☐
50-59 ☐
60-over ☐

10. Are you:

Male ☐
Female ☐

11. Which computer publications do you read regularly? (Please list)

_____
_____
_____
_____
_____
_____
_____
_____
_____

Comments: _____
_____
_____

Fold here and scotch-tape to ma[il]

BUSINESS REPLY MAIL
FIRST-CLASS MAIL PERMIT NO. 9918 INDIANAPOLIS IN

POSTAGE WILL BE PAID BY THE ADDRESSEE

ATTN MARKETING
MACMILLAN COMPUTER PUBLISHING
MACMILLAN PUBLISHING USA
201 W 103RD ST
INDIANAPOLIS IN 46290-9042

NO POSTAGE
NECESSARY
IF MAILED
IN THE
UNITED S[TATES]

END-USER LICENSE AGREEMENT FOR MICROSOFT SOFTWARE

IMPORTANT—READ CAREFULLY: This Microsoft End-User License Agreement ("EULA") is a legal agreement between you (either an individual or a single entity) and Microsoft Corporation for the Microsoft software accompanying this EULA, which includes computer software and associated media and printed materials, and may include "on-line" or electronic documentation ("SOFTWARE PRODUCT" or "SOFTWARE"). By opening the sealed packet(s) OR exercising your rights to make and use copies of Internet Assistant, you agree to be bound by the terms of this EULA. If you do not agree to the terms of this EULA, promptly return this package to the place from which you obtained it.

SOFTWARE PRODUCT LICENSE

The Internet Assistant is protected by copyright laws and international copyright treaties, as well as other intellectual property laws and treaties. The Internet Assistant is licensed, not sold.

1. GRANT OF LICENSE. This EULA grants you the following rights:

- **Installation and Use.** You may install and use an unlimited number of copies of the Internet Assistant.
- **Reproduction and Distribution.** You may reproduce and distribute an unlimited number of copies of the Internet Assistant; provided that each copy shall be a true and complete copy, including all copyright and trademark notices, and shall be accompanied by a copy of the EULA. The copies may be distributed as a stand-alone product or included with your own product.

2. DESCRIPTION OF OTHER RIGHTS AND LIMITATIONS.

- **Limitations on Reverse Engineering, Decompilation, and Disassembly.** You may not reverse-engineer, decompile, or disassemble the Internet Assistant, except and only to the extent that such activity is expressly permitted by applicable law notwithstanding this limitation.
- **Separation of components.** The Internet Assistant is licensed as a single product. Its component parts may not be separated for use on more than one computer.
- **Software Transfer.** You may permanently transfer all of your rights under this EULA, provided the recipient agrees to the terms of this EULA.
- **Termination.** Without prejudice to any other rights, Microsoft may terminate this EULA if you fail to comply with the terms and conditions of this EULA. In such event, you must destroy all copies of the Internet Assistant and all of its component parts.

3. COPYRIGHT. All titles and copyrights in and to the Internet Assistant (including but not limited to any images, photographs, animations, video, audio, music, text, and "applets" incorporated into the Internet Assistant), the accompanying printed materials, and any copies of the Internet Assistant are owned by Microsoft or its suppliers. The SOFTWARE PRODUCT is protected by copyright laws and international treaty provisions. Therefore, you must treat the SOFTWARE PRODUCT like any other copyrighted material.

4. U.S. GOVERNMENT RESTRICTED RIGHTS. The Internet Assistant and documentation are provided with RESTRICTED RIGHTS. Use, duplication, or disclosure by the Government is subject to restrictions as set forth in subparagraph (c)(1)(ii) of the Rights in Technical Data and Computer Software clause at DFARS 252.227-7013 or subparagraphs (c)(1) and (2) of the Commercial Computer Software—Restricted Rights at 48 CFR 52.227-19, as applicable. Manufacturer is Microsoft Corporation/One Microsoft Way/Redmond, WA 98052-6399.

(continues)

LIMITED WARRANTY

NO WARRANTIES. Microsoft expressly disclaims any warranty for the Internet Assistant. The Internet Assistant and any related documentation is provided "as is" without warranty of any kind, either express or implied, including, without limitation, the implied warranties or merchantablility, fitness for a particular purpose, or noninfringement. The entire risk arising out of use or performance of the Internet Assistant remains with you.

NO LIABILITY FOR CONSEQUENTIAL DAMAGES. In no event shall Microsoft or its suppliers be liable for any damages whatsoever (including, without limitation, damages for loss of business profits, business interruption, loss of business information, or any other pecuniary loss) arising out of the use of or inability to use this Microsoft product, even if Microsoft has been advised of the possibility of such damages. Because some states/jurisdictions do not allow the exclusion or limitation of liability for consequential or incidental damages, the above limitation may not apply to you.

MISCELLANEOUS

If you acquired this product in the United States, this EULA is governed by the laws of the State of Washington.

If this product was acquired outside the United States, then local laws may apply.

Should you have any questions concerning this EULA, or if you desire to contact Microsoft for any reason, please contact the Microsoft subsidiary serving your country, or write: Microsoft Sales Information Center/ One Microsoft Way/Redmond, WA 98052-6399

This program was reproduced by Macmillan Computer Publishing under a special arrangement with Microsoft Corporation. For this reason, Macmillan Computer Publishing is responsible for the product warranty and for support. If your diskette is defective, please return it to Macmillan Computer Publishing, which will arrange for its replacement. PLEASE DO NOT RETURN IT TO MICROSOFT CORPORATION. End users of this Microsoft program shall not be considered "registered owners" of a Microsoft product and therefore shall not be eligible for upgrades, promotions, or other benefits available to "registered Owners" of Microsoft Products.